University Casebook Series

March, 1989

ACCOUNTING AND THE LAW, Fourth Edition (1978), with Problems Pamphlet (Successor to Dohr, Phillips, Thompson & Warren)

George C. Thompson, Professor, Columbia University Graduate School of Business.
Robert Whitman, Professor of Law, University of Connecticut.
Ellis L. Phillips, Jr., Member of the New York Bar.
William C. Warren, Professor of Law Emeritus, Columbia University.

ACCOUNTING FOR LAWYERS, MATERIALS ON (1980)

David R. Herwitz, Professor of Law, Harvard University.

ADMINISTRATIVE LAW, Eighth Edition (1987), with 1983 Problems Supplement (Supplement edited in association with Paul R. Verkuil, Dean and Professor of Law, Tulane University)

Walter Gellhorn, University Professor Emeritus, Columbia University.
Clark Byse, Professor of Law, Harvard University.
Peter L. Strauss, Professor of Law, Columbia University.
Todd D. Rakoff, Professor of Law, Harvard University.
Roy A. Schotland, Professor of Law, Georgetown University.

ADMIRALTY, Third Edition (1987), with Statute and Rule Supplement

Jo Desha Lucas, Professor of Law, University of Chicago.

ADVOCACY, see also Lawyering Process

AGENCY, see also Enterprise Organization

AGENCY—PARTNERSHIPS, Fourth Edition (1987)

Abridgement from Conard, Knauss & Siegel's Enterprise Organization, Fourth Edition.

AGENCY AND PARTNERSHIPS (1987)

Melvin A. Eisenberg, Professor of Law, University of California, Berkeley.

ANTITRUST: FREE ENTERPRISE AND ECONOMIC ORGANIZATION, Sixth Edition (1983), with 1983 Problems in Antitrust Supplement and 1988 Case Supplement

Louis B. Schwartz, Professor of Law, University of Pennsylvania.
John J. Flynn, Professor of Law, University of Utah.
Harry First, Professor of Law, New York University.

BANKRUPTCY (1985)

Robert L. Jordan, Professor of Law, University of California, Los Angeles.
William D. Warren, Professor of Law, University of California, Los Angeles.

BANKRUPTCY AND DEBTOR–CREDITOR LAW, Second Edition (1988)

Theodore Eisenberg, Professor of Law, Cornell University.

BUSINESS ORGANIZATION, see also Enterprise Organization

BUSINESS PLANNING, Temporary Second Edition (1984)

David R. Herwitz, Professor of Law, Harvard University.

BUSINESS TORTS (1972)

Milton Handler, Professor of Law Emeritus, Columbia University.

CHILDREN IN THE LEGAL SYSTEM (1983) with 1988 Supplement

Walter Wadlington, Professor of Law, University of Virginia.
Charles H. Whitebread, Professor of Law, University of Southern California.
Samuel Davis, Professor of Law, University of Georgia.

CIVIL PROCEDURE, see Procedure

CIVIL RIGHTS ACTIONS (1988), with 1988 Supplement

Peter W. Low, Professor of Law, University of Virginia.
John C. Jeffries, Jr., Professor of Law, University of Virginia.

CLINIC, see also Lawyering Process

COMMERCIAL AND DEBTOR–CREDITOR LAW: SELECTED STATUTES, 1988 EDITION

COMMERCIAL LAW, Second Edition (1987)

Robert L. Jordan, Professor of Law, University of California, Los Angeles.
William D. Warren, Professor of Law, University of California, Los Angeles.

COMMERCIAL LAW, Fourth Edition (1985)

E. Allan Farnsworth, Professor of Law, Columbia University.
John Honnold, Professor of Law, University of Pennsylvania.

COMMERCIAL PAPER, Third Edition (1984)

E. Allan Farnsworth, Professor of Law, Columbia University.

COMMERCIAL PAPER, Second Edition (1987) (Reprinted from COMMERCIAL LAW, Second Edition (1987))

Robert L. Jordan, Professor of Law, University of California, Los Angeles.
William D. Warren, Professor of Law, University of California, Los Angeles.

COMMERCIAL PAPER AND BANK DEPOSITS AND COLLECTIONS (1967), with Statutory Supplement

William D. Hawkland, Professor of Law, University of Illinois.

COMMERCIAL TRANSACTIONS—Principles and Policies (1982)

Alan Schwartz, Professor of Law, University of Southern California.
Robert E. Scott, Professor of Law, University of Virginia.

COMPARATIVE LAW, Fifth Edition (1988)

Rudolf B. Schlesinger, Professor of Law, Hastings College of Law.
Hans W. Baade, Professor of Law, University of Texas.
Mirjan P. Damaska, Professor of Law, Yale Law School.
Peter E. Herzog, Professor of Law, Syracuse University.

COMPETITIVE PROCESS, LEGAL REGULATION OF THE, Third Edition (1986), with 1987 Selected Statutes Supplement

Edmund W. Kitch, Professor of Law, University of Virginia.
Harvey S. Perlman, Dean of the Law School, University of Nebraska.

CONFLICT OF LAWS, Eighth Edition (1984), with 1987 Case Supplement

Willis L. M. Reese, Professor of Law, Columbia University.
Maurice Rosenberg, Professor of Law, Columbia University.

CONSTITUTIONAL LAW, Eighth Edition (1989)

Edward L. Barrett, Jr., Professor of Law, University of California, Davis.
William Cohen, Professor of Law, Stanford University.
Jonathan D. Varat, Professor of Law, University of California, Los Angeles.

CONSTITUTIONAL LAW, CIVIL LIBERTY AND INDIVIDUAL RIGHTS, Second Edition (1982), with 1987 Supplement

William Cohen, Professor of Law, Stanford University.
John Kaplan, Professor of Law, Stanford University.

CONSTITUTIONAL LAW, Eleventh Edition (1985), with 1988 Supplement (Supplement edited in association with Frederick F. Schauer, Professor of Law, University of Michigan)

Gerald Gunther, Professor of Law, Stanford University.

CONSTITUTIONAL LAW, INDIVIDUAL RIGHTS IN, Fourth Edition (1986), (Reprinted from CONSTITUTIONAL LAW, Eleventh Edition), with 1988 Supplement (Supplement edited in association with Frederick F. Schauer, Professor of Law, University of Michigan)

Gerald Gunther, Professor of Law, Stanford University.

CONSUMER TRANSACTIONS (1983), with Selected Statutes and Regulations Supplement and 1987 Case Supplement

Michael M. Greenfield, Professor of Law, Washington University.

CONTRACT LAW AND ITS APPLICATION, Fourth Edition (1988)

Arthur Rosett, Professor of Law, University of California, Los Angeles.

CONTRACT LAW, STUDIES IN, Third Edition (1984)

Edward J. Murphy, Professor of Law, University of Notre Dame.
Richard E. Speidel, Professor of Law, Northwestern University.

CONTRACTS, Fifth Edition (1987)

John P. Dawson, Professor of Law Emeritus, Harvard University.
William Burnett Harvey, Professor of Law and Political Science, Boston University.
Stanley D. Henderson, Professor of Law, University of Virginia.

CONTRACTS, Fourth Edition (1988)

E. Allan Farnsworth, Professor of Law, Columbia University.
William F. Young, Professor of Law, Columbia University.

CONTRACTS, Selections on (statutory materials) (1988)

CONTRACTS, Second Edition (1978), with Statutory and Administrative Law Supplement (1978)

Ian R. Macneil, Professor of Law, Cornell University.

COPYRIGHT, PATENTS AND TRADEMARKS, see also Competitive Process; see also Selected Statutes and International Agreements

COPYRIGHT, PATENT, TRADEMARK AND RELATED STATE DOCTRINES, Second Edition (1981), with 1988 Case Supplement, 1987 Selected Statutes Supplement and 1981 Problem Supplement

Paul Goldstein, Professor of Law, Stanford University.

COPYRIGHT, Unfair Competition, and Other Topics Bearing on the Protection of Literary, Musical, and Artistic Works, Fourth Edition (1985), with 1985 Statutory Supplement

Ralph S. Brown, Jr., Professor of Law, Yale University.
Robert C. Denicola, Professor of Law, University of Nebraska.

CORPORATE ACQUISITIONS, The Law and Finance of (1986), with 1988 Supplement

Ronald J. Gilson, Professor of Law, Stanford University.

CORPORATE FINANCE, Third Edition (1987)

Victor Brudney, Professor of Law, Harvard University.
Marvin A. Chirelstein, Professor of Law, Columbia University.

CORPORATE READJUSTMENTS AND REORGANIZATIONS (1976)

Walter J. Blum, Professor of Law, University of Chicago.
Stanley A. Kaplan, Professor of Law, University of Chicago.

CORPORATION LAW, BASIC, Third Edition (1989), with Documentary Supplement

Detlev F. Vagts, Professor of Law, Harvard University.

CORPORATIONS, see also Enterprise Organization

CORPORATIONS, Sixth Edition—Concise (1988), with Statutory Supplement (1988)

William L. Cary, late Professor of Law, Columbia University.
Melvin Aron Eisenberg, Professor of Law, University of California, Berkeley.

CORPORATIONS, Sixth Edition—Unabridged (1988), with Statutory Supplement (1988)

William L. Cary, late Professor of Law, Columbia University.
Melvin Aron Eisenberg, Professor of Law, University of California, Berkeley.

CORPORATIONS AND BUSINESS ASSOCIATIONS—STATUTES, RULES AND FORMS (1988)

CORPORATIONS COURSE GAME PLAN (1975)

David R. Herwitz, Professor of Law, Harvard University.

CORRECTIONS, SEE SENTENCING

CREDITORS' RIGHTS, see also Debtor-Creditor Law

CRIMINAL JUSTICE ADMINISTRATION, Third Edition (1986), with 1988 Case Supplement

Frank W. Miller, Professor of Law, Washington University.
Robert O. Dawson, Professor of Law, University of Texas.
George E. Dix, Professor of Law, University of Texas.
Raymond I. Parnas, Professor of Law, University of California, Davis.

CRIMINAL LAW, Fourth Edition (1987)

Fred E. Inbau, Professor of Law Emeritus, Northwestern University.
Andre A. Moenssens, Professor of Law, University of Richmond.
James R. Thompson, Professor of Law Emeritus, Northwestern University.

CRIMINAL LAW AND APPROACHES TO THE STUDY OF LAW (1986)

John M. Brumbaugh, Professor of Law, University of Maryland.

CRIMINAL LAW, Second Edition (1986)

Peter W. Low, Professor of Law, University of Virginia.
John C. Jeffries, Jr., Professor of Law, University of Virginia.
Richard C. Bonnie, Professor of Law, University of Virginia.

CRIMINAL LAW, Fourth Edition (1986)

Lloyd L. Weinreb, Professor of Law, Harvard University.

CRIMINAL LAW AND PROCEDURE, Seventh Edition (1989)

Ronald N. Boyce, Professor of Law, University of Utah.
Rollin M. Perkins, Professor of Law Emeritus, University of California, Hastings
College of the Law.

CRIMINAL PROCEDURE, Third Edition (1987), with 1988 Supplement

James B. Haddad, Professor of Law, Northwestern University.
James B. Zagel, Chief, Criminal Justice Division, Office of Attorney General of
Illinois.
Gary L. Starkman, Assistant U. S. Attorney, Northern District of Illinois.
William J. Bauer, Chief Judge of the U.S. Court of Appeals, Seventh Circuit.

CRIMINAL PROCESS, Fourth Edition (1987), with 1988 Supplement

Lloyd L. Weinreb, Professor of Law, Harvard University.

DAMAGES, Second Edition (1952)

Charles T. McCormick, late Professor of Law, University of Texas.
William F. Fritz, late Professor of Law, University of Texas.

DECEDENTS' ESTATES AND TRUSTS, Seventh Edition (1988)

John Ritchie, Late Professor of Law, University of Virginia.
Neill H. Alford, Jr., Professor of Law, University of Virginia.
Richard W. Effland, Professor of Law, Arizona State University.

DISPUTE RESOLUTION, Processes of (1989)

John S. Murray, President and Executive Director of The Conflict Clinic, Inc.,
George Mason University.
Alan Scott Rau, Professor of Law, University of Texas.
Edward F. Sherman, Professor of Law, University of Texas.

DOMESTIC RELATIONS, see also Family Law

DOMESTIC RELATIONS, Successor Edition (1984) with 1988 Supplement

Walter Wadlington, Professor of Law, University of Virginia.

EMPLOYMENT DISCRIMINATION, Second Edition (1987), with 1988 Supplement

Joel W. Friedman, Professor of Law, Tulane University.
George M. Strickler, Professor of Law, Tulane University.

EMPLOYMENT LAW (1987), with 1987 Statutory Supplement and 1988 Case Supplement

Mark A. Rothstein, Professor of Law, University of Houston.
Andria S. Knapp, Adjunct Professor of Law, University of California, Hastings
College of Law.
Lance Liebman, Professor of Law, Harvard University.

ENERGY LAW (1983) with 1986 Case Supplement

Donald N. Zillman, Professor of Law, University of Utah.
Laurence Lattman, Dean of Mines and Engineering, University of Utah.

ENTERPRISE ORGANIZATION, Fourth Edition (1987), with 1987 Corporation and Partnership Statutes, Rules and Forms Supplement

Alfred F. Conard, Professor of Law, University of Michigan.
Robert L. Knauss, Dean of the Law School, University of Houston.
Stanley Siegel, Professor of Law, University of California, Los Angeles.

ENVIRONMENTAL POLICY LAW 1985 Edition, with 1985 Problems Supplement (Supplement in association with Ronald H. Rosenberg, Professor of Law, College of William and Mary)

Thomas J. Schoenbaum, Professor of Law, University of Georgia.

EQUITY, see also Remedies

EQUITY, RESTITUTION AND DAMAGES, Second Edition (1974)

Robert Childres, late Professor of Law, Northwestern University.
William F. Johnson, Jr., Professor of Law, New York University.

ESTATE PLANNING, Second Edition (1982), with 1985 Case, Text and Documentary Supplement

David Westfall, Professor of Law, Harvard University.

ETHICS, see Legal Profession, Professional Responsibility, and Social Responsibilities

ETHICS AND PROFESSIONAL RESPONSIBILITY (1981) (Reprinted from THE LAWYERING PROCESS)

Gary Bellow, Professor of Law, Harvard University.
Bea Moulton, Legal Services Corporation.

EVIDENCE, Sixth Edition (1988 Reprint)

John Kaplan, Professor of Law, Stanford University.
Jon R. Waltz, Professor of Law, Northwestern University.

EVIDENCE, Eighth Edition (1988), with Rules, Statute and Case Supplement (1988)

Jack B. Weinstein, Chief Judge, United States District Court.
John H. Mansfield, Professor of Law, Harvard University.
Norman Abrams, Professor of Law, University of California, Los Angeles.
Margaret Berger, Professor of Law, Brooklyn Law School.

FAMILY LAW, see also Domestic Relations

FAMILY LAW Second Edition (1985), with 1988 Supplement

Judith C. Areen, Professor of Law, Georgetown University.

FAMILY LAW AND CHILDREN IN THE LEGAL SYSTEM, STATUTORY MATERIALS (1981)

Walter Wadlington, Professor of Law, University of Virginia.

FEDERAL COURTS, Eighth Edition (1988)

Charles T. McCormick, late Professor of Law, University of Texas.
James H. Chadbourn, late Professor of Law, Harvard University.
Charles Alan Wright, Professor of Law, University of Texas, Austin.

UNIVERSITY CASEBOOK SERIES—Continued

FEDERAL COURTS AND THE FEDERAL SYSTEM, Hart and Wechsler's Third Edition (1988), with the Judicial Code and Rules of Procedure in the Federal Courts (1988)

Paul M. Bator, Professor of Law, University of Chicago.
Daniel J. Meltzer, Professor of Law, Harvard University.
Paul J. Mishkin, Professor of Law, University of California, Berkeley.
David L. Shapiro, Professor of Law, Harvard University.

FEDERAL COURTS AND THE LAW OF FEDERAL–STATE RELATIONS, Second Edition (1989)

Peter W. Low, Professor of Law, University of Virginia.
John C. Jeffries, Jr., Professor of Law, University of Virginia.

FEDERAL PUBLIC LAND AND RESOURCES LAW, Second Edition (1987), with 1984 Statutory Supplement

George C. Coggins, Professor of Law, University of Kansas.
Charles F. Wilkinson, Professor of Law, University of Oregon.

FEDERAL RULES OF CIVIL PROCEDURE and Selected Other Procedural Provisions, 1988 Edition

FEDERAL TAXATION, see Taxation

FOOD AND DRUG LAW (1980), with Statutory Supplement

Richard A. Merrill, Dean of the School of Law, University of Virginia.
Peter Barton Hutt, Esq.

FUTURE INTERESTS (1958)

Philip Mechem, late Professor of Law Emeritus, University of Pennsylvania.

FUTURE INTERESTS (1970)

Howard R. Williams, Professor of Law, Stanford University.

FUTURE INTERESTS AND ESTATE PLANNING (1961), with 1962 Supplement

W. Barton Leach, late Professor of Law, Harvard University.
James K. Logan, formerly Dean of the Law School, University of Kansas.

GOVERNMENT CONTRACTS, FEDERAL, Successor Edition (1985)

John W. Whelan, Professor of Law, Hastings College of the Law.

GOVERNMENT REGULATION: FREE ENTERPRISE AND ECONOMIC ORGANI-ZATION, Sixth Edition (1985)

Louis B. Schwartz, Professor of Law, Hastings College of the Law.
John J. Flynn, Professor of Law, University of Utah.
Harry First, Professor of Law, New York University.

HEALTH CARE LAW AND POLICY (1988)

Clark C. Havighurst, Professor of Law, Duke University.

HINCKLEY, JOHN W., JR., TRIAL OF: A Case Study of the Insanity Defense (1986)

Peter W. Low, Professor of Law, University of Virginia.
John C. Jeffries, Jr., Professor of Law, University of Virginia.
Richard C. Bonnie, Professor of Law, University of Virginia.

INJUNCTIONS, Second Edition (1984)

Owen M. Fiss, Professor of Law, Yale University.
Doug Rendleman, Professor of Law, College of William and Mary.

INSTITUTIONAL INVESTORS, (1978)

David L. Ratner, Professor of Law, Cornell University.

INSURANCE, Second Edition (1985)

William F. Young, Professor of Law, Columbia University.
Eric M. Holmes, Professor of Law, University of Georgia.

INTERNATIONAL LAW, see also Transnational Legal Problems, Transnational Business Problems, and United Nations Law

INTERNATIONAL LAW IN CONTEMPORARY PERSPECTIVE (1981), with Essay Supplement

Myres S. McDougal, Professor of Law, Yale University.
W. Michael Reisman, Professor of Law, Yale University.

INTERNATIONAL LEGAL SYSTEM, Third Edition (1988), with Documentary Supplement

Joseph Modeste Sweeney, Professor of Law, University of California, Hastings.
Covey T. Oliver, Professor of Law, University of Pennsylvania.
Noyes E. Leech, Professor of Law Emeritus, University of Pennsylvania.

INTRODUCTION TO LAW, see also Legal Method, On Law in Courts, and Dynamics of American Law

INTRODUCTION TO THE STUDY OF LAW (1970)

E. Wayne Thode, late Professor of Law, University of Utah.
Leon Lebowitz, Professor of Law, University of Texas.
Lester J. Mazor, Professor of Law, University of Utah.

JUDICIAL CODE and Rules of Procedure in the Federal Courts, Students' Edition, 1988 Revision

Daniel J. Meltzer, Professor of Law, Harvard University.
David L. Shapiro, Professor of Law, Harvard University.

JURISPRUDENCE (Temporary Edition Hardbound) (1949)

Lon L. Fuller, late Professor of Law, Harvard University.

JUVENILE, see also Children

JUVENILE JUSTICE PROCESS, Third Edition (1985)

Frank W. Miller, Professor of Law, Washington University.
Robert O. Dawson, Professor of Law, University of Texas.
George E. Dix, Professor of Law, University of Texas.
Raymond I. Parnas, Professor of Law, University of California, Davis.

LABOR LAW, Tenth Edition (1986), with 1986 Statutory Supplement

Archibald Cox, Professor of Law, Harvard University.
Derek C. Bok, President, Harvard University.
Robert A. Gorman, Professor of Law, University of Pennsylvania.

LABOR LAW, Second Edition (1982), with Statutory Supplement

Clyde W. Summers, Professor of Law, University of Pennsylvania.
Harry H. Wellington, Dean of the Law School, Yale University.
Alan Hyde, Professor of Law, Rutgers University.

LAND FINANCING, Third Edition (1985)

The late Norman Penney, Professor of Law, Cornell University.
Richard F. Broude, Member of the California Bar.
Roger Cunningham, Professor of Law, University of Michigan.

LAW AND MEDICINE (1980)

Walter Wadlington, Professor of Law and Professor of Legal Medicine, University of Virginia.
Jon R. Waltz, Professor of Law, Northwestern University.
Roger B. Dworkin, Professor of Law, Indiana University, and Professor of Biomedical History, University of Washington.

LAW, LANGUAGE AND ETHICS (1972)

William R. Bishin, Professor of Law, University of Southern California.
Christopher D. Stone, Professor of Law, University of Southern California.

LAW, SCIENCE AND MEDICINE (1984), with 1989 Supplement

Judith C. Areen, Professor of Law, Georgetown University.
Patricia A. King, Professor of Law, Georgetown University.
Steven P. Goldberg, Professor of Law, Georgetown University.
Alexander M. Capron, Professor of Law, University of Southern California.

LAWYERING PROCESS (1978), with Civil Problem Supplement and Criminal Problem Supplement

Gary Bellow, Professor of Law, Harvard University.
Bea Moulton, Professor of Law, Arizona State University.

LEGAL METHOD (1980)

Harry W. Jones, Professor of Law Emeritus, Columbia University.
John M. Kernochan, Professor of Law, Columbia University.
Arthur W. Murphy, Professor of Law, Columbia University.

LEGAL METHODS (1969)

Robert N. Covington, Professor of Law, Vanderbilt University.
E. Blythe Stason, late Professor of Law, Vanderbilt University.
John W. Wade, Professor of Law, Vanderbilt University.
Elliott E. Cheatham, late Professor of Law, Vanderbilt University.
Theodore A. Smedley, Professor of Law, Vanderbilt University.

LEGAL PROFESSION, THE, Responsibility and Regulation, Second Edition (1988)

Geoffrey C. Hazard, Jr., Professor of Law, Yale University.
Deborah L. Rhode, Professor of Law, Stanford University.

LEGISLATION, Fourth Edition (1982) (by Fordham)

Horace E. Read, late Vice President, Dalhousie University.
John W. MacDonald, Professor of Law Emeritus, Cornell Law School.
Jefferson B. Fordham, Professor of Law, University of Utah.
William J. Pierce, Professor of Law, University of Michigan.

LEGISLATIVE AND ADMINISTRATIVE PROCESSES, Second Edition (1981)

Hans A. Linde, Judge, Supreme Court of Oregon.
George Bunn, Professor of Law, University of Wisconsin.
Fredericka Paff, Professor of Law, University of Wisconsin.
W. Lawrence Church, Professor of Law, University of Wisconsin.

LOCAL GOVERNMENT LAW, Second Revised Edition (1986)

Jefferson B. Fordham, Professor of Law, University of Utah.

MASS MEDIA LAW, Third Edition (1987)

Marc A. Franklin, Professor of Law, Stanford University.

MENTAL HEALTH PROCESS, Second Edition (1976), with 1981 Supplement

Frank W. Miller, Professor of Law, Washington University.
Robert O. Dawson, Professor of Law, University of Texas.
George E. Dix, Professor of Law, University of Texas.
Raymond I. Parnas, Professor of Law, University of California, Davis.

MUNICIPAL CORPORATIONS, see Local Government Law

NEGOTIABLE INSTRUMENTS, see Commercial Paper

NEGOTIATION (1981) (Reprinted from THE LAWYERING PROCESS)

Gary Bellow, Professor of Law, Harvard Law School.
Bea Moulton, Legal Services Corporation.

NEW YORK PRACTICE, Fourth Edition (1978)

Herbert Peterfreund, Professor of Law, New York University.
Joseph M. McLaughlin, Dean of the Law School, Fordham University.

OIL AND GAS, Fifth Edition (1987)

Howard R. Williams, Professor of Law, Stanford University.
Richard C. Maxwell, Professor of Law, University of California, Los Angeles.
Charles J. Meyers, Dean of the Law School, Stanford University.
Stephen F. Williams, Judge of the United States Court of Appeals.

ON LAW IN COURTS (1965)

Paul J. Mishkin, Professor of Law, University of California, Berkeley.
Clarence Morris, Professor of Law Emeritus, University of Pennsylvania.

PATENTS AND ANTITRUST (Pamphlet) (1983)

Milton Handler, Professor of Law Emeritus, Columbia University.
Harlan M. Blake, Professor of Law, Columbia University.
Robert Pitofsky, Professor of Law, Georgetown University.
Harvey J. Goldschmid, Professor of Law, Columbia University.

PLEADING AND PROCEDURE, see Procedure, Civil

POLICE FUNCTION, Fourth Edition (1986), with 1988 Case Supplement

Reprint of Chapters 1–10 of Miller, Dawson, Dix and Parnas's CRIMINAL
JUSTICE ADMINISTRATION, Third Edition.

**PREPARING AND PRESENTING THE CASE (1981) (Reprinted from THE LAW-
YERING PROCESS)**

Gary Bellow, Professor of Law, Harvard Law School.
Bea Moulton, Legal Services Corporation.

PROCEDURE (1988), with Procedure Supplement (1988)

Robert M. Cover, late Professor of Law, Yale Law School.
Owen M. Fiss, Professor of Law, Yale Law School.
Judith Resnik, Professor of Law, University of Southern California Law Center.

**PROCEDURE—CIVIL PROCEDURE, Second Edition (1974), with 1979 Supple-
ment**

The late James H. Chadbourn, Professor of Law, Harvard University.
A. Leo Levin, Professor of Law, University of Pennsylvania.
Philip Shuchman, Professor of Law, Cornell University.

UNIVERSITY CASEBOOK SERIES—Continued

PROCEDURE—CIVIL PROCEDURE, Fifth Edition (1984), with 1988 Supplement

Richard H. Field, late Professor of Law, Harvard University.
Benjamin Kaplan, Professor of Law Emeritus, Harvard University.
Kevin M. Clermont, Professor of Law, Cornell University.

PROCEDURE—CIVIL PROCEDURE, Fourth Edition (1985), with 1988 Supplement

Maurice Rosenberg, Professor of Law, Columbia University.
Hans Smit, Professor of Law, Columbia University.
Harold L. Korn, Professor of Law, Columbia University.

PROCEDURE—PLEADING AND PROCEDURE: State and Federal, Fifth Edition (1983), with 1988 Supplement

David W. Louisell, late Professor of Law, University of California, Berkeley.
Geoffrey C. Hazard, Jr., Professor of Law, Yale University.
Colin C. Tait, Professor of Law, University of Connecticut.

PROCEDURE—FEDERAL RULES OF CIVIL PROCEDURE, 1988 Edition

PRODUCTS LIABILITY (1980)

Marshall S. Shapo, Professor of Law, Northwestern University.

PRODUCTS LIABILITY AND SAFETY (1980), with 1985 Case and Documentary Supplement

W. Page Keeton, Professor of Law, University of Texas.
David G. Owen, Professor of Law, University of South Carolina.
John E. Montgomery, Professor of Law, University of South Carolina.

PROFESSIONAL RESPONSIBILITY, Fourth Edition (1987), with 1989 Selected National Standards Supplement

Thomas D. Morgan, Dean of the Law School, Emory University.
Ronald D. Rotunda, Professor of Law, University of Illinois.

PROPERTY, Fifth Edition (1984)

John E. Cribbet, Professor of Law, University of Illinois.
Corwin W. Johnson, Professor of Law, University of Texas.

PROPERTY—PERSONAL (1953)

S. Kenneth Skolfield, late Professor of Law Emeritus, Boston University.

PROPERTY—PERSONAL, Third Edition (1954)

Everett Fraser, late Dean of the Law School Emeritus, University of Minnesota.
Third Edition by Charles W. Taintor, late Professor of Law, University of Pittsburgh.

PROPERTY—INTRODUCTION, TO REAL PROPERTY, Third Edition (1954)

Everett Fraser, late Dean of the Law School Emeritus, University of Minnesota.

PROPERTY—REAL AND PERSONAL, Combined Edition (1954)

Everett Fraser, late Dean of the Law School Emeritus, University of Minnesota.
Third Edition of Personal Property by Charles W. Taintor, late Professor of Law, University of Pittsburgh.

PROPERTY—FUNDAMENTALS OF MODERN REAL PROPERTY, Second Edition (1982), with 1985 Supplement

Edward H. Rabin, Professor of Law, University of California, Davis.

PROPERTY—PROBLEMS IN REAL PROPERTY (Pamphlet) (1969)

Edward H. Rabin, Professor of Law, University of California, Davis.

PROPERTY, REAL (1984), with 1988 Supplement

Paul Goldstein, Professor of Law, Stanford University.

PROSECUTION AND ADJUDICATION, Third Edition (1986), with 1988 Case Supplement

Reprint of Chapters 11–26 of Miller, Dawson, Dix and Parnas's CRIMINAL JUSTICE ADMINISTRATION, Third Edition.

PSYCHIATRY AND LAW, see Mental Health, see also Hinckley, Trial of

PUBLIC REGULATION OF DANGEROUS PRODUCTS (paperback) (1980)

Marshall S. Shapo, Professor of Law, Northwestern University.

PUBLIC UTILITY LAW, see Free Enterprise, also Regulated Industries

REAL ESTATE PLANNING, Second Edition (1980), with 1980 Problems, Statutes and New Materials Supplement

Norton L. Steuben, Professor of Law, University of Colorado.

REAL ESTATE TRANSACTIONS, Revised Second Edition (1988), with Statute, Form and Problem Supplement (1988)

Paul Goldstein, Professor of Law, Stanford University.

RECEIVERSHIP AND CORPORATE REORGANIZATION, see Creditors' Rights

REGULATED INDUSTRIES, Second Edition, (1976)

William K. Jones, Professor of Law, Columbia University.

REMEDIES, Second Edition (1987)

Edward D. Re, Chief Judge, U. S. Court of International Trade.

RESTITUTION, Second Edition (1966)

John W. Wade, Professor of Law, Vanderbilt University.

SALES, Second Edition (1986)

Marion W. Benfield, Jr., Professor of Law, University of Illinois.
William D. Hawkland, Chancellor, Louisiana State Law Center.

SALES AND SALES FINANCING, Fifth Edition (1984)

John Honnold, Professor of Law, University of Pennsylvania.

SALES LAW AND THE CONTRACTING PROCESS (1982)

Reprint of Chapters 1–10 of Schwartz and Scott's Commercial Transactions.

SECURED TRANSACTIONS IN PERSONAL PROPERTY, Second Edition (1987) (Reprinted from COMMERCIAL LAW, Second Edition (1987))

Robert L. Jordan, Professor of Law, University of California, Los Angeles.
William D. Warren, Professor of Law, University of California, Los Angeles.

SECURITIES REGULATION, Sixth Edition (1987), with 1988 Selected Statutes, Rules and Forms Supplement and 1988 Cases and Releases Supplement

Richard W. Jennings, Professor of Law, University of California, Berkeley.
Harold Marsh, Jr., Member of California Bar.

SECURITIES REGULATION, Second Edition (1988), with Statute, Rule and Form Supplement (1988)

Larry D. Soderquist, Professor of Law, Vanderbilt University.

UNIVERSITY CASEBOOK SERIES—Continued

SECURITY INTERESTS IN PERSONAL PROPERTY, Second Edition (1987)

Douglas G. Baird, Professor of Law, University of Chicago.
Thomas H. Jackson, Professor of Law, Stanford University.

SECURITY INTERESTS IN PERSONAL PROPERTY (1985) (Reprinted from Sales and Sales Financing, Fifth Edition)

John Honnold, Professor of Law, University of Pennsylvania.

SENTENCING AND THE CORRECTIONAL PROCESS, Second Edition (1976)

Frank W. Miller, Professor of Law, Washington University.
Robert O. Dawson, Professor of Law, University of Texas.
George E. Dix, Professor of Law, University of Texas.
Raymond I. Parnas, Professor of Law, University of California, Davis.

SOCIAL RESPONSIBILITIES OF LAWYERS, Case Studies (1988)

Philip B. Heymann, Professor of Law, Harvard University.
Lance Liebman, Professor of Law, Harvard University.

SOCIAL SCIENCE IN LAW, Cases and Materials (1985)

John Monahan, Professor of Law, University of Virginia.
Laurens Walker, Professor of Law, University of Virginia.

TAX, POLICY ANALYSIS OF THE FEDERAL INCOME (1976)

William A. Klein, Professor of Law, University of California, Los Angeles.

TAXATION, FEDERAL INCOME (1989)

Stephen B. Cohen, Professor of Law, Georgetown University

TAXATION, FEDERAL INCOME, Second Edition (1988)

Michael J. Graetz, Professor of Law, Yale University.

TAXATION, FEDERAL INCOME, Sixth Edition (1987)

James J. Freeland, Professor of Law, University of Florida.
Stephen A. Lind, Professor of Law, University of Florida and University of California, Hastings.
Richard B. Stephens, Professor of Law Emeritus, University of Florida.

TAXATION, FEDERAL INCOME, Successor Edition (1986), with 1988 Legislative Supplement

Stanley S. Surrey, late Professor of Law, Harvard University.
Paul R. McDaniel, Professor of Law, Boston College.
Hugh J. Ault, Professor of Law, Boston College.
Stanley A. Koppelman, Professor of Law, Boston University.

TAXATION, FEDERAL INCOME, VOLUME II, Taxation of Partnerships and Corporations, Second Edition (1980), with 1988 Legislative Supplement

Stanley S. Surrey, late Professor of Law, Harvard University.
William C. Warren, Professor of Law Emeritus, Columbia University.
Paul R. McDaniel, Professor of Law, Boston College.
Hugh J. Ault, Professor of Law, Boston College.

TAXATION, FEDERAL WEALTH TRANSFER, Successor Edition (1987)

Stanley S. Surrey, late Professor of Law, Harvard University.
Paul R. McDaniel, Professor of Law, Boston College.
Harry L. Gutman, Professor of Law, University of Pennsylvania.

UNIVERSITY CASEBOOK SERIES—Continued

TAXATION, FUNDAMENTALS OF CORPORATE, Second Edition (1987)

Stephen A. Lind, Professor of Law, University of Florida and University of California, Hastings.
Stephen Schwarz, Professor of Law, University of California, Hastings.
Daniel J. Lathrope, Professor of Law, University of California, Hastings.
Joshua Rosenberg, Professor of Law, University of San Francisco.

TAXATION, FUNDAMENTALS OF PARTNERSHIP, Second Edition (1988)

Stephen A. Lind, Professor of Law, University of Florida and University of California, Hastings.
Stephen Schwarz, Professor of Law, University of California, Hastings.
Daniel J. Lathrope, Professor of Law, University of California, Hastings.
Joshua Rosenberg, Professor of Law, University of San Francisco.

TAXATION, PROBLEMS IN THE FEDERAL INCOME TAXATION OF PARTNER-SHIPS AND CORPORATIONS, Second Edition (1986)

Norton L. Steuben, Professor of Law, University of Colorado.
William J. Turnier, Professor of Law, University of North Carolina.

TAXATION, PROBLEMS IN THE FUNDAMENTALS OF FEDERAL INCOME, Second Edition (1985)

Norton L. Steuben, Professor of Law, University of Colorado.
William J. Turnier, Professor of Law, University of North Carolina.

TAXES AND FINANCE—STATE AND LOCAL (1974)

Oliver Oldman, Professor of Law, Harvard University.
Ferdinand P. Schoettle, Professor of Law, University of Minnesota.

TORT LAW AND ALTERNATIVES, Fourth Edition (1987)

Marc A. Franklin, Professor of Law, Stanford University.
Robert L. Rabin, Professor of Law, Stanford University.

TORTS, Eighth Edition (1988)

William L. Prosser, late Professor of Law, University of California, Hastings.
John W. Wade, Professor of Law, Vanderbilt University.
Victor E. Schwartz, Adjunct Professor of Law, Georgetown University.

TORTS, Third Edition (1976)

Harry Shulman, late Dean of the Law School, Yale University.
Fleming James, Jr., Professor of Law Emeritus, Yale University.
Oscar S. Gray, Professor of Law, University of Maryland.

TRADE REGULATION, Second Edition (1983), with 1987 Supplement

Milton Handler, Professor of Law Emeritus, Columbia University.
Harlan M. Blake, Professor of Law, Columbia University.
Robert Pitofsky, Professor of Law, Georgetown University.
Harvey J. Goldschmid, Professor of Law, Columbia University.

TRADE REGULATION, see Antitrust

TRANSNATIONAL BUSINESS PROBLEMS (1986)

Detlev F. Vagts, Professor of Law, Harvard University.

TRANSNATIONAL LEGAL PROBLEMS, Third Edition (1986) with Documentary Supplement

Henry J. Steiner, Professor of Law, Harvard University.
Detlev F. Vagts, Professor of Law, Harvard University.

TRIAL, see also Evidence, Making the Record, Lawyering Process and Preparing and Presenting the Case

TRUSTS, Fifth Edition (1978)

George G. Bogert, late Professor of Law Emeritus, University of Chicago.
Dallin H. Oaks, President, Brigham Young University.

TRUSTS AND SUCCESSION (Palmer's), Fourth Edition (1983)

Richard V. Wellman, Professor of Law, University of Georgia.
Lawrence W. Waggoner, Professor of Law, University of Michigan.
Olin L. Browder, Jr., Professor of Law, University of Michigan.

UNFAIR COMPETITION, see Competitive Process and Business Torts

UNITED NATIONS LAW, Second Edition (1967), with Documentary Supplement (1968)

Louis B. Sohn, Professor of Law, Harvard University.

WATER RESOURCE MANAGEMENT, Third Edition (1988)

Charles J. Meyers, Esq., Denver, Colorado, formerly Dean, Stanford University Law School.
A. Dan Tarlock, Professor of Law, II Chicago-Kent College of Law.
James N. Corbridge, Jr., Chancellor, University of Colorado at Boulder, and Professor of Law, University of Colorado School of Law.
David H. Getches, Professor of Law, University of Colorado School of Law.

WILLS AND ADMINISTRATION, Fifth Edition (1961)

Philip Mechem, late Professor of Law, University of Pennsylvania.
Thomas E. Atkinson, late Professor of Law, New York University.

WORLD LAW, see United Nations Law

WRITING AND ANALYSIS IN THE LAW (1989)

Helene S. Shapo, Professor of Law, Northwestern University
Marilyn R. Walter, Professor of Law, Brooklyn Law School
Elizabeth Fajans, Writing Specialist, Brooklyn Law School

FEDERAL COURTS

AND

THE LAW OF FEDERAL–STATE RELATIONS

SECOND EDITION

By

PETER W. LOW
Hardy Cross Dillard Professor of Law
and John V. Ray Research Professor of Law,
University of Virginia

and

JOHN CALVIN JEFFRIES, JR.
Emerson Spies Professor of Law,
University of Virginia

Westbury, New York
THE FOUNDATION PRESS, INC.
1989

615 Merrick Ave.
Westbury, N.Y. 11590

Library of Congress Cataloging-in-Publication Data

Low, Peter W., 1937–
    Federal courts and the law of federal-state relations / by Peter W.
Low and John Calvin Jeffries, Jr. — 2nd ed.
        p.   cm. — (University casebook series)
    ISBN 0–88277–708–4
    1. Courts—United States—Cases. 2. Judicial power—United
States—Cases. 3. Jurisdiction—United States—Cases. 4. Federal
government—United States—Cases. 5. Conflict of laws—Jurisdiction—
United States—Cases. 6. State action (Civil rights)—United States—
Cases. I. Jeffries, John Calvin, 1948– . II. Title. III. Series.
KF8735.A7L69 1989
347.73'2—dc19
[347.3072]   88–36762
                                                                     CIP

∞

PREFACE

The content of this book was described in the Preface to the first edition:

> Two inquiries dominate this book. First, what are the respective spheres of state and federal law? Second, what are the conditions of access to the federal courts?

> In developing these themes, we have tried not only to provide modern materials for the study of federal courts, but also, to an extent, to present a new agenda. Specifically, we have de-emphasized the traditional intersection with procedure and designed the materials on diversity and federal question jurisdiction with an eye to economy of coverage. We have taken the same approach to some of the technical details of appellate jurisdiction. We deal more fully with the choice between state or federal law and provide the opportunity to examine the use of federal common law in a variety of contexts. We also cover in some detail such traditional topics as the case or controversy limitation, the powers of Congress to limit access to state and federal courts, and Supreme Court review of state court decisions. Most importantly, we have explored at length what we take to be the two most important structures of modern federalism—federal habeas corpus and federal civil rights actions under 42 U.S.C. § 1983. A separate chapter on the 11th amendment is included because of its importance to litigation under § 1983.

These interests have not changed. The only organizational innovation of the second edition is a separate chapter (Ch. IV) on private rights of action. This seemed warranted by the continuing stream of interesting and controversial decisions in the field. Otherwise, the revisions consist chiefly of adding recent decisions—six as new main cases, many more briefly noted and described. We have made every effort to avoid simply adding these decisions to existing materials. Instead, we have tried to integrate the new developments, often with corresponding reduction of older materials, so as to maintain manageability.

As with the first edition, we have presented these subjects in a way to facilitate flexibility of coverage. Not only is there the usual opportunity to select among topics, but individual topics are presented in a way that preserves the option of doing more or doing less. Often the notes following a case are grouped under two or more headings. This is a signal that the separate sets of notes can be assigned or omitted separately.

A good example of this technique is the organization of the materials on standing. The core of our coverage is *Allen v. Wright* and the set of notes immediately following (pages 13–38). One could plausibly stop there. Or one could add the notes on taxpayer standing (pages 39–48), or the notes on standing under federal statutes (pages 48–52), or both. Third-party standing is treated in *Singleton v. Wulff* and the accompanying notes (pages 52–64), which also can be covered or omitted at the instructor's option. Thus, the standing materials invite brief or extensive coverage, as the instructor desires.

Finally, matters of form are dealt with as in the first edition. All citations are conformed to our usage, which is standard save that we omit citations to subsequent history, such as certiorari or rehearing denied. Many citations have been omitted without specific indication, but the deletion of anything more than bare citation to authority is indicated by brackets or ellipses. The original footnote numbers have been retained in all excerpted materials; footnotes by the editors are lettered rather than numbered.

PERMISSION TO DUPLICATE

There are many intersections between this book and its companion volume, Civil Rights Actions: Section 1983 and Related Statutes (Foundation Press, 1988). Occasionally, a teacher using one book may wish to use material from the other or from an annual supplement designed for the other book.

We wish to facilitate such borrowings whenever they would be helpful. To that end, we authorize teachers who have adopted either the Federal Courts book or the Civil Rights book to duplicate limited portions of the other, or of a supplement designed for use with the other, for distribution to their students in a course for which the students are assigned one of the two books.

We are grateful to The Foundation Press, Inc., for agreeing to make this option possible.

PWL
JCJjr

Charlottesville, Virginia
February, 1989

SUMMARY OF CONTENTS

APPENDICES

*

TABLE OF CONTENTS

CHAPTER IV: IMPLIED RIGHTS OF ACTION

CHAPTER V: DISTRICT COURT JURISDICTION

CHAPTER VII: FEDERAL HABEAS CORPUS

CHAPTER VIII: STATE SOVEREIGN IMMUNITY AND THE 11TH AMENDMENT

CHAPTER X: ABSTENTION IN CIVIL RIGHTS CASES

APPENDICES

TABLE OF CONTENTS

TABLE OF CASES

Principal cases are in italic type. Non-principal cases are in roman type. References are to Pages.

TABLE OF SECONDARY AUTHORITIES

References are to Pages.

ABA Project on Standards for Criminal Justice, The Prosecution Function and Defense Function § 5.2, pp. 237–38 (Approved Draft 1971)—p. 762.

Abrams, Reserved Water Rights, Indian Rights and the Narrowing Scope of Federal Jurisdiction: The *Colorado River* Decision, 30 Stan. L. Rev. 1111 (1978)—p. 558.

Adams, The Court of Appeals for the Federal Circuit: More than a National Patent Court, 49 Mo. L. Rev. 43 (1984)—p. C–5.

Albert, Justiciability and Theories of Judicial Review: A Remote Relationship, 50 So. Cal. L. Rev. 1139 (1977)—p. 38.

Albert, Standing to Challenge Administrative Action: An Inadequate Surrogate for Claim for Relief, 83 Yale L.J. 425 (1974)—p. 38.

Aleinikoff, Cover and, Dialectical Federalism: Habeas Corpus and the Court, 86 Yale L. J. 1305 (1977)—pp. 749, 775.

Alsup, Reservations on the Proposal of the Hruska Commission to Establish a National Court of Appeals, 7 U. Tol. L. Rev. 431 (1976)—p. C–7.

Althouse, How to Build a Separate Sphere: Federal Courts and State Power, 100 Harv.L.Rev. 1485 (1987)—pp. 627, 878.

Amar, Of Sovereignty and Federalism, 96 Yale L.J. 1425 (1987)—pp. 245, 804.

American Law Institute, Study of the Division of Jurisdiction Between State and Federal Courts (1969)—pp. 446, 471, 487.

American Law Institute, Study of the Division of Jurisdiction Between State and Federal Courts, Proposed Final Draft No. 1 §§ 1301(b)(2) and 1302(b) (1965)—p. 464.

Amsterdam, Criminal Prosecutions Affecting Federally Guaranteed Civil Rights: Federal Removal and Habeas Corpus Jurisdiction to Abort State Court Trial, 113 U. Pa. L. Rev. 793 (1965)—pp. 579, 591.

Amsterdam, Search, Seizure, and Section 2255: A Comment, 112 U. Pa. L. Rev. 378 (1964)—p. 725.

Arnold, The Power of State Courts to Enjoin Federal Officers, 73 Yale L.J. 1385 (1964)—pp. 246, 247.

Arnold, State Power to Enjoin Federal Court Proceedings, 51 Va. L. Rev. 59 (1965)—p. 250.

Atwood, The Choice-of-Law Dilemma in Mass Tort Litigation: Kicking Around *Erie, Klaxon,* and *Dusen,* 19 Conn.L.Rev. 9 (1986)—p. 362.

Atwood, Domestic Relations Cases in Federal Court: Toward a Principled Exercise of Jurisdiction, 35 Hastings L.J. 571 (1984)—p. 470.

Atwood, State Court Judgments in Federal Litigation: Mapping the Contours of Full Faith and Credit, 58 Ind. L.J. 59 (1982)—p. 1060.

Baker, The Ambiguous Independent and Adequate State Grounds in Criminal Cases: Federalism Along a Mobius Strip, 19 Ga. L. Rev. 799 (1985)—p. 627.

Baker, Hill and, Dam Federal Jurisdiction!, 32 Emory L. J. 1 (1983)—p. 38.

Baker and McFarland, Commentary, The Need for a New National Court, 100 Harv.L.Rev. 1400 (1987)—p. C–7.

Bandes, *Monell, Parratt, Daniels, and Davidson:* Distinguishing a Custom or Policy from a Random, Unauthorized Act, 72 Iowa L.Rev. 101 (1986)—pp. 988, 1009.

Baron, The Evolution of Domestic Relations Cases in Our Federal Courts, 1985 S.Ill.U.L.J. 353 (1985)—p. 470.

Bartels, Avoiding a Comity of Errors: A Model for Adjudicating Federal Civil Rights Suits That "Interfere" with State Civil Proceedings, 29 L. Rev. 27 (1976)—p. 1236.

Bartke, "Finality" Four Years Later—Some Reflections and Recommendations, 9 Baylor L. Rev. 350 (1976)—p. 684.

Batey, Federal Habeas Corpus Relief and the Death Penalty: "Finality with a Capital F," 36 U. Fla. L. Rev. 252 (1984)—p. 799.

Bator, Congressional Power Over the Jurisdiction of the Federal Courts, 72 Vill. L. Rev. 1030 (1982)—pp. 165, 199, 200.

Bator, Finality in Criminal Law and Federal Habeas Corpus for State Prisoners, 76 Harv. L. Rev. 441 (1963)—pp. 728, 738.

FEDERAL COURTS

AND

THE LAW OF
FEDERAL–STATE
RELATIONS

*

Chapter I

THE FEDERAL JUDICIAL POWER

SECTION 1: JUDICIAL REVIEW

MARBURY v. MADISON
Supreme Court of the United States, 1803.
5 U.S. (1 Cranch) 137.

The following opinion of the Court was delivered by the Chief Justice:

At the last term on the affidavits then read and filed with the clerk, a rule was granted in this case, requiring the Secretary of State to show cause why a mandamus should not issue, directing him to deliver to William Marbury his commission as a justice of the peace for the county of Washington, in the District of Columbia.

No cause has been shown, and the present motion is for a mandamus. The peculiar delicacy of this case, the novelty of some of its circumstances, and the real difficulty attending the points which occur in it, require a complete exposition of the principles on which the opinion to be given by the Court is founded.

These principles have been, on the side of the applicant, very ably argued at the bar. In rendering the opinion of the Court, there will be some departure in form, though not in substance, from the points stated in that argument.

In the order in which the Court has viewed this subject, the following questions have been considered and decided:

1st. Has the applicant a right to the commission he demands?

2d. If he has a right, and that right has been violated, do the laws of this country afford him a remedy?

3d. If they do afford him a remedy, is it a mandamus issuing from this Court?

The first object of inquiry is, 1st. Has the applicant a right to the commission he demands?

His right originates in an act of Congress passed in February 1801, concerning the District of Columbia. . . .

It appears, from the affidavits, that in compliance with this law, a commission for William Marbury as a justice of the peace for the county of Washington, was signed by John Adams, then President of the United States; after which the seal of the United States was affixed

1

to it; but the commission has never reached the person for whom it was made out. . . .

It is . . . decidedly the opinion of the Court, that when a commission has been signed by the President, the appointment is made; and that the commission is complete, when the seal of the United States has been affixed to it by the Secretary of State. . . .

Mr. Marbury, then, since his commission was signed by the President and sealed by the Secretary of State, was appointed; and as the law creating the office, gave the officer a right to hold for five years, independent of the executive, the appointment was not revocable, but vested in the officer legal rights, which are protected by the laws of his country.

To withhold his commission, therefore, is an act deemed by the Court not warranted by law, but violative of a vested legal right.

This brings us to the second inquiry; which is, 2dly. If he has a right, and that right has been violated, do the laws of his country afford him a remedy?

The very essence of civil liberty certainly consists in the right of every individual to claim the protection of the laws, whenever he receives an injury. One of the first duties of government is to afford that protection. . . .

The government of the United States has been emphatically termed a government of laws, and not of men. It will certainly cease to deserve this high appellation, if the laws furnish no remedy for the violation of a vested legal right.

If this obloquy is to be cast on the jurisprudence of our country, it must arise from the peculiar character of the case.

It behooves us then to enquire whether there be in its composition any ingredient which shall exempt it from legal investigation, or exclude the injured party from legal redress. . . .

Is it in the nature of the transaction? Is the act of delivering or withholding a commission to be considered as a mere political act, belonging to the executive department alone, for the performance of which entire confidence is placed by our Constitution in the supreme executive; and for any misconduct respecting which, the injured individual has no remedy.

That there may be such cases is not to be questioned; but that every act of duty, to be performed in any of the great departments of government, constitutes such a case, is not to be admitted. . . .

It follows, then, that the question, whether the legality of an act of the head of a department be examinable in a court of justice or not, must always depend on the nature of that act. . . .

By the Constitution of the United States, the President is invested with certain important political powers, in the exercise of which he is to use his own discretion, and is accountable only to his country in his political character, and to his conscience. To aid him in the performance of these duties, he is authorized to appoint certain officers, who act by his authority and in conformity with his orders.

In such cases, their acts are his acts; and whatever opinion may be entertained of the manner in which executive discretion may be used, still there exists, and can exist, no power to control that discretion. The subjects are political. They respect the nation, not individual rights, and being entrusted to the executive, the decision of the executive is conclusive. . . .

But when the legislature proceeds to impose on that officer other duties; when he is directed peremptorily to perform certain acts; when the rights of individuals are dependent on the performance of those acts; he is so far the officer of the law; is amenable to the laws for his conduct; and cannot at his discretion sport away the vested rights of others.

The conclusion from this reasoning is, that where the heads of departments are the political or confidential agents of the executive, merely to execute the will of the President, or rather to act in cases in which the executive professes a constitutional or legal discretion, nothing can be more perfectly clear than that their acts are only politically examinable. But where a specific duty is assigned by law, and individual rights depend upon the performance of that duty, it seems equally clear, that the individual who considers himself injured, has a right to resort to the laws of his country for a remedy. . . .

It is, then, the opinion of the Court [that Marbury has a] right to the commission; a refusal to deliver which is a plain violation of that right, for which the laws of his country afford him a remedy.

It remains to be enquired whether,

3dly. He is entitled to the remedy for which he applies. This depends on,

1st. The nature of the writ applied for, and, 2dly. The power of this Court. . . .

[T]o render the mandamus a proper remedy, the officer to whom it is to be directed, must be one to whom, on legal principles, such writ may be directed; and the person applying for it must be without any other specific and legal remedy. . . .

With respect to the officer to whom it would be directed. The intimate political relation, subsisting between the President of the United States and the heads of the departments, necessarily renders any legal investigation of the acts of one of those high officers peculiarly irksome, as well as delicate; and excites some hesitation with respect to the propriety of entering into such investigation. Impressions are often received without much reflection or examination, and it is not wonderful, that in such a case as this, the assertion, by an indvidual, of his legal claims in a court of justice, to which claims it is the duty of that court to attend, should at first view be considered by some, as an attempt to intrude into the cabinet, and to intermeddle with the prerogatives of the executive.

It is scarcely necessary for the Court to disclaim all pretensions to such a jurisdiction. An extravagance, so absurd and excessive, could not have been entertained for a moment. The province of the Court is, solely, to decide on the rights of individuals, not to enquire how the executive, or executive officers, perform duties in which they have a discretion. Questions in their nature political, or which are, by the Constitution and laws, submitted to the executive, can never be made in this Court.

But if this be not such a question; . . . what is there in the exalted station of the officer, which shall bar a citizen from asserting, in a court of justice, his legal rights, or shall forbid a court to listen to the claim; or to issue a mandamus, directing the performance of a duty, not depending on executive discretion, but on particular acts of Congress and the general principles of law? . . .

It is not by the office of the person to whom the writ is directed, but the nature of the thing to be done that the propriety or impropriety of issuing a mandamus, is to be determined. Where the head of a department acts in a case, in which executive discretion is to be exercised; in which he is the mere organ of executive will; it is again repeated, that any application to a court to control, in any respect, his conduct, would be rejected without hesitation.

But where he is directed by law to do a certain act affecting the absolute rights of individuals, in the performance of which he is not placed under the particular direction of the President, and the performance of which, the President cannot lawfully forbid, and therefore is never presumed to have forbidden; as for example, to record a commission, or a patent for land, which has received all the legal solemnities; or to give a copy of such record; in such cases, it is not perceived on what ground the courts of the country are further excused from the duty of giving judgment, that right be done to an injured individual, than if the same services were to be performed by a person not the head of a department. . . .

This, then, is a plain case for a mandamus, either to deliver the commission, or a copy of it from the record; and it only remains to be enquired,

Whether it can issue from this Court.

The act to establish the judicial courts of the United States authorizes the Supreme Court "to issue writs of mandamus in cases warranted by the principles and usages of law, to any courts appointed, or persons holding office, under the authority of the United States." [a]

---

[a] Section 13 of the Judiciary Act of 1789 provided:

"And be it further enacted, That the Supreme Court shall have exclusive jurisdiction of all controversies of a civil nature, where a state is a party, except between a state and its citizens; and except also between a state and citizens of other states, or aliens, in which later case it shall have original but not exclusive jurisdiction. And shall have exclusively all such jurisdiction of suits or proceedings against ambassadors, or other public ministers, or their domestics, or domestic servants, as a court of law can have or exercise consistently with the law of nations; and original, but not exclusive jurisdiction of all suits brought

The Secretary of State, being a person holding an office under the authority of the United States, is precisely within the letter of the description; and if this Court is not authorized to issue a writ of mandamus to such an officer, it must be because the law is unconstitutional, and therefore absolutely incapable of conferring the authority, and assigning the duties which its words purport to confer and assign.

The Constitution vests the whole judicial power of the United States in one Supreme Court, and such inferior courts as Congress shall, from time to time, ordain and establish. This power is expressly extended to all cases arising under the laws of the United States; and, consequently, in some form, may be exercised over the present case; because the right claimed is given by a law of the United States.

In the distribution of this power it is declared that "the Supreme Court shall have original jurisdiction in all cases affecting ambassadors, other public ministers and consuls, and those in which a state shall be a party. In all other cases, the Supreme Court shall have appellate jurisdiction."

It has been insisted, at the bar, that as the original grant of jurisdiction, to the supreme and inferior courts, is general, and the clause, assigning original jurisdiction to the Supreme Court, contains no negative or restrictive words, the power remains to the legislature, to assign original jurisdiction to that Court in other cases than those specified in the article which has been recited; provided those cases belong to the judicial power of the United States.

If it had been intended to leave it in the discretion of the legislature to apportion the judicial power between the supreme and inferior courts according to the will of that body, it would certainly have been useless to have proceeded further than to have defined the judicial power, and the tribunals in which it should be vested. The subsequent part of the section is mere surplusage, is entirely without meaning, if such is to be the construction. If Congress remains at liberty to give this Court appellate jurisdiction, where the Constitution has declared their jurisdiction shall be original; and original jurisdiction where the Constitution has declared it shall be appellate; the distribution of jurisdiction, made in the Constitution, is form without substance.

Affirmative words are often, in their operation, negative of other objects than those affirmed; and in this case, a negative or exclusive sense must be given to them or they have no operation at all.

by ambassadors, or other public ministers, or in which a consul, or vice consul, shall be a party. And the trial of issues of fact in the Supreme Court, in all actions at law against citizens of the United States, shall be by jury. The Supreme court shall also have appellate jurisdiction from the circuit courts and courts of the several states, in the cases hereinafter specially provided for; and shall have power to issue writs of prohibition to the district courts, when proceeding as courts of admiralty and maritime jurisdiction, and writs of mandamus, in cases warranted by the principles and usages of law, to any courts appointed, or persons holding office, under the authority of the United States." [Footnote by eds.]

It cannot be presumed that any clause in the Constitution is intended to be without effect; and, therefore, such a construction is inadmissible, unless the words require it.

If the solicitude of the convention, respecting our peace with foreign powers, induced a provision that the Supreme Court should take original jurisdiction in cases which might be supposed to affect them; yet the clause would have proceeded no further than to provide for such cases, if no further restriction on the powers of Congress had been intended. That they should have appellate jurisdiction in all other cases, with such exceptions as Congress might make, is no restriction; unless the words be deemed exclusive of original jurisdiction.

When an instrument organizing fundamentally a judicial system, divides into one supreme, and so many inferior courts as the legislature may ordain and establish; then enumerates its powers, and proceeds so far to distribute them, as to define the jurisdiction of the Supreme Court by declaring the cases in which it shall take original jurisdiction, and that in others it shall take appellate jurisdiction; the plain import of the words seems to be, that in one class of cases its jurisdiction is original, and not appellate; in the other it is appellate, and not original. If any other construction would render the clause inoperative, that is an additional reason for rejecting such other construction, and for adhering to their obvious meaning.

To enable this Court, then, to issue a mandamus, it must be shown to be an exercise of appellate jurisdiction, or to be necessary to enable them to exercise appellate jurisdiction.

It has been stated at the bar that the appellate jurisdiction may be exercised in a variety of forms, and that if it be the will of the legislature a mandamus should be used for that purpose, that will must be obeyed. This is true, yet the jurisdiction must be appellate, not original.

It is the essential criterion of appellate jurisdiction, that it revises and corrects the proceedings in a cause already instituted, and does not create that cause. Although, therefore, a mandamus may be directed to courts, yet to issue such a writ to an officer for the delivery of a paper, is in effect the same as to sustain an original action for that paper, and, therefore, seems not to belong to appellate, but to original jurisdiction. Neither is it necessary in such a case as this, to enable the Court to exercise its appellate jurisdiction.

The authority, therefore, given to the Supreme Court, by the act establishing the judicial courts of the United States, to issue writs of mandamus to public officers, appears not to be warranted by the Constitution; and it becomes necessary to enquire whether a jurisdiction, so conferred, can be exercised.

The question, whether an act, repugnant to the Constitution, can become the law of the land, is a question deeply interesting to the United States; but, happily, not of an intricacy proportioned to its interest. It seems only necessary to recognize certain principles, supposed to have been long and well established, to decide it.

That the people have an original right to establish, for their future government, such principles as, in their opinion, shall most conduce to their own happiness, is the basis on which the whole American fabric has been erected. The exercise of this original right is a very great exertion; nor can it, nor ought it, to be frequently repeated. The principles, therefore, so established, are deemed fundamental. And as the authority from which they proceed is supreme and can seldom act, they are designed to be permanent.

This original and supreme will organizes the government, and assigns to different departments their respective powers. It may either stop here, or establish certain limits not to be transcended by those departments.

The government of the United States is of the latter description. The powers of the legislature are defined and limited; and that those limits may not be mistaken, or forgotten, the Constitution is written. To what purpose are powers limited, and to what purpose is that limitation committed to writing, if these limits may, at any time, be passed by those intended to be restrained? The distinction between a government with limited and unlimited powers is abolished, if those limits do not confine the persons on whom they are imposed, and if acts prohibited and acts allowed, are of equal obligation. It is a proposition too plain to be contested, that the Constitution controls any legislative act repugnant to it; or, that the legislature may alter the Constitution by an ordinary act.

Between these alternatives there is no middle ground. The Constitution is either a superior, paramount law, unchangeable by ordinary means, or it is on a level with ordinary legislative acts, and, like other acts, is alterable when the legislature shall please to alter it.

If the former part of the alternative be true, then a legislative act contrary to the Constitution is not law: if the latter part be true, then written constitutions are absurd attempts, on the part of the people, to limit a power in its own nature illimitable.

Certainly all those who have framed written constitutions contemplate them as forming the fundamental and paramount law of the nation, and consequently, the theory of every such government must be, that an act of the legislature, repugnant to the Constitution, is void.

This theory is essentially attached to a written constitution, and is, consequently, to be considered, by this Court, as one of the fundamental principles of our society. It is not therefore to be lost sight of in the further consideration of this subject.

If an act of the legislature, repugnant to the Constitution, is void, does it, notwithstanding its invalidity, bind the courts, and oblige them to give it effect? Or, in other words, though it be not law, does it constitute a rule as operative as if it was a law? This would be to overthrow in fact what was established in theory; and would seem, at first view, an absurdity too gross to be insisted on. It shall, however, receive a more attentive consideration.

It is emphatically the province and duty of the judicial department to say what the law is. Those who apply the rule to particular cases, must of necessity expound and interpret that rule. If two laws conflict with each other, the courts must decide on the operation of each.

So if a law be in opposition to the Constitution; if both the law and the Constitution apply to a particular case, so that the court must either decide that case conformably to the law, disregarding the Constitution; or conformably to the Constitution, disregarding the law; the court must determine which of these conflicting rules governs the case. This is of the very essence of judicial duty.

If, then, the courts are to regard the Constitution, and the Constitution is superior to any ordinary act of the legislature, the Constitution, and not such ordinary act, must govern the case to which both apply.

Those then who controvert the principle that the Constitution is to be considered, in court, as a paramount law, are reduced to the necessity of maintaining that courts must close their eyes on the Constitution, and see only the law.

This doctrine would subvert the very foundation of all written constitutions. It would declare that an act which, according to the principles and theory of our government, is entirely void, is yet, in practice, completely obligatory. It would declare that if the legislature shall do what is expressly forbidden, such act, notwithstanding the express prohibition, is in reality effectual. It would be giving to the legislature a practical and real omnipotence, with the same breath which professes to restrict their powers within narrow limits. It is prescribing limits, and declaring that those limits may be passed at pleasure.

That it thus reduces to nothing what we have deemed the greatest improvement on political institutions—a written constitution—would of itself be sufficient, in America, where written constitutions have been viewed with so much reverence, for rejecting the construction. But the peculiar expressions of the Constitution of the United States furnish additional arguments in favour of its rejection.

The judicial power of the United States is extended to all cases arising under the Constitution.

Could it be the intention of those who gave this power, to say that in using it the Constitution should not be looked into? That a case arising under the Constitution should be decided without examining the instrument under which it arises?

This is too extravagant to be maintained.

In some cases, then, the Constitution must be looked into by the judges. And if they can open it at all, what part of it are they forbidden to read or to obey?

There are many other parts of the Constitution which serve to illustrate this subject. It is declared that "no tax or duty shall be laid on articles exported from any state." Suppose a duty on the export of cotton, of tobacco, or of flour; and a suit instituted to recover it. Ought judgment to be rendered in such a case? Ought the judges to close their eyes on the Constitution and see only the law?

The Constitution declares that "no bill of attainder or ex post facto law shall be passed."

If, however, such a bill should be passed, and a person should be prosecuted under it; must the court condemn to death those victims whom the Constitution endeavors to preserve?

"No person," says the Constitution, "shall be convicted of treason unless on the testimony of two witnesses to the same overt act, or on confession in open court."

Here the language of the Constitution is addressed especially to the courts. It prescribes, directly for them, a rule of evidence not to be departed from. If the legislature should change that rule, and declare *one* witness, or a confession *out* of court, sufficient for conviction, must the constitutional principle yield to the legislative act?

From these, and many other selections which might be made, it is apparent, that the framers of the Constitution contemplated that instrument as a rule for the government of *courts,* as well as of the legislature.

Why otherwise does it direct the judges to take an oath to support it? This oath certainly applies, in an especial manner, to their conduct in their official character. How immoral to impose it on them, if they were to be used as the instruments, and the knowing instruments, for violating what they swear to support!

That oath of office, too, imposed by the legislature, is completely demonstrative of the legislative opinion on this subject. It is in these words: "I do solemnly swear that I will administer justice without respect to persons, and do equal right to the poor and to the rich; and that I will faithfully and impartially discharge all the duties incumbent on me as _____, according to the best of my abilities and understanding, agreeably to *the Constitution,* and laws of the United States."

Why does a judge swear to discharge his duties agreeably to the Constitution of the United States, if that Constitution forms no rule for his government? If it is closed upon him, and cannot be inspected by him?

If such be the real state of things, this is worse than solemn mockery. To prescribe, or to take this oath, becomes equally a crime.

It is also not entirely unworthy of observation that in declaring what shall be the *supreme* law of the land, the *Constitution* itself is first mentioned; and not the laws of the United States generally, but those only which shall be made in *pursuance* of the Constitution, have that rank.

Thus, the particular phraseology of the Constitution of the United States confirms and strengthens the principle, supposed to be essential to all written constitutions, that a law repugnant to the Constitution is void; and that *courts,* as well as other departments, are bound by that instrument.

The rule must be discharged.

NOTES ON *MARBURY v. MADISON*

1. **The Meaning of *Marbury.*** *Marbury* can be read "more or less imperialistically"[a] in its claim of power for the judicial branch. William Van Alstyne, author of A Critical Guide to *Marbury v. Madison*,[b] addresses this issue by identifying three possible "specifications" of the holding of the case.

At its narrowest, *Marbury* could be limited to the kind of "defensive" use of judicial review actually presented by its facts:

> "In litigation before the Supreme Court, the Court may refuse to give effect to an act of Congress where the act pertains to the judicial power itself. In deciding whether to give effect to such an act, the Court may determine its decision according to its own interpretation of constitutional provisions which describe the judicial power."

So described, *Marbury* seeks only to "maintain the Court as a coordinate branch of government" and thus draws "considerable support from the concept of *separated* powers."[c]

Perhaps *Marbury* could have stopped there, but in fact it said much more. Nothing in the text of Marshall's opinion, at least, appears to limit the assertion of the power of judicial review to such a "defensive" context. Perhaps for this reason, a second and broader reading of *Marbury* has come to be generally accepted:

> "In litigation before the Supreme Court, the Court may refuse to give effect to an act of Congress where, in the Court's own view, that act is repugnant to the Constitution."

By this view, *Marbury* stands for the proposition that it is the responsibility of the Supreme Court—and presumably all courts—to apply the Constitution as the "supreme law of the land" to all cases properly presented for decision. Courts may not, in other words, decide cases by the application of principles that offend constitutional limitations.

[a] The phrase is from P. Brest and S. Levinson, Processes of Constitutional Decisionmaking 107 (2d ed. 1983).

[b] 1969 Duke L.J. 1. Van Alstyne's article includes a brief statement of the historical context of the case, a close textual analysis of the opinion, and a selection of excerpts on the legitimacy of judicial review. Also excellent, and widely available, is the review of these issues in G. Gunther, Constitutional Law 10–29 (11th ed. 1985). Those desiring a more detailed exposition of the historical context may consult D. Dewey, Marshall v. Jefferson: The Political Background of *Marbury v. Madison* (1970).

[c] It should be noted that the precise ruling in *Marbury* that Congress may not add to the original jurisdiction of the Supreme Court remains good law. But Marshall's suggestion that Congress also may not confer appellate jurisdiction over cases within the Court's original jurisdiction has been specifically disapproved. See Ames v. Kansas, 111 U.S. 449 (1884).

This view of *Marbury* stops considerably short of the most expansive reading of the opinion. Some read the case as an assertion of "judicial supremacy." Under this view, it is the responsibility of courts, and ultimately the Supreme Court, to provide authoritative interpretations of the Constitution and to ensure the enforcement of constitutional values. Van Alstyne notes that nothing in *Marbury* compels the view that "the only interpretation of the Constitution which all branches of the national government must employ is the interpretation which the Court may provide in the course of litigation." Yet this claim is often made, sometimes by the Supreme Court itself. In Cooper v. Aaron, 358 U.S. 1, 18 (1958), for example, the Court reviewed *Marbury* and announced that:

> "This decision declared the basic principle that the federal judiciary is supreme in the exposition of the law of the Constitution, and that principle has ever since been respected by this Court and the country as a permanent and indispensable feature of our constitutional system."

The same view was taken by Chief Justice Warren in Powell v. McCormack, 395 U.S. 486, 549 (1969) (which appears as a main case at page 95, infra), where he cites *Marbury* in support of the proposition that "it is the responsibility of this Court to act as the ultimate interpreter of the Constitution."

2. Implications of *Marbury*. The second and third of these interpretations of *Marbury* may seem at first only slightly different, but in fact the choice between them is consequential. Many issues of contemporary significance turn, at least in part, on one's view of the meaning of *Marbury*. Is the Supreme Court merely authorized, in deciding cases properly before it, to disregard laws found to conflict with the Constitution? Or is the Court justified in creating for itself a special role as the ultimate and supreme expositor of constitutional principles? These questions arise at numerous points in the materials to follow.

The distinction is important, for example, in the law of standing and in related doctrines of justiciability. If *Marbury* means merely that the Court may consider the Constitution in resolving cases properly before it, there should be no occasion for regret if a constitutional claim is not decided because it is not presented—and perhaps cannot be presented—in the format of a traditional lawsuit. Under narrower readings of *Marbury*, courts are properly concerned with deciding *cases*, not *issues*. If, however, the judiciary enjoys a special role as the ultimate expositor of the Constitution, it may be appropriate for it to ensure that occasions exist for the exercise of that responsibility. If no conventionally appropriate lawsuit can be filed, the courts may be moved to redefine the nature of a constitutional "case" or "controversy" in order that the issue may be heard.[d]

[d] In fact, the Court has from time to time espoused both of these views, as is recounted at pages 13–95, infra, in the materials on standing, ripeness, and mootness.

The meaning of *Marbury* is also relevant to the "political question" doctrine. Chief Justice Marshall said in *Marbury* that, "Questions in their nature political, *or* which are, by the Constitution and laws, submitted to the executive, can never be made in this Court." [Emphasis added.] Does that mean that the courts can properly decline to hear questions that are in some sense "political," even if they are not, by law, committed to the determination of another branch? This position may be hard to square with the view that the power of judicial review is entirely incident to the judicial duty to decide cases according to law. It may, perhaps, more easily be reconciled with the view that the judiciary has a broad (and ultimately political) responsibility to expound constitutional principles. In this broader frame of reference, it may be necessary for the Court to choose its ground. In some situations, the Court may wish to withhold constitutional pronouncements for reasons of political unacceptability. The desirability and legitimacy of such discretion depend in part on one's conception of the nature of judicial review—an inquiry that begins with the opinion in *Marbury*. [e]

One more illustration will suffice. Congress has repeatedly debated the limits on its powers to control the jurisdiction of the Supreme Court and other federal courts. On its face, art. III speaks directly to this question. The appellate jurisdiction of the Supreme Court is subject to "such Exceptions . . . as the Congress may make." And since the implementation of a system of lower federal courts appears to have been left to Congressional discretion, Congress would seem to have complete control over the jurisdiction to be exercised by lower federal courts. An oft-expressed fear is that Congress might seek to influence constitutional adjudication by confining certain classes of cases to state courts. This possibility is, perhaps, not a problem under a narrow reading of *Marbury*. The judicial duty to decide the case at hand in accordance with law is not directly impaired by restrictions on jurisdiction. In contrast, Congressional authority to eliminate a class of cases from the jurisdiction of the Supreme Court obviously could undermine the role of that body as the final and supreme authority on the Constitution. And combined with Congressional authority to eliminate cases from the lower federal courts, the ability of Congress to influence the outcome of constitutional controversies could be complete. One's view of the reach of the Congressional power to eliminate cases from the jurisdiction of the Supreme Court and the lower federal courts thus may depend in part on how the *Marbury* decision is interpreted. [f]

In these and in many other respects, the meaning of *Marbury* remains a live issue today. Its implications lie just beneath the surface of many of the problems considered in this book.

---

[e] Interestingly, the Court itself has from time to time espoused each of these positions, as is recounted more fully at pages 95–112, infra, in the materials on the political question.

[f] The issues raised by these possibilities are examined in more detail at pages 167–208, infra, in materials on congressional control over federal court jurisdiction.

SECTION 2: CASE OR CONTROVERSY

SUBSECTION A: STANDING

INTRODUCTORY NOTE ON STANDING

Traditionally, the law of standing required the plaintiff to show that some "legal interest" had been invaded by the defendant. Put in this way, the issue of standing tended to merge with the merits; standing to sue was subsumed in the question whether the plaintiff had a cause of action for redress of injury to a legally protected interest.

The modern law of standing is, at bottom, a response to changes that have occurred in the objectives that can be accomplished by litigation. No longer is litigation simply a method of resolving disputes between private parties. Today, it is often seen as a vehicle for participating in the governance of the nation. This is especially true of suits challenging the constitutionality of government behavior. Although accomplished within the forms of ordinary litigation, such lawsuits are often importantly different in scope and content. The characteristics of this new kind of lawsuit and its departures from the classical model are summarized in Chayes, Foreword: Public Law Litigation and the Burger Court, 96 Harv. L. Rev. 4, 4–5 (1982):*

"In the classical model, litigation is viewed as a mode of dispute settlement. The dispute is between private parties, and it concerns the consequences of the parties' actions for the legal relationships—rights and obligations—between them. This central focus on the dispute more or less determines the other basic elements of the traditional model. First, litigation is bipolar; two parties are locked in a confrontational, winner-take-all controversy. Second, the process is retrospective, directed to determining the legal consequences of a closed set of past events. Third, right and remedy are linked in a close, mutually defining logical relationship. Fourth, the lawsuit is a self-contained entity. It is bounded in time: judicial involvement ends with the determination of the disputed issues. It is bounded in effect: the impact is limited to the (two) parties before the court. Finally, the whole process is party initiated and party controlled. The judge is passive, a neutral umpire.

. . .

"In the contemporary model, the subject matter of the litigation is not a dispute between private parties, but a grievance about the content or conduct of policy—most often gov-

* Copyright © 1982 by the Harvard Law Review Association. Reprinted with permission of the author and the publication.

ernmental policy, but frequently the policy of nongovernmental aggregates. Again, this characteristic dictates the main features of the litigation. First, the party structure and the matters in controversy are both amorphous, defined ad hoc as the proceedings unfold rather than exogenously determined by legal theories and concepts. Second, the temporal orientation of the lawsuit is prospective rather than historical. Third, because the relief sought looks to the future and is corrective rather than compensatory, it is not derived logically from the rights asserted. Instead, it is fashioned ad hoc, usually by a quasi-negotiating process. Fourth, prospective relief implies continuing judicial involvement. And because the relief is directed at government or corporate policies, it will have a direct impact that extends far beyond the immediate parties to the lawsuit."[a]

The origins of this development cannot be fully canvassed here, but a few factors may be noted:

First, there has been an explosion in the recognition of constitutional rights. The natural by-product has been proliferation of plausible legal theories that can be used to test the validity of government action.

Second, shifts in the manner in which government power is exercised have led to the rise of the administrative state. Typically, administrative agencies are empowered to act in a quasi-legislative manner. Courts, feeling the need to supervise agency power, have accorded review to persons adversely affected by agency action, even where there was no infringement of a traditional common-law interest. As Professor Monaghan put it: "Standing as a constitutional limitation on the exercise of judicial power simply could not survive the onset of the administrative agencies once the courts assumed the task of limiting the agencies' power." Monaghan, Constitutional Adjudication: The Who and When, 82 Yale L.J. 1363, 1381 (1973).

Third, the protracted process of school desegregation educated many judges to the mechanisms of continuing judicial supervision of state and local governments. In many ways, school desegregation suits became the prototype for a new style of litigation, which could then be adapted to other contexts.

Finally, the development of the class action as an effective vehicle for representing group or collective interests facilitated large-scale litigation leading to system-wide judicial relief.

Whatever the causes, by the 1960's a new style of lawsuit—Chayes calls it "public law litigation"—had developed. Such lawsuits were designed to coerce systemic reform or curtailment of government actions, and they created a potential nation of plaintiffs. It therefore

[a] These views are elaborated in Chayes, The Role of the Judge in Public Law Litigation, 89 Harv. L. Rev. 1281 (1976).

became increasingly important to decide who had the power to bring such suits. As Chayes pointed out:

> "The ability to bring such lawsuits is ultimately the ability to elicit judicial pronouncements on the public policies and values implicated in the challenged official actions. Limitations on standing thus translate into limitations on the power of the courts, or at least on the occasions for its exercise." Chayes, Foreword: Public Law Litigation and the Burger Court, 96 Harv. L. Rev. 4, 9–10 (1982).

In the last few decades, therefore, the Supreme Court has become increasingly concerned with issues of standing. Its pronouncements on that subject have not been altogether consistent, but in recent cases, the Court seems to have settled on the rather elaborate rendition of standing doctrine recounted in *Allen v. Wright,* the next main case. The law of standing is said to be a blend of constitutional and prudential considerations.[b] The constitutional minimum derives from the art. III limitation of the judicial power to "cases" and "controversies" and comprises two distinct requirements. First, the plaintiff must have suffered an injury, either actual or threatened. Second, the injury must satisfy the closely related requirements of being "fairly" traceable to the defendant's conduct and "likely" to be redressed by a favorable decision.

ALLEN v. WRIGHT

Supreme Court of the United States, 1984.
468 U.S. 737.

JUSTICE O'CONNOR delivered the opinion of the Court.

Parents of black public school children allege in this nationwide class action that the Internal Revenue Service (IRS) has not adopted sufficient standards and procedures to fulfill its obligation to deny tax-exempt status to racially discriminatory private schools. They assert that the IRS thereby harms them directly and interferes with the ability of their children to receive an education in desegregated public schools. The issue before us is whether plaintiffs have standing to bring this suit. . . . We hold that they do not.

I

The Internal Revenue Service denies tax-exempt status under §§ 501(a) and (c)(3) of the Internal Revenue Code—and hence eligibility to receive charitable contributions deductible from income taxes under §§ 170(a)(1) and (c)(2) of the Code—to racially discriminatory private schools. Rev.Rul. 71–447, 1972–2 Cum. Bull. 230.[1] The IRS policy

---

[b] Perhaps the most important prudential concern is the bar against litigating the rights of another. This subject is considered in connection with *Singleton v. Wulff,* which appears as a main case at page 52, infra.

[1] As the Court explained last term in Bob Jones University v. United States, 461

requires that a school applying for tax-exempt status show that it "admits the students of any race to all the rights, privileges, programs, and activities generally accorded or made available to students at that school and that the school does not discriminate on the basis of race in administration of its educational policies, admissions policies, scholarship and loan programs, and athletic and other school-administered programs." To carry out this policy, the IRS has established guidelines and procedures for determining whether a particular school is in fact racially nondiscriminatory. Rev. Proc. 75–50, 1975–6 Cum. Bull. 587. Failure to comply with the guidelines "will ordinarily result in the proposed revocation of" tax-exempt status.

The guidelines provide that "[a] school must show affirmatively both that it has adopted a racially nondiscriminatory policy as to students that is made known to the general public and that since the adoption of that policy it has operated in a bona fide manner in accordance therewith." The school must state its nondiscrimination policy in its organizational charter, and in all of its brochures, catalogues, and other advertisements to prospective students. The school must make its nondiscrimination policy known to the entire community served by the school and must publicly disavow any contrary representations made on its behalf once it becomes aware of them. The school must have nondiscriminatory policies concerning all programs and facilities, including scholarships and loans, and the school must annually certify, under penalty of perjury, compliance with these requirements.

The IRS rules require a school applying for tax-exempt status to give a breakdown along racial lines of its student body and its faculty and administrative staff, as well as of scholarships and loans awarded. They also require the applicant school to state the year of its organization, and to list "incorporators, founders, board members, and donors of land or buildings," and state whether any of the organizations among these have an objective of maintaining segregated public or private school education. The rules further provide that, once given an exemption, a school must keep specified records to document the extent of compliance with the IRS guidelines. Finally, the rules announce that any information concerning discrimination at a tax-exempt school is officially welcomed.

In 1976 respondents challenged these guidelines and procedures in a suit filed in federal District Court against the Secretary of the Treasury and the Commissioner of Internal Revenue. The plaintiffs named in the complaint are parents of black children who, at the time the complaint was filed, were attending public schools in seven states in school districts undergoing desegregation. They brought this nation-

U.S. 574, 577–79 (1983), the IRS announced this policy in 1970 and formally adopted it in 1971. This change in prior policy was prompted by litigation over tax exemptions for racially discriminatory private schools in the state of Mississippi, litigation that resulted in the entry of an injunction against the IRS largely if not entirely coextensive with the position the IRS had voluntarily adopted. Green v. Connally, 330 F.Supp. 1150 (D.D.C.), summarily aff'd sub nom. Coit v. Green, 404 U.S. 997 (1971) (entering permanent injunction).

wide class action "on behalf of themselves and their children, and . . . on behalf of all other parents of black children attending public school systems undergoing, or which may in the future undergo, desegregation pursuant to court order [or] HEW regulations and guidelines, under state law, or voluntarily." They estimated that the class they seek to represent includes several million persons.

Respondents allege in their complaint that many racially segregated private schools were created or expanded in their communities at the time the public schools were undergoing desegregation. According to the complaint, many such private schools, including 17 schools or school systems identified by name in the complaint (perhaps some 30 schools in all), receive tax exemptions either directly or through the tax-exempt status of "umbrella" organizations that operate or support the schools. Respondents allege that, despite the IRS policy of denying tax-exempt status to racially discriminatory private schools and despite the IRS guidelines and procedures for implementing that policy, some of the tax-exempt racially segregated private schools created or expanded in desegregating districts in fact have racially discriminatory policies. Respondents allege that the IRS grant of tax exemptions to such racially discriminatory schools is unlawful.

Respondents allege that the challenged government conduct harms them in two ways. The challenged conduct

"(a) constitutes tangible federal financial aid and other support for racially segregated educational institutions, and

"(b) fosters and encourages the organization, operation and expansion of institutions providing racially segregated educational opportunities for white children avoiding attendance in desegregating public school districts and thereby interferes with the efforts of federal courts, HEW and local school authorities to desegregate public school districts which have been operating racially dual school systems."

Thus, respondents do not allege that their children have been the victims of discriminatory exclusion from the schools whose tax exemptions they challenge as unlawful. Indeed, they have not alleged at any stage of this litigation that their children have ever applied or would ever apply to any private school. Rather, respondents claim a direct injury from the mere fact of the challenged government conduct and, as indicated by the restriction of the plaintiff class to parents of children in desegregating school districts, injury to their children's opportunity to receive a desegregated education. The latter injury is traceable to the IRS grant of tax exemptions to racially discriminatory schools, respondents allege, chiefly because contributions to such schools are deductible from income taxes . . . and the "deductions facilitate the raising of funds to organize new schools and expand existing schools in order to accommodate white students avoiding attendance in desegregating public school districts."

Respondents request only prospective relief. They ask for a declaratory judgment that the challenged IRS tax-exemption practices are unlawful. They also ask for an injunction requiring the IRS to deny tax exemptions to a considerably broader class of private schools than the class of racially discriminatory private schools. Under the requested injunction, the IRS would have to deny tax-exempt status to all private schools

> "which have insubstantial or non-existent minority enrollments, which are located in or serve desegregating public school districts, and which either—
>
> "(1) were established or expanded at or about the time the public school district in which they are located or which they serve were desegregating;
>
> "(2) have been determined in adversary judicial or administrative proceedings to be racially segregated; or
>
> "(3) cannot demonstrate that they do not provide racially segregated educational opportunities for white children avoiding attendance in desegregating public school systems."

Finally, respondents ask for an order directing the IRS to replace its 1975 guidelines with standards consistent with the requested injunction.

In May 1977 the District Court permitted intervention as a defendant by petitioner Allen, the head of one of the private school systems identified in the complaint. Thereafter, progress in the lawsuit was stalled for several years. During this period, the Internal Revenue Service reviewed its challenged policies and proposed new Revenue Procedures to tighten requirements for eligibility for tax-exempt schools. In 1979, however, Congress blocked any strengthening of the IRS guidelines at least until October 1980.[16] The District Court thereupon considered and granted the defendants' motion to dismiss the complaint, concluding that respondents lack standing, that the judicial task proposed by respondents is inappropriately intrusive for a federal court, and that awarding the requested relief would be contrary to the will of Congress expressed in the 1979 ban on strengthening the IRS guidelines.

The United States Court of Appeals for the District of Columbia reversed, concluding that respondents have standing to maintain this lawsuit. . . . The Court of Appeals also held that the 1979 congressional actions were not intended to preclude judicial remedies and that

---

[16] Section 615 of the act, known as the Dornan amendment, specifically forbade the use of funds to carry out the IRS's proposed Revenue Procedures. Section 103 of the act, known as the Ashbrook amendment, more generally forbade the use of funds to make the requirements for tax-exempt status of private schools more stringent than those in effect prior to the IRS's proposal of its new Revenue Procedures.

These provisions expired on October 1, 1980, but [the] Dornan and Ashbrook amendments were reinstated for the period December 16, 1980, through September 30, 1981. For fiscal year 1982, Congress specifically denied funding for carrying out not only administrative actions but also court orders entered after the date of the IRS's proposal of its first revised Revenue Procedure. No such spending restrictions are currently in force.

the relief requested by respondents could be fashioned "without large scale judicial intervention in the administrative process." . . .

We granted certiorari and now reverse.

II

A

Article III of the Constitution confines the federal courts to adjudicating actual "cases" and "controversies." As the Court [has] explained . . ., the "case or controversy" requirement defines with respect to the judicial branch the idea of separation of powers on which the federal government is founded. The several doctrines that have grown up to elaborate that requirement are "founded in concern about the proper— and properly limited—role of the courts in a democratic society." Warth v. Seldin, 422 U.S. 490, 498 (1975).

> "All of the doctrines that cluster about art. III—not only standing but mootness, ripeness, political question, and the like—relate in part, and in different though overlapping ways, to an idea, which is more than an intuition but less than a rigorous and explicit theory, about the constitutional and prudential limits to the powers of an unelected, unrepresentative judiciary in our kind of government." Vander Jagt v. O'Neill, 699 F.2d 1166, 1178–79 (D.C.Cir. 1982) (Bork, J., concurring).

The case-or-controversy doctrines state fundamental limits on federal judicial power in our system of government.

The art. III doctrine that requires a litigant to have "standing" to invoke the power of a federal court is perhaps the most important of these doctrines. "In essence the question of standing is whether the litigant is entitled to have the court decide the merits of the dispute or of particular issues." *Warth v. Seldin,* supra, at 498. Standing doctrine embraces several judicially self-imposed limits on the exercise of federal jurisdiction, such as the general prohibition on a litigant's raising another person's legal rights, the rule barring adjudication of generalized grievances more appropriately addressed in the representative branches, and the requirement that a plaintiff's complaint fall within the zone of interests protected by the law invoked. The requirement of standing, however, has a core component derived directly from the Constitution. A plaintiff must allege personal injury fairly traceable to the defendant's allegedly unlawful conduct and likely to be redressed by the requested relief.

Like the prudential component, the constitutional component of standing doctrine incorporates concepts concededly not susceptible of precise definition. The injury alleged must be, for example, " 'distinct and palpable,' " and not "abstract" or "conjectural" or "hypothetical." The injury must be "fairly" traceable to the challenged action, and relief from the injury must be "likely" to follow from a favorable decision. See Simon v. Eastern Kentucky Welfare Rights Org., 426 U.S. 26, 38 (1976).

The absence of precise definitions, however, as this Court's extensive body of case law on standing illustrates, hardly leaves courts at sea in applying the law of standing. Like most legal notions, the standing concepts have gained considerable definition from developing case law. In many cases the standing question can be answered chiefly by comparing the allegations of the particular complaint to those made in prior standing cases. More important, the law of art. III standing is built on a single basic idea—the idea of separation of powers. It is this fact which makes possible the gradual clarification of the law through judicial application. Of course, both federal and state courts have long experience in applying and elaborating in numerous contexts the pervasive and fundamental notion of separation of powers.

Determining standing in a particular case may be facilitated by clarifying principles or even clean rules developed in prior cases. Typically, however, the standing inquiry requires careful judicial examination of a complaint's allegations to ascertain whether the particular plaintiff is entitled to an adjudication of the particular claims asserted. Is the injury too abstract, or otherwise not appropriate, to be considered judicially cognizable? Is the line of causation between the illegal conduct and injury too attenuated? Is the prospect of obtaining relief from the injury as a result of a favorable ruling too speculative? These questions and any others relevant to the standing inquiry must be answered by reference to the art. III notion that federal courts may exercise power only "in the last resort, and as a necessity," and only when adjudication is "consistent with a system of separated powers and [the dispute is one] traditionally thought to be capable of resolution through the judicial process." Flast v. Cohen, 392 U.S. 83, 97 (1968).

B

Respondents allege two injuries in their complaint to support their standing to bring this lawsuit. First, they say that they are harmed directly by the mere fact of government financial aid to discriminatory private schools. Second, they say that the federal tax exemptions to racially discriminatory private schools in their communities impair their ability to have their public schools desegregated. . . . We conclude that neither suffices to support respondents' standing. The first fails under clear precedents of this Court because it does not constitute judicially cognizable injury. The second fails because the alleged injury is not fairly traceable to the assertedly unlawful conduct of the IRS.

1

Respondents' first claim of injury can be interpreted in two ways. It might be a claim simply to have the government avoid the violation of law alleged in respondents' complaint. Alternatively, it might be a claim of stigmatic injury, or denigration, suffered by all members of a racial group when the government discriminates on the basis of race.[20] Under neither interpretation is this claim of injury judicially cognizable.

This Court has repeatedly held that an asserted right to have the government act in accordance with law is not sufficient, standing alone, to confer jurisdiction on a federal court. In Schlesinger v. Reservists Committee to Stop the War, 418 U.S. 208 (1974), for example, the Court rejected a claim of citizen standing to challenge Armed Forces Reserve commissions held by members of Congress as violating the incompatibility clause of art. I, § 6, cl. 2 of the Constitution. As citizens, the Court held, plaintiffs alleged nothing but "the abstract injury in nonobservance of the Constitution." . . . Respondents here have no standing to complain simply that their government is violating the law.

Neither do they have standing to litigate their claims based on the stigmatizing injury often caused by racial discrimination. There can be no doubt that this sort of noneconomic injury is one of the most serious consequences of discriminatory government action and is sufficient in some circumstances to support standing. Our cases make clear, however, that such injury accords a basis for standing only to "those persons who are personally denied equal treatment" by the challenged discriminatory conduct.

In Moose Lodge No. 107 v. Irvis, 407 U.S. 163 (1972), the Court held that the plaintiff had no standing to challenge a club's racially discriminatory membership policies because he had never applied for membership. In O'Shea v. Littleton, 414 U.S. 488 (1974), the Court held that the plaintiffs had no standing to challenge racial discrimination in the administration of their city's criminal justice system because they had not alleged that they had been or would likely be subject to the challenged practices. The Court denied standing on similar facts in Rizzo v. Goode, 423 U.S. 362 (1976). In each of those cases, the plaintiffs alleged official racial discrimination comparable to that alleged by respondents here. Yet standing was denied in each case because the plaintiffs were not personally subject to the challenged discrimination. Insofar as their first claim of injury is concerned, respondents are in exactly the same position . . . .

The consequences of recognizing respondents' standing on the basis of their first claim of injury illustrate why our cases plainly hold that such injury is not judicially cognizable. If the abstract stigmatic injury were cognizable, standing would extend nationwide to all members of the particular racial groups against which the government was alleged to be discriminating by its tax exemption to a racially discriminatory school, regardless of the location of that school. A black person in Hawaii could challenge the grant of a tax exemption to a racially discriminatory school in Maine. Recognition of standing in such circumstances would transform the federal courts into "no more than a vehicle for the vindication of the value interests of concerned bystand-

---

[20] [W]e assume, without deciding, that the challenged government tax exemptions are the equivalent of government discrimination.

ers." United States v. SCRAP, 412 U.S. 669, 687 (1973). Constitutional limits on the role of the federal courts preclude such a transformation.

2

It is in their complaint's second claim of injury that respondents allege harm to a concrete, personal interest that can support standing in some circumstances. The injury they identify—their children's diminished ability to receive an education in a racially integrated school—is, beyond any doubt, not only judicially cognizable but . . . one of the most serious injuries recognized in our legal system. Despite the constitutional importance of curing the injury alleged by respondents, however, the federal judiciary may not redress it unless standing requirements are met. In this case, respondents' second claim of injury cannot support standing because the injury alleged is not fairly traceable to the government conduct respondents challenge as unlawful.

The illegal conduct challenged by respondents is the IRS's grant of tax exemptions to some racially discriminatory schools. The line of causation between that conduct and desegregation of respondents' schools is attenuated at best. From the perspective of the IRS, the injury to respondents is highly indirect and "results from the independent action of some third party not before the court," *Simon v. Eastern Kentucky Welfare Rights Org.,* supra, at 42. . . .

The diminished ability of respondents' children to receive a desegregated education would be fairly traceable to unlawful IRS grants of tax exemptions only if there were enough racially discriminatory private schools receiving tax exemptions in respondents' communities for withdrawal of those exemptions to make an appreciable difference in public-school integration. Respondents have made no such allegation. It is, first, uncertain how many racially discriminatory private schools are in fact receiving tax exemptions. Moreover, it is entirely speculative, as respondents themselves conceded in the Court of Appeals, whether withdrawal of a tax exemption from any particular school would lead the school to change its policies. It is just as speculative whether any given parent of a child attending such a private school would decide to transfer the child to public school as a result of any changes in educational or financial policy made by the private school once it was threatened with loss of tax-exempt status. It is also pure speculation whether, in a particular community, a large enough number of the numerous relevant school officials and parents would reach decisions that collectively would have a significant impact on the racial composition of the public schools. . . .

The idea of separation of powers that underlies standing doctrine explains why our cases preclude the conclusion that respondents' alleged injury "fairly can be traced to the challenged action" of the IRS. That conclusion would pave the way generally for suits challenging, not specifically identifiable government violations of law, but the particular programs agencies establish to carry out their legal obligations. Such suits, even when premised on allegations of several instances of violations of law, are rarely if ever appropriate for federal-court adjudication.

> "Carried to its logical end, [respondents'] approach would have the federal courts as virtually continuing monitors of the wisdom and soundness of executive action; such a role is appropriate for the Congress acting through its committees and the 'power of the purse'; it is not the role of the judiciary, absent actual present or immediately threatened injury resulting from unlawful government action." Laird v. Tatum, 408 U.S. 1, 15 (1972).

The same concern for the proper role of the federal courts is reflected in cases like *O'Shea v. Littleton,* supra, *Rizzo v. Goode,* supra, and City of Los Angeles v. Lyons, 461 U.S. 95 (1983). In all three cases plaintiffs sought injunctive relief directed at certain statewide law enforcement practices. The Court held in each case that, absent an allegation of a specific threat of being subject to the challenged practices, plaintiffs had no standing to ask for an injunction. Animating this Court's holdings was the principle that "[a] federal court . . . is not the proper forum to press" general complaints about the way in which government goes about its business. Id. at 111–12.

Case-or-controversy considerations, the Court observed in *O'Shea v. Littleton,* supra, at 499, "obviously shade into those determining whether the complaint states a sound basis for equitable relief." The latter set of considerations should therefore inform our judgment about whether respondents have standing. Most relevant to this case is the principle articulated in *Rizzo v. Goode,* supra, at 378–79:

> "When a plaintiff seeks to enjoin the activity of a government agency . . . his case must contend with 'the well established rule that the government has traditionally been granted the widest latitude in the "dispatch of its own internal affairs." ' "

When transported into the art. III context, that principle, grounded as it is in the idea of separation of powers, counsels against recognizing standing in a case brought not to enforce specific legal obligations whose violation works a direct harm, but to seek a restructuring of the apparatus established by the executive branch to fulfill its legal duties. The Constitution, after all, assigns to the executive branch, and not to the judicial branch, the duty to "take Care that the Laws be faithfully executed." Art. II, § 3. We could not recognize respondents' standing in this case without running afoul of that structural principle.

C

The Court of Appeals relied for its contrary conclusion on Gilmore v. City of Montgomery, 417 U.S. 556 (1974), Norwood v. Harrison, 413 U.S. 455 (1973), and on Coit v. Green, 404 U.S. 997 (1971), summarily affirming Green v. Connally, 330 F.Supp. 1150 (D.D.C.). . . . None of these cases, however, requires that we find standing in this lawsuit.

In *Gilmore v. City of Montgomery,* supra, the plaintiffs asserted a constitutional right, recognized in an outstanding injunction, to use the city's public parks on a nondiscriminatory basis. They alleged that the city was violating that equal protection right by permitting racially discriminatory private schools and other groups to use the public parks. The Court recognized plaintiffs' standing to challenge this city policy insofar as the policy permitted the exclusive use of the parks by racially discriminatory private schools: the plaintiffs had alleged direct cognizable injury to their right to nondiscriminatory access to the public parks.

Standing in *Gilmore* thus rested on an allegation of direct deprivation of a right to equal use of the parks. . . . The *Gilmore* Court did not rest its finding of standing on an abstract denigration injury, and no problem of attenuated causation attended the plaintiffs' claim of injury.

In *Norwood v. Harrison,* supra, parents of public school children in Tunica County, Mississippi, filed a statewide class action challenging the state's provision of textbooks to students attending racially discriminatory private schools in the state. The Court held the state's practice unconstitutional because it breached "the state's acknowledged duty to establish a unitary school system." The Court did not expressly address the basis for the plaintiffs' standing.

In *Gilmore,* however, the Court identified the basis for standing in *Norwood* : "The plaintiffs in *Norwood* were parties to a school desegregation order and the relief they sought was directly related to the concrete injury they suffered." Through the school-desegregation decree, the plaintiffs had acquired a right to have the state "steer clear" of any perpetuation of the racially dual school system that it had once sponsored. The interest acquired was judicially cognizable because it was a personal interest, created by law, in having the state refrain from taking specific actions. The plaintiffs' complaint alleged that the state directly injured that interest by aiding racially discriminatory private schools. Respondents in this lawsuit, of course, have no injunctive rights against the IRS that are allegedly being harmed by the challenged IRS action.

Unlike *Gilmore* and *Norwood, Coit v. Green,* supra, cannot easily be seen to have based standing on an injury different in kind from any asserted by respondents here. The plaintiffs in *Coit,* parents of black school children in Mississippi, sued to enjoin the IRS grant of tax exemptions to racially discriminatory private schools in the state. Nevertheless, *Coit* in no way mandates the conclusion that respondents have standing.

First, the decision has little weight as a precedent on the law of standing. This Court's decision in *Coit* was merely a summary affirmance; for that reason alone it could hardly establish principles contrary to those set out in opinions issued after full briefing and argument. Moreover, when the case reached this Court, the plaintiffs and the IRS were no longer adverse parties; and the ruling that was summarily affirmed did not include a ruling on the issue of standing, which had been briefly considered in a prior ruling of the District Court. . . .

In any event, the facts in the *Coit* case are sufficiently different from those presented in this lawsuit that the absence of standing here is unaffected by the possible propriety of standing there. In particular, the suit in *Coit* was limited to the public schools of one state. Moreover, the District Court found, based on extensive evidence before it . . ., that large numbers of segregated private schools had been established in the state for the purpose of avoiding a unitary public school system; that the tax exemptions were critically important to the ability of such schools to succeed; and that the connection between the grant of tax exemptions to discriminatory schools and desegregation of the public schools in the particular state was close enough to warrant the conclusion that irreparable injury to the interest in desegregated education was threatened if the tax exemptions continued. What made possible those findings was the fact that, when the Mississippi plaintiffs filed their suit, the IRS had a policy of granting tax exemptions to racially discriminatory private schools; thus, the suit was initially brought, not simply to reform executive branch enforcement procedures, but to challenge a fundamental IRS policy decision, which affected numerous identifiable schools in the state of Mississippi.

The limited setting, the history of school desegregation in Mississippi at the time of the *Coit* litigation, the nature of the IRS conduct challenged at the outset of the litigation, and the District Court's particular findings, which were never challenged as clearly erroneous, amply distinguish the *Coit* case from respondents' lawsuit. Thus, we need not consider whether standing was properly found in *Coit*. Whatever the answer to that question, respondents' complaint, which aims at nationwide relief and does not challenge particular identified unlawful IRS actions, alleges no connection between the asserted desegregation injury and the challenged IRS conduct direct enough to overcome the substantial separation-of-powers barriers to a suit seeking an injunction to reform administrative procedures.

"The necessity that the plaintiff who seeks to invoke judicial power stand to profit in some personal interest remains an art. III requirement." *Simon v. Eastern Kentucky Welfare Rights Org.*, supra, at 39. Respondents have not met this fundamental requirement. The judgement of the Court of Appeals is accordingly reversed, and the injunction issued by that court is vacated.

JUSTICE MARSHALL took no part in the decision of this case.

JUSTICE BRENNAN, dissenting. . . .

One could hardly dispute the proposition that art. III of the Constitution, by limiting the judicial power to "cases" or "controversies," embodies the notion that each branch of our national government must confine its actions to those that are consistent with our scheme of separated powers. But simply stating that unremarkable truism provides little, if any, illumination of the standing inquiry that must be undertaken by a federal court faced with a particular action filed by particular plaintiffs. . . .

The Court's attempt to obscure the standing question must be seen, therefore, as no more than a cover for its failure to recognize the nature of the specific claims raised by the respondents in these cases. By relying on generalities concerning our tripartite system of government, the Court is able to conclude that the respondents lack standing to maintain this action without acknowledging the precise nature of the injuries they have alleged. In so doing, the Court displays a startling insensitivity to the historical role played by the federal courts in eradicating race discrimination from our nation's schools . . . . Because I cannot join in such misguided decisionmaking, I dissent.

I

The respondents, suing individually and on behalf of their minor children, are parents of black children attending public schools in various school districts across the nation. Each of these school districts, the respondents allege, was once segregated and is now in the process of desegregating pursuant to court order, federal regulations or guidelines, state law, or voluntary agreement. Moreover, each contains one or more private schools that discriminate against black school children and that operate with the assistance of tax exemptions unlawfully granted to them by the Internal Revenue Service (IRS).

To eliminate this federal financial assistance for discriminating schools, the respondents seek a declaratory judgment that current IRS practices are inadequate both in identifying racially discriminatory schools and in denying requested tax exemptions or revoking existing exemptions for any schools so identified. In particular, they allege that existing IRS guidelines permit schools to receive tax exemptions simply by adopting and certifying—but not implementing—a policy of nondiscrimination. Pursuant to these ineffective guidelines,[2] many private schools that discriminate on the basis of race continue to benefit illegally from their tax-exempt status and the resulting charitable deductions granted to taxpayers who contribute to such schools. The respondents therefore seek a permanent injunction requiring the IRS to deny tax exemptions [as set forth in the opinion of the Court]. The requested relief is substantially similar to the enforcement guidelines

---

[2] [W]e must accept as true the factual allegations made by the respondents. It nonetheless should be noted that significant evidence exists to support the respondents' claim that the IRS guidelines are ineffective. Indeed, the Commissioner of the IRS admitted as much in testimony before Congress:

"This litigation prompted the Service once again to review its procedures in this area. It focused our attention on the adequacy of existing policies and procedures as we moved to formulate a litigation position. *We concluded that the Service's procedures were ineffective in identifying schools which in actual operation discriminate against minority students,* even though the schools may profess an open enrollment policy and comply with the yearly publication requirements of Revenue Procedure 75–50." . . . Tax-Exempt Status of Private Schools: Hearings Before the Subcommittee on Oversight of the House Committee on Ways and Means, 96th Cong., 1st. Sess., 5 (1979) (statement of Jerome Kurtz, Commissioner of Internal Revenue) (emphasis added).

promulated by the IRS itself in 1978 and 1979, before congressional action temporarily stayed, and the agency withdrew, the amended procedures.

II

Persons seeking judicial relief from an art. III court must have standing to maintain their cause of action. At a minimum, the standing requirement is not met unless the plaintiff has "such a personal stake in the outcome of the controversy as to assure that concrete adverseness which sharpens the presentation of issues upon which the court so largely depends . . . ." Baker v. Carr, 369 U.S. 186, 204 (1962). Under the Court's cases, this "personal stake" requirement is satisfied if the person seeking redress has suffered, or is threatened with, some "distinct and palpable injury," and if there is some causal connection between the asserted injury and the conduct being challenged.

A

In these cases, the respondents have alleged at least one type of injury that satisfies the constitutional requirement of "distinct and palpable injury."[3] In particular, they claim that the IRS' grant of tax-exempt status to racially discriminatory private schools directly injures their children's opportunity and ability to receive a desegregated education. . . .

The Court acknowledges that this alleged injury is sufficient to satisfy constitutional standards. It does so only grudgingly, however, without emphasizing the significance of the harm alleged. Nonetheless, we have consistently recognized throughout the last 30 years that the deprivation of a child's right to receive an education in a desegregated school is a harm of special significance . . . .

B

Fully explicating the injury alleged helps to explain why it is fairly traceable to the government conduct challenged by the respondents. . . . Viewed in light of the injuries they claim, the respondents have alleged a direct causal relationship between the government action they challenge and the injury they suffer: their inability to receive an education in a racially integrated school is directly and adversely affected by the tax-exempt status granted by the IRS to racially discriminatory schools in their respective school districts. Common sense alone would recognize that the elimination of tax-exempt status for racially discriminatory private schools would serve to lessen the impact that those institutions have in defeating efforts to desegregate the public schools. . . .

[3] Because I conclude that the second injury alleged by the respondents is sufficient to satisfy constitutional requirements, I do not need to reach what the Court labels the "stigmatic injury." . . .

Moreover, the Court has previously recognized the existence, and constitutional significance, of such direct relationships between unlawfully segregated school districts and government support for racially discriminatory private schools in those districts. In Norwood v. Harrison, 413 U.S. 455 (1973), for example, we considered a Mississippi program that provided textbooks to students attending both public and private schools, without regard to whether any participating school had racially discriminatory policies. In declaring that program constitutionally invalid, we noted that "a state may not induce, encourage or promote private persons to accomplish what it is constitutionally forbidden to accomplish." We then spoke directly to the financial aid provided by the state textbook program and the constitutional rights asserted by the students and their parents:

> "The District Court laid great stress on the absence of a showing by appellants that 'any child enrolled in private school, if deprived of free textbooks, would withdraw from private school and subsequently enroll in the public schools.' . . . *We do not agree with the District Court in its analysis of the legal consequences of this uncertainty, for the Constitution does not permit the state to aid discrimination even when there is no precise causal relationship between state financial aid to a private school and the continued well-being of that school. A state may not grant the type of tangible financial aid here involved if that aid has a significant tendency to facilitate, reinforce, and support private discrimination.*" (Emphasis added.)

Thus, *Norwood* explicitly stands for the proposition that government aid to racially discriminatory schools is a direct impediment to school desegregation.

The Court purports to distinguish *Norwood* from the present litigation because " '[t]he plaintiffs in *Norwood* were parties to a school desegregation order' " and therefore "had acquired a right to have the state 'steer clear' of any perpetuation of the racially dual school system that it had once sponsored," whereas the "[r]espondents in this lawsuit . . . have no injunctive rights against the IRS that are allegedly being harmed." . . . Given that many of the school districts identified in the respondents' complaint have also been the subject of court-ordered integration, the standing inquiry in these cases should not differ. And, although, the respondents do not specifically allege that they are named parties to any outstanding desegregation orders, that is undoubtedly due to the passage of time since the orders were issued, and not to any difference in the harm they suffer.

Even accepting the relevance of the Court's distinction, moreover, that distinction goes to the injury suffered by the respective plaintiffs and not to the causal connection between the harm alleged and the governmental action challenged. The causal relationship existing in

Norwood between the alleged harm (i.e., interference with the plaintiffs' injunctive rights to a desegregated school system) and the challenged government action (i.e., free textbooks provided to racially discriminatory schools) is indistinguishable from the causal relationship existing in the present cases, unless the Court intends to distinguish the lending of textbooks from the granting of tax-exempt status. . . .[8]

Similarly, although entitled to less weight than a decision after full briefing and oral argument on the merits, our summary affirmance in Coit v. Green, 404 U.S. 997 (1971), is directly relevant to the standing of the respondents in this litigation. . . .

Given these precedents, the Court is forced to place primary reliance on our decision in Simon v. Eastern Kentucky Welfare Rights Org., 426 U.S. 26 (1976). In that case, the Court denied standing to plaintiffs who challenged an IRS revenue ruling that granted charitable status to hospitals even though they failed to operate to the extent of their financial ability when refusing medical services for indigent patients. The Court found that the injury alleged was not one "that fairly can be traced to the challenged action of the defendant." In particular, it was "purely speculative" whether the denial of access to hospital services alleged by the plaintiffs fairly could be traced to the government's grant of tax-exempt status to the relevant hospitals, primarily because hospitals were likely making their service decisions without regard to the tax implications.

Even accepting the correctness of the causation analysis included in that decision, however, it is plainly distinguishable from the case at hand. The respondents in this case do not challenge the denial of any service by a tax-exempt institution; admittedly, they do not seek access to racially discriminatory private schools. Rather, the injury they allege, and the injury that clearly satisfies constitutional requirements, is the deprivation to their children's opportunity and ability to receive an education in a racially integrated school district. This injury, as the Court admits, and as we have previously held in *Norwood v. Harrison,* is of a kind that is directly traceable to the governmental action being challenged. The relationship between the harm alleged and the governmental action cannot simply be deemed "purely speculative," as was the causal connection at issue in *Simon.* . . .

III

More than one commentator has noted that the causation component of the Court's standing inquiry is no more than a poor disguise for the Court's view of the merits of the underlying claims.[10] The Court today does nothing to avoid that criticism. What is most disturbing

---

[8] Our subsequent decision in Gilmore v. City of Montgomery, 417 U.S. 556 (1974), heavily relied on our decision in *Norwood.* . . .

[10] See, e.g., L. Tribe, American Constitutional Law § 3–21 (1978); Chayes, Foreword: Public Law Litigation and the Burger Court, 96 Harv. L. Rev. 1, 14–22 (1982); Nichol, Causation as a Standing Requirement: The Unprincipled Use of Judicial Restraint, 69 Ky. L.J. 185 (1980–81); Tushnet, The New Law of Standing: A Plea for Abandonment, 62 Corn. L. Rev. 663 (1977).

about today's decision, therefore, is not the standing analysis applied, but the indifference evidenced by the Court to the detrimental effects that racially segregated schools, supported by tax-exempt status from the federal government, have on the respondents' attempt to obtain an education in a racially integrated school system. I cannot join such indifference, and would give the respondents a chance to prove their case on the merits.

JUSTICE STEVENS, with whom JUSTICE BLACKMUN joins, dissenting.

Three propositions are clear to me: (1) respondents have adequately alleged "injury in fact"; (2) their injury is fairly traceable to the conduct that they claim to be unlawful; and (3) the "separation of powers" principle does not create a jurisdictional obstacle to the consideration of the merits of their claim.

I

Respondents, the parents of black school children, have alleged that their children are unable to attend fully desegregated schools because large numbers of white children in the areas in which respondents reside attend private schools which do not admit minority children. The Court, Justice Brennan, and I all agree that this is an adequate allegation of "injury in fact." . . .

II

In the final analysis, the wrong the respondents allege that the government has committed is to subsidize the exodus of white children from schools that would otherwise be racially integrated. The critical question in this case, therefore, is whether respondents have alleged that the government has created that kind of subsidy.

In answering that question, we must of course assume that respondents can prove what they have alleged. Furthermore, at this stage of the case we must put to one side all questions about the appropriateness of a nationwide class action. The controlling issue is whether the causal connection between the injury and the wrong has been adequately alleged.

. . . Only last term we explained the effect of . . . preferential [tax] treatment:

> "Both tax exemptions and tax deductibility are a form of subsidy that is administered through the tax system. A tax exemption has much the same effect as a cash grant to the organization of the amount of tax it would have to pay on its income. Deductible contributions are similar to cash grants of the amount of a portion of the individual's contributions."
> Regan v. Taxation With Representation of Washington, Inc., 461 U.S. 540, 544 (1983).

The purpose of this scheme, like the purpose of any subsidy, is to promote the activity subsidized . . . . If the granting of preferential tax treatment would "encourage" private segregated schools to conduct their "charitable" activities, it must follow that the withdrawal of the treatment would "discourage" them, and hence promote the process of desegregation.

We have held that when a subsidy makes a given activity more or less expensive, injury can fairly be traced to the subsidy for purposes of standing analysis because of the resulting increase or decrease in the ability to engage in the activity. Indeed, we have employed exactly this causation analysis in the same context at issue here—subsidies given private schools that practice racial discrimination. Thus, in Gilmore v. City of Montgomery, 417 U.S. 556 (1974), we easily recognized the causal connection between official policies that enhanced the attractiveness of segregated schools and the failure to bring about or maintain a desegregated public school system. Similarly, in Norwood v. Harrison, 413 U.S. 455 (1973), we concluded that the provision of textbooks to discriminatory private schools "has a significant tendency to facilitate, reinforce, and support private discrimination.". . .

This causation analysis is nothing more than a restatement of elementary economics: when something becomes more expensive, less of it will be purchased. . . . If racially discriminatory private schools lose the "cash grants" that flow from the operation of the statutes, the education they provide will become more expensive and hence less of their services will be purchased. [T]he withdrawal of the subsidy for segregated schools means the incentive structure facing white parents who seek such schools for their children will be altered. Thus, the laws of economics, not to mention the laws of Congress embodied in §§ 170 and 501(c)(3), compel the conclusion that the injury respondents have alleged—the increased segregation of their children's schools because of the ready availability of private schools that admit whites only—will be redressed if these schools' operations are inhibited through the denial of preferential tax treatment.

III

Considerations of tax policy, economics, and pure logic all confirm the conclusion that respondents' injury in fact is fairly traceable to the government's allegedly wrongful conduct. The Court therefore is forced to introduce the concept of "separation of powers" into its analysis. The Court writes that the separation of powers "explains why our cases preclude the conclusion" that respondents' injury is fairly traceable to the conduct they challenge.

The Court could mean one of three things by its invocation of the separation of powers. First, it could simply be expressing the idea that if the plaintiff lacks art. III standing to bring a lawsuit, then there is no "case or controversy" within the meaning of art. III and hence the matter is not within the area of responsibility assigned to the judiciary by the Constitution. . . . While there can be no quarrel with this proposition, in itself it provides no guidance for determining if the injury respondents have alleged is fairly traceable to the conduct they have challenged.

Second, the Court could be saying that it will require a more direct causal connection when it is troubled by the separation of powers implications of the case before it. That approach confuses the standing doctrine with the justiciability of the issues that respondents seek to raise. The purpose of the standing inquiry is to measure the plaintiff's stake in the outcome, not whether a court has the authority to provide it with the outcome it seeks. . . .

Thus, the " 'fundamental aspect of standing' is that it focuses primarily on the *party* seeking to get his complaint before the federal court rather than 'on the issues he wishes to have adjudicated,' " United States v. Richardson, 418 U.S. 166, 174 (1974) (emphasis in original). The strength of the plaintiff's interest in the outcome has nothing to do with whether the relief it seeks would intrude upon the prerogatives of other branches of government; the possibility that the relief might be inappropriate does not lessen the plaintiff's stake in obtaining that relief. If a plaintiff presents a nonjusticiable issue, or seeks relief that a court may not award, then its complaint should be dismissed for those reasons, and not because the plaintiff lacks a stake in obtaining that relief and hence has no standing. Imposing an undefined but clearly more rigorous standard for redressability for reasons unrelated to the causal nexus between the injury and the challenged conduct can only encourage undisciplined, ad hoc litigation, a result that would be avoided if the Court straightforwardly considered the justiciability of the issues respondents seek to raise, rather than using those issues to obfuscate standing analysis.

Third, the Court could be saying that it will not treat as legally cognizable injuries that stem from an administration decision concerning how enforcement resources will be allocated. This surely is an important point. Respondents do seek to restructure the IRS' mechanisms for enforcing the legal requirement that discriminatory institutions not receive tax-exempt status. Such restructuring would dramatically affect the way in which the IRS exercises its prosecutorial discretion. The executive requires latitude to decide how best to enforce the law, and in general the Court may well be correct that the exercise of that discretion, especially in the tax context, is unchallengeable.

However, as the Court also recognizes, this principle does not apply when suit is brought "to enforce specific legal obligations whose violation works a direct harm." . . . Here, respondents contend that the IRS is violating a specific constitutional limitation on its enforcement discretion. There is a solid basis for that contention. In *Norwood*, we wrote:

"A state's constitutional obligation requires it to steer clear, not only of operating the old dual system of racially segregated schools, but also of giving significant aid to institutions that practice racial or other invidious discrimination."

Gilmore echoed this theme:

"[A]ny tangible state assistance, outside the generalized services government might provide to private segregated schools in common with other schools, and with all citizens, is constitutionally prohibited if it has 'a significant tendency to facilitate, reinforce, and support private discrimination.' " . . .

Respondents contend that these cases limit the enforcement discretion enjoyed by the IRS. They establish, respondents argue, that the IRS cannot provide "cash grants" to discriminatory schools through preferential tax treatment without running afoul of a constitutional duty to refrain from "giving significant aid" to these institutions. Similarly, respondents claim that the Internal Revenue Code itself, as construed in Bob Jones University v. United States, 461 U.S. 574 (1983), constrains enforcement discretion.[12] It has been clear since Marbury v. Madison, 1 Cranch (5 U.S.) 137 (1803), that "[i]t is emphatically the province and duty of the judicial department to say what the law is." Deciding whether the Treasury has violated a specific legal limitation on its enforcement discretion does not intrude upon the prerogative of the executive, for in so deciding we are merely saying "what the law is." Surely the question whether the Constitution or the Code limits enforcement discretion is one within the judiciary's competence, and I do not believe that the question whether the law, as enunciated in *Gilmore, Norwood,* and *Bob Jones,* imposes such an obligation upon the IRS is so insubstantial that respondents' attempt to raise it should be defeated for lack of subject-matter jurisdiction on the ground that it infringes the executive's prerogatives.

In short, I would deal with the question of the legal limitations on the IRS' enforcement discretion on the merits, rather than by making the untenable assumption that the granting of preferential tax treatment to segregated schools does not make those schools more attractive to white students and hence does not inhibit the process of desegregation. I respectfully dissent.

NOTES ON STANDING AS A CONSTITUTIONAL REQUIREMENT

1. The Requirement of Injury: *Schlesinger v. Reservists Committee to Stop the War.* In Schlesinger v. Reservists Committee to Stop the War, 418 U.S. 208 (1974), the Reservists Committee and several of its members challenged the holding of Armed Forces Reserve commissions by members of Congress on the theory that the commissions violated the incompatibility clause.[a] The plaintiffs alleged that members of Congress who held such commissions might be subject to undue influence by the executive branch and therefore might not faithfully execute their legislative duties. The District Court found that the plaintiffs had standing to sue as citizens of the United States. The court acknowledged that the alleged injury was "hypothetical," but

---

[12] In *Bob Jones* we clearly indicated that the Internal Revenue Code not only permits but in fact requires the denial of tax-exempt status to racially discriminatory private schools . . . .

[a] Art. I, § 6, cl. 2 provides in part that "no Person holding any Office under the United States, shall be a Member of either House during his Continuance in Office."

concluded that it was precisely that potential injury, as distinct from any specific harm, that the incompatibility clause was designed to prevent. The court further found that the parties were genuinely adverse and ably represented. Finally, the District Court noted that if these plaintiffs could not raise this issue, "then as a practical matter no one can."

The Court of Appeals affirmed, but the Supreme Court reversed. "[S]tanding to sue," said Chief Justice Burger in his opinion for the Court,

> "may not be predicated upon an interest of the kind alleged here which is held in common by all members of the public, because of the necessarily abstract nature of the injury all citizens share. Concrete injury, whether actual or threatened, is that indispensable element of a dispute which serves in part to cast it in a form traditionally capable of judicial resolution. It adds the essential dimension of specificity to the dispute by requiring that the complaining party have suffered a particular injury caused by the action challenged as unlawful. This personal stake is what the Court has consistently held enables a complainant authoritatively to present to a court a complete perspective upon the adverse consequences flowing from the specific set of facts undergirding his grievance. Such authoritative presentations are an integral part of the judicial process, for a court must rely on the parties' treatment of the facts and claims before it to develop its rules of law. Only concrete injury presents the factual context within which a court, aided by parties who argue within the context, is capable of making decisions.

> "Moreover, when a court is asked to undertake constitutional adjudication, the most important and delicate of its responsibilities, the requirement of concrete injury further serves the function of insuring that such adjudication does not take place unnecessarily. This principle is particularly applicable here, where respondents seek an interpretation of a constitutional provision which has never before been construed by the federal courts. First, concrete injury removes from the realm of speculation whether there is a real need to exercise the power of judicial review in order to protect the interests of the complaining party. . . . Second, the discrete factual context within which the concrete injury occurred or is threatened insures the framing of relief no broader than required by the precise facts to which the court's ruling would be applied."

The Court found that none of the factors cited by the District Court warranted a different conclusion. It specifically rejected reliance on the absence of an alternative plaintiff: "The assumption that if respondents have no standing to sue, no one would have standing, is not a reason to find standing." Justices Douglas, Brennan, and Marshall dissented.

2. Questions and Comments on the Requirement of Injury.
The Court said in *Schlesinger* that standing "may not be predicated
upon an interest . . . which is held in common by all members of the
public." Why not? Did the Court mean that it is impossible for a
citizen to be harmed by the mere fact of government illegality? Or
only that this sort of injury somehow does not count?

What does it mean to say that a suit should be cast "in a form
traditionally capable of judicial resolution?" That an "essential dimension of specificity" was lacking? What kind of "authoritative presentation" did the Court think these plaintiffs unable to make? Do these
matters depend on the nature of the client's injury or on the skill and
dedication of counsel?

Consider also the Court's desire to avoid unnecessary constitutional
adjudication. Was the *Schlesinger* suit unnecessary because the plaintiffs were insufficiently injured? Or because the underlying constitutional provision was not sufficiently important to require a confrontation with the legislative branch?

Now consider the application of *Schlesinger* to *Allen v. Wright.*
Does it follow from *Schlesinger* that the first claim of injury was
inadequate? The entire Court agreed that the second claim of injury
was sufficient. What made it so? Is a cognizable injury that establishes standing the same thing as a legal right giving rise to a cause of
action? If so, why have a separate doctrine of standing?

**3. Questions and Comments on the Requirements of Causa-
tion and Redressability.** Justice Brennan stated in the text accompanying footnote 10 of his *Allen* dissent that "the causation component
of the Court's standing inquiry is no more than a poor disguise for the
Court's view of the merits of the underlying claim." Is Justice Brennan
right that the Court in effect decided these cases on the merits by
denying the plaintiffs the opportunity to prove their allegations? Or
does the requirement of causation perform some independent function?[b]

Consider also the allegations in *Norwood, Gilmore,* and *Coit,* all of
which are extensively discussed in the *Allen* opinions. How did *Allen*
differ from those cases?

[b] For another example of a demanding
approach to allegations of causation, see
Warth v. Seldin, 422 U.S. 490 (1975). The
case involved a claim that the zoning restrictions of a small bedroom community
near Rochester, N.Y., had made "practically and economically impossible" the construction of low-income housing. Plaintiffs
alleged that they wished to live in the
community in question and that *because* of
the zoning restrictions, they had been unable to find affordable housing there. Despite this allegation, the Court held that
the availability of affordable housing depended on intervening factors, such as the
willingness of third-parties to build affordable housing. The plaintiffs' description of
their finances suggested to the Court that
"their inability to reside in [the town] is
the consequence of the economics of the

housing market, rather than of [the town's]
illegal acts." Standing was therefore denied for insufficient allegation of causation. Justices Douglas, Brennan, White,
and Marshall dissented.

For a detailed examination of *Warth,* see
Broderick, The *Warth* Optional Standing
Doctrine: Return to Judicial Supremacy,
25 Cath. U.L. Rev. 467 (1976).

City of Los Angeles v. Lyons, 461 U.S. 95
(1983), is also frequently cited on the causation and redressability elements of
standing. For a comprehensive analysis
that locates *Lyons* in a broader context and
explores its implications for the law of
standing, see Fallon, Of Justiciability,
Remedies, and Public Law Litigation:
Notes on the Jurisprudence of *Lyons,* 59
N.Y.U.L. Rev. 1 (1984).

Finally, note that the Court's statement of the proper standing analysis in part IIA of its *Allen* opinion is that the plaintiff must allege a "personal injury" that is "fairly traceable to the defendant's allegedly unlawful conduct" and that is "likely to be redressed by the requested relief." What does the last requirement add? If causation is lacking, should it suffice that the injury can be redressed by the requested relief?

4. *Duke Power.* Duke Power Co. v. Carolina Environmental Study Group, Inc., 438 U.S. 59 (1978), concerned the constitutionality of the Price-Anderson Act, which imposes an aggregate limit on utility company liability for a nuclear accident. Originally enacted in 1957, the statute was designed to encourage the development of nuclear power by protecting the industry against the uninsurable risk of catastrophic liability in the event of nuclear mishap.

Two environmental organizations and some 40 individuals sued the Duke Power Co. and the Nuclear Regulatory Commission seeking, among other relief, a declaration that the Price-Anderson Act was unconstitutional. The District Court upheld plaintiffs' standing and found the act unconstitutional on two grounds: first, because it violated due process by allowing injuries to occur without assuring adequate compensation to the victims; and, second, because it violated the equal protection component of the fifth amendment by forcing accident victims to bear the burden of injury when society as a whole benefitted from nuclear power. On direct appeal, the Supreme Court affirmed as to standing, but reversed on the merits.

Speaking through Chief Justice Burger, the Court first held that the complaint stated a cause of action over which the District Court had jurisdiction.[c] After repeating the familiar litany that standing requires that the plaintiff have a "personal stake" in the outcome, consisting of an allegation of "distinct and palpable" injury to the plaintiff and a "fairly traceable" causal connection between that injury and the challenged conduct, the Court then faced three aspects of the standing question.

First, the plaintiffs had alleged a number of injuries, including the adverse environmental and aesthetic effects of thermal pollution of the two lakes on which the plants were sited and the fear of damage resulting from low-level radiation. The Court accepted these allegations as sufficient to meet the first part of the standing inquiry.

Second, the Court proceeded to "the more difficult step" of determining whether the injuries " 'fairly can be traced to the challenged action of the defendant,' or put otherwise, [whether] the exercise of the Court's remedial powers would redress the claimed injuries." The District Court had found that "there is a substantial likelihood that Duke would not be able to complete the construction and maintain the

[c] The Court construed the complaint as stating a cause of action based on the fifth amendment. Cf. *Bivens v. Six Unknown Named Agents of the Federal Bureau of Narcotics*, page 395, infra. Jurisdiction was upheld under 28 U.S.C. § 1331(a) (the general federal question statute). Justice Rehnquist, joined by Justice Stevens, construed the complaint as stating a cause of action based on state law, and dissented on the ground that the federal District Court lacked subject matter jurisdiction.

operation of the [plants] but for the protection of the Price-Anderson Act." The Court found this conclusion "not clearly erroneous," based chiefly on the congressional testimony of utility officials in support of the legislation.

Finally and most importantly, the Court rejected the contention that

> "in addition to proof of injury and of a causal link between such injury and the challenged conduct, [plaintiffs] must demonstrate a connection between the injuries they claim and the constitutional rights being asserted. . . . Since the environmental and health injuries claimed by [plaintiffs] are not directly related to the constitutional attack on the Price-Anderson Act, such injuries, the argument continues, cannot supply a predicate for standing."

The Court held that no "subject-matter nexus between the right asserted and the injury alleged" was required. As a constitutional matter, the Court added, litigants are not required to "demonstrate anything more than injury in fact and a substantial likelihood that the judicial relief requested will prevent or redress the claimed injury." Prudential restraints also were not a bar.

Justices Stevens and Stewart wrote separately to dispute the Court's handling of the standing question. Justice Stevens addressed the causation issue:

> "The string of contingencies that supposedly holds this litigation together is too delicate for me. We are told that but for the Price-Anderson Act there would be no financing of nuclear power plants, no development of those plants by private parties, and hence no present injury to persons such as appellees; we are then asked to remedy an alleged due process violation that may possibly occur at some uncertain time in the future, and may possibly injure the appellees in a way that has no significant connection with any present injury. It is remarkable that such a series of speculations is considered sufficient . . . to establish appellees' standing . . . .

> "The Court's opinion will serve the national interest in removing doubts concerning the constitutionality of the Price-Anderson Act. I cannot, therefore, criticize the statesmanship of the Court's decision to provide the country with an advisory opinion on an important subject. Nevertheless, my view of the proper function of this Court, or of any other federal court, in the structure of our government is more limited. We are not statesmen; we are judges. When it is necessary to resolve a constitutional issue in the adjudication of an actual case or controversy, it is our duty to do so. But whenever we are persuaded by reasons of expediency to engage in the business of giving legal advice, we chip away a part of the foundation of our independence and our strength."

Justice Stewart insisted that there should be some connection between the federal claim and the injury alleged for purposes of standing:

"[T]he Court relies on the 'present' injuries of increased water temperatures and low-level radiation emissions [to establish standing]. Even assuming that but for the act the plant would not exist and therefore neither would its effects on the environment, I cannot believe that it follows that the [plaintiffs] have standing to attack the constitutionality of the act. Apart from the but-for connection in the loosest sense of that concept, there is no relationship at all between the injury alleged for standing purposes and the injury alleged [to support the claim on the merits].

"Surely a plaintiff does not have standing simply because his challenge, if successful, will remove the injury relied on for standing purposes *only* because it will put the defendant out of existence. Surely there must be *some* direct relationship between the plaintiff's federal claim and the injury relied on for standing. An interest in the local water temperature does not, in short, give these [plaintiffs] standing . . . to challenge the constitutionality of a law limiting liability in an unrelated and as-yet-to-occur major nuclear accident."

Did the Court reach the right result on the standing question?[d] Is *Duke Power* consistent with *Allen*?

5. Bibliography. The issue of standing has generated an enormous literature. For an account of the demise of the "legal interest" test and a conceptual investigation of the standing issues produced by the advent of public law litigation, see generally J. Vining, Legal Identity: The Coming of Age of Public Law (1978).

Among the many articles criticizing the modern law of standing are Albert, Justiciability and Theories of Judicial Review: A Remote Relationship, 50 So. Cal. L. Rev. 1139 (1977); Albert, Standing to Challenge Administrative Action: An Inadequate Surrogate for Claim for Relief, 83 Yale L.J. 425 (1974); Currie, Misunderstanding Standing, 1981 Sup. Ct Rev. 41 (1981); Doernberg, "We the People": John Locke, Collective Constitutional Rights, and Standing to Challenge Government Action, 73 Calif. L. Rev. 52 (1985); Fallon, Of Justiciability, Remedies, and Public Law Litigation: Notes on the Jurisprudence of *Lyons,* 59 N.Y.U.L. Rev. 1 (1984); Floyd, The Justiciability Decisions of the Burger Court, 60 Notre Dame Law. 862 (1985); Hill and Baker, Dam Federal Jurisdiction!, 32 Emory L.J. 1 (1983); McCormack, The Justiciability Myth and the Concept of Law, 14 Hast.Con.L.Q. 595 (1987); Nichol, Rethinking Standing, 72 Calif.L.Rev. 68 (1984); Nichol, Injury and the Disintegration of Article III, 74 Cal.L.Rev. 1915 (1986); Tushnet, The New Law of Standing: A Plea for Abandonment, 62 Cornell L. Rev. 663 (1977); Winter, The Metaphor of Standing and the Problem of Self-Governance, 40 Stan.L.Rev. 1371 (1988).

------

d The *Duke Power* case is examined and criticized in Varat, Variable Justiciability and the *Duke Power* Case, 58 Tex. L. Rev. 273 (1980).

NOTES ON TAXPAYER STANDING

1. Introduction. Obviously, recognition of "citizen standing" in cases such as *Allen* or *Schlesinger* would obviate the need for a more elaborate standing inquiry. As it is, the Court's refusal to allow litigation by the purely ideological plaintiff necessitates some more particularized allegation of injury by persons seeking to challenge government action. An inviting alternative is "taxpayer standing"— the assertion that a taxpayer is injured in his or her allocable share of tax revenues expended in illegal activity.

"Taxpayer standing" differs from "citizen standing" in that it focuses on an injury that is concrete, though often trivial in dollar amount. Functionally, however, the two are very similar. Under both theories, a vast number of persons would be empowered to contest government action on the basis of an injury shared generally by all taxpayers and not otherwise relevant to any given plaintiff. One might have thought, therefore, that "taxpayer standing" would be categorically disallowed on the same ground that denies standing to the purely ideological plaintiff, but in fact the history of this question has been more complex. The result is a unique doctrine, applicable only in the context of suits by taxpayers.

2. *Frothingham v. Mellon.* In Frothingham v. Mellon, 262 U.S. 447 (1923), Mrs. Frothingham sued to challenge the Maternity Act of 1921, alleging that it was beyond federal legislative power. That legislation provided federal funding to the states for improving infant and maternal health. The alleged injury was the plaintiff's individual share of the tax burden resulting from the assertedly unconstitutional expenditure of federal funds. Despite some history of allowing *municipal* taxpayers to challenge the expenditure of municipal funds, the Court found that Frothingham lacked standing:

> "The administration of any statute, likely to produce additional taxation to be imposed upon a vast number of taxpayers, is essentially a matter of public and not of individual concern. If one taxpayer may champion and litigate such a cause, then every other taxpayer may do the same, not only in respect of the statute here under review but also in respect of every other appropriation act and statute whose administration requires the outlay of public money, and whose validity may be questioned. The bare suggestion of such a result, with its attendant inconveniences, goes far to sustain the conclusion which we have reached, that a suit of this character cannot be maintained."

Unlike municipal taxpayers, a federal taxpayer's interest in the federal treasury "is shared with millions of others; is comparatively minute and indeterminable; and the effect upon future taxation, of any payment out of the funds, so remote, fluctuating and uncertain, that no basis is afforded for an appeal to the preventive powers of a court of equity."

3. ***Flast v. Cohen.*** In Flast v. Cohen, 392 U.S. 83 (1968), suit was brought to challenge certain aspects of the Elementary and Secondary Education Act of 1965. Plaintiffs claimed that federal moneys were disbursed to the benefit of religious and sectarian schools in violation of the establishment clause of the first amendment. Their only connection to the controversy was their status as federal taxpayers.

The Supreme Court found *Frothingham* not controlling. Speaking through Chief Justice Warren, the Court concluded that art. III erected no absolute bar to taxpayer standing and suggested that the *Frothingham* limitation was prudential in nature. The critical issue, said the Court, was the "nexus" between plaintiffs' status as taxpayers and the claim they wished to present:

> "The nexus demanded of federal taxpayers has two aspects to it. First, the taxpayer must establish a logical link between that status and the type of legislative enactment attacked. Thus, the taxpayer will be a proper party to allege the unconstitutionality only of exercises of congressional power under the taxing and spending clause of art. I, § 8, of the Constitution. It will not be sufficient to allege an incidental expenditure of tax funds in the administration of an essentially regulatory statute. . . . Secondly, the taxpayer must establish a nexus between the status and the precise nature of the constitutional infringement alleged. Under this requirement, the taxpayer must show that the challenged enactment exceeds specific constitutional limitations imposed upon the exercise of the congressional taxing and spending power and not simply that the enactment is generally beyond the powers delegated to Congress by art. I, § 8. When both nexuses are established, the litigant will have shown a taxpayer's stake in the outcome of the controversy and will be a proper and appropriate party to invoke a federal court's jurisdiction."

On this analysis, *Frothingham* and *Flast* were distinguishable. Both involved challenges to federal spending programs, and therefore in both cases the first nexus was established. In *Frothingham,* however, the claim was merely that the program exceeded the scope of federal legislative power under art. I, § 8; no *specific* limitation on the taxing and spending power was alleged: "In essence, Mrs. Frothingham was attempting to assert the states' interest in their legislative prerogatives and not a federal taxpayer's interest in being free of taxing and spending in contravention of specific constitutional limitations imposed upon Congress' taxing and spending power." In *Flast,* by contrast, plaintiffs had alleged a specific limitation on the taxing and spending power, namely the establishment clause of the first amendment.

Justice Douglas concurred to say that he would simply overrule *Frothingham.* Justices Fortas and Stewart wrote to suggest that taxpayer standing might be limited to establishment clause cases. Only Justice Harlan dissented. He found the majority's treatment of *Frothingham* unpersuasive. Specifically, he argued that a taxpayer's stake in federal expenditures, such as it is, cannot depend on whether the money is expended under the spending power or incidental to a regulatory program. Harlan also argued that the establishment clause was not in any meaningful sense more "specific" than other constitutional commands and that in any event that criterion was irrelevant to the question of standing. He concluded as follows:

> "The difficulty, with which the Court never comes to grips, is that taxpayers' suits under the establishment clause are not in these circumstances meaningfully different from other public actions. If this case involved a tax specifically designed for the support of religion . . ., I would agree that taxpayers have rights under the religious clauses of the first amendment that would permit them standing to challenge the tax's validity in the federal courts. But this is not such a case, and appellants challenge an expenditure, not a tax. Where no such tax is involved, a taxpayer's complaint can consist only of an allegation that public funds have been, or shortly will be, expended for purposes inconsistent with the Constitution. The taxpayer cannot ask the return of any portion of his previous tax payments, cannot prevent the collection of any existing tax debt, and cannot demand an adjudication of the propriety of any particular level of taxation. His tax payments are received for the general purposes of the United States, and are, upon proper receipt, lost in the general revenues. The interests he represents, and the rights he espouses, are, as they are in all public actions, those held in common by all citizens.

> . . .

> "It seems to me clear that public actions, whatever the constitutional provisions on which they are premised, may involve important hazards for the continued effectiveness of the federal judiciary. Although I believe such actions to be within the jurisdiction conferred upon the federal courts by art. III of the Constitution, there surely can be little doubt that they strain the judicial function and press to the limit judicial authority. There is every reason to fear that unrestricted public actions might well alter the allocation of authority among the three branches of the federal government."

4. *United States v. Richardson.* *Flast* was distinguished in United States v. Richardson, 418 U.S. 166 (1974). There a federal taxpayer sued to coerce disclosure of CIA expenditures. He claimed that the refusal to publish such information, an omission specifically authorized by the Central Intelligence Agency Act of 1949, violated the accounts clause of the federal Constitution.[a] The alleged injury was the impairment of the taxpayer's ability to monitor actions by the political branches.

---

[a] Art. I, § 9, cl. 7 provides as follows:

"No Money shall be drawn from the Treasury, but in Consequence of Appropriations made by Law; and a regular Statement and Account of the Receipts and Expenditures of all public Money shall be published from time to time."

The Third Circuit found standing under *Flast,* but the Supreme Court disagreed. The problem, said Chief Justice Burger for the Court, was that plaintiff failed to allege violation of any specific limitation on the taxing and spending power. He did not claim that funds were expended unlawfully, but only that such expenditures had not been adequately reported. Thus, there was no "logical nexus" between plaintiff's status as a taxpayer and Congress' alleged failure to require public accounts.

Justice Powell filed a lengthy concurrence. He criticized *Flast* as neither sound nor logical, and suggested that it be limited to its facts. Finding no "meaningful stopping point between an all or nothing position with regard to federal taxpayer or citizen standing," Powell opted for the latter:

> "Relaxation of standing requirements is directly related to the expansion of judicial power. It seems to me inescapable that allowing unrestricted taxpayer or citizen standing would significantly alter the allocation of power at the national level, with a shift away from a democratic form of government. I also believe that repeated and essentially head-on confrontations between the lifetenured branch and the representative branches of government will not, in the long run, be beneficial to either. The public confidence essential to the former and the vitality critical to the latter may well erode if we do not exercise self-restraint in the utilization of our power to negative the actions of the other branches."[b]

Justices Douglas, Brennan, and Stewart (joined by Marshall) filed dissenting opinions.

5. Valley Forge. Both "taxpayer" and "citizen" standing were at issue in Valley Forge Christian College v. Americans United for Separation of Church and State, Inc., 454 U.S. 464 (1982). That case posed an establishment clause challenge to the disposition of surplus property under the Federal Property and Administrative Services Act of 1949. Under that statute, the Secretary of Health, Education and Welfare (now the Secretary of Education) is empowered to sell or lease surplus real property to nonprofit, tax-exempt educational institutions for a price that is discounted by the Secretary's evaluation of "any benefit which has accrued or which may accrue to the United States" from the transferee's use of the property.

The Valley Forge General Hospital was built by the Army in 1942. In 1973 the Secretary of Defense decided to close the hospital as a cost-cutting measure, and the facility therefore became surplus property. In 1976 the Secretary of Education conveyed the Hospital and some 77 acres of land to the Valley Forge Christian College, a nonprofit educational institution operating under the supervision of a religious order known as the Assemblies of God and offering "systematic training on the collegiate level to men and women for Christian service as either

---

[b] For a generally favorable review of Powell's position, see Leedes, Mr. Justice Powell's Standing, 11 Rich. L. Rev. 269 (1977).

ministers or laymen." The appraised value of the transferred property was $557,500, but the price was discounted by a 100 per cent public-benefit allowance, so that the college paid nothing.

This action was challenged by Americans United for Separation of Church and State. The complaint described the organization as composed of "taxpayer members" and alleged that each member "would be deprived of the fair and constitutional use of his (her) tax dollar for constitutional purposes in violation of his (her) rights under the first amendment." The Third Circuit found this allegation sufficient to sustain standing, but the Supreme Court reversed.

(i) **The Majority.** Speaking through Justice Rehnquist, the Court found *Frothingham* controlling and *Flast* distinguishable:

> "Unlike the plaintiffs in *Flast*, respondents fail the first prong of the test for taxpayer standing. Their claim is deficient in two respects. First, the source of their complaint is not a congressional action, but a decision by HEW to transfer a parcel of federal property. *Flast* limited taxpayer standing to challenges directed "only [at] exercises of congressional power." . . . Second, and perhaps redundantly, the property transfer about which respondents complain was not an exercise of authority conferred by the taxing and spending clause of art. I, § 8. The authorizing legislation, the Federal Property and Administrative Services Act of 1949, was an evident exercise of Congress' power under the property clause, art. IV, § 3, cl. 2.ᶜ Respondents do not dispute this contention, and it is decisive of any claim of taxpayer standing under the *Flast* precedent."

In a footnote the Court added that the connection between the property transfer and respondents' tax burden was "at best speculative and at worst nonexistent." Respondents' only complaint was that the property had been transferred for inadequate consideration, but it appeared that in any event "the ultimate purchaser would, in all likelihood, have been another non-profit institution or local school district rather than a purchaser for cash."

The Third Circuit had agreed that this case did not precisely meet the precedent of *Flast* but concluded that respondents nevertheless had standing on the basis of "their shared individuated right to a government that 'shall make no law respecting the establishment of religion.'" Unlike other claimants to citizen standing, said the Third Circuit, respondents had alleged "a particular and concrete injury" to a "personal constitutional right." The Supreme Court also rejected this conclusion:

> "This reasoning process merely disguises, we think with a rather thin veil, the inconsistency of the court's results with our decisions in *Schlesinger* and *Richardson*. The plaintiffs in those cases plainly asserted a 'personal right' to have the

---

ᶜ Art. IV, § 3, cl. 2 provides that Congress has "Power to dispose of and make all needful Rules and Regulations respecting the . . . Property belonging to the United States." [Footnote by eds.]

government act in accordance with their views of the Constitution . . . . But assertion of a right to a particular kind of government conduct, which the government has violated by acting differently, cannot alone satisfy the requirements of art. III without draining those requirements of meaning. . . .

"The complaint in this case shares a common deficiency with those in *Schlesinger* and *Richardson*. Although they claim that the Constitution has been violated, they claim nothing else. They fail to identify any personal injury suffered by the plaintiffs *as a consequence* of the alleged constitutional error, other than the psychological consequence presumably produced by observation of conduct with which one disagrees. That is not an injury sufficient to confer standing under art. III, even though the disagreement is phrased in constitutional terms."

Finally, the Court rejected the idea, advanced by the Third Circuit and developed at length by Justice Brennan in dissent, that there is something special about the establishment clause:

"To the extent the Court of Appeals relied on a view of standing under which the art. III burdens diminish as the 'importance' of the claim on the merits increases, we reject that notion. The requirement of standing 'focuses on the party seeking to get his complaint before a federal court and not on the issues he wishes to have adjudicated.' Moreover, we know of no principled basis on which to create a hierarchy of constitutional values or a complementary 'sliding scale' of standing which might permit respondents to invoke the judicial power of the United States."

The fact that statutes claimed to violate the establishment clause might not affect any individual in a way sufficient to establish traditional standing seemed to the Court unimportant:

"Implicit in the [view that respondents should be granted standing in order 'to assure a basis for judicial review'] is the philosophy that the business of the federal courts is correcting constitutional errors, and that 'cases and controversies' are at best merely convenient vehicles for doing so and at worst nuisances that may be dispensed with when they become obstacles to that transcendent scheme. It does not become more palatable when the underlying merits concern the establishment clause. Respondents' claim of standing implicitly rests on the presumption that violations of the establishment clause typically will not cause injury sufficient to confer standing under the 'traditional' view of art. III. But '[t]he assumption that if respondents have no standing to sue, no one would have standing, is not a reason to find standing.' *Schlesinger v. Reservists Committee to Stop the War*, supra, at 227. This view would convert standing into a 'requirement that must be observed only when satisfied.' "

(ii) **The Dissent.** Justice Brennan filed an extensive dissent, in which Justices Marshall and Blackmun joined. Brennan decried the impulse "to decide difficult questions of substantive law obliquely in the course of opinions purporting to do nothing more than determine what the Court labels 'standing.'" The by-product of this practice, said Brennan, is that standing is used "to slam the courthouse door against plaintiffs who are entitled to full consideration of their claims on the merits."

Justice Brennan began his analysis with a general review of standing doctrine. It largely tracked the established emphasis on injury plus causation and redressability, but with the following interpretation:

> "The Constitution requires an art. III court to ascertain that both requirements are met before proceeding to exercise its authority on behalf of any plaintiff, [b]ut the existence of art. III injury 'often turns on the nature and source of the claim asserted.' Neither 'palpable injury' nor 'causation' is a term of unvarying meaning. There is much in the way of 'mutual understandings' and 'common-law traditions' that necessarily guides the definitional inquiry. *In addition,* the Constitution, and by legislation the Congress, may impart a new, and on occasion unique, meaning to the terms 'injury' and 'causation' in particular statutory or constitutional contexts. The Court makes a fundamental mistake when it determines that a plaintiff has failed to satisfy the two-pronged 'injury-in-fact' test, or indeed any other test of 'standing,' without first determining whether the Constitution or a statute defines injury, and creates a cause of action for redress of that injury, in precisely the circumstances presented to the Court. . . .

> "When the Constitution makes it clear that a particular person is to be protected from a particular form of government action, then that person has a 'right' to be free of that action; when that right is infringed, then there is injury, and a personal stake, within the meaning of art. III."

Justice Brennan examined both *Frothingham* and *Flast* at some length. He found the reasoning of *Frothingham* "obscure" but thought that it nevertheless displayed "sound judgment." He distinguished *Flast* on the ground that it involved the establishment clause. After an extensive review of the history of that provision, he concluded that "one of the primary purposes of the establishment clause was to prevent the use of tax monies for religious purposes. *The taxpayer was the direct and intended beneficiary of the prohibition on financial aid to religion.*" On this ground, *Flast* should control:

> "It is at once apparent that the test of standing formulated by the Court in *Flast* sought to reconcile the developing doctrine of taxpayer 'standing' with the Court's historical understanding that the establishment clause was intended to prohibit the federal government from using tax

funds for the advancement of religion, and thus the constitutional imperative of taxpayer standing in certain cases
brought pursuant to the establishment clause. The two-
pronged 'nexus' test offered by the Court, despite its general
language, is best understood as 'a determinant of standing
of plaintiffs alleging only injury as taxpayers who challenge
alleged violations of the establishment and free exercise
clauses of the first amendment,' and not as a general statement of standing principles. . . .

"It may be that Congress can tax for *almost* any reason,
or for no reason at all. There is, so far as I have been able
to discern, but one constitutionally imposed limit on that
authority. Congress cannot use tax money to support a
church, or to encourage religion. That is '*the* forbidden
exaction.' Everson v. Board of Education, 330 U.S. 1, 45
(1947) (Rutledge, J., dissenting) (emphasis added). In absolute terms the history of the establishment clause of the
first amendment makes this clear. History also makes it
clear that the federal taxpayer is a singularly 'proper and
appropriate party to invoke a federal court's jurisdiction' to
challenge a federal bestowal of largesse as a violation of the
establishment clause. Each, and indeed every, federal taxpayer suffers precisely the injury that the establishment
clause guards against when the federal government directs
that funds be taken from the pocketbooks of the citizenry
and placed into the coffers of the ministry."

Finally, Justice Brennan attacked the majority's distinctions of
Flast as at best "specious" and at worst "pernicious to our constitutional heritage." The fact that the plaintiffs had challenged an
executive decision rather than an act of Congress could not be
constitutionally significant: "The first amendment binds the government as a whole, regardless of which branch is at work in a
particular instance." The Court's second distinction was, for Brennan, "equally unavailing":

"The majority finds it 'decisive' that the Federal Property and Administrative Services Act of 1949 'was an evident exercise of Congress' power under the property clause,
art. IV, § 3, cl. 2,' while the government action in *Flast*
was taken under art. I, § 8. . . . It can make no constitutional difference in the case before us whether the donation
to the petitioner here was in the form of a cash grant to
build a facility, or in the nature of a gift of property
including a facility already built. . . . Whether undertaken pursuant to the property clause or the spending clause,
the breach of the establishment clause, and the relationship
of the taxpayer to that breach, [are] precisely the same."

Justice Stevens submitted a brief dissent endorsing Justice Brennan's analysis and recording his view that "the essential holding of

Flast v. Cohen attaches special importance to the establishment clause and does not permit the drawing of a tenuous distinction between the spending clause and the property clause."[d]

6. *Duke Power* **Revisited.** The Court also distinguished *Flast* in the *Duke Power* decision, summarized at page 36, supra. Recall that the injuries alleged in *Duke Power* were unrelated to the legal basis for attacking the constitutionality of the Price-Anderson Act. It was argued that the requirement in *Flast* that there be a "logical nexus" between the alleged injury (to one's status as a taxpayer) and the "precise nature of the constitutional infringement alleged" was generally applicable to the standing issue.

The Court disagreed:

"The major difficulty with the argument is that it implicitly assumes that the nexus requirement formulated in the context of taxpayer suits has general applicability in suits of all other types brought in the federal courts. No cases have been cited outside the context of taxpayer suits where we have demanded this type of subject matter nexus between the right asserted and the injury alleged and we are aware of none. . . . We . . . cannot accept the contention that, outside of taxpayers' suits, a litigant must demonstrate anything more than injury in fact and a substantial likelihood that the judicial relief requested will prevent or redress the claimed injury to satisfy the 'case and controversy' requirement of art. III."

7. Questions and Comments on Taxpayer Standing. Examine the quotation from Chief Justice Warren's *Flast* opinion reproduced at page 40, supra. From what sources did the Chief Justice derive the two aspects of the "nexus" requirement that he established? More broadly, why should such requirements limit taxpayer standing but, as the Court stated in *Duke Power,* not limit standing asserted by another type of claimant? More broadly still, are citizen and taxpayer standing meaningfully different? Should the answer depend on whether the dollar value of the taxpayer's share is de minimis?[e]

Another question concerns whether there is any meaningful basis for distinguishing among instances of taxpayer standing. Several differentiations have been attempted. These include the two-pronged nexus approach of *Flast v. Cohen* and the assertion that the establishment clause is different from other constitutional guarantees. Is either of these approaches persuasive? Is there any other sensible basis for

[d] Reactions to the *Valley Forge* decision may be found in Marshall and Flood, Establishment Clause Standing: The Not Very Revolutionary Decision at *Valley Forge,* 11 Hofstra L. Rev. 63 (1982), and in Nichol, Standing on the Constitution: The Supreme Court and *Valley Forge,* 61 N.C.L. Rev. 798 (1983).

[e] At one time, it was estimated that a federal expenditure of $10 billion would likely impose a cost of approximately $150 million on a major corporation such as General Motors. See Hearings on S. 2097 before the Subcommittee on Constitutional Rights of the Senate Committee on the Judiciary, 89th Cong., 2d Sess., pt. 2, p. 493 (1966) (letter from K.C. Davis).

allowing some but not all instances of taxpayer standing? Should it matter whether any other plaintiff is likely to have traditional standing to raise the same claim? If the choice presented by taxpayer standing is essentially all or nothing, which is better?

———

NOTES ON STANDING UNDER FEDERAL STATUTES

1. **The Zone-of-Interests Test.** The Supreme Court's treatment of standing to sue under federal statutes is arguably different from the analysis developed in the preceding materials. In 1970 the Court decided a pair of cases involving attempts under the Administrative Procedure Act (APA) to seek judicial review of agency action. The APA authorized such suits by any person "aggrieved by agency action within the meaning of a relevant statute." The Court held that standing depended on a two-part inquiry: (i) whether plaintiffs had alleged the constitutional minimum requirement of injury in fact; and (ii) "whether the interest sought to be protected by the complainant is arguably within the zone of interests to be protected or regulated by the statute or constitutional guarantee in question." Association of Data Processing Serv. Orgs. v. Camp, 397 U.S. 150, 152–53 (1970); Barlow v. Collins, 397 U.S. 159 (1970).

The "zone of interests" test was from the start controversial, and whether it survives as a significant test of standing may perhaps be doubted. With respect to constitutional claims, the "zone of interests" inquiry would seem to have been superseded by the more elaborate rendition of standing doctrine in such cases as *Allen v. Wright.* With respect to statutory claims, however, the phrase retains some currency.

The most recent application of the "zone of interests" test came in Clarke v. Securities Industry Association, 479 U.S. 388 (1987). The case involved a decision by the Comptroller of the Currency to allow two national banks to operate discount brokerage subsidiaries. The question was whether the discount brokerage offices would fall within federal legislative restrictions on branch banking. The Comptroller determined that they would not, and his decision was challenged in court by a trade association of securities brokers, underwriters, and investment bankers. Ultimately, the Supreme Court held that the trade association was entitled to seek judicial review of the Comptroller's action. The Court inquired into the "zone of interests," but its analysis cast doubt on whether that inquiry is properly an aspect of "standing." Speaking through Justice White, the Court referred to *Association of Data Processing Serv. Orgs. v. Camp* as raising a question "which the Court described as one of standing." At other points, the *Clarke* opinion referred to the "zone of interests" test as an aspect of "reviewability." And in a footnote, the Court indicated that the "zone of interests" inquiry was "most usefully understood" as a gloss on the judicial review provision of the Administrative Procedure Act.

Whatever the correct taxonomy, the Court provided a clear restatement of the nature of the inquiry:

"The zone of interests test is a guide for deciding whether, in view of Congress' evident intent to make agency action presumptively reviewable, a particular plaintiff should be heard to complain of a particular agency decision. In cases where the plaintiff is not itself the subject of the contested regulatory action, the test denies a right of review if the plaintiff's interests are so marginally related or inconsistent with the purposes implicit in the statute that it cannot reasonably be assumed that Congress intended to permit the suit." [a]

2. The Injury Requirement: The Fair Housing Act Cases. The Fair Housing Act was enacted as title VIII of the Civil Rights Act of 1968 and is codified at 42 U.S.C. §§ 3601–17. That statute forbids racial and certain other kinds of discrimination in housing sales and rentals. Section 810(a) provides that "[a]ny person who claims to have been injured by a discriminatory housing practice or who believes that he will be irrevocably injured by a discriminatory housing practice that is about to occur (hereafter 'person aggrieved')" may file a complaint with the Secretary of Housing and Urban Development. If the Secretary fails to obtain voluntary compliance within 30 days, the "person aggrieved" becomes entitled under § 810(d) to file a civil action "to enforce the rights granted or protected by this title, insofar as such rights relate to the subject of the complaint."

(i) *Trafficante.* In Trafficante v. Metropolitan Life Ins. Co., 409 U.S. 205 (1972), two tenants of a large apartment complex charged that their landlord discriminated against nonwhites and that consequently they had suffered "the loss of important benefits from interracial associations." The lower courts construed the statute to permit complaints only by persons who are the objects of discriminatory housing practices, but the Supreme Court reversed. Speaking for a unanimous Court, Justice Douglas noted that HUD officials endorsed a broad construction of "person aggrieved" and found that discriminatory housing practices injure not merely the immediate victims but also "the whole community." Justice White, joined by Justices Blackmun and Powell, submitted the following concurrence:

"Absent the Civil Rights Act of 1968, I would have great difficulty in concluding that petitioners' complaint in this case presented a case or controversy within the jurisdiction of the District Court under art. III of the Constitution. But with that statute purporting to give all those who are authorized to complain to the agency the right also to sue in court, I would sustain the statute insofar as it extends standing to those in the position of petitioners in this case."

(ii) *Gladstone, Realtors v. Bellwood.* The approach of *Trafficante* was continued in Gladstone, Realtors v. Bellwood, 441 U.S. 91 (1979). The realtors were charged with racial "steering"—that is, with

---

[a] Justice Stevens, joined by Chief Justice Rehnquist and Justice O'Connor, concurred in the judgment on the issue of standing but termed the Court's analysis "a wholly unnecessary exegesis" on the "zone of interests" test.

directing black prospective home buyers to an integrated area of some 12 by 13 blocks and away from other, predominantly white areas. Plaintiffs consisted of the village of Bellwood, a municipal corporation; several individuals who had acted as "testers" by pretending to be prospective home buyers, some of whom lived in the integrated area of Bellwood; and a black resident of a neighboring community. Suit was brought under a different provision of the statute, but the Court, speaking through Justice Powell, concluded that it too was intended to extend standing "as broadly as is permitted by art. III." The Court then found that most plaintiffs had alleged legally cognizable injury under art. III. The village had standing because defendants' alleged practices would affect the community's racial composition and perhaps diminish property values, and the individual plaintiffs who lived in the "target" area had standing to complain of the progressive deprivation of "the social and professional benefits of living in an integrated society," citing *Trafficante.* The fact that the relevant community was defined in terms of city blocks rather than the residents of a particular apartment complex was immaterial.[b]

(iii) *Havens Realty Corp. v. Coleman.* Finally, Havens Realty Corp. v. Coleman, 455 U.S. 363 (1982), was a class action claiming racial "steering" of the sort alleged in *Gladstone, Realtors.* Plaintiffs were an organization called Housing Opportunities Made Equal (HOME) and individual residents of Richmond, Va., and adjacent Henrico County. The relevant individuals[c] were two "testers," one black and one white, each of whom had made inquiries regarding the availability of apartments in order to ascertain whether defendants were engaged in prohibited practices. Speaking through Justice Brennan, a unanimous Court found that all plaintiffs had standing.

HOME had standing, said the Court, in view of the organization's claim that its counseling and referral services for low- and moderate-income persons seeking housing had been impaired by defendants' practices. The black "tester" was found to have standing on the theory that the statute created "an enforceable right to truthful information concerning the availability of housing." Since she alleged that she had been falsely told that no apartment was available, she had alleged "specific injury" within the meaning of art. III. The white "tester," by contrast, had been given truthful information and therefore had no standing under this theory. However, both individuals might have standing, apart from their actions as "testers," based on their allegation of residence in Richmond or Henrico County. It was "implausible," said the Court, that defendants' alleged discrimination "could have palpable effects throughout the *entire* Richmond metropolitan area," but "in the absence of further factual development, we cannot say as a matter of law that no injury could be proved." The case was

b Justice Rehnquist, joined by Justice Stewart, dissented from the majority's construction of the statute.

c An additional plaintiff was a black renter who alleged that he had asked about an apartment at a particular complex and was falsely told that none was available. His standing was not contested.

therefore remanded for determination whether defendants' practices "had an appreciable effect" in the areas where plaintiffs lived.

3. The Causation Requirement: *United States v. SCRAP.*
United States v. SCRAP, 412 U.S. 669 (1973), involved a suit brought by five George Washington law students constituting themselves Students Challenging Regulatory Agency Procedures (SCRAP). They sought an injunction requiring the Interstate Commerce Commission to suspend enforcement of a temporary 2.5 per cent surcharge on rail freight rates. SCRAP claimed that the agency's decision not to suspend the rate increase required preparation of a detailed environmental impact statement in conformity with the National Environmental Policy Act of 1969. The asserted connection between rail freight rates and environmental quality was described by the Court as follows:

> "[A] general rate increase would allegedly cause increased use of nonrecyclable commodities as compared to recyclable goods, thus resulting in the need to use more natural resources to produce such goods, some of which resources might be taken from the Washington area, and resulting in more refuse that might be discarded in national parks in the Washington area."

SCRAP's connection to this chain of events was the allegation that each of its members "uses the forest, rivers, streams, mountains, and other natural resources surrounding the Washington metropolitan area and at his legal residence, for camping, hiking, fishing, sightseeing, and other recreational [and] aesthetic purposes." Additionally, SCRAP alleged that the rate increase would force its members to pay higher prices for finished goods, to suffer from increased air pollution, and to pay higher taxes to clean up waste materials.

Speaking through Justice Stewart, the Supreme Court found that SCRAP had standing. SCRAP's members had alleged "a specific and perceptible harm that distinguishes them from other citizens who had not used the natural resources that were claimed to be affected." The causal link might be "attenuated," but the allegations, if proved, would place SCRAP's members "squarely among those persons injured in fact by the Commission's action" and thus among those persons "adversely affected or aggrieved by agency action" within the meaning of the Administrative Procedure Act and thus entitled to seek judicial review.

Justice White filed a dissent joined by the Chief Justice and Justice Rehnquist. Justice Powell did not participate.

4. Questions and Comments on Standing Under Federal Statutes. Are the injuries alleged in the cases summarized above appreciably different from those alleged in *Allen v. Wright*? Is the causation holding of the *SCRAP* decision consistent with the causation holding in *Allen*?

More particularly, did any of the plaintiffs challenging the Fair Housing Act do more than advance the "generalized grievance" of living in a community burdened by racial discrimination? Is the size of the community important? Would the *Allen v. Wright* plaintiffs have had a better claim to standing if they had confined their attention to a single city rather than proposing a nationwide class action? Or is the critical difference that the Fair Housing Act plaintiffs had the advantage of a statutory provision authorizing a very broad class of persons to seek judicial review? Note that the limitations that the Court found decisive in *Allen v. Wright* purportedly were required by art. III. Does the Court mean that Congress is empowered to relax the requirements of the Constitution?

Consider the views of David Logan, as stated in Standing to Sue: A Proposed Separation of Powers Analysis, 1984 Wis. L. Rev. 37 (1984). Logan asserts that "a plaintiff claiming a violation of constitutional rights is more likely to be denied standing than one claiming a violation of statutory rights," and says that the Court "has done little to explain or justify this anomaly." He suggests that the disparity may be intelligible from a separation-of-powers perspective. Specifically, Logan suggests that the judicial reluctance to hear so-called "generalized grievances" be viewed as a prudential limitation designed to minimize friction with the elected branches. With respect to statutory rights, in contrast, such concerns cut the other way:

> "As a general proposition, the Court should defer to Congress and grant standing to 'any person' who is injured in a way colorably contemplated by the remedial legislation unless express legislative history or a clear failure to meet the minimum content of article III compels a contrary judgment. By deferring in this way to Congress' broad power to act to cure social ills, the Court serves the principle of separation of powers."

SINGLETON v. WULFF
United States Supreme Court, 1976.
428 U.S. 106.

MR. JUSTICE BLACKMUN delivered the opinion of the Court (parts I [and] II–A . . .) together with an opinion (part II–B), in which MR. JUSTICE BRENNAN, MR. JUSTICE WHITE, and MR. JUSTICE MARSHALL joined.

[T]his case involves a claim of a state's unconstitutional interference with the decision to terminate pregnancy. The particular object of the challenge is a Missouri statute excluding abortions that are not "medically indicated" from the purposes for which Medicaid benefits are available to needy persons. In its present posture, [the issue] is whether the plaintiff-appellees, as physicians who perform nonmedically indicated abortions, have standing to maintain the suit, to which we answer that they do.

I

Missouri participates in the so-called Medicaid program, under which the federal government partially underwrites qualifying state plans for medical assistance to the needy. Missouri's plan . . .

includes . . . a list of 12 categories of medical services that are eligible for Medicaid funding. The last is:

> "(12) Family planning services as defined by federal rules and regulations; provided, however, that such family planning services shall not include abortions unless such abortions are medically indicated."

This provision is the subject of the litigation before us.

The suit was filed in the United States District Court for the Eastern District of Missouri by two Missouri-licensed physicians. Each plaintiff avers, in an affidavit filed in opposition to a motion to dismiss, that he "has provided, and anticipates providing abortions to welfare patients who are eligible for Medicaid payments." The plaintiffs further allege in their affidavits that all Medicaid applications filed in connection with abortions performed by them have been refused by the defendant, who is the responsible state official . . . . [E]ach plaintiff states that he anticipates further refusals by the defendant to fund nonmedically indicated abortions. Each avers that such refusals "deter [him] from the practice of medicine in the manner he considers to be most expertise [sic] and beneficial for said patients . . . and chill and thwart the ordinary and customary functioning of the doctor-patient relationship."

The complaint sought a declaration of the statute's invalidity and an injunction against its enforcement. . . . The defendant's sole pleading in District Court was a pre-answer motion to dismiss. [The District Court dismissed the case] "for lack of standing." The court saw no "logical nexus between the status asserted by the plaintiffs and the claim they seek to have adjudicated." The United States Court of Appeals for the Eighth Circuit reversed. . . . We granted certiorari. . . .

II

Although we are not certain that they have been clearly separated in the District Court's and Court of Appeals' opinions, two distinct standing questions are presented. . . . First, whether the plaintiff-respondents allege "injury in fact," that is, a sufficiently concrete interest in the outcome of their suit to make it a case or controversy subject to a federal court's art. III jurisdiction, and, second, whether, as a prudential matter, the plaintiff-respondents are proper proponents of the particular legal rights on which they base their suit.

A. The first of these questions needs little comment, for there is no doubt now that the respondent-physicians suffer concrete injury from the operation of the challenged statute. Their complaint and affidavits, described above, allege that they have performed and will continue to perform operations for which they would be reimbursed under the Medicaid program, were it not for the limitation of reimbursable abortions to those that are "medically indicated." If the physicians prevail in their suit to remove this limitation, they will benefit, for they will then receive payment for the abortions. The state (and federal and government) will be out of pocket by the amount of the payments. The relationship between the parties is classically adverse, and there clearly exists between them a case or controversy in the constitutional sense.

B. The question of what rights the doctors may assert in seeking to resolve that controversy is more difficult. The Court of Appeals adverted to what it perceived to be the doctor's own "constitutional rights to practice medicine." We have no occasion to decide whether such rights exist. Assuming that they do, the doctors, of course, can assert them. It appears, however, that the Court of Appeals also accorded the doctors standing to assert . . . the rights of their patients. We must decide whether this assertion of jus tertii was a proper one.

Federal courts must hesitate before resolving a controversy, even one within their constitutional power to resolve, on the basis of the rights of third persons not parties to the litigation. The reasons are two. First, the courts should not adjudicate such rights unnecessarily, and it may be that in fact the holders of those rights either do not wish to assert them, or will be able to enjoy them regardless of whether the in-court litigant is successful or not. Second, third parties themselves usually will be the best proponents of their own rights. The courts depend on effective advocacy, and therefore should prefer to construe legal rights only when the most effective advocates of those rights are before them. The holders of the rights may have a like preference, to the extent they will be bound by the courts' decisions under the doctrine of stare decisis. These two considerations underlie the Court's general rule: "Ordinarily, one may not claim standing in this Court to vindicate the constitutional rights of some third party."

Like any general rule, however, this one should not be applied where its underlying justifications are absent. With this in mind, the Court has looked primarily to two factual elements to determine whether the rule should apply in a particular case. The first is the relationship of the litigant to the person whose right he seeks to assert. If the enjoyment of the right is inextricably bound up with the activity the litigant wishes to pursue, the court at least can be sure that its construction of the right is not unnecessary in the sense that the right's enjoyment will be unaffected by the outcome of the suit. Furthermore, the relationship between the litigant and the third party may be such that the former is fully, or very nearly, as effective a proponent of the right as the latter. Thus in Griswold v. Connecticut, 381 U.S. 479 (1965), where two persons had been convicted of giving advice on contraception, the Court permitted the defendants, one of whom was a licensed physician, to assert the privacy rights of the married persons whom they advised. The Court pointed to the "confidential" nature of the relationship between the defendants and the married persons, and reasoned that the rights of the latter were "likely to be diluted or adversely affected" if they could not be asserted in such a case. See also Eisenstadt v. Baird, 405 U.S. 438, 445–46 (1972); Barrows v. Jackson, 346 U.S. 249 (1953). . . .

The other factual element to which the Court has looked is the ability of the third party to assert his own right. Even where the relationship is close, the reasons for requiring persons to assert their own rights will generally still apply. If there is some genuine obstacle to such assertion, however, the third party's absence from court loses its tendency to suggest that his right is not truly at stake, or truly important to him, and the party who is in court becomes by default the right's best available proponent. Thus, in NAACP v. Alabama, 357 U.S. 449 (1958), the Court held that the National Association for the Advancement of Colored People, in resisting a court order that it divulge the names of its members, could assert the first and 14th amendment rights of those members to remain anonymous. The Court reasoned that "[t]o require that [the right] be claimed by the members themselves would result in nullification of the right at the very moment of its assertion." See also Eisenstadt v. Baird, 405 U.S., at 446; Barrows v. Jackson, 346 U.S., at 259.[6]

Application of these principles to the present case quickly yields its proper result. The closeness of the relationship is patent, as it was in *Griswold.* . . . A woman cannot safely secure an abortion without the aid of a physician, and an impecunious woman cannot easily secure an abortion without the physician's being paid by the state. The woman's exercise of her right to an abortion, whatever its dimension, is therefore necessarily at stake here. Moreover, the constitutionally protected abortion decision is one in which the physician is intimately involved.

As to the woman's assertion of her own rights, there are several obstacles. For one thing, she may be chilled from such assertion by a desire to protect the very privacy of her decision from the publicity of a court suit. A second obstacle is the imminent mootness, at least in the technical sense, of any individual woman's claim. Only a few months, at the most, after the maturing of the decision to undergo an abortion, her right thereto will have been irrevocably lost, assuming, as it seems fair to assume, that unless the impecunious woman can establish Medicaid eligibility she must forego abortion. It is true that these obstacles are not insurmountable. Suit may be brought under a pseudonym, as so frequently has been done. A woman who is no longer pregnant may nonetheless retain the right to litigate the point because

---

[6] Mr. Justice Powell objects that such an obstacle is not enough, that our prior cases allow assertion of third-party rights only when such assertion by the third parties themselves would be "in all practicable terms impossible." Carefully analyzed, our cases do not go that far. The Negro real-estate purchaser in *Barrows,* if he could prove that the racial covenant alone stood in the way of his purchase (as presumably he could easily have done, given the amicable posture of the seller in that case), could surely have sought a declaration of its invalidity or an injunction against its enforcement. The Association members in *NAACP v. Alabama* could have obtained a similar declaration or injunction, suing anonymously by the use of pseudonyms. The recipients of contraceptives in *Eisenstadt* (or their counterparts in *Griswold* . . ., for that matter) could have sought similar relief as necessary to the enjoyment of their constitutional rights. The point is not that these were easy alternatives, but that they differed only in the degree of difficulty, if they differed at all, from the alternative in this case of the women themselves seeking a declaration or injunction that would force the state to pay the doctors for their abortions.

it is "'capable of repetition yet evading review.'" Roe v. Wade, 410 U.S. 113, 124–25 (1973). And it may be that a class could be assembled, whose fluid membership always included some women with live claims. But if the assertion of the right is to be "representative" to such an extent anyway, there seems little loss in terms of effective advocacy from allowing its assertion by a physician.

For these reasons, we conclude that it generally is appropriate to allow a physician to assert the rights of women patients as against governmental interference with the abortion decision. [T]he judgment of the Court of Appeals is affirmed . . . and the case is remanded with directions that it be returned to the District Court so that petitioner may file an answer to the complaint and the litigation proceed accordingly.

It is so ordered.

MR. JUSTICE STEVENS, concurring in part.

In this case (1) the plaintiff-physicians have a financial stake in the outcome of the litigation, and (2) they claim that the statute impairs their own constitutional rights. They therefore clearly have standing to bring this action.

Because these two facts are present, I agree that the analysis in part II–B of Mr. Justice Blackmun's opinion provides an adequate basis for considering the arguments based on the effect of the statute on the constitutional rights of their patients. Because I am not sure whether the analysis in part II–B would, or should, sustain the doctor's standing, apart from those two facts, I join only parts I [and] II–A . . . of the Court's opinion.

MR. JUSTICE POWELL, with whom THE CHIEF JUSTICE, MR. JUSTICE STEWART, and MR. JUSTICE REHNQUIST join, concurring in part and dissenting in part.

The Court holds that the respondents have standing to bring this suit and to assert their own constitutional rights, if any, in an attack on [the Missouri statute]. I agree with [this holding] and therefore concur in parts I [and] II–A, . . . of Justice Blackmun's opinion, as well as in the first four sentences of part II–B.

The Court further holds that after remand to the District Court the respondents may assert, in addition to their own rights, the constitutional rights of their patients who would be eligible for Medicaid assistance in obtaining elective abortions but for the exclusion of such abortions in [the statute]. I dissent from this holding.

I

As the Court notes, respondents by complaint and affidavit established their art. III standing to invoke the judicial power of the District Court. They have performed abortions for which Missouri's Medicaid system would compensate them directly if the challenged statutory section did not preclude it. Respondents allege an intention to continue to perform such abortions, and that the statute deprives them of compensation. These arguments, if proved, would give respondents a personal stake in the controversy over the statute's constitutionality.

II

[T]he art. III standing inquiry often is only the first of two inquiries necessary to determine whether a federal court should entertain a claim at the instance of a particular party. The art. III question is one of power within our constitutional system, as courts may decide only actual cases and controversies between the parties who stand before the court. Beyond this question, however, lies the further and less easily defined inquiry of whether it is prudent to proceed to decision on particular issues even at the instance of a party whose art. III standing is clear. This inquiry has taken various forms, including the one presented by this case: whether, in defending against or anticipatorily attacking state action, a party may argue that it contravenes someone else's constitutional rights.

This second inquiry is a matter of "judicial self-governance." The usual and wise stance of the federal courts when policing their own exercise of power in this manner is one of cautious reserve. This caution has given rise to the general rule that a party may not defend against or attack governmental action on the ground that it infringes the rights of some third party, and to the corollary that any exception must rest on specific factors outweighing the policies behind the rule itself.[3]

The plurality acknowledges this general rule, but identifies "two factual elements"—thought to be derived from prior cases—that justify the adjudication of the asserted third-party rights: (i) obstacles to the assertion by the third party of her own rights, and (ii) the existence of some "relationship" such as the one between physician and patient. In my view these factors do not justify allowing these physicians to assert their patients' rights.

A

Our prior decisions are enlightening. In *Barrows v. Jackson,* supra, a covenantor who breached a racially restrictive covenant by

---

[3] I agree with the plurality that a fundamental policy behind the general rule is a salutary desire to avoid unnecessary constitutional adjudication. See Ashwander v. TVA, 297 U.S., at 346–48 (Brandeis, J., concurring). The plurality perceives a second basis for the rule in the Court's need for effective advocacy. While this concern is relevant, it should receive no more emphasis in this context than in the context of art. III standing requirements. There the need for effective advocacy or a factual sharpening of issues long was the touchstone of discussion. Perhaps a more accurate formulation of the art. III limitation— one consistent with the concerns underlying the constitutional provision—is that the plaintiff's stake in a controversy must insure that exercise of the court's remedial powers is both necessary and sufficient to give him relief. The Court today uses this formulation. A similar focus upon the proper judicial role, rather than quality of advocacy, is preferable in the area of prudential limitations upon judicial power.

Congress by statute may foreclose any inquiry into competing policy considerations and give a party with art. III standing the right to assert the interests of third parties or even the public interest.

selling to Negroes was permitted to set up the buyers' rights to equal protection in defense against a damages action by the covenantees. See Shelley v. Kraemer, 334 U.S. 1 (1948). The Court considered the general rule outweighed by "the need to protect [these] fundamental rights" in a situation "in which it would be difficult if not impossible for the persons whose rights are asserted to present their grievance before any court." It would indeed have been difficult if not impossible for the rightholders to assert their own rights: the operation of the restrictive covenant and the threat of damages actions for its breach tended to insure they would not come into possession of the land, and there was at the time little chance of a successful suit based on a covenantor's failure to sell to them. In a second case, NAACP v. Alabama, 357 U.S. 449 (1958), an organization was allowed to resist an order to produce its membership list by asserting the associational rights of its members to anonymity because, as the plurality notes, the members themselves would have had to forgo the rights in order to assert them. And in Eisenstadt v. Baird, 405 U.S. 438 (1972), the Court considered it necessary to relax the rule and permit a distributor of contraceptives to assert the constitutional rights of the recipients because the statutory scheme operating to deny the contraceptives to the recipients appeared to offer them no means of challenge.

The plurality purports to derive from these cases the principle that a party may assert another's rights if there is "some genuine obstacle" to the third party's own litigation. But this understates the teaching of those cases: On their facts they indicate that such an assertion is proper, not when there is merely some "obstacle" to the rightholder's own litigation, but when such litigation is in all practicable terms impossible. Thus, in its framing of this principle, the plurality has gone far beyond our major precedents.

Moreover, on the plurality's own statement of this principle and on its own discussion of the facts, the litigation of third-party rights cannot be justified in this case. The plurality virtually concedes, as it must, that the two alleged "obstacles" to the women's assertion of their rights are chimerical. Our docket regularly contains cases in which women, using pseudonyms, challenge statutes that allegedly infringe their right to exercise the abortion decision. Nor is there basis for the "obstacle" of incipient mootness when the plurality itself quotes from the portion of Roe v. Wade, 410 U.S. 113, 124–25 (1973), that shows no such obstacle exists. In short, in light of experience which we share regularly in reviewing appeals and petitions for certiorari, the "obstacles" identified by the plurality as justifying departure from the general rule simply are not significant. Rather than being a logical descendant of *Barrows, NAACP*, and *Eisenstadt*, this case is much closer to Warth v. Seldin, 422 U.S. 490 (1975), in which taxpayers were refused leave to assert the constitutional rights of low-income persons in part because there was no obstacle to those low-income persons' asserting their own rights in a proper case.[4]

---

[4] The plurality retrospectively analyzes the facts in *Barrows, NAACP,* and *Eisen-* *stadt* in an effort to show that litigation by the rightholders was possible in each case.

B

The plurality places primary reliance on a second element, the existence of a "confidential relationship" between the rightholder and the party seeking to assert her rights.[5] Focusing on the professional [relationship] present in *Griswold,* the plurality suggests that allowing the physicians in this case to assert their patients' rights flows natural-ly . . . . Indeed, its conclusion is couched in terms of the general appropriateness of allowing physicians to assert the privacy interests of their patients in attacks on "governmental interference with the abor-tion decision."

With all respect, I do not read [*Griswold*] as merging the physician and his patient for constitutional purposes. The principle [it supports] turns not upon the confidential nature of a physician-patient relation-ship but upon the nature of the state's impact upon the relationship. [T]he state directly interdicted the normal functioning of the physician-patient relationship by criminalizing certain procedures. In the cir-cumstances of direct interference, I agree that one party to the relation-ship should be permitted to assert the constitutional rights of the other, for a judicial rule of self-restraint should not preclude an attack on a state's proscription of constitutionally protected activity. But Missouri has not directly interfered with the abortion decision—neither the physicians nor their patients are forbidden to engage in the procedure. The only impact of [the statute] is that . . . it causes these doctors financial detriment. This affords them art. III standing because they aver injury in fact, but it does not justify abandonment of the salutary rule against assertion of third-party rights.

[See] n.6. While this technically may be true, it also is true that the Court in *Bar-rows* and *NAACP* expressly emphasized the extreme difficulty of such litigation. Moreover, the plurality underestimates the difficulty confronting a would-be Negro vendee in *Barrows* who attempted to prove that race alone blocked his deal with a covenantor. And the plurality denigrates the difficulty of the NAACP members' as-sertion of their own right to anonymity when in the text on the same page it quotes, approvingly, the very language in the *NAACP* case expressing the difficulty of such litigation. As for *Eisenstadt,* al-lowing the assertion of third-party rights there was justified not only because of the difficulty of rightholders' litigation, but al-so because the state directly interdicted a course of conduct that allegedly enjoyed constitutional protection. As explained in-fra, Part II–B, the Court rightly shows special solicitude in that situation.

In any event, as argued above in the text, my basic disagreement with the plu-rality rests on the facts of *this case,* and the application of the plurality's *own* test—"some genuine obstacle" to the rightholder's assertion of her own rights. There simply is *no* such obstacle here.

[5] The plurality's primary emphasis upon this relationship is in marked contrast to the Court's previous position that the rela-tionship between litigant and rightholder was subordinate in importance to "the im-pact of the litigation on the third-party interests." Eisenstadt v. Baird, 405 U.S. 438, 445 (1972). I suspect the plurality's inversion of the previous order results from the weakness of the argument that this litigation is necessary to protect third-party interests. I would keep the empha-sis where it has been before, and would consider the closeness of any "relation-ship" only as a factor imparting confidence that third-party interests will be represent-ed adequately in a case in which allowing their assertion is justified on other grounds.

C

The physicians have offered no special reason for allowing them to assert their patients' rights in an attack on this welfare statute, and I can think of none. Moreover, there are persuasive reasons not to permit them to do so. It seems wholly inappropriate, as a matter of judicial self-governance, for a court to reach unnecessarily to decide a difficult constitutional issue in a case in which nothing more is at stake than remuneration for professional services. And second, this case may well set a precedent that will prove difficult to cabin. No reason immediately comes to mind, after today's holding, why any provider of services should be denied standing to assert his client's or customer's constitutional rights, if any, in an attack on a welfare statute that excludes from coverage his particular transaction.

Putting it differently, the Court's holding invites litigation by those who perhaps have the least legitimate ground for seeking to assert the rights of third parties. Before today I certainly would not have thought that an interest in being compensated for professional services, without more, would be deemed a sufficiently compelling reason to justify departing from a rule of restraint that well serves society and our judicial system. . . .

NOTES ON THIRD–PARTY STANDING

1. **Introduction.** The Supreme Court has often said that a litigant has standing to raise only his or her own rights. This rule is "prudential" only and has many exceptions. In those circumstances in which a litigant is allowed to raise another's rights, "third-party standing" or "jus tertii" is said to exist. The exceptions have been important in constitutional litigation. As the Court notes in *Singleton,* for example, development of the right to marital privacy in the *Griswold* case occurred in a context where such an exception was recognized. Other exceptions are illustrated below.

The rule against third-party standing and the requirement of standing to sue are related but distinguishable. Both bar the litigation of hypotheticals. The requirement of standing to sue ensures that there is an actual case or controversy requiring judicial resolution. The rule against third-party standing ensures that the litigation is restricted to that case or controversy and does not become an excuse for adjudicating unrelated claims. Not surprisingly, therefore, refusal to allow third-party standing is most likely where the injury to third-party rights is imaginary or conjectural.

In other cases, however, the existence of actual injury to the rights of identifiable third parties can scarcely be doubted. In such circumstances, a litigant who has a concrete interest in the dispute and who will benefit from the vindication of third-party rights is sometimes allowed to raise those rights. Such a litigant may be a plaintiff or a defendant. In either case, the litigant typically seeks to avoid enforcement of a rule or statute on the ground that it violates another's rights. The circumstances under which such a claim will be heard are many and varied. Usually, the Supreme Court has been content to approve or deny third-party standing without elaborate explanation. As a result, the issue is characterized by a confusing multiplicity of examples from which there emerges no coherent pattern, save perhaps a tendency toward progressive liberalization.[a]

Are the rationales articulated in *Singleton* for the general rule against third-party standing persuasive? What would be wrong with allowing third-party standing whenever the litigant before the court has a sufficiently concrete interest in the outcome of the suit to present a justiciable case or controversy? If the general rule is sound, is Justice Blackmun's rendition of the exceptions sound? Or is Justice Powell's more restrictive version to be preferred? These questions should be considered in connection with the following cases.

2. The Third Party's Ability to Raise His or Her Own Rights. In *Singleton* both the plurality and the dissenters agreed that the acceptability of third-party standing might turn on the rightholder's ability to raise his or her own rights. This factor has figured largely in several cases.

(i) *Barrows v. Jackson.* In the famous early case of Barrows v. Jackson, 346 U.S. 249 (1953), Los Angeles landowners had entered into a racially restrictive covenant on land in their neighborhood. Some of them brought an action at law for damages against one of their number who had permitted occupancy of her property by non-Caucasians. The Supreme Court had held in Shelley v. Kraemer, 334 U.S. 1 (1948), that although racially restrictive covenants were not illegal per se, they could not be enforced in equity against black purchasers. The Court had reasoned that judicial enforcement of such an agreement constituted state action and converted conduct permissible to private parties into a constitutional violation.

In *Barrows,* however, no one sought to enforce the covenant against blacks. Instead, plaintiffs sued the white landowner for damages. The question thus arose whether the defendant landowner could raise the rights of blacks in order to avoid her obligation under the covenant. The Court upheld third-party standing, describing the case as a "unique situation . . . in which it would be difficult if not impossible for the persons whose rights are asserted to present their grievance before any court." Since the landowner was the only person in a position to resist this particular form of enforcement, the Court held that the "rule of practice" against litigating the rights of another would give way to "the need to protect the fundamental rights which would be denied by permitting the damages action to be maintained."

---

[a] For academic analysis of the issues raised by third-party standing, see Monaghan, Third Party Standing, 84 Colum.L.Rev. 277 (1984); Sedler, The Assertion of Constitutional Jus Tertii: A Substantive Approach, 70 Calif. L. Rev. 1308 (1982); Rohr, Fighting For the Rights of Others: The Troubled Law of Third Party Standing and Mootness in the Federal Courts, 35 U.Miami L.Rev. 393 (1981).

(ii) ***Eisenstadt v. Baird.*** A similar concern surfaced in Eisenstadt v. Baird, 405 U.S. 438 (1972). Baird gave a public lecture on contraception and afterwards distributed a contraceptive foam to unmarried persons in violation of a Massachusetts statute. *Griswold v. Connecticut* had struck down a ban against using contraceptives as an infringement of the right of "marital privacy," but had not decided whether single persons had similar rights. Baird was allowed to raise that issue in his own defense, largely because "unmarried persons denied access to contraceptives in Massachusetts . . . are not themselves subject to prosecution and, to that extent, are denied a forum in which to assert their own rights."

In *Schlesinger v. Reservists Committee to Stop the War* (page 33, supra) and *United States v. Richardson* (page 41, supra), the absence of an alternative plaintiff was deemed irrelevant to the question of standing to sue. Can that conclusion be reconciled with *Barrows* and *Eisenstadt*? On what ground?

3. Relationship Between Litigant and Third Party. *Singleton v. Wulff* also illustrates the significance that a pre-existing relationship between litigant and rightholder may have in allowing third-party standing. The doctor-patient relationship involved in *Singleton* also figured in Doe v. Bolton, 410 U.S. 179 (1973), in which the Court allowed a physician to litigate the constitutionality of restrictions on abortion. In *Doe* the third-party standing issue was "of no great consequence," given that a woman who wanted an abortion was also a party to the suit. In Planned Parenthood v. Danforth, 428 U.S. 52 (1976), however, there was no such party, and the Supreme Court held, with virtually no discussion, that a physician could raise the abortion rights of women patients.

The Court has also allowed schools to raise the constitutional rights of students and their parents. For example, in Pierce v. Society of Sisters, 268 U.S. 510 (1925), private schools successfully challenged mandatory public school attendance as an unreasonable interference with "the liberty of parents and guardians to direct the upbringing and education of children under their control." In the same vein, the Court in Runyon v. McCrary, 427 U.S. 160 (1976), allowed a private school to claim, albeit unsuccessfully, that a law prohibiting racial discrimination in admissions violated the associational and privacy rights of students and their parents.

4. Dilution of Third-Party Rights. In some cases the Court has suggested a much broader explanation for third-party standing—namely, that failure to vindicate the litigant's claim would "dilute" or "adversely affect" enjoyment of claimed rights by the third party. This rationale may obtain where there is no apparent obstacle to the rightholder's assertion of his or her own rights and where there is no pre-existing relationship between the litigant and the third party.

An example is Craig v. Boren, 429 U.S. 190 (1976), where a saloonkeeper was allowed to raise the equal protection rights of young men to buy beer at the same age as young women. The restriction on young men caused the saloon-keeper economic injury and therefore established standing to sue. Further, she was found "entitled to assert those concomitant rights of third parties that would be 'diluted or adversely affected' should her constitutional challenge fail and the statutes remain in force." Accordingly, the saloon-keeper came within the seemingly general rule that "vendors and those in like positions have been uniformly permitted to resist efforts at restricting their operations by acting as advocates for the rights of third parties who seek access to their market or function," citing *Eisenstadt v. Baird* and *Barrows v. Jackson.*

Craig v. Boren might be discounted on the ground that the litigation originally included an underage male (with respect to whom the case became moot when he reached the required age) and that the objection to the saloon-keeper's assertion of third-party rights was made for the first time in the Supreme Court. No such factors were present, however, in Carey v. Population Services International, 431 U.S. 678 (1977), which followed the same approach. In *Carey* a corporate seller of contraceptives challenged a New York statute that prohibited, inter alia, sale of contraceptives to persons under the age of 16. Speaking for a majority of seven, Justice Brennan declared that the corporation's standing to attack the statute, "not only in its own right but also on behalf of its potential customers, is settled by *Craig v. Boren.*"

Potentially, the rationale of *Craig* and *Carey* has a very broad reach. Indeed, is there any case of actual injury to an identifiable third party in which the third-party's rights would not be "diluted or adversely affected" by failure to vindicate the litigant's claim? If not, the bar against third-party standing is reduced to prohibition against litigating purely hypothetical situations. Is that sound? Is it consistent with the Court's decisions on art. III standing to sue?

5. The Overbreadth Doctrine. The instances of third-party standing discussed to this point have in common the allegation of concrete injury to the rights of identifiable third parties. None involves litigation of a purely hypothetical situation. In one context, however, the Supreme Court has endorsed the litigation of hypotheticals and has allowed a litigant to raise the rights of persons whose interest in the matter at hand is entirely conjectural. That context is the first-amendment overbreadth doctrine.[b]

The word "overbreadth" describes the substantive coverage of a statute challenged on first amendment grounds; a law is "overbroad" if it prohibits some protected speech. The heart of the overbreadth doctrine is not the fact of excessive coverage, however, but the resulting posture of judicial review. Under the overbreadth doctrine, a law may be challenged as unconstitutional "on its face." This means that a litigant whose conduct is not constitutionally protected may challenge the validity of the law as it might be applied to one whose conduct would be constitutionally protected. Although overbreadth cases are

---

[b] The overbreadth doctrine is the subject of a substantial literature. For a good introduction, see Monaghan, Overbreadth, 1981 Sup. Ct Rev. 1.

not often cited as such, the overbreadth doctrine is a classic case of third-party standing: a litigant is allowed to attack the validity of a statute by raising someone else's rights. And unlike most instances of third-party standing, the overbreadth claimant is not required to show that there exists some obstacle to the third party's assertion of his or her own rights, or that there is some relationship between the litigant and the third party, or even that there is an identifiable third party whose rights are infringed. In essence, the overbreadth doctrine is the ultimate extension of the dilution-of-rights rationale: the mere existence of an overbroad law is assumed to "dilute or adversely affect" the right of those unidentified persons whose exercise of first-amendment rights may be "chilled" by the threat that the law will be enforced against them.

The Supreme Court has noted that overbreadth review is "strong medicine" and required that the excess coverage "not only be real, but substantial as well, judged in relation to the statute's plainly legitimate sweep." Broadrick v. Oklahoma, 413 U.S. 601, 613, 615 (1973). Even so constrained, however, the overbreadth doctrine is significantly more accommodating to the litigation of another's rights than most of the judicial pronouncements on third-party standing.

The usual explanation for this approach is the societal importance of first-amendment rights. Does that suggest that other instances of third-party standing might also turn on the importance to society of the right being asserted? Does it suggest that a distinction might be made between those rights (such as free speech?) that are significantly societal or "systemic" in their impact and those (perhaps the fourth amendment?) that are primarily "personal" in nature? Is that distinction tenable? Does it cast any light on third-party standing cases in other contexts? Does it cast any light on other standing decisions, for example in establishment clause cases or cases challenging the incompatibility (page 33, supra), accounts (page 41, supra), or property (page 43, supra) clauses of the Constitution?

SUBSECTION B: RIPENESS

POE v. ULLMAN
Supreme Court of the United States, 1961.
367 U.S. 497.

MR. JUSTICE FRANKFURTER announced the judgment of the Court in an opinion in which the CHIEF JUSTICE, MR. JUSTICE CLARK and MR. JUSTICE WHITTAKER join.

These appeals challenge the constitutionality, under the 14th amendment, of Connecticut statutes which, as authoritatively construed by the Connecticut Supreme Court of Errors, prohibit the use of contraceptive devices and the giving of medical advice in the use of such devices. In proceedings seeking declarations of law, not on review of convictions for violation of the statutes, that court has ruled that these statutes would be applicable in the case of married couples and even under claim that conception would constitute a serious threat to the health or life of the female spouse.

[The appeals involved three separate actions for declaratory relief. The first, brought under the names of Paul and Pauline Poe, alleged that Mrs. Poe had given birth to three deformed children, each of whom died shortly thereafter; that the Poes' physician, Dr. Buxton, had determined "that the best and safest medical treatment which could be prescribed for their situation is advice in methods of preventing conception"; but that the Poes had been unable to obtain such information "for the sole reason that its delivery and use may or will be claimed by the defendant State's Attorney (appellee in this Court) to constitute offenses against Connecticut law." The second suit was brought by a married woman who had endured an extremely difficult pregnancy and had similarly been told by Dr. Buxton that she needed contraceptive advice. The third suit was brought by Dr. Buxton, who claimed that the application of the statute to medical advice interfered with his practice in a manner that violated due process.]

Appellants' complaints in these declaratory judgment proceedings do not clearly, and certainly do not in terms, allege that appellee Ullman threatens to prosecute them for use of, or for giving advice concerning, contraceptive devices. The allegations are merely that, in the course of his public duty, he intends to prosecute any offenses against Connecticut law, and that he claims that use of and advice concerning contraceptives would constitute offenses. The lack of immediacy of the threat described by these allegations might alone raise serious questions of nonjusticiability of appellants' claims. See United Public Workers v. Mitchell, 330 U.S. 75 (1947). But even were we to read the allegations to convey a clear threat of imminent prosecutions, we are not bound to accept as true all that is alleged on the face of the complaint and admitted, technically, by demurrer, any more than the Court is bound by stipulation of the parties. Formal agreement between parties that collide with plausibility is too fragile a foundation for indulging in constitutional adjudication.

The Connecticut law prohibiting the use of contraceptives has been on the state's books since 1879. During the more than three-quarters of a century since its enactment, a prosecution for its violation seems never to have been initiated, save in State v. Nelson, 126 Conn. 412, 11 A.2d 856 (1940). The circumstances of that case . . . only prove the abstract character of what is before us. There, a test case was brought to determine the constitutionality of the act as applied against two doctors and a nurse who had allegedly disseminated contraceptive information. After the Supreme Court of Errors sustained the legislation on appeal from a demurrer to the information, the state moved to dismiss the information. Neither counsel nor our own researches have discovered any other attempt to enforce the prohibition of distribution or use of contraceptive devices by criminal process. The unreality of these suits is illuminated by another circumstance. We were advised by counsel for appellants that contraceptives are commonly and notoriously sold in Connecticut drug stores. Yet no prosecutions are recorded; and certainly such ubiquitous, open, public sales would more quickly invite the attention of enforcement officials than the conduct in which the present appellants wish to engage—the giving of private medical advice by a doctor to his individual patients, and their private use of the devices prescribed. The undeviating policy of nullification by Connecticut of its anti-contraceptive laws throughout all the long years that they have been on the statute books bespeaks more than prosecutorial paralysis. What was said in another context is relevant here. "Deeply embedded traditional ways of carrying out state policy . . ."—or not carrying it out—"are often tougher and truer law than the dead words of the written text."

The restriction of our jurisdiction to cases and controversies within the meaning of article III of the Constitution is not the sole limitation on the exercise of our appellate powers, especially in cases raising constitutional questions. The policy reflected in numerous cases and over a long period was thus summarized in the oft-quoted statement of Mr. Justice Brandeis: "The Court [has] developed, for its own governance in the cases confessedly within its jurisdiction, a series of rules under which it has avoided passing upon a large part of all the constitutional questions pressed upon it for decision." Ashwander v. Tennessee Valley Authority, 297 U.S. 288, 341 (1936) (concurring opinion). In part the rules summarized in the *Ashwander* opinion have derived from the historically defined, limited nature and function of courts and from the recognition that, within the framework of our adversary system, the adjudicatory process is most securely founded when it is exercised under the impact of a lively conflict between antagonistic demands, actively pressed, which make resolution of the controverted issue a practical necessity. In part they derive from the fundamental federal and tripartite character of our national government and from the role—restricted by its very responsibility—of the federal courts, and particularly this Court, within that structure.

These considerations press with special urgency in cases challenging legislative action or state judicial action as repugnant to the Constitution. "The best teaching of this Court's experience admonishes us not to entertain constitutional questions in advance of the strictest necessity." The various doctrines of "standing," "ripeness," and "mootness," which this Court has evolved with particular, though not exclusive, reference to such cases are but several manifestations—each having its own "varied application"—of the primary conception that federal judicial power is to be exercised to strike down legislation, whether state or federal, only at the instance of one who is himself immediately harmed, or immediately threatened with harm, by the challenged action. . . .

It is clear that the mere existence of a state penal statute would constitute insufficient grounds to support a federal court's adjudication of its constitutionality in proceedings brought against the state's prose-

cuting officials if real threat of enforcement is wanting. If the prosecutor expressly agrees not to prosecute, a suit against him for declaratory
and injunctive relief is not such an adversary case as will be reviewed
here. Eighty years of Connecticut history demonstrate a similar, albeit
tacit agreement. The fact that Connecticut has not chosen to press the
enforcement of this statute deprives these controversies of the immediacy which is an indispensable condition of constitutional adjudication.
This Court cannot be umpire to debates concerning harmless, empty
shadows. To find it necessary to pass on these statutes now, in order to
protect appellants from the hazards of prosecution, would be to close
our eyes to reality. . . .

Justiciability is of course not a legal concept with a fixed content or
susceptible of scientific verification. Its utilization is the resultant of
many subtle pressures, including the appropriateness of the issues for
decision by this Court and the actual hardship to the litigants of
denying them the relief sought. Both these factors justify withholding
adjudication of the constitutional issue raised under the circumstances
and in the manner in which they are now before the Court.

Dismissed.

MR. JUSTICE BLACK dissents because he believes that the constitutional questions should be reached and decided.

MR. JUSTICE BRENNAN, concurring in the judgment.

I agree that this appeal must be dismissed for failure to present a
real and substantial controversy which unequivocally calls for adjudication of the rights claimed in advance of any attempt by the state to
curtail them by criminal prosecution. I am not convinced, on this
skimpy record, that these appellants are truly caught in an inescapable
dilemma. The true controversy in this case is over the opening of
birth-control clinics on a large scale; it is that which the state has
prevented in the past, not the use of contraceptives by isolated and
individual married couples. It will be time enough to decide the
constitutional questions urged upon us when, if ever, that real controversy flares up again. Until it does, or until the state makes a definite
and concrete threat to enforce these laws against individual married
couples—a threat which it has never made in the past except under the
provocation of litigation—this Court may not be compelled to exercise
its most delicate power of constitutional adjudication.

MR. JUSTICE DOUGLAS, dissenting.

These cases are dismissed because a majority of the members of
this Court conclude, for varying reasons, that this controversy does not
present a justiciable question. That conclusion is too transparent to
require an extended reply. The device of the declaratory judgment is
an honored one. . . . If there is a case where the need for this remedy
in the shadow of a criminal prosecution is shown, it is this one, as Mr.
Justice Harlan demonstrates. . . .

What are these people—doctor and patients—to do? Flout the law
and go to prison? Violate the law surreptitiously and hope they will

not get caught? By today's decision we leave them no other alternatives. It is not the choice they need have under the regime of the declaratory judgment and our constitutional system. It is not the choice worthy of a civilized society. A sick wife, a concerned husband, a conscientious doctor seek a dignified, discrete [sic], orderly answer to the critical problem confronting them. We should not turn them away and make them flout the law and get arrested to have their constitutional rights determined. They are entitled to an answer to their predicament here and now. . . .

MR. JUSTICE HARLAN, dissenting. . . .

There can be no quarrel with the plurality opinion's statement that "Justiciability is of course not a legal concept with a fixed content or susceptible of scientific verification," but, with deference, the fact that justiciability is not precisely definable does not make it ineffable. . . .

[T]he Court, in the course of its decisions on matters of justiciability, has developed and given expression to a number of important limitations on the exercise of its jurisdiction, the presence or absence of which here should determine the justiciability of these appeals. Since all of them are referred to here in one way or another, it is well to proceed to a disclosure of those which are *not* involved in the present appeals, thereby focusing attention on the one factor on which reliance appears to be placed by both the plurality and concurring opinions in this instance.

First: It should by now be abundantly clear that the fact that only constitutional claims are presented in proceedings seeking *anticipatory* relief against state criminal statutes does not for that reason alone make the claims premature. . . .

Second: I do not think these appeals may be dismissed for want of "ripeness" as that concept has been understood in its "varied applications." There is no lack of "ripeness" in the sense that is exemplified by cases such as United Public Workers v. Mitchell, 330 U.S. 75 (1947); International Longshoremen's and Warehousemen's Union v. Boyd, 347 U.S. 222 (1954); [and others]. In all of these cases the lack of ripeness inhered in the fact that the need for some further procedure, some further contingency of application or interpretation, whether judicial administrative or executive, or some further clarification of the intentions of the claimant, served to make remote the issue which was sought to be presented to the Court. Certainly the appellants have stated in their pleadings fully and unequivocally what it is that they intend to do; no clarifying or resolving contingency stands in their way before they may embark on that conduct. Thus, there is no circumstance besides that of detection or prosecution to make remote the particular controversy. And it is clear beyond cavil that the mere fact that a controversy such as this is rendered still more unavoidable by an actual prosecution, is not *alone* sufficient to make the case too remote, not ideally enough "ripe" for adjudication, at the prior stage of anticipatory relief.

. . . I cannot see what further elaboration is required to enable us to decide the appellants' claims, and indeed neither the plurality opinion nor the concurring opinion—notwithstanding the latter's characterization of this record as "skimpy"—suggests what more grist is needed before the judicial mill could turn.

Third: This is not a feigned, hypothetical, friendly or colorable suit such as discloses "a want of a truly adversary contest." . . .

Fourth: The doctrine of the cases dealing with a litigant's lack of standing to raise a constitutional claim is said to justify the dismissal of these appeals. . . . There is no question but that appellants here are asserting rights which are peculiarly their own, and which, if they are to be raised at all, may be raised most appropriately by them. Nor do I understand the argument to be that this is the sort of claim which is too remote ever to be pressed by anyone, because no one is ever sufficiently involved. Thus, in truth, it is not the parties pressing this claim but the occasion chosen for pressing it which is objected to. But as has been shown the fact that it is anticipatory relief which is asked cannot of itself make the occasion objectionable.

We are brought, then, to the precise failing in these proceedings which is said to justify refusal to exercise our mandatory appellate jurisdiction: that there has been but one recorded Connecticut case dealing with a *prosecution* under the statute. The significance of this lack of recorded evidence of prosecutions is said to make the presentation of appellants' rights too remote, too contingent, too hypothetical for adjudication . . . .

As far as the record is concerned, I think it is pure conjecture, and indeed conjecture which to me seems contrary to realities, that an open violation of the statute by a doctor (or more obviously still by a birth-control clinic) would not result in a substantial threat of prosecution. Crucial to the opposite conclusion is the description of the 1940 prosecution instituted in *State v. Nelson* as a "test case" which, as it is viewed, scarcely even punctuates the uniform state practice of nonenforcement of this statute. I read the history of Connecticut enforcement in a very different light. The *Nelson* case, as appears from the state court's opinion, was a prosecution of two doctors and a nurse for aiding and abetting violations of this statute by married women in prescribing and advising the use of contraceptive materials by them. It is true that there is evidence of a customary unwillingness to enforce the statute prior to *Nelson* . . . . What must also be noted is that the prosecutor [in that case] stated that the purpose of the prosecution was:

"the establishment of the constitutional validity and efficacy of the statutes under which these accused are informed against. Henceforth any person, whether a physician or layman, who violates the provisions of these statutes, must expect to be prosecuted and punished in accordance with the literal provisions of the law." . . .

The plurality opinion now finds, and the concurring opinion must assume, that the only explanation of the absence of recorded prosecutions subsequent to the *Nelson* case is that Connecticut has renounced that intention to prosecute and punish "*any* person . . . in accordance with the literal provisions of the law" which it announced in *Nelson*. But if renunciation of the purposes of the *Nelson* prosecution is consistent with a lack of subsequent prosecutions, success of that purpose is no less consistent with that lack. . . .   In short, I fear that the Court has indulged in a bit of sleight of hand to be rid of this case. It has treated the significance of the absence of prosecutions during the 20 years since *Nelson* as identical with that of the absence of prosecutions during the years before *Nelson*. It has ignored the fact that the very purpose of the *Nelson* prosecution was to change defiance into compliance. It has ignored the very possibility that this purpose may have been successful. The result is to postulate a security from prosecution for open defiance of the statute which I do not believe the record supports. . . .

The Court's disposition assumes that to decide the case now, in the absence of any consummated prosecutions, is unwise because it forces a difficult decision in advance of any exigent necessity therefor.   Of course it is abundantly clear that this requisite necessity can exist prior to any actual prosecution, for that is the theory of anticipatory relief, and is by now familiar law. What must be relied on, therefore, is that the historical absence of prosecutions in some way leaves these appellants free to violate the statute without fear of prosecution, whether or not the law is constitutional, and thus absolves us from the duty of deciding if it is. Despite the suggestion of a "tougher and truer law" of immunity from criminal prosecution and despite speculation as to a "tacit agreement" that this law will not be enforced, there is, of course, no suggestion of an estoppel against the state if it should attempt to prosecute appellants. Neither the plurality nor the concurring opinion suggests that appellants have some legally cognizable right not to be prosecuted if the statute is constitutional. What is meant is simply that the appellants are more or less free to act without fear of prosecution because the prosecuting authorities of the state, in their discretion and at their whim, are, as a matter of prediction, unlikely to decide to prosecute.

Here is the core of my disagreement with the present disposition. [T]he most substantial claim which these married persons press is their right to enjoy the privacy of their marital relations free of the enquiry of the criminal law, whether it be in a prosecution of them or of a doctor whom they have consulted. And I cannot agree that their enjoyment of this privacy is not substantially impinged upon, when they are told that . . . the only thing which stands between them and being forced to render criminal account of their marital privacy is the whim of the prosecutor. . . .

I therefore think it is incumbent on us to consider the merits of appellants' constitutional claims. . . .

MR. JUSTICE STEWART, dissenting.

For the reasons so convincingly advanced by both Mr. Justice Douglas and Mr. Justice Harlan, I join them in dissenting from the dismissal of these appeals. . . .[a]

NOTES ON RIPENESS

1. Relation to Standing. The connection between ripeness and standing is traced by Lea Brilmayer in The Jurisprudence of Article III: Perspectives on the "Case or Controversy" Requirement, 93 Harv. L. Rev. 297, 298–99 (1979): *

> "[I]magine a citizen in a town that has recently enacted an ordinance prohibiting the posting of campaign signs on residential property. Assume he believes it is unconstitutional to restrict political expression this way, but has posted no campaign signs himself and therefore has not been prosecuted. In fact, he has no present interest in putting up a sign. He does, however, resent this ordinance. What can he do?
>
> "First, he might initiate litigation by alleging the ordinance infringes the first amendment rights of others. His neighbor would put up signs but for the ordinance. Second, he might attempt to show that his own future first amendment rights are threatened. Next year, he may wish to post campaign signs. The first approach raises standing objections; the second, ripeness objections. The standing doctrine holds that one may not assert the rights of other persons; it is necessary to allege a 'personal stake' in the dispute. If the citizen straightforwardly insists his interests are not involved but the rights of his neighbors are, he will be denied access to federal court, and most state courts also. If the citizen tries the second approach—hypothesizing a personal future interest— then the ripeness requirement must be met. The danger that supposedly motivates him must be real and immediate, rather than distant and speculative. There must be concrete demonstration that some harm really will occur; it must be based on objective evidence and not merely his own assertions. Otherwise the standing limitation could be subverted by self-serving hypotheses about future harm."

What light does this analysis shed on *Poe*? Was the Court concerned that the plaintiffs lacked the "personal stake" required for standing? Or that the controversy was not ripe for adjudication? Are the two concepts distinguishable? Insofar as both derive from art. III,

[a] In 1961, Dr. Buxton served as medical director of a birth-control clinic opened by the Planned Parenthood League in New Haven, Conn. His criminal prosecution and that of the League's executive director led to the invalidation of the Connecticut statutes in Griswold v. Connecticut, 381 U.S. 479 (1965). [Footnote by eds.]

they might be thought duplicative: Presumably, a person who has no actual or threatened redressable injury lacks standing to sue, and the issue posed by that person is not ripe for adjudication. Does that mean that ripeness issues can always be recast as questions of standing, or does each doctrine have independent content?

Is it useful to think of ripeness, as standing is so often described, as having both constitutional and prudential aspects? If so, which was at issue in *Poe* ?

2. *Aetna Life Ins. v. Haworth*. Since "ripeness" is the name given to the issue of prematurity in litigation, it usually arises in suits for anticipatory relief. Of course, anticipatory relief has long been available in the form of an injunction, but the equitable requirements of irreparable harm and no adequate remedy at law typically proved more restrictive than any art. III limitation on the exercise of judicial power. The problem of ripeness, as an issue distinct from the law of equity, is chiefly a product of the suit for declaratory judgment.

The Federal Declaratory Judgment Act, now codified in 28 U.S.C. §§ 2201–2202, was enacted in 1934. Its purpose was to obviate the necessity "to violate or purport to violate a statute in order to obtain a judicial determination of its meaning or validity." S. Rep. No. 1005, 73rd Cong., 2d Sess., pp. 2–3. As originally passed, the statute authorized the courts of the United States "to declare rights and other legal relations" without regard to whether further relief was or could be asked for. This power was expressly limited to "cases of actual controversy."[a]

In Aetna Life Ins. Co. v. Haworth, 300 U.S. 227 (1937), this procedure was challenged as inconsistent with art. III. The case involved a series of insurance policies providing various benefits in the event of total and permanent disability. The insured claimed such disability and so notified his insurer. The company denied the claim and asserted that the policies had lapsed for non-payment of premiums. After some time, the company sued for a declaration of non-liability, contending that otherwise its ability to disprove the claimed disability might be impaired by the disappearance, illness, or death of relevant witnesses. The trial court dismissed the complaint on the ground that it did not set forth a justiciable "controversy." That decision was affirmed by the Court of Appeals, but reversed by the Supreme Court. Speaking for a unanimous Court, Chief Justice Hughes said:

> "The Constitution limits the exercise of the judicial power to 'cases' and 'controversies.' . . . The Declaratory Judgment Act of 1934, in its limitation to 'cases of actual controversy,' manifestly has regard to the constitutional provision and is

[a] Act of June 14, 1934, 48 Stat. 955. The successor provision, 28 U.S.C. § 2201, reads as follows:

"In a case of actual controversy within its jurisdiction, except with respect to federal taxes, any court of the United States, upon the filing of an appropriate pleading, may declare the rights and other legal relations of any interested party seeking such declaration, whether or not further relief is or could be sought. Any such declaration shall have the force and effect of a final judgment or decree and shall be reviewable as such."

operative only in respect to controversies which are such in the
constitutional sense. . . .

"A 'controversy' in this sense must be one that is appropriate for judicial determination. A justiciable controversy is
thus distinguished from a difference or dispute of a hypothetical or abstract character; from one that is academic or moot.
The controversy must be definite and concrete, touching the
legal relations of parties having adverse legal interests. It
must be a real and substantial controversy admitting of specific relief through a decree of a conclusive character, as distinguished from an opinion advising what the law would be upon
a hypothetical state of facts."

Applying these principles to the case at hand, the Court found that
it was "manifestly susceptible of judicial determination." It called "not
for an advisory opinion upon a hypothetical basis, but for an adjudication of present right upon established facts." If the insured had sued
on the policies, the existence of a justiciable controversy would not have
been doubted. That the company brought suit instead was of no
consequence, for "[i]t is the nature of the controversy, not the method of
its presentation or the particular party who presents it, that is determinative."

Is *Poe* consistent with *Haworth*? Was the controversy in *Poe* more
abstract, hypothetical, or academic than the controversy in *Haworth*?
Or is the difference in result attributable to a difference in judicial
attitude toward the claim being raised? Might the Court have been
more chary to rule on the constitutionality of Connecticut's laws than
to resolve the contractual rights of private parties? Is it proper for
such considerations to figure in determinations of ripeness?

3. United Public Workers v. Mitchell. Another early ripeness
case, cited by both sides in *Poe,* is United Public Workers v. Mitchell,
330 U.S. 75 (1947). Federal workers sued to enjoin enforcement of a
provision in the Hatch Act stating that "[n]o officer or employee in the
executive branch of the federal government . . . shall take any active
part in political management or in political campaigns." Only one of
the plaintiffs had actually violated the Hatch Act. The rest alleged
their desire to act contrary to the rule against political activity and
stated their conviction that the statute contravened their constitutional
rights. The Supreme Court found their claim non-justiciable. "We can
only speculate," said Justice Reed, "as to the kinds of political activity
the appellants desire to engage in or as to the contents of their
proposed public statements or the circumstances of their publication."
To this he added an influential statement of the case for judicial self-
restraint:

"The Constitution allots the nation's judicial power to the
federal courts. Unless these courts respect the limits of that
unique authority, they intrude upon powers vested in the
legislative or executive branches. Judicial adherence to the
doctrine of the separation of powers preserves the courts for

the decision of issues, between litigants, capable of effective determination. Judicial exposition upon political proposals is permissible only when necessary to decide definite issues between litigants. When the courts act continually within these constitutionally imposed boundaries of their power, their ability to perform their function as a balance for the people's protection against abuse of power by other branches of government remains unimpaired. Should the courts seek to expand their power so as to bring under their jurisdiction ill-defined controversies over constitutional issues, they would become the organ of political theories. Such abuse of judicial power would properly meet rebuke and restriction from other branches."[b]

Are these remarks persuasive? Do they provide a rationale for the decision in *Poe*?

4. *Duke Power*. In Duke Power Co. v. Carolina Environmental Study Group, Inc., 438 U.S. 59 (1978), environmental activists sought to derail construction of nuclear power plants by attacking the constitutionality of the Price-Anderson Act. That statute limited total compensation to be paid by the utility companies in the event of a major nuclear accident.[c] That no such event had occurred or, in the view of the experts, was likely to, might have been thought to make adjudication of the issue premature, but the Supreme Court disagreed:

"To the extent that issues of ripeness involve, at least in part, the existence of a live 'Case or Controversy,' our conclusion that appellees will sustain immediate injury from the operation of the disputed power plants [chiefly resulting from thermal pollution of lake waters used to cool the reactors] and that such injury would be redressed by the relief requested would appear to satisfy this requirement.

"The prudential considerations embodied in the ripeness doctrine also argue strongly for a prompt resolution of the claims presented. Although it is true that no nuclear accident has yet occurred and that such an occurrence would eliminate much of the existing scientific uncertainty surrounding this subject, it would not, in our view, significantly advance our ability to deal with the legal issues presented nor aid us in their resolution. However, delayed resolution of these issues would foreclose any relief from the present injury suffered by appellees—relief that would be forthcoming if they were to prevail in their various challenges to the act. Similarly, delayed resolution would frustrate one of the key purposes of the Price-Anderson Act—the elimination of doubts concerning the scope of private liability in the event of major nuclear

[b] Justice Douglas dissented.

[c] The case is considered, and the facts are further described, at pages 36–38, supra. Recall that one of the problems with the plaintiffs' standing was that the claim asserted (the constitutionality of limiting compensation in the event of a nuclear accident) was unrelated to the injuries held sufficient for purposes of standing (thermal and environmental pollution resulting from ordinary operation).

accident. In short, all parties would be adversely affected by a decision to defer definitive resolution of the constitutional validity vel non of the Price-Anderson Act. Since we are persuaded that 'we will be in no better position later than we are now' to decide this question, we hold that it is presently ripe for adjudication."

Are these persuasive reasons for resolving the constitutionality of the statute? Did the decision on justiciability depend on a "preliminary" assessment of the merits? Should it have mattered that the alleged constitutional defect had no relation to plaintiffs' present injuries?

Consider the view expressed by Jonathan Varat in Variable Justiciability and the *Duke Power* Case, 58 Tex. L. Rev. 273 (1980). Varat asserts that the "unacknowledged result" of this decision is "to collapse the article III ripeness inquiry into the article III standing inquiry and to alter the primary policy of ripeness from a concern with the issues to a concern with the plaintiff's cognizable injury in fact":

> "If ripeness, in the dimension of reasonable certainty of actual harm, is not to be a redundant inquiry into standing, the Court must focus on harm to the rights claimed to be unlawfully disregarded, not the concrete harm that gives the plaintiff a stake in the litigation. Ripeness is meaningful only if applied to the issue raised in the case. To be sure, relative certainty of harm to the plaintiff in most cases coincides with relative certainty of harm to the rights asserted in the suit. Most suits claim that present rights have been, or are being, unlawfully ignored. In the rare case like *Duke Power,* however, the inquiries are separate and should be treated as such. The Court's job is to protect rights that are threatened—not to redress any injury that incidentally might be redressed by adjudication of rights not in jeopardy and not legally related to that injury."

Does this criticism suggest an independent significance to questions of ripeness and standing? Is the focus here on ripeness, or on the adjudication of third-party rights? Or are they perhaps only two ways of looking at the same thing?[d]

5. Related Doctrines. Ripeness is the main, but not the only, bar to premature litigation. Closely related are the requirements of finality and exhaustion of remedies, both of which operate to prevent premature judicial review of administrative decisions. As used in this context,[e] "finality" describes the usual statutory authorization of judicial review of final agency actions. See, e.g., 15 U.S.C. § 45(c) (authorizing judicial review of final "cease and desist" orders of the Federal

[d] For commentary on these issues, see Nichol, Ripeness and the Constitution, 54 U.Chi.L.Rev. 153 (1987), which suggests that ripeness be treated as a prudential concern.

[e] The word is also used to describe the limitation of appellate jurisdiction in 28 U.S.C. § 1291 to "final decisions" of the District Courts and the specification in 28 U.S.C. § 1257 that the Supreme Court has jurisdiction over "[f]inal judgments or decrees" of the highest state courts. These matters are considered at pages 657–85, infra.

Trade Commission). The generic provision is in the Administrative Procedure Act (APA), 5 U.S.C. § 704, which provides for judicial review of "final agency action for which there is no other adequate remedy in a court." Other agency action may be challenged if "made reviewable by statute." 5 U.S.C. § 701(a).

As the Supreme Court made clear in Abbott Laboratories v. Gardner, 387 U.S. 136 (1967), the APA does not bar pre-enforcement review by means of suits for declaratory or injunctive relief. The Court said that the basic rationale of the ripeness doctrine in this context is "to prevent the courts, through avoidance of premature adjudication, from entangling themselves in abstract disagreements over administrative policies, and also to protect the agencies from judicial interference until an administrative decision has been formalized and its effects felt in a concrete way by the challenging parties." These goals could be served by a "pragmatic" administration of the statutory requirement. Specifically, said the Court, "finality" would depend on an evaluation of "the fitness of the issues for judicial decision" and "the hardship to the parties of withholding court consideration."

Of similar effect is the requirement of exhaustion of administrative remedies. See Myers v. Bethlehem Shipbuilding Corp., 303 U.S. 41 (1938). In that case the Court invoked the "long settled rule of judicial administration that no one is entitled to judicial relief for a supposed or threatened injury until the prescribed administrative remedy has been exhausted." The goal is to avoid disruption of agency action by premature judicial intervention.

For discussion of these doctrines and a comprehensive analysis of prematurity issues in the administrative context, see Vining, Direct Judicial Review and the Doctrine of Ripeness in Administrative Law, 69 Mich. L. Rev. 1445 (1971).

SUBSECTION C: MOOTNESS

INTRODUCTORY NOTES ON MOOTNESS

1. **Introduction.** Mootness has been described as "the doctrine of standing set in a time frame: The requisite personal interest that must exist at the commencement of the litigation (standing) must continue throughout its existence (mootness)." Monaghan, Constitutional Adjudication: The Who and When, 82 Yale L.J. 1363, 1384 (1973).[a] If, during the course of litigation, the requisite live controversy between

---

[a] For further discussion of the relation of mootness and standing, see Brilmayer, The Jurisprudence of Article III: Perspectives on the "Case or Controversy" Requirement, 93 Harv. L. Rev. 297, 298–99 (1979); Fallon, Of Justiciability, Remedies, and Public Law Litigation: Notes on the Jurisprudence of *Lyons*, 59 N.Y.U.L. Rev. 1 (1984).

the contending parties ceases to exist, the case will be dismissed as moot.

So stated, the mootness doctrine is deceptively simple. In fact, however, the doctrine is complicated by a number of exceptions and by a history of uncertainty in its administration.

2. Voluntary Cessation of Illegal Activity. An established exception to mootness is illustrated by United States v. W.T. Grant Co., 345 U.S. 629 (1953). In that case the government brought an antitrust action to enjoin the use of interlocking directorates among competing corporations. The offending directors resigned, and the defendants sought to have the suit dismissed as moot. The Supreme Court disagreed:

> "Both sides agree to the abstract proposition that voluntary cessation of allegedly illegal conduct does not deprive the tribunal of power to hear and determine the case, i.e., does not make the case moot. A controversy may remain to be settled in such circumstances, e.g., a dispute over the legality of the challenged practices. The defendant is free to return to his old ways. This, together with a public interest in having the legality of the practices settled, militates against a mootness conclusion. For to say that the case has become moot means that the defendant is entitled to a dismissal as a matter of right. The courts have rightly refused to grant defendants such a powerful weapon against public law enforcement."

The Court went on to say that the case might nevertheless be moot if the defendants could demonstrate that "there is no reasonable expectation that the wrong will be repeated," but that a mere disclaimer of intention to revive the illegal practice is insufficient.

Is it clear that the *W.T. Grant* case should have been heard on the merits? Is the issue in that case different from any other case in which an injunction is sought against activity in which the defendant has engaged in the past and allegedly will continue in the future?[b]

3. Controversies "Capable of Repetition, Yet Evading Review." Another established exception to the mootness doctrine applies to questions "capable of repetition, yet evading review." The phrase comes from Southern Pacific Terminal Co. v. Interstate Commerce Commission, 219 U.S. 498, 515 (1911), and is typically invoked where the specific case between the plaintiff and the defendant has been mooted by the passage of time, but where the same issue is likely to arise again. As the Court has said, there must be "a 'reasonable expectation' or a 'demonstrated probability' that the same controversy will recur." Murphy v. Hunt, 455 U.S. 478, 482 (1982) (per curiam). Moreover, at least as the doctrine is conventionally applied, it is not

[b] For an application of this principle, see City of Mesquite v. Aladdin's Castle, Inc., 455 U.S. 283 (1982). In that case, a municipal ordinance was declared unconstitutionally vague on the basis of statutory language that had already been repealed when the decision was rendered. The Supreme Court noted that the municipality would be free to reenact the same ordinance if the judgment were vacated and concluded that the case was not moot.

enough that the same issue will arise in the future; the controversy must be "capable of repetition, yet evading review" with respect to the same claimant.

This principle is illustrated by First National Bank of Boston v. Bellotti, 435 U.S. 765 (1978). In that case, Massachusetts businesses attacked a statute forbidding expenditure of corporate funds to influence voter referenda on issues not materially affecting business interests. The statute further provided that no issue concerning the taxation of individuals should be deemed materially to affect a corporation's business interests. The plaintiff corporations wanted to spend money to oppose a state constitutional amendment authorizing a graduated individual income tax. When informed that such expenditures would violate state law, the corporations challenged the statute as a violation of free speech. By the time the case reached the Supreme Court, however, the referendum had been held, and the proposed amendment defeated. The suggestion was therefore made that the case had become moot, but the Supreme Court disagreed.

Similar amendments had been proposed by the legislature on four occasions. In each instance, the time between the legislative action and submission to the voters had been too short to allow complete judicial review. Moreover, there seemed little doubt that the proposal would be revived in the future and that the plaintiff corporations would again be subject to the statutory restriction. The case was therefore found to fall within that category of controversies "capable of repetition, yet evading review," and thus was not moot.[c]

On what ground is this exception justifiable? Can it be squared with the Court's statement, made in *Schlesinger v. Reservists Committee to Stop the War* (page 34, supra) and repeated in other cases, that "[t]he assumption that if [plaintiffs] have no standing to sue, no one would have standing, is not a reason to find standing"?

4. *Honig v. Doe.* The meaning and implications of "capable of repetition, yet evading review" were disputed in Honig v. Doe, ___ U.S. ___ (1988). The case involved the "stay-put" provision of the Education of the Handicapped Act. That provision directs that a disabled child "shall remain in [his or her] then current educational placement" pending administrative and judicial review of proposed changes. The question was whether emotionally disabled children placed in public school could nevertheless be expelled for dangerous or disruptive conduct growing out of their disabilities.

The decision involved two applications of the "stay-put" provision. Both were undoubtedly live controversies in the lower courts but arguably had become moot during the course of litigation. The majori-

---

[c] See also Gannett Co., Inc. v. DePasquale, 443 U.S. 368 (1977); Gerstein v. Pugh, 420 U.S. 103 (1975); Super Tire Engineering Co. v. McCorkle, 416 U.S. 115 (1974); and Roe v. Wade, 410 U.S. 113 (1973). In *Roe,* a pregnant plaintiff was asserting a right to an abortion, but it took much longer than nine months for the case to get through the legal system to the Supreme Court. Similarly, in *Gerstein* criminal defendants were complaining about pre-trial detentions in cases that were long since over by the time the issue could be fully litigated.

ty, however, found that one dispute was "capable of repetition, yet evading review" and therefore was not moot. The student had not returned to school but was still entitled to invoke the protections of the federal statute. Moreover, he still suffered from the emotional instability that had led to his expulsion. The Court therefore found a "reasonable expectation" that the problem would recur and that any resulting claim would likely evade review.

This conclusion was disputed by Justice Scalia, with whom Justice O'Connor joined. Scalia noted that the precedents spoke of "a 'reasonable expectation' or a 'demonstrated probability' that the same controversy will recur" and argued that the two phrases were equivalent. Under that test, the exception to mootness was not shown. Specifically, there was no showing that the student would return to public school or that, if he did, he would be placed in an educational setting unable to accommodate his disruptive behavior. Therefore, Scalia argued, the traditional standard of "capable of repetition" had not been met.

The most interesting opinion was a concurrence by Chief Justice Rehnquist. Rehnquist called for a "reconsideration" of mootness doctrine and of its relation to article III:

> "If it were indeed art. III which—by reason of its requirement of a case or controversy for the exercise of federal judicial power—underlies the mootness doctrine, the 'capable of repetition, yet evading' review exception relied upon by the Court in this case would be incomprehensible. Article III extends the judicial power of the United States only to cases and controversies; it does not except from this requirement other lawsuits which are 'capable of repetition, yet evading review.' If our mootness doctrine were forced upon us by the case or controversy requirement of art. III itself, we would have no more power to decide lawsuits which are 'moot' but which also raise questions which are capable of repetition but evading review than we would to decide cases which are 'moot' but raise no such questions. . . .

> "The logical conclusion to be drawn from [the precedents], and from the historical development of the principle of mootness, is that while an unwillingness to decide moot cases may be connected to the case or controversy requirement of art. III, it is an attenuated connection that may be overridden where there are strong reasons to override it. The 'capable of repetition, yet evading review' exception is an example. So too is our refusal to dismiss as moot those cases in which the defendant voluntarily ceases, at some advanced stage of the appellate proceedings, whatever activity prompted the plaintiff to seek an injunction. I believe we should adopt an additional exception to our present mootness doctrine for those cases where the events which render the case moot have supervened since our grant of certiorari or noting of probable jurisdiction in the case. [Our] resources—the time spent preparing to

decide the case by reading briefs, hearing oral arguments, and conferring—are squandered in every case in which it becomes apparent after the decisional process is underway that we may not reach the question presented. To me [that] is a sufficient reason either to abandon the doctrine of mootness altogether in cases which this Court has decided to review, or at least to relax the doctrine of mootness in such a manner as the dissent accuses the majority of doing here. I would leave the mootness doctrine as established by our cases in full force and effect when applied to the earlier stages of a lawsuit, but I believe that once this Court has undertaken a consideration of a case, an exception to that principle is just as much warranted as where a case is 'capable of repetition, yet evading review.' "

Justice Scalia responded that he did not see how mootness could be "merely prudential," any more than standing. "Both doctrines have equivalently deep roots in the common-law understanding, and hence the constitutional understanding, of what makes a matter appropriate for judicial disposition." As traditionally applied, "capable of repetition, yet evading review" did not argue to the contrary:

"Where the conduct has ceased for the time being but there is a demonstrated probability that it *will* recur, a real-life controversy between parties with a personal stake in the outcome continues to exist, and art. III is no more violated than it is violated by entertaining a declaratory judgment action. But that is the limit of our power. I agree with the Chief Justice to this extent: the 'yet evading review' portion of our 'capable of repetition, yet evading review' test is prudential; whether or not that criterion is met, a justiciable controversy exists. But the probability of recurrence between the same parties is essential to our jurisdiction as a court, and it is that deficiency which the case before us presents."

Which understanding of the "capable of repetition, yet evading review" exception is more persuasive? Is it plausible to think of mootness as less closely related to constitutional requirements than other justiciability doctrines? If not, is there any way to avoid the waste of resources of which Rehnquist spoke?

5. *DeFunis v. Odegaard.* A controversial application of traditional mootness doctrine occurred in DeFunis v. Odegaard, 416 U.S. 312 (1974). Marco DeFunis was an unsuccessful white applicant for admission to the University of Washington Law School. He brought suit in state court, claiming that the school's minority admissions program constituted invidious discrimination on the basis of race in violation of the 14th amendment. DeFunis won in the trial court and was admitted. That decision was overturned by the Washington Supreme Court, but the judgment was stayed pending final decision by the Supreme Court of the United States. By the time the case was argued, DeFunis was in his final term, and the Law School asserted that it would not seek to cancel registration for any term in which DeFunis was already enrolled. The Supreme Court therefore found the case moot. That illness, economic necessity, or academic failure might yet prevent DeFunis' graduation was unimportant, for the Court found that such "speculative contingencies" provided no basis for adjudicating the merits of the case.[d]

Justice Brennan, joined by Justices Douglas, White, and Marshall, dissented:

> "I can . . . find no justification for the Court's straining to rid itself of this dispute. While we must be vigilant to require that litigants maintain a personal stake in the outcome of a controversy to assure that 'the questions will be framed with the necessary specificity, that the issues will be contested with the necessary adverseness and that the litigation will be pursued with the necessary vigor to assure that the constitutional challenge will be made in a form traditionally thought to be capable of judicial resolution,' there is no such want of an adversary contest in this case. Indeed, the Court concedes that, if petitioner has lost his stake in this controversy, he did so only when he registered for the spring term. But petitioner took that action only after the case had been fully litigated in the state courts, briefs had been filed in this Court, and oral argument had been heard. The case is thus ripe for decision on a fully developed factual record with sharply defined and fully canvassed legal issues.

> "Moreover, in endeavoring to dispose of this case as moot, the Court clearly disserves the public interest. The constitutional issues which are avoided today concern vast numbers of people, organizations, and colleges and universities, as evidenced by the filing of 26 amicus curiae briefs. Few constitutional questions in recent history have stirred as much debate, and they will not disappear. They must inevitably return to the federal courts and ultimately again to this Court. . . . Although the Court should, of course, avoid unnecessary decisions of constitutional questions, we should not transform

[d] The Court's disposition was to vacate the state court judgment and remand for "such proceedings as by that court may be deemed appropriate." On remand, DeFunis, who by this time had graduated, moved that the case be redesignated as a class action and that the state supreme court reconsider the merits and overrule its former action. The court denied the motion to convert the lawsuit to a class action and reinstated its judgment on the merits. DeFunis v. Odegaard, 84 Wash. 2d 617, 529 P.2d 438 (1974). On the mootness question, the court held that it was not governed by federal standards and that, under state law, "the fact that an issue is moot does not divest this court of jurisdiction to decide it." Since the case presented "a broad issue of substantial public import," the court thought it appropriate to resolve the merits. One of the dissenting justices made the following observation:

> "[O]ne of our obligations in a federal system is to refrain from actions not commensurate or consistent with the doctrine of judicial review by the Supreme Court. Since reinstatement would impinge upon the viability and efficacy of that review, I do not believe that we would fulfill our obligations to the federal aspects of our dual court system by reinstating our *DeFunis* decision."

principles of avoidance of constitutional decisions into devices for sidestepping resolution of difficult cases."

The issues avoided in *DeFunis* returned to the Supreme Court and were confronted, if not resolved, in University of California Board of Regents v. Bakke, 438 U.S. 265 (1978). Does that suggest that Justice Brennan was right in disparaging the *DeFunis* dismissal? Or does it simply show that mootness is properly a doctrine concerned with particular cases, not the issues they raise? What weight, if any, should be given to the fact that the mootness question arose late in the litigation, after the development of a record and after substantial investment of time by all concerned? Is the societal importance of the issues raised in *DeFunis* a relevant consideration? Does it argue more persuasively for decision or delay?

From another perspective, why was the exception recognized in the *W.T. Grant* case not applicable in *DeFunis*? The reason, said the Court, was that the question of mootness did not arise from a "unilateral change in the *admissions procedures* of the Law School." Here there had been no voluntary cessation of the challenged admissions practices. Instead, mootness resulted from "the simple fact that DeFunis is now in the final quarter of the final year of his course of study, and the settled and unchallenged policy of the Law School to permit him to complete the term for which he is now enrolled."

Is this distinction persuasive? Both cases involved a defendant's representation as to future conduct. Why should that representation render the case moot when it concerns a collateral issue (whether DeFunis will be allowed to complete the term in which he is enrolled), but not when it concerns the allegedly illegal conduct (whether W.T. Grant will reinstall interlocking directorates)? Is it not arguable that the law school's refusal to disavow the challenged admissions practices made *DeFunis* a *less* appropriate case for mootness than was *W.T. Grant*?

UNITED STATES PAROLE COMMISSION v. GERAGHTY

Supreme Court of the United States, 1980.
445 U.S. 388.

MR. JUSTICE BLACKMUN delivered the opinion of the Court.

This case raises the question whether a trial court's denial of a motion for certification of a class may be reviewed on appeal after the named plaintiff's personal claim has become "moot." . . .

I

In 1973, the United States Parole Board adopted explicit Parole Release Guidelines for adult prisoners. These guidelines establish a "customary range" of confinement for various classes of offenders. The guidelines utilize a matrix, which combines a "parole prognosis" score (based on the prisoner's age at first conviction, employment background, and other personal factors) and an "offense severity" rating, to yield the "customary" time to be served in prison.

[Geraghty, who had been convicted of conspiracy to commit extortion and of making false material statements to a grand jury, was twice denied parole under the guidelines. He brought suit on behalf of "all federal prisoners who are or who will become eligible for release on parole" to challenge the guidelines, both generally and as applied to his case. The trial court refused to certify a class action and rejected Geraghty's claims on the merits. While his appeal was pending, Geraghty was mandatorily released, and the parole authorities contended that his claim had become moot. The Third Circuit, however, ruled that class certification should not have been denied and remanded the case for further proceedings.]

II

Article III of the Constitution limits federal "judicial Power," that is, federal-court jurisdiction, to "Cases" and "Controversies." This case-or-controversy limitation serves "two complementary" purposes. Flast v. Cohen, 392 U.S. 83, 95 (1968). It limits the business of federal courts to "questions presented in an adversary context and in a form historically viewed as capable of resolution through the judicial process," and it defines the "role assigned to the judiciary in a tripartite allocation of power to assure that the federal courts will not intrude into areas committed to the other branches of government." Ibid. Likewise, mootness has two aspects: "when the issues presented are no longer 'live' or the parties lack a legally cognizable interest in the outcome." Powell v. McCormack, 395 U.S. 486, 496 (1969).

It is clear that the controversy over the validity of the Parole Release Guidelines is still a "live" one between petitioners and at least some members of the class respondent seeks to represent. This is demonstrated by the fact that prisoners currently affected by the guidelines have moved to be substituted, or to intervene, as "named" respondents before the Court. We therefore are concerned here with the second aspect of mootness, that is, the parties' interest in the litigation. The Court has referred to this concept as the "personal stake" requirement. E.g., Franks v. Bowman Transportation Co., 424 U.S. 747, 755 (1976); Baker v. Carr, 369 U.S. 186, 204 (1962). . . .

III

On several occasions the Court has considered the application of the "personal stake" requirement in the class-action context. In Sosna v. Iowa, 419 U.S. 393 (1975), it held that mootness of the named plaintiff's individual claim *after* a class has been duly certified does not render the action moot. It reasoned that "even though appellees . . . might not again enforce the Iowa durational residence requirement against [the class representative], it is clear that they will enforce it against those persons in the class that appellant sought to represent and that the District Court certified." The Court stated specifically that an art. III case or controversy "may exist . . . between a named defendant and a member of the class represented by the named plaintiff, even though the claim of the named plaintiff has become moot."

Although one might argue that *Sosna* contains at least an implication that the critical factor for art. III purposes is the timing of class certification, other cases, applying a "relation back" approach, clearly demonstrate that timing is not crucial. When the claim on the merits is "capable of repetition, yet evading review," the named plaintiff may litigate the class certification issue despite loss of his personal stake in the outcome of the litigation. E.g., Gerstein v. Pugh, 420 U.S. 103, 110 n.11 (1975). The "capable of repetition, yet evading review" doctrine, to be sure, was developed outside the class-action context. See Southern Pacific Terminal Co. v. ICC, 219 U.S. 498, 514–15 (1911). But it has been applied where the named plaintiff does have a personal stake at the outset of the lawsuit, and where the claim may arise again with respect to that plaintiff; the litigation then may continue notwithstanding the named plaintiff's current lack of a personal stake. See, e.g., Roe v. Wade, 410 U.S. 113, 123–25 (1973). Since the litigant faces some likelihood of becoming involved in the same controversy in the future, vigorous advocacy can be expected to continue.

When, however, there is no chance that the named plaintiff's expired claim will reoccur, mootness still can be avoided through certification of a class prior to expiration of the named plaintiff's claim. E.g., *Franks v. Bowman Transportation Co.,* supra, at 752–57. Some claims are so inherently transitory that the trial court will not have even enough time to rule on a motion for class certification before the proposed representative's individual interest expires. The Court considered this possibility in *Gerstein v. Pugh,* supra at 110. *Gerstein* was an action challenging pretrial detention conditions. The Court assumed that the named plaintiffs were no longer in custody awaiting trial at the time the trial court certified a class of pretrial detainees. There was no indication that the particular named plaintiffs might again be subject to pretrial detention. Nonetheless, the case was held not to be moot because:

> "The length of pretrial custody cannot be ascertained at the outset, and it may be ended at any time by release on recognizance, dismissal of the charges, or a guilty plea, as well as by acquittal or conviction after trial. It is by no means certain that any given individual, named as plaintiff, would be in pretrial custody long enough for a district judge to certify the class. Moreover, in this case the constant existence of a class of persons suffering the deprivation is certain. The attorney representing the named respondents is a public defender, and we can safely assume that he has other clients with a continuing live interest in the case."

In two different contexts the Court has stated that the proposed class representative who proceeds to a judgment on the merits may appeal *denial* of class certification. First, this assumption was "an important ingredient" in the rejection of interlocutory appeals, "as of right," of class certification denials. Coopers & Lybrand v. Livesay, 437 U.S. 463, 469, 470 n.15 (1978). The Court reasoned that denial of class status will not necessarily be the "death knell" of a small-claimant action, since there still remains "the prospect of prevailing on the merits and reversing an order denying class certification."

Second, in United Airlines, Inc. v. McDonald, 432 U.S. 385, 393–95 (1977), the Court held that a putative class member may intervene, for the purpose of appealing the denial of a class certification motion, after the named plaintiffs' claims have been satisfied and judgment entered in their favor. Underlying that decision was the view that "refusal to certify was subject to appellate review after final judgment at the behest of the named plaintiffs." And today, the Court holds that named plaintiffs whose claims are satisfied through entry of judgment over their objections may appeal the denial of a class certification ruling. Deposit Guaranty Nat. Bank v. Roper, 445 U.S. 326 (1980).

Gerstein, McDonald, and *Roper* are all examples of cases found not to be moot, despite the loss of a "personal stake" in the merits of the litigation by the proposed class representative. The interest of the named plaintiffs in *Gerstein* was precisely the same as that of Geraghty here. Similarly, after judgment had been entered in their favor, the named plaintiffs in *McDonald* had no continuing narrow personal stake in the outcome of the class claims. And in *Roper* the Court points out that an individual controversy is rendered moot, in the strict art. III sense, by payment and satisfaction of a final judgment. These cases demonstrate the flexible character of the art. III mootness doctrine.[7]

IV

Perhaps somewhat anticipating today's decision in *Roper,* petitioners argue that the situation presented is entirely different when mootness of the individual claim is caused by "expiration" of the claim, rather than by a judgment on the claim. They assert that a proposed class representative who individually prevails on the merits still has a "personal stake" in the outcome of the litigation, while the named plaintiff whose claim is truly moot does not. In the latter situation,

---

[7] Three of the Court's cases might be described as adopting a less flexible approach. In Indianapolis School Commissioners v. Jacobs, 420 U.S. 128 (1975), and in Weinstein v. Bradford, 423 U.S. 147 (1975), dismissal of putative class suits, as moot, was ordered after the named plaintiffs' claims became moot. And in Pasadena City Bd. of Education v. Spangler, 427 U.S. 424 (1976), it was indicated that the action would have been moot, upon expiration of the named plaintiffs' claims, had not the United States intervened as a party plaintiff. Each of these, however, was a case in which there was an attempt to appeal the merits without first having obtained proper certification of a class. In each case it was the defendant who petitioned this Court for review. As is observed subsequently in the text, appeal from denial of class classification is permitted in some circumstances where appeal on the merits is not. In the situation where the proposed class representative has lost a "personal stake," the merits cannot be reached until a class properly is certified. Although the Court perhaps could have remanded *Jacobs* and *Weinstein* for reconsideration of the class certification issue, as the Court of Appeals did here, the parties in those cases did not suggest "relation back" of class certification. Thus we do not find this line of cases dispositive of the question now before us.

where no class has been certified, there is no party before the court with a live claim, and it follows, it is said, that we have no jurisdiction to consider whether a class should have been certified.

We do not find this distinction persuasive. [T]he fact that a named plaintiff's substantive claims are mooted due to an occurrence other than a judgment on the merits does not mean that all the other issues in the case are mooted. A plaintiff who brings a class action presents two separate issues for judicial resolution. One is the claim on the merits; the other is the claim that he is entitled to represent a class. "The denial of class certification stands as an adjudication of one of the issues litigated." We think that in determining whether the plaintiff may continue to press the class certification claim, after the claim on the merits "expires," we must look to the nature of the "personal stake" in the class certification claim. Determining art. III's "uncertain and shifting contours," see *Flast v. Cohen,* supra, at 97, with respect to nontraditional forms of litigation, such as the class action, requires reference to the purposes of the case-or-controversy requirement.

Application of the personal-stake requirement to a procedural claim, such as the right to represent a class, is not automatic or readily resolved. . . . The justifications that led to the development of the class action include the protection of the defendant from inconsistent obligations, the protection of the interests of absentees, the provision of a convenient and economical means for disposing of similar lawsuits, and the facilitation of the spreading of litigation costs among numerous litigants with similar claims. Although the named representative receives certain benefits from the class nature of the action, . . . these benefits generally are byproducts of the class-action device. In order to achieve the primary benefits of a class suit, the Federal Rules of Civil Procedure give the proposed class representative the right to have a class certified if the requirements of the rules are met. This "right" is more analogous to the private attorney general concept than to the type of interest traditionally thought to satisfy the "personal stake" requirement.

As noted above, the purpose of the "personal stake" requirement is to assure that the case is in a form capable of judicial resolution. The imperatives of a dispute capable of judicial resolution are sharply presented issues in a concrete factual setting and self-interested parties vigorously advocating opposing positions. We conclude that these elements can exist with respect to the class certification issue notwithstanding the fact that the named plaintiff's claim on the merits has expired. The question whether class certification is appropriate remains as a concrete, sharply presented issue. . . .

We therefore hold that an action brought on behalf of a class does not become moot upon expiration of the named plaintiff's substantive claim, even though class certification has been denied. The proposed representative retains a "personal stake" in obtaining class certification sufficient to assure that art. III values are not undermined. If the appeal results in reversal of the class certification denial, and a class subsequently is properly certified, the merits of the class claim then may be adjudicated pursuant to the holding in *Sosna.*

Our holding is limited to the appeal of the denial of the class certification motion. A named plaintiff whose claim expires may not continue to press the appeal on the merits until a class has been properly certified. If, on appeal, it is determined that class certification properly was denied, the claim on the merits must be dismissed as moot.

Our conclusion that the controversy here is not moot does not automatically establish that the named plaintiff is entitled to continue litigating the interests of the class. "[I]t does shift the focus of examination from the elements of justiciability to the ability of the named representative to 'fairly and adequately protect the interests of the class.' Rule 23(a)." *Sosna v. Iowa,* supra, at 403. We hold only that a case or controversy still exists. The question of who is to represent the class is a separate issue. . . .

[The Court held in an omitted portion of its opinion that the remand order by the Court of Appeals should have been modified in a minor respect. Accordingly, the judgment below was vacated and the case was remanded for further proceedings not inconsistent with the Court's opinion.]

MR. JUSTICE POWELL, with whom the CHIEF JUSTICE, MR. JUSTICE STEWART, and MR. JUSTICE REHNQUIST join, dissenting. . . .

The Court's analysis proceeds in two steps. First, it says that mootness is a "flexible" doctrine which may be adapted as we see fit to "nontraditional" forms of litigation. Second, the Court holds that the named plaintiff has a right "analogous to the private attorney general concept" to appeal the denial of class certification even when his personal claim for relief is moot. Both steps are significant departures from settled law that rationally cannot be confined to the narrow issue presented in this case. Accordingly, I dissent.

I

As the Court observes, this case involves the "personal stake" aspect of the mootness doctrine. There undoubtedly is a "live" issue which an appropriate plaintiff could present for judicial resolution. The question is whether respondent, who has no further interest in this action, nevertheless may—through counsel—continue to litigate it. . . .

"In order to satisfy art. III, the plaintiff must show that he personally has suffered some actual or threatened injury as a result of the putatively illegal conduct of the defendant." Gladstone, Realtors v. Village of Bellwood, 441 U.S. 91, 99 (1979). Although noneconomic injuries can confer standing, the Court has rejected all attempts to substitute abstract concern with a subject—or with the rights of third parties—for "the concrete injury required by art. III." Simon v. Eastern Kentucky Welfare Rights Org., 426 U.S. 26, 40 (1976).

As the Court notes today, the same threshold requirement must be satisfied throughout the action. . . . The limitation flows directly from art. III.

Since the question is one of power, the practical importance of review cannot control. Sosna v. Iowa, 419 U.S. 393, 401 (1975). Nor can public interest in the resolution of an issue replace the necessary individual interest in the outcome. DeFunis v. Odegaard, 416 U.S. 312, 316 (1974). Collateral consequences of the original wrong may supply the individual interest in some circumstances. Sibron v. New York, 392 U.S. 40, 53–58 (1968). So, too, may the prospect of repeated future injury so inherently transitory that it is unlikely to outlast the normal course of litigation. Super Tire Engineering Co. v. McCorkle, 416 U.S. 115 (1974). The essential and irreducible constitutional requirement is simply a nonfrivolous showing of continuing or threatened injury at the hands of the adversary.

These cases demonstrate, contrary to the Court's view today, that the core requirement of a personal stake in the outcome is not "flexible." . . . We have insisted upon the personal stake requirement in mootness and standing cases because it is embedded in the case-or-controversy limitation imposed by the Constitution, "founded in concern about the proper—and properly limited—role of the courts in a democratic society." Warth v. Seldin, 422 U.S. 490, 498 (1975). . . .

II

The foregoing decisions establish principles that the Court has applied consistently. These principles were developed outside the class-action context. But art. III contains no exception for class actions. Thus, we have held that a putative class representative who alleges no individual injury "may [not] seek relief on behalf of himself or any other member of the class." O'Shea v. Littleton, 414 U.S. 488, 494 (1974). Only after a class has been certified in accordance with Rule 23 can it "acquir[e] a legal status separate from the interest asserted by [the named plaintiff]." *Sosna v. Iowa,* supra, at 399. "Given a properly certified class," the live interests of unnamed but identifiable class members may supply the personal stake required by art. III when the named plaintiff's individual claim becomes moot.

This case presents a fundamentally different situation. No class has been certified, and the lone plaintiff no longer has any personal stake in the litigation. . . . In these circumstances, art. III and the precedents of this Court require dismissal. But the Court views the case differently, and constructs new doctrine to breathe life into a lawsuit that has no plaintiff. . . .

The cases principally relied upon are Gerstein v. Pugh, 420 U.S. 103, 110–11 n.11 (1975), United Airlines v. McDonald, 432 U.S. 385 (1977), and today's decision in Deposit Guaranty Nat. Bank v. Roper, 445 U.S. 326 (1980). Each case is said to show that a class action is not mooted by the loss of the class representative's personal stake in the outcome of the lawsuit, even though no class has been certified. *Sosna* itself is cited for the proposition that the requirements of art. III may be met "through means other than the traditional requirement of a 'personal stake in the outcome.'" In my view, the Court misreads these precedents.

A

In *Sosna,* the Court simply acknowledged that actual class certification gives legal recognition to additional adverse parties. And in *Gerstein,* the Court applied a rule long established, outside the class action context, by cases that never have been thought to erode the requirement of a personal stake in the outcome. *Gerstein* held that a class action challenging the constitutionality of pretrial detention procedures could continue after the named plaintiffs' convictions had brought their detentions to an end. The Court did not suggest that a personal stake in the outcome on the merits was unnecessary. The action continued only because of the transitory nature of pretrial detention, which placed the claim within "that narrow class of cases" that are "distinctly 'capable of repetition, yet evading review.'"

McDonald and *Roper* sanction some appeals from the denial of class certification notwithstanding satisfaction of the class representative's claim on the merits. But neither case holds that art. III may be satisfied in the absence of a personal stake in the outcome. In *McDonald,* a putative class member intervened within the statutory time limit to appeal the certification ruling.[10] Because the Court found that her claim was not time-barred, the intervenor in *McDonald* possessed the stake necessary to pursue the action. . . .

There is dictum in *McDonald* that the "refusal to certify was subject to appellate review after final judgment at the behest of the named plaintiffs . . . ." That gratuitous sentence, repeated in Coopers & Lybrand v. Livesay, 437 U.S. 463, 469, 470 n.15 (1978), apparently is elevated by the Court's opinion in this case to the status of new doctrine. There is serious tension between this new doctrine and the much narrower reasoning adopted today in *Roper.* In *Roper* the Court holds that the named plaintiffs, who have refused to accept proffered individual settlements, retain a personal stake in sharing anticipated litigation costs with the class. Finding that art. III is satisfied by this alleged economic interest, *Roper* reasons that the rules of federal practice governing appealability permit a party to obtain review of certain procedural rulings that are collateral to a generally favorable judgment. . . .

It is far from apparent how *Roper* can be thought to support the decision in this case. . . . Here, there is not even a speculative interest in sharing costs, and respondent affirmatively denies that he

---

[10] The individual claims of the original named plaintiffs had been settled after judgment on the question of liability.

retains any stake or personal interest in the outcome of his appeal. Thus, a fact that was critical to the analysis in *Roper* is absent in this case. . . .

B

The cases cited by the Court as "less flexible"—and therefore less authoritative—apply established art. III doctrine in cases closely analogous to this one. Indianapolis School Commissioners v. Jacobs, 420 U.S. 128 (1975) (per curiam); Weinstein v. Bradford, 423 U.S. 147 (1975) (per curiam); Pasadena City Bd. of Education v. Spangler, 427 U.S. 424 (1976). As they are about to become second class precedents, these cases are relegated to a footnote. . . .

In *Jacobs*, six named plaintiffs brought a class action to challenge certain high school regulations. The District Court stated on the record that class treatment was appropriate and that the plaintiffs were proper representatives, but the court failed to comply with Rule 23. After this Court granted review, we were informed that the named plaintiffs had graduated. We held that the action was entirely moot because the "class action was never properly certified nor the class properly identified by the District Court." Since the faulty certification prevented the class from acquiring separate legal status, art. III required a dismissal. We reached precisely the same conclusion in *Spangler*, an action saved from mootness only by the timely intervention of a third party. And in *Bradford*, where the District Court had denied certification outright, the Court held that the named plaintiff's release from prison required the dismissal of his complaint about parole release procedures.

The Court suggests that *Jacobs* and *Spangler* may be distinguished because the plaintiffs there were not appealing the denial of class certification. The Court overlooks the fact that in each case the class representatives were defending a judgment on the merits from which the defendants had appealed. The plaintiffs/respondents continued vigorously to assert the claims of the class. They did not take the procedural route of appealing a denial of certification only because the District Court had granted—albeit defectively—class status. We chose not to remand for correction of the oral certification order in *Jacobs* because we recognized that the putative class representative had suffered no injury that could be redressed by adequate certification. . . . .

III

. . . The Court makes no effort to identify any injury to respondent that may be redressed by, or any benefit to respondent that may accrue from, a favorable ruling on the certification question. Instead, respondent's "personal stake" is said to derive from two factors having nothing to do with concrete injury or stake in the outcome. First, the Court finds that the Federal Rules of Civil Procedure create a "right," "analogous to the private attorney general concept," to have a class certified. Second, the Court thinks that the case retains the "imperatives of a dispute capable of judicial resolution," which are identified as (i) a sharply presented issue, (ii) a concrete factual setting, and (iii) a self-interested party actually contesting the case.

The Court's reliance on some new "right" inherent in Rule 23 is misplaced. We have held that even Congress may not confer federal-court jurisdiction when art. III does not. *Gladstone, Realtors,* supra, at 100. Far less so may a rule of procedure which "shall not be construed to extend . . . the jurisdiction of the United States District Courts." Fed. Rule Civ. Proc. 82. Moreover, the "private attorney general concept" cannot supply the personal stake necessary to satisfy art. III. It serves only to permit litigation by a party who has a stake of his own but otherwise might be barred by prudential standing rules.

Since neither Rule 23 nor the private attorney general concept can fill the jurisdictional gap, the Court's new perception of art. III requirements must rest entirely on its tripartite test of concrete adverseness. Although the components of the test are no strangers to our art. III jurisprudence, they operate only in " 'cases confessedly within [the Court's] jurisdiction.' " The Court cites no decision that has premised jurisdiction upon the bare existence of a sharply presented issue in a concrete and vigorously argued case, and I am aware of none. Indeed, each of these characteristics is sure to be present in the typical "private attorney general" action brought by a public-spirited citizen. Although we have refused steadfastly to countenance the "public action," the Court's redefinition of the personal stake requirement leaves no principled basis for that practice. . . .

IV

In short, this is a case in which the putative class representative—respondent here—no longer has the slightest interest in the injuries alleged in his complaint. No member of the class is before the Court; indeed, none has been identified. The case therefore lacks a plaintiff with the minimal personal stake that is a constitutional prerequisite to the jurisdiction of an art. III court. In any realistic sense, the only persons before this Court who appear to have an interest are the defendants and a lawyer who no longer has a client.

I would vacate the decision of the Court of Appeals and remand with instructions to dismiss the action as moot.[a]

NOTES ON MOOTNESS IN CLASS ACTIONS

1. *Sosna v. Iowa.* Explicit differentiation of the class action context began in Sosna v. Iowa, 419 U.S. 393 (1975). *Sosna* involved a challenge to a one-year durational residency requirement for divorce. The plaintiff sought and obtained certification of her suit as a class

---

[a] On remand, the District Court certified a class but rejected the claims on the merits. 552 F.Supp. 276 (M.D.Pa.1982). These determinations were affirmed on appeal. 719 F.2d 1199 (3d Cir. 1983), cert. denied, 465 U.S. 1103 (1984). [Footnote by eds.]

action on behalf of all persons who had been residents of Iowa for less than one year and who desired to sue for divorce. A three-judge court upheld the residency requirement, and appeal was taken directly to the Supreme Court. By the time the case was heard, however, the plaintiff had not only satisfied the Iowa residency requirement but had obtained a divorce in another state. The Supreme Court acknowledged that the case would have been moot had the plaintiff sued individually, but held that the class certification justified a different result. Although the controversy was moot with respect to the named plaintiff, it remained "very much alive" for the class of persons she was certified to represent.

2. *Franks v. Bowman Transportation Co.* Some language in *Sosna* suggested that the decision was limited to class actions raising issues "capable of repetition, yet evading review." Of course, it was unlikely that the same claimant would be able to raise the issue again, but it would arise for other class members and no individual case would last long enough to allow complete judicial review. Any such limitation was discarded, however, in Franks v. Bowman Transportation Co., 424 U.S. 747 (1976), a multiple class-action charging racially discriminatory employment practices in violation of title VII of the 1964 Civil Rights Act. One of the certified classes consisted of blacks who had applied for positions as over-the-road truck drivers prior to a certain date. Only one named plaintiff belonged to that class, and by the time the case came to the Supreme Court, that individual had been hired, given back pay, and subsequently properly discharged for cause.

The issue on the merits was whether the class members would be entitled to an award of seniority when hired pursuant to the District Court's order. The defendants contended that absence of any named plaintiff who would benefit from such relief rendered the issue moot, but the Supreme Court disagreed. *Sosna* was not limited to issues "capable of repetition, yet evading review," the Court held, but applied to class actions generally:

> "The unnamed members of the class are entitled to the relief already afforded [the named plaintiff], hiring and back-pay, and thus to that extent have 'such a personal stake in the outcome of the controversy as to assure that concrete adverseness which sharpens the presentation of issues upon which the court so largely depends for illumination of difficult . . . questions.' Baker v. Carr, 369 U.S. 186, 204 (1962). Given a properly certified class action, *Sosna* contemplates that mootness turns on whether, in the specific circumstances of the given case at the time it is before this Court, an adversary relationship sufficient to fulfill this function exists."

3. *Deposit Guaranty National Bank v. Roper.* In both *Sosna* and *Franks,* the controversy had been live with respect to the named plaintiff at the time class certification occurred. This was not the case in Deposit Guaranty National Bank v. Roper, 445 U.S. 326 (1980), a case decided on the same day as *Geraghty.*

In *Roper,* two BankAmericard holders sued the issuing bank for charging usurious interest.[a] They sought to represent 90,000 cardholders, but the District Court refused to certify a class action. Instead, it entered judgment for the individual plaintiffs for $889.42 and $423.54, respectively, pursuant to a settlement offer made by the defendant. The question was whether the judgment for the plaintiffs for the entire amount to which they were individually entitled mooted the case, or whether the plaintiffs still retained a sufficient interest in representing the class to appeal the denial of class certification. The Court of Appeals held that they could appeal the certification issue, and the Supreme Court agreed.

Chief Justice Burger's opinion for the Court noted that the general rule was that a "party who receives all that he has sought generally is not aggrieved by the judgment affording the relief and cannot appeal from it." But here, "the dismissal of the action over plaintiffs' objection [did not moot] the plaintiffs' claim on the merits so long as they retained an economic interest in class certification." Such an interest can be a sufficient "personal stake in the appeal," which was here satisfied because the plaintiffs claimed "a continuing interest in the resolution of the class certification question in their desire to shift part of the costs of litigation to those who will share in its benefits if the class is certified and ultimately prevails." A contrary ruling, the Chief Justice noted, would reduce the effectiveness of the class action as a device for obtaining relief for a multiplicity of small claims. Justices Rehnquist, Blackmun, and Stevens concurred separately.[b]

Justice Powell, joined by Justice Stewart, dissented. Justice Powell thought that the plaintiffs' " 'injury'—if any exists—is not one that 'fairly can be traced' " to the defendant. The plaintiffs had a 25 per cent contingent fee arrangement with their attorneys, and "no one has explained how [their] obligation to pay 25 per cent of their recovery to counsel could be reduced if a class is certified and its members became similarly obligated to pay 25 per cent of their recovery." The defendant was "merely a bystander" to that arrangement:

> "Apart from the persistence of the lawyers, this has been a noncase since the [defendant] tendered full satisfaction of the [plaintiffs'] individual claims. . . . I know of no decision by any court that holds that a lawyer's interest in a larger fee, to be paid by third persons not present in court, creates the personal stake in the outcome required by art. III."

[a] The cause of action was based on the National Bank Act, which allows recovery of twice the interest paid in excess of that authorized by state law. The alleged violation of state law concerned the method by which monthly interest charges were assessed. The state law was changed to authorize the bank's practice after the suit was filed. Moreover, the statute of limitations for additional claims based on the alleged previous violations expired while the case was in litigation.

[b] Justice Stevens would have permitted the appeal on a ground different from the Court: "In my opinion, when a proper class action is filed, the absent members of the class should be considered parties to the case or controversy at least for the limited purpose of the court's art. III jurisdiction. If the district judge fails to certify the class, I believe they remain parties until a final determination has been made that the action may not be maintained as a class action."

4. Questions and Comments on Mootness in Class Actions.
The progression from *Sosna* to *Geraghty* greatly increases the utility of
the class action as a device for litigating a wide variety of claims that
otherwise would be mooted by the expiration of the representative's
individual claim. But has it done so at the cost of diluting the "case or
controversy" limitations of art. III? As a practical matter, how do
these cases differ from *DeFunis*? Is the designation of the plaintiff as
the "representative" of other litigants more than a formal change in
the characterization of the suit? What difference would it make in
Geraghty, for example, if another prisoner's name were substituted?
Would the issues be different in any material sense?

Geraghty goes a step beyond *Roper* in its holding that Rule 23 gives
the proposed class representative a "right to have the class certified if
the requirements of the rules are met." This "right," the Court
elaborates, creates a sufficient "personal stake" to defeat a mootness
argument, even though the plaintiff has no economic interest in class
certification and the right is "more analogous to the private attorney
general concept than to the type of interest traditionally thought to
satisfy the 'personal stake' requirement." In essence, is the Court
basing the justiciability of class actions on the adequacy with which the
issues will be presented? Is this proper? Why was this criterion not
satisfied in *DeFunis*? Is the adequacy-of-representation approach consistent with other decisions on the requirements of art. III? In particular, compare *Geraghty* with *Allen v. Wright,* page 15, supra. If "sharply presented issues in a concrete factual setting and self-interested
parties vigorously advocating opposing positions" are sufficient to avoid
apparent mootness, why should the same approach not be applied to
ideological plaintiffs who seek standing to object to government non-
enforcement of law?

Consider the views of Richard Greenstein. In Bridging the Mootness Gap in Federal Court Class Actions, 35 Stan. L. Rev. 897 (1983),
Professor Greenstein examined the cases summarized above, including
Geraghty, and explored their relation to the law of standing. He
concluded that restrictions on the presentation of class claims by a
representative party whose individual interest has become moot should
be regarded as prudential only:

"In a class action suit, the function of the named plaintiff,
with respect to the claims of the class, is to represent the
interests of putative class members, not to supply the injury
needed to satisfy the case-or-controversy requirement of article
III. This latter function is served by the class allegations
themselves from the moment they are formally presented to
the court in the pleadings. Because article III concerns are
met by the class claims, the question of the plaintiff's standing
to litigate those claims has no constitutional significance. Nor
does the mooting of the plaintiff's own claims. To be more
precise, while the mooting of the plaintiff's claim does have
constitutional consequences regarding the litigation of those

specific claims, it has none regarding the litigation of the class claims.

"Thus, the question of the plaintiff's standing to present the claims of the class—whether *his* claim is moot—raises purely prudential concerns. These concerns are addressed by the test for class representation set out in Federal Rule of Civil Procedure 23."

Is this analysis persuasive? Is it consistent with the Court's approach to standing?

SECTION 3: THE POLITICAL QUESTION

POWELL v. MCCORMACK
Supreme Court of the United States, 1969.
395 U.S. 486.

MR. CHIEF JUSTICE WARREN delivered the opinion of the Court.

In November 1966, petitioner Adam Clayton Powell, Jr., was duly elected from the 18th Congressional District of New York to serve in the United States House of Representatives for the 90th Congress. However, pursuant to a House resolution, he was not permitted to take his seat. Powell (and some of the voters of his district) then filed suit in federal District Court, claiming that the House could exclude him only if it found he failed to meet the standing requirements of age, citizenship, and residence contained in art. I, § 2, of the Constitution—requirements the House specifically found Powell met—and thus had excluded him unconstitutionally. The District Court dismissed petitioners' complaint . . . . We have determined that it was error to dismiss the complaint and that petitioner Powell is entitled to a declaratory judgment that he was unlawfully excluded from the 90th Congress.

I.

FACTS

During the 89th Congress, a Special Subcommittee on Contracts of the Committee on House Administration conducted an investigation into the expenditures of the Committee on Education and Labor, of which petitioner Adam Clayton Powell, Jr., was chairman. The Special Subcommittee issued a report concluding that Powell and certain staff employees had deceived the House authorities as to travel expenses. The report also indicated there was strong evidence that certain illegal salary payments had been made to Powell's wife at his direction. No formal action was taken during the 89th Congress. . . .

When the 90th Congress met to organize in January 1967, Powell was asked to step aside while the oath was administered to the other members-elect. Following the administration of the oath to the remaining members, the House discussed the procedure to be followed in determining whether Powell was eligible to take his seat. After some debate, by a vote of 363 to 65 the House adopted House Resolution No. 1, which provided that the Speaker appoint a Select Committee to determine Powell's eligibility. . . .

[O]n February 23, 1967, the Committee issued its report, finding that Powell met the standing qualifications of art. I, § 2. However, the Committee further reported that Powell had asserted an unwarranted privilege and immunity from the processes of the courts of New York; that he had wrongfully diverted House funds for the use of others and himself; and that he had made false reports on expenditures of foreign currency to the Committee on House Administration. The Committee recommended that Powell be sworn and seated as a member of the 90th Congress but that he be censured by the House, fined $40,000 and be deprived of his seniority.

The report was presented to the House on March 1, 1967, and the House debated the Select Committee's proposed resolution. At the conclusion of the debate, by a vote of 222 to 202 the House rejected a motion to bring the resolution to a vote. An amendment to the resolution was then offered; it called for the exclusion of Powell and a declaration that his seat was vacant. The Speaker ruled that a majority vote of the House would be sufficient to pass the resolution if it were so amended. After further debate, the amendment was adopted by a vote of 248 to 176. Then the House adopted by a vote of 307 to 116 House Resolution No. 278 in its amended form, thereby excluding Powell and directing that the Speaker notify the Governor of New York that the seat was vacant.

Powell and 13 voters of the 18th Congressional District of New York subsequently instituted this suit in the United States District Court for the District of Columbia. Five members of the House of Representatives were named as defendants individually and "as representatives of a class of citizens who are presently serving . . . as members of the House of Representatives." John W. McCormack was named in his official capacity as Speaker, and the Clerk of the House of Representatives, the Sergeant at Arms and the Doorkeeper were named individually and in their official capacities. The complaint alleged that House Resolution No. 278 violated the Constitution, specifically art. I, § 2, cl. 1,[a] because the resolution was inconsistent with the mandate that the members of the House shall be elected by the people of each state, and art. I, § 2, cl. 2,[b] which, petitioners alleged, sets forth the exclusive qualifications for membership. The complaint further al-

[a] Art. I, § 2, cl. 1, provides in part that "The House of Representatives shall be composed of Members chosen every second Year by the People of the several States . . . ." [Footnote by eds.]

[b] Art. I, § 2, cl. 2, provides: "No Person shall be a Representative who shall not have attained to the Age of twenty five Years, and been seven Years a Citizen of the United States, and who shall not, when elected, be an Inhabitant of that State in which he shall be chosen." [Footnote by eds.]

leged that the Clerk of the House threatened to refuse to perform the service for Powell to which a duly elected Congressman is entitled, that the Sergeant at Arms refused to pay Powell his salary, and that the Doorkeeper threatened to deny Powell admission to the House Chamber. . . .

The District Court granted respondents' motion to dismiss the complaint "for want of jurisdiction of the subject matter." The Court of Appeals for the District of Columbia Circuit affirmed on somewhat different grounds, with each judge of the panel filing a separate opinion. We granted certiorari. While the case was pending on our docket, the 90th Congress officially terminated and the 91st Congress was seated. In November 1968, Powell was again elected as the representative of the 18th Congressional District of New York, and he was seated by the 91st Congress. The resolution seating Powell also fined him $25,000. . . .

Respondents press upon us a variety of arguments to support the court below; they will be considered in the following order. (1) Events occurring subsequent to the grant of certiorari have rendered this litigation moot. (2) The speech or debate clause of the Constitution, art. I, § 6, insulates respondents' action from judicial review. (3) The decision to exclude petitioner Powell is supported by the power granted to the House of Representatives to expel a member. (4) This Court lacks subject matter jurisdiction over petitioners' action. (5) Even if subject matter jurisdiction is present, this litigation is not justiciable either under the general criteria established by this Court or because a political question is involved.

[The Court determined in Part II of its opinion that Powell's claim for back salary remained viable and that the case was therefore not moot. In Part III, it held as to the speech or debate clause that "though this action may be dismissed against the Congressmen[,] petitioners are entitled to maintain their action against House employees and to judicial review of the propriety of the decision to exclude petitioner Powell." The Court's analysis of the remaining issues is excerpted below.]

IV.

EXCLUSION OR EXPULSION

The resolution excluding petitioner Powell was adopted by a vote in excess of two-thirds of the 434 members of Congress—307 to 116. Article I, § 5,[c] grants the House authority to expel a member "with the Concurrence of two thirds."[27] Respondents assert that the House may

[c] Art. I, § 5, cl. 2, provides: "Each House may determine the Rules of its Proceedings, punish its Members for disorderly Behavior, and, with the Concurrence of two thirds, expel a Member." [Footnote by eds.]

[27] Powell was "excluded" from the 90th Congress, i.e., he was not administered the oath of office and was prevented from taking his seat. If he had been allowed to take the oath and subsequently had been required to surrender his seat, the House's action would have constituted an "expulsion." Since we conclude that Powell was excluded from the 90th Congress, we express no view on what limitations may

expel a member for any reason whatsoever and that, since a two-thirds vote was obtained, the procedure by which Powell was denied his seat in the 90th Congress should be regarded as an expulsion not an exclusion. . . .

After a motion to bring the Select Committee's proposed resolution to an immediate vote had been defeated, an amendment was offered which mandated Powell's exclusion. Mr. Celler, chairman of the Select Committee, then posed a parliamentary inquiry to determine whether a two-thirds vote was necessary to pass the resolution if so amended "in the sense that it might amount to an expulsion." The Speaker replied that "action by a majority vote would be in accordance with the rules." Had the amendment been regarded as an attempt to expel Powell, a two-thirds vote would have been constitutionally required. The Speaker ruled that the House was voting to exclude Powell, and we will not speculate what the result might have been if Powell had been seated and expulsion proceedings subsequently instituted.

Nor is the distinction between exclusion and expulsion merely one of form. The misconduct for which Powell was charged occurred prior to the convening of the 90th Congress. On several occasions the House has debated whether a member can be expelled for actions taken during a prior congress and the House's own manual of procedure applicable in the 90th Congress states that "both Houses have distrusted their power to punish in such cases." [W]e will not assume that two-thirds of its members would have expelled Powell for his prior conduct had the Speaker announced that House Resolution No. 278 was for expulsion rather than exclusion. . . .

V.

SUBJECT MATTER JURISDICTION

As we pointed out in Baker v. Carr, 369 U.S. 186 (1962), there is a significant difference between determining whether a federal court has "jurisdiction of the subject matter" and determining whether a cause over which a court has subject matter jurisdiction is "justiciable." The District Court determined that "to decide this case on the merits . . . would constitute a clear violation of the doctrine of separation of powers." However, as the Court of Appeals correctly recognized, the doctrine of separation of powers is more properly considered in determining whether the case is "justiciable." . . .

[T]his case clearly is one "arising under" the Constitution as the Court has interpreted that phrase. Any bar to federal courts reviewing the judgments made by the House or Senate in excluding a member arises from the allocation of powers between the two branches of the federal government (a question of justiciability), and not from the petitioners' failure to state a claim based on federal law. [Accordingly,

exist on Congress' power to expel or otherwise punish a member once he has been seated.

subject matter jurisdiction was held properly founded on 28 U.S.C. § 1331.]

VI.

JUSTICIABILITY

Having concluded that the Court of Appeals correctly ruled that the District Court had jurisdiction over the subject matter, we turn to the question whether the case is justiciable. Two determinations must be made in this regard. First, we must decide whether the claim presented and the relief sought are of the type which admit of judicial resolution. Second, we must determine whether the structure of the federal government renders the issue presented a "political question"— that is, a question which is not justiciable in federal court because of the separation of powers provided by the Constitution.

A. General Considerations

In deciding generally whether a claim is justiciable, a court must determine whether "the duty asserted can be judicially identified and its breach judicially determined, and whether protection for the right asserted can be judicially molded." *Baker v. Carr,* supra, at 198. Respondents do not seriously contend that the duty asserted and its alleged breach cannot be judicially determined. If petitioners are correct, the House had a duty to seat Powell once it determined he met the standing requirements set forth in the Constitution. It is undisputed that he met those requirements and that he was nevertheless excluded.

Respondents do maintain, however, that this case is not justiciable because, they assert, it is impossible for a federal court to "mold effective relief for resolving this case." Respondents emphasize that petitioners asked for coercive relief against the officers of the House, and, they contend, federal courts cannot issue mandamus or injunctions compelling officers or employees of the House to perform specific official acts. Respondents rely primarily on the speech or debate clause to support this contention.

We need express no opinion about the appropriateness of coercive relief in this case, for petitioners sought a declaratory judgment, a form of relief the District Court could have issued. The Declaratory Judgment Act, 28 U.S.C. § 2201, provides that a district court may "declare the rights . . . of any interested party . . . whether or not further relief is or could be sought." The availability of declaratory relief depends on whether there is a live dispute between the parties, and a request for declaratory relief may be considered independently of whether other forms of relief are appropriate. We thus conclude that in terms of the general criteria of justiciability, this case is justiciable.

B. Political Question Doctrine

1. Textually Demonstrable Constitutional Commitment.

Respondents maintain that even if this case is otherwise justiciable, it presents only a political question. It is well established that the federal courts will not adjudicate political questions. See, e.g., Coleman v. Miller, 307 U.S. 433 (1939); Oetjen v. Central Leather Co., 246 U.S. 297 (1918). In *Baker v. Carr*, supra, we noted that political questions are not justiciable primarily because of the separation of powers within the federal government. After reviewing our decisions in this area, we concluded that on the surface of any case held to involve a political question was at least one of the following formulations:

> "a textually demonstrable constitutional commitment of the issue to a coordinate political department; or a lack of judicially discoverable and manageable standards for resolving it; or the impossibility of deciding without an initial policy determination of a kind clearly for nonjudicial discretion; or the impossibility of a court's undertaking independent resolution without expressing lack of respect due coordinate branches of government; or an unusual need for unquestioning adherence to a political decision already made; or the potentiality of embarrassment from multifarious pronouncements by various departments on one question." 369 U.S. at 217.

Respondents' first contention is that this case presents a political question because under art. I, § 5,[d] there has been a "textually demonstrable constitutional commitment" to the House of the "adjudicatory power" to determine Powell's qualifications. Thus it is argued that the House, and the House alone, has power to determine who is qualified to be a member.

In order to determine whether there has been a textual commitment to a co-ordinate department of the government, we must interpret the Constitution. In other words, we must first determine what power the Constitution confers upon the House through art. I, § 5, before we can determine to what extent, if any, the exercise of that power is subject to judicial review. Respondents maintain that the House has broad power under § 5, and, they argue, the House may determine which are the qualifications necessary for membership. On the other hand, petitioners allege that the Constitution provides that an elected representative may be denied his seat only if the House finds he does not meet one of the standing qualifications expressly prescribed by the Constitution.

If examination of § 5 disclosed that the Constitution gives the House judicially unreviewable power to set qualifications for membership and to judge whether prospective members meet those qualifications, further review of the House determination might well be barred by the political question doctrine. On the other hand, if the Constitu-

---

[d] Art. I, § 5, cl. 1, provides in part: "Each House shall be the Judge of the Elections, Returns and Qualifications of its own Members . . . ." [Footnote by eds.]

tion gives the House power to judge only whether elected members possess the three standing qualifications set forth in the Constitution, further consideration would be necessary to determine whether any of the other formulations of the political question doctrine are "inextricable from the case at bar."[42] *Baker v. Carr,* supra, at 217.

In other words, whether there is a "textually demonstrable constitutional commitment of the issue to a coordinate political department" of government and what is the scope of such commitment are questions we must resolve for the first time in this case. For, as we pointed out in *Baker v. Carr,* supra, "[d]eciding whether a matter has in any measure been committed by the Constitution to another branch of government, or whether the action of that branch exceeds whatever authority has been committed, is itself a delicate exercise in constitutional interpretation, and is a responsibility of this Court as ultimate interpreter of the Constitution." Id. at 211.

In order to determine the scope of any "textual commitment" under art. I, § 5, we necessarily must determine the meaning of the phrase to "be the Judge of the Qualifications of its own Members." Petitioners argue that the record of the debates during the Constitutional Convention; available commentary from the post-Convention, pre-ratification period; and early congressional applications of art. I, § 5, support their construction of the section. Respondents insist, however, that a careful examination of the pre-Convention practices of the English Parliament and American colonial assemblies demonstrates that by 1787, a legislature's power to judge the qualifications of its members was generally understood to encompass exclusion or expulsion on the ground that an individual's character or past conduct rendered him unfit to serve. When the Constitution and the debates over its adoption are thus viewed in historical perspective, argue respondents, it becomes clear that the "qualifications" expressly set forth in the Constitution were not meant to limit the long-recognized legislative power to exclude or expel at will, but merely to establish "standing incapacities," which could be altered only by a constitutional amendment. Our examination of the relevant historical materials leads us to the conclusion that petitioners are correct and that the Constitution leaves the House without authority to *exclude* any person, duly elected by his constituents, who meets all the requirements for membership expressly prescribed in the Constitution.

[At this point the Court extensively examined historical materials. It concluded as follows:]

Had the intent of the framers emerged from these materials with less clarity, we would nevertheless have been compelled to resolve any ambiguity in favor of a narrow construction of the scope of Congress' power to exclude members-elect. A fundamental principle of our representative democracy is, in Hamilton's words, "that the people

---

[42] Consistent with this interpretation, federal courts might still be barred by the political question doctrine from reviewing the House's factual determinaton that a member did not meet one of the standing qualifications. This is an issue not presented in this case and we express no view as to its resolution.

should choose whom they please to govern them." 2 Elliot's Debates 257. As Madison pointed out at the Convention, this principle is undermined as much by limiting whom the people can select as by limiting the franchise itself. In apparent agreement with this basic philosophy, the Convention adopted his suggestion limiting the power to expel. To allow essentially that same power to be exercised under the guise of judging qualifications, would be to ignore Madison's warning . . . . Moreover, it would effectively nullify the Convention's decision to require a two-thirds vote for expulsion. Unquestionably, Congress has an interest in preserving its institutional integrity, but in most cases that interest can be sufficiently safeguarded by the exercise of its power to punish its members for disorderly behavior and, in extreme cases, to expel a member with the concurrence of two-thirds. In short, both the intention of the framers, to the extent it can be determined, and an examination of the basic principles of our democratic system persuade us that the Constitution does not vest in the Congress a discretionary power to deny membership by a majority vote.

For these reasons, we have concluded that art. I, § 5, is at most a "textually demonstrable commitment" to Congress to judge only the qualifications expressly set forth in the Constitution. Therefore, the "textual commitment" formulation of the political question doctrine does not bar federal courts from adjudicating petitioners' claims.

2.   Other Considerations.

Respondents' alternate contention is that the case presents a political question because judicial resolution of petitioners' claim would produce a "potentially embarrassing confrontation between coordinate branches" of the federal government. But, as our interpretation of art. I, § 5, discloses, a determination of petitioner Powell's right to sit would require no more than an interpretation of the Constitution. Such a determination falls within the traditional role accorded courts to interpret the law, and does not involve a "lack of the respect due [a] coordinate [branch] of government," nor does it involve an "initial policy determination of a kind clearly for nonjudicial discretion." *Baker v. Carr,* supra, at 217. Our system of government requires that federal courts on occasion interpret the Constitution in a manner at variance with the construction given the document by another branch. The alleged conflict that such an adjudication may cause cannot justify the courts' avoiding their constitutional responsibility.

Nor are any of the other formulations of a political question "inextricable from the case at bar." *Baker v. Carr,* supra, at 217. Petitioners seek a determination that the House was without power to exclude Powell from the 90th Congress, which, we have seen, requires an interpretation of the Constitution—a determination for which clearly there are "judicially . . . manageable standards." Finally, a judicial resolution of petitioners' claim will not result in "multifarious pronouncements by various departments on one question." For, as we noted in *Baker v. Carr,* supra, at 211, it is the responsibility of this Court to act as the ultimate interpreter of the Constitution. Marbury

v. Madison, 5 U.S. (1 Cranch) 137 (1803). Thus, we conclude that petitioners' claim is not barred by the political question doctrine, and, having determined that the claim is otherwise justiciable, we hold that the case is justiciable.

VII.

CONCLUSION

[A]nalysis of the "textual commitment" under art. I, § 5 . . ., has demonstrated that in judging the qualifications of its members Congress is limited to the standing qualifications prescribed in the Constitution. Respondents concede that Powell met these. Thus, there is no need to remand this case to determine whether he was entitled to be seated in the 90th Congress. Therefore, we hold that, since Adam Clayton Powell, Jr., was duly elected by the voters . . . and was not ineligible to serve under any provision of the Constitution, the House was without power to exclude him from its membership.

Petitioners seek additional forms of equitable relief, including mandamus for the release of Powell's back pay. The propriety of such remedies, however, is more appropriately considered in the first instance by the courts below. Therefore, as to [the Congressional] respondents . . ., the judgment of the Court of Appeals . . . is affirmed. As to [the House employee] respondents . . ., the judgment of the Court of Appeals . . . is reversed and the case is remanded to the District Court . . . with instructions to enter a declaratory judgment and for further proceedings consistent with this opinion.

It is so ordered.

[Justice Douglas filed a concurring opinion. Justice Stewart dissented on the ground that the case had become moot and that the Court "should therefore refrain from deciding the novel, difficult, and delicate constitutional questions which the case presented at its inception."]

NOTES ON THE POLITICAL QUESTION DOCTRINE

1. *Luther v. Borden.* The political question doctrine has a long history. The leading early case arose out of the Dorr Rebellion against the 'charter' government of Rhode Island. Dorr was elected governor under the purported authority of a new state constitution in 1842. The charter government, however, refused to admit the validity of these proceedings. Dorr tried to take power by force, but was repulsed. The charter government then called a constitutional convention, and a peaceful transition to the new government was made in May, 1843.

In 1842 Borden and other state officers, acting under the authority of martial law, broke into Luther's house. Luther sued for trespass. He claimed that the charter government had been displaced in 1842 and therefore could not authorize the defendants' acts. In this way, Luther sought to litigate the existence and authority of the charter government in the interval between the purported approval of a new constitution in May 1842 and the actual transfer of authority to the new government in May 1843. The lower court, however, declined to consider this issue and entered a verdict for defendants. In Luther v. Borden, 48 U.S. (7 How.) 1 (1849), the Supreme Court affirmed.

Speaking through Chief Justice Taney, the Court offered several reasons for refusing to inquire into the continued validity of the charter government. For one thing, grave practical difficulties would follow if all acts of the established government could be called into question. Moreover, the state courts had approved the charter government's authority during that period and accepted its acts as valid. Finally, insofar as the federal Constitution might speak to this issue through art. IV, § 4,[a] Taney said that Congress, not the Court, was the proper authority:

> "Congress must necessarily decide what government is established in the state before it can determine whether it is republican or not. And when the senators and representatives of a state are admitted into the councils of the Union, the authority of the government under which they are appointed, as well as its republican character, is recognized by the proper constitutional authority. And its decision is binding on every other department of the government, and could not be questioned in a judicial tribunal."

2. *Baker v. Carr.* After *Luther v. Borden,* guarantee clause questions were usually held non-justiciable.[b] This position eventually assumed great importance, for it blocked attempts to litigate the constitutionality of legislative malapportionment. In Colegrove v. Green, 328 U.S. 549 (1946), for example, the Court refused to reach the merits of a constitutional attack on Illinois' congressional districting. Speaking for a plurality of the Court, Justice Frankfurter described the issue as one "of a peculiarly political nature and therefore not meet for judicial determination." The controversy concerned "matters that bring courts into immediate and active relations with party contests," an involvement from which the courts have "traditionally remained aloof." The power to correct the situation lay with Congress. "Courts ought not to enter this political thicket." In subsequent cases, the Court followed *Colegrove* in turning aside constitutional attacks on legislative districting. See, e.g., South v. Peters, 339 U.S. 276 (1950).

All this was changed by Baker v. Carr, 369 U.S. 186 (1962). Plaintiffs claimed that the malapportionment of the Tennessee General Assembly denied equal protection to voters in the more populous

---

[a] Art. IV, § 4 provides: "The United States shall guarantee to every State a Republican Form of Government . . . ."

[b] See, e.g., Taylor & Marshall v. Beckham, 178 U.S. 548 (1900) (refusing to adjudicate the claim that state resolution of a disputed gubernatorial election deprived the voters of a republican form of government); Pacific States Tel. & Tel. Co. v. Oregon, 223 U.S. 118 (1912) (refusing to adjudicate company's claim that a special tax imposed by initiative and referendum rather than by the usual legislative process violated the guarantee clause). For a comprehensive treatment, see Bonfield, The Guarantee Clause of Article IV, Section 4: A Study in Constitutional Desuetude, 46 Minn. L. Rev. 513 (1962).

districts. The trial court dismissed the suit on the authority of *Colegrove*, but the Supreme Court reversed. Speaking for the Court, Justice Brennan said that "the mere fact that the suit seeks protection of a political right does not mean it presents a political question." That objection was "little more than a play on words."

Furthermore, the guarantee clause cases were irrelevant. The nonjusticiability of such claims had "nothing to do with their touching upon matters of state governmental organization." Their only significance was in holding that the guarantee clause was "not a repository of judicially manageable standards." The equal protection clause was different.

Justice Brennan recast the political question doctrine as exclusively concerned with separation of powers: "[I]t is the relationship between the judiciary and the coordinate branches of the federal government, and not the federal judiciary's relationship to the states, which gives rise to the 'political question.'" Finally, in a famous passage quoted in *Powell*, Justice Brennan identified the ingredients of a "political question":

> "Prominent on the surface of any case held to involve a political question is found a textually demonstrable constitutional commitment of the issue to a coordinate political department; or a lack of judicially discoverable and manageable standards for resolving it; or the impossibility of deciding without an initial policy determination of a kind clearly for nonjudicial discretion; or the impossibility of a court's undertaking independent resolution without expressing lack of the respect due coordinate branches of government; or an unusual need for unquestioning adherence to a political decision already made; or the potentiality of embarrassment from multifarious pronouncements by various departments on one question."

Unless one of these factors is "inextricable from the case at bar," said the Court, "there should be no dismissal for nonjusticiability" on the ground of a political question. Accordingly, the case was remanded for trial on the merits.[c]

3. The Political Question Doctrine and Judicial Review. The fundamental issue underlying the political question doctrine is its relation to judicial review. Is it a sensible restraint on judicial activism or an unprincipled evasion of judicial responsibility? This question has drawn the attention of leading academic lawyers.

The debate begins with Herbert Wechsler, who argued, partly in rebuttal to Learned Hand, that the power of judicial review is no mere invention of necessity but is "grounded in the language of the Constitution." Wechsler, Toward Neutral Principles of Constitutional Law, 73

---

[c] Two years later, in Reynolds v. Sims, 377 U.S. 533 (1964), the Court ruled that both houses of a state legislature must be elected from districts "as nearly of equal population as is practicable."

Harv. L. Rev. 1, 3 (1959). This premise led Wechsler to a narrow view of the doctrine of the political question:

> "[A]ll the doctrine can defensibly imply is that the courts are called upon to judge whether the Constitution has committed to another agency of government the autonomous determination of the issue raised, a finding that itself requires interpretation. [T]he only proper judgment that may lead to an abstention from decision is that the Constitution has committed the determination of the issue to another agency of government than the courts. Difficult as it may be to make that judgment wisely, whatever factors may be rightly weighed in situations where the answer is not clear, what is involved is itself an act of constitutional interpretation, to be made and judged by standards that should govern the interpretive process generally. This, I submit, is toto caelo different from a broad discretion to abstain or intervene." Id. at 7–8, 9.

This pronouncement produced a response from Alexander Bickel:

> "[O]nly by means of a play on words can the broad discretion that the courts have in fact exercised be turned into an act of constitutional interpretation. The political-question doctrine simply resists being domesticated in this fashion. There is something different about it, in kind, not in degree, from the general 'interpretive process'; something greatly more flexible, something of prudence, not construction and not principle. And it is something that cannot exist within the four corners of *Marbury v. Madison.* "

Bickel, The Supreme Court, 1960 Term—Foreword: The Passive Virtues, 75 Harv. L. Rev. 40, 46 (1961).[d]

For Bickel, as for Wechsler, the scope of the political question doctrine was intimately related to the rationale for judicial review. For Bickel, however, judicial review was not so much a *duty,* imposed by the Constitution on an obedient Court, as a *power,* to be used or withheld on the basis of discerning judgment. In Bickel's view, the task of the Court was to safeguard principle in a world of political expediency. "[T]he role of the Court and its raison d'etre are to evolve, to defend, and to protect principle." In some circumstances, it would be appropriate for the Court to attempt to coerce adherence to principle by the political branches. In others, "there ought to be discretion free of principled rules." After all, "no society, certainly not a large and heterogeneous one, can fail in time to explode if it is deprived of the arts of compromise, if it knows no way to muddle through." In such situations, the Court may have to tolerate unprincipled actions, but it should at least avoid "legitimating" them by pronouncements of constitutionality.

It is in this frame of reference that Bickel placed his view of a political question:

---

[d] Bickel later expanded these views in his book, The Least Dangerous Branch (1962).

"Such is the basis of the political question doctrine: the Court's sense of lack of capacity, compounded in unequal part of the strangeness of the issue and the suspicion that it will have to yield more often and more substantially to expediency than to principle; the sheer momentousness of it, which unbalances judgment and prevents one from subsuming the normal calculations of probabilities; the anxiety not so much that judicial judgment will be ignored, as that perhaps it should be, but won't; finally and in sum ('in a mature democracy'), the inner vulnerability of an institution which is electorally irresponsible and has no earth to draw strength from."

These views drew a riposte from Gerald Gunther, who accused Bickel of a "100 per cent insistence on principle, 20 per cent of the time." Gunther, The Subtle Vices of the "Passive Virtues"—A Comment on Principle and Expediency in Judicial Review, 64 Colum. L. Rev. 1 (1964). In Gunther's view, Bickel's reliance on prudential considerations was "ultimately law-debasing."

4. Questions and Comments on *Powell v. McCormack*. With which of these perspectives is *Powell v. McCormack* more nearly consistent? Which represents the better view of the nature of a political question? And what, if anything, does *Powell* reveal about the Court's conception of the nature of judicial review?

Consider in this connection the remarks of Terrance Sandalow in Comments on *Powell v. McCormack*, 17 U.C.L.A. L. Rev. 164, 168 (1969):

"Throughout, the opinion reflects a conception of the Court as the ultimate interpreter and defender of the Constitution. In *Marbury v. Madison,* the power of the Court to declare Congressional legislation unconstitutional was justified as a necessary incident of the Court's duty to decide cases in conformity to law, including the Constitution as the 'supreme law.' *Powell* demonstrates how far the Court has moved from that rationale. In *Powell,* it is the existence of a constitutional question which leads the Court to conclude that a justiciable controversy is presented. The determination of constitutional questions becomes not merely an incident of the exercise of judicial power, but a reason for it."

Is Dean Sandalow right? If so, is any version of the political question doctrine consistent with the Court's role as "ultimate interpreter and defender of the Constitution?"

5. *Gilligan v. Morgan*. Although *Powell v. McCormack* was thought by some to signal the death of the political question doctrine, subsequent cases have proved that not to be so. Gilligan v. Morgan, 413 U.S. 1 (1973), arose in the aftermath of the shootings at Kent State University in May 1970. Members of the student government sued to enjoin the governor from premature use of the National Guard and to enjoin the Guard from violating students' rights. Most aspects of the suit were dismissed, but the Court of Appeals ordered a trial on the claim that the training and leadership of the Ohio National Guard made "inevitable" the unnecessary use of deadly force. The Supreme Court reversed.

Chief Justice Burger characterized the complaint as a "broad call on judicial power to assume continuing regulatory jurisdiction over the activities of the Ohio National Guard." He concluded that this claim presented a political question within the meaning of *Baker v. Carr,* and added:

> "[I]t is difficult to conceive of an area of governmental activity in which the courts have less competence. The complex, subtle, and professional decisions as to the composition, training, equipping, and control of a military force are essentially professional military judgments, subject *always* to civilian control of the legislative and executive branches. The ultimate responsibility for these decisions is appropriately vested in branches of the government which are periodically subject to electoral responsibility."

Four Justices took the view that the case had become moot and should be remanded for dismissal on that ground.[e]

6. *Goldwater v. Carter.* The political question doctrine also arose when members of Congress sued President Carter to challenge the President's power to terminate a mutual defense treaty with Taiwan. The treaty included a power of termination, but it did not specify how that power could be exercised. The District Court held that the President could not act unilaterally. The Court of Appeals reversed. In Goldwater v. Carter, 444 U.S. 996 (1979), the Supreme Court vacated the judgment below and remanded with instructions to dismiss the complaint.

Speaking for himself and three others, Justice Rehnquist found the case to involve a political question. The Constitution did not speak to the question of congressional participation in the termination of treaties, and the issue should therefore "be controlled by political standards." This was especially so, because the question involved foreign relations, an area in which the courts have traditionally been reluctant to intervene.

Justice Powell disagreed:

> "In my view, reliance upon the political question doctrine is inconsistent with our precedents. As set forth in the seminal case of *Baker v. Carr,* the doctrine incorporates three inquiries: (i) Does the issue involve resolution of questions

[e] An unsuccessful attempt to invoke the political question doctrine was made in Davis v. Bandemer, 478 U.S. 109 (1986). Plaintiffs were Indiana Democrats who claimed that they had been unlawfully disadvantaged by partisan gerrymandering. A majority found that this claim was justiciable, but that plaintiffs had not met the appropriate standard for relief on the merits. (Justices Powell and Stevens dissented on the latter point.) Justice O'Connor, joined by Chief Justice Burger and Justice Rehnquist, dissented on justiciability, arguing that "the legislative business of apportionment is fundamentally a political affair, and challenges to the manner in which an apportionment has been carried out . . . present a political question in the truest sense of the term."

committed by the text of the Constitution to a coordinate branch of government? (ii) Would resolution of the question demand that a court move beyond areas of judicial expertise? (iii) Do prudential considerations counsel against judicial intervention? . . .

"First, the existence of 'a textually demonstrable constitutional commitment of the issue to a coordinate political department,' turns on an examination of the constitutional provisions governing the exercise of the power in question. Powell v. McCormack, 395 U.S. 486, 519 (1969). No constitutional provision explicitly confers upon the President the power to terminate treaties. Further, art. II, § 2, of the Constitution authorizes the President to make treaties with the advice and consent of the Senate. Article VI provides that treaties shall be a part of the supreme law of the land. These provisions add support to the view that the text of the Constitution does not unquestionably commit the power to terminate treaties to the President alone.

"Second, there is no 'lack of judicially discoverable and manageable standards for resolving' this case; nor is a decision impossible without an initial policy determination of a kind clearly for nonjudicial discretion. *Baker v. Carr,* supra. We are asked to decide whether the President may terminate a treaty under the Constitution without congressional approval. Resolution of the question may not be easy, but it only requires us to apply normal principles of interpretation to the constitutional provisions at issue. See *Powell v. McCormack,* supra. The present case involves neither review of the President's activities as Commander in Chief nor impermissible interference in the field of foreign affairs. . . . This case 'touches' foreign relations, but the question presented to us concerns only the constitutional division of power between Congress and the President. . . .

"Finally, the political-question doctrine rests in part on prudential concerns calling for mutual respect among the three branches of government. [But interpretation] of the Constitution does not imply lack of respect for a coordinate branch. *Powell v. McCormack,* supra. [F]inal disposition of the question presented by this case would eliminate, rather than create, multiple constitutional interpretations. The specter of the federal government brought to a halt because of the mutual intransigence of the President and the Congress would require this Court to provide a resolution pursuant to our duty ' "to say what the law is." ' United States v. Nixon, 418 U.S. 683, 703 (1974), quoting Marbury v. Madison, 1 Cranch 137, 177 (1803)."

Justice Powell concluded that the case, although presenting no political question, would nevertheless not be ripe for adjudication "unless and until each branch has taken action asserting its constitutional authority" and the conflict has reached a state of "constitutional impasse."

Justice Marshall concurred in the result without opinion. Justices Blackmun and White voted to set the case for oral argument. Justice Brennan voted to affirm the judgment of the Court of Appeals on the ground that the President's action was supported by the established presidential authority to recognize foreign governments.

7. The Political Question Doctrine and Foreign Affairs. Successful resort to the political question doctrine in purely domestic disputes is increasingly rare. Today, most "political questions" involve foreign affairs. Courts often, if not typically, invoke the political question doctrine to deflect attempts to litigate the legality of U.S. foreign policy. The chief example has been the Vietnam War. See, e.g., Atlee v. Richardson, 411 U.S. 911 (1973). More recent efforts to challenge American military actions abroad have usually met the same fate. For example, in Crockett v. Reagan, 720 F.2d 1355 (D.C. Cir. 1983), several United States Congressmen sought to challenge American military involvement in El Salvador. The District Court dismissed the suit as involving a political question, and the D.C. Circuit affirmed in a brief per curiam opinion. Two years later, the same court reached the same result in dismissing a suit by Congressmen, among others, to contest the legality of United States aid to the Nicaraguan "Contras." Sanchez-Espinoza v. Reagan, 770 F.2d 202 (D.C. Cir. 1985).

Even in foreign affairs cases, however, the political question doctrine does not always prevail. A notable example is Ramirez de Arellano v. Weinberger, 745 F.2d 1500 (D.C. Cir. 1984), in which the D.C. Circuit found the suit justiciable despite obvious foreign policy implications. Ramirez was a U.S. citizen who, through corporate intermediaries, owned and operated a large cattle ranch in Honduras. Part of his land was used to establish a U.S.-sponsored regional training center for the army of El Salvador. When negotiations with American representatives broke down, Ramirez brought suit, not in Honduras, but in the United States District Court for the District of Columbia. He claimed that the U.S. action was unconstitutional because not authorized by federal law and that it deprived him and his corporations of their property without due process of law. The suit sought injunctive and declaratory relief against continued occupation of the Ramirez ranch.

The District Court dismissed this suit as presenting a non-justiciable political question. This decision was initially affirmed by the D.C. Circuit, but on a different ground. Ramirez de Arellano v. Weinberger, 724 F.2d 143 (D.C. Cir. 1983). Writing for the panel, then-Judge Scalia declined to decide the political question issue. He reasoned that in any event traditional principles of equity, also applicable to declaratory judgments, provided ample grounds for withholding relief. An injunction would intrude into foreign affairs, and it would be extremely difficult to monitor compliance. Ramirez had not sought relief in Honduras, and in any event he seemed to have a damage remedy against the United States under the Tucker Act. Given these circumstances, plaintiff had not shown a persuasive case for the exercise of equity power.

This decision was vacated on petition for rehearing en banc, and the full D.C. Circuit held the case justiciable and remanded for further proceedings. This time Scalia was in dissent. In an opinion joined by Judges Bork and Starr, Scalia again declined to invoke the political question doctrine but disputed the majority on a wide range of other issues.[f] In a separate dissent, Judge Tamm argued that the case did present a political question. Although the complaint was styled as merely a dispute over land, said Tamm, the requested relief "would essentially dictate to the executive branch the proper situs or scope of a Central American military training facility and severely restrict the executive's authority to determine the use and disposition of military operations." Additionally, the suit might detrimentally affect U.S. relations with Honduras, which supported or at least allowed construction of the training camp.

To the majority, however, these considerations were unpersuasive. Speaking for the Court, Judge Wilkey dismissed the political question doctrine as "a tempting refuge from the adjudication of difficult constitutional claims." Here the complaint did not purport to challenge the conduct of American foreign policy, but merely asserted the right of a U.S. citizen to be free from illegal occupation and seizure of his property. In Wilkey's view, the suit presented "a paradigmatic issue for resolution by the judiciary." To dismiss it as a political question "would mean that virtually *anything* done by United States officials to United States citizens on foreign soil is nonjusticiable." "That," said Wilkey, "is not the law."[g]

Who has the better of this argument? Note that the chief difference between this case and the others seems to be the way in which the issue was framed. The *Ramirez* complaint did not directly challenge the legality of U.S. policy in Central America; rather, it merely sought equitable relief against invasion of the property rights of a U.S. citizen. Yet it seems plain that this claim could not be heard without implicating foreign affairs. Is the political question doctrine more sensibly based on the nature of the *issue* presented in the case or, as Judge Tamm argued in dissent, on the *consequences* that would flow from judicial action? In other words, does the political question variant of

[f] Among the issues discussed were whether the Tucker Act provided a damages remedy for Ramirez's claim and therefore barred any other relief; whether Ramirez as sole shareholder had standing to raise the legal rights of his corporations; whether the traditionally discretionary considerations governing injunctive and declaratory relief should cause the court to stay its hand; whether litigation in the United States for trespass to land located elsewhere should be barred by the local action rule; and whether the initiation of expropriation proceedings by the Honduran government against the Ramirez property triggered the act of state doctrine. The last point was the subject of a separate dissent by Judge Starr, with whom Judge Scalia joined.

[g] The Supreme Court subsequently granted certiorari, vacated the judgment below, and remanded for reconsideration in light of subsequent developments. Weinberger v. Ramirez de Arellano, 471 U.S. 1113 (1985).

non-justiciability properly turn on the nature of the question presented or on the political context in which it is raised?

8. Bibliography. There is a considerable literature on the political question doctrine and on the major cases decided under its authority. In addition to the works already cited, see Scharpf, Judicial Review and the Political Question: A Functional Analysis, 75 Yale L.J. 517 (1966) (describing and analyzing both the "classical," i.e. Wechsler, and "prudential," i.e., Bickel, versions of the doctrine); Henkin, Is There a "Political Question" Doctrine?, 85 Yale L.J. 597 (1976) (arguing that the political question doctrine is "an unnecessary, deceptive packaging" of several established limitations on the judicial role, none of which depends on any extraordinary notion of nonjusticiability); and Redish, Judicial Review and the "Political Question," 79 Nw. U.L. Rev. 1031 (1985) (arguing, in partial response to Professor Henkin, that there is, but that there should not be, a political question doctrine). For comments on *Powell v. McCormack,* see the Symposium in 17 U.C.L.A. L. Rev. 1 (1969).

An interesting and original analysis of the political question doctrine in the foreign affairs context appears in a recent article by Linda Champlin and Alan Schwarz, Political Question Doctrine and Allocation of the Foreign Affairs Power, 13 Hofstra L. Rev. 215 (1985). The authors argue that the political question doctrine is properly not viewed as an aspect of justiciability, but as an adjudication on the merits. The only difference between a political question and an ordinary decision on the merits is that in the former case the constitutionality of the challenged action is *assumed* rather than *decided.* In their view, such an assumption of constitutionality is warranted only where there is an extraordinary need for finality in the pronouncements of a coordinate branch—in the words of *Baker v. Carr,* where there is "an unusual need for unquestioning adherence to a political decision already made." Such situations will rarely, if ever, arise in purely domestic litigation. But in foreign affairs cases, it may be essential that the nation speak with one voice, even if that voice is wrong. Thus, Champlin and Schwarz contemplate that the political question doctrine should be at least "theoretically applicable" to some foreign affairs controversies, although even this context they argue that the need to respect the finality of a political decision will ordinarily be outweighed by the need for judicial determination of the respective competencies of the executive and legislative branches in foreign affairs.

SECTION 4: ARTICLE I COURTS

NORTHERN PIPELINE CONSTRUCTION CO. v. MARATHON PIPE LINE CO.

Supreme Court of the United States, 1982.
458 U.S. 50.

JUSTICE BRENNAN announced the judgment of the Court and delivered an opinion, in which JUSTICE MARSHALL, JUSTICE BLACKMUN, and JUSTICE STEVENS joined.

The question presented is whether the assignment by Congress to bankruptcy judges of the jurisdiction granted in 28 U.S.C. § 1471 by § 241(a) of the Bankruptcy Act of 1978 violates art. III of the Constitution.

I

A

In 1978, after almost 10 years of study and investigation, Congress enacted a comprehensive revision of the bankruptcy laws. The Bankruptcy Act of 1978 (act) made significant changes in both the substantive and procedural law of bankruptcy. It is the changes in the latter that are at issue in this case.

Before the act, federal district courts served as bankruptcy courts and employed a "referee" system. Bankruptcy proceedings were generally conducted before referees,[2] except in those instances in which the district court elected to withdraw a case from a referee. The referee's final order was appealable to the district court. The bankruptcy courts were vested with "summary jurisdiction"—that is, with jurisdiction over controversies involving property in the actual or constructive possession of the court. And, with consent, the bankruptcy court also had jurisdiction over some "plenary" matters—such as disputes involving property in the possession of a third person.

The act eliminates the referee system and establishes "in each judicial district, as an adjunct to the district court for such district, a bankruptcy court which shall be a court of record known as the United States Bankruptcy Court for the district." The judges of these courts are appointed to office for 14–year terms by the President, with the advice and consent of the Senate. They are subject to removal by the "judicial council of the circuit" on account of "incompetency, misconduct, neglect of duty or physical or mental disability." In addition, the salaries of the bankruptcy judges are set by statute and are subject to adjustment under the Federal Salary Act.

---

[2] Bankruptcy referees were redesignated as "judges" in 1973. For purposes of clarity, however, we refer to all judges under the old act as "referees."

The jurisdiction of the bankruptcy courts created by the act is much broader than that exercised under the former referee system. Eliminating the distinction between "summary" and "plenary" jurisdiction, the act grants the new courts jurisdiction over all "civil proceedings arising under title 11 [the bankruptcy title] or arising in or *related to* cases under title 11." This jurisdictional grant empowers bankruptcy courts to entertain a wide variety of cases involving claims that may affect the property of the estate once a petition has been filed under title 11. Included within the bankruptcy courts' jurisdiction are suits to recover accounts, controversies involving exempt property, actions to avoid transfers and payments as preferences or fraudulent conveyances, and causes of action owned by the debtor at the time of the petition for bankruptcy. The bankruptcy courts can hear claims based on state law as well as those based on federal law.[4]

The judges of the bankruptcy courts are vested with all of the "powers of a court of equity, law, and admiralty," except that they "may not enjoin another court or punish a criminal contempt not committed in the presence of the judge of the court or warranting a punishment of imprisonment." In addition to this broad grant of power, Congress has allowed bankruptcy judges the power to hold jury trials; to issue declaratory judgments; to issue writs of habeas corpus under certain circumstances; to issue all writs necessary in aid of the bankruptcy court's expanded jurisdiction; and to issue any order, process or judgment that is necessary or appropriate to carry out the provisions of title 11.

The act also establishes a special procedure for appeals from orders of bankruptcy courts. The circuit council is empowered to direct the chief judge of the circuit to designate panels of three bankruptcy judges to hear appeals. These panels have jurisdiction of all appeals from final judgments, orders, and decrees of bankruptcy courts, and, with leave of the panel, of interlocutory appeals. If no such appeals panel is designated, the district court is empowered to exercise appellate jurisdiction. The court of appeals is given jurisdiction over appeals from the appellate panels or from the district court. If the parties agree, a direct appeal to the court of appeals may be taken from a final judgment of a bankruptcy court.[5] . . .

B

This case arises out of proceedings initiated in the United States Bankruptcy Court for the District of Minnesota after appellant Northern Pipeline Construction Co. (Northern) filed a petition for reorganization in January 1980. In March 1980, Northern, pursuant to the act,

---

[4] . . . Although the act does not in terms indicate the extent to which bankruptcy judges may exercise personal jurisdiction, it has been construed to allow the constitutional maximum. . . .

[5] Although no particular standard of review is specified in the act, the parties in the present cases seem to agree that the appropriate one is the clearly erroneous standard, employed in the old Bankruptcy Rule 810 for review of findings of facts made by a referee.

filed in that court a suit against appellee Marathon Pipe Line Co. (Marathon). Appellant sought damages for alleged breaches of contract and warranty, as well as for alleged misrepresentation, coercion, and duress. Marathon sought dismissal of the suit, on the ground that the act unconstitutionally conferred art. III judicial power upon judges who lacked life tenure and protection against salary diminution. The United States intervened to defend the validity of the statute.

The bankruptcy judge denied the motion to dismiss. But on appeal the District Court entered an order granting the motion, on the ground that "the delegation of authority in 28 U.S.C. § 1471 to the bankruptcy judges to try cases which are otherwise relegated under the Constitution to article III judges" was unconstitutional. Both the United States and Northern filed notices of appeal in this Court. We noted probable jurisdiction.

II

A

Basic to the constitutional structure established by the framers was their recognition that "The accumulation of all powers, legislative, executive, and judiciary, in the same hands, whether of one, a few, or many, and whether hereditary, self-appointed, or elective, may justly be pronounced the very definition of tyranny." The Federalist No. 47, p. 300 (H. Lodge ed. 1888) (J. Madison). To ensure against such tyranny, the framers provided that the federal government would consist of three distinct branches, each to exercise one of the governmental powers recognized by the framers as inherently distinct. "The framers regarded the checks and balances that they had built into the tripartite federal government as a self-executing safeguard against the encroachment or aggrandizement of one branch at the expense of the other." Buckley v. Valeo, 424 U.S. 1, 122 (1976) (per curiam).

The federal judiciary was therefore designed by the framers to stand independent of the executive and legislature—to maintain the checks and balances of the constitutional structure, and also to guarantee that the process of adjudication itself remained impartial. Hamilton explained the importance of an independent judiciary:

> "Periodical appointments, however regulated, or by whomsoever made, would, in some way or other, be fatal to [the courts'] necessary independence. If the power of making them was committed either to the executive or legislature, there would be danger of an improper complaisance to the branch which possessed it; if to both, there would be an unwillingness to hazard the displeasure of either; if to the people, or to persons chosen by them for the special purpose, there would be too great a disposition to consult popularity, to justify a reliance that nothing would be consulted but the Constitution and the laws." The Federalist No. 78, p. 489 (H. Lodge ed. 1888). . . .

As an inseparable element of the constitutional system of checks and balances, and as a guarantee of judicial impartiality, art. III both defines the power and protects the independence of the judicial branch. . . . The inexorable command of [art. III] is clear and definite: The judicial power of the United States must be exercised by courts having the attributes prescribed in art. III. . . .

The "good Behaviour" clause guarantees that art. III judges shall enjoy life tenure, subject only to removal by impeachment. The compensation clause guarantees art. III judges a fixed and irreducible compensation for their services. Both of these provisions were incorporated into the Constitution to ensure the independence of the judiciary from the control of the executive and legislative branches of government.[10] . . . In sum, our Constitution unambiguously enunciates a fundamental principle—that the "judicial Power of the United States" must be reposed in an independent judiciary. It commands that the independence of the judiciary be jealously guarded, and it provides clear institutional protections for that independence.

B

It is undisputed that the bankruptcy judges whose offices were created by the Bankruptcy Act of 1978 do not enjoy the protections constitutionally afforded to art. III judges. The bankruptcy judges do not serve for life subject to their continued "good Behaviour." Rather, they are appointed for 14–year terms, and can be removed by the judicial council of the circuit in which they serve on grounds of "incompetency, misconduct, neglect of duty, or physical or mental disability." Second, the salaries of bankruptcy judges are not immune from diminution by Congress. In short, there is no doubt that the bankruptcy judges created by the act are not art. III judges. . . .

Appellants suggest two grounds for upholding the act's conferral of broad adjudicative powers upon judges unprotected by art. III. First, it is urged that "pursuant to its enumerated art. I powers, Congress may establish legislative courts that have jurisdiction to decide cases to which the art. III judicial power of the United States extends." . . . Second, appellants contend that even if the Constitution does require that this bankruptcy-related action be adjudicated in an art. III court, the act in fact satisfies this requirement. . . .We consider these arguments in turn.

[10] These provisions serve other institutional values as well. The independence from political forces that they guarantee helps to promote public confidence in judicial determinations. The security that they provide to members of the judicial branch helps to attract well qualified persons to the federal bench. The guarantee of life tenure insulates the individual judge from improper influences not only by other branches but by colleagues as well, and thus promotes judicial individualism. See Kaufman, Chilling Judicial Independence, 88 Yale L.J. 681, 713 (1979). See generally Note, Article III Limits on Article I Courts: The Constitutionality of the Bankruptcy Court and the 1979 Magistrate Act, 80 Colum. L. Rev. 560, 583–85 (1980).

III

Congress did not constitute the bankruptcy courts as legislative courts.[13]   Appellants contend, however, that the bankruptcy courts could have been so constituted, and that as a result the "adjunct" system in fact chosen by Congress does not impermissibly encroach upon the judicial power.   In advancing this argument, appellants rely upon cases in which we have identified certain matters that "Congress may or may not bring within the cognizance of [art. III courts], as it may deem proper."   Murray's Lessee v. Hoboken Land & Improvement Co., 59 U.S. (18 How.) 272, 284 (1856).[14]   But when properly understood, these precedents represent no broad departure from the constitutional command that the judicial power of the United States must be vested in art. III courts.[15]   Rather, they reduce to three narrow situations not subject to that command, each recognizing a circumstance in which the grant of power to the legislative and executive branches was historically and constitutionally so exceptional that the congressional assertion of a power to create legislative courts was consistent with, rather than threatening to, the constitutional mandate of separation of powers.
. . .

Appellants first rely upon a series of cases in which this Court has upheld the creation by Congress of non-art. III "territorial courts." This exception from the general prescription of art. III dates from the earliest days of the Republic, when it was perceived that the framers intended that as to certain geographical areas, in which no state operated as sovereign, Congress was to exercise the general powers of government.   For example, in American Ins. Co. v. Canter, 26 U.S. (1 Pet.) 511 (1828), the Court observed that art. IV bestowed upon Congress alone a complete power of government over territories not within the states that comprised the United States. . . .   The Court followed the same reasoning when it reviewed Congress' creation of non-art. III courts in the District of Columbia. . . .

[13] The act designates the bankruptcy court in each district as an "adjunct" to the district court. . . .

[14] At one time, this Court suggested a rigid distinction between those subjects that could be considered only in art. III courts and those that could be considered only in legislative courts. See Williams v. United States, 289 U.S. 553 (1933). But this suggested dichotomy has not withstood analysis. Our more recent cases clearly recognize that legislative courts may be granted jurisdiction over some cases and controversies to which the art. III judicial power might also be extended. E.g., Palmore v. United States, 411 U.S. 389 (1973).

[15] Justice White's dissent finds particular significance in the fact that Congress could have assigned all bankruptcy matters to the state courts. But, of course, virtually all matters that might be heard in art. III courts could also be left by Congress to state courts. This fact is simply irrelevant to the question before us. Congress has no control over state-court judges; accordingly the principle of separation of powers is not threatened by leaving the adjudication of federal disputes to such judges. See Krattenmaker, Article III and Judicial Independence: Why the New Bankruptcy Courts are Unconstitutional, 70 Geo. L.J. 297, 304–05 (1981). The framers chose to leave to Congress the precise role to be played by the lower federal courts in the administration of justice. But the Framers did not leave it to Congress to define the character of those courts—they were to be independent of the political branches and presided over by judges with guaranteed salary and life tenure.

Appellants next advert to a second class of cases—those in which this Court has sustained the exercise by Congress and the executive of the power to establish and administer courts-martial. The situation in these cases strongly resembles the situation with respect to territorial courts: It too involves a constitutional grant of power that has been historically understood as giving the political branches of government extraordinary control over the precise subject matter at issue. . . .

Finally, appellants rely on a third group of cases, in which this Court has upheld the constitutionality of legislative courts and administrative agencies created by Congress to adjudicate cases involving "public rights." The "public rights" doctrine was first set forth in Murray's Lessee v. Hoboken Land & Improvement Co., 59 U.S. (18 How.) 272, 284 (1856):

> "[W]e do not consider Congress can either withdraw from judicial cognizance any matter which, from its nature, is the subject of a suit at the common law, or in equity, or admiralty; nor, on the other hand, can it bring under the judicial power a matter which, from its nature is not a subject for judicial determination. At the same time there are matters, *involving public rights,* which may be presented in such form that the judicial power is capable of acting on them, and which are susceptible of judicial determination, but which Congress may or may not bring within the cognizance of the courts of the United States, as it may deem proper." (emphasis added).

This doctrine may be explained in part by reference to the traditional principle of sovereign immunity, which recognizes that the government may attach conditions to its consent to be sued. But the public-rights doctrine also draws upon the principle of separation of powers, and a historical understanding that certain prerogatives were reserved to the political branches of government. The doctrine extends only to matters arising "between the government and persons subject to its authority in connection with the performance of the constitutional functions of the executive or legislative departments," Crowell v. Benson, 285 U.S. 22, 50 (1932), and only to matters that historically could have been determined exclusively by those departments, see Ex parte Bakelite Corp., 279 U.S. 438, 458 (1929). The understanding of these cases is that the framers expected that Congress would be free to commit such matters completely to nonjudicial executive determination, and that as a result there can be no constitutional objection to Congress' employing the less drastic expedient of committing their determination to a legislative court or administrative agency.

The public-rights doctrine is grounded in a historically recognized distinction between matters that could be conclusively determined by the executive and legislative branches and matters that are "inherently . . . . judicial." For example, the Court in *Murray's Lessee* looked to the law of England and the states at the time the Constitution was adopted, in order to determine whether the issue presented was customarily cognizable in the courts. Concluding that the matter had not traditionally been one for judicial determination, the Court perceived no bar to Congress' establishment of summary procedures, outside of art. III courts, to collect a debt due to the government from one of its customs agents.[20] On the same premise, the Court in *Ex parte Bakelite Corp.,* supra, held that the Court of Customs Appeals had been properly constituted by Congress as a legislative court:

> "The *full* province of the court under the act creating it is that of determining matters arising between the government and others in the executive administration and application of the customs laws. . . . The appeals include nothing which inherently or necessarily requires judicial determination, but only matters the determination of *which may be, and at times has been, committed exclusively to executive officers.*" (emphasis added).

The distinction between public rights and private rights has not been definitively explained by our precedents. Nor is it necessary to do so in the present cases, for it suffices to observe that a matter of public rights must at a minimum arise "between the government and others." In contrast, "the liability of one individual to another under the law as defined" is a matter of private rights. Our precedents clearly establish that *only* controversies in the former category may be removed from art. III courts and delegated to legislative courts or administrative agencies for their determination.[24] Private rights disputes, on the other hand, lie at the core of the historically recognized judicial power.

In sum, this Court has identified three situations in which art. III does not bar the creation of legislative courts. In each of these situations, the Court has recognized certain exceptional powers bestowed upon Congress by the Constitution or by historical consensus. Only in the face of such an exceptional grant of power has the Court declined to hold the authority of Congress subject to the general prescriptions of art. III.[25]

[20] Doubtless it could be argued that the need for independent judicial determination is greatest in cases arising between the government and an individual. But the rationale for the public-rights line of cases lies not in political theory, but rather in Congress' and this Court's understanding of what power was reserved to the judiciary by the Constitution as a matter of historical fact.

[24] Of course, public rights doctrine does not extend to any criminal matters, although the government is a proper party.

[25] The "unifying principle" that Justice White's dissent finds lacking in all of these cases is to be found in the exceptional constitutional grants of power to Congress with respect to certain matters. Although the dissent is correct that these grants are not explicit in the language of the Constitution, they are nonetheless firmly established in our historical understanding of the constitutional structure. When these three exceptional grants are properly constrained, they do not threaten the framers' vision of an independent federal judiciary. What clearly remains subject to art. III are all private adjudications in federal courts within the states—matters from their nature subject to "a suit at common law or in equity or admiralty"—and all criminal matters, with the narrow exception of military crimes. There is no doubt that when the Framers assigned the "judicial Power" to an independent art. III branch, these matters lay at what they perceived to be the protected core of that power.

Although the dissent recognizes that the framers had something important in mind when they assigned the judicial power of the United States to art. III courts, it concludes that our cases and subsequent practice have eroded this conception. Unable to find a satisfactory theme in our

We discern no such exceptional grant of power applicable to the cases before us. The courts created by the Bankruptcy Act of 1978 do not lie exclusively outside the states of the federal union, like those in the District of Columbia and the territories. Nor do the bankruptcy courts bear any resemblance to courts-martial, which are founded upon the Constitution's grant of plenary authority over the nation's military forces to the legislative and executive branches. Finally, the substantive legal rights at issue in the present action cannot be deemed "public rights." Appellants argue that a discharge in bankruptcy is indeed a "public right," similar to such congressionally created benefits as "radio station licenses, pilot licenses, or certificates for common carriers" granted by administrative agencies. But the restructuring of debtor-creditor relations, which is at the core of the federal bankruptcy power, must be distinguished from the adjudication of state-created private rights, such as the right to recover contract damages that is at issue in this case. The former may well be a "public right," but the latter obviously is not. Appellant Northern's right to recover contract damages to augment its estate is "one of private right, that is, of the liability of one individual to another under the law as defined." *Crowell v. Benson,* supra, at 51.

Recognizing that the present cases may not fall within the scope of any of our prior cases permitting the establishment of legislative courts, appellants argue that we should recognize an additional situation beyond the command of art. III, sufficiently broad to sustain the act. Appellants contend that Congress' constitutional authority to establish "uniform Laws on the subject of Bankruptcies throughout the United States," art. I, § 8, cl. 4, carries with it an inherent power to establish legislative courts capable of adjudicating "bankruptcy-related controversies." In support of this argument, appellants rely primarily upon a quotation from the opinion in Palmore v. United States, 411 U.S. 389, 407–08 (1973), in which we stated that

> "both Congress and this Court have recognized that . . . the requirements of art. III, which are applicable where laws of national applicability and affairs of national concern are at stake, must in proper circumstances give way to accommodate plenary grants of power to Congress to legislate with respect to specialized areas having particularized needs and warranting distinctive treatment."

Appellants cite this language to support their proposition that a bankruptcy court created by Congress under its art. I powers is constitutional, because the law of bankruptcy is a "specialized area," and Congress has found a "particularized need" that warrants "distinctive treatment." . . .

precedents for analyzing these cases, the dissent rejects all of them, as well as the historical understanding upon which they were based, in favor of an ad hoc balancing approach in which Congress can essentially determine for itself whether art. III courts are required. But even the dissent recognizes that the notion that Congress rather than the Constitution should determine whether there is a need for independent federal courts cannot be what the framers had in mind.

The flaw in appellants' analysis is that it provides no limiting principle. It thus threatens to supplant completely our system of adjudication in independent art. III tribunals and replace it with a system of "specialized" legislative courts. True, appellants argue that under their analysis Congress could create legislative courts pursuant only to some "specific" art. I power, and "only when there is a particularized need for distinctive treatment." They therefore assert that their analysis would not permit Congress to replace the independent art. III judiciary through a "wholesale assignment of federal judicial business to legislative courts." But these "limitations" are wholly illusory. For example, art. I, § 8, empowers Congress to enact laws, inter alia, regulating interstate commerce and punishing certain crimes. On appellants' reasoning Congress could provide for the adjudication of these and "related" matters by judges and courts within Congress' exclusive control. The potential for encroachment upon the powers reserved to judicial branch through the device of "specialized" legislative courts is dramatically evidenced in the jurisdiction granted to the courts created by the act before us. The broad range of questions that can be brought into a bankruptcy court because they are "related to cases under title 11," 28 U.S.C. § 1471(b), is the clearest proof that even when Congress acts through a "specialized" court, and pursuant to only one of its many art. I powers, appellants' analysis fails to provide any real protection against the erosion of art. III jurisdiction by the unilateral action of the political branches. In short, to accept appellants' reasoning, would require that we replace the principles delineated in our precedents, rooted in history and the Constitution, with a rule of broad legislative discretion that could effectively eviscerate the constitutional guarantee of an independent judicial branch of the federal government.[26]

Appellants' reliance upon *Palmore* for such broad legislative discretion is misplaced. In the context of the issue decided in that case, the language quoted from the *Palmore* opinion, supra, offers no substantial support for appellants' argument. *Palmore* was concerned with the

----

[26] Justice White's suggested "limitations" on Congress' power to create art. I courts are even more transparent. Justice White's dissent suggests that art. III "should be read as expressing one value that must be balanced against competing constitutional values and legislative responsibilities," and that the Court retains the final word on how the balance is to be struck. The dissent would find the art. III "value" accommodated where appellate review to art. III courts is provided and where the art. I courts are "designed to deal with issues likely to be of little interest to the political branches." But the dissent's view that appellate review is sufficient to satisfy either the command or the purpose of art. III is incorrect. And the suggestion that we should consider whether the art. I courts are designed to

deal with issues likely to be of interest to the political branches would undermine the validity of the adjudications performed by most of the administrative agencies, on which validity the dissent so heavily relies.

In applying its ad hoc balancing approach to the facts of this case, the dissent relies on the justification that these courts differ from standard art. III courts because of their "extreme specialization." As noted above, "extreme specialization" is hardly an accurate description of bankruptcy courts designed to adjudicate the entire range of federal and state controversies. Moreover, the special nature of bankruptcy adjudication is in no sense incompatible with performance of such functions in a tribunal afforded the protection of art. III. . . .

courts of the District of Columbia, a unique federal enclave. . . . The "plenary authority" under the District of Columbia clause, art. I, § 8, cl. 17, was the subject of the quoted passage and the powers granted under that clause are obviously different in kind from the other broad powers conferred on Congress: Congress' power over the District of Columbia encompasses the *full* authority of government, and thus, necessarily, the executive and judicial powers as well as the legislative. This is a power that is clearly possessed by Congress only in limited geographic areas. [O]ur reference in *Palmore* to "specialized areas having particularized needs" referred only to *geographic* areas, such as the District of Columbia or territories outside the states of the federal union. In light of the clear commands of art. III, nothing held or said in *Palmore* can be taken to mean that in every area in which Congress may legislate, it may also create non-art. III courts with art. III powers.

In sum, art. III bars Congress from establishing legislative courts to exercise jurisdiction over all matters related to those arising under the bankruptcy laws. The establishment of such courts does not fall within any of the historically recognized situations in which the general principle of independent adjudication commanded by art. III does not apply. Nor can we discern any persuasive reason, in logic, history, or the Constitution, why the bankruptcy courts here established lie beyond the reach of art. III.

IV

Appellants advance a second argument for upholding the constitutionality of the act: that "viewed within the entire judicial framework set up by Congress," the bankruptcy court is merely an "adjunct" to the district court, and that the delegation of certain adjudicative functions to the bankruptcy court is accordingly consistent with the principle that the judicial power of the United States must be vested in art. III courts. As support for their argument, appellants rely principally upon Crowell v. Benson, 285 U.S. 22 (1931), and United States v. Raddatz, 447 U.S. 667 (1980), cases in which we approved the use of administrative agencies and magistrates as adjuncts to art. III courts. The question to which we turn, therefore, is whether the act has retained "the essential attributes of the judicial power" in art. III tribunals. . . .

The use of administrative agencies as adjuncts was first upheld in *Crowell v. Benson,* supra. The congressional scheme challenged in *Crowell* empowered an administrative agency, the United States Employees' Compensation Commission, to make initial factual determinations pursuant to a federal statute requiring employers to compensate their employees for work-related injuries occurring upon the navigable waters of the United States. The Court began its analysis by noting that the federal statute administered by the Compensation Commission provided for compensation of injured employees "irrespective of fault," and that the statute also prescribed a fixed and mandatory schedule of compensation. The agency was thus left with the limited role of determining "questions of fact as to the circumstances, nature, extent and consequences of the injuries sustained by the employee for which compensation is to be made." The agency did not possess the power to enforce any of its compensation orders: On the contrary, every compensation order was appealable to the appropriate federal district court, which had the sole power to enforce it or set it aside, depending upon whether the court determined it to be "in accordance with law" and supported by evidence in the record. The Court found that in view of these limitations upon the Compensation Commission's functions and powers, its determinations were "closely analogous to findings of the amount of damages that are made, according to familiar practice, by commissioners or assessors." Observing that "there is no requirement that, in order to maintain the essential attributes of the judicial power, all determinations of fact in constitutional courts shall be made by judges," the Court held that art. III imposed no bar to the scheme enacted by Congress.

Crowell involved the adjudication of congressionally created rights. But this Court has sustained the use of adjunct factfinders even in the adjudication of constitutional rights—so long as those adjuncts were subject to sufficient control by an art. III district court. In *United States v. Raddatz,* supra, the Court upheld the [1976 amendments to the 1968] Federal Magistrates Act, which permitted district court judges to refer certain pretrial motions, including suppression motions based on alleged violations of constitutional rights, to a magistrate for initial determination. The Court observed that the magistrate's proposed findings and recommendations were subject to de novo review by the district court, which was free to rehear the evidence or to call for additional evidence. Moreover, it was noted that the magistrate considered motions only upon reference from the district court, and that the magistrates were appointed, and subject to removal, by the district court. In short, the ultimate decisionmaking authority respecting all pretrial motions clearly remained with the district court. Under these circumstances, the Court held that the act did not violate the constraints of art. III.[31]

[31] Appellants and Justice White's dissent also rely on the broad powers exercised by the bankruptcy referees immediately before the Bankruptcy Act of 1978. But those particular adjunct functions, which represent the culmination of years of gradual expansion of the power and authority of the bankruptcy referee, have never been explicitly endorsed by this Court. In Katchen v. Landy, 382 U.S. 323 (1966), on which the dissent relies, there was no discussion of the art. III issue. . . .

We note, moreover, that the 1978 act made at least three significant changes from the bankruptcy practice that immediately preceded it. First, of course, the jurisdiction of the bankruptcy courts was "substantially expanded" by the act. Before the act the referee had no jurisdiction, except with consent, over controversies beyond those involving property in the actual or constructive possession of the court. . . . Second, the bankruptcy judges have broader powers than those exercised by the referees. Finally, and perhaps most significantly, the relationship between the district court and the bankruptcy court was changed under the 1978 act. Before the act, bankruptcy referees were "subordinate adjuncts of the district courts." H.R. Rep. No. 95–595, p. 12 nn. 63–68 (1977). In contrast the new bankruptcy courts are "independent of the United States district courts." Ibid. Before the act, bankruptcy referees were appointed and removable only by the district court. And the district court retained control over the reference by his power to withdraw the case from the referee. Thus even at the trial stage, the parties had access to an independent judi-

Together these cases establish two principles that aid us in determining the extent to which Congress may constitutionally vest traditionally judicial functions in non-art. III officers. First, it is clear that when Congress creates a substantive federal right, it possesses substantial discretion to prescribe the manner in which that right may be adjudicated—including the assignment to an adjunct of some functions historically performed by judges.[32] Thus *Crowell* recognized that art. III does not require "all determinations of fact [to] be made by judges"; with respect to congressionally created rights, some factual determinations may be made by a specialized factfinding tribunal designed by Congress, without constitutional bar. Second, the functions of the adjunct must be limited in such a way that "the essential attributes" of judicial power are retained in the art. III court. Thus in upholding the adjunct scheme challenged in *Crowell,* the Court emphasized that "the reservation of full authority to the court to deal with matters of law provides for the appropriate exercise of the judicial function in this class of cases." And in refusing to invalidate the Magistrates Act at issue in *Raddatz,* the Court stressed that under the congressional scheme " '[t]he authority—and the responsibility—to make an informed, final determination . . . remains with the judge"; the statute's delegation of power was therefore permissible, since "the ultimate decision is made by the district court."

These two principles assist us in evaluating the "adjunct" scheme presented in these cases. Appellants assume that Congress' power to create "adjuncts" to consider all cases related to those arising under title 11 is as great as it was in the circumstances of *Crowell.* But while *Crowell* certainly endorsed the proposition that Congress possesses broad discretion to assign factfinding functions to an adjunct created to aid in the adjudication of congressionally created statutory rights, *Crowell* does not support the further proposition necessary to appellants' argument—that Congress possess the same degree of discretion in assigning traditionally judicial power to adjuncts engaged in the adjudication of rights *not* created by Congress. Indeed, the validity of this proposition was expressly denied in *Crowell,* when the Court rejected "the untenable assumption that the constitutional courts may be deprived in all cases of the determination of facts upon evidence even though a *constitutional* right may be involved" (emphasis added), and stated that

cial officer. Although Congress could still lower the salary of the referees, they were not dependent on the political branches of government for their appointment. To paraphrase Justice Blackmun's observation in *Raddatz,* supra, the primary "danger of a 'threat' to the 'independence' of the [adjunct came] from within, rather than without the judicial department." 447 U.S., at 685 (concurring opinion).

[32] Contrary to Justice White's suggestion, we do not concede that "Congress may provide for initial adjudications by art. I courts or administrative judges of all rights and duties arising under otherwise valid federal laws." Rather we simply reaffirm the holding of *Crowell*—that Congress may assign to non-art. III bodies some adjudicatory functions. *Crowell* itself spoke of "specialized" functions. These cases do not require us to specify further any limitations that may exist with respect to Congress' power to create adjuncts to assist in the adjudication of federal statutory rights.

"the essential independence of the exercise of the judicial power of the United States in the enforcement of *constitutional* rights requires that the federal court should determine . . . an issue [of agency jurisdiction] upon its own record and the facts elicited before it." (Emphasis added.)[34]

Appellants' proposition was also implicitly rejected in *Raddatz.* Congress' assignment of adjunct functions under the Federal Magistrates Act was substantially narrower than under the statute challenged in *Crowell.* Yet the Court's scrutiny of the adjunct scheme in *Raddatz*— which played a role in the adjudication of *constitutional* rights—was far stricter than it had been in *Crowell.* Critical to the Court's decision to uphold the Magistrates Act was the fact that the ultimate decision was made by the district court.

Although *Crowell* and *Raddatz* do not explicitly distinguish between rights created by Congress and other rights, such a distinction underlies in part *Crowell*'s and *Raddatz*' recognition of a critical difference between rights created by federal statute and rights recognized by the Constitution. Moreover, such a distinction seems to us to be necessary in light of the delicate accommodations required by the principle of separation of powers reflected in art. III. The constitutional system of checks and balances is designed to guard against "encroachment or aggrandizement" by Congress at the expense of the other branches of government. But when Congress creates a statutory right, it clearly has the discretion, in defining that right, to create presumptions, or assign burdens of proof, or prescribe remedies; it may also provide that persons seeking to vindicate that right must do so before particularized tribunals created to perform the specialized adjudicative tasks related to that right. Such provisions do, in a sense, affect the exercise of judicial power, but they are also incidental to Congress' power to define the right it has created. No comparable justification exists, however, when the right being adjudicated is not of congressional creation. In such a situation, substantial inroads into functions that have traditionally been performed by the judiciary cannot be characterized merely as incidental extensions of Congress' power to define rights that it has created. Rather, such inroads suggest unwarranted encroachments upon the judicial power of the United States, which our Constitution reserves for art. III courts.

We hold that the Bankruptcy Act of 1978 carries the possibility of such an unwarranted encroachment. Many of the rights subject to adjudication by the act's bankruptcy courts, like the rights implicated in *Raddatz,* are not of Congress' creation. Indeed, the cases before us, which center upon appellant Northern's claim for damages for breach of contract and misrepresentation, involve a right created by *state* law, a right independent of and antecedent to the reorganization petition

---

[34] *Crowell*'s precise holding, with respect to the review of "jurisdictional" and "constitutional" facts that arise within ordinary administrative proceedings, has been undermined by later cases. . . . But the general principle of *Crowell*—distinguishing between congressionally created rights and constitutionally recognized rights—remains valid . . . .

that conferred jurisdiction upon the bankruptcy court. Accordingly, Congress' authority to control the manner in which the right is adjudicated, through assignment of historically judicial functions to a non-art. III "adjunct," plainly must be at a minimum. Yet it is equally plain that Congress has vested the "adjunct" bankruptcy judges with powers over appellant's state-created right that far exceed the powers that it has vested in administrative agencies that adjudicate only rights of Congress' own creation.

Unlike the administrative scheme that we reviewed in *Crowell*, the act vests all "essential attributes" of the judicial power of the United States in the "adjunct" bankruptcy court. First, the agency in *Crowell* made only specialized, narrowly confined factual determinations regarding a particularized area of law. In contrast, the subject-matter jurisdiction of the bankruptcy courts encompasses not only traditional matters of bankruptcy, but also "all civil proceedings arising under title 11 or arising in or *related to* cases under title 11." (Emphasis added.) Second, while the agency in *Crowell* engaged in statutorily channeled factfinding functions, the bankruptcy courts exercise "*all* of the jurisdiction" conferred by the act on the district courts. Third, the agency in *Crowell* possessed only a limited power to issue compensation orders pursuant to specialized procedures, and its orders could be enforced only by order of the district court. By contrast, the bankruptcy courts exercise all ordinary powers of district courts, including the power to preside over jury trials, the power to issue declaratory judgments, the power to issue writs of habeas corpus, and the power to issue any order, process, or judgment appropriate for the enforcement of the provisions of title 11. Fourth, while orders issued by the agency in *Crowell* were to be set aside if "not supported by the evidence," the judgments of the bankruptcy courts are apparently subject to review only under the more deferential "clearly erroneous" standard. Finally, the agency in *Crowell* was required by law to seek enforcement of its compensation orders in the district court. In contrast, the bankruptcy courts issue final judgments, which are binding and enforceable even in the absence of an appeal. In short, the "adjunct" bankruptcy courts created by the act exercise jurisdiction behind the facade of a grant to the district court, and are exercising power far greater than those lodged in the adjuncts approved in either *Crowell* or *Raddatz*.[39]

---

[39] Appellants suggest that *Crowell* and *Raddatz* stand for the proposition that art. III is satisfied so long as some degree of appellate review is provided. But that suggestion is directly contrary to the text of our Constitution: "The Judges, *both* of the supreme and inferior Courts, shall hold their Offices during good Behaviour, and shall . . . receive [undiminished] Compensation." Art. III, § 1 (emphasis added). Our precedents make it clear that the constitutional requirements for the exercise of the judicial power must be met at all stages of adjudication, and not only on appeal, where the court is restricted to considerations of law, as well as the nature of the case as it has been shaped at the trial level. . . .

Justice White's dissent views the function of the third branch as interpreting the Constitution in order to keep the other two branches in check, and would accordingly find the purpose, if not the language, of art. III satisfied where there is an appeal to an art. III court. But in the framers' view, art. III courts would do a good deal more than, in an abstract way, announce guidelines for the other two branches. While "expounding" the Constitution was

We conclude that 28 U.S.C. § 1471 as added by § 241(a) of the Bankruptcy Act of 1978, has impermissibly removed most, if not all, of "the essential attributes of the judicial power" from the art. III district court, and has vested those attributes in a non-art. III adjunct. Such a grant of jurisdiction cannot be sustained as an exercise of Congress' power to create adjuncts to art. III courts.

V

Having concluded that the broad grant of jurisdiction to the bankruptcy courts contained in 28 U.S.C. § 1471 is unconstitutional, we must now determine whether our holding should be applied retroactively to the effective date of the act.[40] Our decision in Chevron Oil v. Huson, 404 U.S. 97 (1971), sets forth the three considerations recognized by our precedents as properly bearing upon the issue of retroactivity. They are, first, whether the holding in question "decid[ed] an issue of first impression whose resolution was not clearly foreshadowed" by earlier cases; second, "whether retrospective operation will further or retard [the] operation" of the holding in question; and third, whether retroactive application "could produce substantial inequitable results" in individual cases. In the present case, all of these considerations militate against the retroactive application of our holding today. It is plain that Congress' broad grant of judicial power to non-art. III bankruptcy judges presents an unprecedented question of interpretation of art. III. It is equally plain that retroactive application would not further the operation of our holding, and would surely visit substantial injustice and hardship upon those litigants who relied upon the act's vesting of jurisdiction in the bankruptcy courts. We hold, therefore, that our decision today shall apply only prospectively.

The judgment of the District Court is affirmed. However, we stay our judgment until October 4, 1982. This limited stay will afford Congress an opportunity to reconstitute the bankruptcy courts or to adopt other valid means of adjudication, without impairing the interim administration of the bankruptcy laws.

surely one vital function of the art. III courts in the framers' view, the tasks of those courts, for which independence was an important safeguard, included the mundane as well as the glamorous, matters of common law and statute as well as constitutional law, issues of fact as well as issues of law. . . .

[40] It is clear that, at the least, the new bankruptcy judges cannot constitutionally be vested with jurisdiction to decide this state-law contract claim against Marathon. As part of a comprehensive restructuring of the bankruptcy laws, Congress has vested jurisdiction over this and all matters related to cases under title 11 in a single non-art. III court, and has done so pursuant to a single statutory grant of jurisdiction. In these circumstances we cannot conclude that if Congress were aware that the grant of jurisdiction could not constitutionally encompass this and similar claims, it would simply remove the jurisdiction of the bankruptcy court over these matters, leaving the jurisdictional provision and adjudicatory structure intact with respect to other types of claims, and thus subject to art. III constitutional challenge on a claim-by-claim basis. Indeed, we note that one of the express purposes of the act was to ensure adjudication of all claims in a single forum and to avoid the delay and expense of jurisdictional disputes. . . . We think that it is for Congress to determine the proper manner of restructuring the Bankruptcy Act of 1978 to conform to the requirements of art. III, in the way that will best effectuate the legislative purpose.

JUSTICE REHNQUIST, with whom JUSTICE O'CONNOR joins, concurring in the judgment.

Were I to agree with the plurality that the question presented by this case is "whether the assignment by Congress to bankruptcy judges of the jurisdiction granted in 28 U.S.C. § 1471 by § 241(a) of the Bankruptcy Act of 1978 violates art. III of the Constitution," I would with considerable reluctance embark on the duty of deciding this broad question. But appellee Marathon Pipe Line Co. has not been subjected to the full range of authority granted bankruptcy courts by § 1471. . . .

Marathon has simply been named defendant in a lawsuit about a contract, a lawsuit initiated by appellant Northern after having previously filed a petition for reorganization under the Bankruptcy Act. Marathon may object to proceeding further with this lawsuit on the grounds that if it is to be resolved by an agency of the United States, it may be resolved only by an agency which exercises "[t]he judicial power of the United States" described by art. III of the Constitution. But resolution of any objections it may make on this ground to the exercise of a different authority conferred on bankruptcy courts by the 1978 act should await the exercise of such authority. . . .

From the record before us, the lawsuit in which Marathon was named defendant seeks damages for breach of contract, misrepresentation, and other counts which are the stuff of the traditional actions at common law tried by the courts at Westminster in 1789. There is apparently no federal rule of decision provided for any of the issues in the lawsuit; the claims of Northern arise entirely under state law. No method of adjudication is hinted, other than the traditional common-law mode of judge and jury. The lawsuit is before the bankruptcy court only because the plaintiff has previously filed a petition for reorganization in that court.

The cases dealing with the authority of Congress to create courts other than by use of its power under art. III do not admit of easy synthesis. . . . I need not decide whether these cases in fact support a general proposition and three tidy exceptions, as the plurality believes, or whether instead they are landmarks on a judicial "darkling plain" where ignorant armies have clashed by night, as Justice White apparently believes them to be. None of the cases has gone so far as to sanction the type of adjudication to which Marathon will be subjected against its will under the provisions of the 1978 act. To whatever extent different powers granted under that act might be sustained under the "public rights" doctrine . . ., I am satisfied that the adjudication of Northern's lawsuit cannot be so sustained.

I am likewise of the opinion that the extent of review by art. III courts provided on appeal from a decision of bankruptcy court in a case such as Northern's does not save the grant of authority to the latter under the rule espoused in Crowell v. Benson, 285 U.S. 22 (1932). All matters of fact and law in whatever domains of the law to which the parties' dispute may lead are to be resolved by the bankruptcy court in the first instance, with only traditional appellate review apparently contemplated by art. III courts. Acting in this manner the bankruptcy court is not an "adjunct" of either the district court or the court of appeals.

I would, therefore, hold so much of the Bankruptcy Act of 1978 as enables a bankruptcy court to entertain and decide Northern's lawsuit over Marathon's objection to be violative of art. III of the United States Constitution. Because I agree with the plurality that this grant of authority is not readily severable from the remaining grant of authority to bankruptcy courts under § 1471, I concur in the judgment. I also agree with the discussion in Part V of the plurality opinion respecting retroactivity and the staying of the judgment of this Court.

CHIEF JUSTICE BURGER, dissenting.

I join Justice White's dissenting opinion, but I write separately only to emphasize that, notwithstanding the plurality opinion, the Court does *not* hold today that Congress' broad grant of jurisdiction to the new bankruptcy courts is generally inconsistent with art. III of the Constitution. Rather, the Court's holding is limited to the proposition stated by Justice Rehnquist in his concurrence in the judgment—that a "traditional" state common-law action, not made subject to a federal rule of decision, and related only peripherally to an adjudication of bankruptcy under federal law, must, absent the consent of the litigants, be heard by an "art. III court" if it is to be heard by any court or agency of the United States. This limited holding, of course, does not suggest that there is something inherently unconstitutional about the new bankruptcy courts . . . .

It will not be necessary for Congress, in order to meet the requirements of this Court's holding, to undertake a radical restructuring of the present system of bankruptcy adjudication. The problems arising from today's judgment can be resolved simply by providing that ancillary common law actions, such as the one involved in this case, be routed to the United States district court of which the bankruptcy court is an adjunct.

JUSTICE WHITE, with whom THE CHIEF JUSTICE and JUSTICE POWELL join, dissenting.

. . . Any reader could easily take [the text of art. III] to mean that although Congress was free to establish such lower courts as it saw fit, any court that it did establish would be an "inferior" court exercising "judicial Power of the United States" and so must be manned by judges possessing both life-tenure and a guaranteed minimum income. This would be an eminently sensible reading and one that, as the plurality shows, is well founded in both the documentary sources and the political doctrine of separation of powers that stands behind much of our constitutional structure.

If this simple reading were correct and we were free to disregard 150 years of history, these would be easy cases and the plurality opinion could end with its observation that "[i]t is undisputed that the bankruptcy judges whose offices were created by the Bankruptcy Act of 1978 do not enjoy the protections constitutionally afforded to art. III judges." The fact that the plurality must go on to deal with what has been characterized as one of the most confusing and controversial areas of constitutional law itself indicates the gross oversimplification implicit in the plurality's claim that "our Constitution unambiguously enunciates a fundamental principle—that the 'judicial Power of the United States' must be reposed in an independent judiciary [and] provides clear institutional protections for that independence." While this is fine rhetoric, analytically it serves only to put a distracting and superficial gloss on a difficult question.

That question is what limits art. III places on Congress' ability to create adjudicative institutions designed to carry out federal policy established pursuant to the substantive authority given Congress elsewhere in the Constitution. Whether fortunate or unfortunate, at this point in the history of constitutional law that question can no longer be answered by looking only to the constitutional text. This Court's cases construing that text must also be considered. In its attempt to pigeonhole these cases, the plurality does violence to their meaning and creates an artificial structure that itself lacks coherence.

I

There are, I believe, two separate grounds for today's decision. First, non-art. III judges, regardless of whether they are labelled "adjuncts" to art. III courts or "art. I judges," may consider only controversies arising out of federal law. Because the immediate controversy in these cases—Northern Pipeline's claim against Marathon—arises out of state law, it may only be adjudicated, within the federal system, by an art. III court.[2] Second, regardless of the source of law that governs the controversy, Congress is prohibited by art. III from establishing art. I courts, with three narrow exceptions. Adjudication of bankruptcy proceedings does not fall within any of these exceptions. I shall deal with the first of these contentions in this section.

The plurality concedes that Congress may provide for initial adjudications by art. I courts or administrative judges of all rights and duties arising under otherwise valid federal law. There is no apparent reason why this principle should not extend to matters arising in federal bankruptcy proceedings. The plurality attempts to escape the reach of prior decisions by contending that the bankrupt's claim against Marathon arose under state law. Non-article III judges, in its view, cannot be vested with authority to adjudicate such issues. It then proceeds to strike down 28 U.S.C. § 1471 on this ground. For several reasons, the Court's judgment is unsupportable.

First, clearly this ground alone cannot support the Court's invalidation of § 1471 on its face. The plurality concedes that in adjudications and discharges in bankruptcy, "the restructuring of debtor-creditor relations, which is at the core of the federal bankruptcy power," and

---

[2] Because this is the sole ground relied upon by the Justices concurring in the judgment this is the effective basis for today's decision.

"the manner in which the rights of debtors and creditors are adjusted," are matters of federal law. Under the plurality's own interpretation of the cases, therefore, these matters could be heard and decided by art. I judges. But because the bankruptcy judge is also given authority to hear a case like that of appellant Northern against Marathon, which the Court says is founded on state law, the Court holds that the section must be stricken down on its face. This is a grossly unwarranted emasculation of the scheme Congress has adopted. Even if the Court is correct that such a state-law claim cannot be heard by a bankruptcy judge, there is no basis for doing more than declaring the section unconstitutional as applied to the claim against Marathon, leaving the section otherwise intact. . . .

Second, the distinction between claims based on state law and those based on federal law disregards the real character of bankruptcy proceedings. The routine in ordinary bankruptcy cases now, as it was before 1978, is to stay actions against the bankrupt, collect the bankrupt's assets, require creditors to file claims or be forever barred, allow or disallow claims that are filed, adjudicate preferences and fraudulent transfers, and make pro rata distributions to creditors, who will be barred by the discharge from taking further actions against the bankrupt. The crucial point to be made is that in the ordinary bankruptcy proceeding the great bulk of creditor claims are claims that have accrued under state law prior to bankruptcy—claims for goods sold, wages, rent, utilities, and the like. . . . Hence the bankruptcy judge is constantly enmeshed in state-law issues.

The new aspect of the Bankruptcy Act of 1978, in this regard, therefore, is not the extension of federal jurisdiction to state-law claims, but its extension to particular kinds of state-law claims, such as contract cases against third parties or disputes involving property in the possession of a third person. Prior to 1978, a claim of a bankrupt against a third party, such as the claim against Marathon in this case, was not within the jurisdiction of the bankruptcy judge. The old limits were based, of course, on the restrictions implicit within the concept of in rem jurisdiction; the new extension is based on the concept of in personam jurisdiction. . . . The difference between the new and old act, therefore, is not to be found in a distinction between state-law and federal-law matters; rather, it is in a distinction between in rem and in personam jurisdiction. The majority at no place explains why this distinction should have constitutional implications.

Third, all that can be left of the majority's argument in this regard is that state-law claims adjudicated within the federal system must be heard in the first instance by art. III judges. I shall argue below that any such attempt to distinguish art. I from art. III courts by the character of the controversies they may adjudicate fundamentally misunderstands the historical and constitutional significance of art. I courts. Initially, however, the majority's proposal seems to turn the separation-of-powers doctrine, upon which the majority relies, on its head: Since state-law claims would ordinarily not be heard by art. III judges—i.e., they would be heard by state judges—one would think that there is little danger of a diminution of, or intrusion upon, the power of art. III courts, when such claims are assigned to a non-art. III court. The plurality misses this obvious point because it concentrates on explaining how it is that federally created rights can ever be adjudicated in art. I courts—a far more difficult problem under the separation-of-powers doctrine. The plurality fumbles when it assumes that the rationale it develops to deal with the latter problem must also govern the former problem. In fact, the two are simply unrelated and the majority never really explains the separation-of-powers problem that would be created by assigning state-law questions to legislative courts or to adjuncts of art. III courts.

One need not contemplate the intricacies of the separation-of-powers doctrine, however, to realize that the majority's position on adjudication of state-law claims is based on an abstract theory that has little to do with the reality of bankruptcy proceedings. Even prior to the present act, bankruptcy cases were generally referred to bankruptcy judges, previously called referees. . . . The referee would initially hear and decide practically all matters arising in the proceedings, including the allowance and disallowance of the claims of creditors. If a claim was disallowed by the bankruptcy judge and the decision was not reversed on appeal, the creditor was forever barred from further action against the bankrupt. As pointed out above, all of these matters could and usually did involve state-law issues. Initial adjudication of state-law issues by non-art. III judges is, then, hardly a new aspect of the 1978 act. . . .

Furthermore, . . . we approved the authority of the referee to allow or disallow claims in Katchen v. Landy, 382 U.S. 323 (1966). . . . We also recognized that the referee could adjudicate counterclaims against a creditor who files his claim against the estate. . . . Hence, if Marathon had filed a claim against the bankrupt in this case, the trustee could have filed and the bankruptcy judge could have adjudicated a counterclaim seeking the relief that is involved in this case.

Of course, all such adjudications by a bankruptcy judge or referee were subject to review in the district court on the record. Bankruptcy Rule 810, transmitted to Congress by this Court, provided that the district court "shall accept the referee's findings of fact unless they are clearly erroneous." As the plurality recognizes, the 1978 act provides for appellate review in art. III courts and presumably under the same "clearly erroneous standard." In other words, under both the old and new acts, initial determinations of state-law questions were to be made by non-art. III judges, subject to review by art. III judges. Why the differences in the provisions for appeal in the two acts are of constitutional dimension remains entirely unclear.

In theory and fact, therefore, I can find no basis for that part of the majority's argument that rests on the state-law character of the claim involved here. Even if prior to 1978, the referee could not generally participate in cases aimed at collecting the assets of a bankrupt estate, he nevertheless repeatedly adjudicated issues controlled by state law.

There is very little reason to strike down § 1471 on its face on the ground that it extends, in a comparatively minimal way, the referees' authority to deal with state-law questions. To do so is to lose all sense of proportion.

II

The plurality unpersuasively attempts to bolster its case for facial invalidity by asserting that the bankruptcy courts are now "exercising powers far greater than those lodged in the adjuncts approved in either *Crowell* or *Raddatz.*" In support of this proposition, it makes five arguments in addition to the "state-law" issue. Preliminarily, I see no basis for according standing to Marathon to raise any of these additional points. The state-law objection applies to the Marathon case. Only that objection should now be adjudicated.

I also believe that the major premise of the plurality's argument is wholly unsupported: There is no explanation of why *Crowell* and *Raddatz* define the outer limits of constitutional authority. Much more relevant to today's decision are first, the practice in bankruptcy prior to 1978, which neither the majority nor any authoritative case has questioned, and second, the practice of today's administrative agencies. Considered from this perspective, all of the plurality's arguments are unsupportable abstractions, divorced from the realities of modern practice.

The first three arguments offered by the plurality focus on the narrowly defined task and authority of the agency considered in *Crowell:* The agency made only "specialized, narrowly confined factual determinations" and could issue only a narrow class of orders. Regardless of whether that was true of the Compensation Board at issue in *Crowell,* it certainly was not true of the old bankruptcy courts, nor does it even vaguely resemble current administrative practice. . . .

The plurality's fourth argument fails to point to any difference between the new and old bankruptcy acts. While the administrative orders in *Crowell* may have been set aside by a court if "not supported by the evidence," under both the new and old acts at issue here, orders of the bankruptcy judge are reviewed under the "clearly erroneous" standard. Indeed, judicial review of the orders of bankruptcy judges is more stringent than that of many modern administrative agencies. Generally courts are not free to set aside the finding of administrative agencies, if supported by substantial evidence. But more importantly, courts are also admonished to give substantial deference to the agency's interpretation of the statute it is enforcing. No such deference is required with respect to decisions on the law made by bankruptcy judges.

Finally, the plurality suggests that, unlike the agency considered in *Crowell,* the orders of the post–1978 bankruptcy judge are final and binding even though not appealed. To attribute any constitutional significance to this, unless the plurality intends to throw into question a large body of administrative law, is strange. More directly, this simply does not represent any change in bankruptcy practice. It was hornbook law prior to 1978 that the authorized judgments and orders of referees, including turnover orders, were final and binding and res judicata unless appealed and overturned. . . .

Even if there are specific powers now vested in bankruptcy judges that should be performed by art. III judges, the great bulk of their functions are unexceptionable and should be left intact. Whatever is invalid should be declared to be such; the rest of the 1978 act should be left alone. I can account for the majority's inexplicably heavy hand in this case only by assuming that the Court has once again lost its conceptual bearings when confronted with the difficult problem of the nature and role of art. I courts. To that question I now turn.

III

A

The plurality contends that the precedents upholding art. I courts can be reduced to three categories. First, there are territorial courts, which need not satisfy art. III constraints because the "framers intended that as to certain geographical areas . . . Congress was to exercise the general powers of government." Second, there are courts-martial, which are exempt from art. III limits because of a constitutional grant of power that has been "historically understood as giving the political branches of government extraordinary control over the precise subject matter at issue." Finally, there are those legislative courts and administrative agencies that adjudicate cases involving public rights—controversies between the government and private parties—which are not covered by art. III because the controversy could have been resolved by the executive alone without judicial review. Despite the plurality's attempt to cabin the domain of art. I courts, it is quite unrealistic to consider these to be only three "narrow" limitations on or exceptions to the reach of art. III. In fact, the plurality itself breaks the mold in its discussion of "adjuncts" in part IV, when it announces that "when Congress creates a substantive federal right, it possesses substantial discretion to prescribe the manner in which that right may be adjudicated." Adjudications of federal rights may, according to the plurality, be committed to administrative agencies, as long as provision is made for judicial review.

The first principle introduced by the plurality is geographical: Art. I courts presumably are not permitted within the states. The problem, of course, is that both of the other exceptions recognize that art. I courts can indeed operate within the states. The second category relies upon a new principle: Art. I courts are permissible in areas in which the Constitution grants Congress "extraordinary control over the precise subject matter." Preliminarily, I do not know how we are to distinguish those areas in which Congress' control is "extraordinary" from those in which it is not. Congress' power over the armed forces is established in art. I, § 8, cls. 13, 14. There is nothing in those clauses that creates congressional authority different in kind from the authority granted to legislate with respect to bankruptcy. But more importantly, in its third category, and in its treatment of "adjuncts," the plurality itself recognizes that Congress can create art. I courts in virtually all the areas in which Congress is authorized to act, regardless of the quality of the constitutional grant of authority. At the same time, territorial courts or the courts of the District of Columbia, which are art. I courts, adjudicate private, just as much as public or federal, rights.

Instead of telling us what it is art. I courts can and cannot do, the plurality presents us with a list of art. I courts. When we try to distinguish those courts from their art. III counterparts, we find—apart from the obvious lack of art. III judges—a series of non-distinctions. By the plurality's own admission, art. I courts can operate throughout the country, they can adjudicate both private and public rights, and they can adjudicate matters arising from congressional actions in those areas in which congressional control is "extraordinary." I cannot distinguish this last category from the general "arising under" jurisdiction of art. III courts.

The plurality opinion has the appearance of limiting art. I courts only because it fails to add together the sum of its parts. Rather than limiting each other, the principles relied upon complement each other; together they cover virtually the whole domain of possible areas of adjudication. Without a unifying principle, the plurality's argument reduces to the proposition that because bankruptcy courts are not sufficiently like any of these three exceptions, they may not be either art. I courts or adjuncts to art. III courts. But we need to know why bankruptcy courts cannot qualify as art. I courts in their own right.

B

The plurality opinion is not the first unsuccessful attempt to articulate a principled ground by which to distinguish art. I from art. III courts. The concept of a legislative, or art. I, court was introduced by an opinion authored by Chief Justice Marshall. Not only did he create the concept, but at the same time he started the theoretical controversy that has ever since surrounded the concept:

"The judges of the Superior Courts of Florida hold their offices for four years. These courts, then, are not constitutional courts, in which the judicial power conferred by the Constitution on the general government, can be deposited. They are incapable of receiving it. They are legislative courts, created in virtue of the general right of sovereignty which exists in the government, or in virtue of that clause which enables Congress to make all needful rules and regulations, respecting the territory belonging to the United States. The jurisdiction with which they are invested, is not a part of that judicial power which is defined in the third article of the Constitution, but is conferred by Congress, in the execution of those general powers which that body possesses over the territories of the United

States." American Ins. Co. v. Canter, 26 U.S. (1 Pet.) 511, 546
(1828).

The proposition was simple enough: Constitutional courts exercise the
judicial power described in art. III of the Constitution; legislative
courts do not and cannot.

There were only two problems with this proposition. First, *Canter*
itself involved a case in admiralty jurisdiction, which is specifically
within the "judicial power of the United States" delineated in art. III.
How, then, could the territorial court not be exercising art. III judicial
power? Second, and no less troubling, if the territorial courts could not
exercise art. III power, how could their decisions be subject to appellate
review in art. III courts, including this one, that can exercise only art.
III "judicial" power? Yet from early on this Court has exercised such
appellate jurisdiction. The attempt to understand the seemingly unex-
plainable was bound to generate "confusion and controversy." The
analytic framework, however—the search for a principled distinction—
has continued to burden this Court.

The first major elaboration on the *Canter* principle was in Murray's
Lessee v. Hoboken Land & Improvement Co., 59 U.S. (18 How.) 272
(1856). The plaintiff in that case argued that a proceeding against a
customs collector for the collection of moneys claimed to be due to the
United States was an exercise of "judicial power" and therefore had to
be carried out by art. III judges. The Court accepted this premise [and]
went on to delineate those matters which could be determined only by
an art. III court, i.e., those matters that fall within the non-delegable
"judicial power" of the United States. The Court's response to this was
twofold. First, it suggested that there are certain matters which are
inherently "judicial": "[W]e do not consider Congress can either withdraw from judicial cognizance any matter which, from its nature, is the
subject of a suit at common law, or in equity, or admiralty." Second, it
suggested that there is another class of issues that, depending upon the
form in which Congress structures the decisionmaking process, may or
may not fall within "the cognizance of the courts of the United States."
This latter category consisted of the so-called "public rights." Apparently, the idea was that Congress was free to structure the adjudication
of "public rights" without regard to art. III.

Having accepted the plaintiff's premise, it is hard to see how the
Court could have taken too seriously its first contention. The Court
presented no examples of such issues that are judicial "by nature" and
simply failed to acknowledge that art. I courts already sanctioned by
the Court—e.g., territorial courts—were deciding such issues all the
time. . . .

[I]n the next major case to consider the distinction between art. I
and art. III courts, Ex parte Bakelite Corp., 279 U.S. 438 (1929), . . .
the Court concluded that the Court of Customs Appeals was a legislative court. The Court there directly embraced the principle also
articulated in *Murray's Lessee* that art. I courts may not consider any
matter "which inherently or necessarily requires judicial determina-

tion," but only such matters as are "susceptible of legislative or executive determination." . . .

The distinction between public and private rights as the principle delineating the proper domains of legislative and constitutional courts respectively received its death blow, I had believed, in Crowell v. Benson, 285 U.S. 22 (1932). In that case, the Court approved an administrative scheme for the determination, in the first instance, of maritime employee compensation claims. Although acknowledging the framework set out in *Murray's Lessee* and *Ex parte Bakelite Corp.,* the Court specifically distinguished the case before it: "The present case does not fall within the categories just described but is one of private right, that is, of the liability of one individual to another under the law as defined."[11] Nevertheless, the Court approved of the use of an art. I adjudication mechanism on the new theory that "there is no requirement that, in order to maintain the essential attributes of the judicial power, all determinations of fact in constitutional courts shall be made by judges." Article I courts could deal not only with public rights, but also, to an extent, with private rights. The Court now established a distinction between questions of fact and law: "[T]he reservation of full authority to the court to deal with matters of law provides for the appropriate exercise of the judicial function in this class of cases."[12]

Whatever sense *Crowell* may have seemed to give to this subject was exceedingly short-lived. One year later, the Court returned to this subject, abandoning both the public/private and the fact/law distinction and replacing both with a simple literalism. In O'Donoghue v. United States, 289 U.S. 516 (1933), considering the courts of the District of Columbia, and in Williams v. United States, 289 U.S. 553 (1933), considering the Court of Claims, the Court adopted the principle that if a federal court exercises jurisdiction over cases of the type listed in art. III, § 2, as falling within the "judicial power of the United States," then that court must be an art. III court. . . . In order to apply this . . . principle and yet hold the Court of Claims to be a legislative court, the Court found it necessary in *Williams* to conclude that the phrase "Controversies to which the United States shall be a party" in art. III must be read as if it said "Controversies to which the United States shall be a party plaintiff or petitioner."

By the time of the *Williams* decision, this area of the law was mystifying to say the least. What followed helped very little, if at all. In the next two major cases the Court could not agree internally on a majority position. In National Ins. Co. v. Tidewater Co., 337 U.S. 582 (1949), the Court upheld a statute giving federal district courts jurisdiction over suits between citizens of the District of Columbia and citizens

---

[11] The plurality is clearly wrong in citing *Crowell* in support of the proposition that matters involving private, as opposed to public, rights may not be considered in a non-art. III court.

[12] *Crowell* also suggests that certain facts-constitutional or jurisdictional—must also be subject to de novo review in an art. III court. I agree with the plurality that this aspect of *Crowell* has been "undermined by later cases."

of a state. A majority of the Court, however, rejected the plurality position that Congress had the authority to assign art. I powers to art. III courts, at least outside the District of Columbia. Only Chief Justice Vinson in dissent reflected on the other side of this problem: whether art. I courts could be assigned art. III powers. He entirely disagreed with the conceptual basis for *Williams* and *O'Donoghue,* noting that to the extent that art. I courts consider non-art. III matters, appellate review by an art. III court would be precluded. Or conversely, since appellate review is exercised by this Court over art. I courts, art. I courts must "exercise federal question jurisdiction." . . .

Another chapter in this somewhat dense history of a constitutional quandary was provided by Justice Harlan's plurality opinion in Glidden Co. v. Zdanok, 370 U.S. 530 (1962), in which the Court, despite *Bakelite* and *Williams*—and relying on an act of Congress enacted since those decisions—held the Court of Claims and the Court of Customs and Patent Appeals to be art. III courts. Justice Harlan continued the process of intellectual repudiation begun by Chief Justice Vinson in *Tidewater.* First, it was clear to him that Chief Justice Marshall could not have meant what he said in *Canter* on the inability of art. I courts to consider issues within the jurisdiction of art. III courts: "Far from being 'incapable of receiving' federal-question jurisdiction, the territorial courts have long exercised a jurisdiction commensurate in this regard with that of the regular federal courts and have been subjected to the appellate jurisdiction of this Court precisely because they do so." Second, exceptions to the requirements of art. III, he thought, have not been founded on any principled distinction between art. I issues and art. III issues; rather, a "confluence of practical considerations" accounts for this Court's sanctioning of art. I courts:

> "The touchstone of decision in all these cases has been the need to exercise the jurisdiction then and there and for a transitory period. Whether constitutional limitations on the exercise of judicial power have been held inapplicable has depended on the particular local setting, the practical necessities, and the possible alternatives."

Finally, recognizing that there is frequently no way to distinguish between art. I and art. III courts on the basis of the work they do, Justice Harlan suggested that the only way to tell them apart is to examine the "establishing legislation" to see if it complies with the requirements of art. III. This, however, comes dangerously close to saying that art. III courts are those with art. III judges; art. I courts are those without such judges. One hundred and fifty years of constitutional history, in other words, had led to a simple tautology.

IV

The complicated and contradictory history of the issue before us leads me to conclude that Chief Justice Vinson and Justice Harlan reached the correct conclusion: There is no difference in principle between the work that Congress may assign to an art. I court and that which the Constitution assigns to art. III courts. Unless we want to overrule a large number of our precedents upholding a variety of art. I courts—not to speak of those art. I courts that go by the contemporary name of "administrative agencies"—this conclusion is inevitable. It is too late to go back that far; too late to return to the simplicity of the principle pronounced in art. III and defended so vigorously and persuasively by Hamilton in The Federalist Nos. 78–82.

To say that the Court has failed to articulate a principle by which we can test the constitutionality of a putative art. I court, or that there is no such abstract principle, is not to say that this Court must always defer to the legislative decision to create art. I, rather than art. III courts. Article III is not to read out of the Constitution; rather, it should be read as expressing one value that must be balanced against competing constitutional values and legislative responsibilities. This Court retains the final word on how that balance is to be struck.

Despite the principled, although largely mistaken, rhetoric [expounded] by the Court in this area over the years, such a balancing approach stands behind many of the decisions upholding art. I courts. . . .

This was precisely the approach taken to this problem in Palmore v. United States, 411 U.S. 389 (1973), which, contrary to the suggestion of the plurality, did not rest on any theory of territorial or geographical control. Rather, it rested on an evaluation of the strength of the legislative interest in pursuing in this manner one of its constitutionally assigned responsibilities—a responsibility not different in kind from numerous other legislative responsibilities. Thus, *Palmore* referred to the wide variety of art. I courts, not just territorial courts. It is in this light that the critical statement of the case must be understood:

> "[T]he requirements of art. III, which are applicable where laws of national applicability and affairs of national concern are at stake, must in proper circumstances give way to accommodate plenary grants of power to Congress to legislate with respect to specialized areas having particularized needs and warranting distinctive treatment." 411 U.S., at 407–08.

I do not suggest that the Court should simply look to the strength of the legislative interest and ask itself if that interest is more compelling than the values furthered by art. III. The inquiry should, rather, focus equally on those art. III values and ask whether and to what extent the legislative scheme accommodates them or, conversely, substantially undermines them. The burden on art. III values should then be measured against the values Congress hopes to serve through the use of art. I courts.

To be more concrete: *Crowell* suggests that the presence of appellate review by an art. III court will go a long way toward insuring a proper separation of powers. Appellate review of the decisions of legislative courts, like appellate review of state-court decisions, provides a firm check on the ability of the political institutions of government to ignore or transgress constitutional limits on their own authority. Obviously, therefore, a scheme of art. I courts that provides for appellate review by art. III courts should be substantially less controversial than a legislative attempt entirely to avoid judicial review in a constitutional court.

Similarly, as long as the proposed art. I courts are designed to deal with issues likely to be of little interest to the political branches, there is less reason to fear that such courts represent a dangerous accumulation of power in one of the political branches of government. Chief Justice Vinson suggested as much when he stated that the Court should guard against any congressional attempt "to transfer jurisdiction . . . for the purpose of emasculating" constitutional courts. National Ins. Co. v. Tidewater Co., 337 U.S. 582, 644 (1949).

V

I believe the new bankruptcy courts established by the Bankruptcy Act of 1978 satisfy this standard.

First, ample provision is made for appellate review by art. III courts. [T]here is in every instance a right of appeal to at least one art. III court. Had Congress decided to assign all bankruptcy matters to the state courts, a power it clearly possesses, no greater review in an art. III court would exist. Although I do not suggest that this analogy means that Congress may establish an art. I court wherever it could have chosen to rely upon the state courts, it does suggest that the critical function of judicial review is being met in a manner that the Constitution suggests is sufficient.

Second, no one seriously argues that the Bankruptcy Act of 1978 represents an attempt by the political branches of government to aggrandize themselves at the expense of the third branch or an attempt to undermine the authority of constitutional courts in general. Indeed, the congressional perception of a lack of judicial interest in bankruptcy matters was one of the factors that led to the establishment of the bankruptcy courts: Congress feared that this lack of interest would lead to a failure to the federal district court to deal with bankruptcy matters in an expeditious manner. Bankruptcy matters are, for the most part, private adjudications of little political significance. Although some bankruptcies may indeed present politically controversial circumstances or issues, Congress has far more direct ways to involve itself in such matters than through some sort of subtle, or not so subtle, influence on bankruptcy judges. Furthermore, were such circumstances to arise, the due process clause might very well require that the matter be considered by an art. III judge: Bankruptcy proceedings remain, after all, subject to all of the strictures of that constitutional provision.

Finally, I have no doubt that the ends that Congress sought to accomplish by creating a system of non-art. III bankruptcy courts were at least as compelling as the ends found to be satisfactory in Palmore v. United States, 411 U.S. 389 (1973), or the ends that have traditionally justified the creation of legislative courts. The stresses placed upon the old bankruptcy system by the tremendous increase in bankruptcy cases were well documented and were clearly a matter to which Congress could respond.[16] I do not believe it is possible to challenge Congress' further determination that it was necessary to create a specialized court to deal with bankruptcy matters. That was the nearly uniform conclusion of all those that testified before Congress on the question of reform of the bankruptcy system, as well as the conclusion of the Commission on Bankruptcy Laws established by Congress in 1970 to explore possible improvements in the system.

The real question is not whether Congress was justified in establishing a specialized bankruptcy court, but rather whether it was justified in failing to create a specialized, art. III bankruptcy court. My own view is that the very fact of extreme specialization may be enough, and certainly has been enough in the past, to justify the creation of a legislative court. Congress may legitimately consider the effect on the federal judiciary of the addition of several hundred specialized judges: We are, on the whole, a body of generalists. The addition of several hundred specialists may substantially change, whether for good or bad, the character of the federal bench. Moreover, Congress may have desired to maintain some flexibility in its possible future responses to the general problem of bankruptcy. There is no question that the existence of several hundred bankruptcy judges with life tenure would have severely limited Congress' future options. Furthermore, the number of bankruptcies may fluctuate producing a substantially reduced need for bankruptcy judges. Congress may have thought that, in that event, a bankruptcy specialist should not as a general matter serve as a judge in the countless nonspecialized cases that come before the federal district courts. It would then face the prospect of large numbers of idle federal judges. Finally, Congress may have believed that the change from the bankruptcy referees to art. I judges was far less dramatic, and so less disruptive of the existing bankruptcy and constitutional court systems, than would be a change to art. III judges.

For all of these reasons, I would defer to the congressional judgment. Accordingly, I dissent.

NOTES ON ARTICLE I COURTS

1. **Introduction.** The Bankruptcy Reform Act of 1978 was the legislative response to a system in crisis. The chief problem under the old act was the distinction between "summary" and "plenary" jurisdiction. Claims involving the disposition to creditors of property in the possession of the court came within "summary" jurisdiction and were heard in the first instance by a bankruptcy referee. Other claims, including those for debts owed to the bankrupt by third parties, fell under "plenary" jurisdiction and could be heard by the referee only

---

[16] "During the past 30 years, the number of bankruptcy cases filed annually has increased steadily from 10,000 to over 254,000." H.R. Rep. No. 95–595, p. 21 (1977).

with the defendant's consent. Otherwise, such claims were tried separately in federal district court or in state court. This division resulted in costly and time-consuming jurisdictional disputes and in other inconveniences of administration. Additionally, because referees' recommendations had to be approved by a judge, bankruptcy proceedings were subject to long delays due to crowded district court dockets.

The 1978 act responded to these problems by expanding the jurisdiction of the bankruptcy courts and by making them functionally independent tribunals, able to control their own dockets and to enter and enforce final judgments. After long consideration, Congress decided not to accord to bankruptcy judges the protections of article III and to maintain at least a nominal superintendency by the district courts. Prominent among the concerns that led to this result was the fear that staffing an independent court of equal rank would dilute the prestige and influence of the district judges.[a]

Thus, the statute invalidated in *Northern Pipeline* was neither unimportant nor unconsidered. Instead, it was a recent act of Congress, passed after years of study and debate, and intended to accomplish major structural reform of the law of bankruptcy. For the Court to strike down such a statute was, by any reckoning, a notable exercise of judicial review.[b] One might expect, therefore, that the fatal defect in the statutory scheme could be clearly stated. As is so often true in the arcane and confusing area of "legislative courts," however, the essential rationale of the decision is far from clear.

2. The Rationale. It may be well, therefore, to begin with a simple question: What was the problem that the invalidation of the bankruptcy act was meant to solve? Put another way, what was the constitutional concern or value that this statute was found to offend? At least four possible rationales may be suggested, each of which has some support in the decisions and in the literature, but none of which seems entirely free from difficulty.

(i) Vindication of the Text. An obvious rationale for *Northern Pipeline* is simply vindication of the constitutional text. Article III is precise and apparently mandatory. Thus, it may be enough to say that the bankruptcy courts exercised the "judicial Power of the United States" without conforming to the requirements of article III. The

---

[a] This background is economically summarized in Fullerton, No Light at the End of the Pipeline: Confusion Surrounds Legislative Court, 49 Brooklyn L. Rev. 207, 216–19 (1983); and Finley, Article III Limits on Article I Courts: The Constitutionality of the Bankruptcy Court and the 1979 Magistrate Act, 80 Colum. L. Rev. 560, 562–65 (1980). A comprehensive history is available in Klee, Legislative History of the New Bankruptcy Law, 28 De Paul L. Rev. 941 (1979).

[b] Since the 1930's the Court has rarely declared acts of Congress unconstitutional for a non-civil liberties reason. One such case was Oregon v. Mitchell, 400 U.S. 112 (1970) (Congress could not extend the vote to 18–year-olds in state elections), which was superseded six months later by the 26th amendment. Another was National League of Cities v. Usery, 426 U.S. 833 (1976) (Congress could not impose wage and hour restrictions on state employees), which was overruled by Garcia v. San Antonio Metropolitan Transit Authority, 469 U.S. 528 (1985). See also United States ex rel. Toth v. Quarles, 350 U.S. 11 (1955) (holding that an ex-serviceman could not constitutionally be tried by court-martial).

difficulty with this rationale is not that it is in any demonstrable way wrong, but that its invocation is unaccountably selective. On its face, article III admits of no exceptions. Neither is there textual basis for distinguishing among Congress' powers under article I. Thus, if the constitutional text is sufficient to condemn non-article III bankruptcy courts, it would seem equally conclusive with respect to non-article III territorial courts, District of Columbia local courts, military courts, and so forth. But if such exceptions are to be recognized, what reliance can fairly be placed on the language of article III as a sufficient ground for invalidating the bankruptcy courts?[c]

　　(ii) Separation of Powers. The phrase "separation of powers" has varied meanings, but as used in this context it typically invokes a concern for judicial independence. Thus, Justice Brennan describes article III as enunciating the "fundamental principle" that the judiciary must be independent and identifies life tenure and guaranteed compensation as "institutional protections" designed to secure that independence. In this light, the problem with article I courts is that they are not adequately shielded from legislative or executive interference. The ultimate evil to be avoided is tyrannous overreaching by the political branches.

　　Is this a persuasive rationale for *Northern Pipeline*? Is this a plausible context in which to raise the fear of outside meddling in judicial decision-making? In particular, is this fear more plausible here than in other contexts where non-article III adjudication has been upheld?

　　Consider especially the military courts. Military judges not only lack life tenure and guaranteed compensation; they are dependent for career advancement on the evaluation of their superiors and in some respects subject to direct command influence. See O'Callahan v. Parker, 395 U.S. 258, 264 (1969). Is it plausible to believe that a prophylaxis against executive interference is more necessary in bankruptcy courts than in the administration of military justice?[d]

　　Consider also the distinction between "public" and "private" rights. Justice Brennan said that it was not permissible for an article I court to settle a contract claim between private parties, in part because private-rights disputes "lie at the core of the historically recognized judicial power." In contrast, "when Congress creates a substantive federal right, it possesses substantial discretion to prescribe the manner in which that right may be adjudicated." At a minimum, the precedents seem to authorize non-article III adjudication of suits "between the government and others."

　　Can this distinction be reconciled with a concern for judicial independence? Consider the views of Maryellen Fullerton. She noted

[c] One commentator has suggested a return to a literal reading of article III, despite the consequences. See Redish, Legislative Courts, Administrative Agencies, and the *Northern Pipeline* Decision, 1983 Duke L.J. 197 (1983).

[d] For a call for article III courts in an unusual but analogous context, see Maryellen Fullerton, Hijacking Trials Overseas: The Need for an Article III Court, 28 Wm. & Mary L.Rev. 1 (1986).

that the *Northern Pipeline* plurality treated private adjudication as the "core" of art. III power and responded:

> "[A] strong argument can be made that the core of judicial power includes public rights cases challenging the validity of legislative or executive actions. This broader description of the core of federal judicial power finds particular support in the checks and balances structure of the Constitution. A major role of the federal judiciary is to declare unlawful congressional or executive actions that exceed their powers under the Constitution. The article III guarantees protect the judiciary in its exercise of the power to invalidate legislative or executive action. . . . Because the need to check unlawful acts by the executive or legislature is more likely to arise in suits challenging government actions rather than in litigation between private parties, allowing legislative courts to adjudicate public rights cases thwarts the policy of checks and balances."

Fullerton, No Light at the End of the Pipeline: Confusion Surrounds Legislative Courts, 49 Brooklyn L. Rev. 207, 230–31 (1983). See also the more pointed comment by Martin Redish that if the dichotomy between public and private rights is to be used at all, "it would make considerably more sense to reverse it." Redish, Legislative Courts, Administrative Agencies, and the *Northern Pipeline* Decision, 1983 Duke L.J. 197, 214 (1983).[e]

(iii) **Fairness to Litigants.** A distinguishable rationale relates the requirements of article III to an underlying concern for fairness to litigants. Judges who are inadequately shielded from political pressure may be less able to provide fair adjudication. In essence, this argument conflates article III and due process of law.

Does this rationale explain *Northern Pipeline*? Does the decision suggest that fundamental fairness requires judicial life tenure and guaranteed compensation? Note that state judges typically lack these protections, and no one suggests that state court adjudications are for that reason unconstitutional. Congress could have left the resolution of "plenary" bankruptcy disputes to state courts, in which case they would have been resolved by judges who have no greater guarantee of judicial independence than do federal bankruptcy judges. Does that sufficiently answer the concern for fairness to litigants?

(iv) **Federalism.** Lastly, there is some suggestion in the literature that the protections of article III were designed not only to protect the federal judiciary against political interference, but also to guard the states against encroachment by the national government. The idea seems to be that life tenure and guaranteed compensation for federal judges would assure an "impartial and independent forum" for

---

[e] Justice Brennan's answer to this suggestion, contained in footnote 20 of his opinion, is that "the rationale for the public-rights line of cases lies not in political theory, but rather in Congress' and this Court's understanding of what power was reserved to the judiciary by the Constitution as a matter of historical fact." What "historical fact" did he have in mind?

adjudication of suits concerning the states and "ensure that any limitation of state prerogatives will occur by proper operation of law, rather than through legislative or executive coercion." Finley, Article III Limits on Article I Courts: The Constitutionality of the Bankruptcy Court and the 1979 Magistrate Act, 80 Colum. L. Rev. 560, 582–83 (1980).

Does federalism make sense as a rationale for *Northern Pipeline*? Perhaps some support for this view is implicit in the observation, made both by the plurality and the concurrence, that Congress did not create a federal rule of decision for Northern Pipeline's claim against Marathon, but merely authorized resolution of this state-law claim in a federal bankruptcy court. Yet it is hard to see *Northern Pipeline* as a meaningful vindication of states' rights. Everyone seems to agree that Congress could have authorized adjudication of this claim in a federal district court, and it also seems clear that Congress could have propounded a federal rule of decision governing this dispute. Indeed, the plurality suggest that had Congress done so, it could then have committed resolution of the dispute to a non-article III tribunal. In light of these possibilities, what federalism interest can *Northern Pipeline* be said to vindicate?

3. The Aftermath. The Supreme Court announced its decision in *Northern Pipeline* on June 28, 1982, but stayed its judgment until October 4 of that year. Arguing that Congress was unable to meet this deadline due to election-year pressures, the Solicitor General persuaded the Court to extend its stay until December 24, 1982. When it became clear that the second deadline would expire before Congressional action, the Solicitor General asked for another extension, but the Court refused. The Judicial Conference of the United States then attempted to restore order to the bankruptcy system by promulgating emergency rules. The interim rules were subsequently enacted by Congress, but not in exactly the form suggested by the Conference. Despite some resulting confusion, the emergency rules provided the operational basis for bankruptcy proceedings through 1984.

Almost exactly two years after the Court announced *Northern Pipeline*, Congress passed the Bankruptcy Amendments and Federal Judgeship Act of 1984. Pub. L. No. 98–353, 98 Stat. 333 (1984). As amended by that legislation, 28 U.S.C. § 157 states that each district court "*may* provide that any or all cases under title 11 and any or all proceedings arising under title 11 or arising in or related to a case under title 11 shall be referred to the bankruptcy judges for the district." (Emphasis added.) The statute then distinguishes between "core" and "non-core" proceedings. Core proceedings, as specified in § 157(b)(2), roughly correspond to the old "summary" jurisdiction. These matters the bankruptcy court may "hear and determine." In non-core proceedings, the bankruptcy judge makes proposed findings of fact and conclusions of law; any final order or judgment is entered by the district court after "reviewing de novo" those matters to which timely objection is made. Finally, the statute provides that "personal injury tort and wrongful death claims" must be tried in district court.[f]

Does this revision cure the defect identified in *Northern Pipeline*? Is the new scheme significantly more protective of the interests underlying article III?

4. ***Thomas v. Union Carbide Agricultural Products.*** In a case decided soon after *Northern Pipeline*, the Supreme Court rejected a related challenge to non-article III adjudication. Thomas v. Union Carbide Agricultural Products Co., 473 U.S. 568 (1985), involved a challenge to statutorily imposed binding arbitration. The Federal Insecticide, Fungicide, and Rodenticide Act established mandatory sharing of research data submitted to the Environmental Protection Agency to support new pesticide registration. The originator of a new pesticide was required, after a period of ten years, to allow competitors to use previously submitted research data for approval of their new products, but was entitled to compensation for the use of such data. Disputes about the appropriate amount of compensation proved extremely difficult for the EPA to handle, so in 1978 Congress amended the statute to require binding arbitration of compensation disputes, with judicial review only for "fraud, misrepresentation or other misconduct."

Following *Northern Pipeline*, several chemical companies charged that the mandatory arbitration procedure violated article III. The Supreme Court disagreed. Speaking through Justice O'Connor, the Court explained that *Northern Pipeline* "establishes only that Congress may not vest in a non-article III court the power to adjudicate, render final judgment, and issue binding orders in a traditional contract action arising under state law, without the consent of the litigants and subject only to ordinary appellate review." So construed, *Northern Pipeline* was distinguishable. Here the right to compensation did not arise under state law but was federally created. Moreover, although arguably a "private right" within the meaning of *Northern Pipeline*, it was enmeshed in a federal regulatory scheme and thus had "many characteristics of a 'public' right." Binding arbitration was therefore upheld. "To hold otherwise would be to erect a rigid and formalistic restraint on the ability of Congress to adopt innovative measures such as negotiation and arbitration with respect to rights created by a regulatory scheme." Justice Brennan, joined by Justices Marshall and Blackmun, and Justice Stevens concurred in the judgment in separate opinions.

5. ***Commodity Futures Trading Commission v. Schor.*** The Supreme Court again considered the implications of *Northern Pipeline* a year later. Commodity Futures Trading Commission v. Schor, 478 U.S. 833 (1986), involved the scope of the Commission's jurisdiction in "reparation" proceedings brought under the Commodity Exchange Act. "Reparation" proceedings are brought by customers of professional

---

[f] For analysis of the 1984 legislation, see Snider, Rochkind, Green, Stein, and Welford, The Bankruptcy Amendments and Federal Judgeship Act of 1984, 83 Mich. L. Rev. 775 (1984). See also Thomas C. Galligan, Jr., Article III and the "Related To" Bankruptcy Jurisdiction: A Case Study in Protective Jurisdiction, 11 U.Puget Sound L.Rev. 1 (1987).

commodity brokers for prohibited forms of fraudulent or manipulative conduct. The Commission, which is organized as an independent federal agency, is empowered to resolve such claims as an "inexpensive and expeditious" alternative to litigation. In 1976, the Commission by regulation authorized itself also to hear all counterclaims "aris[ing] out of the same transaction or occurrence" as the claim for reparations. After *Northern Pipeline,* questions arose concerning the constitutionality of non-article III adjudication of state-law counterclaims, but the Supreme Court approved the procedure.

Speaking through Justice O'Connor, the Court distinguished between the "personal" and "structural" interests protected by article III. Any "personal" interest in securing article III adjudication would be waived by the act of bringing a "reparation" proceeding rather than filing a lawsuit. A commodity customer who elected to forego litigation in favor of the quicker and less expensive administrative procedure "effectively agreed" to administrative adjudication of the entire controversy. To the extent, however, that article III protects "structural" interests, the right to article III adjudication could not be waived. Nevertheless, the Court saw no constitutional violation:

> "The CFTC's adjudicatory powers depart from the traditional agency model in just one respect: the CFTC's jurisdiction over common law counterclaims. . . . The counterclaim asserted in this case is a 'private' right for which state law provides the rule of decision. It is therefore a claim of the kind assumed to be at the 'core' of matters normally reserved to article III courts. Yet this conclusion does not end our inquiry; just as this Court has rejected any attempt to make determinative for article III purposes the distinction between public and private rights, *Thomas,* supra, there is no reason inherent in separation of powers principles to accord the state law character of a claim talismanic power in article III inquiries. . . .

> "[W]here private, common law rights are at stake, our examination of the congressional attempt to control the manner in which those rights are adjudicated has been searching. See, e.g., *Northern Pipeline,* supra. In this case, however, '[l]ooking beyond form to the substance of what' Congress has done, we are persuaded that the congressional authorization of limited CFTC jurisdiction over a narrow class of common law claims as an incident to the CFTC's primary, and unchallenged, adjudicative function does not create a substantial threat to the separation of powers.

> "It is clear that Congress has not attempted to 'withdraw from judicial cognizance' the determination of [the counterclaim]. Congress gave the CFTC the authority to adjudicate such matters, but the decision to invoke this forum is left entirely to the parties and the power of the federal judiciary to take jurisdiction of these matters is unaffected. In such circumstances, separation of powers concerns are diminished, for

it seems self-evident that just as Congress may encourage parties to settle a dispute out of court or resort to arbitration without impermissible incursions on the separation of powers, Congress may make available a quasi-judicial mechanism through which willing parties may, at their option, elect to resolve their differences. . . .

"In such circumstances, the magnitude of any intrusion on the judicial branch can only be termed de minimis. Conversely, were we to hold that the legislative branch may not permit such limited cognizance of common law counterclaims at the election of the parties, it is clear that we would 'defeat the obvious purpose of the legislation to furnish a prompt, continuous, expert and inexpensive method for dealing with a class of questions of fact which are peculiarly suited to examination and determination by an administrative agency specially assigned to that task.' We do not think article III compels this degree of prophylaxis."

Justice Brennan, with whom Justice Marshall joined, dissented. He urged that non-article III adjudication be limited to the "few, well-established exceptions" detailed in his opinion for the plurality in *Northern Pipeline* and charged that the majority had "far exceed[ed] the analytic framework of our precedents." In his view, the Court had improperly subordinated the command of article III to the dictates of convenience.

6. Questions and Comments on Article I Courts. Are *Thomas* and *Schor* fairly distinguishable from *Northern Pipeline*? Are the differences among them responsive to any plausible account of the purposes of article III?

Consider, in this connection, the views of Judith Resnik. In The Mythic Meaning of Article III, 56 U. Colo. L. Rev. 581 (1985), Resnik explores the various inroads made on article III and asks why, in light of these precedents, the Supreme Court nevertheless was concerned to "hold the line" in *Northern Pipeline*. She concludes that, despite the "murkiness" of the decisions, the Court's opinions reflect "strongly held convictions" based on "a deep-seated myth about the role of judges." That myth is exemplified by the battle of Lord Coke against King James—a classic judicial confrontation of executive authority. In Resnik's view, this image of the judge standing up to executive overreaching "animates the Court's work in article III" and explains the outcome in *Northern Pipeline*:

"I believe that the potential battle—Lord Coke v. King James—animated the discussions of both Justices Brennan and White in *Northern Pipeline*. Justice White claimed that bankruptcy cases were not those in which a battle would occur. Justice Brennan must either have thought the opposite or been unsure. Hence, the 'hold that line' stance, because we can never know when issues which appear apolitical will become charged with concern. If Justice Brennan did in fact make the

implicit prediction that bankruptcy cases were potential bat-
tlegrounds, he has been proved correct. Bankruptcy courts
today are where major social policy issues—compensation for
victims of asbestosis, toxic waste cleanups, and labor relations—are being played out."

Has Resnik made sense of *Northern Pipeline*?

Consider also the views of Richard Fallon. In Of Legislative
Courts, Administrative Agencies, and Article III, 101 Harv.L.Rev. 915
(1988), Fallon argues that the best accommodation of article III values
with the "functional imperatives of contemporary government" would
focus on appellate review of non-article III judgments. Fallon believes
that "sufficiently searching" appellate review in a constitutional court
should be both necessary and sufficient to satisfy article III.

Applying this theory, Fallon concludes that both *Northern Pipeline*
and *Thomas v. Union Carbide* were wrongly decided. In *Northern
Pipeline*, "[t]he available appellate review by article III courts offered
sufficient protection for article III values." In *Thomas*, by contrast, the
arbitrator's decisions were reviewed only for fraud, misrepresentation,
or other misconduct. "In the absence of broader judicial review," says
Fallon, the requirement of binding arbitration should have been struck
down. Finally, Fallon approves the result in *Schor*, both "because the
statute provided for de novo review of questions of law in an article III
court" and because the consent of the parties alleviated any concern
about unfairness to them.

For additional analysis of these cases, see George D. Brown, Article
III as a Fundamental Value—The Demise of *Northern Pipeline* and Its
Implications for Congressional Power, 49 Ohio St. L.J. 55 (1988) (relating *Northern Pipeline* to general themes of the Burger Court, including
the impulse to restrain the role of the federal courts); and Richard B.
Saphire and Michael E. Solimine, Shoring Up Article III: Legislative
Court Doctrine in the Post *CFTC v. Schor* Era, 68 B.U.L.Rev. 85 (1988)
(advancing a framework for evaluating the validity of non-art. III courts
and emphasizing in particular the importance of meaningful art. III
review of the factual and legal determinations of non-art. III courts).

NOTES ON ADMINISTRATIVE AGENCIES

1. Introduction. Lurking behind the debate over article I courts
is the problem of administrative agencies. Of course, many federal
agencies exercise rule-making or licensing authority not directly comparable to judicial decision-making. Others, however, make case-by-case
determinations of the rights and liabilities of private parties. In a
literal sense, such agencies would seem to be exercising the "judicial
Power of the United States" within the meaning of article III, that is,
they are deciding "cases" arising under federal law. Plausibly, therefore, they should be subject to the constraints imposed on constitutional
courts. In fact, however, administrative agencies operate very differ-

ently from article III courts and yet are widely accepted as constitutionally valid mechanisms of dispute resolution. Why? What is it about agency adjudication that makes article III inapplicable?

2. An Example: The NLRB. Consider, for example, the National Labor Relations Board.[a] The Board administers and interprets the unfair labor practice and representation provisions of the National Labor Relations Act. As provided in 29 U.S.C. § 153, the Board consists of five members appointed by the president for staggered, five-year terms. The Board itself sits as an appellate body, ordinarily in panels of three. Trial is had before an administrative law judge, who is a civil service officer permanently assigned to hear Board cases. The administrative law judge issues a recommended decision and order, which is automatically issued as a Board order if no one objects. If objection is raised, the case is transferred to the Board for final decision. Although charges of unfair labor practices are made by private parties, no case is brought to the Board unless a "complaint" is filed. This prosecutorial function is fulfilled by a General Counsel appointed by the president and by regional directors appointed by, and responsible to, the General Counsel.

The Board itself has no coercive power. Instead, Board orders are enforced in the United States Courts of Appeals on petition by the Board or by any person aggrieved by a final Board order. Under the statute, a Board finding of fact is conclusive "if supported by substantial evidence." 29 U.S.C. § 160(e) and (f). As elaborated in Universal Camera Corp. v. NLRB, 340 U.S. 474 (1951), this means that courts must give special deference to findings within the Board's area of expertise. Even outside that area, a court is not free to "displace the Board's choice between fairly conflicting views, even though the court would justifiably have made a different choice had the matter been before it de novo." Id. at 488. The standard of review for application of law to fact and for unmixed questions of law is not specified in the statute, and the approach of reviewing courts varies with context. As one authority put it, "All that can be said with confidence is that courts tend to believe that their own competence matches that of the Board, and finally surpasses it, as the finding moves from 'pure' fact, to mixed questions to issues of 'pure' statutory construction and then finally to issues of constitutional dimension." R. Gorman, Basic Text on Labor Law 13 (1976).[b]

Interestingly, the NLRB also has rule-making authority, but is notoriously reluctant to use it. Despite repeated pleas from judges, practitioners, and academics,[c] the Board consistently eschews formal

---

[a] An overview of the organization and function of the NLRB may be found in D. Leslie, Labor Law in a Nutshell 9–18 (1979).

[b] Elaboration of the relationship between administrative agencies and the institution of judicial review can be found in Monaghan, *Marbury* and the Administrative State, 83 Colum. L. Rev. 1 (1983).

[c] See, e.g., H. Friendly, The Federal Administrative Agencies 146–47 (1962); K. Davis, Administrative Law Treatise, 1970 Supplement 278 (1970); Bernstein, The NLRB's Adjudication-Rule Making Dilemma Under the Administrative Procedure Act, 79 Yale L.J. 571, 589–98 (1970); Peck, The Atrophied Rule Making Powers of the National Labor Relations Board, 70 Yale

rule-making in favor of case-by-case adjudication. The reasons for this practice are no doubt many, but one factor repeatedly cited by experts is the agency's desire to insulate itself from effective judicial review by submerging its judgments in the facts of particular cases.[d] Perhaps not entirely unrelated is the widespread perception that NLRB adjudication is ideological and politicized, characterized by sharp swings in enforcement perspective as annual presidential appointments remake the Board's composition.[e]

Obviously, the National Labor Relations Board falls far short of the model of judicial independence established by article III. Indeed, the Board's structure suggests, and the history of the National Labor Relations Act confirms,[f] that the Board was not intended to provide impartial, apolitical adjudication of labor disputes. Instead, it was created to enforce certain policy objectives and constituted so that the

---

L.J. 729, 730–35 (1961); 89 Repts. of the ABA 256–57 (1964) (reporting resolution of the House of Delegates of the American Bar Association).

[d] A sustained and thoughtful analysis of this general issue appears in Shapiro, The Choice of Rulemaking or Adjudication in the Development of Administrative Policy, 78 Harv. L. Rev. 921, 942–58 (1965). Professor Shapiro suggests that "there are times when an agency will not make *any* formal announcement of policy, either by way of adjudication or in rulemaking, perhaps because of uncertainty as to the validity of the policy and a consequent desire to avoid judicial review," and concludes that "by eschewing regulations in favor of the declaration of rules by adjudication, an agency is likely to regard itself as freer, and will in fact be given greater freedom by the courts, to ignore or depart from those rules in specific instances without giving sufficient reasons."

Similar comments made with particular reference to the NLRB include Peck, A Critique of the National Labor Relations Board's Performance in Policy Formulation: Adjudication and Rule Making, 117 U. Pa. L. Rev. 254, 274–75 (1968) (emphasizing the "maneuverability of the adjudicatory process" as a factor in the Board's avoidance of rule-making); Bernstein, The NLRB's Adjudication-Rule Making Dilemma under the Administrative Procedure Act, 79 Yale L.J. 571, 597 (1970) (surmising that the Board has "adopt[ed] the mechanism least subject to attack").

[e] So, for example, the "Reagan Board" has recently been criticized for the "sheer volume of changes in the law which it has effected" and the "devastating effect" with which it has revised labor law. 118 Labor

Rel. Rptr. 282–83, 285 (April 15, 1985) (comments of Professor Charles J. Morris and attorney David Van Os, respectively). See also the comments of labor lawyers Jules Bernstein and Laurence E. Gold, who accuse the Reagan administration of having "packed the Board . . . to an unprecedented degree" and the Board itself of "pursuing an aggressive agenda, reversing precedents at an alarming rate." 119 Labor Rel. Rptr. 114 (June 10, 1985). But however unwelcome such sudden changes might be, few would contend that they are different in kind from earlier "pendulum swings" in Board policies. See, e.g., Bernstein, The NLRB's Adjudication-Rule Making Dilemma Under the Administrative Procedure Act, 79 Yale L.J. 571, 597 (1970) (describing the "extensive overruling" of prior decisions by the "Eisenhower Board" and the "Kennedy-Johnson Board" and the way in which "new Board majorities . . . have gobbled up precedents with relish"). Indeed, Professor Peck recounts that the change following consolidation of the new "Kennedy Board" was so rapid that "one of the labor law reporting services found it appropriate to make a new index entry entitled 'Prior decisions overruled by the Board.'" Peck, A Critique of the National Labor Relations Board's Performance in Policy Formulation: Adjudication and Rule Making, 117 U. Pa. L. Rev. 254, 256 (1968).

[f] As the National Labor Relations Act was originally enacted in 1935, the specification of unfair labor practices applied only to employers. The proscription of certain union activities was added by the Taft-Hartley Act in 1947. See D. Leslie, Labor Law in a Nutshell, 5–8 (1979).

president, acting with the advice and consent of the Senate, can assert relatively short-term political control over Board membership.[g]

3. Questions and Comments on Agency Adjudication and Article III. Given the incentive and opportunity for political interference, why is the Court so tolerant of NLRB adjudication? Or, to put the same question another way, if the Court is prepared to countenance adjudication by the NLRB and other administrative agencies, why is it so concerned with the structure of the bankruptcy courts?

One answer is that the NLRB is not a court and that article III only pertains to courts. This kind of nominalism is not often stated, but some such notion seems implicit in any argument against the constitutionality of an article I court that does not take account of the impact of article III on administrative agencies. Is there reason to suppose that article III should limit only institutions called courts?

A related argument identifies functional differences between courts and agencies. The chief difference is usually said to be that administrative agencies typically lack enforcement authority.[h] Most agencies, like the compensation commission in *Crowell v. Benson* and like the NLRB, must go to court to have their orders enforced. The argument is developed most fully in Krattenmaker, Article III and Judicial Independence: Why the New Bankruptcy Courts are Unconstitutional, 70 Geo. L.J. 297, 308–09 (1981): *

> "Prior to the enactment of the Bankruptcy Reform Act, bankruptcy cases were handled by bankruptcy judges who . . . operated under the supervision of article III district court judges and were empowered to rule only on a limited range of cases. The new bankruptcy judges, however, will function independently of any article III judges [and will] have the power to conduct jury trials, to punish certain contempts of court, and to enter final judgments and issue writs of execution.
>
> "The significance of these increased powers and duties is great; it explains not only why the former bankruptcy system did not present the same constitutional issues as the new one, but also why these new bankruptcy courts are not analogous to the federal administrative agencies. Proponents of the Bankruptcy Reform Act would be correct to argue that no neat, bright-line distinction exists—or could be tolerated in the modern bureaucratic state—between executive and judicial power.

[g] Thus, not surprisingly, those who wish to de-emphasize political influence on Board decisions often call for longer tenure for Board members. See, e.g., ABA Panel Discussion, 119 Lab. Rel. Rptr. 5 (July 22, 1985) (remarks of former Board Chairman John H. Fanning calling for terms of 10 years without possibility of reappointment).

[h] See, e.g., Currie, Bankruptcy Judges and the Independent Judiciary, 16 Creigh-

ton L. Rev. 441, 456 (1983) (distinguishing *Crowell v. Benson* as at most "allow[ing] Congress under certain circumstances, in response to the demonstrated inadequacy of judicial processes, to enlist the aid of nonjudicial agencies without the power to enforce their own orders").

* Reprinted with the permission of the author and of the publisher, © 1981 The Georgetown Law Journal Association.

Many officials must be charged with interpreting congressional statutes and determining violations of them. These determinations, practically viewed, will have important effects on individual citizens. Not all people exercising such authority need be tenured or protected from salary cuts. Were article III so broadly construed, it would hinder significantly congressional efforts to create a rational, efficient system of government.

"But article III, § 1 speaks only of "Courts" exercising "judicial Power." Looking to the purposes the framers had in mind in crafting that section, only a virtually willful inattention to detail could cause one to miss the difference between officers who are and officers who are not empowered to issue final judgments, to enforce their own monetary awards, to conduct all manner of civil proceedings that federal district courts may conduct, including jury trials, and to exercise all these powers in disputes over liabilities between private citizens."

Is Krattenmaker persuasive? Consider the rebuttal in Redish, Legislative Courts, Administrative Agencies, and the *Northern Pipeline* Decision, 1983 Duke L.J. 197, 217–18 (1983). Redish acknowledges that the chief difference between administrative agencies and legislative courts is that agencies "generally cannot issue automatically enforceable orders," but argues that "elevating this distinction to a status of constitutional significance places form over substance":

"When an agency seeks enforcement of an order in federal court, the court is required by both statute and precedent to defer to the findings and conclusions of the agency. . . . [O]ne may question whether there is any difference, in terms of satisfying the article III provisions, between the requirement that the non-article III agency seek enforcement in an article III court where that agency's findings are subject to a minimal level of review, and the roughly comparable appellate review of the automatically enforceable orders of a bankruptcy or other legislative court. . . . In both situations, the non-article III body conducts the primary adjudication, makes the basic legal and factual findings, and is subject to some level of review in an article III court."

Finally, consider whether the constitutional tolerance of administrative adjudication might be justified on other grounds. Would NLRB cases, for example, fall within Justice Brennan's conception of "public rights?" Charges of unfair labor practices arise "between the government and others" in the sense that the regional director must decide to prosecute a complaint. Additionally, the agency is a party to judicial enforcement proceedings. On the other hand, NLRB cases do not involve claims against the government. On the contrary, the underlying dispute is between private parties, and Board adjudication determines their rights and liabilities "under the law as defined."

Even if unfair labor practice cases do not involve "public rights," they do arise under federal law. Recall Justice Brennan's comment that "when Congress creates a substantive federal right, it possesses substantial discretion to prescribe the manner in which that right may be adjudicated—including the assignment to an adjunct of some functions historically performed by judges." Does that explain why agency adjudication is constitutional? If so, what is left of article III? Is article III an effective limit only where a federal agency or legislative court adjudicates cases arising under state law? If so, the strictures of article III may serve little purpose other than to invalidate the Bankruptcy Reform Act of 1978. Does such a limited role for article III make sense?

NOTES ON INTERNAL DELEGATION OF JUDICIAL AUTHORITY: U.S. MAGISTRATES

1. Introduction. As Justice Brennan recounts in the plurality opinion in *Northern Pipeline,* the Bankruptcy Act of 1978 did not actually purport to create legislative courts. Instead, the statute designated the bankruptcy courts as "adjuncts" to the district courts and provided that they "shall exercise" the bankruptcy jurisdiction conferred in the first instance on the district courts. This indirection was designed to take advantage of a second tradition that might have been thought to support the constitutionality of the new bankruptcy courts— namely, the internal delegation of judicial authority to untenured assistants. Officials that have been used in this way include commissioners and masters, but modern federal practice has increasingly concentrated the delegated exercise of judicial responsibility in the hands of a magistrate.[a] Recent federal statutes have expanded the duties of magistrates and brought into question the conformity of this practice with the dictates of article III.

2. The Magistrates Act of 1968. The Federal Magistrates Act of 1968, codified at 28 U.S.C. §§ 631 et seq., created the office of magistrate with the power of appointment in the district court. The specification of a magistrate's duties was intentionally open-ended. Magistrates were authorized to serve as special masters under Federal Rule of Civil Procedure 53, to assist district judges in pretrial or discovery proceedings, to review prisoner applications for post-conviction relief, and to perform "such additional duties as are not inconsistent with the Constitution and laws of the United States." The usual mode of operation was a judicial reference to the magistrate who, after holding the necessary hearings or inquiries, reported back a recommended disposition.

The use of this procedure in habeas cases was temporarily curtailed in Wingo v. Wedding, 418 U.S. 461 (1974), which held that habeas corpus evidentiary hearings had to be conducted by federal judges

---

[a] The history of this practice, both in England and in the United States, is reviewed in Silberman, Masters and Magistrates, Part I: The English Model, 50 N.Y. U.L. Rev. 1070 (1975), and Silberman, Masters and Magistrates, Part II: The American Analogue, 50 N.Y.U.L. Rev. 1297 (1975).

personally. The Court based this conclusion on the habeas corpus statute and interpreted the more recently enacted Magistrates Act to have made no change in that requirement.[b]

3. **The 1976 Amendments.** Congress evidently disagreed, for it promptly amended the Magistrates Act to overrule *Wingo.* In addition to specifying that magistrates could hold evidentiary hearings on habeas corpus applications, the 1976 amendments also clarified magistrates' powers with respect to pretrial and other matters. Magistrates were allowed to "hear and determine" non-dispositive pretrial motions, subject only to overruling where the magistrate's order was "clearly erroneous or contrary to law." So-called "dispositive" motions, however, could be referred to magistrates only for proposed findings of fact and recommended disposition; the presiding judge was required to make a "de novo determination" of any matter to which objection was made.[c] Thus, the 1976 amendments sanctioned the recommended disposition procedure, but with an important limitation in certain cases.

4. *United States v. Raddatz.* The constitutionality of the recommended disposition procedure was contested in United States v. Raddatz, 447 U.S. 667 (1980). *Raddatz* involved a criminal prosecution that hinged on the admissability of a confession. The defendant moved to suppress on the ground that the confession was involuntary. This motion was referred to a magistrate, who found that the statements had been made knowingly and voluntarily and recommended that the suppression motion be denied. The District Court accepted this recommendation after reviewing the transcript and receiving arguments of counsel, but without hearing live testimony on the controverted issue. The Court of Appeals found this procedure authorized by statute and consistent with article III, but violative of due process. The Supreme Court reversed.

Speaking for the Court, Chief Justice Burger found first that the statute required only a de novo *determination* of the suppression motion, not a de novo *hearing.* This requirement was satisfied if the "ultimate adjudicatory determination" was reserved to the judge, who was entitled to give the magistrate's proposed findings and recommendation as much weight as "sound judicial discretion" might indicate. The Court also found no violation of due process. The Court drew attention to the common administrative practice, as in the NLRB, of agency findings of fact based on evidence presented to a hearing officer. The Court concluded that an analogous procedure was acceptable for a suppression motion. The Court noted that the district judge retrained broad discretion to hear live witnesses and to accept, reject, or modify proposed findings. Finally, the Court found no violation of article III.

[b] *Wingo v. Wedding* is reviewed and analyzed in Tushnet, Invitation to a Wedding: Some Thoughts on Article III and a Problem of Statutory Interpretation, 60 Iowa L. Rev. 937 (1975).

[c] This procedure is required for motions for injunctive relief, for judgment on the pleadings, for summary judgment, to dismiss or quash an indictment, to suppress evidence in a criminal case, to certify or dismiss a class action, to dismiss for failure to state a claim upon which relief can be granted, and to dismiss involuntarily, as well as for applications for post-conviction relief. 28 U.S.C. § 636(b)(1).

Congress had not attempted to vest final disposition of a suppression motion in a non-article III officer. On the contrary, the district court had "plenary discretion" to decide to use a magistrate and to review a magistrate's recommendation. "Therefore, the entire process takes place under the district court's total control and jurisdiction."

There were several dissents. Justice Stewart, joined by Justices Brennan and Marshall, dissented on the ground that a trial judge could not make a "de novo determination," as required by the statute, "without being exposed to the one kind of evidence that no written record can ever reveal—the demeanor of the witnesses." Justice Marshall, joined by Justice Brennan, argued that, where, as here, the critical question was witness credibility, judicial resolution of the suppression motion without live testimony would violate due process. Of course, the magistrate had heard the witnesses, but judicial reliance on the magistrate's evaluation would violate article III. Justice Marshall acknowledged the general acceptability of agency factfinding, but argued that a suppression hearing is "one of the admittedly few contexts in which independent factfinding by an art. III judge is constitutionally required." Justice Powell dissented, taking the view that due process requires the court to "rehear crucial witnesses when, as in this case, a suppression hearing turns *only* on credibility."

5. The 1979 Magistrate Act. The year before *Raddatz* was announced, Congress again expanded the duties of magistrates. The Magistrates Act of 1979 authorizes civil trial by magistrate upon consent of the parties. See 28 U.S.C. § 636(c).[d] The district court selects those cases appropriate for trial by magistrate, and the parties are notified of their opportunity to consent. Procedures are required to protect the voluntariness of the parties' choice. The district court can later revoke the reference for "good cause," but otherwise will not supervise the proceeding. The magistrate's determination leads automatically to entry of judgment. Appeal may be had as of right to the court of appeals or, if all parties have previously agreed thereto, an expedited appeal is available in the district court.

This practice of consensual reference has received a mixed reception among commentators.[e] The most elaborate criticism appears in Kraakman, Article III Constraints and the Expanding Civil Jurisdiction of Federal Magistrates: A Dissenting View, 88 Yale L.J. 1023, 1047–59 (1979). Professor Kraakman argues that, "[t]he magistrate system differs from older solutions to court overcrowding in its unique flexibility and political convenience." Given the rising federal caseload, he anticipates "an inherent expansionist dynamic" that will lead to routine reference of large numbers of cases for trial by magistrate. Kraak-

---

[d] The original 1968 legislation had authorized magistrates to try minor criminal cases upon waiver by the accused of right to trial by an article III judge. See 18 U.S.C. § 3401.

[e] Compare Silberman, Masters and Magistrates, Part II: The American Analogue, 50 N.Y.U.L. Rev. 1297, 1350–54 (1975) (de-

fending the constitutionality of consensual reference), with Finley, Article III Limits on Article I Courts: The Constitutionality of the Bankruptcy Court and the 1979 Magistrate Act, 80 Colum. L. Rev. 1980 (attacking the Magistrate Act as unconstitutional).

man argues that such references will involve chiefly "simple cases and needy litigants," with a resulting discrimination among classes of persons before the federal courts and a progressive judicial inattention to certain areas of law.

Professor Kraakman also foresees a dangerous role confusion arising from the magistrate's "dual position as judicial subordinate and independent adjudicator":

"The premise of the 1979 consensual-reference provision is that litigant consent permits the magistrate to assume the full judicial function. The integrity of magistrate decisions is insulated by the same standard of review that safeguards judicial decisionmaking. Yet the magistrate is not a judge. In addition to the familiar 'control' of appellate review that all higher federal tribunals exercise over the judges of lower courts, the magistrate is also subject to a qualitatively different form of bureaucratic control that may attend district court authority to determine his reappointment prospects and, more importantly, the day-to-day contents of his docket. Moreover, district judges must evaluate the magistrate's decisional record in the course of exercising their administrative functions, if only in order to maintain the standards of the court. This ongoing, informal oversight creates the risk of impermissible intrusion on the magistrate's substantive decisions. The danger is not that magistrates will come to function as judicial alter egos, but rather that they may be encouraged to adopt a risk-averse strategy of adjudication by the pressure of judicial scrutiny, a strategy eschewing unconventional decisions that might otherwise be prompted by novel legal claims or by pressing factual idiosyncracies. Such 'judicious' decisionmaking would be inconsistent with the . . . policy of autonomous adjudication within the federal courts that underlies the article III judicial office."

The reaction in the courts, however, has been largely favorable.[f] Perhaps the leading case is Pacemaker Diagnostic Clinic of America v. Instromedix, 725 F.2d 537 (9th Cir. 1984), in which the Ninth Circuit, sitting en banc, reversed an earlier determination by a panel that consensual reference was unconstitutional. Speaking for the court, Judge Kennedy identified two components of the separation-of-powers concept underlying article III. First, article III protects the rights of the litigants by guaranteeing an independent judiciary. But this protection, in common with other constitutional rights, can be validly waived. Second, article III protects "the whole constitutional structure by requiring that each branch retain its essential powers and independence." This interest was served by vesting the article III judiciary with "extensive administrative control over the management, composition, and operation of the magistrate system" and by permitting article

[f] See, e.g., Goldstein v. Kelleher, 728 F.2d 32 (1st Cir.1984), cert. denied, 469 U.S. 852 (1984); Collins v. Foreman, 729 F.2d 108 (2d Cir.), cert. denied, 469 U.S. 870 (1984); Wharton-Thomas v. United States, 721 F.2d 922 (3d Cir. 1983).

III "control over specific cases by the resumption of district court jurisdiction on the court's own initiative":

> "The power to cancel a reference, taken together with the retention by article III judges of the power to designate magistrate positions and to select and remove individual magistrates, provides article III courts with continuing, plenary responsibility for the administration of the judicial business of the United States. This responsibility sufficiently protects the judiciary from the encroachment of other branches to satisfy the separation of powers embodied in article III."

Three judges dissented.

6. 1983 Amendments to Rule 53. Finally, note that Rule 53 of the Federal Rules of Civil Procedure was amended in 1983 to take account of developing practices with respect to magistrates. Specifically, Rule 53(b) was changed to say that a magistrate could be appointed to serve as a special master "upon the consent of the parties" without reference to the earlier limitation to "exceptional circumstances." Additionally, a new subsection was added to make clear that the restrictions imposed by Rule 53 apply only to appointments made under that rule and do not purport to limit the statutory scheme covering the responsibilities of magistrates.

7. Bibliography. In addition to the many recent articles already cited, see, for an influential early treatment of this subject, Katz, Federal Legislative Courts, 43 Harv. L. Rev. 894 (1930). Also of interest is Kurland, The Constitution and the Tenure of Federal Judges: Some Notes from History, 36 U. Chi. L. Rev. 665 (1969).

On the related issue of judicial discipline as a possible threat to judicial independence, see Kaufman, Chilling Judicial Independence, 88 Yale L.J. 680 (1979); Kaufman, The Essence of Judicial Independence, 80 Colum. L. Rev. 671 (1980); and the review of recent legislation authorizing the judicial councils to deal with complaints of judicial misconduct or disability in Burbank, Procedural Rulemaking under the Judicial Councils Reform and Judicial Conduct and Disability Act of 1980, 131 U. Pa. L. Rev. 283 (1982).

For an entertaining romp through the cases bearing on the constitutionality of U.S. Magistrates, see Ralph U. Whitten, Consent, Caseload, and Other Justifications for Non-article III Courts and Judges: A Comment on *Commodities Futures Trading Commission v. Schor*, 20 Creighton L.Rev. 11 (1986).

Chapter II

CONSTITUTIONAL LIMITS ON CONGRESSIONAL ALLOCATION OF JURISDICTION

SECTION 1: CONGRESSIONAL LIMITATION OF THE JURISDICTION OF THE FEDERAL COURTS

INTRODUCTORY NOTES ON THE SOURCES OF FEDERAL COURT JURISDICTION

1. The Constitutional Text. Article III of the Constitution provides in relevant part:

"SECTION 1. The judicial Power of the United States, shall be vested in <u>one</u> supreme Court, and in such inferior Courts as the Congress may from time to time ordain and establish. The Judges, both of the supreme and inferior Courts, shall hold their Offices during good Behavior, and shall, at stated Times, receive for their Services, a Compensation, which shall not be diminished during their continuance in Office.

"SECTION 2. The judicial Power shall extend to all Cases, in Law and Equity, arising under this Constitution, the Laws of the United States, and Treaties made, or which shall be made, under their Authority;—to all Cases affecting Ambassadors, other Public Ministers and Consuls;—to all cases of admiralty and maritime Jurisdiction;—to Controversies to which the United States shall be a Party;—to Controversies between two or more States;—between a State and Citizens of another State;—between Citizens of different States;—between Citizens of the same State claiming Lands under Grants of different States, and between a State, or the Citizens thereof, and foreign States, Citizens or Subjects.

"In all Cases affecting Ambassadors, other public Ministers and Consuls, and those in which a State shall be a Party, the supreme Court shall have original Jurisdiction. In all the other Cases before mentioned, the supreme Court shall have appellate Jurisdiction, both as to Law and Fact, with such Exceptions, and under such Regulations as the Congress shall make."

Article I, § 8, cl. 9 also gives Congress the power "To constitute Tribunals inferior to the supreme Court."

2. Analysis of the Constitutional Text. The constitutional text can usefully be examined from at least three perspectives.

(i) **The Supreme Court.** Section 1 of art. III vests the "judicial Power of the United States" in one supreme court. Section 2 then seems to confer jurisdiction on the Supreme Court over the entire range of subjects to which the judicial power extends. It proceeds in two steps: first, by describing the scope of the judicial power; and second, by saying that the Supreme Court "shall have original Jurisdiction" over certain subjects and "shall have appellate Jurisdiction" over all the rest.

Note, however, that the appellate jurisdiction is conferred "with such Exceptions, and under such Regulations as the Congress shall make." One of the questions considered in the materials that follow is whether the power of Congress to make exceptions to the appellate jurisdiction of the Supreme Court is plenary or whether it is limited by art. III itself, by other provisions of the Constitution, or by inferences drawn from the constitutional structure.

Argument over this question must take into account the fact that the Supreme Court has never had authority over the entire range of subjects to which the judicial power extends. For example, it does not today review, and never has reviewed, diversity cases coming from state courts. Moreover, the First Judiciary Act[a] limited Supreme Court review of cases coming from state courts to instances in which a federal question was decided *against* the federal claimant. The decision by a state court of a federal question *in favor of* the federal claimant was not then (though it is now) subject to review in the Supreme Court.

(ii) **The Lower Federal Courts.** The power of Congress to create lower federal courts is stated in art. I, § 8, cl. 9 and in the first sentence of art. III, § 1. The Constitution is not explicit, however, as to the scope of the jurisdiction to be exercised by courts created under this power. It could be argued from the text that the entire judicial power is vested by the Constitution itself in all lower federal courts. The document says that the power "shall be vested" in such lower courts as Congress may create. And nowhere does it say explicitly, as it does in the case of the Supreme Court, that Congress has the power to make exceptions to the jurisdiction conferred on lower courts.

From the beginning, however, the Supreme Court has never taken the above argument seriously. No lower federal court has ever possessed jurisdiction over the entire range of subjects to which the "judicial Power" could constitutionally extend. The First Judiciary Act, for example, created lower federal trial courts with the power to hear diversity cases, but only if a jurisdictional amount was satisfied. That statute gave *no* federal trial court the power to hear cases arising generally under federal law. What is today known as the general

---

[a] The First Judiciary Act was adopted in 1789. Its provisions and its contemporary significance are summarized in Appendix C, infra.

federal question statute (28 U.S.C. § 1331) was first enacted in 1875. And it too contained a jurisdictional amount until 1980, a tradition that has been continued to this day in the general diversity statute (28 U.S.C. § 1332).

If Congress need not confer the entire judicial power on every lower federal court it creates, does this mean that there are no limits on Congressional control over the jurisdiction of the lower federal courts? The materials below address this question.

(iii) **The Federal Court System.** It can also be argued from the text of art. III that Congress is obligated to create a system to which the entire federal judicial power is distributed. That is, there must be at least one federal court—either the Supreme Court or some lower federal court—to which any litigant whose case falls within the judicial power as enumerated in art. III may go. It should be noted, however— as the illustrations given above suggest—that at no time in the history of the country has every case to which the federal judicial power extends been conferred on at least one court in the federal system. If one assumes that the present system is constitutional, the challenge is to determine whether Congress' power over the jurisdiction of the federal courts is unlimited, or if not, where the limits come from and to what kinds of cases they apply.

INTRODUCTORY NOTES ON CONGRESSIONAL LIMITATION OF THE JURISDICTION OF STATE AND FEDERAL COURTS

1. **Unfavorable Congressional Reaction to Supreme Court Decisions.** Politically unpopular Supreme Court decisions have often been met in the Congress by the proposal of legislation to make an "exception" from the Supreme Court's appellate jurisdiction. Such laws were first proposed in the 1820's in reaction to decisions by the Marshall Court.[a] In the late 1950's, bills were introduced to curb the Court's jurisdiction over contempt proceedings against congressional witnesses, dismissal of government employees for national security reasons, state subversive activities legislation, and state bar admission requirements.[b] Decisions by the Warren Court in the areas of reapportionment, criminal procedure, and school desegregation prompted similar proposals.[c] And decisions on school prayer, abortion, and school busing led to a series of new proposals in the early 1980's.[d]

[a] See Gunther, Congressional Power to Curtail Federal Court Jurisdiction: An Opinionated Guide to the Ongoing Debate, 36 Stan. L. Rev. 895, 896–97 & n.5 (1984). See also Nagel, Court-Curbing Periods in American History, 18 Vand. L. Rev. 925 (1965).

[b] See Ratner, Congressional Power over the Appellate Jurisdiction of the Supreme Court, 109 U. Pa. L. Rev. 157, 159 (1960).

[c] See G. Gunther, Constitutional Law: Cases and Materials 58–59 (9th ed. 1975).

[d] In the article cited in note a, supra, Professor Gunther reports that 30 such bills were proposed in 1981 and 1982 alone.

None of these proposals has been adopted. As a consequence, the modern Supreme Court has never been called upon to confront the constitutionality of an effort by Congress to deny it jurisdiction to hear cases involving newly established constitutional rights. There is, however, an enormous body of academic literature on the subject, literature that has reached such a state of repetitiveness as to lead one scholar to describe it as "choking on redundancy."[e] Given the rarity of Supreme Court consideration of the constitutionality of such legislation and the voluminous academic literature, most discussion of the issues presented begins and ends with arguments about the various theories advanced in the literature for limiting (or not limiting) Congress' power.

2. *Marbury v. Madison*. All commentators accept the proposition that the power to control jurisdiction does not include the power to dictate unconstitutional outcomes in cases that are to be decided. It is one thing for a court not to decide a case at all; it is quite another for it to decide a case but be required to render a result that is inconsistent with the Constitution. For example, Congress might have the power to exclude all state criminal cases from Supreme Court review. But Congress clearly would not have the power to withhold jurisdiction to decide all due process issues in state criminal cases which the Court otherwise will decide on the merits.

This proposition is thought to follow from even the most limited view of *Marbury v. Madison*. Whatever one thinks that case stands for, it at least supports the conclusion that the courts cannot decide cases inconsistently with constitutional limitations. *Marbury* may or may not say anything about what kinds of cases courts should resolve, and it may or may not address their ultimate role in the constitutional plan. What it plainly does say is that courts are not free to ignore applicable constitutional limitations in rendering decisions on the merits of cases that come before them.

One context in which it is helpful to think about the meaning of this limitation is the provision of remedies for the violation of constitutional rights. Consider, for example, a statute that permitted federal courts to decide school desegregation cases but that denied them jurisdiction to compel busing as a remedy. Would such a statute be constitutional? How about a statute that provided for liquidated damages for unconstitutional searches and seizures by state officials, that permitted the continued review of state criminal cases, but that denied the Supreme Court jurisdiction to reverse because of *Mapp v. Ohio*?

---

[e] The comment was made by William Van Alstyne in a letter to Gerald Gunther. See Gunther, Congressional Power to Curtail Federal Court Jurisdiction: An Opinionated Guide to the Ongoing Debate, 36 Stan. L. Rev. 895, 897 n.9 (1984). There also have been extensive legislative hearings on the issues raised by such proposals. Citations are collected at page 895 n.2 of the Gunther article. For comprehensive citations to the literature, see Clinton, A Mandatory View of Federal Court Jurisdiction: A Guided Quest for the Original Understanding of Article III, 132 U.Pa.L.Rev. 741, 742–46 nn. 3–10 (1984), and Clinton, A Mandatory View of Federal Court Jurisdiction: Early Implementation of and Departures from the Constitutional Plan, 86 Colum.L.Rev. 1515, 1519–20 n.10 (1986).

Or how about a statute that permitted Supreme Court review of state criminal cases but denied jurisdiction if *Miranda* issues were raised?

3. A Problem in the Context of Abortion. The questions for resolution in the remainder of this section are whether there are limits on the power of Congress to control the jurisdiction of the federal courts and, if so, where they come from and what their content should be. It is helpful to think about this problem in a specific context.

Assume a client who has a clear constitutional right to an abortion under Roe v. Wade, 410 U.S. 113 (1973), and its progeny. Assume further that Congress has passed a statute that denies to all courts—the Supreme Court, the lower federal courts, and the state courts—the power to decide any constitutional claim founded upon the right recognized in *Roe.* Assume finally that the state in which the client lives has passed a statute making abortions criminal in the circumstances faced by the client. If the client came to a lawyer seeking advice on her legal rights before obtaining an abortion, what advice should be given? The next two notes are specifically addressed to this problem.

4. Congressional Power to Limit the Jurisdiction of State Courts. All states have trial courts of general jurisdiction and at least one court with statewide jurisdiction to hear appeals from such courts. This jurisdiction is fixed by state constitutional and statutory provisions. To what extent does Congress have the authority to provide that a particular case cannot be heard in state courts?

The answer is that Congress has considerable authority in this regard. It is provided in 28 U.S.C. § 1338 that the jurisdiction of federal courts to hear patent and copyright cases "shall be exclusive of the courts of the states." It is also provided in 28 U.S.C. § 1446(e) that once a civil case has been removed from a state court to a federal district court "the State court shall proceed no further unless and until the case is remanded." Numerous other examples could be given, and today the constitutionality of such provisions is clear.

Do these examples mean that Congress could deprive the state courts of jurisdiction to hear the abortion issue in the problem posed above? What advice about the possibility of asserting the client's constitutional right to an abortion in state court should the lawyer give?

5. The Traditional View of Congressional Power to Limit the Jurisdiction of the Federal Courts. Assume that the state courts have heard the client's abortion claim on the merits, but have decided the case in direct contravention to the decision in *Roe v. Wade.* Could the Supreme Court reverse if Congress had specifically removed its jurisdiction to review such a case?

Many respected commentators—enough so that this view can be labeled the traditional view—take the position that the exceptions clause in art. III means exactly what it says. Congress has the power to make exceptions to the jurisdiction of the Supreme Court over any category of cases, constitutional or otherwise. Most of these commentators conclude that the wisdom of using this power to exclude categories of constitutional cases from the Court's docket is quite another matter and oppose its use for this purpose as a matter of policy. But they do not doubt that the power is there if Congress wants to use it.

Those who take this position believe, essentially, that Congress has plenary power over the appellate jurisdiction of the Supreme Court (as well as the jurisdiction of the lower federal courts) as part of the checks and balances built into the constitutional framework. They believe, however, that the supremacy clause forbids Congress from depriving the state courts of jurisdiction to decide constitutional questions that come before them in the ordinary course of litigation. Thus, in spite of the modern mindset that looks to federal courts as the primary source of federal constitutional decisions, under this view state courts may become the ultimate protectors of federal constitutional values.

Representative of this position are the following comments in Wechsler, The Courts and the Constitution, 65 Colum. L. Rev. 1001, 1005–06 (1965): *

> "There is, to be sure, a school of thought that argues that 'exceptions' has a narrow meaning, not including cases that have constitutional dimension; or that the supremacy clause or the due process clause of the fifth amendment would be violated by an alteration of the jurisdiction motivated by hostility to the decisions of the Court. I see no basis for this view and think it antithetical to the plan of the Constitution for the courts—which was quite simply that the Congress would decide from time to time how far the federal judicial institution should be used within the limits of the federal judicial power; or, stated differently, how far judicial jurisdiction should be left to the state courts, bound as they are by the Constitution as 'the supreme Law of the Land . . . any Thing in the Constitution or Laws of any State to the Contrary notwithstanding.' Federal courts, including the Supreme Court, do not pass on constitutional questions because there is a special function vested in them to enforce the Constitution or police the other agencies of the government. They do so rather for the reason that they must decide a litigated issue that is otherwise within their jurisdiction and in doing so must give effect to the supreme law of the land. That is, at least, what *Marbury v. Madison* was all about. I have not heard that it has yet been superseded, though I confess I read opinions on occasion that do not exactly make its doctrine clear."

Compare the conclusion of Professor Hart's famous dialogue, first published in Hart, The Power of Congress to Limit the Jurisdiction of Federal Courts: An Exercise in Dialectic, 66 Harv. L. Rev. 1362 (1953). In response to the objection that Congress might leave constitutional rights without a remedy, the answer was:

"A. The state courts. In the scheme of the Constitution, they are the primary guarantors of constitutional rights, and in many cases they may be the ultimate ones. If they were to fail, and if Congress had taken away the Supreme Court's appellate jurisdiction and been upheld in doing so, then we really would be sunk.

"Q. But Congress can regulate the jurisdiction of state courts, too, in federal matters.

"A. Congress can't do it unconstitutionally. The state courts always have a general jurisdiction to fall back on. And the supremacy clause binds them to exercise that jurisdiction in accordance with the Constitution.

"Q. But the Supreme Court could reverse their decisions.

"A. Not lawfully, if the decisions were in accordance with the Constitution. Congress can't shut the Supreme Court off from the merits and give it jurisdiction simply to reverse. Not, anyway, if I'm right . . . that jurisdiction always is jurisdiction only to decide constitutionally."[f]

Is this view persuasive? What consequences would it have for the meaning of constitutional rights? For the uniformity of their enforcement? How could state courts be expected to react if the continuing vitality of *Roe v. Wade* or some other controversial constitutional decision were left to them to resolve? One objection frequently made to the traditional view is that Congress would be given the power to amend the Constitution without following the prescribed procedures.[g] Is the objection well taken?

It is frequently noted in the literature that one reason Congress has not enacted jurisdiction-stripping legislation is that it needs the federal courts to carry out its programs. Consider, for example, the

[f] Hart's Dialogue is perhaps the most famous entry in the literature concerning the powers of Congress over the federal court system. It is well worth reading in full.

For other articles that also take essentially the position described above, see Gunther, Congressional Power to Curtail Federal Court Jurisdiction: An Opinionated Guide to the Ongoing Debate, 36 Stan. L. Rev. 895 (1984); Rossum, Congress, the Constitution, and the Appellate Jurisdiction of the Supreme Court: The Letter and Spirit of the Exceptions Clause, 24 W. & M. L. Rev. 385 (1983); Bator, Congressional Power Over the Jurisdiction of the Federal Courts, 27 Vill. L. Rev. 1030 (1982); Redish, Congressional Power to Regulate Supreme Court Appellate Jurisdiction Under the Exceptions Clause: An Internal and External Examination, 27 Vill. L. Rev. 900 (1982); Van Alstyne, A Critical Guide to Ex Parte McCardle, 15 Ariz. L. Rev. 229 (1973).

There is also support in the literature for the proposition that judicial review of the constitutionality of legislation is justifiable *because* Congress has ultimate control through the power to make exceptions to the jurisdiction of the courts. See, e.g., M. Perry, The Constitution, The Courts, and Human Rights 125–39 (1982). Perry rejects congressional control over "interpretevist" decisions, i.e, decisions "enforcing value judgments constitutionalized by the framers." But he justifies judicial review in modern human rights cases—cases where the value judgments expressed by the courts cannot be found in the intent of the framers—on the premise that the democratic process ultimately can prevail through the exercise of control over jurisdiction.

[g] See, e.g., Mickenberg, Abusing the Exceptions and Regulations Clause: Legislative Attempts to Divest the Supreme Court of Appellate Jurisdiction, 32 Am. U. L. Rev. 497 (1983).

following comments in Sager, What is a Nice Court Like You Doing in a Democracy Like This?, 36 Stan. L. Rev. 1087, 1102 (1984):

> "Suppose, for example, that the New Deal Congress had deprived the federal judiciary of jurisdiction over constitutional challenges to economic recovery legislation. The result would have been a disaster from any standpoint. The courts of the 48 states would then have been solely responsible for construing that legislation and determining its constitutional validity. The constitutional doctrines that had plagued the recovery effort before 1937 certainly would have played a significant part in some state adjudications. To the disruption of these *Lochner* progeny, there would have been added the chaos of radical nonuniformity. It is hard to imagine a more certain road to the collapse of the economic recovery program. Had the Roosevelt administration been foolhardy enough to travel this road, the result would have been a vivid illustration of two major problems with the regulation of jurisdiction as a means of surmounting federal judicial doctrine. First, federal legislation generally depends on federal judicial implementation for its effectiveness. Second, a congressional denial of jurisdiction necessarily exposes those programs to the critical review of state courts."

As apt as these comments might be for the context in which they were made, would similar constraints be operative in the abortion example discussed above? Does the answer to this question suggest a greater need for constitutionally required supervision in federal courts of the validity of state laws than for similar supervision of federal laws?

6. Concluding Comments. The traditional view described above is not necessarily the correct resolution of the questions raised. It may be that the hypothetical client not only has a constitutional right to an abortion but also has a constitutional right to assert that claim in the Supreme Court or in a lower federal court. The notes above are designed merely to introduce the problem. They do not purport to resolve it. The remaining materials in this section consider whether a contrary conclusion can or should be derived from cases decided by the Supreme Court or from different assumptions about the nature of our constitutional system.

SUBSECTION A: APPELLATE JURISDICTION OF THE SUPREME COURT

EX PARTE McCARDLE

United States Supreme Court, 1868.
74 U.S. (7 Wall.) 506.

[McCardle was editor of the Vicksburg Times. He was arrested by U.S. Army officials under the Military Reconstruction Act of 1867, a major piece of Reconstruction legislation establishing military jurisdiction over much of the South following the Civil War. He was charged with disturbance of the peace, inciting to insurrection, libel, and impeding reconstruction[a] for writing and publishing inflammatory editorials. He sought his release by bringing an action for habeas corpus in the federal Circuit Court for the Southern District of Mississippi. The Circuit Court dismissed the writ and remanded McCardle to military custody. He was then released on bail subject to the disposition of an appeal of that decision to the Supreme Court. His appeal raised a number of contentions, among them a frontal attack on the constitutionality of the Military Reconstruction Act itself.[b] The government moved to dismiss the appeal, but after argument and opinion the Court upheld its jurisdiction. Ex parte McCardle, 73 U.S. (6 Wall.) 318 (1868). The case was then argued on the merits, after which the statute authorizing the appeal was repealed by Congress. The opinion reproduced below is the Court's reaction to the repealing statute.

[Consideration of the opinion, however, requires an understanding of its procedural background. The First Judiciary Act authorized federal trial courts to issue writs of habeas corpus, but only for persons in *federal* custody. There was no provision specifically authorizing appeals from lower federal courts in habeas actions, but appeals to the Supreme Court were generally available in civil cases (habeas corpus has always been regarded as a "civil" case) if a jurisdictional amount of $2000 was satisfied. Because the jurisdictional amount limitation appeared to be a bar to appellate review of habeas actions, the Court, which itself was authorized to issue writs of habeas corpus, developed the practice of issuing "original" writs of habeas corpus to review the work of lower federal courts in this area. The practice was reconciled with the limitations of art. III by the rationalization that since the work of a lower court was being reviewed, the issuance of an "original" writ

---

[a] See Ex parte McCardle, 73 U.S. (6 Wall.) 318, 320 (1868).

[b] His major argument in this respect was that the trial of civilians by court martial was unconstitutional given the fact that the civil courts were then functioning. See Van Alstyne, A Critical Guide to Ex parte McCardle, 15 Ariz. L. Rev. 229, 238 n.46 (1973), which quotes a letter written by Chief Justice Chase to the effect that "had the merits of the *McCardle* case been decided the Court would doubtless have held that this imprisonment for trial before a military commission was illegal." Professor Van Alstyne's article contains an elaborate discussion of the historical context of the *McCardle* decision, as well as a thorough treatment of the Court's opinion. It is well worth reading.

was nonetheless an exercise of "appellate" jurisdiction. The common law writ of certiorari was often used in this procedure, and it too, being a writ used by appellate courts to call up the record from the court below, gave an "appellate" flavor to the proceedings.

[In February of 1867, Congress expanded the writ of habeas corpus to encompass persons in the custody of *state* officials. It also specifically authorized appeals to the Supreme Court in habeas cases. The argument in the first *McCardle* decision was that McCardle's case was not appealable under this provision, in part because the new statute was limited by its context to appeals from decisions concerning detentions by *state* officials. The Court rejected the argument, holding that the 1867 statute authorizing appeals in habeas cases applied generally to any habeas decision by the lower courts. Thus, McCardle's case was properly before the Court on appeal.

[As noted above, the case was then argued on the merits. Three days after the argument, Congress repealed that part of the 1867 statute authorizing appeals in habeas cases. Two weeks later, President Johnson (who then was facing impeachment proceedings) vetoed the repealing statute, but the veto was overridden two days later (in March of 1868). Argument on the effect of the repealing statute was postponed in the Supreme Court while the Chief Justice presided over the impeachment proceedings, but a year later the Court, after further argument, delivered the following opinion.]

The CHIEF JUSTICE delivered the opinion of the Court.

The first question necessarily is that of jurisdiction; for, if the act of March, 1868, takes away the jurisdiction defined by the act of February, 1867, it is useless, if not improper, to enter into any discussion of other questions.

It is quite true, as was argued by the counsel for the petitioner, that the appellate jurisdiction of this Court is not derived from acts of Congress. It is, strictly speaking, conferred by the Constitution. But it is conferred "with such exceptions and under such regulations as Congress shall make."

It is unnecessary to consider whether, if Congress had made no exceptions and no regulations, this Court might not have exercised general appellate jurisdiction under rules prescribed by itself. For among the earliest acts of the first Congress, at its first session, was the act of September 24th, 1789, to establish the judicial courts of the United States. That act provided for the organization of this Court, and prescribed regulations for the exercise of its jurisdiction.

The source of that jurisdiction, and the limitations of it by the Constitution and by statute, have been on several occasions subjects of consideration here. In the case of Durousseau v. United States, 10 U.S. (6 Cranch) 307 (1810), particularly, the whole matter was carefully examined, and the Court held, that while "the appellate powers of this Court are not given by the judicial act, but are given by the Constitution," they are, nevertheless, "limited and regulated by that act, and by such other acts as have been passed on the subject." The court said, further, that the judicial act was an exercise of the power given by the Constitution to Congress "of making exceptions to the appellate jurisdiction of the Supreme Court." "They have described affirmatively," said the Court, "its jurisdiction, and this affirmative description has been understood to imply a negation of the exercise of such appellate power as is not comprehended within it."

The principle that the affirmation of appellate jurisdiction implies the negation of all such jurisdiction not affirmed having been thus established, it was an almost necessary consequence that acts of Congress, providing for the exercise of jurisdiction, should come to be spoken of as acts granting jurisdiction, and not as acts making exceptions to the constitutional grant of it.

The exception to appellate jurisdiction in the case before us, however, is not an inference from the affirmation of other appellate jurisdiction. It is made in terms. The provision of the act of 1867, affirming the appellate jurisdiction of this Court in cases of habeas corpus is expressly repealed. It is hardly possible to imagine a plainer instance of positive exception.

We are not at liberty to inquire into the motives of the legislature. We can only examine into its power under the Constitution; and the power to make exceptions to the appellate jurisdiction of this Court is given by express words.

What, then, is the effect of the repealing act upon the case before us? We cannot doubt as to this. Without jurisdiction the Court cannot proceed at all in any cause. Jurisdiction is power to declare the law, and when it ceases to exist, the only function remaining to the Court is that of announcing the fact and dismissing the cause. And this is not less clear upon authority than upon principle.

Several [state] cases were cited by the counsel for the petitioner in support of the position that jurisdiction of this case is not affected by the repealing act. But none of them, in our judgment, [affords] any support to it. They are all cases of the exercise of judicial power by the legislature, or of legislative interference with courts in the exercising of continuing jurisdiction.

On the other hand, the general rule, supported by the best elementary writers, is, that "when an act of the legislature is repealed, it must be considered, except as to transactions past and closed, as if it never existed." And the effect of repealing acts upon suits under acts repealed, has been determined by the adjudications of this Court. The subject was fully considered in [two decisions, both of which] held that no judgment could be rendered in a suit after the repeal of the act under which it was brought and prosecuted.

It is quite clear, therefore, that this Court cannot proceed to pronounce judgment in this case, for it has no longer jurisdiction of the appeal; and judicial duty is not less fitly performed by declining ungranted jurisdiction than in exercising firmly that which the Constitution and the laws confer.

Counsel seem to have supposed, if effect be given to the repealing act in question, that the whole appellate power of the Court, in cases of habeas corpus, is denied. But this is an error. The act of 1868 does not except from that jurisdiction any cases but appeals from Circuit Courts under the act of 1867. It does not affect the jurisdiction which was previously exercised.*

The appeal of the petitioner in this case must be dismissed for want of jurisdiction.

NOTES ON CONGRESSIONAL POWER TO LIMIT THE APPELLATE JURISDICTION OF THE SUPREME COURT

1. **The Source of Supreme Court Jurisdiction.** The description of the source of Supreme Court jurisdiction contained at the beginning of the *McCardle* opinion is now generally accepted. As the opinion states, the Constitution itself appears to confer appellate jurisdiction on the Supreme Court in all of the cases and controversies listed in art. III over which the Court does not have original jurisdiction. But Congress is now taken to have "excepted" from the Court's jurisdiction all cases that do not fall within an affirmative statutory grant. Thus if one wants to take a case to the Supreme Court, one must assert jurisdiction grounded in a specific act of Congress. It is not sufficient simply to rely on the constitutional text.

In view of this structure, one might ask why the scope of the congressional power to make exceptions to the jurisdiction of the Court has not been more frequently litigated. After all, Congress has never authorized the Court to hear all of the cases that fall within art. III. Part of the reason, undoubtedly, is that the Court has not felt institutional pressure to decide most of the questions that have been excluded. For example, the Court has never had authority to review questions of state law decided by state supreme courts in cases where diversity of citizenship existed between the parties. But there is little reason why the Court would want to decide such questions, and there are good arguments that it would be unconstitutional for it even to try. Moreover, in cases where the Court has felt an obligation to act, it has sometimes been inventive in finding a way around statutory limitations. A good example, illustrated in the *McCardle* litigation, is the development of "original" habeas corpus as a mechanism for appellate review in early federal habeas corpus cases. Today, in any event, any federal question litigated in the state courts can get to the Supreme

* Ex parte McCardle, 73 U.S. (6 Wall.) 318, 324 (1868). [The Court's reference is to that part of the first *McCardle* holding which discusses the former practice of reviewing lower federal court habeas decisions by issuing original writs of habeas corpus, supplemented by common law writs of certiorari. Indeed, in Ex parte Yerger, 75 U.S. (8 Wall.) 85 (1869), decided after *McCardle*, the Court upheld its jurisdiction to review habeas corpus decisions by the lower federal courts, holding that the repealing statute had no affect on this alternative form of appellate review. *Yerger* was also a challenge to the Military Reconstruction Act by an arrested newspaper editor, but the merits were again left unresolved because the military released Yerger before the Court reached a decision.—Addition to footnote by eds.]

Court by at least one mechanism of review, as can any question litigated in a lower federal court. The issue could arise, therefore, only if Congress were to make a specific exclusion from the prevailing statutory pattern.

2. The Significance of *McCardle*. On its face, the *McCardle* opinion seems to affirm a broad power in the Congress to make exceptions to the appellate jurisdiction of the Supreme Court. Yet *McCardle* can be read more narrowly.

The Court was not anxious to hear the case. The Reconstruction legislation at stake was central to congressional planning for the South following the Civil War, and the case arose in an atmosphere of great political sensitivity. The legislation had been passed over a presidential veto, and the President himself was facing impeachment. For the Court to have declared the legislation unconstitutional would have invited a major institutional confrontation between the Court and Congress at a time when the country was just beginning to emerge from the most unsettling period in its history.

The Court had, in fact, avoided decision on the constitutionality of Reconstruction legislation in two prior cases, Mississippi v. Johnson, 71 U.S. (4 Wall.) 475 (1867), and Georgia v. Stanton, 73 U.S. (6 Wall.) 50 (1868), and was to do so again in Ex parte Yerger, 75 U.S. (8 Wall.) 85 (1869). There thus may have been some appeal to the idea of not resolving the merits, so long as a ground for decision could be found that would not do institutional damage to the Court. And the Court was well aware, as William Van Alstyne has pointed out,[a] that no serious unfairness was being done to McCardle in the meantime. He was free on bail and had gone back to publishing his critical editorials.

These factors may help to explain the significance of the last full paragraph of the Court's opinion. This paragraph suggests that the Court knew perfectly well that it was not giving up much. The act of 1868 cut off only one of two possible ways of getting a case such as McCardle's before the Supreme Court, leaving the other one intact. Thus, one could argue that the Court ducked a sensitive constitutional problem at a propitious time, preserved its authority to adjudicate similar cases, and muted the effect of the repealing statute by limiting the decision to approval of the undoubted authority of Congress to foreclose one of two possible avenues of review.

Note that if such a view of *McCardle* is accepted, the case neither supports nor refutes the traditional view of Congress' power described at pages 163–66, supra. But if the last paragraph of the opinion is not given special significance and the rest of *McCardle* means what it says, the case provides direct Supreme Court authority in support of the traditional view.

[a] See Van Alstyne, A Critical Guide to Ex Parte McCardle, 15 Ariz. L. Rev. 229, 248 (1973). Van Alstyne also points out that the Court itself was under attack in the Congress at the time. The Court had been reduced from 10 to seven members two years before, and a bill had recently passed the House to require an extraordinary majority to invalidate an act of Congress.

3. Limiting Theories. As noted above, the academic literature contains extensive discussion of the scope of the power of Congress to make exceptions to Supreme Court jurisdiction. In addition to the traditional view, there are two major theories that enjoy current support.[b]

(i) **The Essential Functions Thesis.** Professor Hart cryptically suggested at the beginning of his dialogue[c] that "exceptions" presuppose a rule, and cannot be so broad as to engulf the rule itself. The result, he suggested, is that "the exceptions must not be such as will destroy the essential role of the Supreme Court in the constitutional plan." He did not elaborate, but others have.

The best known proponent of what has come to be known as the "essential functions thesis" is Leonard Ratner, who has set forth his views in two major articles.[d] In the more recent, he stated the essential functions of the Supreme Court as:

> "(i) ultimately to resolve inconsistent or conflicting interpretations of federal law, and particularly of the Constitution, by state and federal courts; (ii) to maintain the supremacy of federal law, and particularly the Constitution, when it conflicts with state law or is challenged by state authority. Interpreted in this context, the exceptions and regulations clause means, as Henry Hart first suggested: with such exceptions and under such regulations as Congress may make, not inconsistent with the essential functions of the Supreme Court under the Constitution."

Ratner conceded that this does not mean that a Supreme Court decision is needed in every case that presents a constitutional question. "But an avenue must remain open," he argued, "to permit ultimate resolution by the Supreme Court of persistent conflicts between the Constitution and state law or in the interpretation of federal law by lower courts."

In his earlier article, Ratner defended his thesis by relying on inferences from the constitutional debates and from early Supreme Court decisions. He also suggested that the term "exception" meant to the framers "that in a legal context an exception cannot destroy the

[b] Other theories have been advanced from time to time. Several commentators have argued, for example, that historical evidence supports the view that the "exceptions" clause modifies the word "Fact" rather than the words "appellate jurisdiction." E.g., R. Berger, Congress v. The Supreme Court 285–96 (1969); Brant, Appellate Jurisdiction: Congressional Abuse of the Exceptions Clause, 53 Ore. L. Rev. 3 (1973); Merry, Scope of the Supreme Court's Appellate Jurisdiction: Historical Basis, 47 Minn. L. Rev. 53 (1962). Thus, the argument goes, Congress may regulate the manner in which the Court reviews questions of fact, or may make exceptions from its power to review questions of fact, but may not exclude questions of law from its appellate jurisdiction. Recent commentary uniformly rejects this view. See, e.g., Gunther, Congressional Power to Curtail Federal Court Jurisdiction: An Opinionated Guide to the Ongoing Debate, 36 Stan. L. Rev. 895, 901 (1984).

[c] See page 164, supra.

[d] See Ratner, Majoritarian Constraints on Judicial Review: Congressional Control of Supreme Court Jurisdiction, 27 Vill. L. Rev. 929 (1982); Ratner, Congressional Power Over the Appellate Jurisdiction of the Supreme Court, 109 U. Pa. L. Rev. 157 (1960).

essential characteristics of the subject to which it applies" and the term "regulation" meant that "authority to prescribe [regulations] does not ordinarily include the power to prohibit the entire sphere of activity that is subject to regulation." He also extensively analyzed the early jurisdictional structure under which the Court operated and concluded that, "[d]espite some impediments in early statutes, the Supreme Court from its inception has performed the essential constitutional functions of maintaining the uniformity and supremacy of federal law."

Support for a version of this thesis is presented by Lawrence Sager in Forward: Constitutional Limitations on Congress' Authority to Regulate the Jurisdiction of the Federal Courts, 95 Harv. L. Rev. 17 (1981). Sager relied on "the firm commitment to federal judicial supervision of the states reflected in the history and logic of the Constitution" to defend the "argument that supervision of state conduct to ensure general compliance with the Constitution is an essential function of the Supreme Court . . . ."[e] He also buttressed his argument by reliance on the art. III tenure and salary provisions. Congress does not have unlimited authority, he argued, to allow cases within the federal judicial power to be decided by judges who do not have this art. III protection. Since state judges are not so protected, Congress may not rely exclusively on state courts to decide such cases. This does not mean, he continued, that no art. III cases may be assigned to state courts. Diversity cases, for example, could surely be excluded from all federal courts. But "there must be limits," he concluded, and "those limits are surely crossed when Congress attempts to divest the Supreme Court, and all other federal courts, of jurisdiction at least to review state court decisions on constitutional challenges to governmental behavior."[f]

Those who hold the traditional view have not been kind to the essential functions thesis. Martin Redish calls it "constitutional wishful thinking,"[g] and Gerald Gunther calls it "question-begging" reasoning that confuses the familiar with the necessary.[h] But is the essential functions thesis any more question-begging than the traditional view? How does one discover the premises from which to build an argument about the scope of the congressional power? Does argument about the meaning of *Marbury v. Madison* help? Is removing jurisdiction any more "unconstitutional" than controlling outcomes by packing the Court or refusing to fill vacancies?

[e] Sager modified this statement somewhat in his subsequent discussion: "The Court must be available to superintend state compliance with federal law unless Congress provides effective review elsewhere within the federal judiciary."

[f] Another variation of the essential functions thesis is presented in Forkosch, The Exceptions and Regulations Clause of Article III and A Person's Constitutional Rights: Can the Latter Be Limited by Congressional Power Under the Former?, 72 W. Va. L. Rev. 238 (1970).

[g] Redish, Congressional Power to Regulate Supreme Court Appellate Jurisdiction Under the Exceptions Clause: An Internal and External Examination, 27 Vill. L. Rev. 900, 911 (1982).

[h] Gunther, Congressional Power to Curtail Federal Court Jurisdiction: An Opinionated Guide to the Ongoing Debate, 36 Stan. L. Rev. 895, 908 (1984).

If one views the essential functions theory favorably, how are the "essential functions" of the Supreme Court discovered? Does Ratner or Sager identify the right functions? Should they have included an obligation by the Court to act as a check on the majoritarian branches of government and thereby protect minority rights? [i]

(ii) **Independent Unconstitutionality.** Most commentators accept the proposition that the congressional power to make exceptions to the Supreme Court's jurisdiction is, like all other congressional powers, subject to the specific limitations contained in other parts of the Constitution, for example, in art. I, § 9 and the Bill of Rights. Thus, it would be unconstitutional for the Congress to exclude jurisdiction over a particular litigant by name, or to exclude all cases brought by members of a disfavored race. However, there is considerable dispute over how far this limitation extends. For example, suppose the Congress excluded all blacks from litigation in the Supreme Court *and* denied the Court jurisdiction to hear all cases alleging racial discrimination. Would the second part of this law, standing alone, be unconstitutional? If not, would the two provisions together be unconstitutional?[j]

Several commentators argue that jurisdiction-stripping legislation is virtually always unconstitutional when its object is to remove a particular class of constitutional litigants from the federal courts. Particular attention in recent years has been focused on the equal protection component of the fifth amendment,[k] but the argument could be made in terms of substantive due process as well. The argument, essentially, is that congressional exclusion of particular classes of litigation from the Supreme Court's jurisdiction, identified by the nature of the constitutional claim (e.g., abortion), having an impact only on the class of litigants who would assert that claim, and motivated by congressional hostility to the underlying constitutional rights involved, should be subject to the same strict scrutiny as any other substantive regulation of that subject matter. In particular, the Court should closely examine the rationale underlying the congressional exclusion and should uphold the excision from jurisdiction only if it serves a legitimate and compelling state interest.[l] It goes without saying that dissatisfaction with the constitutional right itself would not satisfy this standard, in this context any more than any other.

[i] Cf. Redish, Congressional Power to Regulate Supreme Court Appellate Jurisdiction Under the Exceptions Clause: An Internal and External Examination, 27 Vill. L. Rev. 900, 911–12 (1982) (criticizing this position).

[j] This hypothetical was suggested by Kenneth R. Kay in a Symposium discussion reported in 27 Vill. L. Rev. 1042, 1044 (1982).

[k] See, e.g., Tribe, Jurisdictional Gerrymandering: Zoning Disfavored Rights Out of the Federal Courts, 16 Harv. C.R.-C.L. L. Rev. 129 (1981). See also Van Alstyne, A Critical Guide to Ex Parte McCardle, 15 Ariz. L. Rev. 229, 263–69 (1973).

[l] For an analysis of the necessary and proper clause as the source of limits on congressional power to control federal court jurisdiction for "illegitimate" ends, see Gressman and Gressman, Necessary and Proper Roots of Exceptions to Federal Jurisdiction, 51 Geo. Wash. L. Rev. 495 (1983).

The ultimate difficulty with this view, the critics respond, is that it too is question-begging.[m] Those who believe that the exceptions power is essentially plenary believe that dissatisfaction with Supreme Court decisions *is* a legitimate basis for the Congress to enact a jurisdictional limitation. The original constitutional plan, they argue, left it up to Congress to allocate judicial business among the state and federal courts, and if Congress chooses to leave certain named constitutional rights to state courts, that was a choice explicitly given to Congress to make.

UNITED STATES v. KLEIN

United States Supreme Court, 1872.
80 U.S. (13 Wall.) 128.

[In 1863, Congress passed one of a series of acts governing property seized by the government during the Civil War. The statute covered "captured or abandoned property" and provided specifically that:

> "[A]ny person claiming to have been the owner of any such abandoned or captured property may, at any time within two years after the suppression of the rebellion, prefer his claim to the proceeds thereof in the Court of Claims; and on proof to the satisfaction of said court of his ownership of said property, of his right to the proceeds thereof, and that he has never given any aid or comfort to the present rebellion, to receive the residue of such proceeds after the deduction of any [expenses]."

[V.F. Wilson was the owner of more than $125,000 worth of cotton that the government had seized. He had assisted the confederate cause by standing as surety on the official bonds of several army officers. In United States v. Padelford, 76 U.S. (9 Wall.) 531 (1870), such conduct was held to constitute "aid and comfort to the . . . rebellion" within the meaning of the statute. After the cotton was seized, Wilson was pardoned by the President, as a condition of which he subscribed to a loyalty oath. He kept the terms of the oath until he died in 1865. Thereafter, Klein, the administrator of his estate, filed suit in the Court of Claims seeking recovery of the proceeds of the cotton. That Court decided in Klein's favor in 1869, and the government docketed an appeal in the Supreme Court later the same year.

[The *Padelford* case came to decision before *Klein*. Padelford had been pardoned and had subscribed to the loyalty oath *before* his cotton was seized. The Court of Claims held that the pardon and the oath cured his participation in the rebellion and awarded relief. The Supreme Court affirmed on April 30, 1870. On July 12, 1870, Congress added a rider to an appropriations bill that purported to deprive the Court of jurisdiction to decide the *Klein* case. For purposes of analysis, it is useful to divide the statute into three parts. The first part provided:

---

[m] See, e.g., Gunther, Congressional Power to Curtail Federal Court Jurisdiction: An Opinionated Guide to the Ongoing Debate, 36 Stan. L. Rev. 895, 916–21 (1984).

"[N]o pardon or amnesty granted by the President . . . shall be admissible in evidence on the part of any claimant in the Court of Claims as evidence in support of any claim against the United States . . .; nor shall any such pardon . . . heretofore offered or put in evidence on behalf of any claimant . . ., be used or considered by said court, or by the appellate court on appeal . . ., in deciding upon the claim . . ., or any appeal therefrom, as any part of the proof to sustain the claim . . ., or to entitle [the claimant] to maintain his action in said Court of Claims, or on appeal therefrom; but the proof of loyalty required by the Abandoned and Captured Property Act . . . shall be made by proof of the matters required, irrespective of any executive . . . pardon . . . ."

The statute then continued:

"And in all cases where judgment shall have been heretofore rendered in the Court of Claims in favor of any claimant, on any other proof of loyalty than such is above required and provided, and which is hereby declared to have been and to be the true intent and meaning of [the Abandoned and Captured Property Act], the Supreme Court shall, on appeal, have no further jurisdiction of the cause, and shall dismiss the same for want of jurisdiction."

Finally, the statute concluded:

"[W]henever any pardon shall have heretofore been granted by the President . . . and such pardon shall have been accepted . . . without an express disclaimer of . . . guilt . . ., such pardon . . . shall be taken . . . in the said Court of Claims, and on appeal therefrom, [as] conclusive evidence that such person did take part in, and give aid and comfort to, the late rebellion . . .; and on proof of such pardon . . ., the jurisdiction of the court in the case shall cease, and the court shall forthwith dismiss the suit of such claimant."

Shortly thereafter, the government moved on the authority of this statute that *Klein* be remanded to the Court of Claims with instructions to dismiss the case for want of jurisdiction. The Court responded to this motion as follows.]

The CHIEF JUSTICE delivered the opinion of the Court.

The general question in this case is whether or not the proviso relating to suits for the proceeds of abandoned and captured property in the Court of Claims, contained in the appropriation act of July 12th, 1870, debars the defendant in error from recovering, as administrator of V.F. Wilson, deceased, the proceeds of certain cotton belonging to the decedent, which came into the possession of agents of the Treasury Department as captured or abandoned property, and the proceeds of which were paid by them according to law into the Treasury of the United States.

The answer to this question requires a consideration of the rights of property, as affected by the late civil war, in the hands of citizens engaged in hostilities against the United States. . . .

[The Court here summarized the various statutes by which property was seized by the government during the war. It then continued:]

It is thus seen that, except to property used in actual hostilities, . . . no titles were divested in the insurgent states unless in pursuance of a judgment rendered after due legal proceedings. The government recognized to the fullest extent the humane maxims of the modern law of nations, which exempt private property of non-combatant enemies from capture as booty of war. . . .

The [Abandoned and Captured Property Act] directs the officers of the Treasury Department to take into their possession and make sale of all property abandoned by its owners or captured by the national forces, and to pay its proceeds into the national treasury.

That it was not the intention of Congress that the title to these proceeds should be divested absolutely out of the original owners of the property seems clear upon a comparison of different parts of the act. . . .

[I]t is reasonable to infer that it was the purpose of Congress that the proceeds of the property . . . should go into the treasury without change of ownership. Certainly such was the intention in respect to the property of loyal men. That the same intention prevailed in regard to the property of owners who, though then hostile, might subsequently become loyal, appears probable from the circumstance that no provision is anywhere made for confiscation of it . . . .

[After elaboration of this point, the Court referred to an 1862 statute authorizing the President to extend pardons "to persons who may have participated in the existing rebellion . . . on such conditions as he may deem expedient for the public welfare." This statute was repealed in 1867, but the Court noted that this was after the war was over and "after the decision by this Court that the President's power of pardon 'is not subject to legislation'; that 'Congress can neither limit the effect of his pardon, nor exclude from its exercise any class of offenders.'" The Court continued:]

It is not important, therefore, to refer to this repealing act further than to say that it is impossible to believe, while the repealed provision was in full force, and the faith of the legislature as well as the executive was engaged to the restoration of the rights of property promised by the latter, that the proceeds of property of persons pardoned, which had been paid into the treasury, were to be withheld from them. The repeal of the section in no respect changes the national obligation, for it does not alter at all the operation of the pardon, or reduce in any degree the obligations of Congress under the Constitution to give full effect to it, if necessary, by legislation.

We conclude, therefore, that the title to the proceeds of the property which came to the possession of the government by capture or abandonment . . . was in no case divested out of the original owner. It was for the government itself to determine whether these proceeds should be restored to the owner or not. The promise of restoration of all rights of property decides that question affirmatively as to all persons who availed themselves of the proferred pardon. It was competent for the President to annex to his offer of pardon any conditions or qualifications he should see fit; but after those conditions and qualifications had been satisfied, the pardon and its connected promises took full effect. The restoration of the proceeds became the absolute right of the persons pardoned, on application within two years from the close of the war. It was, in fact promised for an equivalent. "Pardon and restoration of political rights" were "in return" for the oath and its fulfillment. To refuse it would be a breach of faith not less "cruel and astounding" than to abandon the freed people whom the executive had promised to maintain in their freedom.

What, then, was the effect of the provision of the act of 1870 upon the right of the owner of the cotton in this case? He had done certain acts which this Court has adjudged to be acts in aid of the rebellion; but he abandoned the cotton to the agent of the Treasury Department, by whom it has been sold and the proceeds paid into the Treasury of the United States; and he took, and has not violated, the amnesty oath under the President's [pardon] proclamation. Upon this case the Court of Claims pronounced him entitled to a judgment for the net proceeds in the treasury. . . .

It was urged in argument that the right to sue the government in the Court of Claims is a matter of favor; but this seems not entirely accurate. It is as much the duty of the government as of individuals to fulfil its obligations. . . . The Court of Claims is . . . constituted one of those inferior courts which Congress authorizes, and has jurisdiction of contracts between the government and the citizen, from which appeal regularly lies to this Court.

Undoubtedly the legislature has complete control over the organization and existence of that court and may confer or withhold the right of appeal from its decisions. And if this act did nothing more, it would be our duty to give it effect. If it simply denied the right of appeal in a particular class of cases, there could be no doubt that it must be regarded as an exercise of the power of Congress to make "such exceptions from the appellate jurisdiction" as should seem to it expedient.

But the language of the [statute] shows plainly that it does not intend to withhold jurisdiction except as a means to an end. Its great and controlling purpose is to deny to pardons granted by the President the effect which this Court had adjudged them to have. The [statute] declares that pardons shall not be considered by this Court on appeal. We had already decided that it was our duty to consider them and give them effect, in cases like the present, as equivalent to proof of loyalty. It provides that whenever it shall appear that any judgment of the Court of Claims shall have been founded on such pardons, without other proof of loyalty, the Supreme Court shall have no further jurisdiction of the case and shall dismiss the same for want of jurisdiction. The proviso further declares that every pardon granted to any suitor in the Court of Claims . . . shall . . . be taken as conclusive evidence in that court and on appeal [of the disloyalty of the claimant]; and on proof of pardon . . ., the jurisdiction of the court shall cease and the suit shall be forthwith dismissed.

It is evident from this statement that the denial of jurisdiction to this Court, as well as the Court of Claims, is founded solely on the application of a rule of decision, in cases pending, prescribed by Congress. The court has jurisdiction of the cause to a given point; but when it ascertains that a certain state of things exists, its jurisdiction is to cease and it is required to dismiss the cause for want of jurisdiction.

It seems to us that this is not an exercise of the acknowledged power of Congress to make exceptions and prescribe regulations to the appellate power.

The court is required to ascertain the existence of certain facts and thereupon to declare that its jurisdiction on appeal has ceased, by dismissing the bill. What is this but to prescribe a rule for the decision of a cause in a particular way? In the case before us, the Court of Claims has rendered judgment for the claimant and an appeal has been taken to this Court. We are directed to dismiss the appeal, if we find that the judgment must be affirmed, because of a pardon granted to the intestate of the claimants. Can we do so without allowing one party to the controversy to decide it in its own favor? Can we do so without allowing that the legislature may prescribe rules of decision to the judicial department of the government in cases pending before it?

We think not; and thus thinking, we do not at all question what was decided in the case of Pennsylvania v. Wheeling Bridge Company, 59 U.S. (18 How.) 421 (1856). In that case, after a decree in this Court that the bridge, in the then state of the law, was a nuisance and must be abated as such, Congress passed an act legalizing the structure and making it a post-road; and the Court, on a motion for process to enforce the decree, held that the bridge had ceased to be a nuisance by the exercise of the constitutional powers of Congress, and denied the motion. No arbitrary rule of decision was prescribed in that case, but the Court was left to apply its ordinary rules to the new circumstances created by the act. In the case before us no new circumstances have been created by legislation. But the Court is forbidden to give the effect to evidence which, in its own judgment, such evidence should have, and is directed to give it an effect precisely contrary.

We must think that Congress has inadvertently passed the limit which separates the legislative from the judicial power.

It is of vital importance that these powers be kept distinct. The Constitution provides that the judicial power of the United States shall be vested in one Supreme Court and such inferior courts as the Congress shall from time to time ordain and establish. The same instrument, in the last clause of the same article, provides that in all cases other than those of original jurisdiction, "the Supreme Court shall have appellate jurisdiction both as to law and fact, with such exceptions and under such regulations as the Congress shall make."

Congress has already provided that the Supreme Court shall have jurisdiction of the judgments of the Court of Claims on appeal. Can it prescribe a rule in conformity with which the Court must deny to itself the jurisdiction thus conferred, because and only because its decision, in accordance with settled law, must be adverse to the government and favorable to the suitor? This question seems to us to answer itself.

The rule prescribed is also liable to just exception as impairing the effect of a pardon, and thus infringing the constitutional power of the executive.

It is the intention of the Constitution that each of the great co-ordinate departments of the government—the legislative, the executive, and the judicial—shall be, in its sphere, independent of the others. To the executive alone is intrusted the power of pardon; and it is granted without limit. Pardon includes amnesty. It blots out the offence pardoned and removes all its penal consequences. It may be granted on conditions. In these particular pardons, that no doubt might exist as to their character, restoration of property was expressly pledged, and the pardon was granted on condition that the person who availed himself of it should take and keep a prescribed oath.

Now it is clear that the legislature cannot change the effect of such a pardon any more than the executive can change a law. Yet this is attempted by the provision under consideration. The court is required to receive special pardons as evidence of guilt and to treat them as null and void. It is required to disregard pardons granted by proclamation on condition, though the condition has been fulfilled, and to deny them their legal effect. This certainly impairs the executive authority and directs the court to be instrumental to that end.

We think it unnecessary to enlarge. The simplest statement is the best.

We [think] that it is impossible to believe that this provision was not inserted in the appropriation bill through inadvertence; and that we shall not best fulfil the deliberate will of the legislature by denying the motion to dismiss and affirming the judgment of the Court of Claims; which is accordingly done.

MR. JUSTICE MILLER (with whom concurred MR. JUSTICE BRADLEY), dissenting.

I cannot agree to the opinion of the Court just delivered in an important matter; and I regret this the more because I do agree to the proposition that the . . . act of July 12th, 1870, is unconstitutional, so far as it attempts to prescribe to the judiciary the effect to be given to an act of pardon or amnesty by the President. This power of pardon is confided to the President by the Constitution, and whatever may be its extent or its limits, the legislative branch of the government cannot impair its force or effect in a judicial proceeding in a constitutional court. But I have not been able to bring my mind to concur in the proposition that, under the act concerning captured and abandoned property, there remains in the former owner, who had given aid and comfort to the rebellion, any interest whatever in the property or its proceeds when it had been sold and paid into the treasury or had been converted to the use of the public under that act. I must construe this act, as all others should be construed, by seeking the intention of its framers, and the intention to restore the proceeds of such property to the loyal citizen, and to transfer it absolutely to the government in the case of those who had given active support to the rebellion, is to me too apparent to be disregarded. In the one case the government is converted into a trustee for the former owner; in the other it appropriates it to its own use as the property of a public enemy captured in war. Can it be inferred from anything found in the statute that Congress intended that this property should ever be restored to the disloyal? I am unable to discern any such intent. But if it did, why was not some provision made by which the title of the government could at some time be made perfect, or that of the owner established? Some judicial proceeding for confiscation would seem to be necessary if there remains in the disloyal owner any right or interest whatever. But there is no such provision, and unless the *act* intended to forfeit absolutely the right of the disloyal owner, the proceeds remain in a condition where the owner cannot maintain a suit for its recovery, and the United States can obtain no perfect title to it. . . .

[In United States v. Padelford, 76 U.S. (9 Wall.) 531 (1870),] the opinion makes a labored and successful effort to show that Padelford, the owner of the property, had secured the benefit of the amnesty proclamation *before* the property was seized under the same statute we are now considering. And it bases the right of Padelford to recover its proceeds in the treasury on the fact that *before the capture* his *status* as a loyal citizen had been restored, and with it all his rights of property, although he had previously given aid and comfort to the rebellion. In this view I concurred with all my brethren. And I hold now that as long as the possession or title of property remains in the party, the pardon or the amnesty remits all right in the government to forfeit or confiscate it. But where the property has already been seized and sold, and the proceeds paid into the treasury, and it is clear that the statute contemplates no further proceeding as necessary to divest the right of the former owner, the pardon does not and cannot restore that which has thus completely passed away. And if such was not the view of the court when Padelford's case was under consideration I am at a loss to discover a reason for the extended argument in that case, in the opinion of the court, to show that he had availed himself of the amnesty before the seizure of the property. If the views now advanced are sound, it was wholly immaterial whether Padelford was pardoned before or after the seizure.

———

NOTE ON *KLEIN*

Klein is the only Supreme Court decision to hold unconstitutional an effort by Congress to make an "exception" to the Supreme Court's jurisdiction.[a] It is therefore of importance in evaluating the limits of the congressional power.

Analysis of the significance of *Klein* can usefully begin with what the statute purports to do. The first and third parts of the statute in effect direct the Court of Claims and the Supreme Court to decide a question of fact in a litigated case in a particular manner. Were these portions of the statute at issue in *Klein*? Assume for the moment that they were. Does Congress normally have the power to provide rules of evidence that may have the effect of resolving a question of fact in litigation? If so, is there anything about its direction with respect to this particular question of fact that the Court regards as unconstitutional? And if so, is the constitutional problem with these parts of the statute that they direct the courts to reach an unconstitutional result in a case to be litigated on its merits? Consider the *Wheeling Bridge* case in this respect. Why was Congress permitted to direct the courts how to decide that case but not permitted to direct the courts how to decide *Klein*? Are the two situations distinguishable?

The second part of the statute is quite different. It purports to direct the Supreme Court not to exercise jurisdiction over a certain class of cases. Yet the Supreme Court affirmed the judgment below, in direct contravention of the statutory command. Did it therefore hold this portion of the statute unconstitutional? Does *Klein* stand for the proposition that Congress does not have the authority to exclude a constitutionally-based claim from the jurisdiction of the Supreme Court? After concluding that Wilson's property rights in the cotton were not extinguished by the seizure, the Court said:

> "Undoubtedly the legislature has complete control over the organization and existence of that court and may confer or withhold the right of appeal from its decisions. And if this act did nothing more, it would be our duty to give it effect. If it simply denied the right of appeal in a particular class of cases, there could be no doubt that it must be regarded as an exercise of the power of Congress to make "such exceptions from the appellate jurisdiction" as should seem to it expedient.

> "But the language of the [statute] shows plainly that it does not intend to withhold jurisdiction except as a means to an end. Its great and controlling purpose is to deny to pardons granted by the President the effect which this Court had adjudged them to have."

What does this passage mean?

[a] For an extensive treatment of *Klein*, see Young, Congressional Regulations of Federal Court's Jurisdiction and Processes: *United States v. Klein* Revisited, 1981 Wis. L. Rev. 1189.

Consider the fact that Klein had won in the Court of Claims. If the Court had followed the direction of the second part of the statute, it would have dismissed the case, the effect of which would have been to uphold the Court of Claims' judgment. What relief did the government seek in *Klein?* Would that relief have involved the Court in examining the merits and, in effect, resolving the case in an unconstitutional manner? If so, was the Court's opinion more a response to the relief sought by the government than to the literal wording of the statute? Is *Klein* for that reason *not* a holding that Congress is precluded from excluding a class of cases involving constitutional rights from the Court's jurisdiction?

Finally, consider the relevance of the Court's conclusion that Wilson retained property rights in the cotton after its seizure. Justices Miller and Bradley disagreed with this conclusion, and their disagreement on this point is the basis of their dissent. Why was this matter so important? Does it explain what the Court thought was unconstitutional about the attempt by Congress to interfere with the president's pardoning power? Is this the Court's pivotal constitutional holding, from which it follows that Congress was seeking an unconstitutional objective in the legislation at issue? But if so, what unconstitutional objective was Congress seeking to accomplish? If the answer is that it was trying to force the courts to resolve a case on its merits in an unconstitutional manner, then *Klein* is an unremarkable application of *Marbury v. Madison.* On this reading, it would be consistent with the traditional view of the power of Congress outlined on pages 163–66, supra. But if the answer is that Congress' objective was unconstitutional because it was trying to remove a class of constitutional litigation from the jurisdiction of the Supreme Court, then *Klein* is a rejection of the traditional view. Which is the more accurate reading? If the Court meant to reject the traditional view, what theory did it mean to adopt?

SUBSECTION B: JURISDICTION OF THE DISTRICT COURTS

SHELDON v. SILL
United States Supreme Court, 1850.
49 U.S. (8 How.) 441.

MR. JUSTICE GRIER delivered the opinion of the court.

The only question which it will be necessary to notice in this case is, whether the Circuit Court has jurisdiction.

Sill, the complainant below, a citizen of New York, filed his bill in the Circuit Court of the United States for Michigan, against Sheldon [a citizen of Michigan], claiming to recover the amount of a bond and mortgage, which had been assigned to him by Hastings, the President of the Bank of Michigan.

Sheldon, in his answer, among other things, pleaded that "the bond and mortgage in controversy, having been originally given by a citizen of Michigan to another citizen of the same state, and the complainant being assignee of them, the Circuit Court had no jurisdiction."

The 11th section of the Judiciary Act, which defines the jurisdiction of the circuit court restrains them from taking "cognizance of any suit to recover the contents of any promissory note or other chose in action, in favor of an assignee, unless a suit might have been prosecuted in such court to recover the contents, if no assignment had been made, except in cases of foreign bills of exchange."

The third article of the Constitution declares that "the judicial Power of the United States shall be vested in one Supreme Court, and such inferior Courts as the Congress may, from time to time, ordain and establish." The second section of the same article enumerates the cases and controversies of which the judicial power shall have cognizance, and, among others, it specifies "controversies between Citizens of different States."

It has been alleged, that this restriction of the Judiciary Act, with regard to assignees of choses in action, is in conflict with this provision of the Constitution, and therefore void.[a]

It must be admitted, that if the Constitution had ordained and established the inferior courts, and distributed to them their respective powers, they could not be restricted or divested by Congress. But as it has made no such distribution, one of two consequences must result,— either that each inferior court created by Congress must exercise all the judicial powers not given to the Supreme Court, or that Congress, having the power to establish the courts, must define their respective jurisdictions. The first of these inferences has never been asserted, and could not be defended with any show of reason, and if not, the latter

[a] Counsel for Sill had argued as follows:

"Now we would remark, first, the case before the Circuit Court was a controversy between citizens of different states, and to such a controversy the judicial power of the courts of the United States extends by the Constitution, and by the same Constitution that power is vested, except where the Supreme Court has original jurisdiction by the Constitution, in the inferior courts created by Congress. This judicial power, therefore, to take cognizance of this case, is, by the Constitution, vested in the Circuit Court, and the plaintiff claims the constitutional right to have his controversy with Mr. Sheldon . . ., decided by that court. . . . Where does Congress get the power or authority to deprive the courts of the United States of the judicial power with which the Constitution has invested them? Congress may create the courts, but they are clothed with their powers by the Constitution, and we submit that the provision of the act of Congress, enlarging the jurisdiction of the Supreme Court beyond the terms of the Constitution, is void. Marbury v. Madison, 5 U.S. (1 Cranch) 137 (1803). Can it any more take away a constitutional power than it can confer an unconstitutional one? We submit that it cannot. The jurisdiction of this class of controversies is in the Circuit Court. The Constitution makes no such distinction as the act of Congress does, and we respectfully submit, that it is of the utmost importance to citizens of the different states that the whole judicial power granted by the Constitution to the courts of the United States should be exercised." [Footnote by eds.]

would seem to follow as a necessary consequence. And it would seem to follow, also, that, having a right to prescribe, Congress may withhold from any court of its creation jurisdiction of any of the enumerated controversies. Courts created by statute can have no jurisdiction but such as the statute confers. No one of them can assert a just claim to jurisdiction exclusively conferred on another, or withheld from all.

The Constitution has defined the limits of the judicial power of the United States, but has not prescribed how much of it shall be exercised by the circuit court; consequently, the statute which does prescribe the limits of their jurisdiction, cannot be in conflict with the Constitution, unless it confers powers not enumerated therein.

Such has been the doctrine held by this Court since its first establishment. To enumerate all the cases in which it has been either directly advanced or tacitly assumed would be tedious and unnecessary.
. . .

[The Court then held that Sill was an "assignee" of a chose in action within the meaning of the statute.]

The judgment of the Circuit Court must therefore be reversed, for want of jurisdiction.

WEBSTER v. DOE

Supreme Court of the United States, 1988.
486 U.S. ___.

CHIEF JUSTICE REHNQUIST delivered the opinion of the Court.

Section 102(c) of the National Security Act of 1947, as amended, provides that:

> "[T]he Director of Central Intelligence may, in his discretion, terminate the employment of any officer or employee of the Agency whenever he shall deem such termination necessary or advisable in the interests of the United States. . . ."
> 50 U.S.C. § 403(c).

In this case we decide whether, and to what extent, the termination decisions of the Director under § 102(c) are judicially reviewable.

I

Respondent John Doe was first employed by the Central Intelligence Agency (CIA or Agency) in 1973 as a clerk-typist. He received periodic fitness reports that consistently rated him as an excellent or outstanding employee. By 1977, respondent had been promoted to a position as a covert electronics technician.

In January 1982, respondent voluntarily informed a CIA security officer that he was a homosexual. Almost immediately, the Agency placed respondent on paid administrative leave pending an investigation of his sexual orientation and conduct. On February 12 and again on February 17, respondent was extensively questioned by a polygraph officer concerning his homosexuality and possible security violations.

Respondent denied having sexual relations with any foreign nationals and maintained that he had not disclosed classified information to any of his sexual partners. After these interviews, the officer told respondent that the polygraph tests indicated that he had truthfully answered all questions. The polygraph officer then prepared a five-page summary of his interviews with respondent, to which respondent was allowed to attach a two-page addendum.

On April 14, 1982, a CIA security agent informed respondent that the Agency's Office of Security had determined that respondent's homosexuality posed a threat to security, but declined to explain the nature of the danger. Respondent was then asked to resign. When he refused to do so, the Office of Security recommended to the CIA Director (petitioner's predecessor) that respondent be dismissed. After reviewing respondent's records and the evaluations of his subordinates, the Director "deemed it necessary and advisable in the interests of the United States to terminate [respondent's] employment with this Agency pursuant to § 102(c) of the National Security Act. . . ." Respondent was also advised that, while the CIA would give him a positive recommendation in any future job search, if he applied for a job requiring a security clearance the Agency would inform the prospective employer that it had concluded that respondent's homosexuality presented a security threat.

Respondent then filed an action against petitioner in the United States District Court for the District of Columbia. Respondent's amended complaint asserted a variety of statutory and constitutional claims against the Director. Respondent alleged that petitioner's decision to terminate his employment violated § 706 of the Administrative Procedure Act (APA), because it was arbitrary and capricious, represented an abuse of discretion, and was reached without observing the procedures required by law and CIA regulations. He also complained that the Director's termination of his employment deprived him of constitutionally protected rights to property, liberty, and privacy in violation of the first, fourth, fifth, and ninth amendments. Finally, he asserted that his dismissal transgressed the procedural due process and equal protection of the laws guaranteed by the fifth amendment. Respondent requested a declaratory judgment that petitioner had violated the APA and the Constitution, and asked the District Court for an injunction ordering petitioner to reinstate him to the position he held with the CIA prior to his dismissal. As an alternative remedy, he suggested that he be returned to paid administrative leave and that petitioner be ordered to reevaluate respondent's employment termination and provide a statement of the reasons for any adverse final determination. Respondent sought no monetary damages in his amended complaint.

Petitioner moved to dismiss respondent's amended complaint on the ground that § 102(c) of the National Security Act (NSA) precludes judicial review of the Director's termination decisions under §§ 701, 702, and 706 of the APA. Section 702 provides judicial review to any "person suffering legal wrong because of agency action, or adversely affected or aggrieved by agency action within the meaning of a relevant statute." The section further instructs that "[a]n action in a court of the United States seeking relief other than money damages and stating a claim that an agency or an officer or employee thereof acted or failed to act in an official capacity or under color of legal authority shall not be dismissed nor relief therein denied on the ground that it is against the United States or that the United States is an indispensable party." The [availability] of judicial review under § 702, however, . . . is predicated on satisfying the requirements of § 701, which provide:

> "(a) This chapter applies, according to the provisions thereof, except to the extent that—

> "(1) statutes preclude judicial review; or

> "(2) agency action is committed to agency discretion by law."

The District Court denied petitioner's motion to dismiss, and granted respondent's motion for partial summary judgment. The court determined that the APA provided judicial review of petitioner's termination decisions made under § 102(c) of the NSA, and found that respondent had been unlawfully discharged because the CIA had not followed the procedures described in its own regulations. The District Court declined, however, to address respondent's constitutional claims. . . .

A divided panel of the Court of Appeals for the District of Columbia Circuit vacated the District Court's judgment and remanded the case for further proceedings. The Court of Appeals first decided that judicial review under APA of the Agency's decision to terminate respondent was not precluded by §§ 701(a)(1) or (a)(2). Turning to the merits, the Court of Appeals found that, while an agency must normally follow its own regulations, the CIA regulations cited by respondent do not limit the Director's discretion in making termination decisions. Moreover, the regulations themselves state that, with respect to terminations pursuant to § 102(c), the Director need not follow standard discharge procedures, but may direct that an employee "be separated immediately and without regard to any suggested procedural steps." The majority thus concluded that the CIA regulations provide no independent source of procedural or substantive protection.

The Court of Appeals went on to hold that respondent must demonstrate that the Director's action was an arbitrary and capricious exercise of his power to discharge employees under § 102(c).[6] Because the record below was unclear on certain points critical to respondent's claim for relief, the Court of Appeals remanded the case to the District Court for a determination of the reason for the Director's termination of respondent. We granted certiorari to decide the question whether the Director's decision to discharge a CIA employee under § 102(c) of the NSA is judicially reviewable under the APA.

---

[6] This "arbitrary and capricious" standard is derived from § 706(2)(a) [stating that a reviewing court shall set aside agency action found to be "arbitrary, capricious, an abuse of discretion, or otherwise not in accordance with law"].

II

The APA's comprehensive provisions, set forth in 5 U.S.C. §§ 701–706, allow any person "adversely affected or aggrieved" by agency action to obtain judicial review thereof, so long as the decision challenged represents a "final agency action for which there is no other adequate remedy in a court." Typically, a litigant will contest an action (or failure to act) by an agency on the ground that the agency has neglected to follow the statutory directives of Congress. Section 701(a), however, limits application of the entire APA to situations in which judicial review is not precluded by statute, see § 701(a)(1), and the agency action is not committed to agency discretion by law, see § 701(a)(2).

In Citizens to Preserve Overton Park v. Volpe, 401 U.S. 402 (1971), this Court explained the distinction between §§ 701(a)(1) and (a)(2). Subsection (a)(1) is concerned with whether Congress expressed an intent to prohibit judicial review; subsection (a)(2) applies "in those rare instances where 'statutes are drawn in such broad terms that in a given case there is no law to apply.'"

[*Overton Park*] emphasized that § 701(a)(2) requires careful examination of the statute on which the claim of agency illegality is based . . . . In the present case, respondent's claims against the CIA arise from the Director's asserted violation of § 102(c) of the National Security Act. As an initial matter, it should be noted that § 102(c) allows termination of an Agency employee whenever the Director "shall *deem* such termination necessary or advisable in the interests of the United States" (emphasis added), not simply when the dismissal *is* necessary or advisable to those interests. This standard fairly exudes deference to the Director, and appears to us to foreclose the application of any meaningful judicial standard of review. Short of permitting cross-examination of the Director concerning his views of the nation's security and whether the discharged employee was inimical to those interests, we see no basis on which a reviewing court could properly assess an Agency termination decision. The language of § 102(c) thus strongly suggests that its implementation was "committed to agency discretion by law."

So too does the overall structure of the National Security Act. Passed shortly after the close of the Second World War, the NSA created the CIA and gave its Director the responsibility "for protecting intelligence sources and methods from unauthorized disclosure." Section 102(c) is an integral part of that statute, because the Agency's efficacy, and the nation's security, depend in large measure on the reliability and trustworthiness of the Agency employees. As we recognized in Snepp v. United States, 444 U.S. 507, 510 (1980), employment with the CIA entails a high degree of trust that is perhaps unmatched in government service . . . .

We thus find that the language and structure of § 102(c) indicate that Congress meant to commit individual employee discharges to the

Director's discretion, and that § 701(a)(2) accordingly precludes judicial review of these decisions under the APA. We reverse the Court of Appeals to the extent that it found such terminations reviewable by the courts.

III

In addition to his claim that the Director failed to abide by the statutory dictates of § 102(c), respondent also alleged a number of constitutional violations in his amended complaint. Respondent charged that petitioner's termination of his employment deprived him of property and liberty interests under the due process clause, denied him equal protection of the laws, and unjustifiably burdened his right to privacy. Respondent asserts that he is entitled, under the APA, to judicial consideration of the claimed violations.[8]

Petitioner maintains that, no matter what the nature of respondent's constitutional claim, judicial review is precluded by the language and intent of § 102(c). In petitioner's view, all Agency employment termination decisions, even those based on policies normally repugnant to the Constitution, are given over to the absolute discretion of the Director, and are hence unreviewable under the APA. We do not think that § 102(c) can be read to exclude review of constitutional claims. We emphasized in Johnson v. Robison, 415 U.S. 361 (1974), that where Congress intends to preclude judicial review of constitutional claims its intent to do so must be clear. In Weinberger v. Salfi, 422 U.S. 749 (1975), we reaffirmed that view. We require this heightened showing in part to avoid the "serious constitutional question" that would arise if a federal statute were construed to deny any judicial forum for a colorable constitutional claim. See Bowen v. Michigan Academy of Family Physicians, 476 U.S. 667, 681 n.12 (1986).

Our review of § 102(c) convinces us that it cannot bear the preclusive weight petitioner would have it support. As detailed above, the section does commit employment termination decisions to the Director's discretion, and precludes challenges to these decisions based upon the statutory language of § 102(c). A discharged employee thus cannot complain that his termination was not "necessary or advisable in the interests of the United States," since that assessment is the Director's alone. Subsections (a)(1) and (a)(2) of § 701, however, remove from judicial review only those determinations specifically identified by Congress or "committed to agency discretion by law." Nothing in § 102(c) persuades us that Congress meant to preclude consideration of colorable constitutional claims arising out of the actions of the Director pursuant to that section; we believe that a constitutional claim based

---

[8] We understand that petitioner concedes that the Agency's failure to follow its *own* *regulations* can be challenged under the APA as a violation of § 102(c). The Court of Appeals, however, found that the CIA's own regulations plainly protect the discretion granted the Director by § 102(c), and that the regulations "provide[ ] no independent source of procedural or substantive protections." Thus, since petitioner prevailed on this ground below and does not seek further review of the question here, we do not reach that issue.

on an individual discharge may be reviewed by the District Court.[9] We agree with the Court of Appeals that there must be further proceedings in the District Court on this issue.

Petitioner complains that judicial review even of constitutional claims will entail extensive "rummaging around" in the Agency's affairs to the detriment of national security. But petitioner acknowledges that title VII claims attacking the hiring and promotion policies of the Agency are routinely entertained in federal court, and the inquiry and discovery associated with those proceedings would seem to involve some of the same sort of rummaging. Furthermore, the District Court has the latitude to control any discovery process which may be instituted so as to balance respondent's need for access to proof which would support a colorable constitutional claim against the extraordinary needs of the CIA for confidentiality and the protection of its methods, sources, and mission.

Petitioner also contends that even if respondent has raised a colorable constitutional claim arising out of his discharge, Congress in the interests of national security may deny the courts the authority to decide the claim and to order respondent's reinstatement if the claim is upheld. For the reasons previously stated, we do not think Congress meant to impose such restrictions when it enacted § 102(c) of the NSA. Even without such prohibitory legislation from Congress, of course, traditional equitable principles requiring the balancing of public and private interests control the grant of declaratory or injunctive relief in the federal courts. On remand, the District Court should thus address respondent's constitutional claims and the propriety of the equitable remedies sought.

The judgment of the Court of Appeals is affirmed in part, reversed in part, and the case is remanded for further proceedings consistent with this opinion.

JUSTICE KENNEDY took no part in the consideration or decision of this case.

JUSTICE O'CONNOR, concurring in part and dissenting in part.

I agree that the Administrative Procedure Act (APA) does not authorize judicial review of the employment decisions referred to in § 102(c) of the National Security Act . . . .

I disagree, however, with the Court's conclusion that a constitutional claim challenging the validity of an employment decision covered by § 102(c) may nonetheless be brought in a federal district court. Whatever may be the exact scope of Congress' power to close the lower federal courts to constitutional claims in other contexts, I have no doubt about its authority to do so here. The functions performed by the Central Intelligence Agency and the Director of Central Intelli-

---

[9] Petitioner asserts that respondent fails to present a colorable constitutional claim when he asserts that there is a general CIA policy against employing homosexuals. Petitioner relies on our decision in Bowers v. Hardwick, 478 U.S. 186 (1986), to support this view. This queston was not presented in the petition for certiorari, and we decline to consider it at this stage of the litigation.

gence lie at the core of "the very delicate, plenary and exclusive power of the President as the sole organ of the federal government in the field of international relations." The authority of the Director of Central Intelligence to control access to sensitive national security information by discharging employees deemed to be untrustworthy flows primarily from this constitutional power of the President, and Congress may surely provide that the inferior federal courts are not used to infringe on the President's constitutional authority. Section 102(c) plainly indicates that Congress has done exactly that, and the Court points to nothing in the structure, purpose, or legislative history of the National Security Act that would suggest a different result. Accordingly, I respectfully dissent from the Court's decision to allow this lawsuit to go forward.

JUSTICE SCALIA, dissenting.

I agree with the Court's apparent holding in part II of its opinion that the Director's decision to terminate a CIA employee is "committed to agency discretion by law" within the meaning of 5 U.S.C. § 701(a)(2). But because I do not see how a decision can, either practically or legally, be both unreviewable and yet reviewable for constitutional defect, I regard part III of the opinion as essentially undoing part II. I therefore respectfully dissent from the judgment of the Court.

I

[Part I of Justice Scalia's dissent outlined his view that interpretation of § 701(a)(2) of the Administrative Procedure Act should be informed by reference to "the 'common law' of judicial review of agency action." Determination of matters "committed to agency discretion by law" would not be limited to the text and structure of the statute authorizing agency action. Also relevant, in Scalia's view, would be factors such as whether the agency decision involved "a sensitive and inherently discretionary judgment call," whether the decision was of a type traditionally thought unreviewable, and whether judicial review would have "disruptive practical consequences."]

II

Before taking the reader through the terrain of the Court's holding that respondent may assert some constitutional claims in this suit, I would like to try to clear some of the underbrush, consisting primarily of the Court's ominous warning that "[a] 'serious constitutional question' . . . . would arise if a federal statute were construed to deny any judicial forum for a colorable constitutional claim."

The first response to the Court's grave doubt about the constitutionality of denying all judicial review to a "colorable constitutional claim" is that the denial of all judicial review is not at issue here, but merely the denial of review in the United States district courts. As to that, the law is, and has long been, clear. Article III, § 2 of the Constitution extends the judicial power to "all Cases . . . arising under this Constitution." But article III, § 1 provides that the judicial power shall be vested "in one supreme Court, *and in such inferior Courts as the Congress may from time to time ordain and establish*" (emphasis added). We long ago held that the power not to create any lower federal courts at all includes the power to invest them with less than all of the judicial power.

> "The Constitution has defined the limits of the judicial power of the United States, but has not prescribed how much of it shall be exercised by the Circuit Court; consequently, the statute which does prescribe the limits of their jurisdiction, cannot be in conflict with the Constitution, unless it confers powers not enumerated therein." Sheldon v. Sill, 49 U.S. (8 How.) 441, 449 (1850).

Thus, if there is any truth to the proposition that judicial cognizance of constitutional claims cannot be eliminated, it is, at most, that they cannot be eliminated from state courts, and from this Court's appellate jurisdiction over cases from state courts (or cases from federal courts, should there be any) involving such claims. Narrowly viewed, therefore, there is no shadow of a constitutional doubt that we are free to hold that the present suit, whether based on constitutional grounds or not, will not lie.

It can fairly be argued, however, that our interpretation of § 701(a)(2) indirectly implicates the constitutional question whether state courts can be deprived of jurisdiction, because if they cannot, then interpreting § 701(a)(2) to exclude relief here would impute to Congress the peculiar intent to let state courts review federal government action that it is unwilling to let federal district courts review—or, alternatively, the peculiar intent to let federal district courts review, upon removal from state courts pursuant to 28 U.S.C. § 1442(a)(1), claims that it is unwilling to let federal district courts review in original actions. I turn, then, to the substance of the Court's warning that judicial review of all "colorable constitutional claims" arising out of the respondent's dismissal may well be constitutionally required. What could possibly be the basis for this fear? Surely not some general principle that *all* constitutional violations must be remediable in the courts. The very text of the Constitution refutes that principle, since it provides that "[e]ach House shall be the Judge of the Elections, Returns and Qualifications of its own Members," art. I, § 5, and that "for any Speech or Debate in either House, [the Senators and Representatives] shall not be questioned in any other Place," art. I, § 6. Claims concerning constitutional violations committed in these contexts—for example, the rather grave constitutional claim that an election has been stolen—cannot be addressed to the courts. See, e.g., Morgan v. United States, 801 F.2d 445 (D.C.Cir.1986). Even apart from the strict text of the Constitution, we have found some constitutional claims to be beyond judicial review because they involve "political questions." See, e.g., Coleman v. Miller, 307 U.S. 433, 446–53 (1939). The doctrine of sovereign immunity—not repealed by the Constitution, but to the contrary at least partly reaffirmed as to the states by the 11th amendment—is a monument to the principle that some constitutional claims can go unheard. No one would suggest that, if Congress had not passed the Tucker Act, 28 U.S.C. § 1491(a)(1), the courts would be able to order disbursements from the treasury to pay for property taken under lawful authority (and subsequently destroyed) without just compensation. See Schillinger v. United States, 155 U.S. 163, 166–69 (1894). And finally, the doctrine of equitable discretion, which permits a court to refuse relief, even where no relief at law is available, when that would unduly impair the public interest, does not stand aside simply because the basis for the relief is a constitutional claim. In sum, it is simply untenable that there must be a judicial remedy for every constitutional violation. Members of Congress and the supervising officers of the executive branch take the same oath to uphold the Constitution that we do, and sometimes they are left to perform that oath unreviewed, as we always are.

Perhaps, then, the Court means to appeal to a more limited principle, that although there may be areas where judicial review of a constitutional claim will be denied, the scope of those areas is fixed by the Constitution and judicial tradition, and cannot be affected by *Congress*, through the enactment of a statute such as § 102(c). That would be a rather counter-intuitive principle, especially since Congress has in reality been the principal determiner of the scope of review, for constitutional claims as well as all other claims, through its waiver of the pre-existing doctrine of sovereign immunity. On the merits of the point, however: It seems to me clear that courts would not entertain, for example, an action for backpay by a dismissed Secretary of State claiming that the reason he lost his government job was that the President did not like his religious views—surely a colorable violation of the first amendment. I am confident we would hold that the President's choice of his Secretary of State is a "political question." But what about a similar suit by the Deputy Secretary of State? Or one of the Under Secretaries? Or an Assistant Secretary? Or the head of the European Desk? Is there really a constitutional line that falls at some immutable point between one and another of these offices at which the principle of unreviewability cuts in, and which cannot be altered by congressional prescription? I think not. I think Congress can prescribe, at least within broad limits, that for certain jobs the dismissal decision will be unreviewable—that is, will be "committed to agency discretion by law."

Once it is acknowledged, as I think it must be, (1) that not all constitutional claims require a judicial remedy, and (2) that the identification of those that do not can, even if only within narrow limits, be determined by Congress, then it is clear that the "serious constitutional question" feared by the Court is an illusion. . . . I think it entirely beyond doubt that if Congress intended, by § 701(a)(2) of the APA, to exclude judicial review of the President's decision (through the Director of Central Intelligence) to dismiss an officer of the Central Intelligence Agency, that disposition would be constitutionally permissible.

III

I turn, then, to whether that executive action is, within the meaning of § 701(a)(2), "committed to agency discretion by law." My discussion of this point can be brief, because the answer is compellingly obvious. Section 102(c) of the National Security Act of 1947 states:

> "*Notwithstanding . . . the provisions of any other law,* the Director of Central Intelligence, *may, in his discretion,* terminate the employment of any officer or employee of the Agency *whenever he shall deem* such termination necessary or advisable in the interests of the United States . . ." (emphasis added).

Further, as the Court declares, § 102(c) is an "integral part" of the National Security Act, which throughout exhibits "extraordinary deference to the Director." Given this statutory text, and given . . . that the area to which the text pertains is one of predominant executive authority and traditional judicial abstention, it is difficult to conceive a statutory scheme that more clearly reflects that "commit[ment] to agency discretion by law" to which § 701(a)(2) refers.

It is baffling to observe that the Court seems to agree with the foregoing assessment, holding that "the language and structure of § 102(c) indicate that Congress meant to commit individual employee discharges to the Director's discretion." Nevertheless, without explanation the Court reaches the conclusion that "a constitutional claim based on an individual discharge may be reviewed by the District Court." It seems to me that the Court is attempting the impossible feat of having its cake and eating it too. The opinion states that "[a] discharged employee . . . cannot complain that his termination was not 'necessary or advisable in the interests of the United States,' *since that assessment is the Director's alone.*" (Emphasis added.) But two sentences later it says that "[n]othing in § 102(c) persuades us that Congress meant to preclude consideration of colorable constitutional claims arising out of the actions of the Director pursuant to that section." Which are we to believe? If the former, the case should be at an end. If the § 102(c) assessment is really "the Director's alone," the only conceivable basis for review of respondent's dismissal (which is what this case is about) would be that the dismissal was not *really* the result of a § 102(c) assessment by the Director. But respondent has never contended that, nor could he. Not only was his counsel formally advised, by letter of May 11, 1982, that "the Director has deemed it necessary and advisable in the interests of the United States to terminate your client's employment with this Agency pursuant to § 102(c)," but the petitioner filed with the court an affidavit by the Director, dated September 17, 1982, stating that "[a]fter careful consideration of the matter, I determined that the termination of Mr. Doe's employment was necessary and advisable in the interests of the United States and, exercising my discretion under the authority granted by § 102(c) . . . I terminated Mr. Doe's employment." Even if the basis for the Director's assessment was the respondent's homosexuality, and even if the connection between that and the interests of the United States is an irrational and hence an unconstitutional one, if that assessment is really "the Director's alone" there is nothing more to litigate about. I cannot imagine what the Court expects the "further proceedings in the District Court" which it commands to consist of, unless an academic seminar on the relationship of homosexuality to security risk. For even were the District Court persuaded that no such relationship exists, "that assessment is the Director's alone."

Since the court's disposition contradicts its fair assurances, I must assume that the § 102(c) judgment is no longer "the Director's alone," but rather only "the Director's alone except to the extent it is colorably claimed that his judgment is unconstitutional." I turn, then to the question of where this exception comes from. As discussed at length earlier, the Constitution assuredly does not require it. Nor the text of the statute. True, it only gives the Director absolute discretion to dismiss "[n]otwithstanding . . . the provisions of any other *law*" (emphasis added). But one would hardly have expected it to say "[n]otwithstanding the provisions of any other law *or of the Constitution.*" What the provision directly addresses is the authority to dismiss, not the authority of the courts to review the dismissal. And the Director does *not* have the authority to dismiss in violation of the Constitution, nor could Congress give it to him. The implication of nonreviewability in this text, its manifestation that the action is meant to be "committed to agency discretion," is no weaker with regard to constitutional claims than nonconstitutional claims . . . .

Perhaps, then a constitutional right is by its nature so much more important to the claimant than a statutory right that a statute which plainly excludes the latter should not be read to exclude the former unless it says so. That principle has never been announced—and with good reason, because its premise is not true. An individual's contention that the government has reneged on a $100,000 debt owing under a contract is much more important to him—both financially and, I suspect, in the sense of injustice that he feels—than the same individual's claim that a particular federal licensing provision requiring a $100 license denies him equal protection of the laws, or that a particular state tax violates the commerce clause. A citizen would much rather have his statutory entitlement correctly acknowledged after a constitutionally inadequate hearing, than have it incorrectly denied after a proceeding that fulfills all the requirements of the due process clause. The *only* respect in which a constitutional claim is necessarily more significant than any other kind of claim is that, regardless of how trivial its real-life importance may be in the case at hand, it can be asserted against the action of the legislature itself, whereas a nonconstitutional claim (no matter how significant) cannot. That is an important distinction, and one relevant to the constitutional analysis that I conducted above. But it has no relevance to the question whether, as between executive violations of statute and executive violations of the Constitution—both of which are equally unlawful, and neither of which can be said, a priori, to be more harmful or more unfair to the plaintiff—one or the other category should be favored by a presumption against exclusion of judicial review.

Even if we were to assume, however, contrary to all reason, that every constitutional claim is ipso facto more worthy, and every statutory claim less worthy, of judicial review, there would be no basis for writing that preference into a statute that makes no distinction between the two. We have rejected such judicial rewriting of legislation even in the more appealing situation where particular applications of a statute are not merely less desirable but in fact raise "grave constitutional doubts." That, we have said, only permits us to adopt one rather than another permissible reading of the statute, but not, by altering its terms, "to ignore the legislative will in order to avoid constitutional adjudication." Commodity Futures Trading Comm'n v. Schor, 478 U.S. 833, 841 (1986). There is no more textual basis for reading this statute as barring only nonconstitutional claims than there is to read it as barring only claims with a monetary worth of less than $1 million. Neither of the two decisions cited by the Court to sustain its power to read in a limitation for constitutional claims remotely supports that proposition. In Johnson v. Robison, 415 U.S. 361 (1974), we considered a statute precluding judicial review of " 'the *decisions* of the Administrator on any question of law or fact *under* any law administered by the Veterans' Administration.' " (Quoting 38 U.S.C. § 211(a).) We concluded that this statute did not bar judicial review of a challenge to the constitutionality of the statute itself, since that was a challenge not to a decision of the administrator but to a decision of Congress. Our holding was based upon the text, and not upon some judicial power to read in a "constitutional claims" exception. And in Weinberger v. Salfi, 422 U.S. 749 (1975), we held that 42 U.S.C. § 405(h), a statute depriving district courts of federal-question jurisdiction over "any claim arising under" Title II of the Social Security Act, *did* embrace even constitutional challenges, since its language was "quite different" from that at issue in *Johnson,* and "extend[ed] to any 'action' seeking 'to recover on any [Social Security] claim'—irrespective of whether resort to judicial processes is necessitated by . . . allegedly unconstitutional statutory restrictions." In *Salfi,* to be sure, another statutory provision was available that would enable judicial review of the constitutional claim, but as just observed, that distinction does not justify drawing a line that has no basis in the statute.

The Court seeks to downplay the harm produced by today's decision by observing that "petitioner acknowledges that title VII claims attacking the hiring and promotion policies of the Agency are routinely entertained in federal court." Assuming that those suits are statutorily authorized, I am willing to accept the Director's assertion that, while suits regarding hiring or promotion are tolerable, a suit regarding dismissal is not. Like the Court, I have no basis of knowledge on which I could deny that—especially since it is obvious that if the Director thinks that a particular hiring or promotion suit is genuinely contrary to the interests of the United States he can simply make the hiring or grant the promotion, and then dismiss the prospective litigant under § 102(c).

The harm done by today's decision is that, contrary to what Congress knows is preferable, it brings a significant decisionmaking process of our intelligence services into a forum where it does not belong. Neither the Constitution, nor our laws, nor common sense gives an individual a right to come into court to litigate the reasons for his dismissal as an intelligence agent. It is of course not just *valid* constitutional claims that today's decision makes the basis for judicial review of the Director's action, but all *colorable* constitutional claims, whether meritorious or not. And in determining whether what is colorable is in fact meritorious, a court will necessarily have to review the entire decision. If the Director denies, for example, respondent's contention in the present case that he was dismissed because he was a homosexual, how can a court possibly resolve the dispute without knowing what other good, intelligence-related reasons there might have been? I do not see how any "latitude to control the discovery process" could justify the refusal to permit such an inquiry, at least in camera. Presumably, the court would be expected to evaluate whether the agent really did fail in this or that secret mission. The documents needed will make interesting reading for district judges (and perhaps others) throughout the country. Of course the Agency can seek to protect iself, ultimately, by an authorized assertion of executive privilege, United States v. Nixon, 418 U.S. 683 (1974), but that is a power to be invoked only in extremis, and any scheme of judicial review of which it is a central feature is extreme. I would, in any event, not like to be the agent who has to explain to the intelligence services of other nations, with which we sometimes cooperate, that they need have no worry that the secret information they give us will be subjected to the notoriously broad discovery powers of our courts, because, although we have to litigate the dismissal of our spies, we have available a protection of somewhat uncertain scope known as executive privilege, which the President can invoke if he is willing to take the political damage that it often entails.

Today's result, however, will have ramifications far beyond creation of the world's only secret intelligence agency that must litigate the dismissal of its agents. If constitutional claims can be raised in this highly sensitive context, it is hard to imagine where they cannot. The assumption that there are any executive decisions that cannot be hauled into the courts may no longer be valid . . . .

I respectfully dissent.

NOTES ON CONGRESSIONAL POWER TO LIMIT THE JURISDICTION OF THE DISTRICT COURTS

1. Questions and Comments on *Sheldon v. Sill.* Section 11 of the First Judiciary Act contained the so-called "assignee" clause that was the subject of debate in *Sheldon v. Sill.*[a] The purpose of the provision was to prevent parties from collusively creating federal diversity jurisdiction by selling or assigning their claims to citizens of other states. It seems clear that Congress has the authority to enact such a provision to protect the integrity of diversity jurisdiction, and for that reason *Sheldon* did not present a difficult issue. *Sheldon* nonetheless is the best known early case delineating the power of Congress to limit the jurisdiction of the lower federal courts.

The Court describes the powers of Congress in seemingly unlimited terms. It says that Congress "may withhold from any court of its creation jurisdiction of *any* of the enumerated controversies" (emphasis added), that no federal court can exercise jurisdiction "withheld from all" federal courts, and that a statute prescribing limits on lower federal court jurisdiction "cannot be in conflict with the Constitution, unless it confers powers not enumerated therein." Did the Court mean these statements for all they are worth? Are there indeed no limits on the power of Congress to exclude controversies from litigation in the lower federal courts? Could one take the position that Congress no longer has the option not to continue the existence of the lower federal courts with at least a constitutional minimum of jurisdiction? Alternatively, could one argue that, while Congress may abolish the lower federal courts completely, so long as they exist they must at least be open to hear certain kinds of questions? *Webster* raises these questions in a modern context.

2. Limiting Theories. Before addressing *Webster*, however, one should consider the various theories that have been advanced to control Congress' power to limit the jurisdiction of the lower federal courts. Note that the theory described as the traditional view, pages 163–66, supra, holds that Congress may exclude any class of controversies from the jurisdiction of the lower federal courts. By contrast, the theory labeled "independent unconstitutionality", page 174, supra, would hold that Congress may not make exclusions from the jurisdiction of the lower federal courts based on hostility to a constitutional right. The major additional arguments made in the literature are summarized below. None of them has been authoritatively embraced—or rejected—by the Supreme Court, primarily because it has never had occasion directly to confront the problem in a controversial context.

(i) Justice Story. It is traditional to begin consideration of congressional power to limit the jurisdiction of the lower federal courts with the views expressed by Justice Story in Martin v. Hunter's Lessee, 14 U.S. (1 Wheat.) 304 (1816). Relying mainly on the text of art. III, Justice Story took the position in dicta that Congress

"might establish one or more inferior courts; they might parcel out the jurisdiction among such courts from time to time, at their own pleasure. But the whole judicial power of

---

[a] That provision is found today, in considerably modified form, in 28 U.S.C. § 1359.

the United States should be, at all times, vested, either in an original or an appellate form, in some courts created under its authority."

It has often been noted that Story apparently thought the obligation to which he referred was "moral" and not legal—that is, what he viewed as the mandatory language of art. III was not a legally enforceable obligation of the Congress.[b] And whatever view one takes of what Story meant, it is now clear, given cases such as *Sheldon v. Sill* and given that Congress has never conferred the entire judicial power on the federal courts, that the Supreme Court would not today take this view. This fact led Paul Bator to say that Justice Story's view "no longer deserves to be taken seriously."[c]

    (ii) The Essential Functions Thesis. Versions of the "essential functions" thesis [d] also have been advanced as a limit on the power of Congress to control the jurisdiction of the lower federal courts.[e] The broadest statement of this position appears in Eisenberg, Congressional Authority to Restrict Lower Federal Court Jurisdiction, 83 Yale L.J. 498 (1974).

    Eisenberg argues that the contemporary understanding by the framers was "that the federal courts, whatever their form, could be expected to hear any litigant whose case was within the federal constitutional jurisdiction, either at trial or on appeal." The framers assumed, he continued, that Supreme Court review could accomplish this objective. But with the increased caseloads of modern times, this assumption is no longer practical:

[b] See, e.g., G. Gunther, Constitutional Law: Cases and Materials 60–61 (11th ed. 1985); H. Hart and H. Wechsler, The Federal Courts and the Federal System 292 (1953). Both of these sources point out that Story, while sitting as a Circuit Judge, dismissed a case that was not within the congressional grant of diversity jurisdiction, stating that the Circuit Court "has no jurisdiction which is not given by some statute."

[c] Bator, Congressional Power over the Jurisdiction of the Federal Courts, 27 Vill. L.Rev. 1030, 1035 (1982). A recent article, however, takes issue with this comment. In A Neo-Federalist View of Article III: Separating the Two Tiers of Federal Jurisdiction, 65 Boston U.L.Rev. 205 (1985), Akhil Amar argues that prior commentators have not sufficiently focused on the word "all" in art. III, § 2. Amar notes that art. III requires that "all" cases arising under federal law, "all" cases affecting ambassadors, and "all" cases of admiralty or maritime jurisdiction must be vested, either as an original or an appellate matter, in some federal court. The remaining controversies—since art. III does not say

that they must "all" be vested in a federal court—may be excluded from the federal courts in Congress' discretion. Justice Story was thus partly right, Amar concludes, and his argument "deserves to be taken very seriously indeed."

For another recent defense of a view akin to Story's, see Robert N. Clinton, A Mandatory View of Federal Court Jurisdiction: A Guided Quest for the Original Understanding of Article III, 132 U.Pa.L.Rev. 741 (1984). See also Clinton, A Mandatory View of Federal Court Jurisdiction: Early Implementation of and Departures from the Constitutional Plan, 86 Colum.L.Rev. 1515 (1986).

[d] See page 172, supra.

[e] See, e.g., Sager's views, summarized at page ___, supra. The "essential function" identified by Sager—"supervision of state conduct to ensure general compliance with the Constitution"—must be performed, he argues, by the federal judicial system as a whole. Congress may, therefore, withdraw Supreme Court jurisdiction over such an issue, but it must then provide for jurisdiction in a lower federal court.

"It is thus no longer reasonable to assert that Congress may simply abolish the lower federal courts. When Supreme Court review of all cases within art. III jurisdiction was possible, lower federal courts were perhaps unnecessary. As federal caseloads grew, however, lower federal courts became necessary components of the national judiciary if the constitutional duty of case by case consideration of all federal cases was to be fulfilled. It can now be asserted that their existence in some form is constitutionally required."

Eisenberg does not argue, however, that Congress must therefore vest the entire art. III power in some federal court. He concludes, for example, that Congress may exclude cases from federal jurisdiction for "neutral" policy reasons, such as to avoid case overloads or to promote the efficiency of federal justice. Thus, a jurisdictional amount limitation is defensible, as is the failure to provide for federal trial of state criminal cases in which federal issues might, but need not, arise.[f] He also concludes that Congress "has unfettered power to enact jurisdictional laws that accomplish what it could have accomplished by means of a substantive rule." This means, he asserts, that "it may enact any jurisdictional statute that does not prevent vindication of a constitutional right" but that it "cannot withdraw jurisdiction to issue any constitutionally required remedy."[g]

(iii) Due Process: Access to Courts. Many commentators recognize that due process sometimes means judicial process—that is, that there are some kinds of cases to which access to the courts cannot, as a matter of due process, be foreclosed. Paul Bator—who adheres to the traditional view of Congress' power—accepts this proposition. But he argues that "the Constitution is indifferent to whether that access is to a federal or a state court."[h] Hence, he concludes, where state courts will remain available, Congress may freely foreclose access to lower federal courts.

Martin Redish and Curtis Woods disagree with this conclusion.[i] They argue that "[t]here exists a due process right to an independent judicial determination of constitutional rights," and that state courts under some circumstances are *not* open to hear such claims. They therefore argue that due process requires access in such cases to a federal court.

Redish and Woods's claim that state courts are not open to hear some kinds of federal claims is based on *Tarble's Case,* which is

---

[f] He is comforted in this latter conclusion by the availability of federal habeas corpus for the assertion of federal claims by those convicted of state crimes.

[g] Eisenberg's views are extensively criticized in Redish, Congressional Power to Control the Jurisdiction of Lower Federal Courts: A Critical Review and a New Synthesis, 124 U.Pa.L.Rev. 45, 67–75 (1975). See also Gunther, Congressional Power to Curtail Federal Court Jurisdiction: An Opinionated Guide to the Ongoing Debate, 36 Stanford L.Rev. 895, 913–14 (1984).

[h] Bator, Congressional Power Over the Jurisdiction of the Federal Courts, 27 Vill. L.Rev. 1030, 1034 (1982).

[i] Redish and Woods, Congressional Power to Control the Jurisdiction of Lower Federal Courts: A Critical Review and a New Synthesis, 124 U.Pa.L.Rev. 45 (1975).

considered at page 242, infra. *Tarble's Case* held that a state court could not issue a writ of habeas corpus for a person in federal custody. The opinion can be interpreted as a constitutional holding, but is best understood as a federal common law decision. Be that as it may, Redish and Woods read *Tarble's Case* and related decisions to foreclose state court injunctive (or habeas corpus) relief against federal officials. Although they admit that Congress could overrule this line of decisions, they nonetheless conclude that *Tarble's Case* and its progeny remain good law, and that these cases limit the Congressional power to foreclose lower federal court jurisdiction—though only in cases where injunctive or similar relief is sought against federal officials. In other classes of cases, they agree that access to the state courts would be sufficient to satisfy due process.

In a later article,[j] Redish advances a broader contention. He builds on Lawrence Sager's thesis that the art. III salary and tenure provisions require access to federal courts over cases involving challenges to the constitutionality of state official conduct.[k] Redish suggests that the due process clause could be construed—though it has not been—to preclude final adjudicatory authority by state judges over the constitutionality of actions by state government. The argument in support of this construction would be that state judges are not sufficiently "independent" of the government they are expected to supervise. And since Supreme Court review in every case is unavailable as a practical matter, it would follow that due process requires access to lower federal courts to hear these cases.

(iv) Discrimination Against Constitutional Claims. In Congressional Obligation to Provide a Forum for Constitutional Claims: Discriminatory Jurisdictional Rules and the Conflict of Laws, 69 Va.L. Rev. 819 (1983), Lea Brilmayer and Stefan Underhill argue that a series of conflict-of-laws cases stands for the proposition that Congress may not discriminate against constitutional claims when it enacts jurisdictional legislation.[l] They argue that "*in no other legal context* within our federal system has the power to establish and regulate courts carried with it the power to enact jurisdictional statutes that discriminate against claims arising from other sources of law within that system." This means, they conclude, that "door-closing rules that single out constitutional claims without valid reason are prohibited." Congressional hostility to a constitutional right, they argue, is not a "valid reason" to enact a jurisdiction-stripping statute. Nor can they think of a valid reason if a statute were facially to discriminate

[j] Redish, Constitutional Limitations on Congressional Power to Control Federal Jurisdiction: A Reaction to Professor Sager, 77 Nw.U.L.Rev. 143 (1982).

[k] See page 173, supra.

[l] They primarily rely on Hughes v. Fetter, 341 U.S. 609 (1951) (considered at page 354, infra), Testa v. Katt, 330 U.S. 386 (1947) (considered at page 231, infra), and a series of FELA cases (considered at pages 235–38, infra). *Hughes* held that one state was obligated to hear a statutory claim asserted under the laws of another state. *Testa* and the FELA cases held that state courts were obligated to hear federal statutory claims. Each of the cases is perhaps best characterized as a federal common law decision. See the discussion at pages 280–83, infra.

between some constitutional rights and others, or between constitutional rights and other federal rights.

(v) Institutional Characteristics of State and Federal Courts. Consideration of these theories may be advanced by thinking about the respective institutional characteristics of the state and federal courts. In The Myth of Parity, 90 Harv.L.Rev. 1105 (1977), Burt Neuborne argues that state courts "are less likely [than federal courts] to be receptive to vigorous enforcement of federal constitutional doctrine" even though he disclaims "any intent to cast aspersions on the good faith of state judges." He first notes that the proper institutional comparison is between state and federal trial courts, both because of the importance of fact-finding in constitutional litigation and because the expense and delay of relying on appellate courts may deter prospective litigants from testing their claims.

Neuborne argues that federal trial judges tend to be more competent than their state counterparts, largely because of sheer numbers. There are about twice as many trial judges in California as there are in the entire federal system, and it is necessarily more difficult to maintain a high level of quality with so many positions. Moreover, he continues, federal judges tend to receive higher pay and there is greater prestige associated with the office. They also get better staff support, particularly in the number and quality of law clerks.

Neuborne next focuses on a series of psychological and attitudinal characteristics. He argues that federal judges seem to have a better sense of tradition and institutional mission and that they feel closer to, and more receptive to the trends that seem to be motivating, the Supreme Court. They are also less jaundiced by the fact patterns presented by the daily grist of their cases, and tend to be chosen from a successful, homogeneous socioeconomic class that tends to be receptive to constitutional claims. Additionally, he notes that the life tenure granted to federal judges insulates them from the majoritarian pressures to which elected state judges are subject.

Finally, Neuborne identifies three disadvantages of constitutional litigation in federal courts. First, federal judges may be "less sensitive to the social milieu" into which their decisions must fit. Second, federal courts are overburdened with litigation. And third, channeling important constitutional cases into the federal courts may perpetuate the "second-class status and performance" of the state trial courts.

Neuborne made these arguments in the context of explaining why civil liberties lawyers are likely to choose federal rather than state court.[m] He did not address the extent to which, if at all, his conten-

---

[m] For related inquiries, see Brilmayer and Lee, State Sovereignty and the Two Faces of Federalism: A Comparative Study of Federal Jurisdiction and the Conflict of Laws, 60 Notre Dame L.Rev. 833 (1985); Marvell, The Rationales for Federal Question Jurisdiction: An Empirical Examination of Student Rights Litigation, 1984 Wis. L.Rev. 1315; Solimine and Walker, Constitutional Litigation in Federal and State Courts: An Empirical Analysis of Judicial Parity, 10 Hastings Const. L.Q. 213 (1983). For consideration of the case for litigation of federal constitutional issues in state courts, see Bator, The State Courts and Federal Constitutional Litigation, 22 Wm. & Mary L.Rev. 605 (1981).

tions are relevant to questions of congressional power to limit the jurisdiction of the federal courts. Are they relevant? Are they right?

3. *Webster* Revisited. Justice Scalia revisited his *Webster* dissent in Reed v. Collyer, 837 F.2d 1091 (6th Cir.1988), cert. denied, ___ U.S. ___ (1988). Reed filed unfair labor charges, which the General Counsel of the National Labor Relations Board declined to pursue. Reed then sued the General Counsel, claiming that her dismissal of the charges violated the Constitution. The District Court dismissed the suit on the ground that the General Counsel's prosecutorial decisions were not subject to judicial review, and the Sixth Circuit affirmed without opinion. When the Supreme Court denied the petition for certiorari, Justice Scalia took the opportunity to renew his attack on *Webster:*

> "While this petition for certiorari was pending, this Court decided Webster v. Doe, 486 U.S. ___ (1988), applying for the first time the principle that Congress' intent to preclude judicial review of 'constitutional claims' must be expressed with greater clarity than its intent to preclude judicial review of other claims . . . . The statute at issue in the present case pertains to the NLRB, and provides that the General Counsel 'shall have final authority, on behalf of the Board, in respect of the investigation of charges and issuance of complaints under § 160 of this title, and in respect of the prosecution of such complaints before the Board . . . .' 29 U.S.C. § 153(d). The present case, involving constitutional claims, is unquestionably a prime candidate for application of the new principle we adopted in *Webster*. While the area of administrative activity to which the suit pertains (enforcement discretion) is one in which agencies have traditionally been accorded broad insulation from judicial review, so was the area of managing the nation's intelligence services at issue in *Webster*. And the text of the statute in *Webster* was much more suggestive of total unreviewability . . . . I would grant certiorari in this case in order to begin the necessary process of limiting *Webster* to its facts." [n]

4. Questions and Comments on *Webster*. Was Justice Scalia right that the principle for which *Webster* seems to stand might apply to the issue in *Reed*? How might the two cases be distinguished? At a different level, what constitutional theory did the *Webster* Court have in mind as a counterpoint to Justice Scalia's dissenting arguments?

----

[n] Justice Scalia also expressed puzzlement at the Court's "departure from our standard practice of *remanding* (without opinion) pending cases whose outcome could well be affected by a decision we have promulgated after the judgment below."

ADDITIONAL NOTES ON CONGRESSIONAL POWER TO LIMIT THE JURISDICTION OF THE DISTRICT COURTS

1. *Oestereich v. Selective Service.* A constitutional right of access to the lower federal courts was presented, and avoided, in Oestereich v. Selective Service System, Local Board No. 11, 393 U.S. 233 (1968). The issue was the judicial review of retaliatory reclassification of anti-draft protestors by local Selective Service Boards.

The Selective Service Act of 1940 stated that "decisions of . . . local boards shall be final except where an [administrative] appeal is authorized . . . ." This provision was read to bar pre-induction judicial review of draft classifications. Review was allowed only (1) as a defense to criminal prosecution for refusal to be inducted or (2) on a post-induction petition for habeas corpus. In Wolff v. Selective Service Board, 372 F.2d 817 (2d Cir.1967), however, the Second Circuit allowed pre-induction review of the reclassification of two students who had demonstrated against the war in Vietnam. Congress responded by enacting § 10(b)(3) of Selective Service Act of 1967, which expressly barred judicial review "of the classification or processing of any registrant . . ., except as a defense to a criminal prosecution . . . after the registrant has responded either affirmatively or negatively to an order to report for induction." Since no criminal prosecution would result from an affirmative response to induction, the statute was taken to continue judicial review both as a defense to criminal prosecution and in post-induction habeas corpus. But judicial review of draft classifications in any other context seemed clearly proscribed.

Oestereich was a divinity student and accordingly entitled to classification under § 6(d), which provided that "students preparing for the ministry" in qualified schools "shall be exempt from training and service." When Oestereich mailed in his registration certificate as an anti-draft protest, his local board retaliated with a "delinquency" proceeding, in which he was found not in possession of his certificate and reclassified as I–A. After he took and lost an administrative appeal, Oestereich was ordered to report for induction. He then brought suit in federal District Court, which dismissed the complaint on the authority of § 10(b)(3). The Court of Appeals affirmed, but the Supreme Court reversed.

Speaking for the Court, Justice Douglas saw a "clash" between the exemption granted by § 6(d) and the preclusion of judicial review in § 10(b)(3). He resolved the difficulty by finding an exception to the latter provision:

> "Selective Service has promulgated regulations governing delinquency and uses them to deprive registrants of their statutory exemption, because of various activities and conduct and without any regard to the exemptions provided by law.
>
> "We can find no authorization for that use of delinquency . . . . Once a person registers and qualifies for a statutory exemption, we find no legislative authority to deprive him of

that exemption because of conduct or activities unrelated to the merits of granting or continuing that exemption. The Solicitor General confesses error on the use by Selective Service of delinquency proceedings for that purpose.

"We deal with conduct of a local Board that is basically lawless. It is no different in constitutional implications from a case where induction of an ordained minister or other clearly exempt person is ordered (a) to retaliate against the person because of his political views or (b) to bear down on him for his religious views or his racial attitudes or (c) to get him out of town so that the amorous interests of a Board member be better served. In such instances as in the present one, there is no exercise of discretion by a Board in evaluating evidence and in determining whether a claimed exemption is deserved. The case we decide today involves a clear departure by the Board from its statutory mandate. To hold that a person deprived of his statutory exemption in such a blatantly lawless manner must either be inducted and raise his protest through habeas corpus or defy induction and defend his refusal in a criminal prosecution is to construe the act with unnecessary harshness . . . . Our construction leaves § 10(b)(3) unimpaired in the normal operations of the act."

Justice Harlan concurred in the result. He emphasized that the case did not involve the "numerous discretionary, factual, and mixed law-fact determinations" involved in classification decisions, but instead challenged the facial validity of Selective Service regulations. The validity of those regulations was "beyond the competence of Selective Service Boards to hear and determine." Therefore, to deny pre-induction review in this case would deprive Oestereich of his liberty without the prior opportunity to present his claim to any competent forum, whether court or agency. Such a procedure, said Justice Harlan, "would raise serious constitutional problems." He therefore agreed that § 10(b)(3) did not bar pre-induction review in this case.

Justice Stewart, joined by Justices Brennan and White, dissented. He argued that the intent to preclude review was clear and that the "harshness" of the result was not a ground for rewriting the statute. "[I]f the statute is constitutional," said Justice Stewart, "we have no power to disregard it simply because we think it is harsh." And Stewart plainly thought the statute constitutional.

2. *Clark v. Gabriel.* The Court decided Clark v. Gabriel, 393 U.S. 256 (1968), on the same day as *Oestereich.* Gabriel's draft board had rejected his claim as a conscientious objector, had classified him I–A, and had ordered him to report for induction. He sought an injunction in a federal District Court on the grounds that rejection of his conscientious objector claim had no basis in fact, that the board had misapplied the statutory definition of conscientious objector, and that the members of the board were biased against conscientious objector claimants. The District Court held § 10(b)(3) unconstitutional, and the government appealed directly to the Supreme Court. In a per curiam opinion, the Court reversed, holding that "the result here is dictated by the principles enunciated" in *Oestereich:*

> "Here . . . there is no doubt of the board's statutory authority to take [the] action which [Gabriel] challenges, and that action inescapably involves a determination of fact and an exercise of judgment . . . . To allow preinduction judicial review of such determinations would be to permit precisely the kind of 'litigious interruptions of procedures to provide necessary military manpower' which Congress sought to prevent when it enacted § 10(b)(3).

> "We find no constitutional objection to Congress' thus requiring that assertion of a conscientious objector's claims such as those advanced by [Gabriel] be deferred until after induction, if that is the course he chooses, whereupon habeas corpus would be an available remedy, or until defense of the criminal prosecution which would follow should he press his objections to his classification to the point of refusing to submit to induction."

Justice Douglas concurred on the ground that Gabriel's claim turned "on the weight and credibility of testimony." He would take a different view, he said, if Gabriel had been reclassified because he made an unpopular speech or the board took other "lawless" action.

3. Questions and Comments on *Oestereich* and *Gabriel.* Does *Gabriel* obscure or clarify the decision in *Oestereich?*[a] Taken together, what, if anything, do these cases say about the power of Congress to restrict the jurisdiction of the lower federal courts? Does the decision in *Webster* bring these cases into sharper focus? Or are the cases completely distinguished by the fact that *Webster* involved a constitutional claim, rather than a statutory entitlement? Could Oestereich's claim have been recharacterized as constitutional? Would that have mattered?

Note also that Oestereich had two other means by which he could have asserted his claim. He could have refused induction and raised his claim as a defense to criminal charges, or he could have submitted to induction and sought release on habeas corpus. On what theory is Congress required to provide more than one avenue of relief in a federal court? Would state courts also have been open to hear his claim?

4. *United States v. Mendoza-Lopez.* For another recent decision touching these issues, see United States v. Mendoza-Lopez, 481 U.S. 828 (1987). The question was whether the legality of a deportation order could be challenged only in the deportation proceedings themselves or whether an alien subsequently prosecuted for illegal entry following deportation could then raise the illegality of the order as a

[a] For a general discussion of the history of judicial review of selective service decisions and the avenues of review open after *Oestereich* and *Gabriel,* see Winick, Direct Judicial Review of the Selective Service System, 69 Mich.L.Rev. 55 (1970).

defense. Speaking through Justice Marshall, the Court determined that Congress in the relevant statutes had in fact intended to preclude this form of collateral attack on deportation orders. But that, said the Court, "does not end our inquiry":

> "Our cases establish that where a determination made in an administrative proceeding is to play a critical role in the subsequent imposition of a criminal sanction, there must be *some* meaningful review of the administrative proceeding [citing cases]. This principle means at the very least that where the defects in an administrative proceeding foreclose judicial review of that proceeding, an alternate means of obtaining judicial review must be made available before the administrative order may be used to establish conclusively an element of a criminal offense."

The Court concluded that the original deportation proceeding had been unfair in ways that effectively precluded judicial review at that time and that the opportunity to challenge its validity in the subsequent criminal prosecution was therefore constitutionally required.

Chief Justice Rehnquist, joined by Justices White and O'Connor, dissented. Justice Scalia filed a separate dissent in which he argued, inter alia, that other forms of direct and collateral attack were available and that the Court either must have thought them unavailable or regarded them as irrelevant.[b]

5. *Schweiker v. Chilicky*. In a series of decisions recounted elsewhere in these materials,[c] the Supreme Court has confronted the question whether to imply a right of action for damages under the Constitution in situations where there either was no other effective remedy or where existing remedies were assertedly incomplete. Schweiker v. Chilicky, ___ U.S. ___ (1988), which appears as a main case at page 408, infra, involved claimants of disability benefits under the Social Security Act. The plaintiffs' benefits had been improperly terminated, but they were reinstated and awarded retroactive benefits as a result of administrative proceedings. They sought additional money damages for "emotional distress and for loss of food, shelter, and other necessities" against officials who had allegedly violated their constitutional rights in the initial termination of their benefits.

The Supreme Court held that no cause of action for such damages could be asserted, even though it recognized that the "belated restoration of back benefits" did not fully compensate the plaintiffs for the harm they had suffered: "When the design of a government program suggests that Congress has provided what it considers adequate remedial mechanisms for constitutional violations that may occur in the course of its administration, we have not created additional . . .

---

[b] For related earlier decisions that concerned the preclusion of ordinary judicial review in the Emergency Price Control Act of 1942, see Lockerty v. Phillips, 319 U.S. 182 (1943), and Yakus v. United States, 321 U.S. 414 (1944).

[c] See pages 395–430, infra.

remedies." One of the issues before the Court was the meaning of 42 U.S.C. § 405(h), which provides:

> "The findings and decision of the Secretary after a hearing shall be binding upon all individuals who were parties to such hearing. No findings of fact or decision of the Secretary shall be reviewed by any person, tribunal, or governmental agency except as herein provided. No action against the United States, the Secretary, or any officer or employee thereof shall be brought under section 1331 or 1346 of title 28 to recover on any claim arising under [title II]."

It was argued that the last sentence of this provision prevented the federal courts from recognizing a constitutional cause of action in this context. The Court thought the meaning of the last sentence of § 405(h) "not free from doubt" and said that "because we hold on other grounds that a [constitutional] remedy is precluded in this case, we need not decide whether § 405(h) would have the same effect." Justice Brennan, joined by Marshall and Blackmun, dissented. They would have recognized the constitutional cause of action asserted by the plaintiffs. They found the last sentence of § 405(h) not dispositive:

> "In isolation, the sentence might well suggest such a broad preclusion, for it bars resort to federal-question jurisdiction— the jurisdictional basis of actions [such as the one asserted here]—for recovery on any claims arising under title II. The sentence, however, does not appear in isolation, but is rather part of a subsection governing a discrete category of claims: those brought to findings of fact or final decisions of the Secretary after a hearing to which the claimant was a party. Read in context, therefore, the final sentence serves as an adjunct to the exhaustion requirement established in the first two sentences by channeling any and all challenges to benefits determinations through the administrative process and thereby forestalling attempt to circumvent that process under the guise of independent constitutional challenges. Respondents here do not contest any benefits determination, nor have they attempted to bypass the administrative review process: rather, having exhausted the remedies that process provides, they now seek relief for constitutional injuries they suffered in the course of their benefits determinations which the administrative scheme left unredressed. [B]ecause I do not believe that the sentence in question applies to claims such as those respondents assert, I conclude that Congress has not expressly precluded the . . . remedy respondents seek."

Is it plausible that the Court could have recognized the cause of action but held that § 405(h) precluded its assertion? On what principle might the holding in *Schweiker* that the plaintiffs have no cause of action to assert for the violation of their constitutional rights be reconciled with *Webster?*

SECTION 2: CONGRESSIONAL AUTHORITY TO CONFER FEDERAL QUESTION JURISDICTION ON THE DISTRICT COURTS

INTRODUCTORY NOTES ON CONGRESSIONAL AUTHORITY TO CONFER FEDERAL QUESTION JURISDICTION ON THE DISTRICT COURTS

1. Preliminary Comments. The focus now shifts from the limits on congressional power to withhold jurisdiction from the federal courts to the limits on its power to confer jurisdiction. The materials that follow concern the so-called "arising-under" or "federal question" jurisdiction of the federal district courts.

Note that the authorizing language in article III [a] and the authorizing language in the general federal question statute [b] are practically identical. It is settled, however, that the two provisions have different meanings. The constitutional language, augmented by the general powers of Congress and by the necessary and proper clause, confers a broad authority on the Congress to use the federal district courts to decide disputes involving federal policy. By contrast, the statutory language has, at least in modern times, been construed quite differently and far more narrowly so as not to confer all of the constitutionally permissible power to decide federal cases.[c]

2. *Osborn v. Bank of the United States.* Any consideration of the scope of the congressional power to confer "arising-under" jurisdiction on the federal courts must begin with Chief Justice Marshall's opinion in Osborn v. Bank of the United States, 22 U.S. (9 Wheat.) 738 (1824). Congress created the second Bank of the United States in 1816. In his famous opinion in McCulloch v. Maryland, 17 U.S. (4 Wheat.) 316 (1819), Chief Justice Marshall wrote for the Court in upholding the power of Congress to establish the bank and in denying the power of the states to tax it. The state of Ohio, however, did not give in easily. It assessed an annual tax of $50,000 on each office of the bank. The bank filed suit in federal court to enjoin collection of the tax. After an injunction was issued, a state agent broke into an office of the bank and took more than $120,000, most of which was given to the state treasurer. The federal Circuit Court then issued an injunction ordering the return of the money, and the defendants appealed to the Supreme Court. The ground of appeal was that the Circuit Court did not have jurisdiction to hear the case.

[a] "Cases, in Law and Equity, arising under this Constitution, the Laws of the United States, and Treaties made, or which shall be made, under their Authority."

[b] 28 U.S.C. § 1331: "The district courts shall have original jurisdiction of all civil actions arising under the Constitution, laws, or treaties of the United States."

[c] The meaning of the federal question statute is postponed to Chapter V, beginning at page 431, infra. The concern here, as noted, is with the meaning of the constitutional authority contained in article III.

Recall that the general federal question statute, now found in 28 U.S.C. § 1331, was not enacted until 1875. Since there was no diversity in the *Osborn* case, it was necessary for the bank to rely on a special jurisdictional statute to authorize its suit in federal court. The statute on which it relied provided that the bank was "able and capable" to "sue and be sued, plead and be pleaded, answer and be answered, defend and be defended, in all state courts having competent jurisdiction, and in any circuit court of the United States." It was argued that this statute merely conferred capacity to sue. The Court held, however, that it also established jurisdiction in the circuit courts over *any* suit involving the bank.

Chief Justice Marshall began his opinion with the following general observations:

"In support of [jurisdiction], it is said, that the legislative, executive and judicial powers of every well-constructed government, are co-extensive with each other; that is, they are potentially co-extensive. The executive department may constitutionally execute every law which the legislature may constitutionally make, and the judicial department may receive from the legislature the power of construing every such law. All governments which are not extremely defective in their organization, must possess, within themselves, the means of expounding, as well as enforcing, their own laws. If we examine the Constitution of the United States, we find that its framers kept this great political principle in view. [Article III] enables the judicial department to receive jurisdiction to the full extent of the Constitution, laws, and treaties of the United States, when any question respecting them shall assume such a form that the judicial power is capable of acting on it. That power is capable of acting only when the subject is submitted to it by a party who asserts his rights in the form prescribed by law. It then becomes a case, and the Constitution declares, that the judicial power shall extend to all cases arising under the Constitution, laws and treaties of the United States."

Marshall next considered the argument that cases may not be heard in federal court if questions are presented for decision "which depend upon the general principles of the law, not on any act of Congress." He held that the presence of such "general" questions did not matter:

"A cause may depend on several questions of fact and law. Some of these may depend on the construction of a law of the United States; others on principles unconnected with that law. If it be a sufficient foundation for jurisdiction, that the title or right set up by the party, may be defeated by one construction of the Constitution or law of the United States, and sustained by the opposite construction, provided the facts necessary to support the action be made out, then all the other questions must be decided as incidental to this, which gives that jurisdiction. . . . We think, then, that when a question to which the judicial power of the union is extended by the constitution, forms an ingredient of the original cause, it is in the power of Congress to give the circuit courts jurisdiction of that cause, although other questions of fact or of law may be involved in it."

Marshall then noted that in every case brought by the bank a series of federal questions would necessarily be involved—its capacity to sue as an entity, its capacity to engage in the behavior on which the suit is based, etc. These questions "exist in every possible case" brought by the bank, and even though they had been settled by prior decision, they form "an original ingredient in every cause." "The right of the plaintiff to sue," he continued,

"cannot depend on the defence which the defendant may choose to set up. His right to sue is anterior to that defence, and must depend on the state of things when the action is brought. The question which the case involved, then, must determine its character, whether those questions be made in the cause or not."

Finally, Marshall answered an argument raised by the dissent that the same reasoning could give every naturalized citizen the general right to sue in federal court, even though the suit involved state law only and even though diversity of citizenship was lacking. Marshall's answer was that:

"A naturalized citizen is, indeed, made a citizen under an act of Congress, but the act does not proceed to give, to regulate, or to prescribe his capacities. He becomes a member of the society, possessing all the rights of a native citizen, and standing, in the view of the Constitution, on the footing of a native. The Constitution does not authorize Congress to enlarge or abridge those rights. The simple power of the national legislature is, to prescribe a uniform rule of naturalization, and the exercise of this power exhausts it, so far as respects the individual. The Constitution then takes him up, and, among other rights, extends to him the capacity of suing in the courts of the United States, precisely under the same circumstances under which a native might sue. . . . There is, then, no resemblance between the act incorporating the bank, and the general naturalization law."

The Court therefore upheld the jurisdiction of the court below.

Justice Johnson dissented. He agreed that once a lower federal court properly had jurisdiction it could decide all questions that arose in the suit: "No one can question, that the court which has jurisdiction of the principal question, must exercise jurisdiction over every question." But the courts should not assume jurisdiction "on a mere hypothesis." Cases do not arise under federal law until such a question "actually arise[s]." Justice Johnson also criticized the full reach of the Marshall opinion. He could not distinguish the case of the naturalized citizen so easily. He also posed a situation where Congress passed a tax voiding all contracts not written upon stamped paper and a jurisdictional statute permitting all suits upon such contracts to be filed in federal court. Could such a law, he asked, be constitutional? Could it be distinguished from the theory on which Marshall relies? He thought the answer to both questions was "no."

Was Justice Johnson correct? Is the Chief Justice's theory too broad to be acceptable? Or is it consistent with sound constitutional principles? The remaining materials in this section explore the implications of the Marshall theory.

3. The Concept of Protective Jurisdiction. Chief Justice Marshall's theory of decision in *Osborn* reached far beyond the particular circumstances of the case. On the facts of *Osborn,* Marshall could have held that Congress had the power to confer jurisdiction on the circuit courts to enforce the federal right of the bank not to be taxed. This would not have been a remarkable holding. But the theory Marshall actually used seemed to justify federal court jurisdiction over *any* suit brought by the bank, including an action based entirely on state law. Indeed, in a companion case decided on the same day,[d] the Court upheld a suit by the bank in federal court to collect on negotiable notes issued by a state bank.

The constitutional problem to which these holdings gave rise was whether Congress could authorize suit in federal court in the absence of diversity and in the absence of a substantive federal claim by the bank. Congress clearly may confer jurisdiction on the federal trial courts where it has validly created a substantive federal basis for the suit. The question is whether, if Congress has the power to create federal substantive rights, it may take the (lesser?) step of permitting suit in federal court under state law if it believes that pre-empting state law is not a "necessary and proper" solution to the problem before it. In *Osborn* Chief Justice Marshall seemed to avoid the problem by holding that any suit brought by the bank would "arise under" federal law.

The broader question is whether Congress may use a similar technique in cases not involving a federal instrumentality. The issue is whether Congress may confer "protective jurisdiction" on the federal courts, that is, whether Congress may provide access to federal courts for state-law claims asserted by non-diversity plaintiffs believed to need the "protection" of a federal forum because the neutrality of state courts might be suspect, because of procedural advantages to be found in federal court, or for any other reason that Congress may think good and sufficient.

The argument that Congress may not rely on a theory of "protective jurisdiction" begins with the language of article III. Cases must actually arise under federal law to fall under the "arising under" language, the argument goes, and those cases where Congress may use

---

[d] Bank of United States v. Planter's Bank of Georgia, 22 U.S. (9 Wheat.) 904 (1824).

the federal courts simply to "protect" suitors from the hazards or disadvantages of state courts are specifically, and exclusively, listed in article III itself. Those who believe that "protective jurisdiction" is beyond the power of Congress conclude that the diversity clause and the other provisions of article III based on the status of the parties exhaust the capacity of Congress to provide for the "protection" of litigants who are not actually asserting federal rights.

Was *Osborn* in the end based on a "protective jurisdiction" theory? Justice Johnson in his *Osborn* dissent recognized the policy basis of the Marshall opinion:

> "I have very little doubt, that the public mind will be easily reconciled to the decision of the Court here rendered: for, whether necessary or unnecessary, originally, a state of things has grown up, in some of the states, which renders all the protection necessary, that the general government can give to this bank. The policy of the decision is obvious, that is, if the bank is to be sustained; and few will bestow upon its legal correctness, the reflection that it is necessary to test it by the Constitution and laws, under which it is rendered."

Did Chief Justice Marshall, as Justice Johnson implied, sacrifice the Constitution for expediency? Or is congressional concern over the survival of the bank a sufficient (and constitutional) reason for not subjecting its lawsuits to state courts? Could Congress have provided that all legal rights of the bank would be governed by federal law? If so, should Congress have been required by article III to choose this course in order to permit suits by the bank in federal court? Which solution is the greater intrusion upon the states? The following case and its notes raise these and similar questions in a modern context.

TEXTILE WORKERS UNION v. LINCOLN MILLS

United States Supreme Court, 1957.
353 U.S. 448.

[Section 301 of the Labor Management Relations Act of 1947 provided:

> "(a) Suits for violation of contracts between an employer and a labor organization representing employees in an industry affecting commerce as defined in this chapter, or between any such labor organizations, may be brought in any district court of the United States having jurisdiction of the parties, without respect to the amount in controversy or without regard to the citizenship of the parties.

> "(b) Any labor organization which represents employees in an industry affecting commerce as defined in this chapter and any employer whose activities affect commerce as defined in this chapter shall be bound by the acts of its agents. Any such labor organization may sue or be sued as an entity and in

behalf of the employees whom it represents in the courts of the United States. Any money judgment against a labor organization in a district court of the United States shall be enforceable only against the organization as an entity and its assets, and shall not be enforceable against any individual member or his assets."

The Textile Workers Union entered into a collective bargaining agreement with Lincoln Mills. The agreement contained a no-strike clause and a grievance procedure, the last step of which was compulsory arbitration. The union filed several grievances against the employer, which were processed through the grievance procedure but ultimately denied by the employer. The union requested arbitration under the terms of the contract, but the employer refused. This suit was then brought by the union to compel arbitration. The District Court ordered arbitration, but the Court of Appeals reversed. It held that the District Court had no authority under either state or federal law to grant such relief. The Supreme Court granted certiorari.

[In a majority opinion written by Justice Douglas, the Court held that § 301(a) was in effect a command to the federal courts to develop a body of federal common law to enforce labor contracts. The specific enforcement of arbitration agreements, moreover, was part of the federal common law that the courts were meant to enforce. The Court accordingly reversed the Court of Appeals' judgment.

[Justice Frankfurter dissented. He disagreed that the statute should be interpreted as a directive to fashion a body of federal common law out of whole cloth, and suggested that the courts might lack the power to do so even if that is what Congress meant. For him, therefore, the case presented the question whether Congress could confer jurisdiction on the federal district courts to hear non-diversity suits turning on questions of state law. The portion of his opinion in which he addressed this issue is reproduced below.]

Since I do not agree with the Court's conclusion that federal substantive law is to govern in actions under § 301, I am forced to consider . . . the constitutionality of a grant of jurisdiction to federal courts over contracts that came into being entirely by virtue of state substantive law, a jurisdiction not based on diversity of citizenship, yet one in which a federal court would, as in diversity cases, act in effect merely as another court of the state in which it sits. The scope of allowable federal judicial power that this grant must satisfy is constitutionally described as "Cases, in Law and Equity, arising under this Constitution, the Laws of the United States, and Treaties made, or which shall be made, under their Authority." Art. III, § 2. While interpretive decisions are legion under general statutory grants of jurisdiction strikingly similar to this constitutional wording, it is generally recognized that the full constitutional power has not been exhausted by these statutes. See, e.g., Mishkin, The Federal "Question" in the District Courts, 53 Colum. L. Rev. 157, 160 (1953); Shulman and Jaegerman, Some Jurisdictional Limitations on Federal Procedure, 45

Yale L.J. 393, 405 n.47 (1936); Wechsler, Federal Jurisdiction and the Revision of the Judicial Code, 13 Law & Contemp. Prob. 216, 224–25 (1948).

Almost without exception, decisions under the general statutory grants have tested jurisdiction in terms of the presence, as an integral part of plaintiff's cause of action, of an issue calling for interpretation or application of federal law. E.g., Gully v. First National Bank, 299 U.S. 109 (1936). Although it has sometimes been suggested that the "cause of action" must derive from federal law, see American Well Works Co. v. Layne & Bowler Co., 241 U.S. 257, 260 (1916), it has been found sufficient that some aspect of federal law is essential to plaintiff's success. Smith v. Kansas City Title & Trust Co., 255 U.S. 180 (1921). The litigation-provoking problem has been the degree to which federal law must be in the forefront of the case and not collateral, peripheral or remote.

In a few exceptional cases, arising under special jurisdictional grants, the criteria by which the prominence of the federal question is measured against constitutional requirements have been found satisfied under circumstances suggesting a variant theory of the nature of these requirements. The first, and the leading case in the field, is Osborn v. Bank of the United States, 22 U.S. (9 Wheat.) (1824). There, Chief Justice Marshall sustained federal jurisdiction in a situation—hypothetical in the case before him but presented by the companion case of Bank of the United States v. Planters' Bank, 22 U.S. (9 Wheat.) 904 (1824)—involving suit by a federally incorporated bank upon a contract. Despite the assumption that the cause of action and the interpretation of the contract would be governed by state law, the case was found to "arise under the laws of the United States" because the propriety and scope of a federally granted authority to enter into contracts and to litigate might well be challenged. This reasoning was subsequently applied to sustain jurisdiction in actions against federally chartered railroad corporations. Pacific Railroad Removal Cases, 115 U.S. 1 (1885). The traditional interpretation of this series of cases is that federal jurisdiction under the "arising" clause of the Constitution, though limited to cases involving potential federal questions, has such flexibility that Congress may confer it whenever there exists in the background some federal proposition that might be challenged, despite the remoteness of the likelihood of actual presentation of such a federal question.[4]

The views expressed in *Osborn* and the *Pacific Railroad Removal Cases* were severely restricted in constructing general grants of jurisdiction. But the Court later sustained this jurisdictional section of the Bankruptcy Act of 1893 [§ 23]:

> The United States district courts shall have jurisdiction of
> all controversies at law and in equity, as distinguished from

---

[4] *Osborn* might possibly be limited on the ground that a federal instrumentality, the Bank of the United States, was involved, see n.5, infra, but such an explanation could not suffice to narrow the holding in the *Pacific Railroad Removal Cases*.

> proceedings in bankruptcy, between trustees as such and adverse claimants concerning the property acquired or claimed by the trustees, in the same manner and to the same extent only as though bankruptcy proceedings had not been instituted and such controversies had been between the bankrupts and such adverse claimants."

Under this provision the trustee could pursue in a federal court a private cause of action arising under and wholly governed by state law. Schumacher v. Beeler, 293 U.S. 367 (1934); Williams v. Austrian, 331 U.S. 642 (1947). To be sure, the cases did not discuss the basis of jurisdiction. It has been suggested that they merely represent an extension of the approach of the *Osborn* case; the trustee's right to sue might be challenged on obviously federal grounds—absence of bankruptcy or irregularity of the trustee's appointment or of the bankruptcy proceedings. National Mutual Ins. Co. v. Tidewater Transfer Co., 337 U.S. 582, 611–13 (1949) (Rutledge, J., concurring). So viewed, this type of litigation implicates a potential federal question. . . .

With this background, many theories have been proposed to sustain the constitutional validity of § 301. In Textile Workers Union of America v. American Thread Co., 113 F. Supp. 137, 140 (1953), Judge Wyzanski suggested, among other possibilities, that § 301 might be read as containing a direction that controversies affecting interstate commerce should be governed by federal law incorporating state law by reference, and that such controversies would then arise under a valid federal law as required by article III. Whatever may be said of the assumption regarding the validity of federal jurisdiction under an affirmative declaration by Congress that state law should be applied as federal law by federal courts to contract disputes affecting commerce, we cannot argumentatively legislate for Congress when Congress has failed to legislate. To do so disrespects legislative responsibility and disregards judicial limitations.

Another theory, relying on *Osborn* and the bankruptcy cases, has been proposed [in] H. Hart & H. Wechsler, The Federal Courts and the Federal System 744–47 (1953) [and] Wechsler, Federal Jurisdiction and the Revision of the Judicial Code, 13 Law & Contemp. Prob. 216, 224–25 (1948). Called "protective jurisdiction," the suggestion is that in any case for which Congress has the constitutional power to prescribe federal rules of decision and thus confer "true" federal question jurisdiction, it may, without so doing, enact a jurisdictional statute, which will provide a federal forum for the application of state statute and decisional law. Analysis of the "protective jurisdiction" theory might also be attempted in terms of the language of article III—construing "laws" to include jurisdictional statutes where Congress could have legislated substantively in a field. This is but another way of saying that because Congress could have legislated substantively and thereby could give rise to litigation under a statute of the United States, it can provide a federal forum for state-created rights although it chose not to adopt state law as federal law or to originate federal rights.

Surely the truly technical restrictions of article III are not met or respected by a beguiling phrase that the greater power here must necessarily include the lesser. In the compromise of federal and state interests leading to distribution of jealously guarded judicial power in a federal system, it is obvious that very different considerations apply to cases involving questions of federal law and those turning solely on state law. It may be that the ambiguity of the phrase "arising under the laws of the United States" leaves room for more than traditional theory could accommodate. But, under the theory of "protective jurisdiction," the "arising under" jurisdiction of the federal courts would be vastly extended. For example, every contract or tort arising out of a contract affecting commerce might be a potential cause of action in the federal courts, even though only state law was involved in the decision of the case. At least in *Osborn* and the bankruptcy cases, a substantive federal law was present somewhere in the background. But this theory rests on the supposition that Congress could enact substantive federal law to govern the particular case. It was not held in those cases, nor is it clear, that federal law could be held to govern the transactions of all persons who subsequently become bankrupt, or of all suits of a bank of the United States. See Mishkin, The Federal "Question" in the District Courts, 53 Colum. L. Rev. 157, 189 (1953).

"Protective jurisdiction," once the label is discarded, cannot be justified under any view of the allowable scope to be given to article III. "Protective jurisdiction" is a misused label for the statute we are here considering. That rubric is properly descriptive of safeguarding some of the indisputable, staple business of the federal courts. It is a radiation of an existing jurisdiction. "Protective jurisdiction" cannot generate an independent source for adjudication outside of the article III sanctions and what Congress has defined. The theory must have as its sole justification a belief in the inadequacy of state tribunals in determining state law. The Constitution reflects such a belief in the specific situation within which the diversity clause was confined. The intention to remedy such supposed defects was exhausted in this provision of article III.[5] That this "protective" theory was not adopted by Chief Justice Marshall at a time when conditions might have presented more substantial justification strongly suggests its lack of constitutional merit. Moreover, Congress in its consideration of § 301 nowhere suggested dissatisfaction with the ability of state courts to administer state law properly. Its concern was to provide access to the federal courts for easier enforcement of state-created rights.

---

[5] To be sure, the Court upheld the removal statute for suits or prosecutions commenced in a state court against federal revenue officers on account of any act committed under color of office. Tennessee v. Davis, 100 U.S. 257 (1879). The Court, however, construed the action of Congress in defining the powers of revenue agents as giving them a substantive defense against prosecution under state law for commission of acts "warranted by the federal authority they possess." That put federal law in the forefront as a defense. In any event, the fact that officers of the federal government were parties may be considered sufficient to afford access to the federal forum. See Mishkin, 53 Colum. L. Rev., at 193: "Without doubt, a federal forum should be available for all suits involving the government, its agents and instrumentalities, regardless of the source of the substantive rule."

Another theory also relies on *Osborn* and the bankruptcy cases as an implicit recognition of the propriety of the exercise of some sort of "protective jurisdiction" by the federal courts. Mishkin, 53 Colum. L.Rev. 157, 184 et seq. Professor Mishkin tends to view the assertion of such a jurisdiction, in the absence of any exercise of substantive powers, as irreconcilable with the "arising" clause since the case would then arise only under the jurisdictional statute itself, and he is reluctant to find a constitutional basis for the grant of power outside article III. Professor Mishkin also notes that the only purpose of such a statute would be to insure impartiality to some litigant, an objection inconsistent with article III's recognition of "protective jurisdiction" only in the specified situation of diverse citizenship. But where Congress has "an articulated and active federal policy regulating a field, the 'arising under' clause of article III apparently permits the conferring of jurisdiction on the national courts of all cases in the area—including those substantively governed by state law." In such cases, the protection being offered is not to the suitor, as in diversity cases, but to the "congressional legislative program." Thus he supports § 301: "even though the rules governing collective bargaining agreements continue to be state-fashioned nonetheless the mode of their application and enforcement may play a very substantial part in the labor-management relations of interstate industry and commerce—an area in which the national government has labored long and hard."

Insofar as state law governs the case, Professor Mishkin's theory is quite similar to that advanced by Professors Hart and Wechsler and followed by the Court of Appeals for the First Circuit: The substantive power of Congress, although not exercised to govern the particular "case," gives "arising under" jurisdiction to the federal courts despite governing state law. The second "protective jurisdiction" theory has the dubious advantage of limiting incursions on state judicial power to situations in which the state's feelings may have been tempered by early substantive federal invasions.

Professor Mishkin's theory of "protective jurisdiction" may find more constitutional justification if there is not merely an "articulated and active" congressional policy regulating the labor field but also federal rights existing in the interstices of actions under § 301. See Wollett and Wellington, Federalism and Breach of the Labor Agreement, 7 Stan. L. Rev. 445, 475–79 (1955). Therefore, before resting on an interpretation of § 301 that would compel a declaration of unconstitutionality, we must . . . defer to the strong presumption—even as to such technical matters as federal jurisdiction—that Congress legislated in accordance with the Constitution. . . .

Legislation must, if possible, be given a meaning that will enable it to survive. This rule of constitutional adjudication is normally invoked to narrow what would otherwise be the natural but constitutionally dubious scope of the language. Here the endeavor of some lower courts and of this Court has resulted in adding to the section substantive congressional regulation even though Congress saw fit not to exercise such power or to give the courts any concrete guidance for defining such regulation. . . .

There is a point, however, at which the search may be ended with less misgiving regarding the propriety of judicial infusion of substantive provisions into § 301. The contribution of federal law might consist in postulating the right of a union, despite its amorphous status as an unincorporated association, to enter into binding collective-bargaining contracts with an employer. The federal courts might also give sanction to this right by refusing to comply with any state law that does not admit that collective bargaining may result in an enforceable contract. It is hard to see what serious federal-state conflicts could arise under this view. At most, a state court might dismiss the action, while a federal court would entertain it. Moreover, such a function of federal law is closely related to the removal of the procedural barriers to suit. Section 301 would be futile if the union's status as a contracting party were not recognized. The statement in § 301(b) that the acts of the agents of the union are to be regarded as binding upon the union may be used in support of this conclusion. This provision, not confined in its application to suits in the district court under § 301(a), was primarily directed to responsibility of the union for its agents' actions in authorizing strikes or committing torts. It can be construed, however, as applicable to the formation of a contract. So applied, it would imply that a union must be regarded as contractually bound by the acts of its agents, which in turn presupposes that the union is capable of contract relations.

Of course, the possibility of a state's law being counter to such a limited federal proposition is hypothetical, and to base an assertion of federal law on such a possibility, one never considered by Congress, is an artifice. And were a state ever to adopt a contrary attitude, its reasons for so doing might be such that Congress would not be willing to disregard them. But these difficulties are inherent in any attempt to expand § 301 substantively to meet constitutional requirements.

Even if this limited federal "right" were read into § 301, a serious constitutional question would still be present. It does elevate the situation to one closely analogous to that presented in *Osborn*.[6] Section 301 would, under this view, imply that a union is to be viewed as a juristic entity for purposes of acquiring contract rights under a collective-bargaining agreement, and that it has the right to enter into such a contract and to sue upon it. This was all that was immediately and expressly involved in the *Osborn* case, although the historical setting was vastly different, and the juristic entity in that case was completely the creature of federal law, one engaged in carrying out essential governmental functions. Most of these special considerations had dis-

---

[6] Enunciation of such a requirement could in fact bring federal law somewhat further to the forefront than was true of *Osborn,* the *Pacific Railroad Removal Cases,* or the bankruptcy cases in the few cases where an assertion could be made that state law did not sufficiently recognize collective agreements as contracts. But there appears to be no state that today possesses such a rule. Most and probably all cases arising under § 301—certainly the present ones—would never present such a problem.

appeared, however, at the time and in the circumstances of the decision of the *Pacific Railroad Removal Cases.* There is force in the view that regards the latter as a "sport" and finds that the Court has so viewed it. See Mishkin, 53 Colum. L. Rev., at 160, n.24. The question is whether we should now so consider it and refuse to apply its holding to the present situation.

I believe that we should not extend the precedents of *Osborn* and the *Pacific Railroad Removal Cases* to this case, even though there be some elements of analytical similarity. *Osborn,* the foundation for the *Removal Cases,* appears to have been based on premises that today, viewed in the light of the jurisdictional philosophy of *Gully v. First National Bank* are subject to criticism. The basic premise was that every case in which a federal question might arise must be capable of being commenced in the federal courts, and when so commenced it might, because jurisdiction must be judged at the outset, be concluded there despite the fact that the federal question was never raised. Marshall's holding was undoubtedly influenced by his fear that the bank might suffer hostile treatment in the state courts that could not be remedied by an appeal on an isolated federal question. There is nothing in article III that affirmatively supports the view that original jurisdiction over cases involving federal questions must extend to every case in which there is the potentiality of appellate jurisdiction. We also have become familiar with removal procedures that could be adapted to alleviate any remaining fears by providing for removal to a federal court whenever a federal question was raised. In view of these developments, we would not be justified in perpetuating a principle that permits assertion of original federal jurisdiction on the remote possibility of presentation of a federal question. Indeed, Congress, by largely withdrawing the jurisdiction that the *Pacific Railroad Removal Cases* recognized, and this Court, by refusing to perpetuate it under general grants of jurisdiction, see *Gully v. First National Bank,* have already done much to recognize the changed atmosphere.

Analysis of the bankruptcy power also reveals a superficial analogy to § 301. The trustee enforces a cause of action acquired under state law by the bankrupt. Federal law merely provides for the appointment of the trustee, vests the cause of action in him, and confers jurisdiction on the federal courts. Section 301 similarly takes the rights and liabilities which under state law are vested distributively in the individual members of a union and vests them in the union for purposes of actions in federal courts, wherein the unions are authorized to sue and be sued as an entity. While the authority of the trustee depends on the existence of a bankrupt and on the propriety of the proceedings leading to the trustee's appointment, both of which depend on federal law, there are similar federal propositions that may be essential to an action under § 301. Thus, the validity of the contract may in any case be challenged on the ground that the labor organization negotiating it was not the representative of the employees concerned, a question that has been held to be federal, or on the ground that subsequent change in the representative status of the union has affected the continued validity of the agreement. . . .   Consequently, were the bankruptcy cases to be viewed as dependent solely on the background existence of federal questions, there would be little analytical basis for distinguishing actions under § 301.   But the bankruptcy decisions may be justified by the scope of the bankruptcy power, which may be deemed to sweep within its scope interests analytically outside the "federal question" category, but sufficiently related to the main purpose of bankruptcy to call for comprehensive treatment.   Also, although a particular suit may be brought by a trustee in a district other than the one in which the principal proceedings are pending, if all the suits by the trustee, even though in many federal courts, are regarded as one litigation for the collection and apportionment of the bankrupt's property, a particular suit by the trustee, under state law, to recover a specific piece of property might be analogized to the ancillary or pendent jurisdiction cases in which, in the disposition of a cause of action, federal courts may pass on state grounds for recovery that are joined to federal grounds.

If there is in the phrase "arising under the laws of the United States" leeway for expansion of our concepts of jurisdiction, the history of article III suggests that the area is not great and that it will require the presence of some substantial federal interest, one of greater weight and dignity than questionable doubt concerning the effectiveness of state procedure.   The bankruptcy cases might possibly be viewed as such an expansion.   But even so, not merely convenient judicial administration but the whole purpose of the congressional legislative program—conservation and equitable distribution of the bankrupt's estate in carrying out the constitutional power over bankruptcy—required the availability of federal jurisdiction to avoid expense and delay.   Nothing pertaining to § 301 suggests vesting the federal courts with sweeping power under the commerce clause comparable to that vested in the federal courts under the bankruptcy power.

In the wise distribution of governmental powers, this Court cannot do what a President sometimes does in returning a bill to Congress. We cannot return this provision to Congress and respectfully request that body to face the responsibility placed upon it by the Constitution to define the jurisdiction of the lower courts with some particularity and not to leave these courts at large.   Confronted as I am, I regretfully have no choice.   For all the reasons elaborated in this dissent, even reading into § 301 the limited federal rights consistent with the purposes of that section, I am impelled to the view that it is unconstitutional in cases such as the present ones where it provides the sole basis for exercise of jurisdiction by the federal courts.

NOTES ON THE CONSTITUTIONALITY OF
PROTECTIVE JURISDICTION

1. ***Verlinden B.V. v. Central Bank of Nigeria.***   In the Foreign
Sovereign Immunities Act of 1976, Congress added 28 U.S.C. § 1330 to
the federal code.   That provision states:

"(a) The district courts shall have original jurisdiction
without regard to amount in controversy of any nonjury civil
action against a foreign state as defined in section 1603(a) of
this title as to any claim for relief in personam with respect to
which the foreign state is not entitled to immunity either
under sections 1605–1607 of this title or under any applicable
international agreement."

In Verlinden B.V. v. Central Bank of Nigeria, 461 U.S. 480 (1983), the
Court granted certiorari "to consider whether [this statute], by authorizing a foreign plaintiff to sue a foreign state in a United States
district court on a non-federal cause of action, violates article III of the
Constitution."

Verlinden was a Dutch corporation which contracted with Nigeria
for the delivery of a large quantity of cement.   The contract specified
that Dutch law would control its interpretation and that disputes would
be resolved in a French forum.   Verlinden filed suit in a federal district
court for anticipatory breach of the contract.   The defendant was the
Nigerian instrumentality responsible for the financial aspects of the
transaction.   The District Court held that § 1330(a) authorized the suit,
subject to whether the defendant was entitled to sovereign immunity
under the explicit terms of the statute.   The court then upheld the
defense of sovereign immunity, and accordingly dismissed the case.
The Court of Appeals affirmed on the entirely different ground that
§ 1330(a) was unconstitutional.

The Supreme Court upheld the statute.   It first reviewed the
history of the sovereign immunity granted to foreign governments
under federal law.   An early opinion by Chief Justice Marshall established complete immunity for foreign sovereigns, depending—as the
doctrine developed over the years—on a request by the State Department in each individual case.   In 1952, the Department adopted the
policy that foreign sovereigns would remain immune for their public
acts but would no longer be immune for strictly commercial transactions.   Decisions were still made on a case-by-case basis, however,
which led to diplomatic pressure and consequent inconsistencies.   The
Foreign Sovereign Immunities Act was passed in 1976 to regularize the
law in this area.   In general, it follows the policy adopted in 1952.   It
continues the immunity of foreign governments from the jurisdiction of
federal and state courts, unless a specified exception is satisfied.   Suits
that satisfy one of the exceptions can be brought either in state or
federal court, although the defendant may remove any action from
state to federal court.   The House Report stated that the removal
authority was granted "in view of the political sensitivity of actions

against foreign states and the importance of developing a uniform body of law in this area."

The Court interpreted the statute to permit suits by foreign plaintiffs against a foreign sovereign. This gave rise to the constitutional question, as to which the Court unanimously held:

"This Court's cases firmly establish that Congress may not expand the jurisdiction of the federal courts beyond the bounds established by the Constitution. Within article III of the Constitution, we find two sources authorizing the grant of jurisdiction in the Foreign Sovereign Immunities Act: the diversity clause and the 'arising under' clause.[17] The diversity clause, which provides that the judicial power extends to controversies between 'a State, or the Citizens thereof, and foreign States,' covers actions by citizens of states. Yet diversity jurisdiction is not sufficiently broad to support a grant of jurisdiction over actions by foreign plaintiffs . . . . We conclude, however, that the 'arising under' clause of article III provides an appropriate basis for the statutory grant of subject matter jurisdiction to actions by foreign plaintiffs under the act.

"The controlling decision on the scope of article III 'arising under' jurisdiction is Chief Justice Marshall's opinion for the Court in *Osborn v. Bank of the United States.* In *Osborn,* the Court upheld the constitutionality of a statute that granted the Bank of the United States the right to sue in federal court on causes of action based upon state law. . . . *Osborn* . . . reflects a broad conception of 'arising under' jurisdiction, according to which Congress may confer on the federal courts jurisdiction over any case or controversy that might call for the application of federal law. The breadth of that conclusion has been questioned. It has been observed that, taken at its broadest, *Osborn* might be read as permitting 'assertion of original federal jurisdiction on the remote possibility of presentation of a federal question.' [Citing Frankfurter's dissent in *Lincoln Mills.*] We need not now resolve that issue or decide the precise boundaries of article III jurisdiction, however, since the present case does not involve a mere speculative possibility that a federal question may arise at some point in the proceeding. Rather, a suit against a foreign state under this act necessarily raises questions of substantive federal law at the very outset, and hence clearly 'arises under' federal law, as that term is used in article III.

"By reason of its authority over foreign commerce and foreign relations, Congress has the undisputed power to decide, as a matter of federal law, whether and under what circum-

---

[17] "In view of our conclusion that proper actions by foreign plaintiffs under the Foreign Sovereign Immunities Act are within article III 'arising under' jurisdiction, we need not consider petitioner's alternative argument that the act is constitutional as an aspect of so-called 'protective jurisdiction.'"

stances foreign nations should be amenable to suit in the United States. Actions against foreign sovereigns in our courts raise sensitive issues concerning the foreign relations of the United States, and the primacy of federal concerns is evident.

"To promote these federal interests, Congress exercised its article I powers by enacting a statute comprehensively regulating the amenability of foreign nations to suit in the United States. The statute must be applied by the district courts in every action against a foreign sovereign, since subject matter jurisdiction in any such action depends on the existence of one of the specified exceptions to foreign sovereign immunity. At the threshold of every action, therefore, the court must satisfy itself that one of the exceptions applies—and in doing so it must apply the detailed federal law standards set forth in the act. Accordingly, an action against a foreign sovereign arises under federal law, for purposes of article III jurisdiction."

The Court then responded to two arguments deemed dispositive by the Court of Appeals. The first was that decisions interpreting § 1331, in particular the line of cases requiring that the federal issue appear on the face of the plaintiff's well-pleaded complaint, required dismissal of the case. The Court of Appeals had reasoned that any issue of sovereign immunity would enter the case by way of defense, not on the face of Verlinden's well-pleaded complaint. The Supreme Court responded:

"Although the language of § 1331 parallels that of the 'arising under' clause of article III, this Court never has held that statutory 'arising under' jurisdiction is identical to article III 'arising under' jurisdiction. Quite the contrary is true. '[T]he many limitations which have been placed on jurisdiction under § 1331 are not limitations on the constitutional power of Congress to confer jurisdiction on the federal courts.' . . . Article III 'arising under' jurisdiction is broader than federal question jurisdiction under § 1331 . . . ."

The second argument accepted by the Court of Appeals was that a jurisdictional provision could not itself provide the basis for 'arising under' jurisdiction—that this kind of bootstrapping should not be permitted. The Supreme Court rejected this argument on the ground that the Sovereign Immunities Act was more than a jurisdictional provision:

"The act . . . does not merely concern access to the federal courts. Rather, it governs the types of actions for which foreign sovereigns may be held liable in a court in the United States, federal or state. The act codifies the standards governing foreign sovereign immunity as an aspect of substantive federal law, and applying those standards will generally require interpretation of numerous points of federal law. . . . That the inquiry into foreign sovereign immunity is labeled under the act as a matter of jurisdiction does not affect the constitutionality of Congress' action in granting the federal courts jurisdiction over cases calling for application of this comprehensive regulatory statute.

"Congress, pursuant to its unquestioned article I powers, has enacted a broad statutory framework governing assertions of foreign sovereign immunity. In so doing, Congress deliberately sought to channel cases against foreign sovereigns away from the state courts and into federal courts, thereby reducing the potential for a multiplicity of conflicting results among the courts of 50 states. The resulting jurisdictional grant is within the bounds of article III, since every action against a foreign sovereign necessarily involves application of a body of substantive federal law, and accordingly 'arises under' federal law, within the meaning of article III."

2. Questions and Comments on *Lincoln Mills* and *Verlinden*. In spite of the disclaimer in footnote 17, did the Court in *Verlinden* uphold a kind of protective jurisdiction to which Justice Frankfurter, at least, would have objected? Suppose the foreign sovereign conceded that it was not entitled to immunity and the merits of the case involved no propositions of federal law. Would that matter? Since one cannot tell until the defendant has filed an answer whether sovereign immunity will be raised as a defense, is the Court upholding the Foreign Sovereign Immunities Act because of the *probability* that federal questions will arise? Can distinctions be drawn among *Osborn*, Frankfurter's version of the *Lincoln Mills* statute, and *Verlinden* based on the degree of likelihood that federal questions actually will arise? Or is the critical question the nature of the interests involved, that is, are the foreign relations stakes in *Verlinden* and the survival of the bank in *Osborn* more weighty than the policies involved in Frankfurter's version of *Lincoln Mills*? Or is there no difference among these cases?

Justice Frankfurter's opinion in *Lincoln Mills* is a virtual hornbook on the various theories that have been used to justify protective jurisdiction in the federal courts.[a] Are they singly or collectively persuasive? More persuasive than Frankfurter's responses?

In April of 1969, a bill was introduced to give the federal district courts jurisdiction, regardless of the amount in controversy and regardless of the citizenship of the parties, of civil class actions brought by consumers to redress "the violations of consumers' rights under State or Federal statutory or decisional law." Would this statute have been constitutional? A subsequent version of the bill responded to constitutional concerns by explicitly incorporating as federal law any state

[a] More recent discussion of the issues can be found in Brown, Beyond *Pennhurst*—Protective Jurisdiction, the Eleventh Amendment, and the Power of Congress to Enlarge Federal Jurisdiction in Response to the Burger Court, 71 Va. L. Rev. 343 (1985), Goldberg-Ambrose, The Protective Jurisdiction of the Federal Courts, 30 U.C.L.A. L. Rev. 542 (1983), and Note, The Theory of Protective Jurisdiction, 57 N.Y.U.L. Rev. 933 (1982).

statutes or decisions relating to consumers' rights. Would that ploy
have saved the statute? Neither version of the bill was enacted.[b]

3. *National Mutual Insurance Co. v. Tidewater Transfer Co.*
The general diversity statute, 28 U.S.C. § 1332, provides that citizens of
the District of Columbia are citizens of a state for purposes of diversity
jurisdiction. The constitutionality of the predecessor to this provision
was challenged in National Mutual Insurance Co. v. Tidewater Transfer
Co., 337 U.S. 582 (1949).

The plaintiff, a corporation organized under District of Columbia
law, sued the defendant, a corporation chartered in Virginia, in a
Maryland federal district court. The action sought monetary relief for
breach of an insurance contract. The District Court held that the
statute exceeded the powers of Congress to confer diversity jurisdiction
on the federal courts. The Court of Appeals affirmed, and the Supreme
Court reversed by an oddly aligned vote.

The first question was whether the provision in article III permitting suits in federal court "between Citizens of different States" included suits where one of the parties was a citizen of the District of
Columbia. In an opinion by Chief Justice Marshall, the Supreme Court
had held in Hepburn & Dundas v. Ellzey, 6 U.S. (2 Cranch) 445 (1804),
that a citizen of the District of Columbia was not a citizen of a state
within the diversity statute then in force.[c] The federal courts remained closed to such suits until 1940, when Congress amended the
diversity statute to include District of Columbia citizens. It was this
statute that was before the Court in *Tidewater.*

The *Tidewater* Court upheld Marshall's view by a seven to two
vote. Thus a substantial majority of the Court regarded a citizen of the
District of Columbia as not a citizen of a state for purposes of the
diversity jurisdiction provided in article III.

The question then became whether there was an alternate theory
by which Congress could authorize such a suit. Justice Jackson was
equal to the occasion.[d] His consideration of the merits of the statute
began with the following observations:

---

[b] The text of the bills and a discussion of
the constitutional issues raised are contained in Note, Federal Jurisdiction—Protective Jurisdiction and Adoption as Alternative Techniques for Conferring
Jurisdiction on Federal Courts in Consumer Class Actions, 69 Mich. L. Rev. 710
(1971). See also Note, Consumer Protection—The Class Action Jurisdiction Act, 44
Tulane L. Rev. 580 (1970).

[c] In his opinion in *Tidewater*, Justice
Jackson described *Hepburn* as follows:

"To be sure, nothing was before that
Court except interpretation of a statute
which conferred jurisdiction substantially in the words of the Constitution with
nothing in the text or context to show
that Congress intended to regard the District as a state. But Marshall resolved

the statutory question by invoking the
analogy of the constitutional provisions
of the same tenor and reasoned that the
District was not a state for purposes of
the Constitution and, hence, was not for
purposes of the act."

[d] Justice Jackson's opinion was joined by
two other justices. However, two different
justices had accepted the argument that
the District of Columbia was a "state" for
purposes of the article III diversity provision. Thus five justices voted to uphold
the statute, albeit on quite different theories, and the Court entered a judgment
holding that the suit could go forward.

The Court has not addressed this issue
again. Hence the fractured vote in *Tidewater* remains the basis upon which citi-

"Before concentrating on detail, it may be well to place the general issue in a larger perspective. This constitutional issue affects only the mechanics of administering justice in our federation. It does not involve an extension or a denial of any fundamental right or immunity which goes to make up our freedoms. Those rights and freedoms do not include immunity from suit by a citizen of Columbia or exemption from process of the federal courts. Defendant concedes that it can presently be sued in some court of law, if not this one, and it grants that Congress may make it suable at plaintiff's complaint in some, if not this, federal court. Defendant's contention only amounts to this: that it cannot be made to answer this plaintiff in the particular court which Congress has decided is the just and convenient forum.

"The considerations which bid us strictly to apply the Constitution to congressional enactments which invade fundamental freedoms or which reach for powers that would substantially disturb the balance between the union and its component states, are not present here. In mere mechanics of government and administration we should, so far as the language of the great charter fairly will permit, give Congress freedom to adapt its machinery to the needs of changing times. . . .

"It is elementary that the exclusive responsibility of Congress for the welfare of the District includes both power and duty to provide its inhabitants and citizens with courts adequate to adjudge not only controversies among themselves but also their claims against, as well as suits brought by, citizens of the various states. . . . The defendant here does not challenge the power of Congress to assure justice to the citizens of the District by means of federal instrumentalities, or to empower a federal court within the District to run its process to summon defendants here from any part of the country. And no reason has been advanced why a special statutory court for cases of District citizens could not be authorized to proceed elsewhere in the United States to sit, where necessary or proper, to discharge the duties of Congress toward District citizens.

"However, it is contended that Congress may not combine this function, under article I, with those under article III, in district courts of the United States. . . ."

Justice Jackson then addressed this contention. He argued first that:

"Of course there are limits to the nature of duties which Congress may impose on the constitutional courts vested with the federal judicial power. The doctrine of separation of

zens of the District of Columbia can be parties to diversity suits in federal courts.

powers is fundamental in our system. . . . And this statute reflects that doctrine. It does not authorize or require either the district courts or this Court to participate in any legislative, administrative, political or other nonjudicial function or to render any advisory opinion. The jurisdiction conferred is limited to controversies of a justiciable nature, the sole feature distinguishing them from countless other controversies handled by the same courts being the fact that one party is a District citizen. Nor has the Congress by this statute attempted to usurp any judicial power. It has deliberately chosen the district courts as the appropriate instrumentality through which to exercise part of the judicial functions incidental to exertion of sovereignty over the District and its citizens.

"Unless we are to deny to Congress the same choice of means through which to govern the District of Columbia that we have held it to have in exercising other legislative powers . . ., we cannot hold that Congress lacked the power it sought to exercise in the act before us."

At this point, Justice Jackson took the position that Congress was empowered to confer authority on the district courts to hear controversies falling within Congress' article I powers even though they were not within the "cases" and "controversies" listed in article III. He justified this conclusion both on the basis of the principles quoted above and on the basis of the "consistent" practice of the Court in upholding such exercises of jurisdiction. Over the objection of his dissenting colleagues, he construed numerous prior decisions as examples of this practice. One illustration was the power of bankruptcy courts to hear non-diversity suits based on state law between the trustee in bankruptcy and persons alleged to owe money to the bankrupt. Justice Jackson continued:

"We conclude that where Congress in the exercise of its powers under article I finds it necessary to provide those on whom its power is exerted with access to some kind of court or tribunal for determination of controversies that are within the traditional concept of the justiciable, it may open the regular federal courts to them regardless of lack of diversity of citizenship. . . .

"We therefore hold that Congress may exert its power to govern the District of Columbia by imposing the judicial function of adjudicating justiciable controversies on the regular federal courts . . . . The practical issue here is whether, if defendant is to be suable at all by District citizens, he must be compelled to come to the courts of the District of Columbia or perhaps to a special statutory court sitting outside of it, or whether Congress may authorize the regular federal courts to entertain the suit. We see no justification for holding that Congress in accomplishing an end admittedly within its power is restricted to those means which are most cumbersome and burdensome to a defendant. Since it may provide the District citizen with a federal forum in which to sue the citizens of one of the states, it is hard to imagine a fairer or less prejudiced one than the regular federal courts sitting in the defendant's own state. To vest the jurisdiction in them rather than in courts sitting in the District of Columbia would seem less harsh to defendants and more consistent with the principles of venue that prevail in our system under which defendants are generally suable in their home forums.

". . . Congress is reaching permissible ends by a choice of means which certainly are not expressly forbidden by the Constitution. No good reason is advanced for the Court to deny them by implication. . . . Such a law of Congress should be stricken down only on a clear showing that it transgresses constitutional limitations. We think no such showing has been made. . . ."

4. Questions and Comments on *Tidewater*. One way to resolve the *Tidewater* controversy is to overrule Marshall's *Hepburn* opinion and hold that citizens of the District of Columbia are within the sense, if not the literal language, of the diversity provisions of article III. But if this is inappropriate, how should the case be decided? Should Congress have the power to permit federal courts to hear suits by and against District of Columbia citizens?

The rationale adopted by Justice Jackson in *Tidewater* has been widely criticized in the literature [e] and has never been adopted by a majority of the Court. One ground for objection has been that it was inconsistent for Justice Jackson to claim that article III limits federal courts to the decision of "cases or controversies," but provides no independent limit on the subject matter over which they can be given jurisdiction. Another is that it would never have occurred to Chief Justice Marshall or to the framers that cases that could not be fitted within the "arising under" jurisdiction—nor within any other provision in article III—could be heard by the federal courts. The traditional view of the matter is that article III, not article I, provides the subject matter limitations on suits in a federal court. If these arguments are accepted, can Justice Jackson's result, if not his theory, be defended on the ground that the statute before the Court invoked a kind of protective jurisdiction and that the case could therefore be held to "arise under" federal law? Should it be enough if Congress believed "that citizens of the United States should be entitled to equal access to federal fora?" [f] Is there any other way to defend Justice Jackson's result? Or is this all too much?

5. The Bankruptcy Cases. Congress enacted a new system for bankruptcies in 1978. It created a new bankruptcy court as an adjunct

---

[e] See, e.g., Mishkin, The Federal "Question" in the District Courts, 53 Colum. L. Rev. 157, 190–92 (1953).

[f] Note, The Theory of Protective Jurisdiction, 57 N.Y.U. L. Rev. 933, 985 (1982).

to each federal district court, with jurisdiction to hear all "civil proceedings arising under title 11 [bankruptcy] or arising in or related to cases under title 11." [g] The statute also created nationwide service of process, thus consolidating in a single court all proceedings "related to" a bankruptcy. It is clear from the legislative history of the statute that Congress meant the courts to exercise jurisdiction to the full extent permitted by the Constitution. If one lays aside problems with how the court was constituted,[h] can this jurisdiction be justified? [i]

SECTION 3: THE POWER AND DUTY OF STATE COURTS TO HEAR FEDERAL QUESTIONS

INTRODUCTORY NOTE ON THE POWER OF STATE COURTS TO HEAR FEDERAL QUESTIONS

The focus now shifts to the litigation of federal questions in state courts. The first issue to be confronted is when state courts have the authority to hear cases arising under federal law. The long-established law on this issue was summarized in Gulf Offshore Co. v. Mobil Oil Corp., 453 U.S. 473 (1981).

The Texas courts had adjudicated a personal injury claim arising under the Outer Continental Shelf Lands Act (OCSLA). The plaintiff was injured while working on an oil drilling platform in the Gulf of Mexico. OCSLA provides that federal law applies to such matters, in some instances borrowing "applicable and not inconsistent" laws of the adjacent states. It also confers jurisdiction on federal courts to hear all claims "arising out of or in connection with any operations conducted on the outer Continental Shelf." It was argued in the Supreme Court that this federal jurisdiction was exclusive and that the Texas courts therefore were not free to hear the case. The Court held that the Texas courts could hear the case, and in the course of its opinion described the prevailing law as follows:

> "The general principle of state-court jurisdiction over cases arising under federal laws is straightforward: state courts may assume subject matter jurisdiction over a federal cause of action absent provision by Congress to the contrary or disabling incompatibility between the federal claim and state-court adjudication. This rule is premised on the relation between

---

[g] 28 U.S.C. § 1471(a).

[h] See Northern Pipeline Construction Co. v. Marathon Pipe Line Co., 458 U.S. 50 (1982), which appears as a main case at page 113, supra.

[i] For discussions of the validity of jurisdiction exercised under the "relating to" portion of this statute, see Note, Bankruptcy and the Limits of Federal Jurisdiction, 95 Harv. L. Rev. 703 (1982), and Note, The Theory of Protective Jurisdiction, 57 N.Y.U. L. Rev. 933, 1026–30 (1982).

the states and the national government within our federal system. The two exercise concurrent sovereignty, although the Constitution limits the powers of each and requires the states to recognize federal law as paramount. Federal law confers rights binding on state courts, the subject matter jurisdiction of which is governed in the first instance by state laws.

"In considering the propriety of state-court jurisdiction over any particular federal claim, the Court begins with the presumption that state courts enjoy concurrent jurisdiction. Congress, however, may confine jurisdiction to the federal courts either explicitly or implicitly. Thus, the presumption of concurrent jurisdiction can be rebutted by an explicit statutory directive, by unmistakable implication from legislative history, or by a clear incompatibility between state-court jurisdiction and federal interests."

The Court then interpreted the relevant provisions of OCSLA not to foreclose state-court jurisdiction.[a]

Of course, once a state court assumes jurisdiction over a claim based on federal law, it is obligated by the supremacy clause to resolve the matter consistently with federal policies. It follows, moreover, that federal defenses raised in state court must be decided in accordance with federal law and that state courts cannot decline to hear federal defenses on the ground that they are inconsistent with state policy. All this being true, it may be regarded as a different matter whether state courts are required to hear a suit filed by a federal claimant. The next main case addresses this question.

TESTA v. KATT

Supreme Court of the United States, 1947.
330 U.S. 386.

Mr. Justice Black delivered the opinion of the Court.

Section 205(e) of the Emergency Price Control Act provides that a buyer of goods at above the prescribed ceiling price may sue the seller "in any court of competent jurisdiction" for not more than three times the amount of the overcharge plus costs and a reasonable attorney's fee. Section 205(c) provides that federal district courts shall have jurisdiction of such suits "concurrently with state and territorial courts." Such a suit under § 205(e) must be brought "in the district or county in which the defendant resides or has a place of business. . . ."

---

[a] For a similar conclusion in the context of federal common law actions under § 301 of the Labor Management Relations Act of 1947, see Charles Dowd Box Co. v. Courtney, 368 U.S. 502 (1962). See also the Court's reference to Martinez v. California, 444 U.S. 277 (1980), at page 1017 n.1, infra. The early history of state court enforcement of federal causes of action, including some federal criminal proceedings, is discussed in Note, 73 Harv. L. Rev. 1551 (1960), and Note, 60 Harv. L. Rev. 966 (1947).

The respondent was in the automobile business in Providence, Providence County, Rhode Island. In 1944 he sold an automobile to petitioner Testa, who also resides in Providence, for $1100, $210 above the ceiling price. The petitioner later filed this suit against respondent in the state District Court in Providence. Recovery was sought under § 205(e). The court awarded a judgment of treble damages and costs to petitioner. On appeal to the state Superior Court, where the trial was de novo, the petitioner was again awarded judgment, but only for the amount of the overcharge plus attorney's fees. Pending appeal from this judgment, the Price Administrator was allowed to intervene. On appeal, the state Supreme Court reversed. It interpreted § 205(e) to be "a penal statute in the international sense." It held that an action for violation of § 205(e) could not be maintained in the courts of that state. The state Supreme Court rested its holding on [an] earlier decision in which it had reasoned that: A state need not enforce the penal laws of a government which is foreign in the international sense; § 205(e) is treated by Rhode Island as penal in that sense; the United States is "foreign" to the state in the "private international" as distinguished from the "public international" sense; hence Rhode Island courts, though their jurisdiction is adequate to enforce similar Rhode Island "penal" statutes, need not enforce § 205(e). Whether state courts may decline to enforce federal laws on these grounds is a question of great importance. For this reason, and because the Rhode Island Supreme Court's holding was alleged to conflict with this Court's previous holding in Mondou v. New York, N.H. & H.R. Co., 223 U.S. 1 (1912), we granted certiorari.

For the purposes of this case, we assume, without deciding, that § 205(e) is a penal statute in the "public international," "private international," or any other sense. So far as the question of whether the Rhode Island courts properly declined to try this action, it makes no difference into which of these categories the Rhode Island court chose to place the statute which Congress has passed. For we cannot accept the basic premise on which the Rhode Island Supreme Court held that it has no more obligation to enforce a valid penal law of the United States than it has to enforce a penal law of another state or a foreign country. Such a broad assumption flies in the face of the fact that the states of the Union constitute a nation. It disregards the purpose and effect of article VI of the Constitution which provides:

> "This Constitution, and the Laws of the United States which shall be made in Pursuance thereof; and all Treaties made, or which shall be made, under the Authority of the United States, shall be the supreme Law of the Land; and the Judges in every State shall be bound thereby, any Thing in the Constitution or Laws of any State to the Contrary notwithstanding."

It cannot be assumed, the supremacy clause considered, that the responsibilities of a state to enforce the laws of a sister state are identical with its responsibilities to enforce federal laws. Such an assumption represents an erroneous evaluation of the statutes of Congress and the prior decisions of this Court in their historic setting.

Those decisions establish that state courts do not bear the same relation to the United States that they do to foreign countries. The first Congress that convened after the Constitution was adopted conferred jurisdiction upon the state courts to enforce important federal civil laws, and succeeding Congresses conferred on the states jurisdiction over federal crimes and actions for penalties and forfeitures.

Enforcement of federal laws by state courts did not go unchallenged. Violent public controversies existed throughout the first part of the 19th century until the 1860's concerning the extent of the constitutional supremacy of the federal government. During that period there were instances in which this Court and state courts broadly questioned the power and duty of state courts to exercise their jurisdiction to enforce United States civil and penal statutes or the power of the federal government to require them to do so. But after the fundamental issues over the extent of federal supremacy had been resolved by war, this Court took occasion in 1876 to review the phase of the controversy concerning the relationship of state courts to the federal government. Claflin v. Houseman, 93 U.S. (3 Otto) 130 (1876). The opinion of a unanimous Court in that case was strongly buttressed by historic references and persuasive reasoning. It repudiated the assumption that federal laws can be considered by the states as though they were laws emanating from a foreign sovereign. Its teaching is that the Constitution and the laws passed pursuant to it are the supreme laws of the land, binding alike upon states, courts, and the people, "any Thing in the Constitution or Laws of any State to the Contrary notwithstanding." It asserted that the obligation of states to enforce these federal laws is not lessened by reason of the form in which they are cast or the remedy which they provide. And the Court stated that "If an act of Congress gives a penalty to a party aggrieved, without specifying a remedy for its enforcement, there is no reason why it should not be enforced, if not provided otherwise by some act of Congress, by a proper action in a state court."

The *Claflin* opinion thus answered most of the arguments theretofore advanced against the power and duty of state courts to enforce federal penal laws. And since that decision, the remaining areas of doubt have been steadily narrowed. There have been statements in cases concerned with the obligation of states to give full faith and credit to the proceedings of sister states which suggested a theory contrary to that pronounced in the *Claflin* opinion. But when in *Mondou v. New York, N.H. & H.R. Co.*, supra, this Court was presented with a case testing the power and duty of states to enforce federal laws, it found the solution in the broad principles announced in the *Claflin* opinion.

The precise question in the *Mondou* case was whether rights arising under the Federal Employers' Liability Act, could "be enforced, as of right, in the courts of the states when their jurisdiction, as fixed by local laws, is adequate to the occasion. . . ." The Supreme Court of Connecticut had decided that they could not. Except for the penalty feature, the factors it considered and its reasoning were strikingly similar to that on which the Rhode Island Supreme Court declined to enforce the federal law here involved. But this Court held that the Connecticut court could not decline to entertain the action. The contention that enforcement of the congressionally created right was contrary to Connecticut policy was answered as follows:

> "The suggestion that the act of Congress is not in harmony with the policy of the state, and therefore that the courts of the state are free to decline jurisdiction, is quite inadmissible, because it presupposes what in legal contemplation does not exist. When Congress, in the exertion of the power confided to it by the Constitution, adopted that act, it spoke for all the people and all the states, and thereby established a policy for all. That policy is as much the policy of Connecticut as if the act had emanated from its own legislature, and should be respected accordingly in the courts of the state." Mondou v. New York, N.H. & H.R. Co., 223 U.S. 1, 57 (1912).

So here, the fact that Rhode Island has an established policy against enforcement by its courts of statutes of other states and the United States which it deems penal, cannot be accepted as a "valid excuse." Cf. Douglas v. New York, N.H. & H.R. Co., 279 U.S. 377, 388 (1929). For the policy of the federal act is the prevailing policy in every state. Thus, in a case which chiefly relied upon the *Claflin* and *Mondou* precedents, this Court stated that a state court cannot "refuse to enforce the right arising from the law of the United States because of conceptions of impolicy or want of wisdom on the part of Congress in having called into play its lawful powers." Minneapolis & St. L.R.R. Co. v. Bombolis, 241 U.S. 211, 222 (1916).

The Rhode Island court . . . cites cases of this Court which have held that states are not required by the full faith and credit clause of the Constitution to enforce judgments of the courts of other states based on claims arising out of penal statutes. But those holdings have no relevance here, for this case raises no full faith and credit question. Nor need we consider in this case prior decisions to the effect that federal courts are not required to enforce state penal laws. For whatever consideration they may be entitled to in the field in which they are relevant, those decisions did not bring before us our instant problem of the effect of the supremacy clause on the relation of federal laws to state courts. Our question concerns only the right of a state to deny enforcement to claims growing out of a valid federal law.

It is conceded that this same type of claim arising under Rhode Island law would be enforced by that state's courts. Its courts have enforced claims for double damages growing out of the Fair Labor Standards Act. Thus the Rhode Island courts have jurisdiction adequate and appropriate under established local law to adjudicate this action. Under these circumstances the state courts are not free to refuse enforcement of petitioners' claim. See McKnett v. St. Louis & S.F.R Co., 292 U.S. 230 (1934). The case is reversed and the cause is remanded for proceedings not inconsistent with this opinion.

Reversed.

NOTES ON THE DUTY OF STATE COURTS TO HEAR FEDERAL QUESTIONS

1. *Claflin v. Houseman.* In Claflin v. Houseman, 93 U.S. (3 Otto) 130 (1876), the state courts granted relief on a federal cause of action. On appeal to the Supreme Court, it was unsuccessfully argued that the judgment should be reversed because federal causes of action "can only be prosecuted in the courts of the United States." [a] The *Claflin* Court explicitly commented on the possibility that state courts might decline to exercise jurisdiction over federal claims. But the issue of an obligation to hear federal cases was not before the Court and was not mentioned. Nonetheless, Justice Black regarded *Claflin* as having "answered most of the arguments" against the power "and duty" of state courts to hear a case such as *Testa.*

2. The FELA Cases. Although *Claflin* may have provided questionable precedent for Justice Black's opinion in *Testa,* there was a line of decisions under the Federal Employer's Liability Act more directly on point. These decisions, together with *Testa,* led Terrance Sandalow to describe the "prevailing doctrine" in 1965 as: "a state court may not decline to adjudicate a federal claim if it would enforce an analogous state-created right." "It is still an open question," he continued, "whether it must provide a forum for enforcement of the federal claim even when it does not entertain similar suits arising under local law." [b]

(i) *Mondou.* The first FELA case to address the question was Mondou v. New York, N.H. & H. R. Co., 223 U.S. 1 (1912). The case involved a broadside challenge to the constitutionality of the FELA under the commerce clause and the fifth amendment. It also presented the following question, as phrased by the Court: "May rights arising under [the FELA] be enforced, as of right, in the courts of the states when their jurisdiction, as fixed by local laws, is adequate to the occasion?" The Court answered "yes" without dissent. The Connecticut courts had declined jurisdiction in *Mondou* because

> "the policy manifested by [the FELA] is not in accord with the policy of the state respecting the liability of employers to employees for injuries received by the latter while in the service of the former, and [because] it would be inconvenient and confusing for the same court, in dealing with cases of the same general class, to apply in some the standards of right established by the congressional act and in others the different standards recognized by the laws of the state."

The Court responded:

> "[T]here is not here involved any attempt by Congress to enlarge or regulate the jurisdiction of state courts or to control

---

[a] *Claflin* was an early statement of the principles recited by the Court in the *Gulf Offshore* case, quoted supra at pages 230–31, and was cited approvingly by the Court in *Gulf Offshore.* For an extensive treatment of *Claflin,* see Redish and Muench, Adjudication of Federal Causes of Action in State Court, 75 Mich. L. Rev. 311, 313–40 (1976).

[b] Sandalow, *Henry v. Mississippi* and the Adequate State Ground: Proposals for a Revised Doctrine, 1965 Sup. Ct. Rev. 187, 203.

or affect their modes of procedure, but only a question of the duty of such a court, when its ordinary jurisdiction as prescribed by local laws is appropriate to the occasion and is invoked in conformity with those laws, to take cognizance of an action to enforce a right of civil recovery arising under the act of Congress and susceptible of adjudication according to the prevailing rules of procedure. We say 'when its ordinary jurisdiction as prescribed by local laws is appropriate to the occasion,' because we are advised by the decisions of the [Connecticut courts] that [courts such as the trial court involved here] are courts of general jurisdiction, are empowered to take cognizance of actions to recover for personal injuries and for death, and are accustomed to exercise that jurisdiction, not only in cases where the right of action arose under the laws of that state, but also in cases where it arose in another state, under its laws, and in circumstances in which the laws of Connecticut give no right of recovery, as where the causal negligence was that of a fellow servant." [c]

At this point, the paragraph quoted by Justice Black in *Testa* appears, followed by a lengthy quotation from *Claflin*. The Court then concluded:

"We are not disposed to believe that the exercise of jurisdiction by the state courts will be attended by any appreciable inconvenience or confusion; but, be this as it may, it affords no reason for declining a jurisdiction conferred by law. The existence of the jurisdiction creates an implication of duty to exercise it, and that its exercise may be onerous does not militate against that implication. Besides, it is neither new nor unusual in judicial proceedings to apply different rules of law to different situations. [I]t never has been supposed that courts are at liberty to decline cognizance of cases of a particular class merely because the rules of law to be applied in their adjudication are unlike those applied in other cases.

"We conclude that rights arising under the act in question may be enforced, as of right, in the courts of the states when their jurisdiction, as prescribed by local laws, is adequate to the occasion."

(ii) *Douglas.* Douglas v. New York, N.H. & H.R. Co., 279 U.S. 377 (1929), involved a refusal by the New York courts to hear an FELA case. The injuries were inflicted in Connecticut upon a plaintiff who was a citizen and resident of that state. The defendant was a Connecticut corporation, although it was doing sufficient business in New York to be sued there. The New York courts exercised a discretion available under local law to dismiss the suit under a statute that limited the occasions when a nonresident could sue a foreign corporation. The principal argument in the Supreme Court was that the privileges and

---

[c] The FELA abolished the fellow-servant rule. [Footnote by eds.]

immunities clause of article IV of the Constitution required reversal of the judgment. The unanimous opinion by Justice Holmes rejected this argument and treated the obligation of the New York courts to hear the case in a single paragraph:

> "As to the grant of jurisdiction in the Employers' Liability Act, that statute does not purport to require state courts to entertain suits arising under it, but only to empower them to do so, so far as the authority of the United States is concerned. It may very well be that if the Supreme Court of New York were given no discretion, being otherwise competent, it would be subject to a duty. But there is nothing in the act of Congress that purports to force a duty upon such courts as against an otherwise valid excuse."

(iii) *McKnett.*   McKnett v. St. Louis & S.F.R. Co., 292 U.S. 230 (1934), involved an FELA action brought in an Alabama state court to recover for injuries incurred in Tennessee. The plaintiff was a resident of Tennessee and the defendant a foreign corporation doing business in Alabama. Alabama courts had consistently refused to take jurisdiction of transitory causes of action arising in another state if the defendant was a foreign corporation. Prior to the suit in question, however, the Alabama legislature enacted a statute that required its courts to accept jurisdiction over all such cases if the cause of action arose "by common law or the statutes of another state."

The Alabama courts construed this statute as not applicable to causes of action arising in another state under *federal* law, since the statute was "in plain terms" limited to suits arising under the law of another *state*. The suit was accordingly dismissed. The Supreme Court reversed in a unanimous opinion by Justice Brandeis:

> "Alabama has granted to its circuit courts general jurisdiction of the class of actions to which that here brought belongs, in cases between litigants situated like those in the case at bar. The court would have had jurisdiction of the cause between these parties if the accident had occurred in Alabama. It would have had jurisdiction although the accident occurred in Tennessee, if the defendant had been a domestic corporation. . . . Thus, the ordinary jurisdiction of the Alabama [trial] court is appropriate to enforce the right against this defendant conferred upon the plaintiff by the [FELA]. And its jurisdiction was invoked according to the rules of procedure prevailing in that court.

> "The power of a state to determine the limits of the jurisdiction of its courts and the character of the controversies which shall be heard in them is, of course, subject to the restrictions imposed by the federal Constitution. . . . While Congress has not attempted to compel states to provide courts for the enforcement of the [FELA], the federal Constitution prohibits state courts of general jurisdiction from refusing to do so solely because the suit is brought under a federal law.

The denial of jurisdiction by the Alabama court is based solely upon the source of law sought to be enforced. The plaintiff is cast out because he is suing to enforce a federal act. A state may not discriminate against rights arising under federal laws."

(iv) *Pitcairn* and *Mayfield.* Finally, consider Herb v. Pitcairn, 324 U.S. 117 (1945), and Missouri ex rel. Southern R. Co. v. Mayfield, 340 U.S. 1 (1950). In *Pitcairn* the Court upheld the authority of an Illinois city court to dismiss an FELA action because its jurisdiction was limited to causes of action arising inside the city. In *Mayfield* the Court upheld the authority of a state court to apply its local doctrine of forum non conveniens to dismiss an FELA suit brought by a nonresident against a foreign corporation based on an out-of-state cause of action. In both cases the forum-closing doctrines applied to state and federal causes of action alike.

3. **Comments and Questions.** Consider first whether *Congress* has the power to require state courts to hear federal statutory claims. Congress was not, of course, obligated to create lower federal courts, and perhaps for that reason it should have the power to use the state courts to enforce federal rights. But if Congress wants to create judicially enforceable rights, one could argue that it must also provide a forum for their assertion. And having provided lower federal courts, Congress might be required to use them rather than compel the state courts to hear such cases. How should the powers of Congress in this respect be assessed? How serious is the intrusion upon state sovereignty if state courts are required by Congress to hear federal claims?

Now consider the powers of the Supreme Court. Surely the Court may not force the state courts to hear federal claims if Congress may not. But if Congress has the power, what should the Court do when Congress has *permitted* the states to exercise concurrent jurisdiction but has not clearly indicated that they *must*? At least three solutions seem possible: the Court could compel state courts to hear federal claims only when Congress explicitly imposed the obligation; the Court could impose the obligation when the purposes of the particular federal statute would be advanced by state court enforcement; or the Court could create a general obligation that state courts hear all federal claims over which there is concurrent state and federal jurisdiction. Which course should it take?

Consider the views of Terrence Sandalow in *Henry v. Mississippi* and the Adequate State Ground: Proposals for a Revised Doctrine, 1965 Sup. Ct. Rev. 187, 206–07:*

"[*Testa* may] be taken to mean that the Constitution, presumably through the supremacy clause, directly imposes upon the states an obligation to enforce federal claims that Congress has not committed to the exclusive jurisdiction of the federal courts. Yet it is difficult to perceive the federal interest that justifies so substantial an intrusion upon the power of the states to determine the purposes to be served by agencies of state government. Article III of the Constitution confers upon Congress the power to establish a federal judicial system adequate to enforce claims of federal right. In . . . *Testa* a federal court was open to the plaintiff, so that a decision sustaining the refusal to adjudicate would in no way have interfered with the vindication of federal rights. Conceding, therefore, that a state may not pursue a policy inconsistent with that established by federal law, it is by no means apparent that the state [court] in . . . *Testa* had done so. Federal policy was substantive, that recovery should be permitted under specified circumstances. State policy, on the other hand, was concerned only with the use to be made of state courts, a matter not touched by the federal policy.

"The Court's reliance on the supremacy clause appears to come to no more than it would be unseemly for the state to refuse recognition to rights conferred by federal law—particularly if similar rights under state law are adjudicated in state courts. In view of the rather substantial burden that the Court's current doctrine imposes upon the states, that does not seem an adequate justification. It is, of course, true that if the states are free to decline jurisdiction over federal claims and if they exercise that option, the resulting burden on the federal courts may be extremely heavy. But the allocation of burdens between state and federal judiciaries seems peculiarly a matter for determination by Congress. Recognition of congressional power to require the exercise of jurisdiction by state courts would permit ample protection of any federal interests. In the absence of a declaration by Congress that state courts must enforce rights that Congress has created, there appears to be no substantial reason why the Supreme Court should impose such an obligation."

A contrary position is taken in Redish and Muench, Adjudication of Federal Causes of Action in State Court, 75 Mich. L. Rev. 311, 347–48 (1976). They conclude that "congressional silence should not be construed to authorize state courts to reject federal cases at will." In support of this position, they argue, inter alia, that if the state courts were free to decide for themselves whether to hear federal causes of action "there would be no way to regulate the allocation of burdens between state and federal courts. The resulting unpredictability in the federal judiciary's caseload could conceivably hinder congressional decision-making concerning the structure and jurisdiction of the federal courts."

If state courts are required to hear federal claims, should they be permitted to decline jurisdiction if they have a "valid excuse"? Consider again the comments of Terrance Sandalow: [d]

> "If the duty of the state courts to accept jurisdiction flows from the obligation to respect federal policy, there is no apparent reason why the state should not be required to accept jurisdiction even though it would not entertain an analogous forum-created right. Federal policy is the same whatever lines the state has drawn in defining the jurisdiction of its courts over local claims. If the state may not assert a policy at variance with that expressed by the federal law, adjudication of the claim would seem to be required even in the absence of discrimination since, insofar as the local jurisdictional rule prevents adjudication, it is to that extent, under the reasoning of *Mondou,* inconsistent with the policy underlying the federal claim. Some support for this view may be found in *Testa.*" [e]

Is Sandalow right? [f]

4. *General Oil v. Crain.* *Testa* and the FELA cases present the question whether state courts are obligated to hear federal *statutory* claims in the face of contrary state law. Are the stakes different when *constitutional* rights are presented to a reluctant state court?

This situation was thought by the Court to be presented in General Oil v. Crain, 209 U.S. 211 (1908), which is widely regarded as the case most directly in point. Crain was an oil inspector employed by the state of Tennessee. His job was to inspect stored oil and to collect a fee of 25 cents per barrel. General Oil objected to the inspection fee with respect to oil that was temporarily stored in Tennessee en route to other states for sale, taking the position that it violated the commerce clause for Tennessee to tax goods in transit. General Oil accordingly filed suit in a Tennessee state court to enjoin collection of the fees. The Tennessee trial court entered an injunction covering part of the oil in controversy, but on appeal the Tennessee Supreme Court held the trial court without jurisdiction to entertain the suit because of a state statute which it construed to forbid injunctions against state officials in such circumstances.

On the same day that *Crain* was announced, the Supreme Court decided Ex parte Young, 209 U.S. 123 (1908), in which it held that a

---

[d] Sandalow, *Henry v. Mississippi* and the Adequate State Ground: Proposals for a Revised Doctrine, 1965 Sup. Ct. Rev. 187, 205.

[e] Compare Gordon and Gross, Justiciability of Federal Claims in State Court, 59 Notre Dame L. Rev. 1145 (1984), where it is argued that "the supremacy clause . . . requires state courts to vindicate federal rights, even when similar rights under state law are held to be non-justiciable."

[f] There are, of course, many contexts in which state and federal court jurisdiction is concurrent and in which the meaning of *Testa* and the FELA cases accordingly can arise. For an illustration, see Steven Steinglass, The Emerging State Court § 1983 Action: A Procedural Review, 38 U. Miami L. Rev. 381, 439–53 (1984). For an application of *Testa* in the context of requiring a state administrative agency to adjudicate disputes under federal standards, see Federal Energy Regulatory Comm'n v. Mississippi, 456 U.S. 742 (1982).

federal equitable cause of action could be asserted in *federal* court to enjoin violations of the constitution by a state official.[g] In *Crain,* the Court seemed to say that the same cause of action could be asserted in state court, irrespective, it appeared, of subject matter limitations imposed by the state on its own courts. Justice Harlan disagreed with this view in a separate concurrence:

"The oil company seeks a reversal of the decree of the state court, contending that it was denied a right arising under the commerce clause of the Constitution. But back of any question of that kind was the question before the Supreme Court of Tennessee whether the inferior state court, under the law of its organization, that is, under the law of Tennessee, could entertain jurisdiction of the suit. The question, we have seen, was determined adversely to jurisdiction. That certainly is a state, not a federal question. Surely, Tennessee has the right to say of what class of suits its own courts may take cognizance, and it was peculiarly the function of the Supreme Court of Tennessee to determine such a question. When, therefore, its highest court has declared that the Tennessee statute referred to in argument did not allow the inferior state court to take cognizance of a suit like this, that decision must be accepted as the interpretation to be placed on the local statute. Otherwise, this Court will adjudge that the Tennessee court *shall* take jurisdiction of a suit of which the highest court of the state adjudges that it cannot do consistently with the laws of the state which created it and which established its jurisdiction. It seems to me that this Court, accepting the decision of the highest court of Tennessee, as to the meaning of the Tennessee statute in question, as I think it must, has no alternative but to affirm the judgment, on the ground simply that the ground upon which it is placed is broad enough to support the judgment without any reference to any question raised or discussed [concerning the commerce clause]." [h]

By contrast, the opinion of the Court said:

"Necessarily to give adequate protection to constitutional rights a distinction must be made between valid and invalid

[g] *Ex parte Young* involved a complex series of issues, one of which was whether the 11th amendment precluded such suits in federal courts, on the ground that they were suits against the state. These issues are considered in Chapter VIII. Suffice it to say for now that the Court found the 11th amendment not a bar to suits of this type.

[h] Cf. Brown v. Gerdes, 321 U.S. 178, 188 (1944) (Frankfurter, dissenting):

"Since 1789, rights derived from federal law could be enforced in state courts unless Congress confined their enforcement to the federal courts. This has

been so precisely for the same reason that rights created by the British Parliament or by the legislature of Vermont could be enforced in the New York courts. Neither Congress nor the British Parliament nor the Vermont legislature has power to confer jurisdiction upon the New York courts. But the jurisdiction conferred upon them by the only authority that has power to create them and to confer jurisdiction upon them—namely the law-making power of the state of New York—enables them to enforce rights no matter what the legislative source of the right may be."

state laws, as determining the character of the suit against state officers. And the suit at bar illustrates the necessity. If a suit against state officers is precluded in the national courts by the 11th amendment to the Constitution, and may be forbidden by a state to its courts, as it is contended in the case at bar that it may be, without power of review by this Court, it must be evident that an easy way is open to prevent the enforcement of many provisions of the Constitution, and the 14th amendment, which is directed at state action, could be nullified as to much of its operation. And it will not do to say that the argument is drawn from extremes. Constitutional provisions are based on the possibility of extremes. There need not, however, be imagination of extremes, if by extremes be meant a deliberate purpose to prevent the assertion of constitutional rights. . . .

"It being then the right of a party to be protected against a law which violates a constitutional right, whether by its terms or the manner of its enforcement, it is manifest that a decision which denies such protection gives effect to the law, and the decision is reviewable by this court."

The Court held on the merits, however, that the Tennessee inspection law did not violate the commerce clause. Accordingly, the judgment of the Tennessee Supreme Court was affirmed.

Does the Supreme Court have a special obligation to assure that federal constitutional rights can be used as a sword as well as a shield? Are the implications of *Crain* justified on this ground? Of what relevance to these questions is the conclusion in *Ex parte Young* that such suits can be brought in federal courts?

_____

NOTES ON PRECLUDING STATE COURTS FROM HEARING FEDERAL QUESTIONS

1. **Background.** State courts are precluded from hearing suits based on a federal claim if Congress has provided that federal jurisdiction is exclusive.[a] The Court noted in *Gulf Offshore* (page 230, supra) that state jurisdiction is also precluded if there is a "disabling incompatibility between the federal claim and state court adjudication." The Court gave no examples of a "disabling incompatibility," but presumably it had in mind occasions where the jurisdiction of state courts has been foreclosed without explicit statutory support. Some examples of this practice are given below.[b]

2. *Tarble's Case.* Tarble's Case, 80 U.S. (13 Wall.) 397 (1872), involved a habeas corpus petition filed before a state court commissioner in Dane County, Wisconsin. The defendant was a recruiting officer

_____

[a] For an example, see 28 U.S.C. § 1338.

[b] For a general discussion, see Redish and Muench, Adjudication of Federal

Causes of Action in State Court, 75 Mich. L. Rev. 311 (1976).

of the United States Army. The petition was filed by a father who alleged that his son, who was less than 18 years old, had enlisted under a false name without the father's consent and that the enlistment was therefore illegal. The commissioner issued the writ, and the Supreme Court of Wisconsin affirmed the order discharging the son from the custody of the Army.

The Supreme Court stated the issue as:

". . . whether a state court commissioner has jurisdiction, upon habeas corpus, to inquire into the validity of the enlistment of soldiers into the military service of the United States, and to discharge them from such service when, in his judgment, their enlistment has not been made in conformity with the laws of the United States. The question presented may be more generally stated thus: Whether any judicial officer of a state has jurisdiction to issue a writ of habeas corpus, or to continue proceedings under the writ when issued, for the discharge of a person held under the authority, or under claim and color of the authority, of the United States, by an officer of that government."

The Court gave a categorical response: "[N]o state can authorize one of its judges or courts to exercise judicial power, by habeas corpus or otherwise, within the jurisdiction of another and independent government." It explained:

"There are within the territorial limits of each state two governments, restricted in their spheres of action, but independent of each other, and supreme within their respective spheres. . . . Neither government can intrude within the jurisdiction . . . of the other. The two governments in each state stand in their respective spheres of action in the same independent relation to each other, except in one particular, that they would if their authority embraced distinct territories. That particular consists in the supremacy of the authority of the United States when any conflict arises between the two governments. . . . Whenever . . . any conflict arises . . . the national government must have supremacy until the validity of the different enactments and authorities can be finally determined by the tribunals of the United States. This temporary supremacy until judicial decision by the national tribunals, and the ultimate determination of the conflict by such decision, are essential to the preservation of order and peace, and the avoidance of forcible collision between the two governments.

"Such being the distinct and independent character of the two governments, . . . it follows that neither can intrude with its judicial process into the domain of the other, except so far as such intrusion may be necessary on the part of the national government to preserve its rightful supremacy in cases of conflict of authority."

At this point the Court shifted to more practical considerations:

"Now, among the powers assigned to the national government, is the power 'to raise and support Armies' and the power 'to [make Rules] for the Government and Regulation of the land and naval Forces.' The execution of these powers falls within the line of its duties; and its control over the subject is plenary and exclusive. . . . No interference with the execution of this power of the national government in the formation, organization, and government of its armies by any state officials could be permitted without greatly impairing the efficiency, if it did not utterly destroy, this branch of the public service. Probably in every county and city in the several states there are one or more officers authorized by law to issue writs of habeas corpus on behalf of persons alleged to be illegally restrained of their liberty; and if soldiers could be taken from the army of the United States, and the validity of their enlistment inquired into by any one of these officers, such proceeding could be taken by all of them, and no movement could be made by the national troops without their commanders being subjected to constant annoyance and embarrassment from this source. The experience of the late rebellion has shown us that, in times of great popular excitement, there may be found in every state large numbers ready and anxious to embarrass the operations of the government, and easily persuaded to believe every step taken for the enforcement of its authority illegal and void. Power to issue writs of habeas corpus for the discharge of soldiers in the military service, in the hands of parties thus disposed, might be used, and often would be used, to the great detriment of the public service. In many exigencies the measures of the national government might in this way be entirely bereft of their efficacy and value. An appeal in such cases to this Court, to correct the erroneous action of these officers, would afford no adequate remedy. Proceedings on habeas corpus are summary, and the delay incident to bringing the decision of a state officer, through the highest tribunal of the state, to this Court for review, would necessarily occupy years, and in the meantime, where the soldier was discharged, the mischief would be accomplished. It is manifest that the powers of the national government could not be exercised with energy and efficiency at all times, if its acts could be interfered with and controlled for any period by officers or tribunals of another sovereignty.

"It is true similar embarrassment might sometimes be occasioned, though in a less degree, by the exercise of the authority to issue the writ possessed by judicial officers of the United States, but the ability to provide a speedy remedy for any inconvenience following from this source would always exist with the national legislature. . . .

"This limitation upon the power of state tribunals and state officers furnishes no just ground to apprehend that the liberty of the citizen will thereby be endangered. [The courts of the United States] are clothed with the power to issue the writ of habeas corpus in all cases, where a party is illegally restrained of his liberty by an officer of the United States . . . . And there is no just reason to believe that they will exhibit any hesitation to exert their power, when it is properly invoked. . . ."

3. Questions and Comments on _Tarble's Case_. In a sense, _Tarble's Case_ involves the converse of _Testa v. Katt_. Both cases concern whether the Supreme Court is justified, in the absence of Congressional guidance, in restricting state control over the cases to be heard in its own court system. In _Testa_ the question was whether a reluctant state court should be required to exercise jurisdiction to hear a federal claim; in _Tarble_ the question was whether a state court that wanted to hear a federal claim should be foreclosed from doing so.

What is the basis for the Court's conclusion in _Tarble_? Would the Court have reacted differently if habeas were unavailable in the lower federal courts? If _Tarble_ arose today, the defendant-official could remove the case to a federal court. See 28 U.S.C. § 1442a, passed in 1956. Should this statute affect the result if the same situation comes up again? [c]

4. _McClung v. Silliman_. McClung claimed an interest in land owned by the federal government, and sought to compel Silliman, the federal officer in charge of the local land office, to make a formal conveyance. Silliman refused, on the ground that the interest had already been conveyed to another. McClung first filed an action for mandamus in the local federal trial court. That court held that it did not have jurisdiction to award mandamus against a federal officer, and the Supreme Court affirmed. McIntire v. Wood, 11 U.S. (7 Cranch) 504 (1813). McClung then filed an action seeking the same relief in a state court. Jurisdiction of the state courts to issue mandamus against a federal officer was upheld, but McClung lost on the merits. The Supreme Court then affirmed the judgment on the ground that the state courts lacked the authority to issue a writ of mandamus against a federal officer. McClung v. Silliman, 19 U.S. (6 Wheat.) 598 (1821). The Court reasoned:

"It is not easy to conceive, on what legal ground, a state tribunal can, in any instance, exercise the power of issuing a mandamus to the register of a land-office. The United States have not thought proper to delegate that power to their own courts. But when, in the cases of Marbury v. Madison, 5 U.S. (1 Cranch) 137 (1803), and McIntire v. Wood, 11 U.S. (7 Cranch)

[c] For a criticism of the result in _Tarble_ and an elaboration of the argument that "each constitutionally limited government can deploy its powers to police the constitutional limits on the other's powers and remedy the other's constitutional violations," see Amar, Of Sovereignty and Federalism, 96 Yale L.J. 1425, 1492–1519 (1987).

504 (1813), this Court decided against the exercise of that power, the idea never presented itself to any one, that it was not within the scope of the judicial powers of the United States, although not vested by law in the courts of the general government. And no one will seriously contend, it is presumed, that it is among the reserved powers of the states, because not communicated by law to the courts of the United States.

"There is but one shadow of a ground on which such a power can be contended for, which is, the general rights of legislation which the states possess over the soil within their respective territories. It is not now necessary to consider that power, as to the soil reserved to the United States, in the states respectively. The question in this case is, as to the power of the state courts, over the officers of the general government, employed in disposing of that land, under the laws passed for that purpose. [The] conduct [of such an officer] can only be controlled by the power that created him; since, whatever doubts have from time to time been suggested, as to the supremacy of the United States in its legislative, judicial or executive powers, no one has ever contested its supreme right to dispose of its own property in its own way. And when we find it withholding from its own courts, the exercise of this controlling power over its ministerial officers, employed in the appropriation of its lands, the inference clearly is, that all violations of private right, resulting from the acts of such officers, should be the subject of actions for damages, or to recover the specific property (according to circumstances), in courts of competent jurisdiction. That is, that parties should be referred to the ordinary mode of obtaining justice, instead of resorting to the extraordinary and unprecedented mode of trying such questions on a motion for a mandamus."

Did the Court mean to say that it is inconsistent with the constitutional structure for a state court to issue a writ of mandamus against a federal officer? Or did the Court mean that Congress, by not conferring mandamus jurisdiction on federal courts, meant to deny the same power to state courts? Note that Congress did not by affirmative legislation deny mandamus jurisdiction to the federal courts. Rather, the denial resulted from the lack of an affirmative grant, that is, from Congressional silence.

In any event, *McClung* is taken to have established that the state courts do not have the authority to award mandamus against a federal officer. See Arnold, The Power of State Courts to Enjoin Federal Officers, 73 Yale L.J. 1385, 1391–93 (1964). Note, however, that Congress authorized federal courts to issue writs of mandamus against federal officers in 1962. See 28 U.S.C. § 1361.[d]

[d] The Supreme Court had held in Kendall v. Stokes, 37 U.S. (12 Pet.) 524 (1838), that the District of Columbia courts had the authority to issue a writ of mandamus against a federal officer, but until 1962 Washington was the only place one

5. Other Types of Suits Against Federal Officials in State Courts. Note the reference near the end of the Court's opinion in *McClung* to the availability of more "ordinary" forms of relief against federal officers. Does this mean that state courts can award damages against a federal officer? Specific performance? An injunction? Or does the reasoning of *Tarble* and *McClung* extend to these forms of relief as well?

The authority of state courts to try cases against federal officers is summarized in Arnold, The Power of State Courts to Enjoin Federal Officers, 73 Yale L.J. 1385, 1397 (1964): *

"[T]he decided cases on state court power to entertain proceedings against federal officers are in confusion. Jurisdiction to award damages or possession of specific property, and to punish for crime, is clear. At the other extreme are mandamus and habeas corpus, which, whether for good reasons or not, state courts may not grant. In the middle is injunctive relief. Many cases assume its availability; some explicitly declare it; but most express rulings on the point deny it. Since no Supreme Court case squarely deals with the point, the matter cannot be resolved purely by reference to authority."

Should state courts be permitted to issue an injunction against a federal officer? In an argument that rejects much of the reasoning of *Tarble's Case* and *McClung,* though not necessarily their specific results, Arnold concluded that the state courts should have such jurisdiction. He started with the point that it is normal for state courts to hear cases involving federal questions, and that they are obligated by the supremacy clause to do so with fidelity to the federal Constitution and laws. Moreover, he argued, it is normal for state courts to exercise jurisdiction concurrently with federal courts over any subject matter not reserved by statute to the federal courts. It also follows in the normal course that the *failure* of Congress to speak to the question will leave the general jurisdiction of the state courts intact. He continued:

"Federal and state law are inseparable parts of one system of jurisprudence, binding alike on all persons within the boundaries of any given state. . . . For a state court, accordingly, to order a federal official to act according to federal law, or to obey valid state law that Congress has not displaced, is no usurpation, nor any assertion that state courts are superior to federal courts or federal officials. It is rather an assertion of the supremacy of law, and especially of federal law."

Are there practical reasons why state courts should not be allowed to interfere with federal officials by injunction? Are the state courts not to be trusted to follow federal law faithfully? Any fears in this respect, Arnold concluded, are adequately resolved by one of four responses:

could go to obtain such relief. See Byse and Fiocca, Section 1361 of the Mandamus and Venue Act of 1962 and "Nonstatutory" Judicial Review of Federal Administrative Action, 81 Harv. L. Rev. 308 (1967).

* This and subsequent excerpts from the same work are reprinted by permission of The Yale Law Journal Company and Fred B. Rothman & Company from The Yale Law Journal, Vol. 73, pp. 1385, 1397.

Supreme Court review; removal, which is now permitted by any federal officer sued in a state court "for any act under color of office or in the performance of his duties" [e]; federal habeas, which is now available whenever any person is in custody in violation of the federal Constitution or laws [f]; or specification by Congress that the jurisdiction of the federal courts in a particular respect is exclusive. Given these potential sources of control and given the already extensive jurisdiction of state courts over federal officers in actions at law, he concluded, a prohibition of jurisdiction to issue an injunction (or for that matter mandamus or habeas corpus) cannot be defended:

> "It might be suggested that the existing precedents can be rationalized on the theory that state courts have 'law' jurisdiction over federal officials (replevin, damages), but not 'equity' jurisdiction (injunctions, mandamus). Judgments at law, the argument would run, are less of an interference with the functioning of the federal government. Habeas corpus, involving as it does a particularly striking form of interference, would, in this view, be classified with the 'equity' cases. Apart from the fact that this suggested rationale exalts form over substance—a replevin judgment, for example, may in practice be the equivalent of an injunction—it fails to give full application to the underlying principle that state courts as well as federal have a duty to enforce the limitations that federal law imposes on federal officials. The law-equity distinction, furthermore, has the additional weakness that it fails to explain state court criminal jurisdiction over federal officers—a jurisdiction potentially productive of the most drastic interference of all. The impact of this criminal jurisdiction has not, perhaps, been great, since federal officers have the protection of removal and federal habeas corpus. But its undoubted existence is inconsistent with the suggested law-equity distinction."

Is there anything more to be said?

6. *Donovan v. Dallas.* Contrast with the foregoing discussion the situation in Donovan v. Dallas, 377 U.S. 408 (1964). The question presented, as stated by the Court, was "whether a state court can validly enjoin a person from prosecuting an action in personam in a district or appellate court of the United States which has jurisdiction both of the parties and of the subject matter."

The city of Dallas proposed to build an additional runway on Love Field, its municipal airport, and to issue revenue bonds to raise the money. A class suit was filed in state court against the city by 46 Dallas citizens to prevent this action on a number of grounds. Summary judgment was rendered for the city in this suit, the Texas appellate courts affirmed, and the United States Supreme Court denied certiorari. Knowing that the bonds could not be issued until all litigation involving their validity had concluded, 120 Dallas citizens, including 27 of the same people involved in the state suit, filed a similar suit in a

[e] 28 U.S.C. § 1442(a)(3).   [f] 28 U.S.C. § 2441(c)(3).

federal district court on the day bids for the sale of the bonds were to be opened. The city's response was twofold: it filed a motion to dismiss the federal suit on grounds of res judicata and it applied to a Texas court for a writ of prohibition to bar the plaintiffs in the federal suit from pursuing it further. The Texas courts initially denied relief, but the Texas Supreme Court ordered that the writ be issued.

The state-court plaintiffs not only opposed the city's motion to dismiss the federal suit but filed another action, this time against the city and all of the Texas judges who had been involved in issuing the writ, seeking a federal injunction against enforcement of the state-court writ of prohibition. The federal District Court then dismissed the first federal case and held the second one moot. Some of the plaintiffs in the federal suit filed an appeal. The Texas courts promptly held the plaintiffs in contempt. Donovan served 20 days in jail, and the other plaintiffs were fined $200 each. The federal appeal was then dismissed on a motion "made under duress." The Supreme Court then granted certiorari to review both the initial Texas Supreme Court decision ordering that the writ be issued and the subsequent contempt citations.

Justice Black wrote an opinion for a six-three majority holding that the state courts had no authority to issue the writ of prohibition. He reasoned:

"Early in the history of our country a general rule was established that state and federal courts would not interfere with or try to restrain each other's proceedings. That rule has continued substantially unchanged to this time. An exception has been made in cases where a court has custody of property, that is, proceedings in rem or quasi in rem. In such cases this Court has said that the state or federal court having custody of such property has exclusive jurisdiction to proceed. . . . It may be that a full hearing in an appropriate court would justify a finding that the state-court judgment in favor of Dallas in the first suit barred the issues raised in the second suit, a question as to which we express no opinion. But plaintiffs in the second suit chose to file that case in the federal court. They had a right to do this, a right which is theirs by reason of congressional enactments passed pursuant to congressional policy. And whether or not a plea of res judicata in the second suit would be good is a question for the federal courts to decide. While Congress has seen fit to authorize courts of the United States to restrain state-court proceedings in some special circumstances, it has in no way relaxed the old and well-established judicially declared rule that state courts are completely without power to restrain federal-court proceedings in in personam actions like the one here. And it does not matter that the prohibition here was addressed to the parties rather than to the federal court itself. . . .

"Petitioners being properly in the federal court had a right granted by Congress to have the court decide the issues they presented, and to appeal to the Court of Appeals from the District Court's dismissal. They have been punished both for prosecuting their federal-court case and for appealing it. [T]he propriety of a state court's punishment of a federal-court litigant for pursuing his right to federal-court remedies is [now before us]. That right was granted by Congress and cannot be taken away by the state. The Texas courts were without power to take away this federal right by contempt proceedings or otherwise."

Is this persuasive? Justice Harlan, whose dissent was joined by Justices Clark and Stewart, first restated the question presented: "May a state court enjoin resident state-court suitors from prosecuting in the federal courts vexatious, duplicative litigation which has the effect of thwarting a state-court judgment already rendered against them?" He noted that the Texas Supreme Court made unchallenged findings amply supported by the record that the controversy had "reached the point of vexatious and harassing litigation." He then noted that:

> "The power of a court in equity to enjoin persons subject to its jurisdiction from conducting vexatious and harassing litigation in another forum has not been doubted until now. . . . This Court, in 1941, expressly recognized the power of a state court to do precisely what the Texas court did here. In *Baltimore & Ohio R. Co. v. Kepner*, 314 U.S. 44, 51–52 (1941), the Court, although denying the state court's power to issue an injunction in that case, said:
>
>> 'The real contention of petitioner is that . . . respondent is acting in a vexatious and inequitable manner . . . .. Under such circumstances, petitioner asserts power, abstractly speaking, in the Ohio court to prevent a resident under its jurisdiction from doing inequity. *Such power does exist.*' " [Emphasis supplied by Justice Harlan.]

Justice Harlan then noted that none of the cases relied on by the majority was concerned with vexatious litigation, and concluded:

> "There can be no dispute, therefore, that all the weight of authority . . . is contrary to the position which the Court takes in this case. It is not necessary to comment on the Court's assertion that the petitioners 'had a right granted by Congress' to maintain their suit in the federal court, for that is the very question at issue. In any event, the statutory boundaries of federal jurisdiction are hardly to be regarded as a license to conduct litigation in the federal courts for the purpose of harassment. The exception which the Court recognizes for in rem actions demonstrates that no such view of federal jurisdiction is tenable; for in those cases, too, the federal courts have statutory jurisdiction to proceed."

7. Questions and Comments on *Donovan*. It is concluded in Arnold, State Power to Enjoin Federal Court Proceedings, 51 Va. L.

Rev. 59 (1965), that Justice Black had the best of it in terms of precedent.[g] A number of cases in the mid–1800's squarely held the state courts without power to enjoin prosecution of a federal suit; the *Kepner* dicta in 1941 did not consider those decisions nor thoroughly canvass the issue; and such authority as there was after *Kepner* followed the old rule. But, as Arnold argued, the more interesting issue is whether the result is correct. Arnold concluded that a state court injunction should be permitted only if adequate relief could not be obtained in a federal court. He defended this result as a proper "federal common law" solution, mainly on the ground that it would avoid unnecessary friction between the two court systems.

What should the answer be in the *Donovan* situation? Is it relevant that Congress has forbidden the federal courts to enjoin state court suits in 28 U.S.C. § 2283? But note that § 2283 forbids injunctions only against *pending* litigation; it does not foreclose an injunction against the *institution* of litigation. Note also that § 2283 permits the federal courts to enjoin pending state-court proceedings in three situations, including "to protect or effectuate its judgments" and "where necessary in aid of its jurisdiction." Would these exceptions permit a federal injunction against a pending state court suit if the facts in *Donovan* were reversed, that is, if the first suit had been filed in a federal court and the second in a state court? The answer is probably "yes." [h] Does that matter? [i]

8. Extradition Proceedings: *California v. Superior Court.*
A different kind of limitation on the power of state courts to conduct judicial proceedings arose in California v. Superior Court, __ U.S. __ (1987). The case involved a complex custody dispute between divorced parents. After protracted proceedings, the father obtained a California judgment awarding him custody of the children. The children were then in Louisiana with their mother, and the father—after two years of further legal wrangling—picked up the children one day as they were waiting for a school bus and took them back to California. The mother

[g] For a contrary reading of the precedents, see Comment, 32 U. Chi. L. Rev. 471 (1965). See also Note, 75 Yale L.J. 150 (1965).

[h] The meaning of § 2283 is discussed further at pages 526–41, infra.

[i] The holding in *Donovan* was reaffirmed in General Atomic Co. v. Felter, 434 U.S. 12 (1977) (per curiam). The Court granted certiorari and summarily reversed an injunction approved by the New Mexico Supreme Court without hearing oral argument. It held that it was "clear from *Donovan* that the rights conferred by Congress to bring in personam actions in federal courts are not subject to abridgment by state-court injunctions, regardless of whether the federal litigation is pending or prospective." It also noted that "[f]ederal courts are fully capable of preventing their misuse for purposes of harassment."

Justice Rehnquist dissented. He argued that *Donovan* should be re-examined, and that a "general rule of parity" should be adopted under which "where a federal district court has power to enjoin the institution of proceedings in a state court, a state court must have a similar power to forbid the initiation of vexatious litigation in federal court." He thought that § 2283 indicated that Congress could not have intended to deny to state courts the authority therein granted to federal courts. And "[n]either the supremacy clause . . . nor the congressional grants of jurisdiction to federal courts in any way militate against the conclusion that *both* state and federal courts possess the authority to protect jurisdiction which they have acquired from being undercut or nullified by suits later instituted in the courts of the other jurisdiction."

persuaded Louisiana authorities to file kidnapping charges against the father, pursuant to which Louisiana sought to have the father extradited. Appropriate papers were filed in California, after which the father sought habeas corpus from a California state court to prevent the extradition. The California Supreme Court upheld the grant of the writ on the ground that the father was the lawful custodian and hence could not be guilty of kidnapping under Louisiana law.

The Supreme Court reversed. It held that extradition was a "summary procedure" under the Constitution and that a 1793 federal extradition statute permitted only four questions to be asked by courts of the asylum state: whether the extradition documents on their face were in order; whether the person had been charged with a crime by the demanding state; whether the person before the court is the person sought by the demanding state; and whether the person is a fugitive from the demanding state. These four prerequisites being satisfied, "this ends the inquiry." The Court adhered to this view even though it may have been true that Louisiana was required by federal law to respect the California custody decree and that therefore there could have been no crime under Louisiana law. It may be, the Court added, that the father was "innocent of the charges" and a victim "of a possible abuse of the criminal process." "But, under the Extradition Act, it is for the Louisiana courts to do justice in this case, not the California courts: 'surrender is not to be interfered with by the summary process of habeas corpus upon speculations as to what ought to be the result of a trial in the place where the Constitution provides for its taking place.'"

Justice Stevens, joined by Justice Brennan, dissented. He could not "agree that respect for the criminal laws of other states requires the state of California indiscriminately to render as fugitives those citizens who are conclusorily charged with simple kidnapping for their exercise of a right conferred upon them by a valid custody decree issued by a California court."

DICE v. AKRON, CANTON & YOUNGSTOWN RAILROAD CO.

United States Supreme Court, 1952.
342 U.S. 359.

Opinion of the Court by MR. JUSTICE BLACK, announced by MR. JUSTICE DOUGLAS.

Petitioner, a railroad fireman, was seriously injured when an engine in which he was riding jumped the track. Alleging that his injuries were due to respondent's negligence, he brought this action for damages under the Federal Employers' Liability Act in an Ohio Court of Common Pleas. Respondent's defenses were (1) a denial of negligence and (2) a written document signed by petitioner purporting to release respondent in full for $924.63. Petitioner admitted that he had signed several receipts for payments made him in connection with his injuries but denied that he had made a full and complete settlement of all his claims. He alleged that the purported release was void because he had signed it relying on respondent's deliberately false statement that the document was nothing more than a mere receipt for back wages.

After both parties had introduced considerable evidence the jury found in favor of petitioner and awarded him a $25,000 verdict. The trial judge later entered judgment notwithstanding the verdict. In doing so he reappraised the evidence as to fraud, found that petitioner had been "guilty of supine negligence" in failing to read the release, and accordingly held that the facts did not "sustain either in law or equity the allegations of fraud by clear, unequivocal and convincing evidence."* This judgment notwithstanding the verdict was reversed by the Court of Appeals of Summit County, Ohio, on the ground that under federal law, which controlled, the jury's verdict must stand because there was ample evidence to support its finding of fraud. The Ohio Supreme Court, one judge dissenting, reversed the Court of Appeals' judgment and sustained the trial court's action, holding that: (1) Ohio, not federal, law governed; (2) under that law petitioner, a man of ordinary intelligence who could read, was bound by the release even though he had been induced to sign it by the deliberately false statement that it was only a receipt for back wages; and (3) under controlling Ohio law factual issues as to fraud in the execution of this release were properly decided by the judge rather than by the jury. We granted certiorari because the decision of the Supreme Court of Ohio appeared to deviate from previous decisions of this Court that federal law governs cases arising under the Federal Employers' Liability Act.

First. We agree with the Court of Appeals of Summit County, Ohio, and the dissenting judge in the Ohio Supreme Court and hold that validity of releases under the Federal Employers' Liability Act raises a federal question to be determined by federal rather than state law. Congress in § 1 of the act granted petitioner a right to recover against his employer for damages negligently inflicted. State laws are not controlling in determining what the incidents of this federal right shall be. Manifestly the federal rights affording relief to injured railroad employees under a federally declared standard could be defeated if states were permitted to have the final say as to what defenses could and could not be properly interposed to suits under the act. Moreover, only if federal law controls can the federal act be given that uniform application throughout the country essential to effectuate its purposes. Releases and other devices designed to liquidate or defeat injured employees' claims play an important part in the federal act's administration. Their validity is but one of the many interrelated questions that must constantly be determined in these cases according to a uniform federal law.

---

* The trial judge had charged the jury that petitioner's claim of fraud must be sustained "by clear and convincing evidence," but since the verdict was for peti-tioner, he does not here challenge this charge as imposing too heavy a burden under controlling federal law.

Second. In effect the Supreme Court of Ohio held that an employee trusts his employer at his peril, and that the negligence of an innocent worker is sufficient to enable his employer to benefit by its deliberate fraud. Application of so harsh a rule to defeat a railroad employee's claim is wholly incongruous with the general policy of the act to give railroad employees a right to recover just compensation for injuries negligently inflicted by their employers. And this Ohio rule is out of harmony with modern judicial and legislative practice to relieve injured persons from the effect of releases fraudulently obtained. We hold that the correct federal rule is that announced by the Court of Appeals of Summit County, Ohio, and the dissenting judge in the Ohio Supreme Court—a release of rights under the act is void when the employee is induced to sign it by the deliberately false and material statements of the railroad's authorized representatives made to deceive the employee as to the contents of the release. The trial court's charge to the jury correctly stated this rule of law.

Third. Ohio provides and has here accorded petitioner the usual jury trial of factual issues relating to negligence. But Ohio treats factual questions of fraudulent releases differently. It permits the judge trying a negligence case to resolve all factual questions of fraud "other than fraud in the factum." The factual issue of fraud is thus split into fragments, some to be determined by the judge, others by the jury.

It is contended that since a state may consistently with the federal Constitution provide for trial of cases under the act by a nonunanimous verdict, Minneapolis & St. Louis R. Co. v. Bombolis, 241 U.S. 211 (1916), Ohio may lawfully eliminate trial by jury as to one phase of fraud while allowing jury trial as to all other issues raised. The *Bombolis* case might be more in point had Ohio abolished trial by jury in all negligence cases including those arising under the federal act. But Ohio has not done this. It has provided jury trials for cases arising under the federal act but seeks to single out one phase of the question of fraudulent releases for determination by a judge rather than by a jury. Compare Testa v. Katt, 330 U.S. 386 (1947).

We have previously held that "[t]he right to trial by jury is 'a basic and fundamental feature of our system of federal jurisprudence'" and that it is "part and parcel of the remedy afforded railroad workers under the Employers' Liability Act." Bailey v. Central Vermont R. Co., 319 U.S. 350, 354 (1943). We also recognized in that case that to deprive railroad workers of the benefit of a jury trial where there is evidence to support negligence "is to take away a goodly portion of the relief which Congress has afforded them." It follows that the right to trial by jury is too substantial a part of the rights accorded by the act to permit it to be classified as a mere "local rule of procedure" for denial in the manner that Ohio has here used. Brown v. Western R. Co., 338 U.S. 294 (1949).

The trial judge and the Ohio Supreme Court erred in holding that petitioner's rights were to be determined by Ohio law and in taking away petitioner's verdict when the issues of fraud had been submitted to the jury on conflicting evidence and determined in petitioner's favor. The judgment of the Court of Appeals of Summit County, Ohio, was correct and should not have been reversed by the Supreme Court of Ohio. The cause is reversed and remanded to the Supreme Court of Ohio for further action not inconsistent with this opinion.

It is so ordered.

MR. JUSTICE FRANKFURTER, whom MR. JUSTICE REED, MR. JUSTICE JACKSON and MR. JUSTICE BURTON join, concurring for reversal but dissenting from the Court's opinion.

Ohio, as do many other states, maintains the old division between law and equity as to the mode of trying issues, even though the same judge administers both. The Ohio Supreme Court has told us what, on one issue, is the division of functions in all negligence actions brought in the Ohio courts: "Where it is claimed that a release was induced by fraud (other than fraud in the factum) or by mistake, it is necessary, before seeking to enforce a cause of action which such release purports to bar, that equitable relief from the release be secured." Thus, in all cases in Ohio, the judge is the trier of fact on this issue of fraud, rather than the jury. It is contended that the Federal Employers' Liability Act requires that Ohio courts send the fraud issue to a jury in the cases founded on that act. To require Ohio to try a particular issue before a different fact-finder in negligence actions brought under the Employers' Liability Act from the fact-finder on the identical issue in every other negligence case disregards the settled distribution of judicial power between federal and state courts where Congress authorizes concurrent enforcement of federally-created rights.

It has been settled ever since the Second Employers' Liability Cases, 223 U.S. 1 (1912), that no state which gives its courts jurisdiction over common law actions for negligence may deny access to its courts for a negligence action founded on the Federal Employers' Liability Act. Nor may a state discriminate disadvantageously against actions for negligence under the federal act as compared with local causes of action in negligence. McKnett v. St. Louis & S.F.R. Co., 292 U.S. 230, 234 (1934); Missouri ex rel. Southern R. Co. v. Mayfield, 340 U.S. 1, 4 (1950). Conversely, however, simply because there is concurrent jurisdiction in federal and state courts over actions under the Employers' Liability Act, a state is under no duty to treat actions arising under that act differently from the way it adjudicates local actions for negligence, so far as the mechanics of litigation, the forms in which law is administered, are concerned. This surely covers the distribution of functions as between judge and jury in the determination of the issues in a negligence case.

In 1916 the Court decided without dissent that states in entertaining actions under the Federal Employers' Liability Act need not provide a jury system other than that established for local negligence actions. States are not compelled to provide the jury required of federal courts by the seventh amendment. Minneapolis & St. L. R. Co. v. Bombolis,

241 U.S. 211 (1916). In the 36 years since this early decision after the enactment of the Federal Employers' Liability Act, the *Bombolis* case has often been cited by this Court but never questioned. Until today its significance has been to leave to states the choice of fact-finding tribunal in all negligence actions, including those arising under the federal act. Mr. Chief Justice White's opinion cannot bear any other meaning: . . .

> "And it was of course presumably an appreciation of the principles so thoroughly settled which caused Congress in the enactment of the Employers' Liability Act to clearly contemplate the existence of a concurrent power and duty of both federal and state courts to administer the rights conferred by the statute in accordance with the modes of procedure prevailing in such courts." 241 U.S., at 218. . . .

Although a state must entertain negligence suits under the Federal Employers' Liability Act if it entertains ordinary actions for negligence, it need conduct them only in the way in which it conducts the run of negligence litigation. The *Bombolis* case directly establishes that the Employers' Liability Act does not impose the jury requirements of the seventh amendment on the states pro tanto for Employers' Liability litigation. If its reasoning means anything, the *Bombolis* decision means that, if a state chooses not to have a jury at all, but to leave questions of fact in all negligence actions to a court, certainly the Employers' Liability Act does not require a state to have juries for negligence actions brought under the federal act in its courts. Or, if a state chooses to retain the old double system of courts, common law and equity—as did a good many states until the other day, and as four states still do—surely there is nothing in the Employers' Liability Act that requires traditional distribution of authority for disposing of legal issues as between common law and chancery courts to go by the board. And, if states are free to make a distribution of functions between equity and common law courts, it surely makes no rational difference whether a state chooses to provide that the same judge preside on both the common law and the chancery sides in a single litigation, instead of in separate rooms in the same building. So long as all negligence suits in a state are treated in the same way, by the same mode of disposing equitable, non-jury and common law, jury issues, the state does not discriminate against Employers' Liability suits nor does it make any inroad upon substance.

Ohio and her sister states with a similar division of functions between law and equity are not trying to evade their duty under the Federal Employers' Liability Act; nor are they trying to make it more difficult for railroad workers to recover, than for those suing under local law. The states merely exercise a preference in adhering to historic ways of dealing with a claim of fraud; they prefer the traditional way of making unavailable through equity an otherwise valid defense. The state judges and local lawyers who must administer the Federal Employers' Liability Act in state courts are trained in the ways of local practice; it multiplies the difficulties and confuses the administration of justice to require, on purely theoretical grounds, a hybrid of state and federal practice in the state courts as to a single class of cases. Nothing in the Employers' Liability Act or in the judicial enforcement of the act for over 40 years forces such judicial hybridization upon the states. The fact that Congress authorized actions under the Federal Employers' Liability Act to be brought in state as well as in federal courts seems a strange basis for the inference that Congress overrode state procedural arrangements controlling all other negligence suits in a state, by imposing upon state courts to which plaintiffs choose to go the rules prevailing in the federal courts regarding juries. Such an inference is admissible, so it seems to me, only on the theory that Congress included as part of the right created by the Employers' Liability Act an assumed likelihood that trying all issues to juries is more favorable to plaintiffs. At least, if a plaintiff's right to have all issues decided by a jury rather than the court is "part and parcel of the remedy afforded railroad workers under the Employers' Liability Act," the *Bombolis* case should be overruled explicitly instead of left as a derelict bound to occasion collisions on the waters of the law. We have put the questions squarely because they seem to be precisely what will be roused in the minds of lawyers properly pressing their clients' interests and in the minds of trial and appellate judges called upon to apply this Court's opinion. It is one thing not to borrow trouble from the morrow. It is another thing to create the trouble for the morrow.

Even though the method of trying the equitable issue of fraud which the state applies in all other negligence cases governs Employers' Liability cases, two questions remain for decision: Should the validity of the release be tested by a federal or a state standard? And if by a federal one, did the Ohio courts in the present case correctly administer the standard? If the states afford courts for enforcing the federal act, they must enforce the substance of the right given by Congress. They cannot depreciate the legislative currency issued by Congress—either expressly or by local methods of enforcement that accomplish the same result. In order to prevent diminution of railroad workers' nationally-uniform right to recover, the standard for the validity of a release of contested liability must be federal. We have recently said: "One who attacks a settlement must bear the burden of showing that the contract he has made is tainted with invalidity, either by fraud practiced upon him or by a mutual mistake under which both parties acted." Such proof of fraud need be only by a preponderance of relevant evidence. The admitted fact that the injured worker signed the release is material in tending to show the release to be valid, but presumptions must not be drawn from that fact so as to hobble the plaintiff's showing that it would be unjust to allow a formally good defense to prevail.

The judgment of the Ohio Supreme Court must be reversed for it applied the state rule as to validity of releases, and it is not for us to interpret Ohio decisions in order to be assured that on a matter of substance the state and federal criteria coincide. Moreover, we cannot say with confidence that the Ohio trial judge applied the federal standard correctly. He duly recognized that "the federal law controls as to the validity of a release pleaded and proved in bar of the action, and the burden of showing that the alleged fraud vitiates the contract or compromise or release rests upon the party attacking the release." And he made an extended analysis of the relevant circumstances of the release, concluding, however, that there was no "clear, unequivocal and convincing evidence" of fraud. Since these elusive words fail to assure us that the trial judge followed the federal test and did not require some larger quantum of proof, we would return the case for further proceedings on the sole question of fraud in the release.

NOTES ON SUBSTANCE AND PROCEDURE WHEN STATE COURTS APPLY FEDERAL LAW

1. **Background.** *Dice* is better understood against the background of two lines of FELA decisions. The first, summarized at pages 235–38, supra, concerned the obligation of state courts to hear FELA claims. In general, those decisions required state courts to entertain FELA suits, but did not speak to the procedures under which the cases must be heard. This issue was dealt with in the second line of cases:

(i) *Central Vermont Ry. v. White.* One of the assignments of error in Central Vermont Ry. v. White, 238 U.S. 507 (1915), was that the jury had been improperly instructed on which party bore the burden of proof on contributory negligence. The local Vermont rule was that the plaintiff must prove freedom from contributory negligence. The Vermont courts held, however, that federal law controlled this issue and that under federal law the burden of proof was on the defendant-railroad to prove the plaintiff's decedent contributorily negligent. The jury returned a verdict for the plaintiff. The railroad's appeal was unanimously rejected by the Supreme Court. It said:

"As long as the question involves a mere matter of procedure as to the time when and the order in which evidence should be submitted the state court can . . . follow their own practice even in the trial of suits arising under the federal law.

"But it is a misnomer to say that the question as to the burden of proof as to contributory negligence is a mere matter of state procedure. For, in Vermont, and in a few other states, proof of plaintiff's freedom from fault is a part of the very substance of his case. [It cannot] be said [in these states] that the burden is imposed by a rule of procedure, since it arises out of the general obligation imposed upon every plaintiff, to establish all of the facts necessary to make out his cause of action. But the United States courts have uniformly held that as a matter of general law the burden of proving contributory negligence is on the defendant. . . . Congress in passing the [FELA] evidently intended that the federal statute should be construed in the light of these and other decisions of the federal courts. . . . There was, therefore, no error in failing to enforce what the defendant calls the Vermont rule of procedure as to the burden of proof."

 (ii) *Minneapolis & St. Louis R. Co. v. Bombolis.*   Minneapolis & St. Louis R. Co. v. Bombolis, 241 U.S. 211 (1916), concerned the obligation of the state courts in FELA cases to follow the seventh amendment requirement of a unanimous jury of 12. *Bombolis* concerned a Minnesota law that permitted a verdict by agreement of five-sixths of the jurors if the jury had been unable to achieve unanimous agreement after 12 hours of deliberation. A verdict for the plaintiff in an FELA case was returned under this provision, and the railroad "objected on the ground that as the cause of action against it arose under the [FELA] the defendant was by the seventh amendment to the Constitution entitled to have its liability determined by a jury constituted . . . according to the . . . common law . . . ."

 The Supreme Court agreed that the seventh amendment required a unanimous verdict, but held that:

> "The one question to be decided is . . . reduced to this: Did the seventh amendment apply to the action of the state legislature and to the conduct of the state court . . .?

> "Two propositions as to the operation and effect of the seventh amendment [are controlling]. (a) That the first ten amendments, including of course the seventh, are not concerned with state action and deal only with federal action. . . . And, as a necessary corollary, (b) that the seventh amendment applies only to proceedings in courts of the United States and does not in any manner whatever govern or regulate trials by jury in state courts or the standards which must be applied concerning the same. . . ."

Bombolis was cited without elaboration to uphold the practices involved in companion cases decided on the same day. St. Louis & San Francisco R. Co. v. Brown, 241 U.S. 223 (1916) (three-fourths of the jury returned a verdict for the plaintiff); Chesapeake & Ohio Ry. v. Carnahan, 241 U.S. 241 (1916) (jury of seven returned a verdict for the plaintiff); Louisville and Nashville R. Co. v. Stewart, 241 U.S. 261 (1916) (three-fourths of the jury returned a verdict for the plaintiff).

 (iii) *Bailey v. Central Vermont Ry.*   Bailey v. Central Vermont Ry., 319 U.S. 350 (1943), was the first of a series of decisions in which the Supreme Court reversed a state court judgment directing a verdict for the defendant in an FELA case. The Court carefully reviewed the meagre evidence of negligence in the case, and held that the "jury is the tribunal under our legal system to decide that type of issue . . . . To withdraw such a question from the jury is to usurp its functions." Justice Douglas elaborated for the Court:

> "The right to trial by jury is 'a basic and fundamental feature of our system of federal jurisprudence.' It is part and parcel of the remedy afforded railroad workers under the [FELA]. Reasonable care and cause and effect are as elusive here as in other fields. But the jury has been chosen as the

appropriate tribunal to apply those standards to the facts of these personal injuries. That method of determining the liability of the carriers and of placing on them the cost of these industrial accidents may be crude, archaic, and expensive as compared with the more modern systems of workmen's compensation. But however inefficient and backward it may be, it is the system which Congress has provided. To deprive these workers of the benefit of a jury trial in close or doubtful cases is to take away a goodly portion of the relief which Congress has afforded them."

Justice Roberts, joined by Justice Frankfurter, added a statement to the effect that he thought the case an inappropriate exercise of the Court's discretionary reviewing authority, a theme repeated by Justices Frankfurter and Harlan in later cases involving the review of fact-oriented claims under the FELA.[a] Justice Roberts concluded his statement in *Bailey* with a surmise as to what the Court was up to:

"Finally, I cannot concur in the intimation, which I think the opinion gives, that, as Congress has seen fit not to enact a workmen's compensation law, this Court will strain the law of negligence to accord compensation where the employer is without fault. I yield to none in my belief in the wisdom and equity of workmen's compensation laws, but I do not conceive it to be within our judicial function to write the policy which underlies compensation laws into acts of Congress when Congress has not chosen that policy but, instead, has adopted the common law doctrine of negligence."

Chief Justice Stone added that, though he agreed that certiorari should not have been granted, "as we have adhered to our long standing practice of granting certiorari upon the affirmative vote of four Justices, the case is properly here for decision and is, I think, correctly decided."

(iv) ***Brown v. Western Ry. of Alabama.*** Brown v. Western Ry. of Alabama, 338 U.S. 294 (1949), the Court was faced with the dismissal of an FELA complaint by the Georgia courts on the ground that it failed to set forth a cause of action and was "otherwise insufficient in law." The dismissal was a final judgment on the merits, precluding any further assertion of a related claim. The plaintiff had been injured when he stepped on a large "clinker" lying beside a track in a railroad yard. The Georgia courts, in accordance with local practice, had construed the complaint "most strongly against the pleader" and concluded, in effect, that the "clinker" was in plain view and the plaintiff should have avoided stepping on it. They also found no

---

[a] See, e.g., Rogers v. Missouri Pacific R. Co., 352 U.S. 500, 524, 559 (1957), where the state Supreme Court had set aside a jury verdict in favor of an FELA plaintiff on the ground of insufficient evidence of negligence and the Supreme Court reversed. Justice Frankfurter wrote a 35-page dissent, and listed in an Appendix some 125 FELA cases since 1911 in which the Court had decided sufficiency of the evidence questions. See also Wilkerson v. McCarthy, 336 U.S. 53 (1949) (directed verdict for defendant set aside in FELA case; debate between Justices Frankfurter and Douglas over propriety of granting certiorari).

precise allegation in the complaint that the particular "clinker" was sitting beside the tracks due to the railroad's negligence.

The Supreme Court reversed in an opinion by Justice Black:

"It is contended that this construction of the complaint is binding on us. [But a] long series of cases previously decided, from which we see no reason to depart, makes it our duty to construe the allegations of this complaint ourselves in order to determine whether petitioner has been denied a right of trial granted him by Congress. This federal right cannot be defeated by the forms of local practice. And we cannot accept as final a state court's interpretation of allegations in a complaint asserting it. This rule applies to FELA cases no less than to other types."

The Court then construed the complaint for itself and found it to have sufficiently alleged negligence. It concluded:

"Strict local rules of pleading cannot be used to impose unnecessary burdens upon rights of recovery authorized by federal laws. 'Whatever springes the state may set for those who are endeavoring to assert rights that the state confers, the assertion of federal rights, when plainly and reasonably made, is not to be defeated under the name of local practice.' Should this Court fail to protect federally created rights from dismissal because of over-exacting local requirements for meticulous pleadings, desirable uniformity in adjudication of federally created rights could not be achieved.

"Upon trial of this case the evidence offered may or may not support inferences of negligence. We simply hold that under the facts alleged it was error to dismiss the complaint and that petitioner should be allowed to try his case. . . ."

Justice Frankfurter, joined by Justice Jackson, dissented:

"Have the Georgia courts disrespected the law of the land in the judgment under review? Since Congress empowers state courts to entertain suits under the [FELA], a state cannot wilfully shut its courts to such cases. But the courts so empowered are creatures of the states, with such structures and functions as the states are free to devise and define. Congress has not imposed jurisdiction on state courts for claims under the act 'as against an otherwise valid excuse.' Again, if a state has dispensed with the jury in civil suits or has modified the common-law requirements for trial by jury, a plaintiff must take the jury system as he finds it if he chooses to bring his suit under the [FELA] in a court of that state. After all, the federal courts are always available.

"So also, states have varying systems of pleading and practice. One state may cherish formalities more than another, one state may be more responsive than another to procedural reforms. If a litigant chooses to enforce a federal right in a state court, he cannot be heard to object if he is treated exactly as are plaintiffs who press like claims arising under state law with regard to the form in which the claim must be stated—the particularity, for instance, with which a cause of action must be described. Federal law, though invoked in a state court, delimits the federal claim—defines what gives a right to recovery and what goes to prove it. But the form in which the claim must be stated need not be different from what the state exacts in the enforcement of like obligations created by it, so long as such a requirement does not add to, or diminish, the right as defined by federal law, nor burden the realization of this right in the actualities of litigation. . . .

"The crucial question for this Court is whether the Georgia courts have merely enforced a local requirement of pleading, however finicky, applicable to all such litigation in Georgia without qualifying the basis of recovery under the [FELA] or weighting the scales against the plaintiff. Georgia may adhere to its requirements of pleading, but it may not put 'unreasonable obstacles in the way' of a plaintiff who seeks its courts to obtain what the federal act gives him.

"These decisive differences are usually conveyed by the terms 'procedure' and 'substance.' The terms are not meaningless even though they do not have fixed undeviating meanings. They derive content from the functions they serve here in precisely the same way in which we have applied them in reverse situations—when confronted with the problem whether the federal courts respected the substance of state-created rights, as required by the rule in Erie R. Co. v. Tompkins, 304 U.S. 64 (1938), or impaired them by professing merely to enforce them by the mode in which the federal courts do business. Review on this aspect of state court judgments in [FELA] cases presents essentially the same kind of problem as that with which this Court dealt in Guaranty Trust Co. v. York, 326 U.S. 99 (1945) . . . . Congress has authorized state courts to enforce federal rights, and federal courts state-created rights. Neither system of courts can impair these respective rights, but both may have their own requirements for stating claims (pleading) and conducting litigation (practice)."

Justice Frankfurter then noted that he would have upheld the Georgia decision because the local rule of pleading was conscientiously and straightforwardly applied.

2. Questions and Comments on *Dice*. Does *Dice* turn on particular substantive policies derived from the FELA, or does it state a general principle to be applied to any federal claim asserted in state court?[b] Does Justice Frankfurter disagree about what the FELA

---

[b] For a related exploration of the procedural consequences of trying a federal claim in state court undertaken in the context of actions under 42 U.S.C. § 1983, see Neuborne, Toward Procedural Parity in Constitutional Litigation, 22 W. & M.L. Rev. 725 (1981). For a comprehensive treatment of the litigation of § 1983 claims

means or about the general obligations of state courts with respect to federal claims?

Consider the cases summarized in the preceding note. First, are *Bombolis, Bailey* and *Dice* consistent? If, as *Bailey* says, the right to a trial by jury is "part and parcel of the remedy" afforded by the FELA, how could Justice Black imply in *Dice* that Ohio might have been able to dispense with a jury trial entirely? And if Ohio could have dispensed entirely with a jury trial, why can it not dispense with a jury trial on one issue?

Second, consider *White* and *Brown*. Justice Frankfurter says in *Brown* that the substance/procedure problems when federal courts apply state law and when state courts apply federal law are "reverse situations," implying that the considerations governing when each court must displace its own procedures in order to maintain fidelity to the governing substantive law are similar if not identical. Were they in 1949 (after *Guaranty Trust* but before *Byrd* and *Hanna* ᶜ)? Are they today?

3. *Felder v. Casey*. Plaintiffs filed a federal civil rights action under 42 U.S.C. § 1983 in state court, but failed to comply with a notice-of-claim statute that required written notice of the circumstances of the claim within 120 days of any incident giving rise to a suit against a governmental subdivision or its officers. The state supreme court held that the action should have been dismissed. In Felder v. Casey, ___ U.S. ___ (1988), the Supreme Court reversed.

Justice Brennan's opinion for the Court relied, inter alia, on *Brown v. Western Ry. of Alabama* in holding that "the application of the notice requirement burdens the exercise of the federal right" in a manner that is "inconsistent in both design and effect with the compensatory aims of the federal civil rights laws." Among the arguments in support of enforcing the state requirement was the following:

> "Respondents and their supporting amici urge that we approve the application of the notice-of-claim statute to § 1983 actions brought in state court as a matter of equitable federalism. They note that " '[t]he general rule, bottomed deeply in belief in the importance of state control of state judicial procedure, is that federal law takes the state courts as it finds them.' " Litigants who chose to bring their civil rights actions in state courts presumably do so in order to obtain the benefit of certain procedural advantages in those courts, or to draw their juries from urban populations. Having availed themselves of these benefits, civil rights litigants must comply as well with those state rules they find less to their liking."

in a state court, see Steven Steinglass, The Emerging State Court § 1983 Action: A Procedural Review, 38 U.Miami L.Rev. 381 (1984).

ᶜ See pages 490–99, infra.

Justice Brennan responded:

"However equitable this bitter-with-the-sweet argument may appear in the abstract, it has no place under our supremacy clause analysis. Federal law takes state courts as it finds them only insofar as those courts employ rules that do not 'impose unnecessary burdens upon rights of recovery authorized by federal laws.' *Brown v. Western Ry. of Alabama,* 338 U.S., at 298–299. States may make the litigation of federal rights as congenial as they see fit—not as a quid pro quo for compliance with other, incongenial rules, but because such congeniality does not stand as an obstacle to the accomplishment of Congress' goals. [E]nforcement of the notice-of-claim statute in § 1983 actions brought in state court so interferes with and frustrates the substantive right Congress created that, under the supremacy clause, it must yield to the federal interest. . . .

"Civil rights victims often do not appreciate the constitutional nature of their injuries and thus will fail to file a notice of injury or claim within the requisite time period, which in Wisconsin is a mere four months. Unless such claimants . . . file an itemized claim for damages, they must bring their § 1983 suits in federal court or not at all. Wisconsin, however, may not alter the outcome of federal claims it chooses to entertain in its courts by demanding compliance with outcome-determinative rules that are inapplicable when such claims are brought in federal court, for ' "[w]hatever spring[s] the state may set for those who are endeavoring to assert rights that the state confers, the assertion of federal rights, when plainly and reasonably made, is not to be defeated under the name of local practice." ' *Brown v. Western Ry. of Alabama,* supra at 299. The state notice-of-claim statute is more than a mere rule of procedure: . . . the statute is a substantive condition on the right to sue governmental officials and entities, and the federal courts have therefore correctly recognized that the notice statute governs the adjudication of state-law claims in diversity actions. In Guaranty Trust Co. v. York, 326 U.S. 99 (1945), we held that, in order to give effect to a state's statute of limitations, a federal court could not hear a state-law action that a state court would deem time-barred. Conversely, a state court may not decline to hear an otherwise properly presented federal claim because that claim would be barred under a state law requiring timely filing of notice. State courts simply are not free to vindicate the substantive interests underlying a state rule of decision at the expense of the federal right.

"Finally, in Wilson v. Garcia, 471 U.S. 261 (1985), we characterized § 1983 suits as claims for personal injuries because such an approach ensured that the same limitations period would govern all § 1983 actions brought in any given state, and thus comported with Congress' desire that the federal civil rights laws be given a uniform application within each state. A law that predictably alters the outcome of § 1983 claims depending solely on whether they are brought in state or federal court within the same state is obviously inconsistent with this federal interest in intra-state uniformity."

Justice O'Connor, joined by Chief Justice Rehnquist, dissented.[d] She saw no substantive conflict between § 1983 and the state notice requirement. She thought *Brown* distinguishable because "the statute at issue does not diminish or alter any substantive right cognizable under § 1983. As the majority concedes, the Wisconsin courts 'will hear the entire § 1983 cause of action once a plaintiff complies with the notice-of-claim statute.'" She dismissed the Court's references to *Erie* and *Guaranty Trust* on the ground that the Court's theory seemed "to be based on a sort of upside-down theory of federalism, which the Court attributes to Congress on the basis of no evidence at all."

4. Federal Claims Raised by Defendant. *Dice* and the FELA cases involved *plaintiffs* who asserted federal claims in a state court. Are the issues different when a *defendant* in state court raises a federal claim? Consider two illustrations:

(i) *Jackson v. Denno.* Jackson v. Denno, 378 U.S. 368 (1964), concerned the New York procedure by which the voluntariness of a confession was tried. Under its then prevailing practice, New York required the trial judge to make a preliminary determination and to exclude the confession if it could under no circumstances be regarded as voluntary. But if there were disputed facts or if reasonable people could disagree about the inference of coercion to be drawn from undisputed facts, the judge was required to submit the issue of voluntariness to the jury. The issue was submitted, moreover, along with all of the other evidence in the case. The jury was told to consider a confession found to be voluntary and to ignore a confession found to be involuntary, but no separate findings had to be stated. The jury was required only to return a general verdict of guilty or not guilty.

The Supreme Court held that a "defendant objecting to the admission of a confession is entitled to a fair hearing in which both the underlying factual issues and the voluntariness of his confession are actually and reliably determined." It then held that the New York procedure did not meet this standard and hence violated the due process clause of the 14th amendment. Henceforth it was required that the judge hold an independent hearing, resolve all factual disputes, and make an independent determination of voluntariness before a confession was submitted to the jury for its consideration.

(ii) *Chapman v. California.* In Chapman v. California, 386 U.S. 18 (1967), the prosecutor had commented on the defendants' failure to take the stand, and the jury was charged that it could take such comments into account. Subsequently the Supreme Court held such practices unconstitutional. The question before the Court in

[d] Justice White concurred on a different rationale.

Chapman was whether California had properly applied its harmless error doctrine to uphold the convictions in spite of the constitutional error. Justice Black wrote for the Court:

"Before deciding the two questions here—whether there can ever be harmless constitutional error and whether the error here was harmless—we must first decide whether state or federal law governs. The application of a state harmless-error rule is, of course, a state question where it involves only errors of state procedure or state law. But the error from which these petitioners suffered was a denial of rights guaranteed against invasion by the fifth and 14th amendments . . . . Whether a conviction for crime should stand when a state has failed to accord federal constitutionally guaranteed rights is every bit as much of a federal question as what particular federal constitutional provisions themselves mean, what they guarantee, and whether they have been denied. With faithfulness to the constitutional union of the states, we cannot leave to the states the formulation of the authoritative laws, rules, and remedies designed to protect people from infractions by the states of federally guaranteed rights. We have no hesitation in saying that the right of these [defendants] not to be punished for exercising their fifth and 14th amendment right to be silent—expressly created by the federal Constitution itself—is a federal right which, in the absence of appropriate congressional action, it is our responsibility to protect by fashioning the necessary rule."

The Court went on to hold, over Justice Stewart's dissent, that federal constitutional errors of this type do not always require reversal. It then held that "before a federal constitutional error can be held harmless, the court must be able to declare a belief that it was harmless beyond a reasonable doubt." Applying that standard, it reversed the conviction.

Justice Harlan dissented. He interpreted the majority opinion as embracing the authority to formulate a federal rule of decision even though the state's harmless error procedure did not itself constitute an independent violation of constitutional standards. He then said that:

"I regard the Court's assumption of what amounts to a general supervisory power over the trial of federal constitutional issues in state courts as a startling constitutional development that is wholly out of keeping with our federal system and completely unsupported by the 14th amendment where the source of such a power must be found.

"[T]he Court has always been especially reluctant to interfere with state procedural practices. From the beginning of the federal union, state courts have had power to decide issues of federal law and to formulate 'authoritative laws, rules, and remedies' for the trial of those issues. The primary responsibility for the trial of state criminal cases still rests upon the states, and the only constitutional limitation upon these trials is that the laws, rules, and remedies applied must meet constitutional requirements. If they do not, this Court may hold them invalid. The Court has no power, however, to declare which of many admittedly constitutional alternatives a state may choose. To impose uniform national requirements when alternatives are constitutionally permissible would destroy that opportunity for broad experimentation which is the genius of our federal system."

Justice Harlan then went on to measure the California harmless error rule against constitutional standards and found it acceptable.

(iii) **Questions and Comments.** Are *Jackson* and *Chapman* exercises of the same kind of authority involved in *Dice*? Arguably the answer is "yes," since all three cases require the states to modify the "procedures" by which they resolve federal substantive questions and none holds the "procedures" unconstitutional independent of the underlying federal substantive policy at stake. Does it matter where the underlying federal substantive policy comes from, whether it is derived from the Constitution or a statute? Is the Court more justified in the one case than the other in displacing state procedures? Note that a criminal defendant has no choice but to litigate any federal claims in state court. Does this make it more justifiable for the Court to assure itself that "fair" procedures are used that will respect the underlying federal policies? Or is Justice Harlan right when he says in *Chapman* that the Court cannot displace state procedures unless they are independently unconstitutional?

5. *Engel v. Davenport.* Engel v. Davenport, 271 U.S. 33 (1926), was a damage claim by a seaman against a shipowner for injuries allegedly caused by the owner's negligence in furnishing defective equipment aboard ship. The claim was based on § 33 of the Merchant Marine Act of 1920, a federal statute which incorporated by reference numerous provisions of the FELA, including in particular a two-year statute of limitations for negligence actions. The suit was filed in a California state court, which dismissed the claim because the California statute of limitations for personal injury actions was one year.

The Supreme Court reversed. The unanimous opinion by Justice Sanford first observed that it was "clear that the state courts have jurisdiction concurrently with the federal courts, to enforce the right of action established by the Merchant Marine Act . . . ." The opinion then continued:

"This brings us to the question whether a suit brought in a state court to enforce the right of action granted by the Merchant Marine Act may be commenced within two years after the cause of action accrues, or whether a state statute fixing a shorter period of limitation will apply. [The federal provision establishing a two-year limitation] is one of substantive right, setting a limit to the existence of the obligation which the act creates. And it necessarily implies that the action may be maintained, as a substantive right, if commenced within the two years. . . .

"[P]lainly, Congress in incorporating the provisions of the Employer's Liability Act into the Merchant Marine Act did not intend . . . to permit the uniform operation of the Merchant Marine Act to be destroyed by the varying provisions of the state statutes of limitation.

"We conclude that . . . as a provision affecting the substantive right created by Congress in the exercise of its paramount authority in reference to the maritime law, [the federal statute of limitations] must control in an action brought in a state court under the Merchant Marine Act, regardless of any statute of limitations of the state." [e]

Does *Engel* present the same issue as *Dice*? It also seems clear that state courts cannot hear an action based on federal law if it is barred by an explicit federal statute of limitations, even if it is filed within the period set by a longer state statute. See Atlantic Coast Line R. Co. v. General Burnette, 239 U.S. 199 (1915). Is this result surprising?

---

[e] The Court reached a similar result on the authority of *Engel* in McAllister v. Magnolia Petroleum Co., 357 U.S. 221 (1958).

Chapter III

CHOICE OF LAW IN THE FEDERAL SYSTEM

SECTION 1: THE OBLIGATION OF FEDERAL COURTS TO FOLLOW STATE LAW

ERIE RAILROAD COMPANY v. TOMPKINS
Supreme Court of the United States, 1938.
304 U.S. 64.

MR. JUSTICE BRANDEIS delivered the opinion of the Court.

The question for decision is whether the oft-challenged doctrine of Swift v. Tyson, 41 U.S. (16 Pet.) 1 (1842), shall now be disapproved.

Tompkins, a citizen of Pennsylvania, was injured on a dark night by a passing freight train of the Erie Railroad Company while walking along its right of way at Hughestown in that state. He claimed that the accident occurred through negligence in the operation, or maintenance, of the train; that he was rightfully on the premises as licensee because on a commonly used beaten footpath which ran for a short distance alongside the tracks; and that he was struck by something which looked like a door projecting from one of the moving cars. To enforce that claim he brought an action in the federal court for southern New York, which had jurisdiction because the company is a corporation of that state. It denied liability; and the case was tried by a jury.

The Erie insisted that its duty to Tompkins was no greater than that owed to a trespasser. It contended, among other things, that its duty to Tompkins, and hence its liability, should be determined in accordance with the Pennsylvania law; that under the law of Pennsylvania, as declared by its highest court, persons who use pathways along the railroad right of way—that is a longitudinal pathway as distinguished from a crossing—are to be deemed trespassers; and that the railroad is not liable for injuries to undiscovered trespassers resulting from its negligence, unless it be wanton or wilful. Tompkins denied that any such rule had been established by the decisions of the Pennsylvania courts; and contended that, since there was no statute of the state on the subject, the railroad's duty and liability is to be determined in federal courts as a matter of general law.

The trial judge refused to rule that the applicable law precluded recovery. The jury brought in a verdict of $30,000; and the judgment

269

entered thereon was affirmed by the Circuit Court of Appeals, which held that it was unnecessary to consider whether the law of Pennsylvania was as contended, because the question was one not of local, but of general, law and that

> "upon questions of general law the federal courts are free, in the absence of a local statute, to exercise their independent judgment as to what the law is; and it is well settled that the question of the responsibility of a railroad for injuries caused by its servants is one of general law. . . . Where the public has made open and notorious use of a railroad right of way for a long period of time and without objection, the company owes to persons on such permissive pathway a duty of care in the operation of its trains. . . . It is likewise generally recognized law that a jury may find that negligence exists toward a pedestrian using a permissive path on the railroad right of way if he is hit by some object projecting from the side of the train."

The Erie had contended that application of the Pennsylvania rule was required, among other things, by § 34 of the Federal Judiciary Act of September 24, 1789 [now 28 U.S.C. § 1652], which provides:

> "The laws of the several states, except where the Constitution, treaties, or statutes of the United States otherwise require or provide, shall be regarded as rules of decisions in trials at common law, in the courts of the United States, in cases where they apply."

Because of the importance of the question whether the federal court was free to disregard the alleged rule of the Pennsylvania common law, we granted certiorari.

First. *Swift v. Tyson* held that federal courts exercising jurisdiction on the ground of diversity of citizenship need not, in matters of general jurisprudence, apply the unwritten law of the state as declared by its highest court; that they are free to exercise an independent judgment as to what the common law of the state is—or should be; and that, as there stated by Mr. Justice Story:

> "The true interpretation of the 34th section limited its application to state laws strictly local, that is to say, to the positive statutes of the state, and the construction thereof adopted by the local tribunals, and to rights and titles to things having a permanent locality, such as the rights and titles to real estate, and other matters immovable and intraterritorial in their nature and character. It never has been supposed by us, that the section did apply, or was intended to apply, to questions of a more general nature, not at all dependent upon local statutes or local usages of a fixed and permanent operation, as, for example, to the construction of ordinary contracts or other written instruments, and especially to questions of general commercial law, where the state tribunals are called upon to perform the like functions as ourselves, that is, to

ascertain upon general reasoning and legal analogies, what is the true exposition of the contract or instrument, or what is the just rule furnished by the principles of commercial law to govern the case."

The Court in applying the rule of § 34 to equity cases, in Mason v. United States, 260 U.S. 545, 559 (1923), said: "The statute, however, is merely declarative of the rule which would exist in the absence of the statute." The federal courts assumed, in the broad field of "general law," the power to declare rules of decision which Congress was confessedly without power to enact as statutes. Doubt was repeatedly expressed as to the correctness of the construction given § 34, and as to the soundness of the rule which it introduced. But it was the more recent research of a competent scholar, who examined the original document, which established that the construction given to it by the Court was erroneous; and that the purpose of the section was merely to make certain that, in all matters except those in which some federal law is controlling, the federal courts exercising jurisdiction in diversity of citizenship cases would apply as their rules of decision the law of the state, unwritten as well as written.[5]

Criticism of the doctrine became widespread after the decision of Black & White Taxicab & Transfer Co. v. Brown & Yellow Taxicab & Transfer Co., 276 U.S. 518 (1928). There, Brown and Yellow, a Kentucky corporation owned by Kentuckians, and the Louisville and Nashville Railroad, also a Kentucky corporation, wished that the former

---

[5] Warren, New Light on the History of the Federal Judiciary Act of 1789, 37 Harv. L. Rev. 49, 51–52, 81–88, 108 (1923).

[Professor Warren's principal evidence for this conclusion was a slip of paper he found in the Senate archives containing the original version of § 34, handwritten by Senator (later Chief Justice) Oliver Ellsworth:

"And be it further enacted, That the ~~statute law~~ [laws] of the several states ~~in force for the time being and their unwritten or common law now in use; whether by adoption from the common law of England, the ancient statutes of the same or otherwise~~, except where the Constitution, treaties or statutes of the United States shall otherwise require or provide, shall be regarded as rules of decision in the trials at common law in the courts of the United States in cases where they apply."

Before he submitted his proposal, Senator Ellsworth inserted the word "laws" where it appears in brackets above, and crossed out the words that are struck out above. Warren concluded:

"The meaning of this change was probably as follows: that the word[s] 'laws of the several states' [were] intended to be a concise expression and a summary of the more detailed enumeration of the different forms of state law, set forth in the original draft. It seems clear that the word 'laws' was not intended to be confined to 'statute law,' because Ellsworth expressly and evidently intentionally struck out the words 'statute law' from his original draft, and broadened it by inserting the word 'laws'; having so broadened it, he evidently concluded that the specific enumeration which followed in his original draft was unnecessary."

Warren further argued that unless the change from "statute law" to "laws" was meant to include both statutes and common law,

"then no meaning whatever can be given to the change. If Ellsworth had simply meant to strike out the provision that the state common law should be a rule of decision in federal courts and had intended to have only the state statute law apply, he would have left his original draft just as it stood, and would simply have struck out the clause following the words 'the several states,' in which case the section would have read precisely as Judge Story construed it . . . ."—Addition to footnote by eds.]

should have the exclusive privilege of soliciting passenger and baggage transportation at the Bowling Green, Kentucky, railroad station; and that the Black and White, a competing Kentucky corporation, should be prevented from interfering with that privilege. Knowing that such a contract would be void under the common law of Kentucky, it was arranged that the Brown and Yellow reincorporate under the law of Tennessee, and that the contract with the railroad should be executed there. The suit was then brought by the Tennessee corporation in the federal court for western Kentucky to enjoin competition by the Black and White; an injunction issued by the district court was sustained by the Court of Appeals; and this Court, citing many decisions in which the doctrine of *Swift v. Tyson* had been applied, affirmed the decree.

Second. Experience in applying the doctrine of *Swift v. Tyson* had revealed its defects, political and social; and the benefits expected to flow from the rule did not accrue. Persistence of state courts in their own opinions on questions of common law prevented uniformity; and the impossibility of discovering a satisfactory line of demarcation between the province of general law and that of local law developed a new well of uncertainties.[8]

On the other hand, the mischievous results of the doctrine had become apparent. Diversity of citizenship jurisdiction was conferred in order to prevent apprehended discrimination in state courts against those not citizens of the state. *Swift v. Tyson* introduced grave discrimination by non-citizens against citizens. It made rights enjoyed under the unwritten "general law" vary according to whether enforcement was sought in the state or in the federal court; and the privilege of selecting the court in which the right should be determined was conferred upon the non-citizen. Thus, the doctrine rendered impossible equal protection of the law. In attempting to promote uniformity of law throughout the United States, the doctrine had prevented uniformity in the administration of the law of the state.

The discrimination resulting became in practice far-reaching. This resulted in part from the broad province accorded to the so-called "general law" as to which federal courts exercised an independent judgment. In addition to questions of purely commercial law, "general law" was held to include the obligations under contracts entered into and to be performed within the state; the extent to which a carrier operating within a state may stipulate for exemption from liability for his own negligence or that of his employee; the liability for torts committed within the state upon persons resident or property located there, even where the question of liability depended upon the scope of a property right conferred by the state; and the right to exemplary or

---

[8] Compare 2 C. Warren, The Supreme Court in United States History 89 (rev. ed. 1935):

"Probably no decision of the Court has ever given rise to more uncertainty as to legal rights; and though doubtless intended to promote uniformity in the operation of business transactions, its chief effect has been to render it difficult for business men to know in advance to what particular topic the Court would apply the doctrine. . . ."

The Federal Digest, through the 1937 volume, lists nearly 1000 decisions involving the distinction between questions of general and of local law.

punitive damages. Furthermore, state decisions construing local deeds, mineral conveyances, and even devises of real estate were disregarded.

In part the discrimination resulted from the wide range of persons held entitled to avail themselves of the federal rule by resort to the diversity of citizenship jurisdiction. Through this jurisdiction individual citizens willing to remove from their own state and become citizens of another might avail themselves of the federal rule. And, without even change of residence, a corporate citizen of the state could avail itself of the federal rule by re-incorporating under the laws of another state, as was done in the Taxicab Case.

The injustice and confusion incident to the doctrine of *Swift v. Tyson* have been repeatedly urged as reasons for abolishing or limiting diversity of citizenship jurisdiction. Other legislative relief has been proposed. If only a question of statutory construction were involved, we should not be prepared to abandon a doctrine so widely applied throughout nearly a century. But the unconstitutionality of the course pursued has now been made clear and compels us to do so.

Third. Except in matters governed by the federal Constitution or by acts of Congress, the law to be applied in any case is the law of the state. And whether the law of the state shall be declared by its legislature in a statute or by its highest court in a decision is not a matter of federal concern. There is no federal general common law. Congress has no power to declare substantive rules of common law applicable in a state whether they be local in their nature or "general," be they commercial law or a part of the law of torts. And no clause in the Constitution purports to confer such a power upon the federal courts. As stated by Mr. Justice Field when protesting in Baltimore & Ohio R. Co. v. Baugh, 149 U.S. 368, 401 (1893), against ignoring the Ohio common law of fellow servant liability:

> "I am aware that what has been termed the general law of the country—which is often little less than what the judge advancing the doctrine thinks at the time should be the general law on a particular subject—has been often advanced in judicial opinions of this court to control a conflicting law of a state. I admit that learned judges have fallen into the habit of repeating this doctrine as a convenient mode of brushing aside the law of a state in conflict with their views. And I confess that, moved and governed by the authority of the great names of those judges, I have myself, in many instances, unhesitatingly and confidently, but I think now erroneously, repeated the same doctrine. But, notwithstanding the great names which may be cited in favor of the doctrine, and notwithstanding the frequency with which the doctrine has been reiterated, there stands, as a perpetual protest against its repetition, the Constitution of the United States, which recognizes and preserves the autonomy and independence of the states—independence in their legislative and independence in their judicial departments. Supervision over either the legislative or the judicial

action of the states is in no case permissible except as to matters by the Constitution specifically authorized or delegated to the United States. Any interference with either, except as thus permitted is an invasion of the authority of the state and, to that extent, a denial of its independence."

The fallacy underlying the rule declared in *Swift v. Tyson* is made clear by Mr. Justice Holmes.[15] The doctrine rests upon the assumption that there is "a transcendental body of law outside of any particular state but obligatory within it unless and until changed by statute," that federal courts have the power to use their judgment as to what the rules of common law are; and that in the federal courts "the parties are entitled to an independent judgment on matters of general law":

> "But law in the sense in which courts speak of it today does not exist without some definite authority behind it. The common law so far as it is enforced in a state, whether called common law or not, is not the common law generally but the law of that state existing by the authority of that state without regard to what it may have been in England or anywhere else.
>
> . . .
>
> "The authority and only authority is the state, and if that be so, the voice adopted by the state as its own [whether it be of its legislature or of its Supreme Court] should utter the last word."

Thus the doctrine of *Swift v. Tyson* is, as Mr. Justice Holmes said, "an unconstitutional assumption of powers by courts of the United States which no lapse of time or respectable array of opinion should make us hesitate to correct." In disapproving that doctrine we do not hold unconstitutional § 34 of the Federal Judiciary Act of 1789 or any other act of Congress. We merely declare that in applying the doctrine this Court and the lower courts have invaded rights which in our opinion are reserved by the Constitution to the several states.

Fourth. The defendant contended that by the common law of Pennsylvania as declared by its highest court, the only duty owed to the plaintiff was to refrain from wilful or wanton injury. The plaintiff denied that such is the Pennsylvania law. In support of their respective contentions the parties discussed and cited many decisions of the Supreme Court of the state. The Circuit Court of Appeals ruled that the question of liability is one of general law; and on that ground declined to decide the issue of state law. As we hold this was error, the judgment is reversed and the case remanded to it for further proceedings in conformity with our opinion.

Reversed.

MR. JUSTICE CARDOZO took no part in the consideration or decision of this case.

---

[15] Kuhn v. Fairmont Coal Co., 215 U.S. 349, 370–72 (1910); Black & White Taxicab Co. v. Brown & Yellow Taxicab Co., 276 U.S. 518, 532–36 (1929).

[JUSTICE BUTLER, joined by JUSTICE MCREYNOLDS, concurred in the result, but on the ground that the plaintiff was contributorily negligent as a matter of law. Justice Butler observed that "[n]o constitutional question was suggested or argued below or here" and that "[a]gainst the protest of those joining in this opinion, the Court declines to assign the case for reargument."]

MR. JUSTICE REED.

I concur in the conclusion reached in this case, in the disapproval of the doctrine of *Swift v. Tyson,* and in the reasoning of the majority opinion except in so far as it relies upon the unconstitutionality of the "course pursued" by the federal courts.

The "doctrine of *Swift v. Tyson,* " as I understand it, is that the words "the laws," as used in § 34 . . . do not include in their meaning "the decisions of the local tribunals." . . .

To decide the case now before us and to "disapprove" the doctrine of *Swift v. Tyson* requires only that we say that the words "the laws" include in their meaning the decisions of the local tribunals. As the majority opinion shows . . . that this Court is now of the view that "laws" includes "decisions," it is unnecessary to go further and declare that the "course pursued" was "unconstitutional," instead of merely erroneous.

The "unconstitutional" course referred to in the majority opinion is apparently the ruling in *Swift v. Tyson* that the supposed omission of Congress to legislate as to the effect of decisions leaves federal courts free to interpret general law for themselves. I am not at all sure whether, in the absence of federal statutory direction, federal courts would be compelled to follow state decisions. . . . Mr. Justice Holmes evidently saw nothing "unconstitutional" which required the overruling of *Swift v. Tyson,* for he said in the very opinion quoted by the majority, "I should leave *Swift v. Tyson* undisturbed, . . . but I would not allow it to spread the assumed dominion into new fields." If the opinion commits this Court to the position that the Congress is without power to declare what rules of substantive law shall govern the federal courts, that conclusion also seems questionable. The line between procedural and substantive law is hazy but no one doubts federal power over procedure. Wayman v. Southard, 23 U.S. (10 Wheat.) 1 (1825). The Judiciary Article and the "necessary and proper" clause may fully authorize legislation, such as this section of the Judiciary Act.

In this Court, stare decisis, in statutory construction, is a useful rule, not an inexorable command. It seems preferable to overturn an established construction of an act of Congress, rather than, in the circumstances of this case, to interpret the Constitution.

There is no occasion to discuss further the range or soundness of these few phrases of the opinion. It is sufficient now to call attention to them and express my own non-acquiescence.

———

NOTES ON THE OBLIGATION OF THE FEDERAL COURTS TO FOLLOW STATE LAW

1. **The Regime of *Swift v. Tyson*.** *Swift v. Tyson* involved an issue of commercial law. Tyson had purchased lands in Maine from Nathaniel Norton and Jarius Keith. In return, Tyson became the obligor on a negotiable instrument executed in favor of Norton. The instrument became payable to Swift when Norton endorsed it to him in payment of a prior obligation. Tyson refused to pay, claiming that Norton and Keith had defrauded him in the original transaction because they did not have title to the lands they purported to convey. Swift then sued Tyson in a federal court, basing jurisdiction on diversity of citizenship. The issue was whether Tyson's defense against Norton and Keith was also good against Swift. The defense would fail if Swift could establish several conditions, among them that he was a purchaser for value. This turned on whether satisfaction of the pre-existing debt owed by Norton to Swift constituted sufficient consideration.

The Supreme Court held that this question should be decided by reference to "the general principles and doctrines of commercial jurisprudence." In reaching this conclusion, Justice Story had to confront the meaning of § 34 of the Judiciary Act of 1789, and in particular whether the obligation of the federal courts to follow the "laws of the several states" included state decisional law. Story argued that "[i]n the ordinary use of language, it will hardly be contended that the decisions of courts constitute laws. They are, at most, only evidence of what the laws are, and are not, of themselves, laws." As revealed in the passage from *Swift* quoted in *Erie,* he construed the word "laws" as limited to "state laws strictly local," which included controversies involving statutes, titles to land, and the like. Section 34 therefore did not apply to the issue in *Swift,* and Justice Story felt free to decide the case by independent inquiry into general commercial law.

The doctrine of *Swift v. Tyson* was significantly extended some 50 years later when the Court held in Baltimore & Ohio RR. v. Baugh, 149 U.S. 368 (1893), that questions of tort liability were included in the "general" common law. This decision prompted an extensive dissent by Justice Field which was quoted by Brandeis in *Erie.* *Swift* was expanded still further in Kuhn v. Fairmont Coal Co., 215 U.S. 349 (1910), which held that rights deriving from a deed to land were also within the "general" common law powers of the federal courts. Justice Holmes' dissent in this case is also quoted in *Erie.* Justice Holmes submitted another forceful dissent in Black & White Taxicab Co. v. Brown & Yellow Taxicab Co., 276 U.S. 518 (1928), which is fully described in *Erie.*

The *Taxicab* case became a focus of criticism. In the decade between that decision and *Erie* there were some indications that the regime of *Swift* was weakening. *Swift* had been extended far beyond its original domain of commercial law and, as indicated in footnote 8 of the *Erie* opinion, the distinction between "local" and "general" law had become increasingly troublesome.

2. The Constitutional Premises of *Erie:* Introduction. Brandeis observed at the end of the second part of his *Erie* opinion that:

"If only a question of statutory construction were involved, we should not be prepared to abandon a doctrine so widely applied throughout nearly a century. But the unconstitutionality of the course pursued has now been made clear and compels us to do so."

The following notes draw out some of the possible grounds upon which Brandeis could have believed that "the course pursued" under *Swift* was unconstitutional.[a] It is helpful to bear in mind the year that *Erie* was decided (1938) and the other issues that were before the Court of that day.

3. Equal Protection. Near the end of the paragraph beginning "On the other hand" in part "Second" of his opinion, Brandeis said that the doctrine of *Swift* "rendered impossible equal protection of the law." Did the Court mean that the concept of equal protection forbids the application of different legal principles depending on the forum?

The answer is almost surely "no,"[b] for at least two historical reasons. First, although some state laws had been invalidated on an equal protection rationale before *Erie*,[c] the inequalities involved in *Swift* plainly were not unconstitutional under those precedents.[d] Modern equal protection doctrine developed long after *Erie*. Second, if equal protection was being denied during the regime of *Swift*, it was the federal courts—to whom the 14th amendment in terms does not apply—that were the culprits. It was not until Bolling v. Sharpe, 347 U.S. 497 (1954) (school desegregation in the District of Columbia), that equal protection principles were explicitly applied to the federal government through the fifth amendment due process clause.

There is a sense, moreover, in which *Erie* merely substituted one kind of inequality for another. *Erie* severely limited forum shopping between state and federal courts, but the decision does not prevent forum shopping between the courts of one state and the courts of another. Then, as now, personal jurisdiction frequently could be obtained over a defendant in more than one state, and conflict-of-laws

---

[a] It was suggested in some of the early literature that the constitutional discussion in *Erie* was "dictum" not central to the real ground of decision. This literature is summarized in Friendly, In Praise of *Erie*—And of the New Federal Common Law, 39 N.Y.U. L. Rev. 383, 384–86 (1964). Judge Friendly's response was that a "court's stated and, on its view, necessary basis for deciding does not become dictum because a critic would have decided on another basis."

[b] John Hart Ely refers to the Court's language as "surely . . . a metaphor."

Ely, The Irrepressible Myth of *Erie*, 87 Harv. L. Rev. 693, 713 (1974).

[c] E.g., Strauder v. West Virginia, 100 U.S. 303 (10 Otto) (1879) (exclusion of blacks from a jury); Yick Wo v. Hopkins, 118 U.S. 356 (1886) (purposeful discrimination against Chinese laundries).

[d] The Court's receptivity to equal protection claims in the years before *Erie* is illustrated by the well-known statement by Justice Holmes that equal protection was "the usual last resort of constitutional arguments." Buck v. Bell, 274 U.S. 200 (1927).

principles often would permit each state to apply its own law. And, as confirmed in the subsequent decision that federal courts are to apply conflict-of-laws principles of the state in which they sit,[e] *Erie* does not prevent forum shopping between a federal court in one state and a federal court in another. The modern expansion of in personam jurisdiction has greatly exacerbated this kind of forum shopping, and even today equal protection arguments are unavailing against the practice.

4. Limits of Federal Power Under Article I. Brandeis seems to indicate in the first paragraph of the "Third" part of his opinion that the Court was purporting to exercise power that Congress lacked:

> "Congress has no power to declare substantive rules of common law applicable in a state whether they be local in their nature or 'general,' be they commercial law or a part of the law of torts. And no clause in the Constitution purports to confer such a power on the federal courts."

Congress has today—and more importantly had when *Erie* was decided—considerable authority to pass laws governing commercial law, torts, and the like. Indeed, it seems clear that Congress would have had authority under the commerce clause to regulate the issue involved in *Erie* itself.[f] Is there nonetheless a sense in which the Court in *Swift* authorized the federal courts to exercise a power that the Congress lacked?

The answer is subtle, but "yes." It was clear at the time of *Erie* that the Congress did not have the authority to regulate *all* activity that fell outside the "local" category, that is, that Congress did not have the authority to regulate *all* activity that could be called commercial, or—perhaps more importantly—*all* tortious behavior. Yet *Swift* authorized the federal courts to do just that. In other words, even though *Erie* itself was not one of them, there were cases decided under the regime of *Swift* in which federal courts supplied the rule of decision when Congress could not have done so. This may have been, as Brandeis said, the "course of conduct" in which the courts were acting unconstitutionally.[g] The courts were failing to ask in each instance

---

[e] See Klaxon Co. v. Stentor Electric Manufacturing Co., Inc., 313 U.S. 487 (1941), which is reproduced as a main case at page 358, infra.

[f] Long before *Erie* was decided, the Court had taken a generous view of Congress' power to regulate railroads. See, e.g., Railroad Commission of Wisconsin v. Chicago, Burlington & Quincy RR., 257 U.S. 563 (1922) (railroad rates); Houston E. & W. Texas Ry. Co. v. United States (the Shreveport Rate Case), 234 U.S. 342 (1914) (upholding federal authority to regulate intrastate rail rates that discriminated against interstate traffic); Southern Railway Co. v. United States, 222 U.S. 20 (1911) (upholding federal safety regulation of cars moving in intrastate traffic).

[g] This may explain the importance of the philosophical "fallacy" of *Swift* to which Brandeis referred in part "Third" of his opinion. Article I and the 10th amendment, the argument would go, represented a careful allocation of legislative power between the states and the federal government. Federal law had to find its source in some power delegated to the national government. The Constitution may have contemplated, in other words, an Austinian view of law (i.e., that law does not exist without some definite governmental authority behind it) at least as far as federal law was concerned, rather than the kind of natural law on which *Swift* was premised.

that they supplied "general" federal common law whether Congress had the authority to regulate the behavior in question.[h]

The modern importance of this argument is limited. Today, particularly after National League of Cities v. Usery, 426 U.S. 833 (1976), was overruled in Garcia v. San Antonio Metropolitan Transit Authority, 469 U.S. 528 (1985), it is hard to think of a subject that lies beyond the commerce power. Perhaps Congress cannot regulate some aspects of the law of domestic relations, or perhaps some aspects of the law of wills or intestate succession fall beyond the congressional regulatory power. But it is hard to come up with an example of modern activity that does not affect the economy in some marginal manner, and modern decisions make plain that a marginal effect is enough to justify congressional intervention. It thus may be that the constitutional basis of *Erie* is no longer important.[i]

5. Federalism and Separation of Powers. There is another line of argument, however, that may explain the constitutional foundation of *Erie*. Brandeis observed in the first paragraph of part "Third" of his opinion that there "is no federal general common law" and that "no clause in the Constitution" confers power on the federal courts to "declare substantive rules of common law applicable in a state." Did the Court mean that the "course pursued" was unconstitutional because federal courts cannot "make" law, at least in the absence of constitutional or statutory authorization?

Henry Monaghan has observed in a book review, 87 Harv. L. Rev. 889, 892 (1974), that:

> "[It should be made] clear to students at the outset that *Erie* is, fundamentally, a limitation on the federal court's power to displace state law absent some relevant constitutional or statutory mandate which neither the general language of article III nor the [diversity] jurisdictional statute provides."

Paul Mishkin agrees. In Some Further Last Words on *Erie*—The Thread, 87 Harv. L. Rev. 1682, 1683–86 (1974)*, he argues that the Constitution "imposes a distinctive, independently significant limit on the authority of the federal courts to displace state law." In particular, "[p]rinciples related to the separation of powers impose [a] limit on the authority of federal courts to engage in lawmaking on their own (unauthorized by Congress)." He explains:

> "The point may perhaps be made most easily by example. I take it there is little doubt that Congress could validly enact 'no-fault' liability for all automobile accidents in the country— and no doubt at all about accidents on public thoroughfares

---

[h] For elaboration of this idea, see Ely, The Irrepressible Myth of *Erie*, 87 Harv. L. Rev. 693, 702–04 (1974); Friendly, In Praise of *Erie*—and of the New Federal Common Law, 39 N.Y.U. L. Rev. 383, 394–95 (1964).

[i] For a wide-ranging theoretical defense of the decline of judicial concern for limit-

ing federal power, see La Pierre, Political Accountability in the National Political Process—The Alternative to Judicial Review of Federalism Issues, 80 Nw.U.L.Rev. 577 (1985).

* Copyright © 1974 by The Harvard Law Review Association. Reprinted with permission of the author and the publication.

carrying interstate traffic. At the same time I take it as equally clear that the federal courts would currently not seriously entertain the contention that they should adopt a federal 'no-fault' liability rule even if the particular accident clearly involved interstate traffic. . . . I submit that this conclusion is of constitutional dimension, that any other course would be 'unconstitutional' in the sense that term was used in the *Erie* opinion . . . .

"In my judgment, the clarity and strength with which the inappropriateness of federal judicial lawmaking on such a base is perceived (even when congressional power is pellucid) is itself significant evidence of the constitutional nature of the limitation. On a more theoretical level, I base my position in part on a consideration of how differently the allocation of power between the states and the federal government would appear if a contrary conception were adopted, and how remote that allocation and that conception would be from any accepted view from the time of the Framers to the present. Even more importantly, I base it on the structure established by the Constitution whereby the states, and their interests as such, are represented in the Congress but not in the federal courts. [T]his weighting of state interests in the Congress, more significantly than in the Court (or judicial appointees), was a fulfillment of the institutional structure established in the Constitution."

Professor Mishkin concludes that at least "where Congress has . . . spoken [e.g., in the Rules of Decision Act] in terms which are not only unambiguously consistent with an underlying constitutional principle but actually affirmatively restate its meaning and implications and thus reinforce it—proper construction of the congressional language should be most hospitable to giving it full range."

Consider Mishkin's argument carefully. Does he base his position on principles of federalism, principles of separation of powers, or both? Is his argument consistent with what Brandeis said in *Erie*? With what can fairly be implied from the opinion? Is the argument persuasive? In Westen and Lehman, Is There Life for *Erie* After the Death of Diversity?, 78 Mich. L. Rev. 311, 340–41 (1980), the authors suggest that the trouble with the argument "is that it converts every judicial mistake of legislative interpretation into a constitutional violation." Westen and Lehman ask "why would one ever want to elevate judicial errors of this kind into matters of constitutional magnitude?" Is this a dispositive criticism of Mishkin's position? The following notes should be considered in answering these questions.

6. Examples of Federal Common Law. As Mishkin recognized, there are occasions when the federal courts make federal common law and where it is generally accepted that they should do so.[j] One can

---

[j] For extensive analyses of the powers of federal courts to make federal common law touching on many of the questions raised in this chapter, see Field, Sources of Law:

only assess the current validity of a federalism/separation-of-powers limitation on their capacity to do so in light of an understanding of these situations. The next section of these materials, beginning on page 289, infra, contains a series of cases in which whether to make federal common law was the issue before the Court. Four situations are discussed below, however, in order to aid consideration of the constitutional foundations of *Erie*.

(i) **Lawsuits Between States.** On the same day *Erie* was decided, Justice Brandeis wrote a unanimous opinion for the Court in which he said that the apportionment of water rights in a stream controlled by an interstate compact approved by Congress presented "a question of 'federal common law' upon which neither the statutes nor the decisions of either state can be conclusive."[k] The same principle is involved where one state sues another, for example, over water rights or a boundary dispute. The Court's power in this respect was defended by Henry Monaghan as follows:

> "The interstate dispute cases present a good example of authority to create federal common law gleaned by implication from the federal structure of the United States. Some tribunal must exist for settling interstate controversies; but it is a basic presumption of the Constitution that the state courts may be too parochial to administer fairly disputes in which important state interests are at issue. Nor does it seem appropriate to restrict the choice of controlling substantive law to that of one of the contending states. An acceptable accommodation of interstate, to say nothing of national, interests in a given dispute dictates that the Supreme Court must possess power to fashion substantive law not tied to that of any particular state. Thus the authority to create federal common law springs of necessity from the structure of the Constitution, from its basic division of authority between the national government and the states."[l]

Is it clear that the "structure of the Constitution" leaves the Court with no choice but to fashion common law rules of decision to resolve a suit by one state against another? Do the same arguments work for the interpretation of interstate compacts? Are there other situations where the constitutional structure requires the exercise of a similar power?

(ii) *McCulloch v. Maryland.* In McCulloch v. Maryland, 17 U.S. (4 Wheat.) 316 (1819), Chief Justice Marshall wrote one of his great nationalizing opinions upholding the power of Congress to create a

The Scope of Federal Common Law, 99 Harv. L. Rev. 881 (1986), and Merrill, The Common Law Powers of Federal Courts, 52 U. Chi. L. Rev. 1 (1985). On the history, see Jay, Origins of Federal Common Law: Part One, 133 U. Pa. L. Rev. 1003 (1985), Jay, Origins of Federal Common Law: Part Two, 133 U. Pa. L. Rev. 1231 (1985), and Fletcher, The General Common Law and Section 34 of the Judiciary Act of 1789: The Example of Marine Insurance, 97 Harv. L. Rev. 1513 (1984).

[k] Hinderlider v. La Plata River & Cherry Creek Ditch Co., 304 U.S. 92 (1938).

[l] Monaghan, The Supreme Court, 1974 Term, Forward: Constitutional Common Law, 89 Harv. L. Rev. 1, 14 (1975).

national bank. The case involved a prohibitive tax imposed by Maryland on all banks not chartered by the state legislature. Marshall held that Maryland could not impose the tax: "That the power to tax involves the power to destroy; that the power to destroy may defeat and render useless the power to create . . . are propositions not to be denied."

Marshall asserted several times that the Maryland tax was "unconstitutional," but cited no authority in the Constitution for his statements. On what constitutional provision(s) might he have relied? It seems clear that Congress could have responded to the decision by passing a statute authorizing the tax and that such a statute would have effectively overruled the decision. Can Congress overrule *constitutional* decisions by the Supreme Court? Or is the case better characterized as one that developed a "federal common law" rule to govern this particular aspect of federal-state relations?

(iii) The Negative Commerce Clause Cases. On occasion, the Supreme Court has set aside state legislation because it is inconsistent with unexercised federal power under the commerce clause. These decisions are often called "dormant" or "negative" commerce clause cases. Invariably, the Court says that the stricken legislation is "unconstitutional."

Is the Court using the term "unconstitutional" in the usual sense? Consider the views of Professor Monaghan:

"To my mind, the most satisfactory explanation of the commerce clause cases is that the Supreme Court is fashioning federal common law on the authority of the commerce clause. That clause embodies a national, free-trade philosophy which can be read as requiring the Court, in limited circumstances, to displace state-created trade barriers. . . . I do not see why the Court is not making constitutionally inspired common law. The ultimate source of judicial lawmaking authority is the constitutional text; and like the . . . interstate boundary . . . cases, the negative impact [commerce clause] cases are wholly subject to congressional revision."[m]

Is this an accurate characterization? Is the Court's power in this area capable of rationalization on the same grounds as in the interstate dispute cases? As in *McCulloch?*

(iv) *Dice v. Akron, Canton & Youngstown Railroad.* In Dice v. Akron, Canton & Youngstown Railroad Co., 342 U.S. 359 (1952), the plaintiff was a railroad employee who sued the railroad under the FELA. The railroad defended in part on the ground that the employee had signed a release. The employee admitted that he had received the payments and that he had signed receipts for them, but argued that he had relied on the railroad's deliberately false statement that the document he had signed was merely a receipt for back wages. He had

---

[m] Id. at 17. For a contrary view of the negative commerce cases in the context of an extensive criticism of Monaghan's the- sis, see Schrock and Welsh, Reconsidering the Constitutional Common Law, 91 Harv.L.Rev. 1117, 1138–41 (1978).

not read the document, however, and it purported to be a complete release.

The case was litigated in state court, and the jury awarded the plaintiff $25,000. This verdict was set aside on appeal within the state system, and the Supreme Court granted certiorari. Three issues were before the Court: whether federal or state law governed the validity of the release; if federal law governed, what the content of the law should be; and whether the defendant was entitled to a jury trial on the issue of fraud. *Dice* is reproduced in full beginning on page 252, supra, in order to explore the third of these issues. The first two, however, are of interest now.

On the first issue—whether federal or state law controlled the validity of the purported release—the Court said:

"We . . . hold that validity of releases under the Federal Employers' Liability Act raises a federal question to be determined by federal rather than state law. Congress in § 1 of the act granted petitioner a right to recover against his employer for damages negligently inflicted. State laws are not controlling in determining what the incidents of this federal right shall be. Manifestly the federal rights affording relief to injured railroad employees under a federally declared standard could be defeated if states were permitted to have the final say as to what defenses could and could not be properly interposed to suits under the act. Moreover, only if federal law controls can the federal act be given that uniform application throughout the country essential to effectuate its purposes. Releases and other devices designed to liquidate or defeat injured employees' claims play an important part in the federal act's administration. Their validity is but one of the many interrelated questions that must constantly be determined in these cases according to a uniform federal law."

The Court then determined the content of the applicable federal rule. It held that the position adopted by the state courts was "wholly incongruous with the general policy of the act" and was "out of harmony with modern judicial and legislative practice." It accordingly substituted the "correct federal rule," which was: "[A] release of rights under the act is void when the employee is induced to sign it by the deliberately false and material statements of the railroad's authorized representatives made to deceive the employee as to the contents of the release."

What the Court did in *Dice* has often been called "intersticial" lawmaking; the Court fills in the gaps of a comprehensive federal statutory scheme in a manner consistent with the policies Congress is seeking to promote. Is the Court wrong to exercise such powers? How is *Dice* different from the situations summarized above?

7. Concluding Comments and Questions. Can the four examples given in the preceding note be reconciled with Mishkin's argument that *Erie* stands for a federalism/separation-of-powers limitation on the capacity of the federal courts to make law? Can they be reconciled with the Rules of Decision Act?

Consider these comments by Judge Henry Friendly:

"My view is that, by banishing the spurious uniformity of *Swift* . . . and by leaving to the states what ought be left to them, *Erie* led to the emergence of a federal decisional law in areas of national concern that is truly uniform because, under the supremacy clause, it is binding in every forum . . . . The clarion yet careful pronouncement of *Erie,* 'There is no federal general common law,' opened the way to what, for want of a better term, we may call specialized federal common law. . . .

". . . By focusing judicial attention on the nature of the right being enforced, *Erie* caused the principle of a specialized federal common law, binding in all courts because of its source, to develop within a quarter century into a powerful unifying force. Just as federal courts now conform to state decisions on issues properly for the states, state courts must conform to federal decisions in areas where Congress, acting within powers granted to it, has manifested, be it ever so lightly, an intention to that end. . . .

"[The Supreme Court] has employed a variety of techniques—spontaneous generation as in the cases of government contracts or interstate controversies, implication of a private federal cause of action from a statute providing other sanctions, construing a jurisdictional grant as a command to fashion federal law, and the normal filling of statutory interstices.
. . .

"The complementary concepts—that federal courts must follow state decisions on matters of substantive law appropriately cognizable by the states whereas state courts must follow federal decisions on subjects within national legislative power where Congress has so directed [or the basic scheme of the Constitution demands]—seem so beautifully simple, and so simply beautiful, that we must wonder why a century and a half were needed to discover them, and must wonder even more why anyone should want to shy away once the discovery was made. . . ."[n]

The converse of this position is that the federal courts lack the power to make law where both the Constitution and Congress are silent. Consider Mishkin's example of a court-created national no-fault law. The argument is that the federal courts lack authority to displace state law in this situation because no constitutional values are implicated and because no established congressional policies would be fur-

[n] Friendly, In Praise of *Erie*—and of the New Federal Common Law, 39 N.Y.U. L. Rev. 383, 405, 407–08, 421–22 (1964), also printed in H. Friendly, Benchmarks 155, 178, 180, 194–95 (1967). The bracketed phrase in the last paragraph appears in the later book but not the essay as originally published in the N.Y.U. L. Review. These exercepts are reprinted by permission from The New York University Law Review, Vol. 39, pp. 405, 407–08, 421–22.

thered. The Court is permitted, in other words, to protect constitutional values and to implement programs and policies established by the Congress. It is not, the argument concludes, permitted to create common law out of whole cloth.

NOTES ON THE ADMINISTRATION OF *ERIE*

1. **Introduction.** *Erie* does not say exactly how far its directive to apply state law extends. Perhaps the most important issue left open by the opinion is the range of authority remaining to the federal courts to develop federal common law. This issue is treated in detail in the next section of these materials. There are, however, several technical matters that should be noticed first.

2. **Substance and Procedure.** It seems clear, as Justice Reed pointed out in his *Erie* concurrence, that the federal government retains plenary power to provide for its own judicial procedures. The Federal Rules of Civil Procedure are premised on such authority. The question of how far that power extends, as well as the relationship between Congress and the courts in its exercise, has spawned a long line of decisions that are considered at pages 487–526, infra.

3. **Relation to Diversity Jurisdiction.** *Erie* was a diversity case, and this has sometimes led to the mistaken impression that it applies only in that context. It is plain, however, that the obligation of federal courts to apply state substantive law of its own force [a] is not limited to diversity cases.

The most obvious example is provided by United States Supreme Court review of state court decisions. The Court held long before *Erie* that such review is limited to questions that are controlled by federal law. Murdock v. Memphis, 87 U.S. (20 Wall.) 590 (1875), considered more fully at pages 597–600, infra. While *Murdock* did not purport to be a constitutional decision (and did not consider the relationship of appellate review of state decisions to the power exercised in *Swift*), it seems clear that the relationship between state and federal law envisioned by *Erie* applies no matter in what court the litigation first arises.

[a] It has become common to refer to state law as applying "of its own force" in *Erie* situations. It is argued in Westen and Lehman, Is There Life for *Erie* After the Death of Diversity, 78 Mich. L. Rev. 311, 315–16, 357–59, 389 (1980), that this is inaccurate. They suggest that state law applies "because Congress has chosen to apply it, the choice being explicitly reflected in the Rules of Decision Act itself." The strongest case for this position occurs where Congress could, if it chose, displace state law with a federal rule of decision. But even in cases where the Constitution requires the application of state law, they conclude, there is always the option of declining to exercise jurisdiction. Thus it is more accurate, they argue, to refer to the application of state law by a federal court as a situation where Congress "chooses to borrow [state law] to achieve a federal purpose," namely—in a diversity case—to provide an alternate forum which will nonetheless reach the same result that would have been reached in a state court. This "federal purpose," they continue, can then be weighed against other federal purposes that may conflict in a given situation and that may suggest that state law not be applied.

Another example is provided by United Mine Workers of America v. Gibbs, 383 U.S. 715 (1966). The plaintiff in *Gibbs* asserted in federal district court two claims arising out of the same factual situation. One was governed by federal law and was properly within the court's federal question jurisdiction. The issue before the Supreme Court was whether the plaintiff could also assert a claim governed by state law, a claim over which the federal courts did not have independent jurisdiction (diversity was lacking). The Court held that such "pendent jurisdiction" did exist, and spelled out its terms and limitations. While the issue was not before the Court, it is clear that the *Erie* doctrine would apply fully to the state claim, even though federal district court jurisdiction was based on a theory other than diversity. As subsequent materials illustrate,[b] moreover, it is also clear that state law can apply to some aspects of a claim that is itself a sufficient basis for federal question jurisdiction.

4. Federal Law in Diversity Cases. The converse of the proposition considered in the previous note is also true, i.e., the mere fact that diversity is the basis of jurisdiction does not guarantee that state law will be applied to all issues in the case. The two best-known illustrations are Francis v. Southern Pacific Co., 333 U.S. 445 (1948), and Sola Electric Co. v. Jefferson Electric Co., 317 U.S. 173 (1942).

Francis was a diversity case based on common law negligence. The plaintiff's decedent was an employee of the railroad who was killed while riding as a passenger on a free pass. The Court in effect gave the defendant-railroad a federal defense, holding that a complex series of federal decisions and statutes precluded recovery for ordinary negligence. *Sola* was a suit by a patentee under a licensing agreement. The agreement was governed by state law, and jurisdiction was based on diversity of citizenship. The defendant asserted that the patent covered by the license was invalid and that in any event the licensing agreement violated the Sherman Antitrust Act. Both defenses were controlled by federal law.

5. Ascertaining State Law. In the second sentence of part "Third" of his *Erie* opinion, Justice Brandeis said that state law must be followed whether "declared by its legislature in a statute or by its highest court in a decision." What happens if there is no relevant decision by the state's highest court? Should lower court decisions be followed?

The answer to these questions seems plain in principle. The federal court should do its best to predict what the state's highest court would say if faced with the question (which, indeed, is exactly the posture in which a lower state court judge is likely to be). Lower court decisions should be followed if they are consistent with the recent pattern of decisions by the highest court and if they appear to be

---

[b] See Smith v. Kansas City Title & Trust Co., 255 U.S. 180 (1921), discussed further at pages 434–35, infra.

accurate forecasts of what that court would say if presented with the issue.

The Supreme Court has not always followed this course. Its most severe departure was referred to in Friendly, In Praise of *Erie*—And of the New Federal Common Law, 39 N.Y.U. L. Rev. 383, 400 (1964), as "the excesses of 311 U.S. as to the respect that federal judges must pay to decisions of lower state courts." Judge Friendly had in mind a series of cases decided by the Supreme Court in 1940. The "nadir," Judge Friendly said, was Fidelity Union Trust Co. v. Field, 311 U.S. 169 (1940), which has been "properly excoriated" in subsequent literature which he cites, id. at 400 n.77. In *Field,* the Court required adherence to the decisions of two New Jersey trial judges with statewide jurisdiction, even though the decisions had no precedential effect on other judges of equal (or superior) status and even though they appeared rather plainly to be wrong.[c]

Later decisions are more in accord with the position advanced above. See, e.g., Commissioner v. Estate of Bosch, 387 U.S. 456, 465 (1967), where the Court said:

> "[T]he state's highest court is the best authority on its own law. If there be no decision by that court then federal authorities must apply what they find to be the state law after giving 'proper regard' to relevant rulings of other courts of the state. In this respect, it may be said to be, in effect, sitting as a [lower] state court."

6. Remedies for Uncertain State Law. One difference between federal courts making guesses about state law and lower state courts making such guesses is that the lower state courts are subject to review within the state system. Errors can be corrected on direct review. There is, of course, no system for direct review of federal court decisions by state courts. There are, however, several possible courses of action open to a federal court faced with uncertainty about a controlling question of state law.

(i) Decline Jurisdiction. One is to refuse to adjudicate the case and to remit the parties to a new lawsuit in state court. There are at least two problems with this solution. First, the Supreme Court has said that lower federal courts cannot refuse to decide a case merely because of uncertainty as to the meaning of state law. See Meredith v. Winter Haven, 320 U.S. 228, 236, 238 (1943):

> "Congress having adopted the policy of opening the federal courts to suitors in all diversity cases involving the jurisdictional amount, we can discern in its action no recognition of a policy which would exclude cases from the jurisdiction merely

---

[c] See the discussion in C. Wright, Law of Federal Courts 370–71 (4th ed. 1983). Professor Wright points out that later New Jersey cases followed the Third Circuit decision reversed by the Supreme Court and that New Jersey law today is what the Third Circuit thought it then was. Wright also cites as the "highpoint" of the influence of the *Field* decision a Sixth Circuit case where the court felt required to follow an unreported decision of an intermediate Ohio court which, because it was unreported, was denied precedential effect under applicable state law.

because they involve state law or because the law is uncertain or difficult to determine. . . .

"*Erie* did not free the federal courts from the duty of deciding questions of state law in diversity cases. Instead it placed on them a greater responsibility for determining and applying state laws in all cases within their jurisdiction in which federal law does not govern."

The second problem with this solution has to do with the practicalities of litigation. Often one cannot determine until proceedings are well under way whether a particular proposition of state law will be dispositive or even relevant. It would be difficult to make this prediction at the outset of litigation, and inefficient to abort litigation in progress once an uncertain proposition of state law becomes determinative.

(ii) **Abstention.** A second answer might be to stay litigation in the federal court until a declaratory judgment proceeding, or some other suitable lawsuit in state court, can resolve the uncertain question of state law. The inefficiencies of proceeding in this manner should be obvious. Yet the Supreme Court has authorized this procedure in some contexts, consideration of which have been postponed to pages 562–72, infra. Suffice it to say for the present that the Court has never authorized abstention in a routine diversity case, nor in a case where the only relevant consideration was the difficulty of resolving an uncertain question of state law.

(iii) **Certified Questions.** About half of the states permit the federal courts to certify an uncertain question of state law to the state supreme court for resolution.[d] The Supreme Court has sanctioned use of this procedure. Lehman Brothers v. Schein, 416 U.S. 386 (1974), for example, was a shareholder's derivative suit filed in a New York federal court against a Florida corporation. Jurisdiction was based on diversity of citizenship. The District Court decided that Florida law would govern, and that the controlling issue was whether the Florida courts would follow a New York precedent that supplied the theory of the plaintiff's cause of action. The District Court dismissed the complaint, but the Second Circuit reversed on the ground that Florida would "probably" follow the New York case. The Supreme Court vacated the judgment and remanded for a determination whether the controlling issue of Florida law should be certified to the Florida Supreme Court for decision. The Court noted that *Meredith*

"teaches that the mere difficulty in ascertaining local law is no excuse for remitting the parties to a state tribunal for the start of another lawsuit. We do not suggest that where there is doubt as to local law and where the certification procedure is available, resort to it is obligatory. It does, of course, in the

[d] The laws are collected in 17 C. Wright, A. Miller & E. Cooper, Treatise on Federal Practice and Procedure, Jurisdiction § 4248 (1978). The conflicting literature on the practice is cited in C. Wright, The Law of Federal Courts 313–14 n.53 (4th ed. 1983).

long run save time, energy, and resources and helps build a cooperative judicial federalism. Its use in a given case rests in the sound discretion of the federal court.

"Here resort to it would seem particularly appropriate in view of the novelty of the question and the great unsettlement of Florida law, Florida being a distant state. When federal judges in New York attempt to predict uncertain Florida law, they act, as we have referred to ourselves on this Court in matters of state law, as 'outsiders' lacking the common exposure to local law which comes from sitting in the jurisdiction."

Justice Rehnquist concurred, stating that "in a purely diversity case such as this one, the use of such a procedure is more a question of the considerable discretion of the federal court in going about the decision-making process than it is a question of a choice trenching upon the fundamentals of our federal-state jurisprudence." He also pointed out that the "other side of the certification coin is that it does in fact engender delay and create additional expense for litigants." [e]

(iv) Concluding Questions. Is the best answer in this situation simply to go forward and do as well as possible at forecasting what the highest state court would say? A federal injunction based on an inaccurate prediction of state law can always be modified in the event of a subsequent inconsistent state decision. Could this solution work if damages had been awarded?

SECTION 2: THE POWER OF THE FEDERAL COURTS TO MAKE FEDERAL COMMON LAW

SUBSECTION A: RIGHTS AND DUTIES OF THE UNITED STATES

UNITED STATES v. LITTLE LAKE MISERE LAND CO., INC.

Supreme Court of the United States, 1973.
412 U.S. 580

MR. CHIEF JUSTICE BURGER delivered the opinion of the Court.

We granted the writ in this case to consider whether state law may retroactively abrogate the terms of written agreements made by the United States when it acquires land for public purposes explicitly authorized by Congress.

[e] For a recent use by the Supreme Court of the certification procedure, see Virginia v. American Booksellers Association, Inc., ___ U.S. ___ (1988).

The United States initiated this litigation in 1969 in the United States District Court for the Western District of Louisiana, seeking to quiet title to two adjacent parcels of land in Cameron Parish, Louisiana, which the government had acquired pursuant to the Migratory Bird Conservation Act as part of the Lacassine Wildlife Refuge. Title to one parcel was acquired by the United States by purchase on July 23, 1937; to the other parcel by a judgment of condemnation entered August 30, 1939. Both the 1937 act of sale and the 1939 judgment of condemnation reserved to the respondent Little Lake Misere oil, gas, sulphur, and other minerals for a period of 10 years from the date of vesting of title in the United States. The reservation was to continue in effect "as long [after the initial 10–year period] as oil, gas, sulphur or other mineral is produced . . . or so long thereafter as [respondents] shall conduct drilling or reworking operations thereon with no cessation of more than 60 days consecutively until production results; and, if production results, so long as such mineral is produced." The deed and the judgment of condemnation further recited that at the end of 10 years or at the end of any period after 10 years during which the above conditions had not been met, "the right to mine, produce and market said oil, gas, sulphur or other mineral shall terminate . . . and the complete fee title to said lands shall thereby become vested in the United States."

The parties stipulated, and the District Court found, that as to both the parcels in issue here, no drilling, reworking, or other operations were conducted and no minerals were obtained for a period of more than 10 years following the act of sale and judgment of condemnation, respectively. Thus, under the terms of these instruments, fee title in the United States ripened as of 1947 and 1949, respectively—10 years from the dates of creation. In 1955, the United States issued oil and gas leases applicable to the lands in question.

Respondents, however, continued to claim the mineral rights and accordingly entered various transactions purporting to dispose of those rights. Respondents relied upon Louisiana Act 315 of 1940, which provides:

"When land is acquired by conventional deed or contract, condemnation or expropriation proceedings by the United States of America, or any of its subdivisions or agencies from any person, firm or corporation, and by the act of acquisition, order or judgment, oil, gas or other minerals or royalties are reserved, or the land so acquired is by the act of acquisition conveyed subject to a prior sale or reservation of oil, gas or other minerals or royalties, still in force and effect, the rights so reserved or previously sold shall be imprescriptible."

Respondents contended that the 1940 enactment rendered inoperative the conditions set forth in 1937 and 1939 for the extinguishment of the reservations. . . .

I

[In this section of its opinion, the Court summarized more than 25 years of complex litigation dealing with federal land rights in Louisiana.]

II

The essential premise of the Court of Appeals' decision in [a related] case was that state law governs the interpretation of a federal land acquisition authorized by the Migratory Bird Conservation Act. The Court of Appeals did not set forth in detail the basis for this premise, but that court's opinion seems to say that state law governs this land acquisition because, at bottom, it is an "ordinary" "local" land transaction to which the United States happens to be a party. The suggestion is that this Court's decision in Erie R. Co. v. Tompkins, 304 U.S. 64 (1938), compels application of state law here because the Rules of Decisions Act requires application of state law in the absence of an explicit congressional command to the contrary. We disagree.

The federal jurisdictional grant over suits brought by the United States is not in itself a mandate for applying federal law in all circumstances. This principle follows from *Erie* itself, where, although the federal courts had jurisdiction over diversity cases, we held that the federal courts did not possess the power to develop a concomitant body of general federal law. It is true, too, that "[t]he great body of law in this country which controls acquisition, transmission, and transfer of property, and defines the rights of its owners in relation to the state or to private parties, is found in the statutes and decisions of the state." Even when federal general law was in its heyday, an exception was carved out for local laws of real property. Indeed, before *Erie*, this Court's opinions left open the possibility that even "the United States, while protected by the Constitution from discriminatory state action, and perhaps certain other special forms of state control, was nevertheless governed generally in its ordinary proprietary relations by state law." Hart, The Relations Between State and Federal Law, 54 Colum. L. Rev. 489, 533 (1954). See, e.g., Mason v. United States, 260 U.S. 545, 558 (1923).

Despite this arguable basis for its reasoning the Court of Appeals in the instant case seems not to have recognized that this land acquisition . . . is one arising from and bearing heavily upon a federal regulatory program. Here, the choice-of-law task is a federal task for federal courts, as defined by Clearfield Trust Co. v. United States, 318 U.S. 363 (1943). Since *Erie*, and as a corollary of that decision, we have consistently acted on the assumption that dealings which may be "ordinary" or "local" as between private citizens raise serious questions of national sovereignty when they arise in the context of a specific constitutional or statutory provision; particularly is this so when transactions undertaken by the federal government are involved, as in this case.[10] In such cases, the Constitution or acts of Congress "require" otherwise than that state law govern of its own force.

There will often be no specific federal legislation governing a particular transaction to which the United States is a party; here, for example, no provision of the Migratory Bird Conservation Act guides us to choose state or federal law in interpreting federal land acquisition agreements under the act. But silence on that score in federal legislation is no reason for limiting the reach of federal law. . . . To the contrary, the inevitable incompleteness presented by all legislation means that interstitial federal lawmaking is a basic responsibility of the federal courts. "At the very least, effective constitutionalism requires recognition of power in the federal courts to declare, as a matter of common law or 'judicial legislation,' rules which may be necessary to fill in interstitially or otherwise effectuate the statutory patterns enacted in the large by Congress. In other words, it must mean recognition of federal judicial competence to declare the governing law in an area comprising issues substantially related to an established program of government operation." Mishkin, The Variousness of "Federal Law": Competence and Discretion in the Choice of National and State Rules for Decision, 105 U. Pa. L. Rev. 797, 800 (1957).

This, then, is what has aptly been described as the "first" of the two holdings of *Clearfield Trust*—that the right of the United States to seek legal redress for duly authorized proprietary transactions "is a federal right, so that the courts of the United States may formulate a rule of decision." Friendly, In Praise of *Erie*—And of the New Federal Common Law, 39 N.Y.U.L. Rev. 383, 410 (1964). At least this first step of the *Clearfield* analysis is applicable here. We deal with the interpretation of a land acquisition agreement (a) explicitly authorized, though not precisely governed, by the Migratory Bird Conservation Act and (b) to which the United States itself is a party. Cf. Bank of America v. Parnell, 352 U.S. 29, 33 (1956). As in *Clearfield* and its progeny, "[t]he duties imposed upon the United States and the rights acquired by it . . . find their roots in the same federal sources. . . . In absence of

---

[10] This is not a case where the United States seeks to oust state substantive law on the basis of "an amorphous doctrine of national sovereignty" divorced from any specific constitutional or statutory provision and premised solely on the argument "that every authorized activity of the United States represents an exercise of its governmental power," see United States v. Burnison, 339 U.S. 87, 91, 92 (1950); United States v. Fox, 94 U.S. 315 (1877). *Burnison* and *Fox* stand at the opposite end of the spectrum from cases where Congress explicitly displaces state law in the course of exercising clear constitutional regulatory power over a particular subject matter. See, e.g., Sunderland v. United States, 266 U.S. 226, 232–33 (1924) (United States may displace Oklahoma law by imposing restrictions on alienation of Indian property despite the "general rule . . . that the tenure, transfer, control and disposition of real property are matters which rest exclusively with the state where the property lies"). The present case falls between the poles of *Burnison* and *Sunderland.* Here we deal with an unquestionably appropriate and specific exercise of congressional regulatory power which fails to specify whether or to what extent it contemplates displacement of state law.

an applicable act of Congress it is for the federal courts to fashion the governing rule of law according to their own standards."

III

The next step in our analysis is to determine whether the 1937 and 1939 land acquisition agreements in issue should be interpreted according to "borrowed" state law—Act 315 of 1940. The availability of this choice was explicitly recognized in *Clearfield Trust* itself and fully elaborated some years later in United States v. Standard Oil Co., 332 U.S. 301 (1947). There we acknowledged that "in many situations, and apart from any supposed influence of the *Erie* decision, rights, interests and legal relations of the United States are determined by application of state law, where Congress has not acted specifically." We went on to observe that whether state law is to be applied is a question "of federal policy, affecting not merely the federal judicial establishment and the groundings of its action, but also the government's legal interests and relations, a factor not controlling in the types of cases producing and governed by the *Erie* ruling. And the answer to be given necessarily is dependent upon a variety of considerations always relevant to the nature of the specific governmental interests and to the effects upon them of applying state law."

The government urges us to decide, virtually without qualification, that land acquisition agreements of the United States should be governed by federally created federal law. We find it unnecessary to resolve this case on such broad terms. For even if it be assumed that the established body of state property law should generally govern federal land acquisitions, we are persuaded that the particular rule of law before us today—Louisiana's Act 315 of 1940, as retroactively applied—may not. The "reasons which may make state law at times the appropriate federal rule are singularly inappropriate here."

The Court in the past has been careful to state that, even assuming in general terms the appropriateness of "borrowing" state law, specific aberrant or hostile state rules do not provide appropriate standards for federal law. In De Sylva v. Ballentine, 351 U.S. 570 (1956), we held that whether an illegitimate child was a "child" of the author entitled under the Copyright Act to renew the author's copyright was to be determined by whether, under state law, the child would be an heir of the author. But Mr. Justice Harlan's opinion for the Court took pains to caution that the Court's holding "does not mean that a state would be entitled to use the word 'children' in a way entirely strange to those familiar with its ordinary usage . . . ." In RFC v. Beaver County, 328 U.S. 204 (1946), the issue was whether the definition of "real property," owned by the RFC and authorized by Congress to be subject to state and local taxation, was to be derived from state law or to be fashioned as an independent body of federal law. The Court concluded that "the congressional purpose can best be accomplished by application of settled state rules as to what constitutes 'real property' "—but again the Court foresaw that its approach would be acceptable only "so long as it is plain, as it is here, that the state rules do not effect a discrimination against the government, or patently run counter to the terms of the act."

Under Louisiana's Act 315, land acquisitions of the United States, explicitly authorized by the Migratory Bird Conservation Act, are made subject to a rule of retroactive imprescriptibility, a rule that is plainly hostile to the interests of the United States. As applied to a consummated land transaction under a contract which specifically defined conditions for prolonging the vendor's mineral reservation, retroactive application of Act 315 to the United States deprives it of bargained-for contractual interests.

To permit state abrogation of the explicit terms of a federal land acquisition would deal a serious blow to the congressional scheme contemplated by the Migratory Bird Conservation Act and indeed all other federal land acquisition programs. These programs are national in scope. They anticipate acute and active bargaining by officials of the United States charged with making the best possible use of limited federal conservation appropriations. Certainty and finality are indispensable in any land transaction, but they are especially critical when, as here, the federal officials carrying out the mandate of Congress irrevocably commit scarce funds.

The legislative history of the Migratory Bird Conservation Act confirms the importance of contractual certainty to the federal land acquisition program it authorizes. As originally enacted in 1929, the act provided that land acquisitions might include reservations, easements, and rights of way but that these were to be subject to "such rules and regulations" as the Secretary of Agriculture might prescribe "from time to time." This sweeping statement of the Secretary's power to modify contract terms in favor of the government had an unsettling effect on potential vendors; in 1935, the act was amended to require the Secretary either to include his rules or regulations in the contract itself or to state in the contract that the reservation or easement would be subject to rules and regulations promulgated "from time to time." A Congress solicitous of the interests of private vendors in the certainty of contract would hardly condone state modification of the contractual terms specified by the United States itself as vendee, whether or not those terms may be characterized as "rules and regulations" within the meaning of the act.

Conceivably, our conclusion might be influenced if Louisiana's Act 315 of 1940, as applied retroactively, served legitimate and important state interests the fulfillment of which Congress might have contemplated through application of state law. But that is not the case. We do not deprecate Louisiana's concern with facilitating federal land acquisitions by removing uncertainty on the part of reluctant vendors over the duration of mineral reservations retained by them. From all appearances, this concern was a significant force behind the enactment of the 1940 legislation. But today we are not asked to consider Act 315 on its face, or as applied to transactions consummated after 1940; we are concerned with the application of Act 315 to a pair of acquisition agreements in 1937 and 1939. And however legitimate the state's interest in facilitating federal land acquisitions, that interest has no application to transactions already completed at the time of the enactment of Act 315: the legislature cannot "facilitate" transactions already consummated.

The Louisiana Supreme Court has candidly acknowledged two additional purposes which help to explain retroactive application of Act 315: to clarify the taxability by the state of mineral interests in the large federal land holdings in Louisiana, otherwise in doubt by virtue of the arcane and fluctuating doctrines of intergovernmental tax immunity; and to ensure that federal mineral interests could be subjected to state mineral conservation laws without federal pre-emption. We are not unsympathetic to Louisiana's concern for the consequences of a continuing substantial, even if contingent, federal interest in Louisiana minerals. Congress, however, could scarcely have viewed that concern as a proper justification for retroactive application of state legislation which effectively deprives the government of its bargained-for contractual interests. Our federal union is a complicated organism, but its legal processes cannot legitimately be simplified through the inviting expedient of special legislation which has the effect of confiscating interests of the United States. . . .

Were the terms of the mineral reservations at issue here less detailed and specific, it might be said that the government acknowledged and intended to be bound by unforeseeable changes in state law. But the mineral reservations before us are flatly inconsistent with the respondents' suggestion that the United States in fact expected that these reservations would be wholly subject to retroactive modification. Nor, given the absence of any reliable contemporaneous Louisiana signpost and the absence even today of any final resolution of the pertinent state law question, can we say that the United States ought to have anticipated that its deed contained an empty promise. . . . Years after the fact, state law may not redefine federal contract terminology "in a way entirely strange to those familiar with its ordinary usage. . . ."

IV

In speaking of the choice of law to be applied, the alternatives are plain although in this case identifying them in fixed categories is somewhat elusive. One "choice" would be to apply the law urged on us by respondents, i.e., Louisiana Act 315 of 1940. In some circumstances, . . . state law may be found an acceptable choice, possibly even when the United States itself is a contracting party. However, in a setting in which the rights of the United States are at issue in a contract to which it is a party and "the issue's outcome bears some relationship to a federal program, no rule may be applied which would not be wholly in accord with that program." Mishkin, 105 U. Pa. L. Rev. at 805–06.

Since Act 315 is plainly not in accord with the federal program implemented by the 1937 and 1939 land acquisitions, state law is not a permissible choice here. The choice of law merges with the constitutional demands of controlling federal legislation; we turn away from state law by default. Once it is clear that Act 315 has no application here, we need not choose between "borrowing" some residual state rule of interpretation or formulating an independent federal "common law" rule; neither rule is the law of Louisiana yet either rule resolves this dispute in the government's favor. The contract itself is unequivocal; the District Court concluded, and it is not disputed here, that by the clear and explicit terms of the contract reservations, "[respondents'] interests in the oil, gas, sulphur and other minerals terminated . . . no later than July 23, 1947, and August 30, 1949, unless Act 315 of 1940 has caused the reservations of the servitudes in favor of [respondents] to be imprescriptible."

We hold that, under settled principles governing the choice of law by federal courts, Louisiana's Act 315 of 1940 has no application to the mineral reservations agreed to by the United States and respondents in 1937 and 1939, and that, as a result, any contract interests of respondents expired on the dates identified by the District Court. Accordingly, we reverse the judgment of the Court of Appeals and remand the case for entry of an order consistent with this opinion.

Reversed and remanded.

MR. JUSTICE STEWART, concurring in the judgment.

I cannot agree with the Court that the mineral reservations agreed to by the United States and the respondents in 1937 and 1939 are governed by some brooding omnipresence labeled federal common law. It seems clear to me, as a matter of law, not a matter of "choice" or "borrowing," that when anyone, including the federal government, goes into a state and acquires real property, the nature and extent of the rights created are to be determined, in the absence of a specifically applicable federal statute, by the law of the state.

Since I think the government's property acquisitions here are controlled by state law, the decisive question for me is whether the retroactive application of Louisiana Act 315 of 1940 to those acquisitions is constitutional. The 1937 deed of purchase and the 1939 condemnation judgment were unequivocal: the mineral rights were reserved to the former owners of the land for a 10–year period, after which time—if certain conditions regarding exploration and production were not met—the reserved rights were to terminate, and complete fee title to the land, including the mineral rights, was to become vested in the United States. The federal government bargained for this contingent future interest in the minerals; it was clearly agreed to in the conveyances, and was thus reflected in the consideration paid by the government to the former owners.

Yet the Court of Appeals held that Louisiana Act 315, which was enacted subsequent to those conveyances, operated to abrogate the agreed-upon terms of the mineral reservations by eliminating the government's future interest. This retroactive application of Act 315, I believe, is a textbook example of a violation of art. I, § 10, cl. 1, of the Constitution, which provides that no state shall pass any law "impairing the Obligation of Contracts."[2]

Accordingly, I concur in the judgment of the Court.

MR. JUSTICE REHNQUIST concurring in the judgment.

I agree with my Brother Stewart that the central question presented by this case is whether Louisiana has the constitutional power to make Act 315 applicable to this transaction, and not whether a judicially created rule of decision, labeled federal common law, should displace state law. The Migratory Bird Conservation Act does not establish a federal rule controlling the rights of the United States under the reservation. Whether Congress could enact such a provision is a question not now before us. In *Clearfield Trust,* this Court held that federal common law governed the rights and duties of the United States "on commercial paper which it issues. . . ." The interest in having those rights governed by a rule which is uniform across the nation was the basis of that decision. But the interest of the federal government in having real property acquisitions that it makes in the states pursuant to a particular federal program governed by a similarly uniform rule is too tenuous to invoke the *Clearfield* principle, especially in light of the consistent statements by this Court that state law governs real property transactions.

What for my Brother Stewart, however, is a "textbook example" of a violation of the obligation of contracts clause, is for me something more difficult. The scope of this clause has been restricted by past decisions of the Court such as Home Building & Loan Ass'n v. Blaisdell, 290 U.S. 398 (1934), in which a Minnesota statute extending the period of time in which the mortgagor might redeem his equity following foreclosure was upheld in the face of vigorous arguments that the statute impaired a valid contract. Were there no simpler ground for disposing of the case, it would be necessary to resolve this very debatable question.

I believe that such another ground is present here, in view of the fact that Act 315 enacted by Louisiana by its terms applies only to transactions in which "the United States of America, or any of its subdivisions or agencies" is a party. While it is argued that Louisiana by other legislation made the same principle applicable to the state government, this proposition is . . . by no means demonstrated. And in any event the change in the period of prescriptibility was not made applicable to nongovernmental grantees.

Implicit in the holdings of a number of our cases dealing with state taxation and regulatory measures applied to the federal government is that such measures must be nondiscriminatory.

---

[2] This case is a far cry from Home Building & Loan Ass'n v. Blaisdell, 290 U.S. 398 (1934), which upheld, in the face of a challenge based on the contract clause, emergency state legislation enacted to cope with the extraordinary economic depression existing in 1934. The retroactive application of Louisiana Act 315 serves no such paramount state interest. Cf. City of El Paso v. Simmons, 379 U.S. 497 (1965).

The doctrine of intergovernmental immunity enunciated in McCulloch v. Maryland, 17 U.S. (4 Wheat.) 316 (1819), however it may have evolved since that decision, requires at least that the United States be immune from discriminatory treatment by a state which in some manner interferes with the execution of federal laws. If the state of Pennsylvania could not impose a nondiscriminatory property tax on property owned by the United States, United States v. Allegheny County, 322 U.S. 174 (1944), a fortiori, the state of Louisiana may not enforce Act 315 against the property of the United States involved in this case. I therefore concur in the judgment of the Court.

NOTES ON THE LAW GOVERNING THE RIGHTS AND DUTIES OF THE UNITED STATES

1. Background. Chief Justice Burger said in part II of his opinion that pre-*Erie* decisions "left open the possibility" that the United States, with certain exceptions, was governed by state law in its ordinary proprietary relations. Although the matter was not carefully analyzed in the early decisions, this appears to be a considerable understatement.

Two of the best known early cases are Cotton v. United States, 52 U.S. (11 How.) 229 (1850), and Mason v. United States, 260 U.S. 545 (1923). In *Cotton*, the United States brought a civil trespass action against Cotton for cutting timber from federal lands. Cotton claimed that the United States had no civil remedy for damage to public lands, but the Supreme Court disagreed. The Court reasoned that it would be a "strange anomaly" if, "having the power to make contracts and hold property as other persons," the United States were not equally "entitled to the same remedies for their protection." Thus, whatever the constitutional limitations on the federal government as sovereign, the federal government as landowner was entitled to the protections of state law. "As an owner of property in almost every state of the Union, they have the same right to have it protected by the local laws that other persons have."

Mason v. United States was a suit brought by the United States for an accounting for oil and gas extracted by the defendants from public lands in Louisiana. One of the issues was whether federal law supplied the measure of damages for a suit in equity. The Supreme Court held that the "entire cause of action is . . . local, and the matter of damages within the controlling scope of state legislation."

The impression that state law governed the rights of the United States in the acquisition of property was confirmed by a pair of famous cases involving probate. The earlier decision was United States v. Fox, 94 U.S. (4 Otto) 315 (1877). Fox lived in New York City. He left all his real and personal property to the United States for the purpose of reducing the debt from the Civil War. His heirs challenged the devise, and the New York probate courts held that under state law the United States could not take property by will. The Supreme Court affirmed.

The Court reasoned that the United States could acquire and hold real property as needed for the exercise of governmental powers and, where appropriate, could exercise a right of eminent domain. But otherwise state law governed: "It is an established principle of law, everywhere recognized, arising from the necessity of the case, that the disposition of immovable property, whether by deed, descent, or any other mode, is exclusively subject to the government within whose jurisdiction the property is situated."

Fox was reaffirmed in United States v. Burnison, 339 U.S. 87 (1950). Two California decedents left property to the United States by will. The California Supreme Court voided both wills pursuant to a state statute prohibiting testamentary gifts to the United States, even though it did not prohibit such gifts to California or its subdivisions. The Supreme Court upheld the state law. It reasoned that, "Within broad limits, the state has power to say what is devisable and to whom it may be given." The Court further found that it was not unconstitutional for California to discriminate against the United States in its regulation of testamentary dispositions. The decision to forbid inheritance by the United States but not by the state and its subdivisions was

> "based on a permissible distinction. It is justified by reason of the state's close relationship with its residents and their property. A state may by statute properly prefer itself in this way, just as states have always preferred themselves in escheat."

There was no discussion of the line of cases relied on in Justice Rehnquist's concurrence in *Lake Misere*.

2. *Clearfield Trust Co. v. United States.* As a general proposition, as the foregoing well-known cases attest, the law used to be that the United States entered the marketplace as an ordinary citizen. Except where federal statutes explicitly displaced state law, the law governing the rights and duties of the United States in proprietary transactions was the same state law that would govern the rights and duties of a private party to the same transaction. Thus, if the Internal Revenue Service leased office space or if the United States bought or sold land or issued negotiable paper, the assumption was that state law would govern the rights and obligations that flowed from the transaction. If anything, *Erie* might be thought to have reinforced that tradition.

The best known break with this tradition was Clearfield Trust Co. v. United States, 318 U.S. 363 (1943). *Clearfield Trust* involved a check issued by the United States in 1936 for services rendered to the WPA. The check was stolen and presented by an unknown person to a J.C. Penney's store. Penney's cashed the check, endorsing it over to Clearfield Trust for payment. Clearfield in turn collected on the check through the Federal Reserve System. The original payee then informed the WPA that he had not been paid, and a second check was issued and paid. The United States sued Clearfield Trust in a federal court, invoking jurisdiction under what is now 28 U.S.C. § 1345. The question before the Supreme Court concerned the effect of the government's delay in giving notice to Penney's and Clearfield of the theft and forgery of the original payee's signature. The District Court held that Pennsylvania law governed, and that recovery was accordingly barred by an unreasonable delay in giving notice. The Circuit Court reversed. The reasoning on the choice-of-law question in Justice Douglas' opinion was:

> "We agree with the Circuit Court of Appeals that the rule of Erie Railroad Co. v. Tompkins, 304 U.S. 64 (1938), does not apply to this action. The rights and duties of the United States on commercial paper which it issues are governed by federal rather than local law. When the United States disburses its funds or pays its debts, it is exercising a constitutional function or power. This check was issued for services performed under the Federal Emergency Relief Act of 1935. The authority to issue the check had its origin in the Constitution and the statutes of the United States and was in no way dependent on the laws of Pennsylvania or of any other state. The duties imposed upon the United States and the rights acquired by it as a result of the issuance find their roots in the same federal sources.[2] In absence of an applicable act of Congress it is for the federal courts to fashion the governing rule of law according to their own standards. . . .

> "In our choice of the applicable federal rule we have occasionally selected state law. But reasons which may make state law at times the appropriate federal rule are singularly inappropriate here. The issuance of commercial paper by the United States is on a vast scale and transactions in that paper from issuance to payment will commonly occur in several states. The application of state law, even without the conflict of laws rules of the forum, would subject the rights and duties of the United States to exceptional uncertainty. It would lead to great diversity in results by making identical transactions subject to the vagaries of the laws of the several states. The desirability of a uniform rule is plain. And while the federal law merchant, developed for about a century under the regime of *Swift v. Tyson,* represented general commercial law rather than a choice of a federal rule designed to protect a federal right, it nevertheless stands as a convenient source of reference for fashioning federal rules applicable to these federal questions."

At this point the Court examined the commercial precedents and held that the lack of prompt notice was a defense only if Clearfield and Penney's could show actual damages resulting from the lack of notification. Ironically, the Court said during this discussion that the

---

[2] "Various Treasury Regulations govern the payment and endorsement of government checks and warrants and the reimbursement of the Treasurer of the United States by Federal Reserve banks and member bank depositories on payment of checks or warrants bearing a forged endorsement. Forgery of the check was an offense against the United States."

"fact[s] that the drawee is the United States and the laches those of its employees are not material. The United States as drawee of commercial paper stands in no different light than any other drawee. As stated in [a prior case], '[t]he United States does business on business terms.' It is not excepted from the general rules governing the rights and duties of drawees . . . ."

There was no dissent (two Justices did not participate).

3. Federal or State Law. The first step in a case concerning the legal rights and obligations of the United States is to determine whether state or federal law applies. This is the question to which part II of the Court's opinion in *Lake Misere* is devoted. It is the question answered in favor of federal law by the "first" of the two holdings of *Clearfield Trust.* [a] And it is the question answered in favor of state law in *Cotton, Mason, Fox,* and *Burnison.*

Note that the answer to this question is not affected by the court in which the lawsuit is initiated. As Chief Justice Burger said in *Lake Misere,* 28 U.S.C. § 1345 (United States a plaintiff) does not automatically mean that federal law applies. *Fox* and *Burnison* involved the rights of the United States in suits initiated in state courts, while *Cotton* and *Mason* started in federal court. In none of the cases did the Supreme Court make anything of the court in which the suit was filed.

Why did the Supreme Court hold in part II of *Lake Misere* that federal law applied? Is it the Constitution, the Congress, or the Court that has displaced the application of state law to this transaction? Can *Cotton* and *Mason* or *Fox* and *Burnison* be distinguished? Do *Clearfield Trust* and *Lake Misere* mean that federal law *always* governs the rights and obligations of the United States? Recall that the Chief Justice repeatedly referred to the fact that the Migratory Bird Act "explicitly authorized" the transactions in question. Does this limit the reach of the decision?

4. Content of Federal Law. If the Court decides that federal law governs, the next question is what the content of the federal law should be. If it reaches this stage, the Court is likely to do one of two things.

First, it may develop a rule of federal common law that will apply uniformly throughout the country. This is what the Court did in *Clearfield Trust* and *Dice* (page 252, supra). The Court is free in making this determination to look to such Congressional policies as it can discern, to the common law or statutory policies used by any state to solve related problems, or to any other source. The Court is acting

---

[a] The "first" holding of *Clearfield Trust* is that federal law will apply. The reference is to the first full paragraph quoted from the opinion on page 300, supra. The "second" holding is that state law will not be "borrowed" but an independent rule of federal common law will be formulated. The reference here is to the second full paragraph quoted on page 300, supra. Designation of these two paragraphs as concerning the "first" and "second" holdings of *Clearfield Trust* originated in the article by Judge Friendly cited on page 284, supra, and has passed into the vocabulary in which the *Clearfield Trust* case is commonly discussed.

in this instance just as any common law court would act. Its job is to formulate the wisest solution to the problem before it, consistent with any controlling legislative policy.

Second, the Court may incorporate or "borrow" state law as the federal rule of decision. This is the option to which the Court referred at the beginning of part III of its *Lake Misere* opinion. If this option is selected, the federal law will differ depending on the state in which the controversy arises. The controlling federal policy, therefore, will be that it is better for federal law to mirror local law in each different state than for there to be a uniform federal rule.

(i) **Should State Law Be Borrowed?** The Federal Tort Claims Act provides that the United States can be sued, under certain conditions, for the negligent acts of its employees. Specifically, 28 U.S.C. § 1346(b) says that the United States can be sued in a federal district court

> "for money damages . . . for injury or loss of property, or personal injury or death caused by the negligent or wrongful act or omission of any employee of the government while acting within the scope of his office or employment, *under circumstances where the United States, if a private person, would be liable to the claimant in accordance with the law of the place where the act or omission occurred.*" (Emphasis added.)[b]

Why did Congress incorporate state law in this statute? Because federal employees ought to observe local laws? Because it is fair to local citizens that they be allowed to recover against the federal government under the same conditions that apply to anyone else who injures them?

The Federal Tort Claims Act presents an easy situation for the courts because the statute is explicit that state law should be borrowed. A more difficult problem is presented when Congress has given no guidance on how the federal law should be formulated. This was the case in DeSylva v. Ballentine, 351 U.S. 570 (1956), which, although it does not involve the rights and obligations of the United States, was cited by the Chief Justice in *Lake Misere* because it is one of the best known instances of the Court borrowing state law.

DeSylva involved the federal Copyright Act, which provided that a copyright extended for 28 years and could be renewed for an additional 28 years on application by "the author of such work, if still living, or the widow, widower, or children of the author, if he be dead . . . ." The author of the work in question had died, leaving a widow and an illegitimate child. The widow had renewed the copyright, but proposed not to share the proceeds with the illegitimate child. The case was brought by the mother of the child against the widow, and raised two questions: whether the widow and children took as a class or in the

[b] Important limitations are placed on this cause of action by the provisions in 28 U.S.C. §§ 2671–2680.

order of enumeration in the statute; and, if they took as a class, whether the word "children" in the statute encompassed illegitimate children. Both issues, obviously, were controlled by federal law since the interpretation of a federal statute was at stake.

The Court first decided that both the widow and any "children" were entitled to share in the renewal term of the copyright. It was then faced with what the word "children" meant:

> "The scope of a federal right is, of course, a federal question, but that does not mean that its content is not to be determined by state, rather than federal law. This is especially true where a statute deals with a familial relationship; there is no federal law of domestic relations, which is primarily a matter of state concern.
>
> "If we look at the other persons who . . . are entitled to renew the copyright after the author's death, it is apparent that this is the general scheme of the statute. To decide who is the widow or widower of a deceased author, or who are his executors or next of kin, requires a reference to the law of the state which created those legal relationships. The word 'children,' although it to some extent describes a purely physical relationship, also describes a legal status not unlike the others. To determine whether a child has been legally adopted, for example, requires a reference to state law. We think it proper, therefore, to draw on the ready-made body of state law to define the word 'children' . . . . This does not mean that a state would be entitled to use the word 'children' in a way entirely strange to those familiar with its ordinary usage, but at least to the extent that there are permissible variations in the ordinary concept of 'children' we deem state law controlling.
>
> ". . . The evident purpose of [the copyright provisions] is to provide for the family of the author after his death. Since the author cannot assign his family's renewal rights, [the provision] takes the form of a compulsory bequest of the copyright to the designated persons. This is really a question of the descent of property, and we think the controlling question under state law should be whether the child would be an heir of the author. It is clear [under the applicable California law that] the child is . . . included within the term 'children.'"

Justice Douglas, joined by Justice Black, concurred in the judgment. He argued:

> "The meaning of the word 'children' as used in . . . the Copyright Act is a federal question. Congress could of course give the word the meaning it has under the laws of the several states. But I would think the statutory policy of protecting dependents would be better served by uniformity, rather than by the diversity which would flow from incorporating into the

act the laws of 48 states. Cf. Clearfield Trust Co. v. United States, 318 U.S. 363 (1943).

"An illegitimate child was given the benefits of the Federal Death Act by Middleton v. Luckenbach S.S. Co., 70 F.2d 326, 329–30 (2d Cir. 1934), where the court . . . said:

'There is no right of inheritance involved here. It is a statute that confers recovery upon dependents, not for the benefit of an estate, but for those who by our standards are legally or morally entitled to support. Humane considerations and the realization that children are such no matter what their origin alone might compel us to the construction that, under present day conditions, our social attitude warrants a construction different from that of the early English view. The purpose and object of the statute is to continue the support of dependents after a casualty. To hold that these children . . . do not come within the terms of the act would be to defeat the purposes of the act. The benefit conferred beyond being for such beneficiaries is for society's welfare in making provision for the support of those who might otherwise become dependent. . . .'

"I would take the same approach here and, regardless of state law, hold that illegitimate children were 'children' within the meaning . . . of the Copyright Act, whether or not state law would allow them dependency benefits."

Should the Court have incorporated state law in *DeSylva* ? What factors should the Court use in making such a decision? Is the question entirely contextual, or are there valid generalizations one could make about when state law ought to be borrowed?

Contrast *Clearfield Trust* with *DeSylva* and the Federal Tort Claims Act. The "second" holding in *Clearfield* (see footnote a on page 301, supra) was that a uniform federal law was required by the federal interests at stake. But exactly what federal policy requires a uniform federal rule governing the rights and obligations of the United States on its commercial paper? Consider in this respect United States v. Kimbell Foods, 440 U.S. 715 (1979), where the Court elaborated the criteria relevant to this decision:

"Undoubtedly, federal programs that 'by their nature are and must be uniform in character throughout the nation' necessitate formulation of controlling federal rules. Conversely, when there is little need for a nationally uniform body of law, state law may be incorporated as the federal rule of decision. Apart from considerations of uniformity, we must also determine whether application of state law would frustrate specific objectives of the federal programs. If so, we must fashion special rules solicitous of those federal interests. Finally, our choice-of-law inquiry must consider the extent to which application of a federal rule would disrupt commercial relationships predicated on state law."

Does this help?

Finally, note that in both *DeSylva* and the Federal Tort Claims Act, there is no question of state law applying of its own force. The meaning of a federal statute is necessarily a matter of federal law. Contrast a case, such as *Lake Misere* or *Clearfield Trust*, where the Court decides as a matter of federal common law that federal law applies. Would the reasons for holding that federal law applies necessarily support the conclusion that a uniform rule of decision should be developed? Conversely, if state law is to be borrowed, does that suggest that federal law should not apply in the first place?

(ii) Does It Matter How State Law Applies? Assume a case where everyone agrees that state law should apply to a particular issue involving the rights and obligations of the United States. The theories used by Justices Stewart and Rehnquist in *Lake Misere* would reach this result by holding that state law applies unless and until displaced by an applicable federal statute or by the Constitution. The theory used by Chief Justice Burger, on the other hand, would reach the result by holding that federal law applies but state law should in this instance be borrowed as the applicable federal law.

Does anything turn on which theory is chosen? Is this an example of theory run amuck, or are there practical consequences that flow from whether state law applies of its own force or is borrowed by federal law? Why did Chief Justice Burger explain the result in *Lake Misere* as he did?

Now consider a situation, such as that in *Lake Misere,* where everyone agrees that state law should not apply. Is there any advantage in reaching this conclusion by approaching it from the theoretical perspective adopted by the Chief Justice rather than that of Justices Stewart or Rehnquist? Would it have been better simply to hold that this particular Louisiana law could not apply under the supremacy clause because it was inconsistent with the policies of the Migratory Bird Act?

SUBSECTION B: RIGHTS AND DUTIES OF PRIVATE PARTIES

BOYLE v. UNITED TECHNOLOGIES CORP.
Supreme Court of the United States, 1988.
__ U.S. __.

JUSTICE SCALIA delivered the opinion of the Court.

This case requires us to decide when a contractor providing military equipment to the federal government can be held liable under state tort law for injury caused by a design defect.

I

On April 27, 1983, David A. Boyle, a United States Marine helicopter pilot, was killed when the CH–53D helicopter in which he was flying crashed off the coast of Virginia Beach, Virginia, during a training exercise. Although Boyle survived the impact of the crash, he was unable to escape from the helicopter and drowned. Boyle's father, petitioner here, brought this diversity action in federal District Court against the Sikorsky Division of United Technologies Corporation (Sikorsky), which built the helicopter for the United States.

At trial, petitioner presented two theories of liability under Virginia tort law that were submitted to the jury. First, petitioner alleged that Sikorsky had defectively repaired a device called the servo in the helicopter's automatic flight control system, which allegedly malfunctioned and caused the crash. Second, petitioner alleged that Sikorsky had defectively designed the copilot's emergency escape system: the escape hatch opened out instead of in (and was therefore ineffective in a submerged craft because of water pressure), and access to the escape hatch handle was obstructed by other equipment. The jury returned a general verdict in favor of petitioner and awarded him $725,000. The District Court denied Sikorsky's motion for judgment notwithstanding the verdict.

The Court of Appeals reversed and remanded with directions that judgment be entered for Sikorsky. It found, as a matter of Virginia law, that Boyle had failed to meet his burden of demonstrating that the repair work performed by Sikorsky, as opposed to work that had been done by the Navy, was responsible for the alleged malfunction of the flight control system. It also found, as a matter of federal law, that Sikorsky could not be held liable for the allegedly defective design of the escape hatch because, on the evidence presented, it satisfied the requirements of the "military contractor defense," which the court had recognized the same day in Tozer v. LTV Corp., 792 F.2d 403 (4th Cir.1986).

Petitioner sought review here, challenging the Court of Appeals' decision on three levels: First, petitioner contends that there is no justification in federal law for shielding government contractors from liability for design defects in military equipment. Second, he argues in the alternative that even if such a defense should exist, the Court of Appeals' formulation of the conditions for its application is inappropriate. Finally, petitioner contends that the Court of Appeals erred in not remanding for a jury determination of whether the elements of the defense were met in this case. We granted certiorari.

II

Petitioner's broadest contention is that, in the absence of legislation specifically immunizing government contractors from liability for design defects, there is no basis for judicial recognition of such a defense. We disagree. In most fields of activity, to be sure, this Court has refused to find federal pre-emption of state law in the absence of either a clear statutory prescription or a direct conflict between federal and state law. But we have held that a few areas, involving "uniquely federal interests," Texas Industries, Inc. v. Radcliff Materials, Inc., 451 U.S. 630, 640 (1981), are so committed by the Constitution and laws of the United States to federal control that state law is pre-empted and replaced where necessary, by federal law of a content prescribed (absent explicit statutory directive) by the courts—so-called "federal common law." See, e.g., Howard v. Lyons, 360 U.S. 593, 597 (1959); Clearfield Trust Co. v. United States, 318 U.S. 363, 366–67 (1943).

The dispute in the present case borders upon two areas that we have found to involve such "uniquely federal interests." We have held that obligations to and rights of the United States under its contracts are governed exclusively by federal law. See, e.g., United States v. Little Lake Misere Land Co., 412 U.S. 580, 592–94 (1973); *Clearfield Trust,* supra. The present case does not involve an obligation to the United States under its contract, but rather liability to third persons. That liability may be styled one in tort, but it arises out of performance of the contract—and traditionally has been regarded as sufficiently related to the contract that until 1962 Virginia would generally allow design defect suits only by the purchaser and those in privity with the seller.

Another area that we have found to be of peculiarly federal concern, warranting the displacement of state law, is the civil liability of federal officials for actions taken in the course of their duty. We have held in many contexts that the scope of that liability is controlled by federal law. See, e.g., Westfall v. Erwin, 484 U.S. __, __ (1988); *Howard v. Lyons,* supra, at 597; Barr v. Mateo, 360 U.S. 564 (1959). The present case involves an independent contractor performing its obligation under a procurement contract, rather than an official performing his duty as a federal employee, but there is obviously implicated the same interest in getting the government's work done.[2]

We think the reasons for considering these closely related areas to be of "uniquely federal" interest apply as well to the civil liabilities arising out of the performance of federal procurement contracts. [I]t is plain that the federal government's interest in the procurement of equipment is implicated by suits such as the present one—even though the dispute is one between private parties. It is true that where "litigation is purely between private parties and does not touch the rights and duties of the United States," Bank of American Nat. Trust & Savings Ass'n v. Parnell, 352 U.S. 29, 33 (1956), federal law does not govern. Thus, for example, in Miree v. DeKalb County, 433 U.S. 25, 30 (1977), which involved the question whether certain private parties could sue as third-party beneficiaries to an agreement between a

---

[2] The dissent misreads our discussion here to "intimat[e] that the immunity [of federal officials] might extend . . . to nongovernment employees" such as a government contractor. But we do not address this issue, as it is not before us. We cite these cases merely to demonstrate that the liability of independent contractors performing work for the federal government, like the liability of federal officials, is an area of uniquely federal interest.

municipality and the Federal Aviation Administration, we found that state law was not displaced because "the operations of the United States in connection with FAA grants such as these . . . would [not] be burdened" by allowing state law to determine whether third-party beneficiaries could sue, and because "any federal interest in the outcome of the [dispute] before us '[was] far too speculative, far too remote a possibility to justify the application of federal law to transactions essentially of local concern.' "   [S]ee also Wallis v. Pan American Petroleum Corp., 384 U.S. 63, 69 (1966).[3] But the same is not true here. The imposition of liability on government contractors will directly affect the terms of government contracts: either the contractor will decline to manufacture the design specified by the government, or it will raise its price. Either way the interests of the United States will be directly affected.

That the procurement of equipment by the United States is an area of uniquely federal interest does not, however, end the inquiry. That merely establishes a necessary, not a sufficient, condition for the displacement of state law.[4] Displacement will occur only where, as we have variously described, a "significant conflict" exists between an identifiable "federal policy or interest and the [operation] of state law," *Wallis,* supra, at 68, or the application of state law would "frustrate specific objectives" of federal legislation, *Kimbell Foods,* supra, at 728. The conflict with federal policy need not be as sharp as that which must exist for ordinary preemption when Congress legislates "in a field which the states have traditionally occupied." Rice v. Santa Fe Elevator Corp., 331 U.S. 218, 230 (1947). Or to put the point differently, the fact that the area in question *is* one of unique federal concern changes what would otherwise be a conflict that cannot produce pre-emption into one that can. But conflict there must be. In some cases, for example where the federal interest requires a uniform rule, the entire body of state law applicable to the area conflicts and is replaced by federal rules. See, e.g., *Clearfield Trust,* supra, at 366–67 . . . .   In others, the conflict is more narrow, and only particular elements of state law are superseded. See, e.g., *Little Lake Misere Land Co.,* supra, at 595 . . .; *Howard v. Lyons,* supra, at 597 . . . .

In *Miree,* supra, the suit was not seeking to impose upon the person contracting with the government a duty contrary to the duty imposed

---

[3] As this language shows, the dissent is simply incorrect to describe *Miree* and other cases as declining to apply federal law despite the assertion of interests "comparable" to those before us here.

[4] We refer here to the displacement of state law, although it is possible to analyze it as the displacement of federal-law reference to state law for the rule of decision. Some of our cases appear to regard the area in which a uniquely federal interest exists as being entirely governed by federal law, with federal law deigning to "borro[w]," United States v. Little Lake Misere

Land Co., 412 U.S. 580, 594 (1973), or "incorporat[e]" or "adopt," United States v. Kimbell Foods, Inc., 440 U.S. 715, 728, 729, 730 (1979), state law except where a significant conflict with federal policy exists. We see nothing to be gained by expanding the theoretical scope of the federal pre-emption beyond its practical effect, and so adopt the more modest terminology. If the distinction between displacement of state law and displacement of federal law's incorporation of state law ever makes a practical difference, it at least does not do so in the present case.

by the government contract. Rather, it was the contractual duty *itself* that the private plaintiff (as third party beneficiary) sought to enforce. Between *Miree* and the present case, it is easy to conceive of an intermediate situation, in which the duty sought to be imposed on the contractor is not identical to one assumed under the contract, but is also not contrary to any assumed. If, for example, the United States contracts for the purchase and installation of an air conditioning unit, specifying the cooling capacity but not the precise manner of construction, a state law imposing upon the manufacturer of such units a duty of care to include a certain safety feature would not be a duty identical to anything promised the government, but neither would it be contrary. The contractor could comply with both its contractual obligations and the state-prescribed duty of care. No one suggests that state law would generally be pre-empted in this context.

The present case, however, is at the opposite extreme from *Miree*. Here the state-imposed duty of care that is the asserted basis of the contractor's liability (specifically, the duty to equip helicopters with the sort of escape-hatch mechanism petitioner claims was necessary) is precisely contrary to the duty imposed by the government contract (the duty to manufacture and deliver helicopters with the sort of escape-hatch mechanism shown by the specifications). Even in this sort of situation, it would be unreasonable to say that there is always a "significant conflict" between the state law and a federal policy or interest. If, for example, a federal procurement officer orders, by model number, a quantity of stock helicopters that happen to be equipped with escape hatches opening outward, it is impossible to say that the government has a significant interest in that particular feature. That would be scarcely more reasonable than saying that a private individual who orders such a craft by model number cannot sue for the manufacturer's negligence because he got precisely what he ordered . . . .

There is . . . a statutory provision that demonstrates the potential for, and suggests the outlines of, "significant conflict" between federal interests and state law in the context of government procurement. In the Federal Tort Claims Act (FTCA), Congress authorized damages to be recovered against the United States for harm caused by the negligent or wrongful conduct of government employees, to the extent that a private person would be liable under the law of the place where the conduct occurred. 28 U.S.C. § 1346(b). It excepted from this consent to suit, however,

> "[a]ny claim . . . based upon the exercise or performance or the failure to exercise or perform a discretionary function or duty on the part of a federal agency or an employee of the Government, whether or not the discretion involved be abused." 28 U.S.C. § 2680(a).

We think that the selection of the appropriate design for military equipment to be used by our Armed Forces is assuredly a discretionary function within the meaning of this provision. It often involves not merely engineering analysis but judgment as to the balancing of many technical, military, and even social considerations, including specifically the trade-off between greater safety and greater combat effectiveness. And we are further of the view that permitting "second-guessing" of these judgments through state tort suits against contractors would produce the same effect sought to be avoided by the FTCA exemption. The financial burden of judgments against the contractors would ultimately be passed through, substantially if not totally, to the United States itself, since defense contractors will predictably raise their prices to cover, or to insure against, contingent liability for the government-ordered designs. To put the point differently: It makes little sense to insulate the government against financial liability for the judgment that a particular feature of military equipment is necessary when the government produces the equipment itself, but not when it contracts for the production. In sum, we are of the view that state law which holds government contractors liable for design defects in military equipment does in some circumstances present a "significant conflict" with federal policy and must be displaced.

We agree with the scope of displacement adopted by the Fourth Circuit here . . . . Liability for design defects in military equipment cannot be imposed, pursuant to state law, when (1) the United States approved reasonably precise specifications; (2) the equipment conformed to those specifications; and (3) the supplier warned the United States about the dangers in the use of the equipment that were known to the supplier but not to the United States. The first two of these conditions assure that the suit is within the area where the policy of the "discretionary function" would be frustrated—i.e., they assure that the design feature in question was considered by a government officer, and not merely by the contractor itself. The third condition is necessary because, in its absence, the displacement of state tort law would create some incentive for the manufacturer to withhold knowledge of risks, since conveying that knowledge might disrupt the contract but withholding it would produce no liability. We adopt this provision lest our effort to protect discretionary functions perversely impedes them by cutting off information highly relevant to the discretionary decision.

We have considered [an] alternative formulation of the government contractor defense, urged upon us by petitioner . . . . That would preclude suit only if (1) the contractor did not participate, or participated only minimally, in the design of the defective equipment; *or* (2) the contractor timely warned the government of the risks of the design and notified it of alternative designs reasonably known by it, *and* the government, although forewarned, clearly authorized the contractor to proceed with the dangerous design. While this formulation may represent a perfectly reasonable tort rule, it is not a rule designed to protect the federal interest embodied in the "discretionary function" exemption. The design ultimately selected may well reflect a significant policy judgment by government officials whether or not the contractor rather than those officials developed the design. In addition, it does not seem to us sound policy to penalize, and thus deter, active contractor participation in the design process, placing the contractor at risk unless it identifies all design defects.

III

[In this part of his opinion, Justice Scalia determined that a remand was necessary for the Court of Appeals to determine whether the case should have gone to the jury or whether the evidence was such that no reasonable jury could find the government contractor defense inapplicable.]

So ordered.

JUSTICE BRENNAN, with whom JUSTICE MARSHALL and JUSTICE BLACK-MUN join, dissenting.

Lieutenant David A. Boyle died when the CH–53D helicopter he was copiloting spun out of control and plunged into the ocean. We may assume, for purpose of this case, that Lt. Boyle was trapped under water and drowned because respondent United Technologies negligently designed the helicopter's escape hatch. We may further assume that any competent engineer would have discovered and cured the defects, but that they inexplicably escaped respondent's notice. Had respondent designed such a death trap for a commercial firm, Lt. Boyle's family could sue under Virginia tort law and be compensated for his tragic and unnecessary death. But respondent designed the helicopter for the federal government, and that, the Court tells us today, makes all the difference: Respondent is immune from liability so long as it obtained approval of "reasonably precise specifications"—perhaps no more than a rubberstamp from a federal procurement officer who might or might not have noticed or cared about the defects, or even had the expertise to discover them.

If respondent's immunity "bore the legitimacy of having been prescribed by the people's elected representatives," we would be duty bound to implement their will, whether or not we approved. United States v. Johnson, 481 U.S. ___, ___ (1987) (dissenting opinion of Scalia, J.). Congress, however, has remained silent—and conspicuously so, having resisted a sustained campaign by government contractors to legislate for them some defense.[1] The Court—unelected and unaccountable to the people—has unabashedly stepped into the breach to legislate a rule denying Lt. Boyle's family the compensation that state law assures them. This time the injustice is of this Court's own making.

Worse yet, the injustice will extend far beyond the facts of this case, for the Court's newly discovered government contractor defense is breathtakingly sweeping. It applies not only to military equipment like the CH–53D helicopter, but (so far as I can tell) to any made-to-order gadget that the federal government might purchase after previewing plans—from NASA's Challenger space shuttle to the Postal Service's old mail cars. The contractor may invoke the defense in suits

---

[1] [Justice Brennan cited six bills that failed of passage.]

brought not only by military personnel like Lt. Boyle, or government employees, but by anyone injured by a government contractor's negligent design, including, for example, the children who might have died had respondent's helicopter crashed on the beach. It applies even if the government has not intentionally sacrificed safety for other interests like speed or efficiency, and, indeed, even if the equipment is not of a type that is typically considered dangerous; thus, the contractor who designs a government building can invoke the defense when the elevator cable snaps or the walls collapse. And the defense is invocable regardless of how blatant or easily remedied the defect, so long as the contractor missed it and the specifications approved by the government, however unreasonably dangerous, were "reasonably precise."

In my view, this Court lacks both authority and expertise to fashion such a rule, whether to protect the Treasury of the United States or the coffers of industry. Because I would leave that exercise of legislative power to Congress, where our Constitution places it, I would reverse the Court of Appeals and reinstate petitioner's jury award.

I

Before our decision in Erie R. Co. v. Tompkins, 304 U.S. 64 (1938), federal courts sitting in diversity were generally free, in the absence of a controlling state statute, to fashion rules of "general" federal common law. *Erie* renounced the prevailing scheme: "Except in matters governed by the federal Constitution or by acts of Congress, the law to be applied in any case is the law of the state." The Court explained that the expansive power that federal courts had theretofore exercised was an unconstitutional "invasion of the authority of the state and, to that extent, a denial of its independence." Thus, *Erie* was deeply rooted in notions of federalism, and is most seriously implicated when, as here, federal judges displace the state law that would ordinarily govern with their own rules of federal common law. See, e.g., United States v. Standard Oil Co., 332 U.S. 301, 307 (1947).[2]

In pronouncing that "[t]here is no federal general common law," *Erie* put to rest the notion that the grant of diversity jurisdiction to federal courts is itself authority to fashion rules of substantive law. As the author of today's opinion for the Court pronounced for a unanimous Court just two months ago, " ' " 'we start with the assumption that the historic police powers of the states were not to be superseded . . . unless that was the clear and manifest purpose of Congress.' " ' " Puerto Rico Dept. of Consumer Affairs v. Isla Petroleum Corp., 485 U.S. __, __ (1988). Just as "[t]here is no federal pre-emption in vacuo, without a constitutional text or a federal statute to assert it," id., at

---

[2] Not all exercises of our power to fashion federal common law displace state law in the same way. For example, our recognition of federal causes of action based upon either the Constitution, see, e.g., Bivens v. Six Unknown Fed. Narcotics Agents, 403 U.S. 388 (1971), or a federal statute, see Cort v. Ash, 422 U.S. 66 (1975), supplements whatever rights state law might provide, and therefore does not implicate federalism concerns in the same way as does pre-emption of a state-law rule of decision or cause of action. Throughout this opinion I use the word "displace" in the latter sense.

___, federal common law cannot supersede state law in vacuo out of no more than an idiosyncratic determination by five Justices that a particular area is "uniquely federal."

Accordingly, we have emphasized that federal common law can displace state law in "few and restricted" instances. Wheeldin v. Wheeler, 373 U.S. 647, 651 (1963). "[A]bsent some congressional authorization to formulate substantive rules of decision, federal common law exists only in such narrow areas as those concerned with the rights and obligations of the United States, interstate and international disputes implicating conflicting rights of states or our relations with foreign nations, and admiralty cases." Texas Industries, Inc. v. Radcliff Materials, Inc., 451 U.S. 630, 641 (1981). The enactment of a federal rule in an area of national concern, and the decision whether to displace state law in doing so, is generally made not by the federal judiciary, purposefully insulated from democratic pressures, but by the people through their elected representatives in Congress." Milwaukee v. Illinois, 451 U.S. 304, 312–13 (1981). See also Wallis v. Pan American Petroleum Corp., 384 U.S. 63, 68 (1966); Miree v. DeKalb County, 433 U.S. 25, 32 (1977). State laws "should be overridden by the federal courts only where clear and substantial interests of the national government, which cannot be served consistently with respect for such state interests, will suffer major damage if the state law is applied." United States v. Yazell, 382 U.S. 341, 352 (1966).

II

Congress has not decided to supersede state law here (if anything, it has decided not to, see n.1 supra) and the Court does not pretend that its newly manufactured "government contractor defense" fits within any of the handful of "narrow areas," Texas Industries, supra, at 641, of "uniquely federal interests" in which we have heretofore done so. Rather, the Court creates a new category of "uniquely federal interests" out of a synthesis of two whose origins predate Erie itself: the interest in administering the "obligations to and rights of the United States under its contracts" and the interest in regulating the "civil liability of federal officials for actions taken in the course of their duty." This case is, however, simply a suit between two private parties. We have steadfastly declined to impose federal contract law on relationships that are collateral to a federal contract, or to extend the federal employee's immunity beyond federal employees. And the Court's ability to list two, or 10, inapplicable areas of "uniquely federal interest" does not support its conclusion that the liability of government contractors is so "clear and substantial" an interest that this Court must step in lest state law does "major damage." Yazell, supra, at 352.

A

The proposition that federal common law continues to govern the "obligations to and rights of the United States under its contracts" is nearly as old as Erie itself. Federal law typically controls when the federal government is a party to a suit involving its rights or obligations under a contract, whether the contract entails procurement, see Priebe & Sons v. United States, 332 U.S. 407 (1947), a loan, see United States v. Kimbell Foods, Inc., 440 U.S. 715, 726 (1979), a conveyance of property, see *Little Lake Misere*, supra, at 591–594, or a commercial instrument issued by the government, see Clearfield Trust Co. v. United States, 318 U.S. 363, 366 (1943), or assigned to it, see D'Oench, Duhme & Co. v. FDIC, 315 U.S. 447, 457 (1942). But it is by now established that our power to create federal common law controlling the *federal government's* contractual rights and obligations does not translate into a power to prescribe rules that cover all transactions or contractual relationships collateral to government contracts.

In *Miree v. DeKalb County*, supra, for example, the county was contractually obligated under a grant agreement with the Federal Aviation Administration (FAA) to " 'restrict the use of land adjacent to . . . the airport to activities and purposes compatible with normal airport operations including landing and takeoff of aircraft.' " At issue was whether the county breached its contractual obligation by operating a garbage dump adjacent to the airport, which allegedly attracted the swarm of birds that caused a plane crash. Federal common law would undoubtedly have controlled in any suit by the federal government to enforce the provision against the county or to collect damages for its violation. The diversity suit, however, was brought not by the government, but by assorted private parties injured in some way by the accident. We observed that "the operations of the United States in connection with FAA grants such as these are undoubtedly of considerable magnitude," and that "the United States has a substantial interest in regulating aircraft travel and promoting air travel safety." Nevertheless, we held that state law should govern the claim because "only the rights of private litigants are at issue here" and the claim against the county "will have *no direct effect upon the United States or its Treasury.*"

Miree relied heavily on *Parnell*, supra, and *Wallis*, supra, the former involving commercial paper issued by the United States and the latter involving property rights in federal land. In the former case, Parnell cashed certain government bonds that had been stolen from their owner, a bank. It is beyond dispute that federal law would have governed the United States' duty to pay the value bonds upon presentation; we held as much in *Clearfield Trust*, supra. But the central issue in *Parnell*, a diversity suit, was whether the victim of the theft could recover the money paid to Parnell. That issue, we held, was governed by state law, because the "litigation [was] purely between private parties and [did] *not touch the rights and duties of the United States.*" (Emphasis added.)

The same was true in *Wallis*, which also involved a government contract—a lease issued by the United States to a private party under the Mineral Leasing Act of 1920, 30 U.S.C. § 181 et seq.—governed entirely by federal law. Again, the relationship at issue in this diversity case was collateral to the government contract: it involved the validity of contractual arrangements between the lessee and other private parties, not between the lessee and the federal government. Even though a federal statute authorized certain assignments of lease rights and imposed certain conditions on their validity, we held that state law, not federal common law, governed their validity because application of state law would present "no significant threat to any identifiable federal policy or interest."

Here, as in *Miree, Parnell,* and *Wallis,* a government contract governed by federal common law looms in the background. But here, too, the United States is not a party to the suit and the suit neither "touch[es] the rights and duties of the United States," *Parnell,* supra, at 33, nor has a "direct effect upon the United States or its Treasury," *Miree,* supra, at 29. The relationship at issue is at best collateral to the government contract.[3] We have no greater power to displace state law governing the collateral relationship in the government procurement realm than we had to dictate federal rules governing equally collateral relationships in the areas of aviation, government-issued commercial paper, or federal lands.

That the government might "have to pay higher prices for what it orders if delivery in accordance with the contract exposes the seller to potential liability" does not distinguish this case. Each of the cases just discussed declined to extend the reach of federal common law despite the assertion of comparable interests that would have affected the terms of the government contract—whether its price or its substance— just as "directly" (or indirectly). Third-party beneficiaries can sue under a county's contract with the FAA, for example, even though—as the Court's focus on the absence of "*direct* effect on the United States or its Treasury," 433 U.S., at 29 (emphasis added), suggests—counties will likely pass on the costs to the government in future contract negotiations. Similarly, we held that state law may govern the circumstances under which stolen federal bonds can be recovered, notwithstanding Parnell's argument that "the value of bonds to the first purchaser and hence their salability by the government would be materially affected." Brief for Respondent Parnell in Bank of America Nat. Trust & Savings Ass'n v. Parnell, O.T. 1956, No. 21, pp. 10–11. As in each of the cases declining to extend the traditional reach of federal law of contracts beyond the rights and duties of the *federal government,* "any federal interest in the outcome of the question before us 'is far too speculative, far too remote a possibility to justify the application of federal law to transactions essentially of local concern.'" *Miree,* 433 U.S., at 32–33, quoting *Parnell,* 352 U.S., at 33–34.

---

[3] True, in this case the collateral relationship is the relationship between victim and tortfeasor, rather than between contractors, but that distinction makes no difference. We long ago established that the principles governing application of federal common law in "contractual relations of the government . . . are equally applicable . . . where the relations affected are noncontractual or tortious in character." United States v. Standard Oil Co., 332 U.S. 301, 305 (1947).

B

Our "uniquely federal interest" in the tort liability of affiliates of the federal government is equally narrow. The immunity we have recognized has extended no further than a subset of "officials of the federal government" and has covered only "discretionary" functions within the scope of their legal authority. See, e.g., Westfall v. Erwin, 484 U.S. ___ (1988); Howard v. Lyons, 360 U.S. 593 (1959); Barr v. Mateo, 360 U.S. 564, 571 (1959). Never before have we so much as intimated that the immunity (or the "uniquely federal interest" that justifies it) might extend beyond that narrow class to cover also nongovernment employees whose authority to act is independent of any source of federal law and that are as far removed from the "functioning of the federal government" as is a government contractor, *Howard*, supra, at 597.

The historical narrowness of the federal interest and the immunity is hardly accidental. A federal officer exercises statutory authority, which not only provides the necessary basis for the immunity in positive law, but also permits us confidently to presume that interference with the exercise of discretion undermines congressional will. In contrast, a government contractor acts independently of any congressional enactment. Thus, immunity for a contractor lacks both the positive law basis and the presumption that it furthers congressional will.

Moreover, even within the category of congressionally authorized tasks, we have deliberately restricted the scope of immunity to circumstances in which "the contributions of immunity to effective government in particular contexts outweigh the perhaps recurring harm to individual citizens," Doe v. McMillan, 412 U.S. 306, 320 (1973), because immunity "contravenes the basic tenet that individuals be held accountable for their wrongful conduct," *Westfall*, supra, at ___. The extension of immunity to government contractors skews the balance we have historically struck. On the one hand, whatever marginal effect contractor immunity might have on the "effective administration of policies of government," its "harm to individual citizens" is more severe than in the government-employee context. Our observation that "there are . . . other sanctions than civil tort suits available to deter the executive official who may be prone to exercise his functions in an unworthy and irresponsible manner," *Barr*, supra, at 576, offers little deterrence to the government contractor. On the other hand, a grant of immunity to government contractors could not advance "the fearless, vigorous, and effective administration of policies of government" nearly as much as does the current immunity for government employees. Id., at 571. In the first place, the threat of a tort suit is less likely to influence the conduct of an industrial giant than that of a lone civil servant, particularly since the work of a civil servant is significantly less profitable, and significantly more likely to be the subject of a vindictive lawsuit. In fact, were we to take seriously the Court's assertion that contractors pass their costs—including presumably litigation costs—through, "substantially if not totally, to the United States," the threat of a tort suit should have only marginal impact on the conduct of government contractors. More importantly, inhibition of the government official who actually sets government policy presents a greater threat to the "administration of policies of government," than does inhibition of a private contractor, whose role is devoted largely to assessing the technological feasibility and cost of satisfying the government's predetermined needs. Similarly, unlike tort suits against government officials, tort suits against government contractors would rarely "consume time and energies" that "would otherwise be devoted to governmental service." Id., at 571.

In short, because the essential justifications for official immunity do not support an extension to the government contractor, it is no surprise that we have never extended it that far . . . .

III

[T]he Court invokes the discretionary function exception of the Federal Tort Claims Act (FTCA), 28 U.S.C. § 2680(a). The Court does not suggest that the exception has any direct bearing here, for petitioner has sued a private manufacturer (not the federal government) under Virginia law (not the FTCA). [T]he Court [reasons] that federal common law must immunize government contractors from state tort law to prevent erosion of the discretionary function exception's *policy* of foreclosing judicial " 'second-guessing' " of discretionary governmental decisions. The erosion the Court fears apparently is rooted not in a concern that suits against government contractors will prevent them from designing, or the government from commissioning the design of, precisely the product the government wants, but in the concern that such suits might preclude the government from purchasing the desired product at the price it wants: "The financial burden of judgments against the contractors," the Court fears, "would ultimately be passed through, substantially if not totally, to the United States itself."

Even granting the Court's factual premise, which is by no means self-evident, the Court cites no authority for the proposition that burdens imposed on government contractors, but passed on to the government, burden the government in a way that justifies extension of its immunity. However substantial such indirect burdens may be, we have held in other contexts that they are legally irrelevant.

Moreover, the statutory basis on which the Court's rule of federal common law totters is more unstable than any we have ever adopted. In the first place, we rejected an analytically similar attempt to construct federal common law out of the FTCA when we held that the government's waiver of sovereign immunity for the torts of its employees does not give the government an implied right of indemnity from them, even though "[t]he financial burden placed on the United States by the Torts Claims Act [could conceivably be] so great that government employees should be required to carry part of the burden." United States v. Gilman, 347 U.S. 507, 510 (1954). So too here, the FTCA's retention of sovereign immunity for the government's discretionary acts does not imply a defense for the benefit of contractors who participate in those acts, even though they might pass on the financial burden to the United States. In either case, the most that can be said is that the position "asserted, though the product of a law Congress passed, is a matter on which Congress has not taken a position." Id., at 511.

Here, even that much is an overstatement, for the government's immunity for discretionary functions is not even "a product of" the FTCA. Before Congress enacted the FTCA (when sovereign immunity barred any tort suit against the federal government) we perceived no need for a rule of federal common law to reinforce the government's immunity by shielding also parties who might contractually pass costs on to it. Nor did we (or any other court of which I am aware) identify a special category of "discretionary" functions for which sovereign immunity was so crucial that a government contractor who exercised discretion should share the government's immunity from state tort law.

Now, as before the FTCA's enactment, the federal government is immune from "[a]ny claim . . . based upon the exercise or performance [of] a discretionary function," including presumably any claim that petitioner might have brought against the federal government based upon respondent's negligent design of the helicopter in which Lt. Boyle died. There is no more reason for federal common law to shield contractors now that the government is liable for some torts than there was when the government was liable for none. The discretionary function exception does not support an immunity for the discretionary acts of government *contractors* any more than the exception for "[a]ny claim [against the government] arising out of assault," § 2680(h), supports a personal immunity for government employees who commit assaults. In short, while the Court purports to divine whether Congress would object to this suit, it inexplicably begins and ends its sortilege with an exception to a statute that is itself inapplicable and whose repeal would leave unchanged every relationship remotely relevant to the accident underlying this suit . . . .

IV

At bottom, the Court's analysis is premised on the proposition that any tort liability indirectly absorbed by the government so burdens governmental functions as to compel us to act when Congress has not. That proposition is by no means uncontroversial. The tort system is premised on the assumption that the imposition of liability encourages actors to prevent any injury whose expected cost exceeds the cost of prevention. If the system is working as it should, government contractors will design equipment to avoid certain injuries (like the deaths of soldiers or government employees), which would be certain to burden the government. The Court therefore has no basis for its assumption that tort liability will result in a net burden on the government (let alone a clearly excessive net burden) rather than a net gain.

Perhaps tort liability is an inefficient means of ensuring the quality of design efforts, but "[w]hatever the merits of the policy" the Court wishes to implement, "its conversion into law is a proper subject for congressional action, not for any creative power of ours." *Standard Oil*, 332 U.S., at 314–15. It is, after all, "Congress, not this Court or the other federal courts, [that] is the custodian of the national purse. By the same token [Congress] is the primary and most often the exclusive arbiter of federal fiscal affairs. And these comprehend, as we have said, securing the treasury or the government against financial losses *however inflicted* . . . ." Ibid. (emphasis added). If Congress shared the Court's assumptions and conclusion it could readily enact "A BILL to place limitations on the civil liability of government contractors to ensure that such liability does not impede the ability of the United States to procure necessary goods and services," H.R. 4765, 99th Cong., 2d Sess. (1986). It has not.

Were I a legislator, I would probably vote against any law absolving multibillion dollar private enterprises from answering for their tragic mistakes, at least if that law were justified by no more than the unsupported speculation that their liability might ultimately burden the United States Treasury. Some of my colleagues here would evidently vote otherwise (as they have here), but that should not matter here. We are judges not legislators, and the vote is not ours to cast.

I respectfully dissent.

JUSTICE STEVENS, dissenting.

When judges are asked to embark on a lawmaking venture, I believe they should carefully consider whether they, or a legislative body, are better equipped to perform the task at hand. There are instances of so-called interstitial lawmaking that inevitably become part of the judicial process.[1] But when we are asked to create an entirely new doctrine—to answer "questions of policy on which Congress has not spoken," United States v. Gilman, 347 U.S. 507, 511 (1954)—we have a special duty to identify the proper decisionmaker before trying to make the proper decision.

When the novel question of policy involves a balancing of the conflicting interests in the efficient operation of a massive governmental program and the protection of the rights of the individual—whether in the social welfare context, the civil service context, or the military procurement context—I feel very deeply that we should defer to the expertise of the Congress. That is the central message of the unanimous decision in Bush v. Lucas, 462 U.S. 367 (1983);[2] that is why I

---

[1] "I recognize without hesitation that judges do and must legislate, but they can do so only interstitially; they are confined from molar to molecular motions. A common-law judge could not say I think the doctrine of consideration a bit of historical nonsense and shall not enforce it in my court. No more could a judge exercising the limited jurisdiction of admiralty say I think well of the common-law rules of mas-ter and servant and propose to introduce them here en bloc." Southern Pacific Co. v. Jensen, 244 U.S. 205, 221 (1917) (Holmes, J., dissenting).

[2] "[W]e decline to create a new substantive legal liability without legislative aid and as at the common law, because we are convinced that Congress is in a better position to decide whether or not the public

joined the majority in Schweiker v. Chilicky, ___ U.S. ___ (1988),[3] a case decided only three days ago, and that is why I am so distressed by the majority's decision today. For in this case, as in *United States v. Gilman*, supra: "The selection of that policy which is most advantageous to the whole involves a host of considerations that must be weighed and appraised. That function is more appropriately for those who write the laws, rather than for those who interpret them."

I respectfully dissent.

NOTES ON THE LAW GOVERNING THE RIGHTS AND DUTIES OF PRIVATE PARTIES

1. **Background: Suits Between Private Parties.** Three major cases involving suits between private parties provide the background for the decision in *Boyle.*

(i) *Bank of America v. Parnell.* The first is a counterpoint to the Court's decision in Clearfield Trust Co. v. United States, 318 U.S. 363 (1943).[a] Bank of America Nat. Trust & Savings Ass'n v. Parnell, 352 U.S. 29 (1956), was the Court's first major elaboration of the implications of *Clearfield* for suits between private parties. *Parnell* was a diversity case brought by Bank of America for the conversion of 73 government-issued bearer bonds held by four defendants, among them Parnell. The bonds had been stolen while Bank of America was getting them ready for presentation for payment.

It was not alleged that Parnell and the other defendants stole the bonds. To the contrary, they apparently were acting for people who received them for value. The question, therefore, was whether they were "holders in due course" and as such were entitled to extinguish the rights of the original owner. The main issue at trial was whether the defendants took the bonds in the requisite good faith without notice of the defect in their chain of title. The trial judge, following state law and treating the suit as an ordinary diversity case, charged that the defendants had the burden of persuasion on their good faith and lack of notice. A divided Court of Appeals disagreed. It held in an en banc decision that *Clearfield Trust* required that federal law apply and that federal law placed the burden of persuasion on the plaintiff to show notice and lack of good faith by the defendants.

Justice Frankfurter's opinion for the Court reasoned:

"The Court of Appeals misconceived the nature of this litigation in holding that the *Clearfield Trust* case controlled . . . . The basis for [*Clearfield*] was stated with unclouded explicitness:

interest would be served by creating it." [*Bush* appears as a note case at pages 425–28, infra.—Addition to footnote by eds.]

[3] "Congressional competence at 'balancing governmental efficiency and the rights of [individuals],' *Bush*, supra, at 389, is no more questionable in the social welfare context than it is in the civil service context." [*Schweiker* is a main case at page 408, infra.—Addition to footnote by eds.]

[a] *Clearfield* is excerpted at pages 299–301, supra.

'The issuance of commercial paper by the United States is on a vast scale and transactions in that paper from issuance to payment will commonly occur in several states.   The application of state law, even without the conflict of laws rules of the forum, would subject the rights and duties of the United States to exceptional uncertainty.'

"Securities issued by the government generate immediate interests of the government.   These were dealt with in *Clearfield Trust* . . . .   But they also radiate interests in transactions between private parties.   The present litigation is purely between private parties and does not touch the rights and duties of the United States.   The only possible interest of the United States in a situation like the one here, exclusively involving the transfer of government paper between private persons, is that the floating of securities of the United States might somehow or other be adversely affected by the local rule of a particular state regarding the liability of a converter. This is far too speculative, far too remote a possibility to justify the application of federal law to transactions essentially of local concern.

"We do not mean to imply that litigation with respect to government paper necessarily precludes the presence of a federal interest, to be governed by federal law, in all situations merely because it is a suit between private parties, or that it is beyond the range of federal legislation to deal comprehensively with government paper.   We do not of course foreclose such judicial or legislative action in appropriate situations by concluding that this controversy over burden of proof and good faith represents too essentially a private transaction not to be dealt with by the local law of Pennsylvania where the transactions took place.   Federal law of course governs the interpretation of the nature of the rights and obligations created by the government bonds themselves.[b] . . . ."

Justice Black, joined by Justice Douglas (the author of *Clearfield Trust*), dissented:

"We believe that the 'federal law merchant,' which *Clearfield Trust* held applicable to transactions in the commercial paper of the United States, should be applicable to all transactions in that paper . . . .   Not until today has a distinction been drawn between suits by the United States on that paper and suits by other parties to it.   But the Court does not stop there.   Because this is 'essentially a private transaction,' it is to be governed by local law.   Yet the nature of the rights and obligations created by commercial paper of the

[b] This point should be emphasized. If an issue arose as to when the bonds were due for payment or as to the nature of the government's obligation to pay, the Court made it clear that the fact that the suit was between private parties would not mean that state law would control. In that event the holding of *Clearfield* would require the application of federal law. [Footnote by eds.]

United States government is said to be controlled by federal law. Thus, federal law is to govern some portion of a dispute between private parties, while that portion of the dispute which is 'essentially of local concern' is to be governed by local law. The uncertainties which inhere in such a dichotomy are obvious.

"The virtue of a uniform law governing bonds, notes, and other paper issued by the United States is that it provides a certain and definite guide to the rights of all parties rather than subjecting them to the vagaries of the laws of many states. The business of the United States will go on without that uniformity. But the policy surrounding our choice of law is concerned with the convenience, certainty, and definiteness in having one set of rules governing the rights of all parties to government paper, as contrasted to multiple rules. If the rule of the *Clearfield Trust* case is to be abandoned as to some parties, it should be abandoned as to all and we should start afresh on this problem."

(ii) *Wallis v. Pan American Petroleum Corp.* Wallis v. Pan American Petroleum Corp., 384 U.S. 63 (1966), is well known for its statement of the criteria for determining when federal law will apply in suits between private parties. Justice Harlan wrote for the Court:

"The question before us is whether in general federal or state law should govern the dealings of private parties in an oil and gas lease validly issued under the Mineral Leasing Act of 1920 . . . .

"In deciding whether rules of federal common law should be fashioned, normally the guiding principle is that a significant conflict between some federal policy or interest and the use of state law in the premises must first be specifically shown. It is by no means enough that, as we may assume, Congress could under the Constitution readily enact a complete code of law governing transactions in federal mineral leases among private parties. Whether latent federal power should be exercised to displace state law is primarily a decision for Congress. Even where there is related federal legislation in an area, as is true in this instance, it must be remembered that 'Congress acts . . . against the background of the total corpus juris of the states . . . .' H. Hart & H. Wechsler, The Federal Courts and the Federal System 435 (1953).[c] Because

---

[c] The full passage from which this quotation is taken is well known. It reads:

"Federal law is generally interstitial in nature. It rarely occupies a legal field completely, totally excluding all participation by the legal systems of the states. This was plainly true in the beginning when the federal legislative product (including the Constitution) was extremely small. It is significantly true today, de-spite the volume of Congressional enactments, and even within areas where Congress has been very active. Federal legislation, on the whole, has been conceived and drafted on an ad hoc basis to accomplish limited objectives. It builds upon legal relationships established by the states, altering or supplanting them only so far as necessary for the special purpose. Congress acts, in short, against

we find no significant threat to any identifiable federal policy or interest, we do not press on to consider other questions relevant to invoking federal common law, such as the strength of the state interest in having its own rules govern, cf. United States v. Yazell, 382 U.S. 341, 351–353 (1966),[d] the feasibility of creating a judicial substitute, cf. U.A.W. v. Hoosier Cardinal Corp., 383 U.S. 696, 701 (1966),[e] and other similar factors.

"If there is a federal statute dealing with the general subject, it is a prime repository of federal policy and a starting point for federal common law. We find nothing in the Mineral Leasing Act of 1920 expressing policies inconsistent with state law in the area that concerns us here."

As the last sentence implies, the remainder of Justice Harlan's opinion closely examined the policies of the Mineral Leasing Act and determined that none required the application of federal law to the controversy before the Court.

(iii) *Miree v. DeKalb County.* The facts of Miree v. DeKalb County, 433 U.S. 25 (1977), are described in Justice Brennan's dissent in *Boyle.* The survivors of deceased passengers, the assignee of the airplane involved, and a burn victim sought to recover as third-party beneficiaries to a federal contract between the Federal Aviation Administration (FAA) and a County airport. Georgia law permitted the suit, but the County argued that federal law precluded third-party suits on FAA contracts. Justice Rehnquist wrote the opinion for a unanimous Court: [f]

"The litigation before us raises no question regarding the liability of the United States or the responsibilities of the United States under the contracts. The relevant inquiry is a

the background of the total corpus juris of the states in much the same way that a state legislature acts against the background of the common law, assumed to govern unless changed by legislation."

[Footnote by eds.]

[d] *Yazell* involved an effort by the Small Business Administration to foreclose on a disaster loan. The question was whether the Texas law of "coverture" prevented the government from seizing Mrs. Yazell's separate property. The Court held that the state law applied, which had the effect of insulating Mrs. Yazell's property even though she had signed the note when the money was borrowed. Among the factors emphasized by the Court were that these loans tend to be negotiated in light of local law, that there was no overriding interest in nationwide uniformity on the issue, and that the state had a strong interest in regulating property arrangements of this type. The Court expressly refrained from deciding whether state law would apply of its own force or would be borrowed and applied as federal law.

That *Yazell* may have been a "widows and orphans" case was revealed in the opening line to Justice Fortas' opinion: "[T]he question presented is whether the . . . federal government, in its zealous pursuit of the balance due on a disaster loan made by the Small Business Administration, may obtain judgment against Ethel Mae Yazell of Lampass, Texas." [Footnote by eds.]

[e] *Hoosier Cardinal* concerned the statute of limitations applicable to a suit brought under § 301 of the Taft-Hartley Act. The suit involved a federal cause of action to be governed entirely by "federal common law." But the Court held that state law should be looked to for the statute of limitations, in part because of the difficulty the Court itself would have in determining a particular period of limitation. [Footnote by eds.]

[f] Chief Justice Burger concurred in the judgment in a separate opinion.

narrow one: whether petitioners as third-party beneficiaries of the contracts have standing to sue respondent. While federal common law may govern even in diversity cases [3] where a uniform national rule is necessary to further the interests of the federal government, Clearfield Trust Co. v. United States, 318 U.S. 363 (1943), the application of federal common law to resolve the issue presented here would promote no federal interests even approaching the magnitude of those found in *Clearfield Trust. . . .*

"[I]n this case, the resolution of petitioners' breach-of-contract claim against respondent will have no direct effect upon the United States or its Treasury. The Solicitor General, waiving his right to respond in these cases, advised us:

'In the course of the proceedings below, the United States determined that its interests would not be directly affected by the resolution of these issue[s] and therefore did not participate in briefing or argument in the Court of Appeals. In view of these considerations, the United States does not intend to respond to the petitions unless it is requested to do so by the Court.'

The operations of the United States in connection with FAA grants such as these are undoubtedly of considerable magnitude. However, we see no reason for concluding that these operations would be burdened or subjected to uncertainty by variant state-law interpretations regarding whether those with whom the United States contracts might be sued by third-party beneficiaries to the contracts. Since only the rights of private litigants are at issue here, we find the *Clearfield Trust* rationale inapplicable.

"We think our conclusion that these cases do not fit within the *Clearfield Trust* rule follows from the Court's later decision in Bank of America Nat. Trust & Savings Ass'n v. Parnell, 352 U.S. 29 (1956), in which the Court declined to apply that rule in a fact situation analogous to this one. . . . The parallel between *Parnell* and these cases is obvious. The question of whether petitioners may sue respondent does not require decision under federal common law since the litigation is among private parties and no substantial rights or duties of the United States hinge on its outcome. On the other hand, nothing we say here forecloses the applicability of federal common law in interpreting the rights and duties of the United States under federal contracts.

"Nor is the fact that the United States has a substantial interest in regulating aircraft travel and promoting air travel

---

[3] "The *Clearfield Trust* rule may apply in diversity cases. See Sola Electric Co. v. Jefferson Electric Co., 317 U.S. 173 (1942); Bank of America Nat. Trust & Savings Ass'n v. Parnell, 352 U.S. 29 (1956); Wallis v. Pan American Petroleum Corp., 384 U.S. 63 (1966)."

safety sufficient, given the narrow question before us, to call into play the rule of *Clearfield Trust*. In Wallis v. Pan American Petroleum Corp., 384 U.S. 63, 68 (1966), the Court discussed the nature of a federal interest sufficient to bring forth the application of federal common law:

> 'In deciding whether rules of federal common law should be fashioned, normally the guiding principle is that a *significant conflict between some federal policy or interest and the use of state law in the premises must first be specifically shown.* It is by no means enough that, as we may assume, Congress could under the Constitution readily enact a complete code of law governing transactions in federal mineral leases among private parties. Whether latent federal power should be exercised to displace state law is primarily a decision for Congress.' (Emphasis added.)

The question of whether private parties may, as third-party beneficiaries, sue a municipality for breach of the FAA contracts involves this federal interest only insofar as such lawsuits might be thought to advance federal aviation policy by inducing compliance with FAA safety provisions. However, even assuming the correctness of this notion, we adhere to the language in *Wallis*, cited above, stating that the issue of whether to displace state law on an issue such as this is primarily a decision for Congress. Congress has chosen not to do so in this case.[5] Actually the application of federal common law, as interpreted by the Court of Appeals here would frustrate this federal interest pro tanto, since that court held that this breach-of-contract lawsuit would not lie under federal law. On the other hand, at least in the opinion of the majority of the panel below, Georgia law would countenance the action. Even assuming that a different result were to be reached under federal common law, we think this language from *Wallis* all but forecloses its application to these cases:

> 'Apart from the highly abstract nature of [the federal] interest, there has been no showing that state law is not adequate to achieve it.'

We conclude that any federal interest in the outcome of the question before us 'is far too speculative, far too remote a possibility to justify the application of federal law to transactions essentially of local concern.' *Parnell*, supra, at 33–34."

2. Suits Against Federal Officers. Also relevant to the decision in *Boyle* is a line of cases developing a federal defense to tort suits against federal officials based on state law. Three of the Court's prior decisions warrant elaboration.

[5] "The Congress has considered, but not passed, a bill to provide for a federal cause of action arising out of aircraft disasters."

(i) ***Howard v. Lyons.***   Howard v. Lyons, 360 U.S. 593 (1959), involved an action for defamation filed against the Commander of the Boston Naval Shipyard by two civilian employees.   Justice Harlan's opinion for the Court first addressed the question "whether the extent of the privilege in respect of civil liability for statements allegedly defamatory under state law which may be claimed by officers of the federal government, acting in the course of their duties, is a question as to which the federal courts are bound to follow state law."   His response was brief:

> "We think that the very statement of the question dictates a negative answer.   The authority of a federal officer to act derives from federal sources, and the rule which recognizes a privilege under appropriate circumstances as to statements made in the course of duty is one designed to promote the effective functioning of the federal government.   No subject could be one of more peculiarly federal concern, and it would deny the very considerations which give the rule of privilege its being to leave determination of its extent to the vagaries of the laws of the several states.   Cf.   Clearfield Trust Co. v. United States, 318 U.S. 363 (1943).   We hold that the validity of petitioner's claim of absolute privilege must be judged by federal standards, to be formulated by the courts in the absence of legislative action by Congress."

The Court then held the Commander's statements absolutely privileged because made " 'in the discharge of [his] official duties and in relation to matters committed to him for determination.' "

(ii) ***Barr v. Mateo.***   Barr v. Mateo, 360 U.S. 564 (1959), was a companion case to *Howard* involving a similar situation.   In that case, Justice Harlan's plurality opinion summarized the reasons for judicial recognition of a federal defense to tort suits based on state law:

> "It has been thought important that officials of government should be free to exercise their duties unembarrassed by the fear of damage suits in respect of acts done in the course of those duties—suits which would consume time and energies which would otherwise be devoted to governmental service and the threat of which might appreciably inhibit the fearless, vigorous, and effective administration of policies of government.   The matter has been admirably expressed by Judge Learned Hand:
>
>> 'It does indeed go without saying that an official, who is in fact guilty of using his powers to vent his spleen upon others, or for any other personal motive not connected with the public good, should not escape liability for the injuries he may cause; and, if it were possible in practice to confine such complaints to the guilty, it would be monstrous to deny recovery.   The justification for doing so is that it is impossible to know whether the claim is well founded until the case has been tried, and that to submit

all officials, the innocent as well as the guilty, to the burden of a trial and to the inevitable danger of its outcome, would dampen the ardor of all but the most resolute, or the most irresponsible, in the unflinching discharge of their duties. Again and again the public interest calls for action which may turn out to be founded on mistake, in the face of which an official may later find himself hard put to it to satisfy a jury of his good faith. There must indeed be means of punishing public officers who have been truant to their duties; but that is quite another matter from exposing such as have been honestly mistaken to suit by anyone who has suffered from their errors. As is so often the case, the answer must be found in a balance between the evils inevitable in either alternative. In this instance it has been thought in the end better to leave unredressed the wrongs done by dishonest officers than to subject those who try to do their duty to the constant dread of retaliation. . . .' Gregoire v. Biddle, 177 F.2d 579, 581 (2d Cir. 1949)."

The Court held that the privilege should not be restricted to high-ranking officials, although the occasions for its invocation may increase with the rank of the official. "[T]hat is because," Harlan added, "the higher the post, the broader the range of responsibilities and duties, and the wider the scope of discretion it entails. It is not the title of the office but the duties with which the particular officer sought to be made to respond in damages is entrusted . . . which must provide the guide in delineating the scope of the [defense]." Harlan concluded:

"We are told that we should forbear from sanctioning any such rule of absolute privilege lest it open the door to whole-sale oppression and abuses on the part of unscrupulous government officials. It is perhaps enough to say that fears of this sort have not been realized within the wide area of government where a judicially formulated absolute privilege of broad scope has long existed. It seems to us wholly chimerical to suggest that what hangs in the balance here is the maintenance of high standards of conduct among those in the public service. To be sure, as with any rule of law which attempts to reconcile fundamentally antagonistic social policies, there may be occasional instances of actual injustice which will go unredressed, but we think that price a necessary one to pay for the greater good. And there are of course other sanctions than civil tort suits available to deter the executive official who may be prone to exercise his functions in an unworthy and irresponsible manner. We think that we should not be deterred from establishing the rule which we announce today by any such remote forebodings." [g]

[g] Justice Harlan wrote for a plurality of four. Justice Black would have gone further: "So far as I am concerned, if federal employees are to be subjected to such suits in reporting their views about how to run the government better, the restraint will

(iii) *Westfall v. Erwin.* In Westfall v. Erwin, ___ U.S. ___ (1988), Erwin and his wife brought a state-law tort suit for injuries allegedly suffered through the negligence of federal officials. Erwin was a civilian warehouseman at an Army depot. The defendant-officials were supervisors at the depot. As the suit came to the Supreme Court, the issue was "whether these federal officials are absolutely immune from liability under state tort law for conduct within the scope of their employment without regard to whether the challenged conduct was discretionary in nature."

Justice Marshall wrote the opinion for a unanimous Court. The Court held that "absolute immunity does not shield official functions from state tort liability unless the challenged conduct is within the outer perimeter of an official's duties and is discretionary in nature." Justice Marshall elaborated:

> "The purpose of such official immunity is not to protect an erring official, but to insulate the decisionmaking process from the harassment of prospective litigation. The provision of immunity rests on the view that the threat of liability will make federal officials unduly timid in carrying out their official duties, and that effective government will be promoted if officials are freed of the costs of vexatious and often frivolous damages suits. See *Barr v. Mateo.* This Court always has recognized, however, that official immunity comes at a great cost. An injured party with an otherwise meritorious tort claim is denied compensation simply because he had the misfortune to be injured by a federal official. Moreover, absolute immunity contravenes the basic tenet that individuals be held accountable for their wrongful conduct. We therefore have held that absolute immunity for federal officials is justified only when 'the contributions of immunity to effective government in particular contexts outweigh the perhaps recurring harm to individual citizens.' Doe v. McMillan, 412 U.S. 306, 320 (1973).[3] . . .
>
> The central purpose of official immunity, promoting effective government, would not be furthered by shielding an official from state-law tort liability without regard to whether the alleged tortious conduct is discretionary in nature. When an official's conduct is not the product of independent judgment, the threat of liability cannot detrimentally inhibit that con-

have to be imposed expressly by Congress and not by the general libel laws of the states. . . ." Chief Justice Warren and Justices Brennan and Stewart wrote separate dissents. Justice Douglas joined the dissent of the Chief Justice.

[3] "In determining the propriety of shielding an official from suit under the circumstances, this Court has long favored a 'functional' inquiry—immunity attaches to particular official functions, not to particular offices. The adoption of this functional approach reflects the Court's concern . . . that federal officials be granted absolute immunity only insofar as the benefits of immunity outweigh the costs. Because the benefits of official immunity lie principally in avoiding disruption of governmental functions, the inquiry into whether absolute immunity is warranted in a particular context depends on the degree to which the official function would suffer under the threat of prospective litigation."

duct. It is only when officials exercise decisionmaking discretion that potential liability may shackle 'the fearless, vigorous, and effective administration of policies of government.' Barr v. Mateo, 360 U.S. 564, 571 (1959). Because it would not further effective governance, absolute immunity for nondiscretionary functions finds no support in the traditional justification for official immunity."

3. Questions and Comments. By the time of *Clearfield* and *Parnell*, every state had adopted the Uniform Negotiable Instruments Law, later to be superseded by Article 3 of the Uniform Commercial Code. Given this body of relatively uniform state law, does the *Clearfield-Parnell* dichotomy make sense? Whatever the theory, would it be better simply to let state law apply to the rights and obligations of the federal government on its checks and bonds, as well as to the rights and obligations of private parties on the same instruments? Black and Douglas apparently would have preferred for federal law to apply across the board. Is that a better answer?

One might conclude from *Parnell, Wallis,* and *Miree* that the law could be summarized as follows: federal law applies to the rights and obligations of the federal government itself and state law, except where displaced by Congress, applies to the rights and obligations of private parties. The line of cases concerning the immunity of federal officials from suits based on state tort law illustrates the error of such a generalization. And *Boyle* seems further to confuse the issue. By what criteria does the Court determine when "federal common law" should apply to disputes among private parties? Is the Court consistent? Has it been right?

In the end, should the question be whether the Constitution requires a uniform federal law (as in the case of admiralty, for example) or whether there are valid federal policies that require this result? If so, how is the Court to determine the relevant federal policies? Should the problem be regarded as entirely contextual?

NOTES ON STATUTES OF LIMITATIONS FOR FEDERAL CLAIMS

1. *Agency Holding Corp. v. Malley-Duff & Associates.* There are many situations in which Congress has explicitly provided a federal remedy that can be asserted by one private party against another. Questions arising in suits based on such statutes are controlled by federal law, and the federal courts often are called on to resolve unanticipated disputes. One recurrent problem has been how the courts should deal with time limitations for such actions in cases where Congress has provided no explicit limit. The Court has been reluctant to conclude that no period of limitation should apply, and has been equally reluctant to specify a limitation in the absence of congressional guidance. Thus, it normally has turned to state law.

Agency Holding Corp. v. Malley-Duff & Associates, __ U.S. __ (1987), involved the statute of limitations applicable to a civil RICO claim.[a] Justice O'Connor's opinion for the Court summarized the prevailing approach to such issues as follows: "Given our longstanding practice of borrowing state law, and the congressional awareness of this practice, we can generally assume that Congress intends by its silence that we borrow state law." The question in such cases is which state limitations period to borrow, and that problem is compounded where the federal statute, as does RICO, covers many different types of behavior. Thus, the appropriate analogy to state law in one case might be different from the appropriate analogy in another case arising within the same state. The Court's response to this problem in other cases [b] has been to adopt a rule of uniformity within each state—that is, to adopt a single state statute of limitations in each state that applies to all claims under the federal statute arising in that state. This solution, however, was regarded by the Court as inappropriate for civil RICO. Here the Court thought that another *federal* statute offered the "closest analogy," and it therefore held that a civil RICO claim should be measured against the limitations period adopted by Congress in a different statute: "The federal policies at stake and the practicalities of litigation suggest that the limitations period of the Clayton Act [c] is a significantly more appropriate statute of limitations than any state limitations period."

Justice Scalia disagreed. He described the history of the Court's treatment of this issue as going through two phases. In the first, which he regarded as the theoretically correct approach to the problem, state statutes of limitation applied of their own force to federal claims in the absence of an intention by Congress to pre-empt state law:

> "So understood, the borrowing doctrine involves no borrowing at all. Instead, it only requires us to engage in two everyday interpretive exercises: the determination of which state statute of limitations applies to a federal claim as a matter of state law, and the determination of whether the federal statute creating the cause of action pre-empts the state limitations period. We need not embark on a quest for an 'appropriate' statute of limitations except to the limited extent that making those determinations may entail judgments as to which statute the state would believe 'appropriate' and as to

---

[a] The reference is to the Racketeer Influenced and Corrupt Organizations Act, 18 U.S.C. §§ 1962–68. RICO is a criminal statute providing severe penalties against enterprises that engage in a pattern of activity involving a wide variety of listed criminal offenses. Section 1964(c) provides a private treble damages remedy that can be asserted by "[a]ny person injured in his business or property by reason of a violation of" the criminal provisions. No statute of limitations for such an action is explicitly provided.

[b] See, e.g., Wilson v. Garcia, 471 U.S. 261 (1985).

[c] Congress provided a four-year limitations period in the Clayton Act. 15 U.S.C. § 15b. The Court buttressed its conclusion by references to legislative history, at one point observing that the " 'clearest current' in the legislative history of RICO 'is the reliance on the Clayton Act model.' Sedima, S.P.R.L. v. Imrex Co., 473 U.S. 479, 489 (1985)." [Footnote by eds.]

whether federal policy nevertheless makes that statute 'inappropriate.' Finally, if we determine that the state limitations period that would apply under state law is pre-empted because it is inconsistent with the federal statute, that is the end of the matter, and there is no limitation on the federal cause of action.

"In my view, that is the best approach to the question before us, and if a different historical practice had not intervened I would adhere to it. For many years, however, we have used a different analysis. In the second phase of development of the borrowing doctrine, perhaps forgetting its origins, the Court adopted the view that we borrow the 'appropriate' state statute of limitations when Congress fails to provide one because that is Congress' directive, implied by its silence on the subject. As an original matter, this is not a very plausible interpretation of congressional silence. If one did not believe that state limitations periods applied of their own force, the most natural intention to impute to a Congress that enacted no limitations period would be that it wished none. However, after a century and a half of the Court's reacting to congressional silence by applying state statutes—first for the right reason, and then for the wrong one—by now at least it *is* reasonable to say that such a result is what Congress must expect and hence intend, by its silence. The approach therefore has some legitimacy, and in any event generally produces the same results as the one I believe to be correct."

Applying this approach to the case at hand, Justice Scalia concluded that there should be no limitations period for civil RICO claims: "[I]f the basis of the rule is, in some form, that Congress knows that we will borrow state statutes of limitations unless it directs otherwise, it also knows that it has to direct otherwise if it wants us to do something else. In addition, . . . should we discover that there is no appropriate state statute to borrow, because [as here] all available ones run afoul of federal policy, we ought to conclude that there is no limitations period."

Justice Scalia objected strongly to the Court's solution:

"In the case before us, . . . the Court does not require any showing of congressional intent at all before departing from our practice of borrowing state statutes, prowling hungrily through the Statutes at Large for an appetizing federal limitations period, and pouncing on the Clayton Act. Of course, a showing of actual congressional intent that we depart from tradition and borrow a federal statute is quite impossible. Under ordinary principles of construction, the very identity between the language and structure of the Clayton Act and RICO's private civil-remedy provisions relied on by the Court as arguments for borrowing 15 U.S.C. § 15b, would, when coupled with Congress' enactment of a limitations period for the former and failure to enact one for the latter, demon-

strate—if any intent to depart from the state borrowing rule—
a desire for no limitations period at all."

Justice Scalia thought the choice of an analogous federal limitations
period inappropriate for two reasons. First, he could "find no legitimate source for the new rule." His second reason was more fundamental: the choice of an analogous federal limit "involves us in a very
different kind of enterprise from that required when we borrow state
law":

> "In general, the type of decision we face in the latter context is
> how to choose among various statutes of limitations, each of
> which was intended by the state legislature to apply to a whole
> category of causes of action. Federal statutes of limitations, on
> the other hand, are almost invariably tied to specific causes of
> action. [One] consequence of this distinction is that in practice
> the inquiry as to which state statute to select will be very close
> to the traditional kind of classification question courts deal
> with all the time. . . . In deciding whether to borrow a
> federal statute that clearly does not apply by its own terms,
> however, we genuinely will have to determine whether, for
> example, the Clayton Act's limitations period will better serve
> the policies underlying civil actions under RICO than the
> limitations period covering criminal actions under RICO, or
> whether either will do the job better than state limitations
> upon actions for economic injury. That seems to me quintes-
> sentially the kind of judgment to be made by a legisla-
> ture. . . .
>
> "Thus, while I can accept the reasons the Court gives for
> refusing to apply state statutes of limitations to the civil RICO
> claims at issue here, they lead me to a very different conclu-
> sion from that reached by the Court. I would hold that if state
> codes do not furnish an 'appropriate' limitations period, there
> is none to apply. Such an approach would promote uniformity
> as effectively as the borrowing of a federal statute, and would
> do a better job of avoiding litigation over limitations issues
> than the Court's approach. . . . Indeed, it might even
> prompt Congress to enact a limitations period that it believes
> 'appropriate,' a judgment far more within its competence than
> ours."

2. **Questions and Comments.** As the preceding discussion reveals, there were at least five options before the Court in the choice of a
statute of limitations for civil RICO actions: (i) the Court could have
left the matter entirely to state law applied of its own force; (ii) it could
have "borrowed" state law; (iii) it could have used federal standards to
select a particular limitations statute in each state, thus achieving
uniformity on all civil RICO actions within a particular state regardless
of subject matter; (iv) it could have held that there was no statute of
limitations; or (v) it could have, as it did, applied an analogous federal
statute of limitations. Did the Court make the right choice? Is what

the Court did any more beyond the appropriate competence of the Supreme Court, as Justice Scalia charges, than the decision in *Boyle?*

SECTION 3: CHOICE AMONG STATE LAWS

SUBSECTION A: CHOICE BY STATE COURTS

ALLSTATE INSURANCE CO. v. HAGUE
Supreme Court of the United States, 1981.
449 U.S. 302.

JUSTICE BRENNAN announced the judgment of the Court and delivered an opinion, in which JUSTICE WHITE, JUSTICE MARSHALL, and JUSTICE BLACKMUN joined.

This Court granted certiorari to determine whether the due process clause of the 14th amendment or the full faith and credit clause of art. IV, § 1, of the United States Constitution bars the Minnesota Supreme Court's choice of substantive Minnesota law to govern the effect of a provision in an insurance policy issued to respondent's decedent.

I

Respondent's late husband, Ralph Hague, died of injuries suffered when a motorcycle on which he was a passenger was struck from behind by an automobile. The accident occurred in Pierce County, Wis., which is immediately across the Minnesota border from Red Wing, Minn. The operators of both vehicles were Wisconsin residents, as was the decedent, who, at the time of the accident, resided with respondent in Hager City, Wis., which is one and one-half miles from Red Wing. Mr. Hague had been employed in Red Wing for the 15 years immediately preceding his death and had commuted daily from Wisconsin to his place of employment.

Neither the operator of the motorcycle nor the operator of the automobile carried valid insurance. However, the decedent held a policy issued by petitioner Allstate Insurance Co. covering three automobiles owned by him and containing an uninsured motorist clause insuring him against loss incurred from accidents with uninsured motorists. The uninsured motorist coverage was limited to $15,000 for each automobile.[3]

After the accident, but prior to the initiation of this lawsuit, respondent moved to Red Wing. Subsequently, she married a Minnesota resident and established residence with her new husband in Savage, Minn. At approximately the same time, a Minnesota Registrar of

---

[3] Ralph Hague paid a separate premium for each automobile including an addition-al separate premium for each uninsured motorist coverage.

Probate appointed respondent personal representative of her deceased husband's estate. Following her appointment, she brought this action in Minnesota District Court seeking a declaration under Minnesota law that the $15,000 uninsured motorist coverage on each of her late husband's three automobiles could be "stacked" to provide total coverage of $45,000. Petitioner defended on the ground that whether the three uninsured motorist coverages could be stacked should be determined by Wisconsin law, since the insurance policy was delivered in Wisconsin, the accident occurred in Wisconsin, and all persons involved were Wisconsin residents at the time of the accident.

The Minnesota District Court disagreed. Interpreting Wisconsin law to disallow stacking, the court concluded that Minnesota's choice-of-law rules required the application of Minnesota law permitting stacking. The court refused to apply Wisconsin law as "inimical to the public policy of Minnesota" and granted summary judgment for respondent.

The Minnesota Supreme Court, sitting en banc, affirmed the District Court. The court, also interpreting Wisconsin law to prohibit stacking, applied Minnesota law after analyzing the relevant Minnesota contacts and interests within the analytical framework developed by Professor Leflar. See Leflar, Choice-Influencing Considerations in Conflicts Law, 41 N.Y.U.L. Rev. 267 (1966). The state court, therefore, examined the conflict-of-laws issue in terms of (1) predictability of result, (2) maintenance of interstate order, (3) simplification of the judicial task, (4) advancement of the forum's governmental interests, and (5) application of the better rule of law. Although stating that the Minnesota contacts might not be, "in themselves sufficient to mandate application of [Minnesota] law,"[8] under the first four factors, the court concluded that the fifth factor—application of the better rule of law— favored selection of Minnesota law. The court emphasized that a majority of states allow stacking and that legal decisions allowing stacking "are fairly recent and well considered in light of current uses of automobiles." In addition, the court found the Minnesota rule superior to Wisconsin's "because it requires the cost of accidents with uninsured motorists to be spread more broadly through insurance premiums than does the Wisconsin rule." Finally, after rehearing en banc, the court buttressed its initial opinion by indicating "that contracts of insurance on motor vehicles are in a class by themselves" since an insurance company "knows the automobile is a movable item which will be driven from state to state." From this premise the court concluded that application of Minnesota law was "not so arbitrary and unreasonable as to violate due process."

II

It is not for this Court to say whether the choice-of-law analysis suggested by Professor Leflar is to be preferred or whether we would

---

[8] The court apparently was referring to sufficiency as a matter of choice-of-law and not as a matter of constitutional limitation on its choice-of-law decision.

make the same choice-of-law decision if sitting as the Minnesota Supreme Court. Our sole function is to determine whether the Minnesota Supreme Court's choice of its own substantive law in this case exceeded federal constitutional limitations. Implicit in this inquiry is the recognition, long accepted by this Court, that a set of facts giving rise to a lawsuit, or a particular issue within a lawsuit, may justify, in constitutional terms, application of the law of more than one jurisdiction. As a result, the forum state may have to select one law from among the laws of several jurisdictions having some contact with the controversy.

In deciding constitutional choice-of-law questions, whether under the due process clause or the full faith and credit clause,[10] this Court has traditionally examined the contacts of the state, whose law was applied, with the parties and with the occurrence or transaction giving rise to the litigation. In order to ensure that the choice of law is neither arbitrary nor fundamentally unfair, the Court has invalidated the choice of law of a state which has had no significant contact or significant aggregation of contacts, creating state interests, with the parties and the occurrence or transaction.[11]

Two instructive examples of such invalidation are Home Ins. Co. v. Dick, 281 U.S. 397 (1930), and John Hancock Mutual Life Ins. Co. v. Yates, 299 U.S. 178 (1936). In both cases, the selection of forum law rested exclusively on the presence of one nonsignificant forum contact.

[10] This Court has taken a similar approach in deciding choice-of-law cases under both the due process clause and the full faith and credit clause. In each instance, the Court has examined the relevant contacts and resulting interests of the state whose law was applied. Although at one time the Court required a more exacting standard under the full faith and credit clause than under the due process clause for evaluating the constitutionality of choice-of-law decisions, see Alaska Packers Assn. v. Industrial Accident Comm'n, 294 U.S. 532, 549–50 (1935) (interest of state whose law was applied was no less than interest of state whose law was rejected), the Court has since abandoned the weighing-of-interests requirement. Different considerations are of course at issue when full faith and credit is to be accorded to acts, records, and proceedings outside the choice-of-law area, such as in the case of sister state-court judgments.

[11] Prior to the advent of interest analysis in the state courts as the "dominant mode of analysis in modern choice of law theory," the prevailing choice-of-law methodology focused on the jurisdiction where a particular event occurred. For example, in cases characterized as contract cases, the law of the place of contracting controlled the determination of such issues as capacity, fraud, consideration, duty, performance, and the like. In the tort context, the law of the place of the wrong usually governed traditional choice-of-law analysis.

Hartford Accident and Indemnity Co. v. Delta & Pine Land Co., 292 U.S. 143 (1934), can, perhaps, best be explained as an example of that period. In that case, the Court struck down application by the Mississippi courts of Mississippi law which voided the limitations provision in a fidelity bond written in Tennessee between a Connecticut insurer and Delta, both of which were doing business in Tennessee and Mississippi. By its terms, the bond covered misapplication of funds "by any employee 'in any position, anywhere. . . . '" After Delta discovered defalcations by one of its Mississippi-based employees, a lawsuit was commenced in Mississippi.

That case, however, has scant relevance for today. It implied a choice-of-law analysis which, for all intents and purposes, gave an isolated event—the writing of the bond in Tennessee—controlling constitutional significance, even though there might have been contacts with another state (there Mississippi) which would make application of its law neither unfair nor unexpected.

Home Ins. Co. v. Dick involved interpretation of an insurance policy which had been issued in Mexico, by a Mexican insurer, to a Mexican citizen, covering a Mexican risk. The policy was subsequently assigned to Mr. Dick, who was domiciled in Mexico and "physically present and acting in Mexico," although he remained a nominal, permanent resident of Texas. The policy restricted coverage to losses occurring in certain Mexican waters and, indeed, the loss occurred in those waters. Dick brought suit in Texas against a New York reinsurer. Neither the Mexican insurer nor the New York reinsurer had any connection to Texas.[12] The Court held that application of Texas law to void the insurance contract's limitation-of-actions clause violated due process.

The relationship of the forum state to the parties and the transaction was similarly attenuated in *John Hancock Mutual Life Ins. Co. v. Yates.* There, the insurer, a Massachusetts corporation, issued a contract of insurance on the life of a New York resident. The contract was applied for, issued, and delivered in New York where the insured and his spouse resided. After the insured died in New York, his spouse moved to Georgia and brought suit on the policy in Georgia. Under Georgia law, the jury was permitted to take into account oral modifications when deciding whether an insurance policy application contained material misrepresentations. Under New York law, however, such misrepresentations were to be evaluated solely on the basis of the written application. The Georgia court applied Georgia law. This Court reversed, finding application of Georgia law to be unconstitutional.

Dick and *Yates* stand for the proposition that if a state has only an insignificant contact with the parties and the occurrence or transaction, application of its law is unconstitutional. *Dick* concluded that nominal residence—standing alone—was inadequate; *Yates* held that a post occurrence change of residence to the forum state—standing alone— was insufficient to justify application of forum law. Although instructive as extreme examples of selection of forum law, neither *Dick* nor *Yates* governs this case. For in contrast to those decisions, here the Minnesota contacts with the parties and the occurrence are obviously significant. Thus, this case is like cases where this Court sustained choice-of-law decisions based on the contacts of the state, whose law was applied, with the parties and occurrence.

In Alaska Packers Assn. v. Industrial Accident Comm'n, 294 U.S. 532 (1935), the Court upheld California's application of its Workmen's Compensation Act, where the most significant contact of the worker with California was his execution of an employment contract in California. The worker, a nonresident alien from Mexico, was hired in California for seasonal work in a salmon canning factory in Alaska. As

[12] Dick sought to obtain quasi-in-rem jurisdiction by garnishing the reinsurance obligation of the New York reinsurer. The reinsurer had never transacted business in Texas, but it "was cited by publication, in accordance with a Texas statute; attorneys were appointed for it by the trial court; and they filed on its behalf an answer which denied liability." There would be no jurisdiction in the Texas Courts to entertain such a lawsuit today. See Rush v. Savchuk, 444 U.S. 320 (1980); Shaffer v. Heitner, 433 U.S. 186 (1977).

part of the employment contract, the employer, who was doing business in California, agreed to transport the worker to Alaska and to return him to California when the work was completed. Even though the employee contracted to be bound by the Alaska Workmen's Compensation Law and was injured in Alaska, he sought an award under the California Workmen's Compensation Act. The Court held that the choice of California law was not "so arbitrary or unreasonable as to amount to a denial of due process," because "[w]ithout a remedy in California [he] would be remediless," and because of California's interest that the worker not become a public charge.[15]

Similarly, Clay v. Sun Insurance Office, Ltd., 377 U.S. 179 (1964), upheld the constitutionality of the application of forum law. There, a policy of insurance had issued in Illinois to an Illinois resident. Subsequently the insured moved to Florida and suffered a property loss in Florida. Relying explicitly on the nationwide coverage of the policy and the presence of the insurance company in Florida and implicitly on the plaintiff's Florida residence and the occurrence of the property loss in Florida, the Court sustained the Florida court's choice of Florida law.

The lesson from *Dick* and *Yates*, which found insufficient forum contacts to apply forum law, and from *Alaska Packers* . . . and *Clay*, which found adequate contacts to sustain the choice of forum law, is that for a state's substantive law to be selected in a constitutionally permissible manner, that state must have a significant contact or significant aggregation of contacts, creating state interests, such that choice of its law is neither arbitrary nor fundamentally unfair. Application of this principle to the facts of this case persuades us that the Minnesota Supreme Court's choice of its own law did not offend the federal Constitution.

III

Minnesota has three contacts with the parties and the occurrence giving rise to the litigation. In the aggregate, these contacts permit selection by the Minnesota Supreme Court of Minnesota law allowing the stacking of Mr. Hague's uninsured motorist coverages.

First, and for our purposes a very important contact, Mr. Hague was a member of Minnesota's workforce, having been employed by a Red Wing, Minn., enterprise for the 15 years preceding his death. While employment status may implicate a state interest less substantial than does resident status, that interest is nevertheless important. The state of employment has police power responsibilities towards the nonresident employee that are analogous, if somewhat less profound, than towards residents. Thus, such employees use state services and amenities and may call upon state facilities in appropriate circumstances.

---

[15] The Court found no violation of the full faith and credit clause, since California's interest was considered to be no less than Alaska's, even though the injury occurred in Alaska while the employee was performing his contract obligations there. While *Alaska Packers* balanced the interests of California and Alaska to determine the full faith and credit issue, such balancing is no longer required.

In addition, Mr. Hague commuted to work in Minnesota . . . and was presumably covered by his uninsured motorist coverage during the commute. The state's interest in its commuting nonresident employees reflects a state concern for the safety and well-being of its work force and the concomitant effect on Minnesota employers.

That Mr. Hague was not killed while commuting to work or while in Minnesota does not dictate a different result. To hold that the Minnesota Supreme Court's choice of Minnesota law violated the Constitution for that reason would require too narrow a view of Minnesota's relationship with the parties and the occurrence giving rise to the litigation. An automobile accident need not occur within a particular jurisdiction for that jurisdiction to be connected to the occurrence. Similarly, the occurrence of a crash fatal to a Minnesota employee in another state is a Minnesota contact. If Mr. Hague had only been injured and missed work for a few weeks, the effect on the Minnesota employer would have been palpable and Minnesota's interest in having its employee made whole would be evident. Mr. Hague's death affects Minnesota's interest still more acutely, even though Mr. Hague will not return to the Minnesota work force. Minnesota's work force is surely affected by the level of protection the state extends to it, either directly or indirectly. Vindication of the rights of the estate of a Minnesota employee, therefore, is an important state concern.

Mr. Hague's residence in Wisconsin does not—as Allstate seems to argue—constitutionally mandate application of Wisconsin law to the exclusion of forum law.[21] If, in the instant case, the accident had occurred in Minnesota between Mr. Hague and an uninsured Minnesota motorist, if the insurance contract had been executed in Minnesota covering a Minnesota registered company automobile which Mr. Hague was permitted to drive, and if a Wisconsin court sought to apply Wisconsin law, certainly Mr. Hague's residence in Wisconsin, his commute between Wisconsin and Minnesota, and the insurer's presence in Wisconsin should be adequate to apply Wisconsin's law.[22] Employment

[21] Petitioner's statement that the instant dispute involves the interpretation of insurance contracts which were "underwritten, applied for, and paid for by Wisconsin residents and issued covering cars garaged in Wisconsin," is simply another way of stating that Mr. Hague was a Wisconsin resident. Respondent could have replied that the insurance contract was underwritten, applied for and paid for by a Minnesota worker and issued covering cars that were driven to work in Minnesota and garaged there for a substantial portion of the day. The former statement is hardly more significant than the latter since the accident in any event did not involve any of the automobiles which were covered under Mr. Hague's policy. Recovery is sought pursuant to the uninsured motorist coverage.

In addition, petitioner's statement that the contracts were "underwritten . . . by Wisconsin residents" is not supported by the stipulated facts if petitioner means to include itself within that phrase. Indeed, the policy, which is part of the record, recites that Allstate signed the policy in Northbrook, Ill. Under some versions of the hoary rule of lex loci contractus, and depending on the precise sequence of events, a sequence which is unclear from the record before us, the law of Illinois arguably might apply to govern contract construction, even though Illinois would have less contact with the parties and the occurrence than either Wisconsin or Minnesota. No party sought application of Illinois law on that basis in the court below.

[22] Of course Allstate could not be certain that Wisconsin law would necessarily govern any accident which occurred in Wisconsin, whether brought in the Wisconsin courts or elsewhere. Such an expectation

status is not a sufficiently less important status than residence, when combined with Mr. Hague's daily commute across state lines and the other Minnesota contacts present, to prohibit the choice-of-law result in this case on constitutional grounds.

Second, Allstate was at times present and doing business in Minnesota.[23] By virtue of its presence, Allstate can hardly claim unfamiliarity with the laws of the host jurisdiction and surprise that the state courts might apply forum law to litigation in which the company is involved. "Particularly since the company was licensed to do business in [the forum], it must have known it might be sued there, and that [the forum] courts would feel bound by [forum] law."[24] Moreover, Allstate's presence in Minnesota gave Minnesota an interest in regulating the company's insurance obligations insofar as they affected both a Minnesota resident and court-appointed representative—respondent—and a longstanding member of Minnesota's work force—Mr. Hague.

Third, respondent became a Minnesota resident prior to institution of this litigation. The stipulated facts reveal that she first settled in Red Wing, Minn., the town in which her late husband had worked.[26]

would give controlling significance to the wooden lex loci delicti doctrine. While the place of the accident is a factor to be considered in choice-of-law analysis, to apply blindly the traditional, but now largely abandoned, doctrine, would fail to distinguish between the relative importance of various legal issues involved in a lawsuit as well as the relationship of other jurisdictions to the parties and the occurrence or transaction. If, for example, Mr. Hague had been a Wisconsin resident and employee who was injured in Wisconsin and was then taken by ambulance to a hospital in Red Wing, Minn., where he languished for several weeks before dying, Minnesota's interest in ensuring that its medical creditors were paid would be obvious. Moreover, under such circumstances, the accident itself might be reasonably characterized as a bistate occurrence beginning in Wisconsin and ending in Minnesota. Thus, reliance by the insurer that Wisconsin law would necessarily govern any accident that occurred in Wisconsin, or that the law of another jurisdiction would necessarily govern any accident that did not occur in Wisconsin, would be unwarranted.

If the law of a jurisdiction other than Wisconsin did govern, there was a substantial likelihood, with respect to uninsured motorist coverage, that stacking would be allowed. Stacking was the rule in most states at the time the policy was issued. Indeed, the Wisconsin Supreme Court identified 29 states, including Minnesota, whose law it interpreted to allow stacking, and only nine states whose law it interpreted to prohibit stacking. Clearly then, Allstate could not have expected that an antistacking rule would govern any particular accident in which the insured might be involved and thus cannot claim unfair surprise from the Minnesota Supreme Court's choice of forum law.

[23] The Court has recognized that examination of a state's contacts may result in divergent conclusions for jurisdiction and choice-of-law purposes. Nevertheless, "both inquiries 'are often closely related and to a substantial degree depend upon similar considerations.'" Here, of course, jurisdiction in the Minnesota courts is unquestioned, a factor not without significance in assessing the constitutionality of Minnesota's choice of its own substantive law.

[24] There is no element of unfair surprise or frustration of legitimate expectations as a result of Minnesota's choice of its law. Because Allstate was doing business in Minnesota and was undoubtedly aware that Mr. Hague was a Minnesota employee, it had to have anticipated that Minnesota law might apply to an accident in which Mr. Hague was involved. Indeed, Allstate specifically anticipated that Mr. Hague might suffer an accident either in Minnesota or elsewhere in the United States, outside of Wisconsin, since the policy it issued offered continental coverage. At the same time, Allstate did not seek to control construction of the contract since the policy contained no choice-of-law clause dictating application of Wisconsin law.

[26] The stipulated facts do not reveal the date on which Mrs. Hague first moved to Red Wing.

She subsequently moved to Savage, Minn., after marrying a Minnesota resident who operated an automobile service station in Bloomington, Minn. Her move to Savage occurred "almost concurrently" with the initiation of the instant case.[27] There is no suggestion that Mrs. Hague moved to Minnesota in anticipation of this litigation or for the purpose of finding a legal climate especially hospitable to her claim.[28] The stipulated facts, sparse as they are, negate any such inference.

While *John Hancock Mutual Life Ins. Co. v. Yates,* supra, held that a postoccurrence change of residence to the forum state was insufficient in and of itself to confer power on the forum state to choose its law, that case did not hold that such a change of residence was irrelevant. Here, of course, respondent's bona fide residence in Minnesota was not the sole contact Minnesota had with this litigation. And in connection with her residence in Minnesota, respondent was appointed personal representative of Mr. Hague's estate by the Registrar of Probate for the County of Goodhue, Minn. Respondent's residence and subsequent appointment in Minnesota as personal representative of her late husband's estate constitute a Minnesota contact which gives Minnesota an interest in respondent's recovery, an interest which the court below identified as full compensation for "resident accident victims" to keep them "off welfare rolls" and able "to meet financial obligations."

In sum, Minnesota had a significant aggregation[29] of contacts with the parties and the occurrence, creating state interests, such that application of its law was neither arbitrary nor fundamentally unfair. Accordingly, the choice of Minnesota law by the Minnesota Supreme Court did not violate the due process clause or the full faith and credit clause.

Affirmed.

JUSTICE STEWART took no part in the consideration or decision of this case.

JUSTICE STEVENS, concurring in the judgment.

As I view this unusual case—in which neither precedent nor constitutional language provides sure guidance—two separate questions must be answered. First, does the full faith and credit clause *require* Minnesota, the forum state, to apply Wisconsin law? Second, does the due process clause of the 14th amendment *prevent* Minnesota from applying its own law? The first inquiry implicates the federal interest in ensuring that Minnesota respect the sovereignty of the state of

---

[27] These proceedings began on May 28, 1976. Mrs. Hague was remarried on June 19, 1976.

[28] The dissent suggests that considering respondent's postoccurrence change of residence as one of the Minnesota contacts will encourage forum shopping. This overlooks the fact that her change of residence was bona fide and not motivated by litigation considerations.

[29] We express no view whether the first two contacts, either together or separately, would have sufficed to sustain the choice of Minnesota law made by the Minnesota Supreme Court.

Wisconsin; the second implicates the litigants' interest in a fair adjudication of their rights.[3]

I realize that both this Court's analysis of choice-of-law questions and scholarly criticism of those decisions have treated these two inquiries as though they were indistinguishable. Nevertheless, I am persuaded that the two constitutional provisions protect different interests and that proper analysis requires separate consideration of each.

I

The full faith and credit clause is one of several provisions in the federal Constitution designed to transform the several states into a single, unified nation. The full faith and credit clause implements this design by directing that a state, when acting as the forum for litigation having multistate aspects or implications, respect the legitimate interests of other states and avoid infringement upon their sovereignty. The clause does not, however, rigidly require the forum state to apply foreign law whenever another state has a valid interest in the litigation. On the contrary, in view of the fact that the forum state is also a sovereign in its own right, in appropriate cases it may attach paramount importance to its own legitimate interests. Accordingly, the fact that a choice-of-law decision may be unsound as a matter of conflicts law does not necessarily implicate the federal concerns embodied in the full faith and credit clause. Rather, in my opinion, the clause should not invalidate a state court's choice of forum law unless that choice threatens the federal interest in national unity by unjustifiably infringing upon the legitimate interests of another state.

In this case, I think the Minnesota courts' decision to apply Minnesota law was plainly unsound as a matter of normal conflicts law. Both the execution of the insurance contract and the accident giving rise to the litigation took place in Wisconsin. Moreover, when both of those events occurred, the plaintiff, the decedent, and the operators of both vehicles were all residents of Wisconsin. Nevertheless, I do not believe that any threat to national unity or Wisconsin's sovereignty ensues from allowing the substantive question presented by this case to be determined by the law of another state.

The question on the merits is one of interpreting the meaning of the insurance contract. Neither the contract itself, nor anything else in the record, reflects any express understanding of the parties with respect to what law would be applied or with respect to whether the

---

[3] The two questions presented by the choice-of-law issue arise only after it is assumed or established that the defendant's contacts with the forum state are sufficient to support personal jurisdiction. Although the choice-of-law concerns—respect for another sovereign and fairness to the litigants—are similar to the two functions performed by the jurisdictional inquiry, they are not identical. In World-Wide Volkswagen Corp. v. Woodson, 444 U.S. 286, 291–92 (1980), we stated:

"The concept of minimum contacts, in turn, can be seen to perform two related, but distinguishable, functions. It protects the defendant against the burdens of litigating in a distant or inconvenient forum. And it acts to ensure that the states, through their courts, do not reach out beyond the limits imposed on them by their status as coequal sovereigns in a federal system."

separate uninsured motorist coverage for each of the decedent's three cars could be "stacked." Since the policy provided coverage for accidents that might occur in other states, it was obvious to the parties at the time of contracting that it might give rise to the application of the law of states other than Wisconsin. Therefore, while Wisconsin may have an interest in ensuring that contracts formed in Wisconsin in reliance upon Wisconsin law are interpreted in accordance with that law, that interest is not implicated in this case.

Petitioner has failed to establish that Minnesota's refusal to apply Wisconsin law poses any direct or indirect threat to Wisconsin's sovereignty. In the absence of any such threat, I find it unnecessary to evaluate the forum state's interest in the litigation in order to reach the conclusion that the full faith and credit clause does not require the Minnesota courts to apply Wisconsin law to the question of contract interpretation presented in this case.

II

It may be assumed that a choice-of-law decision would violate the due process clause if it were totally arbitrary or if it were fundamentally unfair to either litigant. I question whether a judge's decision to apply the law of his own state could ever be described as wholly irrational. For judges are presumably familiar with their own state law and may find it difficult and time consuming to discover and apply correctly the law of another state. The forum state's interest in the fair and efficient administration of justice is therefore sufficient, in my judgment, to attach a presumption of validity to a forum state's decision to apply its own law to a dispute over which it has jurisdiction.

The forum state's interest in the efficient operation of its judicial system is clearly not sufficient, however, to justify the application of a rule of law that is fundamentally unfair to one of the litigants. Arguably, a litigant could demonstrate such unfairness in a variety of ways. Concern about the fairness of the forum's choice of its own rule might arise if that rule favored residents over nonresidents, if it represented a dramatic departure from the rule that obtains in most American jurisdictions, or if the rule itself was unfair on its face or as applied.

The application of an otherwise acceptable rule of law may result in unfairness to the litigants if, in engaging in the activity which is the subject of the litigation, they could not reasonably have anticipated that their actions would later be judged by this rule of law. A choice-of-law decision that frustrates the justifiable expectations of the parties can be fundamentally unfair. This desire to prevent unfair surprise to a litigant has been the central concern in this Court's review of choice-of-law decisions under the due process clause.[16]

16 Upon careful analysis, most of the decisions of this Court that struck down on due process grounds a state court's choice of forum law can be explained as attempts to prevent a state with a minimal contact with the litigation from materially enlarging the contractual obligations of one of the parties where the party had no reason to anticipate the possibility of such enlargement.

Neither the "stacking" rule itself, nor Minnesota's application of that rule to these litigants, raises any serious question of fairness. As the plurality observes, "[s]tacking was the rule in most states at the time the policy was issued." Moreover, the rule is consistent with the economics of a contractual relationship in which the policyholder paid three separate premiums for insurance coverage for three automobiles, including a separate premium for each uninsured motorist coverage. Nor am I persuaded that the decision of the Minnesota courts to apply the "stacking" rule in this case can be said to violate due process because that decision frustrates the reasonable expectations of the contracting parties.

Contracting parties can, of course, make their expectations explicit by providing in their contract either that the law of a particular jurisdiction shall govern questions of contract interpretation, or that a particular substantive rule, for instance "stacking" shall or shall not apply. In the absence of such express provisions, the contract nonetheless may implicitly reveal the expectations of the parties. For example, if a liability insurance policy issued by a resident of a particular state provides coverage only with respect to accidents within that state, it is reasonable to infer that the contracting parties expected that their obligations under the policy would be governed by that state's law.

In this case, no express indication of the parties' expectations is available. The insurance policy provided coverage for accidents throughout the United States; thus, at the time of contracting, the parties certainly could have anticipated that the law of states other than Wisconsin would govern particular claims arising under the policy.[22] By virtue of doing business in Minnesota, Allstate was aware that it could be sued in the Minnesota courts; Allstate also presumably was aware that Minnesota law, as well as the law of most states, permitted "stacking." Nothing in the record requires that a different inference be drawn. Therefore, the decision of the Minnesota courts to apply the law of the forum in this case does not frustrate the reasonable expectations of the contracting parties, and I can find no fundamental unfairness in that decision requiring the attention of this Court.[23]

[22] In Clay v. Sun Ins. Office, Ltd., 377 U.S. 179 (1964), the loss to which the insurance applied actually occurred in the forum state, whereas the accident in this case occurred in Wisconsin, not Minnesota. However, as the dissent recognizes, because the question on the merits is one of contract interpretation rather than tort liability, the actual site of the accident is not dispositive with respect to the due process inquiry. More relevant is the fact that the parties, at the time of contracting, anticipated that an accident covered by the policy could occur in a "stacking" state. The fact that this particular accident did not occur in Minnesota does not undercut the expectations formed by the parties at the time of contracting.

[23] Comparison of this case with Home Ins. Co. v. Dick, 281 U.S. 397 (1930); confirms my conclusion that the application of Minnesota law in this case does not offend the due process clause. In *Home Ins. Co.,* the contract expressly provided that a particular limitations period would govern claims arising under the insurance contract and that Mexican law was to be applied in interpreting the contract; in addition, the contract was limited in effect to certain Mexican waters. The parties could hardly have made their expectations with respect to the applicable law more plain. In this case, by way of contrast, nothing in the contract suggests that Wisconsin law should be applied or that Minnesota's "stacking" rule should not be applied. In

In terms of fundamental fairness, it seems to me that two factors relied upon by the plurality—the plaintiff's post-accident move to Minnesota and the decedent's Minnesota employment—are either irrelevant to or possibly even tend to undermine the plurality's conclusion. When the expectations of the parties at the time of contracting are the central due process concern, as they are in this case, an unanticipated post-accident occurrence is clearly irrelevant for due process purposes. The fact that the plaintiff became a resident of the forum state after the accident surely cannot justify a ruling in her favor that would not be made if the plaintiff were a nonresident. Similarly, while the fact that the decedent regularly drove into Minnesota might be relevant to the expectations of the contracting parties,[24] the fact that he did so because he was employed in Minnesota adds nothing to the due process analysis. The choice-of-law decision of the Minnesota courts is consistent with due process because it does not result in unfairness to either litigant, not because Minnesota now has an interest in the plaintiff as resident or formerly had an interest in the decedent as employee.

III

Although I regard the Minnesota courts' decision to apply forum law as unsound as a matter of conflicts law, and there is little in this record other than the presumption in favor of the forum's own law to support that decision, I concur in the plurality's judgment. It is not this Court's function to establish and impose upon state courts a federal choice-of-law rule, nor is it our function to ensure that state courts correctly apply whatever choice-of-law rules they have themselves adopted. Our authority may be exercised in the choice-of-law area only to prevent a violation of the full faith and credit or the due process clause. For the reasons stated above, I find no such violation in this case.

JUSTICE POWELL, with whom THE CHIEF JUSTICE and JUSTICE REHNQUIST join, dissenting.

My disagreement with the plurality is narrow. I accept with few reservations Part II of the plurality opinion, which sets forth the basic principles that guide us in reviewing state choice-of-law decisions under the Constitution. The Court should invalidate a forum state's decision to apply its own law only when there are no significant contacts between the state and the litigation. This modest check on state power

---

this case, unlike *Home Ins. Co.*, the court's choice of forum law results in no unfair surprise to the insurer.

[24] Even this factor may not be of substantial significance. At the time of contracting, the parties were aware that the insurance policy was effective throughout the United States and that the law of any state, including Minnesota, might be applicable to particular claims. The fact that the decedent regularly drove to Minnesota, for whatever purpose, is relevant only to the extent that it affected the parties' evaluation, at the time of contracting, of the likelihood that Minnesota law would actually be applied at some point in the future. However, because the applicability of Minnesota law was perceived as possible at the time of contracting, it does not seem especially significant for due process purposes that the parties may also have considered it likely that Minnesota law would be applied. This factor merely reinforces the expectation revealed by the policy's national coverage.

is mandated by the due process clause of the 14th amendment and the full faith and credit clause of art. IV, § 1. I do not believe, however, that the plurality adequately analyzes the policies such review must serve. In consequence, it has found significant what appear to me to be trivial contacts between the forum state and the litigation.

I

[T]he Court has recognized that both the due process and the full faith and credit clauses are satisfied if the forum has such significant contacts with the litigation that it has a legitimate state interest in applying its own law. The significance of asserted contacts must be evaluated in light of the constitutional policies that oversight by this Court should serve. Two enduring policies emerge from our cases.

First, the contacts between the forum state and the litigation should not be so "slight and casual" that it would be fundamentally unfair to a litigant for the forum to apply its own state's law. The touchstone here is the reasonable expectation of the parties. Thus, in Clay v. Sun Ins. Office, Ltd., 377 U.S. 179 (1964), the insurer sold a policy to Clay "with knowledge that he could take his property anywhere in the world he saw fit without losing the protection of his insurance." When the insured moved to Florida with the knowledge of the insurer, and a loss occurred in that state, this Court found no unfairness in Florida's applying its own rule of decision to permit recovery on the policy. The insurer "must have known it might be sued there."[1]

Second, the forum state must have a legitimate interest in the outcome of the litigation before it. The full faith and credit clause addresses the accommodation of sovereign power among the various states. Under limited circumstances, it requires one state to give effect to the statutory law of another state. To be sure, a forum state need not give effect to another state's law if that law is in "violation of its own legitimate public policy." Nonetheless, for a forum state to further its legitimate public policy by applying its own law to a controversy, there must be some connection between the facts giving rise to the litigation and the scope of the state's lawmaking jurisdiction.

Both the due process and full faith and credit clauses ensure that the states do not "reach out beyond the limits imposed on them by their status as coequal sovereigns in a federal system." As the Court [has] stated: "[T]he full faith and credit clause does not require one state to substitute for its own statute, *applicable to persons and events within it,* the conflicting statute of another state." The state has a legitimate

---

[1] Home Ins. Co. v. Dick, 281 U.S. 397 (1930), is a case where the reasonable expectations of a litigant were frustrated. The insurance contract confined the risk to Mexico, where the loss occurred and where both the insurer and the insured resided until the claim accrued. This Court found a violation of the due process clause when Texas, the forum state, applied a local rule to allow the insured to gain a recovery unavailable under Mexican law. Because of the geographic limitation on the risk, and because there were no contacts with the forum state until the claim accrued, the insurer could have had no reasonable expectation that Texas law would be applied to interpret its obligation under the contract.

interest in applying a rule of decision to the litigation only if the facts to which the rule will be applied have created effects within the state, toward which the state's public policy is directed. To assess the sufficiency of asserted contacts between the forum and the litigation, the Court must determine if the contacts form a reasonable link between the litigation and a state policy. In short, examination of contacts addresses whether "the state has an interest in the application of its policy in this instance."

John Hancock Mut. Ins. Co. v. Yates, 299 U.S. 178 (1936), illustrates this principle. A life insurance policy was executed in New York, on a New York insured with a New York beneficiary. The insured died in New York; his beneficiary moved to Georgia and sued to recover on the policy. The insurance company defended on the ground that the insured, in the application for the policy, had made materially false statements that rendered it void under New York law. This Court reversed the Georgia court's application of its contrary rule that all questions of the policy's validity must be determined by the jury. The Court found a violation of the full faith and credit clause, because "[i]n respect to the accrual of the right asserted under the contract . . . there was no occurrence, nothing done, to which the law of Georgia could apply." In other words, the Court determined that Georgia had no legitimate interest in applying its own law to the legal issue of liability. Georgia's contacts with the contract of insurance were nonexistent.

In summary, the significance of the contacts between a forum state and the litigation must be assessed in light of these two important constitutional policies.[3] A contact, or a pattern of contacts, satisfies the Constitution when it protects the litigants from being unfairly surprised if the forum state applies its own law, and when the application of the forum's law reasonably can be understood to further a legitimate public policy of the forum state.

II

Recognition of the complexity of the constitutional inquiry requires that this Court apply these principles with restraint. Applying these principles to the facts of this case, I do not believe, however, that Minnesota had sufficient contacts with the "persons and events" in this litigation to apply its rule permitting stacking. I would agree that no reasonable expectations of the parties were frustrated. The risk insured by petitioner was not geographically limited. The close proximity of Hager City, Wis., to Minnesota, and the fact that Hague commuted daily to Red Wing, Minn., for many years should have led the

---

[3] The plurality today apparently recognizes that the significance of the contacts must be evaluated in light of the policies our review serves. It acknowledges that the sufficiency of the same contacts sometimes will differ in jurisdiction and choice-of-law questions. The plurality, however, pursues the rationale for the requirement of sufficient contacts in choice-of-law cases no further than to observe that the forum's application of its own law must be "neither arbitrary nor fundamentally unfair." But this general prohibition does not distinguish questions of choice of law from those of jurisdiction, or from much of the jurisprudence of the 14th amendment.

insurer to realize that there was a reasonable probability that the risk would materialize in Minnesota. Under our precedents, it is plain that Minnesota could have applied its own law to an accident occurring within its borders. The fact that the accident did not, in fact, occur in Minnesota is not controlling because the expectations of the litigants *before* the cause of action accrues provide the pertinent perspective.

The more doubtful question in this case is whether application of Minnesota's substantive law reasonably furthers a legitimate state interest. The plurality attempts to give substance to the tenuous contacts between Minnesota and this litigation. Upon examination, however, these contacts are either trivial or irrelevant to the furthering of any public policy of Minnesota.

First, the post-accident residence of the plaintiff-beneficiary is constitutionally irrelevant to the choice-of-law question. The plurality today insists that *Yates* only held that a post-occurrence move to the forum state could not "in and of itself" confer power on the forum to apply its own law, but did not establish that such a change of residence was irrelevant. What the *Yates* Court held, however, was that "there was no occurrence, *nothing* done, to which the law of Georgia could apply." Any possible ambiguity in the Court's view of the significance of a post-occurrence change of residence is dispelled by *Home Ins. Co. v. Dick,* cited by the *Yates* Court, where it was held squarely that Dick's post-accident move to the forum state was "without significance."

This rule is sound. If a plaintiff could choose the substantive rules to be applied to an action by moving to a hospitable forum, the invitation to forum shopping would be irresistible. Moreover, it would permit the defendant's reasonable expectations at the time the cause of action accrues to be frustrated, because it would permit the choice-of-law question to turn on a post-accrual circumstance. Finally, post-accrual residence has nothing to do with facts to which the forum state proposes to apply its rule; it is unrelated to the substantive legal issues presented by the litigation.

Second, the plurality finds it significant that the insurer does business in the forum state. The state does have a legitimate interest in regulating the practices of such an insurer. But this argument proves too much. The insurer here does business in all 50 states. The forum state has no interest in regulating that conduct of the insurer unrelated to property, persons or contracts executed within the forum state.[4] The plurality recognizes this flaw and attempts to bolster the significance of the local presence of the insurer by combining it with the other factors deemed significant: the presence of the plaintiff and the fact that the deceased worked in the forum state. This merely restates the basic question in the case.

[4] The petitioner in *Yates* did business in Georgia, the forum state, at the time of that case. Also, Georgia extensively regulated insurance practices within the state at that time. This Court did not hint in *Yates* that this fact was of the slightest significance to the choice-of-law question, although it would have been crucial for the exercise of in personam jurisdiction.

Third, the plurality emphasizes particularly that the insured worked in the forum state.[5] The fact that the insured was a nonresident employee in the forum state provides a significant contact for the furtherance of some local policies. [E.g., compensation for employment related injuries.] The insured's place of employment is not, however, significant in this case. Neither the nature of the insurance policy, the events related to the accident, nor the immediate question of stacking coverage is in any way affected or implicated by the insured's employment status. The plurality's opinion is understandably vague in explaining how trebling the benefits to be paid to the estate of a nonresident employee furthers any substantial state interest relating to employment. Minnesota does not wish its workers to die in automobile accidents, but permitting stacking will not further this interest. The substantive issue here is solely one of compensation, and whether the compensation provided by this policy is increased or not will have no relation to the state's employment policies or police power.

Neither taken separately nor in the aggregate do the contacts asserted by the plurality today indicate that Minnesota's application of its substantive rule in this case will further any legitimate state interest.[6] The plurality focuses only on physical contacts vel non, and in doing so pays scant attention to the more fundamental reasons why our precedents require reasonable policy-related contacts in choice-of-law cases. Therefore, I dissent.

NOTES ON CHOICE OF LAW AND THE CONSTITUTION

1. **Background on Choice of Law.** As Justice Brennan indicates in footnote 11 of his plurality opinion in *Hague,* the common law governing choice of law has undergone dramatic change. The traditional theory was quite rigid, at least in form. It went something like this: Each state has the power to determine the legal effect of acts within its territory, and conversely no power to attach legal effects to

[5] The Court exacts double service from this fact, by finding a separate contact in that the insured commuted daily to his job. This is merely a repetition of the facts that the insured lived in Wisconsin and worked in Minnesota. The state does have an interest in the safety of motorists who use its roads. This interest is not limited to employees, but extends to all nonresident motorists on its highways. This safety interest, however, cannot encompass, either in logic or in any practical sense, the determination whether a nonresident's estate can stack benefit coverage in a policy written in another state regarding an accident that occurred on another state's roads.

[6] The opinion of Justice Stevens concurring in the judgment supports my view that the forum state's application of its own law to this case cannot be justified by the existence of relevant minimum contacts. As Justice Stevens observes, the principal factors relied on by the plurality are "either irrelevant or possibly even tend to undermine the [plurality's] conclusion." The interesting analysis he proposes to uphold the state's judgment is, however, difficult to reconcile with our prior decisions and may create more problems than it solves. For example, it seems questionable to measure the interest of a state in a controversy by the degree of conscious reliance on that state's law by private parties to a contract. Moreover, scrutinizing the strength of the interests of a nonforum state may draw this Court back into the discredited practice of weighing the relative interests of various states in a particular controversy.

acts outside its territory. Whether a tort is committed or a contract made therefore turns on whether events given that significance occurred in a particular state. Once they have occurred, the law of that state governs no matter where litigation might arise. The theory was that "vested rights" were created when the events occurred, "rights" that could not be disturbed by another sovereign. This theory drew on notions of "territorial sovereignty" that governed the powers of one state as they related to the powers of another.

Thus stated, the theory sounds deceptively simple. The problems are well illustrated by the facts of Alabama Great Southern R.R. v. Carroll, 97 Ala. 126, 11 So. 803 (1892). Carroll, who lived in Alabama, was a brakeman on a freight train that ran from Birmingham, Alabama, to Meridian, Mississippi. His employer was an Alabama corporation. He was injured when a link between two cars of the train broke. The break was caused by a defect that existed when the train left Birmingham, a defect that should have been discovered by railroad employees whose specific job it was to inspect for such defects at various points along the train's route. The link broke and the injury occurred after the train had entered Mississippi. Recovery was sought in an Alabama state court under an Alabama workman's compensation statute. Mississippi had no such statute, but followed the traditional common law rule that precluded recovery for the negligence of fellow servants.

Whose law should apply in this situation? Mississippi's, because the injury occurred there and Mississippi is therefore the place of the tort? Or should Alabama law apply because the suit is not really a tort action at all, but a contract action based on an employment relation established in Alabama? Does the action *really* sound in tort or contract, or might the characterization depend on where one wanted to come out?

As Justice Brennan also indicates in footnote 11 of his *Hague* opinion, the old "territorial" or "vested rights" approach to choice of law problems has in large part been replaced by various forms of "interest analysis." The basic approach was invented by Professor Brainard Currie, whose major articles have been collected in a book entitled "Selected Essays on Conflict of Laws" published in 1963.

The key to Currie's approach is to ask what governmental policies are at stake among those jurisdictions with a connection to the controversy. When one does so, the cases will fall into one of three categories: (1) cases in which no state's policy would be advanced by the decision ("no interest" cases); (2) cases in which one state's policy can be advanced without impairing the policies of any other state ("false conflict" cases, so named because there is no conflict among the applicable policies in such a situation); and (3) cases in which the policies of more than one state are implicated and where a decision in favor of the policies of one state would necessarily undermine the policies of another ("true conflict" cases).

How would Currie's approach be applied to the *Carroll* situation? It is clear that Alabama has several significant interests, including those of compensating its citizens and regulating employer-employee relationships within its borders. Does Mississippi have any interest in the outcome of the litigation? If not, the case presents a false conflict, and Alabama law should apply. Would it matter if Carroll were hospitalized in Mississippi and as a result had accumulated significant debts there? Would it change the analysis if Mississippi permitted a more generous recovery than Alabama? If some of the acts of negligence occurred in Mississippi?

It is clear at some point that a "true" conflict can be developed by various hypothetical variations on the facts of *Carroll.* What is to be done in such a case? This is a question with which Currie was never able to come to rest. Do the questions suggested by Leflar and adopted by the Minnesota Supreme Court in *Hague* help? More importantly for present purposes, would an "interest analysis" applied by a Mississippi court in a "true conflict" situation be likely to produce the same answer as would be reached by an Alabama court in the same case? Would it be surprising if both courts applied their own law?

2. Background on the Constitution. The old "vested rights" theory held out the promise that the same state's law would apply no matter where the controversy was litigated. In fact, this was unlikely to be the case for at least three reasons: the doctrines were subject to manipulation (as by characterizing *Carroll* as a contracts case rather than a torts case); they were subject to numerous exceptions (such as, the forum will not enforce a law that is contrary to its deeply held public policy); and the forum remained free to apply its own procedural rules to any litigation (which opened an opportunity for more characterization and manipulation).

The Supreme Court nonetheless flirted with adoption of the vested rights theory as a matter of constitutional compulsion. For example, New York Life Ins. Co. v. Dodge, 246 U.S. 357 (1918), was essentially a substantive due process holding that a New York insurance company could insist on the application of New York law to insurance agreements "made" there even though they affected the rights of insureds who lived in other states. Perhaps the last significant decision of this genre was Hartford Accident & Indemnity Co. v. Delta & Pine Land Co., 292 U.S. 143 (1934), which Justice Brennan distinguishes from *Hague* in footnote 11 of his opinion.

The turning point came in the *Alaska Packers* decision, discussed in Justice Brennan's opinion in *Hague* at footnote 15 and its accompanying text. Most of the cases since then have taken the position that any state with a sufficient interest in the litigation can apply its own law if it chooses to do so. And in spite of all the sophisticated variations in interest analysis that have emerged, most states, as did the Minnesota Supreme Court in *Hague,* make that choice most of the time.

3. The Role of the Supreme Court. In his Benjamin Cardozo lecture before the Association of the Bar of the City of New York in 1945, Justice Jackson outlined the options available to the Supreme Court in the choice-of-law area:

> "That the Supreme Court should impose uniformity in choice-of-law problems is a prospect comforting to none, least of all to a member of that body. . . . But the available courses from which our choice may be made seem to me limited. One is that we will leave choice of law in all cases to the local policy of the state. This seems to me to be at odds with the implication of our federal system that the mutual limits of the states' powers are defined by the Constitution. It also seems productive of confusion, for it means that choice among conflicting substantive rules depends only upon which state happens to have the last word. . . . A second course is that we will adopt no rule, permit a good deal of overlapping and confusion, but interfere now and then, without imparting to the bar any reason by which the one or the other course is to be guided or predicted. This seems to me about where our present decisions leave us. Third, we may candidly recognize that choice-of-law questions, when properly raised, ought to and do present constitutional questions under the full faith and credit clause which the Court may properly decide and as to which it ought at least to mark out reasonably narrow limits of permissible variation in areas where there is confusion. . . ."

Jackson, Full Faith and Credit—The Lawyer's Clause of the Constitution, 45 Colum. L. Rev. 1, 26–27 (1945).

Though he indicated that he was inclined towards the third choice, Justice Jackson was vague about its implementation. What should the Court do in this area? Is it tolerable to permit the disuniformity, and consequent forum-shopping, to which decisions like *Hague* lead? Professor Baxter, in Choice of Law and the Federal System, 16 Stan. L. Rev. 1, 23 (1963), suggests by way of analogy that "[b]aseball's place as the favorite American pastime would not long survive if the responsibilities of the umpire were transferred to the first team member who managed to rule on a disputed event."

On the other hand, consider the alternatives. It is clear that Congress has the authority under the full faith and credit clause to enact a uniform system of choice of law. Would it be easy to draft legislation that would get the right answer in both *Carroll* and *Hague*, as well as the thousands of other variations that will arise? Would it be better for the Supreme Court to resolve the situations on a case-by-case basis?

Consider the burden on the Court were it to do so. How many transactions in American society today have contacts with more than one state and therefore potentially involve a choice-of-law question? How many conflicts cases can the Supreme Court review? Is it likely that the district courts and circuit courts could aid in enforcement of the principles the Supreme Court might develop? Could the state courts be expected to do so?

From another perspective, would it be proper for the Court to allocate law-making competence among the several states? Is that what it would be doing if it adopted a uniform system of choice of law? What would be its source of authority for such a step?

Finally, if one were persuaded that the Court should take an approach that is more limited than dictating a comprehensive, uniform choice-of-law system, what more limited role should the Court play? Should it adopt Justice Jackson's first approach and stay out of the area entirely? Should it adopt one or the other of the approaches in *Hague?* [a]

NOTE ON RECOGNITION OF JUDGMENTS

In the last sentence of footnote 10 of his opinion in *Hague*, Justice Brennan recognizes that "different considerations" govern when recognition of state court judgments is at stake. Some background on this issue may help to put Justice Brennan's point in perspective.

The Court has taken an entirely different approach when a cause of action has been reduced to judgment and the meaning of that judgment becomes relevant to subsequent litigation. The rule it follows can be stated simply: A second court is obligated to give the same effect to a prior judgment as the court that rendered the judgment would give it. There are, of course, exceptions, such as a holding that the first court lacked jurisdiction. But the basic structure is simple and straightforward and totally unlike the structure governing choice of law in initial litigation. Fundamentally, the Court has adopted a hands-off policy (subject to whatever limits can be derived from cases such as *Hague*) to recognition of the *laws* of another state, but has adopted a hands-on policy requiring full recognition (with limited exceptions) of the *judgments* of the courts of another state.

Why should this be so? The answer requires consideration of 28 U.S.C. § 1738. Today that statute reads in relevant part:

> "The acts of the legislature of any State, Territory, or Possession of the United States, [and the] records and judicial proceedings of any court of any such State, Territory or Possession . . . shall have the same full faith and credit in every court within the United States and its Territories and Possessions as they have by law or usage in the courts of such State, Territory or Possession from which they are taken."

---

[a] For discussion of the problem presented by *Hague*, see Patricia Youngblood, Constitutional Constraints on Choice of Law: the Nexus Between *World Wide Volkswagon Corp. v. Woodson* and *Allstate Insurance Co. v. Hague*, 50 Albany L. Rev. 1 (1985).

For a more general argument that constitutional limitations on choice-of-law decisions should be taken seriously, see James R. Pielemeier, Why We Should Worry About Full Faith and Credit to Laws, 60 S.Cal.L.Rev. 1299 (1987).

Note that this statute requires both state and federal courts ("*every court* within the United States") to give full faith and credit to prior state court judgments.[a] The statute is also explicit about the recognition that is due: it must be "the same" as the judgment would "have by law or usage in the courts" by which it was rendered.[b] The result, therefore, is that the local law of res judicata is given extraterritorial application; the preclusive effect that obtains locally must be recognized in any subsequent litigation in which the judgment becomes relevant.

One reason the Court has adopted an interventionist position with respect to prior judgments is that Congress by statute has required that result.[c] There are, moreover, at least three additional reasons that can be advanced in support of the Court's position:

(i) The problems associated with recognition of judgments are less controversial and easier to solve than are choice-of-law issues that arise during litigation. It seems clear that res judicata is in general a sound policy, and that it is right to require courts to enforce prior judgments. Unlike general choice-of-law problems, in other words, this issue has an easy answer.

(ii) Half a loaf is better than none. Uniformity is a desirable goal, and the fact that the courts cannot or will not achieve that objective in the general choice-of-law system is not a reason to abandon that goal with respect to recognition of judgments.

(iii) Inconsistent judgments, enforceable by contempt, would put litigants in an intolerable position. It is bad

---

[a] The meaning of federal court judgments is dictated by principles of federal common law, which other federal courts are required to respect and which are binding on state courts by virtue of the supremacy clause. The net result is that essentially the same approach is required no matter what court rendered the first judgment and no matter what court is to give effect to that judgment.

[b] Some of the exceptions to the recognition requirement can easily be reconciled with this statutory language. For example, a state judgment entered without in personam jurisdiction over the defendant could not constitutionally be given effect by the rendering court. It follows that no other court need respect such a judgment. It is less clear how some of the other exceptions can be reconciled. For example, a judgment in excess of state-imposed subject-matter limitations on a state court's jurisdiction may not have to be recognized in another state or federal court even though it is not subject to collateral attack under state law. See Thompson v. Whitman, 85 U.S. (18 Wall.) 457 (1873).

[c] Notice that the statute could also be interpreted to require that the "same effect" be given to local *laws*, i.e., that Congress meant to enjoin the Court to create and enforce a uniform national choice-of-law system. The statute has not been so interpreted, however, as the *Hague* case illustrates. One reason for this, perhaps, is technical. The statute was first enacted in 1790, and originally required that full faith and credit be given only to "records and judicial proceedings." The word "acts" was added in 1948, without debate and with no apparent intent to do more than conform the statute to the constitutional language of the full faith and credit clause. Thus, for a long period of our history, it was possible to regard Congress as not having spoken to the choice-of-laws issue. When Congress did speak to the issue in 1948, moreover, it did not explicitly direct the Court to develop a uniform national choice-of-law system. In any event, it seems likely that the Court has chosen for policy reasons not to become embroiled in the problem of creating and enforcing such a system.

enough, to be sure, that one may not be able to predict rights and obligations in advance of litigation. It would be more plainly intolerable if one were not able to do so *after* litigation.

Is it therefore clear that judgments should be treated differently than laws? Is it rational to have a system that requires full faith and credit to another state's judgments, but that in other respects effectively allows each state to pursue its own policy goals in litigation before its courts even though the goals of other states might thereby be undermined?[d]

NOTES ON THE DUTY OF STATE COURTS TO HEAR STATE CASES

1. *Hughes v. Fetter.* In Hughes v. Fetter, 341 U.S. 609 (1951), an administrator brought an action based on the Illinois wrongful death statute in a Wisconsin state court against an allegedly negligent automobile driver and his insurance company. The accident occurred in Illinois. The Wisconsin trial court dismissed the complaint "on the merits"[a] based on a Wisconsin statute "which creates a right of action only for deaths caused in that state [and which] establishes a local public policy against Wisconsin's entertaining suits brought under the wrongful death acts of other states." The dismissal was affirmed by the Wisconsin Supreme Court.

The Supreme Court reversed five-four in an opinion by Justice Black:

"We are called upon to decide the narrow question whether Wisconsin . . . can close the doors of its courts to the cause of action created by the Illinois wrongful death act.[4] Prior decisions have established that the Illinois statute is a 'public act' within the provision of art. IV, § 1 that 'Full Faith and Credit shall be given in each State to the public Acts . . . of every other State." It is also settled that Wisconsin cannot escape this constitutional obligation to enforce the rights and duties validly created under the laws of other states by the simple device of removing jurisdiction from courts otherwise competent. We have recognized, however, that full faith and credit does not automatically compel a forum state to subordinate its own statutory policy to a conflicting public act of another state; rather, it is for this Court to choose in each case between the competing public policies involved. The clash of

---

[d] For discussion of the differences in the constitutional treatment of judgments and laws, see Lea Brilmayer, Credit Due Judgments and Credit Due Laws: The Respective Roles of Due Process and Full Faith and Credit in the Interstate Context, 70 Iowa L. Rev. 95 (1984).

[a] The Supreme Court did not explain why the dismissal was "on the merits" or exactly what "on the merits" meant in this context.

[4] "The parties concede, as they must, that if the same cause of action had previously been reduced to judgment, the full faith and credit clause would compel the courts of Wisconsin to entertain an action to enforce it."

interests in cases of this type has usually been described as a conflict between the public policies of two or more states. The more basic conflict involved in the present appeal, however, is as follows: On the one hand is the strong unifying principle embodied in the full faith and credit clause looking toward maximum enforcement in each state of the obligations or rights created or recognized by the statutes of sister states; on the other hand is the policy of Wisconsin, as interpreted by its highest court, against permitting Wisconsin courts to entertain this wrongful death action.[10]

"We hold that Wisconsin's policy must give way. That state has no real feeling of antagonism against wrongful death suits in general. To the contrary, a forum is regularly provided for cases of this nature, the exclusionary rule extending only so far as to bar actions for death not caused locally. The Wisconsin policy, moreover, cannot be considered as an application of the forum non conveniens doctrine, whatever effect that doctrine might be given if its use resulted in denying enforcement to public acts of other states. Even if we assume that Wisconsin could refuse, by reason of particular circumstances, to hear foreign controversies to which nonresidents were parties, the present case is not one lacking a close relationship with the state. For not only were appellant, the decedent and the individual defendant all residents of Wisconsin, but also appellant was appointed administrator and the corporate defendant was created under Wisconsin laws. We also think it relevant, although not crucial here, that Wisconsin may well be the only jurisdiction in which service could be had as an original matter on the insurance company defendant. And while in the present case jurisdiction over the individual defendant apparently could be had in Illinois by substituted service, in other cases Wisconsin's exclusionary statute might amount to a deprivation of all opportunity to enforce valid death claims created by another state.

"Under these circumstances, we conclude that Wisconsin's statutory policy which excludes this Illinois cause of action is forbidden by the national policy of the full faith and credit clause. The judgment is reversed and the cause is remanded to the Supreme Court of Wisconsin for proceedings not inconsistent with this opinion."[b]

Justice Frankfurter wrote a dissent for himself and for Justices Reed, Jackson, and Minton. He wrote:

[10] "The present case is not one where Wisconsin, having entertained appellant's lawsuit, chose to apply its own instead of Illinois' statute to measure the substantive rights involved. This distinguishes the present case from those where we have said that 'Prima facie every state is entitled to enforce in its own courts its own statutes, lawfully enacted.' Alaska Packers Assn. v. Industrial Accident Comm'n, 294 U.S. 532, 547 (1935)."

[b] The Court reached a similar result in reliance on *Hughes* in First National Bank v. United Air Lines, 342 U.S. 396 (1952). [Footnote by eds.]

"This Court has, with good reason, gone far in requiring that the courts of a state respect judgments entered by courts of other states. But the extent to which a state must recognize and enforce the rights of action created by other states is not so clear. . . .

"This Court should certainly not require that the forum deny its own law and follow the tort law of another state where there is a reasonable basis for the forum to close its courts to the foreign cause of action. The decision of Wisconsin to open its courts to actions for wrongful deaths within the state but close them to actions for deaths outside the state may not satisfy everyone's notion of wise policy. But it is neither novel nor without reason. Compare the similar Illinois statute. . . . Wisconsin may be willing to grant a right of action where witnesses will be available in Wisconsin and the courts are acquainted with a detailed local statute and cases construing it. It may not wish to subject residents to suit where out-of-state witnesses will be difficult to bring before the court, and where the court will be faced with the alternative of applying a complex foreign statute—perhaps inconsistent with that of Wisconsin on important issues—or fitting the statute to the Wisconsin pattern. The legislature may well feel that it is better to allow the courts of the state where the accident occurred to construe and apply its own statute, and that the exceptional case where the defendant cannot be served in the state where the accident occurred does not warrant a general statute allowing suit in the Wisconsin courts. The various wrongful death statutes are inconsistent on such issues as beneficiaries, the party who may bring suit, limitations on liability, comparative negligence, and the measure of damages.

"No claim is made that Wisconsin has discriminated against the citizens of other states and thus violated art. IV, § 2 of the Constitution. Nor is a claim made that the lack of a forum in Wisconsin deprives the plaintiff of due process. Nor is it argued that Wisconsin is flouting a federal statute. The only question before us is how far the full faith and credit clause undercuts the purpose of the Constitution, made explicit by the 10th amendment, to leave the conduct of domestic affairs to the states. Few interests are of more dominant local concern than matters governing the administration of law. This vital interest of the states should not be sacrificed in the interest of a merely literal reading of the full faith and credit clause.

"There is no support, either in reason or in the cases, for holding that this Court is to make a de novo choice between the policies underlying the laws of Wisconsin and Illinois. . . ."

Is *Hughes* consistent with *Hague?* How is it possible for the Court to hold that Wisconsin can apply its own law to the controversy, as apparently would follow from *Hague* and *Alaska Packers* (see the Court's footnote 10 in *Hughes*), but that it cannot refuse to adjudicate the suit? Does it matter that the Wisconsin judgment appears to have been "on the merits"? Would it matter if Wisconsin were the only place all of the potential defendants could be sued in one proceeding? Or is *Hughes* simply wrong by modern standards?

2. *Wells v. Simonds Abrasive Co.* Wells was killed in Alabama by a grinding wheel with which he was working. The wheel had been manufactured by the Simonds Abrasive Company, a Pennsylvania corporation. Wells' administratrix was unable under then-prevailing Alabama law to serve Simonds in Alabama, so she sued in a federal District Court in Pennsylvania alleging diversity of citizenship. The action was filed more than one year after the accident, but less than two years. The limitations period on the Alabama statutory wrongful death action was two years. The Pennsylvania limitations period was only one year.

The District Court granted summary judgment for the defendant. Its rationale was that it was required to apply the conflicts rules of Pennsylvania and that Pennsylvania required that the Pennsylvania and not the Alabama statute of limitations be applied. The District Court accordingly dismissed the complaint. The Circuit Court affirmed. In Wells v. Simonds Abrasive Co., 345 U.S. 514 (1953), the Supreme Court affirmed. The opinion by Chief Justice Vinson reasoned:

> "The states are free to adopt such rules of conflict of laws as they choose, subject to the full faith and credit clause and other constitutional restrictions. The full faith and credit clause does not compel a state to adopt any particular set of rules of conflict of laws; it merely sets certain minimum requirements which each state must observe when asked to apply the law of a sister state. . . .

> "The rule that the limitations of the forum apply . . . is the usual conflicts rule of the states. However, there have been divergent views when a foreign statutory right unknown to the common law has a period of limitation included in the section creating the right. The Alabama statute here involved creates such a right and contains a built-in limitation. The view is held in some jurisdictions that such a limitation is so intimately connected with the right that it must be enforced in the forum state along with the substantive right.

> "We are not concerned with the reasons which have led some states for their own purposes to adopt the foreign limitation, instead of their own, in such a situation. The question here is whether the full faith and credit clause compels them to do so. Our prevailing rule is that the full faith and credit clause does not compel the forum state to use the period of

limitation of a foreign state. We see no reason in the present situation to graft an exception onto it. Differences based upon whether the foreign right was known to the common law or upon the arrangement of the code of the foreign state are too unsubstantial to form the basis for constitutional distinctions under the full faith and credit clause. . . .

"Our decisions in *Hughes v. Fetter* and *First National Bank v. United Airlines* [see page 355 n.b, supra] do not call for a change in the well-established rule that the forum state is permitted to apply its own period of limitation. The crucial factor in those two cases was that the forum laid an uneven hand on causes of action arising within and without the forum state. Causes of action arising in sister states were discriminated against. Here Pennsylvania applies her one-year limitation to all wrongful death actions wherever they may arise. . . ."

Justice Jackson, joined by Justices Black and Minton, argued in dissent that the District Court was not required to follow the Pennsylvania conflicts rule.

Assume that the District Court was obligated to follow the conflicts rules of Pennsylvania and that a Pennsylvania court would have dismissed the action, applying its own period of limitations. Could a Pennsylvania court do so consistently with *Hughes?* Is it rational to force a state to hear an action based on a statute of another state, but then allow it to decide the case under its own law or dismiss it under its own statute of limitations? Are *Hughes* and *Wells* as readily distinguishable as Chief Justice Vinson's opinion makes out? Why is it discrimination not to hear the case, but not discrimination to dismiss it under the local statute of limitations?

Whether the federal District Court should have applied the Pennsylvania conflicts rules in the first place is the subject of the next main case.

SUBSECTION B: CHOICE BY FEDERAL COURTS

KLAXON CO. v. STENTOR ELECTRIC MANUFACTURING CO., INC.
United States Supreme Court, 1941.
313 U.S. 487.

MR. JUSTICE REED delivered the opinion of the Court.

The principal question in this case is whether in diversity cases the federal courts must follow conflict of laws rules prevailing in the states in which they sit. . . .

In 1918 respondent, a New York corporation, transferred its entire business to petitioner, a Delaware corporation. Petitioner contracted to use its best efforts to further the manufacture and sale of certain patented devices covered by the agreement, and respondent was to have a share of petitioner's profits. The agreement was executed in New York, the assets were transferred there, and petitioner began performance there although later it moved its operations to other states. Respondent was voluntarily dissolved under New York law in 1919. Ten years later it instituted this action in the United States District Court for the District of Delaware, alleging that petitioner had failed to perform its agreement to use its best efforts. Jurisdiction rested on diversity of citizenship. In 1939 respondent recovered a jury verdict of $100,000, upon which judgment was entered. Respondent then moved to correct the judgment by adding interest at the rate of six per cent from June 1, 1929, the date the action had been brought. The basis of the motion was the provision in the New York Civil Practice Act directing that in contract actions interest be added to the principal sum "whether theretofore liquidated or unliquidated." The District Court granted the motion, taking the view that the rights of the parties were governed by New York law and that under New York law the addition of such interest was mandatory. The Circuit Court of Appeals affirmed and we granted certiorari, limited to the question whether the New York Civil Practice Act is applicable to an action in the federal court in Delaware.

The Circuit Court of Appeals was of the view that under New York law the right to interest before verdict went to the substance of the obligation, and that proper construction of the contract in suit fixed New York as the place of performance. It then concluded that [New York law] was applicable to the case because:

> "it is clear by what we think is undoubtedly the better view of the law that the rules for ascertaining the measure of damages are not a matter of procedure at all, but are matters of substance which should be settled by reference to the law of the appropriate state according to the type of case being tried in the forum. The measure of damages for breach of a contract is determined by the law of the place of performance."

The court referred also to [a section] of the Restatement,[a] which makes interest part of the damages to be determined by the law of the place of performance. Application of the New York statute apparently followed from the court's independent determination of the "better view" without regard to Delaware law, for no Delaware decision or statute was cited or discussed.

We are of opinion that the prohibition declared in Erie Railroad Co. v. Tompkins, 304 U.S. 64 (1938), against such independent determinations by the federal courts, extends to the field of conflict of laws. The conflict of laws rules to be applied by the federal court in Delaware

[a] The reference is to the first Restatement of Conflict of Laws, which adopts the "vested rights" approach to choice of law issues. [Footnote by eds.]

must conform to those prevailing in Delaware's state courts. Otherwise the accident of diversity of citizenship would constantly disturb equal administration of justice in co-ordinate state and federal courts sitting side by side. Any other ruling would do violence to the principle of uniformity within a state, upon which the *Tompkins* decision is based. Whatever lack of uniformity this may produce between federal courts in different states is attributable to our federal system, which leaves to a state, within the limits permitted by the Constitution, the right to pursue local policies diverging from those of its neighbors. It is not for the federal courts to thwart such local policies by enforcing an independent "general law" of conflict of laws. Subject only to review by this Court on any federal question that may arise, Delaware is free to determine whether a given matter is to be governed by the law of the forum or some other law. This Court's views are not the decisive factor in determining the applicable conflicts rule. And the proper function of the Delaware federal court is to ascertain what the state law is, not what it ought to be. . . .

Accordingly, the judgment is reversed and the case remanded to the Circuit Court of Appeals for decision in conformity with the law of Delaware.

Reversed.

———

NOTES ON CHOICE OF LAW BY FEDERAL COURTS

1. **Comments and Questions on *Klaxon*.** *Klaxon* has come to stand for the proposition that when federal courts are bound by *Erie* to use state law they are also obligated to use the conflict of laws rules of the forum state. The Court has not wavered from this conclusion. Is this the right answer? One way to think about the problem is to consider the alternatives. Is this a situation where the Court was forced to an undesirable solution only because the other possible solutions were even more unacceptable?

Consider the situation in Sampson v. Channell, 110 F.2d 754 (1st Cir. 1940), a pre-*Klaxon* case in which the court anticipated the holding in *Klaxon*. *Sampson* involved the burden of proof on contributory negligence. The suit was brought in a federal court in Massachusetts based on diversity jurisdiction, and concerned an automobile accident that occurred in Maine. It was clear that Maine put the burden of proof on the plaintiff and Massachusetts on the defendant. But it was also clear that Massachusetts, though it would have followed Maine law on the "substantive" issues in the case, regarded the burden of proof as "procedural" under its conflicts rules and hence would have put the burden on the defendant had the suit been filed in a Massachusetts state court. The First Circuit concluded that it was required by *Erie* to follow state law on the questions of substantive law involved in the case, and that allocation of the burden of proof was "substantive" in this sense. The question then was which state's law should be used, Massachusetts or Maine? Anticipating the result in *Klaxon*, the court held that it must apply the conflicts rules of the forum state. It then held that Massachusetts law must be applied on the burden of proof question because the Massachusetts conflicts rules classified it as "procedural." The court noted that it might seem "to present a surface incongruity" to apply Massachusetts law first because it was "substantive" and then because it was "procedural," but concluded that it had no choice given the policies of *Erie.*

Is something funny going on, or is the court's analysis correct? Is this what the Supreme Court would have done after *Klaxon?*

2. ***Griffin v. McCoach.*** Griffin v. McCoach, 313 U.S. 498 (1941), was decided on the same day as *Klaxon* and was also written by Justice Reed for a unanimous Court (Justice Frankfurter concurred in the result without opinion). The suit was filed in a federal District Court in Texas by the personal representatives of a decedent against the Prudential Life Insurance Company to collect on a life insurance policy. Prudential invoked statutory interpleader, naming various other claimants to the money, paying the money into court, and withdrawing from the suit. Some of the claimants lacked an "insurable interest" in the decedent under Texas law. They acquired their interests in New York under contracts that apparently were valid there.

The lower courts held that the contracts were to be interpreted according to the laws of New York, and enforced the claimants' interests accordingly. The Supreme Court reversed. It held first that for the reasons given in *Klaxon* :

> "[W]e are of the view that the federal courts in diversity of citizenship cases are governed by the conflict of laws rules of the courts in which they sit. In deciding that the . . . laws of Texas could not be applied to a foreign contract in Texas courts, the [lower] courts were applying rules of law in a way which may or may not have been consistent with Texas decisions. [I]t is for Texas to say whether its public policy permits a beneficiary of an insurance policy on the life of a Texas citizen to recover where no insurable interest in the decedent exists in the beneficiary. . . . The decision must be reversed and remanded to the Circuit Court of Appeals for determination of the law of Texas as applied to the circumstances of this case."

The Court went on to hold that it would not be unconstitutional for Texas to refuse to enforce the New York contract if it offended the public policy of Texas.

The reason the *Griffin* case is interesting is that it appears that one or more of the claimants to the policy had insufficient contacts with Texas to have justified an in personam suit against them in the courts of that state. An ordinary in personam action to cut off their interests in the policy therefore could not have been brought against them in a Texas state or federal court. But since service of process is nationwide in federal statutory interpleader cases, they were amenable to this procedure in a federal district court in Texas. The irony, therefore, is that Texas law could be applied to foreclose their interests in a situation where that result could not have obtained had they been sued in Texas directly by the other claimants to the policy. The Court's opinion in *Griffin* made no mention of this anomaly, nor did it mention the fact that some of the parties may have been beyond the power of the Texas courts.

Note that there are at least two other situations where this situation might arise. The first results from the so-called "bulge" provision of Rule 4(f) of the Federal Rules of Civil Procedure. That provision applies in impleader cases under Rule 14, that is, in situations where the defendant seeks to implead as a third-party defendant someone who is or may be liable to the defendant if the plaintiff prevails. Additionally, the bulge provision applies to joinder of necessary parties under Rule 19. In these situations, Rule 4(f) permits the third-party defendant to be served at any place within a 100–mile radius of the place where the action was commenced or to which it has been transferred, whether or not a state line must be crossed. The second situation is a suit filed on a federal cause of action where nationwide service of process is permitted, in which claims based on state law are also asserted based on a theory of pendent jurisdiction. It is possible in both of these cases for a person to be required to defend in a federal court in a state which could not—under either its own statutory policies or by reason of constitutional limitations—independently assert in personam jurisdiction. If *Klaxon* applies, as *Griffin* apparently contemplates, the law of a state that could not itself get control over the defendant might be applied to the detriment of the defendant's interests.

Does it make sense to apply *Klaxon* to these situations? What else could a federal court do? Suppose a defendant who is sued in federal court in state X could also have been sued in two other states, and that the law the two states would apply is different. If the forum's conflicts law is not to be used by the federal court, by what criteria could that court select a law to be applied?

A related context in which the same problems can arise is mass tort litigation in which multiple lawsuits are consolidated in a single federal court. Barbara Ann Atwood has addressed this situation in The Choice-of-Law Dilemma in Mass Tort Litigation: Kicking Around *Erie*, *Klaxon*, and *Van Dusen*, 19 Conn.L.Rev. 9 (1986). Her solution is the abandonment of *Klaxon* in this context and the development of a federal common law under which applicable state rules of law would be chosen. See also Rowe and Sibley, Beyond Diversity: Federal Multiparty, Multiforum Jurisdiction, 135 U.Pa.L.Rev. 7, 37–41 (1986). For the more extreme suggestion that Congress "should authorize the creation of a federal common law of torts for mass-tort cases," see Linda Mullenix, Class Resolution of the Mass-Tort Case: A Proposed Federal Procedure Act, 64 Texas L.Rev. 1039, 1077 (1986).

3. *Van Dusen v. Barrack.* Section 1404(a) of Title 28 provides that "[f]or the convenience of parties and witnesses, in the interest of justice, a district court may transfer any civil action to any other district or division where it might have been brought." Normally, motions to transfer under this section are made by defendants. Van Dusen v. Barrack, 376 U.S. 612 (1964), was such a case. It involved claims by the personal representatives of 40 Pennsylvania decedents killed in a plane crash in Boston. They filed an action in a Pennsylvania federal District Court. More than 100 actions against the same defendants were pending in a Massachusetts District Court. Massachusetts placed a $20,000 ceiling on any recovery for wrongful death, whereas Pennsylvania law permitted recovery based on compensation for losses incurred without any prescribed limitation. It was unclear whether the Pennsylvania state courts would apply their own law to the limitation question—as cases from some other states had done—or whether they would apply the law of the place where the accident occurred (Massachusetts).

One of the questions before the Supreme Court was whether, if the case were transferred to Massachusetts, the conflicts principles of the transferor forum (Pennsylvania) or the transferee forum (Massachusetts) should be applied. The Court's answer was that Pennsylvania conflicts principles should be applied—that plaintiffs should be entitled to retain whatever advantages they are entitled to by virtue of the forum they selected, and correspondingly that defendants should not be entitled to secure a change of law by a successful motion to change the location of the suit. It followed that the criteria governing whether a transfer was appropriate would have to take the applicable law into account. If, for example, Pennsylvania would apply its own law, consolidation of the cases might be less desirable, since a single jury would have to be instructed under two applicable legal systems. And the testimony of witnesses located in Pennsylvania on the damages suffered by each estate would be more relevant if Pennsylvania law was to control.

Did the Court get the right answer? The Court reserved decision on what would happen if the plaintiff requested transfer, if it appeared that the transferor forum would have dismissed the action on grounds of forum non conveniens, or if application of the transferor forum's law would offend constitutional limitations on choice of law. The Court also did not address the choice of law implications of a transfer under 28 U.S.C. § 1406(a) ("The district court of a district in which is filed a case laying venue in the wrong division or district shall dismiss, or if it be in the interest of justice, transfer such case to any district or division in which it could have been brought"). How should these situations be resolved? [a]

4. Borrowed State Law. Federal courts occasionally borrow state law to be applied as the federal rule of decision. Thus, for example, the Court in DeSylva v. Ballentine, 351 U.S. 570 (1956), held

---

[a] For extensive consideration of a related problem, see Joan Steinman, Law of the Case: A Judicial Puzzle in Consolidated and Transferred Cases and in Multidistrict Litigation, 135 Pa.L.Rev. 595 (1987).

that the word "children" in the federal copyright statute should include an illegitimate child if the state courts would so interpret the word.

But how does a federal court decide which state's law to borrow? And once the state has been chosen, how does it decide which part of that state's law is to govern? Is it possible, for example, that an illegitimate is one's "child" for some purposes under state law but not others?

The Court has not spoken definitively to these questions, although the issues have been noticed in *DeSylva* and numerous other cases. Should *Klaxon* control? Or are the questions different enough so that they should be controlled by different principles?

————

Chapter IV

IMPLIED RIGHTS OF ACTION

SECTION 1: SUITS BY PRIVATE PARTIES TO ENFORCE FEDERAL STATUTES

TEXAS INDUSTRIES, INC. v. RADCLIFF MATERIALS, INC.

Supreme Court of the United States, 1981.
451 U.S. 630.

CHIEF JUSTICE BURGER delivered the opinion of the Court.

This case presents the question whether the federal antitrust laws allow a defendant, against whom civil damages, costs, and attorney's fees have been assessed, a right to contribution from other participants in the unlawful conspiracy on which recovery was based. . . .

I

Petitioner and the three respondents manufacture and sell ready-mix concrete in the New Orleans, La., area. In 1975, the Wilson P. Abraham Construction Corp., which had purchased concrete from petitioner, filed a civil action in the United States District Court for the Eastern District of Louisiana naming petitioner as defendant; the complaint alleged that petitioner and certain unnamed concrete firms had conspired to raise prices in violation of § 1 of the Sherman Act, which provides in relevant part:

> "Every contract, combination in the form of trust or otherwise, or conspiracy, in restraint of trade or commerce among the several States, or with foreign nations, is declared to be illegal."

The complaint sought treble damages plus attorney's fees under § 4 of the Clayton Act, which provides:

> "Any person who shall be injured in his business or property by reason of anything forbidden in the antitrust laws may sue therefor in any district court of the United States in the district in which the defendant resides or is found or has an agent, without respect to the amount in controversy, and shall recover threefold the damages by him sustained, and the cost of suit, including a reasonable attorney's fee."

Through discovery, petitioner learned that Abraham believed respondents were the other concrete producers that had participated in the alleged price-fixing scheme. Petitioner then filed a third-party complaint against respondents seeking contribution from them should it be held liable in the action filed by Abraham. The District Court dismissed the third-party complaint for failure to state a claim upon which relief could be granted, holding that federal law does not allow an antitrust defendant to recover in contribution from co-conspirators. The District Court also determined there was no just reason for delay with respect to that aspect of the case and entered final judgment under Federal Rule of Civil Procedure 54(b).

On appeal, the Court of Appeals for the Fifth Circuit affirmed, holding that, although the Sherman and the Clayton Acts do not expressly afford a right to contribution, the issue should be resolved as a matter of federal common law. The court then examined what it perceived to be the benefits and the difficulties of contribution and concluded that no common-law rule of contribution should be fashioned by the courts.

II

The common law provided no right to contribution among joint tortfeasors. In part, at least, this common-law rule rested on the idea that when several tortfeasors have caused damage, the law should not lend its aid to have one tortfeasor compel others to share in the sanctions imposed by way of damages intended to compensate the victim. Since the turn of the century, however, 39 states and the District of Columbia have fashioned rules of contribution in one form or another, ten initially through judicial action and the remainder through legislation. Because courts generally have acknowledged that treble-damages actions under the antitrust laws are analogous to common-law actions sounding in tort, we are urged to follow this trend and adopt contribution for antitrust violators.

The parties and amici representing a variety of business interests—as well as a legion of commentators—have thoroughly addressed the policy concerns implicated in the creation of a right to contribution in antitrust cases. With potentially large sums at stake, it is not surprising that the numerous and articulate amici disagree strongly over the basic issue raised: whether sharing of damages liability will advance or impair the objectives of the antitrust laws.

Proponents of a right to contribution advance concepts of fairness and equity in urging that the often massive judgments in antitrust actions be shared by all the wrongdoers. In the abstract, this position has a certain appeal: collective fault, collective responsibility. But the efforts of petitioner and supporting amici to invoke principles of equity presuppose a legislative intent to allow parties violating the law to draw upon equitable principles to mitigate the consequences of their wrongdoing. Moreover, traditional equitable standards have something to say about the septic state of the hands of such a suitor in the courts, and, in the context of one wrongdoer suing a co-conspirator, these standards similarly suggest that parties generally in pari delicto should be left where they are found.

The proponents of contribution also contend that, by allowing one violator to recover from co-conspirators, there is a greater likelihood that most or all wrongdoers will be held liable and thus share the consequences of the wrongdoing. It is argued that contribution would thus promote more vigorous private enforcement of the antitrust laws and thereby deter violations, one of the important purposes of the treble-damages action under § 4 of the Clayton Act. Independent of this effect, a right to contribution may increase the incentive of a single defendant to provide evidence against co-conspirators so as to avoid bearing the full weight of the judgment. Realization of this possibility may also deter one from joining an antitrust conspiracy.

Respondents and amici opposing contribution point out that an even stronger deterrent may exist in the possibility, even if more remote, that a single participant could be held fully liable for the total amount of the judgment. In this view, each prospective co-conspirator would ponder long and hard before engaging in what may be called a game of "Russian roulette." Moreover, any discussion of this problem must consider the problem of "overdeterrence," i.e., the possibility that severe antitrust penalties will chill wholly legitimate business agreements.

The parties and amici also discuss at length how a right to contribution should be structured and, in particular, how to treat problems that may arise with the allocation of damages among the wrongdoers and the effect of settlements. Dividing or apportioning damages among a cluster of co-conspirators presents difficult issues, for the participation of each in the conspiracy may have varied. Some may have profited more than others; some may have caused more damage to the injured plaintiff. Some may have been "leaders" and others "followers"; one may be a "giant," others "pygmies." Various formulae are suggested: damages may be allocated according to market shares, relative profits, sales to the particular plaintiff, the role in the organization and operation of the conspiracy, or simply pro rata, assessing an equal amount against each participant on the theory that each one is equally liable for the injury caused by collective action. In addition to the question of allocation, a right to contribution may have a serious impact on the incentive of defendants to settle. Some amici and commentators have suggested that the total amount of the plaintiff's claim should be reduced by the amount of any settlement with any one co-conspirator; others strongly disagree. Similarly, vigorous arguments can be made for and against allowing a losing defendant to seek contribution from co-conspirators who settled with the plaintiff before trial. Regardless of the particular rule adopted for allocating damages or enforcing settlements, the complexity of the issues involved may result in additional trial and pretrial proceedings, thus adding new complications to what already is complex litigation.

III

The contentions advanced indicate how views diverge as to the "unfairness" of not providing contribution, the risks and trade-offs perceived by decisionmakers in business, and the various patterns for contribution that could be devised. In this vigorous debate over the advantages and disadvantages of contribution and various contribution schemes, the parties, amici, and commentators have paid less attention to a very significant and perhaps dispositive threshold question: whether courts have the power to create such a cause of action absent legislation and, if so, whether that authority should be exercised in this context.

[A] right to contribution may arise in either of two ways: first, through the affirmative creation of a right of action by Congress, either expressly or by clear implication; or, second, through the power of federal courts to fashion a federal common law of contribution.

A

There is no allegation that the antitrust laws expressly establish a right of action for contribution. Nothing in these statutes refers to contribution, and if such a right exists it must be by implication. Our focus, as it is in any case involving the implication of a right of action, is on the intent of Congress. Touche Ross & Co. v. Redington, 442 U.S. 560 (1979). Congressional intent may be discerned by looking to the legislative history and other factors: e.g., the identity of the class for whose benefit the statute was enacted, the overall legislative scheme, and the traditional role of the states in providing relief. See Cort v. Ash, 422 U.S. 66 (1975).

Petitioner readily concedes that "there is nothing in the legislative history of the Sherman Act or the Clayton Act to indicate that Congress considered whether contribution was available to defendants in antitrust actions." Moreover, it is equally clear that the Sherman Act and the provision for treble-damages actions under the Clayton Act were not adopted for the benefit of the participants in a conspiracy to restrain trade. On the contrary, petitioner "is a member of the class whose activities Congress intended to regulate for the protection and benefit *of an entirely distinct class.*" Piper v. Chris-Craft Industries, Inc., 430 U.S. 1, 37 (1977) (emphasis added). The very idea of treble damages reveals an intent to punish past, and to deter future, unlawful conduct, not to ameliorate the liability of wrongdoers. The absence of any reference to contribution in the legislative history or of any possibility that Congress was concerned with softening the blow on joint wrongdoers in this setting makes examination of other factors unnecessary. We therefore conclude that Congress neither expressly nor implicitly intended to create a right to contribution. If any right to contribution exists, its source must be federal common law.

B

There is, of course, "no federal general common law." Erie R. Co. v. Tompkins, 304 U.S. 64, 78 (1938). Nevertheless, the Court has recognized the need and authority in some limited areas to formulate what has come to be known as "federal common law." These instances are "few and restricted," and fall into essentially two categories: those in which a federal rule or decision is "necessary to protect uniquely federal interests," and those in which Congress has given the courts the power to develop substantive law.

(1)

The vesting of jurisdiction in the federal courts does not in and of itself give rise to authority to formulate federal common law, nor does the existence of congressional authority under art. I mean that federal courts are free to develop a common law to govern those areas until Congress acts. Rather, absent some congressional authorization to formulate substantive rules of decision, federal common law exists only in such narrow areas as those concerned with the rights and obligations of the United States, interstate and international disputes implicating the conflicting rights of states or our relations with foreign nations, and admiralty cases. In these instances, our federal system does not permit the controversy to be resolved under state law, either because the authority and duties of the United States as sovereign are intimately involved or because the interstate or international nature of the controversy makes it inappropriate for state law to control.

In areas where federal common law applies, the creation of a right to contribution may fall within the power of the federal courts. For example, in Cooper Stevedoring Co. v. Fritz Kopke, Inc., 417 U.S. 106 (1974), we held that contribution is available among joint tortfeasors for injury to a longshoreman. But that claim arose within admiralty jurisdiction, one of the areas long recognized as subject to federal common law; our decision there was based, at least in part, on the traditional division of damages in admiralty not recognized at common law. *Cooper Stevedoring* thus does not stand for a general federal common-law right to contribution.

The antitrust laws were enacted pursuant to the power of Congress under the commerce clause to regulate interstate and foreign trade, and the case law construing the Sherman Act now spans nearly a century. Nevertheless, a treble-damages action remains a private suit involving the rights and obligations of private parties. Admittedly, there is a federal interest in the sense that vindication of rights arising out of these congressional enactments supplements federal enforcement and fulfills the objects of the statutory scheme. Notwithstanding that nexus, contribution among antitrust wrongdoers does not involve the duties of the federal government, the distribution of powers in our federal system, or matters necessarily subject to federal control even in the absence of statutory authority. Cf. Bank of America v. Parnell, 352 U.S. 29, 33 (1956). In short, contribution does not implicate "uniquely federal interests" of the kind that oblige courts to formulate federal common law.

(2)

Federal common law also may come into play when Congress has vested jurisdiction in the federal courts and empowered them to create governing rules of law. In this vein, this Court has read § 301(a) of the Labor Management Relations Act not only as granting jurisdiction over defined areas of labor law but also as vesting in the courts the power to develop a common law of labor-management relations within that jurisdiction. Textile Workers v. Lincoln Mills, 353 U.S. 448 (1957). A similar situation arises with regard to the first two sections of the Sherman Act, which in sweeping language forbid "[e]very contract, combination . . ., or conspiracy, in restraint of trade" and "monopoliz[ing], or attempt[ing] to monopolize, . . . any part of the trade or commerce . . . ." We noted in National Society of Professional Engineers v. United States, 435 U.S. 679, 688 (1978):

> "Congress, however, did not intend the text of the Sherman Act to delineate the full meaning of the statute or its application in concrete situations. The legislative history makes it perfectly clear that it expected the courts to give shape to the statute's broad mandate by drawing on common-law tradition."

It does not necessarily follow, however, that Congress intended to give courts as wide discretion in formulating remedies to enforce the provisions of the Sherman Act or the kind of relief sought through contribution. The intent to allow courts to develop governing principles of law, so unmistakably clear with regard to substantive violations, does not appear in debates on the treble-damages action created in § 7 of the original act.[16] In the Senate debates of 1890, Senator Morgan described the type of authority given the courts:

> "Now, whoever recovers upon this statute, in whatever court he may go to, will recover upon the statute. It is very true that we use common-law terms here and common-law definitions in order to define an offense which is in itself comparatively new, *but it is not a common-law jurisdiction that we are conferring upon the circuit courts of the United States.* " (emphasis added).

The Senator added that common-law actions in state courts might still exist, but recovery of treble damages would not be available, for its source is federal, not state, law. This description of the power of federal courts under the act suggests a sharp distinction between the lawmaking powers conferred in defining violations and the ability to fashion the relief available to parties claiming injury.[17]

---

[16] Section 4 of the Clayton Act, which provides the private treble-damages action, derives from § 7 of the Sherman Act as originally enacted. Congress repealed the original § 7 in 1955, as being redundant to Clayton Act § 4.

[17] Courts, of course, should be wary of relying on the remarks of a single legislator, and Senator Morgan's comments are not unambiguous. Yet it is clear that when the Sherman Act was adopted the common law did not provide a right to

In contrast to the sweeping language of §§ 1 and 2 of the Sherman Act, the remedial provisions defined in the antitrust laws are detailed and specific: (1) violations of §§ 1 and 2 are crimes; (2) Congress has expressly authorized a private right of action for treble damages, costs, and reasonable attorney's fees; (3) other remedial sections also provide for suits by the United States to enjoin violations or for injury to its "business or property," and parens patriae suits by state attorneys general; (4) Congress has provided that a final judgment or decree of an antitrust violation in one proceeding will serve as prima facie evidence in any subsequent action or proceeding; and (5) the remedial provisions in the antimerger field, not at issue here, are also quite detailed. "The presumption that a remedy was deliberately omitted from a statute is strongest when Congress has enacted a comprehensive legislative scheme including an integrated system of procedures for enforcement." Northwest Airlines, Inc. v. Transport Workers, 451 U.S. 77, 97 (1981).[a] That presumption is strong indeed in the context of antitrust violations; the continuing existence of this statutory scheme for 90 years without amendments authorizing contribution is not without significance. There is nothing in the statute itself, in its legislative history, or in the overall regulatory scheme to suggest that Congress intended courts to have the power to alter or supplement the remedies enacted.

Our cases interpreting the treble-damages action do not suggest that, in the past, we have invoked some broad-ranging common-law source for creating a cause of action. Nor does the judicial determination that defendants should be jointly and severally liable suggest that courts also may order contribution, since joint and several liability simply ensures that the plaintiffs will be able to recover the full amount of damages from some, if not all participants. These cases do no more than identify the scope of the remedy Congress itself has provided. "In almost any statutory scheme, there may be a need for judicial interpretation of ambiguous or incomplete provisions. But the authority to construe a statute is fundamentally different from the authority to fashion a new rule or to provide a new remedy which Congress has decided not to adopt." Ibid. We are satisfied that neither the Sherman Act nor the Clayton Act confers on federal courts the broad power to formulate the right to contribution sought here.

IV

The policy questions presented by petitioner's claimed right to contribution are far-reaching. In declining to provide a right to contribution, we neither reject the validity of those arguments nor adopt the views of those opposing contribution. Rather, we recognize that, re-

contribution among tortfeasors participating in proscribed conduct. One permissible, though not mandatory, inference is that Congress relied on courts continuing to apply principles in effect at the time of enactment.

[a] The Court refused in the *Northwest Airlines* case to find a right of contribution for sex discrimination in violation of the Equal Pay Act of 1963 and Title VII of the Civil Rights Act of 1964. Contribution was sought by the Airlines against employee unions who were alleged to be at least partly responsible for pay discrimination against female cabin attendants. [Footnote by eds.]

gardless of the merits of the conflicting arguments, this is a matter for Congress, not the courts, to resolve.

The range of factors to be weighed in deciding whether a right to contribution should exist demonstrates the inappropriateness of judicial resolution of this complex issue. Ascertaining what is "fair" in this setting calls for inquiry into the entire spectrum of antitrust law, not simply the elements of a particular case or category of cases. Similarly, whether contribution would strengthen or weaken enforcement of the antitrust laws, or what form a right to contribution should take, cannot be resolved without going beyond the record of a single lawsuit. As in Diamond v. Chakrabarty, 447 U.S. 303, 317 (1980):

> "The choice we are urged to make is a matter of high policy for resolution within the legislative process after the kind of investigation, examination, and study that legislative bodies can provide and courts cannot. That process involves the balancing of competing values and interests, which in our democratic system is the business of elected representatives. Whatever their validity, the contentions now pressed on us should be addressed to the political branches of the government, the Congress and the Executive, and not to the courts."

Because we are unable to discern any basis in federal statutory or common law that allows federal courts to fashion the relief urged by petitioner, the judgment of the Court of Appeals is

Affirmed.

––––––––

NOTES ON SUITS BY PRIVATE PARTIES TO ENFORCE FEDERAL STATUTES

1. ***J.I. Case v. Borak.*** Since 1964, federal courts have often been asked to recognize a remedy for the violation of a federal statute that did not explicitly create a private right of action. The Supreme Court's response to such requests has changed considerably.

The story begins with J.I. Case v. Borak, 377 U.S. 426 (1964). Section 14(a) of the Securities and Exchange Act of 1934 provided that it "shall be unlawful for any person . . . to solicit . . . any proxy . . . in contravention of such rules and regulations as the [Securities and Exchange] Commission may prescribe as necessary or appropriate in the public interest or for the protection of investors." Rule 14a–9 promulgated by the Commission provided that "[n]o solicitation . . . shall be made by means of any proxy statement . . . containing any statement which . . . is false or misleading . . . ." Additionally § 27 of the act provided that the "district courts . . . shall have exclusive jurisdiction of violations of this title or the rules and regulations thereunder, and of all suits in equity and actions at law brought to enforce any liability or duty created by this title or the rules and regulations thereunder."

Borak owned stock in the J.I. Case Co. He filed a stockholders' derivative action against J.I. Case to challenge the terms of its merger with another corporation. As the case came to the Supreme Court, the issue was "whether § 27 of the act authorizes a federal cause of action for recision or damages to a corporate stockholder with respect to a consummated merger which was authorized pursuant to the use of a proxy statement alleged to contain false and misleading statements violative of § 14(a) of the act." In a brief and unanimous opinion, the Court held that a federal cause of action could be asserted. Justice Clark wrote:

> "It appears clear that private parties have a right under § 27 to bring suit for violation of § 14(a) of the act. Indeed, this section specifically grants the appropriate district courts jurisdiction over 'all suits in equity and actions at law brought to enforce any liability or duty created' under the Act.[a] [J.I. Case emphasizes] that Congress made no specific reference to a private right of action in § 14(a). . . .

> "The purpose of § 14(a) is to prevent management or others from obtaining authorization for corporate action by means of deceptive or inadequate disclosure in proxy solicitation. . . . While [it] makes no specific reference to a private right of action, among its chief purposes is 'the protection of investors,' which certainly implies the availability of judicial relief where necessary to achieve that result.

> ". . . Private enforcement of the proxy rules provides a necessary supplement to Commission action. As in antitrust treble damage litigation, the possibility of civil damages or injunctive relief serves as a most effective weapon in the enforcement of the proxy requirements. The Commission advises [in an amicus brief supporting the existence of a private cause of action] that it examines over 2,000 proxy statements annually and each of them must necessarily be expedited. Time does not permit an independent examination of the facts set out in the proxy material and this results in the Commission's acceptance of the representations contained therein at their face value, unless contrary to other material on file with it. Indeed, on the allegations of [Borak's] complaint, the proxy material failed to disclose alleged unlawful market manipulation of the stock [of the company with which J.I. Case merged], and this unlawful manipulation would not have been apparent to the Commission until after the merger.

> "We, therefore, believe that under the circumstances here it is the duty of the courts to be alert to provide such remedies as are necessary to make effective the congressional purpose. . . ."

---

[a] Private suits for damages were authorized explicitly in prescribed circumstances (not applicable here) by other sections of the securities laws. [Footnote by eds.]

2. *Cort v. Ash.* In the decade following *J.I. Case*, the lower federal courts routinely recognized private rights of action to enforce federal regulatory provisions. The Supreme Court's next major pronouncement in the area came in Cort v. Ash, 422 U.S. 66 (1975). Although the Court reversed the creation of a private right of action by the Court of Appeals in *Cort*, its rationale did little to stem the tide begun in *J.I. Case.*

Cort was a stockholders' derivative action to enforce 18 U.S.C. § 610, a criminal statute prohibiting corporations from making contributions or expenditures in connection with any presidential or vice-presidential election. The Court held that a private cause of action could not be asserted, and thus avoided the necessity of determining whether the statute prohibited the particular expenditures involved in the case and, if so, whether it was constitutional.

Justice Brennan wrote for a unanimous Court. The opinion began by stating four criteria for recognition of a private right of action:

> "In determining whether a private remedy is implicit in a statute not expressly providing one, several factors are relevant. First, is the plaintiff 'one of the class for whose *especial* benefit the statute was enacted'—that is, does the statute create a right in favor of the plaintiff? Second, is there any indication of legislative intent, explicit or implicit, either to create such a remedy or to deny one? Third, is it consistent with the underlying purposes of the legislative scheme to imply such a remedy for the plaintiff? And finally, is the cause of action one traditionally relegated to state law, in an area basically the concern of the states, so that it would be inappropriate to infer a cause of action based solely on federal law?"

Justice Brennan then noted that in *J.I. Case* and several other cases, "there was at least a statutory basis for inferring that a civil cause of action of some sort lay in favor of someone." [b] "Here," by contrast, "there was nothing more than a bare criminal statute, with absolutely no indication that civil enforcement of any kind was available to anyone."

Justice Brennan then applied the four criteria to the situation before the Court. He noted first that the statute was motivated by two concerns: the desire to restrain the influence of corporations over elections; and the feeling that corporations had no moral right to use corporate funds for such a purpose without stockholder consent. Justice Brennan thought the legislative history demonstrated that concern for stockholders was secondary. "In contrast," he continued, "in those

---

[b] He added in a footnote that:

"In *Borak*, § 27 of the Securities and Exchange Act of 1934 specifically granted jurisdiction to the district courts over civil actions to 'enforce any liability or duty created by this title or the rules and regulations thereunder,' and there seemed to be no dispute over the fact that at least a private suit for declaratory relief was authorized; the question was whether a derivative suit for recision and damages was also available. Further it was clear that the Securities and Exchange Commission could sue to enjoin violations of § 14(a) of the Act, the section involved in *Borak*."

situations in which we have inferred a private cause of action not expressly provided, there has generally been a clearly articulated federal right in the plaintiff [citing *Bivens*, page 395, infra] or a pervasive legislative scheme governing the relationship between the plaintiff class and the defendant class in a particular regard [citing *J.I. Case*]."

Second, Justice Brennan noted:

"[T]here is no indication whatever in the legislative history of § 610 which suggests a congressional intention to vest in corporate shareholders a federal right to damages for violation of § 610. True, in situations in which it is clear that federal law has granted a class of persons certain rights, it is not necessary to show an intention to *create* a private cause of action, although an explicit purpose to *deny* such cause of action would be controlling. But where, as here, it is at least dubious whether Congress intended to vest in the plaintiff class rights broader than those provided by state regulation of corporations, the fact that there is no suggestion at all that § 610 may give rise to a suit for damages or, indeed, to any civil cause of action, reinforces the conclusion that the expectation, if any, was that the relationship between corporations and their stockholders would continue to be entrusted entirely to state law."

Third, Justice Brennan observed that the remedy sought would not aid the primary congressional goal, that is, it "would not cure the influence which the use of corporate funds in the first instance may have had on a federal election." Finally, he noted that the internal affairs of corporations are regulated primarily by state law and that leaving the matter to the states would not undermine the "primary goal" of the federal statute.

3.   *Cannon v. University of Chicago.* In both *J.I. Case v. Borak* and *Cort v. Ash*, the Supreme Court assumed that it had the power to recognize private rights of action where appropriate. Attention focused chiefly on the circumstances justifying the exercise of that power. The antecedent question of the scope of judicial authority was not seriously debated until Cannon v. University of Chicago, 441 U.S. 677 (1979).

In *Cannon*, the plaintiff alleged that she had been denied admission to medical school in violation of § 901 of title IX of the Education Amendments of 1972. That statute provided that:

"No person in the United States shall, on the basis of sex, be excluded from participation in, be denied the benefits of, or be subjected to discrimination under any education program or activity receiving federal financial assistance . . .."

The District Court held that no private suit for an injunction could be asserted for a violation of this provision, and the Circuit Court agreed. The Supreme Court was divided. Justice Stevens wrote the opinion of the Court reversing the Circuit Court and finding an implied cause of action. Chief Justice Burger concurred without opinion, while Justice

Rehnquist, joined by Justice Stewart, wrote a separate concurrence. Justice White, joined by Justice Blackmun, and Justice Powell wrote separate dissents.

(i) **The Majority.** Justice Stevens began by applying the four *Cort* criteria. The first, he noted, was easily satisfied: the statute clearly created a right not to be discriminated against on the basis of sex. Second, Stevens thought Congress "rather plainly . . . intended to create" a private remedy. Title IX was patterned after title VI of the Civil Rights Act of 1964, and the courts had already recognized a private remedy under title VI when title IX was being considered. "Moreover," he continued,

> "during the period between the enactment of title VI in 1964 and the enactment of title IX in 1972, this Court had consistently found implied remedies—often in cases much less clear than this. It was *after* 1972 that this Court decided *Cort v. Ash* [and several other cases] cited by the Court of Appeals in support of its strict construction of the remedial aspects of the statute. We, of course, adhere to the strict approach followed in our recent cases, but our evaluation of congressional action in 1972 must take into account its contemporary legal context."

He then considered other indications in the legislative history that Congress intended to create a private remedy.

Third, Justice Stevens noted that Congress had two purposes in enacting title IX: to avoid the use of federal funds to support discriminatory practices; and to protect individual citizens against discrimination. Funds cut-off may be an effective means of serving the first purpose, but it is a severe remedy and one not likely to be invoked for an isolated violation. An injunction might be more effective, and there is no inconsistency in permitting both remedies. The federal agency charged with enforcing the statute, moreover, had expressed its support of the private remedy as a supplementary means of enforcement.

Finally, the last *Cort* factor also supported recognition of a federal remedy. Ever since the Civil War, he said, the federal government has been the primary protector against discrimination. "In sum," he concluded, "there is no need in this case to weigh the four *Cort* factors, all of them support the same result."

Justice Rehnquist wrote to emphasize that the Court's approach was "quite different from the analysis in earlier cases such as [*J.I.*] *Case*. The question of the existence of a private right of action is basically one of statutory construction." He concluded that while Congress may well have had reason in the past to believe that the courts would readily infer a private cause of action, the situation now was different. The lawmaking branch should be apprised "that the ball, so to speak, may well now be in its court. [T]his Court in the future should be extremely reluctant to imply a cause of action absent . . . specificity on the part of the legislative branch."

(ii) The Powell Dissent. Justice Powell's dissent is worth particular attention since it has been influential in subsequent decisions. In his separate dissent, Justice White argued that Congress specifically intended that there *not* be a private cause of action. Justice Powell agreed, but added that the "mode of analysis we have applied in the recent past cannot be squared with the doctrine of separation of powers. The time has come to reappraise our standards for the judicial implication of private causes of action":

> "Under article III, Congress alone has the responsibility for determining the jurisdiction of the lower federal courts. As the legislative branch, Congress also should determine when private parties are to be given causes of action under legislation it adopts. . . . When Congress chooses not to provide a private civil remedy, federal courts should not assume the legislative role of creating such a remedy and thereby enlarge their jurisdiction.

> ". . . The 'four factor' analysis of *Cort* is an open invitation to federal courts to legislate causes of action not authorized by Congress. It is an analysis not faithful to constitutional principles and should be rejected. Absent the most compelling evidence of affirmative congressional intent, a federal court should not infer a private cause of action."

Justice Powell then reviewed past decisions, concluding that *J.I. Case* "constituted a singular and, I believe, aberrant interpretation of a federal regulatory statute." [c]

Justice Powell then turned to further criticism of *Cort:*

> "[A]s the opinion of the Court today demonstrates, the *Cort* analysis too easily may be used to deflect inquiry away from the intent of Congress, and to permit a court instead to substitute its own views as to the desirability of private enforcement.

> "Of the four factors mentioned in *Cort*, only one refers expressly to legislative intent. The other three invite independent judicial lawmaking. Asking whether a statute creates a right in favor of a private party, for example, begs the question at issue. What is involved is not the mere existence of a legal right, but a particular person's right to invoke the power of the courts to enforce that right. Determining whether a private action would be consistent with the 'underlying purposes' of a legislative scheme permits a court to decide for itself what the goals of a scheme should be, and how those goals should be advanced. Finally, looking to state law for parallels to the federal right simply focuses inquiry on a particular policy

[c] He did recognize that there had been occasions where private remedies had been legitimately inferred—as, for example, where the failure to imply a remedy would leave a federal statutory command otherwise unenforceable by any means. He also approved of cases in the voting rights area, which were justified by "this Court's special and traditional concern for safeguarding the electoral process."

consideration that Congress already may have weighed in deciding not to create a private action.

"That the *Cort* analysis too readily permits courts to override the decision of Congress not to create a private action is demonstrated conclusively by the flood of lower-court decisions applying it. Although from the time *Cort* was decided until today this Court consistently has turned back attempts to create private actions, other federal courts have tended to proceed in exactly the opposite direction. In the four years since we decided *Cort*, no less than 20 decisions by the courts of appeals have implied private actions from federal statutes. It defies reason to believe that in each of these statutes Congress absent mindedly forgot to mention an intended private action. Indeed, the accelerating trend evidenced by these decisions attests to the need to re-examine the *Cort* analysis."

Justice Powell then echoed the famous passage in *Erie* by stating that "[i]f only a matter of statutory construction were involved," he might be inclined to refine the *Cort* factors so as better to reflect congressional intent. " 'But the unconstitutionality of the course pursued has now been made clear' and compels us to abandon the implication doctrine of *Cort*." He continued:

"*Cort* allows the judicial branch to assume a policymaking authority vested by the Constitution in the legislative branch. It also invites Congress to avoid resolution of the often controversial question whether a new regulatory statute should be enforced through private litigation. Rather than confronting the hard political choices involved, Congress is encouraged to shirk its constitutional obligation and leave the issue to the courts to decide. When this happens, the legislative process with its public scrutiny and participation has been bypassed, with attendant prejudice to everyone concerned. . . .

"The Court's implication doctrine encourages, as a corollary to the political default by Congress, an increase in the governmental power exercised by the federal judiciary. The dangers posed by judicial arrogation of the right to resolve general societal conflicts have been manifest to this Court throughout its history. . . .

"It is true that the federal judiciary necessarily exercises substantial powers to construe legislation, including, when appropriate, the power to prescribe substantive standards of conduct that supplement federal legislation. But this power normally is exercised with respect to disputes over which a court already has jurisdiction, and in which the existence of the asserted cause of action is established. Implication of a private cause of action, in contrast, involves a significant additional step. By creating a private action, a court of limited jurisdiction necessarily extends its authority to embrace a dispute Congress has not assigned it to resolve. This runs contrary to the established principle that '[t]he jurisdiction of the federal courts is carefully guarded against expansion by judicial interpretation . . .,' and conflicts with the authority of Congress under art. III to set the limits of federal jurisdiction.

"The facts of this case illustrate how the implication of a right of action not authorized by Congress denigrates the democratic process. Title IX embodies a national commitment to the elimination of discrimination based on sex, a goal the importance of which has been recognized repeatedly by our decisions. But because title IX applies to most of our nation's institutions of higher learning, it also trenches on the authority of the academic community to govern itself, an authority the free exercise of which is critical to the vitality of our society. Arming frustrated applicants with the power to challenge in court his or her rejection inevitably will have a constraining effect on admissions programs. The burden of expensive, vexatious litigation upon institutions whose resources often are severely limited may well compel an emphasis on objectively measured academic qualifications at the expense of more flexible admissions criteria that bring richness and diversity to academic life. If such a significant incursion into the arena of academic polity is to be made, it is the constitutional function of the legislative branch, subject as it is to the checks of the political process, to make this judgment.

". . . Henceforth, we should not condone the implication of any private action from a federal statute absent the most compelling evidence that Congress in fact intended such an action to exist. Where a statutory scheme expressly provides for an alternative mechanism for enforcing the rights and duties created, I would be especially reluctant ever to permit a federal court to volunteer its services for enforcement purposes. Because the Court today is enlisting the federal judiciary in just such an enterprise, I dissent."

4. Post-*Cannon* Decisions. Justice Powell's opinion seemed to have some effect, for in the aftermath of *Cannon*, the Court became decidedly, if not consistently, more restrictive.

(i) *Touche Ross & Co. v. Redington*. Slightly more than a month after *Cannon*, the Court refused to infer a private remedy for damages in a complex securities case. Touche Ross & Co. v. Redington, 442 U.S. 560 (1979), all but rejected the four *Cort* factors in favor of congressional intent as the sole inquiry. Section 17(a) of the 1934 Act imposed a duty on broker-dealers and certain others to maintain and report such records and reports "as the Commission by its rules and regulations may prescribe as necessary or appropriate in the public interest or for the protection of investors." Touche Ross was a firm of public accountants that audited the books and records of Weis Securities Inc. and prepared required reports. Weis became insolvent and went through a liquidation procedure pursuant to which a trustee (Redington) and a federal agency were subrogated to all rights of Weis' customers. The argument was that a private right of action should be implied from § 17(a) against Touche Ross in favor of the Weis customers, and that this cause of action could be asserted by the trustee and the agency.

Justice Rehnquist began his opinion for the Court by asserting that the "question of the existence of a statutory cause of action is, of course, one of statutory construction." "[O]ur task," he continued, "is limited solely to determining whether Congress intended to create the private right of action asserted . . . .." He then noted that the statute did not, "by its terms, purport to create a private cause of action in favor of anyone" and that the legislative history was "entirely silent." As to the relevance of the four *Cort* factors, he said:

> "[T]he Court did not decide that each [factor] is entitled to equal weight. The central inquiry remains whether Congress intended to create, either expressly or by implication, a private cause of action. Indeed, the first three factors discussed in *Cort*—the language and focus of the statute, its legislative history, and its purpose—are ones traditionally relied upon in determining legislative intent. Here, the statute by its terms grants no private rights to any identifiable class and proscribes no conduct as unlawful. And the parties . . . agree that the legislative history . . . simply does not speak to the issue of private remedies . . . . At least in such a case as this, the inquiry ends there: The question whether Congress, either expressly or by implication, intended to create a private right of action, has been definitely answered in the negative. . . . The ultimate question is one of congressional intent, not one of whether this Court thinks it can improve upon the statutory scheme that Congress enacted into law."

Justice Powell did not participate. Justice Brennan wrote a concurrence in which he agreed that the first two *Cort* factors were not satisfied here, and that "the remaining two *Cort* factors cannot by themselves be a basis for implying a right of action." Justice Marshall was alone in dissent. He thought that "straightforward application of the four *Cort* factors" compelled recognition of a private cause of action.

(ii) ***Transamerica Mortgage Advisors, Inc. v. Lewis.*** Transamerica Mortgage Advisors, Inc. (TAMA) v. Lewis, 444 U.S. 11 (1979), involved a suit under the Investment Advisers Act of 1940. Section 206 of the act broadly proscribes fraudulent practices by investment advisers. Section 215 provides that contracts in violation of the act "shall be void . . . as regards the rights of" the violator and knowing successors in interest. The plaintiff was a shareholder of the Mortgage Trust of America. TAMA was the trust's investment adviser. The plaintiff brought a derivative action on behalf of the trust and a class action on behalf of other shareholders. The suit sought an injunction to restrain further performance of the investment adviser's contract between the trust and TAMA and damages and other relief for various alleged frauds and breaches of fiduciary duty.

The Court's opinion, by Justice Stewart, began with the now customary notations that "[t]he question whether a statute creates a cause of action, either expressly or by implication, is basically a matter of statutory construction" and "what must ultimately be determined is whether Congress intended to create the private remedy asserted." Justice Stewart recognized that §§ 206 and 215 of the act were intended to benefit the clients of investment advisers, but said that "whether Congress intended additionally that these provisions would be enforced through private litigation is a different question." The opinion continued:

"On this question the legislative history of the act is entirely silent—a state of affairs not surprising when it is remembered that the act concededly does not explicitly provide any private remedies whatever.[d] But while the absence of anything in the legislative history that indicates an intention to confer any private right is hardly helpful to the [plaintiff], it does not automatically undermine his position. This Court has held that the failure of Congress expressly to consider a private remedy is not inevitably inconsistent with an intent on its part to make such a remedy available [citing *Cannon*]. Such an intent may appear implicitly in the language or structure of the statute, or in the circumstances of its enactment.

"In the case of § 215, we conclude that the statutory language itself fairly implies a right to specific and limited relief in a federal court. By declaring certain contracts void, § 215 by its terms necessarily contemplates that the issue of voidness under its criteria may be litigated somewhere. At the very least Congress must have assumed that § 215 could be raised defensively in private litigation to preclude the enforcement of an investment advisers contract. But the legal consequences of voidness are typically not so limited. A person with the power to void a contract ordinarily may resort to a court to have the contract rescinded and to obtain restitution of consideration paid. And this Court has previously recognized that a comparable provision of the Securities Exchange Act of 1934 confers a 'right to rescind' a contract void under the criteria of the statute. Moreover, the federal courts in general have viewed such language as implying an equitable cause of action for recision or similar relief.

"For these reasons we conclude that when Congress declared in § 215 that certain contracts are void, it intended that the customary legal incidents of voidness would follow, includ-

---

[d] Several specific remedies were provided in the act itself. The Securities and Exchange Commission was expressly authorized to bring suits to enjoin violations of the act or regulations under it; the Commission was authorized to impose various administrative sanctions on violators; and a wilful violation of the act was a criminal offense. [Footnote by eds.]

ing the availability of a suit for recision or for an injunction against continued operation of the contract, and for restitution.[8] Accordingly, we hold that . . . the [plaintiff] may maintain an action on behalf of the trust seeking to void the investment advisers contract.

"We view quite differently, however, the [plaintiff's] claim for damages and other monetary relief under § 206. Unlike § 215, § 206 simply proscribes certain conduct, and does not in terms create or alter any civil liabilities. If monetary liability to a private plaintiff is to be found, it must be read into the act. Yet it is an elementary canon of statutory construction that where a statute expressly provides a particular remedy or remedies, a court must be chary of reading others into it. . . ."

In the remainder of his opinion, Justice Stewart argued that the provision of other remedies in the act made it unlikely that Congress intended that § 206 be enforced by a private damage remedy and emphasized that the "dispositive question remains whether Congress intended to create any such remedy."

Justice Powell concurred with the notation that he regarded the Court's opinion "as compatible with my dissent in *Cannon*." Justice White, joined by Justices Brennan, Marshall, and Stevens, dissented. The dissent argued that the four *Cort* factors justified the damages remedy to enforce § 206.

(iii) *Thompson v. Thompson*. Thompson v. Thompson, ___ U.S. ___ (1988), involved the Parental Kidnapping and Prevention Act of 1980 (PKPA), 28 U.S.C. § 1738A, which requires states to enforce the child custody decrees of other states if certain conditions are met in the rendering court.[e] The statute focuses on enforcing custody decrees in *state* court; while it mandates interstate cooperation, it makes no explicit provision for resort to federal court in the event that two state courts ultimately disagree.

Thompson v. Thompson involved conflicting custody decrees entered by California and Louisiana state courts. The father filed suit in a federal court in Califonia seeking an injunction against enforcement of the Louisiana decree. The District Court dismissed the action, and the Court of Appeals held that the PKPA "does not create a private right of action in federal court to determine the validity of two conflicting custody decrees." The Supreme Court unanimously affirmed, but two Justices disagreed with Justice Marshall's opinion for the Court. Marshall said:

---

[8] "One possibility, of course, is that Congress intended that claims under § 215 would be raised in state court. But we decline to adopt such an anomalous construction without some indication that Congress in fact wished to remit the litigation of a federal right to the state courts."

[e] For a wide-ranging analysis of the many federalism concerns implicated by enforcement of the PKPA, see Michael Finch and Jerome Kasriel, Federal Court Correction of State Court Error: The Singular Case of Interstate Custody Disputes, 48 Ohio St. L.J. 927 (1987).

"In determining whether to infer a private cause of action from a federal statute, our focal point is Congress' intent in enacting the statute. As guides to discerning that intent, we have relied on the four factors set out in *Cort v. Ash*, along with other tools of statutory construction. Our focus on congressional intent does not mean that we require evidence that members of Congress, in enacting the statute, actually had in mind the creation of a private cause of action. The implied cause of action doctrine would be a virtual dead letter were it limited to correcting drafting errors when Congress simply forgot to codify its evident intention to provide a cause of action. Rather, as an *implied* cause of action doctrine suggests, 'the legislative history of a statute that does not expressly create or deny a private remedy will typically be equally silent or ambiguous on the question' [quoting *Cannon*]. We therefore have recognized that Congress' 'intent may appear implicitly in the language or structure of the statute, or in the circumstances of its enactment' [quoting *TAMA*]. The intent of Congress remains the ultimate issue, however, and 'unless this congressional intent can be inferred from the language of the statute, the statutory structure, or some other source, the essential predicate for implication of a private remedy simply does not exist.' "

Justice O'Connor joined all but this paragraph of the Court's opinion for reasons stated in part I of Justice Scalia's opinion. In that part, Scalia made three points. First, he was "at a loss to imagine what congressional intent to create a private right of action might mean, if it does not mean that Congress had in mind the creation of a private right of action." Second, he objected to the emphasis on *Cort v. Ash*, for "[i]t could not be plainer that we effectively overruled the *Cort* analysis in *Touche Ross* and *Transamerica*, converting one of its four factors (congressional intent) into *the determinative factor*, with the other three merely indicative of its presence or absence." Finally, Scalia objected to the Court's examination in later portions of its opinion of the "context" of the legislation "after having found no [intent to create a private right of action] in either text or legislative history." For him, "context alone cannot suffice."

In part II of his opinion, Justice Scalia went further:

"I have found the Court's dicta in the present case particularly provocative because it is my view that, if the current state of the law were to be changed, it should be moved in precisely the opposite direction—away from our current congressional intent test to the categorical position that federal private rights of action will not be implied.

". . . It is, to be sure, not beyond imagination that in a particular case Congress may intend to create a private right of action, but choose to do so by implication. One must wonder, however, whether the good produced by a judicial rule that accommodates this remote possibility is outweighed by its adverse effects. An enactment by implication cannot realistically be regarded as the product of the difficult lawmaking process our Constitution has prescribed. It is . . . dangerous to assume that, even with the utmost self-discipline, judges can prevent the implications they see from mirroring the policies they favor.

"I suppose all this could be said, to a greater or lesser degree, of *all* implications that courts derive from statutory language . . .. But as the likelihood that Congress would leave the matter to implication decreases, so does the justification for bearing the risk of distorting the constitutional process. A legislative act so significant, and so separable from the remainder of the statute, as the creation of a private right of action seems to me so implausibly left to implication that the risk should not be endured.

"If we were to announce a flat rule that private rights of action will not be implied in statutes hereafter enacted, the risk that that course would occasionally frustrate genuine legislative intent would decrease from its current level of minimal to virtually zero. . . . If change is to be made, we should get out of the business of implied private rights of action altogether."

(iv) Less Restrictive Decisions. Are there any situations today in which the Court will create a cause of action for damages to enforce a federal statute? The Court has done so twice since the decision in *Texas Industries*.

The first case was Merrill Lynch, Pierce, Fenner & Smith v. Curran, 456 U.S. 353 (1982), which involved the Commodity Futures Trading Commission Act. The statute had been amended in 1974, and the Court reasoned that the focus must be on the judicial climate at the time Congress acted. Since at that time "the federal courts routinely and consistently had recognized an implied private cause of action on behalf of plaintiffs seeking to enforce" related provisions and everyone, the Supreme Court included, "simply assumed the remedy was available, . . . the fact that a comprehensive reexamination and significant amendment of [the statute] left intact the statutory provisions under which the federal courts had implied a cause of action is itself evidence that Congress affirmatively intended to preserve the remedy." In addition, the fact that Congress had amended the statute twice without speaking to the question meant that "[t]he inference that Congress intended to preserve the preexisting remedy is compelling." Justice Powell, joined by Chief Justice Burger and by Justices Rehnquist and O'Connor, dissented.

The second case was Herman & MacLean v. Huddleston, 459 U.S. 375 (1983), where a unanimous Court (Justice Powell not participating) inferred a cause of action from § 10(b) of the 1934 Securities Exchange Act in spite of the existence of an overlapping, though not completely congruent, civil remedy under § 11 of the 1933 Act. The Court noted that "a private right of action [in this area] has been consistently recognized for more than 35 years. The existence of this implied remedy is simply beyond peradventure." The Court added that in 1975 Congress had enacted the "most substantial and significant revision of this country's federal securities laws since the passage of the Securities Exchange Act in 1934," and had left unchanged the well-established judicial interpretation of a private right of action to enforce § 10(b). To the Court, this suggested Congressional ratification of the § 10(b) private action.

5. Questions and Comments. Judicial recognition of private rights of action presents two distinct issues. First, there is the question of power: whether courts have the authority to create private rights of action to enforce federal statutes where Congress has not done so. This question was disputed most vigorously in *Cannon v. University of Chicago.* Was Justice Powell right in suggesting that the approach of *Cort v. Ash* is *unconstitutional?* Are there valid grounds for thinking that judicial creativity should be more limited here than with respect to other issues of federal common law?

Second, there is a question of policy. If courts have the power to create private remedies, what are the proper criteria to guide its exercise? Are the *Cort* factors inadequate or inappropriate? If they are, what guidelines should take their place?

In this connection, it may be useful to focus on the intersection between private rights of action and administrative law. The issue of judicial creation of private rights of action is largely a product of the administrative state. The problem usually arises when Congress authorizes administrative regulation of private activity without expressly allowing or forbidding private law suits. The question then becomes whether judicial recognition of a private right of action will aid or disrupt agency enforcement.

In some circumstances—*J.I. Case v. Borak* seems a good example— there is no conflict. Given the numbers of the proxy statements that the Securities and Exchange Commission must review and the limited opportunity the Commission has to know if those statements are false or misleading, a private right of action to enforce the proxy rules seemed a "necessary supplement" to agency action. No doubt that is why the Commission itself urged that result.

In other cases, a private right of action may disrupt agency action. This is especially likely where the underlying statute provides only vague and indefinite specification of substantive standards. In these circumstances, the effective role in defining substantive law, at least in the first instance, is left to the administrative agency. Agencies are typically expert and specialized; they usually have a centralized enforcement agenda; and they may be structured to be politically accountable. A private right of action by-passes the administrative structure in favor of direct resort to the courts. In a private enforcement action, the courts have no specialized expertise; the enforcement agenda is decentralized among private plaintiffs; and the decisionmaking process is insulated from political pressure. These may be desirable characteristics in some cases, but they are importantly different from administrative action. In such circumstances, judicial recognition of a private right of action may well be viewed as disruptive of the role assigned to the administrative agency in the enabling legislation.[f]

Note that *Texas Industries* presents an unusual situation in this respect. Unlike most of the other cases described above, *Texas Industries* does not turn on whether an administrative enforcement structure should be supplemented by a private right of action. The antitrust statutes were already enforced in judicial proceedings. Moreover, over the years the Supreme Court has played the primary role in developing the relevant substantive standards in this area. And however the Court decides *Texas Industries*, the contribution issue is resolved on the merits—there is no right to contribution unless and until Congress creates one. In the cases involving the intersection of private and agency enforcement, by contrast, the formal legality of the defendant's behavior is unaffected by the Court's decision—other remedies may be available, and the legality of the defendant's behavior is not resolved on the merits. Do these considerations effectively differentiate *Texas Industries* from the rest of the cases described above? Do they perhaps suggest a different result?

A further complexity—in addition to the intersection of implied private rights of action with the administrative state—is the extent to which the difficulty of the policy questions to be resolved should inhibit judicial creation of a private remedy. In *Cannon*, for example, part of Justice Powell's argument was that it was not clear, at least to him, that the cost of defending individual sex discrimination suits should be placed on institutions of higher learning. Most of Chief Justice Burger's opinion in *Texas Industries* was devoted to a demonstration of the difficulty of the contribution issue. Of what relevance is the difficulty of the policy questions raised by recognition of a private right of action?

6. 42 U.S.C. § 1983: A Comparison. The Supreme Court's restrictive approach to creating private rights of action to enforce federal statutes stands in apparent contrast to the Court's decisions in a doctrinally distinct, but functionally similar line of cases involving 42 U.S.C. § 1983. That statute creates a civil action for damages or injunctive relief against any person acting "under color of" state law who deprives any person of "any rights, privileges, or immunities secured by the Constitution *and laws*. . . ." (emphasis added).

---

[f] For an extended analysis of these issues, see Richard Stewart and Cass Sunstein, Public Programs and Private Rights, 95 Harv.L.Rev. 1191 (1982). Stewart and Sunstein locate the controversy over implied rights of action in the larger context of judicial control of the administrative state. Specifically, they relate the private right of action to other potential remedies for administrative deficiencies. These include a right of defense against agency action, a right to a hearing on distribution of government benefits, and a right of private initiation to compel agency action. Each of these rights is a "judicially created corrective for defective administrative performance." Stewart and Sunstein argue that judicial creativity to vindicate statutory norms is generally valid, but they also examine the circumstances under which the exercise of that power may be inappropriate.

In Maine v. Thiboutot, 448 U.S. 1 (1980), the Supreme Court said that the words "and laws" should be read literally and comprehensively to create a private cause of action for damages or injunctive relief against any state officer who violated any federal statute, regardless of whether that statute contemplated private enforcement. The apparent effect of this decision was to recognize a host of new private rights of action against state and local officials who violate federal statutory standards. Such standards appear in a variety of statutes that do not authorize private enforcement. Examples include joint federal-state regulatory programs, resource management programs administered co-operatively by state and federal agencies (such as national parks and forests), and, most importantly, federal statutes that fund state and local programs that meet federal standards.

Many commentators noted the inconsistency between the Court's restrictive and particularistic approach to private rights of action under most federal statutes and *Maine v. Thiboutot*'s categorical approval of private enforcement of other federal statutes. Subsequently, however, the divergence between these two lines of cases has narrowed, as the Court has cut back on *Maine v. Thiboutot.* See, e.g., Middlesex County Sewerage Authority v. National Sea Clammers Association, 453 U.S. 1 (1981). Today, the fact that a particular federal statute applies to persons acting "under color of" state law and hence covered by 42 U.S.C. § 1983 makes a difference in the availability of private enforce-ment, but just how much a difference is hard to say. *Maine v. Thiboutot* is excerpted, and the whole issue discussed in the materials on the civil rights acts, infra, pages 1017–40.

7. Bibliography. The subject of implied rights of action has generated an enormous literature. Among the prominent recent works of general interest is George D. Brown, Of Activism and *Erie*—Implica-tion Doctrine's Implications for the Nature and Role of the Federal Courts, 69 Iowa L.Rev. 617 (1984). Brown relates the recent judicial hostility to implied rights of action to a "new" *Erie* doctrine—that is, a renewed emphasis on *Erie* as a limitation on the creativity of the federal courts. Brown portrays this hostility as "fundamentally at odds with the vanguard of academic thinking," but "[f]or those who take the separation of powers doctrine seriously," nonetheless the "correct path." A sharply different view is expressed by Linda Sheryl Greene in Judicial Implication of Remedies for Federal Statutory Violations: The Separation of Powers Concerns, 53 Temple L. Q. 469 (1980). Greene argues that the separation of powers is not violated by judicial poli-cymaking regarding remedies for violations of federal rights. There-fore, for Greene, "the important inquiry becomes not the existence of power, but the proper exercise of judicial discretion."

For additional perspectives on the same theme, see Richard W. Creswell, The Separation of Powers Implications of Implied Rights of Action, 34 Mercer L.Rev. 973 (1983), which relates the recent judicial focus on congressional intent to separation-of-powers principles; H. Miles Foy, III, Some Reflections on Legislation, Adjudication, and Implied Private Actions in the State and Federal Courts, 71 Corn. L.

Rev. 501 (1986), which examines the history of this issue and concludes that recognizing private actions vindicates the "powerful and valuable political principle" of judicial availability to provide adequate remedies for all wrongs defined by law; Tamar Frankel, Implied Rights of Action, 67 Va. L. Rev. 553 (1981), which argues that "no constitutional principle bars federal courts from recognizing by implication claims by private plaintiffs who are clearly members of the class the statute was designed to protect"; Thomas L. Hazen, Implied Private Remedies Under Federal Statutes: Neither a Death Knell Nor a Moratorium— Civil Rights, Securities Regulation, and Beyond, 33 Vand. L. Rev. 1333 (1983), which suggests that the proper approach, and the one generally followed by the Supreme Court, is one of "general restraint with room for implication in compelling cases"; Marc I. Steinberg, Implied Private Rights of Action Under Federal Law, 55 Notre Dame Law. 33 (1979), which advocates a modified version of *Cort v. Ash* that is "more stringent" than the original, but nevertheless "receptive to the implication of private remedies in appropriate circumstances"; and Donald Zeigler, Rights Require Remedies: A New Approach to the Enforcement of Rights in the Federal Courts, 38 Hast. L.J. 665 (1987), which criticizes restrictive standards for recognition of private rights of action.

Additionally, there are many articles that address private rights of action with particular reference to specific statutes. For analysis of this issue under §§ 503 and 504 of the Rehabilitation Act of 1973, see Michael P. Seng, Private Rights of Action, 27 DePaul L. Rev. 1117 (1978); Michael A. Wolff, Protecting the Disabled Minority: Rights and Remedies Under Sections 503 and 504 of the Rehabilitation Act of 1973, 22 St. Louis L.J. 25 (1978); Harvey Boller, Unlawful Treatment of the Handicapped by Federal Contractors and an Implied Private Cause of Action: Shall Silence Reign?, 33 Hastings L.J. 1294 (1982). Discussion of private right of action issues under federal securities statutes may be found in Mark J. Loewenstein, Implied Contribution Under the Federal Securities Laws: A Reassessment, 1982 Duke L.J. 543; Mary Siegel, The Interplay Between the Implied Remedy Under Section 10(b) and the Express Causes of Action of the Federal Securities Laws, 62 B.U.L. Rev. 385 (1982); and Marc I. Steinberg, The Propriety and Scope of Cumulative Remedies Under the Federal Securities Laws, 67 Cornell L. Rev. 557 (1982).

Treatment of this issue in other contexts may be found in James M. Fischer, The Availability of Private Remedies for Acid Rain Damage, 9 Ecology L.Q. 429 (1981); C. Douglas Floyd, Contribution Among Antitrust Violators: A Question of Legal Process, 1980 B.Y.U.L.Rev. 183; Julia Lamber, Private Causes of Action under Federal Agency Nondiscrimination Statutes, 10 Conn.L.Rev. 859 (1978); John E. Noyes, Executive Orders, Presidential Intent, and Private Rights of Action, 59 Tex.L.Rev. 837 (1981) (examining and analyzing judicial refusal to infer private rights of action from executive orders); Dinah Shelton and Dorothy Berndt, Sex Discrimination in Vocational Education: Title IX and Other Remedies, 62 Calif.L.Rev. 1121 (1974); and Mary Siegel, The

Implication Doctrine and the Foreign Corrupt Practices Act, 79
Colum.L.Rev. 1085 (1979).

SECTION 2: SUITS BY THE UNITED STATES SEEKING COMMON LAW REMEDIES

UNITED STATES v. GILMAN

Supreme Court of the United States, 1954.
347 U.S. 507.

MR. JUSTICE DOUGLAS delivered the opinion of the Court.

The single question in the case is whether the United States may
recover indemnity from one of its employees after it has been held
liable under the Federal Tort Claims Act, 28 U.S.C. §§ 1346, 2671 et
seq., for the negligence of the employee.

Respondent, an employee of the United States, had a collision with
the car of one Darnell, while respondent was driving a government
automobile. Darnell sued the United States under the Tort Claims Act.
The United States filed a third-party complaint against respondent,
asking that if it should be held liable to Darnell, it have indemnity
from respondent. The District Court found that Darnell's injuries were
caused solely by the negligence of respondent, acting within the scope
of his employment. It entered judgment against the United States for
$5,500 and judgment over for the United States in the same amount.
The Court of Appeals reversed the judgment against respondent by a
divided vote. The case is here on writ of certiorari.

Petitioner's argument is that the right of indemnity, though not
expressly granted by the Tort Claims Act, is to be implied. A private
employer, it is said, has a common-law right of indemnity against an
employee whose negligence has made the employer liable. The Tort
Claims Act, by imposing liability on the United States for the negligent
acts of its employees, has placed it in the general position of a private
employer. Therefore, it should have the comparable right of indemnity
against the negligent employee which private employers have. . . .

The relations between the United States and its employees have
presented a myriad of problems with which the Congress over the years
has dealt. Tenure, retirement, discharge, veterans' preferences, the
responsibility of the United States to some employees for negligent acts
of other employees—these are a few of the aspects of the problem on
which Congress has legislated. Government employment gives rise to
policy questions of great import, both to the employees and the executive and legislative branches. On the employee side are questions of
considerable import. Discipline of the employee, the exactions which
may be made of him, the merits or demerits he may suffer, the rate of
his promotion are of great consequence to those who make government
service their career. The right of the employer to sue the employee is a

form of discipline. Perhaps the suits which would be instituted under the rule which petitioner asks would mostly be brought only when the employee carried insurance. But the decision we could fashion could have no such limitations, since we deal only with a rule of indemnity which is utterly independent of any underwriting of the liability. Moreover, the suits that would be brought would haul the employee to court and require him to find a lawyer, to face his employer's charge, and to submit to the ordeal of a trial. The time out for the trial and its preparation, plus the out-of-pocket expenses, might well impose on the employee a heavier financial burden than the loss of his seniority or a demotion in rank. When the United States sues an employee and takes him to court, it lays the heavy hand of discipline on him, as onerous to the employee perhaps as any measure the employer might take, except discharge itself.

On the government side are questions of employee morale and fiscal policy. We have no way of knowing what the impact of the rule of indemnity we are asked to create might be. But we do know the question has serious aspects—considerations that pertain to the financial ability of employees, to their efficiency, to their morale. These are all important to the executive branch. The financial burden placed on the United States by the Tort Claims Act also raises important questions of fiscal policy. A part of that fiscal problem is the question of reimbursement of the United States for the losses it suffers as a result of the waiver of its sovereign immunity. Perhaps the losses suffered are so great that government employees should be required to carry part of the burden. Perhaps the cost in the morale and efficiency of employees would be too high a price to pay for the rule of indemnity the petitioner now asks us to write into the Tort Claims Act.

We had an analogous problem before us in United States v. Standard Oil Co., 332 U.S. 301 (1947), where the United States sued the owner and driver of a truck for the negligent injury of a soldier in the Army of the United States, claiming damages for loss of the soldier's service during the period of his disability. We were asked to extend the common-law action of per quod servitium amisit to the government-soldier relation. We declined, stating that the problem involved federal fiscal affairs over which Congress, not the Court, should formulate the policy.

The reasons for following that course in the present case are even more compelling. Here a complex of relations between federal agencies and their staffs is involved. Moreover, the claim now asserted, though the product of a law Congress has passed, is a matter on which Congress has not taken a position. It presents questions of policy on which Congress has not spoken.[2] The selection of that policy which is most advantageous to the whole involves a host of considerations that must be weighed and appraised. That function is more appropriately for those who write the laws, rather than for those who interpret them.

Affirmed.

---

[2] Though the legislative history of the act is not too helpful on this issue, such indications as there are point toward the result we reach.

NOTES ON SUITS BY THE UNITED STATES SEEKING COMMON LAW REMEDIES

1. *United States v. Hudson & Goodwin.* The question in United States v. Hudson & Goodwin, 11 U.S. (7 Cranch) 32 (1812), was whether the federal trial courts had authority to punish common law crimes against the United States. The Court held that they did not, a position from which there has been no subsequent departure. The Court stated:

> "The course of reasoning which leads to this conclusion is simple, obvious, and admits of but little illustration. The powers of the general government are made up of concessions from the several states—whatever is not expressly given to the former, the latter expressly reserve. The judicial power of the United States is a constituent part of those concessions; that power is to be exercised by courts organized for the purpose, and brought into existence by an effort of the legislative power of the union. . . .
>
> "It is not necessary to inquire, whether the general government, in any and what extent, possesses the power of conferring on its courts a jurisdiction in cases similar to the present; it is enough, that such jurisdiction has not been conferred by any legislative act, if it does not result to those courts as a consequence of their creation. . . .
>
> "Certain implied powers must necessarily result to our courts of justice, from the nature of their institution. But jurisdiction of crimes against the state is not among those powers. To fine for contempt, imprison for contumacy, enforce the observance of order, etc., are powers which cannot be dispensed with in a court, because they are necessary to the exercise of all others: and so far our courts, no doubt, possess powers not immediately derived from statute; but all exercise of criminal jurisdiction in common-law cases, we are of opinion, is not within their implied powers." [a]

2. *United States v. Standard Oil.* United States v. Standard Oil Co. of California, 332 U.S. 301 (1947), referred to in the *Gilman* opinion, arose out of an automobile accident in Los Angeles. A Standard Oil truck hit a soldier, who was hospitalized and disabled for a

---

[a] On its facts, *Hudson & Goodwin* involved an indictment for criminal libel on the President and the Congress published in a Connecticut newspaper. United States v. Coolidge, 14 U.S. (1 Wheat.) 415 (1816), involved an indictment for an offense committed on the high seas. The case came to the Supreme Court because the judges of the Circuit Court were divided on whether they had authority to punish common law offenses against the United States. The Attorney General took the position that the issue was settled by *Hudson & Goodwin* and declined to argue the case. The Court said:

"Upon the question now before the Court a difference of opinion has existed, and still exists, among the members of the Court. We should, therefore, have been willing to have heard the question discussed upon solemn argument. But the Attorney General has declined to argue the cause; and no counsel appears for the defendant. Under these circumstances, the Court would not choose to review their former decision in [*Hudson & Goodwin*] or draw it into doubt. They will, therefore, certify an opinion to the Circuit Court in conformity with that decision."

short period of time. The soldier settled his claim with Standard Oil. Thereafter, the United States filed a lawsuit against Standard Oil seeking compensation for the pay the injured soldier received while incapacitated as well as the cost of the medical services supplied by a military hospital. The amount involved was less than $200, but the government sought to establish the principle that it was entitled to such recoveries because it was faced at the time with about 40 such incidents a month.

The District Court made findings in favor of the government on all issues but the Circuit Court reversed, holding that state law governed and that (1) the government had no independent cause of action under California law and (2) the soldier's release of Standard Oil foreclosed any right of subrogation which the government might assert.

The Supreme Court affirmed, but on a different theory. Its opinion can be divided into three parts. In the first, the Court concluded that federal and not state law applied:

> "Perhaps no relation between the government and a citizen is more distinctively federal in character than that between it and members of its armed forces. To whatever extent state law may apply to govern the relations between soldiers . . . and persons outside [the armed forces], the scope, nature, legal incidents and consequences of the relation between persons in service and the government are fundamentally derived from federal sources and governed by federal authority. So also we think are interferences with that relationship such as the facts of this case involve. For, as the federal government has the exclusive power to establish and define the relationship by virtue of its military and other powers, equally clearly it has power in execution of the same functions to protect the relation once formed from harms inflicted by others.
>
> "Since also the government's purse is affected, as well as its power to protect the relationship, its fiscal powers, to the extent that they are available to protect it against financial injury, add their weight to the military basis for excluding state intrusion. Indeed, in this aspect the case is not greatly different from the *Clearfield* case [b] . . . .."

In the second part of its opinion, the Court noted that sometimes borrowed state law supplies the substantive content of federal common law. This course was, however, inappropriate here:

> "[W]e . . . are of opinion that state law should not be selected as the federal rule for governing the matter in issue. Not only is the government-soldier relation distinctively and exclusively a creation of federal law, but we know of no good reason why the government's right to be indemnified in these circumstances, or the lack of such a right, should vary in accordance with the different rulings of the several states,

[b] *Clearfield* is discussed at pages 299–301, supra. [Footnote by eds.]

simply because the soldier marches or today perhaps as often flies across state lines.

"Furthermore, the liability sought is not essential or even relevant to protection of the state's citizens against tortious harms, nor indeed for the soldier's personal indemnity or security . . . since his personal rights against the wrongdoer may be fully protected without reference to any indemnity for the government's loss. It is rather a liability the principal, if not the only, effect of which would be to make whole the federal treasury for financial losses sustained, flowing from the injuries inflicted and the government's obligations to the soldier. The question, therefore, is chiefly one of federal fiscal policy, not of special or peculiar concern to the states or their citizens. And because those matters ordinarily are appropriate for uniform national treatment rather than diversified local disposition, as well where Congress has not acted affirmatively as where it has, they are more fittingly determinable by independent federal judicial decision than by reference to varying state policies."

Up to this point, the government's position had been fully accepted. The government argued further that growth "is the life of the law" and that "the special problem here has roots in the ancient soil of tort law, wherein the chief plowman has been the judge, notwithstanding his furrow may be covered up or widened by legislation." The government also cited analogous causes of action that had been recognized by common law decisions. In the third part of its opinion, the Court responded:

"But we forego the tendered opportunity. For we think the argument ignores factors of controlling importance distinguishing the present problem . . .. These are centered in the very fact that it is the government's interests and relations that are involved . . . and in the narrower scope, as compared with that allowed courts of general common-law jurisdiction, for the action of federal courts in such matters.

"We would not deny the government's basic premise of the law's capacity for growth, or that it must include the creative work of judges. . . . But in the federal scheme our part in that work, and the part of the other federal courts, outside the constitutional area is more modest than that of state courts, particularly in the freedom to create new common-law liabilities, as *Erie* itself witnesses. See also United States v. Hudson & Goodwin, 11 U.S. (7 Cranch) 32 (1812).

"Moreover, . . . we have not here simply a question of creating a new liability in the nature of a tort. For grounded though the argument is in analogies drawn from that field, the issue comes down in final consequence to a question of federal fiscal policy, coupled with considerations concerning the need for and the appropriateness of means to be used in executing the policy sought to be established. The tort law analogy is brought forth . . . as the instrument for determining and establishing the federal fiscal and regulatory policies which the government's executive arm thinks should prevail in a situation not covered by traditionally established liabilities.

"Whatever the merits of the policy, its conversion into law is a proper subject for congressional action, not for any creative power of ours. Congress, not this Court or the other federal courts, is the custodian of the national purse. By the same token it is the primary and most often the exclusive arbiter of federal fiscal affairs. And these comprehend . . . securing the treasury or the government against financial losses however inflicted . . . . Until it acts to establish the liability, this Court and others should withhold creative touch."

Justice Frankfurter concurred in the result without opinion, and Justice Jackson was alone in dissent.

3. Questions and Comments. Cases such as *Lake Misere* (page 289, supra) and *Clearfield Trust* (page 299, supra) focus on whether state or federal law applies in suits where the United States is the plaintiff without asking about the source of the remedy—without asking, in other words, where the government's "cause of action" comes from. In situations where state law has been displaced and where the United States is allowed to recover, it would seem to follow that the cause of action as well as the controlling substantive principles must come from federal law. By contrast, *Gilman* and *Standard Oil*—and in a different context *Hudson & Goodwin*—present situations where the remedy or "cause of action" question was explicitly raised and where the Court held that the United States had no remedy to assert. What explains the difference between these two lines of cases? Can the Court consistently permit recovery in *Lake Misere* and *Clearfield Trust* but deny relief in *Gilman* and *Standard Oil*? Is *Hudson & Goodwin* different because it involved the criminal law, or does it stand for principles that are also applicable to civil suits?

Consider also the relation between the implication of a remedy in favor of the United States and the implication of a remedy in favor of private parties. Is the *Texas Industries'* problem (page 365, supra) analytically similar to the *Gilman* problem? Or do the two lines of cases involve contexts so different that one cannot inform the other?

SECTION 3: SUITS BY PRIVATE PARTIES TO ENFORCE THE CONSTITUTION

BIVENS v. SIX UNKNOWN NAMED AGENTS OF FEDERAL BUREAU OF NARCOTICS

Supreme Court of the United States, 1971.
403 U.S. 388.

MR. JUSTICE BRENNAN delivered the opinion of the Court. . . .

This case has its origin in an arrest and search carried out on the morning of November 26, 1965. Petitioner's complaint alleged that on that day respondents, agents of the Federal Bureau of Narcotics acting under claim of federal authority, entered his apartment and arrested him for alleged narcotics violations. The agents manacled petitioner in front of his wife and children, and threatened to arrest the entire family. They searched the apartment from stem to stern. Thereafter, petitioner was taken to the federal courthouse in Brooklyn, where he was interrogated, booked, and subjected to a visual strip search.

On July 7, 1967, petitioner brought suit in federal District Court. In addition to the allegations above, his complaint asserted that the arrest and search were effected without a warrant, and that unreasonable force was employed in making the arrest; fairly read, it alleges as well that the arrest was made without probable cause. Petitioner claimed to have suffered great humiliation, embarrassment, and mental suffering as a result of the agents' unlawful conduct, and sought $15,000 damages from each of them. The District Court, on respondents' motion, dismissed the complaint on the ground, inter alia, that it failed to state a cause of action.[2] The Court of Appeals . . . affirmed on that basis. We granted certiorari. We reverse.

I

Respondents do not argue that petitioner should be entirely without remedy for an unconstitutional invasion of his rights by federal agents. In respondents' view, however, the rights that petitioner asserts—primarily rights of privacy—are creations of state and not of federal law. Accordingly, they argue, petitioner may obtain money damages to redress invasion of these rights only by an action in tort, under state law, in the state courts. In this scheme the fourth amendment would serve merely to limit the extent to which the agents could defend the state law tort suit by asserting that their actions were a valid exercise of federal power: if the agents were shown to have violated the fourth amendment, such a defense would be lost to them and they would stand before the state law merely as private individu-

---

[2] The agents were not named in petitioner's complaint, and the District Court ordered that the complaint be served upon "those federal agents who it is indicated by the records of the United States Attorney participated in the November 25, 1965, arrest of the [petitioner]." Five agents were ultimately served.

als. Candidly admitting that it is the policy of the Department of Justice to remove all such suits from the state to the federal courts for decision,[4] respondents nevertheless urge that we uphold dismissal of petitioner's complaint in federal court, and remit him to filing an action in the state courts in order that the case may properly be removed to the federal court for decision on the basis of state law.

We think that respondents' thesis rests upon an unduly restrictive view of the fourth amendment's protection against unreasonable searches and seizures by federal agents, a view that has consistently been rejected by this Court. Respondents seek to treat the relationship between a citizen and a federal agent unconstitutionally exercising his authority as no different from the relationship between two private citizens. In so doing, they ignore the fact that power, once granted, does not disappear like a magic gift when it is wrongfully used. An agent acting—albeit unconstitutionally—in the name of the United States possesses a far greater capacity for harm than an individual trespasser exercising no authority other than his own. Accordingly, as our cases make clear, the fourth amendment operates as a limitation upon the exercise of federal power regardless of whether the state in whose jurisdiction that power is exercised would prohibit or penalize the identical act if engaged in by a private citizen. It guarantees to citizens of the United States the absolute right to be free from unreasonable searches and seizures carried out by virtue of federal authority. And "where federally protected rights have been invaded, it has been the rule from the beginning that courts will be alert to adjust their remedies so as to grant the necessary relief."

First. Our cases have long since rejected the notion that the fourth amendment proscribes only such conduct as would, if engaged in by private persons, be condemned by state law. [R]espondents' argument that the fourth amendment serves only as a limitation on federal defenses to a state law claim, and not as an independent limitation upon the exercise of federal power, must [therefore] be rejected.

Second. The interests protected by state laws regulating trespass and the invasion of privacy, and those protected by the fourth amendment's guarantee against unreasonable searches and seizures, may be inconsistent or even hostile. Thus, we may bar the door against an unwelcome private intruder, or call the police if he persists in seeking entrance. The availability of such alternative means for the protection of privacy may lead the state to restrict imposition of liability for any consequent trespass. A private citizen, asserting no authority other

---

[4] "[S]ince it is the present policy of the Department of Justice to remove to the federal courts all suits in state courts against federal officers for trespass or false imprisonment, a claim for relief, whether based on state common law or directly on the fourth amendment, will ultimately be heard in a federal court." Brief for Respondents 13. In light of this, it is difficult to understand our Brother Blackmun's complaint that our holding today "opens the door for another avalanche of new federal cases." In estimating the magnitude of any such "avalanche," it is worth noting that a survey [in 1968] of comparable actions against state officers under 42 U.S.C. § 1983 found only 53 reported cases in 17 years (1951–1967) that survived a motion to dismiss. Increasing this figure by 900% to allow for increases in rate and unreported cases, every federal district judge could expect to try one such case every 13 years.

than his own, will not normally be liable in trespass if he demands, and is granted, admission to another's house. But one who demands admission under a claim of federal authority stands in a far different position. The mere invocation of federal power by a federal law enforcement official will normally render futile any attempt to resist an unlawful entry or arrest by resort to the local police; and a claim of authority to enter is likely to unlock the door as well. "In such cases there is no safety for the citizen, except in the protection of the judicial tribunals, for rights which have been invaded by the officers of the government, professing to act in its name. There remains to him but the alternative of resistance, which may amount to crime." Nor is it adequate to answer that the state may take into account the different status of one clothed with the authority of the federal government. For just as state law may not authorize federal agents to violate the fourth amendment, neither may state law undertake to limit the extent to which federal authority can be exercised. The inevitable consequence of this dual limitation on state power is that the federal question becomes not merely a possible defense to the state law action, but an independent claim both necessary and sufficient to make out the plaintiff's cause of action.

Third. That damages may be obtained for injuries consequent upon a violation of the fourth amendment by federal officials should hardly seem a surprising proposition. Historically, damages have been regarded as the ordinary remedy for an invasion of personal interests in liberty. Of course, the fourth amendment does not in so many words provide for its enforcement by an award of money damages for the consequences of its violation. But "it is . . . well settled that where legal rights have been invaded, and a federal statute provides for a general right to sue for such invasion, federal courts may use any available remedy to make good the wrong done." The present case involves no special factors counselling hesitation in the absence of affirmative action by Congress. We are not dealing with a question of "federal fiscal policy," as in United States v. Standard Oil Co., 332 U.S. 301, 311 (1947). In that case we refused to infer from the government-soldier relationship that the United States could recover damages from one who negligently injured a soldier and thereby caused the government to pay his medical expenses and lose his services during the course of his hospitalization. Noting that Congress was normally quite solicitous where the federal purse was involved, we pointed out that "the United States [was] the party plaintiff to the suit. And the United States has power at any time to create the liability." Nor are we asked in this case to impose liability upon a congressional employee for actions contrary to no constitutional prohibition, but merely said to be in excess of the authority delegated to him by the Congress. Wheeldin v. Wheeler, 373 U.S. 647 (1963). Finally, we cannot accept respondents' formulation of the question as whether the availability of money damages is necessary to enforce the fourth amendment. For we have here no explicit congressional declaration that persons injured by a federal officer's violation of the fourth amendment may not recover money damages from the agents, but must instead be remitted to another remedy, equally effective in the view of Congress. The question is merely whether petitioner, if he can demonstrate an injury consequent upon the violation by federal agents of his fourth amendment rights, is entitled to redress his injury through a particular remedial mechanism normally available in the federal courts. Cf. J.I. Case Co. v. Borak, 377 U.S. 426, 433 (1964). "The very essence of civil liberty certainly consists in the right of every individual to claim the protection of the laws, whenever he receives an injury." Marbury v. Madison, 5 U.S. (1 Cranch) 137, 163 (1803). Having concluded that petitioner's complaint states a cause of action under the fourth amendment, we hold that petitioner is entitled to recover money damages for any injuries he has suffered as a result of the agents' violation of the amendment.

II

In addition to holding that petitioner's complaint had failed to state facts making out a cause of action, the District Court ruled that in any event respondents were immune from liability by virtue of their official position. This question was not passed upon by the Court of Appeals, and accordingly we do not consider it here.[a] The judgment of the Court of Appeals is reversed and the case is remanded for further proceedings consistent with this opinion.

So ordered.

MR. JUSTICE HARLAN, concurring in the judgment. . . .

Chief Judge Lumbard's opinion [for the court below] reasoned, in essence, that: (1) the framers of the fourth amendment did not appear to contemplate a "wholly new federal cause of action founded directly on the fourth amendment," and (2) while the federal courts had power under a general grant of jurisdiction to imply a federal remedy for the enforcement of a constitutional right, they should do so only when the absence of alternative remedies renders the constitutional command a "mere 'form of words.'" The government takes essentially the same position here. And two members of the Court add the contention that we lack the constitutional power to accord Bivens a remedy for damages in the absence of congressional action creating "a federal cause of action for damages for an unreasonable search in violation of the fourth amendment."

For the reasons set forth below, I am of the opinion that federal courts do have the power to award damages for violation of "constitutionally protected interests" and I agree with the Court that a traditional judicial remedy such as damages is appropriate to the vindication of the personal interests protected by the fourth amendment.

---

[a] The question of immunity is dealt with in these materials in connection with § 1983, pages 898–927, infra. [Footnote by eds.]

I

I turn first to the contention that the constitutional power of federal courts to accord Bivens damages for his claim depends on the passage of a statute creating a "federal cause of action." Although the point is not entirely free of ambiguity, I do not understand either the government or my dissenting Brothers to maintain that Bivens' contention that he is entitled to be free from the type of official conduct prohibited by the fourth amendment depends on a decision by the state in which he resides to accord him a remedy. Such a position would be incompatible with the presumed availability of federal equitable relief, if a proper showing can be made in terms of the ordinary principles governing equitable remedies. However broad a federal court's discretion concerning equitable remedies, it is absolutely clear—at least after Erie R. Co. v. Tompkins, 304 U.S. 64 (1938)—that in a nondiversity suit a federal court's power to grant even equitable relief depends on the presence of a substantive right derived from federal law.

Thus the interest which Bivens claims—to be free from official conduct in contravention of the fourth amendment—is a federally protected interest. Therefore, the question of judicial *power* to grant Bivens damages is not a problem of the "source" of the "right"; instead, the question is whether the power to authorize damages as a judicial remedy for the vindication of a federal constitutional right is placed by the Constitution itself exclusively in Congress' hands.

II

The contention that the federal courts are powerless to accord a litigant damages for a claimed invasion of his federal constitutional rights until Congress explicitly authorizes the remedy cannot rest on the notion that the decision to grant compensatory relief involves a resolution of policy considerations not susceptible of judicial discernment. Thus, in suits for damages based on violations of federal statutes lacking any express authorization of a damage remedy, this Court has authorized such relief where, in its view, damages are necessary to effectuate the congressional policy underpinning the substantive provisions of the statute. J.I. Case Co. v. Borak, 377 U.S. 426 (1964).[4]

---

[4] The *Borak* case is an especially clear example of the exercise of federal judicial power to accord damages as an appropriate remedy in the absence of any express statutory authorization of a federal cause of action. There we "implied"—from what can only be characterized as an "exclusively procedural provision" affording access to a federal forum—a private cause of action for damages for violation of § 14(a) of the Securities Exchange Act of 1934. We did so in an area where federal regulation has been singularly comprehensive and elaborate administrative enforcement machin-

ery had been provided. The exercise of judicial power involved in *Borak* simply cannot be justified in terms of statutory construction, see Hill, Constitutional Remedies, 69 Colum. L. Rev. 1109, 1120–21 (1969); nor did the *Borak* Court purport to do so. The notion of "implying" a remedy, therefore, as applied to cases like *Borak*, can only refer to a process whereby the federal judiciary exercises a choice among *traditionally available* judicial remedies according to reasons related to the substantive social policy embodied in an act of positive law.

If it is not the nature of the remedy which is thought to render a judgment as to the appropriateness of damages inherently "legislative," then it must be the nature of the legal interest offered as an occasion for invoking otherwise appropriate judicial relief. But I do not think that the fact that the interest is protected by the Constitution rather than statute or common law justifies the assertion that federal courts are powerless to grant damages in the absence of explicit congressional action authorizing the remedy. Initially, I note that it would be at least anomalous to conclude that the federal judiciary—while competent to choose among the range of traditional judicial remedies to implement statutory and common law policies, and even to generate substantive rules governing primary behavior in furtherance of broadly formulated policies articulated by statute or Constitution, see Textile Workers v. Lincoln Mills, 353 U.S. 448 (1957); United States v. Standard Oil Co., 332 U.S. 301, 304–11 (1947); Clearfield Trust Co. v. United States, 318 U.S. 363 (1943)—is powerless to accord a damages remedy to vindicate social policies which, by virtue of their inclusion in the Constitution, are aimed predominantly at restraining the government as an instrument of the popular will.

More importantly, the presumed availability of federal equitable relief against threatened invasions of constitutional interests appears entirely to negate the contention that the status of an interest as constitutionally protected divests federal courts of the power to grant damages absent express congressional authorization. . . .

If explicit congressional authorization is an absolute prerequisite to the power of a federal court to accord compensatory relief regardless of the necessity or appropriateness of damages as a remedy simply because of the status of a legal interest as constitutionally protected, then it seems to me that explicit congressional authorization is similarly prerequisite to the exercise of equitable remedial discretion in favor of constitutionally protected interests. Conversely, if a general grant of jurisdiction to the federal courts by Congress is thought adequate to empower a federal court to grant equitable relief for all areas of subject-matter jurisdiction enumerated therein, then it seems to me that the same statute is sufficient to empower a federal court to grant a traditional remedy at law.[6] Of course, the special historical traditions governing the federal equity system, might still bear on the comparative appropriateness of granting equitable relief as opposed to money damages. That possibility, however, relates, not to whether the federal courts have the power to afford one type of remedy as opposed to the

---

[6] Chief Judge Lumbard's opinion for the Court of Appeals in the instant case is, as I have noted, in accord with this conclusion:

"Thus even if the Constitution itself does not give rise to an inherent injunctive power to prevent its violation by governmental officials there are strong reasons for inferring the existence of this power under any general grant of jurisdiction to the federal courts by Congress."

The description of the remedy as "inferred" cannot, of course, be intended to assimilate the judicial decision to accord such a remedy to any process of statutory construction. Rather, as with the cases concerning remedies, implied from statutory schemes, see n.4, supra, the description of the remedy as "inferred" can only bear on the reasons offered to explain a judicial decision to accord or not to accord a particular remedy.

other, but rather to the criteria which should govern the exercise of our power. To that question, I now pass.

III

The major thrust of the government's position is that, where Congress has not expressly authorized a particular remedy, a federal court should exercise its power to accord a traditional form of judicial relief at the behest of a litigant, who claims a constitutionally protected interest has been invaded, only where the remedy is "essential," or "indispensable for vindicating constitutional rights." While this "essentiality" test is most clearly articulated with respect to damages remedies, apparently the government believes the same test explains the exercise of equitable remedial powers. It is argued that historically the Court has rarely exercised the power to accord such relief in the absence of an express congressional authorization and that "[i]f Congress had thought that federal officers should be subject to a law different than state law, it would have had no difficulty in saying so, as it did with respect to state officers. . . ." See 42 U.S.C. § 1983. Although conceding that the standard of determining whether a damage remedy should be utilized to effectuate statutory policies is one of "necessity" or "appropriateness," see J.I. Case Co. v. Borak, 377 U.S. 426, 432 (1964), the government contends that questions concerning congressional discretion to modify judicial remedies relating to constitutionally protected interests warrant a more stringent constraint on the exercise of judicial power with respect to this class of legally protected interests.

These arguments for a more stringent test to govern the grant of damages in constitutional cases[7] seem to be adequately answered by the point that the judiciary has a particular responsibility to assure the vindication of constitutional interests such as those embraced by the fourth amendment. To be sure, "it must be remembered that legislatures are ultimate guardians of the liberties and welfare of the people in quite as great a degree as the courts." But it must also be . recognized that the Bill of Rights is particularly intended to vindicate the interests of the individual in the face of the popular will as expressed in legislative majorities; at the very least, it strikes me as no more appropriate to await express congressional authorization of traditional judicial relief with regard to these legal interests than with respect to interests protected by federal statutes.

The question then, is, as I see it, whether compensatory relief is "necessary" or "appropriate" to the vindication of the interest asserted. In resolving that question, it seems to me that the range of policy considerations we may take into account is at least as broad as the range of those a legislature would consider with respect to an express statutory authorization of a traditional remedy. In this regard I agree with the Court that the appropriateness of according Bivens compensa-

---

[7] I express no view on the government's suggestion that congressional authority to simply discard the remedy the Court today authorizes might be in doubt; nor do I understand the Court's opinion today to express any view on that particular question.

tory relief does not turn simply on the deterrent effect liability will have on federal official conduct.[8] Damages as a traditional form of compensation for invasion of a legally protected interest may be entirely appropriate even if no substantial deterrent effects on future official lawlessness might be thought to result. Bivens, after all, has invoked judicial processes claiming entitlement to compensation for injuries resulting from allegedly lawless official behavior, if those injuries are properly compensable in money damages. I do not think a court of law—vested with the power to accord a remedy—should deny him his relief simply because he cannot show that future lawless conduct will thereby be deterred.

And I think it is clear that Bivens advances a claim of the sort that, if proved, would be properly compensable in damages. The personal interests protected by the fourth amendment are those we attempt to capture by the notion of "privacy"; while the Court today properly points out that the type of harm which officials can inflict when they invade protected zones of an individual's life are different from the types of harm private citizens inflict on one another, the experience of judges in dealing with private trespass and false imprisonment claims supports the conclusion that courts of law are capable of making the types of judgment concerning causation and magnitude of injury necessary to accord meaningful compensation for invasion of fourth amendment rights.[9]

On the other hand, the limitations on state remedies for violation of common-law rights by private citizens argue in favor of a federal damages remedy. The injuries inflicted by officials acting under color of law, while no less compensable in damages than those inflicted by private parties, are substantially different in kind, as the Court's opinion today discusses in detail. It seems to me entirely proper that these injuries be compensable according to uniform rules of federal law, especially in light of the very large element of federal law which must in any event control the scope of official defenses to liability. Certainly, there is very little to be gained from the standpoint of federalism by preserving different rules of liability for federal officers dependent on the state where the injury occurs.

[8] And I think it follows from this point that today's decision has little, if indeed any, bearing on the question whether a federal court may properly devise remedies—other than traditionally available forms of judicial relief—for the purpose of enforcing substantive social policies embodied in constitutional or statutory policies. Compare today's decision with Mapp v. Ohio, 367 U.S. 643 (1961), and Weeks v. United States, 232 U.S. 383 (1914). The Court today simply recognizes what has long been implicit in our decisions concerning equitable relief and remedies implied from statutory schemes; i.e., that a court of law vested with jurisdiction over the subject matter of a suit has the power—and therefore the duty—to make principled choices among traditional judicial remedies. Whether special prophylactic measures—which at least arguably the exclusionary rule exemplifies—are supportable on grounds other than a court's competence to select among traditional judicial remedies to make good the wrong done is a separate question.

[9] The same, of course, may not be true with respect to other types of constitutionally protected interests, and therefore the appropriateness of money damages may well vary with the nature of the personal interest asserted.

Putting aside the desirability of leaving the problem of federal official liability to the vagaries of common-law actions, it is apparent that some form of damages is the only possible remedy for someone in Bivens' alleged position. It will be a rare case indeed in which an individual in Bivens' position will be able to obviate the harm by securing injunctive relief from any court. However desirable a direct remedy against the government might be as a substitute for individual official liability, the sovereign still remains immune to suit. Finally, assuming Bivens' innocence of the crime charged, the "exclusionary rule" is simply irrelevant. For people in Bivens' shoes, it is damages or nothing.

The only substantial policy consideration advanced against recognition of a federal cause of action for violation of fourth amendment rights by federal officials is the incremental expenditure of judicial resources that will be necessitated by this class of litigation. There is, however, something ultimately self-defeating about this argument. For if, as the government contends, damages will rarely be realized by plaintiffs in these cases because of jury hostility, the limited resources of the official concerned, etc., then I am not ready to assume that there will be a significant increase in the expenditure of judicial resources on these claims. Few responsible lawyers and plaintiffs are likely to choose the course of litigation if the statistical chances of success are truly de minimis. And I simply cannot agree with my Brother Black that the possibility of "frivolous" claims—if defined simply as claims with no legal merit—warrants closing the courthouse doors to people in Bivens' situation. There are other ways, short of that, of coping with frivolous lawsuits.

On the other hand, if—as I believe is the case with respect, at least, to the most flagrant abuses of official power—damages to some degree will be available when the option of litigation is chosen, then the question appears to be how fourth amendment interests rank on a scale of social values compared with, for example, the interests of stockholders defrauded by misleading proxies. See *J.I. Case Co. v. Borak,* supra. Judicial resources, I am well aware, are increasingly scarce these days. Nonetheless, when we automatically close the courthouse door solely on this basis, we implicitly express a value judgment on the comparative importance of classes of legally protected interests. And current limitations upon the effective functioning of the courts arising from budgetary inadequacies should not be permitted to stand in the way of the recognition of otherwise sound constitutional principles.

Of course, for a variety of reasons, the remedy may not often be sought. And the countervailing interests in efficient law enforcement of course argue for a protective zone with respect to many types of fourth amendment violations. But, while I express no view on the immunity defense offered in the instant case, I deem it proper to venture the thought that at the very least such a remedy would be available for the most flagrant and patently unjustified sorts of police conduct. Although litigants may not often choose to seek relief, it is important, in a civilized society, that the judicial branch of the nation's government stand ready to afford a remedy in these circumstances. It goes without saying that I intimate no view on the merits of petitioner's underlying claim.

For these reasons, I concur in the judgment of the Court.

MR. CHIEF JUSTICE BURGER, dissenting.

I dissent from today's holding which judicially creates a damage remedy not provided for by the Constitution and not enacted by Congress. We would more surely preserve the important values of the doctrine of separation of powers—and perhaps get a better result—by recommending a solution to the Congress as the branch of government in which the Constitution has vested the legislative power. Legislation is the business of the Congress, and it has the facilities and competence for that task—as we do not. Professor Thayer, speaking of the limits on judicial power, albeit in another context, had this to say:[1]

> "And if it be true that the holders of legislative power are careless or evil, yet the constitutional duty of the court remains untouched; it cannot rightly attempt to protect the people, by undertaking a function not its own. On the other hand, by adhering rigidly to its own duty, the court will help, as nothing else can, to fix the spot where responsibility lies, and to bring down on that precise locality the thunderbolt of popular condemnation. . . . For that course—the true course of judicial duty always—will powerfully help to bring the people and their representatives to a sense of their own responsibility."

[At this point Chief Justice Burger undertook an extensive analysis of the exclusionary rule, concluding that it had failed to accomplish its objectives and should be abandoned.]

I do not question the need for some remedy to give meaning and teeth to the constitutional guarantees against unlawful conduct by government officials. Without some effective sanction, these protections would constitute little more than rhetoric. Beyond doubt the conduct of some officials requires sanctions. . . . But the hope that this objective could be accomplished by the exclusion of reliable evidence from criminal trials was hardly more than a wistful dream. Although I would hesitate to abandon it until some meaningful substitute is developed, the history of the suppression doctrine demonstrates that it is both conceptually sterile and practically ineffective in accomplishing its stated objective. This is illustrated by the paradox that an unlawful act against a totally innocent person—such as petitioner claims to be—has been left without an effective remedy, and hence the Court finds it necessary now . . . to construct a remedy of its own.

. . .

Today's holding seeks to fill one of the gaps of the suppression doctrine—at the price of impinging on the legislative and policy func-

[1] J. Thayer, O. Holmes, & F. Frankfurter, John Marshall 87–88 (Phoenix ed. 1967).

tions that the Constitution vests in Congress. Nevertheless, the holding serves the useful purpose of exposing the fundamental weaknesses of the suppression doctrine. Suppressing unchallenged truth has set guilty criminals free but demonstrably has neither deterred deliberate violations of the fourth amendment nor decreased those errors in judgment that will inevitably occur given the pressures inherent in police work having to do with serious crimes. . . .

The problems of both error and deliberate misconduct by law enforcement officials call for a workable remedy. Private damage actions against individual police officers concededly have not adequately met this requirement, and it would be fallacious to assume today's work of the Court in creating a remedy will really accomplish its stated objective. There is some validity to the claims that juries will not return verdicts against individual officers except in those unusual cases where the violation has been flagrant or where the error has been complete, as in the arrest of the wrong person or the search of the wrong house. There is surely serious doubt, for example, that a drug peddler caught packaging his wares will be able to arouse much sympathy in a jury on the ground that the police officer did not announce his identity and purpose fully or because he failed to utter a "few more words." Jurors may well refuse to penalize a police officer at the behest of a person they believe to be a "criminal" and probably will not punish an officer for honest errors of judgment. In any event an actual recovery depends on finding non-exempt assets of the police officer from which a judgment can be satisfied.

I conclude, therefore, that an entirely different remedy is necessary but it is one that in my view is as much beyond judicial power as the step the Court takes today. Congress should develop an administrative or quasi-judicial remedy against the government itself to afford compensation and restitution for persons whose fourth amendment rights have been violated. [At this point Chief Justice Burger sketched some of the details of the remedy he had in mind.]

MR. JUSTICE BLACK, dissenting. . . .

There can be no doubt that Congress could create a federal cause of action for damages for an unreasonable search in violation of the fourth amendment. Although Congress has created such a federal cause of action against *state* officials acting under color of state law [42 U.S.C. § 1983], it has never created such a cause of action against federal officials. If it wanted to do so, Congress could, of course, create a remedy against federal officials who violate the fourth amendment in the performance of their duties. But the point of this case and the fatal weakness in the Court's judgment is that neither Congress nor the state of New York has enacted legislation creating such a right of action. For us to do so is, in my judgment, an exercise of power that the Constitution does not give us.

Even if we had the legislative power to create a remedy, there are many reasons why we should decline to create a cause of action where none has existed since the formation of our government. The courts of the United States as well as those of the states are choked with lawsuits. The number of cases on the docket of this Court have reached an unprecedented volume in recent years. A majority of these cases are brought by citizens with substantial complaints—persons who are physically or economically injured by torts or frauds or governmental infringement of their rights; persons who have been unjustly deprived of their liberty or their property; and persons who have not yet received the equal opportunity in education, employment, and pursuit of happiness that was the dream of our forefathers. Unfortunately, there have also been a growing number of frivolous lawsuits, particularly actions for damages against law enforcement officers whose conduct has been judicially sanctioned by state trial and appellate courts and in many instances even by this Court. My fellow Justices on this Court and our brethren throughout the federal judiciary know only too well the time-consuming task of conscientiously poring over hundreds of thousands of pages of factual allegations of misconduct by police, judicial, and corrections officials. Of course, there are instances of legitimate grievances, but legislators might well desire to devote judicial resources to other problems of a more serious nature.

We sit at the top of a judicial system accused by some of nearing the point of collapse. Many criminal defendants do not receive speedy trials and neither society nor the accused are assured of justice when inordinate delays occur. Citizens must wait years to litigate their private civil suits. Substantial changes in correctional and parole systems demand the attention of the lawmakers and the judiciary. If I were a legislator I might well find these and other needs so pressing as to make me believe that the resources of lawyers and judges should be devoted to them rather than to civil damage actions against officers who generally strive to perform within constitutional bounds. There is also a real danger that such suits might deter officials from the *proper* and honest performance of their duties.

All of these considerations make imperative careful study and weighing of the arguments both for and against the creation of such a remedy under the fourth amendment. I would have great difficulty for myself in resolving the competing policies, goals, and priorities in the use of resources, if I thought it were my job to resolve those questions. But that is not my task. The task of evaluating the pros and cons of creating judicial remedies for particular wrongs is a matter for Congress and the legislatures of the state. Congress has not provided that any federal court can entertain a suit against a federal officer for violations of fourth amendment rights occurring in the performance of his duties. A strong inference can be drawn from creation of such actions against state officials that Congress does not desire to permit such suit against federal officials. Should the time come when Congress desires such lawsuits, it has before it a model of valid legislation, 42 U.S.C. § 1983, to create a damage remedy against federal officers. Cases could be cited to support the legal proposition which I assert, but it seems to me to be a matter of common understanding that the business of the judiciary is to interpret the laws and not to make them.

I dissent.

MR. JUSTICE BLACKMUN, dissenting.

I, too, dissent. I do so largely for the reasons expressed in Chief Judge Lumbard's thoughtful and scholarly opinion for the Court of Appeals. But I also feel that the judicial legislation, which the Court by its opinion today concededly is effectuating, opens the door for another avalanche of new federal cases. Whenever a suspect imagines, or chooses to assert, that a fourth amendment right has been violated, he will now immediately sue the federal officer in federal court. This will tend to stultify proper law enforcement and to make the day's labor for the honest and conscientious officer even more onerous and more critical. Why the Court moves in this direction at this time of our history, I do not know. The fourth amendment was adopted in 1791, and in all the intervening years neither the Congress nor the Court has seen fit to take this step. I had thought that for the truly aggrieved person other quite adequate remedies have always been available. If not, it is the Congress and not this Court that should act.

NOTE ON *BIVENS*

Prior to *Bivens*, it was well accepted that a cause of action for an *injunction* based on a violation of the federal Constitution could be asserted in a federal court, notwithstanding the lack of any express statutory authority.[a] This cause of action stemmed from the decision in Ex parte Young, 209 U.S. 123 (1908), which is reproduced as a main case at page 809, infra. It was also established that the Court could infer a federal cause of action for recission or damages from a federal statute which, although it stated a standard of conduct, did not specifically authorize private relief. See J.I. Case Co. v. Borak, 377 U.S. 426 (1964), discussed further at pages 372–73, supra. And of course, the Court had created the exclusionary rule for federal courts in 1914 and applied that rule to state courts in 1961. See Mapp v. Ohio, 367 U.S. 643 (1961); Weeks v. United States, 232 U.S. 383 (1914).

Does it follow from these decisions that the Court had the constitutional authority to do what it did in *Bivens?* The *Borak* decision was unanimous. On what basis could Justice Black join in that decision and take the position in *Bivens* that "[f]or us [to create the cause of action is] an exercise of power that the Constitution does not give us?"

On the other hand, several Justices, most notably Justice Powell in the *Cannon* decision (see pages 377–79, supra), have more recently taken the position that the Court should not—and perhaps constitutionally cannot—infer a cause of action from a federal statute in the

---

[a] The availability of remedies against *state* officials or units of local government for the violation of the 14th amendment and other constitutional limitations on state power is considered in connection with § 1983. See chapter IX, infra.

absence of a clear indication of congressional intent that it be done. If this position is correct, does it follow that *Bivens* is wrong? Or is the Court arguably more justified in supplying a remedy for a constitutional violation than for the violation of a federal statute?[b]

SCHWEIKER v. CHILICKY

Supreme Court of the United States, 1988.
___ U.S. ___.

JUSTICE O'CONNOR delivered the opinion of the Court.

This case requires us to decide whether the improper denial of social security disability benefits, allegedly resulting from violations of due process by government officials who administered the federal social security program, may give rise to a cause of action for money damages against those officials. We conclude that such a remedy, not having been included in the elaborate remedial scheme devised by Congress, is unavailable.

I

A

Under title II of the Social Security Act, the federal government provides disability benefits to individuals who have contributed to the social security program and who, because of a medically determinable physical or mental impairment, are unable to engage in substantial gainful work. A very similar program for disabled indigents is operated under title XI of the act, but those provisions are technically not at issue in this case. Title II . . . provides benefits only while an individual's statutory disability persists. In 1980, Congress noted that existing administrative procedures provided for reexamination of eligibility "only under a limited number of circumstances." Congress responded by enacting legislation requiring that most disability determinations be reviewed at least once every three years. Although the statute did not require this program for "continuing disability review" (CDR) to become effective before January 1, 1982, the Secretary of Health and Human Services initiated CDR in March 1981.

[A]n individual whose case is selected for review bears the burden of demonstrating the continuing existence of a statutory disability. . . . Under the original CDR procedures, benefits were usually terminated after a state agency found a claimant ineligible, and were not available during administrative appeals.

Finding that benefits were too often being improperly terminated by state agencies, only to be reinstated by a federal administrative law judge (ALJ), Congress enacted temporary emergency legislation in 1983. This law provided for the continuation of benefits, pending review by

[b] For a thoughtful argument in favor of the approach of *Bivens,* see Walter E. Dellinger, Of Rights and Remedies: The Constitution as a Sword, 85 Harv. L. Rev. 1532 (1972).

an ALJ, after a state agency determined that an individual was no longer disabled. In the Social Security Disability Benefits Reform Act of 1984 (1984 Reform Act), Congress extended this provision until January 1, 1988, and provided for a number of other significant changes in the administration of CDR. In its final form, this legislation was enacted without a single opposing vote in either Chamber.

The problems to which Congress responded so emphatically were widespread. One of the cosponsors of the 1984 Reform Act, who had conducted hearings on the administration of CDR, summarized evidence from the General Accounting Office as follows:

> "[T]he message perceived by the state agencies, swamped with cases, was to deny, deny, deny, and I might add, to process cases faster and faster and faster. In the name of efficiency, we have scanned our computer terminals, rounded up the disabled workers in the country, pushed the discharge button, and let them go into a free [f]all toward economic chaos."

Other legislators reached similar conclusions. Such conclusions were based, not only on anecdotal evidence, but on compellingly forceful statistics. The Social Security Administration itself apparently reported that about 200,000 persons were wrongfully terminated, and then reinstated, between March 1981 and April 1984. In the first year of CDR, half of those who were terminated appealed the decision, and "an amazing two-thirds of those who appealed were being reinstated."

Congress was also made aware of the terrible effects on individual lives that CDR had produced. The chairman of the Senate's Special Committee on Aging pointed out that "[t]he human dimension of the crisis—the unnecessary suffering, anxiety, and turmoil—has been graphically exposed by dozens of congressional hearings and in newspaper articles all across the country." Termination could also lead to the cut-off of Medicare benefits, so that some people were left without adequate medical care. There is little doubt that CDR led to many hardships and injuries that could never be adequately compensated.

B

Respondents were three individuals whose disability benefits under title II were terminated pursuant to the CDR program in 1981 and 1982. Respondents Spencer Harris and Dora Adelerte appealed these determinations through the administrative process, were restored to disabled status, and were awarded full retroactive benefits. Respondent James Chilicky did not pursue these administrative remedies. Instead, he filed a new application for benefits about a year and a half after his benefits were stopped. His application was granted, and he was awarded one year's retroactive benefits; his application for the restoration of the other six months benefits is apparently still pending. Because the terminations in these three cases occurred before the 1983 emergency legislation was enacted, respondents experienced delays of many months in receiving disability benefits to which they were entitled. All the respondents had been wholly dependent on their disability benefits, and all allege that they were unable to maintain themselves or their families in even a minimally adequate fashion after they were declared ineligible. Respondent James Chilicky was in the hospital recovering from open-heart surgery when he was informed that his heart condition was no longer disabling.

In addition to pursuing administrative remedies, respondents (along with several other individuals who have since withdrawn from the case) filed this lawsuit in the United States District Court for the District of Arizona. They alleged that petitioners—one Arizona[1] and two federal officials who had policymaking roles in the administration of the CDR program—had violated respondents' due process rights. The thrust of the complaint, which named petitioners in their official and individual capacities, was that petitioners had adopted illegal policies that led to the wrongful termination of benefits by state agencies. . . . Respondents sought injunctive and declaratory relief, and money damages for "emotional distress and for loss of food, shelter and other necessities proximately caused by [petitioners'] denial of benefits without due process."

The District Court dismissed the case . . . . Respondents appealed, pressing only their claims for money damages against petitioners in their individual capacities. These claims, noted the Court of Appeals, are "predicated on the constitutional tort theory of Bivens v. Six Unknown Fed. Narcotics Agents, 403 U.S. 388 (1971)." [The Court of Appeals reversed and remanded for further proceedings.] The petition for certiorari presented one question: "Whether a *Bivens* remedy should be implied for alleged due process violations in the denial of social security disability benefits." We granted the petition and now reverse.

II

A

. . . In 1971, this Court held that the victim of a fourth amendment violation by federal officers acting under color of their authority may bring suit for money damages against the officers in federal court. *Bivens v. Six Unknown Fed. Narcotics Agents,* supra. The Court noted that Congress had not specifically provided for such a remedy and that "the fourth amendment does not in so many words provide for its enforcement by an award of money damages for the consequences of its violation." Nevertheless, finding "no special factors counselling hesitation in the absence of affirmative action by Congress," and "no explicit congressional declaration" that money damages may not be awarded,

---

[1] Petitioner William R. Sims is director of the Arizona Disability Determination Service, which participates in the administration of title II under the supervision of the Secretary of Health and Human Services. The Court of Appeals concluded, for jurisdictional purposes only, that Sims "was acting under color of federal law as an agent of the Secretary." We may as-sume, arguendo, that if an action akin to the one recognized in Bivens v. Six Unknown Fed. Narcotics Agents, 403 U.S. 388 (1971), would be available against the petitioners who were federal employees, it would also be available against Sims. In light of our disposition of the case, however, we need not decide the question.

the majority relied on the rule that " 'where legal rights have been invaded, and a federal statute provides for a general right to sue for such invasion, federal courts may use any available remedy to make good the wrong done.' "

So-called "*Bivens* actions" for money damages against federal officers have subsequently been permitted under 28 U.S.C. § 1331 for violations of the due process clause of the fifth amendment, Davis v. Passman, 442 U.S. 228 (1979) and the cruel and unusual punishment clause of the eighth amendment, Carlson v. Green, 446 U.S. 14 (1980). In each of these cases, as in *Bivens* itself, the Court found that there were no "special factors counselling hesitation in the absence of affirmative action by Congress," no explicit statutory prohibition against the relief sought, and no exclusive statutory alternative remedy.

Our more recent decisions have responded cautiously to suggestions that *Bivens* remedies be extended into new contexts. The absence of statutory relief for a constitutional violation, for example, does not by any means necessarily imply that courts should award money damages against the officers responsible for the violation. Thus, in Chappell v. Wallace, 462 U.S. 296 (1983), we refused—unanimously—to create a *Bivens* action for enlisted military personnel who alleged that they had been injured by the unconstitutional actions of their superior officers and who had no remedy against the government itself:

"The special nature of military life—the need for unhesitating and decisive action by military officers and equally disciplined responses by enlisted personnel—would be undermined by a judicially created remedy exposing officers to personal liability at the hands of those they are charged to command. . . .

"Also, Congress, the constitutionally authorized source of authority over the military system of justice, has not provided a damages remedy for claims by military personnel that constitutional rights have been violated by superior officers. *Any action to provide a judicial response by way of such a remedy would be plainly inconsistent with Congress' authority in this field.*

"Taken together, the unique disciplinary structure of the military establishment and Congress' activity in the field constitute 'special factors' which dictate that it would be inappropriate to provide enlisted military personnel a *Bivens*-type remedy against their superior officers." (Emphasis added).

See also United States v. Stanley, 483 U.S. ___, ___ (1987) (disallowing *Bivens* actions by military personnel "whenever the injury arises out of activity 'incident to service' ").

Similarly, we refused—again unanimously—to create a *Bivens* remedy for a first amendment violation "aris[ing] out of an employment relationship that is governed by comprehensive procedural and substantive provisions giving meaningful remedies against the United States." Bush v. Lucas, 462 U.S. 367, 368 (1983). In that case, a federal employee was demoted, allegedly in violation of the first amendment, for making public statements critical of the agency for which he worked. He was reinstated through the administrative process, with retroactive seniority and full backpay, but he was not permitted to recover for any loss due to emotional distress or mental anguish, or for attorney's fees. Concluding that the administrative system created by Congress "provides meaningful remedies for employees who may have been unfairly disciplined for making critical comments about their agencies," the Court refused to create a *Bivens* action even though it assumed a first amendment violation and acknowledged that "existing remedies do not provide complete relief for the plaintiff." See also id., at 385, n. 28 (no remedy whatsoever for short suspensions or for adverse personnel actions against probationary employees). The Court stressed that the case involved policy questions in an area that had received careful attention from Congress. Noting that the legislature is far more competent than the judiciary to carry out the necessary "balancing [of] government efficiency and the rights of employees," we refused to "decide whether or not it would be good policy to permit a federal employee to recover damages from a supervisor who has improperly disciplined him for exercising his first amendment rights."

In sum, the concept of "special factors counselling hesitation in the absence of affirmative action by Congress" has proved to include an appropriate judicial deference to indications that congressional inaction has not been inadvertent. When the design of a government program suggests that Congress has provided what it considers adequate remedial mechanisms for constitutional violations that may occur in the course of its administration, we have not created additional *Bivens* remedies.

B

. . . The steps provided for under title II are essentially identical for new claimants and for persons subject to CDR. An initial determination of a claimant's eligibility for benefits is made by a state agency, under federal standards and criteria. Next, a claimant is entitled to de novo reconsideration by the state agency, and additional evidence may be presented at that time. If the claimant is dissatisfied with the state agency's decision, review may then be had by the Secretary of Health and Human Services, acting through a federal ALJ; at this stage, the claimant is again free to introduce new evidence or raise new issues. If the claimant is still dissatisfied, a hearing may be sought before the Appeals Council of the Social Security Administration. Once these elaborate administrative remedies have been exhausted, a claimant is entitled to seek judicial review, including review of constitutional claims. The act, however, makes no provision for remedies in money damages against officials responsible for unconstitutional conduct that leads to the wrongful denial of benefits. As respondents concede, claimants whose benefits have been fully restored through the administrative process would lack standing to invoke the Constitution under the statute's administrative review provision.

The case before us cannot reasonably be distinguished from *Bush v. Lucas.* Here, exactly as in *Bush,* Congress has failed to provide for "complete relief": respondents have not been given a remedy in damages for emotional distress or for other hardships suffered because of delays in their receipt of social security benefits. The creation of a *Bivens* remedy would obviously offer the prospect of relief for injuries that must now go unredressed. Congress, however, has not failed to provide meaningful safeguards or remedies for the rights of persons situated as respondents were. Indeed, the system for protecting their rights is, if anything, considerably more elaborate than the civil service system considered in *Bush.* The prospect of personal liability for official acts, moreover, would undoubtedly lead to new difficulties and expense in recruiting administrators for the programs Congress has established. Congressional competence at "balancing governmental efficiency and the rights of [individuals]" is no more questionable in the social welfare context than it is in the civil service context.

Congressional attention to problems that have arisen in the administration of CDR (including the very problems that gave rise to this case) has, moreover, been frequent and intense. Congress itself required that the CDR program be instituted. Within two years after the program began, Congress enacted emergency legislation providing for the continuation of benefits even after a finding of ineligibility by a state agency. Less than two years after passing that law, and fully aware of the results of extensive investigations of the practices that led to respondents' injuries, Congress again enacted legislation aimed at reforming the administration of CDR; that legislation again specifically addressed the problem that had provoked the earlier emergency legislation. At each step, Congress chose specific forms and levels of protection for the rights of persons affected by incorrect eligibility determinations under CDR. At no point did Congress choose to extend to any person the kind of remedies that respondents seek in this lawsuit. Thus, congressional unwillingness to provide consequential damages for unconstitutional deprivations of a statutory right is at least as clear in the context of this case as it was in *Bush.*

Respondents nonetheless contend that *Bush* should be confined to its facts, arguing that it applies only in the context of what they call "the special nature of federal employee relations." Noting that the parties to this case did "not share the sort of close, collaborative, continuing juridical relationship found in the federal civil service," respondents suggest that the availability of *Bivens* remedies would create less "inconvenience" to the social security system than it would in the context of the civil service. The Solicitor General is less sanguine, arguing that the creation of *Bivens* remedy in this context would lead to "a complete disruption of [a] carefully crafted and constantly monitored congressional scheme."

We need not choose between these competing predictions, which have little bearing on the applicability of *Bush* to this case. The decision in *Bush* did not rest on this Court's belief that *Bivens* actions would be more disruptive the civil service than they are in other contexts where they have been allowed, such as federal law enforcement agencies (*Bivens* itself) or the federal prisons (Carlson v. Green, 446 U.S. 14 (1980)). Rather, we declined in *Bush* " 'to create a new substantive legal liability . . .' because we are convinced that Congress is in a better position to decide whether or not the public interest would be served by creating it." That reasoning applies as much, or more, in this case as it did in *Bush* itself.

Respondents also suggest that this case is distinguishable from *Bush* because the plaintiff in that case received compensation for the constitutional violation itself, while these respondents have merely received that to which they would have been entitled had there been no constitutional violation. The *Bush* opinion, however, drew no distinction between compensation for a "constitutional wrong" and the restoration of statutory rights that had been unconstitutionally taken away. Nor did it suggest that such labels would matter. Indeed, the Court appeared to assume that civil service employees would get "precisely the same thing whether or not they were victims of constitutional deprivation." *Bush* thus lends no support to the notion that statutory violations caused by unconstitutional conduct necessarily require remedies in addition to the remedies provided generally for such statutory violations. Here, as in *Bush*, it is evident that if we were "to fashion an adequate remedy for every wrong that can be proved in a case [the complaining party] would obviously prevail." In neither case, however, does the presence of alleged unconstitutional conduct that is not *separately* remedied under the statutory scheme imply that the statute has provided "no remedy" for the constitutional wrong at issue.

The remedy sought in *Bush* was virtually identical to the one sought by respondents in this case: consequential damages for hardships resulting from an allegedly unconstitutional denial of a statutory right (social security benefits in one instance and employment in a particular government job in the other). In light of the comprehensive statutory schemes involved, the harm resulting from the alleged constitutional violation can in neither case be separated from the harm resulting from the denial of the statutory right. Respondents' effort to separate the two does not distinguish this case from *Bush* in any analytically meaningful sense.

In the end, respondents' various arguments are rooted in their insistent and vigorous contention that they simply have not been adequately recompensed for their injuries . . . . We agree that suffering months of delay in receiving the income on which one has depended for the very necessities of life cannot be fully remedied by the "belated restoration of back benefits." The trauma to respondents, and thousands of others like them, must surely have gone beyond what anyone of normal sensibilities would wish to see imposed on innocent disabled citizens. Nor would we care to "trivialize" the nature of the wrongs alleged in this case. Congress, however, has addressed the problems created by state agencies' wrongful termination of disability benefits. Whether or not we believe that its response was the best response, Congress is the body charged with making the inevitable compromises required in the design of a massive and complex welfare benefits program. Congress has discharged that responsibility to the extent that it affects the case before us, and we see no legal basis that would allow us to revise its decision.

Because the relief sought by respondents is unavailable as a matter of law, the case must be dismissed. The judgment of the Court of Appeals to the contrary is therefore

Reversed.

[The concurring opinion of Justice Stevens has been omitted.]

JUSTICE BRENNAN, with whom JUSTICE MARSHALL and JUSTICE BLACK-MUN join, dissenting. . . .

I

[In part I of his dissent, Justice Brennan, inter alia, recounted respondents' allegations: "that in the course of their review proceedings, state and federal officials violated their due process rights by judging their eligibility in light of impermissible quotas, disregarding dispositive favorable evidence, selecting biased physicians, purposely using unpublished criteria and rules inconsistent with statutory standards, arbitrarily reversing favorable decisions, and failing impartially to review adverse decisions." He added that the merits of these allegations were not before the Court, although it was common ground that "the CDR program was in total disarray."]

II

A

In *Bivens* itself, we noted that, although courts have the authority to provide redress for constitutional violations in the form of an action for money damages, the exercise of that authority may be inappropriate where Congress has created another remedy that it regards as equally effective, or where "special factors counse[l] hesitation [even] in the absence of affirmative action by Congress." . . . The cases setting forth the "special factors" analysis upon which the Court relies, however, reveal, by way of comparison, both the inadequacy of title II's "remedial mechanism" and the wholly inadvertent nature of Congress' failure to provide any statutory remedy for constitutional injuries inflicted during the course of previous review proceedings.

In Chappell v. Wallace, 462 U.S. 296 (1983), where we declined to permit an action for damages by enlisted military personnel seeking redress from their superior officers for constitutional injuries, we noted that Congress, in the exercise of its "plenary constitutional authority over the military, has enacted statutes regulating military life, and has established a comprehensive internal system of justice to regulate military life . . . . The resulting system provides for the review and remedy of complaints and grievances such as [the equal protection claim] presented by respondents." That system not only permits aggrieved military personnel to raise constitutional challenges in administrative proceedings, it authorizes recovery of significant consequential damages, notably retroactive promotions. Similarly, in Bush v. Lucas, 462 U.S. 367 (1983), we concluded that, in light of the "elaborate, comprehensive scheme" governing federal employment relations, recognition of any supplemental judicial remedy for constitutional wrongs was inappropriate. Under that scheme—which Congress has "constructed step-by-step, with careful attention to conflicting policy considerations," over the course of nearly 100 years—"[c]onstitutional challenges . . . are fully cognizable" and prevailing employees are entitled not only to full backpay, but to retroactive promotions, seniority, pay raises, and accumulated leave. Indeed, Congress expressly "intended [to] put the employee 'in the same position he would have been in had the unjustified or erroneous personnel action not taken place.' "

It is true that neither the military justice system nor the federal employment relations scheme affords aggrieved parties full compensation for constitutional injuries: nevertheless, the relief provided in both is far more complete than that available under title II's review process. Although federal employees may not recover damages for any emotional or dignitary harms they might suffer as a result of a constitutional injury, they, like their military counterparts, are entitled to redress for most economic consequential damages, including, most significantly, consequential damage to their government careers. Here, by stark contrast, title II recipients cannot even raise constitutional challenges to agency action in any of the four tiers of administrative review, and if they ultimately prevail on their eligibility claims in those administrative proceedings they can recover no consequential damages whatsoever. The only relief afforded persons unconstitutionally deprived of their disability benefits is retroactive payment of the very benefits they should have received all along. Such an award, of course, fails miserably to compensate disabled persons illegally stripped of the income upon which, in many cases, their very subsistence depends.

The inadequacy of this relief is by no means a product of "the inevitable compromises required in the design of a massive and complex welfare benefits program." In *Chappell* and *Bush*, we dealt with elaborate administrative systems in which Congress anticipated that federal officials might engage in unconstitutional conduct, and in which it accordingly sought to afford injured persons a form of redress as complete as the government's institutional concerns would allow. In the federal employment context, for example, Congress carefully "balanc[ed] governmental efficiency and the rights of employees," paying "careful attention to conflicting policy considerations," *Bush*, supra, at 388–89, and in the military setting it "established a comprehensive internal system of justice to regulate military life, taking into account the special patterns that define the military structure." *Chappell*, supra, at 302.

Here, as the legislative history of the 1984 Reform Act makes abundantly clear, Congress did not attempt to achieve a delicate balance between the constitutional rights of title II beneficiaries on the one hand, and administrative concerns on the other. Rather than finetuning "an elaborate remedial scheme that ha[d] been constructed step by step" over the better part of a century, Congress confronted a paralyzing breakdown in a vital social program, which it sought to rescue from near-total anarchy. Although the legislative debate surrounding the 1984 Reform Act is littered with references to "arbitrary," "capricious," and "wrongful" terminations of benefits, it is clear that neither Congress nor anyone else identified unconstitutional conduct by state agencies as the cause of this paralysis. . . .

At no point during the lengthy legislative debate . . . did any member of Congress so much as hint that the substantive eligibility criteria, notice requirements, and interim payment provisions that would govern *future* disability reviews adequately redressed the harms that beneficiaries may have suffered as a result of the unconstitutional actions of individual state and federal officials in *past* proceedings, or that the constitutional rights of those unjustly deprived of benefits in the past had to be sacrificed in the name of administrative efficiency or any other governmental interest. The Court today identifies no legislative compromise . . . in which lawmakers expressly declined to afford a remedy for such past wrongs. Nor can the Court point to any legislator who suggested that state and federal officials should be shielded from liability for any unconstitutional acts taken in the course of administering the review program, or that exposure to liability for such acts would be inconsistent with Congress' comprehensive and carefully crafted remedial scheme. . . .

The mere fact, that Congress was aware of the prior injustices and failed to provide a form of redress for them, standing alone, is simply not a "special factor counselling hesitation" in the judicial recognition of a remedy. Inaction, we have repeatedly stated, is a notoriously poor indication of congressional intent, all the more so where Congress is legislating in the face of a massive breakdown calling for prompt and sweeping corrective measures. In 1984, Congress undertook to resuscitate a disability review process that had ceased functioning: that the prospective measures it prescribed to prevent future dislocations included no remedy for past wrongs in no way suggests a conscious choice to leave those wrongs unremedied. I therefore think it altogether untenable to conclude, on the basis of mere legislative silence and inaction, that Congress intended an administrative scheme that does not even take cognizance of constitutional claims to displace a damages action for constitutional deprivations that might arise in the administration of the disability insurance program.

B

Our decisions in *Chappell* and *Bush* reveal yet another flaw in the "special factors" analysis the Court employs today. In both those cases, we declined to legislate in areas in which Congress enjoys a special expertise that the judiciary clearly lacks. Thus, in *Chappell*, we dealt with military affairs, a subject over which "[i]t is clear that the

Constitution contemplated that the legislative branch have plenary control." Indeed, as we reaffirmed:

> " '[I]t is difficult to conceive of an area of governmental activity in which the courts have less competence. The complex, subtle, and professional designs as to the composition, training, equipping, and control of a military force are essentially professional military judgments, subject *always* to civilian control of the legislative and executive branches.' "   Id., at 302.

Similarly, in *Bush* we dealt with the unique area of federal employment relations, where the government acts not as governor but as employer. We observed that Congress had devoted a century to studying the problems peculiar to this subject, during the course of which it had "developed considerable familiarity with balancing governmental efficiency and the rights of employees." In addition, Congress "has a special interest in informing itself about the efficiency and morale of the executive branch," and is far more capable than courts of apprising itself of such matters "through factfinding procedures such as hearings that are not available to the courts." In declining to recognize a cause of action for constitutional violations that might arise in the civil service context, therefore, we reasoned that the recognition of such an action could upset Congress' careful structuring of federal employment relations, and concluded that "Congress is in a far better position to evaluate the impact of a new species of litigation between federal employees on the efficiency of the civil service."

Ignoring the unique characteristics of the military and civil service contexts that made judicial recognition of a *Bivens* action inappropriate in those cases, the Court today observes that "[c]ongressional competence at 'balancing governmental efficiency and the rights of [individuals]' is no more questionable in the social welfare context than it is in the civil service context." This observation, however, avails the Court nothing, for in *Bush* we declined to create a *Bivens* action for aggrieved federal employees not because Congress is simply competent to legislate in the area of federal employment relations, but because Congress is far more capable of addressing the special problems that arise in those relations than are courts. Thus, I have no quarrel with the Court's assertion that in *Bush* we did not decline to create a *Bivens* action because we believed such an action would be more disruptive in the civil service context than elsewhere, but because we are " 'convinced that Congress is in a better position to decide whether or not the public interest would be served by creating [such an action.]' " That conviction, however, flowed not from mere congressional competence to legislate in the area of federal employment relations, but from our recognition that we lacked the special expertise Congress had developed in such matters, as well as the ability to evaluate the impact such a right of action would have on the civil service.

The Court's suggestion, therefore, that congressional authority over a given subject is itself a "special factor" that "counsel[s] hesitation [even] in the absence of affirmative action by Congress" is clearly mistaken. In Davis v. Passman, 442 U.S. 228 (1979), we recognized a cause of action under the fifth amendment's due process clause for a congressional employee who alleged that she had been discriminated against on the basis of her sex, even though Congress is competent to pass legislation governing the employment relations of its own members. Likewise, in Carlson v. Green, 446 U.S. 14 (1980), we created a *Bivens* action for redress of injuries flowing from the allegedly unconstitutional conduct of federal prison officials, notwithstanding the fact that Congress had expressly (and competently) provided a statutory remedy in the Federal Tort Claims Act for injuries inflicted by such officials. In neither case was it necessary to inquire into Congress' competence over the subject matter. Rather, we permitted the claims because they arose in areas in which congressional competence is no greater than that of the courts, and in which, therefore, courts need not fear to tread even in the absence of congressional action.

The same is true here. Congress, of course, created the disability insurance program and obviously may legislate with respect to it. But unlike the military setting, where Congress' authority is plenary and entitled to considerable judicial deference, or the federal employment context, where Congress enjoys special expertise, social welfare is hardly an area in which the courts are largely incompetent to act. The disability insurance program is concededly large, but it does not involve necessarily unique relationships like those between enlisted military personnel and their superior officers, or government workers and their federal employers. Rather, like the federal law enforcement and penal systems that gave rise to the constitutional claims in *Bivens* and *Carlson,* the constitutional issues that surface in the social welfare system turn on the relationship of the government and those it governs—the relationship that lies at the heart of constitutional adjudication. Moreover, courts do not lack familiarity or expertise in determining what the dictates of the due process clause are. In short, the social welfare context does not give rise to the types of concerns that make it an area where courts should refrain from creating a damages action even in the absence of congressional action.

III

Because I do not agree that the scope and design of title II's administrative review process is a "special factor" precluding recognition of a *Bivens* action, I turn to petitioners' [argument] that the sheer size of the disability insurance program is a special factor militating against recognition of a *Bivens* action for respondents' claims. SSA is "probably the largest adjudicative agency in the western world," Heckler v. Campbell, 461 U.S. 458, 461, n. 2 (1983), responsible for processing over two million disability claims each year. Accordingly, petitioners argue, recognition of a *Bivens* action for any due process violations that might occur in the course of this processing would have an intolerably disruptive impact on the administration of the disability insurance program. Thousands of such suits could potentially be brought, diverting energy and money from the goals of the program itself, discouraging public service in the agency, and deterring those officials brave enough to accept such employment from "legitimate efforts" to ensure that only those truly unable to work receive benefits.

Petitioners' dire predictions are overblown in several respects. To begin with, Congress' provision for interim payments in both the 1983 emergency legislation and the 1984 Reform Act dramatically reduced the number of recipients who suffered consequential damages as a result of initial unconstitutional benefits termination. Similarly, the various other corrective measures incorporated in the 1984 legislation, which petitioners champion here as a complete remedy for past wrongs, should forestall future constitutional deprivations. Moreover, in order to prevail in any *Bivens* action, recipients such as respondents must both prove a deliberate abuse of governmental power rather than mere negligence, see Daniels v. Williams, 474 U.S. 327 (1986), and overcome the defense of qualified immunity. See Harlow v. Fitzgerald, 457 U.S. 800 (1982). Indeed, these very requirements are designed to protect government officials from liability for their "legitimate" actions; the prospect of liability for deliberate violations of known constitutional rights, therefore, will not dissuade well-intentioned civil servants either from accepting such employment or from carrying out the legitimate duties that employment imposes.

Petitioners' argument, however, is more fundamentally flawed. Both the federal law enforcement system involved in *Bivens* and the federal prison system involved in Carlson v. Green, 446 U.S. 14 (1980), are vast undertakings, and the possibility that individuals who come in contact with these government entities will consider themselves aggrieved by the misuse of official power is at least as great as that presented by the social welfare program involved here. Yet in neither case did we even hint that such factors might legitimately counsel against recognition of a remedy for those actually injured by the abuse of such authority . . . . That the authority wielded by officials in this case may be used to harm an especially large number of innocent citizens . . . militates in *favor* of a cause of action, not against one, and petitioners' argument to the contrary perverts the entire purpose underlying our recognition of *Bivens* actions. In the modern welfare society in which we live, where many individuals such as respondents depend on government benefits for their sustenance, the due process clause stands as an essential guarantee against arbitrary governmental action. The scope of any given welfare program is relevant to determining what process is due those dependent upon it, but it can never free the administrators of that program from all constitutional restraints, and should likewise not excuse those administrators from liability when they act in clear contravention of the due process clause's commands.

IV

After contributing to the disability insurance program throughout their working lives, respondents turned to it for essential support when disabling medical conditions prevented them from providing for themselves. If the allegations of their complaints are true, they were unjustly deprived of this essential support by state and federal officials acting beyond the bounds of their authority and in violation of respondents' constitutional rights. That respondents suffered grievous harm as a result of these actions—harm for which the belated restoration of disability benefits in no way compensated them—is undisputed and indisputable. Yet the Court today declares that respondents and others like them may recover nothing from the officials allegedly responsible for these injuries because Congress failed to include such a remedy among the reforms it enacted in an effort to rescue the disability insurance program from a paralyzing breakdown. Because I am convinced that Congress did not intend to preclude judicial recognition of a cause of action for such injuries, and because I believe there are no special factors militating against the creation of such a remedy here, I dissent.

———

NOTES ON PRIVATE RIGHTS OF ACTION TO ENFORCE THE CONSTITUTION AFTER *BIVENS*

1. **Cases Upholding *Bivens* Actions in Other Contexts.** There were two major decisions prior to *Schweiker* where the Court had extended *Bivens* relief to other contexts.

(i) *Davis v. Passman.* In Davis v. Passman, 442 U.S. 228 (1979), the issue was "whether a cause of action and a damages remedy can . . . be implied directly under the Constitution when the due process clause of the fifth amendment is violated." The suit was brought against Congressman Otto Passman by Shirley Davis, an administrative assistant who alleged that she had been discharged because she was a woman. The Supreme Court upheld her cause of action in an opinion by Justice Brennan:

> "The Constitution . . . speaks . . . with a majestic simplicity. One of 'its important objects' is the designation of rights. And in 'its great outlines' the judiciary is clearly discernible as the primary means through which these rights may be enforced. . . .

> "At least in the absence of 'a textually demonstrable constitutional commitment of [an] issue to a coordinate political department,' we presume that justiciable constitutional rights are to be enforced through the courts. And, unless such rights are to become merely precatory, the class of those litigants who allege that their own constitutional rights have been violated, and who at the same time have no effective means other than the judiciary to enforce these rights, must be able to invoke the existing jurisdiction of the courts for the protection of their justiciable constitutional rights."

Justice Brennan also noted that since Passman was no longer in Congress, "there are available no other alternative forms of judicial relief. For Davis, as for Bivens, 'it is damages or nothing.'" He added that a suit against a member of Congress for allegedly unconstitutional action taken in the course of official conduct "does raise special concerns counselling hesitation," but that these concerns "are coextensive with the protections afforded by the speech or debate clause." And since the Court of Appeals had not addressed the applicability of the speech or debate clause, the Court remanded for consideration of that issue.

The *Davis* Court upheld the cause of action for damages in spite of the provisions of § 717 of title VII of the Civil Rights Act of 1964. That statute protects federal employees from sex discrimination, but specifically exempts congressional employees. The Court found that exclusion of congressional employees from the coverage of title VII did not reflect an "*explicit* congressional declaration" that persons in her situation should not recover. The Court also made it clear that it was speaking only to the question of damages, and that it expressed no view on whether equitable relief in the form of reinstatement would ever be an appropriate remedy.

Four Justices dissented in three separate opinions. Chief Justice Burger, joined by Justices Powell and Rehnquist, argued that "the case presents very grave questions of separation of powers," independent of any speech or debate clause issue.[a] He noted that a president could appoint persons on racial, ethnic, religious, or gender grounds and that presidents "have done so since the beginning of the Republic." Members of Congress "occup[y] a position in the legislative branch comparable to that of the President in the executive branch" and should have the same authority. "[L]ong accepted concepts of separation of powers dictate," he concluded, "that until Congress legislates otherwise as to employment standards for its own staffs, judicial power in this area is circumscribed."

Justice Powell, joined by the Chief Justice and Justice Rehnquist, wrote separately "to emphasize that no prior decision of this Court justifies today's intrusion upon the legitimate powers of members of Congress." He "thought it clear that federal courts must exercise a principled discretion when called upon to infer a private cause of action directly from the language of the Constitution. In the present case, for reasons well summarized by the Chief Justice, principles of comity and separation of powers should require a federal court to stay its hand." He thought it clear enough that the Court should not interfere, but especially so in light of the fact that Congress "took pains to exempt itself" from the coverage of title VII.

(ii) *Carlson v. Green.* In Carlson v. Green, 446 U.S. 14 (1980), Marie Green filed suit on behalf of the estate of her deceased son

---

[a] Justice Stewart, joined by Justice Rehnquist, said that the Court should have addressed the speech or debate clause issue first. He voted to remand for a determination of that question before addressing the availability of a cause of action.

against the Director of the Federal Bureau of Prisons and other prison officials. She claimed that her son had suffered personal injuries from which he died because the federal officials violated his due process, equal protection, and eighth amendment rights. The question before the Supreme Court was whether "a remedy [was] available directly under the Constitution, given that [Green's] allegations could also support a suit against the United States under the Federal Tort Claims Act." Justice Brennan's opinion for the Court reasoned:

"*Bivens* established that the victims of a constitutional violation by a federal agent have a right to recover damages against the official in federal court despite the absence of any statute conferring such a right. Such a cause of action may be defeated in a particular case, however, in two situations. The first is when defendants demonstrate 'special factors counseling hesitation in the absence of affirmative action by Congress.' The second is when defendants show that Congress has provided an alternative remedy which it explicitly declared to be a *substitute* for recovery directly under the Constitution and viewed it as equally effective.

"Neither situation obtains in this case. First, the case involves no special factors counselling hesitation in the absence of affirmative action by Congress. [Federal prison officials] do not enjoy such independent status in our constitutional scheme as to suggest that judicially created remedies against them might be inappropriate. Moreover, even if requiring them to defend respondent's suit might inhibit their efforts to perform their official duties, the qualified immunity accorded them under Butz v. Economou, 438 U.S. 478 (1978), provides adequate protection.[b]

"Second, we have here no explicit congressional declaration that persons injured by federal officers' violations of the eighth amendment may not recover money damages from the agents but must be remitted to another remedy, equally effective in the view of Congress. [The federal officers] point to nothing in the Federal Tort Claims Act (FTCA) or its legislative history to show that Congress meant to preempt a *Bivens* remedy or to create an equally effective remedy for constitutional violations. The FTCA was enacted long before *Bivens* was decided, but when Congress amended FTCA in 1974 to create a cause of action against the United States for intentional torts committed by federal law enforcement officers, the congressional comments accompanying that amendment made it crystal clear that Congress views FTCA and *Bivens* as parallel, complementary causes of action . . . . [The FTCA] thus contemplates that victims of the kind of intentional

[b] *Butz* held that a reasonable, good faith belief can sometimes provide a defense to a *Bivens* action. *Butz* is considered in conjunction with the immunity issue as it arises in § 1983 suits against state officials. See pages 916–18, infra. [Footnote by eds.]

wrongdoing alleged in this complaint shall have an action under FTCA against the United States as well as a *Bivens* action against the individual officials alleged to have infringed their constitutional rights."

Justice Brennan added that Congress had made the FTCA exclusive when it wanted that result, and that other bills that would have expanded the exclusivity of the FTCA had not been enacted. Finally, he elaborated on four additional factors suggesting that the *Bivens* remedy was more effective than the FTCA remedy and should therefore be retained: (1) the *Bivens* remedy is likely to act as a greater deterrent; (2) punitive damages might be available in a *Bivens* action,[c] but are precluded by statute in an FTCA action; (3) jury trial is not available by statute in an FTCA action, but is available in a *Bivens* action; and (4) the FTCA incorporates state law as the measure of liability, and thus would preclude an action if none was available under state law. "Yet it is obvious," Justice Brennan continued, "that the liability of federal officials for violations of citizens' constitutional rights should be governed by uniform federal rules [absent] a contrary congressional resolution." For these reasons, he concluded, "[p]lainly FTCA is not a sufficient protector of the citizens' constitutional rights, and without a clear congressional mandate we cannot hold that Congress relegated respondents exclusively to the FTCA remedy."[d]

Justice Powell, joined by Justice Stewart, concurred in the judgment. He disagreed strongly with the majority statement that the *Bivens* cause of action may be defeated only if one of two conditions obtains. He thought this too rigid and that the Court should have more discretion to refuse to create a cause of action to enforce the Constitution, especially when alternative remedies existed. He concluded, however, that the FTCA "simply is not an adequate remedy" and that "there are reasonably clear indications that Congress did not intend that statute to displace *Bivens* claims. . . . I therefore agree that a private damages remedy properly is inferred from the Constitution in this case."

Separate dissents were filed by Chief Justice Burger and by Justice Rehnquist. The Chief Justice said that the FTCA "provides an adequate remedy for prisoners' claims of medical mistreatment. For me, that is the end of the matter." Justice Rehnquist argued at length that *Bivens* was an unconstitutional assumption of power and that the Court was here compounding the error. "In my view," he stated, "the

---

[c] Cf. Smith v. Wade, 461 U.S. 30 (1983), which held that punitive damages were available against state officials in a § 1983 action.

[d] On a second question—whether state or federal law should control the survival of a *Bivens* cause of action—Justice Brennan began by observing that "*Bivens* actions are a creation of federal law and, therefore, the question whether [Green's] action survived [the] death [of her son] is a question of federal law." He explicitly refused to borrow state law, moreover, holding that "only a uniform federal rule of survivorship will suffice to redress the constitutional deprivation here alleged and to protect against repetition of such conduct." He concluded that the "liability of federal agents for violation of constitutional rights should not depend upon where the violation occurred."

authority of federal courts to fashion remedies based on the 'common law' of damages for constitutional violations . . . falls within the legislative domain, and does not exist where not conferred by Congress. The determination by federal courts of the scope of such a remedy involves the creation of a body of common law analogous to that repudiated in *Erie* and *Hudson & Goodwin.*"ᵉ He also observed:

> "While federal courts have historically had broad authority to fashion equitable remedies, it does not follow that absent congressional authorization they may also grant damages awards for constitutional violations that would traditionally be regarded as remedies at law. The broad power of federal courts to grant equitable relief for constitutional violations has long been established. . . . Thus, for example, in Ex parte Young, 209 U.S. 123 (1908), it was held that a federal court may enjoin a state officer from enforcing penalties and remedies provided by an unconstitutional statute.

> "No similar authority of federal courts to award damages for violations of constitutional rights had ever been recognized prior to *Bivens.* And no statutory grant by Congress supports the exercise of such authority by federal courts. . . . Neither [the Rules of Decision Act], nor § 1331, authorizes federal courts to create a body of common-law damages remedies for constitutional violations or any other legal wrong. And . . . federal courts do not have the authority to act as general courts of common law absent authorization by Congress."

Justice Rehnquist also disagreed at length with the Court's analysis of the four differences between an FTCA action and a *Bivens* action, and argued that the provision of the FTCA action by Congress was "dispositive." He concluded this part of his dissent with the observation that the "policy questions at issue in the creation of any tort remedies, constitutional or otherwise, involve judgments as to diverse factors that are more appropriately made by the legislature than by this Court in an attempt to fashion a constitutional common law." Finally, Justice Rehnquist agreed with Justice Powell that the Court's two-part "canon of divining legislative intention" was unprecedented and too rigid.

2. Cases Rejecting *Bivens* Actions in Other Contexts. There were three major cases prior to *Schweiker,* all decided after *Davis* and *Carlson,* in which *Bivens* relief was denied. The first, Chappell v. Wallace, 462 U.S. 296 (1983), is adequately detailed in *Schweiker.* The other two warrant further elaboration.

(i) ***Bush v. Lucas.*** In Bush v. Lucas, 462 U.S. 367 (1983), Bush, a federal employee, sued Lucas, his supervisor, alleging that Lucas fired him because of public statements he made about the agency in which they worked. As the case came to the Supreme Court, the question was whether Bush could assert an implied right of action

---

ᵉ *Hudson & Goodwin* is considered at page 391, supra. [Footnote by eds.]

based on a deprivation of his first amendment rights. Bush argued that available civil service remedies (reinstatement with back pay and restoring the employee to the position he or she would have been in had the unconstitutional action not been taken) were inadequate because punitive damages, attorneys fees, and a jury trial were unavailable, because the deterrence provided by such relief was inadequate, and because emotional and dignitary harms could not be compensated. The Court was prepared to "assume that, as [Bush] asserts, civil service remedies were not as effective as an individual damages remedy and did not fully compensate him for the harm he suffered." But, in an opinion by Justice Stevens, it nonetheless held that a cause of action was not available:

> "This much is established by our prior cases. The federal courts' statutory jurisdiction to decide federal questions confers adequate power to award damages to the victim of a constitutional violation. When Congress provides an alternative remedy, it may, of course, indicate its intent, by statutory language, by clear legislative history, or perhaps even by the statutory remedy itself, that the Court's power should not be exercised. In the absence of such a congressional directive, the federal courts must make the kind of remedial determination that is appropriate for a common-law tribunal, paying particular heed, however, to any special factors counselling hesitation before authorizing a new kind of federal litigation.

> "Congress has not resolved the question presented by this case by expressly denying [Bush] the judicial remedy he seeks or by providing him with an equally effective substitute.[14] There is, however, a good deal of history that is relevant to the question whether a federal employee's attempt to recover damages from his superior for violation of his first amendment rights involves any 'special factors counselling hesitation.'. . ."

Justice Stevens then reviewed the decisions in *Standard Oil* (see page 391, supra) and *Gilman* (see page 389, supra) and concluded that:

> "The special factors counselling hesitation in the creation of a new remedy in *Standard Oil* and *Gilman* did not concern the merits of the particular remedy that was sought. Rather, they related to the question of who should decide whether such a remedy should be provided. We should therefore begin by considering whether there are reasons for allowing Congress to prescribe the scope of relief that is made available to federal employees whose first amendment rights have been violated by their supervisors."

[14] "We need not reach the question whether the Constitution itself requires a judicially fashioned damages remedy in the absence of any other remedy to vindicate the underlying right, unless there is an express textual command to the contrary. The existing civil service remedies for a demotion in retaliation for protected speech are clearly constitutionally adequate."

Justice Stevens then noted that the case concerned "federal personnel policy" and reviewed in detail the growth of the various civil service remedies available to Bush. He concluded:

"Given the history of the development of civil service remedies and the comprehensive nature of the remedies currently available, it is clear that the question we confront today is quite different from the typical remedial issue confronted by a common-law court. The question is not what remedy the court should provide for a wrong that would otherwise go unredressed. It is whether an elaborate remedial system that has been constructed step by step, with careful attention to conflicting policy considerations, should be augmented by the creation of a new judicial remedy for the constitutional violation at issue. That question obviously cannot be answered simply by noting that existing remedies do not provide complete relief for the plaintiff. The policy judgment should be informed by a thorough understanding of the existing regulatory structure and the respective costs and benefits that would result from the addition of another remedy for violation of employees' first amendment rights.

"The costs associated with the review of disciplinary decisions are already significant—not only in monetary terms, but also in the time and energy of managerial personnel who must defend their decisions. [The government] argues that supervisory personnel are already more hesitant than they should be in administering discipline, because the review that ensues inevitably makes the performance of their regular duties more difficult. Whether or not this assessment is accurate, it is quite probable that if management personnel face the added risk of personal liability for decisions that they believe to be a correct response to improper criticism of the agency, they would be deterred from imposing discipline in future cases. In all events, Congress is in a far better position than a court to evaluate the impact of a new species of litigation between federal employees on the efficiency of the civil service. Not only has Congress developed considerable familiarity with balancing governmental efficiency and the rights of employees, but it also may inform itself through factfinding procedures such as hearings that are not available to the courts.

"Nor is there any reason to discount Congress' ability to make an evenhanded assessment of the desirability of creating a new remedy for federal employees who have been demoted or discharged for expressing controversial views. Congress has a special interest in informing itself about the efficiency and morale of the executive branch. In the past it has demonstrated its awareness that lower level government employees are a valuable source of information, and that supervisors might improperly attempt to curtail their subordinates' freedom of expression.

"Thus, we do not decide whether or not it would be good policy to permit a federal employee to recover damages from a supervisor who has improperly disciplined him for exercising his first amendment rights. As we did in *Standard Oil*, we decline 'to create a new substantive legal liability without legislative aid and as at the common law,' because we are convinced that Congress is in a better position to decide whether or not the public interest would be served by creating it."

Justice Marshall, joined by Justice Blackmun, wrote a concurring opinion emphasizing that he thought the civil service remedies were "substantially as effective as a damage action." He also pointed out that there were several advantages provided by the administrative remedies that would be unavailable under a *Bivens* claim. For example, the burden of proof is on the agency in the administrative proceedings, there are no immunity doctrines available, and the civil service remedies are faster and less costly. There was no dissent.[f]

(ii) *United States v. Stanley.* In United States v. Stanley, ___ U.S. ___ (1987), Stanley, a sergeant in the Army, "volunteered to participate in a program ostensibly designed to test the effectiveness of protective clothing and equipment as defenses against chemical warfare." He was transferred to the test site, and there, over a period of one month, "was secretly administered doses of [LSD], pursuant to an Army plan to study the effects of the drug on human subjects." His complaint alleged that he suffered severe adverse effects, leading among other things to violent behavior towards his wife and children and his subsequent divorce. He discovered the fact that he had been given LSD when, in 1975, the Army sent him a letter asking him to participate "in a study of the long-term effects of LSD on 'volunteers who participated' in the 1958 tests."

After an administrative claim for compensation was denied, he filed suit in a federal District Court in 1979. Protracted proceedings followed. The question whether he could assert a *Bivens* claim on these facts came before the Supreme Court in 1987. The Court, in an opinion by Justice Scalia, held that he could not.

The rationale for that conclusion can best be understood against the background of the Court's decision a month earlier in United States v. Johnson, ___ U.S. ___ (1987). *Johnson* involved a suit by the wife of a Coast Guard officer who was killed in the line of duty by the alleged negligence of officials employed by a civilian agency of the federal government. The issue was whether a Federal Tort Claims Act (FTCA) claim could be asserted against the government for such negligence. In a five-four decision, with Justice Scalia authoring the dissent, the Court held that "the government is not liable under the Federal Tort Claims Act for injuries to servicemen where the injuries arise out of or are in the course of activity incident to service," even if the injuries are caused by the alleged negligence of government officials unconnected

---

[f] For a detailed analysis of *Bush,* see Note, *Bivens* Doctrine in Flux: Statutory Preclusion of a Constitutional Cause of Action, 101 Harv.L.Rev. 1251 (1988).

with the service. This decision was not based on explicit language in the FTCA, nor on its legislative history. Instead, it was derived from policies concerning the appropriate relationship of the judiciary to the military.

In *Stanley,* the Court thought that the same policies should control in the *Bivens* context and that the same exception to liability should apply. As Justice Scalia explained:

> "Today, no more than when we wrote Chappell v. Wallace, 462 U.S. 296 (1983), do we see any reason why our judgment in the *Bivens* context should be any less protective of military concerns than it has been with respect to FTCA suits, where we adopted an 'incident to service' rule. In fact, if anything we might have felt more free to compromise military concerns in the latter context, since we were confronted with an explicit congressional authorization for judicial involvement that was, on its face, unqualified; whereas here we are confronted with an explicit constitutional authorization for *Congress* '[t]o make Rules for the Government and Regulation of the land and naval Forces,' U.S. Const. art. I, § 8, cl. 14, and rely upon inference for our own authority to allow money damages. This is not to say . . . that all matters within congressional power are exempt from *Bivens.* What is distinctive here is the specificity of that . . . grant of power, and the insistence (evident from the number of clauses devoted to the subject) with which the Constitution confers authority over the Army, Navy, and militia upon the political branches. All this counsels hesitation in our creation of damages remedies in this field."

Accordingly the Court held "that no *Bivens* remedy is available for injuries that 'arise out of or are in the course of activity incident to service.' "[g]

Justice O'Connor dissented in part. She agreed that "generally" *Bivens* actions were unavailable to service personnel under the Court's standard, but she thought that this case was different:

> "[T]he *Chappell* exception to the availability of a *Bivens* action applies only to 'injuries that "arise out of or are in the course of activity incident to service." ' In my view, conduct of the type alleged in this case is so far beyond the bounds of human decency that as a matter of law it simply cannot be considered a part of the military mission. The bar created by *Chappell*—a judicial exception to an implied remedy for the violation of constitutional rights—surely cannot insulate defendants from liability for deliberate and calculated exposure of

---

[g] The Court also held it "irrelevant . . . whether the laws currently on the books afford Stanley, or any other particular serviceman, an 'adequate' federal remedy for his injuries. The 'special facto[r]' that 'counsel[s] hesitation' is not the fact that Congress has chosen to afford some manner of relief in the particular case, but the fact that congressionally uninvited intrusion into military affairs by the judiciary is inappropriate."

otherwise healthy military personnel to medical experimentation without their consent, outside of any combat, combat training, or military exigency, and for no other reason than to gather information on the effect of [LSD] on human beings.

"No judicially crafted rule should insulate from liability the involuntary and unknowing human experimentation alleged to have occurred in this case. Indeed, as Justice Brennan observes, the United States military played an instrumental role in the criminal prosecution of Nazi officials who experimented with human subjects during the Second World War, and the standards that the Nuernberg Military Tribunals developed to judge the behavior of the defendants stated that the 'voluntary consent of the human subject is absolutely essential . . . to satisfy moral, ethical and legal concepts.' If this principle is violated the very least that society can do is to see that the victims are compensated, as best they can be, by the perpetrators. I am prepared to say that our Constitution's promise of due process of law guarantees this much. Accordingly, I would permit James Stanley's *Bivens* action to go forward, and I therefore dissent."

Justice Brennan, joined by Justice Marshall and in part by Justice Stevens, also dissented. He pointed out that the allegations were that Stanley "was one of 1,000 soldiers covertly administered LSD by Army Intelligence between 1955 and 1958" and that the Army "recognized the moral and legal implications of its conduct" by seeking to avoid "legal liability . . . by covering up the LSD experiments." On the question of legal liability, he noted that one of the two factors emphasized in *Chappell*—the presence of an alternative remedial mechanism—was entirely absent here. As to the other factor—the proper relationship of the courts to the military—he thought that concern outweighed by the need for a remedy for the intentional violation of constitutional rights in a context where the "special requirements of command that concerned us in *Chappell* are not implicated . . . ."

3. Questions and Comments. Has the Court substantially retreated from *Bivens?*[h] Are the factors emphasized in *Schweiker, Bush,* and *Stanley* irrelevant to whether a cause of action should have been implied in *Bivens*? Or is the critical difference that in *Bivens* (and *Davis*) it was "damages or nothing?" If so, how does the holding in *Carlson* fit with the holdings in *Schweiker, Bush,* and *Stanley*? Are there distinctive features of the contexts in which each of these cases were decided that make them consistent?

---

[h] For a critical review of *Chappell* and *Bush*, see Joan Steinman, Backing Off *Bivens* and the Ramifications of this Retreat for the Vindication of First Amendment Rights, 83 Mich.L.Rev. 269 (1984).

Chapter V

DISTRICT COURT JURISDICTION

SECTION 1: THE GENERAL FEDERAL QUESTION STATUTE

INTRODUCTORY NOTES ON THE GENERAL FEDERAL QUESTION STATUTE

1. The Statute. The general federal question statute, 28 U.S.C. § 1331, provides that "[t]he district courts shall have original jurisdiction of all civil actions arising under the Constitution, laws, or treaties of the United States." Section 1331 is a broad, catch-all provision governing cases arising under federal law.[a] There are many more specific provisions. Indeed, most federal question cases filed in district courts are based on special statutes dealing with narrower classes of litigation.[b]

2. The Face-of-the-Complaint Rule. The first step in determining whether a case arises under federal law within 28 U.S.C. § 1331 is to determine those matters which the plaintiff must plead in order to state a claim against the defendant. This is called the "face-of-the-complaint rule." It requires that jurisdiction be judged solely on the basis of allegations that would appear on the face of well-pleaded complaint.

A famous articulation of this rule came in Louisville & Nashville Railroad Co. v. Mottley, 211 U.S. 149 (1908). Mr. and Mrs. Mottley had received lifetime passes on the L&N Railroad in settlement of a personal injury claim. Thereafter Congress passed legislation outlawing free passes. The railroad then refused to honor the settlement contract, and the Mottleys sued in federal court for specific performance. Their arguments were, first, that the statute did not affect their previously agreed-upon contract of settlement and, second, if it did, it

---

[a] Does the word "laws" as used in § 1331 only refer to legislation, or does it also encompass cases that "arise under" federal common law? The question was answered in Illinois v. Milwaukee, 406 U.S. 91, 100 (1972), where the Court said, "We see no reason not to give 'laws' its natural meaning, and therefore conclude that § 1331 jurisdiction will support claims founded upon federal common law as well as those of a statutory origin."

[b] For example, suits "arising under any act of Congress regulating commerce" may be brought under 28 U.S.C. § 1337; suits "arising under any act of Congress relating to patents, plant variety protection, copyrights, and trademarks" may be brought under 28 U.S.C. § 1338; suits "arising under any act of Congress relating to the postal service" may be brought under 28 U.S.C. § 1339; and so on. Moreover, most acts of Congress that create substantive rights also contain jurisdictional provisions permitting claims under the statute to be asserted in federal court.

431

was to that extent unconstitutional. They grounded jurisdiction on these federal questions and won their suit in the trial court.

The Supreme Court raised the jurisdictional question on its own motion and ordered the suit dismissed. The Court said:

> "There was no diversity of citizenship and it is not and cannot be suggested that there was any ground of jurisdiction, except that the case was a 'suit . . . arising under the Constitution and laws of the United States.' It is the settled interpretation of these words, as used in this statute, conferring jurisdiction, that a suit arises under the Constitution and laws of the United States only when the plaintiff's statement of his own cause of action shows that it is based upon those laws or that Constitution. It is not enough that the plaintiff alleges some anticipated defense to his cause of action and asserts that the defense is invalidated by some provision of the Constitution of the United States. Although such allegations show that very likely, in the course of the litigation, a question under the Constitution would arise, they do not show that the suit, that is, the plaintiff's original cause of action, arises under the Constitution."

Note that what the complaint actually said was not determinative. It was what a properly pleaded complaint should have said that mattered. A court is thus required to reformulate the allegations in the complaint and to identify those matters that form the plaintiff's "cause of action"—that is, the minimum allegations that would justify a default judgment in favor of the plaintiff if the defendant declined to answer the complaint. In the *Mottley* case, for example, this would consist of allegations that the parties had a valid contract and that the defendant had refused to honor its terms. Whether the reason the defendant refused to honor the contract was a justification for its behavior is no part of a properly pleaded complaint, but would enter the case only when issue is joined on the defense.

What is the justification for this rule? Note the statement by Chief Justice Marshall in Osborn v. Bank of the United States, 22 U.S. (9 Wheat.) 738 (1824): "The right of the plaintiff to sue cannot depend on the defence which the defendant may choose to set up. His right to sue is anterior to that defence, and must depend on the state of things when the action is brought."[c] Does that adequately explain the rule? [d]

3. The Case Law. The face-of-the-complaint rule requires three analytical steps to determine whether a case "arises under" federal law within the meaning of § 1331. First, one must determine whether the plaintiff's cause of action is based on state or federal law. Second, one

---

[c] *Osborn* is more fully considered at pages 209–12, supra.

[d] For a detailed consideration of the evolution of the *Mottley* rule, see Donald Doernberg, There's No Reason For It; It's Just Our Policy: Why the Well-Pleaded Complaint Rule Sabotages the Purposes of Federal Question Jurisdiction, 38 Hastings L.J. 597 (1987). As his title suggests, Doernberg is no fan of *Mottley*. His article canvasses and criticizes the possible justifications for the rule and discusses in some detail most of the cases considered in the remainder of this section.

must identify the sources of the various legal propositions that are necessary components of the cause of action. It is possible, as will be illustrated, for a state cause of action to incorporate a federal-law ingredient or for a federal cause of action to incorporate a state-law ingredient. Third, one must ascertain whether the case "arises under" federal law. Of course, if the cause of action is based on state law and its legal basis consists entirely of propositions of state law, the case cannot be filed in federal court under § 1331. That was the situation in *Mottley*. But if the cause of action is federal or if a state cause of action has a federal component, the case might then "arise under" federal law. Whether it will be held to do so involves a number of factors. Consideration of four well known cases will help frame the issue.

(i) *American Well Works.* Analysis of whether a case arises under federal law usually starts with the opinion by Justice Holmes in American Well Works Co. v. Layne & Bowler Co., 241 U.S. 257 (1916). The plaintiff manufactured and sold pumps on which it held, or had applied for, patents. The defendant claimed that the plaintiff's pump infringed defendant's patent. The defendant had filed suits against some users of the plaintiff's pump and had threatened suit against all who used it. The plaintiff sued for libel and slander to the plaintiff's title to its pump. The question was whether the case arose under the predecessor to 28 U.S.C. § 1338, which provides for exclusive jurisdiction in federal district courts over "any civil action arising under any Act of Congress relating to patents."

The Court held that the case did not arise under the patent laws. Justice Holmes said that "[a] suit arises under the law that creates the cause of action." Whether business libel by the defendant was actionable was entirely up to state law; there was nothing in the federal patent laws that made the defendant liable to the plaintiff for the relief sought. Hence the case did not "arise under" federal law.

(ii) *Shoshone Mining Co. v. Rutter.* Most cases litigated under statutes such as §§ 1331 and 1338 involve causes of action created by federal law. It does not follow, however, that every cause of action created by federal law presents a case arising under federal law. As a test of inclusion, the Holmes test does not always work.

An example is Shoshone Mining Co. v. Rutter, 177 U.S. 505 (1900). Congress created a system for issuing patents to miners on federal lands in the West. It provided that an "adverse suit" could be filed "in a court of competent jurisdiction" by a person who claimed a right of possession to a mine that was also claimed by another person. The dispute between them was to be resolved by "local customs or rules of miners in the several mining districts, so far as the same are applicable and not inconsistent with the laws of the United States" and "by the statute of limitations for mining claims of the State or Territory where the same may be situated." The question was whether an adverse claim filed under these provisions could be brought under the general federal question statute.

Following an earlier decision, the Court held that it could not:

"[T]he 'adverse suit' to determine the right of possession may not involve any question as to the construction or effect of the Constitution or laws of the United States, but may present simply a question of fact as to the time of the discovery of mineral, the location of the claim on the ground, or a determination of the meaning and effect of certain local rules and customs prescribed by the miners of the district, or the effect of state statutes . . . ."

(iii) *Smith v. Kansas City Title & Trust Co.* The Holmes test also does not always work as a test of exclusion. The leading case is Smith v. Kansas City Title & Trust Co., 255 U.S. 180 (1921). A stockholder in a corporation created by state law sued to enjoin the corporation from investing in certain federally authorized bonds. The federal statute provided that the bonds were lawful investments for corporations such as the defendant, and state law authorized the corporation to invest in all lawfully issued government bonds. The plaintiff's position was that the federal statute authorizing the sale of the bonds was unconstitutional.

Predictably, Justice Holmes argued that the case did not arise under federal law. The right of the stockholder to sue the corporate defendant, he reasoned, derived solely from state law:

"It is evident that the cause of action arises not under any law of the United States but wholly under Missouri law. The defendant is a Missouri corporation and the right claimed is that of a stockholder to prevent the directors from doing an act, that is, making an investment, alleged to be contrary to their duty. But the scope of their duty depends upon the charter of their corporation and other laws of Missouri. . . . If the Missouri law authorizes or forbids the investment according to the determination of this Court upon a point under the Constitution or acts of Congress, still that point is material only because the Missouri law saw fit to make it so. The whole foundation of the duty is Missouri law, which at its sole will incorporated the other law as it might incorporate a document. . . .

"But it seems to me that a suit cannot be said to arise under any other law than that which creates the cause of action. It may be enough that the law relied upon creates a part of the cause of action although not the whole, as held in *Osborn v. Bank of United States* . . . . I am content to assume this to be so, although the *Osborn* case has been criticized and regretted. But the law must create at least a part of the cause of action by its own force, for it is the suit, not a question in the suit, that must arise under the law of the United States. The mere adoption by a state law of a United States law as a criterion or test, when the law of the United States has no force ex proprio vigore, does not cause a case under the state law to be also a case under the law of the United States. . . ."

These words, however, were written in dissent. The majority held that the case arose under federal law:

"The general rule is that, where it appears from the bill or statement of the plaintiff that the right to relief depends upon the construction or application of the Constitution or laws of the United States, and that such federal claim is not merely colorable, and rests upon a reasonable foundation, the district court has jurisdiction . . . ..

". . . In the instant case the averments of the bill show that the directors were proceeding to make the investments in view of the act authorizing the bonds about to be purchased, maintaining that the act authorizing them was constitutional and the bonds valid and desirable investments. The objecting shareholder avers in the bill that the securities were issued under an unconstitutional law, and hence of no validity. It is therefore apparent that the controversy concerns the constitutional validity of an act of Congress which is directly drawn in question. The decision depends upon the determination of this issue."

(iv) *Moore v. Chesapeake & Ohio Ry.* One might infer from *Smith* that federal question jurisdiction normally can be founded upon a state cause of action that incorporates a question of federal law. The Court reached the opposite conclusion, however, in Moore v. Chesapeake & Ohio Ry. Co., 291 U.S. 205 (1934).

Moore was a railroad worker. He filed an action against the railroad under a Kentucky statute covering injuries in *intrastate* commerce. He alleged that portions of the Federal Safety Appliance Act had been violated by the railroad:

"The Kentucky Act provided that no employee should be held 'to have been guilty of contributory negligence' or 'to have assumed the risk of his employment' in any case 'where the violation by such common carrier of any statute, state or federal, enacted for the safety of employees contributed to the injury . . . .' [A] violation of the acts for the safety of employees was to constitute negligence per se in applying the state statute and was to furnish the ground for precluding the defense of contributory negligence as well as that of assumption of risk."

The Court noted that questions concerning the meaning of the Federal Safety Appliance Act arising in such a context in state court litigation were reviewable in the Supreme Court.[e] But the case nonetheless did not arise under federal law:

[e] This aspect of the decision is considered at page 612, infra.

"[I]t does not follow that a suit brought under the state statute which defines liability to employees who are injured while engaged in intrastate commerce, and brings within the purview of the statute a breach of the duty imposed by the federal statute, should be regarded as a suit arising under the laws of the United States and cognizable in the federal court in the absence of diversity of citizenship. The Federal Safety Appliance Acts, while prescribing absolute duties, and thus creating correlative rights in favor of injured employees, did not attempt to lay down rules governing actions for enforcing these rights. . . .

"The Safety Appliance Acts having prescribed the duty in this fashion, the right to recover damages sustained by the injured employee through the breach of duty sprang from the principle of the common law and was left to be enforced accordingly. . . . When the Federal Employers' Liability Act was enacted, it drew to itself the right of action for injuries or death to the employees who were engaged in interstate commerce, including those cases in which injuries were due to a violation of the Safety Appliance Acts. . . . With respect to injuries sustained in intrastate commerce, nothing in the Safety Appliance Acts precluded the state from incorporating in its legislation applicable to local transportation the paramount duty which the Safety Appliance Acts imposed as to the equipment of cars used on interstate railroads. . . .

"We are of the opinion that . . . the suit is not to be regarded as one arising under the laws of the United States. . . ."

4. Questions and Comments. How can these cases be reconciled? Consider the comments by William Cohen in The Broken Compass: The Requirement that a Case Arise "Directly" under Federal Law, 115 U. Pa. L. Rev. 890 (1967). Cohen argues that the search for analytical or verbal formulas to determine when a case arises under federal law is misguided. Instead, he suggests, what the courts have done (and should have done) is establish "pragmatic standards for a pragmatic problem":

"In stockholders' derivative suits presenting substantial federal constitutional objections to federal statutes, taken as a class, the federal constitutional issues are likely to be among the most significant in the litigation. In cases like *Smith v. Kansas City Title & Trust Co.,* it is certain that the federal constitutional issues will form the core of the litigation. Those issues require the same expert and sympathetic federal forum at the trial level as they would if presented in an injunction suit against a federal official. On the other hand, there is little reason to fear that the sustaining of jurisdiction in this class of litigation would add significantly to the workload of an overburdened federal judiciary. By contrast, the practical reasons for refusing jurisdiction in *Shoshone Mining Co. v. Rutter* were overwhelming. The congressional directive that controversies between rival claimants for mineral rights be decided by 'local customs or rules of miners' meant that most of these lawsuits would turn on a combination of factual issues and interpretation of local law or custom, not requiring the expertise of a federal trial forum. There was no significant federal government interest in the choice between the rival claimants which would require the protective jurisdiction of a federal trial court. Finally, and most important, accepting jurisdiction in *Shoshone* would have added significantly to the business of overburdened federal trial courts in the West.[f]

"It is not startling that these practical considerations precipitated the results in *Smith* and *Shoshone*. Nor is it unusual that the Court in the two cases applied contradictory analytical formulas to explain the results, rather than resting squarely on those factors which, no doubt, influenced the actual decisions. What is surprising is the continuing belief that there is, or should be, a single, all-purpose, neutral analytical concept which marks out federal question jurisdiction. A frank recognition of the pragmatic nature of the decision-making process would help throw light on the factors which actually induce decision. It would, moreover, reduce the danger that a judge would be beguiled by one of the numerous analytical tests into reaching an indefensible result."

Is Cohen right? Can *Smith* and *Moore* be reconciled by applying his thesis?[g] Could it be argued that a verbal formula that is easy to apply is precisely what is needed in determining questions of subject matter jurisdiction? If so, what formula should be used?[h]

---

[f] And, as the Court itself noted in *Shoshone*, would in many cases have moved the site of the litigation many miles from the locale of the claim. [Footnote by eds.]

[g] The Court adverted to the "widely perceived 'irreconcilable' conflict" between *Smith* and *Moore* in Merrell Dow Pharmaceuticals, Inc. v. Thompson, 478 U.S. 804, 814 n.12 (1986), and suggested that "the difference in results can be seen as manifestations of the difference in the nature of the federal issues at stake." In *Smith*, the Court explained, "the issue was the constitutionality of an important federal statute." In *Moore*, on the other hand, "the violation of the federal standard as an element of state tort recovery did not fundamentally change the state tort nature of the action." The Court also observed, citing *Shoshone*, that the "importance of the nature of the federal issue in federal question jurisdiction is highlighted by the fact that . . . this Court has sometimes found that formally federal causes of action were not properly brought under federal-question jurisdiction because of the overwhelming predominance of state-law issues."

Justice Brennan, joined by Justices White, Marshall, and Blackmun, disagreed. They thought *Smith* and *Moore* "irreconcilable" but were not troubled by the observation because *Moore* "was a 'sport' at the time it was decided and [has] long been in a state of innocuous desuetude. . . . *Moore* simply has not survived the test of time; it is presently moribund, and, to the extent that it is inconsistent with the well-established rule of the *Smith* case, it ought to be overruled."

[h] In Whose Law is it Anyway? A Reconsideration of Federal Question Jurisdiction over Cases of Mixed State and Federal Law, 60 Ind.L.J. 17 (1984), Linda Hirshman supports a return to the Holmes test. For a general essay on uncertainty and complexity in many aspects of federal jurisdiction (including federal question, diversity, *Pullman* abstention, and *Younger v. Harris*), see Martha Field, The Uncertain Na-

Consider in this respect the following well-known passage from Justice Cardozo's opinion in Gully v. First National Bank in Meridian, 299 U.S. 109 (1936):

"How and when a case arises 'under the Constitution or laws of the United States' has been much considered in the books. Some tests are well established. To bring a case within the statute, a right or immunity created by the Constitution or laws of the United States must be an element, and an essential one, of the plaintiff's cause of action. . . . The right or immunity must be such that it will be supported if the Constitution or laws of the United States are given one construction or effect, and defeated if they receive another. . . . A genuine and present controversy, not merely a possible or conjectural one, must exist with reference thereto . . . and the controversy must be disclosed upon the face of the complaint. . . ."

Does this help? Would it always work?

5. *Merrell Dow Pharmaceuticals, Inc. v. Thompson.*   The Court was faced with the meaning of *Smith* in a different context in Merrell Dow Pharmaceuticals, Inc. v. Thompson, 478 U.S. 804 (1986). The plaintiffs had filed actions in state court seeking relief from the defendant for birth defects caused by a mother's use of a drug during pregnancy. One of the theories of relief was common law negligence, which was in part based on an allegation that the drug was "misbranded" in violation of the Federal Food, Drug, and Cosmetic Act (FDCA) because its label did not contain adequate warnings. The defendant removed the case to federal court in reliance on *Smith*. The District Court upheld jurisdiction, but the Circuit Court reversed.

The Supreme Court held that the case could not originally have been filed in federal court under § 1331 and that removal was accordingly improper.[i] Justice Stevens' opinion for the Court first noted that no federal cause of action was explicitly available under the FDCA and that both parties agreed that this was not a situation where the federal courts would create a cause of action in the face of congressional silence. The Court agreed for purposes of its decision that the recognition of such a cause of action would be improper. The Court held:

"The significance of the . . . assumption that there is no federal private cause of action . . . cannot be overstated. For the ultimate import of such a conclusion . . . is that it would flout congressional intent to provide a private remedy for the violation of the federal statute. We think it would similarly flout, or at least undermine, congressional intent to conclude that the federal courts might nevertheless exercise federal-question jurisdiction and provide remedies for violation of that federal statute solely because the violation of the federal stat-

ture of Federal Jurisdiction, 22 Wm & M. L. Rev. 683 (1981).

[i] 28 U.S.C. § 1441(b) permits removal only if the plaintiff's claim could originally have been filed in federal court.

ute is said to be [an element of a state cause of action], rather than a federal action under federal law.

". . . Given the significance of the assumed congressional determination to preclude federal private remedies, the presence of the federal issue as an element of the state tort is not the kind of adjudication for which jurisdiction would serve congressional purposes and the federal system. We simply conclude that the congressional determination that there should be no federal remedy for the violation of this federal statute is tantamount to a congressional conclusion that the presence of a claimed violation of this statute as an element of a state cause of action is insufficiently 'substantial' to confer federal question jurisdiction."

Justice Brennan, joined by Justices White, Marshall, and Blackmun, dissented. He thought the case appropriately in federal court under *Smith.* As to the relevance of the line of cases dealing with the implication of private causes of action, he noted first that the FDA was given no independent enforcement authority, but was required to ask the Justice Department to seek an injunction in federal court, institute federal criminal proceedings, or take other actions in federal court to enforce the statute. Justice Brennan then reasoned:

"It may be that a decision by Congress not to create a private remedy is intended to preclude all private enforcement. If that is so, then a state cause of action that makes relief available to private individuals for violations of the FDCA is pre-empted. But if Congress' decision not to provide a private federal remedy does *not* pre-empt such a state remedy, then, in light of the FDCA's clear policy of relying on the federal courts for enforcement, it also should not foreclose federal jurisdiction over that state remedy. Both § 1331 and the enforcement provisions of the FDCA reflect Congress' strong desire to utilize the federal courts to interpret and enforce the FDCA, and it is therefore at odds with both these statutes to recognize a private state law remedy for violating the FDCA but to hold that this remedy cannot be adjudicated in the federal courts.

"The Court's contrary conclusion requires inferring from Congress' decision not to create a private federal remedy that, while some private enforcement is permissible in state courts, it is 'bad' if that enforcement comes from the *federal* courts. But that is simply illogical. Congress' decision to withhold a private right of action and to rely instead on public enforcement reflects congressional concern with obtaining more accurate implementation and more coordinated enforcement of a regulatory scheme. These reasons are closely related to the Congress' reasons for giving federal courts original federal question jurisdiction. Thus, if anything, Congress' decision not to create a private remedy *strengthens* the argument in favor of finding federal jurisdiction over a state remedy that is not pre-empted."

6. *United Mine Workers v. Gibbs.* Once jurisdiction has been properly obtained over a case arising under federal law, the plaintiff may assert additional state claims based on a theory of pendent jurisdiction. The leading case is United Mine Workers of America v. Gibbs, 383 U.S. 715 (1966).

Gibbs divided the issue into two questions. The first concerned the power of federal courts to exercise pendent jurisdiction:

> "Pendent jurisdiction, in the sense of judicial *power,* exists whenever there is a claim 'arising under [the] Constitution, the Laws of the United States, and Treaties made, or which shall be made, under their Authority . . .', U.S. Const., art. III, § 2, and the relationship between that claim and the state claim permits the conclusion that the entire action before the court comprises but one constitutional 'case.' The federal claim must have substance sufficient to confer subject matter jurisdiction on the court.[j] The state and federal claims must derive from a common nucleus of operative fact. But if, considered without regard to their federal or state character, a plaintiff's claims are such that he would ordinarily be expected to try them all in one judicial proceeding, then, assuming substantiality of the federal issues, there is *power* in federal courts to hear the whole."

The second question concerned when this power should be exercised:

> "That power need not be exercised in every case in which it is found to exist. It has consistently been recognized that pendent jurisdiction is a doctrine of discretion, not of plaintiff's right. Its justification lies in considerations of judicial economy, convenience and fairness to litigants; if these are not present a federal court should hesitate to exercise jurisdiction over state claims, even though bound to apply state law to them. Needless decisions of state law should be avoided both as a matter of comity and to promote justice between the parties, by procuring for them a surer-footed reading of applicable law. Certainly, if the federal claims are dismissed before trial, even though not insubstantial in a jurisdictional sense, the state claims should be dismissed as well. Similarly, if it appears that the state issues substantially predominate, whether in terms of proof, of the scope of the issues raised, or of the comprehensiveness of the remedy sought, the state claims may be dismissed without prejudice and left for resolution to state tribunals. . . . Finally, there may be reasons independent of

[j] The reference here is to the doctrine that any federal question must be "substantial," that is, non-frivolous, in order to confer jurisdiction on a federal court. See Zucht v. King, 260 U.S. 174 (1922). See also Matasar, Rediscovering "One Constitutional Case": Procedural Rules and the Rejection of the *Gibbs* Test for Supplemental Jurisdiction, 71 Calif.L.Rev. 1401, 1417–38 (1983). [Footnote by eds.]

jurisdictional considerations, such as the likelihood of jury confusion in treating divergent legal theories of relief, that would justify separating state and federal claims for trial. If so, jurisdiction should ordinarily be refused.

"The question of power will ordinarily be resolved on the pleadings. But the issue whether pendent jurisdiction has been properly assumed is one which remains open throughout the litigation. . . ." [k]

There are many situations when federal courts, once having assumed proper jurisdiction over a claim, are entitled to hear related claims. Frequently such exercises of jurisdiction are called "ancillary" rather than "pendent," but the underlying concept is the same.[l] Perhaps the most familiar example is the compulsory counterclaim, which under traditional doctrine need not independently satisfy jurisdictional prerequisites in order to be asserted. Thus, if the plaintiff's case properly arises under federal law, a state claim that would not itself justify the exercise of federal question jurisdiction (and over which there was no other available basis of jurisdiction) could nonetheless be raised in federal court (i) under the theory of pendent jurisdiction if asserted as an additional claim by the plaintiff; or (ii) under the theory of ancillary jurisdiction if asserted as a compulsory counterclaim by the defendant. Note in this respect that the test for when a counterclaim is compulsory under Rule 13(a) of the Federal Rules of Civil Procedure—a claim that "arises out of the transaction or occurrence that is the subject matter of the opposing party's claim"—is closely related to, if not the same as, the test for when the federal courts have power to hear "pendent" claims asserted by a plaintiff.

---

[k] The authority of the district courts to refuse to hear pendent state claims when the federal claim has been disposed of early in the litigation was reaffirmed in Carnegie-Mellon University v. Cohill, ___ U.S. ___ (1988). The case had originally been filed in state court, but had been removed by the defendant. The plaintiff later amended the complaint to delete the federal claim that provided the basis for the removal. The issue was whether the District Court could then remand the case to the state courts or whether the only options were dismissal or the retention of jurisdiction. In spite of language in Thermetron Products, Inc. v. Hermansdorfer, 423 U.S. 336 (1976), to the effect that remand was only permissible in situations specifically authorized by the removal statute, the Court voted five to three to permit the remand.

[l] See Freer, A Principled Statutory Approach to Supplemental Jurisdiction, 1987 Duke L.J. 34; Matasar, A Pendent and Ancillary Jurisdiction Primer: The Scope and Limits of Supplemental Jurisdiction, 17 U.C.Davis L.Rev. 103 (1983); Miller, Ancillary and Pendent Jurisdiction, 26 South Texas L.J. 1 (1985).

FRANCHISE TAX BOARD OF CALIFORNIA v. CONSTRUCTION LABORERS VACATION TRUST FOR SOUTHERN CALIFORNIA

United States Supreme Court, 1983.
463 U.S. 1.

JUSTICE BRENNAN delivered the opinion of the Court.

The principal question in dispute between the parties is whether the Employment Retirement Income Security Act of 1974 (ERISA), codified at 29 U.S.C. §§ 1001 et seq., permits state tax authorities to collect unpaid state income taxes by levying on funds held in trust for the taxpayers under an ERISA-covered vacation benefit plan. The issue is an important one, which affects thousands of federally regulated trusts and all non-federal tax collection systems, and it must eventually receive a definitive, uniform resolution. Nevertheless, for reasons involving perhaps more history than logic, we hold that the lower federal courts had no jurisdiction to decide the question in the case before us, and we vacate the judgment and remand the case with instructions to remand it to the state court from which it was removed.

I

None of the relevant facts is in dispute. Appellee Construction Laborers Vacation Trust for Southern California (CLVT) is a trust established by an agreement between four associations of employers active in the construction industry in Southern California and the Southern California District Council of Laborers, an arm of the District Council and affiliated locals of the Laborers' International Union of North America. The purpose of the agreement and trust was to establish a mechanism for administering the provisions of a collective bargaining agreement that grants construction workers a yearly paid vacation.[2] The trust agreement expressly proscribes any assignment, pledge, or encumbrance of funds held in trust by CLVT. The plan that CLVT administers is unquestionably an "employee welfare benefit plan" within the meaning of § 3 of ERISA, and CLVT and its individual trustees are thereby subject to extensive regulation under titles I and III of ERISA.

Appellant Franchise Tax Board is a California agency charged with enforcement of that state's personal income tax law. California law authorizes appellant to require any person in possession of "credits or other personal property belonging to a taxpayer" "to withhold . . . the amount of any tax, interest, or penalties due from the taxpayer . . . and to transmit the amount withheld to the Franchise Tax Board." Cal. Rev. & Tax. Code Ann. § 18817. Any person who, upon notice by the Franchise Tax Board, fails to comply with its request to

---

[2] As part of the hourly compensation due bargaining unit members, employers pay a certain amount to CLVT, which places the money in an account for each employee. Once a year, CLVT distributes the money in each account to the employee for whom it is kept. . . . This system was set up in large part because union members typically work for several employers during the course of a year.

withhold and to transmit funds becomes personally liable for the amounts identified in the notice.

In June 1980, the Franchise Tax Board filed a complaint in state court against CLVT and its trustees. Under the heading "First Cause of Action," appellant alleged that CLVT had failed to comply with three levies issued under § 18817,[4] concluding with the allegation that it had been "damaged in a sum . . . not to exceed $380.56 plus interest from June 1, 1980." Under the heading "Second Cause of Action," appellant incorporated its previous allegations and added:

> "There was at the time of the levies alleged above and continues to be an actual controversy between the parties concerning their respective legal rights and duties. The board [appellant] contends that defendants [CLVT] are obligated and required by law to pay over to the board all amounts held . . . in favor of the board's delinquent taxpayers. On the other hand, defendants contend that § 514 of ERISA preempts state law and that the trustees lack the power to honor the levies made upon them by the state of California.

> "[D]efendants will continue to refuse to honor the board's levies in this regard. Accordingly, a declaration by this court of the parties' respective rights is required to fully and finally resolve this controversy."

In a prayer for relief, appellant requested damages for defendants' failure to honor the levies and a declaration that defendants are "legally obligated to honor all future levies by the board."

CLVT removed the case to the United States District Court for the Central District of California, and the court denied the Franchise Tax Board's motion for remand to the state court. On the merits, the District Court ruled that ERISA did not preempt the state's power to levy on funds held in trust by CLVT. CLVT appealed, and the Court of Appeals reversed. On petition for rehearing, the Franchise Tax Board

---

[4] At several points in 1977 and 1978, appellant issued notices to CLVT requesting it to withhold and to transmit approximately $380 in unpaid taxes, interest, and penalties due from three individuals. CLVT did not dispute that the individuals in question were beneficiaries of its trust or that it was then holding vacation benefit funds for them. In each case, however, it acknowledged receipt of appellant's notice and informed appellant that it had requested an opinion letter from the Administrator for Pension and Welfare Benefit Programs of the United States Department of Labor as to whether it was permitted under ERISA to honor appellant's levy. CLVT also informed appellant that it would withhold the funds from the individual workers until it received an opinion from the Department of Labor, but that it would not transmit the funds to the Franchise Tax Board.

Appellant took no immediate action to enforce its levy, and in January 1980 CLVT finally received the opinion letter it had requested. The opinion letter concluded "[I]t is the position of the Department of Labor that the process of any state judicial or administrative agency seeking to levy for unpaid taxes or unpaid unemployment insurance contributions upon benefits due a participant or beneficiary under the Plan is pre-empted under ERISA § 514." Accordingly, on January 7, 1980, counsel for CLVT furnished appellant a copy of the opinion letter, informed appellant that CLVT lacked the power to honor appellant's levies, and stated their intention to recommend that CLVT should disburse the funds it had withheld to the employees in question.

renewed its argument that the District Court lacked jurisdiction over the complaint in this case. The petition for rehearing was denied, and an appeal was taken to this Court. We postponed consideration of our jurisdiction pending argument on the merits. We now hold that this case was not within the removal jurisdiction conferred by 28 U.S.C. § 1441, and therefore we do not reach the merits of the preemption question.

II

The jurisdictional structure at issue in this case has remained basically unchanged for the past century. With exceptions not relevant here, "any civil action brought in a state court of which the district courts of the United States have original jurisdiction, may be removed by the defendant or the defendants, to the district court of the United States for the district and division embracing the place where such action is pending." 28 U.S.C. § 1441. If it appears before final judgment that a case was not properly removed, because it was not within the original jurisdiction of the United States district courts, the district court must remand it to the state court from which it was removed. See § 1447(c). For this case—as for many cases where there is no diversity of citizenship between the parties—the propriety of removal turns on whether the case falls within the original "federal question" jurisdiction of the United States district courts: "The district courts shall have jurisdiction of all civil actions arising under the Constitution, laws, or treaties of the United States." 28 U.S.C. § 1331.[7]

Since the first version of § 1331 was enacted [in 1875], the statutory phrase "arising under the Constitution, laws, or treaties of the United States" has resisted all attempts to frame a single, precise definition for determining which cases fall within, and which cases fall outside, the original jurisdiction of the district courts. Especially when considered in light of § 1441's removal jurisdiction, the phrase "arising under" masks a welter of issues regarding the interrelation of federal and state authority and the proper management of the federal judicial system.[8]

The most familiar definition of the statutory "arising under" limitation is Justice Holmes' statement, "A suit arises under the law that creates the cause of action." *American Well Works Co. v. Layne & Bowler Co.*, 241 U.S. 257, 260 (1916). However, it is well settled that

---

[7] ERISA may also be an "Act of Congress regulating commerce" within the meaning of 28 U.S.C. § 1337, but we have not distinguished between the "arising under" standards of § 1337 and § 1331. See, e.g., *Skelly Oil Co. v. Phillips Petroleum Co.*, 339 U.S. 667 (1950).

[8] The statute's "arising under" language tracks similar language in art. III, § 2 of the Constitution, which has been construed as permitting Congress to extend federal jurisdiction to any case of which federal law potentially "forms an ingredient," see *Osborn v. Bank of the United States*, 22 U.S. (9 Wheat.) 738, 823 (1824), and its limited legislative history suggests that the 44th Congress may have meant to "confer the whole power which the Constitution conferred," 2 Cong. Rec. 4986 (1874) (remarks of Sen. Carpenter). Nevertheless, we have only recently reaffirmed what has long been recognized—that "article III 'arising under' jurisdiction is broader than federal question jurisdiction under § 1331." *Verlinden B.V. v. Central Bank of Nigeria*, 461 U.S. 480, 495 (1983).

Justice Holmes' test is more useful for describing the vast majority of cases that come within the district courts' original jurisdiction than it is for describing which cases are beyond district court jurisdiction. We have often held that a case "arose under" federal law where the vindication of a right under state law necessarily turned on some construction of federal law, see, e.g., Smith v. Kansas City Title & Trust Co., 255 U.S. 180 (1921), and even the most ardent proponent of the Holmes test has admitted that it has been rejected as an exclusionary principle, see Flournoy v. Wiener, 321 U.S. 253, 270–72 (1944) (Frankfurter, J., dissenting). See also T.B. Harms Co. v. Eliscu, 339 F.2d 823, 827 (2d Cir. 1964) (Friendly, J.). Leading commentators have suggested that for purposes of § 1331 an action "arises under" federal law "if in order for the plaintiff to secure the relief sought he will be obliged to establish both the correctness and the applicability to his case of a proposition of federal law." P. Bator, P. Mishkin, D. Shapiro & H. Wechsler, Hart & Wechsler's The Federal Courts and the Federal System 889 (2d ed. 1973); cf. *T.B. Harms Co.,* supra ("a case may 'arise under' a law of the United States if the complaint discloses a need for determining the meaning or application of such a law").

One powerful doctrine has emerged, however—the "well-pleaded complaint" rule—which as a practical matter severely limits the number of cases in which state law "creates the cause of action" that may be initiated in or removed to federal district court, thereby avoiding more-or-less automatically a number of potentially serious federal-state conflicts.

> "[W]hether a case is one arising under the Constitution or a law or treaty of the United States, in the sense of the jurisdictional statute, . . . must be determined from what necessarily appears in the plaintiff's statement of his own claim in the bill or declaration, unaided by anything alleged in anticipation of avoidance of defenses which it is thought the defendant may interpose." Taylor v. Anderson, 234 U.S. 74, 75–76 (1914).

Thus, a federal court does not have original jurisdiction over a case in which the complaint presents a state-law cause of action, but also asserts that federal law deprives the defendant of a defense he may raise, Louisville & Nashville R. Co. v. Mottley, 211 U.S. 149 (1908), or that a federal defense the defendant may raise is not sufficient to defeat the claim, Tennessee v. Union & Planters' Bank, 152 U.S. 454 (1894). "Although such allegations show that very likely, in the course of the litigation, a question under the Constitution would arise, they do not show that the suit, that is, the plaintiff's original cause of action, arises under the Constitution." *Louisville & Nashville R. Co. v. Mottley,* supra at 152. For better or worse, under the present statutory scheme as it has existed since 1887, a defendant may not remove a case to federal court unless the plaintiff's complaint establishes that the case "arises under" federal law.[9] "[A] right or immunity created by the

---

[9] The well-pleaded complaint rule applies to the original jurisdiction of the district courts as well as to their removal jurisdiction. [Footnote continued on p. 446.]

Constitution or laws of the United States must be an element, and an essential one, of the plaintiff's cause of action." Gully v. First National Bank, 299 U.S. 109, 112 (1936).

For many cases in which federal law becomes relevant only insofar as it sets bounds for the operation of state authority, the well-pleaded complaint rule makes sense as a quick rule of thumb. Describing the case before the Court in *Gully*,[10] Justice Cardozo wrote:

> "Petitioner will have to prove that the state law has been obeyed before the question will be reached whether anything in its provisions or in administrative conduct under it is inconsistent with the federal rule. If what was done by the taxing officers in levying the tax in suit did not amount in substance under the law of Mississippi to an assessment of the shareholders, but in substance as well as in form was an assessment of the bank alone, the conclusion will be inescapable that there was neither tax nor debt, apart from any barriers Congress may have built. On the other hand, a finding upon evidence that the Mississippi law has been obeyed may compose the controversy altogether, leaving no room for a contention that the federal law has been infringed. The most that one can say is that a question of federal law is lurking in the background, just as farther in the background there lurks a question of constitutional law, the question of state power in our federal form of government. A dispute so doubtful and conjectural, so far removed from plain necessity, is unavailing to extinguish the jurisdiction of the states." 299 U.S., at 117.

The rule, however, may produce awkward results, especially in cases in which neither the obligation created by state law nor the defendant's factual failure to comply are in dispute, and both parties admit that the only question for decision is raised by a federal preemption defense. Nevertheless, it has been correctly understood to apply in

---

It is possible to conceive of a rational jurisdictional system in which the answer as well as the complaint would be consulted before a determination was made whether the case "arose under" federal law, or in which original and removal jurisdiction were not co-extensive. Indeed, until the 1887 amendments to the 1875 Act, the well-pleaded complaint rule was not applied in full force to cases removed from state court; the defendant's petition for removal could furnish the necessary guarantee that the case necessarily presented a substantial question of federal law. See Railroad Co. v. Mississippi, 102 U.S. 135, 140 (1880); Gold-Washing & Water Co. v. Keyes, 96 U.S. 199, 203–204 (1877). Commentators have repeatedly proposed that some mechanism be established to permit removal of cases in which a federal defense may be dispositive. See, e.g., American Law Institute, Study of the Division of Jurisdiction Between State and Federal Courts § 1312, at 188–94 (1969) (ALI Study); Wechsler, Federal Jurisdiction and the Revision of the Judicial Code, 13 Law & Contemp. Prob. 216, 233–34 (1948). But those proposals have not been adopted.

[10] *Gully* was a suit by Mississippi tax authorities, claiming that the First National Bank had failed to make good on a contract with its predecessor corporation whereby, according to the state, the bank had promised to pay the predecessor's tax liabilities. It had been removed to federal court, and the motion for remand had been defeated, on the ground that the state's "power to lay a tax upon the shares of national banks has its origin and measure in the provisions of a federal statute" and that "by necessary implication a plaintiff counts upon the statute in suing for the tax."

such situations. As we said in *Gully,* "By unimpeachable authority, a suit brought upon a state statute does not arise under an act of Congress or the Constitution of the United States because prohibited thereby." 299 U.S., at 116.[12]

III

Simply to state these principles is not to apply them to the case at hand. Appellants' complaint sets forth two "causes of action," one of which expressly refers to ERISA; if either comes within the original jurisdiction of the federal courts, removal was proper as to the whole case. See U.S.C. § 1441(c). Although appellant's complaint does not specifically assert any particular statutory entitlement for the relief it seeks, the language of the complaint suggests (and the parties do not dispute) that appellant's "first cause of action" states a claim under Cal. Rev. & Tax. Code § 18818, and its "second cause of action" states a claim under California's Declaratory Judgment Act, Cal. Civ. Proc. Code § 1060. As an initial proposition, then, the "law that creates the cause of action" is state law, and original federal jurisdiction is unavailable unless it appears that some substantial, disputed question of federal law is a necessary element of one of the well-pleaded state claims, or that one or the other claim is "really" one of federal law.

A

Even though state law creates appellant's causes of action, its case might still "arise under" the laws of the United States if a well-pleaded complaint established that its right to relief under state law requires resolution of a substantial question of federal law in dispute between the parties. For appellant's first cause of action—to enforce its levy, under § 18818—a straightforward application of the well-pleaded complaint rule precludes original federal court jurisdiction. California law establishes a set of conditions, without reference to federal law, under which a tax levy may be enforced; federal law becomes relevant only by way of a defense to an obligation created entirely by state law, and then only if appellant has made out a valid claim for relief under state law. The well-pleaded complaint rule was framed to deal with precisely such a situation. As we discuss above, since 1887 it has been settled law that a case may not be removed to federal court on the basis of a federal defense, including the defense of preemption, even if the defense is anticipated in the plaintiff's complaint, and even if both parties admit that the defense is the only question truly at issue in the case.

Appellant's declaratory judgment action poses a more difficult problem. Whereas the question of federal preemption is relevant to appellant's first cause of action only as a potential defense, it is a necessary element of the declaratory judgment claim. Under Cal. Proc.

---

[12] Note, however, that a claim of federal preemption does not always arise as a defense to a coercive action. See infra, n.20. And, of course, the absence of original jurisdiction does not mean that there is no federal forum in which a preemption defense may be heard. If the state courts reject a claim of federal preemption, that decision may ultimately be reviewed on appeal by this Court.

Code § 1060, a party with an interest in property may bring an action for a declaration of another party's legal rights and duties with respect to that property upon showing that there is an "actual controversy relating to the respective rights and duties" of the parties. The only questions in dispute between the parties in this case concern the rights and duties of CLVT and its trustees under ERISA. Not only does appellant's request for a declaratory judgment under California law clearly encompass questions governed by ERISA, but appellant's complaint identifies no other questions as a subject of controversy between the parties. Such questions must be raised in a well-pleaded complaint for a declaratory judgment. Therefore, it is clear on the face of its well-pleaded complaint that appellant may not obtain the relief it seeks in its second cause of action ("[t]hat the court declare defendants legally obligated to honor all future levies by the board upon [CLVT]") without a construction of ERISA and/or an adjudication of its preemptive effect and constitutionality—all questions of federal law.

Appellant argues that original federal court jurisdiction over such a complaint is foreclosed by our decision in Skelly Oil Co. v. Phillips Petroleum Co., 339 U.S. 667 (1950). As we shall see, however, *Skelly Oil* is not directly controlling.

In *Skelly Oil*, Skelly Oil and Phillips had a contract, for the sale of natural gas, that entitled the seller—Skelly Oil—to terminate the contract at any time after December 1, 1946, if the Federal Power Commission had not yet issued a certificate of convenience and necessity to a third party, a pipeline company to whom Phillips intended to resell the gas purchased from Skelly Oil. Their dispute began when the Federal Power Commission informed the pipeline company on November 30 that it would issue a conditional certificate, but did not make its order public until December 2. By this time Skelly Oil had notified Phillips of its decision to terminate their contract. Phillips brought an action in United States District Court under the federal Declaratory Judgment Act, 28 U.S.C. § 2201, seeking a declaration that the contract was still in effect.

There was no diversity between the parties, and we held that Phillips' claim was not within the federal question jurisdiction conferred by § 1331. We reasoned:

> " '[T]he operation of the Declaratory Judgment Act is procedural only.' Congress enlarged the range of remedies available in the federal courts but did not extend their jurisdiction. When concerned as we are with the power of the inferior federal courts to entertain litigation within the restricted area to which the Constitution and acts of Congress confine them, 'jurisdiction' means the kinds of issues which give right of entrance to federal courts. Jurisdiction in this sense was not altered by the Declaratory Judgment Act. Prior to that act, a federal court would entertain a suit on a contract only if the plaintiff asked for an immediate enforceable remedy like money damages or an injunction, but such relief could only be

given if the requisites of jurisdiction, in the sense of a federal right or diversity, provided foundation for the resort to the federal courts. The Declaratory Judgment Act allowed relief to be given by way of recognizing the plaintiff's right even though no immediate enforcement of it was asked. But the requirements of jurisdiction—the limited subject matters which alone Congress had authorized the district courts to adjudicate—were not impliedly repealed or modified." 339 U.S., at 671–72.

We then observed that, under the well-pleaded complaint rule, an action by Phillips to enforce its contract would not present a federal question. *Skelly Oil* has come to stand for the proposition that "if, but for the availability of the declaratory judgment procedure, the federal claim would arise only as a defense to a state created action jurisdiction is lacking." 10A C. Wright, A. Miller & M. Kane, Federal Practice and Procedure § 2767, at 744–745 (2d ed. 1983). Cf. Public Service Comm'n v. Wycoff, 344 U.S. 237, 248 (1952) (dictum).[14]

1. As an initial matter, we must decide whether the doctrine of *Skelly Oil* limits original federal court jurisdiction under § 1331—and by extension removal jurisdiction under § 1441—when a question of federal law appears on the face of a well-pleaded complaint for a state law declaratory judgment. Apparently, it is a question of first impression. As the passage quoted above makes clear, *Skelly Oil* relied significantly on the precise contours of the federal Declaratory Judgment Act as well as of § 1331. . . . The Court's emphasis that the Declaratory Judgment Act was intended to affect only the remedies available in a federal district court, not the court's jurisdiction, was critical to the Court's reasoning. Our interpretation of the federal Declaratory Judgment Act in *Skelly Oil* does not apply of its own force to *state* declaratory judgment statutes, many of which antedate the federal statute.

Yet while *Skelly Oil* itself is limited to the federal Declaratory Judgment Act, fidelity to its spirit leads us to extend it to state declaratory judgment actions as well. If federal district courts could take jurisdiction, either originally or by removal, of state declaratory judgment claims raising questions of federal laws, without regard to the doctrine of *Skelly Oil*, the federal Declaratory Judgment Act—with the limitations *Skelly Oil* read into it—would become a dead letter. For

---

[14] In *Wycoff,* [we said]:

"Where the complaint in an action for declaratory judgment seeks in essence to assert a defense to an impending or threatened state court action, it is the character of the threatened action, and not of the defense, which will determine whether there is federal-question jurisdiction in the district court. If the cause of action, which the declaratory defendant threatens to assert, does not itself involve a claim under federal law, it is doubtful if a federal court may entertain an action for a declaratory judgment establishing a defense to that claim. This is dubious even though the declaratory complaint sets forth a claim of federal right, if that right is in reality in the nature of a defense to a threatened cause of action. Federal courts will not seize litigations from state courts merely because one, normally a defendant, goes to federal court to begin his federal-law defense before the state court begins the case under state law."

any case in which a state declaratory judgment action was available, litigants could get into federal court for a declaratory judgment despite our interpretation of § 2201, simply by pleading an adequate state claim for a declaration of federal law. Having interpreted the Declaratory Judgment Act of 1934 to include certain limitations on the jurisdiction of federal district courts to entertain declaratory judgment suits, we should be extremely hesitant to interpret the Judiciary Act of 1875 and its 1887 amendments in a way that renders the limitations in the later statute nugatory. Therefore, we hold that under the jurisdictional statutes as they now stand[17] federal courts do not have original jurisdiction, nor do they acquire jurisdiction on removal, when a federal question is presented by a complaint for a state declaratory judgment, but *Skelly Oil* would bar jurisdiction if the plaintiff had sought a federal declaratory judgment.

2. The question, then, is whether a federal district court could take jurisdiction of appellant's declaratory judgment claim had it been brought under 28 U.S.C. § 2201.[18] The application of *Skelly Oil* to such a suit is somewhat unclear. Federal courts have regularly taken original jurisdiction over declaratory judgment suits in which, if the declaratory judgment *defendant* brought a coercive action to enforce its rights, that suit would necessarily present a federal question.[19] Section 502(a)(3) of ERISA specifically grants trustees of ERISA-covered plans like CLVT a cause of action for injunctive relief when their rights and duties under ERISA are at issue, and that action is exclusively governed by federal law.[20] If CLVT could have sought an injunction under

[17] It is not beyond the power of Congress to confer a right to a declaratory judgment in a case or controversy arising under federal law—within the meaning of the Constitution or of § 1331—without regard to *Skelly Oil*'s particular application of the well-pleaded complaint rule. The 1969 ALI report strongly criticized the *Skelly Oil* doctrine: "If no other changes were to be made in federal question jurisdiction, it is arguable that such language, and the historical test it seems to embody, should be repudiated." ALI Study § 1311, at 170–71. Nevertheless, Congress has declined to make such a change. At this point, any adjustment in the system that has evolved under the *Skelly Oil* rule must come from Congress.

[18] It may seem odd that, for purposes of determining whether removal was proper, we analyze a claim brought under state law, in state court, by a party who has continuously objected to district court jurisdiction over its case, as if that party had been trying to get original federal court jurisdiction all along. That irony, however, is a more-or-less constant feature of the removal statute, under which a case is removable if a federal district court could have taken jurisdiction had the same complaint been filed. See Wechsler, Federal Jurisdiction and the Revision of the Judicial Code, 13 Law & Contemp. Prob. 216, 234 (1948).

[19] For instance, federal courts have consistently adjudicated suits by alleged patent infringers to declare a patent invalid, on the theory that an infringement suit by the declaratory judgment defendant would raise a federal question over which the federal courts have exclusive jurisdiction. See Hart & Wechsler 896–97. Taking jurisdiction over this type of suit is consistent with the dictum in *Public Service Comm'n of Utah v. Wycoff Co.*, see supra, n.14, in which we stated only that a declaratory judgment plaintiff could not get original federal jurisdiction if the anticipated lawsuit by the declaratory judgment defendant would *not* "arise under" federal law. It is also consistent with the nature of the declaratory remedy itself, which was designed to permit adjudication of either party's claims of right. See E. Borchard, Declaratory Judgments 15, 18, 23, 25 (1984).

[20] . . . See . . . infra, n.26 (federal jurisdiction over suits under § 502 is exclusive, and they are governed entirely by federal common law).

Even if ERISA did not expressly provide jurisdiction, CLVT might have been able to

ERISA against application to it of state regulations that require acts inconsistent with ERISA,[21] does a declaratory judgment suit by the state "arise under" federal law?

We think not. We have always interpreted what *Skelly Oil* called "the current of jurisdictional legislation since the Act of March 3, 1875" with an eye to practicality and necessity. "What is needed is something of that common-sense accommodation of judgment to kaleidoscopic situations which characterizes the law in its treatment of causation . . . a selective process which picks the substantial causes out of the web and lays the other ones aside." Gully v. First National Bank, 299 U.S., at 117–18. There are good reasons why the federal courts should not entertain suits by the states to declare the validity of their regulations despite possibly conflicting federal law. States are not significantly prejudiced by an inability to come to federal court for a declaratory judgment in advance of a possible injunctive suit by a person subject to federal regulation. They have a variety of means by which they can enforce their own laws in their own courts, and they do not suffer if the preemption questions such enforcement may raise are tested there.[22] The express grant of federal jurisdiction in ERISA is limited to suits brought by certain parties, as to whom Congress presumably determined that a right to enter federal court was necessary to further the statute's purposes.[23] It did not go so far as to provide that any suit *against* such parties must also be brought in federal court when they themselves did not choose to sue. The situation presented by a state's suit for a declaration of the validity of state law is sufficiently removed from the spirit of necessity and careful limitation of district court jurisdiction that informed our statutory interpretation in *Skelly Oil* and *Gully* to convince us that, until Congress informs us otherwise, such a

obtain federal jurisdiction under the doctrine applied in some cases that a person subject to a scheme of federal regulation may sue in federal court to enjoin application to him of conflicting state regulations, and a declaratory judgment action by the same person does not necessarily run afoul of the *Skelly Oil* doctrine. See, e.g., Lake Carriers' Assn. v. MacMullan, 406 U.S. 498, 506–08 (1972).

[21] We express no opinion, however, whether a party in CLVT's position could sue under ERISA to enjoin or to declare invalid a state tax levy, despite the Tax Injunction Act, 28 U.S.C. § 1341. See California v. Grace Brethren Church, ___ U.S. ___ (1982). To do so, it would have to show either that state law provided no "speedy and efficient remedy" or that Congress intended § 502 of ERISA to be an exception to the Tax Injunction Act.

[22] Indeed, as appellant's strategy in this case shows, they may often be willing to go to great lengths to avoid federal-court resolution of a preemption question. Realistically, there is little prospect that states will flood the federal courts with declaratory judgment actions; most questions will arise, as in this case, because a state has sought a declaration in state court and the defendant has removed the case to federal court. Accordingly, it is perhaps appropriate to note that considerations of comity make us reluctant to snatch cases which a state has brought from the courts of that state, unless some clear rule demands it.

[23] Alleged patent infringers, for example, have a clear interest in swift resolution of the federal issue of patent validity—they are liable for damages if it turns out they are infringing a patent, and they frequently have a delicate network of contractual arrangements with third parties that is dependent on their right to sell or license a product. Parties subject to conflicting state and federal regulatory schemes also have a clear interest in sorting out the scope of each government's authority, especially where they face a threat of liability if the application of federal law is not quickly made clear.

suit is not within the original jurisdiction of the United States district courts. Accordingly, the same suit brought originally in state court is not removable either.

B

CLVT also argues that appellant's "causes of action" are, in substance, federal claims. Although we have often repeated that "the party who brings the suit is master to decide what law he will rely upon," The Fair v. Kohler Die & Specialty Co., 228 U.S. 22, 25 (1913), it is an independent corollary of the well-pleaded complaint rule that a plaintiff may not defeat removal by omitting to plead necessary federal questions in a complaint, see Avco Corp. v. Aero Lodge No. 735, Int'l Assn. of Machinists, 376 F.2d 337, 339–40 (6th Cir. 1967), aff'd, 390 U.S. 557 (1968).

CLVT's best argument stems from our decision in *Avco Corp. v. Aero Lodge No. 735.* In that case, the petitioner filed suit in state court alleging simply that it had a valid contract with the respondent, a union, under which the respondent had agreed to submit all grievances to binding arbitration and not to cause or sanction any "work stoppages, strikes, or slowdowns." The petitioner further alleged that the respondent and its officials had violated the agreement by participating in and sanctioning work stoppages, and it sought temporary and permanent injunctions against further breaches. It was clear that, had petitioner invoked it, there would have been a federal cause of action under § 301 of the Labor Management Relations Act of 1947 (LMRA), see Textile Workers v. Lincoln Mills, 353 U.S. 448 (1957), and that, even in state court, any action to enforce an agreement within the scope of § 301 would be controlled by federal law, see Teamsters Local 174 v. Lucas Flour Co., 369 U.S. 95, 103–04 (1962). It was also clear, however, under the law in effect at the time, that independent limits on federal jurisdiction made it impossible for a federal court to grant the injunctive relief petitioner sought. See Sinclair Refining Co. v. Atkinson, 370 U.S. 195 (1962) (later overruled in Boys Markets, Inc. v. Retail Clerks Local 770, 398 U.S. 235 (1970)).

The Court of Appeals held and we affirmed that the petitioner's action "arose under" § 301, and thus could be removed to federal court, although the petitioner had undoubtedly pleaded an adequate claim for relief under the state law of contracts and had sought a remedy available *only* under state law. The necessary ground of decision was that the preemptive force of § 301 is so powerful as to displace entirely any state cause of action "for violation of contracts between an employer and a labor organization."[25] Any such suit is purely a creature of federal law, notwithstanding the fact that state law would provide a

---

[25] To similar effect is Oneida Indian Nation v. County of Oneida, 414 U.S. 661, 677 (1974), in which we held that—unlike all other ejectment suits in which the plaintiff derives its claim from a federal grant—an ejectment suit based on Indian title is within the original "federal question" jurisdiction of the district courts, because Indian title creates a federal possessory right to tribal lands, "wholly apart from the application of state law principles which normally and separately protect a valid right of possession."

cause of action in the absence of § 301. *Avco* stands for the proposition that if a federal cause of action completely preempts a state cause of action any complaint that comes within the scope of the federal cause of action necessarily "arises under" federal law.

CLVT argues by analogy that ERISA, like § 301, was meant to create a body of federal common law, and that "any state court action which would require the interpretation or application of ERISA to a plan document 'arises under' the laws of the United States." ERISA contains provisions creating a series of express causes of action in favor of participants, beneficiaries, and fiduciaries of ERISA-covered plans, as well as the Secretary of Labor. § 502(a).[26] It may be that, as with § 301 as interpreted in *Avco*, any state action coming within the scope of § 502(a) of ERISA would be removable to federal district court, even if an otherwise adequate state cause of action were pleaded without reference to federal law. It does not follow, however, that either of appellant's claims in this case comes within the scope of one of ERISA's causes of action.

The phrasing of § 502(a) is instructive. Section 502(a) specifies which persons—participants, beneficiaries, fiduciaries, or the Secretary of Labor—may bring actions for particular kinds of relief. It neither creates nor expressly denies any cause of action in favor of state governments, to enforce tax levies or for any other purpose. It does not purport to reach every question relating to plans covered by ERISA. Furthermore, § 514(b)(2)(A) of ERISA makes clear that Congress did not intend to preempt entirely every state cause of action relating to such plans. With important, but express limitations, it states that "nothing in this subchapter shall be construed to relieve any person from any law of any state which regulates insurance, banking, or securities."

Against this background, it is clear that a suit by state tax authorities under a statute like § 18818 does not "arise under" ERISA. Unlike the contract rights at issue in *Avco*, the state's right to enforce its tax levies is not of central concern to the federal statute. For that reason, as in *Gully*, on the face of a well-pleaded complaint there are many reasons completely unrelated to the provisions and purposes of ERISA why the state may or may not be entitled to the relief it seeks.[29] Furthermore, ERISA does not provide an alternative cause of action in favor of the state to enforce its rights, while § 301 expressly supplied

---

[26] The statute further states that "the district courts of the United States shall have exclusive jurisdiction of civil actions under the subchapter brought by the Secretary or by a participant, beneficiary, or fiduciary," except for actions by a participant or beneficiary to recover benefits due, to enforce rights under the terms of a plan, or to clarify rights to future benefits, over which state courts have concurrent jurisdiction. § 502(e)(1). "[A] body of federal substantive law will be developed by the courts to deal with issues involving rights and obligations under private welfare and pension plans." 120 Cong. Rec. 29, 942 (1974) (remarks of Sen. Javits).

[29] In theory (looking only at the complaint), it may turn out that the levy was improper under state law, or that in fact the defendant had complied with the levy. Furthermore, a levy on CLVT might be for something like property taxes on real estate it owned. CLVT's trust agreement authorizes its trustees to pay such taxes.

the plaintiff in *Avco* with a federal cause of action to replace its preempted state contract claim. Therefore, even though the Court of Appeals may well be correct that ERISA precludes enforcement of the state's levy in the circumstances of this case, an action to enforce the levy is not itself preempted by ERISA.

Once again, appellant's declaratory judgment cause of action presents a somewhat more difficult issue. The question on which a declaration is sought—that of the CLVT trustees' "power to honor the levies made upon them by the state of California"—is undoubtedly a matter of concern under ERISA. It involves the meaning and enforceability of provisions in CLVT's trust agreement forbidding the trustees to assign or otherwise to alienate funds held in trust, and thus comes within the class of questions for which Congress intended that federal courts create federal common law.[30] Under § 502(a)(3)(B) of ERISA, a participant, beneficiary, or fiduciary of a plan covered by ERISA may bring a declaratory judgment action in federal court to determine whether the plan's trustees may comply with a state levy on funds held in trust.[31] Nevertheless, CLVT's argument that the appellant's second cause of action arises under ERISA fails for the second reason given above. ERISA carefully enumerates the parties entitled to seek relief under § 502; it does not provide anyone other than participants, beneficiaries, or fiduciaries with an express cause of action for a declaratory judgment on the issues in this case. A suit for similar relief by some other party does not "arise under" that provision.

IV

Our concern in this case is consistent application of a system of statutes conferring original federal court jurisdiction, as they have been interpreted by this Court over many years. Under our interpretations, Congress has given the lower federal courts jurisdiction to hear, originally or by removal from a state court, only those cases in which a well-pleaded complaint establishes either that federal law creates the cause of action or that the plaintiff's right to relief necessarily depends on resolution of a substantial question of federal law. We hold that a suit by state tax authorities both to enforce its levies against funds held in trust pursuant to an ERISA-covered employee benefit plan, and to declare the validity of the levies notwithstanding ERISA, is neither a creature of ERISA itself nor a suit of which the federal courts will take

---

[30] Of course, in suggesting that the trustees' power to comply with a state tax levy is—as a subset of the trustees' general duties with respect to CLVT—a matter of concern under ERISA, we express no opinion as to whether ERISA forbids the trustees to comply with the levies in this case or otherwise preempts the state's power to levy on funds held in trust. The same is true of our holding that ERISA does not preempt the state's causes of action entirely. Merely to hold that ERISA does not have the same effect on appellant's suit in

this case that § 301 of the LMRA had on the petitioner's contract suit in *Avco* is not to prejudge the merits of CLVT's preemption claim.

[31] See n.19, supra. Section 502(a)(3)(B) of ERISA has been interpreted as creating a cause of action for a declaratory judgment. See Cutaiar v. Marshall, 590 F.2d 523, 527 (3d Cir. 1979). We repeat, however, the caveat expressed in n.21, supra, as to the effect of the Tax Injunction Act.

jurisdiction because it turns on a question of federal law. Accordingly, we vacate the judgment of the Court of Appeals and remand so that this case may be remanded to the Superior Court of the state of California for the county of Los Angeles.

It is so ordered.[a]

NOTES ON DECLARATORY JUDGMENTS AND THE GENERAL FEDERAL QUESTION STATUTE

1. The Federal Declaratory Judgment Statute. The federal declaratory judgment statute, now found in 28 U.S.C. §§ 2201–2202, permits a federal court, "[i]n a case of actual controversy within its jurisdiction," to "declare the rights and other legal relations of any interested party seeking such declaration, whether or not further relief is or could be sought." As the *Franchise Tax Board* case reveals, the interaction between this statute and § 1331 has become a problem of some complexity. The leading case is Skelly Oil Co. v. Phillips Petroleum Co., 339 U.S. 667 (1950), which is detailed in *Franchise Tax Board.* A plaintiff who seeks a declaratory judgment must establish the jurisdiction of the court under some other statute. The declaratory judgment statute merely creates a federal cause of action; it does not contain independent authority to exercise jurisdiction. The problem, therefore, is how to determine whether a complaint seeking declaratory relief states a case arising under federal law such that jurisdiction is authorized by § 1331.

2. Questions and Comments. Consider the following comments on *Skelly Oil* in Cohen, The Broken Compass: The Requirement That a Case Arise "Directly" Under Federal Law, 115 U. Pa. L. Rev. 890, 910 (1967): *

> "In cases like *Skelly,* arguably there is some need for an expert federal forum in interpreting federal law, even though that law has been incorporated in a private contract. But, obviously, that need is counterbalanced. First, there is the real possibility that the contract may be construed, once the merits of the controversy are reached, to render the issue of federal law irrelevant or inconclusive; there was in *Skelly* a real question whether the contract used the term 'certificate of public convenience and necessity' in the same sense the Natural Gas Act used the term for entirely different purposes. Second, in most cases where issues of federal law are relevant only because incorporated in a private contract, there will be little federal

---

[a] On the merits of the pre-emption question before the Court, see Mackey v. Lanier Collections Agency & Service, Inc., __ U.S. __ (1988). *Mackey* held that Georgia garnishment procedures could be used by a collection agency to reach employee welfare benefits covered by ERISA. [Footnote by eds.]

* Reprinted by permission of The University of Pennsylvania Law Review, Fred B. Rothman & Company, and the author from The University of Pennsylvania Law Review, Vol. 115, p. 910.

interest in providing the protective jurisdiction of a sympathetic federal forum. And, finally, there would be real reason to fear a 'vast current of litigation' in the federal courts if parties could, in effect, specify federal court jurisdiction by privately agreeing that their disputes would be governed by federal law. There may be some cases in which federal law is relevant only as incorporated in a private contract, and in which there would be sufficient federal interest to justify a conclusion favoring federal question jurisdiction. Arguably *Skelly* itself might be such a case. But a general rule applied to all cases in which federal law is incorporated in private contracts will work well in most cases, and provide an administrable and predictable standard for that group of cases. For that reason, I agree . . . that controversies as to the meaning of contractual terms incorporating federal standards do not arise . . . under federal law."

Should *Skelly Oil* have been decided, as the opinion itself suggests, on the principle that federal declaratory judgment proceedings arise under federal law only if one of the parties could have brought a coercive action that would support jurisdiction? Or should it have been decided, as Professor Cohen would have it, on the ground that cases where private contracts incorporate federal law do not belong in the federal courts? Is it really necessary to turn jurisdiction on whether a different kind of suit could have been brought, or is it sufficient if the same factors that generally govern federal question jurisdiction also apply to declaratory judgment proceedings?

Consider, for example, the facts of *Mottley,* supra, page 431. It is clear that the lawsuit turned exclusively on the resolution of an important federal question, probable that numerous prior settlements would have been affected by its decision, and unlikely that upholding jurisdiction would have opened the floodgates to numerous federal suits. It also seems clear that no coercive lawsuit could have been filed by either party that would present a case arising under federal law. Does the rationale underlying district court jurisdiction in *Smith v. Kansas City Title* suggest that a declaratory judgment proceeding should be heard in federal court if filed by either party?

Assume that the Court's view of *Skelly Oil* is right, or at least should be followed until Congress provides for a different result. Does *Franchise Tax Board* follow from this premise? Consider the following argument. As the Court recognizes, a plaintiff should be able to seek a declaratory judgment in situations where the defendant could have brought a coercive action that would arise under federal law. Since the trust fund could have filed an action under ERISA for an injunction to prevent the tax assessments, the taxing authority should therefore have been able to seek declaratory relief. This result is supported, not undermined, by the fact that Congress has provided a cause of action to covered trust funds. Such actions are governed by federal common law and are to be heard exclusively in federal courts. Presumably this means that Congress believes it important that the *questions* involved in such lawsuits be heard in federal courts. Whatever the reasons for this judgment, are they not equally applicable if the same questions arise in a declaratory judgment proceeding brought by the party who would be a defendant in a coercive action? Why was this argument rejected?

Finally, consider the facts of Stone & Webster Engineering Corp. v. Ilsley, 690 F.2d 323 (2d Cir. 1982). Ilsley was an employee of Stone & Webster. He was injured on the job and was awarded workmen's compensation. Before Ilsley was injured, Stone & Webster had paid 75 cents for each hour he had worked into a fund established pursuant to a collective bargaining agreement for the provision of medical, surgical, and life insurance benefits. Under the terms of a Connecticut statute, Stone & Webster was obligated to continue payments into the fund after the injury. A state administrator issued a "finding and award" requiring Stone & Webster to make such payments. Stone & Webster appealed this decision to the Workmen's Compensation Commission and simultaneously instituted suit in federal court against Ilsley, the unions involved, and various state officials charged with enforcement of the Connecticut statute. Its claim was that the Connecticut law was preempted by ERISA. Both a declaratory judgment and injunctive relief were sought.

The District Court awarded the declaratory relief sought by Stone & Webster. On appeal, the state officials argued that since "only participants, beneficiaries or fiduciaries are empowered to institute an action for civil enforcement of ERISA in district court," the federal court lacked jurisdiction to award the declaratory judgment. The Court of Appeals affirmed. On the jurisdictional question, it said:

> "Here not only is a right being asserted on the face of the complaint, but an injunction is also being affirmatively sought to prevent interference with that right. This claim raises federal question jurisdiction. Ex parte Young, 209 U.S. 123 (1908). Regardless of whether . . . the equitable considerations necessary to support the issuance of an injunction are sufficiently alleged, jurisdiction under § 1331(a) clearly exists since a declaratory judgment action may be entertained even where further relief is unavailable. Thus, the historical test in *Mottley* has been satisfied. The declaratory claim asserted is not merely a defense, but affirmative coercive relief is sought by way of injunction."

Stone & Webster was decided by the Court of Appeals on September 30, 1982. The Supreme Court decided *Franchise Tax Board* on June 24, 1983, and on July 6, 1983, it summarily affirmed an appeal by the Connecticut officials in *Stone & Webster*. Is this result surprising?

3. Footnote on *American Well Works*. In footnote 19 in its opinion in the *Vacation Trust* case, the Court approves a line of lower court patent cases that would now allow the *American Well Works* dispute to be heard in federal district court if the case were filed as a declaratory judgment seeking a determination of the validity of the defendant's patent. If *Skelly Oil* is right, is this an unwarranted extension of the declaratory judgment procedure? Could the plaintiff in *American Well Works* seek such declaratory relief and then justify district court jurisdiction over its slander of title claim on a theory of pendent jurisdiction?

4. Digression on Preemption, Federal Question Jurisdiction, and Removal: *Metropolitan Life Ins. Co. v. Taylor.* Justice Brennan said in *Franchise Tax Board* that although normally " 'the party who brings the suit is master to decide what law he will rely upon,' it is an independent corollary of the well-pleaded complaint rule that a plaintiff may not defeat removal by omitting to plead necessary federal questions in a complaint." The tension between these two statements in the context of ERISA came before the Court in Metropolitan Life Ins. Co. v. Taylor, 481 U.S. 58 (1987).

Taylor was an employee of General Motors, which had established a disability plan insured by Metropolitan. A dispute arose about whether Taylor was disabled from working. General Motors took the position that Taylor was malingering and fired him. Taylor responded by filing suit in state court against both General Motors and Metropolitan for breach of his employment contract, for wrongful termination, for the insurance benefits to which he believed himself entitled, and for other grievances. General Motors and Metropolitan removed the case to federal court, alleging that the claim for disability benefits presented a federal claim by virtue of ERISA and asserting pendent jurisdiction over the other claims. The District Court found the case removable and granted summary judgment for the defendants. The Court of Appeals reversed on the ground that "Taylor's complaint stated only state law causes of action subject to the federal defense of ERISA preemption, and that the 'well-pleaded complaint' rule of *Mottley* precluded removal on the basis of a federal defense." The Supreme Court granted certiorari and, in an opinion by Justice O'Connor, reversed.

The Court had held in a companion case, Pilot Life Ins. Co. v. Dedeaux, 481 U.S. 41 (1987), that state common law causes of action claiming benefits under plans regulated by ERISA were preempted by ERISA. It followed that Taylor's claim for disability benefits, "as a suit by a beneficiary to recover benefits from a covered plan . . . falls directly under § 502(a)(1)(B) of ERISA, which provides an exclusive federal cause of action for resolution of such disputes." The Court continued:

> "Federal pre-emption is ordinarily a federal defense to the plaintiff's suit. As a defense, it does not appear on the face of a well-pleaded complaint, and, therefore, does not authorize removal to a federal court. One corollary of the well-pleaded complaint rule developed in the case law, however, is that Congress may so completely pre-empt a particular area, that any civil complaint raising this select group of claims is necessarily federal in character. . . .

> "There is no dispute in this case that Taylor's complaint, although pre-empted by ERISA, purported to raise only state law causes of action. The question, therefore, resolves itself into whether or not the *Avco* principle [see pages 452–54, supra] can be extended to statutes other than the [Labor Management Relations Act] in order to recharacterize a state law complaint displaced by § 502(a)(1)(B) as an action arising under federal law. In *Franchise Tax Board,* the Court held that ERISA pre-emption, without more, does not convert a claim into an action arising under federal law. The Court suggested, however, that a state action that was not only pre-empted by ERISA, but also came 'within the scope of § 502 of ERISA' might fall within the *Avco* rule. The claim in this case, unlike the state tax collection suit in *Franchise Tax Board,* is within the scope of § 502(a) and we therefore must face the question specifically reserved by *Franchise Tax Board.*"

The Court observed that "[i]n the absence of explicit direction from Congress, this question would be a close one." But it found in the legislative history of ERISA express references to the Labor Management Relations Act and inferred from this that Congress wanted the two statutes to be interpreted similarly. The Court also held that it did not matter how "obvious" it was at the time Taylor filed suit that federal law had this effect:

> "[T]he touchstone of the federal district court's removal jurisdiction is not the 'obviousness' of the pre-emption defense but the intent of Congress. Indeed, . . . even an 'obvious' pre-emption defense does not, in most cases, create removal jurisdiction. In this case, however, Congress has clearly manifested an intent to make causes of action within the scope of the civil enforcement provisions of § 502(a) removable to a federal court. . . . Accordingly, this suit, though it purports to raise only state law claims, is necessarily federal in character by virtue of the clearly manifested intent of Congress."

Justice Brennan, joined by Justice Marshall, concurred. He said:

> "While I join the Court's opinion, I note that our decision should not be interpreted as adopting a broad rule that *any* defense premised on congressional intent to pre-empt state law is sufficient to establish removal jurisdiction. The Court holds only that removal jurisdiction exists when, as here, 'Congress has *clearly* manifested an intent to make causes of action . . . *removable to federal court.*' In future cases involving other statutes, the prudent course for a federal court that does not find a *clear* congressional intent to create removal jurisdiction will be to remand the case to state court." [a]

---

[a] Justice Brennan authored the Court's unanimous opinion in the later case of Caterpillar, Inc. v. Williams, ___ U.S. ___ (1987), where the Court held that a particu- lar labor dispute did not come within the Court's *Avco* decision and was therefore not removable. The Court held that the *Avco* rule extended to claims founded upon

The assertion of a federal pre-emption defense to a state law claim filed in state court is likely to occur with some frequency. After *Taylor,* how are the lower courts to determine whether such a claim is removable? Must they decide the merits of the pre-emption claim before they can determine whether they have jurisdiction? Although the Court was unanimous in *Pilot Life* that ERISA pre-empted claims of the sort raised in *Taylor,* the answer to that question, as Justice Brennan said in his *Taylor* concurrence, "was not obvious." How would the Supreme Court have decided *Taylor* had it not decided *Pilot Life* on the same day?

For an analysis of how the issue had been approached prior to *Taylor,* see Mary Twitchell, Characterizing Federal Claims: Preemption, Removal, and the Arising-Under Jurisdiction of the Federal Courts, 54 Geo.Wash.L.Rev. 812 (1986).[b] Twitchell proposes a three-part test: "whether Congress has given plaintiff an express cause of action" for some of the relief sought in state court; if so, "whether defendant could reasonably argue that Congress intended that the regulatory scheme preempt plaintiff's asserted state law claim"; and if so, whether in fact the state claim is pre-empted. Applying her approach, she correctly predicted the result in *Taylor.* Did the Court apply the same approach?

---

collective bargaining agreements, and not to claims—such as those before the Court—founded upon individual employment contracts. The employer did have other pre-emption arguments, namely that the individual contracts were pre-empted by the principle of exclusive union representation protected by federal law, that enforcement of the individual contracts were pre-empted as an unfair labor practice, and that state law claims were pre-empted by federal defenses that required interpretation of a collective bargaining agreement. The Court responded:

"It is true that when a defense to a state claim is based on the terms of a collective-bargaining agreement, the state court will have to interpret that agreement to decide whether the state claim survives. But the presence of a federal question, even a § 301 question, in a defensive argument does not overcome the paramount policies embodied in the well-pleaded complaint rule—that the plaintiff is the master of the complaint, that a federal question must appear on the face of the complaint, and that the plaintiff may, by eschewing claims based on federal law, choose to have the cause heard in state court.

When a plaintiff invokes a right created by a collective-bargaining agreement, the plaintiff has *chosen* to plead what we have held must be regarded as a federal claim, and removal is at the defendant's option. But a *defendant* cannot, merely by injecting a federal question into an action that asserts what is plainly a state-law claim, transform the action into one arising under federal law, thereby selecting the forum in which the claim shall be litigated. If a defendant could do so, the plaintiff would be master of nothing. Congress has long since decided that federal defenses do not provide a basis for removal."

[b] See also Segreti, The Federal Preemption Question—A Federal Question? An Analysis of Federal Jurisdiction over Supremacy Clause Issues, 33 Cleve.State L.Rev. 653 (1984–85). Although he admits that it is too late to turn the clock back, in The Unhappy History of Federal Question Removal, 71 Iowa L.Rev. 717 (1986), Michael G. Collins has undertaken an extensive demonstration as an historical matter that the Court's federal defense removal cases incorrectly interpret the congressional intent.

SECTION 2: THE DIVERSITY STATUTE

SUBSECTION A: FUNCTION AND INTERPRETATION

UNITED STEELWORKERS OF AMERICA AFL–CIO v. R.H. BOULIGNY, INC.

United States Supreme Court, 1965.
382 U.S. 145.

MR. JUSTICE FORTAS delivered the opinion of the Court.

Respondent, a North Carolina corporation, brought this action in a North Carolina state court. It sought $200,000 in damages for defamation alleged to have occurred during the course of the United Steelworkers' campaign to unionize respondent's employees. The Steelworkers, an unincorporated labor union whose principal place of business purportedly is Pennsylvania, removed the case to a federal District Court.[1] The union asserted . . . that for purposes of . . . diversity jurisdiction it was a citizen of Pennsylvania, although some of its members were North Carolinians.

The corporation sought to have the case remanded to the state courts, . . . relying upon the generally prevailing principle that an unincorporated association's citizenship is that of each of its members. But the District Court retained jurisdiction. The district judge noted "a trend to treat unincorporated associations in the same manner as corporations and to treat them as citizens of the state wherein the principal office is located." Divining "no common sense reason for treating an unincorporated national labor union differently from a corporation," he declined to follow what he styled "the poorer reasoned but more firmly established rule" of Chapman v. Barney, 129 U.S. 677 (1889).

On interlocutory appeal the Court of Appeals for the Fourth Circuit reversed and directed that the case be remanded to the state courts. Certiorari was granted, so that we might decide whether an unincorporated labor union is to be treated as a citizen for purposes of federal diversity jurisdiction, without regard to the citizenship of its members. Because we believe this properly a matter for legislative consideration which cannot adequately or appropriately be dealt with by this Court, we affirm the decision of the Court of Appeals.

Article III, § 2, of the Constitution provides:

[1] 28 U.S.C. § 1441(a) provides:

"Except as otherwise expressly provided by Act of Congress, any civil action brought in a State court of which the district courts of the United States have original jurisdiction, may be removed by the defendant or the defendants, to the district court of the United States for the district and division embracing the place where such action is pending."

"The judicial Power shall extend . . . to Controversies . . .
between Citizens of different States . . . ."

Congress lost no time in implementing the grant. In 1789 it provided
for federal jurisdiction in suits "between a citizen of the State where
the suit is brought, and a citizen of another State." There shortly arose
the question as to whether a corporation—a creature of state law—is to
be deemed a "citizen" for purposes of the statute. This Court, through
Chief Justice Marshall, initially responded in the negative, holding that
a corporation was not a "citizen" and that it might sue and be sued
under the diversity statute only if none of its shareholders was a co-
citizen of any opposing party. Bank of the United States v. Deveaux, 9
U.S. (5 Cranch) 61 (1809). In 1844 the Court reversed itself and ruled
that a corporation was to be treated as a citizen of the state which
created it. Louisville, C. & C.R. Co. v. Letson, 43 U.S. (2 How.) 497
(1844). Ten years later, the Court reached the same result by a
different approach. In a compromise destined to endure for over a
century,[4] the Court indulged in the fiction that, although a corporation
was not itself a citizen for diversity purposes, its shareholders would
conclusively be presumed citizens of the incorporating state. Marshall
v. Baltimore & O.R. Co., 57 U.S. (16 How.) 314 (1853).

Congress re-entered the lists in 1875, significantly expanding diversity jurisdiction by deleting the requirement imposed in 1789 that one
of the parties must be a citizen of the forum state. The resulting
increase in the quantity of diversity litigation, however, cooled enthusi-
asts of the jurisdiction, and in 1887 and 1888 Congress enacted sharp
curbs. It quadrupled the jurisdictional amount, confined the right of
removal to non-resident defendants, reinstituted protections against
jurisdiction by collusive assignment, and narrowed venue.[6]

It was in this climate that the Court in 1889 decided *Chapman v.
Barney,* supra. On its own motion the Court observed that plaintiff was
a joint stock company and not a corporation or natural person. It held
that although plaintiff was endowed by New York with capacity to sue,
it could not be considered a "citizen" for diversity purposes.

In recent years courts and commentators have reflected dissatisfaction with the rule of *Chapman v. Barney.* [8] The distinction between the
"personality" and "citizenship" of corporations and that of labor unions
and other unincorporated associations, it is increasingly argued, has
become artificial and unreal. The mere fact that a corporation is
endowed with a birth certificate is, they say, of no consequence. In
truth and in fact, they point out, many voluntary associations and labor

---

[4] See 28 U.S.C. § 1332(c), providing that:

"For the purposes of this section and
section 1441 of this title, a corporation
shall be deemed a citizen of any State by
which it has been incorporated and of
the State where it has its principal place
of business."

[6] On the historical background of these
changes in the diversity jurisdiction see
generally, Moore and Weckstein, Diversity

Jurisdiction: Past, Present, and Future, 43
Tex. L. Rev. 1 (1964); Moore and Weckstein, Corporations and Diversity of Citizenship Jurisdiction: A Supreme Court
Fiction Revisited, 77 Harv. L. Rev. 1426
(1964); Hart and Wechsler, The Federal
Courts and the Federal System 891–943
(1953).

[8] See [e.g.,] Note, Unions as Juridical
Persons, 66 Yale L.J. 712, 742–49 (1957).

unions are indistinguishable from corporations in terms of the reality of function and structure, and to say that the latter are juridical persons and "citizens" and the former are not is to base a distinction upon an inadequate and irrelevant difference. They assert, with considerable merit, that it is not good judicial administration, nor is it fair, to remit a labor union or other unincorporated association to vagaries of jurisdiction determined by the citizenship of its members and to disregard the fact that unions and associations may exist and have an identity and a local habitation of their own.

The force of these arguments in relation to the diversity jurisdiction is particularized by petitioner's showing in this case. Petitioner argues that one of the purposes underlying the jurisdiction—protection of the nonresident litigant from local prejudice—is especially applicable to the modern labor union. According to the argument, when the nonresident defendant is a major union, local juries may be tempted to favor local interests at its expense. Juries may also be influenced by the fear that unionization would adversely affect the economy of the community and its customs and practices in the field of race relations. In support of these contentions, petitioner has exhibited material showing that during organizational campaigns like that involved in this case, localities have been saturated with propaganda concerning such economic and racial fears. Extending diversity jurisdiction to unions, says petitioner, would make available the advantages of federal procedure, article III judges less exposed to local pressures than their state court counterparts, juries selected from wider geographical areas, review in appellate courts reflecting a multi-state perspective, and more effective review by this Court.

We are of the view that these arguments, however appealing, are addressed to an inappropriate forum, and that pleas for extension of the diversity jurisdiction to hitherto uncovered broad categories of litigants ought to be made to the Congress and not to the courts. . . .

If we were to accept petitioner's urgent invitation to amend diversity jurisdiction so as to accommodate its case, we would be faced with difficulties which we could not adequately resolve. Even if the record here were adequate, we might well hesitate to assume that petitioner's situation is sufficiently representative or typical to form the predicate of a general principle. We should, for example, be obliged to fashion a test for ascertaining of which state the labor union is a citizen. Extending the jurisdiction to corporations raised no such problem, for the state of incorporation was a natural candidate, its arguable irrelevance in terms of the policies underlying the jurisdiction being outweighed by its certainty of application. But even that easy and apparent solution did not dispose of the problem; in 1958 Congress thought it necessary to enact legislation providing that corporations are citizens both of the state of incorporation and of the state in which their principal place of business is located.[11] Further, in contemplating a rule which would accommodate petitioner's claim, we are acutely aware of the complica-

[11] See note 4, supra.

tions arising from the circumstance that petitioner, like other labor unions, has local as well as national organizations and that these perhaps, should be reckoned with in connection with "citizenship" and its jurisdictional incidents.[12]

Whether unincorporated labor unions ought to be assimilated to the status of corporations for diversity purposes, how such citizenship is to be determined, and what if any related rules ought to apply, are decisions which we believe suited to the legislative and not the judicial branch, regardless of our views as to the intrinsic merits of petitioner's argument—merits stoutly attested by widespread support for the recognition of labor unions as juridical personalities.

We affirm the decision below.

NOTES ON DIVERSITY JURISDICTION

1. The Abolition Debate. As the Court indicates in *Bouligny*, Congress conferred diversity jurisdiction on the federal courts when it first created those courts in the Judiciary Act of 1789. Although restrictive modifications have been adopted from time to time, and although there have been frequent calls over the years for its abolition,[a] the jurisdiction still persists. Perhaps the most remarkable feature of the tenacity of diversity jurisdiction is that there is no consensus as to why the authorizing clause was included in article III, why the first Congress included diversity cases in the Judiciary Act of 1789, or whether the diversity jurisdiction should be retained today.

The generally accepted rationale for diversity jurisdiction is the one stated in *Bouligny:* "protection of the nonresident litigant from local prejudice."[b] Yet Henry Friendly reported in an influential article that the diversity clause "was not a product of difficulties that had been

[12] The American Law Institute has proposed that for diversity purposes unincorporated associations be deemed citizens of the states in which their principal places of business are located, but that they be disabled from initiating diversity litigation in states where they maintain "local establishments." ALI, Study of the Division of Jurisdiction Between State and Federal Courts, Proposed Final Draft No. 1 §§ 1301(b)(2) and 1302(b) (1965). . . .

[a] For example, extensive hearings were held on bills that proposed abolition in the House of Representatives in 1977 and the Senate in 1978. See Hearings before the Subcommittee on Courts, Civil Liberties, and the Administration of Justice of the Committee on the Judiciary, House of Representatives, 95th Cong., 1st Sess., Ser. No. 21 (1977); Hearings before the Subcommittee on Improvements in Judicial Machinery of the Committee on the Judiciary, United States Senate, 95th Cong., 2d Sess.

(1978). The House actually voted to abolish the jurisdiction on two occasions in 1978, but neither bill came to a vote in the Senate. See C. Wright, The Law of Federal Courts 137 & n.50 (4th ed. 1983).

[b] See, for example, the frequently quoted statement by Chief Justice Marshall in Bank of the United States v. Deveaux, 9 U.S. (5 Cranch) 61, 87 (1809):

"However true the fact may be, that the tribunals of the states will administer justice as impartially as those of the nation, to parties of every description, it is not less true that the Constitution itself either entertains apprehensions on this subject, or views with such indulgence the possible fears and apprehensions of suitors, that it has established national tribunals for the decision of controversies between aliens and a citizen, or between citizens of different states."

acutely felt under the Confederation" and that "such information as we are able to gather . . . entirely fails to show the existence of prejudice on the part of the state judges."[c] Friendly did find, however, two grounds for concern.

The first was that "a careful reading of the arguments of the time will show that the real fear was not of state courts so much as of state legislatures." In particular, the concern was that local legislatures would pass laws favorable to resident debtors: "the desire to protect creditors against legislation favorable to debtors was a principal reason for the grant of diversity jurisdiction, and that . . . reason . . . was by no means without validity."

Second, although hostility to out-of-state litigants was not apparent, "there were other grounds for distrust of the local courts. The method of appointment and the tenure of the judges were not of the sort to invite confidence." In all but two states, judges were selected by the legislatures, and in many they were also removable by legislative action. The "practical workings of the system" also were suspect. In Connecticut, for example, all judges were appointed by members of the Council, who then felt free to appear as advocates before the courts. In addition, the Council acted as the Supreme Court, thus reviewing cases which some of its members had tried. To make matters worse, Council members would occasionally argue their cases before the Council itself, and on some occasions Council members were appointed judges of lower courts and later permitted to sit in review of their own decisions. Friendly concluded:

> "Not unnaturally the commercial interests of the country were reluctant to expose themselves to the hazards of litigation before such courts as these. They might be good enough for the inhabitants of their respective states, but merchants from abroad felt themselves entitled to something better. There was a vague feeling that the new courts would be strong courts, creditors' courts, business men's courts."

Both of the concerns voiced by Friendly have been translated into modern arguments for the retention of diversity jurisdiction. It is true, of course, that avoidance of local law cannot be achieved by resort to federal courts today.[d] Some argue, however, that cases should be channelled to federal courts because they are "so much better" than state courts,[e] and that since out-of-state litigants have no opportunity to

---

[c] Friendly, The Historic Basis of Diversity Jurisdiction, 41 Harv. L. Rev. 483 (1928). Friendly acknowledged that fear of local prejudice is the "classical" or "orthodox" theory underlying diversity jurisdiction, even though he argued that such fears "had only a speculative existence in 1789, and are still less real today." John Frank has argued in response, as he put it, that fear of local prejudice "was largely a gloomy anticipation of things to come rather than an experienced evil . . . ." Frank, The Case for Diversity Jurisdiction,

16 Harv. J. Legis. 403, 406 (1979), referring to Frank, Historical Bases of the Federal Judicial System, 13 Law & Contemp. Probs. 3 (1948). See also Moore & Weckstein, Diversity Jurisdiction: Past, Present, and Future, 43 Texas L. Rev. 1, 15 (1964).

[d] See *Erie v. Tompkins,* page 269, supra, and *Klaxon v. Stentor,* page 358, supra.

[e] See C. Wright, The Law of Federal Courts 134 (4th ed. 1983). It should be noted that Professor Wright is merely reporting the argument, not advocating it.

participate in reforms of local courts, they should not be required to appear before them.[f] Moreover, it is still argued that "diversity jurisdiction is an indispensable condition to the free flow of capital from one part of the nation to another."[g]

Perhaps the most frequent spokesman for the retention of diversity jurisdiction is John P. Frank, an influential practicing attorney from Arizona.[h] He reports that there "is no reason to suppose that any appreciable group of private practitioners in the United States" supports abolition; the "position of the private practitioners is solid regardless of the interests they represent."[i] He elaborates:

> "There is no substantial reason that is or can be advanced for [abolition of diversity jurisdiction] except the commendable desire to lighten the load on the federal courts. The difficulty with lightening that load is that necessarily the load must be increased on the state courts. Yet there is no profit in transferring cases from one logjam to another. Diversity jurisdic-

In the Senate hearings cited in footnote a, supra, he strongly supported abolition. His reasoning is summarized below, pages 467–68.

[f] See Shapiro, Federal Diversity Jurisdiction: A Survey and A Proposal, 91 Harv. L. Rev. 317, 329 (1977). Professor Shapiro adds that there "may also be warrant for affording an out-of-state lawyer a procedure with which he is likely to be familiar because it is in force in the federal court in his own state."

[g] C. Wright, The Law of Federal Courts 136 (4th ed. 1983). Chief Justice Taft argued before the American Bar Association in 1922 that "no single element in our governmental system has done so much to secure capital for the legitimate development of enterprise, throughout the West and South." 47 Reports of the American Bar Association 250, 259 (1922).

Compare the comments made by Adrienne Marsh in Diversity Jurisdiction: Scapegoat of Overcrowded Federal Courts, 48 Brooklyn L. Rev. 197, 208–09 (1982):

"In the 1980's, the corporate entity is a major force in interstate investments and development. Large corporations have come to rely on the unified system of federal jurisprudence. They customarily retain major law firms, who, from time-to-time, are called upon to represent their corporate clients in federal courts throughout the country. If national corporations were compelled to litigate in state courts, it would become necessary for them to retain numerous local attorneys. The inconvenience and increased costs of litigation caused by the use of correspondent attorneys would be compounded by trials held in county

courthouses, which are often remote from air terminals."

[h] See, e.g., Frank, The Case for Diversity Jurisdiction, 16 Harv. J. Legis. 403 (1979). Other articles supporting retention are collected in C. Wright, The Law of Federal Courts 130 n.17 (4th ed. 1983). Articles supporting abolition are collected in id, at 130 n.16. See also the extensive collection of citations in Marsh, Diversity Jurisdiction: Scapegoat of Overcrowded Federal Courts, 48 Brooklyn L. Rev. 197 n.1 (1982).

[i] He also reports that the ABA Board of Governors was one vote short of unanimity in opposing the abolition bill that passed the House in 1978, and that the American Trial Lawyers Association strongly opposed it.

Charles Allen Wright has characterized the strong support of diversity by the practicing bar as follows:

"I believe the basis for their position is not that they love the state courts less but that they love a choice of forum more. Of course it is tactically advantageous to be able to choose, and to pick for each case the system of courts in which a favorable result seems more likely. But surely our dual court structure was created to serve some loftier purpose than tactical maneuvering. It is dismaying to see respected bar groups asserting a vested interest in preserving jurisdictional statutes that have developed quite fortuitously and that are demonstrably irrational, unclear, inefficient, and productive of unnecessary friction."

Wright, Restructuring Federal Jurisdiction: The American Law Institute Proposals, 26 Wash. & Lee L. Rev. 185, 207 (1969).

tion must be seen for what it is, a social service of the federal government provided for the people of the United States. A primary function of the legal profession is to settle disputes. The diversity jurisdiction provides an opportunity for settling those disputes. In one sense, it can be compared to the school lunch program or the federal highway program or any other program by which the federal government serves the general public. . . . It is the oldest single federal social service. It comes to us quite literally from the hands of George Washington, James Madison, and Oliver Ellsworth."[j]

In addition to making some of the points noted above, Frank advances two major arguments in favor of retaining the jurisdiction. First, there is the number of cases disposed of, on the order of 30,000 in 1979.[k] Sometimes federal courts are better, he contends, and sometimes they are worse. But the general manner in which these cases have been tried and settled has led to the "general feeling that justice in federal courts is being well administered. There is no widespread, obvious abuse to be corrected." Second, there is "the educational value of having two systems in interaction." The development of the Federal Rules of Civil Procedure has had a positive impact on state procedures and, he continues, the fact that federal courts must constantly look to state law has led to positive changes in federal procedures. Moreover, the diversity jurisdiction "puts the whole litigation bar" into federal courts, rather than limiting dual exposure to those specialists who tend to litigate federal question cases. This in turn, he concludes, has an educational effect on the bar, which feeds law reform in both systems.

Charles Allen Wright stated the case against diversity jurisdiction in testimony before the Senate in 1978.[l] He made three major points. The first was the burden that diversity cases place on federal courts. A time study in 1969–70, he pointed out, showed that while diversity cases constituted 26.2 per cent of the civil docket of the district courts, 37.9 per cent of the time district judges spent on civil cases was devoted to diversity litigation. Given the other demands on the federal courts, he concluded, "diversity cases are a luxury we can no longer afford." Second, he argued that prejudice against out-of-state litigants is no longer a significant factor in the administration of justice in state court

---

[j] He contended elsewhere that "no serious argument can be made that diversity conflicts with the theory of federalism for it is of the essence of the theory of federalism; it is at least as traditionally federal as the Flag and the 4th of July." Frank, Federal Diversity Jurisdiction—An Opposing View, 17 S.C.L. Rev. 677, 682 (1965).

[k] In 1984, the number was 54,339. Annual Report of the Director of the Administrative Office of the United States Courts 283 (1984).

[l] Hearings before the Subcommittee on Improvements in Judicial Machinery of the Committee on the Judiciary, United States Senate, 95th Cong., 2d Sess. 45–48

(1978). For an important addition to the abolition side of the debate, see Thomas Rowe, Abolished Diversity Jurisdiction: Positive Side Effects and Potential for Further Reforms, 92 Harv.L.Rev. 963 (1979). Professor Rowe argues that "the considerable simplification in federal practice resulting from abolition would be an important benefit," as would "decisional developments and statutory and rule reforms that are now difficult or impossible because of problems that flow from diversity jurisdiction." See also Sheran and Isaacman, State Cases Belong in State Courts, 12 Creighton L.Rev. 1 (1978).

systems, even though there may be anecdotal evidence of an occasional abuse. Finally, he argued that the complexity of diversity cases is largely a function of their litigation in federal courts; many such cases could be much more straightforwardly resolved in state court:

> "It was Mr. Frank himself . . . who made the penetrating insight that a case is a series of decision points, and that the goal of law reform must be to reduce the number and complexity of these decision points.
>
> "Whether a case is properly within the diversity jurisdiction of the federal courts is a wholly useless decision point that vanishes if the case is brought in state court. This is a decision point of great complexity, because the rules of federal jurisdiction are far from being bright lines. Lawyers can easily be mistaken about those rules, and judges frequently must spend much time deciding and writing lengthy opinions about whether jurisdiction exists. In my multi-volume treatise, my collaborators and I devote 414 pages to the rules on diversity jurisdiction. . . . Amount in controversy has always been almost entirely a problem in diversity litigation . . . . [These rules] detain us for another 156 pages. We have a 32–page section on removal in diversity cases, and much of the rest of the 257–page chapter on removal deals with problems that are peculiar to diversity cases. . . ."

Professor Wright continued by noting that most of the 199 pages in his treatise devoted to venue concerned diversity problems, and that the task of ascertaining local law under *Erie* presents perhaps the most imposing difficulty. He concluded that abolition of diversity jurisdiction would mean "that litigants and judges no longer need be concerned about these problems and can go immediately to the merits of the case, rather than wasting time on unnecessary preliminary issues of this kind."

Finally, note the concluding observations, which could as well have been written yesterday, made by Henry Friendly in his 1928 article quoted above:

> "The steady expansion of the jurisdiction of the federal courts, especially since Reconstruction days, has been but a reflex of the general growth of federal political power. That growth will not abate, since it is responsive to deep social and economic causes. Only one aspect of the work of the federal courts is out of the current of these nationalizing forces—the jurisdiction based on diversity of citizenship. . . . The unifying tendencies of America here make for a recession of jurisdiction to the states, rather than an extension of federal authority. The pressure of distinctly federal litigation may call for relief of business that intrinsically belongs to the state courts. How far, if at all, the United States courts should be left with jurisdiction merely because the parties are citizens of different

states is a question which calls for critical re-examination of the practical bases of diversity jurisdiction."

2. *Strawbridge v. Curtiss*. The decision that gave rise to the problem in *Bouligny* was Strawbridge v. Curtiss, 7 U.S. (3 Cranch) 267 (1806). *Strawbridge* involved a suit brought by citizens of Massachusetts against a citizen of Vermont and other citizens of Massachusetts. The question was whether "complete" diversity was required, that is, whether the presence of Massachusetts citizens on both sides of the case was fatal to the jurisdiction. In a brief and cryptic opinion, the Court held that complete diversity was required. This holding has survived as an interpretation of the diversity statute until the present day.[m] Thus, the facts that the plaintiff was a citizen of North Carolina and that some of the defendant-union's members were also citizens of North Carolina was fatal to the exercise of diversity jurisdiction in *Bouligny* unless the union itself could attain an independent citizenship.

3. Questions and Comments on *Bouligny*. Bouligny is an illustration of the kind of technical problem in the administration of diversity jurisdiction to which Professor Wright referred in his Senate testimony. The entire course of litigation could have been avoided had the case been filed in state court. Are cases raising such issues a good reason for the abolition of diversity jurisdiction? Are the other reasons for abolition persuasive? Or is the case for retention stronger?

Bouligny also illustrates another pervasive problem in the administration of diversity jurisdiction, namely the attitude the courts should bring to the resolution of questions unanswered by statute. The Supreme Court, as the opinion in *Bouligny* states, took the lead in making the jurisdiction available to corporate litigants, although its decision was subsequently ratified by Congress. Should the Court have accepted the analogy to corporations offered by the union in *Bouligny*?[n] Or should the Court have declined, as it unanimously did, to expand the

---

[m] The Court has observed many times that the requirement of "complete" diversity is not of constitutional magnitude. See, e.g., footnote 13 of the *Kroger* opinion, page 476, infra. Indeed, the one context in which everyone agrees that diversity jurisdiction should be retained does not require "complete" diversity. Interpleader suits typically involve an effort to resolve multiple claims to a single fund in one lawsuit. Since the multiple claimants may be from different states and may not all be subject to service of process in any single state, sometimes no state court can adjudicate such a suit. The Federal Interpleader Act, by contrast, provides for nationwide service of process. See 28 U.S.C. §§ 1335, 2361. It has been interpreted, moreover, to require "minimal" diversity, that is, diversity between any two adverse claimants. See State Farm Fire & Cas. Co. v. Tashire, 386 U.S. 523 (1967). For discussion of the theory and mechanics of interpleader, see Hazard and Moscovitz, An Historical and Critical Analysis of Interpleader, 52 Calif. L. Rev. 706 (1964); Ilsen and Sardell, Interpleader in the Federal Courts, 35 St. John's L. Rev. 1 (1960). For the proposal of a new type of diversity jurisdiction for complex multi-state tort and products liability claims, see Rowe and Sibley, Beyond Diversity: Federal Multiparty, Multiform Jurisdiction, 135 U.Pa.L.Rev. 7 (1986).

[n] Cf. Currie, The Federal Courts and the American Law Institute, 36 U. Chi. L. Rev. 1, 35 (1968):

"In view of the Court's initial willingness to find a niche for corporations in the diversity statute this deference to Congress is remarkable. The application of statutes to situations not anticipated by the legislature is a pre-eminently judicial function, and the Court's refusal to decide constituted a decision against jurisdiction without considering the relevant arguments."

scope of diversity litigation? What were its reasons for doing so? Separation of powers? Federalism? Hostility to diversity? Hostility to unincorporated associations?

Note that the Court held in Supreme Tribe of Ben-Hur v. Cauble, 255 U.S. 356 (1921), that in a class action it is the citizenship of the representatives of the class that count for diversity purposes, not the citizenship of all members of the class. Is this decision consistent with *Bouligny*? Would the Court permit its holding in *Bouligny* to be undermined by the class action device? Should it?[o]

4. Interpretation of the Diversity Statute. As alluded to by Professor Wright in his Senate testimony, the details of litigation concerning when diversity jurisdiction exists involve complex and often arcane issues that would require many pages to unfold, too many to justify complete treatment here. There may be value, however, in a brief overview of the general principles that have emerged.

The problem of aliens aside, a person must be a "citizen of a state" in order to invoke diversity jurisdiction. Citizenship for this purpose has two prerequisites: one must be a citizen of the United States, and must be domiciled in a particular state. A person can have only one domicile at a time.[p] Diversity is determined as of the time the suit is filed, and must be alleged in the pleadings and proved if challenged. A later change of domicile will not affect the court's jurisdiction. As with any question of subject-matter jurisdiction, a failure of diversity can be noticed at any point in the litigation—even on appeal—and requires dismissal of the case. With three exceptions—in rem actions involving property already in the custody of a state court, domestic relations cases, and probate cases[q]—a diversity action can involve any kind of

[o] The Supreme Court has not had occasion to address this issue, although several lower courts have upheld jurisdiction over class actions in this context. See, e.g., Kerney v. Fort Griffin Fandangle Assoc., 624 F.2d 717 (5th Cir. 1980); Oskoian v. Canuel, 269 F.2d 311 (1st Cir. 1959); Philadelphia Local 192 of American Federation of Teachers v. American Federation of Teachers, 44 F. Supp. 345 (E.D. Pa. 1982). See also Lumbermen's Underwriting Alliance v. Mobil Oil Corp., 612 F. Supp. 1166 (D. Idaho 1985).

[p] Determination of domicile is often a difficult matter. Its formal definition is "that place where he has his true, fixed, and permanent home and principal establishment, and to which he has the intention of returning whenever he is absent therefrom." C. Wright, The Law of Federal Courts 146 (4th ed. 1983). A citizen of the United States who is domiciled abroad cannot be a "citizen of a state" for purposes of diversity. A citizen of the United States who has two homes and who divides his or her time equally between them must nonetheless be found to be "domiciled" in one of them. For discussion of some of the difficulties of the concept, see Weckstein, Citizenship for Purposes of Diversity Jurisdiction, 26 Sw. L.J. 360 (1972); Currie, The Federal Courts and the American Law Institute, 36 U. Chi. L. Rev. 1, 8–12 (1968).

[q] See, e.g., Atwood, Domestic Relations Cases in Federal Court: Toward a Principled Exercise of Jurisdiction, 35 Hastings L.J. 571 (1984); Baron, The Evolution of Domestic Relations Cases in Our Federal Courts, 1985 S.Ill.U.L.J. 353 (1985); Vestal and Foster, Implied Limitations on the Diversity Jurisdiction of Federal Courts, 41 Minn. L. Rev. 1 (1956); Wand, A Call for the Repudiation of the Domestic Relations Exception to Federal Jurisdiction, 30 Vill. L.Rev. 307 (1985). For a modern judicial effort to rationalize the probate exception, see Dragan v. Miller, 679 F.2d 712 (7th Cir. 1982).

dispute; it is the status of the parties rather than the subject matter of the lawsuit that determines jurisdiction.[r]

As *Bouligny* indicates, corporations are regarded as citizens of each state of incorporation, as well as of the state in which their principal place of business is located.[s] This rule extends to municipal corporations, but not to the state itself. Unincorporated associations, as *Bouligny* holds, are citizens of each state of which any member is a citizen.

There are many rules about whose citizenship counts. For example, in Navarro Savings Association v. Lee, 446 U.S. 458 (1980), the Supreme Court was faced with the question "whether the trustees of a business trust may invoke the diversity jurisdiction of the federal courts on the basis of their own citizenship, rather than that of the trust's beneficial shareholders." The Court held that the trustees could sue because they were the real parties in interest: they held legal title to the trust assets, managed the assets, and had legal power to control the litigation.[t] A similar problem has arisen in the context of estate administration, specifically, whether the citizenship of the decedent, the beneficiaries, or the representatives of the estate should control.[u]

It is also clear that the alignment of the parties in the pleadings is not conclusive. The court is obligated to examine the "real interests" of the parties, place them on one side or another of the dispute, and determine the existence of complete diversity based on the proper

[r] Many have argued that it makes no sense to permit a local plaintiff to file a diversity action in federal court against an out-of-state defendant. Some have estimated that perhaps as many as 50 per cent of the current diversity litigation would be eliminated if this rule were changed. See Marsh, Diversity Jurisdiction: Scapegoat of Overcrowded Federal Courts, 48 Brooklyn L. Rev. 197, 222 (1982). The statute permits such suits to be filed in federal court even though, if it were filed in state court, removal by an in-state defendant on grounds of diversity is prohibited.

[s] Corporations can have only one principal place of business. The case law on where "the" principal place of business of major interstate or international corporations is located is imposingly difficult. See, e.g., Kelly v. United States Steel Corp., 284 F.2d 850 (3rd Cir. 1960). See also Moore and Weckstein, Corporations and Diversity of Citizenship: A Supreme Court Fiction Revisited, 77 Harv. L. Rev. 1426 (1964); Note, Alien Corporations and Federal Diversity Jurisdiction, 84 Colum. L. Rev. 177 (1984); Note, A Corporation's Principal Place of Business for Federal Diversity Jurisdiction, 38 N.Y.U. L. Rev. 148 (1963).

The ALI proposed that a corporation's citizenship be expanded to include places where it maintains a "local establishment" of business. See ALI, Study of the Division of Jurisdiction Between State and Federal Courts § 1302(b) (Official Draft, 1969). The proposal is criticized in Currie, The Federal Courts and the American Law Institute, 36 U. Chi. L. Rev. 1, 47–49 (1968), and defended in Field, Proposals on Federal Diversity Jurisdiction, 17 S.C.L. Rev. 669, 673–74 (1965).

[t] It is unclear whether the rule of *Navarro* or the rule of *Bouligny* applies to suits by general partners on behalf of a limited partnership. The two leading pre-*Navarro* cases were split. See Carlsberg Resources Corp. v. Cambria Savings & Loan Association, 554 F.2d 1254 (3d Cir. 1977) (citizenship of all partners taken into account); Colonial Realty Corp. v. Bache & Co., 358 F.2d 178 (2d Cir. 1966) (citizenship of limited partners not taken into account). For pre-*Navarro* consideration of the question, see Comment, 45 U. Chi. L. Rev. 384 (1978); Note, 56 Tex. L. Rev. 243 (1978). For post-*Navarro* consideration, see Note, 71 Iowa L. Rev. 235 (1985).

[u] Linda Mullenix extensively considered this question in Creative Manipulation of Federal Jurisdiction: Is There Diversity After Death?, 70 Corn. L. Rev. 1011 (1985). It was resolved by statute in 1988. See 28 U.S.C. § 1332(c)(2).

alignment. The leading case is City of Indianapolis v. Chase National Bank, 314 U.S. 63 (1941). A gas company had issued bonds, which were secured by a mortgage on which the bank was trustee. The bank, a citizen of New York, sued the gas company, a citizen of Indiana, and the city of Indianapolis, also a citizen of Indiana. The issue was whether the city had become a party to a lease from the gas company that made it, the city, liable for interest on the bonds. The Court held that the "primary" issue was whether the city was bound by the lease, and that on this issue the bank and the gas company were on the same side. Hence it realigned the parties and held that diversity jurisdiction did not exist.[v]

Finally, note must be taken of the jurisdictional amount. The original diversity statute in 1789 fixed a jurisdictional amount of $500, a figure that has been raised over the years to its present level of $50,000. It is not required that the plaintiff actually recover that amount—such a requirement would make the initial jurisdiction of the court turn on the ultimate resolution of the merits of the controversy. What is required is that the plaintiff make a good faith claim for a sum in excess of $50,000.

One of the most complicated issues in determining whether the jurisdictional amount has been met is when multiple claims can be aggregated. A plaintiff may aggregate as many claims as he or she has against a defendant. But multiple parties may not aggregate claims against a single defendant, even in the context of class actions, if the claims are "separate and distinct" as opposed to claims in which the parties have a "common undivided interest."[w]

---

[v] Four Justices dissented on the grounds that other issues in the case made the realignment inappropriate and that it was unfair for the Court to withhold federal jurisdiction after it had denied certiorari on the question three years earlier.

The major difficulties of realignment today occur in shareholder's derivative suits, more particularly on the question of whether a corporation named as a defendant should be realigned as a plaintiff. See Smith v. Sperling, 354 U.S. 91 (1957); Comment, Director's Failure to Bring Suit, Demand, and the Business Judgment Rule, 3 J. Corp. L. 208 (1977).

[w] For elaboration of the aggregation issue, see Bell, Jurisdictional Requirements in Suits for which Class Action Status is Sought Under Rule 23(b)(3), 8 Valparaiso L. Rev. 237 (1974); Coiner, Class Actions: Aggregation of Claims for Federal Jurisdiction, 4 Memphis St. L. Rev. 427 (1974); Mattis and Mitchell, The Trouble With *Zahn*: Progeny of *Snyder v. Harris* Further Cripples Class Actions, 53 Neb. L. Rev. 137 (1974); Theis, *Zahn v. International Paper Co.*: The Non-Aggregation Rule in Jurisdictional Amount Cases, 35 La. L. Rev. (1974); Note, Ancillary Jurisdiction and the Jurisdictional Amount Requirement, 50 Notre Dame Law. 346 (1974); Note, The Federal Jurisdictional Amount and Rule 20 Joinder of Parties: Aggregation of Claims, 53 Minn. L. Rev. 94 (1968); Note, Aggregation of Plaintiff's Claims to Meet the Jurisdictional Minimum Amount Requirement of the Federal District Courts, 80 U. Pa. L. Rev. 106 (1931).

OWEN EQUIPMENT & ERECTION CO. v. KROGER, ADMINISTRATRIX

Supreme Court of the United States, 1978.
437 U.S. 365.

MR. JUSTICE STEWART delivered the opinion of the Court.

In an action in which federal jurisdiction is based on diversity of citizenship, may the plaintiff assert a claim against a third-party defendant when there is no independent basis for federal jurisdiction over that claim? The Court of Appeals for the Eighth Circuit held in this case that such a claim is within the ancillary jurisdiction of the federal courts. We granted certiorari, because this decision conflicts with several recent decisions of other Courts of Appeals.

I

On January 18, 1972, James Kroger was electrocuted when the boom of a steel crane next to which he was walking came too close to a high-tension electric power line. The respondent (his widow, who is the administratrix of his estate) filed a wrongful-death action in the United States District Court for the District of Nebraska against the Omaha Public Power District (OPPD). Her complaint alleged that OPPD's negligent construction, maintenance, and operation of the power line had caused Kroger's death. Federal jurisdiction was based on diversity of citizenship, since the respondent was a citizen of Iowa and OPPD was a Nebraska corporation.

OPPD then filed a third-party complaint pursuant to Fed. Rule Civ. Proc. 14(a)[2] against the petitioner, Owen Equipment and Erection Co. (Owen), alleging that the crane was owned and operated by Owen, and that Owen's negligence had been the proximate cause of Kroger's death.[3] OPPD later moved for summary judgment on the respondent's

[2] Rule 14(a) provides in relevant part:

"At any time after commencement of the action a defending party, as a third-party plaintiff, may cause a summons and complaint to be served upon a person not a party to the action who is or may be liable to him for all or part of the plaintiff's claim against him. . . . The person served with the summons and third-party complaint, hereinafter called the third-party defendant, shall make his defenses to the third-party plaintiff's claim as provided in Rule 12 and his counterclaim against the third-party plaintiff and cross-claims against other third-party defendants as provided in Rule 13. The third-party defendant may assert against the plaintiff any defenses which the third-party plaintiff has to the plaintiff's claim. The third-party defendant may also assert any claim against the plaintiff arising out of the transaction or occurrence that is the subject matter of the plaintiff's claim against the third-party plaintiff. The plaintiff may assert any claim against the third-party defendant arising out of the transaction or occurrence that is the subject matter of the plaintiff's claim against the third-party plaintiff, and the third-party defendant thereupon shall assert his defenses as provided in Rule 12 and his counter-claims and cross-claims as provided in Rule 13."

[3] Under Rule 14(a), a third-party defendant may not be impleaded merely because he may be liable to the *plaintiff*. While the third-party complaint in this case alleged merely that Owen's negligence caused Kroger's death, and the basis of Owen's alleged liability to *OPPD* is nowhere spelled out, OPPD evidently relied upon the state common-law right of contribution among joint tortfeasors. The petitioner has never challenged the propriety of the third-party complaint as such.

complaint against it. While this motion was pending, the respondent was granted leave to file an amended complaint naming Owen as an additional defendant. Thereafter, the District Court granted OPPD's motion for summary judgment . . . .[4] The case thus went to trial between the respondent and the petitioner alone.

The respondent's amended complaint alleged that Owen was "a Nebraska corporation with its principal place of business in Nebraska." Owen's answer admitted that it was "a corporation organized and existing under the laws of the state of Nebraska," and denied every other allegation of the complaint. On the third day of trial, however, it was disclosed that the petitioner's principal place of business was in Iowa, not Nebraska,[5] and that petitioner and the respondent were thus both citizens of Iowa. The petitioner then moved to dismiss the complaint for lack of jurisdiction. The District Court reserved decision on the motion, and the jury thereafter returned a verdict in favor of the respondent. In an unreported opinion issued after the trial, the District Court denied the petitioner's motion to dismiss the complaint.

The judgment was affirmed on appeal. The Court of Appeals held that under this Court's decision in Mine Workers v. Gibbs, 383 U.S. 715 (1966), the District Court had jurisdictional power, in its discretion, to adjudicate the respondent's claim against the petitioner because that claim arose from the "core of 'operative facts' giving rise to both [respondent's] claim against OPPD and OPPD's claim against Owen." It further held that the District Court had properly exercised its discretion in proceeding to decide the case even after summary judgment had been granted to OPPD, because the petitioner had concealed its Iowa citizenship from the respondent. Rehearing en banc was denied by an equally divided court.

II

It is undisputed that there was no independent basis of federal jurisdiction over the respondent's state-law tort action against the petitioner, since both are citizens of Iowa. And although Fed. Rule Civ. Proc. 14(a) permits a plaintiff to assert a claim against a third-party defendant, it does not purport to say whether or not such a claim requires an independent basis of federal jurisdiction. Indeed, it could not determine that question, since it is axiomatic that the Federal Rules of Civil Procedure do not create or withdraw federal jurisdiction.

In affirming the District Court's judgment, the Court of Appeals relied upon the doctrine of ancillary jurisdiction, whose contours it believed were defined by this Court's holding in *Mine Workers v. Gibbs*, supra. The *Gibbs* case differed from this one in that it involved

---

[4] Judgment was entered pursuant to Fed. Rule Civ. Proc. 54(b), and the Court of Appeals affirmed.

[5] The problem apparently was one of geography. Although the Missouri River generally marks the boundary between Iowa and Nebraska, Carter Lake, Iowa, where the accident occurred and where Owen had its main office, lies west of the river, adjacent to Omaha, Neb. Apparently the river once avulsed at one of its bends, cutting Carter Lake off from the rest of Iowa.

pendent jurisdiction, which concerns the resolution of a plaintiff's federal- and state-law claims against a single defendant in one action. By contrast, in this case there was no claim based upon substantive federal law, but rather state-law tort claims against two different defendants. Nonetheless, the Court of Appeals was correct in perceiving that *Gibbs* and this case are two species of the same generic problem: Under what circumstances may a federal court hear and decide a state-law claim arising between citizens of the same state?[8] But we believe that the Court of Appeals failed to understand the scope of the doctrine of the *Gibbs* case.

The plaintiff in *Gibbs* alleged that the defendant union had violated the common law of Tennessee as well as the federal prohibition of secondary boycotts. This Court held that, although the parties were not of diverse citizenship, the District Court properly entertained the state-law claim as pendent to the federal claim. The crucial holding was stated as follows:

> "Pendent jurisdiction, in the sense of judicial *power,* exists whenever there is a claim 'arising under [the] Constitution, the laws of the United States, and Treaties made, or which shall be made, under their Authority. . . .,' U.S. Const., art. III, § 2, and the relationship between that claim and the state claim permits the conclusion that the entire action before the court comprises but one constitutional 'case.' . . . The state and federal claims must derive from a common nucleus of operative fact. But if, considered without regard to their federal or state character, a plaintiff's claims are such that he would ordinarily be expected to try them all in one judicial proceeding, then, assuming substantiality of the federal issues, there is *power* in federal courts to hear the whole." 383 U.S., at 725 (emphasis in original).[9]

It is apparent that *Gibbs* delineated the constitutional limits of federal judicial power. But even if it be assumed that the District Court in the present case had constitutional power to decide the respondent's lawsuit against the petitioner,[10] it does not follow that the decision of the Court of Appeals was correct. Constitutional power is merely the first hurdle that must be overcome in determining that a federal court has jurisdiction over a particular controversy. For the

---

[8] No more than in Aldinger v. Howard, 427 U.S. 1, 13 (1976), is it necessary to determine here "whether there are any 'principled' differences between pendent and ancillary jurisdiction; or, if there are, what effect *Gibbs* had on such differences."

[9] The Court further noted that even when such power exists, its exercise remains a matter of discretion based upon "considerations of judicial economy, convenience and fairness to litigants," and held that the District Court had not abused its discretion in retaining jurisdiction of the state-law claim.

[10] Federal jurisdiction in *Gibbs* was based upon the existence of a question of federal law. The Court of Appeals in the present case believed that the "common nucleus of operative fact" test also determines the outer boundaries of constitutionally permissible federal jurisdiction when that jurisdiction is based upon diversity of citizenship. We may assume without deciding that the Court of Appeals was correct in this regard. See also n.13, infra.

jurisdiction of the federal courts is limited not only by the provisions of art. III of the Constitution, but also by acts of Congress.

That statutory law as well as the Constitution may limit a federal court's jurisdiction over nonfederal claims[11] is well illustrated by two recent decisions of this Court, Aldinger v. Howard, 427 U.S. 1 (1976), and Zahn v. International Paper Co., 414 U.S. 291 (1973). In *Aldinger* the Court held that a federal district court lacked jurisdiction over a state-law claim against a county, even if that claim was alleged to be pendent to one against county officials under 42 U.S.C. § 1983. In *Zahn* the Court held that in a diversity class action under Fed. Rule Civ. Proc. 23(b)(3), the claim of each member of the plaintiff class must independently satisfy the minimum jurisdictional amount set by 28 U.S.C. § 1332(a), and rejected the argument that jurisdiction existed over those claims that involved $10,000 or less as ancillary to those that involved more. In each case, despite the fact that federal and nonfederal claims arose from a "common nucleus of operative fact," the Court held that the statute conferring jurisdiction over the federal claim did not allow the exercise of jurisdiction over the nonfederal claims.[12]

The *Aldinger* and *Zahn* cases thus make clear that a finding that federal and nonfederal claims arise from a "common nucleus of operative fact," the test of *Gibbs*, does not end the inquiry into whether a federal court has power to hear the nonfederal claims along with the federal ones. Beyond this constitutional minimum, there must be an examination of the posture in which the nonfederal claim is asserted and of the specific statute that confers jurisdiction over the federal claim, in order to determine whether "Congress in [that statute] has . . . expressly or by implication negated" the exercise of jurisdiction over the particular nonfederal claim. *Aldinger v. Howard,* supra, at 18.

III

The relevant statute in this case, 28 U.S.C. § 1332(a)(1), confers upon federal courts jurisdiction over "civil actions where the matter in controversy exceeds the sum or value of $10,000 . . . and is between . . . citizens of different States." [a] This statute and its predecessors have consistently been held to require complete diversity of citizenship.[13] That is, diversity jurisdiction does not exist unless *each* defen-

---

[11] As used in this opinion, the term "nonfederal claim" means one as to which there is no independent basis for federal jurisdiction. Conversely, a "federal claim" means one as to which an independent basis for federal jurisdiction exists.

[12] In Monell v. New York City Dept. of Social Services, 436 U.S. 658 (1978), we have overruled Monroe v. Pape, 365 U.S. 167 (1961), insofar as it held that political subdivisions are never amenable to suit under 42 U.S.C. § 1983—the basis of the holding in *Aldinger* that 28 U.S.C. § 1343(3) does not allow pendent jurisdiction of a state-law claim against a county. But *Monell* in no way qualifies the holding

of *Aldinger* that the jurisdictional questions presented in a case such as this one are statutory as well as constitutional, a point on which the dissenters in *Aldinger* agreed with the Court.

[a] Title 28 of the United States Code, § 1332, was amended in 1988 to raise the jurisdictional amount from $10,000 to $50,000. [Footnote by eds.]

[13] E.g., Strawbridge v. Curtiss, 7 U.S. (3 Cranch) 267 (1806); Coal Co. v. Blatchford, 78 U.S. (11 Wall.) 172 (1870); Indianapolis v. Chase Nat. Bank, 314 U.S. 63, 69 (1941); American Fire & Cas. Co. v. Finn, 341 U.S. 6, 17 (1951). It is settled that complete

dant is a citizen of a different state from *each* plaintiff. Over the years Congress has repeatedly re-enacted or amended the statute conferring diversity jurisdiction, leaving intact this rule of complete diversity. Whatever may have been the original purposes of diversity-of-citizenship jurisdiction, this subsequent history clearly demonstrates a congressional mandate that diversity jurisdiction is not to be available when any plaintiff is a citizen of the same state as any defendant.

Thus it is clear that the respondent could not originally have brought suit in federal court naming Owen and OPPD as codefendants, since citizens of Iowa would have been on both sides of the litigation. Yet the identical lawsuit resulted when she amended her complaint. Complete diversity was destroyed just as surely as if she had sued Owen initially. In either situation, in the plain language of the statute, the "matter in controversy" could not be "between . . . citizens of different States."

It is a fundamental precept that federal courts are courts of limited jurisdiction. The limits upon federal jurisdiction, whether imposed by the Constitution or by Congress, must be neither disregarded nor evaded. Yet under the reasoning of the Court of Appeals in this case, a plaintiff could defeat the statutory requirement of complete diversity by the simple expedient of suing only those defendants who were of diverse citizenship and waiting for them to implead nondiverse defendants.[17] If, as the Court of Appeals thought, a "common nucleus of operative fact" were the only requirement for ancillary jurisdiction in a diversity case, there would be no principled reason why the respondent in this case could not have joined her cause of action against Owen in her original complaint as ancillary to her claim against OPPD. Congress' requirement of complete diversity would thus have been evaded completely.

It is true, as the Court of Appeals noted, that the exercise of ancillary jurisdiction over nonfederal claims has often been upheld in situations involving impleader, cross-claims or counterclaims.[18] But in determining whether jurisdiction over a nonfederal claim exists, the

diversity is not a constitutional requirement. State Farm Fire & Cas. Co. v. Tashire, 386 U.S. 523, 530–31 (1967).

[17] This is not an unlikely hypothesis, since a defendant in a tort suit such as this one would surely try to limit his liability by impleading any joint tortfeasors for indemnity or contribution. Some commentators have suggested that the possible abuse of third-party practice could be dealt with under 28 U.S.C. § 1359, which forbids collusive attempts to create federal jurisdiction. Note, Rule 14 Claims and Ancillary Jurisdiction, 57 Va. L. Rev. 265, 274–75 (1971). The dissenting opinion today also expresses this view. But there is nothing necessarily collusive about a plaintiff's selectively suing only those tortfeasors of diverse citizenship, or about the named defendants' desire to implead joint tort-

feasors. Nonetheless, the requirement of complete diversity would be eviscerated by such a course of events.

[18] The ancillary jurisdiction of the federal courts derives originally from cases such as Freeman v. Howe, 65 U.S. (24 How.) 450 (1860), which held that when federal jurisdiction "effectively controls the property or fund under dispute, other claimants thereto should be allowed to intervene in order to protect their interest, without regard to jurisdiction." *Aldinger v. Howard*, 427 U.S., at 11. More recently, it has been said to include cases that involve multiparty practice, such as compulsory counterclaims, e.g., Moore v. New York Cotton Exchange, 270 U.S. 593 (1926), impleader, or intervention as of right, e.g., Phelps v. Oaks, 117 U.S. 236, 241 (1886). [Other citations omitted—eds.]

context in which the nonfederal claim is asserted is crucial. And the claim here arises in a setting quite different from the kinds of nonfederal claims that have been viewed in other cases as falling within the ancillary jurisdiction of the federal courts.

First, the nonfederal claim in this case was simply not ancillary to the federal one in the same sense that, for example, the impleader by a defendant of a third-party defendant always is. A third-party complaint depends at least in part upon the resolution of the primary lawsuit. See n.3, supra. Its relation to the original complaint is thus not mere factual similarity but logical dependence. The respondent's claim against the petitioner, however, was entirely separate from her original claim against OPPD, since the petitioner's liability to her depended not at all upon whether or not OPPD was also liable. Far from being an ancillary and dependent claim, it was a new and independent one.

Second, the nonfederal claim here was asserted by the plaintiff, who voluntarily chose to bring suit upon a state-law claim in a federal court. By contrast, ancillary jurisdiction typically involves claims by a defending party haled into court against his will, or by another person whose rights might be irretrievably lost unless he could assert them in an ongoing action in a federal court. A plaintiff cannot complain if ancillary jurisdiction does not encompass all of his possible claims in a case such as this one, since it is he who has chosen the federal rather than the state forum and must thus accept its limitations. "[T]he efficiency plaintiff seeks so avidly is available without question in the state courts." Kenrose Mfg. Co. v. Fred Whitaker Co., 512 F.2d 890, 894 (4th Cir. 1972).[20]

It is not unreasonable to assume that, in generally requiring complete diversity, Congress did not intend to confine the jurisdiction of federal courts so inflexibly that they are unable to protect legal rights or effectively to resolve an entire, logically entwined lawsuit. Those practical needs are the basis of the doctrine of ancillary jurisdiction. But neither the convenience of litigants nor considerations of judicial economy can suffice to justify extension of the doctrine of ancillary jurisdiction to a plaintiff's cause of action against a citizen of the same state in a diversity case. Congress has established the basic rule that diversity jurisdiction exists under 28 U.S.C. § 1332 only when there is complete diversity of citizenship. "The policy of the statute calls for its strict construction." Snyder v. Harris, 394 U.S. 332, 340 (1968). To allow the requirement of complete diversity to be circumvented as it was in this case would simply flout the congressional command.[21]

Accordingly, the judgment of the Court of Appeals is reversed.

---

[20] Whether Iowa's statute of limitations would now bar an action by the respondent in an Iowa court is, of course, entirely a matter of state law.

[21] Our holding is that the District Court lacked power to entertain the respondent's lawsuit against the petitioner. Thus, the asserted inequity in the respondent's alleged concealment of its citizenship is irrelevant. Federal judicial power does not depend upon "prior action or consent of the parties." American Fire & Cas. Co. v. Finn, 341 U.S. 6, 17–18 (1951).

It is so ordered.

MR. JUSTICE WHITE, with whom MR. JUSTICE BRENNAN joins, dissenting.

The Court today states that "[i]t is not unreasonable to assume that, in generally requiring complete diversity, Congress did not intend to confine the jurisdiction of federal courts so inflexibly that they are unable . . . effectively to resolve an entire, logically entwined lawsuit." In spite of this recognition, the majority goes on to hold that in diversity suits federal courts do not have the jurisdictional power to entertain a claim asserted by a plaintiff against a third-party defendant, no matter how entwined it is with the matter already before the court, unless there is an independent basis for jurisdiction over that claim. Because I find no support for such a requirement in either art. III of the Constitution or in any statutory law, I dissent from the Court's "unnecessarily grudging" approach.

The plaintiff below, Mrs. Kroger, chose to bring her lawsuit against the Omaha Public Power District (OPPD) in federal district court. No one questions the power of the District Court to entertain this claim, for Mrs. Kroger at the time was a citizen of Iowa, OPPD was a citizen of Nebraska, and the amount in controversy was greater than $10,000; jurisdiction therefore existed under 28 U.S.C. § 1332(a). As permitted by Fed. Rule Civ. Proc. 14(a), OPPD impleaded petitioner Owen Equipment & Erection Co. (Owen). Although OPPD's claim against Owen did not raise a federal question and although it was alleged that Owen was a citizen of the same state as OPPD, the parties and the court apparently believed that the District Court's ancillary jurisdiction encompassed this claim. Subsequently, Mrs. Kroger asserted a claim against Owen, everyone believing at the time that these two parties were citizens of different states. Because it later came to light that Mrs. Kroger and Owen were in fact both citizens of Iowa, the Court concludes that the District Court lacked jurisdiction over the claim.

In Mine Workers v. Gibbs, 383 U.S. 715, 725 (1966), we held that once a claim has been stated that is of sufficient substance to confer subject-matter jurisdiction on the federal district court, the court has judicial power to consider a nonfederal claim if it and the federal claim[2] are derived from "a common nucleus of operative fact." Although the specific facts of that case concerned a state claim that was said to be pendent to a federal-question claim, the Court's language and reasoning were broad enough to cover the instant factual situation: "[I]f, considered without regard to their federal or state character, a plaintiff's claims are such that he would ordinarily be expected to try them all in one judicial proceeding, then, assuming substantiality of the federal issues, there is *power* in federal courts to hear the whole." In the present case, Mrs. Kroger's claim against Owen and her claim against OPPD derived from a common nucleus of fact; this is necessarily so

[2] I use the terms "federal claim" and "nonfederal claim" in the same sense that the majority uses them. See n.11.

because in order for a plaintiff to assert a claim against a third-party defendant, Fed. Rule Civ. Proc. 14(a) requires that it "aris[e] out of the transaction or occurrence that is the subject matter of the plaintiff's claim against the third-party plaintiff. . . ." Furthermore, the substantiality of the claim Mrs. Kroger asserted against OPPD is unquestioned. Accordingly, as far as art. III of the Constitution is concerned, the District Court had power to entertain Mrs. Kroger's claim against Owen.

The majority correctly points out, however, that the analysis cannot stop here. As Aldinger v. Howard, 427 U.S. 1 (1976), teaches the jurisdictional power of the federal courts may be limited by Congress, as well as by the Constitution. In *Aldinger,* although the plaintiff's state claim against Spokane County was closely connected with her 42 U.S.C. § 1983 claim against the county treasurer, the Court held that the District Court did not have pendent jurisdiction over the state claim, for, under the Court's precedents at that time, it was thought that Congress had specifically determined not to confer on the federal courts jurisdiction over civil rights claims against cities and counties. That being so, the Court refused to allow "the federal courts to fashion a jurisdictional doctrine under the general language of art. III enabling them to circumvent this exclusion . . . ." 427 U.S., at 16.

In the present case, the only indication of congressional intent that the Court can find is that contained in the diversity jurisdictional statute, 28 U.S.C. § 1332(a), which states that "district courts shall have original jurisdiction of all civil actions where the matter in controversy exceeds the sum or value of $10,000 . . . and is between . . . citizens of different States. . . ." Because this statute has been interpreted as requiring complete diversity of citizenship between each plaintiff and each defendant, Strawbridge v. Curtiss, 7 U.S. (3 Cranch) 267 (1806), the Court holds that the District Court did not have ancillary jurisdiction over Mrs. Kroger's claim against Owen. In so holding, the Court unnecessarily expands the scope of the complete-diversity requirement while substantially limiting the doctrine of ancillary jurisdiction.

The complete-diversity requirement, of course, could be viewed as meaning that in a diversity case, a federal district court may adjudicate only those claims that are between parties of different states. Thus, in order for a defendant to implead a third-party defendant, there would have to be diversity of citizenship; the same would also be true for cross-claims between defendants and for a third-party defendant's claim against a plaintiff. Even the majority, however, refuses to read the complete-diversity requirement so broadly; it recognizes with seeming approval the exercise of ancillary jurisdiction over nonfederal claims in situations involving impleader, cross-claims, and counterclaims. Given the Court's willingness to recognize ancillary jurisdiction in these contexts, despite the requirements of § 1332(a), I see no justification for the Court's refusal to approve the District Court's exercise of ancillary jurisdiction in the present case.

It is significant that a plaintiff who asserts a claim against a third-party defendant is not seeking to add a new party to the lawsuit. In the present case, for example, Owen had already been brought into the suit by OPPD, and, that having been done, Mrs. Kroger merely sought to assert against Owen a claim arising out of the same transaction that was already before the court. Thus the situation presented here is unlike that in *Aldinger,* supra, wherein the Court noted:

> "[I]t is one thing to authorize two parties, already present in federal court by virtue of a case over which the court has jurisdiction, to litigate in addition to their federal claim a state-law claim over which there is no independent basis of federal jurisdiction. But it is quite another thing to permit a plaintiff, who has asserted a claim against one defendant with respect to which there is federal jurisdiction, to join an entirely different defendant on the basis of a state-law claim over which there is no independent basis of federal jurisdiction, simply because his claim against the first defendant and his claim against the second defendant 'derive from a common nucleus of operative fact.'. . . True, the same considerations of judicial economy would be served insofar as plaintiff's claims 'are such that he would ordinarily be expected to try them all in one judicial proceeding. . . .' [*Gibbs,* 383 U.S., at 725.] But the addition of a completely new party would run counter to the well-established principle that federal courts, as opposed to state trial courts of general jurisdiction, are courts of limited jurisdiction marked out by Congress." 427 U.S., at 14–15.

Because in the instant case Mrs. Kroger merely sought to assert a claim against someone already a party to the suit, considerations of judicial economy, convenience, and fairness to the litigants—the factors relied upon in *Gibbs*—support the recognition of ancillary jurisdiction here. Already before the court was the whole question of the cause of Mr. Kroger's death. Mrs. Kroger initially contended that OPPD was responsible; OPPD in turn contended that Owen's negligence had been the proximate cause of Mr. Kroger's death. In spite of the fact that the question of Owen's negligence was already before the District Court, the majority requires Mrs. Kroger to bring a separate action in state court in order to assert that very claim. Even if the Iowa statute of limitations will still permit such a suit, considerations of judicial economy are certainly not served by requiring such duplicate litigation.[4]

[4] It is true that prior to trial OPPD was dismissed as a party to the suit and that, as we indicated in *Gibbs,* the dismissal prior to trial of the federal claim will generally require the dismissal of the nonfederal claim as well. Given the unusual facts of the present case, however—in particular, the fact that the actual location of Owen's principal place of business was not revealed until the third day of trial—fairness to the parties would lead me to conclude that the District Court did not abuse its discretion in retaining jurisdiction over Mrs. Kroger's claim against Owen. Under the Court's disposition, of course, it would not matter whether or not the federal claim is tried, for in either situation the court would have no jurisdiction over the plaintiff's nonfederal claim against the third-party defendant.

The majority, however, brushes aside such considerations of convenience, judicial economy, and fairness because it concludes that recognizing ancillary jurisdiction over a plaintiff's claim against a third-party defendant would permit the plaintiff to circumvent the complete-diversity requirement and thereby "flout the congressional command." Since the plaintiff in such a case does not bring the third-party defendant into the suit, however, there is no occasion for deliberate circumvention of the diversity requirement, absent collusion with the defendant. In the case of such collusion, of which there is absolutely no indication here,[5] the court can dismiss the action under the authority of 28 U.S.C. § 1359.[6] In the absence of such collusion, there is no reason to adopt an absolute rule prohibiting the plaintiff from asserting those claims that he may properly assert against the third-party defendant pursuant to Fed. Rule Civ. Proc. 14(a). The plaintiff in such a situation brings suit against the defendant only, with absolutely no assurance that the defendant will decide or be able to implead a particular third-party defendant. Since the plaintiff has no control over the defendant's decision to implead a third party, the fact that he could not have originally sued that party in federal court should be irrelevant. Moreover, the fact that a plaintiff in some cases may be able to foresee the subsequent chain of events leading to the impleader does not seem to me to be a sufficient reason to declare that a district court does not have the *power* to exercise ancillary jurisdiction over the plaintiff's claims against the third-party defendant.[7]

We have previously noted that "[s]ubsequent decisions of this Court indicate that *Strawbridge* is not to be given an expansive reading." State Farm Fire & Cas. Co. v. Tashire, 386 U.S. 523, 531 n.6 (1967). In light of this teaching, it seems to me appropriate to view § 1332 as requiring complete diversity only between the plaintiff and those parties he actually brings into the suit. Beyond that, I would hold that in a diversity case the district court has power, both constitutional and statutory, to entertain all claims among the parties arising from the same nucleus of operative fact as the plaintiff's original, jurisdiction-conferring claim against the defendant. Accordingly, I dissent from the Court's disposition of the present case.

----

[5] When Mrs. Kroger brought suit, it was believed that Owen was a citizen of Nebraska, not Iowa. Therefore, had she desired at that time to make Owen a party to the suit, she would have done so directly by naming Owen as a defendant.

[6] Section 1359 states: "A district court shall not have jurisdiction of a civil action in which any party, by assignment or otherwise, has been improperly or collusively made or joined to invoke the jurisdiction of such court."

[7] Under the *Gibbs* analysis, recognition of the district court's power to hear a plaintiff's nonfederal claim against a third-party defendant in a diversity suit would not mean that the court would be required to entertain such claims in all cases. The district court would have the discretion to dismiss the nonfederal claim if it concluded that the interests of judicial economy, convenience, and fairness would not be served by the retention of the claim in the federal lawsuit. Accordingly, the majority's concerns that lead it to conclude that ancillary jurisdiction should not be recognized in the present situation could be met on a case-by-case basis, rather than by the absolute rule it adopts.

FURTHER NOTES ON DIVERSITY JURISDICTION

1. Ancillary Jurisdiction. As the Court observes in footnote 18, Freeman v. Howe, 65 U.S. (24 How.) 450 (1860), was an important early recognition of the concept of ancillary jurisdiction. *Freeman* held that a state court could not entertain an action brought by claimants to property if the property had previously been attached in a federal suit grounded on diversity jurisdiction. The state-court plaintiffs had objected to the possibility of this holding by arguing that they otherwise would be without any remedy, since their joinder in the federal suit would destroy complete diversity of citizenship. The Court responded that the state-court plaintiffs could nonetheless join the federal suit since their claim was "ancillary and dependent, supplementary entirely to the original suit."

The Court in *Freeman* was faced with a dilemma. Permitting the state-court suit to go forward would have allowed the state court to interfere with property already before the federal court. But forbidding the continuation of the state suit would leave claimants to the property without a remedy in any court, unless they could become parties to the pending federal suit. The Court's response was to permit the state-court parties to join the federal suit, even though their presence destroyed complete diversity.

The doctrine of *Freeman*, born of necessity, has since become a doctrine of convenience and efficiency. For example, as the Court notes in *Kroger*, a defendant who asserts a compulsory counterclaim in a diversity action may do so even though the requirements of diversity jurisdiction—specifically, the jurisdictional amount—are not independently satisfied.[a] And under Rule 14, a defendant may implead a third party even though the defendant and the third party are citizens of the same state. The rationale for these exceptions to the normal requirements of diversity jurisdiction obviously goes beyond *Freeman*, but there are substantial reasons that support extension of the doctrine to these situations. Both, for example, will involve litigation of closely related issues that will arise in a subsequent lawsuit if not the present one. The time of courts, parties, and witnesses, and the other expenses of litigation, strongly suggest the desirability of disposing of the matter in one suit. In the case of impleader, moreover, there is a possibility of inconsistent results that cannot be dealt with by the traditional doctrines of res judicata or collateral estoppel.[b]

Is the argument for ancillary jurisdiction in *Kroger* as strong as it is in the compulsory counterclaim and impleader situations? Does the

[a] This proposition was recognized by the Supreme Court in an analogous situation before adoption of the federal rules. See Moore v. New York Cotton Exchange, 270 U.S. 593 (1926).

[b] Assume, for example, that *A* asserts a claim against *B*, and *B* claims that *C* is liable to *B* if *B* is liable to *A*. Assume further that *B* is not allowed to add *C* to the lawsuit. If *A* wins against *B*, *B* will not be able to use collateral estoppel against *C* to preclude relitigation of any of the issues. *C* may therefore be able to prevail against *B* by securing an inconsistent verdict on an issue already adjudicated.

Court effectively distinguish these two contexts? Or does the dissent have the better of the argument? Consider two variations of the *Kroger* situation:

(i) The third-party defendant files a claim against the original plaintiff arising from the same transaction as the plaintiff's claim against the defendant. Plaintiff and defendant are from different states. The plaintiff and the third-party defendant are from the same state.

(ii) The plaintiff files suit in state court against an out-of-state defendant. Defendant removes to a federal court, and then impleads a third-party defendant who is from the same state as the plaintiff. The plaintiff now seeks to file a claim against the third-party defendant arising from the same transaction as the original claim.

How should *Kroger* be applied to these two situations?[c]

Consider also the precedents relied on by the majority. *Aldinger* arose at a time when 42 U.S.C. § 1983 had been interpreted not to permit suit against a unit of local government, even though it did permit suits against officials of that government.[d] What the plaintiffs sought was the joinder of a state-law claim against the county with their federal claim against the county officials. This, as the dissent in *Kroger* notes, seemed to fly in the face of the determination that federal courts did not have jurisdiction over claims against counties. *Zahn* also involved a situation where the recognition of ancillary jurisdiction arguably would have undermined a prior Supreme Court decision. The Court had held in Snyder v. Harris, 394 U.S. 332 (1969), that the separate claims of class-action plaintiffs could not be aggregated in order to satisfy the jurisdictional amount requirement of the diversity statute. In *Zahn*, the District Court found that the claims of those who purported to represent the class exceeded $10,000, as the jurisdictional amount then was, but that there were other class members whose claims were smaller. It found that it was not feasible to define a class of plaintiffs with claims in excess of $10,000, and accordingly refused to

---

[c] These variations were suggested by John Garvey in The Limits of Ancillary Jurisdiction, 57 Texas L. Rev. 697 (1979). Professor Garvey concludes that "the line drawn by the Court in *Kroger* is likely to be particularly mischievous and is inconsistent with the justifications of fairness, convenience, and economy generally advanced to support the doctrine of ancillary jurisdiction."

Consider another comment by Professor Garvey:

"In Phelps v. Oaks, 117 U.S. 236 (1886), . . . plaintiffs, citizens of Pennsylvania, had brought an action of ejectment in federal court against Oaks, a citizen of Missouri. Oaks, however, was a tenant of John and Maria Zeidler—both of Pennsylvania—and had been paying them the rent the plaintiffs sought. Today Oaks normally would implead the Zeidlers, and plaintiffs then might wish to settle the entire question by asserting their claims against the landlords. Instead, the Zeidlers intervened as defendants to protect their own claim to title, and the Court permitted the action to proceed with Pennsylvanians on both sides. If permitting plaintiffs to claim against intervening defendants differs from allowing them to claim against impleaded defendants on these facts, that difference eludes me."

The Court cited *Phelps* in footnote 18 of its *Kroger* opinion. Did the difference elude the Court as well?

[d] This issue is treated in detail at pages 927–92, infra.

permit the suit to proceed as a class action. It also refused to permit ancillary jurisdiction over those members of the class whose claims were smaller. Having held in *Snyder* that a class action could not be maintained to enforce claims for less than the jurisdictional minimum, the Supreme Court extended the holding in *Zahn* to a case where some claims exceeded $10,000 but others did not.

Why did the Court refuse to permit ancillary jurisdiction in *Alding-er* and *Zahn*? Is the case for not recognizing ancillary jurisdiction in *Kroger* as strong? Would a contrary decision have undermined the rule of "complete" diversity? Any more than other decisions already had done?[e]

2. Collusion: *Kramer v. Caribbean Mills*. The dissenters in *Kroger* suggested that 28 U.S.C. § 1359, which they quote in footnote 6,[f] could be invoked to prevent collusion between the plaintiff and the defendant to manufacture jurisdiction on facts such as those presented by the *Kroger* case. The majority, as it states in footnote 17, thought § 1359 an insufficient protection.

Kramer v. Caribbean Mills, Inc., 394 U.S. 823 (1969), illustrates the classic situation to which § 1359 applies. *Kramer* involved a contract in which a Haitian corporation agreed to purchase stock in a Panamanian corporation for $85,000 in cash and $165,000 in 12 annual installments. The installment payments were not made. The Panamanian corporation assigned its entire interest in the installment payments to a Texas attorney for $1. On the same day, the Texas attorney agreed to pay 95 per cent of any net recovery to the Panamanian corporation "solely as a bonus." A diversity suit was then filed by the Texas attorney in a Texas federal district court.

The Supreme Court had little difficulty with the case. Justice Harlan's opinion for a unanimous Court found that the assignment fell "within [the] very core" of § 1359:

> "If federal jurisdiction could be created by assignments of this kind, which are easy to arrange and involve few disadvantages for the assignor, then a vast quantity of ordinary contract and tort litigation could be channeled into the federal courts at the will of one of the parties. Such 'manufacture of federal juris-

[e] There is an extensive literature on *Kroger* and the problem of ancillary jurisdiction. In addition to the Garvey article discussed above in footnote c, see, e.g., Freer, A Principled Statutory Approach to Supplemental Jurisdiction, 1987 Duke L.J. 34; Miller, Ancillary and Pendent Jurisdiction, 26 S. Tex. L.J. 1 (1985); Matasar, A Pendent and Ancillary Jurisdiction Primer: The Scope and Limits of Supplemental Jurisdiction, 17 U.C. Davis L.Rev. 103 (1983); Stephens, Ancillary Jurisdiction: Plaintiffs' Claims Against Nondiverse Third-Party Defendants, 14 Loy. U. Chi. L.J. 419 (1983); Brill, Federal Rule of Civil Procedure 14 and Ancillary Jurisdiction, 59 Neb. L. Rev. 631 (1980); Berch, The Erection of a Barrier Against Assertion of Ancillary Claims: An Examination of *Owen Equipment and Erection Company v. Kroger*, 1979 Ariz. St. L.J. 253.

[f] Section 1359 was enacted in 1948 as a consolidation of two former statutes. The first, the so-called "assignee clause," had been enacted in the Judiciary Act of 1789. See *Sheldon v. Sill*, page 183, supra. The second, originally enacted in 1875, dealt with parties "improperly or collusively joined."

diction' was the very thing which Congress intended to prevent when it enacted § 1359 and its predecessors."[g]

3. Sandbagging. Owen admitted in its pleadings in the *Kroger* case that it was a citizen of Nebraska, but then moved on the third day of trial (after it realized that it was losing?) to dismiss the case because it really was a citizen of Iowa. Should it have been permitted to make such a motion? The majority of the Supreme Court seemed unconcerned. In footnote 21, it said that "the asserted inequity in the respondent's alleged concealment of its citizenship is irrelevant." In footnote 20, it said that whether the plaintiff's suit was now barred by the state statute of limitations "is, of course, entirely a matter of state law."

Compare American Fire & Casualty Co. v. Finn, 341 U.S. 6 (1951), cited by the Court in footnote 21. Finn had filed suit for a fire loss against his insurance company in a Texas state court. The insurance company removed the case to federal court over Finn's objection. The case went to trial, and Finn won. The *insurance company* then appealed on the ground that the removal was improper. The Supreme Court agreed, vacated the judgment, and ordered that, if the jurisdictional error were not cured,[h] the case be remanded to the state courts. Three Justices dissented on the ground that the insurance company "having asked for and obtained the removal of the case to the federal District Court, and having lost its case in that court, is now estopped from having it remanded to the state court."

The standard doctrine, as the majority in the *Finn* case explained, is that the conduct of the parties cannot confer subject-matter jurisdiction on the federal courts:

> "The jurisdiction of the federal courts is carefully guarded against expansion by judicial interpretation or by prior action or consent of the parties. To permit a federal trial court to enter a judgment . . . where the federal court could not have original jurisdiction . . . would by the act of the parties work a wrongful extension of federal jurisdiction and give district courts power the Congress has denied them."

The American Law Institute disagrees. See ALI, Study of the Division of Jurisdiction Between State and Federal Courts § 1386 (Official Draft, 1969). With certain exceptions in cases of collusion or where the facts were unavailable before trial, it proposed that neither the parties nor the courts be able to raise objections going to subject-matter jurisdiction after the beginning of the trial on the merits. It

[g] Section 1359 figures prominently in the dispute over whose citizenship should count in suits brought on behalf of a decedent's estate. See page 471, supra. For an extensive treatment of *Kramer* in this context, see Mullenix, Creative Manipulation of Federal Jurisdiction: Is there Diversity After Death, 70 Corn. L. Rev. 1011 (1985). On collusion generally, see Daniels, Judicial Control of Manufactured Diversity Pursuant to § 1359, 9 Rutgers-Camden L.J. 1 (1977).

[h] As it happened, the jurisdictional error was easily cured on remand by dismissing an additional party who had destroyed complete diversity of citizenship. Judgment was accordingly entered in favor of Finn. See Finn v. American Fire & Cas. Co., 207 F.2d 113 (5th Cir. 1953).

also proposed that state statutes of limitation be tolled for claims asserted in a federal suit while the suit was pending and for a prescribed period after a jurisdictional dismissal.[i]

Would the American Law Institute proposal be constitutional if adopted by Congress and applied to a case such as *Kroger*? To other cases that might arise? Would it be desirable? Should the Supreme Court adopt the ALI view even if Congress does not? Could it constitutionally do so?

SUBSECTION B: THE SUBSTANCE/PROCEDURE PROBLEM

INTRODUCTORY NOTES ON SUBSTANCE AND PROCEDURE IN DIVERSITY CASES

1. **Background.** Two important changes occurred in 1938. The first was the decision in Erie Railroad Co. v. Tompkins, 304 U.S. 64 (1938), which held that federal courts were required to look to state substantive rules of decision in cases not covered by the Constitution, acts of Congress, or rules of federal common law.[a] The second was the adoption of the Federal Rules of Civil Procedure, which for the first time provided uniform rules of procedure for the federal district courts.[b]

The federal rules were adopted pursuant to the Rules Enabling Act, now found in 28 U.S.C. § 2072. As it then was, § 2072 provided:

"The Supreme Court shall have the power to prescribe by general rules, the forms of process, writs, pleadings, and mo-

---

[i] After observing that "a wily defendant may conceal a known jurisdictional defect until the period of the statute of limitations has run, then obtain dismissal, and achieve total immunity from suit" and that "[s]ome decisions indicate that he may even do this by controverting jurisdictional facts previously alleged or admitted," the ALI commentary concludes that "this fetish of federal jurisdiction is wholly inconsistent with sound judicial administration and can only serve to diminish respect for a system that tolerates it." ALI, Study of the Division of Jurisdiction Between State and Federal Courts § 1386, p. 366 (Official Draft, 1969). The commentary cites Page v. Wright, 116 F.2d 449 (7th Cir. 1940), and Ramsey v. Mellon Nat'l Bank & Trust Co., 350 F.2d 874 (3d Cir. 1965), as enforcing the "fetish," and DiFrischia v. New York Cent. R.R. Co., 279 F.2d 141 (3d Cir. 1960), as running counter to the trend. For additional commentary, see Dobbs, Beyond Bootstrap: Foreclosing the Issue of Sub-ject-Matter Jurisdiction Before Final Judgment, 51 Minn. L. Rev. 491 (1967); Stephens, Estoppel to Deny Jurisdiction—*Klee* and *DiFrischia* Break Ground, 68 Dick. L. Rev. 39 (1963).

[a] *Erie* is treated fully at pages 269–89, supra.

[b] The effect of *Erie* and the new federal rules was to reverse the former practice with respect to both substantive and procedural questions. As to substance, federal courts had been free under *Swift v. Tyson* to develop independent substantive rules of decision in many cases that would have been controlled by state law if litigated in a state court. As to procedure, the Conformity Act of 1872 had provided that federal rules of procedure in district court cases, other than equity and admiralty, should "conform, as near as may be" to the procedures of the state in which the court sat.

tions, and the practice and procedure of the district courts and courts of appeals of the United States in civil actions, including admiralty and maritime cases, and appeals therein . . . .

"Such rules shall not abridge, enlarge or modify any substantive right and shall preserve the right of trial by jury as at common law and as declared by the Seventh Amendment to the Constitution. . . .

"All laws in conflict with such rules shall be of no further force or effect after such rules have taken effect. . . ."[c]

Erie commands that state "substantive" law be applied to certain classes of cases tried in federal district court.[d] Yet the "procedures" to be followed in federal courts are within the power of the federal government to determine,[e] and the federal rules are obviously meant to be followed when applicable. Should the federal rules be interpreted narrowly to avoid conflicts with state law? What is to be done if a federal rule of civil procedure is in unavoidable conflict with a state "substantive" rule? What is to be done in cases where a "procedure" is needed but the Federal Rules of Civil Procedure are silent? The answers to these questions have provoked decades of litigation, to which the materials in this section are devoted.

2. *Sibbach v. Wilson.* The first serious challenge to the validity of a federal rule of civil procedure occurred in Sibbach v. Wilson & Co., 312 U.S. 1 (1941). Sibbach sued in an Illinois federal district court for bodily injuries suffered in an accident in Indiana. The defendant moved for an order requiring the plaintiff to submit to a physical examination by court-appointed physicians to determine the nature and extent of her injuries. The court ordered the examination, but the plaintiff refused. The court held her in contempt, and she appealed. The Court of Appeals affirmed and the Supreme Court granted certiorari.

The Court and the parties assumed that the substantive law of Indiana would apply to the merits of the case, since that is where the cause of action arose.[f] For this reason, Sibbach was forced to concede that rules concerning physical examinations were "procedural" in nature. If they were "substantive," the laws of Indiana would control, and they permitted the physical examination Sibbach was trying to avoid. The problem she then faced was that Rules 35 and 37 of the

---

[c] The Enabling Act was passed in 1934, and four years later the Supreme Court promulgated the new Federal Rules of Civil Procedure. The Enabling Act provided that the rules as adopted by the Supreme Court should be laid before the Congress, and that they should become effective 90 days thereafter unless Congress acted to the contrary.

In 1988, the Rules Enabling Act was revised. The provisions formerly codified in § 2072 now appear in §§ 2072, 2073, and 2074, all of which are quoted in Appendix B.

[d] This requirement is reinforced by the provision in the Rules Enabling Act that federal rules of procedure "shall not abridge, enlarge, or modify any substantive right."

[e] This has been settled at least since Chief Justice Marshall's opinion in Wayman v. Southard, 23 U.S. (10 Wheat.) 1 (1825).

[f] *Sibbach* was decided before Klaxon Co. v. Stentor Electric Mfg. Co., 313 U.S. 487 (1941), which appears as a main case at page 358, supra.

Federal Rules of Civil Procedure also permitted the court to order a party to take a physical examination. Her response was that even though the matter was one to be governed by court "procedures," the invasion of her person from a compelled physical examination denied her such an important freedom that Congress could not have meant to authorize it in the Rules Enabling Act. Her contention, therefore, was that the provisions of Rules 35 and 37 on this question were invalid.[g]

The Court began by observing that "Congress has undoubted authority to regulate the practice and procedure of federal courts, and may exercise that power by delegating to this or other federal courts authority to make rules . . . ." The Court continued:

> "The suggestion that the rule offends the important right to freedom from invasion of the person ignores the fact that, as we hold, no invasion of freedom from personal restraint attaches to refusal so to comply with its provisions. If we were to adopt the suggested criterion of the importance of the alleged right we should invite endless litigation and confusion worse confounded. The test must be whether a rule really regulates procedure,—the judicial process for enforcing rights and duties recognized by substantive law and for justly administering remedy and redress for disregard or infraction of them. That the rules in question are such is admitted.

> "Finally, it is urged that Rules 35 and 37 work a major change of policy and that this was not intended by Congress. [I]t is to be noted that the authorization of a comprehensive system of court rules was a departure in policy, and that the new policy envisaged in the enabling act of 1934 was that the whole field of court procedure be regulated in the interest of speedy, fair and exact determination of the truth. The challenged rules comport with this policy. . . ."

The Court did hold, however, that it was improper under the terms of the federal rules themselves to hold Sibbach in contempt. The judgment was therefore reversed and remanded for entry of a more appropriate sanction.

Justice Frankfurter, joined by Justices Black, Douglas, and Murphy, dissented. He argued, inter alia, that "a drastic change in public policy, in a matter deeply touching the sensibilities of people or even their prejudices as to privacy, ought not to be inferred from a general authorization to formulate rules for the more uniform and effective dispatch of business on the civil side of the federal courts."

3. Early Decisions on Substance v. Procedure. Even though *Sibbach* settled the general validity of the federal rules, the Court was forced in other early decisions to address the implications of *Erie* on the obligation of the federal courts to follow state law on matters that arguably could be termed "procedural." In Cities Service Oil Co. v.

---

[g] The rules in Illinois (where the federal court sat) did not permit the court to order a physical examination.

Dunlap, 308 U.S. 208 (1939), for example, the Court held that a Texas rule on burden of proof must be followed because it "relate[d] to a substantial right" and was not merely "one of practice."[h] And in Palmer v. Hoffman, 318 U.S. 109 (1943), the Court interpreted the provision in Rule 8(c) that contributory negligence must be pleaded as an affirmative defense. The question was whether this meant that the defendant also had the burden of proving contributory negligence. The Court held that "Rule 8(c) covers only the matter of pleading. The question of the burden of establishing contributory negligence is a question of local law which federal courts in diversity of citizenship cases must apply."

These early cases did not make an effort to develop general guidelines for interpreting the federal rules or for administering the line between substance and procedure. In *Guaranty Trust v. York,* the next main case, the Court took occasion to address some aspects of the problem in more general terms.

GUARANTY TRUST CO. v. YORK

Supreme Court of the United States, 1945.
326 U.S. 99.

MR. JUSTICE FRANKFURTER delivered the opinion of the Court. . . .

In May, 1930, Van Sweringen Corporation issued notes to the amount of $30,000,000. Under an indenture of the same date, petitioner, Guaranty Trust Co., was named trustee with power and obligations to enforce the rights of the noteholders in the assets of the corporation and of the Van Sweringen brothers. In October, 1931, when it was apparent that the corporation could not meet its obligations, Guaranty cooperated in a plan for the purchase of the outstanding notes on the basis of cash for 50 per cent of the face value of the notes and 20 shares of Van Sweringen Corporation's stock for each $1,000 note. This exchange offer remained open until December 15, 1931.

Respondent York received $6,000 of the notes as a gift in 1934, her donor not having accepted the offer of exchange. [This] suit, instituted as a class action on behalf of non-accepting noteholders and brought in a federal court solely because of diversity of citizenship, is based on an alleged breach of trust by Guaranty in that it failed to protect the interests of the noteholders in assenting to the exchange offer and failed to disclose its self-interest when sponsoring the offer. Petitioner moved for summary judgment, which was granted. . . . On appeal, the Circuit Court of Appeals, one judge dissenting, . . . held that in a suit brought on the equity side of a federal district court that court is not required to apply the state statute of limitations that would govern like suits in the courts of a state where the federal court is sitting even though the exclusive basis of federal jurisdiction is diversity of citizen-

---

[h] The federal rules contain no provisions on burden of proof in civil cases.

ship. The importance of the question for the disposition of litigation in the federal courts led us to bring the case here.

In view of the basis of the decision below, it is not for us to consider whether the New York statute would actually bar this suit were it brought in a state court. Our only concern is with the holding that the federal courts in a suit like this are not bound by local law.

We put to one side the considerations relevant in disposing of questions that arise when a federal court is adjudicating a claim based on a federal law. Our problem only touches transactions for which rights and obligations are created by one of the states, and for the assertion of which, in case of diversity of the citizenship of the parties, Congress has made a federal court another available forum.

Our starting point must be the policy of federal jurisdiction which Erie R. Co. v. Tompkins, 304 U.S. 64 (1938), embodies. In overruling Swift v. Tyson, 41 U.S. (16 Pet.) 1 (1842), *Erie* did not merely overrule a venerable case. It overruled a particular way of looking at law which dominated the judicial process long after its inadequacies had been laid bare. Law was conceived as a "brooding omnipresence" of reason, of which decisions were merely evidence and not themselves the controlling formulations. Accordingly, federal courts deemed themselves free to ascertain what Reason, and therefore Law, required wholly independent of authoritatively declared state law, even in cases where a legal right as the basis for relief was created by state authority and could not be created by federal authority and the case got into a federal court merely because it was "between Citizens of different States" under art. III, § 2 of the Constitution of the United States.

This impulse to freedom from the rules that controlled state courts regarding state-created rights was so strongly rooted in the prevailing views concerning the nature of law, that the federal courts almost imperceptibly were led to mutilating construction even of the explicit command given to them by Congress to apply state law in cases purporting to enforce the law of a state. See § 34 of the Judiciary Act of 1789.[a] The matter was fairly summarized by the statement that "During the period when *Swift v. Tyson* (1842–1938) ruled the decisions of the federal courts, its theory of their freedom in matters of general law from the authority of state courts pervaded opinions of this Court involving even state statutes or local law." Vandenbark v. Owens-Illinois Co., 311 U.S. 538, 540 (1941).

In relation to the problem now here, the real significance of *Swift v. Tyson* lies in the fact that it did not enunciate novel doctrine. Nor was it restricted to its particular situation. It summed up prior attitudes and expressions in cases that had come before this Court and lower federal courts for at least 30 years, at law as well as in equity.[1]

---

[a] Now 28 U.S.C. § 1652. [Footnote by eds.]

[1] In Russell v. Southard, 53 U.S. (12 How.) 139, 147 (1851), Mr. Justice Curtis, refusing to be bound by Kentucky law barring the reception of oral evidence to show that an absolute bill of sale was in reality a mortgage, declared that "upon the principles of general equity jurisprudence, this court must be governed by its own views of those principles." To support this statement, he cited, among others, . . . *Swift*

The short of it is that the doctrine was congenial to the jurisprudential climate of the time. Once established, judicial momentum kept it going. Since it was conceived that there was "a transcendental body of law outside of any particular state but obligatory within it unless and until changed by statute," state court decisions were not "the law" but merely someone's opinion—to be sure an opinion to be respected—concerning the content of this all-pervading law. Not unnaturally, the federal courts assumed power to find for themselves the content of such a body of law. The notion was stimulated by the attractive vision of a uniform body of federal law. To such sentiments for uniformity of decision and freedom from diversity in state law the federal courts gave currency, particularly in cases where equitable remedies were sought, because equitable doctrines are so often cast in terms of universal applicability when close analysis of the source of legal enforceability is not demanded.

In exercising their jurisdiction on the ground of diversity of citizenship, the federal courts, in the long course of their history, have not differentiated in their regard for state law between actions at law and suits in equity. Although § 34 of the Judiciary Act of 1789 directed that the "laws of the several states . . . shall be regarded as rules of decision in trials at common law . . .," this was deemed, consistently for over a hundred years, to be merely declaratory of what would in any event have governed the federal courts and therefore was equally applicable to equity suits. Indeed, it may fairly be said that the federal courts gave greater respect to state-created "substantive rights" in equity than they gave them on the law side, because rights at law were usually declared by state courts and as such increasingly flouted by extension of the doctrine of *Swift v. Tyson,* while rights in equity were frequently defined by legislative enactment and as such known and respected by the federal courts.

Partly because the states in the early days varied greatly in the manner in which equitable relief was afforded and in the extent to which it was available, Congress provided that "the forms and modes of proceeding in suits . . . of equity" would conform to the settled uses of courts of equity. 1 Stat. 275, 276. But this enactment gave the federal courts no power that they would not have had in any event when courts were given "cognizance," by the First Judiciary Act, of suits "in equity." From the beginning there has been a good deal of talk in the cases that federal equity is a separate legal system. And so it is, properly understood. The suits in equity of which the federal courts have had "cognizance" ever since 1789 constituted the body of law which had been transplanted to this country from the English Court of Chancery. But this system of equity "derived its doctrines, as well as its powers, from its mode of giving relief." Langdell, Summary of Equity Pleading (1877) xxvii. In giving federal courts "cognizance" of equity suits in cases of diversity jurisdiction, Congress never gave, nor

v. Tyson, supra. This commingling of law and equity cases indicates that the same views governed both and that *Swift v. Ty-* son was merely another expression of the ideas put forth in the equity cases.

did the federal courts ever claim, the power to deny substantive rights created by state law or to create substantive rights denied by state law.

This does not mean that whatever equitable remedy is available in a state court must be available in a diversity suit in a federal court, or conversely, that a federal court may not afford an equitable remedy not available in a state court. Equitable relief in a federal court is of course subject to restrictions: the suit must be within the traditional scope of equity as historically evolved in the English Court of Chancery; a plain, adequate and complete remedy at law must be wanting; explicit Congressional curtailment of equity powers must be respected; the constitutional right to trial by jury cannot be evaded. That a state may authorize its courts to give equitable relief unhampered by any or all such restrictions cannot remove these fetters from the federal courts. State law cannot define the remedies which a federal court must give simply because a federal court in diversity jurisdiction is available as an alternative tribunal to the state's courts. Contrariwise, a federal court may afford an equitable remedy for a substantive right recognized by a state even though a state court cannot give it. Whatever contradiction or confusion may be produced by a medley of judicial phrases severed from their environment, the body of adjudications concerning equitable relief in diversity cases leaves no doubt that the federal courts enforced state-created substantive rights if the mode of proceeding and remedy were consonant with the traditional body of equitable remedies, practice and procedure, and in so doing they were enforcing rights created by the states and not arising under any inherent or statutory federal law.

Inevitably, therefore, the principle of *Erie R. Co. v. Tompkins,* an action at law, was promptly applied to a suit in equity. Ruhlin v. N.Y. Life Ins. Co., 304 U.S. 202 (1938).

And so this case reduces itself to the narrow question whether, when no recovery could be had in a state court because the action is barred by the statute of limitations, a federal court in equity can take cognizance of the suit because there is diversity of citizenship between the parties. Is the outlawry, according to state law, of a claim created by the states a matter of "substantive rights" to be respected by a federal court of equity when that court's jurisdiction is dependent on the fact that there is a state-created right, or is such statute of "a mere remedial character" which a federal court may disregard?

Matters of "substance" and matters of "procedure" are much talked about in the books as though they defined a great divide cutting across the whole domain of law. But, of course, "substance" and "procedure" are the same key-words to very different problems. Neither "substance" nor "procedure" represents the same invariants. Each implies different variables depending upon the particular problem for which it is used. And the different problems are only distantly related at best, for the terms are in common use in connection with situations turning on such different considerations as those that are relevant to questions pertaining to ex post facto legislation, the impairment of the obligations of contract, the enforcement of federal rights in the state courts and the multitudinous phases of the conflict of laws.

Here we are dealing with a right to recover derived not from the United States but from one of the states. When, because the plaintiff happens to be a non-resident, such a right is enforceable in a federal as well as in a state court, the forms and mode of enforcing the right may at times, naturally enough, vary because the two judicial systems are not identical. But since a federal court adjudicating a state-created right solely because of the diversity of citizenship of the parties is for that purpose, in effect, only another court of the state, it cannot afford recovery if the right to recover is made unavailable by the state nor can it substantially affect the enforcement of the right as given by the state.

And so the question is not whether a statute of limitations is deemed a matter of "procedure" in some sense. The question is whether such a statute concerns merely the manner and the means by which a right to recover, as recognized by the state, is enforced, or whether such statutory limitation is a matter of substance in the aspect that alone is relevant to our problem, namely, does it significantly affect the result of a litigation for a federal court to disregard a law of a state that would be controlling in an action upon the same claim by the same parties in a state court?

It is therefore immaterial whether statutes of limitation are characterized either as "substantive" or "procedural" in state court opinions in any use of those terms unrelated to the specific issue before us. *Erie R. Co. v. Tompkins* was not an endeavor to formulate scientific legal terminology. It expressed a policy that touches vitally the proper distribution of judicial power between state and federal courts. In essence, the intent of that decision was to insure that, in all cases where a federal court is exercising jurisdiction solely because of the diversity of citizenship of the parties, the outcome of the litigation in the federal court should be substantially the same, so far as legal rules determine the outcome of a litigation, as it would be if tried in a state court. The nub of the policy that underlies *Erie R. Co. v. Tompkins* is that for the same transaction the accident of a suit by a non-resident litigant in a federal court instead of in a state court a block away should not lead to a substantially different result. And so, putting to one side abstractions regarding "substance" and "procedure," we have held that in diversity cases the federal courts must follow the law of the state as to burden of proof, Cities Service Co. v. Dunlap, 308 U.S. 208 (1939), as to conflict of laws, Klaxon Co. v. Stentor Co., 313 U.S. 487 (1941), as to contributory negligence, Palmer v. Hoffman, 318 U.S. 109, 117 (1943). And see Sampson v. Channell, 110 F.2d 754 (1st Cir. 1940). *Erie R. Co. v. Tompkins* has been applied with an eye alert to essentials in avoiding disregard of state law in diversity cases in the federal courts. A policy so important to our federalism must be kept free from entanglements with analytical or terminological niceties.

Plainly enough, a statute that would completely bar recovery in a suit if brought in a state court bears on a state-created right vitally and not merely formally or negligibly.　As to consequences that so intimately affect recovery or non-recovery a federal court in a diversity case should follow state law.　The fact that under New York law a statute of limitations might be lengthened or shortened, that a security may be foreclosed though the debt be barred, that a barred debt may be used as a set-off, are all matters of local law properly to be respected by federal courts sitting in New York when their incidence comes into play there. Such particular rules of local law, however, do not in the slightest change the crucial consideration that if a plea of the statute of limitations would bar recovery in a state court, a federal court ought not to afford recovery.

Prior to *Erie R. Co. v. Tompkins* it was not necessary, as we have indicated, to make the critical analysis required by the doctrine of that case of the nature of jurisdiction of the federal courts in diversity cases. But even before *Erie R. Co. v. Tompkins,* federal courts relied on statutes of limitations of the states in which they sat.　In suits at law state limitations statutes were held to be "rules of decision" within § 34 of the Judiciary Act of 1789 and as such applied in "trials at common law."　While there was talk of freedom of equity from such state statutes of limitations, the cases generally refused recovery where suit was barred in a like situation in the state courts, even if only by way of analogy.　However in Kirby v. Lake Shore & M.S. R. Co., 120 U.S. 130 (1887), the Court disregarded a state statute of limitations where the Court deemed it inequitable to apply it.

To make an exception to *Erie R. Co. v. Tompkins* on the equity side of a federal court is to reject the considerations of policy which, after long travail, led to that decision.　Judge Augustus N. Hand thus summarized below the fatal objection to such inroad upon *Erie R. Co. v. Tompkins* :

> "In my opinion it would be a mischievous practice to disregard state statutes of limitation whenever federal courts think that the result of adopting them may be inequitable.　Such procedure would promote the choice of United States rather than of state courts in order to gain the advantage of different laws. The main foundation for the criticism of *Swift v. Tyson* was that a litigant in cases where federal jurisdiction is based only on diverse citizenship may obtain a more favorable decision by suing in the United States courts."

Diversity jurisdiction is founded on assurance to non-resident litigants of courts free from susceptibility to potential local bias.　The framers of the Constitution, according to Marshall, entertained "apprehensions" lest distant suitors be subjected to local bias in state courts, or, at least, viewed with "indulgence the possible fears and apprehensions" of such suitors.　Bank of the United States v. Deveaux, 9 U.S. (5 Cranch) 61, 87 (1809).　And so Congress afforded out-of-state litigants another tribunal, not another body of law.　The operation of a double system of conflicting laws in the same state is plainly hostile to the reign of law.　Certainly, the fortuitous circumstance of residence out of a state of one of the parties to a litigation ought not to give rise to a discrimination against others equally concerned but locally resident. The source of substantive rights enforced by a federal court under diversity jurisdiction, it cannot be said too often, is the law of the states. Whenever that law is authoritatively declared by a state, whether its voice be the legislature or its highest court, such law ought to govern in litigation founded on that law, whether the forum of application is a state or a federal court and whether the remedies be sought at law or may be had in equity.

Dicta may be cited characterizing equity as an independent body of law. To the extent that we have indicated, it is. But insofar as these general observations go beyond that, they merely reflect notions that have been replaced by a sharper analysis of what federal courts do when they enforce rights that have no federal origin. And so, before the true source of law that is applied by the federal courts under diversity jurisdiction was fully explored, some things were said that would not now be said. But nothing that was decided, unless it be the *Kirby* case, needs to be rejected.

The judgment is reversed and the case is remanded for proceedings not inconsistent with this opinion.

So ordered.

MR. JUSTICE ROBERTS and MR. JUSTICE DOUGLAS took no part in the consideration or decision of this case.

MR. JUSTICE RUTLEDGE.

I dissent. [T]he Court . . . overturns a rule of decision which has prevailed in the federal courts from almost the beginning. . . . One may give full adherence to the rule of Erie R. Co. v. Tompkins, 304 U.S. 64 (1938), and its extension to cases in equity in so far as they affect clearly substantive rights, without conceding or assuming that the long tradition, both federal and state, which regards statutes of limitations as falling within the category of remedial rather than substantive law, necessarily must be ruled in the same way; and without conceding further that only a different jurisprudential climate or a kind of "brooding omnipresence in the sky" has dictated the hitherto unvaried policy of the federal courts in their general attitude toward the strict application of local statutes of limitations in equity causes.

If any characteristic of equity jurisprudence has descended unbrokenly from and within "the traditional scope of equity as historically evolved in the English Court of Chancery," it is that statutes of limitations, often in terms applying only to actions at law, have never been deemed to be rigidly applicable as absolute barriers to suits in equity as they are to actions at law. That tradition, it would seem, should be regarded as having been incorporated in the various acts of Congress which have conferred equity jurisdiction upon the federal courts. . . .

More is at stake in the implications of the decision, if not in the words of the opinion, than simply bringing federal and local law into accord upon matters clearly and exclusively within the constitutional power of the state to determine. It is one thing to require that kind of an accord in diversity cases when the question is merely whether the federal court must follow the law of the state as to burden of proof, Cities Service Co. v. Dunlap, 308 U.S. 208 (1939); contributory negligence, Palmer v. Hoffman, 318 U.S. 109, 117 (1943); or perhaps in application of the so-called parol evidence rule. These ordinarily involve matters of substantive law, though nominated in terms of procedure. But in some instances their application may lie along the border between procedure or remedy and substance, where the one may or may not be fact but another name for the other. It is exactly in this borderland, where procedural or remedial rights may or may not have the effect of determining the substantive ones completely, that caution is required in extending the rule of the *Erie* case by the very rule itself.

The words "substantive" and "procedural" or "remedial" are not talismanic. Merely calling a legal question by one or the other does not resolve it otherwise than as a purely authoritarian performance. But they have come to designate in a broad way large and distinctive legal domains within the greater one of the law and to mark, though often indistinctly or with overlapping limits, many divides between such regions.

One of these historically has been the divide between the substantive law and the procedural or remedial law to be applied by the federal courts in diversity cases, a division sharpened but not wiped out by *Erie R. Co. v. Tompkins* and subsequent decisions extending the scope of its ruling. The large division between adjective law and substantive law still remains, to divide the power of Congress from that of the states and consequently to determine the power of the federal courts to apply federal law or state law in diversity matters.

This division, like others drawn by the broad allocation of adjective or remedial and substantive, has areas of admixture of these two aspects of the law. In these areas whether a particular situation or issue presents one aspect or the other depends upon how one looks at the matter. As form cannot always be separated from substance in a work of art, so adjective or remedial aspects cannot be parted entirely from substantive ones in these borderland regions.

Whenever this integration or admixture prevails in a substantial measure, so that a clean break cannot be made, there is danger either of nullifying the power of Congress to control not only how the federal courts may act, but what they may do by way of affording remedies, or of usurping that function, if the *Erie* doctrine is to be expanded judicially to include such situations to the utmost extent.

It may be true that if the matter were wholly fresh the barring of rights in equity by statutes of limitation would seem to partake more of the substantive than of the remedial phase of law. But the matter is not fresh and it is not without room for debate. A long tradition, in the states and here, as well as in the common law which antedated both state and federal law, has emphasized the remedial character of statutes of limitations, more especially in application to equity causes, on many kinds of issues requiring differentiation of such matters from more clearly and exclusively substantive ones. . . .

Applicable statutes of limitations in state tribunals are not always the ones which would apply if suit were instituted in the courts of the state which creates the substantive rights for which enforcement is sought. The state of the forum is free to apply its own period of limitations, regardless of whether the state originating the right has barred suit upon it. Whether or not *the action* will be held to be barred depends therefore not upon the law of the state which creates the substantive right, but upon the law of the state where suit may be brought. . . .

MR. JUSTICE MURPHY joins this opinion.

———

NOTES ON *GUARANTY TRUST*

1. **Comments and Questions on *Guaranty Trust Co. v. York*.** There was no federal rule of civil procedure that governed the problem before the Court in *Guaranty Trust*. Thus, the problem reduced itself to whether district courts were free to fashion their own statutes of limitations to apply to such cases or whether the state statutes should be followed. The problem was complicated, as Justice Frankfurter noted, by the fact that federal equity had its own tradition of independence from state law. At least one pre-*Erie* case, Kirby v. Lake Shore & M.S. R. Co., 120 U.S. 130 (1887), had held that a state statute of limitations need not be followed by a federal equity court.

One might have thought the question nonetheless to be straightforward. In the absence of an applicable federal rule on the question, and in the absence of any federal policies suggesting the need for the courts to fashion one, the easy answer would be to follow state law. Yet neither the majority nor the dissent followed such a simple course. Why not? What are the implications of the respective approaches of Justice Frankfurter and Justice Rutledge? What are their objectives? Did Justice Frankfurter mean for the questions he asked to be controlling in a case where there is a federal rule of procedure on point? If he did, how would *Sibbach* have been decided under this approach?

2. **The Varied Meanings of Substance and Procedure.** In Sun Oil Co. v. Wortman, __ U.S. __ (1988), the Court held that it was appropriate for Kansas courts to apply a Kansas statute of limitations to a controversy the substance of which was constitutionally required to be determined by the laws of other states. Justice Scalia's opinion for the Court stated the issue as follows:

"Since the procedural rules of its courts are surely matters on which a state is competent to legislate, it follows that a state may apply its own procedural rules to actions litigated in its courts. The issue here, then, can be characterized as whether a statute of limitations may be considered as a procedural matter for purposes of the full faith and credit clause."

It was argued that *Guaranty Trust* was relevant to the answer to this question. Justice Scalia responded:

"*Guaranty Trust* itself rejects the notion that there is an equivalence between what is substantive under the *Erie* doctrine and what is substantive for purposes of conflict of laws. Except at the extremes, the terms 'substance' and 'procedure' precisely describe very little except a dichotomy, and what they mean in a particular context is largely determined by the purposes for which the dichotomy is drawn. In the context of our *Erie* jurisprudence, that purpose is to establish (within the limits of applicable federal law, including the prescribed rules of federal procedure) substantial uniformity of predictable outcome between cases tried in a federal court and cases tried in the courts of the state in which the federal court sits. The purpose of the substance-procedure dichotomy in the context of the full faith and credit clause, by contrast, is not to establish uniformity but to delimit spheres of state legislative competence. How different the two purposes (and hence the appropriate meanings) are is suggested by this: It is never the case under *Erie* that either federal *or* state law—if the two differ— can properly be applied to a particular issue; but since the legislative jurisdictions of the states overlap, it is frequently the case under the full faith and credit clause that a court can lawfully apply either the law of one state or the contrary law of another. Today, for example, we do not hold that Kansas must apply its own statute of limitations to a claim governed in its substance by another state's law, but only that it may."

Is Justice Scalia correct in attributing different purposes to the "substance-procedure dichotomy" in the *Erie* and the full faith and credit contexts? Are there other reasons why the two terms ought to mean different things in the two situations?

NOTES ON THE CASES DECIDED BETWEEN *GUARANTY TRUST* AND *HANNA*

1. *Ragan, Woods,* and *Cohen*. Four years after *Guaranty Trust*, the Court decided three cases dealing with the interaction of *Erie, Guaranty Trust,* and the federal rules in diversity cases. These cases represent the high water mark of deference to state law in the progression of cases on the "substance/procedure" question.

(i) *Ragan.* Ragan v. Merchants Transfer & Warehouse Co., 337 U.S. 530 (1949), involved an automobile accident that occurred on October 1, 1943. Rule 3 of the federal rules provides that "a civil action is commenced by filing a complaint with the court." This was done on September 4, 1945, well within the two-year statute of limita-

tions established by the applicable Kansas law. A summons was issued
on September 7, and duly served. But it was later quashed, presumably because of some irregularity. A valid summons was finally served
on December 28, 1945, after the statute of limitations had expired.

Under Kansas law, service of the summons had to occur within the
two-year statute of limitations in order for the suit to go forward. The
plaintiff claimed that "the Federal Rules of Civil Procedure determine
the manner in which an action is commenced in the federal courts—a
matter of procedure which the principle of *Erie* does not control."
Accordingly, the plaintiff argued, the suit should be allowed to continue
since it was properly filed in federal court within the statute of
limitations.

The Supreme Court disagreed. It held that the "theory of *Guaranty Trust*" required that the Kansas rule be followed:

> "[T]here can be no doubt that the suit was properly com-
> menced in the federal court. But in the present case we look
> to local law to find the cause of action on which the suit is
> brought. Since that cause of action is created by local law, the
> measure of it is to be found only in local law. It carries the
> same burden and is subject to the same defenses in federal
> court as in the state court. It accrues and comes to an end
> when local law so declares. Where local law qualifies or
> abridges it, the federal court must follow suit. . . . We
> cannot give it longer life in the federal court than it would
> have had in the state court without adding something to the
> cause of action. We may not do that consistently with *Erie.*
> . . ."

(ii) *Woods.* In Woods v. Interstate Realty Co., 337 U.S. 535
(1949), a Tennessee corporation brought suit for a broker's commission
in a Mississippi federal court. The corporation had failed to comply
with a Mississippi statute requiring appointment of a local agent for
service of process as a condition of doing business in the state. The
statute provided that "[a]ny corporation failing to comply with the
above provisions shall not be permitted to bring or maintain any action
or suit in any of the courts of this state."

The Supreme Court held that this statute also closed the doors of
the Mississippi federal court:

> "The *York* case was premised on the theory that a right which
> local law creates but which it does not supply with a remedy is
> no right at all for purposes of enforcement in a federal court in
> a diversity case; that where in such cases one is barred from
> recovery in the state court, he should likewise be barred in the
> federal court. The contrary result would create discrimina-
> tions against citizens of the state in favor of those authorized to
> invoke the diversity jurisdiction of the federal courts. It was
> that element of discrimination that *Erie* was designed to elimi-
> nate."

Three Justices dissented. They argued that the Court was "giving the state law a different meaning in federal court than the state courts would have given it." They elaborated:

"The Mississippi statute follows a pattern among the states in requiring qualification and payment of fees by foreign corporations. State courts have generally held such acts to do no more than to withhold state help from the noncomplying corporation but to leave their rights otherwise unimpaired. This interpretation left such corporations a basis on which to get the help of any other court—federal or state—that could otherwise take jurisdiction . . . . The penalty thus suffered . . . results in the unjust enrichment of the debtor, who has suffered no injury from the creditor's default in qualification. [T]he Court's action in refusing to accept the state court's determination of the effect of its own statute is a perversion of the *Erie* doctrine."[a]

(iii) *Cohen*. In Cohen v. Beneficial Industrial Loan Corporation, 337 U.S. 541 (1949), the plaintiff and an intervenor held 250 of the more than two million shares of the outstanding stock of the defendant corporation.[b] They brought a stockholder's derivative action in a New Jersey federal court, claiming mismanagement and fraud over a period of 18 years and seeking the recovery of more than $100 million. Under a New Jersey statute,[c] plaintiffs in stockholder's derivative actions were required to post a bond as security for the expenses and attorney's fees of the defendant if they failed to make good their complaint.[d] The question was whether this statute applied to a suit in federal court.

The Supreme Court held that it did:

"The only substantial argument that this New Jersey statute is not applicable here is that its provisions are mere rules of procedure rather than rules of substantive law.

"Even if we were to agree that the New Jersey statute is procedural, it would not determine that it is not applicable. Rules which lawyers call procedural do not always exhaust their effect by regulating procedure. But this statute is not merely a regulation of procedure. With it or without it the main action takes the same course. However, it creates a new liability where none existed before, for it makes a stockholder who institutes a derivative action liable for the expense to

---

[a] Note Rule 17(b): "The capacity of a corporation to sue or be sued shall be determined by the law under which it was organized." Neither the majority nor the dissent mentioned the possible relevance of this provision. Laura Little has extensively discussed the relevance of Rule 17(b) to the problem in *Woods* in Out of *Woods* and Into the Rules: The Relationship Between State Foreign Corporation Door-Closing Statutes and Federal Rule of Civil Procedure 17(b), 72 Va.L.Rev. 767 (1986).

[b] This represented 0.0125 per cent of the corporation's stock, with a market value of less than $9,000.

[c] The statute became effective after the suit was filed, but was explicitly made applicable to pending litigation. The Supreme Court held the statute constitutional, and found nothing untoward about its retroactive application in this context.

[d] In this case the bond was in the amount of $125,000.

which he puts the corporation and other defendants, if he does not make good his claims. . . . We do not think a statute which so conditions the stockholder's action can be disregarded by the federal court as a mere procedural device."

The plaintiffs had argued that Rule 23 of the federal rules "deals with [the] right to maintain such an action in federal court and that therefore the subject is recognized as procedural and the federal rule alone prevails."[e] After summarizing the provisions of the rule, the Court responded:

"None conflict[s] with the statute in question and all may be observed by a federal court, even if not applicable in state court. We see no reason why the policy stated in *Guaranty Trust* should not apply."

Justice Douglas, joined by Justice Frankfurter, dissented. He argued that:

"The measure of the cause of action is the claim which the corporation has against the alleged wrongdoers. This New Jersey statute does not add one iota to nor subtract one iota from that cause of action. It merely prescribes the method by which stockholders may enforce it. [Such statutes] do not fall under the principle of *Erie* unless they define, qualify or delimit the cause of action or otherwise relate to it.

"This New Jersey statute . . . regulates only the procedure for instituting a particular cause of action and hence need not be applied in this diversity suit in the federal court. Rule 23 . . . defines that procedure for the federal courts."

(iv) The Rutledge Dissent. The three cases summarized above were decided by the Supreme Court on the same day. Justice Rutledge was the only dissenter from all three. He argued that "the three decisions taken together demonstrate the extreme extent to which the Court is going in submitting the control of diversity litigation to the states rather than to Congress, where it properly belongs." He continued:

"What is being applied is a gloss on the *Erie* rule, not the rule itself. [T]he *Erie* case made no ruling that in . . . deciding diversity cases a federal court is 'merely another court of the state in which it sits,' and hence that in every situation

---

[e] Rule 23(b) at the time provided:

"In an action brought to enforce a secondary right on the part of one or more shareholders in an association, incorporated or unincorporated, because the association refuses to enforce rights which may properly be asserted by it, the complaint shall be verified by oath and shall aver (1) that the plaintiff was a shareholder at the time of the transaction of which he complains or that his share thereafter devolved upon him by operation of law and (2) that the action is not a collusive one to confer on a court of the United States jurisdiction of any action of which it would not otherwise have jurisdiction. The complaint shall also set forth with particularity the efforts of the plaintiff to secure from the managing directors or trustees and, if necessary, from the shareholders such action as he desires, and the reasons for his failure to obtain such action or the reasons for not making such effort."

in which the doors of state courts are closed to a suitor, so must be also those of the federal courts. . . .

"The accepted dichotomy is the familiar 'procedural-substantive' one. [A]s the matter stands, it is Congress which has the power to govern the procedure of the federal courts in diversity cases, and the states which have that power over matters clearly substantive in nature. Judges . . . cannot escape making the division."

The only case on which he commented specifically was *Cohen*, which he thought controlled by Rule 23:

"In my view Rule 23 . . . is valid and governs in the *Cohen* case. If, however, the state of New Jersey has the power to govern federal diversity suits within its borders as to all matters having a substantive tinge or aspect, then it may be questioned whether, in the event of conflict with some local policy, a federal court sitting in that state could give effect to the Rule's requirement[s]. . . . For in any strict and abstract sense that provision would seem to be as much a 'substantive' one as the New Jersey requirements for bond, etc. And, if so, then it would seem highly doubtful, on any automatic or mechanical application of the substantive-procedural dichotomy, that either Congress or this Court could create such a limitation on diversity litigation, since as a substantive matter this would be for the states to control.

"For myself I have no doubt of the validity of Rule 23 or of the power of Congress to enact such a rule, even though it has a substantive aspect. Notwithstanding that aspect, the rule is too closely related to procedural and other matters affecting litigation in the federal courts for me to conceive of its invalidity. So also in the present cases I think the state regulations, though each may be regarded as having a substantive aspect, are too closely related to the modes and methods of conducting litigation in the federal courts to be capable of displacing Congress' power of regulation in those respects or the federal courts' power to hear and determine the respective controversies."

2. Byrd. Byrd v. Blue Ridge Rural Electric Cooperative, Inc., 356 U.S. 525 (1958), was the next significant decision in the substance/procedure line. The plaintiff was injured while installing an electrical power line. He worked for a contractor that, under agreement with the defendant, was responsible for installing some 24 miles of new lines. The question before the Court concerned one of the defenses to the suit, namely whether the plaintiff was a "statutory employee" of the defendant under South Carolina law.[f] If he was, then he was entitled only to workmen's compensation for his injury. If he was not, he was permitted to sue for negligence.

---

[f] This turned on the nature of the work the plaintiff was performing and on whether the same type of work was performed by employees of the defendant.

The Court addressed two questions. The first was whether the Court of Appeals had been mistaken in directing the entry of judgment for the defendant without giving the plaintiff an opportunity to introduce further evidence. The Court reversed the Court of Appeals on this point. The second question was whether the plaintiff was entitled to a jury trial on remand. In a decision rendered after the Court of Appeals decision in *Byrd,* the South Carolina Supreme Court had held in Adams v. Davison-Paxon Co., 230 S.C. 532, 96 S.E.2d 566 (1957), that the "statutory-employee" question should be resolved by the judge and not the jury. The issue was the effect of this decision in a federal diversity action.

Justice Brennan's opinion for the Court on this issue was divided into three parts. In the first he said:

"It was decided in *Erie* that the federal courts in diversity cases must respect the definition of state-created rights and obligations by the state courts. We must, therefore, first examine the rule in *Adams v. Davison-Paxon Co.* to determine whether it is bound up with these rights and obligations in such a way that its application in the federal court is required.

". . . The South Carolina Supreme Court states no reasons in *Adams v. Davison-Paxon Co.* why, although the jury decides all other factual issues raised by the cause of action and defenses, the jury is displaced as to the factual issue raised [in this case.] A state may, of course, distribute the functions of its judicial machinery as it sees fit. . . . The conclusion is inescapable that the *Adams* holding is grounded in the practical consideration that the question had theretofore come before the South Carolina courts from the Industrial Commission and the courts had become accustomed to deciding the factual issue . . . without the aid of juries. We find nothing to suggest that this rule was announced as an integral part of the special relationship created by the statute. Thus the requirement appears to be merely a form and mode of enforcing the immunity, Guaranty Trust Co. v. York, 326 U.S. 99, 108 (1945), and not a rule intended to be bound up with the definition of the rights and obligations of the parties. The situation is therefore not analogous to that in Dice v. Akron, C & Y. R. Co., 342 U.S. 359 (1952),[g] where this Court held that the right to trial by jury is so substantial a part of the cause of action created by the Federal Employers' Liability Act that the Ohio courts could not apply, in an action under that statute, the Ohio rule that the question of fraudulent release was for determination by a judge rather than by a jury."

In part two of his opinion, Justice Brennan turned to a different inquiry:

"But cases following *Erie* have evinced a broader policy to the effect that the federal courts should conform as near as

[g] See page 252, supra. [Footnote by eds.]

may be—in the absence of other considerations—to state rules even of form and mode where the state rules may bear substantially on the question whether the litigation would come out one way in the federal court and another way in the state court if the federal court failed to apply a particular local rule. E.g., *Guaranty Trust v. York,* supra. Concededly the nature of the tribunal which tries issues may be important in the enforcement of the parcel of rights making up a cause of action or defense, and bear significantly upon achievement of uniform enforcement of the right. It may well be that in the instant personal-injury case the outcome would be substantially affected by whether the issue . . . is decided by a judge or a jury. Therefore, were 'outcome' the only consideration, a strong case might appear for saying that the federal court should follow the state practice.

"But there are affirmative countervailing considerations at work here. The federal system is an independent system for administering justice to litigants who properly invoke its jurisdiction. An essential characteristic of that system is the manner in which, in civil common-law actions, it distributed trial functions between judge and jury and, under the influence—if not the command[10]—of the seventh amendment, assigns the decisions of disputed questions of fact to the jury. The policy of uniform enforcement of state-created rights and obligations, see, e.g., *Guaranty Trust v. York,* supra, cannot in every case exact compliance with a state rule—not bound up with rights and obligations—which disrupts the federal system of allocating functions between judge and jury. . . ."

At this point, Justice Brennan discussed the "strong policy against allowing state rules to disrupt the judge-jury relationship in the federal courts," concluding that state law "could not disrupt or alter the essential character or function of a federal court." He then moved to the third part of his analysis:

"We have discussed the problem upon the assumption that the outcome of the litigation may be substantially affected by whether the issue of immunity is decided by a judge or a jury. But clearly there is not present here the certainty that a different result would follow, or even the strong possibility that this would be the case. There are factors present here which might reduce that possibility. The trial judge in the federal system has powers denied the judges of many states to comment on the weight of evidence and credibility of witnesses, and discretion to grant a new trial if the verdict appears . . . to be against the weight of the evidence. We do not think the

---

[10] "Our conclusion makes unnecessary the consideration of—and we intimate no view upon—the constitutional question whether the right of jury trial protected in the federal courts by the seventh amendment embraces the factual issue of statutory immunity when asserted, as here, as an affirmative defense in a common-law negligence action."

likelihood of a different result is so strong as to require the federal practice of jury determination of disputed factual issues to yield to the state rule in the interest of uniformity of outcome. . . ."

Justice Whittaker dissented on the ground that the "outcome" formula of *Guaranty Trust* required the federal court to follow the South Carolina practice. Justices Frankfurter and Harlan also dissented, but they did not reach the *Erie* question.

HANNA v. PLUMER

Supreme Court of the United States, 1965.
380 U.S. 460.

MR. CHIEF JUSTICE WARREN delivered the opinion of the Court.

The question to be decided is whether, in a civil action where the jurisdiction of the United States district court is based upon diversity of citizenship between the parties, service of process shall be made in the manner prescribed by state law or that set forth in Rule 4(d)(1) of the Federal Rules of Civil Procedure.

On February 6, 1963, petitioner, a citizen of Ohio, filed her complaint in the District Court for the District of Massachusetts, claiming damages in excess of $10,000 for personal injuries resulting from an automobile accident in South Carolina, allegedly caused by the negligence of one Louise Plumer Osgood, a Massachusetts citizen deceased at the time of the filing of the complaint. Respondent, Mrs. Osgood's executor and also a Massachusetts citizen, was named as defendant. On February 8, service was made by leaving copies of the summons and the complaint with respondent's wife at his residence, concededly in compliance with Rule 4(d)(1), which provides:

"The summons and complaint shall be served together. The plaintiff shall furnish the person making service with such copies as are necessary. Service shall be made as follows:

"(1) Upon an individual other than an infant or an incompetent person, by delivering a copy of the summons and of the complaint to him personally or by leaving copies thereof at his dwelling house or usual place of abode with some person of suitable age and discretion then residing therein. . . ."

Respondent filed his answer on February 26, alleging, inter alia, that the action could not be maintained because it had been brought "contrary to and in violation of the provisions of Massachusetts General Laws Chapter 197, Section 9." That section provides:

"Except as provided in this chapter, an executor or administrator shall not be held to answer to an action by a creditor of the deceased which is not commenced within one year from the time of his giving bond for the performance of his trust, or to such an action which is commenced within said year unless before the expiration thereof the writ in such action has been served by delivery in hand upon such executor or administrator or service thereof accepted by him or a notice stating the name of the estate, the name and address of the creditor, the amount of the claim and the court in which the action has been brought has been filed in the proper registry of probate. . . ."

On October 17, 1963, the District Court granted respondent's motion for summary judgment, citing Ragan v. Merchants Transfer Co., 337 U.S. 530 (1949), and Guaranty Trust Co. v. York, 326 U.S 99 (1945), in support of its conclusion that the adequacy of the service was to be measured by § 9, with which, the court held, petitioner had not complied. On appeal, petitioner admitted noncompliance with § 9, but argued that Rule 4(d)(1) defines the method by which service of process is to be effected in diversity actions. The Court of Appeals for the First Circuit, finding that "[r]elatively recent amendments [to § 9] evince a clear legislative purpose to require personal notification within the year,"[1] concluded that the conflict of state and federal rules was over "a substantive rather than a procedural matter," and unanimously affirmed. Because of the threat to the goal of uniformity of federal procedure posed by the decision below,[2] we granted certiorari.

We conclude that the adoption of Rule 4(d)(1), designed to control service of process in diversity actions,[3] neither exceeded the congressional mandate embodied in the Rules Enabling Act nor transgressd constitutional bounds, and that the Rule is therefore the standard against which the District Court should have measured the adequacy of the service. Accordingly, we reverse the decision of the Court of Appeals.

The Rules Enabling Act, 28 U.S.C. § 2702, provides, in pertinent part:

[1] Section 9 is in part a statute of limitations, providing that an executor need not "answer to an action . . . which is not commenced within one year from the time of his giving bond. . . ." This part of the statute, the purpose of which is to speed the settlement of estates, is not involved in this case, since the action clearly was timely commenced. (Respondent filed bond on March 1, 1962; the complaint was filed February 6, 1963; and the service—the propriety of which is in dispute—was made on February 8, 1963.)

Section 9 also provides for the manner of service. Generally, service of process must be made by "delivery in hand," although there are two alternatives: acceptance of service by the executor, or filing of a notice of claim, the components of which are set out in the statute, in the appropriate probate court. The purpose of this part of the statute, which is involved here, is, as the court below noted, to insure that executors will receive actual notice of claims. Actual notice is of course also the goal of Rule 4(d)(1); however, the federal rule reflects a determination that this goal can be achieved by a method less cumbersome than that prescribed in § 9. In this case the goal seems to have been achieved; although the affidavit filed by respondent in the District Court asserts that he had not been served in hand nor had he accepted service, it does not allege lack of actual notice.

[2] There are a number of state service requirements which would not necessarily be satisfied by compliance with Rule 4(d)(1). [Citations omitted.]

[3] "These rules govern the procedure in the United States district court in all suits of a civil nature whether cognizable as cases at law or in equity, with the exceptions stated in Rule 81. . . ." Fed. Rules Civ. Proc. 1.

This case does not come within any of the exceptions noted in Rule 81.

"The Supreme Court shall have the power to prescribe, by general rules, the forms of process, writs, pleadings, and motions, and the practice and procedure of the district courts of the United States in civil actions.

"Such rules shall not abridge, enlarge or modify any substantive right and shall preserve the right of trial by jury. . . ."

Under the cases construing the scope of the Enabling Act, Rule 4(d)(1) clearly passes muster. Prescribing the manner in which a defendant is to be notified that a suit has been instituted against him, it relates to the "practice and procedure of the district courts."

"The test must be whether a rule really regulates procedure,— the judicial process for enforcing rights and duties recognized by substantive law and for justly administering remedy and redress for disregard or infraction of them." Sibbach v. Wilson & Co., 312 U.S. 1, 14 (1941).

In Mississippi Pub. Corp. v. Murphree, 326 U.S. 438 (1946), this Court upheld Rule 4(f), which permits service of a summons anywhere within the state (and not merely the district) in which a district court sits:

"We think that Rule 4(f) is in harmony with the Enabling Act. . . . Undoubtedly most alterations of the rules of practice and procedure may and often do affect the rights of litigants. Congress' prohibition of any alteration of substantive rights of litigants was obviously not addressed to such incidental effects as necessarily attend the adoption of the prescribed new rules of procedure upon the rights of litigants who, agreeably to rules of practice and procedure, have been brought before a court authorized to determine their rights. Sibbach v. Wilson & Co., 312 U.S. 1, 11–14 (1941). The fact that the application of Rule 4(f) will operate to subject petitioner's rights to adjudication by the District Court for Northern Mississippi will undoubtedly affect those rights. But it does not operate to abridge, enlarge or modify the rules of decision by which that court will adjudicate its rights."

Thus were there no conflicting state procedure, Rule 4(d)(1) would clearly control. However, respondent, focusing on the contrary Massachusetts rule, calls to the Court's attention another line of cases, a line which—like the Federal Rules—had its birth in 1938. Erie R. Co. v. Tompkins, 304 U.S. 64 (1938), overruling Swift v. Tyson, 41 U.S. (16 Pet.) 1 (1842), held that federal courts sitting in diversity cases, when deciding questions of "substantive" law, are bound by state court decisions as well as state statutes. The broad command of *Erie* was therefore identical to that of the Enabling Act: federal courts are to apply state substantive law and federal procedural law. However, as subsequent cases sharpened the distinction between substance and procedure, the line of cases following *Erie* diverged markedly from the line construing the Enabling Act. Guaranty Trust Co. v. York, 326 U.S. 99 (1945), made it clear that *Erie*-type problems were not to be solved by reference to any traditional or common-sense substance-procedure distinction:

> "And so the question is not whether a statute of limitations is deemed a matter of 'procedure' in some sense. The question is . . . does it significantly affect the result of a litigation for a federal court to disregard a law of a state that would be controlling in an action upon the same claim by the same parties in a state court?" 326 U.S. at 109.

Respondent, by placing primary reliance on *York* and *Ragan* suggests that the *Erie* doctrine acts as a check on the Federal Rules of Civil Procedure, that despite the clear command of Rule 4(d)(1), *Erie* and its progeny demand the application of the Massachusetts rule. Reduced to essentials, the argument is: (1) *Erie,* as refined in *York,* demands that federal courts apply state law whenever application of federal law in its stead will alter the outcome of the case. (2) In this case, a determination that the Massachusetts service requirements obtain will result in immediate victory for respondent. If, on the other hand, it should be held that Rule 4(d)(1) is applicable, the litigation will continue, with possible victory for petitioner. (3) Therefore, *Erie* demands application of the Massachusetts rule. The syllogism possesses an appealing simplicity, but is for several reasons invalid.

In the first place, it is doubtful that, even if there were no federal rule making it clear that in-hand service is not required in diversity actions, the *Erie* rule would have obligated the District Court to follow the Massachusetts procedure. "Outcome-determination" analysis was never intended to serve as a talisman. Byrd v. Blue Ridge Cooperative, 356 U.S. 525, 537 (1958). Indeed, the message of *York* itself is that choices between state and federal law are to be made not by application of any automatic "litmus paper" criterion, but rather by reference to the policies underlying the *Erie* rule. *Guaranty Trust Co. v. York,* supra, at 108–12.

The *Erie* rule is rooted in part in a realization that it would be unfair for the character or result of a litigation materially to differ because the suit had been brought in a federal court.

> "Diversity of citizenship jurisdiction was conferred in order to prevent apprehended discrimination in state courts against those not citizens of the state. *Swift v. Tyson* introduced grave discrimination by non-citizens against citizens. It made rights enjoyed under the unwritten 'general law' vary according to whether enforcement was sought in the state or in the federal court; and the privilege of selecting the court in which the right should be determined was conferred upon the non-citizen. Thus, the doctrine rendered impossible equal protection of the law." *Erie R. Co. v. Tompkins,* supra, at 74–75.

The decision was also in part a reaction to the practice of "forum-shopping" which had grown up in response to the rule of *Swift v. Tyson.* That the *York* test was an attempt to effectuate these policies is demonstrated by the fact that the opinion framed the inquiry in terms of "substantial" variations between state and federal litigation. Not only are nonsubstantial, or trivial, variations not likely to raise the sort of equal protection problems which troubled the Court in *Erie*; they are also unlikely to influence the choice of a forum. The "outcome-determination" test therefore cannot be read without reference to the twin aims of the *Erie* rule: discouragement of forum-shopping and avoidance of inequitable administration of the laws.[9]

The difference between the conclusion that the Massachusetts rule is applicable, and the conclusion that it is not, is of course at this point "outcome-determinative" in the sense that if we hold the state rule to apply, respondent prevails, whereas if we hold that Rule 4(d)(1) governs, the litigation will continue. But in this sense *every* procedural variation is "outcome-determinative." For example, having brought suit in a federal court, a plaintiff cannot then insist on the right to file subsequent pleadings in accord with the time limits applicable in the state courts, even though enforcement of the federal timetable will, if he continues to insist that he must meet only the state time limit, result in determination of the controversy against him. So it is here. Though choice of the federal or state rule will at this point have a marked effect upon the outcome of the litigation, the difference between the two rules would be of scant, if any, relevance to the choice of a forum. Petitioner, in choosing her forum, was not presented with a situation where application of the state rule would wholly bar recovery;[10] rather, adherence to the state rule would have resulted only in altering the way in which process was served.[11] Moreover, it is difficult to argue that permitting service of defendant's wife to take the place of in-hand service of defendant himself alters the mode of enforcement of state-created rights in a fashion sufficiently "substantial" to raise the sort of equal protection problems to which the *Erie* opinion alluded.

[9] The Court of Appeals seemed to frame the inquiry in terms of how "important" § 9 is to the state. In support of its suggestion that § 9 serves some interest the state regards as vital to its citizens, the court noted that something like § 9 has been on the books in Massachusetts a long time, that § 9 has been amended a number of times, and that § 9 is designed to make sure that executors receive actual notice. See note 1, supra. The apparent lack of relation among these three observations is not surprising, because it is not clear to what sort of question the Court of Appeals was addressing itself. One cannot meaningfully ask how important something is without first asking "important for what purpose?" *Erie* and its progeny make clear that when a federal court sitting in a diversity case is faced with a question of whether or not to apply state law, the importance of a state rule is indeed relevant, but only in the context of asking whether application of the rule would make so important a difference to the character or result of the litigation that failure to enforce it would unfairly discriminate against citizens of the forum state, or whether application of the rule would have so important an effect upon the fortunes of one or both of the litigants that failure to enforce it would be likely to cause a plaintiff to choose the federal court.

[10] Similarly, a federal court's refusal to enforce the New Jersey rule involved in Cohen v. Beneficial Loan Corp., 337 U.S. 541 (1949), requiring the posting of security by plaintiffs in stockholders' derivative actions, might well impel a stockholder to choose to bring suit in the federal, rather than the state, court.

[11] We cannot seriously entertain the thought that one suing an estate would be led to choose the federal court because of a belief that adherence to Rule 4(d)(1) is less likely to give the executor actual notice than § 9, and therefore more likely to produce a default judgment. Rule 4(d)(1) is well designed to give actual notice, as it did in this case. See note 1, supra.

There is, however, a more fundamental flaw in respondent's syllogism: the incorrect assumption that the rule of *Erie R. Co. v. Tompkins* constitutes the appropriate test of the validity and therefore the applicability of a Federal Rule of Civil Procedure. The *Erie* rule has never been invoked to void a federal rule. It is true that there have been cases where this Court has held applicable a state rule in the face of an argument that the situation was governed by one of the Federal Rules. But the holding of each such case was not that *Erie* commanded displacement of a federal rule by an inconsistent state rule, but rather that the scope of the federal rule was not as broad as the losing party urged, and therefore, there being no federal rule which covered the point in dispute, *Erie* commanded the enforcement of state law.

> "Respondent contends, in the first place, that the charge was correct because of the fact that Rule 8(c) of the Rules of Civil Procedure makes contributory negligence an affirmative defense. We do not agree. Rule 8(c) covers only the manner of pleading. The question of the burden of establishing contributory negligence is a question of local law which federal courts in diversity of citizenship cases must apply." Palmer v. Hoffman, 318 U.S. 109, 117 (1943).

(Here, of course, the clash is unavoidable; Rule 4(d)(1) says—implicitly, but with unmistakable clarity—that in-hand service is not required in federal courts.) At the same time, in cases adjudicating the validity of federal rules, we have not applied the *York* rule or other refinements of *Erie*, but have to this day continued to decide questions concerning the scope of the Enabling Act and the constitutionality of specific federal rules in light of the distinction set forth in *Sibbach*. E.g., Schlagenhauf v. Holder, 379 U.S. 104 (1964).

Nor has the development of two separate lines of cases been inadvertent. The line between "substance" and "procedure" shifts as the legal context changes. "Each implies different variables depending upon the particular problem for which it is used." *Guaranty Trust Co. v. York,* supra, at 108. It is true that both the Enabling Act and the *Erie* rule say, roughly, that federal courts are to apply state "substantive" law and federal "procedural" law, but from that it need not follow that the tests are identical. For they were designed to control very different sorts of decisions. When a situation is covered by one of the federal rules, the question facing the court is a far cry from the typical, relatively unguided *Erie* choice: the court has been instructed to apply the federal rule, and can refuse to do so only if the Advisory Committee, this Court, and Congress erred in their prima facie judgment that the rule in question transgresses neither the terms of the Enabling Act nor constitutional restrictions.

We are reminded by the *Erie* opinion that neither Congress nor the federal courts can, under the guise of formulating rules of decision for federal courts, fashion rules which are not supported by a grant of federal authority contained in article I or some other section of the Constitution; in such areas state law must govern because there can be no other law. But the opinion in *Erie*, which involved no federal rule and dealt with a question which was "substantive" in every traditional sense (whether the railroad owed a duty of care to Tompkins as a trespasser or a licensee), surely neither said nor implied that measures like Rule 4(d)(1) are unconstitutional. For the constitutional provision for a federal court system (augmented by the necessary and proper clause) carries with it congressional power to make rules governing the practice and pleading in those courts, which in turn includes a power to regulate matters which, though falling within the uncertain area between substance and procedure, are rationally capable of classification as either. Cf. M'Culloch v. Maryland, 17 U.S. (4 Wheat.) 316, 421 (1819). Neither *York* nor the cases following it ever suggested that the rule there laid down for coping with situations where no federal rule applies is coextensive with the limitation on Congress to which *Erie* had adverted. Although this Court has never before been confronted with a case where the applicable federal rule is in direct collision with the law of the relevant state,[15] courts of appeals faced with such clashes have rightly discerned the implications of our decisions.

> "One of the shaping purposes of the Federal Rules is to bring about uniformity in the federal courts by getting away from local rules. This is especially true of matters which relate to the administration of legal proceedings, an area in which federal courts have traditionally exerted strong inherent power, completely aside from the powers Congress expressly conferred in the rules. The purpose of the *Erie* doctrine, even as extended in *York* and *Ragan*, was never to bottle up federal courts with 'outcome-determinative' and 'integral-relations' stoppers—when there are 'affirmative countervailing [federal] considerations' and when there is a Congressional mandate (the rules) supported by constitutional authority." Lumbermen's Mutual Casualty Co. v. Wright, 322 F.2d 759, 764 (5th Cir. 1963).

Erie and its offspring cast no doubt on the long-recognized power of Congress to prescribe housekeeping rules for federal courts even though some of those rules will inevitably differ from comparable state rules. "When, because the plaintiff happens to be a non-resident, such a right is enforceable in a federal as well as in a state court, the forms and mode of enforcing the right may at times, naturally enough, vary because the two judicial systems are not identic." *Guaranty Trust Co. v. York*, supra, at 108. Thus, though a court, in measuring a federal rule against the standards contained in the Enabling Act and the Constitution, need not wholly blind itself to the degree to which the rule makes the character and result of the federal litigation stray from the course it would follow in state courts, *Sibbach v. Wilson & Co.*,

---

[15] In *Sibbach v. Wilson & Co.*, supra, the law of the forum state (Illinois) forbade the sort of order authorized by Rule 35. However, *Sibbach* was decided before Klaxon Co. v. Stentor Co., 313 U.S. 487 (1941), and the *Sibbach* opinion makes clear that the Court was proceeding on the assumption that if the law of any state was relevant, it was the law of the state where the tort occurred (Indiana), which, like Rule 35, made provision for such orders.

supra, at 13–14, it cannot be forgotten that the *Erie* rule, and the guidelines suggested in *York*, were created to serve another purpose altogether. To hold that a Federal Rule of Civil Procedure must cease to function whenever it alters the mode of enforcing state-created rights would be to disembowel either the Constitution's grant of power over federal procedure or Congress' attempt to exercise that power in the Enabling Act. Rule 4(d)(1) is valid and controls the instant case.

Reversed.

MR. JUSTICE BLACK concurs in the result.

MR. JUSTICE HARLAN, concurring.

It is unquestionably true that up to now *Erie* and the cases following it have not succeeded in articulating a workable doctrine governing choice of law in diversity actions. I respect the Court's effort to clarify the situation in today's opinion. However, in doing so I think it has misconceived the constitutional premises of *Erie* and has failed to deal adequately with those past decisions upon which the courts below relied.

Erie was something more than an opinion which worried about "forum-shopping and avoidance of inequitable administration of the laws," although to be sure these were important elements of the decision. I have always regarded that decision as one of the modern cornerstones of our federalism, expressing policies that profoundly touch the allocation of judicial power between the state and federal systems. *Erie* recognized that there should not be two conflicting systems of law controlling the primary activity of citizens, for such alternative governing authority must necessarily give rise to a debilitating uncertainty in the planning of everyday affairs.[1] And it recognized that the scheme of our Constitution envisions an allocation of law-making functions between state and federal legislative processes which is undercut if the federal judiciary can make substantive law affecting state affairs beyond the bounds of congressional legislative powers in this regard. Thus, in diversity cases *Erie* commands that it be the state law governing primary private activity which prevails.

The shorthand formulations which have appeared in some past decisions are prone to carry untoward results that frequently arise from oversimplification. The Court is quite right in stating that the "outcome-determinative" test of *Guaranty Trust Co. v. York*, if taken literally proves too much, for any rule, no matter how clearly "procedural," can affect the outcome of litigation if it is not obeyed. In turning from the "outcome" test of *York* back to the unadorned forum-shopping rationale of *Erie*, however, the Court falls prey to like oversimplification, for a simple forum-shopping rule also proves too much; litigants often choose a federal forum merely to obtain what they consider the advantages of the Federal Rules of Civil Procedure or to try their cases before a supposedly more favorable judge. To my mind the proper line of approach in determining whether to apply a state or a federal rule,

---

[1] Since the rules involved in the present case are parallel rather than conflicting, this first rationale does not come into play here.

whether "substantive" or "procedural," is to stay close to basic principles by inquiring if the choice of rule would substantially affect those primary decisions respecting human conduct which our constitutional system leaves to state regulation.[2] If so, *Erie* and the Constitution require that the state rule prevail, even in the face of a conflicting federal rule.

The Court weakens, if indeed it does not submerge, this basic principle by finding, in effect, a grant of substantive legislative power in the constitutional provision for a federal court system (compare Swift v. Tyson, 41 U.S. (16 Pet.) 1 (1842)), and through it, setting up the federal rules as a body of law inviolate.

> "[T]he constitutional provision for a federal court system . . . carries with it congressional power . . . to regulate matters which, though falling within the uncertain area between substance and procedure, *are rationally capable of classification as either.*" (Emphasis supplied.)

So long as a reasonable man could characterize any duly adopted federal rule as "procedural," the Court, unless I misapprehend what is said, would have it apply no matter how seriously it frustrated a state's substantive regulation of the primary conduct and affairs of its citizens. Since the members of the Advisory Committee, the Judicial Conference, and this Court who formulated the federal rules are presumably reasonable men, it follows that the integrity of the federal rules is absolute. Whereas the unadulterated outcome and forum-shopping tests may err too far toward honoring state rules, I submit that the Court's "arguably procedural, ergo constitutional" test moves too fast and far in the other direction.

The courts below relied upon this Court's decisions in Ragan v. Merchants Transfer Co., 337 U.S. 530 (1949), and Cohen v. Beneficial Loan Corp., 337 U.S. 541 (1949). Those cases deserve more attention than this Court has given them, particularly *Ragan* which, if still good law, would in my opinion call for affirmance of the result reached by the Court of Appeals. Further, a discussion of these two cases will serve to illuminate the "diversity" thesis I am advocating.

In *Ragan* a Kansas statute of limitations provided that an action was deemed commenced when service was made on the defendant. Despite Federal Rule 3 which provides that an action commences with the filing of the complaint, the Court held that for purposes of the Kansas statute of limitations a diversity tort action commenced only when service was made upon the defendant. The effect of this holding was that although the plaintiff has filed his federal complaint within the state period of limitations, his action was barred because the federal marshal did not serve a summons on the defendant until after the limitations period had run. I think that the decision was wrong. At

---

[2] Byrd v. Blue Ridge Coop., Inc., 356 U.S. 525, 536–40 (1958), indicated that state procedures would apply if the state had manifested a particularly strong interest in their employment. Compare Dice v. Akron, C. & Y. R. Co., 342 U.S. 359 (1952). However, this approach may not be of constitutional proportions.

most, application of the federal rule would have meant that potential Kansas tort defendants would have to defer for a few days the satisfaction of knowing that they had not been sued within the limitations period. The choice of the federal rule would have had no effect on the primary stages of private activity from which torts arise, and only the most minimal effect on behavior following the commission of the tort. In such circumstances the interest of the federal system in proceeding under its own rules should have prevailed.

Cohen v. Beneficial Loan Corp. held that a federal diversity court must apply a state statute requiring a small stockholder in a stockholder derivative suit to post a bond securing payment of defense costs as a condition to prosecuting an action. Such a statute is not "outcome-determinative"; the plaintiff can win with or without it. The Court now rationalizes the case on the ground that the statute might affect the plaintiff's choice of forum (n.10), but as has been pointed out, a simple forum-shopping test proves too much. The proper view of *Cohen* is, in my opinion, that the statute was meant to inhibit small stockholders from instituting "strike suits," and thus it was designed and could be expected to have a substantial impact on private primary activity. Anyone who was at the trial bar during the period when *Cohen* arose can appreciate the strong state policy reflected in the statute.[a] I think it wholly legitimate to view Federal Rule 23 as not purporting to deal with the problem. But even had the Federal Rules purported to do so, and in so doing provided a substantially less effective deterrent to strike suits, I think the state rule should still have prevailed. That is where I believe the Court's view differs from mine; for the Court attributes such overriding force to the federal rules that it is hard to think of a case where a conflicting state rule would be allowed to operate, even though the state rule reflected policy considerations which, under *Erie*, would lie within the realm of state legislative authority.

It remains to apply what has been said to the present case. The Massachusetts rule provides that an executor need not answer suits unless in-hand service was made upon him or notice of the action was filed in the proper registry of probate within one year of his giving bond. The evident intent of this statute is to permit an executor to distribute the estate which he is administering without fear that further liabilities may be outstanding for which he could be held personally liable. If the Federal District Court in Massachusetts applies Rule 4(d)(1) of the Federal Rules of Civil Procedure instead of the Massachusetts service rule, what effect would that have on the speed and assurance with which estates are distributed? As I see it, the effect would not be substantial. It would mean simply that an executor would have to check at his own house or the federal courthouse as well as the registry of probate before he could distribute the estate with impunity. As this does not seem enough to give rise to any real

[a] Justice Harlan, then a practicing lawyer in New York, argued *Cohen* in the Supreme Court on behalf of the corporate defendant. [Footnote by eds.]

impingement on the vitality of the state policy which the Massachusetts rule is intended to serve, I concur in the judgment of the Court.

NOTES ON SUBSTANCE AND PROCEDURE
AFTER *HANNA*

1. **Questions and Comments on *Hanna*.** Chief Justice Warren's opinion in *Hanna* can be read as dealing with two distinct issues. The first is what the federal courts should do when a rule of federal civil procedure conflicts with state law. The question then, Warren says, is whether the federal rule is "rationally capable of classification" as procedure.[a] If so, the federal rule is valid and must be applied.

Does the Court mean to say that a federal rule of procedure can override state substantive policies? Suppose, if it is still possible, that a state enacted a substantive law that fell within its exclusive constitutional prerogative. Congress could not pass a contrary substantive law. Could it nonetheless undermine the state law by passing a contrary rule of procedure? Does Warren mean to say that it could? Or does he assume that this situation could not arise today? Even if the subject matter was within the reach of the federal legislative power, should Congress be taken to have exercised its power to displace a state substantive law by approving a rule of federal procedure? How does the Rules Enabling Act bear on this question?

The second issue to which *Hanna* speaks is what should be done in a situation where there is no federal rule of civil procedure on the subject. Warren's discussion of the "twin aims" of *Erie* in footnote 9 and its accompanying text suggests that the test for determining whether to follow state law in such a situation is twofold. State law is to be followed if

> "the rule would make so important a difference to the character of the litigation that failure to enforce it would unfairly discriminate against citizens of the forum state, or . . . application of the rule would have so important an affect upon the fortunes of one or both of the litigants that failure to enforce it would be likely to cause a plaintiff to choose a federal court."

Is this a meaningful inquiry? Is Harlan correct that this inquiry, like the "outcome" test, "proves too much"?

How should the Court in *Hanna* have approached these two issues? Could the rules be this simple: (i) If there is an applicable federal rule of civil procedure, follow it; (ii) If there is not, follow state law? These rules of course would not work in cases where there are federal

----

[a] This formulation and the citation to *M'Culloch*, see page 512, supra, is reminiscent of the Court's modern approach to questions concerning the scope of Congress' commerce clause power. For a recent application of this standard, see Burlington Northern R.R. Co. v. Woods, 480 U.S. 1 (1987). For a detailed criticism of the result in *Burlington*, see Ralph Whitten, *Erie* and the Federal Rules: A Review and Reappraisal After *Burlington Northern Railroad v. Woods*, 21 Creighton L.Rev. 1 (1987).

substantive policies that must be taken into account. But would they work in diversity cases where all of the applicable substantive law is derived from state sources? Consider these questions further in connection with the following cases.

Consider also a third problem, not mentioned in *Hanna,* namely the attitude the federal courts should bring to interpretation of the federal rules. Should the federal rules be narrowly interpreted in order to avoid conflicts with state law? Or is the desirability of a uniform system of federal procedure—applicable to diversity and federal question cases alike—so strong that the possibility of conflict with state law should be ignored? If so, can any guidelines to interpretation be given?

2. *Walker v. Armco Steel Corp.* The Court revisited the *Ragan* issue in Walker v. Armco Steel Corp., 446 U.S. 740 (1980). Walker, a carpenter, injured his eye when a nail he was hammering shattered. He filed a federal diversity suit against the manufacturer of the nail. The injury occurred on August 22, 1975. The complaint was filed on August 19, 1977.[b] The record is ambiguous as to whether the summons was issued on August 19 or August 20, but in any event it was not delivered to the marshall for service until December 1, 1977.[c] It was served on the defendant the day the marshall received it.

The applicable Oklahoma statute of limitations was two years. Oklahoma law provided that an action was "commenced" for purposes of tolling the statute of limitations by service of the summons, or in the alternative by filing the complaint if the summons was served within 60 days. The plaintiff conceded that the Oklahoma law was not followed, but argued in response to the defendant's motion to dismiss that Rule 3 should govern in federal court. The District Court dismissed the complaint, citing *Ragan,* and the Court of Appeals affirmed. The Supreme Court granted certiorari and affirmed.

Justice Marshall wrote for a unanimous Court. After reviewing *Erie, Guaranty Trust, Ragan,* and *Hanna,* Marshall noted that "the instant action is barred by the statute of limitations unless *Ragan* is no longer good law." He continued:

> "This Court in *Hanna* distinguished *Ragan* rather than overruled it, and for good reason. Application of the *Hanna* analysis is premised on a 'direct collision' between the federal rule and the state law. In *Hanna* itself the 'clash' between Rule 4(d)(1) and the state in-hand service requirement was 'unavoidable.' The first question must therefore be whether the scope of the federal rule in fact is sufficiently broad to control the issue before the Court. It is only if that question is answered affirmatively that the *Hanna* analysis applies.[9]

[b] Recall the provisions of Rule 3: "A civil action is commenced by filing a complaint with the court."

[c] Counsel for the plaintiff stated in oral argument before the Supreme Court that the summons was found "in an unmarked folder in the filing cabinet" in counsel's office about 90 days after the complaint was filed. The record did not show how it got there.

[9] "This is not to suggest that the Federal Rules of Civil Procedure are to be narrowly

". . . There is no indication that [Rule 3] was intended to toll a state statute of limitations, much less that it purported to displace state tolling rules for purposes of state statutes of limitations. In our view, in diversity actions[11] Rule 3 governs the date from which various timing requirements of the federal rules begin to run, but does not affect state statutes of limitations.

"In contrast to Rule 3, the Oklahoma statute is a statement of a substantive decision by that state that actual service on, and accordingly actual notice by, the defendant is an integral part of the several policies served by the statute of limitations. The statute of limitations establishes a deadline after which the defendant may legitimately have peace of mind; it also recognizes that after a certain period of time it is unfair to require the defendant to attempt to piece together his defense to an old claim. A requirement of actual service promotes both of those functions of the statute. It is these policy aspects which make the service requirement an 'integral' part of the statute of limitations both in this case and in *Ragan*. As such, the service rule must be considered part and parcel of the statute of limitations. Rule 3 does not replace such policy determinations found in state law. Rule 3 and [the Oklahoma law] can exist side-by-side, therefore, each controlling its own intended sphere of coverage without conflict.

"Since there is no direct conflict between the federal rule and the state law, the *Hanna* analysis does not apply.[14] Instead, the policies behind *Erie* and *Ragan* control the issue whether, in the absence of a federal rule directly on point, state service requirements which are an integral part of the state statute of limitations should control in an action based on state law which is filed in federal court under diversity jurisdiction. The reasons for the application of such a state service requirement in a diversity action in the absence of a conflicting federal rule are well explained in *Erie* and *Ragan,* and need not be repeated here. It is sufficient to note that although in this case failure to apply the state service law might not create any problem of forum shopping,[15] the result would be an

construed in order to avoid a 'direct collision' with state law. The Federal Rules should be given their plain meaning. If a direct collision with state law arises from that plain meaning, then the analysis developed in *Hanna v. Plumer* applies."

[11] "The Court suggested in *Ragan* that in suits to enforce rights under a federal statute Rule 3 means that the filing of the complaint tolls the applicable statute of limitations. We do not here address the role of Rule 3 as a tolling provision for a statute of limitations, whether set by federal law or borrowed from state law, if the cause of action is based on federal law."

[14] "Since we hold that Rule 3 does not apply, it is unnecessary for us to address the second question posed by the *Hanna* analysis: whether Rule 3, if applied, would be outside the scope of the Rules Enabling Act or beyond the power of Congress under the Constitution."

[15] "There is no indication that when petitioner filed his suit in federal court he had any reason to believe that he would be unable to comply with the service requirements of Oklahoma law or that he chose to sue in federal court in an attempt to avoid those service requirements."

'inequitable administration' of the law. Hanna v. Plumer, 380 U.S. 460, 468 (1965). There is simply no reason why, in the absence of a controlling federal rule, an action based on state law which concededly would be barred in the state courts by the statute of limitations should proceed through litigation to judgment in federal court solely because of the fortuity that there is diversity of citizenship between the litigants. The policies underlying diversity jurisdiction do not support such a distinction between state and federal plaintiffs, and *Erie* and its progeny do not permit it."

Does *Walker* clear up all the problems?

3. *Stewart Organization, Inc. v. Ricoh Corporation.* Stewart, an Alabama corporation, signed a dealership agreement with Ricoh to market its copier products. The agreement contained a "forum selection" clause which stated that any suit arising out of the contract could be filed only in a federal or state court located in Manhattan. Stewart brought a diversity action based on the contractual relationship in an Alabama federal court.[d] Ricoh moved to transfer the case to the Southern District of New York under 28 U.S.C. § 1404(a).[e] The basis for its motion was the forum selection clause in the contract.

The District Court denied the motion, reasoning that Alabama law applied and that an Alabama court would not enforce such a contractual provision. The 11th Circuit Court of Appeals reversed, holding that venue in a federal court was controlled by federal law and that the forum selection clause was enforceable as a matter of federal law. This judgment was sustained by a divided 11th Circuit sitting en banc. In Stewart Organization, Inc. v. Ricoh Corporation, ___ U.S. ___ (1988), the Supreme Court agreed that Alabama law did not apply, but remanded the case to the District Court so that it could "determine in the first instance the appropriate effect under federal law of the parties' forum selection clause . . . ."

Justice Marshall wrote the Court's opinion. Under the analytical structure of *Hanna,* the first question was whether § 1404(a) was "sufficiently broad to control the issue before the Court." If so, then the only remaining question was "whether the statute represents a valid exercise of Congress' authority under the Constitution."

On the first question, the Court held that the "flexible and individual analysis Congress prescribed in § 1404(a) . . . encompasses consideration of the parties' private expression of their venue preferences." Thus such matters as "the convenience of a Manhattan forum given the parties' expressed preference for that venue, and the fairness of transfer in light of the forum selection clause and the parties' relative bargaining power" should control the discretion of the district court in

---

[d] The complaint included claims based on state law and on federal antitrust law, but the Supreme Court analyzed the case as though only state-law claims were presented and diversity the only basis for federal jurisdiction.

[e] Section 1404(a) provides: "For the convenience of the parties and witnesses, in the interest of justice, a district court may transfer any civil action to any other district or division where it might have been brought."

considering the transfer motion.[f] The forum selection clause was not to be automatically enforced without considering the normal range of factors relevant to a motion to change venue. The Alabama policy against enforcement of such clauses was not dispositive because it conflicted with the "discretionary mode of operation" of the federal law. Having concluded that § 1404(a) was broad enough to apply to the present dispute, the Court had no difficulty with the second part of its analysis: "The constitutional authority of Congress to enact § 1404(a) is not subject to serious question."[g]

Justice Scalia dissented. He argued that § 1404(a) did not apply and that the federal courts could not, consistent with the "twin-aims" test of *Erie*, "fashion a judge-made rule to govern this issue of contract validity." He thought § 1404(a) inapplicable for three reasons. First, the text of the statute suggests that the district court's discretion should be directed to present and future factors governing the justice of a change of venue.[h] Section 1404(a) is not concerned, he argued, with retrospective factors such as the relative bargaining powers of the parties and the presence or absence of overreaching at the time the contract was made. Second, "§ 1404(a) was enacted against the background that issues of contract, including a contract's validity, are nearly always governed by state law. It is simply contrary to the practice of our system that such an issue should be wrenched from state control in absence of a clear conflict with federal law or explicit statutory provision." Justice Scalia continued:

> "Third, it has been common ground in this Court, since *Erie*, that when a federal procedural statute or rule of procedure is not on point, substantial uniformity of predictable outcome between federal and state courts in adjudicating claims should be striven for. This rests upon a perception of the constitutional and congressional plan underlying the creation of diversity and pendent jurisdiction in the lower federal courts, which should quite obviously be carried forward into our interpretation of ambiguous statutes relating to the exer-

[f] The Court added that the district court was also required to consider "the convenience of the witnesses and those public-interest factors of systemic integrity and fairness that, in addition to private concerns, come under the heading of 'the interest of justice.'"

[g] Justice Kennedy, joined by Justice O'Connor, concurred. He thought that forum selection clauses should be more generously received by the federal courts:

> "The federal judicial system has a strong interest in the correct resolution of these questions, not only to spare litigants unnecessary costs but also to relieve courts of time consuming pretrial motions. Courts should announce and encourage rules that support private parties who negotiate such clauses. Though

state policies should be weighed in the balance, the authority and prerogative of the federal courts to determine the issue, as Congress has directed by § 1404(a), should be exercised so that a valid forum selection clause is given controlling weight in all but the most exceptional cases."

[h] "Accordingly, the courts in applying § 1404(a) have examined a variety of factors, each of which pertains to facts that currently exist or will exist: e.g., the forum actually chosen by the plaintiff, the current convenience of the parties and witnesses, the current location of pertinent books and records, similar litigation pending elsewhere, current docket conditions, and familiarity of the potential courts with governing state law."

cise of that jurisdiction. We should assume, in other words, when it is fair to do so, that Congress is just as concerned as we have been to avoid significant differences between state and federal courts in adjudicating claims. Thus, in deciding whether a federal procedural statute or rule of procedure encompasses a particular issue, a broad reading that would create significant disuniformity between state and federal courts should be avoided if the text permits. [T]he interpretation given § 1404(a) by the Court today is neither plain nor the more natural meaning; at best, § 1404(a) is ambiguous. I would therefore construe it to avoid the significant encouragement in forum shopping that will inevitably be provided by the interpretation the Court adopts today."

Justice Scalia then observed that "[s]ince no federal statute or rule of procedure governs the validity of a forum-selection clause, the remaining issue is whether federal courts may fashion a judge-made rule to govern the question." He had no difficulty concluding that the answer was "no." He saw a significant forum shopping problem: in a state such as Alabama that disfavored forum selection clauses, nonresident defendants would be encouraged to remove actions filed in state court; in a state that encouraged such clauses, plaintiffs would try to avoid their effect by suing in federal court. He also thought a judge-made rule in this context would produce inequitable administration of the laws by turning the decision of an important question of law on the accident of diversity. "Nor," he concluded, "can or should courts ignore that issues of contract validity are traditionally matters governed by state law."

4. *Szantay v. Beech Aircraft Corp.* Szantay purchased a Beech Aircraft in Nebraska, flew it to Miami, Fla., and from there flew to Columbia, S.C. It was serviced in Columbia by the Dixie Aviation Co., a South Carolina corporation. Szantay and his passengers left for Chicago the following day, but the plane crashed en route in Tennessee. The personal representatives of all the victims were citizens of Illinois. They brought wrongful death actions against Dixie and Beech in the Eastern District of South Carolina. Jurisdiction was based on diversity. Beech was incorporated in Delaware and had its principal place of business in Kansas.

South Carolina had a "door closing" statute that prohibited the state courts from exercising jurisdiction over a suit brought by a nonresident against a foreign corporation on a cause of action arising in another state. Beech moved to dismiss on the ground that *Erie* and its progeny required the federal courthouse in South Carolina also to be closed to such a case. The District Court denied the motion to dismiss, and in Szantay v. Beech Aircraft Corp., 349 F.2d 60 (4th Cir. 1965), the Court of Appeals affirmed.

The court held that the "spirit" of *Erie, York,* and *Byrd* required the following analysis:

"1. If the state provision, whether legislatively adopted or judicially declared, is the substantive right or obligation at issue, it is constitutionally controlling.

"2. If the state provision is a procedure intimately bound up with the state right or obligation, it is likewise constitutionally controlling.

"3. If the state procedural provision is not intimately bound up with the right being enforced but its application would substantially affect the outcome of the litigation, the federal diversity court must still apply it unless there are affirmative countervailing federal considerations. This is not deemed a constitutional requirement but one dictated by comity."

Applying this analysis, the court found the first two questions easily resolved:

"[A]s the right asserted is one arising under the laws of Tennessee, it cannot be contended that the South Carolina rule is intimately bound up with that right. It follows from this that the constitutional compulsions of the *Erie* doctrine are not applicable here."

The court then turned to the third question. It was reduced to speculation as to the reasons for the South Carolina statute. There was no helpful legislative history, and there were no relevant state court decisions.[i] In any event, there was another side of the debate:

"The countervailing federal considerations, however, are explicit, and they are numerous. The most fundamental is that expressed in the constitutional extension of subject-matter jurisdiction to the federal courts in suits between citizens of different states. The purpose of this jurisdictional grant was to avoid discrimination against nonresidents. The South Carolina 'door-closing' statute permits its residents to sue foreign corporations on foreign causes of action yet denies this privilege to nonresidents. While such discrimination may not be unconstitutional, it is the role of diversity jurisdiction . . . to make certain that:

'[a] nonresident litigant in resorting to the federal diversity jurisdiction should obtain the same relief a resident litigant asserting the same cause of action would receive in the state courts.' Markham v. City of Newport News, 292 F.2d 711, 718 (4th Cir. 1961).

"A further federal consideration, likewise expressed in the Constitution itself, is that underlying the full faith and credit

---

[i] The court guessed that it could be akin to a local policy of forum non conveniens, or that it might have been designed to relieve docket congestion—though that was hardly a problem in 1870 when the statute was passed. Beech argued that it was de- signed to encourage foreign corporations to do business in South Carolina, though the court doubted this because of other provisions enacted at the same time that placed burdens on such corporations.

clause. That clause expresses a national interest 'looking toward maximum enforcement of the obligations or rights created or recognized by the statutes of sister states.' Hughes v. Fetter, 341 U.S. 609 (1951). While the South Carolina 'door-closing' statute may not directly violate the demands of this constitutional principle, it is contrary to its implicit policy in that it prevents enforcement of the Tennessee wrongful death action in the South Carolina courts.

"The plaintiffs' choice of a South Carolina forum was not frivolous. One of the defendants, Dixie, could be served only in that state. It is a federal policy to encourage efficient joinder in multi-party actions. . . . Furthermore, if the plaintiffs had brought suit against Beech alone in the federal forum where the accident occurred, the district judge there would have been free to transfer the case to a South Carolina district court pursuant to the federal doctrine of forum non conveniens, 28 U.S.C. § 1404(a), even though South Carolina law denies the plaintiffs access to state courts. Van Dusen v. Barrack, 376 U.S. 612 (1964).[j] . . .

"South Carolina has no policy against the particular plaintiffs, as Mississippi had against nonregistered foreign corporations in Woods v. Interstate Realty Co., 337 U.S. 535 (1949) . . . . The superficiality of the South Carolina policy is demonstrated in this case by the fact that the plaintiffs could have gained access to a South Carolina court by simply qualifying as administrators under South Carolina law.

"Therefore we hold that the conflict here between federal and state policies, if in fact one exists, is to be resolved in favor of the federal interest in providing a convenient forum for the adjudication of the plaintiffs' actions."

Did the court get the right answer? *Szantay* was decided after *Hanna.* If the "twin aims" approach of that case had been taken, would the answer have been the same? Was there "forum shopping" here?

5. *Marshall v. Mulrenin.* Mrs. Marshall fell and injured herself at a business establishment. She learned the identity of the owners by checking the certificate of ownership on file at the town hall, and filed a diversity action in a Massachusetts federal court against Mr. and Mrs. Kirk, the registered owners. After the Massachusetts statute of limitations had run, she discovered that the Kirks had sold the property several years before the accident to Mr. and Mrs. Mulrenin and that, through oversight, the certificate of ownership on file at the town hall had never been changed. She therefore sought to amend her complaint to substitute the Mulrenins for the Kirks as defendants. The problem was whether the statute of limitations had run against the Mulrenins.

---

[j] See page 362, supra. [Footnote by eds.]

Federal Rule 15(c) provides as follows:

"Whenever the claim or defense asserted in the amended pleading arose out of the conduct, transaction, or occurrence set forth or attempted to be set forth in the original pleading, the amendment relates back to the date of the original pleading. An amendment changing the party against whom a claim is asserted relates back if the foregoing provision is satisfied and, within the period provided by law for commencing the action against him, the party to be brought in by amendment (1) has received such notice of the institution of the action that he will not be prejudiced in maintaining his defense on the merits, and (2) knew or should have known that, but for a mistake concerning the identity of the proper party, the action would have been brought against him."

The District Court denied plaintiff's motion to amend because the provisions of Rule 15(c) were not satisfied. Plaintiff argued that the amendment was proper under Massachusetts law, which permitted such amendments as "may enable the plaintiff to sustain the action for the cause for which it was intended to be brought." The question on appeal was whether the "relation back" of the plaintiff's amendment was controlled by Rule 15(c) or by the more liberal provisions of Massachusetts law.

In Marshall v. Mulrenin, 508 F.2d 39 (1st Cir. 1974), the court held that the Massachusetts law controlled. It began its opinion by disagreeing with the Supreme Court's decision in *Hanna*: "Briefly, and with the greatest of respect, our position is that, perhaps because of the way in which issue was joined, the Court misconstrued the state statute [at issue in *Hanna*]." The First Circuit noted that it was the court that had been unanimously overturned in *Hanna,* and explained why it thought the Massachusetts provision at issue there was in fact "substantive" in nature.[k] The court then turned to the relevance of *Hanna* to the case before it:

"Under all the circumstances we conclude it proper to take *Hanna* at its word, as stating a principle for resolving a direct conflict between two strictly procedural rules. We do not accept the . . . view that *Hanna* commands that the federal rules be woodenly applied irrespective of a discoverable substantive, as distinguished from a merely procedural, state purpose. . . . Such a construction . . . means that a rule is not to be applied to the extent, if any, that it would defeat rights arising from state substantive law as distinguished from state procedure."

[k] The court's reasoning was that: "[I]n addition to bringing the executor into court, the Massachusetts legislature felt it so important that he be free to make distributions at the earliest possible moment, that it afforded him the protection of affirmative personal notice within the year during which suit must be commenced . . . ." The court added: "The suggestion by Mr. Justice Harlan in his concurring opinion that last and usual service under Rule 4 affords substantially as good a notice is a direct contravention of the statute."

The court then noted that in this case there was a "true conflict" between the federal rule and the Massachusetts statute. It continued:

> "We believe this to be the clear meaning of [the Massachusetts statute]: an action is commenced within the meaning of the Massachusetts statute of limitations although the wrong defendant is named, so long as it appeared that the correct defendant had been the one intended. We have no question but that the federal court normally must recognize such a provision in a diversity case. . . .
>
> "We do not believe *Hanna* requires us to refuse this recognition. Although Rule 15, on its face, conflicts with [the Massachusetts statute], to apply the rule would mean that the choice of forum 'would wholly bar recovery.' We do not read *Hanna* to mean that although the statute of limitations would be tolled if an action were brought on the state side, because of the civil rules it will run if brought in the federal court. We accordingly hold that [the Massachusetts statute] permits the amendment to relate back for the purpose of the Massachusetts statute of limitations in spite of the contrary provisions of Rule 15. . . ."

Did the court properly read *Hanna*? How in any event should the *Mulrenin* situation be analyzed? Even if the Massachusetts statute was "substantive" in effect, is there anything in *Erie* or any of its progeny that *requires* the federal courts to hear an action that is prohibited by federal statute or the federal rules? For example, if federal venue laws were not satisfied, the fact that a suit could be brought in state court across the street would not mean that a federal diversity court would be required to hear the case. How is the *Mulrenin* situation different? But should the court have been required to foreclose the plaintiff from recovery at a time when no new suit could have been filed in any other court? Did the *Mulrenin* court therefore get the right answer?

6. Bibliography. *Erie* and its progeny have inspired a deluge of literature, much of it on the substance/procedure issue. Two excellent articles that discuss the evolution of doctrine from *Erie* through *Hanna* are John Hart Ely, The Irrepressible Myth of *Erie,* 87 Harv. L. Rev. 693 (1974), and John McCoid, *Hanna v. Plumer* : The *Erie* Doctrine Changes Shape, 51 Va. L. Rev. 884 (1965). These articles also contain comprehensive citations to older literature.

Ely's article provoked two responses and a riposte. See Chayes, The Bead Game, 87 Harv. L. Rev. 741 (1974); Ely, The Necklace, 87 Harv. L. Rev. 753 (1974); Mishkin, Some Further Last Words on *Erie*— The Thread, 87 Harv. L. Rev. 1682 (1974).

For a continuation of the debate, see, e.g., Bourne, Federal Common Law and the *Erie-Byrd* Rule, 12 U. Balt. L. Rev. 426 (1983); Casto, The *Erie* Doctrine and the Structure of Constitutional Revolutions, 62 Tulane L.Rev. 907 (1988); Redish and Phillips, *Erie* and the Rules of

Decision Act: In Search of the Appropriate Dilemma, 91 Harv. L. Rev. 356 (1977); Westen and Lehman, Is There Life for *Erie* After the Death of Diversity?, 78 Mich. L. Rev. 311 (1980); Redish, Continuing the *Erie* Debate: A Response to Westen and Lehman, 78 Mich. L. Rev. 959 (1980); Westen, After "Life for *Erie*"—A Reply, 78 Mich. L. Rev. 971 (1980).

SECTION 3: THE ANTI-INJUNCTION ACT

ATLANTIC COAST LINE RAILROAD CO. v. BROTHERHOOD OF LOCOMOTIVE ENGINEERS
Supreme Court of the United States, 1970.
398 U.S. 281.

MR. JUSTICE BLACK delivered the opinion of the Court.

Congress in 1793, shortly after the American colonies became one united nation, provided that in federal courts "a writ of injunction [shall not] be granted to stay proceedings in any court of a state." Act of March 2, 1793, § 5. Although certain exceptions to this general prohibition have been added, that statute, directing that state courts shall remain free from interference by federal courts, has remained in effect until this time. Today that amended statute provides:

> "A court of the United States may not grant an injunction to stay proceedings in a State court except as expressly authorized by Act of Congress, or where necessary in aid of its jurisdiction, or to protect or effectuate its judgments." 28 U.S.C. § 2283.

Despite the existence of this longstanding prohibition, in this case a federal court did enjoin the petitioner, Atlantic Coast Line Railroad Co. (ACL), from invoking an injunction issued by a Florida state court which prohibited certain picketing by respondent Brotherhood of Locomotive Engineers (BLE). The case arose in the following way.

In 1967 BLE began picketing the Moncrief yard, a switching yard located near Jacksonville, Florida, and wholly owned and operated by ACL.[2] As soon as this picketing began ACL went into federal court seeking an injunction. When the federal judge denied the request, ACL immediately went into state court and there succeeded in obtaining an injunction. No further legal action was taken in this dispute until two years later in 1969, after this Court's decision in Brotherhood of Railroad Trainmen v. Jacksonville Terminal Co., 394 U.S. 369 (1969). In that case the Court considered the validity of a state injunction

---

[2] There is no present labor dispute between the ACL and the BLE or any other ACL employees. ACL became involved in this case as a result of a labor dispute between the Florida East Coast Railway Co. (FEC) and its employees. FEC cars are hauled into and out of Moncrief Yard and switched around to make up trains in that yard. The BLE picketed the yard, encouraging ACL employees not to handle any FEC cars.

against picketing by the BLE and other unions at the Jacksonville Terminal, located immediately next to Moncrief Yard. The Court reviewed the factual situation surrounding the Jacksonville Terminal picketing and concluded that the unions had a federally protected right to picket under the Railway Labor Act, 45 U.S.C. § 151 et seq., and that that right could not be interfered with by state court injunctions. Immediately after a petition for rehearing was denied in that case, the respondent BLE filed a motion in state court to dissolve the Moncrief yard injunction, arguing that under the *Jacksonville Terminal* decision the injunction was improper. The state judge refused to dissolve the injunction, holding that this Court's *Jacksonville Terminal* decision was not controlling. The union did not elect to appeal that decision directly, but instead went back into the federal court and requested an injunction against the enforcement of the state court injunction. The district judge granted the injunction and upon application a stay of that injunction, pending the filing and disposition of a petition for certiorari, was granted. The Court of Appeals summarily affirmed on the parties' stipulation, and we granted a petition for certiorari to consider the validity of the federal court's injunction against the state court.

In this Court the union contends that the federal injunction was proper either "to protect or effectuate" the District Court's denial of an injunction in 1967, or as "necessary in aid of" the District Court's jurisdiction. Although the questions are by no means simple and clear, and the decision is difficult, we conclude that the injunction against the state court was not justified under either of these two exceptions to the anti-injunction statute. We therefore hold that the federal injunction in this case was improper.

I

Before analyzing the specific legal arguments advanced in this case, we think it would be helpful to discuss the background and policy that led Congress to pass the anti-injunction statute in 1793. While all the reasons that led Congress to adopt this restriction on federal courts are not wholly clear, it is certainly likely that one reason stemmed from the essentially federal nature of our national government. When this nation was established by the Constitution, each state surrendered only a part of its sovereign power to the national government. But those powers that were not surrendered were retained by the states and unless a state was restrained by "the supreme Law of the Land" as expressed in the Constitution, laws, or treaties of the United States, it was free to exercise those retained powers as it saw fit. One of the reserved powers was the maintenance of state judicial systems for the decision of legal controversies. Many of the framers of the Constitution felt that separate federal courts were unnecessary and that the state courts could be entrusted to protect both state and federal rights. Others felt that a complete system of federal courts to take care of federal legal problems should be provided for in the Constitution itself. This dispute resulted in compromise. One "supreme Court" was created by the Constitution, and Congress was given the power to create other federal courts. In the first Congress this power was exercised and a system of federal trial and appellate courts with limited jurisdiction was created by the Judiciary Act of 1789.

While the lower federal courts were given certain powers in the 1789 act, they were not given any power to review directly cases from state courts, and they have not been given such powers since that time. Only the Supreme Court was authorized to review on direct appeal the decisions of state courts. Thus from the beginning we have had in this country two essentially separate legal systems. Each system proceeds independently of the other with ultimate review in this Court of the federal questions raised in either system. Understandably this dual court system was bound to lead to conflicts and frictions. Litigants who foresaw the possibility of more favorable treatment in one or the other system would predictably hasten to invoke the powers of whichever court it was believed would present the best chance of success. Obviously this dual system could not function if state and federal courts were free to fight each other for control of a particular case. Thus, in order to make the dual system work and "to prevent needless friction between state and federal court," it was necessary to work out lines of demarcation between the two systems. Some of these limits were spelled out in the 1789 act. Others have been added by later statutes as well as judicial decisions. The 1793 anti-injunction act was at least in part a response to these pressures.

On its face the present act is an absolute prohibition against enjoining state court proceedings, unless the injunction falls within one of three specifically defined exceptions. The respondents here have intimated that the act only establishes a "principle of comity," not a binding rule on the power of the federal courts. The argument implies that in certain circumstances a federal court may enjoin state court proceedings even if that action cannot be justified by any of the three exceptions. We cannot accept any such contention. In 1955 when this Court interpreted this statute, it stated: "This is not a statute conveying a broad general policy for appropriate ad hoc application. Legislative policy is here expressed in a clear-cut prohibition qualified only by specifically defined exceptions." Amalgamated Clothing Workers v. Richman Bros., 348 U.S. 511, 515–16 (1955). Since that time Congress has not seen fit to amend the statute and we therefore adhere to that position and hold that any injunction against state court proceedings otherwise proper under general equitable principles must be based on one of the specific statutory exceptions to § 2283 if it is to be upheld. Moreover since the statutory prohibition against such injunctions in part rests on the fundamental constitutional independence of the states and their courts, the exceptions should not be enlarged by loose statutory construction. Proceedings in state courts should normally be allowed to continue unimpaired by intervention of the lower federal courts, with relief from error, if any, through the state appellate courts and ultimately this Court.

II

In this case the Florida Circuit Court enjoined the union's intended picketing, and the United States District Court enjoined the railroad "from giving effect to or availing [itself] of the benefits of" that state court order. Both sides agree that although this federal injunction is in terms directed only at the railroad it is an injunction "to stay proceedings in a State court." It is settled that the prohibition of § 2283 cannot be evaded by addressing the order to the parties or prohibiting utilization of the results of a completed state proceeding. Oklahoma Packing Co. v. Gas Co., 309 U.S. 4, 9 (1940); Hill v. Martin, 296 U.S. 393, 403 (1935). Thus if the injunction against the Florida court proceedings is to be upheld, it must be "expressly authorized by Act of Congress," "necessary in aid of [the District Court's] jurisdiction," or "to protect or effectuate [that court's] judgments."

Neither party argues that there is any express congressional authorization for injunctions in this situation and we agree with that conclusion. The respondent does contend that the injunction was proper either as a means to protect or effectuate the District Court's 1967 order, or in aid of that court's jurisdiction. We do not think that either alleged basis can be supported.

A

[The federal District Court declined to enjoin the picketing in 1967 in part on the ground that under federal law the union was "free to engage in self-help." The union asserted in the Supreme Court that the] determination that it was "free to engage in self-help" was a determination that it had a federally protected right to picket and that state law could not be invoked to negate that right. The railroad, on the other hand, argues that the order merely determined that the *federal* court could not enjoin the picketing, in large part because of the general prohibition in the Norris-LaGuardia Act, 29 U.S.C. § 101 et seq., against issuance by federal courts of injunctions in labor disputes. Based solely on the state of the record when the order was entered, we are inclined to believe that the District Court did not determine whether federal law precluded an injunction based on state law. Not only was that point never argued to the court, but there is no language in the order that necessarily implies any decision on that question. In short we feel that the District Court in 1967 determined that federal law could not be invoked to enjoin the picketing at Moncrief Yard, and that the union did have a right "to engage in self-help" as far as the federal courts were concerned. But that decision is entirely different from a decision that the Railway Labor Act precludes state regulation of the picketing as well, and this latter decision is an essential prerequisite for upholding the 1969 injunction as necessary "to protect or effectuate" the 1967 order. [W]e think it highly unlikely that the brief statements in the order conceal a determination of a disputed legal point that later was to divide this Court in a four to three vote in *Jacksonville Terminal,* supra, in opinions totaling 29 pages. . . .

This record, we think, conclusively shows that neither the parties themselves nor the District Court construed the 1967 order as the union now contends it should be construed. Rather we are convinced that the union in effect tried to get the federal District Court to decide that the state court judge was wrong in distinguishing the *Jacksonville Terminal* decision.[a] Such an attempt to seek appellate review of a state decision in the federal District Court cannot be justified as necessary "to protect or effectuate" the 1967 order. The record simply will not support the union's contention on this point.

B

This brings us to the second prong of the union's argument in which it is suggested that even if the 1967 order did not determine the union's right to picket free from state interference, once the decision in *Jacksonville Terminal* was announced, the District Court was then free to enjoin the state court on the theory that such action was "necessary in aid of [the District Court's] jurisdiction." [T]he argument is somewhat unclear, but it appears to go in this way: The District Court had acquired jurisdiction over the labor controversy in 1967 when the railroad filed its complaint, and it determined at that time that it did have jurisdiction. The dispute involved the legality of picketing by the union and the *Jacksonville Terminal* decision clearly indicated that such activity was not only legal, but was protected from state court interference. The state court had interfered with that right, and thus a federal injunction was "necessary in aid of [the District Court's] jurisdiction." For several reasons we cannot accept the contention.

First, a federal court does not have inherent power to ignore the limitations of § 2283 and to enjoin state court proceedings merely because those proceedings interfere with a protected federal right or invade an area pre-empted by federal law, even when the interference is unmistakably clear. This rule applies regardless of whether the federal court itself has jurisdiction over the controversy, or whether it is ousted from jurisdiction for the same reason that the state court is. This conclusion is required because Congress itself set forth the only exceptions to the statute, and those exceptions do not include this situation. Second, if the District Court does have jurisdiction, it is not enough that the requested injunction is related to that jurisdiction, but it must be "*necessary in aid of*" that jurisdiction. While this language is admittedly broad, we conclude that it implies something similar to the concept of injunctions to "protect or effectuate" judgments. Both exceptions to the general prohibition of § 2283 imply that some federal injunctive relief may be necessary to prevent a state court from so interfering with a federal court's consideration or disposition of a case as to seriously impair the federal court's flexibility and authority to

---

[a] In an omitted portion of the opinion, the Court stated in a footnote that it was prepared to "assume, without deciding, that the Florida Circuit Court's decision was wrong in light of our decision in *Jacksonville Terminal.*" [Footnote by eds.]

decide that case. Third, no such situation is presented here. Although the federal court did have jurisdiction of the railroad's complaint based on federal law, the state court also had jurisdiction over the complaint based on state law and the union's asserted federal defense as well. While the railroad could probably have based its federal case on the pendent state law claims as well, United Mine Workers v. Gibbs, 383 U.S. 715 (1966), it was free to refrain from doing so and leave the state law questions and the related issue concerning preclusion of state remedies by federal law to the state courts. Conversely, although it could have tendered its federal claims to the state court, it was also free to restrict the state complaint to state grounds alone. In short, the state and federal courts had concurrent jurisdiction in this case, and neither court was free to prevent either party from simultaneously pursuing claims in both courts. Kline v. Burke Constr. Co., 260 U.S. 226 (1922); cf. Donovan v. Dallas, 377 U.S. 408 (1964). Therefore the state court's assumption of jurisdiction over the state law claims and the federal preclusion issue did not hinder the federal court's jurisdiction so as to make an injunction *neccessary* to aid that jurisdiction. Nor was an injunction necessary because the state court may have taken action which the federal court was certain was improper under the *Jacksonville Terminal* decision. Again, lower federal courts possess no power whatever to sit in direct review of state court decisions. If the union was adversely affected by the state court's decision, it was free to seek vindication of its federal right in the Florida appellate courts and ultimately, if necessary, in this Court. Similarly if, because of the Florida Circuit Court's action, the union faced the threat of immediate irreparable injury sufficient to justify an injunction under usual equitable principles, it was undoubtedly free to seek such relief from the Florida appellate courts, and might possibly in certain emergency circumstances seek such relief from this Court as well. Unlike the federal District Court, this Court does have potential appellate jurisdiction over federal questions raised in state court proceedings, and that broader jurisdiction allows this Court correspondingly broader authority to issue injunctions "necessary in aid of its jurisdiction."

III

This case is by no means an easy one. The arguments in support of the union's contentions are not insubstantial. But whatever doubts we may have are strongly affected by the general prohibition of § 2283. Any doubts as to the propriety of a federal injunction against state court proceedings should be resolved in favor of permitting the state courts to proceed in an orderly fashion to finally determine the controversy. The explicit wording of § 2283 itself implies as much, and the fundamental principle of a dual system of courts leads inevitably to that conclusion.

The injunction issued by the District Court must be vacated. Since that court has not yet proceeded to a final judgment in the case, the cause is remanded to it for further proceedings in conformity with this opinion.

It is so ordered.

MR. JUSTICE MARSHALL took no part in the consideration or decision of this case.

MR. JUSTICE HARLAN, concurring.

I join the Court's opinion on the understanding that its holding implies no retreat from Brotherhood of Railroad Trainmen v. Jacksonville Terminal Co., 394 U.S. 369 (1969). Whether or not that case controls the underlying controversy here is a question that will arise only on review of any final judgment entered in the state court proceedings respecting that controversy.

MR. JUSTICE BRENNAN, with whom MR. JUSTICE WHITE joins, dissenting.

My disagreement with the Court in this case is a relatively narrow one. I do not disagree with much that is said concerning the history and policies underlying 28 U.S.C. § 2283. Nor do I dispute the Court's holding on the basis of Amalgamated Clothing Workers v. Richman Bros., 348 U.S. 511 (1955), that federal court courts do not have authority to enjoin state proceedings merely because it is asserted that the state court is improperly asserting jurisdiction in an area preempted by federal law or federal procedures. Nevertheless, in my view the District Court had discretion to enjoin the state proceedings in the present case because it acted pursuant to an explicit exception to the prohibition of § 2283, that is, "to protect or effectuate [the District Court's] judgments." . . .

In my view, what the District Court decided in 1967 was that BLE had a federally protected right to picket at the Moncrief Yard and, by necessary implication, that this right could not be subverted by resort to state proceedings. I find it difficult indeed to ascribe to the district judge the views that the Court now says he held, namely, that ACL, merely by marching across the street to the state court, could render wholly nugatory the district judge's declaration that BLE had a federally protected right to strike at the Moncrief Yard.

Moreover, it is readily apparent from the District Court's 1969 order enjoining the state proceedings that the district judge viewed his 1967 order as delineating the rights of the respective parties, and more particularly, as establishing BLE's right to conduct the picketing in question under paramount federal law. This interpretation should be accepted as controlling, for certainly the district judge is in the best position to render an authoritative interpretation of his own order. . . .

In justifying its niggardly construction of the District Court's orders, the Court takes the position that any doubts concerning the propriety of an injunction against state proceedings should be resolved against the granting of injunctive relief. Unquestionably § 2283 manifests a general design on the part of Congress that federal courts not precipitately interfere with the orderly determination of controversies in state proceedings. However, this policy of nonintervention is by no means absolute, as the explicit exceptions in § 2283 make entirely clear. Thus, § 2283 itself evinces a congressional intent that resort to state proceedings not be permitted to undermine a prior judgment of a federal court. But that is exactly what has occurred in the present case. Indeed, the federal determination that BLE may picket at the Moncrief Yard has been rendered wholly ineffective by the state injunction. The crippling restrictions that the Court today places upon the power of the District Court to effectuate and protect its orders are totally inconsistent with both the plain language of § 2283 and the policies underlying that statutory provision.

Accordingly, I would affirm the judgment of the Court of Appeals sustaining the District Court's grant of injunctive relief against petitioner's giving effect to, or availing itself of, the benefit of the state court injunction.[b]

NOTES ON THE ANTI–INJUNCTION ACT

1. *Toucey v. New York Life Ins. Co.* As Justice Black noted in *Atlantic Coast Line,* the Anti-Injunction Act stems from a 1793 statute that appeared flatly to prohibit federal courts from issuing an injunction to stay proceedings in a state court. The statute, with the three exceptions discussed in *Atlantic Coast Line,* was enacted in its present form in 1948.[a] Prior to 1948, the Supreme Court had permitted the issuance of injunctions in many situations that were literally covered by the prohibition. A sharp break with this practice occurred in Toucey v. New York Life Ins. Co., 314 U.S. 118 (1941).[b]

Toucey had sued the New York Life Insurance Company in state court in order to collect monthly disability benefits. The insurance company removed to a federal District Court, which resolved the case on the merits in its favor. Toucey then assigned his claim to Shay, who

[b] For a comment on *Atlantic Coast Line* shortly after it was decided, see Reaves and Golden, The Federal Anti-Injunction Statute in the Aftermath of *Atlantic Coast Line Railroad,* 5 Ga. L. Rev. 294 (1971). [Footnote by eds.]

[a] There is no helpful legislative history of the original statute, and little in its subsequent re-enactments that explains the intended scope of the present version. Various limiting constructions of the original statute have been suggested in the literature. For example, it is argued in Mayton, Ersatz Federalism Under the Anti-Injunction Statute, 78 Colum. L. Rev. 330 (1978), that it was intended only as a limitation on the powers of an individual Supreme Court justice to grant injunctions. But the accepted judicial view is that stated in *Atlantic Coast Line.*

For other examinations of the history of the statute and its administration prior to

its appearance in its present form, see Taylor and Willis, The Power of Federal Courts to Enjoin Proceedings in State Courts, 42 Yale L.J. 1169 (1933); Durfee and Sloss, Federal Injunctions Against Proceedings in State Courts: The Life History of a Statute, 30 Mich. L. Rev. 1145 (1932); Warren, Federal and State Court Interference, 43 Harv. L. Rev. 345 (1930); Comment, Federal Court Stays of State Court Proceedings: A Re-Examination of Original Congressional Intent, 38 U. Chi. L. Rev. 612 (1971).

[b] At the time *Toucey* was decided, the statute read: "The writ of injunction shall not be granted by any court of the United States to stay proceedings in any court of a State, except in cases where such injunction may be authorized by any law relating to proceedings in bankruptcy." The bankruptcy exception had been added in 1875.

filed a second action on the policy in state court. The insurance company did not enter an appearance in the state court,[c] but instead asked the federal court to enjoin Shay and Toucey from proceeding further in state court. The injunction was issued, and the Court of Appeals affirmed. The Supreme Court granted certiorari in order to decide the following question: "Does a federal court have power to stay a proceeding in a state court simply because the claim in controversy has previously been adjudicated in the federal court?" The Court's answer was "no," in language suggesting that no further exceptions to the statute would be developed and, indeed, that some of the exceptions recognized in the past might no longer be valid. "We must be scrupulous," Justice Frankfurter concluded for the Court, "in our regard for the limits within which Congress has confined the authority of the courts of its own creation."

The codification of the three exceptions to the Anti-Injunction Act in 1948 was a reaction to *Toucey,* and the exception permitting a federal court to issue an injunction "to protect or effectuate its judgments" was designed specifically to overrule *Toucey* on its facts. It was not clear, however, whether the 1948 revision was also meant to overrule the approach adopted in *Toucey,* namely refusal by the Court to recognize exceptions not specifically covered by the statutory language. This issue became the subject of subsequent litigation.

2. **Early Litigation Under the 1948 Revision.** Three cases set the precedential backdrop for the interpretation of the 1948 revision of the Anti-Injunction Act in *Atlantic Coast Line:*

(i) *Capital Service.* The first was Capital Service, Inc. v. NLRB, 347 U.S. 501 (1954). An employer was awarded an injunction in state court against picketing by a union. The employer then filed an unfair labor practice charge against the union with the National Labor Relations Board, and the Board issued a formal complaint. The Board then went to federal court to enjoin the union from picketing until the complaint was adjudicated on the merits, and additionally to restrain the employer from taking any further steps to enforce its state court injunction. The District Court awarded the requested relief, and both the Court of Appeals and the Supreme Court affirmed. The Supreme Court held that the injunction against enforcement of the state court order was "necessary in aid of" the District Court's jurisdiction, since the District Court was required to enforce valid orders by the NLRB and it needed to be free of any restraints set by the state court injunction in order to resolve the case on its merits.

(ii) *Amalgamated Clothing Workers.* The second case was Amalgamated Clothing Workers v. Richman Bros., 348 U.S. 511 (1955), which also involved a labor dispute. The employer obtained a state court injunction against union picketing. The union sued in federal court to enjoin enforcement of the state court order, arguing that the subject matter of the dispute was exclusively within the control of the

---

[c] Removal to federal court would not have been possible because no federal question was involved and there was no diversity of citizenship.

NLRB and that any state court adjudication of the controversy was preempted by the federal labor laws.[d] The federal injunction was denied by the lower courts, and the Supreme Court, speaking through Justice Frankfurter, affirmed:

> "In the face of this carefully considered enactment [the 1948 revision of the Anti-Injunction Act], we cannot accept the argument of petitioner and the Board, as amicus curiae, that § 2283 does not apply whenever the moving party in the district court alleged that the state court is 'wholly without jurisdiction over the subject matter, having invaded a field preempted by Congress.' No such exception had been established by judicial decision under [the former statute]. In any event, Congress has left no justification for its recognition now. This is not a statute conveying a broad general policy for appropriate ad hoc application. Legislative policy is here expressed in a clear-cut prohibition qualified only by specifically defined exceptions."

Justice Frankfurter then considered whether any of the three exceptions applied. He found no "express" exception, and there was no former federal court judgment to be protected. As to the "necessary in aid of jurisdiction" exception, Justice Frankfurter said:

> "In no lawyer-like sense can the present proceeding be thought to be in aid of the District Court's jurisdiction. Under no circumstances has the District Court jurisdiction to enforce rights and duties which call for recognition by the Board. Such non-existent jurisdiction therefore cannot be aided.

> "Insofar as protection is needed for the Board's exercise of its jurisdiction, Congress has . . . specifically provided for resort, but only by the Board, to the District Court's equity powers. [A]ny aid that is needed to protect jurisdiction is the aid which the Board may need for the safeguarding of its authority. Such aid only the Board could seek, and only if, in a case pending before it, it has satisfied itself as to the adequacy of the complaint."[e]

Chief Justice Warren and Justices Black and Douglas dissented. Justice Douglas said:

---

[d] It seems clear that the state-court proceeding in fact was pre-empted under Garner v. Teamsters, Chauffeurs and Helpers Local Union No. 776, 346 U.S. 485 (1953). In any event, the Supreme Court assumed as much in its decision in *Amalgamated Clothing Workers.*

[e] The employer had filed no unfair labor practice charge against the union with the NLRB, and there was no such charge available to the union unless the employer had committed an unfair labor practice by the act of filing the state-court suit. At the time it was unclear whether the act of filing a state-court suit could be considered an unfair labor practice. Hence there may have been no way the union could get the dispute before the Labor Board, and no basis for the Board itself to seek an injunction against the state court proceedings. For later developments on this issue, see Bill Johnson's Restaurants, Inc. v. NLRB, 461 U.S. 731 (1983) (The Board may regard it as an unfair labor practice if a state suit is filed in retaliation for the exercise of federally protected rights *and* if the suit "lacks a reasonable basis in fact or law.")

"The Court has been ready to imply other exceptions to § 2283, where the common sense of the situation required it. Thus, if the federal court first takes possession of a res, it may protect its control over it, even to the extent of enjoining a state court from interfering with the property. That result flies in the face of the literal words of § 2283. Yet the injunction is allowed to issue as the preferable way of avoiding unseemly clashes between state and federal authorities.[f] . . .

"A like exception is needed here, if the state suit is not to dislocate severely the federal regulatory scheme. Under the present decision, an employer can move in the state courts for an injunction against the strike. The injunction, if granted, may for all practical purposes settle the matter. There is no way for the union to transfer the dispute to the federal Board, for it seems to be assumed by both parties that the employer has committed no unfair labor practice. By today's decision the federal court is powerless to enjoin the state action. The case lingers in the state court. There can be no appeal to this Court from the temporary injunction. It may take substantial time in the trial court to prepare a record to support a permanent injunction. Once one is granted, the long, drawn-out appeal through the state hierarchy and on to this Court commences. Yet by the time this Court decides that from the very beginning the state court had no jurisdiction, . . . a year or more has passed; and time alone has probably defeated the claim."

(iii) *Leiter Minerals. Amalgamated Clothing Workers* seemed to put an end to the argument that there were exceptions to § 2283 beyond those specifically stated in the statute. The Court found an additional exception, however, in Leiter Minerals, Inc. v. United States, 352 U.S. 220 (1957). The United States had leased mineral rights under federally owned land to certain private parties. Leiter claimed that it owned the mineral rights and filed an action in state court against the federal lessees. The United States then filed an action against Leiter in federal court to quiet title to the mineral rights, and also sought to enjoin continuation of the state proceedings. The Supreme Court, in an opinion by Justice Frankfurter no less, held that

[f] In spite of Justice Douglas' comments, the established "in rem" exception is normally regarded as comfortably within the "in aid of its jurisdiction" language of § 2283. It is clear, however—as Justice Black said in *Atlantic Coast Line*—that this statutory exception does not permit a federal court to enjoin state court proceedings merely because concurrent in personam actions are in litigation in both court systems. See Vendo Co. v. Lektro-Vend Corp., 433 U.S. 623, 641–43 (1977) (plurality opinion); Kline v. Burke Constr. Co., 260 U.S. 226 (1922); C. Wright, The Law of Federal Courts 283–84 (4th ed. 1983). The situation may be different if the subject matter of state in personam litigation is within the exclusive jurisdiction of the federal courts. See Kochery, Conflict of Jurisdiction: 28 U.S.C.A. § 2283 and Exclusive Federal Jurisdiction, 4 Buff. L. Rev. 269 (1955); Comment, Power of a Federal Court to Enjoin State Court Action in Aid of Its Exclusive Jurisdiction, 48 Nw. L. Rev. 383 (1953).

the injunction could be issued even though it did not fit within any of the statutory exceptions to § 2283:

> "The frustration of superior federal interests that would ensue from precluding the federal government from obtaining a stay of state court proceedings except under the severe restrictions of § 2283 would be so great that we cannot reasonably impute such a purpose to Congress from the general language of § 2283 alone. It is always difficult to feel confident about construing an ambiguous statute . . . but the interpretation excluding the United States from the coverage of the statute seems to us preferable in the context of healthy federal-state relations."

3. *NLRB v. Nash-Finch Co.* Some of the language in *Atlantic Coast Line* may have been intended to restrict the implication of *Leiter Minerals* that further exceptions to § 2283 might be recognized.[g] Yet the rationale of *Leiter Minerals* was extended in NLRB v. Nash-Finch Co., 404 U.S. 138 (1971). In that case an employer again had obtained an injunction restraining picketing by a union. The NLRB then sued in federal court to restrain enforcement of the state court injunction. Its rationale for doing so is contained in the following excerpt from Justice Douglas' opinion for the Court:

> "The action in the instant case does not seek an injunction to restrain specific activities upon which the Board has issued a complaint but is based upon the general doctrine of pre-emption. We therefore do not believe this case falls within the narrow exception contained in § 2283 for matter 'necessary in aid of its jurisdiction.' There is in the act no express authority for the Board to seek injunctive relief against pre-empted state action. The question remains whether there is implied authority to do so.
>
> "It has long been held that the Board, though not granted express statutory remedies, may obtain appropriate and traditional ones to prevent frustration of the purposes of the act. . . . We conclude that there is . . . an implied authority of the Board, in spite of the command of § 2283, to enjoin state action where its federal power pre-empts the field. . . . The purpose of § 2283 was to avoid unseemly conflict between the state and the federal courts where the litigants were private persons, not to hamstring the federal government and its agencies in the use of federal courts to protect federal rights. We can no more conclude here than in *Leiter* that a general statute, limiting the power of federal courts to issue injunctions, had as its purpose the frustration of federal systems of regulation. . . ."

Justices White and Brennan dissented.

[g] See C. Wright, The Law of Federal Courts 281–83 (4th ed. 1983).

4. The Statutory Exceptions. Administration of the exceptions contained in § 2283 has produced important ambiguities.[h] The following cases are illustrative.

(i) *Mitchum v. Foster.* One might think that the "expressly authorized by Act of Congress" exception would be fairly easy to administer. Yet Mitchum v. Foster, 407 U.S. 225 (1972), demonstrates otherwise. The question in *Mitchum* was whether 42 U.S.C. § 1983 contained "express" authority to enjoin state court proceedings in the face of § 2283. Section 1983 provides:

> "Every person who, under color of any statute, ordinance, regulation, custom, or usage, of any state or territory, subjects, or causes to be subjected, any citizen of the United States or other person within the jurisdiction thereof to the deprivation of any rights, privileges, or immunities secured by the Constitution and laws, shall be liable to the party injured in an action at law, suit in equity, or other proper proceeding for redress."

On its face, § 1983 seems to do no more than many federal statutes: it supplies, inter alia, a federal equitable cause of action in general terms. But the Court held that it was an "express" exception to § 2283.

The Court made two preliminary observations. First, "in order to qualify under the 'expressly authorized' exception of the anti-injunction statute, a federal law need not contain an express reference to that statute. . . . Indeed, none of the previously recognized statutory exceptions contains any such reference." Second, "a federal law need not expressly authorize an injunction of a state court proceeding in order to qualify as an exception." Yet not all federal equitable causes of action will be held to be an exception to the prohibition. The relevant inquiry is:

> "[I]n order to qualify as an 'expressly authorized' exception to the anti-injunction statute, an act of Congress must have created a specific and uniquely federal right or remedy, enforceable in a federal court of equity, which could be frustrated if the federal court were not empowered to enjoin a state court proceeding. This is not to say that in order to come within the exception an act of Congress must, on its face and in every one of its provisions, be totally incompatible with the prohibition of the anti-injunction statute. The test, rather, is whether an act of Congress, clearly creating a federal right or remedy enforceable in a federal court of equity, could be given its intended scope only by the stay of a state court proceeding."

The Court then examined the legislative history and function of § 1983 and concluded that it indeed was an "express" exception.[i] Justices

---

[h] For a critique of the Court's treatment of the statutory exceptions, see Redish, The Anti-Injunction Statute Reconsidered, 44 U. Chi. L. Rev. 717 (1977). Problems posed by § 2283 in the class action context are discussed by Steven Larimore in Exploring the Interface Between Rule 23 Class Actions and the Anti-Injunction Act, 18 Ga. L. Rev. 259 (1984).

[i] Section 1983 is the subject of extensive consideration later in these materials, be-

Powell and Rehnquist did not participate in the decision. There was no dissent.

(ii) *Vendo Co. v. Lektro-Vend Corp.* The implications of *Mitchum* for other acts of Congress authorizing equitable relief were raised in Vendo Co. v. Lektro-Vend Corp., 433 U.S. 623 (1977). The case involved an agreement not to compete entered into by a vending machine company (Vendo) and Stoner when Stoner sold his vending machine business to Vendo. Vendo filed a state court suit against Stoner and Lektro-Vend Corp., a competing vending machine company that had entered into a business relationship with Stoner. After nine years of litigation, Vendo won a judgment in excess of $7 million. Shortly after the state suit was filed, Stoner and Lektro-Vend filed an action in federal court against Vendo alleging that the agreement not to compete violated the federal antitrust laws and that the state court suit was filed to harass the plaintiffs and to eliminate their competition with Vendo. This suit lay dormant throughout the state court litigation, but after the state judgment became final, Stoner and Lektro-Vend persuaded the federal judge to enjoin its enforcement. The Court of Appeals affirmed, and the Supreme Court granted certiorari.

The issue was whether § 16 of the Clayton Act was an "express" exception to § 2283. That statute provides:

"Any person . . . shall be entitled to sue for and have injunctive relief, in any court of the United States having jurisdiction over the parties, against threatened loss or damage by violation of the antitrust laws . . . when and under the same conditions and principles as injunctive relief against threatened conduct that will cause loss or damage is granted by courts of equity, under the rules governing such proceedings . . . ."

The divided vote of the Court can best be understood by focusing first on the dissent by Justice Stevens, which was joined by Justices Brennan, White, and Marshall. In Justice Stevens' view, "litigation in state courts may constitute an antitrust violation," and that was exactly what the federal District Court found to have happened in this case. Since this was so, "[t]he language in § 16 of the Clayton Act which expressly authorizes injunctions against violations of the antitrust laws" constitutes an express exception to § 2283 and authorized the federal injunction.

Justice Blackmun, joined by Chief Justice Burger, agreed that § 16 was an express exception to § 2283, but only "under narrowly limited circumstances" that were not satisfied in the present case:

"[N]o injunction may issue against currently pending state court proceedings unless those proceedings are themselves part

ginning on page 880, infra. As noted there, and as the Court was careful to point out in *Mitchum,* even though § 2283 does not preclude an injunction against state court proceedings in a § 1983 suit, the Court has developed other doctrines that in many contexts will preclude such relief. See especially Younger v. Harris, 401 U.S. 37 (1971), and its progeny, pages 1158–1243, infra. *Mitchum* itself is a main case at page 1179, infra.

of a 'pattern of baseless, repetitive claims' that are being used as an anti-competitive device, all the traditional prerequisites for equitable relief are satisfied, and the only way to give the antitrust laws their intended scope is by staying the state proceedings."

Here there was only one state court lawsuit, not a "pattern of baseless, repetitive claims," and hence "§ 16 itself did not authorize the injunction below."

Justice Rehnquist, writing for himself and Justices Stewart and Powell, took a different view of the relationship between § 16 and § 2283. He began by saying that § 2283 "is an absolute prohibition against any injunction of any state court proceedings, unless the injunction falls within one of the three specifically defined exceptions in the act." Section 16 was not an "express" exception for three reasons. First, the last clause in the statute (beginning "under the same conditions and principles") means that § 16, unlike § 1983, "may fairly be read as virtually incorporating the prohibitions of the Anti-Injunction Act . . . ." Second, unlike in *Mitchum,* the legislative history of the Clayton Act could not cure the omission of express reference in the statute to the possibility of enjoining state court proceedings. Third, reading § 16 as an "express" exception would mean that "§ 2283 would be completely eviscerated since the ultimate logic of this position can mean no less than that virtually *all* federal authorizing injunctive relief statutes are exceptions to § 2283."[j]

(iii) *Parsons Steel, Inc. v. First Alabama Bank.* Parsons Steel, Inc. v. First Alabama Bank, 474 U.S. 518 (1986), involved the intersection between § 2283 and 28 U.S.C. § 1738 (requiring that federal courts give full faith and credit to state court judgments). Simultaneous suits on related subjects were pending in both state and federal courts. Parsons was the plaintiff and the bank was the defendant in both actions. The federal suit was concluded first, in favor of the bank. The bank then pleaded res judicata as a defense to the state court action, but the state court held that the federal judgment did not preclude continuation of the state suit. Judgment for some $4 million was then awarded against the bank, after which the bank sought an injunction from the federal court to preclude enforcement of the state court judgment. The injunction was entered and the Court of Appeals affirmed.

[j] At this point Justice Rehnquist cited 26 federal statutes that authorized equitable relief in general terms. Justice Stevens responded:

"I am not now persuaded that the concept of federalism is necessarily inconsistent with the view that the 1793 act should be considered wholly inapplicable to later enacted federal statutes that are enforceable exclusively in federal litigation. If a fair reading of the jurisdictional grant in any such statute does authorize an injunction against state court litigation frustrating the federal policy, nothing in our prior cases would foreclose the conclusion that it is within the 'expressly authorized' exception to § 2283."

He also noted that these other statutes were relatively obscure, and "it is extremely doubtful that they would generate as much, or as significant, litigation as either the Civil Rights Act or the antitrust laws."

The Supreme Court unanimously reversed. It agreed that *Toucey* had been overruled by the 1948 amendment to § 2283, but held that the "relitigation exception" to § 2283 is limited "to those situations in which the state court has not yet ruled on the merits of the res judicata issue." The bank may have been entitled to an injunction while the state court proceeding was pending, but once the res judicata issue was raised in state court and decided against the bank, it could "not return to federal court for another try."

5. Concluding Comments. Two further comments on the reach of § 2283 are warranted. First, it is clear that the statute does not itself preclude relief designed to prevent the institution of litigation in a state court.[k] It is a prohibition on interference with state proceedings that are pending or that have been concluded when the federal suit is filed. Second, the fact that § 2283 does not prohibit federal interference with state court proceedings does not necessarily mean that the federal courts will intervene. The general prerequisites for an injunction must independently be satisfied, and in addition—as noted above in connection with the *Mitchum* case—there are other doctrines that may lead the federal courts to withhold relief.[l]

SECTION 4: DEFERENCE TO STATE COURT LITIGATION

COLORADO RIVER WATER CONSERVATION DISTRICT v. UNITED STATES
Supreme Court of the United States, 1976.
424 U.S. 800.

Mr. Justice Brennan delivered the opinion of the Court.

The McCarran Amendment, 43 U.S.C. § 666, provides that

"consent is hereby given to join the United States as a defendant in any suit

(1) for the adjudication of rights to the use of water of a river system or other source, or

(2) for the administration of such rights, where it appears that the United States is the owner of or is in the process of acquiring water rights by appropriation under State law, by purchase, by exchange, or otherwise, and the United States is a necessary party to such suit."

The questions presented by this case concern the effect of the McCarran Amendment upon the jurisdiction of the federal district courts under 28

---

[k] See Dombrowski v. Pfister, 380 U.S. 479, 484 n.2 (1965).

[l] The premier illustration of "other grounds" that may counsel withholding re- lief is found in Younger v. Harris, 401 U.S. 37 (1971), and its progeny. The *Younger* doctrine is developed in detail beginning at page 1158, infra.

U.S.C. § 1345 over suits for determination of water rights brought by the United States as trustee for certain Indian tribes and as owner of various non-Indian government claims.[1]

I

It is probable that no problem of the southwest section of the nation is more critical than that of scarcity of water. As southwestern populations have grown, conflicting claims to this scarce resource have increased. To meet these claims, several southwestern states have established elaborate procedures for allocation of water and adjudication of conflicting claims to that resource. In 1969, Colorado enacted its Water Rights Determination and Administration Act in an effort to revamp its legal procedures for determining claims to water within the state.

Under the Colorado act, the state is divided into seven water divisions, each division encompassing one or more entire drainage basins for the larger rivers in Colorado. Adjudication of water claims within each division occurs on a continuous basis. Each month, water referees in each division rule on applications for water rights filed within the preceding five months or refer those applications to the water judge of their division. Every six months, the water judge passes on referred applications and contested decisions by referees. A state engineer and engineers for each division are responsible for the administration and distribution of the waters of the state according to the determinations in each division.

Colorado applies the doctrine of prior appropriation in establishing rights to the use of water. Under that doctrine, one acquires a right to water by diverting it from its natural source and applying it to some beneficial use. Continued beneficial use of the water is required in order to maintain the right. In periods of shortage, priority among confirmed rights is determined according to the date of initial diversion.

The reserved rights of the United States extend to Indian reservations, and other federal lands, such as national parks and forests. The reserved rights claimed by the United States in this case affect waters within Colorado Water Division No. 7. On November 14, 1972, the government instituted this suit in the United States District Court for the District of Colorado, invoking the court's jurisdiction under 28 U.S.C. § 1345. The District Court is located in Denver, some 300 miles from Division 7. The suit, against some 1,000 water users, sought declaration of the government's rights to waters in certain rivers and their tributaries located in Division 7. In the suit, the government asserted reserved rights on its own behalf and on behalf of certain Indian tribes, as well as rights based on state law. It sought appointment of a water master to administer any waters decreed to the United

---

[1] . . .Title 28 U.S.C. § 1345 provides:

"Except as otherwise provided by Act of Congress, the district courts shall have original jurisdiction of all civil actions, suits or proceedings commenced by the United States, or by any agency or officer thereof expressly authorized to sue by Act of Congress."

States. Prior to institution of this suit, the government had pursued adjudication of non-Indian reserved rights and other water claims based on state law in Water Divisions 4, 5, and 6, and the government continues to participate fully in those divisions.

Shortly after the federal suit was commenced, one of the defendants in that suit filed an application in the state court for Division 7, seeking an order directing service of process on the United States in order to make it a party to proceedings in Division 7 for the purpose of adjudicating all of the government's claims, both state and federal. On January 3, 1973, the United States was served pursuant to authority of the McCarran Amendment. Several defendants and intervenors in the federal proceeding then filed a motion in the District Court to dismiss on the ground that under the amendment, the court was without jurisdiction to determine federal water rights. Without deciding the jurisdictional question, the District Court, on June 21, 1973, granted the motion in an unreported oral opinion stating that the doctrine of abstention required deference to the proceedings in Division 7. On appeal, the Court of Appeals for the Tenth Circuit reversed, holding that the suit of the United States was within district-court jurisdiction under 28 U.S.C. § 1345, and that abstention was inappropriate. We granted certiorari to consider the important questions of whether the McCarran Amendment terminated jurisdiction of federal courts to adjudicate federal water rights and whether, if that jurisdiction was not terminated, the District Court's dismissal in this case was nevertheless appropriate. We reverse.

II

We first consider the question of district-court jurisdiction under 28 U.S.C. § 1345. That section provides that the district courts shall have original jurisdiction over all civil actions brought by the federal government "[e]xcept as otherwise provided by Act of Congress." It is thus necessary to examine whether the McCarran Amendment is such an act of Congress excepting jurisdiction under § 1345. . . .

In view of the McCarran Amendment's language and legislative history, controlling principles of statutory construction require the conclusion that the amendment did not constitute an exception "provided by Act of Congress" that repealed the jurisdiction of district courts under § 1345 to entertain federal water suits. . . . Not only do the terms and legislative history of the McCarran Amendment not indicate an intent to repeal § 1345, but also there is no irreconcilability in the operation of both statutes. The immediate effect of the amendment is to give consent to jurisdiction in the state courts concurrent with jurisdiction in the federal courts over controversies involving federal rights to the use of water. There is no irreconcilability in the existence of concurrent state and federal jurisdiction. Such concurrency has, for example, long existed under federal diversity jurisdiction. Accordingly, we hold that the McCarran Amendment in no way diminished federal-district-court jurisdiction under § 1345 and that the District Court had jurisdiction to hear this case.[15]

III

We turn next to the question whether this suit nevertheless was properly dismissed in view of the concurrent state proceedings in Division 7.

A

First, we consider whether the McCarran Amendment provided consent to determine federal reserved rights held on behalf of Indians in state court. [G]iven the claims for Indian water rights in this case, dismissal clearly would have been inappropriate if the state court had no jurisdiction to decide those claims. We conclude that the state court had jurisdiction over Indian water rights under the amendment. . . .

B

Next, we consider whether the District Court's dismissal was appropriate under the doctrine of abstention. We hold that the dismissal cannot be supported under that doctrine in any of its forms.

Abstention from the exercise of federal jurisdiction is the exception, not the rule[:]

> "The doctrine of abstention, under which a district court may decline to exercise or postpone the exercise of its jurisdiction, is an extraordinary and narrow exception to the duty of a district court to adjudicate a controversy properly before it. Abdication of the obligation to decide cases can be justified under this doctrine only in the exceptional circumstances where the order to the parties to repair to the state court would clearly serve an important countervailing interest." County of Allegheny v. Frank Mashuda Co., 360 U.S. 185, 188–89 (1959).

> "[I]t was never a doctrine of equity that a federal court should exercise its judicial discretion to dismiss a suit merely because a state court could entertain it." Alabama Pub. Serv. Comm'n v. Southern R. Co., 341 U.S. 341, 361 (1951) (Frankfurter, J., concurring in result).

Our decisions have confined the circumstances appropriate for abstention to three general categories.

(a) Abstention is appropriate "in cases presenting a federal constitutional issue which might be mooted or presented in a different posture by a state court determination of pertinent state law." *County of Allegheny v. Frank Mashuda Co.* supra, at 189. See, e.g., Railroad Comm'n of Texas v. Pullman Co., 312 U.S. 496 (1941). This case, however, presents no federal constitutional issue for decision.

---

[15] The District Court also would have had jurisdiction of this suit under the general federal-question jurisdiction of 28 U.S.C. § 1331. For the same reasons, the McCarran Amendment did not affect jurisdiction under § 1331 either.

(b) Abstention is also appropriate where there have been presented difficult questions of state law bearing on policy problems of substantial public import whose importance transcends the result in the case then at bar. Louisiana Power & Light Co. v. City of Thibodaux, 360 U.S. 25 (1959), for example, involved such a question. In particular, the concern there was with the scope of the eminent domain power of municipalities under state law. See also Kaiser Steel Corp. v. W.S. Ranch Co., 391 U.S. 593 (1968). In some cases, however, the state question itself need not be determinative of state policy. It is enough that exercise of federal review of the question in a case and in similar cases would be disruptive of state efforts to establish a coherent policy with respect to a matter of substantial public concern. In Burford v. Sun Oil Co., 319 U.S. 315 (1943), for example, the Court held that a suit seeking review of the reasonableness under Texas state law of a state commission's permit to drill oil wells should have been dismissed by the District Court. The reasonableness of the permit in that case was not of transcendent importance, but review of reasonableness by the federal courts in that and future cases, where the state had established its own elaborate review system for dealing with the geological complexities of oil and gas fields, would have had an impermissibly disruptive effect on state policy for the management of those fields. See also *Alabama Pub. Serv. Comm'n v. Southern R. Co.*, supra.[21]

The present case clearly does not fall within this second category of abstention. While state claims are involved in the case, the state law to be applied appears to be settled. No questions bearing on state policy are presented for decision. Nor will decision of the state claims impair efforts to implement state policy as in *Burford*. To be sure, the federal claims that are involved in the case go to the establishment of water rights which may conflict with similar rights based on state law. But the mere potential for conflict in the results of adjudications, does not, without more, warrant staying exercise of federal jurisdiction. See Meredith v. Winter Haven, 320 U.S. 228 (1943); Kline v. Burke Constr. Co., 260 U.S. 226 (1922); McClellan v. Carland, 217 U.S. 268 (1910). The potential conflict here, involving state claims and federal claims, would not be such as to impair impermissibly the state's effort to effect its policy respecting the allocation of state waters. . . .

(c) Finally, abstention is appropriate where, absent bad faith, harassment, or a patently invalid state statute, federal jurisdiction has been invoked for the purpose of restraining state criminal proceedings,

---

[21] We note that *Burford v. Sun Oil Co.*, and *Alabama Pub. Serv. Comm'n v. Southern R. Co.*, differ from *Louisiana Power & Light Co. v. City of Thibodaux*, and *County of Allegheny v. Frank Mashuda Co.*, in that the former two cases, unlike the latter two, raised colorable constitutional claims and were therefore brought under federal-question, as well as diversity, jurisdiction. While abstention in *Burford* and *Alabama Pub. Serv.* had the effect of avoiding a federal constitutional issue, the opinions indicate that this was not an additional ground for abstention in those cases. We have held, of course, that the opportunity to avoid decision of a constitutional question does not alone justify abstention by a federal court. See Harman v. Forssenius, 380 U.S. 528 (1965); Baggett v. Bullitt, 377 U.S. 360 (1964). Indeed, the presence of a federal basis for jurisdiction may raise the level of justification needed for abstention. See *Burford v. Sun Oil Co.*, supra, at 318 n. 5; *Hawks v. Hamill*, 288 U.S., at 61.

Younger v. Harris, 401 U.S. 37 (1971); Douglas v. City of Jeannette, 319 U.S. 157 (1943); state nuisance proceedings antecedent to a criminal prosecution, which are directed at obtaining the closure of places exhibiting obscene films, Huffman v. Pursue, Ltd., 420 U.S. 592 (1975); or collections of state taxes, Great Lakes Dredge & Dock Co. v. Huffman, 319 U.S. 293 (1943). Like the previous two categories, this category also does not include this case. We deal here neither with a criminal proceeding, nor such a nuisance proceeding, nor a tax collection. We also do not deal with an attempt to restrain such actions or to seek a declaratory judgment as to the validity of a state criminal law under which criminal proceedings are pending in a state court.

C

Although this case falls within none of the abstention categories, there are principles unrelated to considerations of proper constitutional adjudication and regard for federal-state relations which govern in situations involving the contemporaneous exercise of concurrent jurisdictions, either by federal courts or by state and federal courts. These principles rest on considerations of "[w]ise judicial administration, giving regard to conservation of judicial resources and comprehensive disposition of litigation." Kerotest Mfg. Co. v. C–O–Two Fire Equipment Co., 342 U.S. 180, 183 (1952). Generally, as between state and federal courts, the rule is that "the pendency of an action in the state court is no bar to proceedings concerning the same matter in the federal court having jurisdiction. . . ." McClellan v. Carland, supra, at 282. As between federal district courts, however, though no precise rule has evolved, the general principle is to avoid duplicative litigation. See Kerotest Mfg. Co. v. C–O–Two Fire Equipment Co., supra. This difference in general approach between state-federal concurrent jurisdiction and wholly federal concurrent jurisdiction stems from the virtually unflagging obligation of the federal courts to exercise the jurisdiction given them. Given this obligation, and the absence of weightier considerations of constitutional adjudication and state-federal relations, the circumstances permitting the dismissal of a federal suit due to the presence of a concurrent state proceeding for reasons of wise judicial administration are considerably more limited than the circumstances appropriate for abstention. The former circumstances, though exceptional, do nevertheless exist.

It has been held, for example, that the court first assuming jurisdiction over property may exercise that jurisdiction to the exclusion of other courts. This has been true even where the government was a claimant in existing state proceedings and then sought to invoke district-court jurisdiction under the jurisdictional provision antecedent to 28 U.S.C. § 1345. In assessing the appropriateness of dismissal in the event of an exercise of concurrent jurisdiction, a federal court may also consider such factors as the inconvenience of the federal forum; the desirability of avoiding piecemeal litigation; and the order in which jurisdiction was obtained by the concurrent forums. No one factor is necessarily determinative; a carefully considered judgment taking into account both the obligation to exercise jurisdiction and the combination of factors counselling against that exercise is required. Only the clearest of justifications will warrant dismissal.

Turning to the present case, a number of factors clearly counsel against concurrent federal proceedings. The most important of these is the McCarran Amendment itself. The clear federal policy evinced by that legislation is the avoidance of piecemeal adjudication of water rights in a river system. This policy is akin to that underlying the rule requiring that jurisdiction be yielded to the court first acquiring control of property, for the concern in such instances is with avoiding the generation of additional litigation through permitting inconsistent dispositions of property. This concern is heightened with respect to water rights, the relationships among which are highly interdependent. Indeed, we have recognized that actions seeking the allocation of water essentially involve the disposition of property and are best conducted in unified proceedings. The consent to jurisdiction given by the McCarran Amendment bespeaks a policy that recognizes the availability of comprehensive state systems for adjudication of water rights as the means for achieving these goals.

As has already been observed, the Colorado Water Rights Determination and Administration Act established such a system for the adjudication and management of rights to the use of the state's waters. As the government concedes . . ., the act established a single continuous proceeding for water rights adjudication which antedated the suit in District Court. . . . Additionally, the responsibility of managing the state's waters, to the end that they be allocated in accordance with adjudicated water rights, is given to the state engineer.

Beyond the congressional policy expressed by the McCarran Amendment and consistent with furtherance of that policy, we also find significant (a) the apparent absence of any proceedings in the District Court, other than the filing of the complaint, prior to the motion to dismiss, (b) the extensive involvement of state water rights occasioned by this suit naming 1,000 defendants, (c) the 300–mile distance between the District Court in Denver and the court in Division 7, and (d) the existing participation by the government in Divisions 4, 5, and 6 proceedings. We emphasize, however, that we do not overlook the heavy obligation to exercise jurisdiction. We need not decide, for example, whether, despite the McCarran Amendment, dismissal would be warranted if more extensive proceedings had occurred in the District Court prior to dismissal, if the involvement of state water rights were less extensive than it is here, or if the state proceeding were in some respect inadequate to resolve the federal claims. But the opposing factors here, particularly the policy underlying the McCarran Amendment, justify the District Court's dismissal in this particular case.[26]

The judgment of the Court of Appeals is reversed and the judgment of the District Court dismissing the complaint is affirmed for the reasons here stated.

[26] Whether similar considerations would permit dismissal of a water suit brought by a private party in federal district court is a question we need not now decide.

It is so ordered.

Mr. Justice Stewart, with whom Mr. Justice Blackmun and Mr. Justice Stevens concur, dissenting.

The Court says that the United States District Court for the District of Colorado clearly had jurisdiction over this lawsuit. I agree. The Court further says that the McCarran Amendment "in no way diminished" the District Court's jurisdiction. I agree. The Court also says that federal courts have a "virtually unflagging obligation . . . to exercise the jurisdiction given them." I agree. And finally, the Court says that nothing in the abstention doctrine "in any of its forms" justified the District Court's dismissal of the Government's complaint. I agree. These views would seem to lead ineluctably to the conclusion that the District Court was wrong in dismissing the complaint. Yet the Court holds that the order of dismissal was "appropriate." With that conclusion I must respectfully disagree.

In holding that the United States shall not be allowed to proceed with its lawsuit, the Court relies principally on cases reflecting the rule that where "control of the property which is the subject of the suit [is necessary] in order to proceed with the cause and to grant the relief sought, the jurisdiction of one court must of necessity yield to that of the other." Penn General Casualty Co. v. Pennsylvania ex rel. Schnader, 294 U.S. 189, 195 (1935). But, as [*Penn General* and similar cases] make clear, this rule applies only when exclusive control over the subject matter is necessary to effectuate a court's judgment. Here the federal court did not need to obtain in rem or quasi in rem jurisdiction in order to decide the issues before it. The court was asked simply to determine as a matter of federal law whether federal reservations of water rights had occurred, and, if so, the date and scope of the reservations. The District Court could make such a determination without having control of the river. . . .

The Court's principal reason for deciding to close the doors of the federal courthouse to the United States in this case seems to stem from the view that its decision will avoid piecemeal adjudication of water rights.[6] To the extent that this view is based on the special considera-

---

[6] The Court lists four other policy reasons for the "appropriateness" of the District Court's dismissal of this lawsuit. All of those reasons are insubstantial. First, the fact that no significant proceedings had yet taken place in the federal court at the time of the dismissal means no more than that the federal court was prompt in granting the defendants' motion to dismiss. At that time, of course, no proceedings involving the government's claims had taken place in the state court either. Second, the geographic distance of the federal court from the rivers in question is hardly a significant factor in this age of rapid and easy transportation. Since the basic issues here involve the determination of the amount of water the government intended to reserve rather than the amount it actually appropriated on a given date, there is little likelihood that live testimony by water district residents would be necessary. In any event, the federal District Court in Colorado is authorized to sit at Durango, the headquarters of Water Division 7. Third, the government's willingness to participate in some of the state proceedings certainly does not mean that it had no right to bring this action, unless the Court has today unearthed a new kind of waiver. Finally, the fact that there were many defendants in the federal suit is hardly relevant. It only indicates that the federal court had all the necessary parties before it in order to issue a decree finally settling the government's claims. . . .

tions governing in rem proceedings, it is without precedential basis. . . . To the extent that the Court's view is based on the realistic practicalities of this case, it is simply wrong, because the relegation of the government to the state courts will not avoid piecemeal litigation.

The Colorado courts are currently engaged in two types of proceedings under the state's water-rights law. First, they are processing new claims to water based on recent appropriations. Second, they are integrating these new awards of water rights with all past decisions awarding such rights into one all-inclusive tabulation for each water source. The claims of the United States that are involved in this case have not been adjudicated in the past. Yet they do not involve recent appropriations of water. In fact, these claims are wholly dissimilar to normal state water claims, because they are not based on actual beneficial use of water but rather on an intention formed at the time the federal land use was established to reserve a certain amount of water to support the federal reservations. The state court will, therefore, have to conduct separate proceedings to determine these claims. And only after the state court adjudicates the claims will they be incorporated into the water source tabulations. If this suit were allowed to proceed in federal court the same procedures would be followed, and the federal court decree would be incorporated into the state tabulation, as other federal court decrees have been incorporated in the past. Thus, the same process will occur regardless of which forum considers these claims. Whether the virtually identical separate proceedings take place in a federal court or a state court, the adjudication of the claims will be neither more nor less "piecemeal." Essentially the same process will be followed in each instance.

As the Court says, it is the virtual "unflagging obligation" of a federal court to exercise the jurisdiction that has been conferred upon it. Obedience to that obligation is particularly "appropriate" in this case, for at least two reasons.

First, the issues involved are issues of federal law. A federal court is more likely than a state court to be familiar with federal water law and to have had experience in interpreting the relevant federal statutes, regulations, and Indian treaties. Moreover, if tried in a federal court, these issues of federal law will be reviewable in a federal appellate court, whereas federal judicial review of the state courts' resolution of issues of federal law will be possible only on review by this Court in the exercise of its certiorari jurisdiction.

Second, some of the federal claims in this lawsuit relate to water reserved for Indian reservations. It is not necessary to determine that there is no state-court jurisdiction of these claims to support the proposition that a federal court is a more appropriate forum than a state court for determination of questions of life-and-death importance to Indians. This Court has long recognized that " '[t]he policy of leaving Indians free from state jurisdiction and control is deeply rooted in the Nation's history.' " McClanahan v. Arizona State Tax Comm'n, 411 U.S. 164, 168 (1973), quoting Rice v. Olson, 324 U.S. 786, 789 (1945).

The Court says that "[o]nly the clearest of justifications will warrant dismissal" of a lawsuit within the jurisdiction of a federal court. In my opinion there was no justification at all for the District Court's order of dismissal in this case.

I would affirm the judgment of the Court of Appeals.

MR. JUSTICE STEVENS, dissenting.

While I join Mr. Justice Stewart's dissenting opinion, I add three brief comments:

First, I find the holding that the United States may not litigate a federal claim in a federal court having jurisdiction thereof particularly anomalous. I could not join such a disposition unless commanded to do so by an unambiguous statutory mandate or by some other clearly identifiable and applicable rule of law. The McCarran Amendment . . . announces no such rule.

Second, the federal government surely has no lesser right of access to the federal forum than does a private litigant, such as an Indian asserting his own claim. If this be so, today's holding will necessarily restrict the access to federal court of private plaintiffs asserting water rights claims in Colorado. This is a rather surprising byproduct of the McCarran Amendment; for there is no basis for concluding that Congress intended that amendment to impair the private citizen's right to assert a federal claim in a federal court.

Third, even on the Court's assumption that this case should be decided by balancing the factors weighing for and against the exercise of federal jurisdiction, I believe we should defer to the judgment of the Court of Appeals rather than evaluate those factors in the first instance ourselves. In this case the District Court erroneously dismissed the complaint on abstention grounds and the Court of Appeals found no reason why the litigation should not go forward in a federal court. Facts such as the number of parties, the distance between the courthouse and the water in dispute, and the character of the Colorado proceedings are matters which the Court of Appeals sitting in Denver is just as able to evaluate as are we. . . .

NOTES ON CONCURRENT LITIGATION IN STATE AND FEDERAL COURTS

1. **Background.** Chief Justice Marshall is often quoted in support of the obligation of federal courts to hear cases within their jurisdiction: the federal judiciary has "no more right to decline the exercise of jurisdiction which is given, than to usurp that which is not given. The one or the other would be treason to the Constitution." Cohens v. Virginia, 19 U.S. (6 Wheat.) 264, 404 (1821). There are, however, many situations where litigation within the literal coverage of a jurisdictional statute will not be heard by the federal courts. The three "abstention" doctrines discussed by Justice Brennan in *Colorado River* are examples. These doctrines are examined further in the notes beginning on page

562, infra, and two of them form the focus of Chapter X, infra. For now it is only necessary to note that a separate jurisprudence has developed around each of them, and that they have been confined to particular classes of litigation involving defined situations.

A different issue is of present concern. It involves the general obligation of federal district courts to exercise jurisdiction conferred by the Congress, and in particular whether the existence of concurrent state and federal litigation in any way relaxes that obligation. Three lines of cases had evolved prior to *Colorado River*. Each concerns deference by a federal court to concurrent litigation involving the same parties and the same issues.

The first is where the second suit would interfere with the control of property already in the "custody" of another court. When this principle applies, it is clear that the second court must defer to the court that has control of the property. All of the justices in *Colorado River* accepted the validity of this principle, though they disagreed about its relevance.

The second situation involves declaratory judgments. Federal courts are authorized by 28 U.S.C. §§ 2201 and 2202 to grant declaratory relief in cases of "actual controversy" otherwise within the scope of a jurisdictional statute. These statutes were passed in 1934. Shortly thereafter, the Court made it clear that declaratory relief was discretionary, and that one reason for declining the relief requested might be that the same issues were already pending in a prior proceeding.[a]

Both of these doctrines permit or require a federal court to decline jurisdiction in favor of proceedings pending elsewhere, whether in state or federal court. The third situation is peculiar to the relationship among federal courts. It has long been the rule that the lower federal courts have discretion to defer to pending *federal* litigation involving the same parties and issues.[b] But the rule is generally regarded as different when contemporaneous in personam litigation is being pursued in a *state* court.[c] It is up to state law, of course, to resolve how the state courts should react to such a situation. But the federal rule, as usually formulated, is that the federal court should proceed to judgment, subject to the application of normal res judicata principles if the state proceeding becomes final before the federal suit is concluded. The question before the Court in *Colorado River* concerned the flexibility of this general rule.

2. Questions and Comments on *Colorado River*. Three issues may help to focus study of *Colorado River* and the cases considered in the succeeding notes:

The first is whether it is generally correct to require federal courts to continue in personam litigation when the same parties

---

[a] See Brillhart v. Excess Ins. Co. of America, 316 U.S. 491 (1942).

[b] See, e.g., Kerotest Manufacturing Co. v. C–O–Two Fire Equipment Co., 342 U.S. 180 (1952).

[c] See, e.g., Kline v. Burke Constr. Co., 260 U.S. 226 (1922).

are already litigating the same issues in state court. Would it not be more efficient if the federal judge had discretion to defer to the state proceeding? Should the rule be that the federal judge is *required* to defer to a pending state proceeding unless there are good reasons not to?

The second issue assumes the existence of a general obligation to hear the case in spite of the pending state proceeding, but focuses on possible exceptions to that rule. Should there be exceptions? If so, did the Court identify the right considerations in *Colorado River*? Was the Court right to order deference to the state proceedings in *Colorado River*?

The third issue concerns who should weigh the relevant criteria. One of the problems underlying *Colorado River* is the weight that should be given to the judgment of a district judge to defer to pending state litigation. The dissenters appear to regard exceptions to the "unflagging obligation" of federal courts to hear cases within their jurisdiction as presenting a question of law—they felt free, in other words, to weigh the relevant factors themselves. Did the majority agree on this point? Is this a question on which the deference normally given discretionary decisions by trial courts should be followed? What are the practical consequences on litigation strategy if the decision by a district judge to stay a federal proceeding in favor of concurrent state proceedings is appealable and subject to de novo review?

3. ***Will v. Calvert Fire Ins. Co.*** The Calvert Fire Insurance Co., which specialized in property and casualty insurance, subscribed to a reinsurance pool operated by the American Mutual Reinsurance Co. When Calvert sought to rescind this arrangement, American Mutual filed suit in state court for a declaratory judgment that the recission was ineffective and the reinsurance agreement still in effect. Six months later, Calvert filed an answer claiming that the agreement was unenforceable because American Mutual had violated the Securities Act of 1933, the Securities Exchange Act of 1934, two state securities laws, and the common law of fraud. Calvert also filed a counterclaim seeking $2 million in damages on all of these grounds except the Securities Exchange Act of 1934, the enforcement of which lies within the exclusive jurisdiction of the federal courts. On the same day, Calvert filed a federal suit seeking damages under § 10–b and Rule 10(b)(5) of the 1934 Act.[d] It also added claims based on each of the other defenses asserted in the state suit.

One month later American Mutual moved to dismiss or abate the federal suit. The motion to dismiss was based on the substantive ground that the reinsurance agreement was not a "security" within the 1933 or 1934 acts, and hence that it could not be in violation of federal law. The motion to abate was based on the argument that in any event the federal court should defer to the pending state proceedings. Judge

[d] It is settled that state courts have authority to consider defenses based on the 1934 act, but that only a federal court can give affirmative relief.

Will granted the motion to defer to the state proceedings, noting that a trial date had been set by the state court and that duplicative proceedings in both courts would be wasteful. Judge Will also heard argument on whether the reinsurance agreement was a "security," but did not render a decision on that issue. In effect, therefore, Judge Will decided to await the conclusion of the state proceedings and then, if necessary, try the claim for damages under the 1934 act.

Calvert next sought mandamus in the Court of Appeals to compel Judge Will to proceed with the claim based on the 1934 act. The Court of Appeals issued the writ, and the Supreme Court granted certiorari. It reversed in Will v. Calvert Fire Ins. Co., 437 U.S. 655 (1978), dividing four–one–four on how the case should be decided.

Justice Rehnquist, joined by Justices Stewart, White, and Stevens, wrote for the plurality. Calvert argued, among other things, that a district court could not stay proceedings in deference to a state suit when the federal courts had exclusive jurisdiction over the issue presented. As Justice Rehnquist read the record, however, Judge Will "has not purported to stay consideration of Calvert's claim for damages" under the 1934 act. While it was true, Justice Rehnquist admitted, that the claim had not been ruled on for more than three years, "[s]o far as appears, the delay in adjudicating the damages claim is simply a product of the normal excessive load of business in the District Court, compounded by the 'unfortunate consequence of making the judge a litigant' in this mandamus proceeding." Under the normal standards for reviewing district court proceedings by mandamus, the plurality thus thought the writ should not have been issued.[e]

The real import of Justice Rehnquist's opinion, however, was addressed to the broader issue of the general propriety of federal court deference to contemporaneous state proceedings:

> "It is well established that 'the pendency of an action in the state court is no bar to proceedings concerning the same matter in the federal court having jurisdiction.' McClellan v. Carland, 217 U.S. 268, 282 (1910). It is equally well settled that a district court is 'under no compulsion to exercise that jurisdiction,' Brillhart v. Excess Ins. Co., 316 U.S. 491, 494 (1942), where the controversy may be settled more expeditiously in the state court. Although most of our decisions discussing the propriety of stays or dismissals of duplicative actions have concerned conflicts of jurisdiction between two federal district courts, we have recognized the relevance of these cases in the analogous circumstances presented here. See Colorado River Water Conservation District et al. v. United States, 424 U.S. 800, 817–19 (1976). In both situations, the decision is largely committed to the 'carefully considered judgment,' id. at 18, of the district court. . . .

[e] At one point in the opinion, Justice Rehnquist said that "[a]lthough the District Court's exercise of its discretion may be subject to review and modification in a proper interlocutory appeal, we are convinced that it ought not to be overridden by a writ of mandamus."

"It is true that *Colorado River* emphasized 'the virtually unflagging obligation of the federal courts to exercise the jurisdiction given them.' That language underscores our conviction that a district court should exercise its discretion with this factor in mind, but it in no way undermines the conclusion of *Brillhart* that the decision whether to defer to the concurrent jurisdiction of a state court is, in the last analysis, a matter committed to the district court's discretion. . . . We are loath to rest our analysis on this ubiquitous phrase, for if used carelessly or without a precise definition it may impede rather than assist sound resolution of the underlying issue.

"There are sound reasons for our reiteration of the rule that a district court's decision to defer proceedings because of concurrent state litigation is generally committed to the discretion of that court. No one can seriously contend that a busy federal trial judge confronted both with competing demands on his time for matters properly within his jurisdiction and with inevitable scheduling difficulties because of the unavailability of lawyers, parties, and witnesses, is not entrusted with a wide latitude in setting his own calendar. Had Judge Will simply decided on his own initiative to defer setting this case for trial until the state proceedings were completed, his action would have been the 'equivalent' of granting the motion of American Mutual to defer, yet such action would at best have afforded Calvert a highly dubious claim for mandamus. We think the fact that the judge accomplished this same result by ruling favorably on a party's motion to defer does not change the underlying legal question. . . ."

Justice Brennan, joined by Chief Justice Burger and by Justices Marshall and Powell, sharply disagreed. In his view, *McClellan v. Carland* established a general obligation of federal courts to proceed in spite of concurrent state litigation, especially when federal questions were involved and most particularly when the federal court had exclusive jurisdiction over those questions. *Brillhart* was "completely inapposite," since it involved a diversity action in which no federal question was raised and was based on "the permissive nature of declaratory judgment jurisdiction." Rehnquist's "unpersuasive grope for supporting precedent" was "especially lamentable in light of our decision only two terms ago in *Colorado River.*" *Colorado River* emphasized the "unflagging obligation" of federal courts to exercise jurisdiction as conferred, an obligation that is subject to exceptions only in "rare circumstances" like those present in that case. Brennan accused Rehnquist of "[i]gnoring wholesale the analytical framework set forth in *Colorado River*" and creating an "ominous potential for the abdication of federal-court jurisdiction in the opinion's disturbing indifference" to the teaching of *Colorado River*. He concluded:

"The relevant federal policy here is the precise opposite of that found to require deference to the concurrent state proceeding in *Colorado River*. . . . Even putting aside the opinion's case-reading errors—its flouting of *McClellan,* its misreliance on *Brillhart,* and its misapplication of *Colorado River*—. . . the conclusion is . . . compelled that the District Court had no authority to stay Calvert's 1934 act claims."

With the Court thus divided four to four, Justice Blackmun cast the decisive vote for reversal. He said:

> "The plurality's opinion appears to me to indicate that it now regards as fully compatible the Court's decisions in *Brillhart,* a diversity case, and *Colorado River,* a federal-issue case. I am not at all sure that this is so. I—as were Mr. Justice Stewart and Mr. Justice Stevens—was in dissent in *Colorado River,* and if the holding in that case is what I think it is, and if one assumes, as I do not, that *Brillhart* has any application here, the Court cut back on Mr. Justice Frankfurter's rather sweeping language in *Brillhart.*
>
> "Because Judge Will's stay order was issued prior to this Court's decision in *Colorado River,* and he therefore did not have such guidance as that case affords in this area, I join in the Court's reversal of the Court of Appeals' issuance of a writ of mandamus. The issuance was premature. The Court of Appeals should have done no more than require reconsideration of the case by Judge Will in light of *Colorado River.*"

4. ***Moses H. Cone Memorial Hospital v. Mercury Constr. Corp.*** The message of *Calvert* was, to say the least, unclear. How, for example, were the votes of Justices Stevens and Stewart in *Calvert* to be explained in light of their position in *Colorado River*? What did Justice Blackmun's opinion mean? Were lower courts now free to follow a more liberal policy of deference to pending state proceedings?[f] These questions were clarified in Moses H. Cone Memorial Hospital v. Mercury Constr. Corp., 460 U.S. 1 (1983).

Mercury contracted to build additions to the Hospital. Disputes involving performance of the work or interpretation of the contract were first to be referred to the architect. Either party could invoke arbitration if unsatisfied with the architect's decision. The project was delayed, and Mercury claimed that the Hospital was liable for some of the costs of the delay. After a complicated series of events, the Hospital sued both Mercury and the architect in state court seeking a declaratory judgment that Mercury's claim was without foundation, that Mercury had lost its right to arbitration under the terms of the contract, and that if adjudged liable to Mercury the Hospital was entitled to indemnity from the architect. Shortly thereafter, Mercury filed a diversity action against the Hospital seeking an order compelling arbitration. The District Court stayed the federal suit in favor of the state court proceedings. The Court of Appeals reversed and instructed the District Court to enter an order compelling arbitration. The Supreme Court granted certiorari and affirmed.

---

[f] Some clearly thought so. See Note, Abstention and Mandamus After *Will v. Cal-* *vert Fire Insurance Co.,* 64 Cornell L. Rev. 566, 585 & n.127 (1979).

Justice Brennan wrote the opinion for the Court. The first question was whether the decision to stay was an appealable order. The Court held that it was.[g] The next question was whether the District Court had erred in deferring to the state proceeding. Justice Brennan started with a summary of *Colorado River,* concluding that "the decision whether to dismiss a federal action because of parallel state-court litigation does not rest on a mechanical checklist, but on a careful balancing of the important factors as they apply in a given case, with the balance heavily weighted in favor of the exercise of jurisdiction." Brennan then dismissed the significance of Rehnquist's remarks in *Calvert*:

> "[I]t is clear that a majority of the Court reaffirmed [*Colorado River*'s exceptional-circumstances] test in *Calvert*. Justice Rehnquist's opinion commanded only four votes. It was opposed by the dissenting opinion, in which four justices concluded that the *Calvert* District Court's stay was impermissible under *Colorado River*. Justice Blackmun, although concurring in the judgment, agreed with the dissent that *Colorado River*'s exceptional-circumstances test was controlling; he voted to remand to permit the District Court to apply the *Colorado River* factors in the first instance. On remand, the Court of Appeals correctly recognized that the four dissenting justices and Justice Blackmun formed a majority to require application of the *Colorado River* test."[h]

Justice Brennan then addressed the proper scope of review:

> "The Hospital . . . contends that *Calvert* requires reversal here because the opinions of Justice Rehnquist and Justice Blackmun require greater deference to the discretion of the District Court than was given by the Court of Appeals in this case. Under both *Calvert* and *Colorado River,* of course, the decision whether to defer to the state courts is necessarily left to the discretion of the district court in the first instance. Yet to say that the district court has discretion is not to say that its decision is unreviewable; such discretion must be exercised under the relevant standard prescribed by this Court. In this case, the relevant standard is *Colorado River*'s exceptional-

[g] The question was whether the District Court's order was a "final decision" within 28 U.S.C. § 1291. Justice Rehnquist, joined by Chief Justice Burger and Justice O'Connor, dissented on the appealability issue. He did not reach the merits: "Given my view of appealability, I do not find it necessary to decide whether the District Court's order was proper in this case." No other opinions were filed.

The "final decision" language of § 1291 is considered beginning at page 657, infra. The appealability issue in *Cone* is addressed at pages 668–70, infra. On the appealability of district court orders deny-

ing a motion to stay sought on *Colorado River* grounds, see the note on Gulfstream Aerospace Corp. v. Mayacamas Corp., ____ U.S. ____ (1988), page 673, infra.

[h] Justice Brennan also argued that Justice Rehnquist's opinion in *Calvert* did not control this case even on its own terms: Rehnquist's rationale in *Calvert* had in part rested on the impropriety of using mandamus to control such decisions by lower courts. And he had conceded (see footnote e, page 553, supra) that the scope of review would be different if review were by appeal.

circumstances test, as elucidated by the factors discussed in that case."

Under this standard, according to the Court, the District Court "abused its discretion in granting the stay."

Justice Brennan explained in great detail why the Court came to this conclusion. In brief, he gave five reasons: (1) piecemeal litigation was inevitable here because there were two disputes, only one of which—the claim by Mercury against the Hospital—was subject to arbitration; (2) the fact that the state suit was filed first was irrelevant because the federal suit was farther along on the only issue before the court at the time the stay order was issued; (3) federal law controlled the issue of arbitrability;[i] (4) here the state remedy might be inadequate to protect Mercury's federal rights;[j] and (5) it made no difference that the federal court stayed the action rather than dismissed it. Justice Brennan explained the last point as follows:

> "We have no occasion in this case to decide whether a dismissal or a stay should ordinarily be the preferred course of action when a district court properly finds that *Colorado River* counsels in favor of deferring to a parallel state-court suit. We can say, however, that a stay is as much a refusal to exercise federal jurisdiction as a dismissal. When a district court decides to dismiss or stay under *Colorado River*, it presumably concludes that the parallel state-court action will be an adequate vehicle for the complete and prompt resolution of the issues between the parties. If there is any substantial doubt as to this, it would be a serious abuse of discretion to grant the stay or dismissal at all. Thus, a decision to invoke *Colorado River* necessarily contemplates that the federal court will have nothing further to do in resolving the case, whether it stays or dismisses.

> "Moreover, assuming that for some unexpected reason the state forum does turn out to be inadequate in some respect, [there is] no genuine difference between a stay and a dismissal.

[i] As Justice Brennan explained, the federal Arbitration Act is "something of an anomaly" in that it creates a federal right to compel arbitration, but does not confer federal question jurisdiction to enforce the right. The right is enforceable in federal court only when there is some independent jurisdictional basis for filing a federal suit. Here there was diversity, and it was settled in Prima Paint Corp. v. Flood & Conklin Mfg. Corp., 388 U.S. 395 (1967), that a federal diversity court was required to compel arbitration under the terms of the act even though the relevant state law might forbid it.

[j] It was not clear at the time that the federal Arbitration Act required state courts to compel arbitration, even if the controversy was one that required a federal court to do so. This matter was subsequently clarified in Southland Corp. v. Keating, 465 U.S. 1 (1984), where the Court held that state courts were required to enforce the federal act. The issue in *Southland* was whether the federal act created procedural rights enforceable only in federal court, or whether it announced a federal substantive policy applicable to all contracts "involving commerce." Although the Court concluded, over a dissent by Justice O'Connor (joined by Justice Rehnquist), that the arbitration act created substantive policies enforceable in state court, it adhered to the view that "it does not create any independent federal-question jurisdiction under 28 U.S.C. § 1331 or otherwise."

It is true that Mercury could seek to return to federal court if it proved necessary; but that would be equally true if the District Court had dismissed the case. It is highly questionable whether this Court would have approved a dismissal of a federal suit in *Colorado River* . . . if the federal courts did not remain open to a dismissed plaintiff who later demonstrated the inadequacy of the state forum."

5. Questions, Comments, and Bibliography. The effect of the *Colorado River-Calvert-Cone* trilogy seems to be that under normal circumstances it is an appealable abuse of discretion for a district judge to stay a federal trial because the same issues are already being litigated in state court between the same parties. Has the Court come to the right result? Why is it required that a federal judge spend time litigating issues that are already being heard in state court? Should it matter if the federal plaintiff is also the state plaintiff, i.e., that the plaintiff may be trying to wear the defendant down with multiple lawsuits? If the state court defendant filed the federal action, should it matter whether the suit could have been removed to federal court?[k]

For a consideration of all three decisions, see Sonenshein, Abstention: The Crooked Course of *Colorado River,* 59 Tulane L. Rev. 651 (1985). For searing criticism of *Colorado River* and its progeny, see Linda Mullenix, A Branch Too Far: Pruning the Abstention Doctrine, 75 Geo.L.J. 99 (1986). Mullenix concludes that *Colorado River* abstention is "dangerous, unprincipled, and unfair." *Colorado River* is critically examined in the context of water-rights litigation in Abrams, Reserved Water Rights, Indian Rights and the Narrowing Scope of Federal Jurisdiction: The *Colorado River* Decision, 30 Stan. L. Rev. 1111 (1978). David Shapiro has criticized reflexive invocation of the *Cohens* dictum[l] in Jurisdiction and Discretion, 60 N.Y.U.L. Rev. 543 (1985). He argues that "suggestions of an overriding obligation, subject only and at most to a few narrowly drawn exceptions, are far too grudging in their recognition of judicial discretion in matters of jurisdiction."

NOTES ON RES JUDICATA AND EXCLUSIVE FEDERAL JURISDICTION

1. *Will v. Calvert Ins. Co.* Revisited. One of the subsidiary issues in *Calvert* was whether a final judgment by the state court should be given res judicata or collateral estoppel effect in the federal court. Normally, of course, state court judgments are fully enforceable in federal court, even if they resolve questions of federal law. Section

---

[k] In *Cone,* Mercury attempted to remove the case at the same time that it filed the independent federal suit. The District Court remanded the state court action because both the Hospital and the architect were citizens of the same state and complete diversity thus was lacking. The Court noted in *Cone* that the propriety of the effort to remove was not before it.

[l] See page 550, supra.

1738 of title 28 specifically requires as much.[a] The complication in
Calvert was whether this rule should be applied where Congress has
given the federal courts exclusive jurisdiction to enforce the federal law
in question.[b] No Justice took a position on this issue in *Calvert*, but
Justice Brennan speculated as follows:

> "I confess to serious doubt that it is ever appropriate to accord
> res judicata effect to a state-court determination of a claim
> over which the federal courts have exclusive jurisdiction; for
> surely state-court determinations should not disable federal
> courts from ruling de novo on purely legal questions surround-
> ing such federal claims. As recognized by Judge Learned
> Hand in Lyons v. Westinghouse Elec. Corp., 222 F.2d 184, 189
> (2d Cir. 1955), 'the grant to the district courts of exclusive
> jurisdiction over the action . . . should be taken to imply an
> immunity of their decisions from any prejudgment elsewhere.'
> I recognize that it may make sense, for reasons of fairness and
> judicial economy, to give collateral-estoppel effect to specific
> findings of historical facts by a state court's adjudicating an
> exclusively federal claim raised as a defense, but there are
> reasons why even such a limited preclusive effect should not be
> given state-court determinations. It is at least arguable that,
> in creating and defining a particular federal claim, Congress
> assumed that the claim would be litigated only in the context
> of federal-court procedure—a fair assumption when the claim
> is within exclusive federal jurisdiction. For example, Congress
> may have thought the liberal federal discovery procedures
> crucial to the proper determination of the factual disputes
> underlying the federal claim."[c]

2. *Marrese v. American Academy of Orthopaedic Surgeons.*
A related question came before the Court in Marrese v. American
Academy of Orthopaedic Surgeons, 470 U.S. 373 (1985). The plaintiffs
had been excluded from the defendant association. They filed a state
action claiming violation of associational rights protected by state
common law. They did not assert any claims under state or federal
antitrust laws, and indeed could not have asserted a violation of federal
antitrust laws because of the exclusive jurisdiction of the federal
district courts. They lost on the merits in the state court, and then
filed a federal antitrust action. The District Court denied a motion to
dismiss, and certified its decision for interlocutory review. The Court
of Appeals held that the federal suit was barred by claim preclusion.

[a] See the discussion at pages 352–54, supra.

[b] Even though Congress gave federal
courts exclusive jurisdiction to enforce
claims under the 1934 Securities Act, state
courts may hear defenses based on the
statute.

[c] Justice Brennan thought it unnecessary to resolve this question in *Calvert*. He
reasoned that if res judicata effect were

not to be given to the state court proceeding, the federal court would have to hear
the case anyway and it might as well get
started. If res judicata effect were to be
given, Brennan argued, it would undermine the statute conferring exclusive jurisdiction on the federal courts for the court
to stay its hand while the issues were resolved in state court.

In an opinion by Justice O'Connor, the Supreme Court reversed. It stated the issue as "whether a state court judgment may have preclusive effect on a federal antitrust claim that could not have been raised in the state proceeding." The Court of Appeals had resolved this question by resort to federal common law. The Supreme Court held this improper. What the Court of Appeals should have done was examine state claim-preclusion law first. Section 1738 of title 28 requires that federal courts give the same effect to a state judgment that the state courts themselves would give it. The Court concluded: "We are unwilling to create a special exception to § 1738 for federal antitrust claims that would give state court judgments greater preclusive effect than would the courts of the state rendering the judgment." The Court elaborated:

> "If we had a single system of courts and our only concerns were efficiency and finality, it might be desirable to fashion claim preclusion rules that would require a plaintiff to bring suit initially in the forum of most general jurisdiction, thereby resolving as many issues as possible in one proceeding. The decision of the Court of Appeals approximates such a rule inasmuch as it encourages plaintiffs to file suit initially in federal district court and to attempt to bring any state law claims pendent to their federal antitrust claims. Whether this result would reduce the overall burden of litigation is debatable, and we decline to base our interpretation of § 1738 on our opinion on this question.

> "More importantly, we have parallel systems of state and federal courts, and the concerns of comity reflected in § 1738 generally allow states to determine the preclusive effect of their own courts' judgments. These concerns are certainly not made less compelling because state courts lack jurisdiction over federal antitrust claims. We therefore reject a judicially created exception to § 1738 that effectively holds as a matter of federal law that a plaintiff can bring state law claims initially in state court only at the cost of forgoing subsequent federal antitrust actions."

Justices Blackmun and Stevens did not participate in the decision.

Chief Justice Burger concurred in the judgment. He agreed "that a federal court is not free to accord greater preclusive effect to a state court judgment than the state courts themselves would give to it." But he was concerned with what the District Court should do on remand "if it finds state law silent or indeterminate on the claim preclusion question," a situation he thought "likely." In that event, he said:

> "[I]t may be consistent with § 1738 for a federal court to formulate a federal rule to resolve the matter. If state law is simply indeterminate, the concerns of comity and federalism do not come into play. At the same time, the federal courts have direct interests in ensuring that their resources are used efficiently and not as a means of harassing defendants with

repetitive lawsuits, as well as in ensuring that parties asserting federal rights have an adequate opportunity to litigate those rights. Given the insubstantiality of the state interests and the weight of the federal interests, a strong argument could be made that a federal rule would be more appropriate than a creative interpretation of ambiguous state law. . . . "

What the Chief Justice had in mind was that Marrese could have attached a claim under the state antitrust law to his common law action in state court. If he had done so, it may have been that virtually the same issues would have been litigated in state court as would subsequently be litigated in a federal antitrust action. If the state preclusion law foreclosed a second suit on state antitrust issues because that claim could have been raised in the first suit, then perhaps a federal antitrust suit should also be foreclosed even though state preclusion law did not speak to the effect of the state judgment on matters within the exclusive jurisdiction of the federal courts.

   3. Questions, Comments, and Bibliography. The issues raised in *Marrese* and *Calvert* require consideration of at least two separate questions. The first is whether federal litigants should be barred from raising claims within the exclusive jurisdiction of the federal courts when they have litigated—or could have litigated—related state claims in a prior state proceeding. This was the situation presented by *Marrese*. Was the case correctly resolved? What should the District Court have done on remand if the state law was ambiguous or inconclusive? Suppose the federal plaintiff were a defendant in state court who could have raised a violation of the antitrust laws as a defense to a state cause of action but did not do so. Is that situation different?

   The second question is whether actually litigated in state courts should be given collateral estoppel effect in a subsequent federal suit if they concern matters within the exclusive jurisdiction of the federal courts. This question could arise in several contexts. For example, as fact relevant to federal antitrust pr securities violations could be resolved in a suit between the same parties involving only state questions. Or, as in *Calvert*, the state defendant could rely on plaintiff's violation of federal law in defense to a claim based on state law and later assert a claim for affirmative relief in federal court. How should the issues raised by such situations be resolved? In the latter case, should it matter whether the federal plaintiff won or lost on the state court defense? If the federal plaintiff lost in state court, should collateral estoppel be denied in the federal proceeding for the reasons speculated by Justice Brennan in *Calvert*?

   If collateral estoppel effect is not given to the state court judgment and if the federal court later resolves the disputed issue differently, what effect should the federal judgment have on the prior state judgment? Suppose, for example, a state court rejects a securities act defense on the merits, but the federal court—instructed not to give the state judgment collateral estoppel effect—finds the federal claim meritorious and awards affirmative relief. Should the federal plaintiff still be required to satisfy the state judgment?

For extensive consideration of how § 1738 should be interpreted in the context of state judgments sought to be used in a federal court, see Gene Shreve, Preclusion and Federal Choice of Law, 64 Texas L.Rev. 1209 (1986). Shreve addresses three problems left open by *Marrese*: how the courts should deal with uncertain state law; whether exceptions to the preclusive effect of a state judgment should be recognized; and whether it should ever be permissible for a federal court to give greater preclusive effect to a state judgment than the judgment would receive in the state courts. In Interjurisdictional Preclusion, Full Faith and Credit and Federal Common Law: A General Approach, 71 Cornell L. Rev. 733, 822–29 (1986), Stephen Burbank considered the issues raised in these notes in the context of an elaborate treatment of the relationship between state and federal court judgments. For other discussions, see Degnan, Federalized Res Judicata, 85 Yale L.J. 741 (1976); Note, The Claim Preclusion Effect of State Court Judgments on Federal Antitrust Claims: *Marrese v. American Academy of Orthopaedic Surgeons,* 71 Iowa L. Rev. 609 (1986); Note, The Res Judicata Effect of Prior State Court Judgments in Sherman Act Suits: Exalting Substance Over Form, 51 Fordham L. Rev. 1374 (1983); Note, The Collateral Estoppel Effect of Prior State Court Findings in Cases Within Exclusive Federal Jurisdiction, 91 Harv. L. Rev. 1281 (1978); Note, The Effect of Prior Nonfederal Proceedings on Exclusive Federal Jurisdiction over Section 10–b of the Securities Exchange Act of 1934, 46 N.Y. U.L. Rev. 936 (1971); Note, Res Judicata: Exclusive Federal Jurisdiction and the Effect of Prior State-Court Determinations, 53 Va. L. Rev. 1360 (1967).

NOTES ON THE ABSTENTION DOCTRINES

1. **Introduction.** The generic term "abstention" has been used to refer to a wide variety of doctrines that all have the same effect: deference by a federal court to litigation in state court. In some instances, federal courts will abstain irrespective of the existence or prospect of state proceedings. The judgment in such cases is that the subject matter is simply inappropriate for litigation in federal court.[a] In other instances, deference is triggered by the fact that litigation on the same issues between the same parties is already pending in state court, and the judgment is that the federal court should await the results of that litigation.[b] In still other situations, the purpose of

---

[a] Examples of this form of abstention are the refusal of federal district courts to hear domestic relations and probate cases even though the requirements of diversity jurisdiction are formally satisfied. See page 470 & footnote q, supra. Another example is so-called *Burford* abstention, discussed at pages 564–66, below.

[b] Examples are the *Colorado River* sequence of cases, pages 541–58, supra, and many instances where 28 U.S.C. § 2283 is invoked. See pages 526–41, supra. So-called *Younger* abstention, discussed briefly at page 563, infra, and more fully at pages 1158–1243, infra, is another example.

abstention is to require the institution of litigation in state court to resolve issues central to the federal court proceeding.[c]

As these illustrations confirm, there is no unitary doctrine of "abstention." Instead, there are several doctrines that are specific to particular situations. The purpose of the following notes is to give an overview of the abstention doctrines. More detail on some of them is developed in other parts of the book.[d]

2. *Pullman* **Abstention.** The case most often associated with the term "abstention," perhaps because of its visibility in early civil rights litigation, is Railroad Commission of Texas v. Pullman, 312 U.S. 496 (1941). A federal court enjoined an order by the Texas Railroad Commission that effectively excluded blacks from supervising sleeping cars on trains. In an opinion by Justice Frankfurter, the Supreme Court set the injunction aside and ordered the trial court to hold the federal action in abeyance until the parties could secure a ruling in state court on whether the Railroad Commission's order was authorized by state law. The state law was uncertain, and rather than have the federal court decide a federal constitutional question, perhaps unnecessarily, the Court thought it best to obtain an authoritative ruling on the state law. The effect of the decision was to require the parties to institute litigation in the state courts to resolve the uncertain state issue. In the meantime, the federal court would retain jurisdiction over the controversy and the parties could return to federal court for a ruling on the federal constitutional issue if that proved necessary after the state litigation.

The paradigmatic case in which *Pullman* abstention may be appropriate thus involves an effort to enjoin a state official from engaging in certain behavior where (i) there is doubt as to the official's authority under state law and (ii) the conduct is challenged on federal constitutional grounds. Since *Pullman* abstention primarily arises today in suits filed under 42 U.S.C. § 1983, full consideration of the doctrine is postponed in these materials to pages 1139–58, infra, where it is considered in the context of other issues associated with that statute.

3. *Younger* **Abstention.** The most visible form of abstention today derives from Younger v. Harris, 401 U.S. 37 (1971). *Younger* involved an effort to enjoin a criminal proceeding then pending in state court. The Court held that federal courts ordinarily should permit pending state criminal proceedings to run their course without interference from federal courts. In a companion case, the Court held that the policies underlying *Younger* also precluded federal declaratory relief on issues involved in pending state criminal proceedings. In another

[c] So-called *Pullman* abstention is the prime illustration here. *Pullman* is discussed briefly below, and more fully at pages 1139–58, infra.

[d] Account should also be taken of the possibility of certification. While not normally called "abstention," certification is a form of deference to state court resolution of an issue of state law pending in federal court. Certification is further discussed at pages 288–89, supra. For a recent debate among the Justices on the propriety of certification in a case where abstention was regarded as inappropriate, see Houston v. Hill, __ U.S. __ (1987).

companion case, it directed the federal courts not to interfere by way of injunction or declaratory judgment with the admissibility of evidence in state criminal proceedings.

The paradigm *Younger* situation involves an effort to obtain a federal declaratory judgment or injunction on issues involved in pending state criminal proceedings. Such federal relief will ordinarily be sought under 42 U.S.C. § 1983, and for this reason consideration of *Younger* has been postponed to the materials on that statute. See pages 1158–1243, infra, which also consider the application of *Younger* to certain kinds of state civil litigation. The question of federal *damages* relief in this context is dealt with at pages 1218–23 infra.

4. *Burford* **Abstention.** A third context in which the term "abstention" is frequently used stems from Burford v. Sun Oil Co., 319 U.S. 315 (1943). Sun Oil Co. filed an action in federal court to enjoin an order of the Texas Railroad Commission granting Burford a permit to drill four oil wells. Jurisdiction was based on diversity and the alleged unconstitutionality of the Railroad Commission's order. Over a vigorous dissent by Justice Frankfurter, the Court, in an opinion by Justice Black, decided that the federal suit should have been dismissed. Since "the important constitutional issues have . . . been fairly well settled from the beginning," the Court treated the case as presenting the question whether federal district courts should be permitted to intervene by injunction in ordinary diversity litigation involving the Texas regulatory scheme.

The case involved the East Texas oil field, an area approximately 40 miles long and five to nine miles wide, split into many small tracts and containing more than 26,000 wells. "Since the oil moves through the entire field," the Court explained, "one operator can not only draw the oil from under his own surface area, but can also, if he is advantageously located, drain oil from the most distant parts of the reservoir." It was important, therefore, for the oil field to be regulated as a unit, and for a single regulatory agency to handle the inevitable and complex problems of apportionment. That task had been assigned to the Texas Railroad Commission. The Court examined the state interests in efficient regulation of fields such as this, and concluded:

> "To prevent the confusion of multiple review of the same general issues, the legislature provided for concentration of all direct review of the commission's orders in the state district courts of Travis County. [Yet the] very 'confusion' which the Texas legislature . . . feared might result from review by many state courts of the Railroad Commission's orders has resulted from the exercise of federal equity jurisdiction. As a practical matter, the federal courts can make small contribution to the well organized system of regulation and review which the Texas statutes provide. Texas courts can give fully as great relief . . . as the federal courts. Delay, misunderstanding of local law, and needless federal conflict with the state policy, are the most inevitable product of this double

system of review. [F]ederal court decisions on state law have created a constant task for the Texas Governor, the Texas legislature, and the Railroad Commission. . . . Special sessions of the legislature have been occupied with consideration of federal court decisions. . . . The instant case [raises] a number of problems of no general significance on which a federal court can only try to ascertain state law. . . . These questions of regulation of the industry by the state administrative agency . . . so clearly [involve] basic problems of Texas policy that equitable discretion should be exercised to give the Texas courts the first opportunity to consider them. . . .

"The state provides a unified method for the formation of policy and determination of cases by the commission and by the state courts. The judicial review of the commission's decisions in the state courts is expeditious and adequate. Conflicts in the interpretation of state law, dangerous to the success of state policies, are almost certain to result from the intervention of lower federal courts. On the other hand, if the state procedure is followed from the commission to the state supreme court, ultimate review of the federal questions is fully preserved here. Under such circumstances, a sound respect for the independence of state action requires the federal equity court to stay its hand."

Another case frequently associated with *Burford* abstention is Alabama Public Service Comm'n v. Southern Ry. Co., 341 U.S. 341 (1951). In that case, also based on diversity jurisdiction and the presence of a federal constitutional challenge, the federal court was asked to enjoin the Commission's refusal to permit discontinuance of two local trains. The Court, again over a vigorous dissent by Justice Frankfurter, held that the suit should have been dismissed. The regulation of local train service, Chief Justice Vinson said, is "primarily the concern of the state." As in *Burford,* review of commission decisions was concentrated in a single state court. The Chief Justice characterized the case as involving an "essentially local problem" and concluded that "[a]s adequate state court review of an administrative order based upon predominantly local factors is available . . . ., intervention of a federal court is not necessary for the protection of federal rights."[e]

e See also Prentis v. Atlantic Coast Line Co., 211 U.S. 210 (1908), where the Supreme Court held that a federal court should have refused to review a rate order of the Virginia State Corporation Commission because that body was acting in a legislative capacity and review by the Virginia Supreme Court of Appeals should first have been sought. Review in the Virginia court, which was available as of right, was regarded as a continuation of the legislative process because of the powers of revision which that court had been given. The Court explicitly said, moreover, that—since the Virginia court would act in a legislative capacity—no res judicata effect should be given to its decision in the event of a subsequent federal suit.

The *Prentis* doctrine is analogous to the doctrine of exhaustion of administrative remedies. In effect, because of its power to revise the agency order, the Virginia court was a part of the administrative process.

For a contrasting decision, see Bacon, Public Service Commission of State of Vermont v. Rutland Railroad Co., 232 U.S. 134 (1914). In that case, appeal of an order by

Abstention under *Burford* has not been widely invoked, and there has been very little Supreme Court discussion of the meaning of the doctrine in recent years. For consideration of the doctrine in relation to other grounds of abstention, see Wells, The Role of Comity in the Law of Federal Courts, 60 N.C. L. Rev. 59 (1981), and Bezanson, Abstention: The Supreme Court and the Allocation of Judicial Power, 27 Vand. L. Rev. 1107 (1974). For consideration of the extent to which *Burford* and the other federal abstention doctrines undermine the enforcement of legal rights, see Donald Zeigler, Rights Require Remedies: A New Approach to the Enforcement of Rights in the Federal Courts, 38 Hastings L.J. 665 (1987). For the suggestion that *Burford* abstention should be exercised in a more objective manner that is not responsive to changes in judicial attitudes towards federalism and the substance of federal rights, see Julie Davies, *Pullman* and *Burford* Abstention: Clarifying the Roles of State and Federal Courts in Constitutional Cases, 20 U.C.Davis L.Rev. 1 (1986). The impact of *Burford* in the lower courts is extensively considered in Comment, Abstention by Federal Courts in Suits Challenging State Administrative Decisions: The Scope of the *Burford* Doctrine, 46 U. Chi. L. Rev. 971 (1979), where the author accurately characterizes the doctrine as "a confused and cryptic corner in the law of federal jurisdiction."

5. ***Meredith, Mashuda,* and *Thibodaux.*** Meredith v. City of Winter Haven, 320 U.S. 228 (1943), is well known for the proposition that a federal court is not free to refuse to decide a diversity case because of the difficulty or novelty of the questions of state law that must be resolved.[f] *Meredith* was brought by holders of municipal bonds to restrain the city from redeeming them without paying deferred interest. Two issues were raised: whether the City was authorized by the Florida constitution to issue the bonds without a referendum; and, if the bonds were valid, what recovery was available to the bondholders. Jurisdiction was based solely on diversity. The Circuit Court held that the case should be dismissed without prejudice to suit in a state court. The Supreme Court reversed, holding that dismissal of the suit was improper "merely because the state law is uncertain or difficult to determine."

The meaning of *Meredith* was challenged in two decisions rendered on the same day in 1959. In Allegheny County v. Frank Mashuda Co., 360 U.S. 185 (1959), Mashuda's land had been taken by the county for the purpose of improving and enlarging the Pittsburgh airport. Mashuda was awarded compensation under the applicable state procedure, and both parties appealed the award to the appropriate state court.[g] Mashuda then learned that the land had been leased to a corporation, allegedly for its private business use. It was clear under

a state administrative agency to the state supreme court was available—but had not been taken—at the time a federal suit was initiated. The Supreme Court allowed the federal action to proceed because the state court did not have the revisory powers that the Virginia court had in *Prentis* and

hence the administrative process had concluded before the federal suit was filed.

[f] See pages 287–88, supra.

[g] This appeal was still pending when the diversity suit, described below, reached the Supreme Court.

state law that private property could not be taken for private use under the power of eminent domain. Mashuda filed a diversity action in federal court against the county and the corporation, seeking damages and their ouster from the land. The District Court dismissed the suit on the ground that it should not interfere with the ongoing condemnation proceedings. The Court of Appeals reversed, noting that the validity of the taking could not be challenged in the compensation proceeding and that, since an independent suit was required to be filed anyway, the federal diversity action should proceed. The Supreme Court granted certiorari and affirmed.

Justice Brennan's opinion for the Court said that abstention was "an extraordinary and narrow exception to the duty of a district court to adjudicate a controversy properly before it," justified "only in the exceptional circumstances where the order to the parties to repair to the state court would clearly serve an important countervailing interest." He saw no such circumstances here. The case involved the resolution of a question of fact under settled state law, and could not have been brought as part of the original condemnation proceedings. Moreover, federal courts had routinely heard eminent domain proceedings under the diversity jurisdiction. Neither *Pullman* nor *Burford* was applicable, and there was no unusual likelihood of federal-state friction that would follow from district court resolution of the case.

Mashuda seemed a fairly straightforward application of the *Meredith* principle, but for two complicating factors. The first was that the case provoked a dissent by four Justices. The second was that these four Justices joined with two who were in the *Mashuda* majority to vote for abstention in Louisiana Power & Light Co. v. City of Thibodaux, 360 U.S. 25 (1959).[h]

The city had filed a condemnation proceeding in a state court. The power company removed the case to federal court, invoking diversity jurisdiction. After a pre-trial conference, the District Court, on its own motion, ordered that the case be stayed pending institution of a declaratory judgment proceeding in state court to determine whether the city had the power to make the kind of expropriation that was involved.[i] The city then appealed the District Court's decision. The corporation— the party that had removed the case to federal court in the first place— supported the District Court's decision to defer to additional state proceedings. The Court of Appeals reversed, holding the stay inappropriate. The corporation then successfully obtained certiorari in the Supreme Court, arguing that the stay order was proper. A majority of the Court agreed, and the case was remanded to await the outcome of a state suit.

[h] Specifically, the *Mashuda* majority was composed of Chief Justice Warren and Justices Brennan, Douglas, Stewart, and Whittaker. The dissenters in *Mashuda* were Justices Clark, Frankfurter, Black, and Harlan. Stewart and Whittaker voted for abstention in *Thibodaux* along with the four *Mashuda* dissenters. Brennan, joined by Warren and Douglas, dissented in *Thibodaux*.

[i] It was contemplated that the case would return to federal court for the assessment of compensation if the taking were upheld by the state courts.

Justice Frankfurter wrote the opinion for the Court. He argued that the differences between eminent domain proceedings and ordinary diversity litigation were "relevant and important." Eminent domain cases are of a "special and peculiar nature" that are "intimately involved with sovereign prerogative." This was especially true in this case, where the city's power to condemn was challenged. This issue concerned

> "the apportionment of governmental powers between city and state. . . . The considerations that prevailed in conventional equity suits for avoiding the hazards of serious disruption by federal courts of state government or needless friction between state and federal authorities are similarly appropriate in a state eminent domain proceeding brought in, or removed to, a federal court."

The district judge was "[c]aught between the language of an old but uninterpreted statute [that appeared to authorize the taking] and the pronouncement of the attorney general [which in an analogous case ruled that the city did not have the claimed power]." The judge "was thus exercising a fair and well-considered judicial discretion" in staying the proceedings pending resolution of the question by the state supreme court.

Justice Frankfurter cited *Pullman* as supporting "the wisdom of staying actions in the federal courts pending determination by a state court of decisive issues of state law." He agreed that *Meredith* stood for the proposition that "the mere difficulty of state law does not justify a federal court's relinquishment of jurisdiction in favor of state court action." But the issue in *Meredith* was, "of course, decisively different from the issue now before the Court." Here the question was:

> "whether an experienced district judge, especially conversant with Louisiana law, who, when troubled with the construction which Louisiana courts may give to a Louisiana statute, himself initiates the taking of appropriate measures for securing construction of this doubtful and unsettled statute (and not at all in response to any alleged attempt by [the power company] to delay a decision by that judge), should be jurisdictionally disabled from seeking the controlling light of the Louisiana Supreme Court. The issue in *Winter Haven* was not that. It was whether jurisdiction must be surrendered to the state court. . . . In *Winter Haven* the Court of Appeals directed the action to be dismissed. In this case the Court of Appeals denied a conscientious exercise by the federal district judge of his discretionary power merely to stay disposition of a retained case . . . ."

Justice Frankfurter did not mention *Mashuda*. Among those who voted for abstention, only Justice Stewart spoke to the difference between the two cases. His explanation was:

> "In a conscientious effort to do justice the District Court deferred immediate adjudication of this controversy pending

authoritative clarification of a controlling state statute of highly doubtful meaning. Under the circumstances presented, I think the course pursued was clearly within the District Court's allowable discretion. For that reason I concur in the judgment.

> "This case is totally unlike *Mashuda* . . . except for the coincidence that both cases involve eminent domain proceedings. In *Mashuda* the Court holds that it was error for the District Court to dismiss the complaint. The Court further holds in that case that, since the controlling state law is clear and only factual issues need be resolved, there is no occasion in the interest of justice to refrain from prompt adjudication."

Justice Brennan dissented at length. He began by referring to the "imperative duty" of the District Court "to render prompt justice" in diversity cases: "To order these suitors out of the federal court and into a state court in the circumstances of this case passes beyond disrespect for the diversity jurisdiction to plain disregard of this imperative duty." Abstention was justified only in "exceptional circumstances" where "one of two important countervailing interests" was served: "either the avoidance of a premature and perhaps unnecessary decision of a serious federal constitutional question, or the avoidance of the hazard of unsettling some delicate balance in the area of federal-state relationships." "[U]ntil now" this was "a very narrow corridor through which a district court could escape from its obligation to decide state law questions when federal jurisdiction was properly invoked." Justice Brennan thought that the case

> "does not involve the slightest hazard of friction with a state, the indispensable ingredient for upholding abstention on grounds of comity . . . . Clearly decision of this case, in which the city itself is the party seeking an interpretation of its authority under state law, will not entail the friction in federal-state relations that would result from decision of a suit brought by another party to enjoin the city from acting. . . . There is no more possibility of conflict with the state in this situation than there is in the ordinary negligence or contract case in which a district court applies state law under its diversity jurisdiction. [T]he state of Louisiana, represented by its constituent organ the city of Thibodaux, urges the District Court to adjudicate the state law issue. How, conceivably, can the Court justify the abdication of responsibility to exercise jurisdiction on the ground of avoiding interference and conflict with the state when the state itself desires the federal court's adjudication? It is obvious that the abstention in this case was for the convenience of the District Court, not for the state."

Justice Brennan also argued that the question was not whether there was an abuse of discretion, but whether there was any discretion at all in a case such as this. He concluded that there was not: "It would obviously wreak havoc with federal jurisdiction if the exercise of that jurisdiction was a matter for the ad hoc discretion of the district court in each particular case." As to *Meredith,* Justice Brennan was "unable to see a distinction, so far as concerns non-interference with the exercise of state sovereignty, between decision as to the city of Winter Haven's authority . . . to issue deferred-interest bonds without a referendum, and decision as to the city of Thibodaux's authority . . . to expropriate the Power and Light Company's property." He regarded Justice Frankfurter's effort to distinguish the case as unsuccessful:

"It is perfectly clear that *Winter Haven* did not turn on any difference between an abstention and a dismissal, nor on the fact that it was a court of appeals rather than a district court which initially decided to refrain from adjudicating the state issues. Neither did it turn on this Court's ideas about the competence or experience of the judges below. *Meredith v. Winter Haven* rested squarely on the Court's conclusion that, no matter how intimately related to a state's sovereignty a case is, the district court must adjudicate it if jurisdiction is properly invoked and that adjudication would not entail decision of a serious constitutional question or disruption of state policy."

Justice Brennan concluded with the following comments:

"The Power and Light Company, which escaped a state court decision by removing the city's action to the District Court, is now wholly content with the sua sponte action of the District Court. This is understandable since the longer decision is put off . . . the longer the Power and Light Company will enjoy the possession of [its property]. Resolution of the legal question of the city's authority, already delayed over two years due to no fault of the city, will be delayed . . . a minimum of two additional years before a decision may be obtained from the state supreme court in the declaratory judgment action. [A]t best the District Court will finally dispose of this case only after prolonged delay and considerable additional expense for the parties. . . . I think it is more than coincidence that both in this case and in *Mashuda* the party supporting abstention is the one presently in possession of the property in question. I cannot escape the conclusion in these cases that delay in the reaching of a decision is more important to those parties than the tribunal which ultimately renders the decision. [T]he Power and Light Company's strategy of delay . . . has succeeded, I dare say, past the fondest expectation of counsel who conceived it. . . ."

Seven justices thought that *Mashuda* and *Thibodaux* were indistinguishable, though they disagreed four to three about whether abstention in both cases was appropriate. Two justices thought abstention warranted in one case but not the other. Can the cases be reconciled? If they are inconsistent, which one is right? Consideration of the case discussed in the next note may further confuse the issue.

6. *Kaiser Steel Corp. v. W.S. Ranch Co.* Kaiser Steel Corp v. W.S. Ranch Co., 391 U.S. 593 (1968) (per curiam), was a diversity action seeking damages and an injunction for trespass. Kaiser had entered the plaintiff's land to use water under the authority of a New Mexico statute. The plaintiff claimed that the statute, if construed to permit Kaiser's action, would violate the New Mexico Constitution, which permitted the taking of private property only for a "public use." The District Court resolved the case on the merits, and the Circuit Court reversed. Both courts refused to stay the action pending resolution of the state constitutional issue by the state courts. The Supreme Court granted certiorari and summarily reversed.

The Court devoted a single paragraph to its rationale:

> "The Court of Appeals erred in refusing to stay its hand. The state law issue which is crucial in this case is one of vital concern to the arid state of New Mexico, where water is one of the most valuable natural resources. The issue, moreover, is a truly novel one. The question will eventually have to be resolved by the New Mexico courts, and since a declaratory judgment action is actually pending there, in all likelihood will be forthcoming soon. Sound judicial administration requires that the parties in this case be given the benefit of the same rule of law which will apply to all other businesses and landowners concerned with the use of this vital state resource."

No cases were cited. The Court remanded the case "with directions that the action be stayed . . . . Federal jurisdiction will be retained in the District Court in order to insure a just disposition of this litigation should anything prevent a prompt state court determination."[j]

Is the result in *Kaiser* so clear that it justified summary reversal? What is its rationale? Does it follow from *Burford*? From *Mashuda* and *Thibodaux*? Is it consistent with *Colorado River*?

7. Statutes Requiring Abstention. There are several federal statutes that require a federal court to stay its hand even though the literal prerequisites for jurisdiction are satisfied. The most frequently invoked is 28 U.S.C. § 2283, which is extensively considered at pages 526–41, supra. That statute, with certain exceptions, forbids a federal court from enjoining pending state litigation. Abstention is also required in specified bankruptcy cases by 28 U.S.C. § 1334, reproduced in Appendix B, page B–7, infra. Two other statutes should also be noted. The first is the Tax Injunction Act, found in 28 U.S.C. § 1341. It provides that "[t]he district courts shall not enjoin, suspend or restrain the assessment, levy or collection of any tax under State law where a

---

[j] Justice Brennan, joined by Justices Douglas and Marshall, concurred "solely on the ground that this case presents one of the 'narrowly limited "special circumstances"' which justify the invocation of '[t]he judge-made doctrine of abstention.'" Justice Brennan cited both *Burford* and *Alabama Public Service Comm'n* in support of this resolution. He also noted that he adhered to the view stated in his *Thibodaux* dissent "that in a diversity case abstention from decision of a state law question is improper in the absence of such 'special circumstances.'"

plain, speedy and efficient remedy may be had in the courts of such State." [k] The second is 28 U.S.C. § 1342, which provides:

> "The district courts shall not enjoin, suspend or restrain the operation of, or compliance with any order affecting rates chargeable by a public utility and made by a State administrative agency or a rate-making body of a State political subdivision, where:

> > (1) Jurisdiction is based solely on diversity of citizenship or repugnance of the order to the Federal Constitution; and,

> > (2) The order does no interfere with interstate commerce; and

> > (3) The order has been made after reasonable notice and hearing; and,

> > (4) A plain, speedy and efficient remedy may be had in the courts of such State." [l]

SECTION 5: CIVIL RIGHTS REMOVAL

INTRODUCTORY NOTES ON CIVIL RIGHTS REMOVAL

1. The Statute. Removal in civil rights cases is permitted by 28 U.S.C. § 1443, which provides:

> "Any of the following civil actions or criminal prosecutions, commenced in a State court may be removed by the defendant to the district court of the United States for the district and division embracing the place wherein it is pending:

> > "(1) Against any person who is denied or cannot enforce in the courts of such State a right under any law providing for the equal civil rights of citizens of the United States, or of all persons within the jurisdiction thereof;

> > "(2) For any act under color of authority derived from any law providing for equal rights, or for refusing to do any act on the ground that it would be inconsistent with such law."

2. *Strauder* and *Rives*. The civil rights removal provision was enacted in 1866. The first cases to construe it were Strauder v. West

---

[k] This statute was enacted in 1937. Its relation to 42 U.S.C. § 1983 is further discussed at pages 1079–83, infra. Its legislative history is extensively considered in Rosewell v. LaSalle National Bank, 450 U.S. 503 (1981), which involved the meaning of the words "plain, speedy and efficient" as they applied to an Illinois tax refund procedure.

[l] This statute was originally the Johnson Act of 1934. Contemporaneous comments on the statute can be found in Note, The Johnson Act: Defining a "Plain, Speed and Efficient" Remedy in the State Courts, 50 Harv. L. Rev. 813 (1937), and Comment, Limitation of Lower Federal Court Jurisdiction Over Public Utility Rate Cases, 44 Yale L.J. 119 (1934).

Virginia, 100 U.S. (10 Otto) 303 (1879), and Virginia v. Rives, 100 U.S. (10 Otto) 313 (1879).

In *Strauder* a black man indicted for murder sought removal because a West Virginia statute barred blacks from service on a grand or petit jury. Removal was allowed on the ground that he was denied rights under applicable civil rights laws by the "statute laws of the state." In *Rives* two black men who had been indicted for murder alleged that they could not obtain a fair trial in state court because "strong prejudice existed in the community against them," no blacks had ever served on a jury in the county in which they were to be tried, and their request to put blacks on the jury panel had been denied. The defendants could point to no statute, however, that precluded blacks from serving on juries. Removal was disallowed on the ground that the removal statute only "has reference to a legislative denial or an inability resulting from it."

Numerous other cases involving the civil rights removal statute came before the Court in the next decade. In all of them the Court applied the distinction drawn between *Strauder* and *Rives*. The statute permitting appeal of a remand order by a federal trial court was repealed in 1887, and as a consequence no further cases involving civil rights removal were decided by the Court between 1887 and 1966. A new round of litigation in the appellate courts was begun by the Civil Rights Act of 1964, which specifically permitted appeals of remand orders under § 1443. The first cases to reach the Supreme Court under this provision were Georgia v. Rachel, 384 U.S. 780 (1966), and City of Greenwood v. Peacock, 384 U.S. 808 (1966). Again the Court upheld removal in one case and disallowed it in the other. Justice Stewart wrote both opinions.

3. *Georgia v. Rachel.* *Rachel* involved sit-in demonstrators who sought to remove their state trespass prosecutions on the ground that the Civil Rights Act of 1964 created both a right to engage in the conduct for which they were prosecuted and an independent right not to be prosecuted for that conduct. The Court held that § 1443(1) contained two requirements: the right asserted as the basis for removal must be, in the statutory language, a "right under any law providing for . . . equal civil rights"; and the state defendants must establish that they are "denied or cannot enforce" that right in the state courts.

As to what rights qualified as a "right under any law providing for . . . equal civil rights," the Court held that Congress meant

> "only to include laws comparable in nature to the Civil Rights Act of 1866.[a] . . . The legislative history of the 1866 act clearly indicates that Congress intended to protect a limited category of rights, specifically defined in terms of racial equality. . . . Thus, . . . broad contentions under the first

[a] The original removal provision was § 3 of a statute that in § 1 provided for the protection of certain substantive rights. Section 1 of the 1866 act was the predeces- sor to the provisions now codified in 42 U.S.C. §§ 1981 and 1982. [Footnote by eds.]

amendment and the due process clause of the 14th amendment cannot support a valid claim for removal under § 1443, because the guarantees of those clauses are phrased in terms of general application available to all persons or citizens, rather than in the specific language of racial equality . . . ."[b]

This requirement did not pose a problem in *Rachel* itself because the 1964 Civil Rights Act was clearly designed to protect rights of racial equality.

The next question was how the statutory phrase "is denied or cannot enforce" the protected rights "in the courts of" the state should be construed. On this point the Court reaffirmed the distinction announced in *Strauder* and *Rives*:

"*Strauder* and *Rives* . . . teach that removal is not warranted by an assertion that a denial of rights of equality may take place and go uncorrected at trial. Removal is warranted only if it can be predicted by reference to a law of general application that the defendant will be denied or cannot enforce the specified federal rights in the state courts. A state statute authorizing the denial affords an ample basis for such a prediction."

It then continued:

"The *Strauder-Rives* doctrine . . . required a removal petition to allege, not merely that rights of equality would be denied or could not be enforced, but that the denial would take place in the courts in the state. This doctrine also required that the denial be manifest in a formal expression of state law. This requirement served two ends. It ensured that removal would be available only in cases where the predicted denial appeared with relative clarity prior to trial. It also ensured that the task of prediction would not involve detailed analysis by a federal judge of the likely disposition of particular federal claims by particular state courts. That task not only would have been difficult, but it also would have involved federal judges in the unseemly process of pre-judging their brethren of the state courts. Thus, the Court in *Strauder* and *Rives* concluded that a state enactment, discriminatory on its face, so clearly authorized discrimination that it could be taken as a suitable indication that all courts in that state would disregard the federal right of equality with which the state enactment was precisely in conflict."

By the time of the sit-in prosecutions at issue in *Rachel*, Georgia had no statute denying the rights protected by the Civil Rights Act of 1964. But the Court noted that *Rives* had said that § 1443 referred to the denial of rights that is "primarily, if not exclusively" a product of a discriminatory state statute:

[b] The Court also quoted with approval a Court of Appeals case that identified 42 U.S.C. § 1983 as a statute the violation of which would not support removal.

"The [*Rives*] Court thereby gave some indication that removal might be justified, even in the absence of a discriminatory state enactment, if an equivalent basis could be shown for an equally firm prediction that the defendant would be 'denied or cannot enforce' the specified federal rights in the state court. Such a basis for prediction exists in the present case.

"In the narrow circumstances of this case, *any* proceedings in the courts of the state will constitute a denial of the rights conferred by the Civil Rights Act of 1964 . . ., if the allegations of the removal petition are true. . . . It is no answer in these circumstances that the defendants might eventually prevail in the state court. The burden of having to defend the prosecutions is itself the denial of a right explicitly conferred by the Civil Rights Act of 1964 . . . ."

Accordingly, the Court held that the defendants had stated a valid basis for removal and remanded the case for a hearing on whether the allegations in the removal petition were true.

4. *City of Greenwood v. Peacock.* The *Peacock* case involved numerous defendants charged with a variety of minor offenses.[c] They claimed, inter alia, that their arrest and prosecution were designed to harass them for exercising their constitutionally protected right to object to racial discrimination. They denied violating any valid laws and made vagueness and other constitutional challenges to some of the statutes sought to be enforced against them. Some of them claimed that they were members of a civil rights group engaged in a drive to encourage voter registration and that they were "denied or cannot enforce" rights under 42 U.S.C. § 1971.[d] Others claimed they were "denied or cannot enforce" rights under 42 U.S.C. § 1981.

These allegations, the Court said, made this case "far different" from *Rachel*. The Court first noted that some of the rights claimed by the petitioners clearly did not qualify as rights protected by federal laws providing for "equal civil rights," as that phrase was interpreted in *Rachel*. The Court admitted, however, that §§ 1971 and 1981 were "equal civil rights" laws. Nonetheless, the "fundamental claim" asserted in *Peacock* was that the petitioners were arrested and charged because they were black or because they were engaged in helping blacks assert their rights, that they were innocent of the charges, and that they would be unable to obtain a fair trial in the state court. The Court pointed out two significant differences between this case and *Rachel* : no federal statute conferred any right to engage in the conduct with which the petitioners were charged, and no federal statute con-

[c] They included, among other things, obstructing traffic, disturbing the peace, biting a police officer, reckless driving, operating a vehicle with improper license tags, and profanity.

[d] Section 1971(a)(1) forbids racial discrimination in voting. Section 1971(b) provides that

"No person, whether acting under color of law or otherwise, shall intimidate, threaten, coerce, or attempt to intimidate, threaten, or coerce, any other person for the purpose of interfering with the right of such other person to vote or to vote as he may choose . . . ."

ferred immunity from state prosecution on such charges.[e] The Court held that the case was controlled by

> "one basic proposition: It is not enough to support removal under § 1443(1) to allege or show that the defendant's federal equal rights have been illegally and corruptly denied by state administrative officials in advance of trial, that the charges against the defendant are false, or that the defendant is unable to obtain a fair trial in a particular state court. The motives of the officers bringing the charges may be corrupt, but that does not show that the state trial court will find the defendant guilty if he is innocent, or that in any other manner the defendant will be 'denied or cannot enforce in the courts' of the state any right under a federal law providing for equal civil rights. The civil rights removal statute does not require and does not permit the judges of the federal courts to put their brethren of the state judiciary on trial. Under § 1443(1), the vindication of the defendant's federal rights is left to the state courts except in the rare situations where it can be clearly predicted by reason of the operation of a pervasive and explicit state or federal law that those rights will inevitably be denied by the very act of bringing the defendant to trial in the state court."

The Court noted that it was by no means saying that the petitioners had not alleged serious violations of their federal rights. But other federal remedies were available, including review by the Supreme Court of any state court convictions, habeas corpus, in some situations an injunction against the state proceedings, civil damage suits against offending state officials under 42 U.S.C. § 1983, and criminal prosecution of the officials under 18 U.S.C. § 241. But the removal provisions of § 1443 "do not operate to work a wholesale dislocation of the historic relationship between the state and the federal courts in the administration of the criminal law." The Court continued:

> "[I]f the . . . petitioners should prevail in their interpretation of § 1443(1), then every criminal case in every court of every state—on any charge from a five dollar misdemeanor to first-degree murder—would be removable to a federal court upon a petition alleging (1) that the defendant was being prosecuted because of his race and that he was completely innocent of the charge brought against him, or (2) that he would be unable to obtain a fair trial in the state court. On motion to remand, the federal court would be required in every case to hold a hearing, which would amount to at least a preliminary trial of the motivations of the state officers who

---

[e] The Court elaborated this point by quoting from the statute involved in *Rachel.* The 1964 Civil Rights Act

"explicitly provides that no person shall 'punish or attempt to punish any person for exercising or attempting to exercise

any right or privilege' secured by the public accommodations section of the act. None of the statutes invoked by the defendants in the present case contains any such provision."

> arrested and charged the defendant, of the quality of the state court or judge before whom the charges were filed and of the defendant's innocence or guilt. . . . If [a] remand order were eventually affirmed [on appeal], there might, if the witnesses were still available, finally be a trial in the state court, months or years after the original charge was brought."

The Court said that it had "no doubt that Congress, if it chose, could provide for exactly such a system." But in the absence of affirmative congressional action, this was too big a step for the Court to take.

5. The Douglas Dissent. Justice Douglas, joined by Chief Justice Warren and by Justices Brennan and Fortas, concurred in *Rachel* and dissented in *Peacock*. The purpose of the *Rachel* concurrence was to disassociate these four Justices from the rationale of the majority. The purpose of the dissent in *Peacock* was to assert a different approach to the removal statute.

The operative language of § 1443(1) provides that removal is permitted if the defendant "is denied or cannot enforce in the courts of such State" the equal civil rights at stake. Justice Douglas first separated the statute into two parts, holding it "essential that these two aspects of § 1443(1) be distinguished. The words 'is denied' refer to a *present* deprivation of rights while the language 'cannot enforce' has reference to an *anticipated* state court frustration of civil rights."

(i) "Is Denied." As to the "is denied" portion of the statute, Justice Douglas asserted that a "defendant 'is denied' his federal right when 'disorderly conduct' statutes, 'breach of the peace' ordinances, and the like are used as the instrument to suppress his promotion of civil rights." One could reach this conclusion by reading "is denied" in either of two ways. First, the statute could be read to apply to "any person who is denied . . . a right under any law providing for the equal civil rights of citizens." Under this reading, a right could be denied "by state action at any time—before, as well as during, a trial." Second, the statute could be read to apply to "any person who is denied . . . in the courts of such State a right under any law providing for the equal civil rights of citizens." Under this reading, the courts must be implicated in the denial of rights, an element that is satisfied here,

> "for the judiciary is implicated even prior to actual trial by issuance of a warrant or summons, by commitment of the prisoner, or by accepting and filing of the information or indictment. . . . Prosecution for a federally protected act is punishment for that act."

Thus under either reading of the "is denied" portion of the statute, the defendants had stated a case for removal. Douglas analogized this form of removal to an injunction against the state prosecution:

> "For removal, if allowed, is equivalent to a plea in bar granted by a federal court to protect a federal right.
>
> "The threshold question—whether initiation of the state prosecution has 'denied' a federal right—is resolvable by the

federal court on a hearing on the motion to remove. . . . If
the motion is granted, the removed case is concluded at that
stage, as a case of misuse of a state prosecution has been made
out. In other words, the result of removal is not the transfer
of the trial from the state to the federal courts in this type of
case. If after hearing it does not appear that the state prosecution is being used to deny federal rights, the case is remanded
for trial in the state courts."

(ii) "Cannot Enforce." Justice Douglas also disagreed with
the majority on the meaning of the words "cannot enforce." He agreed
that this portion of the statute "rests on a prediction of the future
performance of the state courts" and that the *Strauder-Rives* line of
cases was applicable. But he read Congress' conferral of appellate
jurisdiction over remand orders in 1964 as an invitation to reconsider
those cases, and concluded that the distinction between them "should
not be followed." He was not impressed with the majority's argument
that the Court should not put the lower federal courts in the position of
trying their state brethren:

"In my view, § 1443(1) requires the federal court to decide
whether the defendant's allegation (that the state court will
not fairly enforce his equal rights) is true. [I]f the federal
court is persuaded that the state court indeed will not make a
good-faith effort to apply the paramount federal law pertaining
to 'equal civil rights,' then the federal court must accept the
removal and try the case on the merits."

He agreed that removal under this provision "would occur only in the
unusual case," that most state courts "try conscientiously to apply the
law of the land," and that "honest differences of opinion are not the
kind of recalcitrance" that come within the removal statute. But
Congress

"realized that considerable damage could be done by even a
single court which harbored such hostility toward federally
protected civil rights as to render it unable to meet its responsibilities. The 'cannot enforce' clause is directed to that rare
case.

"Execution of the legislative mandate calls for particular
sensitivity on the part of federal district judges; but the
delicacy of the task surely does not warrant a refusal to
attempt it. I am confident that the federal district judges
would exercise care and good judgment in passing on 'cannot
enforce' claims. The district judge could not lightly assume
that the state court would shirk its responsibilities, and should
remand the case to the state court unless it appeared by clear
and convincing evidence that the allegations of an inability to
enforce equal civil rights were true."

6. Questions and Comments. At the time of the *Rachel* and
Peacock decisions, a few members of the state judiciary were sufficiently hostile to civil rights demonstrators to warrant a prediction that they

would not fairly try federal claims raised in that context. What should the Court have done about this situation? Should it have adopted Justice Douglas' reading of the removal statute? Or were the costs of adopting his solution too high? Note that Justice Douglas' reading of the "is denied" portion of the statute does not require that the "good faith" of the state judiciary be tried. Would that reading have solved the problem? If not, should the entire provision have been limited in the manner of the majority in *Rachel* and *Peacock*?

Note the logical inconsistency of the majority opinions. The fact that a state statute requires an unconstitutional result does not mean that the state judges will enforce it. Similarly, if, as in *Rachel*, the mere fact of prosecution is a violation of federal law, a conscientious state judge will dismiss the charge. Thus, neither situation presents a case where it can be "predicted" that the defendant "cannot enforce" his or her rights in state court. The only basis for such a "prediction" is an assumption that the state judge will not enforce the paramount federal law. Why did the Court accept this basis for "prediction" but reject the factual inquiry that Douglas would have undertaken? One answer may be that the majority position "provides a limited, easily applied standard to define the scope of civil rights removal jurisdiction."[f] But if this is to be the rule, have *Rachel* and *Peacock* robbed § 1443(1) of any modern utility? Have they reduced its availability to situations where it is least likely to be needed?[g]

7. Relation to Other Remedies. One of the points made by the majority in *Peacock* was that removal was unnecessary because other remedies are available to the federal claimant who cannot enforce his or her rights in state court. A full understanding of the stakes presented by the Court's interpretation of the removal statute requires, therefore, an understanding of the efficacy of these alternative remedies.

With the exception of criminal prosecution under 18 U.S.C. § 241, each of the other remedies mentioned by Justice Stewart is treated at some length in other portions of this book. Direct review in the Supreme Court is the subject of Chapter VI. Habeas corpus is treated in Chapter VII. Injunctions against state criminal proceedings are covered in Chapter X, beginning at page 1158, infra. And civil damage claims under 42 U.S.C. § 1983 form the subject of Chapter IX. Many of the concerns that surface in the debate over the proper meaning of § 1443 are raised again in the discussion of these alternative remedies. It is important to understand now, in any event, that a full appreciation of the *Rachel-Peacock* controversy must await assessment of the relative effectiveness of other methods of attacking the problem.

8. Section 1443(2). *Peacock* also involved the meaning of § 1443(2), which provides a right of removal:

[f] Redish, Revitalizing Civil Rights Removal Jurisdiction, 64 Minn. L. Rev. 523, 530 (1980).

[g] See Amsterdam, Criminal Prosecutions Affecting Federally Guaranteed Civil Rights: Federal Removal and Habeas Corpus Jurisdiction to Abort State Court Trial, 113 U. Pa. L. Rev. 793, 857–58 (1965).

> "For any act under color of authority derived from any law
> providing for equal rights, or for refusing to do any act on the
> ground that it would be inconsistent with such law."

The Court held, without dissent, that the words "[f]or any act under
color of authority derived from any law providing for equal rights" in
§ 1443(2) were inapplicable to the *Peacock* defendants because they
were "available only to federal officers and to persons assisting such
officers in the performance of their official duties." The rationale for
this construction was the legislative history of the original 1866 act and
its subsequent recodifications over the years.

The Court noted that it had not had occasion to construe § 1443(2)
or its predecessors since the enactment of the original act in 1866. It
also took note of the fact that § 1442(a)(1) now permits removal by

> "Any officer of the United States . . . ., or person acting
> under him, for any act under color of such office or on account
> of any right, title or authority claimed under any Act of
> Congress for the apprehension or punishment of criminals or
> the collection of the revenue."

This statute was originally limited to revenue officers, but was expanded to its present scope in 1948. The Court recognized that § 1443(2) as
construed in *Peacock* largely duplicated the coverage of § 1442(a)(1):

> "Thus many, if not all, of the cases presently removable under
> [§ 1443(2)] would now also be removable under § 1442(a)(1).
> The present overlap between the provisions simply reflects the
> separate historical evolution of the removal provision for civil
> rights legislation."

Finally, the Court said that the phrase "for refusing to do any act
on the ground that it would be inconsistent with such law" in § 1443(2)
"has no relevance to this case," but that in any event it was "clear that
removal under that language is available only to state officers."

JOHNSON v. MISSISSIPPI

Supreme Court of the United States, 1975.
421 U.S. 213.

MR. JUSTICE WHITE delivered the opinion of the Court.

This case concerns the application of 28 U.S.C. § 1443(1), permitting defendants in state cases to remove the proceedings to the federal
district courts under certain conditions, in the light of title I of the Civil
Rights Act of 1968, 18 U.S.C. § 245.

I

During March 1972, petitioners, six Negro citizens of Vicksburg,
Miss., along with other citizens of Vicksburg, made various demands
upon certain merchants and city officials generally relating to the
number of Negroes employed or serving in various positions in both

local government and business enterprises. In late March, petitioners began picketing some business establishments in Vicksburg and urging, by word of mouth and through leaflets, that the citizens of Vicksburg boycott those establishments until such time as petitioners' demands were realized. [P]etitioners . . . were arrested on the basis of warrants charging, in general terms, their complicity in a conspiracy unlawfully to bring about a boycott of merchants and businesses. [They] were transported to the city jail where they each remained after processing until the posting of bail. There is no indication . . . that the arrests and subsequent detentions . . . involved the application of any force by the arresting officers beyond the verbal directions issued by those officers and the coercive custody normally incident to arrest, processing, and detention.

On May 25, 1972, those arrested filed a petition in the federal District Court . . . seeking [removal] pursuant to [28 U.S.C. § 1443(1)].[4] . . . In their removal petition, it was alleged, inter alia, that those arrested were being prosecuted under several state conspiracy statutes which were "on their face and as applied repugnant to the Constitution . . .," and that:

> "The charges against petitioners, their arrest, and subsequent prosecution on those charges have no basis in fact and have been effectuated solely and exclusively for the purpose and effect of depriving petitioners of their federally protected rights, including by force or threat of force, punishing, injuring, intimidating, and interferring [sic], or attempting to punish, injure, intimidate, . . . and interfere with petitioners, and the class of persons participating in the . . . boycott and demonstrations, for the exercise of their rights peacefully to protest discrimination and to conduct and publicize a boycott which seeks to remedy the denial of equal civil rights . . . which activities are protected by 18 U.S.C. [§] 245."

On December 29, 1972, after an evidentiary hearing . . ., the District Court remanded the prosecutions to the state courts. The Court of Appeals affirmed, reasoning that § 245, as a criminal statute, "confers no rights whatsoever . . .," and that under this Court's decisions in Georgia v. Rachel, 384 U.S. 780 (1966), and City of Greenwood v. Peacock, 384 U.S. 808 (1966), a federal statute must "provide" for the equal rights of citizens before it can be invoked as a basis for removal of prosecutions under § 1443(1). . . .[7] We granted certiorari . . . and, for reasons stated below, affirm the judgment of the Court of Appeals.

---

[4] Although the petitioners pleaded § 1443 generally, they made no suggestion that any among them was in the position to claim the protection of § 1443(2) as construed by our decision in City of Greenwood v. Peacock, 384 U.S. 808, 815–24 (1966), nor do they press such a claim in this Court.

[7] [T]he Court of Appeals granted . . . a stay . . . until disposition of the case by this Court. Since that time the prosecution of petitioners . . . has not gone forward.

II

Our most recent cases construing § 1443(1) are the companion cases of *Georgia v. Rachel,* supra, and *City of Greenwood v. Peacock,* supra. Those cases established that a removal petition under 28 U.S.C. § 1443(1) must satisfy a two-pronged test. First, it must appear that the right allegedly denied the removal petitioner arises under a federal law "providing for specific civil rights stated in terms of racial equality." Claims that prosecution and conviction will violate rights under constitutional or statutory provisions of general applicability or under statutes not protecting against racial discrimination, will not suffice. That a removal petitioner will be denied due process of law because the criminal law under which he is being prosecuted is allegedly vague or that the prosecution is assertedly a sham, corrupt, or without evidentiary basis does not, standing alone, satisfy the requirements of § 1443(1).

Second, it must appear, in accordance with the provisions of § 1443(1), that the removal petitioner is "denied or cannot enforce" the specified federal rights "in the courts of [the] State." This provision normally requires that the "denial be manifest in a formal expression of state law," such as a state legislative or constitutional provisions, " 'rather than a denial first made manifest at the trial of the case.' " Except in the unusual case where "an equivalent basis could be shown for an equally firm prediction that the defendant would be 'denied or cannot enforce' the specified federal rights in the state court," it was to be expected that the protection of federal constitutional or statutory rights could be effected in the pending state proceedings, civil or criminal. Under § 1443(1),

> "the vindication of the defendant's federal rights is left to the state courts except in the rare situations where it can be clearly predicted by reason of the operation of a pervasive and explicit state or federal law that those rights will inevitably be denied by the very act of bringing the defendant to trial in the state court." *City of Greenwood v. Peacock,* supra, at 828.

In *Rachel,* the allegations of the petition for removal were held to satisfy both branches of the rule. The federal right claimed arose under §§ 201(a) and 203(c) of the Civil Rights Act of 1964, 42 U.S.C. §§ 2000a(a) and 2000a–2(c). Section 201(a) forbids refusals of service in, or exclusions from, public accommodations on account of race or color; and § 203(c) prohibits any "attempt to punish any person for exercising or attempting to exercise any right or privilege secured by section 201 . . . ." The removal petition fairly alleged that the prosecutions sought to be removed from state court were brought and would be tried "solely as the result of peaceful attempts to obtain service at places of public accommodation."[8] We concluded that if the allegations in the removal petition were true, the defendants by being prosecuted under a

---

[8] We had earlier construed § 203(c) as prohibiting "prosecution of any person for seeking service in a covered establishment, because of his race or color." Hamm v. City of Rock Hill, 379 U.S. 306, 311 (1964).

state criminal trespass law would be denied or could not enforce their rights in the courts of Georgia, since the "burden of having to defend the prosecutions is itself the denial of a right explicitly conferred by the Civil Rights Act of 1964."

In *Peacock,* on the contrary, the state-court defendants petitioning for removal were being prosecuted for obstructing public streets, assault and battery, and various other local crimes. The federal rights allegedly being denied were said to arise under the Constitution as well as under 42 U.S.C. §§ 1971 and 1981, the former section guaranteeing the right to vote without discrimination on the grounds of race or color and forbidding interference therewith, and the latter guaranteeing all persons equal access to specified rights enjoyed by white persons. The Court assumed that the claimed statutory rights were within those rights contemplated by § 1443(1), but went on to hold that there had been no showing that petitioners would be denied or could not enforce their rights in the state courts. The removal petitions alleged

> "(1) that the defendants were arrested by state officers and charged with various offenses under state law because they were Negroes or because they were engaged in helping Negroes assert their rights under federal equal civil rights laws, and that they are completely innocent of the charges against them, or

> "(2) that the defendants will be unable to obtain a fair trial in the state court."

The Court held, however, that it was not enough to support removal to allege that "federal equal civil rights have been illegally and corruptly denied by state administrative officials in advance of trial, that the charges against the defendant are false, or that the defendant is unable to obtain a fair trial in a particular state court." Petitioners could point to no federal law conferring on them the right to engage in the specific conduct with which they were charged; and there was no "federal statutory right that no state should even attempt to prosecute them for their conduct."

III

With our prior cases in mind, it is apparent, without further discussion, that removal under § 1443(1) was not warranted here based solely on petitioners' allegations that the statutes underlying the charges against them were unconstitutional, that there was no basis in fact for those charges, or that their arrest and prosecution otherwise denied them their constitutional rights. We are also convinced for the following reasons that § 245,[a] on which petitioners principally rely,

---

[a] Section 245 punishes one who "whether or not acting under color of law, by force or threat of force, willfully injures, intimidates or interferes with, or attempts to injure, intimidate or interfere with" persons engaged in certain activities. Subsection (b)(2)(C) prohibits such acts against a person "because of his race" who has sought or obtained employment. Subsection (b)(5) prohibits such acts directed against a person for "lawfully aiding or encouraging other persons to participate, without discrimination on account of race" in the activities protected by subsection

does not furnish adequate basis for removal under § 1443(1) of these state prosecutions to the federal court.

Whether or not § 245, a federal criminal statute, provides for "specific civil rights stated in terms of racial equality . . .," Georgia v. Rachel, 384, U.S. 780, 792 (1966), it evinces no intention to interfere in any manner with state criminal prosecutions of those who seek to have their cases removed to the federal courts. On the contrary, § 245(a)(1) itself expressly provides:

> "Nothing in this section shall be construed as indicating an intent on the part of Congress to prevent any State . . . from exercising jurisdiction over any offense over which it would have jurisdiction in the absence of this section . . . ."[12]

The Mississippi courts undoubtedly have jurisdiction over conspiracy and boycott cases brought under state law; and § 245(a)(1) appears to disavow any intent to interrupt such state prosecutions, a conclusion that is also implicit in the operative provisions of that section. Section 245(b) makes it a crime for any persons, by "force or threat of force" to injure, intimidate, or interfere with any individual engaged in specified activities. The provision on its face focuses on the use of force, and its legislative history confirms that its central purpose was to prevent and punish *violent* interferences with the exercise of specified rights and that it was not aimed at interrupting or frustrating the otherwise orderly processes of state law.

Section 245, which was title I of the Civil Rights Act of 1968, was the antidote prescribed by Congress to deter and punish those who would forcibly suppress the free exercise of civil rights enumerated in that statute. . . .

The Senate Report . . . explained title I as a measure "to meet the problem of violent interference, for racial or other discriminatory reasons, with a person's free exercise of civil rights." . . . In the debate on the floor of the Senate, frequent references to the bill's being directed at crimes of racial violence were made, the following being particularly relevant here:

> "This new law would provide that when a law enforcement officer totally abandons his duty in order to violently intimidate individuals seeking lawfully to exercise certain enumerated federal rights, he will be punished like any other citizen.
>
> ". . . So long as it appears that an officer reasonably believed he was doing his duty, that is, that the arrest took place because of a perceived violation of a then-valid law, no

(b)(2)(C), or for "participating lawfully in speech or peaceful assembly opposing any denial of the opportunity to participate" in such activities. [Footnote by eds.]

[12] Section 245(a)(1) goes on to negative any intent by Congress to foreclose state prosecution of the acts forbidden by that section:

"nor shall anything in this section be construed as depriving State and local law enforcement authorities of responsibility for prosecuting acts that may be violations of this section and that are violations of State and local law."

case of knowing interference with civil rights could be made against him."

Viewed in this context, it seems quite evident that a state prosecution, proceeding as it does in a court of law, cannot be characterized as an application of "force or threat of force" within the meaning of § 245. That section furnishes federal protection against violence in certain circumstances. But whatever "rights" it may confer, none of them is denied by a state criminal prosecution for conspiracy or boycott. Here, as in *Peacock,* there is no "federal statutory right that no state should even attempt to prosecute them for their conduct."

IV

We think further observations are in order. We stated in *City of Greenwood v. Peacock* :

> "[I]f changes are to be made in the long-settled interpretation of the provisions of this century-old removal statute, it is for Congress and not for this Court to make them. Fully aware of the established meaning the removal statute had been given by a consistent series of decisions in this Court, Congress in 1964 declined to act on proposals to amend the law. All that Congress did was to make remand orders appealable, and thus invite a contemporary judicial consideration of the meaning of the unchanged provisions of 28 U.S.C. § 1443."

When we decided that case, there had been introduced in the Congress no fewer than 12 bills which, if enacted, would have enlarged in one way or another the right of removal in civil rights cases. None of those bills was reported from the cognizant committee of Congress; none has been reported in the intervening years; and the parties have informed us of no comparable bill under active consideration in the present Congress. The absence of any evidence or legislative history indicating that Congress intended to accomplish in § 245 what it has failed or refused to do directly through amendment to § 1443 necessitates our considered rejection of the right of removal in this case. Also, as we noted in *Peacock,* there are varied avenues of relief open to these defendants for vindication of any of their federal rights that may have been or will be violated; and, indeed, it appears from the record in this case that at least one such avenue was pursued early on by them and continues to be pursued.[17]

Affirmed.

MR. JUSTICE DOUGLAS took no part in the consideration or decision of this case.

---

[17] Brief for Petitioners 16 n.9:

"Simultaneously [with the filing of the removal petition sub judice], the petitioners also filed a complaint pursuant to 42 U.S.C. § 1983 seeking injunctive relief against the arrests and prosecutions in a companion action, *Concerned Citizens of* *Vicksburg v. Sills,* but the District Court denied temporary injunctive relief which would have held the prosecutions in status quo pending a final hearing on the merits. A final hearing in that action has not yet been held, and is not part of this appeal."

MR. JUSTICE MARSHALL, with whom MR. JUSTICE BRENNAN joins, dissenting.

I believe the dissenters in City of Greenwood v. Peacock, 384 U.S. 808 (1966), correctly construed the civil rights removal statute, 28 U.S.C. § 1443. On that broader view of the statute, removal would plainly be proper here, and if the federal District Court determined that the state proceedings were being used to deny federally protected rights, it would be required to dismiss the prosecution. Even under *Peacock* and its companion case, Georgia v. Rachel, 384 U.S. 780 (1966), however, I think that removal should have been available on the particular facts of this case.

As the Court today observes, *Rachel* and *Peacock* imposed sharp limitations on the scope of the removal statute. The statute was held to permit removal only in the rare case in which (1) the federal right at issue stemmed from a law providing expressly for equal civil rights; (2) the conduct with which the removal petitioners were charged was arguably protected by the federal law in question; and (3) the federal law granted the further right not only to engage in the conduct in question, but to be free from arrest and prosecution by state officials for that conduct. Focusing on the third requirement, the Court today holds that title I of the 1968 Civil Rights Act, 18 U.S.C. § 245, does not provide a right to be free from arrest and prosecution for engaging in specific federally protected conduct. In my view, the three requirements from *Peacock* were satisfied to the extent necessary to call for a full hearing on the removal petition, and I would therefore vacate the judgment of the Court of Appeals and remand for further proceedings.[1]

I

The Court of Appeals based its ruling on the first of the three requirements, holding that § 245 was not a "law providing for . . . equal civil rights." The court reasoned that the statute failed to meet this requirement because it did not "provide" any substantive rights but merely supplied a criminal sanction for the violation of rights that had been elsewhere created. This misses the point.[2]

Even if § 245 is regarded solely as creating criminal penalties for interference with previously established civil rights, it certainly "provid[es] for" those rights by facilitating their exercise. Congress plainly intended § 245 in part to render certain rights meaningful, even though the rights themselves had in some instances been created

[1] Although the District Court . . . held a hearing, the Court of Appeals disposed of the case without reviewing the findings of the District Court. I would therefore remand the case to the Court of Appeals to review the findings . . . and to order further proceedings if necessary.

[2] The Court of Appeals acknowledged that § 245 met the requirement that the statute under which removal is claimed be a law dealing with "specific civil rights stated in terms of racial equality," Georgia v. Rachel, 384 U.S. 780, 792 (1966). The statute was plainly addressed to problems associated with the exercise and advocacy of minority rights. Like the 1964 Civil Rights Act, and unlike the more general constitutional and statutory provisions that were rejected as bases for removal in *Rachel* and *Peacock*, § 245(b)(2) refers throughout to conduct premised on racial discrimination.

in prior legislation. If Congress had provided private legal or equitable remedies for the vindication of pre-existing rights, such a statute would certainly be deemed one "providing for" equal civil rights. The fact that Congress has invoked the criminal sanction to protect and enforce those rights rather than relying on private remedies should make no difference.

In any event, § 245 does more than enforce pre-existing rights: in several respects it creates rights that had no previous statutory recognition. First, the statute protects not only those participating in the exercise of equal civil rights, but also those "encouraging other persons to participate" and those "participating lawfully in speech or peaceful assembly opposing any denial of the opportunity to so participate," § 245(b)(5). Second, because it is based on § 5 of the 14th amendment rather than the commerce clause, § 245 goes beyond the specific protections of prior civil rights laws in various particulars. . . . Finally, the statute goes beyond protecting against racially motivated misconduct by state officials and those acting in concert with them. It reaches racially motivated conduct by private individuals as well, thus extending both a right against, and a remedy for, certain private misconduct. The inclusion of private individuals within the reach of § 245 was a topic of intense dispute during the congressional debates over the statute. Both the advocates and opponents of the statute recognized that § 245 would criminalize a whole new sphere of conduct and thus significantly expand the scope of federal statutory protection for civil rights. In view of the statute's broad remedial purposes and effects, only on the most grudging reading can it be said not to "provid[e] for equal civil rights."

II

Although neither the Court of Appeals nor this Court has discussed the second requirement for § 1443 removal, I believe that under *Rachel* and *Peacock* a sufficient showing has been made to require further proceedings below. The Court in *Peacock* established that where the state criminal charge includes allegations of conduct clearly unprotected by federal law, removal is not available. In that case, the state charges included obstruction of the streets, assault, and interference with a police officer—all forms of conduct not even arguably protected under federal law.[3]

In *Rachel,* by contrast, the Court observed that the defendants had been charged only with violating the state criminal trespass statute, which required that a person leave a place of business when requested to do so by the owner. The defendants alleged in their removal

---

[3] The Court rejected the argument made in dissent that it was the allegations in the removal petition that should be looked to in determining whether the conduct was arguably protected by federal law, not the charges filed in the state proceeding. As has been suggested elsewhere, relying on the charges to determine whether the conduct is protected would immunize from removal any case in which the state charges included allegations of conduct plainly outside the scope of federal protection. Comment, Civil Rights Removal after *Rachel* and *Peacock*: A Limited Federal Remedy, 121 U. Pa. L. Rev. 351, 368 (1972).

petitions that they had remained on the premises of the privately owned restaurants where they were arrested in the course of seeking service to which they were entitled by the 1964 Civil Rights Act. Thus none of the conduct that the defendants were allegedly engaged in fell plainly outside the protection of federal law, as was the case in *Peacock*. Accordingly, the District Court was instructed to hold a hearing to determine whether the defendants were ordered to leave the restaurant facilities solely for racial reasons, and whether the conduct was in fact within the protection of federal law—in that case by determining whether the restaurants in question were within the coverage of the Civil Rights Act.

On this point, the instant case is controlled by *Rachel* rather than *Peacock*. The arrest affidavits charged merely that the petitioners had conspired to promote a boycott of merchants and businessmen and that they had engaged in and promoted acts "injurious to trade or commerce among the public." In their removal papers, the petitioners alleged that the conduct underlying their arrests on these charges was wholly within the protection of federal law. There is nothing in the arrest affidavits or the statute under which the petitioners were charged that rebuts this claim. The line between *Rachel* and *Peacock* is that between "prosecutions in which the conduct necessary to constitute the state offense is specifically protected by a federal equal rights statute under the circumstances alleged by the petitioner, and prosecutions where the only grounds for removal are that the charge is false and motivated by a desire to discourage the petitioner from exercising or to penalize him for having exercised a federal right." New York v. Davis, 411 F.2d 750, 754 (2d Cir.), cert. denied, 396 U.S. 856 (1969). Like *Rachel*, this case falls into the former category. Accordingly, the courts below should determine whether the petitioners' conduct was in fact protected. If it was, the prosecutions should be dismissed.

III

Finally, the *Rachel-Peacock* test requires that the federal law invoked by the petitioners must do more than merely provide a defense to conviction: it must immunize them from arrest and prosecution for the conduct in question. In *Rachel*, the Court held that this test was met, since § 203 of the 1964 Civil Rights Act provided: "No person shall . . . (c) punish or attempt to punish any person for exercising or attempting to exercise any right or privilege secured by section 201 or 202." The rights protected by § 201 included the right to "full and equal enjoyment of the . . . facilities . . . of any of public accommodation . . . without discrimination . . . on the ground of race." Viewing this language in light of a subsequent construction in Hamm v. City of Rock Hill, 379 U.S. 306, 311 (1964), the Court in *Rachel* concluded that if the facts in the removal petition were found to be true, the defendants would not only be immune from conviction under the Georgia trespass statute, but they would also have a right under the Civil Rights Act of 1964 "not even to be brought to trial on these charges in the Georgia courts."

The Court today distinguishes the language of 18 U.S.C. § 245 from that of § 203(c) of the Civil Rights Act of 1964, holding that the former does not grant the same immunity from prosecution that was implied in the latter. To me, the language of the two statutes is not sufficiently different to support such a distinction. While the statute in *Rachel* provided that no person should "punish or attempt to punish" a person engaged in conduct protected under the act, the statute at issue here provides sanctions against anyone who, "whether or not acting under color of law, by force or threat of force willfully injures, intimidates or interferes with, or attempts to injure, intimidate or interfere with" any person who is engaged in protected civil rights activity or is "lawfully aiding or encouraging other persons to participate" in various protected activities. The use of force or the threat of force to intimidate or interfere with persons engaged in protected activity fairly describes an "attempt to punish" the same persons, and it would seem plainly to include pretextual arrests such as are alleged to have occurred in this case.

Besides the difference in language between § 203(c) and § 245, the Court points to two other factors that it contends provide a further basis for denying removal here. I do not find either to be dispositive.

First, the Court relies on § 245(a)(1), in which Congress emphasized that § 245 was not intended to prevent "any State . . . from exercising jurisdiction over any offense over which it would have jurisdiction in the absence of this section . . . ." The Court argues that this "non-preemption" provision indicates that § 245 "appears to disavow any intent to interrupt . . . state prosecutions [for offenses such as boycotting and conspiracy]." I cannot agree that § 245(a)(1) means to do that much. The legislative history of this subsection indicates that it was intended to avoid the risk that § 245 would be read to bar or interfere with state prosecutions of those who violated § 245 as well as parallel state laws. The fear was that § 245, because of its potential breadth, might appear to give pre-emptive authority to federal law officers in prosecuting a broad spectrum of offenses that were traditionally subject to local criminal jurisdiction. There is no indication in the legislative history that § 245(a)(1) was intended to defeat removal of state prosecutions by those protected under the act, nor is there any suggestion that it was meant to reduce the protection for the beneficiaries of § 245 in any other way.

Second, the Court relies heavily on the main purpose of § 245: to penalize violent interference with the exercise of specific rights. Certainly, violent interference with the exercise of civil rights was a primary target of the statute. But curbing private violence was not the drafters' sole aim. The act was intended to reach law enforcement officers as well as private citizens, and the process of arrest and prosecution in state courts is precisely the means by which state officials, acting under color of state law, can most plausibly exert force or the threat of force to interfere with federally protected rights.

The Court is correct, of course, in noting that Congress did not expressly indicate that § 245 should be available as a means of removing prosecutions to federal courts. But the Court in *Rachel* did not require any showing that Congress had specifically intended the statute in issue to be used as a vehicle for removal. All that was necessary was that the statute protect against the institution of criminal actions against those engaged in protected federal rights, and in my view that standard is met here.[8]

IV

If the facts of this case are as alleged in the removal petition, then the protest effort of the petitioners and their group, although well within the protection of federal law, has been muffled, if not altogether stilled, by discriminatory and cynical misuse of the state criminal process. The Court makes reference to the possibility of federal injunctive relief, which would be available in this case if the petitioners can show that the arrests and prosecutions were instituted in bad faith or for the purpose of harassment. See Dombrowski v. Pfister, 380 U.S. 479, 482, 490 (1965); Younger v. Harris, 401 U.S. 37, 47–50 (1971). I only hope that the recent instances in which this Court has emphasized the values of comity and federalism in restricting the issuance of federal injunctions against state criminal and quasi-criminal proceedings will not mislead the district courts into forgetting that at times these values must give way to the need to protect federal rights from being irremediably trampled. The possibility that the petitioners might be vindicated in state-court criminal actions or through subsequent habeas corpus relief will do little to restore what has been lost: the right to engage in legitimate, if unpopular, protest without being subjected to the inconvenience, the expense, and the ignominy of arrest and prosecution. If the federal courts abandon persons like the petitioners in this case without a fair hearing on the merits of their claims, then in my view comity will have been bought at too great a cost.

I respectfully dissent.

FURTHER NOTES ON CIVIL RIGHTS REMOVAL

1. **Questions and Comments on** *Johnson v. Mississippi.* Does the Court's result follow from the distinction between *Rachel* and *Peacock*? Do the dissenters have a point that § 245 is not that different from the provisions of the Civil Rights Act of 1964 held sufficient to justify removal in *Rachel*? Some of the defendants in *Peacock* unsuccessfully relied on rights claimed under 42 U.S.C. § 1971, quoted in footnote d, page 575, supra. Are there clear differences

----

[8] In its analysis, the Court relies in part on a statement by Senator Kennedy to the effect that a state law enforcement officer reasonably believing that he is doing his duty, would not violate § 245, which re- quires at least knowing interference with civil rights. The interference alleged in the removal petition however is intentional interference, which would fall within the literal terms of the statute.

between the 1964 Civil Rights Act on the one hand and §§ 245 and 1971 on the other?

2. **Bibliography.** The most extensive consideration of § 1443 in the literature is contained in Amsterdam, Criminal Prosecutions Affecting Federally Guaranteed Civil Rights: Federal Removal and Habeas Corpus Jurisdiction to Abort State Court Trial, 113 U. Pa. L. Rev. 793 (1965). This article was written before *Rachel* and *Peacock,* and was characterized by the Court in *Rachel* [a] as "remarkably original and comprehensive," though its thesis as to the meaning of § 1443 was rejected.[b] For other treatments of the provision, see Redish, Revitalizing Civil Rights Removal Jurisdiction, 64 Minn. L. Rev. 523 (1980); Johnson, Removal of Civil Rights Cases from State to Federal Courts: The Matrix of Section 1443, 26 Fed. B.J. 99 (1966); Morse, Civil Rights Removal: "The Letter Killeth, But the Spirit Giveth Life," 11 How. L.J. 149 (1965); Note, Civil Rights Removal After *Rachel* and *Peacock* : A Limited Federal Remedy, 121 U. Pa. L. Rev. 351 (1972); Note, Federal Jurisdiction: The Civil Rights Removal Statute Revisited, 1967 Duke L.J. 136; Note, Civil Rights Removal: *City of Greenwood v. Peacock* and *Georgia v. Rachel,* 14 U.C.L.A. L. Rev. 1159 (1967); Note, A Reexamination of the Civil Rights Removal Statute, 51 Va. L. Rev. 950 (1965).

NOTE ON REMOVAL OF FEDERAL QUESTION AND DIVERSITY CASES

Removal in the ordinary run of cases in the federal courts is governed by 28 U.S.C. § 1441. That statute provides:

"(a) Except as otherwise expressly provided by Act of Congress, any civil action brought in a State court of which the district courts of the United States have original jurisdiction, may be removed by the defendant or the defendants, to the district court of the United States for the district and division embracing the place where such action is pending.

"(b) Any civil action of which the district courts have original jurisdiction founded on a claim or right arising under the Constitution, treaties or laws of the United States shall be removable without regard to the citizenship of the parties. Any other such action shall be removable only if none of the parties in interest properly joined and served as defendants is a citizen of the State in which such action is brought.

"(c) Whenever a separate and independent claim or cause of action, which would be removable if sued upon alone, is joined with one or more otherwise non-removable claims or

---

[a] Amsterdam argued the case for the state court defendants in *Rachel.*

[b] Amsterdam would have allowed removal "wherever a substantive federal civil rights defense is claimed," though he "unhappily" agreed that a claim that federal procedural guarantees would be denied by a state court would require an "inquiry into the probability of their denial by the state courts," which was "the sort of inquiry I regard as ordinarily unfeasible."

causes of action, the entire case may be removed and the district court may determine all issues therein, or, in its discretion, may remand all matters not otherwise within its original jurisdiction. . . .

"(e) The court to which such civil action is removed is not precluded from hearing and determining any claim in such civil action because the State court from which such civil action is removed did not have jurisdiction over that claim."

Subsection (a) states the basic removal authority of the district courts. It requires that the case be one that is within the court's "original jurisdiction." This has the effect of precluding removal based on a federal defense, since a federal question case will not be within the "original jurisdiction" of the district court unless the plaintiff's properly pleaded complaint contains a federal question that justifies jurisdiction under § 1331 or some comparable statute.[a]

Subsection (b) states the relevance of the defendant's citizenship to the removal authorized by subsection (a). Citizenship is said to be irrelevant in federal question cases, but only defendants who do not live in the state where the action is brought can remove a diversity case. Thus, even though a plaintiff can bring a diversity action in his or her own state, a defendant can remove only if he or she is a citizen of a state other than the one in which the suit was filed.

Subsection (c) states a complex exception to the basic structure established by subsections (a) and (b). The provision was severely limited in American Fire & Casualty Co. v. Finn, 341 U.S. 6 (1951), and is of little modern utility. Its history and the effect of *Finn* are described in Cohen, Problems in the Removal of a "Separate and Independent Claim or Cause of Action," 46 Minn. L. Rev. 1 (1961). See also Lewin, The Federal Courts' Hospitable Back Door—Removal of "Separate and Independent" Non-Federal Causes of Action, 66 Harv. L. Rev. 423 (1953).

Subsection (e) was added in 1986. Prior to this enactment, the authority to remove a case under subsection (a) was said to be derivative, that is, a case must have been properly before the state court before it could be removed to a federal court. Thus, anomalously, if a case within the exclusive jurisdiction of the federal court was filed in state court and then sought to be removed to federal court, the federal court was obligated to dismiss (though the case could then be refiled in

---

[a] See page 431, supra. There are, however, more specific statutes that permit removal on the basis of a federal defense. For example, § 1442(a)(1) permits a federal law enforcement officer to remove a state murder prosecution on the ground that he or she acted in self-defense under color of official authority. The limitation in § 1441(a) is thus statutory policy and not constitutional limitation.

Note also that some federal question cases cannot be removed. See, e.g., 28 U.S.C. § 1445. For detailed treatment of the background of removal of federal question cases, see Michael G. Collins, The Unhappy History of Federal Question Removal, 71 Iowa L. Rev. 717 (1986). The reviewability of remand orders is dealt with in detail in Mark Herrmann, *Thermetron* Revisited: When and How Federal Trial Court Remand Orders Are Reviewable, 19 Ariz.St.L.J. 395 (1987).

federal court if the statute of limitations had not expired). The House Report on subsection (e) stated its purpose as follows:

> "The purpose of [the addition of subsection (e)] is to abolish the present judicial rule that an improvidently brought state civil action, the subject matter of which is within the exclusive jurisdiction of a federal district court, must be dismissed when it is removed to the district court. . . . The theory behind the current rule is that removal confers only 'derivative jurisdiction' on the federal courts; and therefore, since the state court lacked subject matter jurisdiction of the civil action, the federal court cannot acquire subject matter jurisdiction by removal. [The addition of subsection (e) to § 1441] eliminates this arcane rule, so wasteful to finite judicial resources. . . .

> "One commentator on the bill (Professor Thomas Rowe of Duke University School of Law) suggested statutory clarification on the question of the impact of the bill on territorial jurisdiction. Federal courts are often confined to the long-arm authority of the courts of the state in which they sit. The Committee does not intend to cure any defect in territorial jurisdiction."

———

Chapter VI

APPELLATE REVIEW

SECTION 1: SUPREME COURT REVIEW OF FEDERAL QUESTIONS

INTRODUCTORY NOTES ON THE POWER OF THE SUPREME COURT TO REVIEW STATE DECISIONS

1. *Martin v. Hunter's Lessee.* The power of the United States Supreme Court to review state-court decisions was settled in Martin v. Hunter's Lessee, 14 U.S. (1 Wheat.) 304 (1816). The case involved when and whether an escheat of land to the state of Virginia had occurred. Hunter's lessee claimed the land under a grant from the state made in 1789. Martin claimed the land through the will of Lord Fairfax, a British subject who had originally owned the land. Two treaties, one in 1783 and one in 1794, prevented state governments from interfering with the normal rights of British subjects to land in the United States. If the escheat of the land to Virginia had occurred before these treaties went into effect, the state's grant of the land was valid, and Hunter's lessee would prevail. If the land had not escheated until the treaties came into effect, then the grant by Virginia was invalid, and Martin would win.

The Virginia Court of Appeals (as the highest court in Virginia was then known) held in favor of Hunter's lessee, in part on the ground that the land had escheated to Virginia in 1782, before either of the treaties came into effect. The United States Supreme Court reversed, but the Virginia Court of Appeals declined to obey its mandate. The Virginia judges expressed their views individually, but joined in the unanimous conclusion "that the appellate power of the Supreme Court of the United States, does not extend to this court." The gist of their position was stated by Judge Cabell:

> [B]efore one court can dictate to another, . . . it must bear, to that other, the relation of an appellate court. The term appellate, however, necessarily includes the idea of superiority. But one court cannot be correctly said to be superior to another, unless both of them belong to the same sovereignty. It would be a misapplication of terms to say that a court of Virginia is superior to a court of Maryland, or vice versa. The courts of the United States, therefore, belonging to one sovereignty, cannot be appellate courts in relation to the state

594

courts, which belong to a different sovereignty—and, of course, their commands or instructions impose no obligation."

The case then came back to the Supreme Court, which held that it had both constitutional and statutory authority to review state court decisions. Justice Story's opinion makes three main arguments. The first was grounded in the text of the Constitution:

"The appellate power is not limited by the terms of the third article to any particular courts. The words are, 'the judicial Power . . . shall extend *to all Cases,* '. . . and 'in all other Cases before mentioned the supreme Court shall have appellate Jurisdiction.' It is the *case,* then, and not *the court,* that gives the jurisdiction. . . .

"If the Constitution meant to limit the appellate jurisdiction to cases pending in the courts of the United States, it would necessarily follow that the jurisdiction of these courts would, in all the cases enumerated in the Constitution, be exclusive of state tribunals. . . . If some of these cases might be entertained by state tribunals, and no appellate jurisdiction as to them should exist, then the appellate power would not extend to *all,* but to *some,* cases. . . .

"On the other hand, if . . . a discretion be vested in Congress to establish, or not to establish, inferior courts at their own pleasure, and Congress should not establish such courts, the appellate jurisdiction of the Supreme Court would have nothing to act upon, unless it could act upon cases pending in the state courts. . . .

"But it is plain that the framers of the Constitution did contemplate that cases within the judicial cognizance of the United States . . . would arise in the state courts . . . . With this view the sixth article declares, that 'This Constitution, and the Laws of the United States which shall be made in Pursuance thereof, and all Treaties made, or which shall be made, under the Authority of the United States, shall be the supreme Law of the Land, and the Judges in every State shall be bound thereby, any Thing in the Constitution or Laws of any State to the Contrary notwithstanding.' . . .

"It must, therefore, be conceded that the Constitution . . . meant to provide for cases within the scope of the judicial power of the United States, which might yet depend before state tribunals. It was foreseen that in the exercise of their ordinary jurisdiction, state courts would incidentally take cognizance of cases arising under the Constitution, the laws, and treaties of the United States. Yet to all these cases the judicial power, by the very terms of the Constitution, is to extend. It cannot extend by original jurisdiction if that was already rightfully and exclusively attached in the state courts . . .; it must, therefore, extend by appellate jurisdiction . . . ."

Story then turned to a series of policy considerations:

"It is further argued, that no great public mischief can result from a construction which shall limit the appellate power of the United States to cases in their own courts: first, because state judges are bound by an oath to support the Constitution of the United States, and must be presumed to be men of learning and integrity; and, secondly, because Congress must have an unquestionable right to remove all cases within the scope of the judicial power from the state courts to the courts of the United States, at any time before final judgment, though not after final judgment. As to the first reason— admitting that the judges of the state courts are, and always will be, of as much learning, integrity, and wisdom, as those of the courts of the United States, . . . it does not aid the argument. The Constitution has presumed . . . that state attachments, state prejudices, state jealousies, and state interests, might sometimes obstruct, or control, or be supposed to obstruct or control, the regular administration of justice. . . .

"This is not all. A motive of another kind, perfectly compatible with the most sincere respect for state tribunals, might induce the grant of appellate power over their decisions. That motive is the importance, and even necessity of *uniformity* of decisions throughout the whole United States, upon all subjects within the purview of the Constitution. Judges of equal learning and integrity, in different states, might differently interpret a statute, or a treaty of the United States, or even the Constitution itself: If there were no revising authority to control these jarring and discordant judgments, and harmonize them into uniformity, the laws, the treaties, and the Constitution of the United States would be different in different states, and might, perhaps, never have precisely the same construction, obligation, or efficacy, in any two states. [T]he appellate jurisdiction must continue to be the only adequate remedy for such evils.

"There is an additional consideration, which is entitled to great weight. The Constitution of the United States was designed for the common and equal benefit of all the people of the United States. The judicial power was granted for the same benign and salutary purposes. It was not to be exercised exclusively for the benefit of parties who might be plaintiffs, and would elect the national forum, but also for the protection of defendants who might be entitled to try their rights, or assert their privileges, before the same forum. Yet, if the construction contended for be correct, it will follow, that as the plaintiff may always elect the state court, the defendant may be deprived of all the security which the Constitution intended in aid of his rights. Such a state of things can, in no respect, be considered as giving equal rights. To obviate this difficulty, we are referred to the power which it is admitted Congress possess to remove suits from state courts to the national courts . . . .

". . . The power of removal . . . presupposes an exercise of original jurisdiction to have attached elsewhere. . . . But [the power of removal] is always deemed . . . an exercise of appellate, and not of original jurisdiction. If, then, the right of removal be included in the appellate jurisdiction, it is only because it is one mode of exercising that power, and as Congress is not limited by the Constitution to any particular mode, . . . it may authorize a removal either before or after judgment. . . . A writ of error is, indeed, but a process which removes the record of one court to the possession of another court, and enables the other to inspect the proceedings, and give such judgment as its own opinion of the law and justice of the case may warrant. . . ."

Finally, Justice Story pointed to history:

"Strong as this conclusion stands upon the general language of the Constitution, it may still derive support from other sources. It is an historical fact, that this exposition of the Constitution, extending its appellate power to state courts, was, previous to its adoption, uniformly and publicly avowed by its friends, and admitted by its enemies . . . . It is an historical fact, that at the time when the judiciary act was submitted to the deliberations of the first Congress, composed, as it was, not only of men who had acted a principal part in framing, supporting, or opposing that Constitution, the same exposition was explicitly declared and admitted by the friends and by the opponents of that system. It is an historical fact, that the Supreme Court of the United States have, from time to time, sustained this appellate jurisdiction in a great variety of cases, brought from the tribunals of many of the most important states in the union, and that no state tribunal has ever breathed a judicial doubt on the subject, or declined to obey the mandate of the Supreme Court, until the present occasion. This weight of contemporaneous exposition by all parties, this acquiescence of enlightened state courts, and these judicial decisions of the Supreme Court through so long a period, do, as we think, place the doctrine upon a foundation of authority which cannot be shaken . . . ."

2. *Murdock v. City of Memphis.* Murdock v. City of Memphis, 87 U.S. (20 Wall.) 590 (1875), is famous for having established the contours of modern appellate review of state decisions. *Murdock* is the *Erie* of appellate review. It held that only questions of federal law are open to Supreme Court decision and that the judgments of the state supreme courts are final on questions of state law. As in *Erie,* a number of subtleties are hidden in such a simple statement of the Court's position. Unlike *Erie,* the Court's decision had no constitutional pretensions: it was based solely on the interpretation of an 1867 statute.

The ancestors of Murdock conveyed land to the city of Memphis in July of 1844 for the location of a naval depot. They provided in the instrument of sale that the land would revert to the grantors or their heirs "in case the same shall not be appropriated by the United States for that purpose." In September of 1844, the city conveyed the land unconditionally to the United States. The federal government took possession of the land for the purpose of establishing the naval depot, and made various improvements. Ten years later, it abandoned the project and, by act of Congress, conveyed the land back to the city "for the use and benefit of said city."

Murdock sued the city in state court, claiming that the abandonment of the naval depot triggered his reversionary interest in the land. The state court held that the deed of July, 1844, established a reversionary interest in Murdock only in the event that the land was never conveyed to the United States for establishment of the depot. It did not contemplate reversion in the event that the depot was abandoned. The state court also held that the act of Congress reconveying the land back to the city was unconditional, and that the city therefore held complete title to the land.

The case came to the Supreme Court by writ of error under a statute passed in 1867. The 1867 act amended the Judiciary Act of 1789, the statute that in § 25 had originally established the appellate jurisdiction of the Supreme Court over state court decisions. Both statutes described certain categories of cases subject to Supreme Court review—e.g., cases where the state court held a federal statute unconstitutional, cases where the state court upheld the constitutionality of a state statute against a federal challenge, and cases where a federal right claimed under the Constitution or a statute was denied. The last sentence of the original § 25 had provided:

> "But no other error shall be assigned or regarded as a ground of reversal in any such case as aforesaid than such as appears on the face of the record and immediately respects the before-mentioned questions of validity or construction of the said Constitution, treaties, statutes, commissions, or authorities in dispute."

The effect of this language, as the Court put it, was expressly to limit review of state decisions to "questions, that for the sake of brevity, though not with strict verbal accuracy, we shall call federal questions, namely, those in regard to the validity or construction of the Constitution, treaties, statutes, commissions, or authority of the federal government." The sentence was omitted in the 1867 revision. The effect of the deletion, Murdock argued, was to open up the entire case for review—including questions of state law. The Court responded:

> "The 25th section of the act of 1789 has been the subject of innumerable decisions, some of which are to be found in almost every volume of the reports from that year down to the

present. These form a system of appellate jurisprudence relating to the exercise of the appellate power of this Court over the courts of the states. That system has been based upon the fundamental principle that this jurisdiction was limited to the correction of errors relating solely to federal law. And though it may be argued with some plausibility that the reason of this is to be found in the restrictive clause of the act of 1789, which is omitted in the act of 1867, yet an examination of the cases will show that it rested quite as much on the conviction of this Court that without that clause and on general principles the jurisdiction extended no further. It requires a very bold reach of thought, and a readiness to impute to Congress a radical and hazardous change of a policy vital in its essential nature to the independence of the state courts, to believe that that body contemplated, or intended, what is claimed, by the mere omission of a clause in the substituted statute, which may well be held to have been superfluous, or nearly so, in the old one.

. . .

"It is not difficult to discover what the purpose of Congress in the passage of this law was. In a vast number of cases the rights of the people of the Union, as they are administered in the courts of the states, must depend upon the construction which those courts gave to the Constitution, treaties, and laws of the United States. The highest courts of the states were sufficiently numerous, even in 1789, to cause it to be feared that, with the purest motives, this construction given in different courts would be various and conflicting. It was desirable, however, that whatever conflict of opinion might exist in those courts on other subjects, the rights which depended on the federal laws should be the same everywhere, and that their construction should be uniform. This could only be done by conferring upon the Supreme Court of the United States—the appellate tribunal established by the Constitution—the right to decide these questions finally and in a manner which would be conclusive on all other courts, state or national. This was the first purpose of the statute, and it does not require that, in a case involving a variety of questions, any other should be decided than those described in the act.

"[In addition, it] was no doubt the purpose of Congress to secure to every litigant whose rights depended on any question of federal law that that question should be decided for him by the highest federal tribunal if he desired it, when the decisions of the state courts were against him on that question. That rights of this character, guaranteed to him by the Constitution and laws of the Union, should not be left to the exclusive and final control of the state courts.

"There may be some plausibility in the argument that these rights cannot be protected in all cases unless the Supreme Court has final control of the whole case. But the experience of 85 years of the administration of the law under the opposite theory would seem to be a satisfactory answer to the argument. It is not to be presumed that the state courts, where the rule is clearly laid down to them on the federal question, and its influence on the case fully seen, will disregard or overlook it, and this is all that the rights of the party claiming under it require. Besides, by the very terms of this statute, when the Supreme Court is of opinion that the question of federal law is of such relative importance to the whole case that it should control the final judgment, that court is authorized to render such judgment and enforce it by its own process. It cannot, therefore, be maintained that it is in any case necessary for the security of the rights claimed under the Constitution, laws, or treaties of the United States that the Supreme Court should examine and decide other questions not of a federal character."

On the merits, the Court held that the deed of conveyance from the United States to the city was unconditional and established no federal rights in Murdock. The question whether Murdock retained a reversionary interest based on the original conveyance from his ancestors to the city was held to be one of state law over which the Supreme Court had no jurisdiction.

3. **Conclusion.** It was established in *Murdock,* and has not been questioned since, that Supreme Court review of state court decisions is limited to federal questions. The Court is not free to re-examine questions of state law decided by a state supreme court and to reverse because the question of state law was wrongly decided.

The next two main cases, Indiana ex rel. Anderson v. Brand, 303 U.S. 95 (1938), and Standard Oil Co. of California v. Johnson, 316 U.S. 481 (1942), concern the scope of this limitation. In *Brand* the Court decided, contrary to the determination of the Indiana Supreme Court, that a contract had been created by state law. In *Johnson* the Court decided, contrary to the determination of the California Supreme Court, that an army post exchange might have fallen within an exemption created by a state tax statute. Both issues, in the end, would seem to be controlled by state law. Whether the Court properly respected the limitations fixed by *Murdock* is the question to be considered in connection with these cases and their accompanying notes.

INDIANA ex rel. ANDERSON v. BRAND

Supreme Court of the United States, 1938.
303 U.S. 95.

MR. JUSTICE ROBERTS delivered the opinion of the Court.

The petitioner sought a writ of mandate to compel the respondent to continue her in employment as a public school teacher. Her complaint alleged that as a duly licensed teacher she entered into a contract in September, 1924, to teach in the township schools and, pursuant to successive contracts, taught continuously to and including the school year 1932–33; that her contracts for the school years 1931–32 and 1932–33 contained this clause: "It is further agreed by the contracting parties that all of the provisions of the Teachers' Tenure Law, approved March 8, 1927, shall be in full force and effect in this contract"; and that by force of that act she had a contract, indefinite in duration, which could be canceled by the respondent only in the manner and for the causes specified in the act. She charged that in July, 1933, the respondent notified her he proposed to cancel her contract for cause; that, after a hearing, he adhered to his decision and the county superintendent affirmed his action; that, despite what occurred in July, 1933, the petitioner was permitted to teach during the school year 1933–34 and the respondent was presently threatening to terminate her employment at the end of that year. The complaint alleged [that] the termination of her employment would be a breach of her contract with the school corporation. The respondent demurred on the grounds that (1) the complaint disclosed [that] the matters pleaded had been submitted to the respondent and the county superintendent who were authorized to try the issues and had lawfully determined them in favor of the respondent; and (2) the Teachers' Tenure Law [of 1927] had been repealed in respect of teachers in township schools. The demurrer was sustained and the petitioner appealed to the state Supreme Court which affirmed the judgment. The court did not discuss the first ground of demurrer relating to the action taken in the school year 1932–33, but rested its decision upon the second, that . . . the Teachers' Tenure Law [of 1927] had been repealed as respects teachers in township schools; and held that the repeal did not deprive the petitioner of a vested property right and did not impair her contract within the meaning of the Constitution. In its original opinion the court said: "The relatrix contends . . . that, having become a permanent teacher under the Teachers' Tenure Law before the amendment, she had a vested property right in her indefinite contract, which may not be impaired under the Constitution. The question is whether there is a vested right in a permanent teacher's contract; whether, under the tenure law, there is a grant which cannot lawfully be impaired by a repeal of the statute." Where the state court does not decide against a petitioner or appellant upon an independent state ground, but deeming the federal question to be before it, actually entertains and decides that question adversely to the federal right asserted, this Court has jurisdiction to review the judgment if, as here, it is a final judgment. We cannot refuse jurisdiction because the state court might have based its decision, consistently with the record, upon an independent and adequate nonfederal ground. And since the amendment of the Judiciary Act of 1789 by the act of February 5, 1867, it has always been held [that] this Court may examine the opinion of the state court to ascertain whether a federal question was raised and decided, and whether the court rested its judgment on an adequate nonfederal ground. Any ambiguity arising from the generality of the court's reference to the

Constitution is resolved by a certificate signed by all the Justices of the court, made a part of the record, to the effect that the reference to the Constitution in the opinion was to article 1, section 10, of the Constitution of the United States. It thus appearing that the constitutional validity of the repealing act was drawn in question and the statute sustained, we issued the writ of certiorari.

The court below holds that in Indiana teachers' contracts are made for but one year; that there is no contractual right to be continued as a teacher from year to year; that the law grants a privilege to one who has taught five years and signed a new contract to continue in employment under given conditions; that the statute is directed merely to the exercise of their powers by the school authorities and the policy therein expressed may be altered at the will of the legislature; that in enacting laws for the government of public schools, the legislature exercises a function of sovereignty and the power to control public policy in respect of their management and operation cannot be contracted away by one legislature so as to create a permanent public policy unchangeable by succeeding legislatures. In the alternative the court declares that if the relationship be considered as controlled by the rules of private contract the provision for re-employment from year to year is unenforceable for want of mutuality.

As in most cases brought to this Court under the contract clause of the Constitution, the question is as to the existence and nature of the contract and not as to the construction of the law which is supposed to impair it. The principal function of a legislative body is not to make contracts but to make laws which declare the policy of the state and are subject to repeal when a subsequent legislature shall determine to alter that policy. Nevertheless, it is established that a legislative enactment may contain provisions which, when accepted as the basis of action by individuals, become contracts between them and the state or its subdivisions within the protection of article 1, § 10. If the people's representatives deem it in the public interest they may adopt a policy of contracting in respect of public business for a term longer than the life of the current session of the legislature. This the petitioner claims has been done with respect to permanent teachers. The Supreme Court has decided, however, that it is the state's policy not to bind school corporations by contract for more than one year.

On such a question, one primarily of state law, we accord respectful consideration and great weight to the views of the state's highest court but, in order that the constitutional mandate may not become a dead letter, we are bound to decide for ourselves whether a contract was made, what are its terms and conditions, and whether the state has, by later legislation, impaired its obligation. This involves an appraisal of the statutes of the state and the decisions of its courts.

The courts of Indiana have long recognized that the employment of school teachers was contractual and have afforded relief in actions upon teachers' contracts. An act adopted in 1899 required all contracts between teachers and school corporations to be in writing, signed by the parties to be charged, and to be made a matter of public record. A statute of 1921 enacted that every such contract should be in writing and should state the date of the beginning of the school term, the number of months therein, the amount of the salary for the term, and the number of payments to be made during the school year.

In 1927 the state adopted the Teachers' Tenure Act under which the present controversy arises. . . . By this act it was provided that a teacher who has served under contract for five or more successive years, and thereafter enters into a contract for further service with the school corporation, shall become a permanent teacher and the contract, upon the expiration of its stated term, shall be deemed to continue in effect for an indefinite period, shall be known as an indefinite contract, and shall remain in force unless succeeded by a new contract or canceled as provided in the act. The corporation may cancel the contract, after notice and hearing, for incompetency, insubordination, neglect of duty, immorality, justifiable decrease in the number of teaching positions, or other good or just cause, but not for political or personal reasons. The teacher may not cancel the contract during the school term nor for a period 30 days previous to the beginning of any term (unless by mutual agreement) and may cancel only upon five days' notice.

By an amendatory act of 1933 township school corporations were omitted from the provisions of the act of 1927. The court below construed this act as repealing the act of 1927 so far as township schools and teachers are concerned and as leaving the respondent free to terminate the petitioner's employment. But we are of opinion that the petitioner had a valid contract with the respondent, the obligation of which would be impaired by the termination of her employment.

Where the claim is that the state's policy embodied in a statute is to bind its instrumentalities by contract, the cardinal inquiry is as to the terms of the statute supposed to create such a contract. The state long prior to the adoption of the act of 1927 required the execution of written contracts between teachers and school corporations, specified certain subjects with which such contracts must deal, and required that they be made a matter of public record. These were annual contracts, covering a single school term. The act of 1927 announced a new policy that a teacher who had served for five years under successive contracts, upon the execution of another was to become a permanent teacher and the last contract was to be indefinite as to duration and terminable by either party only upon compliance with the conditions set out in the statute. The policy which induced the legislation evidently was that the teacher should have protection against the exercise of the right, which would otherwise inhere in the employer, of terminating the employment at the end of any school term without assigned reasons and solely at the employer's pleasure. The state courts in earlier cases so declared.

The title of the act is couched in terms of contract. It speaks of the making and cancelling of indefinite contracts. In the body the word "contract" appears 10 times in section 1, defining the relationship; 11 times in section 2, relating to the termination of the employment by the employer, and four times in section 4, stating the conditions of termination by the teacher.

The tenor of the act indicates that the word "contract" was not used inadvertently or in other than its usual legal meaning. By section 6 it is expressly provided that the act is a supplement to that of March 7, 1921, requiring teachers' employment contracts to be in writing. By section 1 it is provided that the written contract of a permanent teacher "shall be deemed to continue in effect for an indefinite period and shall be known as an indefinite contract." Such an indefinite contract is to remain in force unless succeeded by a new contract signed by both parties or canceled as provided in section 2. No more apt language could be employed to define a contractual relationship. By section 2 it is enacted that such indefinite contracts may be canceled by the school corporation only in the manner specified. The admissible grounds of cancellation, and the method by which the existence of such grounds shall be ascertained and made a matter of record, are carefully set out. Section 4 permits cancellation by the teacher only at certain times consistent with the convenient administration of the school system and imposes a sanction for violation of its requirements. Examination of the entire act convinces us that the teacher was by it assured of the possession of a binding and enforceable contract against school districts.

Until its decision in the present case the Supreme Court of the state had uniformly held that the teacher's right to continued employment by virtue of the indefinite contract created pursuant to the act was contractual.

[For example, in] School City of Elwood v. State ex rel. Griffin, 203 Ind. 626, 634, 180 N.E. 471, 474 (1932), it was said:

> "The position of a teacher in the public schools is not a public office, but an employment by contract between the teacher and the school corporation. The relation remains contractual after the teacher has, under the provisions of a Teachers' Tenure Law, become a permanent teacher—but the terms and conditions of the contract are thereafter governed primarily by the statute." . . .

We think the decision in this case runs counter to the policy evinced by the act of 1927, to its explicit mandate and to earlier decisions construing its provisions. . . .

The respondent urges that every contract is subject to the police power and that in repealing the Teachers' Tenure Act the legislature validly exercised that reserved power of the state. The sufficient answer is found in the statute. By section 2 of the act of 1927 power is given to the school corporation to cancel a teacher's indefinite contract for incompetency, insubordination (which is to be deemed to mean willful refusal to obey the school laws of the state or reasonable rules prescribed by the employer), neglect of duty, immorality, justifiable decrease in the number of teaching positions, or other good and just cause. The permissible reasons for cancellation cover every conceivable basis for such action growing out of a deficient performance of the obligations undertaken by the teacher, and diminution of the school requirements. Although the causes specified constitute in themselves just and reasonable grounds for the termination of any ordinary contract of employment, to preclude the assumption that any other valid ground was excluded by the enumeration, the legislature added that the relation might be terminated for any other good and just cause. Thus in the declaration of the state's policy, ample reservations in aid of the efficient administration of the school system were made. The express prohibitions are that the contract shall not be canceled for political or personal reasons. We do not think the asserted change of policy evidenced by the repeal of the statute is that school boards may be at liberty to cancel a teacher's contract for political or personal reasons. We do not understand the respondent so to contend. The most that can be said for his position is that, by the repeal, township school corporations were again put upon the basis of annual contracts, renewable at the pleasure of the board. It is significant that the act of 1933 left the system of permanent teachers and indefinite contracts untouched as respects school corporations in cities and towns of the state. It is not contended, nor can it be thought, that the legislature of 1933 determined that it was against public policy for school districts in cities and towns to terminate the employment of teachers of five or more years' experience for political or personal reasons and to permit cancellation, for the same reasons, in townships.

Our decisions recognize that every contract is made subject to the implied condition that its fulfillment may be frustrated by a proper exercise of the police power but we have repeatedly said that, in order to have this effect, the exercise of the power must be for an end which is in fact public and the means adopted must be reasonably adapted to that end, and the Supreme Court of Indiana has taken the same view in respect of legislation impairing the obligation of the contract of a state instrumentality. The causes of cancellation provided in the act of 1927 and the retention of the system of indefinite contracts in all municipalities except townships by the act of 1933 are persuasive that the repeal of the earlier act by the later was not an exercise of the police power for the attainment of ends to which its exercise may properly be directed.

As the court below has not passed upon one of the grounds of demurrer which appears to involve no federal question, and may present a defense still open to the respondent, we reverse the judgment and remand the cause for further proceedings not inconsistent with this opinion.

So ordered.

MR. JUSTICE CARDOZO took no part in the consideration or decision of this case.

MR. JUSTICE BLACK, dissenting.

[Justice Black argued, inter alia, that the Court had misread the Indiana cases and that no "contract" under state law had ever been created.]

NOTES ON FEDERAL PROTECTION OF STATE–CREATED RIGHTS

1. **Introduction.** Generically, the issue in *Brand* concerns a situation where the federal Constitution protects a right created by state law. The following notes draw out the implications of such issues for Supreme Court review of state court decisions.

2. **Questions and Comments on *Brand*.** The *Brand* case involves the provision in art. 1, § 10 of the Constitution that "no State shall . . . pass any . . . Law impairing the Obligation of Contracts." In order to administer such a prohibition, one must first decide whether a contractual obligation has been created, and then decide whether it has been impaired. Whose law governs the creation of the contract obligation itself? It has occasionally been suggested that this is an area where federal common law should be created. See, e.g., D'Oench, Duhme & Co. v. Federal Deposit Ins. Corp., 315 U.S. 447, 470 (1942). But this suggestion has not prevailed, and it is settled that state law governs.

Should this mean that the state courts are completely free to determine whether a contract has been created? If that were the Supreme Court's position, would the contract clause have any meaning? If a state court were determined to avoid the constitutional limitation, could it not do so in every case?

It seems clear that *some* review by the Supreme Court is needed to assure that the federal protection is not nullified or evaded by the state courts. But does it follow that the Supreme Court is free to substitute its judgment for that of the state court as to what the state law should be? Does it help to ask what the state law seems to have been at the time the contract was made? Is this different from asking what are the correct policies to follow in determining the rights and obligations that flow from contracts? What question was the Court asking in *Brand*?

The Court has not taken the occasion to address explicitly the criteria that ought to govern in cases such as *Brand*. It has said in a related context, however, that:

> "Whether the state court has denied to rights asserted under local law the protection which the Constitution guarantees is a question upon which the petitioners are entitled to invoke the judgment of this Court. Even though the Constitutional protection invoked be denied on non-federal grounds, it is the province of this Court to inquire whether the decision of

the state court rests upon a fair or substantial basis. If unsubstantial, constitutional obligations may not thus be evaded. But if there is no evasion of the constitutional issue, and the non-federal ground of decision has fair support, this Court will not inquire whether the rule applied by the state court is right or wrong, or substitute its view of what should be deemed the better rule, for that of the state court."

Broad River Power Co. v. South Carolina, 281 U.S. 537, 540 (1930). Does this help? Is the Court in *Broad River* asking the right questions?

3. Procedural Due Process. The issue in *Brand* may seem somewhat dated. Today it is more likely that a teacher in Anderson's situation would make his or her claim in terms of procedural due process. Does this mean that the type of review illustrated by *Brand* is also dated?

The Court's approach to procedural due process cases can involve exactly the same type of issue. The constitutional claim involved in a modern procedural due process case is that the state has deprived a person of "liberty" or "property" without adequate procedural precautions. Whose law creates the rights of "liberty" or "property?" The answer, as in the case of the contract rights in *Brand,* could be federal law. Indeed, some Justices have embraced this notion, as has the Court to some extent. See, e.g., Board of Regents of State Colleges v. Roth, 408 U.S. 564 (1972) (definition of "liberty"). But it is clear at least since *Roth* that state law creates many of the rights and expectations to which the constitutional protection attaches. Recall the language of Justice Stewart's opinion for the Court in *Roth* as to the "property" interests claimed there by an untenured teacher who was fired without a hearing:

> "Property interests, of course, are not created by the Constitution. Rather they are created and their dimensions are defined by existing rules or understandings that stem from an independent source such as state law—rules or understandings that secure certain benefits and that support claims of entitlement to those benefits."

Suppose that the *Brand* case came before the Court today, that Anderson claimed a right to a hearing before she was discharged, and that the school authorities fired her without one in the view that under state law she had no "property" right to her job. Would the Supreme Court reexamine a determination by the Indiana Supreme Court that she was terminable at will? By what standards?

4. Other Constitutional Protections. Are there other federal constitutional protections that are analogous to the contract-clause and procedural-due-process questions involved in cases like *Brand* and *Roth* ? The answer is that there are: "property" is protected against a "taking" by the due process clause of the 14th amendment; "full faith and credit" must be given to the judgments of one state court by another; state courts may not deny fair notice by the retroactive interpretation of criminal statutes. These are all situations where state law plays some part in the determination of the rights to which a federal constitutional protection attaches. Any case in which they arise will involve two analytically distinct steps. First, one must determine which issues are governed by state law and which by federal (constitutional or common) law. Once that is decided, one must determine the content of any state law that is to apply. Whenever the case has been litigated in state court and has come to the Supreme Court on direct review, moreover, the Supreme Court must determine the deference it will give to the state court's determination of the state law issues. And that, of course, is the question in *Brand.*

Are there other federal constitutional protections that may give rise to the same problem? Are all of the examples given above the same? In particular, is the problem presented by a full-faith-and-credit case the same as the problem in *Brand*? How are any differences related to the appropriate scope of review by the Supreme Court over state court decisions?

5. *Martin v. Hunter's Lessee.* Recall the facts of *Martin v. Hunter's Lessee,* discussed beginning on page 594, supra. The question was whether land had escheated to the state prior to the effective date of two treaties. If it had, then a grant of the land by the state to the defendant gave him effective title to the land. If it had not, then the plaintiff held title to the land because it could not be seized by the state according to the terms of the treaties. The Virginia Court of Appeals held that the escheat had occurred prior to the effective date of the treaties, and accordingly rendered judgment for the defendant. The Supreme Court examined common law precedents and the Virginia statutes, and decided that the escheat had not occurred before the treaty came into effect. It therefore reversed, which led to the fuss for which the case is famous.

Whose law determines when land escheats to state government? Is *Martin* like *Brand*? Should the criteria governing the scope of Supreme Court review have been the same in both cases?

STANDARD OIL CO. OF CALIFORNIA v. JOHNSON

Supreme Court of the United States, 1942.
316 U.S. 481.

MR. JUSTICE BLACK delivered the opinion of the Court.

The California Motor Vehicle Fuel License Tax Act imposes a license tax, measured by gallonage, on the privilege of distributing any motor vehicle fuel. Section 10 states that the act is inapplicable "to any motor vehicle fuel sold to the government of the United States or any department thereof for official use of said government." The appellant, a "distributor" within the meaning of the act, sold gasoline to the United States Army Post Exchanges in California. The state levied a tax, and the appellant paid it under protest. The appellant then filed this suit in the Superior Court of Sacramento County seeking to recover the payment on two grounds: (1) that sales to the Exchanges were exempt from tax under § 10; (2) that if construed and applied to require payment of the tax on such sales the act would impose a burden upon instrumentalities or agencies of the United States contrary to the federal Constitution. Holding against the appellant on both grounds, the trial court rendered judgment for the state. The Supreme Court of California affirmed. Since validity of the state statute as construed was drawn in question on the ground of its being repugnant to the Constitution, we think the case is properly here on appeal . . . .

Since § 10 of the California act made the tax inapplicable "to any motor vehicle fuel sold to the government of the United States or any department thereof," it was necessary for the Supreme Court of California to determine whether the language of this exemption included sales to post exchanges. If the court's construction of § 10 of the act had been based purely on local law, this construction would have been conclusive, and we should have to determine whether the statute so construed and applied is repugnant to the federal Constitution. But in deciding that post exchanges were not "the government of the United States or any department thereof," the court did not rely upon the law of California. On the contrary, it relied upon its determination concerning the relationship between post exchanges and the government of the United States, a relationship which is controlled by federal law. For post exchanges operate under regulations of the Secretary of War pursuant to federal authority. These regulations and the practices under them establish the relationship between the post exchange and the United States government, and together with the relevant statutory and constitutional provisions from which they derive, afford the data upon which the legal status of the post exchange may be determined. It was upon a determination of a federal question, therefore, that the Supreme Court of California rested its conclusion that, by § 10, sales to a post exchange were not exempted from the tax. Since this determination of a federal question was by a state court, we are not bound by it. We proceed to consider whether it is correct.

On July 25, 1895, the Secretary of War, under authority of Congressional enactments promulgated regulations providing for the establishment of post exchanges. These regulations have since been amended from time to time and the exchange has become a regular feature of Army posts. That the establishment and control of post exchanges have been in accordance with regulations rather than specific statutory directions does not alter their status, for authorized War Department regulations have the force of law.

Congressional recognition that the activities of post exchanges are governmental has been frequent. Since 1903, Congress has repeatedly made substantial appropriations to be expended under the direction of the Secretary of War for construction, equipment, and maintenance of suitable buildings for post exchanges. In 1933 and 1934, Congress ordered certain moneys derived from disbanded exchanges to be handed over to the federal Treasury. And in 1936, Congress gave consent to state taxation of gasoline sold by or through post exchanges, when the gasoline was not for the exclusive use of the United States.

The commanding officer of an Army Post, subject to the regulations and the commands of his own superior officers, has complete authority to establish and maintain an exchange. He details a post exchange officer to manage its affairs. This officer and the commanding officers of the various company units make up a council which supervises exchange activities. None of these officers receives any compensation other than his regular salary. The object of the exchanges is to provide convenient and reliable sources where soldiers can obtain their ordinary needs at the lowest possible prices. Soldiers, their families, and civilians employed on military posts here and abroad can buy at exchanges. The government assumes none of the financial obligations of the exchange. But government officers, under government regulations, handle and are responsible for all funds of the exchange which are obtained from the companies or detachments composing its membership. Profits, if any, do not go to individuals. They are used to improve the soldiers' mess, to provide various types of recreation, and in general to add to the pleasure and comfort of the troops.

From all of this, we conclude that post exchanges as now operated are arms of the government deemed by it essential for the performance of governmental functions. They are integral parts of the War Department, share in fulfilling the duties entrusted to it, and partake of whatever immunities it may have under the Constitution and federal statutes. In concluding otherwise the Supreme Court of California was in error.

Whether the California Supreme Court would have construed the Motor Vehicle Fuel License Act as applicable to post exchanges if it had decided the issue of legal status of post exchanges in accordance with this opinion, we have no way of knowing. Hence, a determination here of the constitutionality of such an application of the act is not called for by the state of the record. Accordingly, we reverse the judgment and remand the cause to the court below for further proceedings not inconsistent with this opinion.

Reversed.

———

NOTES ON REMOTE FEDERAL PREMISE CASES

1. **Introduction.** The issue on which the *Johnson* decision turned was the meaning of a state tax statute, surely a question of state law. Yet the Supreme Court felt free to examine a premise in the chain of reasoning that led the state court to its conclusion. Cases of this sort can be called "remote federal premise cases."

Why did the Court hold as it did in *Johnson*? Suppose on remand the California court thanked the Supreme Court for its advice as to the meaning of federal law, but held nonetheless that the post exchange was not exempt under the tax statute. What options would then be open if the case came back to the Supreme Court? Would the Supreme Court cite *Marbury v. Madison* and *Martin v. Hunter's Lessee,* and accuse the California Supreme Court of improper conduct? If not, should the Court's decision in *Johnson* be regarded as an advisory opinion? Is it for that reason an unconstitutional exercise of reviewing authority?

   2. *State Tax Comm'n v. Van Cott.* In State Tax Comm'n v. Van Cott, 306 U.S. 511 (1939), an attorney for two federal agencies deducted his federal wages on his state income tax return, relying on an exemption in the state income tax law for all "amounts received as compensation, salaries or wages from the United States . . . for services rendered in connection with the exercise of an essential governmental function." The state taxing authorities denied the exemption. Van Cott filed suit in state court based on two arguments: that his salary was exempt by the terms of the state statute itself, and that it could not in any event be taxed by the state without violating an immunity granted by the federal Constitution. The Utah Supreme Court held that the income was not taxable, but the United States Supreme Court vacated the judgment and remanded the case to the state courts for further proceedings. It reasoned:

> "In holding [Van Cott's] income not taxable, the Supreme Court of Utah said: 'We shall have to be content to follow, as we think we must, the doctrine of [Rogers v. Graves, 299 U.S. 401 (1937)], until such time as a different rule is laid down by the courts, the Congress, or the people through amendment to the Constitution.' The *Graves* case applied the doctrine that the federal Constitution prohibits the application of state income taxes to salaries derived from federal instrumentalities. We granted certiorari, in the present case, because of the importance of the principle of constitutional immunity from state taxation which the Utah court apparently thought controlled its judgment.

> "[Van Cott] contends that the Utah Supreme Court's decision 'was based squarely upon the construction of the Utah taxing statute which was held to omit respondent's salaries as a subject of taxation, and therefore that decision did not and could not reach the federal question and should not be reviewed.' But that decision cannot be said to rest squarely upon a construction of the state statute. The Utah court stated that the question before it was whether [Van Cott's] salaries from the [federal] agencies in question were 'taxable income for the purpose of the state income tax law,' and that the answer depended upon whether these agencies exercised 'essential governmental functions.' But the opinion as a whole shows that the court felt constrained to conclude as it did because of the federal Constitution and this Court's prior adjudications of constitutional immunity. . . ."

As it happened, another decision announced on the same day had overruled *Graves*. The Court explained its disposition as follows:

"Whether the Utah income tax, by its terms, exempts [Van Cott], can now be decided by the state's highest court apart from any question of constitutional immunity, and without the necessity, so far as the federal Constitution is concerned, of attempting to divide functions of government into those which are essential and those which are nonessential."

Assume, as apparently was not entirely clear, that the Utah Supreme Court meant to rest its judgment on its interpretation of the state tax statute, but that it did so because it felt coerced by the *Graves* decision. Could the Supreme Court then have reviewed the case, overruled *Graves*, and remanded for reconsideration? Would it have mattered whether *Graves* was overruled in a separate decision (as in fact was the case) or in *Van Cott* itself?

Now consider the relevance to the scope of Supreme Court review of uncertainty as to the rationale of the decision below. What should the Court do in a case where it cannot tell how the lower court meant to use federal law? In *Van Cott* the Court said on this point:

"If the [Utah] court were only incidentally referring to decisions of this Court in determining the meaning of the state law, and had concluded therefrom that the statute itself was intended to grant exemption to respondent, this Court would have no jurisdiction to review that question. But, if the state court did in fact intend alternatively to base its decision upon the state statute and upon an immunity it thought granted by the Constitution as interpreted by this Court, these two grounds are so interwoven that we are unable to conclude that the judgment rests upon an independent interpretation of the state law. Whatever exemptions the Supreme Court of Utah may find in the terms of this statute, its opinion in the present case only indicates that 'it thought the federal Constitution [as construed by this Court] required' it to hold [Van Cott] not taxable."

Why would the Court not have had "jurisdiction" on its first hypothesis? Could the Court still have vacated and remanded for reconsideration in light of the intervening change in constitutional law? If not, should the Court have clarified the matter before proceeding?[a]

3. *Moore v. Chesapeake & Ohio Ry. Co.* Moore v. Chesapeake & Ohio Ry. Co., 291 U.S. 205 (1934), involved a railroad employee injured while working in intrastate commerce. A Kentucky statute provided the applicable cause of action. It also provided that contributory negligence and assumption of risk could not be asserted by the railroad in any case where the Federal Safety Appliance Acts had been

[a] On remand, the Utah Supreme Court held that it had "correctly interpreted" the intent of the legislature the first time, and that its prior decision was "still correct," even if the Supreme Court had changed the constitutional law. Van Cott v. State Tax Comm'n, 98 Utah 264, 96 P.2d 740 (1939).

violated, and perhaps that violation of these federal laws constituted negligence per se. The question before the Court was whether a case asserting that an intrastate railroad had violated the federal statute arose under federal law for purposes of the federal question jurisdiction of the district courts. The Court held that "the complaint set forth a cause of action under the Kentucky statute and, as to this cause of action, the suit is not to be regarded as one arising under the laws of the United States."[b]

In the course of its opinion, the Court said that "[q]uestions arising in actions in state courts to recover for injuries sustained by employees in intrastate commerce and relating to the scope of the Federal Safety Appliance Acts are, of course, federal questions which may appropriately be reviewed in this Court." On what basis could the Supreme Court review such a question coming from the state courts? There was no requirement in federal law that Kentucky incorporate federal safety standards in state laws designed to redress intrastate injuries. Why is a federal question presented if it voluntarily does so?

Assume that the Supreme Court reviewed such a case and construed the Safety Appliance Acts in a way that the Kentucky courts did not like. Would the Kentucky courts then be free to ignore the Supreme Court's decision and construe the state statute not to incorporate that particular aspect of federal law? If so, would the Supreme Court then have rendered an advisory opinion? Would the Supreme Court decision therefore have been unconstitutional? Is the case for Supreme Court review in a *Moore* situation different from, or stronger or weaker than, the case for review in *Johnson* and *Van Cott*?

4. *California v. Byers*. California v. Byers, 402 U.S. 424 (1971), as Chief Justice Burger's plurality opinion put it, presented:

> "the narrow but important question whether the constitutional privilege against compulsory self-incrimination is infringed by California's so-called 'hit and run' statute which requires the driver of a motor vehicle involved in an accident to stop at the scene and give his name and address. Similar 'hit and run' statutes are in effect in all 50 states and the District of Columbia."

The California Supreme Court had held that compliance with the statute would have confronted Byers with "substantial hazards of self-incrimination" under federal decisions, but upheld the statute by interpreting it to impose a use restriction on the required disclosures. It then held that it would be "unfair" to punish Byers for failing to stop, because he could not have reasonably anticipated judicial creation of the use restriction.

The Supreme Court granted certiorari, again in the words of the plurality opinion, "to assess the validity of the California Supreme Court's premise that without a use restriction [the statute] would violate the privilege against compulsory self-incrimination." Writing

b This aspect of the case is considered at
page 435, supra.

for four Justices, the Chief Justice concluded that the privilege would not be violated by enforcement of the statute without the use restriction, and accordingly voted to vacate the judgment and remand for further proceedings "not inconsistent" with the Supreme Court's judgment. Justice Harlan concurred in this judgment, agreeing that the privilege would not be violated by enforcing the statute without a use restriction but on a different analysis. During the course of his opinion, Justice Harlan observed that:

> "Of course, after the federal law premise has been removed, the state is free to conclude as a matter of state constitutional or legislative policy that continued imposition of use restrictions with respect to this category of cases would still be appropriate in light of the state's own assessment of the relevant regulatory interests at stake and the personal values protected by the privilege against self-incrimination."

Justices Black, Douglas, Brennan, and Marshall dissented on the merits of the self-incrimination analysis.

Does *Byers* involve an exercise of the same reviewing authority approved in *Johnson, Van Cott,* and *Moore*? There is the analytical similarity that each concerned Supreme Court review of a federal "premise" underlying a state court's conclusion on a question of state law. But are all four decisions justified (if at all) by the same factors, or are there different reasons that could be advanced in favor of the Court's authority to review these cases?

SECTION 2: THE ADEQUATE AND INDEPENDENT STATE GROUND DOCTRINE

INTRODUCTORY NOTES ON THE ADEQUATE AND INDEPENDENT STATE GROUND DOCTRINE

1. *Murdock* Revisited. In Murdock v. City of Memphis, 87 U.S. (20 Wall.) 590 (1875), summarized at page 594, supra, the Court concluded that it did not have the statutory authority to review questions of state law arising in cases that also presented federal questions for decision. After reaching this conclusion, it outlined an analysis for dealing with cases involving questions of both state and federal law:

> "[W]e hold the following propositions on this subject as flowing from the statute as it now stands:

> "1. That it is essential to the jurisdiction of this Court over the judgment of a state court, that it shall appear that one of the questions mentioned in the act must have been raised, and presented to the state court.

"2. That it must have been decided by the state court, or that its decision was necessary to the judgment or decree, rendered in the case.

"3. That the decision must have been against the right claimed or asserted by plaintiff in error under the Constitution, treaties, laws, or authority of the United States.

"4. These things appearing, this Court has jurisdiction and must examine the judgment so far as to enable it to decide whether this claim of right was correctly adjudicated by the state court.

"5. If it finds that it was rightly decided, the judgment must be affirmed.

"6. If it was erroneously decided against plaintiff in error, then this court must further inquire, whether there is any other matter or issue adjudged by the state court, which is sufficiently broad to maintain the judgment of that court, notwithstanding the error in deciding the issue raised by the federal question. If this is found to be the case, the judgment must be affirmed without inquiring into the soundness of the decision on such other matter or issue.

"7. But if it be found that the issue raised by the question of federal law is of such controlling character that its correct decision is necessary to any final judgment in the case, or that there has been no decision by the state court of any other matter or issue which is sufficient to maintain the judgment of that court without regard to the federal question, then this Court will reverse the judgment of the state court, and will either render such judgment here as the state court should have rendered, or remand the case to that court, as the circumstances of the cases may require."

2. The Modern Doctrine. The principles advanced in *Murdock* have since been modified by the emergence of the adequate and independent state ground doctrine. That doctrine asks whether the judgment of a state court rests on a proposition of state law that is adequate to support the judgment and that is independent of any proposition of federal law. If both of these conditions obtain, the Court will hold that it lacks jurisdiction over the case. It will not in that instance examine any federal question to see whether it was correctly resolved.

The next two main cases involve the scope and application of this doctrine. Among the questions that are to be addressed are the following: What are the reasons that have led the Court to adopt the rule? Is it a prudential restraint that can be disregarded when the Court perceives strong reasons for reviewing a federal question? If so, what are the prudential reasons for its adoption? If not, is it a constitutional limitation on the Court's power that must be respected no matter how strongly the Court wants to decide a particular federal question? The following note contains introductory comments on these questions.

3. Rationale. The traditional rationale for the adequate and independent state ground doctrine was stated in an opinion for the Court by Justice Jackson in Herb v. Pitcairn, 324 U.S. 117, 125–26 (1945). The passage is frequently, if uncritically, quoted:

> "This Court from the time of its foundation has adhered to the principle that it will not review judgments of state courts that rest on adequate and independent state grounds. The reason is so obvious that it has rarely been thought to warrant statement. It is found in the partitioning of power between the state and federal judicial systems and in the limitations of our own jurisdiction. Our only power over state judgments is to correct them to the extent that they incorrectly adjudge federal rights. And our power is to correct wrong judgments, not to revise opinions. We are not permitted to render an advisory opinion, and if the same judgment would be rendered by the state court after we corrected its views of federal laws, our review could amount to nothing more than an advisory opinion."

Potential rationales for the adequate and independent state ground doctrine are collected and criticized by Richard Matasar and Gregory Bruch in Procedural Common Law, Federal Jurisdictional Policy, and Abandonment of the Adequate and Independent State Grounds Doctrine, 86 Colum.L.Rev. 1291 (1986). They reject the "advisory opinion" argument on the ground that the two principal reasons for that limitation—"ensuring an adversarial presentation of actual disputes" and "promoting finality of judicial action essential to the maintenance of separation of powers within the national government"—would not be undermined even if the adequate and independent state ground doctrine were not followed. They also argue that the adequate and independent state ground limitation is not mandated by the Constitution or by any federal statute. Instead, they conclude, it is a doctrine of federal "procedural common law" and as such "is a judicial creature, subject to judicial modification and experiment." [a]

Compare Justice Harlan's discussion in Fay v. Noia, 372 U.S. 391 (1963) (dissenting opinion):

> "What is the reason for the rule that an adequate and independent state ground of decision bars Supreme Court review of that decision—a rule which, of course, is as applicable to procedural as to substantive grounds? [T]he . . . rule has roots far deeper than the statutes governing our jurisdiction,

---

[a] Other examples of federal "procedural common law" are extensively discussed by way of comparison to the adequate and independent state ground doctrine. They include the "well-pleaded complaint" rule (see pages 431–32, supra), the abstention doctrines (see pages 562–72, supra; 1138– 1243, infra), forum non conveniens (see Margaret Stewart, Forum Non Conveniens: A Doctrine in Search of a Role, 74 Calif.L. Rev. 1259 (1986)), and the exceptions to the "final judgment" rule (see pages 657–85, infra).

and rests on fundamentals that [govern] this Court's . . . direct reviewing power. An examination of the alternatives that might conceivably be followed will, I submit, confirm that the rule is one of constitutional dimensions going to the heart of the division of judicial powers in a federal system."

Justice Harlan considered three possible resolutions of a hypothetical case where a federal claim was not heard by a state court on the merits because a valid state procedure was not followed. The first thing the Court might do, he reasoned, is:

"review and decide any federal questions in the case, even if the determination of nonfederal questions were adequate to sustain the judgment below, and then . . . send the case back to the state court for further consideration. But it needs no extended analysis to demonstrate that such action would exceed this Court's powers under article III."

At this point, Justice Harlan quoted the last three sentences from the passage in *Herb v. Pitcairn* quoted above.

"Another alternative," Justice Harlan continued, "would be to take the entire case and to review on the merits the state court's decision of *every* question in it." But once the Court has determined that a state ground is adequate and independent, "the constitutional limit of our power in this sphere" has been reached:

"The reason why this is so was perhaps most articulately expressed in a different but closely related context by Mr. Justice Field in [an] opinion . . . quoted with approval in the historic decision in *Erie v. Tompkins*:

'[T]he Constitution . . . recognizes and preserves the autonomy and independence of the states,—independence in their legislative and independence in their judicial departments. Supervision over either the legislative or the judicial action of the states is in no case permissible except as to matters by the Constitution specifically delegated to the United States. Any interference with either, except as thus permitted, is an invasion of the authority of the state, and to that extent, a denial of its independence.'

For this Court to go beyond the adequacy of the state ground and to review and determine the correctness of that ground on its merits would . . . be to assume full control over a state's procedures for the administration of its own criminal justice. This is and must be beyond our power if the federal system is to exist in substance as well as form. The right of the state to regulate its own procedures governing the conduct of litigants in its courts, and its interest in supervision of those procedures, stand on the same constitutional plane as its right and interest in framing 'substantive' laws governing other aspects of the conduct of those within its borders."

Finally, Justice Harlan considered a third alternative: the Court could ignore the state ground of decision, decide the federal question, and, if the state court decided it erroneously, enter judgment for the claimant. But in doing so, he argued, the Court would undermine the same values at stake in the second option.

Is Justice Harlan's analysis correct? Are there important constitutional values that underlie the adequate and independent state ground doctrine?

MICHIGAN v. LONG

United States Supreme Court, 1983.
463 U.S. 1032.

JUSTICE O'CONNOR delivered the opinion of the Court.

[In Terry v. Ohio, 392 U.S. 1 (1968), the Supreme Court held that a protective search of the person for weapons could be made in the absence of probable cause to arrest if a police officer had an "articulable suspicion" that an individual was armed and dangerous. *Michigan v. Long* involved whether such a protective search for weapons could extend beyond the person, specifically to the passenger compartment of a car the defendant was driving.

[The Michigan Supreme Court held the search invalid and reversed the resulting conviction for possession of marijuana. The United States Supreme Court granted certiorari. Part II of its opinion, excerpted below, addressed the question whether it was appropriate for the Court to reach the merits of the *Terry* question.]

Before reaching the merits, we must consider Long's argument that we are without jurisdiction to decide this case because the decision below rests on an adequate and independent state ground. The court below referred twice to the state constitution in its opinion, but otherwise relied exclusively on federal law. Long argues that the Michigan courts have provided greater protection from searches and seizures under the state constitution than is afforded under the fourth amendment, and the references to the state constitution therefore establish an adequate and independent ground for the decision below.

It is, of course, "incumbent upon this Court . . . to ascertain for itself . . . whether the asserted non-federal ground independently and adequately supports the judgment." Although we have announced a number of principles in order to help us determine whether various forms of references to state law constitute adequate and independent state grounds,[4] we openly admit that we have thus far not developed a

---

[4] For example, we have long recognized that "where the judgment of a state court rests upon two grounds, one of which is federal and the other nonfederal in character, our jurisdiction fails if the non-federal ground is independent of the federal ground and adequate to support the judgment." Fox Film Corp. v. Muller, 296 U.S. 207, 210 (1935). We may review a state case decided on a federal ground even if it is clear that there was an available state ground for decision on which the state court could properly have relied. Beecher v. Alabama, 389 U.S. 35, 37, n.3 (1967). Also, if, in our view, the state court " 'felt compelled by what it understood to be fed-

satisfying and consistent approach for resolving this vexing issue. In some instances, we have taken the strict view that if the ground of decision was at all unclear, we would dismiss the case. In other instances, we have vacated or continued a case, in order to obtain clarification about the nature of a state court decision. In more recent cases, we have ourselves examined state law to determine whether state courts have used federal law to guide their application of state law or to provide the actual basis for the decision that was reached. In Oregon v. Kennedy, 456 U.S. 667, 670–71 (1982), we rejected an invitation to remand to the state court for clarification even when the decision rested in part on a case from the state court, because we determined that the state case itself rested upon federal grounds. We added that "[e]ven if the case admitted of more doubt as to whether federal and state grounds for decision were intermixed, the fact that the state court relied to the extent it did on federal grounds requires us to reach the merits."

This ad hoc method of dealing with cases that involve possible adequate and independent state grounds is antithetical to the doctrinal consistency that is required when sensitive issues of federal-state relations are involved. Moreover, none of the various methods of disposition that we have employed thus far recommends itself as the preferred method that we should apply to the exclusion of others, and we therefore determine that it is appropriate to reexamine our treatment of this jurisdictional issue in order to achieve the consistency that is necessary.

The process of examining state law is unsatisfactory because it requires us to interpret state laws with which we are generally unfamiliar, and which often, as in this case, have not been discussed at length by the parties. Vacation and continuance for clarification have also been unsatisfactory both because of the delay and decrease in efficiency of judicial administration, see Dixon v. Duffy, 344 U.S. 143 (1952),[5] and, more important, because these methods of disposition place significant burdens on state courts to demonstrate the presence or absence of our jurisdiction. Finally, outright dismissal of cases is clearly not a panacea because it cannot be doubted that there is an important need for uniformity in federal law, and that this need goes unsatisfied when we fail to review an opinion that rests primarily upon

---

eral constitutional considerations to construe . . . its own law in the manner that it did,'" then we will not treat a normally adequate state ground as independent, and there will be no question about our jurisdiction. Delaware v. Prouse, 440 U.S. 648, 653 (1979). Finally, "where the non-federal ground is so interwoven with the [federal ground] as not to be an independent matter, or is not of sufficient breadth to sustain the judgment without any decision of the other, our jurisdiction is plain." Enterprise Irrigation District v. Farmers Mutual Canal Company, 243 U.S. 157, 164 (1917).

[5] Indeed, *Dixon v. Duffy* is also illustrative of another difficulty involved in our requiring state courts to reconsider their decisions for purposes of clarification. In *Dixon,* we continued the case on two occasions in order to obtain clarification, but none was forthcoming. "[T]he California court advised petitioner's counsel informally that it doubted its jurisdiction to render such a determination." We then vacated the judgment of the state court, and remanded.

federal grounds and where the *independence* of an alleged state ground is not apparent from the four corners of the opinion. We have long recognized that dismissal is inappropriate "where there is strong indication . . . that the federal Constitution as judicially construed controlled the decision below."

Respect for the independence of state courts, as well as avoidance of rendering advisory opinions, have been the cornerstones of this Court's refusal to decide cases where there is an adequate and independent state ground. It is precisely because of this respect for state courts, and this desire to avoid advisory opinions, that we do not wish to continue to decide issues of state law that go beyond the opinion that we review, or to require state courts to reconsider cases to clarify the grounds of their decisions. Accordingly, when, as in this case, a state court decision fairly appears to rest primarily on federal law, or to be interwoven with the federal law, and when the adequacy and independence of any possible state law ground is not clear from the face of the opinion, we will accept as the most reasonable explanation that the state court decided the case the way it did because it believed that federal law required it to do so. If a state court chooses merely to rely on federal precedents as it would on the precedents of all other jurisdictions, then it need only make clear by a plain statement in its judgment or opinion that the federal cases are being used only for the purpose of guidance, and do not themselves compel the result that the court has reached. In this way, both justice and judicial administration will be greatly improved. If the state court decision indicates clearly and expressly that it is alternatively based on bona fide separate, adequate, and independent grounds, we, of course, will not undertake to review the decision.

This approach obviates in most instances the need to examine state law in order to decide the nature of the state court decision, and will at the same time avoid the danger of our rendering advisory opinions.[6] It also avoids the unsatisfactory and intrusive practice of requiring state courts to clarify their decisions to the satisfaction of this Court. We believe that such an approach will provide state judges with a clearer opportunity to develop state jurisprudence unimpeded by federal interference, and yet will preserve the integrity of federal law. "It is fundamental that state courts be left free and unfettered by us in interpreting their state constitutions. But it is equally important that ambiguous or obscure adjudications by state courts do not stand as barriers to a determination by this Court of the validity under the federal Constitution of state action." Minnesota v. National Tea Co., 309 U.S. 551, 557 (1940).

The principle that we will not review judgments of state courts that rest on adequate and independent state grounds is based, in part, on "the limitations of our own jurisdiction." Herb v. Pitcairn, 324 U.S.

---

[6] There may be certain circumstances in which clarification is necessary or desirable, and we will not be foreclosed from taking the appropriate action.

117, 125 (1945).[7] The jurisdictional concern is that we not "render an advisory opinion, and if the same judgment would be rendered by the state court after we corrected its views of federal laws, our review could amount to nothing more than an advisory opinion." Our requirement of a "plain statement" that a decision rests upon adequate and independent state grounds does not in any way authorize the rendering of advisory opinions. Rather, in determining, as we must, whether we have jurisdiction to review a case that is alleged to rest on adequate and independent state grounds, we merely assume that there are no such grounds when it is not clear from the opinion itself that the state court relied upon an adequate and independent state ground and when it fairly appears that the state court rested its decision primarily on federal law.[8]

Our review of the decision below under this framework leaves us unconvinced that it rests upon an independent state ground. Apart from its two citations to the state constitution, the court below relied *exclusively* on its understanding of *Terry* and other federal cases. Not a single state case was cited to support the state court's holding that the search of the passenger compartment was unconstitutional. Indeed, the court declared that the search in this case was unconstitutional because "[t]he Court of Appeals erroneously applied the principles of *Terry v. Ohio* . . . to the search of the interior of the vehicle in this case." The references to the state constitution in no way indicate that the decision below rested on grounds in any way *independent* from the state court's interpretation of federal law. Even if we accept that the Michigan Constitution has been interpreted to provide independent

[7] In Herb v. Pitcairn, 324 U.S. 117, 128 (1945), the Court also wrote that it was desirable that state courts "be asked rather than told what they have intended." It is clear that we have already departed from that view in those cases in which we have examined state law to determine whether a particular result was guided or compelled by federal law. Our decision today departs further from *Herb* insofar as we disfavor further requests to state courts for clarification, and we require a clear and express statement that a decision rests on adequate and independent state grounds. However, the "plain statement" rule protects the integrity of state courts for the reasons discussed above. The preference for clarification expressed in *Herb* has failed to be a completely satisfactory means of protecting the state and federal interests that are involved.

[8] . . . In dissent, Justice Stevens proposes the novel view that this Court should never review a state court decision unless the Court wishes to vindicate a federal right that has been endangered. The rationale of the dissent is not restricted to cases where the decision is arguably supported by adequate and independent state grounds. Rather, Justice Stevens appears to believe that even if the decision below rests exclusively on federal grounds, this Court should not review the decision as long as there is no federal right that is endangered.

The state courts handle the vast bulk of all criminal litigation in this country. In 1982, more than 12 million criminal actions (excluding juvenile and traffic charges) were filed in the 50 state court systems and the District of Columbia. See 7 State Court Journal 18 (1983). By comparison, approximately 32,700 criminal suits were filed in federal courts during that same year. See Annual Report of the Director of the Administrative Office of the United States Courts 6 (1982). The state courts are required to apply federal constitutional standards, and they necessarily create a considerable body of "federal law" in the process. It is not surprising that this Court has become more interested in the application and development of federal law by state courts in the light of the recent significant expansion of federally created standards that we have imposed on the states.

protection for certain rights also secured under the fourth amendment, it fairly appears in this case that the Michigan Supreme Court rested its decision primarily on federal law.

Rather than dismissing the case, or requiring that the state court reconsider its decision on our behalf solely because of a mere possibility that an adequate and independent ground supports the judgment, we find that we have jurisdiction in the absence of a plain statement that the decision below rested on an adequate and independent state ground. It appears to us that the state court "felt compelled by what it understood to be federal constitutional considerations to construe . . . its own law in the manner it did."[10]

[The Court then held the search valid under federal standards. Accordingly, it reversed the state court decision and remanded "for further proceedings not inconsistent with this opinion."]

JUSTICE BLACKMUN, concurring in part and concurring in the judgment.

I join [all of the Court's opinion except the discussion reproduced above.] While I am satisfied that the Court has jurisdiction in this particular case, I do not join the Court . . . in fashioning a new presumption of jurisdiction over cases coming here from state courts. Although I agree with the Court that uniformity in federal law is desirable, I see little efficiency and an increased danger of advisory opinions in the Court's new approach.

JUSTICE BRENNAN, with whom, JUSTICE MARSHALL joins, dissenting.

[Justice Brennan's dissent was on the merits of the Terry issue. As to the jurisdictional point, he said in a footnote "I agree that the Court has jurisdiction to decide this case. See ante, at n.10."]

JUSTICE STEVENS, dissenting.

The jurisprudential questions presented in this case are far more important than the question whether the Michigan police officer's search of respondent's car violated the fourth amendment. The case raises profoundly significant questions concerning the relationship between two sovereigns—the state of Michigan and the United States of America.

---

[10] There is nothing unfair about requiring a plain statement of an independent state ground in this case. Even if we were to rest our decision on an evaluation of the state law relevant to Long's claim, as we have sometimes done in the past, our understanding of Michigan law would also result in our finding that we have jurisdiction to decide this case. Under state search and seizure law, a "higher standard" is imposed under art. 1, § 11, of the 1963 Michigan Constitution. If, however, the item seized is, inter alia, a "narcotic drug . . . seized by a peace officer outside the curtilage of any dwelling house in this state," art. 1, § 11 of the 1963 Michigan Constitution, then the seizure is governed by a standard identical to that imposed by the fourth amendment.

. . . At the time that the 1963 Michigan Constitution was enacted, it is clear that marijuana was considered a narcotic drug. We . . . conclude that the seizure of marijuana in Michigan is not subject to analysis under any "higher standard" than may be imposed on the seizure of other items. In the light of our holding in Delaware v. Prouse, supra, that an interpretation of state law in our view compelled by federal constitutional considerations is not an independent state ground, we would have jurisdiction to decide the case.

The Supreme Court of the state of Michigan expressly held "that the deputies' search of the vehicle was proscribed by the fourth amendment of the United States Constitution and *art. 1, § 11 of the Michigan Constitution.*" The state law ground is clearly adequate to support the judgment, but the question whether it is independent of the Michigan Supreme Court's understanding of federal law is more difficult. Four possible ways of resolving that question present themselves: (1) asking the Michigan Supreme Court directly, (2) attempting to infer from all possible sources of state law what the Michigan Supreme Court meant, (3) presuming that adequate state grounds are independent unless it clearly appears otherwise, or (4) presuming that adequate state grounds are *not* independent unless it clearly appears otherwise. This Court has, on different occasions, employed each of the first three approaches; never until today has it even hinted at the fourth. In order to "achieve the consistency that is necessary," the Court today undertakes a reexamination of all the possibilities. It rejects the first approach as inefficient and unduly burdensome for state courts, and rejects the second approach as an inappropriate expenditure of our resources. Although I find both of those decisions defensible in themselves, I cannot accept the Court's decision to choose the fourth approach over the third—to presume that adequate state grounds are intended to be dependent on federal law unless the record plainly shows otherwise. I must therefore dissent.

If we reject the intermediate approaches, we are left with a choice between two presumptions: one in favor of our taking jurisdiction, and one against it. Historically, the latter presumption has always prevailed. The rule, as succinctly stated in Lynch v. New York, 293 U.S. 52, 54–55 (1952), was as follows:

> "Where the judgment of the state court rests on two grounds, one involving a federal question and the other not, or if it does not appear upon which of two grounds the judgment was based, and the ground independent of a federal question is sufficient in itself to sustain it, this Court will not take jurisdiction."

The Court today points out that in several cases we have weakened the traditional presumption by using the other two intermediate approaches identified above. Since those two approaches are now to be rejected, however, I would think that stare decisis would call for a return to historical principle. Instead, the Court seems to conclude that because some precedents are to be rejected, we must overrule them all.

Even if I agreed with the Court that we are free to consider as a fresh proposition whether we may take presumptive jurisdiction over the decisions of sovereign states, I could not agree that an expansive attitude makes good sense. It appears to be common ground that any rule we adopt should show "respect for state courts, and [a] desire to avoid advisory opinions." And I am confident that all members of this Court agree that there is a vital interest in the sound management of scarce federal judicial resources. All of those policies counsel against the exercise of federal jurisdiction. They are fortified by my belief that a policy of judicial restraint—one that allows other decisional bodies to have the last word in legal interpretation until it is truly necessary for this Court to intervene—enables this Court to make its most effective contribution to our federal system of government.

The nature of the case before us hardly compels a departure from tradition. These are not cases in which an American citizen has been deprived of a right secured by the United States Constitution or a federal statute. Rather, they are cases in which a state court has upheld a citizen's assertion of a right, finding the citizen to be protected under both federal and state law. The complaining party is an officer of the state itself, who asks us to rule that the state court interpreted federal rights too broadly and "overprotected" the citizen.

Such cases should not be of inherent concern to this Court. The reason may be illuminated by assuming that the events underlying this case had arisen in another country, perhaps the Republic of Finland. If the Finnish police had arrested a Finnish citizen for possession of marijuana, and the Finnish courts had turned him loose, no American would have standing to object. If instead they had arrested an American citizen and acquitted him, we might have been concerned about the arrest but we surely could not have complained about the acquittal, even if the Finnish Court had based its decision on its understanding of the United States Constitution. That would be true even if we had a treaty with Finland requiring it to respect the rights of American citizens under the United States Constitution. We would only be motivated to intervene if an American citizen were unfairly arrested, tried, and convicted by the foreign tribunal.

In this case the state of Michigan has arrested one of its citizens and the Michigan Supreme Court has decided to turn him loose. The respondent is a United States citizen as well as a Michigan citizen, but since there is no claim that he has been mistreated by the state of Michigan, the final outcome of the state processes offended no federal interest whatever. Michigan simply provided greater protection to one of its citizens than some other state might provide or, indeed, than this Court might require throughout the country.

I believe that in reviewing the decisions of state courts, the primary role of this Court is to make sure that persons who seek to *vindicate* federal rights have been fairly heard. That belief resonates with statements in many of our prior cases. In Abie State Bank v. Bryan, 282 U.S. 765 (1931), the Supreme Court of Nebraska had rejected a federal constitutional claim, relying in part on the state law doctrine of laches. Writing for the Court in response to the Nebraska governor's argument that the Court should not accept jurisdiction because laches provided an independent ground for decision, Chief Justice Hughes concluded that this Court must ascertain for itself whether the asserted nonfederal ground independently and adequately supported the judgment "in order that constitutional guarantees may appropriately be enforced." He relied on our earlier opinion in Union Pacific Railroad Co. v. Public Service Commission of Missouri, 248 U.S. 67 (1918), in which Justice Holmes had made it clear that the Court engaged in such an inquiry so that it would not "be possible for a state to impose an unconstitutional burden" on a private party.   And both *Abie* and *Union Pacific* rely on Creswell v. Knights of Pythias, 225 U.S. 246, 261 (1912), in which the Court explained its duty to review the findings of fact of a state court "where a federal right has been denied."

Until recently we had virtually no interest in cases of this type. Thirty years ago, this Court reviewed only one.   Nevada v. Stacher, 346 U.S. 906 (1953).   Indeed, that appears to have been the only case during the entire 1952 term in which a state even sought review of a decision by its own judiciary.   Fifteen years ago, we did not review any such cases, although the total number of requests had mounted to three. Some time during the past decade, perhaps about the time of the 5–to–4 decision in Zacchini v. Scripps-Howard Broadcasting Co., 433 U.S 562 (1977), our priorities shifted.   The result is a docket swollen with requests by states to reverse judgments that their courts have rendered in favor of their citizens.[3]   I am confident that a future Court will recognize the error of this allocation of resources.   When that day comes, I think it likely that the Court will also reconsider the propriety of today's expansion of our jurisdiction.

The Court offers only one reason for asserting authority over cases such as the one presented today: "an important need for uniformity in federal law [that] goes unsatisfied when we fail to review an opinion that rests primarily upon federal grounds and where the independence of an alleged state ground is not apparent from the four corners of the opinion."   Of course, the supposed need to "review an opinion" clashes directly with our oft-repeated reminder that "our power is to correct wrong judgments, not to revise opinions."   Herb v. Pitcairn, 324 U.S. 117, 126 (1945).   The clash is not merely one of form: the "need for uniformity in federal law" is truly an ungovernable engine.   That same need is no less present when it is perfectly clear that a state ground is both independent and adequate.   In fact, it is equally present if a state prosecutor announces that he believes a certain policy of non-enforcement is commanded by federal law.   Yet we have never claimed jurisdiction to correct such errors, no matter how egregious they may be, and no matter how much they may thwart the desires of the state electorate.   We do not sit to expound our understanding of the Constitution to interested listeners in the legal community; we sit to resolve disputes.   If it is not apparent that our views would affect the outcome of a particular case, we cannot presume to interfere.[4]

[3] This year, we devoted argument time to [13 other cases, one of which was argued twice], as well as this case.   And a cursory survey of the United States Law Week index reveals that so far this term at least 80 petitions for certiorari to state courts were filed by the states themselves.

[4] In this regard, one of the cases overruled today deserves comment.   In Minnesota v. National Tea Co., 309 U.S. 551 (1940), the Court considered a case much like this one—the Minnesota Supreme Court had concluded that both the 14th amendment to the United States Constitution and art. 9, § 1, of the Minnesota Constitution prohibited a graduated income tax on chain store income.   The state court stated that "the[ ] provisions of the federal and state Constitutions impose identical restrictions upon the legislative power of the state in respect to classification for purposes of taxation," and "then adverted

Finally, I am thoroughly baffled by the Court's suggestion that it must stretch its jurisdiction and reverse the judgment of the Michigan Supreme Court in order to show "[r]espect for the independence of state courts." Would we show respect for the Republic of Finland by convening a special sitting for the sole purpose of declaring that its decision to release an American citizen was based upon a misunderstanding of American law?

I respectfully dissent.

NOTES ON *MICHIGAN v. LONG*

1. **Questions and Comments.** Justice O'Connor stated in footnote 4 of her opinion that "[w]e may review a state case decided on a federal ground even if it is clear that there was an available state ground for decision on which the state court could properly have relied." This is standard lore. The Court has traditionally based its jurisdiction to review state court judgments on the actual grounds of decision by the court below, not the potential grounds.[a] Is this practice consistent with the limitation that the Court not render advisory opinions? Is it consistent with the view that the adequate and independent state ground rule has a constitutional foundation? Can it be justified?

briefly to three of its former decisions which had interpreted" the state provision. It then proceeded to conduct a careful analysis of the federal Constitution. It could justly be said that the decision rested primarily on federal law. The majority of the Court reasoned as follows:

"Enough has been said to demonstrate that there is considerable uncertainty as to the precise grounds for the decision. That is sufficient reason for us to decline at this time to review the federal question asserted to be present, consistently with the policy of not passing upon questions of a constitutional nature which are not clearly necessary to a decision of the case."

The Court therefore remanded to the state court for clarification.

Today's Court rejects that approach as intruding unduly on the state judicial process. One might therefore expect it to turn to Chief Justice Hughes's dissenting opinion in *National Tea*. In a careful statement of the applicable principles, he made an observation that I find unanswerable:

"The fact that provisions of the state and federal Constitutions may be similar or even identical does not justify us in disturbing a judgment of a state court which adequately rests upon its application of the provisions of its own constitution. That the state court may be influenced by the reasoning of our opinions makes no difference. The state court may be persuaded by majority opinions in this Court or it may prefer the reasoning of dissenting judges, but the judgment of the state court upon the application of its own constitution remains a judgment which we are without jurisdiction to review. Whether in this case we thought that the state tax was repugnant to the federal Constitution or consistent with it, the judgment of the state court that the tax violated the state constitution would still stand. It cannot be supposed that the Supreme Court of Minnesota is not fully conscious of its independent authority to construe the constitution of the state, whatever reasons it may adduce in so doing."

[a] This position was reaffirmed in Caldwell v. Mississippi, 472 U.S. 320, 327 (1985): "The mere existence of a basis for a procedural bar does not deprive this Court of jurisdiction; the state court must have relied on the procedural bar as an independent basis for its disposition of the case." See also County Court of Ulster County, New York, et al. v. Allen, 442 U.S. 140, 152–54 (1979).

In connection with these questions, consider the following hypothetical. Assume a criminal conviction in state court. Evidence is introduced that was arguably the product of an illegal search and seizure. There is a substantial basis for claiming that admission of the evidence was reversible error under state law. However, the state supreme court reverses the conviction based on federal constitutional principles derived from *Mapp v. Ohio,* without reaching the question of state law. The Supreme Court then grants certiorari and reverses, holding the evidence admissible under federal standards. Would the state court then be free on remand to hold that the conviction must nonetheless be set aside on grounds of state law? The settled answer is "yes." Does this mean that the Supreme Court would then have rendered an advisory opinion? How should the Court deal with a situation such as this?

If one concludes, as the Court has, that the practice of reviewing the actual grounds of decision below is desirable and permissible, how does the practice approved in *Michigan v. Long* differ? Does the presumption that a federal question was resolved by an ambiguous lower court opinion present different constitutional questions? Different policy questions? Does the possibility that the lower court may not have decided a federal question change the calculus?

Consider also the effect of the Supreme Court's decision in *Michigan v. Long* on the options open to the state courts on remand. In the hypothetical discussed above, the state court was free on remand to reinstate its judgment of reversal based on state law. Is the autonomy of the lower court over questions of state law different in the *Michigan v. Long* situation? Do state courts have any basis for complaining that *Michigan v. Long* is an unwarranted intrusion on their prerogatives? Is *Michigan v. Long* consistent with *Erie* and *Murdock*? Is the kind of review exercised in *Michigan v. Long* different from, or more or less legitimate than, the kinds of review exercised in *Standard Oil v. Johnson* (page 608, supra), *Van Cott* (page 611, supra), and *Byers* (page 613, supra)?

Finally, consider the position taken by Justice Stevens. Is Justice Stevens' real objection to the Court's doctrinal approach or to its certiorari policy? Is there any necessary connection between the Court's holding and a decision in favor of or against a federal claimant? How does the Court's approach affect the political accountability of state courts? How does it affect the image of the Supreme Court?

2. Bibliography. *Michigan v. Long* has been the subject of extensive commentary. See, e.g., Althouse, How to Build a Separate Sphere: Federal Courts and State Power, 100 Harv.L.Rev. 1485 (1987); Baker, The Ambiguous Independent and Adequate State Grounds in Criminal Cases: Federalism Along a Mobius Strip, 19 Ga.L.Rev. 799 (1985); O'Neill, The Good, the Bad, and the Burger Court: Victims' Rights and a New Model of Criminal Review, 75 J. Crim. L. & Criminology 363 (1984); Schlueter, Federalism and Supreme Court Review of Expansive State Court Decisions: A Response to Unfortunate Impressions, 11 Hastings Const.L.R. 523 (1984); Schlueter, Judicial Federalism and Supreme Court Review of State Decisions: A Sensible Balance Emerges, 59 N.D. L. Rev. 1079 (1984); Seid, Schizoid Federalism, Supreme Court Power and Inadequate Adequate State Ground Theory: *Michigan v. Long*, 18 Creighton L. Rev. 1 (1984); Welsh, Reconsidering the Constitutional Relationship Between State and Federal Courts: A Critique of *Michigan v. Long*, 59 N.D. L. Rev. 1118 (1984).

In Procedural Common Law, Federal Jurisdictional Policy, and Abandonment of the Adequate and Independent State Grounds Doctrine, 86 Colum.L.Rev. 1291 (1986), Richard Matasar and Gregory Bruch argue that "*Michigan v. Long* is fundamentally indefensible, not because it impinges on state court lawmaking functions, but because it attempts to perfect a doctrine that should be abandoned." Abandoning the adequate and independent state ground doctrine would give "the Court greater flexibility to find the appropriate case for maintaining supremacy and uniformity in federal law," would enhance "its ability to eliminate potential barriers to state democratic processes," and would harmonize "its appellate jurisdiction over state cases with other common law jurisdictional doctrines and Congress' jurisdictional plan." In effect, they suggest a return to the rules adopted in *Murdock v. City of Memphis* (see pages 614–15, supra [b]) : The Court should feel free to review any federal question decided by a state court. If the judgment rendered below is supported by a state ground of decision, the Court would then affirm even though the federal question was wrongly decided. If it was not clear that state grounds required affirmance of the judgment, the Court could remand for proceedings not inconsistent with its decision.[c]

HENRY v. MISSISSIPPI

United States Supreme Court, 1965.
379 U.S. 443.

MR. JUSTICE BRENNAN delivered the opinion of the Court.

Petitioner was convicted of disturbing the peace, by indecent proposals to and offensive contact with an 18–year-old hitchhiker to whom he is said to have given a ride in his car. The trial judge charged the jury that "you cannot find the defendant guilty on the unsupported and uncorroborated testimony of the complainant alone." The petitioner's federal claim derives from the admission of a police officer's testimony, introduced to corroborate the hitchhiker's testimony. The Mississippi Supreme Court held that the officer's testimony was improperly admit-

---

[b] Of the seven propositions stated on pages 614–15, supra, only the third would not be followed. The third of the *Murdock* rules was derived from a statutory limitation contained in the original 1789 act and carried forward until 1914. In 1914, the jurisdictional statute was amended specifically to permit Supreme Court review of state decisions that were based upon federal law but that extended a federal right beyond the requirements of federal law.

[c] For a recent case in which three dissenting Justices thought the Court was following this procedure, see Pennsylvania v. Finley, ___ U.S. ___ (1987).

ted as the fruit of "an unlawful search and was in violation of § 23, Miss. Constitution 1890." The tainted evidence tended to substantiate the hitchhiker's testimony by showing its accuracy in a detail which could have been seen only by one inside the car. In particular, it showed that the right-hand ashtray of the car in which the incident took place was full of Dentyne chewing gum wrappers, and that the cigarette lighter did not function. The police officer testified that after petitioner's arrest he had returned to the petitioner's home and obtained the permission of petitioner's wife to look in petitioner's car. The wife provided the officer with the keys, with which the officer opened the car. He testified that he tried the lighter and it would not work, and also that the ashtray "was filled with red Dentyne chewing gum wrappers."

The Mississippi Supreme Court first filed an opinion which reversed petitioner's conviction and remanded for a new trial. The court held that the wife's consent to the search of the car did not waive petitioner's constitutional rights, and noted that the "[t]estimony of the state's witness . . . is, in effect, uncorroborated without the evidence disclosed by the inspection of defendant's automobile."[2] Acting in the belief that petitioner had been represented by nonresident counsel unfamiliar with local procedure, the court reversed despite petitioner's failure to comply with the Mississippi requirement that an objection to illegal evidence be made at the time it is introduced. The court noted that petitioner had moved for a directed verdict at the close of the state's case, assigning as one ground the use of illegally obtained evidence; it did not mention petitioner's renewal of his motion at the close of all evidence.

After the first opinion was handed down, the state filed a suggestion of error, pointing out that petitioner was in fact represented at his trial by competent local counsel as well as by out-of-state lawyers. Thereupon the Mississippi Supreme Court withdrew its first opinion and filed a new opinion in support of a judgment affirming petitioner's conviction. The new opinion is identical with the first save for the result, the statement that petitioner had local counsel, and the discussion of the effect of failure for whatever reason to make timely objection to the evidence. "In such circumstances, even if honest mistakes of counsel in respect to policy or strategy or otherwise occur, they are binding upon the client as a part of the hazards of courtroom battle." Moreover, the court reasoned, petitioner's cross-examination of the state's witness before the initial motion for directed verdict, and introduction of other evidence of the car's interior appearance afterward, "cured" the original error and estopped petitioner from complaining of the tainted evidence. We granted certiorari. We vacate

[2] The complaining witness also testified as to the last four digits of petitioner's license plate, and to the fact that the first three digits were obscured; these facts were independently substantiated. Since the license plate could be seen from outside the car, and petitioner denied that the complaining witness had ever been in his car, the Mississippi Supreme Court apparently accepted the officer's testimony concerning the Dentyne wrappers and cigarette lighter as the only cogent corroborative evidence.

the judgment of conviction and remand for a hearing on the question whether the petitioner is to be deemed to have knowingly waived decision of his federal claim when timely objection was not made to the admission of the illegally seized evidence.

It is, of course, a familiar principle that this Court will decline to review state court judgments which rest on independent and adequate state grounds, even where those judgments also decide federal questions. The principle applies not only in cases involving state substantive grounds, but also in cases involving state procedural grounds. But it is important to distinguish between state substantive grounds and state procedural grounds. Where the ground involved is substantive, the determination of the federal question cannot affect the disposition if the state court decision on the state law question is allowed to stand. Under the view taken in *Murdock* of the statutes conferring appellate jurisdiction on this Court, we have no power to revise judgments on questions of state law. Thus, the adequate nonfederal ground doctrine is necessary to avoid advisory opinions.

These justifications have no application where the state ground is purely procedural. A procedural default which is held to bar challenge to a conviction in state courts, even on federal constitutional grounds, prevents implementation of the federal right. Accordingly, we have consistently held that the question of when and how defaults in compliance with state procedural rules can preclude our consideration of a federal question is itself a federal question. As Mr. Justice Holmes said:

> "When as here there is a plain assertion of federal rights in the lower court, local rules as to how far it shall be reviewed on appeal do not necessarily prevail. . . . Whether the right was denied or not given due recognition by the [state court] . . . is a question as to which the plaintiffs are entitled to invoke our judgment." Love v. Griffith, 266 U.S. 32, 33–34 (1924).

Only last Term, we reaffirmed this principle, holding that a state appellate court's refusal, on the ground of mootness, to consider a federal claim, did not preclude our independent determination of the question of mootness; that is itself a question of federal law which this Court must ultimately decide. Liner v. Jafco, Inc., 375 U.S. 301 (1964). These cases settle the proposition that a litigant's procedural defaults in state proceedings do not prevent vindication of his federal rights unless the state's insistence on compliance with its procedural rule serves a legitimate state interest. In every case we must inquire whether the enforcement of a procedural forfeiture serves such a state interest. If it does not, the state procedural rule ought not be permitted to bar vindication of important federal rights.

The Mississippi rule requiring contemporaneous objection to the introduction of illegal evidence clearly does serve a legitimate state interest. By immediately apprising the trial judge of the objection, counsel gives the court the opportunity to conduct the trial without using the tainted evidence. If the objection is well taken the fruits of the illegal search may be excluded from jury consideration, and a reversal and new trial avoided. But on the record before us it appears that this purpose of the contemporaneous-objection rule may have been substantially served by petitioner's motion at the close of the state's evidence asking for a directed verdict because of the erroneous admission of the officer's testimony. For at this stage the trial judge could have called for elaboration of the search and seizure argument and, if persuaded, could have stricken the tainted testimony or have taken other appropriate corrective action. For example, if there was sufficient competent evidence without this testimony to go to the jury, the motion for a directed verdict might have been denied, and the case submitted to the jury with a properly worded appropriate cautionary instruction. In these circumstances, the delay until the close of the state's case in presenting the objection cannot be said to have frustrated the state's interest in avoiding delay and waste of time in the disposition of the case. If this is so, and enforcement of the rule here would serve no substantial state interest, then settled principles would preclude treating the state ground as adequate; giving effect to the contemporaneous-objection rule for its own sake "would be to force resort to an arid ritual of meaningless form." Staub v. City of Baxley, 355 U.S. 313, 320 (1958); see also Wright v. Georgia, 373 U.S. 284, 289–91 (1963).[5]

We have no reason, however, to decide that question now or to express any view on the merits of petitioner's substantial constitutional claim. For even assuming that the making of the objection on the motion for a directed verdict satisfied the state interest served by the contemporaneous-objection rule, the record suggests a possibility that petitioner's counsel deliberately bypassed the opportunity to make timely objection in the state court, and thus that the petitioner should be deemed to have forfeited his state court remedies. . . .

[At this point, Justice Brennan noted that there were indications in the record that Henry's attorneys may have deliberately refrained from objecting to the evidence for strategic reasons. They may have wanted the testimony to come in because they thought they could discredit it and thereby weaken the state's case. Or they may have delayed objecting in the hopes of inviting error and obtaining a subsequent reversal of a conviction. Since counsel's reasons for failure to object could not be determined from the record before the Court, however, Justice Brennan concluded that the proper course was to remand the case to give the state courts an opportunity to hold a hearing on whether, in effect, the defense attorney's conduct amounted to a waiver of the constitutional claim.]

[5] We do not rely on the principle that our review is not precluded when the state court has failed to exercise discretion to disregard the procedural default. See Williams v. Georgia, 349 U.S. 375 (1955). We read the second Mississippi Supreme Court opinion as holding that there is no such discretion where it appears that petitioner was represented by competent local counsel familiar with local procedure.

Therefore, the judgment is vacated and the case is remanded to the Mississippi Supreme Court for further proceedings not inconsistent with this opinion.

It is so ordered.[a]

MR. JUSTICE BLACK, dissenting.[b]

Petitioner contends that his conviction was based in part on evidence obtained by an allegedly unlawful search in violation of the United States Constitution. I would decide this federal question here and now. . . .

I [do not] believe that Mississippi's procedural rule concerning the stage of a trial at which constitutional objections should be made is the kind of rule that we should accept as an independent, adequate ground for the state supreme court's refusal to decide the constitutional question raised by petitioner. In Williams v. Georgia, 349 U.S. 375 (1955), this Court held that where a state allows constitutional questions "to be raised at a late stage and be determined by its courts as a matter of discretion, we are not concluded from assuming jurisdiction and deciding whether the state court action in the particular circumstances is, in effect, an avoidance of the federal right." No Mississippi court opinions or state statutes have been called to our attention that I read as denying *power* of the state supreme court, should that court wish to do so, to consider and determine constitutional questions presented at the time this one was. In fact, as I understand counsel for the state, the Supreme Court of Mississippi does have power in its discretion to consider such questions regardless of when they are presented. As that court has said most persuasively:

> "Constitutional rights in serious criminal cases rise above mere rules of procedure. . . . Errors affecting fundamental rights are exceptions to the rule that questions not raised in the trial court cannot be raised for the first time on appeal." Brooks v. State, 209 Miss. 150, 155, 46 So. 2d 94, 97 (1950).

After stating this to be the rule it followed, and citing a number of its past decisions which stated and applied the same rule, the highest court of Mississippi, in the opinion quoted from, because of that rule reversed a conviction obtained through the use of unconstitutionally seized evidence, even though as in the present case there had been no objection made at the time the evidence was presented. The court noted that it had applied this same rule in other cases where proper objection had not been made at the trial. . . . In all of these cases the defendant appears to have been represented by local counsel. Yet this Court now apparently holds that the state court may, if it chooses to do so, depart from its prior cases and apply a new, stricter rule against

---

[a] On remand, the state courts found a waiver and, after some procedural jostling, the Supreme Court denied certiorari without prejudice to Henry's right to bring a federal habeas corpus proceeding. He did so, his claim was upheld, and the conviction was set aside. See Henry v. Williams, 299 F. Supp. 36 (N.D. Miss. 1969). [Footnote by eds.]

[b] The portions of Justice Black's opinion dissenting from the Court's "waiver" holding have been omitted. [Footnote by eds.]

this defendant and thereby prevent this Court from reviewing the case to see that his federal constitutional rights were safeguarded. I do not believe the cherished federal constitutional right of a defendant to object to unconstitutionally seized evidence offered against him can be cut off irrevocably by state-court discretionary rulings which might be different in particular undefined circumstances in other cases. I think such a procedural device for shutting off our review of questions involving constitutional rights is too dangerous to be tolerated.

For these reasons I dissent from the disposition of this case.

MR. JUSTICE HARLAN, with whom MR. JUSTICE CLARK and MR. JUSTICE STEWART join, dissenting.[c] . . .

The Mississippi Supreme Court did not base its ultimate decision upon petitioner's federal claim that his wife's consent could not validate an otherwise improper police search of the family car, but on the procedural ground that petitioner (who was represented by three experienced lawyers) had not objected at the time the fruits of this search were received in evidence. This Court now strongly implies, but does not decide (in view of its remand on the "waiver" issue) that enforcement of the State's "contemporaneous-objection" rule was inadequate as a state of decision because the petitioner's motion for a directed verdict cf acquittal afforded the trial judge a satisfactory opportunity to take "appropriate correction action" with reference to the allegedly inadmissible evidence. Thus, it is suggested, this may be a situation where "giving effect to the contemporaneous-objection rule for its own sake 'would be to force resort to an arid ritual of meaningless form.'"

From the standpoint of the realities of the courtroom, I can only regard the Court's analysis as little short of fanciful. [As the Court suggests,] the trial judge could have denied the motion for a directed verdict, but, sua sponte, called for elaboration of the argument, determined that the search of the automobile was unconstitutional, and given cautionary instructions to the jury to disregard the inadmissible evidence when the case was submitted to it.

The practical difficulties with this approach are manifestly sufficient to show a substantial state interest in their avoidance, and thus to show an "adequate" basis for the state's adherence to the contemporaneous-objection rule. To make my point I must quote the motion for directed verdict in full.

> "Atty Carter: We're going to make a motion, your Honor, for a directed verdict in this case. We are going to base our motion on several grounds. First, we think that this whole process by which this defendant was brought or attempted to be brought into the jurisdiction of this court is illegal and void. There is nothing in the record in this case to show that the warrant that was issued against this defendant was based upon—it must be based in this state and any other state on an

---

[c] The portions of Justice Harlan's opinion dissenting from the Court's "waiver" holding have been omitted. [Footnote by eds.]

affidavit, on a proper affidavit or a proper complaint by any party. True, there is some testimony that some affidavit was made, and the complaining witness said so, but in the record in this case which is before the court, no such affidavit is present and there is a verification from the Justice of the Peace that no such affidavit is present in this case; therefore, we contend that the warrant under which this defendant was subjected to arrest was illegal and without force and effect. Secondly, we contend that the warrant having been issued and the testimony of this Mr. Collins on the stand to the effect that after he had placed this man under arrest, he then proceeded to go and search his car, and clearly, this is a violation of his rights under the fourth amendment, and it is unlawful search and seizure so the evidence that they have secured against this defendant is illegal and unlawful. Finally, we contend that on the basis of these facts that the affidavit under which the defendant was tried before the Justice of the Peace Court, as we contended yesterday, based upon the statement that was sworn to by the County Attorney, not on information and belief, but directly that this is void and defective and could give the Justice of the Peace no jurisdiction in this case. We contend under these circumstances that the state—that this is an illegal process; that this man's rights have been violated under the 14th amendment, and finally, we contend that the state has failed to prove beyond a reasonable doubt to any extent to implicate this man in this case. Now, on these basis [sic] we contend that this whole process is illegal and void, and that it has permeated and contended [sic] the whole process insofar as the jurisdiction of this court is concerned or jurisdiction over this individual is concerned; therefore, he should be released, and we move for a directed verdict.

"Court: Motion overruled. Bring the jury back."

The motion was renewed at the completion of the defense in the following language:

Atty Carter: Your Honor, at this time at the close of the case we want to make a motion for a directed verdict. We base it on the grounds and the reasons which we set forth in our motion for a directed verdict at the close of the state's case. We make it now at the close of the entire case on those grounds and on the grounds that the evidence has not shown beyond any reasonable doubt under the law that the defendant is guilty of the charge. We therefore make a motion for a directed verdict at this time.

"Court: Motion is overruled."

The single sentence in the first motion is the only direct reference to the search and seizure question from beginning to end of the trial.

As every trial lawyer of any experience knows, motions for directed verdicts are generally made as a matter of course at the close of the prosecution's case, and are generally denied without close consideration unless the case is clearly borderline. It is simply unrealistic in this context to have expected the trial judge to pick out the single vague sentence from the directed verdict motion and to have acted upon it with the refined imagination the Court would require of him. Henry's three lawyers apparently regarded the search and seizure claim as makeweight. They had not mentioned it earlier in the trial and gave no explanation for their laxity in raising it. And when they did mention it, they did so in a cursory and conclusional sentence placed in a secondary position in a directed verdict motion. The theory underlying the search and seizure argument—that a wife's freely given permission to search the family car is invalid—is subtle to say the very least, and as the matter was presented to the trial judge it would have been extraordinary had he caught it, or even realized that there was a serious problem to catch. But this is not all the Court would require of him. He must, in addition, realize that despite the inappropriateness of granting the directed verdict requested of him, he could partially serve the cause of the defense by taking it upon himself to frame and give cautionary instructions to the jury to disregard the evidence obtained as fruits of the search.[2]

Contrast with this the situation presented by a contemporaneous objection. The objection must necessarily be directed to the single question of admissibility; the judge must inevitably focus on it; there would be no doubt as to the appropriate form of relief, and the effect of the trial judge's decision would be immediate rather than remote. Usually the proper timing of an objection will force an elaboration of it. Had objection been made in this case during the officer's testimony about the search, it would have called forth of its own force the specific answer that the wife had given her permission and, in turn, the assertion that the permission was ineffective. The issue, in short, would have been advertently faced by the trial judge and the likelihood of achieving a correct result maximized.

Thus the state interest which so powerfully supports the contemporaneous-objection rule is that of maximizing correct decisions and concomitantly minimizing errors requiring mistrials and retrials. The alternative for the state is to reverse a trial judge who, from a long motion, fails to pick out and act with remarkable imagination upon a single vague sentence relating to admissibility of evidence long since admitted. A trial judge is a decision-maker, not an advocate. To force him out of his proper role by requiring him to coax out the arguments and imaginatively reframe the requested remedies for the counsel

---

[2] Furthermore, even if counsel had fully elaborated the argument and had made it in the context of a motion to strike rather than a motion for directed verdict, the trial judge could properly have exercised his discretion (as the Mississippi Supreme Court did) and denied any relief. This power is recognized in trial judges in the federal system in order to prevent the "ambushing" of a trial through the withholding of an objection that should have been made when questionable evidence was first introduced. Federalism is turned upside down if it is denied to judges in the state systems.

before him is to place upon him more responsibility than a trial judge can be expected to discharge.

There was no "appropriate corrective action" that could have realistically satisfied the purposes of the contemporaneous-objection rule. Without question the state had an interest in maintaining the integrity of its procedure, and thus without doubt reliance on the rule in question is "adequate" to bar direct review of petitioner's federal claim by this Court.[3] . . .

Believing that the judgment below rests on an adequate independent state ground, I would dismiss the writ issued in this case as improvidently granted.

NOTES ON THE ADEQUACY AND INDEPENDENCE OF STATE GROUNDS

1. **Questions and Comments on *Henry*.** There are two distinct parts of the *Henry* opinion. The first concerned whether the Mississippi contemporaneous objection rule was adequate to foreclose Supreme Court review of Henry's search and seizure claim. The second was whether the adequate-and-independent-state-ground inquiry should be replaced by an inquiry into whether the defendant had "waived" the federal right.

The "waiver" analysis is derived from the Court's decision in Fay v. Noia, 372 U.S. 391 (1963). *Fay* held that the adequate and independent state ground rule did not apply when state criminal convictions were challenged in federal habeas corpus proceedings. Instead, it asked whether the defendant had "deliberately bypassed" (that is, intentionally waived) the opportunity to raise the federal claim in the state courts. This aspect of *Fay,* which has been modified in subsequent decisions, is dealt with beginning at page 753, infra. For now, it is important to know only that many people, including Justice Harlan, thought that *Henry* was the first step toward applying the "deliberate bypass" inquiry on direct appeal as well as habeas. This did not come to pass, and the "waiver" part of the *Henry* opinion has not been important to subsequent decisions. It is for this reason, and because this aspect of *Henry* cannot be understood apart from *Fay,* that the waiver portions of the *Henry* opinion have been omitted here.

The part of *Henry* reproduced above, in any event, presents an illustration of the adequate and independent state ground in operation. The debate between Justices Brennan, Black, and Harlan is a useful

---

[3] As the first opinion by the Mississippi Supreme Court shows, there is discretion in certain circumstances to lower the procedural bar. It does not follow that this Court is completely free to exercise that discretion. Even in cases from lower federal courts we do so only if there has been an abuse. If, in order to insulate its decisions from reversal by this Court, a state court must strip itself of the discretionary power to differentiate between different sets of circumstances, the rule operates in a most perverse way.

window on when a state ground of decision should be regarded as "adequate" to foreclose direct Supreme Court review.

Consider at the outset the differences between "substantive" and "procedural" state grounds advanced as a basis for foreclosing Supreme Court review. Justice Brennan said that "[w]here the ground involved is substantive, the determination of the federal question cannot affect the disposition if the state court decision on the state law question is allowed to stand." What does this passage mean? A recurring example of a "substantive" state ground of decision occurs when a state law is attacked on the ground that it violates both the federal and the state constitutions. In such a case, a decision by the state court that the state constitution invalidated the law would not be reviewable in the Supreme Court. It would be an "adequate and independent" state substantive ground of decision.[a] Is it possible for such a question to be decided *against* the federal claimant on the state law issue and for that decision to be advanced as an adequate and independent state ground that would foreclose Supreme Court review of the federal question? Does this mean that a state court decision based on a substantive adequate and independent state ground will always result in victory for the person claiming rights under federal law? Are there any situations where this would not be so?

Now contrast the "procedural" state ground. Justice Brennan said that a procedural state ground advanced as adequate and independent "prevents implementation of the federal right." What does Brennan mean here? Consider what happened in *Henry*. The state courts rejected Henry's search and seizure claim because the claim was not properly raised under state law; the decision was against the person claiming rights under federal law without consideration of the merits of the federal claim. Is this an invariable characteristic of the "procedural" adequate and independent state ground? Are there any situations where this would not be so?

Is the difference between substantive and procedural state grounds of decision important? Does the difference have any bearing on the Supreme Court's consideration of the "adequacy" of state procedural grounds? Is there an analogy to *Brand* (page 600, supra)? To *Dice* (page 252, supra)? Would it be important to know that Aaron Henry, the defendant in the *Henry* case, was an active and controversial civil rights leader in Mississippi in the early 1960's?

Focus also on the differences between the approaches of Justices Brennan, Black, and Harlan. Do they disagree about the criteria that should control the "adequacy" of a state procedural ground? Or do they agree about the appropriate criteria and disagree about their

[a] It is possible, of course, that the state court opinion would cite federal cases and rely on propositions of federal law in coming to that decision. In that case, it may be that the decision would be reviewable on the grounds advanced in *Michigan v. Long*, page 618, supra. It would be said in such an instance that the state ground was not "independent" of federal law, and thus the adequate and independent state ground doctrine would not apply. The example in text assumes that the state court has made it clear that the state ground is completely independent of any federal premises.

application to the *Henry* facts? The cases discussed in the following notes describe the precedential background against which *Henry* was decided and several more recent cases. They may inform further consideration of these questions.[b]

2. Procedures That Violate Federal Law. It occasionally happens that the state advances a procedural barrier to Supreme Court review that is itself a violation of due process or some other federal limitation on state procedures. Of course, such a basis for decision cannot serve as an "adequate" state ground to prevent the Supreme Court from reaching the merits of a federal claim.

In Saunders v. Shaw, 244 U.S. 317 (1917), and Brinkerhoff-Faris Trust & Savings Co. v. Hill, 281 U.S. 673 (1930), for example, the Court held that the state rule violated due process by not providing a fair opportunity for a hearing on the federal claims. And in Reece v. Georgia, 350 U.S. 85 (1955), the Court held it a violation of due process to foreclose an illiterate criminal defendant from raising a challenge to the racial composition of the grand jury. The state court rule required that the challenge be before indictment. Counsel had not been appointed until the day after the indictment.

3. *NAACP v. Alabama ex rel. Patterson.* In NAACP v. Alabama ex rel. Patterson, 357 U.S. 449 (1957), the NAACP had been held in civil contempt by the Alabama courts for failing to reveal the names of all of its members and agents to the state attorney general. The NAACP challenged the order on federal constitutional grounds, but the Alabama Supreme Court refused to consider the merits of the claim because the NAACP had sought review by certiorari rather than mandamus. Mandamus, the court held, was the exclusive state remedy in such circumstances.

In the Supreme Court, the Alabama procedural rule was advanced as an adequate and independent state ground. Writing for a unanimous Court, Justice Harlan reached the merits and reversed. On the Court's power to review, he said:

> "We address ourselves first to [the state's] contention that we lack jurisdiction because the denial of certiorari by the Supreme Court of Alabama rests on an independent nonfederal

---

[b] For general treatments of the adequacy of state grounds of decision, see, e.g., Wechsler, The Appellate Jurisdiction of the Supreme Court: Reflections on the Law and Logistics of Direct Review, 34 Wash. & Lee L. Rev. 1043 (1977); Hill, The Inadequate State Ground, 65 Colum. L. Rev. 943 (1965); Sandalow, *Henry v. Mississippi* and the Adequate State Ground: Proposals for a Revised Doctrine, 1965 Sup. Ct. Rev. 187; Note, The Untenable Nonfederal Ground in the Supreme Court, 74 Harv. L Rev. 1375 (1961).

Daniel Meltzer has elaborately considered the adequate and independent state ground doctrine along with the rules of procedural foreclosure that ought to govern in habeas corpus cases. In State Court Forfeitures of Federal Rights, 99 Harv. L. Rev. 1128 (1986), he concludes that there "should be one federal [common law] doctrine governing the permissibility of forfeiting claims in cases originating in state courts, and that doctrine should apply in whichever court"—state or federal— "a case is being considered." Compare Brilmayer, State Forfeiture Rules and Federal Review of State Criminal Convictions, 49 U.Chi.L.Rev. 741 (1982), which also discusses the adequate and independent state ground rule as it relates to procedural foreclosure on habeas corpus.

ground, namely, that [the NAACP] in applying for certiorari had pursued the wrong appellate remedy under state law. [The state] recognizes that our jurisdiction is not defeated if the nonfederal ground relied upon by the state court is 'without any fair or substantial support.' It thus becomes our duty to ascertain, '. . . in order that constitutional guarantees may appropriately be enforced, whether the asserted nonfederal ground independently and adequately supports the judgment.'. . .

"We are unable to reconcile the procedural holding of the Alabama Supreme Court in the present case with its past unambiguous holdings as to the scope of review available upon a writ of certiorari addressed to a contempt judgment. [Justice Harlan then reviewed the prior Alabama decisions, extending back some 50 years.]

"The Alabama cases do indicate . . . that an order [such as this] '. . . *may* be reviewed on petition for mandamus.' But we can discover nothing in the prior state cases which suggests that mandamus is the *exclusive* remedy for reviewing [such orders]. Nor, so far as we can find, do any of these prior decisions indicate that the validity of such orders can be drawn in question by way of certiorari only in instances where a defendant had no opportunity to apply for mandamus. Although the opinion below suggests no such distinction, the state now argues that this was in fact the situation in all of the earlier certiorari cases . . . . Even if that is indeed the rationale of the Alabama Supreme Court's present decision, such a local procedural rule, although it may now appear in retrospect to form part of a consistent pattern of procedures to obtain appellate review, cannot avail the state here, because [the NAACP] could not fairly be deemed to have been apprised of its existence. Novelty in procedural requirements cannot be permitted to thwart review in this Court applied for by those who, in justified reliance upon prior decisions, seek vindication in state courts of their federal constitutional rights. . . ." [c]

What is the justification for what the Court did in *Patterson*? Did it hold the state's rule to be a violation of due process? Must it have done so in order to ignore the rule? Is the Court's holding related to the underlying premises of the decisions in *Brand* (page 600, supra) or *Dice* (page 252, supra)? Do these analogies help in explaining the Court's power to do what it did in *Patterson*?

4. Manner in Which State Rules Applied. Related situations where the Supreme Court will hold a state ground inadequate are where the state has enforced its procedures "with pointless severity" or, as Justice Brennan said in *Henry,* in such a manner as "to force resort

---

[c] Compare Hathorn v. Lovorn, 457 U.S. 255 (1982): "State courts may not avoid deciding federal issues by invoking procedures that they do not apply even-handedly to all similar claims."

to an arid ritual of meaningless form." In each instance, as in *Patterson,* one of the key questions is whether the state's rule has been clearly announced and consistently followed. It is no coincidence that many of these cases have arisen in the civil rights context.

For example, in NAACP v. Alabama ex rel Flowers, 377 U.S. 288 (1964), the Alabama Supreme Court refused to consider constitutional claims by the NAACP related to that state's effort to exclude the NAACP from carrying on activities in Alabama. This was the fourth trip of the case through the Alabama courts to the Supreme Court. The Court said:

> "The Supreme Court of Alabama based its decision entirely on the asserted failure of the [NAACP's] brief to conform to rules of the court. . . . The basis of the decision below was . . . 'a rule of long standing and frequent application that where unrelated assignments of error are argued together and one is without merit, the others will not be considered.' Proceeding to apply that rule to the [NAACP's] brief, the Supreme Court held that at least one of the assignments of error contained in each of the five numbered subdivisions of the 'argument' section of the brief was without merit, and that it would therefore not consider the merit of any of the other assignments. The Attorney General of Alabama argues that this is a nonfederal ground of decision adequate to bar review in this Court of the serious constitutional claims which the [NAACP] presents. We find this position wholly unacceptable."

The Court then said that "it seems to us crystal clear that the rule invoked by [the Alabama Supreme Court] cannot reasonably be deemed applicable to this case." The Court then carefully examined the organization of the brief, concluding that "[w]e are at a loss to understand how it could be concluded that the structure of the brief did not fully meet the requirements" and that "[t]he consideration of asserted constitutional rights may not be thwarted by simple recitation that there has not been observance of a procedural rule with which there has been compliance in both substance and form, in every real sense." Finally, the Court observed that the "Alabama courts have not heretofore applied their rules respecting the preparation of briefs with the pointless severity noted here." The Court then examined prior Alabama cases at length to demonstrate the accuracy of this observation.

Consider also Barr v. City of Columbia, 378 U.S. 146 (1964). Five black sit-in demonstrators had been convicted of trespass and breach of the peace for insisting on service at a drug store lunch counter. The Supreme Court found no evidence in the record to support the breach of the peace conviction (all the defendants did was "politely ask for service") and held that a criminal conviction without evidence violated due process. The city argued, however, that the Court could not reach this question. The South Carolina Supreme Court had refused to pass on the defendants' objections to the breach of the peace conviction because the exceptions taken to the trial court's decision were "too general to be considered." The Court responded:

"We cannot accept the city's argument, since in [another case] decided only a few weeks after the present case, the state Supreme Court had before it the identical two exceptions, and relying on them reversed for insufficiency of evidence the conviction of a peaceful sit-in demonstrator who had been convicted on a charge of resisting arrest. In three other cases decided in the two-month period preceding the present decision it likewise considered these same exceptions enough to raise the question of sufficiency of evidence and in one of those three cases, decided the day before the present one, it reversed on that ground a conviction for interfering with an officer. We have often pointed out that state procedural requirements which are not strictly or regularly followed cannot deprive us of the right to review. We conclude that there is no adequate state ground barring our review of the breach-of-peace convictions."

Compare Wright v. Georgia, 373 U.S. 284 (1963). The defendants were six black youths who were convicted of breach of the peace for playing basketball in a public park. There was no evidence that they did anything more than that. The Georgia Supreme Court refused to consider their due process arguments against the conviction because they were not properly presented. The Supreme Court said in response:

"To ascertain the precise holding of the Georgia court we must examine the brief which the petitioners submitted in connection with their appeal. It specifically assigned as error the overruling of their motions for a new trial. And in the section of the brief devoted to argument it was stated:

'Plaintiffs-in-error had assembled for the purpose of playing basketball and were in fact only playing basketball in a municipally owned park, according to the state's own evidence. Nevertheless, they were arrested and convicted under the said statute which prohibited assemblies for the purpose of "disturbing the public peace or committing any unlawful act." Where a statute is so vague as to make criminal an innocent act, a conviction under it cannot be sustained. [Citing vagueness cases.] Plaintiffs-in-error could not possibly have predetermined from the wording of the statute that it would have punished as a misdemeanor an assembly for the purpose of playing basketball.'

Obviously petitioners did in fact argue the point which they press in this Court. Thus the holding of the Georgia court must not have been that the petitioners abandoned their argument but rather that the argument could not be considered because it was not explicitly identified in the brief with the motions for a new trial. In short the Georgia court would require the petitioners to say something like the following at the end of the paragraph quoted above: 'A fortiori it was error for the trial court to overrule the motions for a new trial.' As was said in a similar case coming to us from the Georgia courts, this 'would be to force resort to an arid ritual of meaningless form.' Staub v. City of Baxley, 355 U.S. 313, 320 (1958). The state may not do that here any more than it could in *Staub.* Here, as in *Staub,* the state ground is inadequate. Its inadequacy is especially apparent because no prior Georgia case which respondent has cited nor which we have found gives notice of the existence of any requirement that an argument in a brief be specifically identified with a motion made in the trial court. '[A] local procedural rule, although it may now appear in retrospect to form part of a consistent pattern of procedures . . ., cannot avail the state here, because petitioner[s] could not fairly be deemed to have been apprised of its existence. Novelty in procedural requirements cannot be permitted to thwart review in this Court . . . .' NAACP v. Alabama ex rel Flowers, 377 U.S. 288 (1964). We proceed to a consideration of the merits of petitioners' constitutional claim."

Whereupon the Court reversed the conviction.

Finally, consider James v. Kentucky, 466 U.S. 341 (1984). The Court had held in Carter v. Kentucky, 450 U.S. 288 (1981), that a trial judge must, if requested, instruct the jury not to draw an adverse inference from the defendant's failure to take the stand. In *James,* the defense attorney requested an "admonition" to this effect rather than an "instruction." The Kentucky Supreme Court held that, because there was a "vast difference" between the two under Kentucky law, the defense request was insufficient. Even though the defendant "was entitled to the instruction" he could not prevail because he "did not ask for it."

The Supreme Court reversed. It first examined the Kentucky distinction between "admonitions" and "instructions," concluding that the "substantive distinction" between them [d] "is not always clear or closely hewn to." It then said:

"There can be no dispute that, for federal constitutional purposes, James adequately invoked his substantive right to jury guidance. The question is whether counsel's passing reference to an 'admonition' is a fatal procedural default under Kentucky law adequate to support the result below and to prevent us from considering petitioner's constitutional claim. [W]e hold that it is not. Kentucky's distinction between admonitions and instructions is not the sort of firmly established and regularly followed state practice that can prevent imple-

---

[d] "Instructions" were "statements of black-letter law . . . governing the outcome of a case," whereas "admonitions" were "cautionary statements regarding the jury's conduct" such as their obligation not to discuss the case during an adjournment. Moreover, "admonitions" were given orally; "instructions" were given orally and also provided to the jury in writing.

mentation of federal constitutional rights. Cf. Barr v. City of Columbia, 378 U.S. 146 (1964). *Carter* holds that if asked to do so the trial court must tell the jury not to draw the impermissible inference. To insist on a particular label for this statement would 'force resort to an arid ritual of meaningless form.' Staub v. City of Baxley, 355 U.S. 313 (1958), and would further no perceivable state interest, Henry v. Mississippi, 379 U.S. 443 (1965). . . ."

5. *Patterson v. Alabama.* In Patterson v. Alabama, 294 U.S. 600 (1934), the Court adopted a different approach. Patterson, Norris, and seven other black youths were convicted of rape in the infamous "Scottsboro Cases." The Supreme Court reversed the convictions. Patterson was retried in another county, was again convicted, and the verdict was set aside as against the weight of the evidence. Patterson was then tried a third time, his conviction was affirmed by the Alabama Supreme Court, and the Supreme Court granted certiorari. At the outset of the third trial, Patterson had objected to both the grand jury and the trial jury on the ground that blacks had been systematically excluded from service. The trial judge denied the motions. Norris was tried immediately after Patterson was convicted, and he made the same motions to the same judge. It was stipulated that the papers and testimony offered by Patterson would be considered in Norris' case too. The trial judge denied Norris' motions in an opinion worded identically to his opinion in Patterson's case.

The state supreme court denied the discrimination claim presented by Norris on the merits. In Patterson's case, however, it refused to reach the merits on the ground that the bill of exceptions, the necessary procedural step to present the issue to that court, had not been filed in time. Whether it had been timely filed—at most it was four days late—presented a complex question of Alabama procedure, but the United States Supreme Court examined the Alabama cases and appeared to conclude that the Alabama court's decision was consistent with those cases.

The Court had, however, upheld the jury discrimination claim in Norris v. Alabama, 294 U.S. 587 (1935), decided on the same day as *Patterson.* The Court then faced the question whether the judgment in Patterson's case should nonetheless be affirmed because the decision "of the state court is based upon a non-federal ground adequate to sustain it." After its discussion of the Alabama cases dealing with the procedural point, it continued:

"While we must have proper regard to this ruling of the state court in relation to its appellate procedure, we cannot ignore the exceptional features of the present case. An important question under the federal Constitution was involved, and, from that standpoint, the case did not stand alone. As the opinion of the state court observes, there was 'being considered along with this cause, the appeal of [Norris] from a conviction under the same indictment.' [The Court here discussed the fact that the same indictment and the same evidence was involved in both cases.] We are not advised that previous state decisions had dealt with a situation having such unusual incidents.

"The decisions in the two cases were announced on the same day. The state court decided the constitutional question against Norris, and it was manifestly with that conclusion in mind that the court approached the decision in the case of Patterson and struck his bill of exceptions. We are not satisfied that the court would have dealt with the case in the same way if it had determined the constitutional question as we have determined it. We are not convinced that the court, in the presence of such a determination of constitutional right, confronting the anomalous and grave situation which would be created by a reversal of the judgment against Norris, and an affirmance of the judgment of death in the companion case of Patterson, who had asserted the same right, and having regard to the relation of the two cases and the other circumstances disclosed by the record, would have considered itself powerless to entertain the bill of exceptions or otherwise to provide appropriate relief. It is always hazardous to apply a judicial ruling, especially in a matter of procedure, to a serious situation which was not in contemplation when the ruling was made. At least the state court should have an opportunity to examine its powers in the light of the situation which has now developed. We should not foreclose that opportunity.

"We have frequently held that in the exercise of our appellate jurisdiction we have power not only to correct error in the judgment under review but to make such disposition of the case as justice requires. And in determining what justice does require, the Court is bound to consider any change, either in fact or in law, which has supervened since the judgment was entered. We may recognize such a change, which may affect the result, by setting aside the judgment and remanding the case so that the state court may be free to act. We have said that to do this is not to review, in any proper sense of the term, the decision of the state court upon a non-federal question, but only to deal appropriately with a matter arising since its judgment and having a bearing upon the right disposition of the case.

"Applying that principle of decision, we vacate the judgment and remand the case to the state court for further proceedings." [e]

[e] On remand, the Alabama Supreme Court vacated the conviction and ordered the indictments against both Norris and Patterson quashed. Both were subsequently reindicted. Patterson was again convicted, and sentenced to 75 years. The conviction was affirmed by the Alabama Supreme Court, and the United States Supreme Court denied certiorari. Patterson v. State, 234 Ala. 342, 175 So. 371, cert. denied, 302 U.S. 733 (1937). Norris was reconvicted and sentenced to death, but his sentence was commuted to life imprisonment. The cases and their outcomes are

6. *Williams v. Georgia.* The *Patterson* case was later invoked in an interesting manner in Williams v. Georgia, 349 U.S. 375 (1955). The *Williams* case is also suggestive as to when the Supreme Court might be justified in ignoring an otherwise adequate state ground of decision, as the use of the *Williams* case in the three opinions in *Henry* indicates.[f]

Williams involved a black defendant convicted of the murder of a white man ard sentenced to death. The trial jury was selected by drawing names from a box, in which the names of white persons appeared on white paper and black persons on yellow paper. More than 120 names were drawn, from which 48 were assigned to criminal duty. Four blacks were in the group of 120, and also in the group of 48. Three of the four were excused for cause, and the state peremptorily challenged the fourth. Williams was thus tried by an all white jury.

Williams' attorney challenged this method of selecting the jury for the first time in an extraordinary motion for new trial filed six weeks after the state supreme court affirmed the conviction. The attorney alleged, as was required in such a motion, that he could not, with due diligence, have learned about the jury selection practices earlier. Whether this was in fact the case, however, was highly doubtful.

A person by the name of Avery had been convicted of rape in the same county a year and a half before Williams had been tried. Avery's all-white jury was selected in the same manner. Avery challenged the array at the proper time, and appealed on the ground of discrimination to the Georgia Supreme Court. That court disapproved of the practice, but held that no actual discrimination had been shown and affirmed the conviction. Certiorari was sought in the Supreme Court in the *Avery* case nine weeks *before* the occurrence of the murder of which Williams was accused. Certiorari was granted the day before the jury selection process for Williams began (and in time for Williams' attorney to raise the constitutional claim). The Supreme Court subsequently held in Avery v. Georgia, 345 U.S. 559 (1953), that the use of different colored tickets made out a prima facie case of unconstitutional discrimination. The extraordinary motion for new trial was filed on behalf of Williams some six months after the Supreme Court's decision in *Avery*.

The Georgia trial court dismissed Williams' extraordinary motion for new trial, and the Georgia Supreme Court affirmed. That court held the objection waived by the failure to raise it at the proper time, and held that counsel had not shown that with due diligence the claim could not have been made in a timely manner. The Supreme Court then granted certiorari. "The question now before us," Justice Frank-

discussed in Boskey and Pickering, Federal Restrictions on State Criminal Procedure, 13 U. Chi. L. Rev. 266, 267–71 (1946).

   f For a recent citation of *Williams* for the proposition that "it is well established that where a state court possesses the power to disregard a procedural default in exceptional cases, the state court's failure to exercise that power in a particular case does not bar review in this Court," see Taylor v. Illinois, ___ U.S. ___, ___ (1988) (Brennan, joined by Marshall and Blackmun, dissenting). The majority in *Taylor* thought that no procedural default had occurred and hence did not address the *Williams* issue.

furter said for the Court, "is whether the ruling of the Georgia Supreme Court rests upon an adequate nonfederal ground, so that this Court is without jurisdiction to review the Georgia court." Justice Frankfurter continued:

"A state procedural rule which forbids the raising of federal questions at late stages in the case, or by any other than a prescribed method, has been recognized as a valid exercise of state power. The principle is clear enough. But the unique aspects of the never-ending new cases that arise require its individual application to particular circumstances. Thus, we would have a different question from that before us if the trial court had no power to consider Williams' constitutional objection at the belated time he raised it. But, where a state allows questions of this sort to be raised at a late stage and be determined by its courts as a matter of discretion, we are not concluded from assuming jurisdiction and deciding whether the state court action in the particular circumstances is, in effect, an avoidance of the federal right. A state court may not, in the exercise of its discretion, decline to entertain a constitutional claim while passing upon kindred issues raised in the same manner."

Justice Frankfurter then examined the Georgia cases in some detail. He noted that such motions were not favored, but that they had been granted in "extraordinary" situations before. Grant or denial of the motion was discretionary with the trial court, and reversal was only for a clear abuse of discretion. Such reversals had occurred in the past, though Justice Frankfurter admitted that virtually all of the cases in which that had happened involved challenges to a particular juror who had participated in the trial (for example, in one it was learned that an ex-convict had obtained a jury seat by impersonating his father; in another, that one of the jurors was distantly related to the prosecutor). Justice Frankfurter discussed at length whether challenges to the entire jury were different from a challenge to a particular juror, and concluded that they were not, at one point observing that it "does not appear rational" to make such a distinction. He then said:

"We conclude that the trial court and the state Supreme Court declined to grant Williams' motion though possessed of power to do so under state law. Since his motion was based upon a constitutional objection, and one the validity of which has in principle been sustained here, the discretionary decision to deny the motion does not deprive this Court of jurisdiction to find that the substantive issue is properly before us.

"But the fact that we have jurisdiction does not compel us to exercise it. In Patterson v. Alabama, 294 U.S. 600 (1935), we remanded a case to the highest court of the state, even though that court had affirmed on state procedural grounds, because after that affirmance we had reversed on constitutional grounds a case having identical substantive facts. . . .

"In the instant case, there is an important factor which has intervened since the affirmance by the Georgia Supreme Court which impels us to remand for that court's further consideration. This is the acknowledgment by the state before this Court that, as a matter of substantive law, Williams has been deprived of his constitutional rights. The Solicitor General of Fulton County . . . had urged before the Georgia Supreme Court that no denial of equal protection was involved, and that court may well have been influenced by the contention. Moreover, if there is another remedy open to Williams, as the Attorney General of the state intimated in his brief to the Georgia Supreme Court, that court should have an opportunity to designate the appropriate remedy.

"The facts of this case are extraordinary, particularly in view of the use of yellow and white tickets . . . almost a year after the state's own Supreme Court had condemned the practice in the *Avery* case. That life is at stake is of course another important factor in creating the extraordinary situation. The difference between capital and non-capital cases is the basis of differentiation in law in diverse ways in which the distinction becomes relevant. We think that orderly procedure requires a remand to the state supreme court for reconsideration of the case. Fair regard for the principles which the Georgia courts have enforced in numerous cases and for the constitutional commands binding on all courts compels us to reject the assumption that the courts of Georgia would allow this man to go to his death as the result of a conviction secured from a jury which the state admits was unconstitutionally impaneled."

Justice Clark, joined by Reed and Minton, dissented.[g]

---

[g] On remand, the Georgia Supreme Court acidly refused to reverse its prior stance. It began by quoting the 10th amendment, and then said:

"Even though executives and legislators, not being constitutional lawyers, might often overstep the foregoing unambiguous constitutional prohibition of federal invasion of state jurisdiction, there can never be an acceptable excuse for judicial failure to strictly observe it. This court bows to the Supreme Court on all federal questions of law but we will not supinely surrender sovereign powers of this state."

The opinion continued in this vein. The court concluded that it would re-enter its prior judgment "[n]ot in recognition of any jurisdiction of the Supreme Court to influence or in any manner to interfere with the functioning of this court on strictly state questions, but solely for the purpose of completing the record" in the case. The Supreme Court then denied certiorari. See Williams v. State, 211 Ga. 763, 88 S.E.2d 376 (1955), cert. denied, 350 U.S. 950 (1956).

WARD v. BOARD OF COUNTY COMMISSIONERS OF LOVE COUNTY, OKLAHOMA

United States Supreme Court, 1920.
253 U.S. 17.

MR. JUSTICE VAN DEVANTER delivered the opinion of the Court.

This is a proceeding by and on behalf of Coleman J. Ward and 66 other Indians to recover moneys alleged to have been coercively collected from them by Love County, Oklahoma, as taxes on their allotments, which under the laws and Constitution of the United States were nontaxable. The county commissioners disallowed the claim and the claimants appealed to the District Court of the county. There the claimants' petition was challenged by a demurrer, which was overruled, and the county elected not to plead further. A judgment for the claimants followed, and this was reversed by the [Oklahoma] Supreme Court. The case is here on writ of certiorari.

The claimants, who were members of the Choctaw tribe and wards of the United States, received their allotments out of the tribal domain under a congressional enactment of 1898, which subjected the right of alienation to certain restrictions and provided that "the lands allotted shall be nontaxable while the title remains in the original allottee, but not to exceed 21 years from date of patent." In the Act of 1906, enabling Oklahoma to become a state, Congress made it plain that no impairment of the rights of property pertaining to the Indians was intended; and the state included in its Constitution a provision exempting from taxation "such property as may be exempt by reason of treaty stipulations, existing between the Indians and the United States government or by federal laws, during the force and effect of such treaties or federal laws." Afterwards Congress, by an act of 1908, removed the restriction on alienation as to certain classes of allottees, including the present claimants, and declared that all land from which the restrictions were removed "shall be subject to taxation . . . as though it were the property of other persons than allottees."

Following the last enactment the officers of Love and other counties began to tax the allotted lands from which restrictions on alienation were removed, and this met with pronounced opposition on the part of the Indian allottees, who insisted, as they had been advised, that the tax exemption was a vested property right which could not be abrogated or destroyed consistently with the Constitution of the United States. Suits were begun in the state courts to maintain the exemption and enjoin the threatened taxation, one of the suits being prosecuted by some 8,000 allottees against the officers of Love and other counties. The suits were resisted, and the state courts, being of opinion that the exemption had been repealed by Congress, sustained the power to tax. The cases were then brought here, and this Court held that the exemption was a vested property right which Congress could not repeal consistently with the fifth amendment, that it was binding on the taxing authorities in Oklahoma, and that the state courts had erred in refusing to enjoin them from taxing the lands.

While those suits were pending the officers of Love County, with full knowledge of the suits and being defendants in one, proceeded with the taxation of the allotments, demanded of these claimants that the taxes on their lands be paid to the county, threatened to advertise and sell the lands unless the taxes were paid, did advertise and sell other lands similarly situated, and caused these claimants to believe that their land would be sold if the taxes were not paid. So, to prevent such a sale and to avoid the imposition of a penalty of 18 per cent, for which the local statute provided, these claimants paid the taxes. They protested and objected at the time that the taxes were invalid, and the county officers knew that all the allottees were pressing the objection in the pending suits.

As a conclusion from these facts the claimants asserted that the taxes were collected by Love County by coercive means, that their collection was in violation of a right arising out of a law of Congress and protected by the Constitution of the United States, and that the county was accordingly bound to repay the moneys thus collected. The total amount claimed is $7,823.35, aside from interest.

Such, in substance, was the case presented by the petition, which also described each tract that was taxed, named the allottee from whom the taxes were collected and stated the amount and date of each payment.

In reversing the judgment which the District Court had given for the claimants the [Oklahoma] Supreme Court held, first, that the taxes were not collected by coercive means, but were paid voluntarily, and could not be recovered back as there was no statutory authority therefor; and, secondly, that there was no statute making the county liable for taxes collected and then paid over to the state and municipal bodies other than the county—which it was assumed was true of a portion of these taxes—and that the petition did not show how much of the taxes was retained by the county, or how much paid over to the state and other municipal bodies, and therefore it could not be the basis of any judgment against the county.

The county challenges our jurisdiction by a motion to dismiss the writ of certiorari and by way of supporting the motion insists that the [Oklahoma] Supreme Court put its judgment entirely on independent nonfederal grounds which were broad enough to sustain the judgment.

As these claimants had not disposed of their allotments and 21 years had not elapsed since the date of the patents, it is certain that the lands were nontaxable. This was settled in [the prior litigation]; and it also was settled . . . that the exemption was a vested property right arising out of a law of Congress and protected by the Constitution of the United States. This being so, the state and all its agencies and political subdivisions were bound to give effect to the exemption. It operated as a direct restraint on Love County, no matter what was said in local statutes. The county did not respect it, but, on the contrary, assessed the lands allotted to these claimants, placed them on the county tax roll, and there charged them with taxes like other property. If a portion of the taxes was to go to the state and other municipal bodies after collection—which we assume was the case—it still was the county that charged the taxes *against these lands* and proceeded to collect them. Payment of all the taxes was demanded by the county, and all were paid to it in the circumstances already narrated.

We accept so much of the [Oklahoma] Supreme Court's decision as held that, if the payment was voluntary, the moneys could not be recovered back in the absence of a permissive statute, and that there was no such statute. But we are unable to accept its decision in other respects.

The right to the exemption was a federal right, and was specially set up and claimed as such in the petition. Whether the right was denied, or not given due recognition, by the [Oklahoma] Supreme Court is a question as to which the claimants were entitled to invoke our judgment, and this they have done in the appropriate way. It therefore is within our province to inquire not only whether the right was denied in express terms, but also whether it was denied in substance and effect, as by putting forward nonfederal grounds of decision that were without any fair or substantial support. Of course, if nonfederal grounds, plainly untenable, may be thus put forward successfully, our power to review easily may be avoided. With this qualification, it is true that a judgment of a state court, which is put on independent nonfederal grounds broad enough to sustain it, cannot be reviewed by us. But the qualification is a material one and cannot be disregarded without neglecting or renouncing a jurisdiction conferred by law and designed to protect and maintain the supremacy of the Constitution and the laws made in pursuance thereof.

The facts set forth in the petition, all of which were admitted by the demurrer whereon the county elected to stand, make it plain, as we think, that the finding or decision that the taxes were paid voluntarily was without any fair or substantial support. The claimants were Indians just emerging from a state of dependency and wardship. Through the pending suits and otherwise they were objecting and protecting that the taxation of their lands was forbidden by a law of Congress. But, notwithstanding this, the county demanded that the taxes be paid, and by threatening to sell the lands of these claimants and actually selling other lands similarly situated made it appear to the claimants that they must choose between paying the taxes and losing their lands. To prevent a sale and to avoid the imposition of a penalty of 18 per cent they yielded to the county's demand and paid the taxes, protesting and objecting at the time that the same were illegal. The moneys thus collected were obtained by coercive means—by compulsion. The county and its officers reasonably could not have regarded it otherwise; much less the Indian claimants. . . .

As the payment was not voluntary, but made under compulsion, no statutory authority was essential to enable or require the county to refund the money. It is a well settled rule that "money got through imposition" may be recovered back; and, as this Court has said on several occasions, "the obligation to do justice rests upon all persons, natural and artificial, and if a county obtains the money or property of others without authority, the law, independent of any statute, will compel restitution or compensation." To say that the county could collect these unlawful taxes by coercive means and not incur any obligation to pay them back is nothing short of saying that it could take or appropriate the property of these Indian allottees arbitrarily and without due process of law. Of course this would be in contravention of the 14th amendment, which binds the county as an agency of the state.

If it be true, as the [Oklahoma] Supreme Court assumed, that a portion of the taxes was paid over, after collection, to the state and other municipal bodies, we regard it as certain that this did not alter the county's liability to the claimants. The county had no right to collect the money, and it took the same with notice that the rights of all who were to share in the taxes were disputed by these claimants and were being contested in the pending suits. In these circumstances it could not lessen its liability by paying over a portion of the money to others whose rights it knew were disputed and were no better than its own. In legal contemplation it received the money for the use and benefit of the claimants and should respond to them accordingly.

The county calls attention to the fact that in the demurrer to the petition the statute of limitation . . . was relied on. This point was not discussed by the [Oklahoma] Supreme Court and we are not concerned with it beyond observing that when the case is remanded it will be open to that court to deal with the point as to the whole claim or any item in it as any valid local law in force when the claim was filed may require.

Motion to dismiss denied.

Judgment reversed.

NOTES ON REMEDIES FOR FEDERAL RIGHTS IN STATE COURTS

1. **Questions and Comments on *Ward v. Love County*.** *Ward v. Love County* is a puzzling case on several levels. It is probably best analyzed by identifying three possible bases for resolution of the controversy in the state courts:

(i) **Voluntary Payment.** The state court held that the taxes were not collected by coercive means, but were paid voluntarily. The Supreme Court responded by asking whether the federal right at stake was "denied in substance and effect, as by putting forward nonfederal grounds of decision that were without any fair or substantial support." This is the language of the adequate and independent state ground doctrine, and seems to suggest that the Court's concern was whether a proposition of state law had been advanced to justify the judgment that for some reason was "not adequate" or "not sufficiently independent." But is that the reason the Court set aside the state judgment on this question? Are the legal elements of the state court's conclusion that the payment was "voluntary" controlled by federal or by state law? Is this a case where a proposition of state law "without fair or substantial support" in prior state cases was used to deny a federal right? Or is it a case where the state court decided a federal question and got it wrong?

        (ii) No Statutory Basis for Recovery. Given that the payment was involuntary, the question is what happens next? Are the Indian plaintiffs entitled to recover from the county for payments involuntarily made? All the state court said on this question was that there was no statute making the county liable for taxes collected, some of which were then paid over to state and municipal bodies other than the county. The Court responded that no statutory authority was needed to permit the Indians to recover for coerced payments, since "the law" compels restitution or compensation. But what law, or more accurately, whose law? And on what basis does the Court reject the relevance of the fact that the county may have paid some of the money over to other governmental units?

        These questions can be analyzed by making two further inquiries. First, what is the source of the cause of action that the Indian plaintiffs can assert to recover tax payments coercively collected in violation of federal law? There are numerous possibilities: the federal Constitution, federal statute, federal common law, state statute, state common law. Which is the most likely source? And what are the implications of the various answers that might be given? If, for example, the cause of action is derived from a federal source, the Court might be remanding to see whether the state courts will hear it, or the remand might be intended as a command that the state court hear it (absent some satisfactory reason in state law for not doing so). On the other hand, the Court might be remanding to see whether there is a cause of action for coerced payments under state law, or the remand might be intended as a command that the state must (by federal compulsion) supply a remedy in this situation. Which of these solutions is more consistent with a proper sense of federal-state relations? Which is it more likely that the Court meant? Is it relevant that *Ward* was decided before *Erie?* In the absence of diversity (which appears to be the case), could a suit have been filed in a federal court in 1920 to recover for these coerced payments? Should the answer to this question have mattered to the resolution of *Ward* as it arose? Could a federal-court suit be filed today? Should that matter if a case like *Ward* were to come before the Supreme Court today?

        Second, if one assumes the existence of a cause of action from some source, what is the relevance of the "payment over" by the county? Is the Court holding as a matter of federal law that this cannot be a defense, no matter the source of the cause of action? Is the Court holding that this is an "inadequate" state ground of decision?

(iii) **Statute of Limitations.** Finally, note that the Court appears to contemplate that a dismissal by the state court may still be possible on remand if the case was filed after the expiration of the state statute of limitations. Is this consistent with the various possible meanings of the case drawn out above?

Note, as held in Holmberg v. Armbrecht, 327 U.S. 392 (1946), that in situations where Congress has been silent as to the statute of limitations that measures an explicitly created federal statutory cause of action, the federal courts normally "borrow" the applicable state statute. Thus, even if a federal cause of action exists in the *Ward* case, it might be permissible for the state to dismiss on statute of limitations grounds, either because the state statute is for present purposes the federal law or because it is an "otherwise valid excuse" [a] for declining to hear the federal cause of action.[b] If the Court means to coerce the state to create a remedy in this situation, would it be consistent to permit a statute of limitations dismissal?

Resolution of the ambiguities in *Ward* may be informed by the cases discussed in the following notes.[c]

2. *Iowa-Des Moines National Bank v. Bennett.* Iowa-Des Moines National Bank v. Bennett, 284 U.S. 239 (1931), involved a tax imposed by the state of Iowa on shares of stock of a national bank and a state bank. A comparable tax collected from corporate competitors of the two banks was from one-fifth to one-seventh as much. The banks complained that this was an illegal discrimination in violation of state law, the equal protection clause of the 14th amendment, and, in the case of the national bank, a federal statute permitting state taxes on national banks only to the extent that they were imposed on other similar entities. The unequal assessment was the result of a mistake by the county auditor in making up the list of tax assessments. The tax assessor had properly imposed the higher tax on all of the corporations involved (including the banks), but the auditor had mistakenly put the competing corporations into a different tax category and had certified an incorrect list to the county treasurer, who collected the taxes. The banks paid the taxes under protest after a threat of seizure of their property. Thereafter, they filed a mandamus action in the Iowa state courts against the appropriate county officials to compel a refund of that portion of the taxes exceeding those imposed on the other corporations.

The state supreme court held that relief was properly denied because, in the words of the United States Supreme Court:

> "[I]t held that the auditor's acts in disregarding assessments properly made were a usurpation of power and a nullity . . . . The court declared that, since the wrongful exaction was made without authority from the state, it did not consti-

---

[a] See page 237, *supra.*

[b] But compare the discussion of Engel v. Davenport, 271 U.S. 33 (1926), pages 267–68, *supra.*

[c] Review of *Testa v. Katt,* page 231, *supra,* may also be helpful to consideration of *Ward.*

tute discrimination by the state; declared that, since neither the auditor nor the treasurer had power to discharge a legally assessed tax, the competing domestic corporations remain, as far as appears, liable for the balance of the assessments; and held that the [banks] had no other remedy than to await action by the taxing authorities to collect the taxes remaining due from their competitors or to initiate proceedings themselves to compel such collection. In other words, it held that no right of [the banks] under the state law was violated, because they were not overassessed; that no right under federal law was violated, because the lower taxation of their competitors due to usurpation by officials was not an act of the state; and that the discrimination thus effected was remediable only by correcting the wrong under the state law in favor of the competitors and not 'by extending . . . the benefits as of a similar wrong' to the [banks]."

The United States Supreme Court held that the state court decision "rests upon a misconception of the scope and effect of the federal rights involved." It first held that the state was indeed responsible for the action of its officials, even though that action may have been in violation of state law. It then held that the fact that the state may have been able to equalize the taxes by collecting the higher tax from the competitors "is not material." The Court continued:

"The [banks'] rights were violated and the causes of action arose, when taxes at the lower rate were collected from their competitors. It may be assumed that all ground for a claim for refund would have fallen if the state, promptly upon discovery of the discrimination, had removed it by collecting the additional taxes from the favored competitors. By such collection the [banks'] grievances would have been redressed, for these are not primarily overassessment. The right invoked is that to equal treatment; and such treatment will be attained if either their competitors' taxes are increased or their own reduced. But it is well settled that a taxpayer who has been subjected to discriminatory taxation through the favoring of others in violation of federal law cannot be required himself to assume the burden of seeking an increase in the taxes which the others should have paid. Nor may he be remitted to the necessity of awaiting such action by the state officials upon their own initiative.

"The [banks] are entitled to obtain in these suits refund of the excess of taxes exacted from them."

Earlier, the Court had said in a footnote:

"The Supreme Court of Iowa held that the right to complain of this discrimination had been lost by failing to avail of the method of review prescribed by the state. We have no occasion to consider this matter, as we hold that the more favorable taxation of the competing domestic corporations entitles the [banks] to the relief sought."

There was no discussion of *Ward* in *Bennett*. Are the two cases related? The Court said in *Bennett* that the "causes of action arose, when taxes at the lower rate were collected from their competitors." Where did the causes of action come from? The state law of mandamus? Federal law? Some other source?

3. *Jackson v. Denno.* Both *Ward* and *Bennett* involve situations where a *plaintiff* sought to assert federal rights in a state court. Is the situation different when remedial action is sought in state court by a *defendant*?

Jackson v. Denno, 378 U.S. 368 (1964), involved the New York procedures for contesting the voluntariness of a confession.[d] *Jackson* is interesting in the present context for two points. First, the Court held that New York was required to hold an independent hearing, out of the presence of the trial jury, at which the voluntariness of confessions would be determined. It thus imposed upon the state the obligation to provide a remedy to test the violation of a federal right before admitting a confession into evidence in a criminal case. Unlike the situations in *Ward* and *Bennett*, in *Jackson* the Court could reverse any conviction in which the separate hearing had not been provided. Is this factor significant?

The second point for which *Jackson* is of present interest is the actual remedy ordered in that case. Jackson had been tried under the invalid procedure. His conviction had been affirmed in appeals through the New York courts. The case came to the Supreme Court following a habeas corpus petition filed in a federal district court. Relief had been denied by the lower federal courts. After holding the New York confession procedures unconstitutional, the Court then faced what should be done in the *Jackson* case itself. After noting that Jackson's allegations required a factual hearing in order to determine what happened at the time the confession was obtained, the Court continued:

> "[W]e think that the further proceedings to which Jackson is entitled should occur initially in the state courts rather than in the federal habeas corpus court. Jackson's trial did not comport with constitutional standards and he is entitled to a determination of the voluntariness of his confession in the state courts in accordance with valid state procedures; the state is also entitled to make this determination before this Court considers a case on direct review or a petition for habeas corpus is filed in a federal district court. . . .
>
> "It is New York, therefore, not the federal habeas corpus court, which should first provide Jackson with that which he has not yet had and to which he is constitutionally entitled—

[d] The prevailing New York procedures and the holding of the Supreme Court in *Jackson* are described at page 265, supra.

an adequate evidentiary hearing productive of reliable results concerning the voluntariness of his confession."

The Court then noted that the state should have the option of retrying Jackson or holding a hearing on the voluntariness of the confession used. If the confession were found involuntary, of course a new trial would be required. But if the confession were found voluntary, the court said that the fact that the voluntariness determination was made by the jury at Jackson's trial could be regarded as harmless error. The Court then concluded:

"Accordingly, the judgment denying [Jackson's] writ of habeas corpus is reversed and the case is remanded to the District Court to allow the state a reasonable time to afford Jackson a hearing or a new trial, failing which Jackson is entitled to his release."

Why was Jackson entitled to release if the state declined to hold a new hearing? Does *Jackson* stand for the proposition that the state must provide an adequate remedy to cure constitutional defects in its criminal processes?

Suppose a defendant convicted in state court claimed that appointed counsel was drunk during the entire trial and otherwise engaged in incompetent representation. Such a claim, if true, obviously entitles the defendant to a new trial, but a hearing must be held in order to determine its truth. If the state affords no procedure by which such a hearing can be held, does it follow from *Jackson* (and/or *Ward* and *Bennett*) that the defendant is automatically entitled to release or a new trial? Is a failure by the state to provide an adequate corrective process—a failure to provide an adequate remedy for an asserted violation of federal law—itself a sufficient basis for Supreme Court reversal of a state criminal conviction? [e] Is the fact that a federal court could hold such a hearing on habeas corpus relevant to the answer? Was it relevant in *Jackson* ? [f]

---

[e] This question—whether the state must provide a post-conviction procedure for the consideration of federal constitutional challenges that could not have been raised at trial—was presented to the Court in *Case v. Nebraska,* 381 U.S. 336 (1965). After the Court granted certiorari and briefs on the merits were submitted, Nebraska enacted a post-conviction procedure. The Court remanded the case for a hearing under the new procedure without deciding what would have happened had the new statute not been enacted.

[f] The Court also remanded for a state court hearing in *Henry v. Mississippi,* page 628, *supra.* The Supreme Court took *Hen-* ry on direct review from the Mississippi Supreme Court and, after holding that a hearing was necessary in order to decide whether Henry's attorney deliberately bypassed the state contemporaneous-objection rule, remanded the case to give the state courts an opportunity to hold the hearing. Unlike *Jackson,* however, *Henry* appears to contemplate that the hearing would be held by a federal habeas court if the state courts declined to do so. In fact, a state court held a hearing and found that a deliberate bypass had occurred. A federal habeas court subsequently disagreed and ordered Henry's release.

SECTION 3: MISCELLANEOUS PROBLEMS OF APPELLATE REVIEW

COOPERS & LYBRAND v. LIVESAY
Supreme Court of the United States, 1978.
437 U.S. 463 (1978).

MR. JUSTICE STEVENS delivered the opinion of the Court.

The question in this case is whether a District Court's determination that an action may not be maintained as a class action pursuant to Fed. Rule Civ. Proc. 23 is a "final decision" within the meaning of 28 U.S.C. § 1291 [1] and therefore appealable as a matter of right. [W]e granted certiorari and now hold that such an order is not appealable under § 1291.

Petitioner, Coopers & Lybrand, is an accounting firm that certified the financial statements in a prospectus issued in connection with a 1972 public offering of securities in Punta Gorda Isles for an aggregate price of over $18 million. Respondents purchased securities in reliance on that prospectus. In its next annual report to shareholders, Punta Gorda restated the earnings that had been reported in the prospectus for 1970 and 1971 by writing down its net income for each year by over $1 million. Thereafter, respondents sold their Punta Gorda securities and sustained a loss of $2,650 on their investment.

Respondents filed this action on behalf of themselves and a class of similarly situated purchasers. They alleged that petitioner and other defendants had violated various sections of the Securities Act of 1933 and the Securities Exchange Act of 1934. The District Court first certified, and then, after further proceedings, decertified the class.

Respondents did not request the District Court to certify its order for interlocutory review under 28 U.S.C. § 1292(b). [5] Rather, they filed a notice of appeal pursuant to § 1291. [6] The Court of Appeals regarded its appellate jurisdiction as depending on whether the decertification order had sounded the "death knell" of the action. After examining

---

[1] "The courts of appeals shall have jurisdiction of appeals from all final decisions of the district courts of the United States . . . except where a direct review may be had in the Supreme Court."

[5] Section 1292(b) provides:

"When a district judge, in making in a civil action an order not otherwise appealable under this section, shall be of the opinion that such order involves a controlling question of law as to which there is substantial ground for difference of opinion and that an immediate appeal from the order may materially advance the ultimate termination of the litigation, he shall so state in writing in such order. The Court of Appeals may thereupon, in its discretion, permit an appeal to be taken from such order, if application is made to it within ten days after the entry of the order: *Provided, however, That* application for an appeal hereunder shall not stay proceedings in the district court unless the district judge or the Court of Appeals or a judge thereof shall so order."

[6] Respondents also petitioned for a writ of mandamus directing the District Court to recertify the class. Since the Court of Appeals accepted appellate jurisdiction, it dismissed the petition for a writ of mandamus.

the amount of respondents' claims in relation to their financial resources and the probable cost of the litigation, the court concluded that they would not pursue their claims individually.[a] The Court of Appeals therefore held that it had jurisdiction to hear the appeal and, on the merits, reversed the order decertifying the class.

Federal appellate jurisdiction generally depends on the existence of a decision by the District Court that "ends the litigation on the merits and leaves nothing for the court to do but execute the judgment." Catlin v. United States, 324 U.S. 229, 233 (1945).[8] An order refusing to certify, or decertifying, a class does not of its own force terminate the entire litigation because the plaintiff is free to proceed on his individual claim. Such an order is appealable, therefore, only if it comes within an appropriate exception to the final-judgment rule. In this case respondents rely on the "collateral order" exception articulated by this Court in Cohen v. Beneficial Industrial Loan Corp., 337 U.S. 541 (1949), and on the "death knell" doctrine adopted by several circuits to determine the appealability of orders denying class certification.

I

In *Cohen,* the District Court refused to order the plaintiff in a stockholder's derivative action to post the security for costs required by a New Jersey statute. The defendant sought immediate review of the question whether the state statute applied to derivative suits in federal court. This Court noted that the purpose of the finality requirement "is to combine in one review all stages of the proceeding that effectively may be reviewed and corrected if and when final judgment results." Because immediate review of the District Court's order was consistent with this purpose, the Court held it appealable as a "final decision" under § 1291. The ruling had "settled conclusively the corporation's claim that it was entitled by state law to require the shareholder to post security for costs [and] concerned a collateral matter that could not be reviewed effectively on appeal from the final judgment."[9]

To come within the "small class" of decisions excepted from the final-judgment rule by *Cohen,* the order must conclusively determine the disputed question, resolve an important issue completely separate

[a] The plaintiffs had an aggregate annual income of $26,000 and a net worth of $75,000, only $4,000 of which was liquid. They had already spent $1,200 on the suit. Accumulated legal expenses had reached $15,000. The case was filed in the Eastern District of Missouri and, if it were to go to trial, would require extensive discovery in Florida and the retention of expert witnesses. [Footnote by eds.]

[8] For a unanimous Court in Cobbledick v. United States, 309 U.S. 323, 325 (1940), Mr. Justice Frankfurter wrote:

"Since the right to a judgment from more than one court is a matter of grace and not a necessary ingredient of justice, Congress from the very beginning has, by

forbidding piecemeal disposition on appeal of what for practical purposes is a single controversy, set itself against enfeebling judicial administration. Thereby is avoided the obstruction to just claims that would come from permitting the harassment and cost of a succession of separate appeals from the various rulings to which a litigation may give rise, from its initiation to entry of judgment. To be effective, judicial administration must not be leaden-footed. Its momentum would be arrested by permitting separate reviews of the component elements in a unified cause."

[9] Eisen v. Carlisle & Jacquelin, 417 U.S. 156, 171 (1974).

from the merits of the action, and be effectively unreviewable on appeal from a final judgment.[10] An order passing on a request for class certification does not fall in that category. First, such an order is subject to revision in the District Court. Fed. Rule Civ. Proc. 23(c)(1).[11] Second, the class determination generally involves considerations that are "enmeshed in the factual and legal issues comprising the plaintiff's cause of action." Mercantile Nat. Bank v. Langdeau, 371 U.S. 555, 558 (1963).[12] Finally, an order denying class certification is subject to effective review after final judgment at the behest of the named plaintiff or intervening class members. For these reasons, . . . the collateral-order doctrine is not applicable to the kind of order involved in this case.

II

Several circuits, including the Court of Appeals in this case, have held that an order denying class certification is appealable if it is likely to sound the "death knell" of the litigation. The "death knell" doctrine assumes that without the incentive of a possible group recovery the individual plaintiff may find it economically imprudent to pursue his lawsuit to a final judgment and then seek appellate review of an adverse class determination. Without questioning this assumption, we hold that orders relating to class certification are not independently appealable under § 1291 prior to judgment.

In addressing the question whether the "death knell" doctrine supports mandatory appellate jurisdiction of orders refusing to certify class actions, the parties have devoted a portion of their argument to the desirability of the small-claim class action. Petitioner's opposition to the doctrine is based in part on criticism of the class action as a vexatious kind of litigation. Respondents, on the other hand, argue that the class action serves a vital public interest and, therefore, special rules of appellate review are necessary to ensure that district judges are subject to adequate supervision and control. Such policy arguments, though proper for legislative consideration, are irrelevant to the issue we must decide.

---

[10] As the Court summarized the rule in *Cohen* :

"This decision appears to fall in that small class which finally determine claims of right separable from, and collateral to, rights asserted in the action, too important to be denied review and too independent of the cause itself to require that appellate consideration be deferred until the whole case is adjudicated."

[11] The rule provides that an order involving class status may be "altered or amended before the decision on the merits." Thus, a district court's order denying or granting class status is inherently tentative.

[12] "Evaluation of many of the questions entering into determination of class action questions is intimately involved with the merits of the claims. The typicality of the representative's claims or defenses, the adequacy of the representative, and the presence of common questions of law or fact are obvious examples. The more complex determinations required in Rule 23(b)(3) class actions entail even greater entanglement with the merits . . . ." 15 C. Wright, A Miller, E. Cooper, Federal Practice and Procedure § 3911, p. 485 n.45 (1976).

There are special rules relating to class actions and, to that extent, they are a special kind of litigation. Those rules do not, however, contain any unique provisions governing appeals. The appealability of any order entered in a class action is determined by the same standards that govern appealability in other types of litigation. Thus, if the "death knell" doctrine has merit, it would apply equally to the many interlocutory orders in ordinary litigation—rulings on discovery, on venue, on summary judgment—that may have such tactical economic significance that a defeat is tantamount to a "death knell" for the entire case.

Though a refusal to certify a class is inherently interlocutory, it may induce a plaintiff to abandon his individual claim. On the other hand, the litigation will often survive an adverse class determination. What effect the economic disincentives created by an interlocutory order may have on the fate of any litigation will depend on a variety of factors.[15] Under the "death knell" doctrine, appealability turns on the court's perception of that impact in the individual case. Thus, if the court believes that the plaintiff has adequate incentive to continue, the order is considered interlocutory; but if the court concludes that the ruling, as a practical matter, makes further litigation improbable, it is considered an appealable final decision.

The finality requirement in § 1291 evinces a legislative judgment that "[r]estricting appellate review to 'final decisions' prevents the debilitating effect on judicial administration caused by piecemeal appeal disposition of what is, in practical consequence, but a single controversy." *Eisen v. Carlisle & Jacquelin,* supra. Although a rigid insistence on technical finality would sometimes conflict with the purposes of the statute, *Cohen v. Beneficial Industrial Loan Corp.,* even adherents of the "death knell" doctrine acknowledge that a refusal to certify a class does not fall in that limited category of orders which, though nonfinal, may be appealed without undermining the policies served by the general rule. It is undisputed that allowing an appeal from such an order in the ordinary case would run "directly contrary to the policy of the final judgment rule embodied in 28 U.S.C. § 1291 and the sound reasons for it. . . ."[16] Yet several Courts of Appeals have sought to identify on a case-by-case basis those few interlocutory orders which, when viewed from the standpoint of economic prudence, may induce a plaintiff to abandon the litigation. These orders, then, become appealable as a matter of right.

In administering the "death knell" rule, the courts have used two quite different methods of identifying an appealable class ruling. Some courts have determined their jurisdiction by simply comparing the claims of the named plaintiffs with an arbitrarily selected jurisdictional

---

[15] E.g., the plaintiff's resources; the size of his claim and his subjective willingness to finance prosecution of the claim; the probable cost of the litigation and the possibility of joining others who will share that cost; and the prospect of prevailing on the merits and reversing an order denying class certification.

[16] Korn v. Franchard Corp., 443 F.2d 1301, 1305 (2d Cir. 1971).

amount;[17] others have undertaken a thorough study of the possible impact of the class order on the fate of the litigation before determining their jurisdiction. Especially when consideration is given to the consequences of applying these tests to pretrial orders entered in non-class-action litigation, it becomes apparent that neither provides an acceptable basis for the exercise of appellate jurisdiction.

The formulation of an appealability rule that turns on the amount of the plaintiff's claim is plainly a legislative, not a judicial, function. While Congress could grant an appeal of right to those whose claims fall below a specific amount in controversy, it has not done so. Rather, it has made "finality" the test of appealability. Without a legislative prescription, an amount-in-controversy rule is necessarily an arbitrary measure of finality because it ignores the variables that inform a litigant's decision to proceed, or not to proceed, in the face of an adverse class ruling.[18] Moreover, if the jurisdictional amount is to be measured by the aggregated claims of the named plaintiffs, appellate jurisdiction may turn on the joinder decisions of counsel rather than the finality of the order.

While slightly less arbitrary, the alternative approach to the "death knell" rule would have a serious debilitating effect on the administration of justice. It requires class-action plaintiffs to build a record in the trial court that contains evidence of those factors deemed relevant to the "death knell" issue and district judges to make appropriate findings. And one Court of Appeals has even required that the factual inquiry be extended to all members of the class because the policy against interlocutory appeals can be easily circumvented by joining "only those whose individual claims would not warrant the cost of separate litigation"; to avoid this possibility, the named plaintiff is required to prove that no member of the purported class has a claim that warrants individual litigation.

A threshold inquiry of this kind may, it is true, identify some orders that would truly end the litigation prior to final judgment; allowing an immediate appeal from those orders may enhance the quality of justice afforded a few litigants. But this incremental benefit is outweighed by the impact of such an individualized jurisdictional inquiry on the judicial system's overall capacity to administer justice.

The potential waste of judicial resources is plain. The district court must take evidence, entertain argument, and make findings; and the court of appeals must review that record and those findings simply to determine whether a discretionary class determination is subject to

[17] Thus, orders denying class certification have been held nonappealable because the plaintiffs alleged damages in the $3,000–$8,000 range. Smaller claims, however, have been held sufficient to support appellate jurisdiction in other cases.

[18] See n.15, supra. Thus, it is not at all clear that the prospect of recovering $3,000 would provide more incentive to sustain complex litigation against corporate defendants than the prospect of recovering $1,000. Yet the amount-in-controversy test allows an appeal in the latter case but not in the former. The arbitrariness of this approach is exacerbated by the fact that the Courts of Appeals have not settled on a specific jurisdictional amount; rather, they have simply determined on an ad hoc basis whether the plaintiff's claim is too small to warrant individual prosecution.

appellate review. And if the record provides an inadequate basis for this determination, a remand for further factual development may be required. Moreover, even if the court makes a "death knell" finding and reviews the class-designation order on the merits, there is no assurance that the trial process will not again be disrupted by interlocutory review. For even if a ruling that the plaintiff does not adequately represent the class is reversed on appeal, the district court may still refuse to certify the class on the ground that, for example, common questions of law or fact do not predominate. Under the "death knell" theory, plaintiff would again be entitled to an appeal as a matter of right pursuant to § 1291. And since other kinds of interlocutory orders may also create the risk of a premature demise, the potential for multiple appeals in every complex case is apparent and serious.

Perhaps the principal vice of the "death knell" doctrine is that it authorizes indiscriminate interlocutory review of decisions made by the trial judge. The Interlocutory Appeals Act of 1958, 28 U.S.C. § 1292(b), was enacted to meet the recognized need for prompt review of certain nonfinal orders. However, Congress carefully confined the availability of such review. Nonfinal orders could never be appealed as a matter of right. Moreover, the discretionary power to permit an interlocutory appeal is not, in the first instance, vested in the courts of appeals.[24] A party seeking review of a nonfinal order must first obtain the consent of the trial judge. This screening procedure serves the dual purpose of ensuring that such review will be confined to appropriate cases and avoiding time-consuming jurisdictional determinations in the court of appeals.[25] Finally, even if the district judge certifies the order under § 1292(b), the appellant still "has the burden of persuading the court of appeals that exceptional circumstances justify a departure from the basic policy of postponing appellate review until after the entry of a final judgment." Fisons, Ltd. v. United States, 458 F.2d 1241, 1248 (7th Cir. 1972). The appellate court may deny the appeal for any reason, including docket congestion. By permitting appeals of right from class-designation orders after jurisdictional determinations that turn on

---

[24] Thus, Congress rejected the notion that the courts of appeals should be free to entertain interlocutory appeals whenever, in their discretion, it appeared necessary to avoid unfairness in the particular case. H.R. Rep. No. 1667, 85th Cong., 2d Sess., 4–6 (1958); Note, Interlocutory Appeals in the Federal Courts under 28 U.S.C. § 1292(b), 88 Harv. L. Rev. 607, 610 (1975).

[25] Rep. No. 1667, supra, at 5–6:

". . . The problem . . . is to provide a procedural screen through which only the desired cases may pass, and to avoid the wastage of a multitude of fruitless applications to invoke the amendment contrary to its purpose.

". . . Requirement that the trial court certify the case as appropriate for

appeal serves the double purpose of providing the appellate court with the best informed opinion that immediate review is of value, and at once protects appellate dockets against a flood of petitions in inappropriate cases. [A]voidance of ill-founded applications in the courts of appeals for piecemeal review is of particular concern. If the consequence of change is to be crowded appellate dockets as well as any substantial number of unjustified delays in the trial court, the benefits to be expected from the amendment may well be outweighed by the lost motion of preparation, consideration, and rejection of unwarranted applications for its benefits."

questions of fact, the "death knell" doctrine circumvents these restrictions.[27]

Additional considerations reinforce our conclusion that the "death knell" doctrine does not support appellate jurisdiction of prejudgment orders denying class certification. First, the doctrine operates only in favor of plaintiffs even though the class issue—whether to certify, and if so, how large the class should be—will often be of critical importance to defendants as well. Certification of a large class may so increase the defendant's potential damages liability and litigation costs that he may find it economically prudent to settle and to abandon a meritorious defense. Yet the courts of appeals have correctly concluded that orders granting class certification are interlocutory. Whatever similarities or differences there are between plaintiffs and defendants in this context involve questions of policy for Congress. Moreover, allowing appeals of right from nonfinal orders that turn on the facts of a particular case thrusts appellate courts indiscriminately into the trial process and thus defeats one vital purpose of the final-judgment rule—"that of maintaining the appropriate relationship between the respective courts. . . . This goal, in the absence of most compelling reasons to the contrary, is very much worth preserving." [29]

Accordingly, we hold that the fact that an interlocutory order may induce a party to abandon his claim before final judgment is not a sufficient reason for considering it a "final decision" within the meaning of § 1291.[30] The judgment of the Court of Appeals is reversed with directions to dismiss the appeal.

It is so ordered.

---

[27] Several courts of appeals have heard appeals from discretionary class determinations pursuant to § 1292(b). As Judge Friendly has noted: "[T]he best solution is to hold that appeals from the grant or denial of class action designation can be taken only under the procedure for interlocutory appeals provided by 28 U.S.C. § 1292(b). . . . Since the need for review of class action orders turns on the facts of the particular case, this procedure is preferable to attempts to formulate standards which are necessarily so vague as to give rise to undesirable jurisdictional litigation with concomitant expense and delay." Parkinson v. April Industries, Inc., 520 F.2d 650, 660 (2d Cir. 1975) (concurring opinion).

[29] *Parkinson v. April Industries, Inc.,* supra at 654.

[30] Respondents also suggest that the Court's decision in Gillespie v. United States Steel Corp., 379 U.S. 148 (1964), supports appealability of a class-designation order as a matter of right. We disagree. In *Gillespie,* the Court upheld an exercise of appellate jurisdiction of what it considered a marginally final order that disposed of an unsettled issue of national significance because review of that issue unquestionably "implemented the same policy Congress sought to promote in § 1292(b)" and the arguable finality issue had not been presented to this Court until argument on the merits, thereby ensuring that none of the policies of judicial economy served by the finality requirement would be achieved were the case sent back with the important issue undecided. In this case, in contrast, respondents sought review of an inherently nonfinal order that tentatively resolved a question that turns on the facts of the individual case; and, as noted above, the indiscriminate allowance of appeals from such discretionary orders is plainly inconsistent with the policies promoted by § 1292(b). If *Gillespie* were extended beyond the unique facts of that case § 1291 would be stripped of all significance.

NOTES ON CIRCUIT COURT REVIEW OF FINAL DECISIONS IN THE DISTRICT COURTS

1. **The "Collateral Order" Doctrine:** *Cohen v. Beneficial Industrial Loan Corp.* The only clearly recognized exception to the finality requirement of § 1291 was created in Cohen v. Beneficial Industrial Loan Corp., 337 U.S. 541 (1949). *Cohen* was a stockholder's derivative action based on diversity jurisdiction. The applicable state law required the plaintiff shareholders to post security for costs in order to discourage harassment by strike suits. The Federal Rules of Civil Procedure did not speak to the issue. The problem on the merits was whether, in a diversity action otherwise governed by state law, the state security-for-costs provision applied.

The District Court refused to require security, and the question was whether this decision was immediately appealable. The Supreme Court held that the District Court's action was a "final" judgment under § 1291:

"The effect of the statute is to disallow appeal from any decision which is tentative, informal or incomplete. Appeal gives the upper court a power of review, not one of intervention. So long as the matter remains open, unfinished or inconclusive, there may be no intrusion by appeal. But the District Court's action upon this application was concluded and closed and its decision final in that sense before the appeal was taken.

"Nor does the statute permit appeals, even from fully consummated decisions, where they are but steps towards final judgment in which they will merge. The purpose is to combine in one review all stages of the proceeding that effectively may be reviewed and corrected if and when final judgment results. But this order of the District Court did not make any step toward final disposition of the merits of the case and will not be merged in final judgment. When that time comes, it will be too late effectively to review the present order and the rights conferred by the statute, if it is applicable, will have been lost, probably irreparably. We conclude that the matters embraced in the decision appealed from are not of such an interlocutory nature as to affect, or to be affected by, decision of the merits of this case.

"This decision appears to fall in that small class which finally determine claims of right separate from, and collateral to, rights asserted in the action, too important to be denied review and too independent of the cause itself to require that appellate consideration be deferred until the whole case is adjudicated. The Court has long given this provision of the statute this practical rather than a technical construction.

"We hold this order appealable because it is a final disposition of a claimed right which is not an ingredient of the cause of action and does not require consideration with it. But we do not mean that every order fixing security is subject to appeal. Here it is the right to security that presents a serious and unsettled question. If the right were admitted or clear and the order involved only an exercise of discretion as to the amount of security, a matter the statute makes subject to reconsideration from time to time, appealability would present a different question."

2. *Gillespie v. United States Steel Corp.* A different approach to § 1291 was taken in Gillespie v. United States Steel Corp., 379 U.S. 148 (1964). Gillespie was the administratrix of her son's estate. She brought suit in federal court alleging that the defendant had negligently caused her son's death while he was working on a docked ship in Ohio. She asserted causes of action based on the Jones Act and on the Ohio wrongful death statute and sought recovery both for herself and for the decedent's surviving brother and sisters.

The District Court dismissed the state cause of action, reasoning that the Jones Act supplied the exclusive remedy in this situation. It also held that the brother and sisters could not recover under the Jones Act while the mother was living, and accordingly struck those portions of the complaint referring to them. Gillespie appealed immediately to the Court of Appeals. The defendant moved to dismiss the appeal on the ground that the District Court decision was not "final" under § 1291. Gillespie responded with a petition for mandamus to coerce the district judge either to reinstate the dismissed charges or certify the issue for interlocutory appeal under § 1292(b). The brother and sisters joined in the mandamus petition.

The Court of Appeals held the appeal proper, denied the petition for mandamus, and upheld the District Court on the merits. As summarized by the Supreme Court, the Court of Appeals said "it was free to [hear the appeal] since its resolution of the merits did not prejudice [the defendant] in any way, because it sustained [the defendant's] contentions by denying the petition for mandamus and affirming the District Court's order." The Supreme Court granted certiorari and affirmed both on the question of appealability and on the merits. On the final judgment issue it said:

> "In this Court respondent joins petitioner in urging us to hold that 28 U.S.C. § 1291 does not require us to dismiss this case and that we can and should decide the validity of the District Court's order to strike. We agree. [A]s this Court has often pointed out, a decision 'final' within the meaning of § 1291 does not necessarily mean the last order possible to be made in a case. Cohen v. Beneficial Industrial Loan Corp., 337 U.S. 541 (1949). And our cases long have recognized that whether a ruling is 'final' . . . is frequently so close a question that decision of that issue either way can be supported with equally forceful arguments, and that it is impossible to devise a formula to resolve all marginal

cases coming within what might well be called the 'twilight zone' of finality. Because of this difficulty this Court has held that the requirement of finality is to be given a 'practical rather than a technical construction.' *Cohen v. Beneficial Industrial Loan Corp.,* supra. . . . Dickenson v. Petroleum Conversion Corp, 338 U.S. 507, 511 (1950), pointed out that in deciding the question of finality the most important competing considerations are 'the inconvenience and costs of piecemeal review on the one hand and the danger of denying justice by delay on the other.' Such competing considerations are shown by the record in the case before us. It is true that the review of this case by the Court of Appeals could be called 'piecemeal'; but it does not appear that the inconvenience and cost of trying this case will be greater because the Court of Appeals decided the issues raised instead of compelling the parties to go to trial with them unanswered. We cannot say that the Court of Appeals chose wrongly under the circumstances. And it seems clear now that the case is before us that the eventual costs, as all parties recognize, will certainly be less if we now pass on the questions presented here rather than send the case back with those issues undecided. Moreover, delay of perhaps a number of years in having the brother's and sisters' rights determined might work a great injustice on them, since the claims for recovery for their benefit have been effectively cut off as long as the district judge's ruling stands. And while their claims are not formally severable so as to make the court's order unquestionably appealable as to them, there certainly is ample reason to view their claims as severable in deciding the issue of finality, particularly since the brother and sisters were separate parties in the petition for extraordinary relief. Furthermore, in United States v. General Motors Corp., 323 U.S. 373, 377 (1945), this Court contrary to its usual practice reviewed a trial court's refusal to permit proof of certain items of damages in a case not yet fully tried, because the ruling was 'fundamental to the further conduct of the case.' . . . We think that the questions presented here are equally 'fundamental to the further conduct of the case.' It is true that if the district judge had certified the case to the Court of Appeals under 28 U.S.C. § 1291(b), the appeal unquestionably would have been proper; in light of the circumstances we believe that the Court of Appeals properly implemented the same policy Congress sought to promote in § 1291(b) by treating this obviously marginal case as final and appealable under 28 U.S.C. § 1291."

Justice Harlan dissented on the appealability question. He thought the issue of finality not close at all, that no injustice would have been done to the brother and sisters by treating them like everybody else, that *Cohen* and *General Motors* [a] were irrelevant, and that the existence of § 1291(b) cut against, not in favor, of the Court's decision. He concluded:

> "Finally, the Court's suggestion that 'it seems clear now that the case is before us that the eventual costs, as all the parties recognize, will certainly be less if we not pass on the questions presented here rather than send the case back with those issues undecided,' furnishes no excuse for avoidance of the finality rule. Essentially such a position would justify review here of any case decided by a court of appeals whenever this Court, as it did in this instance, erroneously grants certiorari and permits counsel to brief and argue the case on the merits. That, I believe, is neither good law nor sound judicial administration."

3. ***Firestone Tire & Rubber Co. v. Risjord.*** Firestone Tire & Rubber Co v. Risjord, 449 U.S. 368 (1981), is a significant post-*Coopers & Lybrand* decision that reinforces its approach to the finality question. Risjord was lead counsel in four product liability cases against Firestone. Firestone was insured for some types of losses by the Home Insurance Co., which was an occasional client of Risjord's firm and for whom Risjord was the defense counsel in an unrelated case. Firestone filed a motion to disqualify Risjord as the plaintiffs' counsel, arguing that he had a conflict of interest that would cause him to structure the claims for relief so that they would not be covered by the insurance. The District Court ordered that Risjord terminate his representation of the plaintiffs unless both the plaintiffs and Home consented to his continuing in the case. The requisite consent was obtained, and the court allowed Risjord to continue. At this point Firestone appealed, arguing that the District Court's decision was "final" within the meaning of § 1291. The Court of Appeals held the order not appealable, but also held that its decision would apply prospectively. It accordingly reached the merits of the disqualification issue.

The Supreme Court granted certiorari. It held that the case would have to come within *Cohen* in order to be appealable, and that it did not do so:

> "An order denying a disqualification motion meets the first part of the 'collateral order' test. It 'conclusively determine[s] the disputed question,' because the only issue is whether challenged counsel will be permitted to continue his representation.[b] In addition, we will assume, although we do not

---

[a] As to *General Motors,* he said:

"The jurisdictional defect in this case arises only from the lack of finality of the District Court's order. In *General Motors, . . .* the District Court had entered a final judgment, but the Court of Appeals reversed and remanded the case for further proceedings. Thus the finality question before this Court was simply whether it should review a nonfinal order of the Court of Appeals, which of course the Court clearly has authority to do under 28 U.S.C. § 1254(1)."

[b] Justice Rehnquist, joined by Chief Justice Burger, filed a separate opinion concurring in the result in which he objected to this statement because it was possible that the trial judge would reconsider his position if an actual incident demonstrating a conflict of interest were to occur at a

decide, that the disqualification question 'resolve[s] an important issue completely separate from the merits of the action.' the second part of the test. Nevertheless, petitioner is unable to demonstrate that an order denying disqualification is 'effectively unreviewable on appeal from a final judgment' within the meaning of our cases."

The Court held that any prejudice that occurred during the trial because of Risjord's participation could, like other errors that may occur during the trial, be corrected on appeal at the conclusion of the case.[c] It also held that the Court of Appeals had been incorrect in not applying this rule to the case before it:

"[T]he finality requirement embraced in § 1291 is jurisdictional in nature. . . . . If the appellate court finds that the order from which a party seeks to appeal does not fall within the statute, its inquiry is over. A court lacks discretion to consider the merits of a case over which it is without jurisdiction, and thus, by definition, a jurisdictional ruling may never be made prospective only."

4. *Moses H. Cone Memorial Hospital v. Mercury Constr. Corp.* Moses H. Cone Memorial Hospital v. Mercury Constr. Corp., 460 U.S. 1 (1983), presented another finality issue. This time the Court held the disputed order "final."

Mercury contracted to build additions to the Hospital. Disputes involving performance of the work or interpretation of the contract were first to be referred to the architect. Either party could invoke arbitration if unsatisfied with the architect's decision. The project was delayed, and Mercury claimed that the Hospital was liable for some of the costs of the delay. After a complicated series of events, the Hospital sued both Mercury and the architect in state court seeking a declaratory judgment that Mercury's claim was without foundation, that Mercury had lost its right to arbitration under the terms of the contract, and that if adjudged liable to Mercury, the Hospital was entitled to indemnity from the architect. Shortly thereafter, Mercury filed a diversity action against the Hospital seeking an order compelling arbitration. The District Court stayed the federal suit in favor of the state court proceedings. The Court of Appeals reversed and instructed the District Court to enter an order compelling arbitration. The Supreme Court granted certiorari.

The question was whether an order by a District Court staying a federal suit in favor of state court proceedings was "final" under § 1291. The Court held that it was. The object of the stay, according

later stage of the proceedings. [Footnote by eds.]

[c] The Court subsequently held unanimously in Flanagan v. United States, 465 U.S. 259 (1984), that pretrial orders disqualifying counsel in criminal cases also did not fit within the *Cohen* collateral order rule and were therefore not appealable

until the conclusion of the trial. The issue returned in Richardson-Merrell, Inc. v. Koller, 472 U.S. 424 (1985), where the Court held, over a dissent by Justice Stevens, that appeal of the disqualification of counsel in a civil case likewise must await the conclusion of the trial.

to the Court, "was to require all or an essential part of the federal suit to be litigated in a state forum." Since the "issue of arbitrability was the only substantive issue present in the federal suit" and since the District Court planned to defer to the state court on the question, "a stay of the federal suit pending resolution of the state suit meant that there would be no further litigation in the federal forum; the state court's judgment on the issue would be res judicata." The stay order thus was final because Mercury was "effectively out of court."

Alternatively, the Court held that the case satisfied the "collateral order" doctrine. As in *Coopers & Lybrand* and *Risjord,* it divided the inquiry into three components: whether the order "conclusively determine[d] the disputed question," whether it "resolve[d] an important issue completely separate from the merits of the action," and whether it was "effectively unreviewable on appeal from a final judgment." The Court's analysis was:

> "There can be no dispute that this order meets the second and third of these criteria. An order that amounts to a refusal to adjudicate the merits plainly presents an important issue separate from the merits. For the same reason, this order would be entirely unreviewable if not appealed now. Once the state court decided the issue of arbitrability, the federal court would be bound to honor that determination as res judicata.

> "The Hospital contends nevertheless that the District Court's stay order did not meet the first of the criteria, namely that it 'conclusively determine the disputed question.' But this is true only in the technical sense that every order short of a final decree is subject to reopening at the discretion of the district judge. In this case, however, there is no basis to suppose that the district judge contemplated any reconsideration of his decision to defer to the parallel state-court suit. He surely would not have made that decision in the first instance unless he had expected the state court to resolve all relevant issues adequately. It is not clear why the judge chose to stay the case rather than to dismiss it outright; for all that the record shows, there was no reason other than the form of the Hospital's motion. Whatever the reason, however, the practical effect of his order was entirely the same for present purposes, and the order was appealable."

The Court then addressed the propriety of the stay order on the merits and reversed.[d]

Justice Rehnquist, joined by Chief Justice Burger and Justice O'Connor, dissented on the appealability question. He characterized the District Court's order as "tentative"—"subject to change on a showing that the state proceedings were being delayed, . . . or that

[d] This aspect of *Cone* is considered beginning at page 555, supra. For a recent entry in the Court's application of the "collateral order" doctrine, see Stringfellow v. Concerned Neighbors in Action, 480 U.S. 370 (1987), holding that the denial of intervention of right accompanied by the grant of permissive intervention under stated restrictions was not appealable.

the state courts were not [following federal law], or that for some other reason a change had arisen." He thus thought the collateral order doctrine inapplicable:

> "The likelihood that a state court of competent jurisdiction may enter a judgment that may determine some issue in a case does not render final a federal district court's decision to take a two day recess, or to order additional briefing by the parties in five days or five months, or to take a case under advisement rather than render an immediate decision from the bench. Such a possibility did not magically change that character of the order the district judge entered in this case. . . .

> "The Court's decision places an unwarranted limitation upon the power of district courts to control their own cases. The Court's opinion does not establish a broad exception to § 1291, but it does create uncertainty about when a district court order in a pending case can be appealed. This uncertainty gives litigants opportunities to disrupt or delay proceedings by taking colorable appeals from interlocutory orders, not only in cases nearly identical to this but in cases which the ingenuity of counsel disappointed by a district court's ruling can analogize to this one. . . . The occasional injustice to a litigant that results from an erroneous district court decision is far outweighed by the far greater systemic disruption created by encouraging parties to attempt interlocutory appeals. . . ."

5. Questions and Comments. The *Cohen* case states a reasonably well-defined and narrow exception to the finality requirement of § 1291, though its malleability is illustrated by the contrast between *Risjord* and *Cone*. *Gillespie*, on the other hand, explicitly proposes a much more open-ended inquiry. Which case states the better approach? What role does the Court's assessment of the importance of the appealed issue have on its determination of finality?

The Court's approach to finality under § 1291 is undoubtedly influenced by the independent availability of interlocutory review.[e]

---

[e] In Van Cauwenberghe v. Biard, ___ U.S. ___ (1988), for example, the Court held that the *Cohen* collateral order doctrine did not permit immediate appeal from a district court order denying a motion to dismiss on the ground of forum non conveniens. It added:

"Our conclusion . . . is fortified by the availability of interlocutory review pursuant to 28 U.S.C. § 1292(b). Under § 1292(b), a district court may certify a nonfinal order for interlocutory review when the order 'involves a controlling question of law as to which there is substantial ground for difference of opinion and . . . an immediate appeal from the order may materially advance the ultimate termination of the litigation.' A court of appeals may then, in its discretion, determine whether the order warrants prompt review. Section 1292(b) therefore provides an avenue for review of forum non conveniens determinations in appropriate cases."

For general treatment of the various methods by which district court judgments can be reviewed, see Redish, The Pragmatic Approach to Appealability in the Federal Courts, 75 Colum. L. Rev. 89 (1975), and Note, Appealability in the Federal Courts, 75 Harv. L. Rev. 351 (1961). See also Theodore Frank's discussion in Requiem for the Final Judgment Rule, 45 Tex. L. Rev. 292 (1966). For a comprehensive effort to restate the law on 28 U.S.C. §§ 1291, 1292, and 1651 with accompany-

Section 1292(a) permits interlocutory review in three sorts of cases: orders of district courts "granting, continuing, modifying, refusing or dissolving injunctions, or refusing to dissolve or modify injunctions," certain orders of district courts concerning receiverships, and certain orders of district courts in admiralty cases. Section 1292(b), the purpose of which is discussed in *Coopers & Lybrand,* permits decision in the court of appeals if the district judge certifies a "controlling question of law" for interlocutory review under criteria stated in the statute.[f]

Two other possibilities for interlocutory review—Rule 54(b) and mandamus—should be noted. Rule 54(b) of the Federal Rules of Civil Procedure provides:

> "When more than one claim for relief is presented in an action, whether as a claim, counterclaim, cross-claim, or third-party claim, or when multiple parties are involved, the court may direct the entry of a final judgment as to one or more but fewer than all the claims or parties only upon an express determination that there is no just reason for delay and upon an express direction for the entry of judgment. In the absence of such determination and direction, any order or other form of decision, however designated, which adjudicates fewer than all the claims or the rights and liabilities of fewer than all the parties shall not terminate the action as to any of the claims or parties, and the order or other form of decision is subject to revision at any time before the entry of judgment adjudicating all the claims and the rights and liabilities of all the parties."

The requirement of an "express determination" by the district judge that the matter is severable and appropriate for appeal lends clarity to the situations governed by this provision.[g]

Depending on the precise nature of the claims, it is possible that Rule 54(b) could have been used by the district judge in *Gillespie*. If not, § 1292(b) may have been available. But both provisions depend on a determination by the district judge that immediate appeal is the efficient way to handle the matter. It is clear that district courts have substantial discretion to invoke either procedure.[h] A district judge who refuses to invoke either procedure can be corrected only by extraordinary writ unless the court of appeals is prepared to hold, as in *Gillespie*, that a "final" decision has been made.

---

ing commentary, see Civil Appellate Jurisdiction, Parts I and II, in the Spring and Summer editions of 47 Law & Contemp. Probs. (1984). Discussion of finality in specific contexts can be found in Note, Interlocutory Appeal of Orders Granting or Denying Stays of Arbitration, 80 Mich. L. Rev. 153 (1981), and Note, A Test for Appealability: The Final Judgment Rule and Closure Orders, 65 Minn. L. Rev. 1110 (1981).

[f] See Note, Interlocutory Appeals in the Federal Courts under 28 U.S.C.A. § 1292(b), 88 Harv. L. Rev. 607 (1975).

[g] The validity of Rule 54(b) was confirmed in Sears, Roebuck & Co. v. Mackey, 351 U.S. 427 (1956).

[h] The Court held in Curtiss Wright Corp. v. General Electric Co., 446 U.S. 1 (1980), that a determination that Rule 54(b) should be invoked to permit an immediate appeal could be overturned by a court of appeals "only if it can say that the judge's conclusion was clearly unreasonable." By the very terms of § 1292(b), of course, the interlocutory appeal must be acceptable to both the district court and the court of appeals before it can go forward.

Mandamus, which the courts of appeal are authorized to grant by 28 U.S.C. § 1651(a), is another way in which an interlocutory appeal can be effected.[i] Obviously, however, if mandamus were routinely available the "final judgment" requirement of § 1291 would be undermined and there would be no point to Rule 54(b) and the opportunities for interlocutory appeal provided in § 1292. It is not surprising, therefore, that the general conception of mandamus is that it is an extraordinary writ designed only for extraordinary situations. The cases defy convenient categorization, although there are pockets of the law where mandamus has been used with some frequency.[j] There is a sense in which the writ functions like the grant or denial of certiorari in the Supreme Court. A litigant who seeks mandamus bears the burden of showing that there are important reasons for *immediate* appellate intervention. It also functions like certiorari in the sense that intervention may be justified in order to correct errors on questions of significance beyond the immediate case.

Will v. United States, 389 U.S. 90 (1967), illustrates the kinds of arguments that might be persuasive. The District Court had ordered the government to give the defendant certain documents in a criminal trial. The government refused. The court then indicated that it would dismiss the indictment, but the government was able to get a writ of mandamus in the Court of Appeals to forestall that action. On certiorari the Supreme Court first recited some of the traditional platitudes about the scope of the writ: "it is clear that only exceptional circumstances amounting to a judicial 'usurpation of power' will justify the invocation of this extraordinary remedy"; mandamus is appropriate only "to confine an inferior court to a lawful exercise of its prescribed jurisdiction or to compel it to exercise its authority when it is its duty to do so." More importantly, the Court seemed to accept the premise of the government's argument, though it held the argument inapplicable to the facts presented. The government argued that the district judge had displayed a "pattern of manifest noncompliance with the rules governing federal criminal trials"—in effect that he had committed the same error in many cases and that it would be expensive and inefficient to correct them one by one. The Court conceded that the writ serves "a vital corrective and didactic function" and that it could be used for "expository and supervisory" purposes. But as noted, the Court rejected the applicability of these arguments to the record in the case before it.

---

[i] For general treatment of the availability of mandamus as a form of interlocutory review, see Griffin Bell's discussion in The Federal Appellate Courts and the All Writs Act, 23 Sw. L.J. 858 (1969). Edmund Kitch addressed the subject in the context of intrajurisdictional transfers in Section 1404(a) of the Judicial Code: In the Interest of Justice or Injustice, 40 Ind. L.J. 99, 110–31 (1965). See also Note, The Use of Extraordinary Writs for Interlocutory Appeals, 44 Tenn. L. Rev. 137 (1976); Note, Supervisory and Advisory Mandamus Under the All Writs Act, 86 Harv. L. Rev. 595 (1973); Note, Mandamus Proceedings in the Federal Courts of Appeals: A Compromise with Finality, 52 Cal. L. Rev. 1036 (1964); Note, The Effect of Mandamus on the Final Decision Rule, 57 Nw. L. Rev. 709 (1963).

[j] For example, the improper denial of a jury trial is usually correctable by application for a writ of mandamus in the court of appeals. See C. Wright, The Law of Federal Courts 712 (4th ed. 1983).

6. *Gulfstream Aerospace Corp. v. Mayacamas Corp.* Gulfstream sued Mayacamas in state court for breach of contract. Mayacamas filed an answer and a counterclaim, declining to remove the case although it could have done so on diversity grounds. One month later Mayacamas filed a diversity action in federal court against Gulf-stream alleging breach of the same contract. Gulfstream moved for a stay or dismissal of the federal court action based on the *Colorado River* decision.[k] The District Court denied the motion. The Court of Appeals held that decision unreviewable on appeal and refused to issue a writ of mandamus. In Gulfstream Aerospace Corp. v. Mayacamas Corp., ___ U.S. ___ (1988), the Supreme Court unanimously affirmed.[l] Three grounds were advanced for review of the District Court decision.

(i) Appeal Under § 1291. First, it was argued that the order was appealable under the "collateral order" doctrine of *Cohen*. After reviewing the decision in *Cone*, the Court held:

"Application of the collateral-order test to an order denying a motion to stay or dismiss an action pursuant to *Colorado River* . . . leads to a different result. We need not decide whether the denial of such a motion satisfies the second and third prongs of the collateral-order test . . . because the order fails to meet the initial requirement of a conclusive determination of the disputed question. A district court that denies a *Colorado River* motion does not 'necessarily contemplate' that the decision will close the matter for all time. In denying such a motion, the district court may well have determined only that it should await further developments before concluding that the balance of factors to be considered under *Colorado River* warrants a dismissal or stay. The district court, for example, may wish to see whether the state-court proceeding becomes more comprehensive than the federal-court action or whether the former begins to proceed at a more rapid pace. Thus, whereas the granting of a *Colorado River* motion necessarily implies an expectation that the state court will resolve the dispute, the denial of such a motion may indicate nothing more than that the district court is not completely confident of the propriety of a stay or dismissal at that time. Indeed, given both the nature of the factors to be considered under *Colorado River* and the natural tendency of courts to attempt to eliminate matters that need not be decided from their dockets, a district court will expect to revisit and reassess an order denying a stay in light of events occurring in the normal course of litigation. Because an order denying a *Colorado River* motion is 'inherently tentative' in this critical sense—because it is not 'made with the expectation that it will be the final word on the subject addressed'—the order is not a conclu-

---

[k] See page 541, supra.

[l] Justice Scalia joined the Court's opinion, but also wrote separately. Justice Kennedy did not participate.

sive determination within the meaning of the collateral-order doctrine and therefore is not appealable under § 1291."

Justice Scalia thought this analysis incomplete. He said it "over-simplifies somewhat to assign as the reason merely that the order is 'inherently tentative.'" *Cohen* was inapplicable, in his view, not only because the motion was likely to be renewed and reconsidered, but also because "the relief will be just as effective, or nearly as effective, if accorded at a later date—that is, the harm caused during the interval between initial denial and reconsideration will not be severe. More-over, since these two conditions will almost always be met when the asserted basis for an initial stay motion is the pendency of state proceedings, the more general conclusion that initial orders denying *Colorado River* motions are never immediately appealable is justified." He also added the following observations:

> "I note that today's result could also be reached by applica-tion of the rule adopted in the First Circuit, that to come within the *Cohen* exception the issue on appeal must involve 'an important and unsettled question of controlling law,' not merely a question of the proper exercise of the trial court's discretion. This approach has some support in our opinions [citing *Cohen* and *Coopers & Lybrand*], as well as in policy. This rationale has not been argued here, and we should not embrace it without full adversarial exploration of its conse-quences. I do think, however, that our finality jurisprudence is sorely in need of further limiting principles, so that *Cohen* appeals will be, as we originally announced they would be, a 'small class [of decisions] too important to be denied review.'"

(ii) Appeal Under § 1292(a)(1). Section 1292(a)(1) of title 28 authorizes appeals from interlocutory orders granting or denying an injunction. Ordinarily, the Court said, "[a]n order by a federal court that relates only to the conduct or progress of litigation before that court . . . is not considered an injunction and therefore is not appeala-ble under § 1292(a)(1)." But the *Enelow-Ettelson* doctrine, it was argued, created an exception to this principle and allowed an appeal in this instance.

This doctrine stemmed from two earlier decisions[m] that were based on the separation of law and equity. If a plaintiff filed an action at law and the defendant sought a stay of the proceedings in order to resolve an equitable defense, the "Court likened the stay to an injunction issued by an equity court to restrain an action at law." On that reasoning, an appeal from the denial of such a stay was allowed under § 1291(a)(1), even after the merger of law and equity.

The Court held in *Gulfstream Aerospace* that the *Enelow-Ettelson* doctrine was a "total fiction" that was "'divorced from any rational or

[m] Enelow v. New York Life Ins. Co., 293 U.S. 379 (1935); Ettelson v. Metropolitan Life Ins. Co., 317 U.S. 188 (1942).

coherent appeals policy.' " It accordingly overruled the cases that gave rise to the doctrine and refused to permit the appeal on this ground.

(iii) **Mandamus.** It was also argued that the Court of Appeals should have reviewed the District Court decision by issuing a writ of mandamus. The Court made short work of this contention. It reiterated the standard doctrine that "mandamus is an extraordinary remedy, to be reserved for extraordinary situations" and held:

> "Petitioner has failed to satisfy this stringent standard. This Court held in *Colorado River* that a federal court should stay or dismiss an action because of the pendency of a concurrent state-court proceeding only in 'exceptional' circumstances and with 'the clearest of justifications.' Petitioner has failed to show that the District Court clearly overstepped its authority in holding that the circumstances of this case were not so exceptional as to warrant a stay or dismissal under *Colorado River*. This Court never has intimated acceptance of petitioner's view that the decision of a party to spurn removal and bring a separate suit in federal court invariably warrants the stay or dismissal of the suit under the *Colorado River* doctrine. Indeed, in *Cone* we held that a District Court's decision to grant a stay pending resolution of an identical matter in state court was an abuse of discretion, notwithstanding that the party who brought the action in federal court could have removed the state-court suit. This holding cannot be reconciled with the notion that the decision of a party to forgo removal and file an independent action in federal court requires a stay or dismissal of the federal-court litigation. Petitioner therefore has failed to show that the District Court's order denying a stay or dismissal of the federal-court suit warranted the issuance of a writ of mandamus."

7. Footnote on Supreme Court Review of Cases in the Courts of Appeals. As Justice Harlan pointed out in *Gillespie* (see page 667, footnote a, supra), review by the Supreme Court of a court of appeals decision is not constrained by a finality requirement. Section 1254 of title 28 provides that cases "in" the courts of appeals may be reviewed by the Supreme Court. Thus, if a court of appeals remands for further proceedings in the district court, review in the Supreme Court is available even though the court of appeals' order is not a "final" disposition of the case. Moreover, once a case has been docketed in a court of appeals, § 1254 provides that certiorari may be granted by the Supreme Court "before or after rendition of judgment or decree." Certiorari before judgment is not, of course, routinely granted.[n]

---

[n] For a study of the frequency of such review and the criteria under which it is exercised, see Lindgren and Marshall, The Supreme Court's Extraordinary Power to Grant Certiorari Before a Judgment of the Court of Appeals, 1986 Sup. Ct. Rev. 259.

NOTES ON SUPREME COURT REVIEW OF FINAL DECISIONS BY STATE COURTS

1. Introduction. The first Congress enacted the Judiciary Act of 1789, which established the federal court system and conferred jurisdiction on the Supreme Court to review state court decisions. That statute gave the Supreme Court jurisdiction over federal questions decided by the highest court of a state against a person claiming a federal right.[a] It was not until 1914 that the successor statute was modified to extend the jurisdiction of the Court to decisions by state courts in favor of federal claimants. The present statutory authority to review state court decisions is contained in 28 U.S.C. § 1257, which provides for review by certiorari of all "[f]inal judgments or decrees rendered by the highest court of a State in which a decision could be had . . . ."

2. *Cox Broadcasting Corp. v. Cohn.* Cox Broadcasting Corp. v. Cohn, 420 U.S. 469 (1975), is well known for its effort to rationalize the law on the question whether a state court decision is "final" for purposes of Supreme Court review. The issue in *Cox,* as the Court stated it, was "whether, consistently with the first and 14th amendments, a state may extend a cause of action for damages for invasion of privacy caused by the publication of the name of a deceased rape victim which was publicly revealed in connection with the prosecution of the crime." A Georgia trial court had recognized such a cause of action and had entered summary judgment on the question of liability against a TV newsman, his station, and its corporate owner. The newsman had learned the identity of the rape victim from the indictments, which were available for public inspection as part of the court records in the criminal case. The state supreme court agreed that a cause of action for publication of the victim's name could be asserted, but reversed the entry of summary judgment and remanded the case for trial on several issues of fact. The Supreme Court reversed on the merits, holding that the first and 14th amendments precluded the state from recognizing a cause of action under these circumstances. The issue of present interest is its holding that the judgment of the Georgia Supreme Court was "final" and that the merits could therefore be reached at this stage of the proceedings.

(i) The Majority. Justice White's opinion for the Court began by summarizing the prior decisions on the finality issue:

> "Since 1789, Congress has granted this Court appellate jurisdiction with respect to state litigation only after the highest state court in which judgment could be had has rendered a '[f]inal judgment or decree.' Title 28 U.S.C. § 1257 retains this limitation on our power to review cases coming from state courts. The Court has noted that '[c]onsiderations of English

---

[a] Review was by writ of error, which is the functional equivalent of appeal as of right. Discretionary jurisdiction to hear certain classes of cases by writ of certiorari was introduced in 1916 and made the exclusive form of review of state court decisions in 1988.

usage as well as those of judicial policy' would justify an interpretation of the final-judgment rule to preclude review 'where anything further remains to be determined by a state court . . . .' Radio Station WOW, Inc. v. Johnson, 326 U.S. 120, 124 (1945). But the Court there observed that the rule had not been administered in such a mechanical fashion and that there were circumstances in which there has been 'a departure from this requirement of finality for federal appellate jurisdiction.'

"These circumstances were said to be 'very few'; but as the cases have unfolded, the Court has recurringly encountered situations in which the highest court of a state has finally determined the federal issue present in a particular case, but in which there are further proceedings in the lower state courts to come. There are now at least four categories of such cases in which the Court has treated the decision on the federal issue as a final judgment for the purposes of 28 U.S.C. § 1257 . . . . In most, if not all, of the cases in these categories, these additional proceedings would not require the decision of other federal questions that might also require review by the Court at a later date, and immediate rather than delayed review would be the best way to avoid 'the mischief of economic waste and of delayed justice,' as well as precipitate interference with state litigation. In the cases in the first two categories considered below, the federal issue would not be mooted or otherwise affected by the proceedings yet to be had because those proceedings have little substance, their outcome is certain, or they are wholly unrelated to the federal question. In the other two categories, however, the federal issue would be mooted if the petitioner or appellant seeking to bring the action here prevailed on the merits in the later state-court proceedings, but there is nevertheless sufficient justification for immediate review of the federal question finally determined in the state courts."

Justice White then described the four categories of cases. The first included

"those cases in which there are further proceedings—even entire trials—yet to occur in the state courts but where for one reason or another the federal issue is conclusive or the outcome of further proceedings preordained. In these circumstances, because the case is for all practical purposes concluded, the judgment of the state court on the federal issue is deemed final."

Justice White's illustration of this first category was Mills v. Alabama, 384 U.S. 214 (1966). As he described that case:

"a demurrer to a criminal complaint was sustained on federal constitutional grounds by a state trial court. The state Supreme Court reversed, remanding for jury trial. This Court took jurisdiction on the reasoning that the appellant had no defense other than his federal claim and could not prevail at trial on the facts or any nonfederal ground. To dismiss the appeal 'would not only be an inexcusable delay of the benefits Congress intended to grant by providing for appeal to this Court, but it would also result in a completely unnecessary waste of time and energy in judicial systems already troubled by delays due to congested dockets.' "

The second category included cases "in which the federal issue, finally decided by the highest court in the state, will survive and require decision regardless of the outcome of future state-court proceedings." Among Justice White's illustrations of this category was Brady v. Maryland, 373 U.S. 83 (1963), in which, as he described it

"the Maryland courts had ordered a new trial in a criminal case but on punishment only, and the petitioner asserted here that he was entitled to a new trial on guilt as well. We entertained the case, saying that the federal issue was separable and would not be mooted by the new trial on punishment ordered in the state courts."

The third category consisted of

"those situations where the federal claim has been finally decided, with further proceedings on the merits in the state courts to come, but in which later review of the federal issue cannot be had, whatever the ultimate outcome of the case. Thus, in these cases, if the party seeking interim review ultimately prevails on the merits, the federal issue will be mooted; if he were to lose on the merits, however, the governing state law would not permit him again to present his federal claims for review."

This category was illustrated by North Dakota State Board of Pharmacy v. Snyder's Drug Stores, Inc., 414 U.S. 156 (1973). There,

"the pharmacy board rejected an application for a pharmacy operating permit relying on a state statute specifying ownership requirements which the applicant did not meet. The state supreme court held the statute unconstitutional and remanded the matter to the board for further consideration of the application, freed from the constraints of the ownership statute. The board brought the case here, claiming that the statute was constitutionally acceptable under modern cases. After reviewing the various circumstances under which the finality requirement has been deemed satisfied despite the fact that litigation had not terminated in the state courts, we entertained the case over claims that we had no jurisdiction. The federal issue would not survive the remand, whatever the result of the state administrative proceedings. The board might deny the license on state-law grounds, thus foreclosing the federal issue, and the Court also ascertained that under state law the board could not bring the federal issue here in the event the applicant satisfied the requirements of state law except for the invalidated ownership statute. Under these circumstances, the issue was ripe for review."

The final category was the one in which *Cox* itself was thought to fit. It was described as

"those situations where the federal issue has been finally decided in the state courts with further proceedings pending in which the party seeking review here might prevail on the merits on nonfederal grounds, thus rendering unnecessary review of the federal issue by this Court, and where reversal of the state court on the federal issue would be preclusive of any further litigation on the relevant cause of action rather than merely controlling the nature and character of, or determining the admissibility of evidence in, the state proceedings still to come. In these circumstances, if a refusal immediately to review the state-court decision might seriously erode federal policy, the Court has entertained and decided the federal issue, which itself has been finally determined by the state courts for purposes of the state litigation."

The Court illustrated this fourth category by reference to Mercantile National Bank at Dallas v. Langdeau, 371 U.S. 555 (1963), where

"two national banks were sued, along with others, in the courts of Travis County, Tex. The claim asserted was conspiracy to defraud an insurance company. The banks as a preliminary matter asserted that a special federal venue statute immunized them from suit in Travis County and that they could properly be sued only in another county. Although trial was still to be had and the banks might well prevail on the merits, the Court, relying on *Curry*, entertained the issue as a 'separate and independent matter, anterior to the merits and not enmeshed in the factual and legal issues comprising the plaintiff's cause of action.' Moreover, it would serve the policy of the federal statute 'to determine now in which state court appellants may be tried rather than to subject them . . . to long and complex litigation which may all be for naught if consideration of the preliminary question of venue is postponed until the conclusion of the proceedings.' "

The Court also referred to Miami Herald Publishing Co. v. Tornillo, 418 U.S. 241 (1974), as "the latest case in this category." As Justice White explained:

"There a candidate for public office sued a newspaper for refusing, allegedly contrary to a state statute, to carry his reply to the paper's editorial critical of his qualifications. The trial court held the act unconstitutional, denying both injunctive relief and damages. The state supreme court reversed, sustaining the statute against the challenge based upon the first and 14th amendments and remanding the case for a trial and appropriate relief, including damages. The newspaper brought the case here. We sustained our jurisdiction, relying on the principles elaborated in the *North Dakota* case and observing:

> 'Whichever way we were to decide on the merits, it would be intolerable to leave unanswered, under these circumstances, an important question of freedom of the press under the first amendment; an uneasy and unsettled constitutional posture of [the state statute] could only further harm the operation of a free press.' "

Against this background, the Court concluded that the judgment before it was final. It reasoned:

> "The Georgia Supreme Court's judgment is plainly final on the federal issue and is not subject to further review in the state courts. Appellants will be liable for damages if the elements of the state cause of action are proved. They may prevail at trial on nonfederal grounds, it is true, but if the Georgia court erroneously upheld the statute, there should be no trial at all. Moreover, even if appellants prevailed at trial and made unnecessary further consideration of the constitutional question, there would remain in effect the unreviewed decision of the state supreme court that a civil action for publishing the name of a rape victim disclosed in a public judicial proceeding may go forward despite the first and 14th amendments. Delaying final decision of the first amendment claim until after trial will "leave unanswered . . . an important question of freedom of the press under the first amendment," "an uneasy and unsettled constitutional posture [that] could only further harm the operation of a free press." *Tornillo,* supra. On the other hand, if we now hold that the first and 14th amendments bar civil liability for broadcasting the victim's name, this litigation ends. Given these factors—that the litigation could be terminated by our decision on the merits and that a failure to decide the question now will leave the press in Georgia operating in the shadow of the civil and criminal sanctions of a rule of law and a statute the constitutionality of which is in serious doubt—we find that reaching the merits is consistent with the pragmatic approach that we have followed in the past in determining finality."

Chief Justice Burger concurred without opinion, and Justices Powell and Douglas wrote separately on the first amendment question.

(ii) **The Dissent.** Justice Rehnquist dissented on the finality issue. He first regretted the gradual erosion of the finality requirement, indicating that he would take a narrower approach to the finality question on review of state court decisions than on review of district court decisions by circuit courts:

> "Were judicial efficiency the only interest at stake there would be less inclination to challenge the Court's resolution in this case, although, as discussed below, I have serious reservations

that the standards the Court has formulated are effective for achieving even this single goal. The case before us, however, is an appeal from a state court, and this fact introduces additional interests which must be accommodated in fashioning any exception to the literal application of the finality requirement. I consider § 1257 finality to be one of a number of congressional provisions reflecting concern that uncontrolled federal judicial interference with state administrative and judicial functions would have untoward consequences for our federal system.[4] . . .

"That comity and federalism are significant elements of § 1257 finality has been recognized by other members of the Court as well, perhaps most notably by Mr. Justice Harlan. In [his dissent in *Langdeau*], he argued that one basis of the finality rule was that it foreclosed 'this Court from passing on constitutional issues that may be dissipated by the final outcome of a case, thus helping to keep to a minimum undesirable federal-state conflicts.' [W]e have in recent years emphasized and re-emphasized the importance of comity and federalism in dealing with a related problem, that of district court interference with ongoing state judicial proceedings. See Younger v. Harris, 401 U.S. 37 (1971). Because these concerns are important, and because they provide "added force" to § 1257's finality requirement, I believe that the Court has erred by [limiting its] concern [to] efficient judicial administration."

Justice Rehnquist then shifted to a different theme, charging that the Court had adopted "a virtually formless exception to the finality requirement, one which differs in kind from those previously carved out." He found five problems with the Court's test. First, it required a preliminary judgment on the merits as part of the finality inquiry. Second, he could not distinguish this case from any other in which a state court had rejected a federal claim at an intermediate stage of the proceedings. Third, he thought the right at stake not important enough to justify a departure from normal procedures. Fourth, he thought the Court had abandoned the salutary "principle that constitutional issues are too important to be decided save when absolutely necessary, and are to be avoided if there are grounds for decision of lesser dimension":

"In this case there has yet to be an adjudication of liability against appellants, and . . . they do not concede that they have no non-federal defenses. Nonetheless, the Court rules on their constitutional defense. Far from eschewing a constitutional holding in advance of the necessity for one, the Court

---

[4] "See, e.g., 28 U.S.C. § 1341 (limitation on power of district courts to enjoin state taxing systems); 28 U.S.C. § 1739 (requiring that state judicial proceedings be accorded full faith and credit in federal courts); 28 U.S.C. §§ 2253–54 (prescribing various restrictions on federal habeas corpus for state prisoners); 28 U.S.C. § 2281 (three judge court requirement); 28 U.S.C. § 2283 (restricting power of federal courts to enjoin state-court proceedings)."

construes § 1257 so that it may virtually rush out and meet the prospective constitutional litigant as he approaches our doors."

Finally, he speculated

"that after the Court has studied briefs and heard oral argument, it has an understandable tendency to proceed to a decision on the merits in preference to dismissing for want of jurisdiction. It is thus especially disturbing that the rule of this case, unlike the more workable and straightforward exceptions which the Court has previously formulated, will seriously compound the already difficult task of accurately determining, at a preliminary stage, whether an appeal from a state-court judgment is a 'final judgment or decree.'"

He elaborated this last point by examining the awkward position in which the Court's rule placed the practicing attorney and the potential impact of the decision on the Court's docket. Faced with an uncertain rule, attorneys could be expected to seek interlocutory review in order to assure that an issue would not be lost for lack of timely filing. "The inevitable result will be totally unnecessary additions to our docket and serious interruptions and delays of the state adjudicatory process."

3. *Southland Corp. v. Keating.* *Cox* was reaffirmed in Southland Corp. v. Keating, 465 U.S. 1 (1984). Owners of 7–Eleven franchises in California sued Southland Corp., the franchisor, alleging violation, inter alia, of the California Franchise Investment Law. Southland requested arbitration under the terms of the franchise contract. The California Supreme Court held that disputes concerning the Franchise Investment Law required judicial resolution, and also held that this interpretation of California law was not inconsistent with the requirements of the Federal Arbitration Act. The case was thus remanded for trial on the merits of the Investment Law claims.

Southland appealed to the Supreme Court, which held that the California Supreme Court decision was "final" under 28 U.S.C. § 1257(2). After summarizing *Cox*, the Court said:

"Without immediate review of the California holding by this Court there may be no opportunity to pass on the federal issue and as a result 'there would remain in effect the unreviewed decision of the state supreme court' holding that the California statute does not conflict with the Federal Arbitration Act. On the other hand, reversal of a state court judgment in this setting will terminate litigation of the merits of this dispute.

"Finally, failure to accord immediate review of the decision of the California Supreme Court might 'seriously erode federal policy.' Plainly the effect of the judgment of the California court is to nullify a valid contract made by private parties under which they agreed to submit all contract disputes to final, binding arbitration. . . . Contracts to arbitrate are not to be avoided by allowing one party to ignore the contract and resort to the courts. Such a course could lead to prolonged litigation, one of the very risks the parties, by contracting for arbitration, sought to eliminate. . . .

"For us to delay review of a state judicial decision denying enforcement of the contract to arbitrate until the state court litigation has run its course would defeat the core purpose of a contract to arbitrate. We hold that the Court has jurisdiction to decide whether the Federal Arbitration Act preempts . . . the California Franchise Investment Law [on the issues in dispute]."

The Court then held that the Federal Arbitration Act required arbitration in this context, that it was enforceable in state court, and that the California Franchise Investment Law violated the supremacy clause. It remanded for entry of an arbitration order. Justices Stevens and O'Connor [b] filed separate dissents on the merits of the arbitration issue. Neither dissent questioned the passages quoted above.

4. *Hathorn v. Lovorn.* Hathorn v. Lovorn, 457 U.S. 255 (1982), involved the requirement in the Voting Rights Act of 1965 that states submit certain changes in election procedures to the federal government for approval. The Mississippi Supreme Court reversed a trial court decision challenging a new election procedure and remanded for further proceedings. The question of compliance with the federal preclearance procedure was raised for the first time in a petition for rehearing. The court denied the petition without comment, and the United States Supreme Court denied certiorari. The state trial court then ordered an election under the new procedure, subject to approval by the United States Attorney General. The Attorney General declined to approve the new procedure, however, and after some complicated maneuvering the case was again appealed to the Mississippi Supreme Court. That court held that its prior decision constituted "the law of the case" upholding the procedure and not conditioning its use on prior approval by federal authorities. It accordingly ordered an election under the new procedure.

The Supreme Court granted certiorari and reversed. Before reaching the merits, it considered the argument that the lower court's reliance on the "law of the case" doctrine barred review at this stage of the proceedings:

"It has long been established . . . that '[w]e have jurisdiction to consider all of the substantial federal questions determined in the earlier stages of [state proceedings] and our right to re-examine such questions is not affected by a ruling that the first decision of the state court became the law of the case . . . .' Reece v. Georgia, 350 U.S. 85 (1955). Because we cannot review a state court judgment until it is final, a contrary rule would insulate interlocutory state court rulings on important federal questions from our consideration.

[b] Justice Rehnquist joined the O'Connor dissent.

"In this case the Mississippi Supreme Court's first decision plainly did not appear final at the time it was rendered. The court's remand . . . together with its failure to address expressly the Voting Rights Act issue, suggested that the [trial court] could still consider the federal issue on remand. . . . Under these circumstances, the Mississippi Supreme Court's subsequent reliance on the law of the case cannot prevent us from reviewing federal questions determined in the first appeal."

5. Questions and Comments. The history of Supreme Court interpretation of the finality requirement of § 1257 is summarized in Justice White's attempt in *Cox* to categorize the exceptional situations where technically non-final state judgments were nonetheless subject to review in the Supreme Court. Does Justice White develop a coherent picture of what constitutes a "final" judgment? In particular, is his fourth category—the one involved in *Cox* and *Southland*—sufficiently well-defined to be meaningful? [c] Consider also the resolution in *Hathorn*. Is it clear that the first decision by the Mississippi Supreme Court would not be reviewable under Justice White's third category? If it would be, does that undermine the Court's reasoning in *Hathorn*? Or is this a situation in which the state court judgment became "final" at two different stages and could be reviewed by the Supreme Court at either? [d]

Section 1291 authorizes courts of appeals to review "final decisions" of district courts. The Supreme Court is authorized by § 1257 to review "final judgments or decrees" of state courts. The Court appears to have given § 1291 a far more rigid construction than § 1257, in spite of Justice Rehnquist's argument that § 1257 should be the more strictly construed. What accounts for the Court's result? Should it matter whether interlocutory review has been permitted within the state system? How important is it that there are established methods of interlocutory review in the federal system?

Also, consider whether *Cox* is consistent with the rationale underlying the adequate and independent state ground rule.[e] If that doctrine

[c] It is suggested in Note, The Finality Rule for Supreme Court Review of State Court Orders, 91 Harv. L. Rev. 1004, 1025 (1978), that the fourth *Cox* category is "virtually limitless" because it turns on one's ad hoc assessment of the importance of various federal rights.

[d] The policies underlying the final judgment requirement are explored by Timothy Dyk in Supreme Court Review of Interlocutory State-Court Decisions: "The Twilight Zone of Finality," 19 Stan. L. Rev. 907 (1967), which was written before *Cox* but which considers many of the cases on which it relies. For post-*Cox* consideration of the same questions, see Note, The Finality Rule for Supreme Court Review of State Court Orders, 91 Harv. L. Rev. 1004,

1025 (1978), and Note, Civil Procedure—New Insight on Finality of State Court Judgments, 1975 Ariz. L.J. 627. See also Bartke, "Finality" Four Years Later—Some Reflections and Recommendations, 9 Baylor L. Rev. 350 (1976); Note, The Requirement of a Final Judgment or Decree for Supreme Court Review of State Courts, 73 Yale L.J. 515 (1964). For the latest developments in the debate over the breadth of the *Cox* exceptions, see Goodyear Atomic Corp. v. Miller, __ U.S. __ (1988) (accepting review under fourth category); Pennsylvania v. Ritchie, 480 U.S. 39 (1987) (5–4 decision on the finality issue).

[e] Cf. Matasar and Bruch, Procedural Common Law, Federal Jurisdictional Policy, and Abandonment of the Adequate and

is based on a constitutional obligation to avoid advisory opinions, should the Court be free to decide federal questions that may not control the outcome of the case if further proceedings are conducted in the state courts?

FURTHER NOTES ON TECHNICAL ASPECTS OF SUPREME COURT REVIEW OF STATE DECISIONS

1. Initiating Review. One of the concerns raised in *Murdock v. City of Memphis*, page 597, supra, was how the Court should deal with frivolous federal issues raised on review of state court decisions. *Murdock* came to the Court on a writ of error, a procedure under which the Court was required to review federal questions properly before it. As the Court noted, cases involving frivolous federal questions had become "such a burden and abuse that we either refuse to hear, or hear only one side of many such, and stop the argument, and have been compelled to adopt a rule that when a motion is made to dismiss it shall only be heard on printed argument." More formal procedures to deal with this problem have since been developed.

The institution of review by writ of certiorari was an early answer.[a] Under Supreme Court Rule 17, "review on writ of certiorari is not a matter of right, but of judicial discretion, and will be granted only when there are special and important reasons therefor." That discretion is exercised after the petitioner has filed a formal "petition for a writ of certiorari" and the respondent has had an opportunity to file a response. The Court then acts on the petition.[b] Full briefs and oral argument will usually follow if the petition is granted.

Until 1988, appeals remained available as of right, at least as a formal matter, in two classes of cases coming from the state courts.[c] Under Supreme Court Rule 12(3), the formal requirements for docketing an appeal included the filing of a "jurisdictional statement" by the appellant. Rule 15 required that this document contain a "statement of the reasons why the questions presented are so substantial as to

---

Independent State Grounds Doctrine, 86 Colum.L.Rev. 1291, 1355 (1986): "[T]he finality exceptions . . . *are* inconsistent with the adequacy doctrine, but justifiably so, because they further the primary mission Congress contemplated for the Court as a vigilant guardian of federal supremacy and uniformity. It is not the finality exceptions, but the adequate and independent state grounds doctrine that flies in the face of federal jurisdictional policy."

[a] For a thoughtful treatment of many of the issues discussed below, and indeed in this entire chapter, see Wechsler, The Appellate Jurisdiction of the Supreme Court: Reflections on the Law and Logistics of Direct Review, 34 Wash. & Lee L. Rev. 1043 (1977).

[b] By tradition, four votes are sufficient to grant the writ. See the quotation from Justice Stone's opinion in the *Bailey* case, page 260, supra. The Court may limit the grant to only some of the issues presented in the petition. Scott Bice has extensively analyzed this practice in The Limited Grant of Certiorari and the Justification of Judicial Review, 1975 Wis. L. Rev. 343.

[c] Specifically, appeals were permitted if "the validity of a treaty or statute of the United States" was drawn in question "and the decision [was] against its validity" and if "the validity of a statute of any state" was drawn in question "on the ground of its being repugnant to the Constitution, treaties or laws of the United States, and the decision [was] in favor of its validity."

require plenary consideration, with briefs on the merits and oral argument, for their resolution." The opposing party was then given an opportunity to file a motion to dismiss or affirm, after which the Court in most cases would either "note probable jurisdiction" (indicating that it most likely would hear the case on the merits) or "dismiss for want of a substantial federal question".[d] The latter disposition was an indication that the standard of Rule 15 had not been met.[e]

Congress amended 28 U.S.C. § 1257 in 1988 to make certiorari the exclusive method of reviewing state court decisions.[f] Thus the Court no longer is compelled by the language of § 1257 to hear any case that comes from a state court.

2. The Meaning of Summary Disposition of Appeals. It is often said that the denial of a petition for certiorari is not a decision on the merits and accordingly has no precedential value.[g] A more difficult question was posed, however, by the pre-1988 requirement that some state court cases (as well as some cases coming from federal courts) be heard on appeal. Many of these cases were disposed of summarily, that is, without full briefing and oral argument. What is the precedential value of such dispositions? Must the Supreme Court and the lower state and federal courts treat these decisions as resolving the merits of the issues presented?

Since both petitions for certiorari and pre-1988 appeals required the filing of a preliminary document on the basis of which the Court decided whether to hear the case, one could have taken the position that the refusal to hear an appeal should be treated the same as the refusal to hear a case on a writ of certiorari. Indeed, for a substantial period of time, many courts and a substantial segment of the bar probably so regarded the summary disposition of an appeal.[h]

[d] Occasionally, the Court would summarily reverse at this stage, a disposition for which it has been criticized. See Hart, Forward: The Time Chart of the Justices, 73 Harv. L. Rev. 84, 89 & n. 13 (1959); cf. Brown, Forward: Process of Law, 72 Harv. L. Rev. 77 (1958).

[e] Arthur Hellman extensively analyzed the Court's management of its docket in The Supreme Court, the National Law, and the Selection of Cases for the Plenary Docket, 44 U. Pitt. L. Rev. 521 (1983), and Error Correction, Lawmaking, and the Supreme Court's Exercise of Discretionary Review, 44 U. Pitt. L. Rev. 795 (1983). In A Managerial Theory of the Supreme Court's Responsibilities, 59 N.Y.U. L. Rev. 681 (1984), Samuel Estreicher and John Sexton addressed the criteria the Court should use in selecting cases for review. Theirs is the lead article in a massive study of the Supreme Court's workload extending over three volumes of the N.Y.U. Law Review.

[f] There were also cases coming from the federal Circuit Courts that 28 U.S.C. § 1254 required to be heard by appeal before the 1988 amendment, specifically where a state statute had been held "invalid as repugnant to the Constitution, treaties or laws of the United States". The 1988 amendment also removed the Court's obligatory jurisdiction over these cases.

[g] Thus, the orthodox view suggests that no inferences can be drawn from denials of certiorari. Peter Linzer undertook an extensive analysis of this proposition in The Meaning of Certiorari Denials, 79 Colum. L. Rev. 1227 (1979). He concluded that "the orthodox view is oversimplified, and in some cases, false" and that "[u]nder standing how to use denials of certiorari can be of great use to writers, practitioners, and judges."

[h] For example, Chief Justice Warren told the American Law Institute in 1954 that it was "only accurate to a degree to say that our jurisdiction in cases on appeal is obligatory as distinguished from discretionary on certiorari." Weiner, The Supreme Court's New Rules, 68 Harv. L. Rev. 20, 51 (1954). And Justice Clark said in a concur-

That situation was clarified, however, in Hicks v. Miranda, 422 U.S. 332 (1975). A three-judge District Court held that it was not bound by a prior Supreme Court dismissal of an appeal. The Court responded:

"[T]he District Court was in error in holding that it could disregard the decision [dismissing the prior case for want of a substantial federal question]. That case was an appeal from a decision by a state court upholding a state statute against federal constitutional attack. A federal constitutional issue was properly presented, it was within our appellate jurisdicion under § 1257(2), and we had no discretion to refuse adjudication of the case on its merits as would have been true had the case been brought here under our certiorari jurisdiction. We were not obligated to grant the case plenary consideration, and we did not; but we were required to deal with its merits. We did so by concluding that the appeal should be dismissed because the constitutional challenge was not a substantial one. The three-judge court was not free to disregard this pronouncement. . . ."

The Supreme Court has been clear that it may reconsider prior summary decisions in the light of subsequent plenary presentation of the issues presented.[i] But there has been no departure from the message of *Hicks* that lower state and federal courts are not free to disregard summary decisions by the Supreme Court.[j]

3. Decision by the "Highest State Court." The requirement in § 1257 that any decision in which review is sought must have been "rendered by the highest court of a State in which a decision could be had" in effect enacts an obligation that the parties exhaust all available

ring opinion in a case on which he was sitting by designation after he retired from the Court that throughout his tenure on the Court, appeals from state courts "received treatment similar to that accorded petitions for certiorari and were given about the same precedential weight." Hogge v. Johnson, 526 F.2d 833, 836 (4th Cir. 1975).

[i] See, e.g., Edelman v. Jordan, 415 U.S. 651 (1974), the relevant passages in which are quoted at pages 823–24, infra. Though *Edelman* was decided before *Hicks*, there is no indication that *Hicks* was intended to modify the Supreme Court's freedom in this regard.

[j] For further elaboration of the requirement and some of the problems presented, see Illinois State Board of Elections v. Socialist Workers Party, 440 U.S. 173 (1979), Mandel v. Bradley, 432 U.S. 173 (1977), and Fusari v. Steinberg, 419 U.S. 379 (1975). Justice Brennan sharply criticized *Hicks* in a dissent from the denial of certiorari in Colorado Springs Amusements, Ltd. v. Rizzo, 428 U.S. 913 (1976).

Hicks has been commented upon widely in the literature. See, e.g., Linzer, The Meaning of Certiorari Denials, 79 Colum. L. Rev. 1227, 1291–99 (1979); Tushnet, The Mandatory Jurisdiction of the Supreme Court—Some Recent Developments, 46 U. Cinn. L. Rev. 347 (1977); Note, The Supreme Court Dismissal of State Court Appeals for Want of a Substantial Federal Question, 15 Creighton L. Rev. 749 (1982); Note, The Precedential Effect of Summary Affirmances and Dismissals for Want of a Substantial Federal Question by the Supreme Court after *Hicks v. Miranda* and *Mandel v. Bradley*, 64 Va. L. Rev. 117 (1978); Comment, The Precedential Weight of a Dismissal by the Supreme Court for Want of a Substantial Federal Question: Some Implications of *Hicks v. Miranda*, 76 Colum. L. Rev. 508 (1976); Note, Summary Disposition of Supreme Court Appeals: The Significance of Limited Discretion and a Theory of Limited Precedent, 52 Boston U. L. Rev. 373 (1972).

judicial remedies in the state courts before seeking review in the United States Supreme Court.[k] Supreme Court review of a state trial court decision is thus permissible if no further (obligatory or discretionary) review is available within the state court system, as happened in the famous "no evidence" case, Thompson v. City of Louisville, 362 U.S. 199 (1960) (police court conviction for minor offense set aside as violation of due process on the ground that there was "no evidence" in the record to support the conviction).

4. Federal Question Raised Properly, Preserved, and Decided. No federal question is open to review unless it has been raised properly, preserved, and decided under the procedures used by the courts from which the case has come. Thus, a question litigated at the trial level may not be open to Supreme Court review if no appeal is sought within the state court system on that question, even though the case is otherwise considered by the state supreme court. And of course if the question is not raised at all at trial or is raised too late, or is raised for the first time on appeal or in a petition for rehearing, review may be unavailable in the United States Supreme Court.

The word "may" has been used advisedly in describing this requirement. There are two reasons why the Court may regard it appropriate to consider an issue even though these rules have not been followed. The first is that if the state courts decide the issue on the merits anyway—in effect overlooking their own procedural requirements—the Supreme Court will not refuse to consider the question on the ground that local procedures have not been followed. Thus, under this doctrine review is unavailable only in those cases where the state courts rely on a "procedural foreclosure," that is, where they foreclose review of the merits of a question because it has not been properly raised and preserved.

The second exception is based on the fairness of the opportunity which the local procedural rules give for raising the question. In effect, if a question is raised at the first realistically available opportunity, if no fair chance is given to the parties to raise the issue, or if it appears that local rules have been applied in a manner that suggests evasion of the federal question, the Supreme Court may overlook the failure and regard the issue as appropriate for review. These conclusions, as explored at pages 628–47, supra, are reached through application of the "adequate and independent state ground" doctrine.

---

[k] It is not required, however, that a discretionary rehearing be sought in a state supreme court after that court has disposed of the case on the merits. See Local 174, Teamster's Union v. Lucas Flour Co., 369 U.S. 95 (1962).

Chapter VII

FEDERAL HABEAS CORPUS

SECTION 1: THE STRUCTURE OF FEDERAL HABEAS CORPUS

INTRODUCTORY NOTES ON FEDERAL HABEAS CORPUS

1. Statutory Authority. There were several forms of the ancient writ of habeas corpus. The one that is most important today tests the legality of the detention of an accused or convicted criminal offender.[a] This form of habeas corpus is a new lawsuit, separate from the underlying criminal prosecution, in which a person who is in custody as a result of a criminal charge or conviction challenges the custodian to defend the legality of the detention.[b]

Statutory authority to hear habeas corpus cases was conferred on the federal courts by the Judiciary Act of 1789—but only for federal prisoners. It was not until 1867 that federal habeas corpus was made available to state prisoners. As currently codified, 28 U.S.C. § 2241(a) authorizes federal courts to grant habeas corpus, but § 2241(c)(3) provides that "the writ of habeas corpus shall not extend to a prisoner" unless the prisoner is "in custody in violation of the Constitution or laws or treaties of the United States." Other important limitations on issuance of the writ are stated in §§ 2242-55, the major features of which are explained in subsequent materials.

2. Section 2255. These materials focus on habeas corpus for state prisoners. A word should be added, however, about 28 U.S.C. § 2255. Section 2255 was adopted in 1948 as an alternative for federal prisoners to the writ of habeas corpus authorized by § 2241. Essentially, it is a venue provision.

The proper venue in a habeas corpus action is the place where the prisoner is in custody. Before the enactment of § 2255, this placed

---

[a] Technically, this is the writ of habeas corpus ad subjiciendum. This writ serves quite a different function from the form of habeas corpus used to remedy executive detention without access to the courts for trial. It was the latter writ that performed such an important role in 17th and 18th century English and American history and that probably was foremost in the minds of the framers when they limited suspension of the writ of habeas corpus in art. I, § 9 of the Constitution. See generally, W. Duker, A Constitutional History of Habeas Corpus (1980).

[b] Because habeas corpus is a separate lawsuit, it is often called "collateral review" or a "collateral attack." A challenge to a criminal charge or conviction through normal appellate channels would be "direct review" or a "direct attack."

690 HABEAS CORPUS Ch. 7

disproportionate burdens on some federal judges: those who sat in districts where federal prisons were located heard all habeas applications by prisoners detained in those prisons; those who sat in districts without federal prisons heard no habeas cases brought by federal prisoners. Moreover, witnesses needed for hearings typically would live near the place where the prisoner was tried, which was often far away from the place of detention. Section 2255 addresses these problems by requiring that any federal prisoner seeking collateral review return to the sentencing court.

As a formal matter, habeas corpus under §§ 2241 and 2254 is still available to a federal prisoner, but the remedy provided by § 2255 must be sought first. Since the relief available under § 2255 is as broad as that available in a habeas action under § 2254, the occasion for resort to § 2254 is unlikely to arise. In consequence, a state prisoner will seek habeas corpus under § 2254, whereas a federal prisoner will file a "2255" proceeding instead. That phrase—a "2255 proceeding"—has now passed into the vernacular of the experienced criminal attorney (and of the experienced federal prisoner). For most purposes, the relief available to a federal prisoner under § 2255 is the same as that available to a state prisoner under § 2254.

3. Habeas Corpus and Res Judicata. Federal habeas corpus for state prisoners presents a complex series of problems concerning the relationship between state and federal courts. The first issue is one of timing: whether federal courts should be authorized to intervene before or during the state judicial proceedings or whether federal intervention should await their conclusion. This issue is addressed in the next main case, which deals with the requirement that state remedies must be exhausted before federal habeas can be sought. Normally habeas intervention by the federal courts before or during a criminal trial is precluded. The defendant may not proceed in federal court until the state proceedings have come to an end.[c]

This rule would leave a small role for the federal courts if normal principles of res judicata applied to a state judgment of conviction. Issues that were raised in prior litigation are normally foreclosed from relitigation in a later suit. It is settled, however, that res judicata does not apply to federal habeas corpus. In some instances even a retrial of the facts is available in federal court. But this does not mean that all issues are open to relitigation. For one thing, the prisoner must demonstrate that he or she is "in custody in violation of the Constitution or laws or treaties of the United States," as required by § 2241(c)(3). This language effectively limits the federal habeas applicant to federal constitutional challenges to the state court conviction. There

[c] Other federal remedies—most notably an injunction against ongoing state criminal proceedings—are usually precluded until the state trial and appellate process has concluded. Other potential federal remedies are considered elsewhere in these materials. Federal injunctions against state criminal proceedings are the subject of Chapter X, beginning at page 1158, infra. The interaction of remedies under 42 U.S.C. § 1983 and federal habeas corpus was dealt with by the Supreme Court in Preiser v. Rodriguez, 411 U.S. 475 (1973), which is a main case beginning at page 1202, infra.

are, moreover, special rules about when a state court judgment will be regarded as final on federal constitutional issues that were, or could have been, raised in the state proceedings.

These matters are dealt with in detail below. For now, three things should be kept in mind. First, in general federal habeas corpus for state prisoners must await the conclusion of the state trial and appellate proceedings—that is, state remedies must be exhausted. Second, res judicata is not applicable to federal habeas corpus. But third, federal habeas corpus has its own doctrines on the finality of state court judgments.

ROSE v. LUNDY
Supreme Court of the United States, 1982.
455 U.S. 509.

JUSTICE O'CONNOR delivered the opinion of the Court, except as to part III–C.

In this case we consider whether the exhaustion rule in 28 U.S.C. §§ 2254(b), (c) requires a federal district court to dismiss a petition for a writ of habeas corpus containing any claims that have not been exhausted in the state courts. Because a rule requiring exhaustion of all claims furthers the purposes underlying the habeas statute, we hold that a district court must dismiss such "mixed petitions," leaving the prisoner with the choice of returning to state court to exhaust his claims or of amending or resubmitting the habeas petition to present only exhausted claims to the district court.

I

Following a jury trial, respondent Noah Lundy was convicted on charges of rape and crime against nature, and sentenced to the Tennessee State Penitentiary.[1] After the Tennessee Court of Criminal Appeals affirmed the convictions and the Tennessee Supreme Court denied review, the respondent filed an unsuccessful petition for postconviction relief in the Knox County Criminal Court.

The respondent subsequently filed a petition in federal District Court for a writ of habeas corpus under 28 U.S.C. § 2254, alleging four grounds for relief: (1) that he had been denied the right to confrontation because the trial court limited the defense counsel's questioning of the victim; (2) that he had been denied the right to a fair trial because the prosecuting attorney stated that the respondent had a violent character; (3) that he had been denied the right to a fair trial because the prosecutor improperly remarked in his closing argument that the state's evidence was uncontradicted; and (4) that the trial judge improperly instructed the jury that every witness is presumed to swear the truth. After reviewing the state court records, however, the Dis-

[1] The court sentenced the respondent to consecutive terms of 120 years on the rape charge and from five to 15 years on the crime against nature charge.

trict Court concluded that it could not consider claims three and four "in the constitutional framework" because the respondent had not exhausted his state remedies for those grounds. The court nevertheless stated that "in assessing the atmosphere of the case taken as a whole these items may be referred to collaterally." [2]

Apparently in an effort to assess the "atmosphere" of the trial, the District Court reviewed the state trial transcript and identified ten instances of prosecutorial misconduct, only five of which the respondent had raised before the state courts.[3] In addition, although purportedly not ruling on the respondent's fourth ground for relief—that the state trial judge improperly charged that "every witness is presumed to swear the truth"—the court nonetheless held that the jury instruction, coupled with both the restriction of counsel's cross-examination of the victim and the prosecutor's "personal testimony" on the weight of the state's evidence, violated the respondent's right to a fair trial. In conclusion the District Court stated:

> "Also, subject to the question of exhaustion of state remedies, where there is added to the trial atmosphere the comment of the Attorney General that the only story presented to the jury was by the state's witnesses there is such mixture of violations that one cannot be separated from and considered independently of the others. . . .
>
> "Under the charge as given, the limitation of cross examination of the victim, and the flagrant prosecutorial misconduct this court is compelled to find that petitioner did not receive a

---

[2] The Tennessee Criminal Court of Appeals had ruled specifically on grounds one and two, holding that although the trial court erred in restricting cross-examination of the victim and the prosecuting attorney improperly alluded to the respondent's violent nature, the respondent was not prejudiced by these errors. Lundy v. State, 521 S.W.2d 591, 595–96 (1974).

[3] In particular, the District Court found that the prosecutor improperly:

(1) misrepresented that the defense attorney was guilty of illegal and unethical misconduct in interviewing the victim before trial;

(2) "testified" that the victim was telling the truth on the stand;

(3) stated his view of the proper method for the defense attorney to interview the victim;

(4) misrepresented the law regarding interviewing government witnesses;

(5) misrepresented that the victim had a right for both private counsel and the prosecutor to be present when interviewed by the defense counsel;

(6) represented that because an attorney was not present, the defense counsel's conduct was inexcusable;

(7) represented that he could validly file a grievance with the bar association on the basis of the defense counsel's conduct;

(8) objected to the defense counsel's cross-examination of the victim;

(9) commented that the defendant had a violent nature; and

(10) gave his personal evaluation of the state's proof.

The petitioner concedes that the state appellate court considered instances 1, 3, 4, 5, and 9, but states without contradiction that the respondent did not object to the prosecutor's statement that the victim was telling the truth (# 2) or to any of the several instances where the prosecutor, in summation, gave his opinion on the weight of the evidence (# 10). The petitioner also notes that the conduct identified in # 6 and # 7 did not occur in front of the jury, and that the conduct in # 8, which was only an objection to cross-examination, can hardly be labeled as misconduct.

fair trial, his sixth amendment rights were violated and the jury poisoned by the prosecutorial misconduct."

In short, the District Court considered several instances of prosecutorial misconduct never challenged in the state trial or appellate courts, or even raised in the respondent's habeas petition.

[T]he Sixth Circuit affirmed . . . .

II

The petitioner urges this Court to apply a "total exhaustion" rule requiring district courts to dismiss every habeas corpus petition that contains both exhausted and unexhausted claims. The petitioner argues at length that such a rule furthers the policy of comity underlying the exhaustion doctrine because it gives the state courts the first opportunity to correct federal constitutional errors and minimizes federal interference and disruption of state judicial proceedings. . . .

In order to evaluate the merits of the petitioner's arguments, we turn to the habeas statute, its legislative history, and the policies underlying the exhaustion doctrine.

III

A

The exhaustion doctrine existed long before its codification by Congress in 1948. In Ex parte Royall, 117 U.S. 241, 251 (1886), this Court wrote that as a matter of comity, federal courts should not consider a claim in a habeas corpus petition until after the state courts have had an opportunity to act:

"The injunction to hear the case summarily, and thereupon 'to dispose of the party as law and justice require' does not deprive the court of discretion as to the time and mode in which it will exert the powers conferred upon it. That discretion should be exercised in the light of the relations existing, under our system of government, between the judicial tribunals of the Union and the states, and the recognition of the fact that the public good requires that those relations be not disturbed by unnecessary conflict between courts equally bound to guard and protect rights secured by the Constitution."

Subsequent cases refined the principle that state remedies must be exhausted except in unusual circumstances. In Ex parte Hawk, 321 U.S. 114, 117 (1944), this Court reiterated that comity was the basis for the exhaustion doctrine: "it is a principle controlling all habeas corpus petitions to the federal courts, that those courts will interfere with the administration of justice in the state courts only 'in rare cases where exceptional circumstances of peculiar urgency are shown to exist.'" None of these cases, however, specifically applied the exhaustion doctrine to habeas petitions containing both exhausted and unexhausted claims.

In 1948, Congress codified the exhaustion doctrine in 28 U.S.C. § 2254, citing *Ex parte Hawk* as correctly stating the principle of exhaustion. Section 2254,[9] however, does not directly address the problem of mixed petitions. To be sure, the provision states that a remedy is not exhausted if there exists a state procedure to raise "the question presented," but we believe this phrase to be too ambiguous to sustain the conclusion that Congress intended to either permit or prohibit review of mixed petitions. Because the legislative history of § 2254, as well as the pre–1948 cases, contains no reference to the problem of mixed petitions, in all likelihood Congress never thought of the problem. Consequently, we must analyze the policies underlying the statutory provision to determine its proper scope.

B

The exhaustion doctrine is principally designed to protect the state courts' role in the enforcement of federal law and prevent disruption of state judicial proceedings. See Braden v. 30th Judicial Circuit Court of Kentucky, 410 U.S. 484, 490–91 (1973). Under our federal system, the federal and state "courts [are] equally bound to guard and protect rights secured by the Constitution." *Ex parte Royall,* supra, at 251. Because "it would be unseemly in our dual system of government for a federal district court to upset a state court conviction without an opportunity to the state courts to correct a constitutional, violation," federal courts apply the doctrine of comity, which "teaches that one court should defer action on causes properly within its jurisdiction until the courts of another sovereignty with concurrent powers, and already cognizant of the litigation, have had an opportunity to pass upon the matter." Darr v. Burford, 339 U.S. 200, 204 (1950).

A rigorously enforced total exhaustion rule will encourage state prisoners to seek full relief first from the state courts, thus giving those courts the first opportunity to review claims of constitutional error. As the number of prisoners who exhaust all of their federal claims increases, state courts may become increasingly familiar with and hospitable toward federal constitutional issues. See *Braden v. 30th Judicial Circuit Court of Kentucky,* supra, at 490. Equally as important, federal claims that have been fully exhausted in state courts will more often be accompanied by a complete factual record to aid the federal courts in their review.

The facts of the present case underscore the need for a rule encouraging exhaustion of all federal claims. In his opinion, the

---

[9] Section 2254 in part provides:

"(b) An application for a writ of habeas corpus in behalf of a person in custody pursuant to the judgment of a State court shall not be granted unless it appears that the applicant has exhausted the remedies available in the courts of the State, or that there is either an absence of available State corrective process or the existence of circumstances rendering such process ineffective to protect the rights of the prisoner.

"(c) An applicant shall not be deemed to have exhausted the remedies available in the courts of the State, within the meaning of this section, if he has the right under the law of the State to raise, by any available procedure, the question presented."

District Court judge wrote that "there is such mixture of violations that one cannot be separated from and considered independently of the others." Because the two unexhausted claims for relief were intertwined with the exhausted ones, the judge apparently considered all of the claims in ruling on the petition. Requiring dismissal of petitions containing both exhausted and unexhausted claims will relieve the district courts of the difficult if not impossible task of deciding when claims are related, and will reduce the temptation to consider unexhausted claims.

In his dissent, Justice Stevens suggests that the District Court properly evaluated the respondent's two exhausted claims "in the context of the entire trial." Unquestionably, however, the District Court erred in considering unexhausted claims, for § 2254(b) expressly requires the prisoner to exhaust "the remedies available in the courts of the state." Moreover, to the extent that exhausted and unexhausted claims are interrelated, the general rule among the courts of appeals is to dismiss mixed habeas petitions for exhaustion of all such claims.

Rather than an "adventure in unnecessary lawmaking" [as Stevens argues in dissent], our holdings today reflect our interpretation of a federal statute on the basis of its language and legislative history, and consistent with its underlying policies. There is no basis to believe that today's holdings will "complicate and delay" the resolution of habeas petitions [as Stevens also argues], or will serve to "trap the unwary pro se prisoner [as Blackmun contends]." On the contrary, our interpretation of §§ 2254(b), (c) provides a simple and clear instruction to potential litigants: before you bring any claims to federal court, be sure that you first have taken each one to state court. Just as pro se petitioners have managed to use the federal habeas corpus machinery, so too should they be able to master this straightforward exhaustion requirement. Those prisoners who misunderstand this requirement and submit mixed petitions nevertheless are entitled to resubmit a petition with only exhausted claims or to exhaust the remainder of their claims.

Rather than increasing the burden on federal courts, strict enforcement of the exhaustion requirement will encourage habeas petitioners to exhaust all of their claims in state court and to present the federal court with a single habeas petition. To the extent that the exhaustion requirement reduces piecemeal litigation, both the courts and the prisoners should benefit, for as a result the district court will be more likely to review all of the prisoner's claims in a single proceeding, thus providing for a more focused and thorough review.

C

The prisoner's principal interest, of course, is in obtaining speedy federal relief on his claims. A total exhaustion rule will not impair that interest since he can always amend the petition to delete the unexhausted claims, rather than returning to state court to exhaust all of his claims. By invoking this procedure, however, the prisoner would risk forfeiting consideration of his unexhausted claims in federal court.

Under 28 U.S.C. § 2254 Rule 9(b), a district court may dismiss subsequent petitions if it finds that "the failure of the petitioner to assert those [new] grounds in a prior petition constituted an abuse of the writ." [a] The Advisory Committee to the Rules notes that Rule 9(b) incorporates the judge-made principle governing the abuse of the writ set forth in Sanders v. United States, 373 U.S. 1 (1963), where this Court stated:

> "[I]f a prisoner deliberately withholds one of two grounds for federal collateral relief at the time of filing his first application, in the hope of being granted two hearings rather than one or for some other such reason, he may be deemed to have waived his right to a hearing on the second application presenting the withheld ground. The same may be true if . . . the prisoner deliberately abandons one of his grounds at the first hearing. Nothing in the traditions of habeas corpus requires the federal courts to tolerate needless piecemeal litigation, or to entertain collateral proceedings whose only purpose is to vex, harass, or delay."

Thus a prisoner who decides to proceed only with his exhausted claims and deliberately sets aside his unexhausted claims risks dismissal of subsequent federal petitions.

IV

In sum, because a total exhaustion rule promotes comity and does not unreasonably impair the prisoner's right to relief, we hold that a district court must dismiss habeas petitions containing both unexhausted and exhausted claims. Accordingly, the judgment of the Court of Appeals is reversed, and the case is remanded for proceedings consistent with this opinion.

It is so ordered.

JUSTICE BLACKMUN, concurring in the judgment.

The important issue before the Court in this case is whether the conservative "total exhaustion" rule espoused now by two courts of appeal . . . is required by 28 U.S.C. §§ 2254(b) and (c), or whether the approach adopted by eight other courts of appeals—that a district court may review the *exhausted* claims of a mixed petition—is the proper interpretation of the statute. On this basic issue, I firmly agree with the majority of the courts of appeals.

I do not dispute the value of comity when it is applicable and productive of harmony between state and federal courts, nor do I deny the principle of exhaustion that §§ 2254(b) and (c) so clearly embrace. What troubles me is that the "total exhaustion" rule, now adopted by

---

[a] Habeas Corpus Rule 9(b) provides:

"A second or successive petition may be dismissed if the judge finds that it fails to allege new or different grounds for relief and the prior determination was on the merits or, if new and different grounds are alleged, the judge finds that the failure of the petitioner to assert those grounds in a prior petition constituted an abuse of the writ." [Footnote by eds.]

this Court, can be read into the statute, as the Court concedes, only by sheer force; that it operates as a trap for the uneducated and indigent pro se prisoner-applicant; that it delays the resolution of claims that are not frivolous; and that it tends to increase, rather than to alleviate, the caseload burdens on both state and federal courts. To use the old expression, the Court's ruling seems to me to "throw the baby out with the bath water." . . .

I

The Court correctly observes that neither the language nor the history of the exhaustion provisions of §§ 2254(b) and (c) mandates dismissal of a habeas petition containing both exhausted and unexhausted claims. Nor does precedent dictate the result reached here. . . .

In reversing the judgment of the Sixth Circuit, the Court focuses, as it must, on the purposes the exhaustion doctrine is intended to serve. . . .

The first interest relied on by the Court involves an offshoot of the doctrine of federal-state comity. The Court hopes to preserve the state courts' role in protecting constitutional rights, as well as to afford those courts an opportunity to correct constitutional errors and—somewhat patronizingly—to "become increasingly familiar with and hospitable toward federal constitutional issues." My proposal, however, is not inconsistent with the Court's concern for comity: indeed, the state courts have occasion to rule first on every constitutional challenge, and have ample opportunity to correct any such error, before it is considered by a federal court on habeas.

In some respects, the Court's ruling appears more destructive than solicitous of federal-state comity. Remitting a habeas petitioner to state court to exhaust a patently frivolous claim before the federal court may consider a serious, exhausted ground for relief hardly demonstrates respect for the state courts. The state judiciary's time and resources are then spent rejecting the obviously meritless unexhausted claim, which doubtless will receive little or no attention in the subsequent federal proceeding that focuses on the substantial exhausted claim. . . .

The second set of interests relied upon by the Court involves those of federal judicial administration—ensuring that a § 2254 petition is accompanied by a complete factual record to facilitate review and relieving the district courts of the responsibility for determining when exhausted and unexhausted claims are interrelated. If a prisoner has presented a particular challenge in the state courts, however, the habeas court will have before it the complete factual record relating to that claim. And the Court's Draconian approach is hardly necessary to relieve district courts of the obligation to consider exhausted grounds for relief when the prisoner also has advanced interrelated claims not yet reviewed by the state courts. When the district court believes, on the facts of the case before it, that the record is inadequate or that full

consideration of the exhausted claims is impossible, it has always been free to dismiss the entire habeas petition pending resolution of unexhausted claims in the state courts. Certainly, it makes sense to commit these decisions to the discretion of the lower federal courts, which will be familiar with the specific factual context of each case.
. . .

The Court's interest in efficient administration of the federal courts therefore does not require dismissal of mixed habeas petitions. In fact, that concern militates *against* the approach taken by the Court today. In order to comply with the Court's ruling, a federal court now will have to review the record in a § 2254 proceeding at least summarily in order to determine whether all claims have been exhausted. In many cases a decision on the merits will involve only negligible additional effort. And in other cases the court may not realize that one of a number of claims is unexhausted until after substantial work has been done. If the district court must nevertheless dismiss the entire petition until all grounds for relief have been exhausted, the prisoner will likely return to federal court eventually, thereby necessitating duplicative examination of the record and consideration of the exhausted claims—perhaps by another district judge. Moreover, when the § 2254 petition does find its way back to federal court, the record on the exhausted grounds for relief may well be stale and resolution of the merits more difficult.

The interest of the prisoner and of society in "preserv[ing] the writ of habeas corpus as a 'swift and imperative remedy in all cases of illegal restraint or confinement,'" Braden v. 30th Judicial Circuit Court of Kentucky, 410 U.S. 484, 490 (1973), is the final policy consideration to be weighed in the balance. Compelling the habeas petitioner to repeat his journey through the entire state and federal legal process before receiving a ruling on his exhausted claims obviously entails substantial delay. And if the prisoner must choose between undergoing that delay and forfeiting unexhausted claims, society is likewise forced to sacrifice either the swiftness of habeas or its availability to remedy all unconstitutional imprisonments. Dismissing only unexhausted grounds for habeas relief, while ruling on the merits of all unrelated exhausted claims, will diminish neither the promptness nor the efficacy of the remedy and, at the same time, will serve the state and federal interests described by the Court.

II

The Court's misguided approach appears to be premised on the specter of "the sophisticated litigious prisoner intent upon a strategy of piecemeal litigation . . .," whose aim is to have more than one day in court. Even if it could be said that the Court's view reflects reality, its ruling today will not frustrate the Perry Masons of the prison populations. To avoid dismissal, they will simply include only exhausted claims in each of many successive habeas petitions. Those subsequent petitions may be dismissed, as Justice Brennan observes, only if the prisoner has "abused the writ" by deliberately choosing, for purposes of delay, not to include all his claims in one petition. And successive habeas petitions that meet the "abuse of the writ" standard have always been subject to dismissal, irrespective of the Court's treatment of mixed petitions today. The Court's ruling in this case therefore provides no additional incentive whatsoever to consolidate all grounds for relief in one § 2254 petition.

Instead of deterring the sophisticated habeas petitioner who understands, and wishes to circumvent, the rules of exhaustion, the Court's ruling will serve to trap the unwary pro se prisoner who is not knowledgeable about the intricacies of the exhaustion doctrine and whose only aim is to secure a new trial or release from prison. He will consolidate all conceivable grounds for relief in an attempt to accelerate review and minimize costs. But, under the Court's approach, if he unwittingly includes in a § 2254 motion a claim not yet presented to the state courts, he risks dismissal of the entire petition and substantial delay before a ruling on the merits of his exhausted claims.

The Court suggests that a prisoner who files a mixed habeas petition will have the option of amending or resubmitting his complaint after deleting the unexhausted claims. To the extent that prisoners are permitted simply to strike unexhausted claims from a § 2254 petition and then proceed as if those claims had never been presented, I fail to understand what all the fuss is about. In that event, the Court's approach is virtually indistinguishable from that of the Court of Appeals, which directs the district court itself to dismiss unexhausted grounds for relief.

I fear, however, that prisoners who mistakenly submit mixed petitions may not be treated uniformly. A prisoner's opportunity to amend a § 2254 petition may depend on his awareness of the existence of that alternative or on a sympathetic district judge who informs him of the option and permits the amendment. If the prisoner is required to refile the petition after striking the unexhausted claims, he may have to begin the process anew and thus encounter substantial delay before his complaint again comes to the district court's attention.

Adopting a rule that will afford knowledgeable prisoners more favorable treatment is, I believe antithetical to the purposes of the habeas writ. Instead of requiring a habeas petitioner to be familiar with the nuances of the exhaustion doctrine and the process of amending a complaint, I would simply permit the district court to dismiss unexhausted grounds for relief and consider exhausted claims on the merits.

III

. . . As the Court notes, the District Court erred in considering both exhausted and unexhausted claims when ruling on Lundy's § 2254 petition. . . . I would therefore remand the case, directing that the courts below dismiss respondent's unexhausted claims and examine those that have been properly presented to the state courts in order to determine whether they are interrelated with the unexhausted grounds and, if not, whether they warrant collateral relief.

JUSTICE BRENNAN, with whom JUSTICE MARSHALL joins, concurring in part and dissenting in part.

I join the opinion of the Court (parts I, II, III–A, III–B, and IV), but I do not join the opinion of the plurality (part III–C). I agree with the Court's holding that the exhaustion requirement of 28 U.S.C. §§ 2254(b), (c) obliges a federal district court to dismiss, without consideration on the merits, a habeas corpus petition from a state prisoner when that petition contains claims that have not been exhausted in the state courts, "leaving the prisoner with the choice of returning to state court to exhaust his claims or of amending or resubmitting the habeas petition to present only exhausted claims to the district court." But I disagree with the plurality's view, in part III–C, that a habeas petitioner must "risk forfeiting consideration of his unexhausted claims in federal court" if he "decides to proceed only with his exhausted claims and deliberately sets aside his unexhausted claims" in the face of the district court's refusal to consider his "mixed" petition. The issue of Rule 9(b)'s proper application to successive petitions brought as the result of our decision today is not before us—it was not among the questions presented by petitioner, nor was it briefed and argued by the parties. Therefore, the issue should not be addressed until we have a case presenting it. In any event, I disagree with the plurality's proposed disposition of the issue. In my view, Rule 9(b) cannot be read to permit dismissal of a subsequent petition under the circumstances described in the plurality's opinion.

The plurality recognizes, as it must, that in enacting Rule 9(b) Congress explicitly adopted the "abuse of the writ" standard announced in Sanders v. United States, 373 U.S. 1 (1963). . . .

It is plain that a proper construction of Rule 9(b) must be consistent with its legislative history. This necessarily entails an accurate interpretation of the *Sanders* standard, on which the rule is based. . . . The relevant language from *Sanders,* quoted by the plurality, is as follows:

> "[I]f a prisoner deliberately withholds one of two grounds for federal collateral relief at the time of filing his first application, in the hope of being granted two hearings rather than one or for some other such reason, he may be deemed to have waived his right to a hearing on a second application presenting the withheld ground. The same may be true if . . . the prisoner deliberately abandons one of his grounds at the first hearing. Nothing in the traditions of habeas corpus requires the federal courts to tolerate needless piecemeal litigation, or to entertain collateral proceedings whose only purpose is to vex, harass, or delay."

From this language the plurality concludes: "Thus a prisoner who decides to proceed only with his exhausted claims and deliberately sets aside his unexhausted claims risks dismissal of subsequent federal petitions."

The plurality's conclusion simply distorts the meaning of the quoted language. *Sanders* was plainly concerned with "a prisoner *deliberately* withhold[ing] one of two grounds" for relief "in the hope of being granted two hearings rather than one or for some other such reason." *Sanders* also notes that waiver might be inferred where "the prisoner *deliberately abandons* one of his grounds at the first hearing." Finally, *Sanders* states that dismissal is appropriate either when the court is faced with "*needless* piecemeal litigation" or with "collateral proceedings *whose only purpose is to vex, harass, or delay.*" Thus, *Sanders* made it crystal clear that dismissal for "abuse of the writ" is *only* appropriate when a prisoner was free to include all of his claims in his first petition, but *knowingly and deliberately* chose not to do so in order to get more than "one bite at the apple." The plurality's interpretation obviously would allow dismissal in a much broader class of cases than *Sanders* permits.

This Court is free, of course, to overrule *Sanders*. But even that course would not support the plurality's conclusion. For Congress incorporated the "judge-made" *Sanders* principle into positive law when it enacted Rule 9(b). . . .

I conclude that when a prisoner's original, "mixed" habeas petition is dismissed without any examination of its claims on the merits, and when the prisoner later brings a second petition based on the previously unexhausted claims that had earlier been refused a hearing, then the remedy of dismissal for "abuse of the writ" cannot be employed against that second petition, absent unusual factual circumstances truly suggesting abuse. . . .

JUSTICE WHITE, concurring in part and dissenting in part.

I agree with most of Justice Brennan's opinion; but like Justice Blackmun, I would not require a "mixed" petition to be dismissed in its entirety, with leave to resubmit the exhausted claims. The trial judge cannot rule on the unexhausted issues and should dismiss them. But he should rule on the exhausted claims unless they are intertwined with those he must dismiss or unless the habeas petitioner prefers to have his entire petition dismissed. In any event, if the judge rules on those issues that are ripe and dismisses those that are not, I would not tax the petitioner with abuse of the writ if he returns with the latter claims after seeking state relief.

JUSTICE STEVENS, dissenting.

This case raises important questions about the authority of federal judges. In my opinion the district judge properly exercised his statutory duty to consider the merits of the claims advanced by respondent that previously had been rejected by the Tennessee courts. The district judge exceeded, however, what I regard as proper restraints on the scope of collateral review of state-court judgments. Ironically, instead of correcting his error, the Court today fashions a new rule of law that will merely delay the final disposition of this case and, as Justice

Blackmun demonstrates, impose unnecessary burdens on both state and federal judges.

An adequate explanation of my disapproval of the Court's adventure in unnecessary lawmaking requires some reference to the facts of this case and to my conception of the proper role of the writ of habeas corpus in the administration of justice in the United States.

I

Respondent was convicted in state court of rape and a crime against nature. The testimony of the victim was corroborated by another eyewitness who was present during the entire sadistic episode. The evidence of guilt is not merely sufficient; it is convincing. As is often the case in emotional, controverted, adversary proceedings, trial error occurred. Two of these errors—a remark by the prosecutor [1] and a limitation on defense counsel's cross-examination of the victim [2]— were recognized by the Tennessee Court of Criminal Appeals, but held to be harmless in the context of the entire case. Because the state appellate court considered and rejected these two errors as a basis for setting aside his conviction, respondent has exhausted his state remedies with respect to those two claims.

In his application in federal court for a writ of habeas corpus, respondent alleged that these trial errors violated his constitutional rights to confront the witnesses against him and to obtain a fair trial. In his petition, respondent also alleged that the prosecutor had imper-

[1] At trial, the prosecutor questioned the eyewitness concerning "difficulties" that her sister had encountered while dating the respondent. In response to an objection to the materiality of the inquiry, the prosecutor explained, in the presence of the jury, that "I would think the defendant's violent nature would be material to this case in the light of what the victim has testified to." The trial court excused the jury to determine the admissibility of the evidence; it ruled that the collateral inquiry was "too far removed to be material and relevant." After the jury had returned, the court instructed it to disregard the prosecutor's remarks. . . .

[2] Defense counsel cross-examined the victim concerning her prior sexual activity. When the victim responded that she could not remember certain activity, counsel attempted to question her concerning statements that she apparently had made in an earlier interview with defense counsel. The prosecutor objected to this questioning on the ground that, during the interview, defense counsel had only disclosed that he was a lawyer involved in the case, and had not told the victim that he was counsel for the defendant. The trial court sustained the objection. The court permitted defense counsel to continue to question the victim

concerning her prior sexual activity, but refused to permit him to refer to his earlier conversation with the victim. On appeal, respondent objected to the trial court's ruling, and also claimed that the prosecutor had prejudiced him by suggesting, before the jury, that defense counsel had acted unethically in not specifically identifying his involvement in the case. The state appellate court rejected respondent's claims, stating:

"We note that the trial judge permitted cross-examination upon the same subject matter, but simply ruled out predicating the cross-examination questions upon the prior questions and answers. From the tender of proof in the record we do not believe that defendant was prejudiced by what we deem to have been too restrictive a ruling. Defense counsel was under no positive duty to affirmatively identify his role in the upcoming case before questioning a witness. He apparently made no misrepresentation, and was apparently seeking the truth. State's counsel was unduly critical of defense counsel in indicating before the jury that state's counsel should have been present at the interview, etc., but we hold this error to be harmless in the context of this case."

missibly commented on his failure to testify [3] and that the trial judge had improperly instructed the jury that "every witness is presumed to swear the truth." [4] Because these two additional claims had not been presented to the Tennessee Court of Criminal Appeals, the federal district judge concluded that he could "not consider them in the constitutional framework." He added, however, that "in assessing the atmosphere of the cause taken as a whole these items may be referred to collaterally."

In considering the significance of respondent's two exhausted claims, the District Court thus evaluated them in the context of the entire trial record. That is precisely what the Tennessee Court of Criminal Appeals did in arriving at its conclusion that these claims, identified as error, were not sufficiently prejudicial to justify reversing the conviction and ordering a new trial. In considering whether an error in these two exhausted claims was sufficient to justify a grant of habeas corpus relief, the federal court—like the state court—had a duty to look at the context in which the error occurred to determine whether it was either aggravated or mitigated by other aspects of the proceeding. The state court and the federal court formed differing judgments based on that broad review. I happen to share the appraisal of the state court on the merits, but I believe that the procedure followed by the federal court was entirely correct.

The Court holds, however, that the District Court committed two procedural errors. "Unquestionably," according to the Court, it was wrong for the District Court to consider the portions of the trial record described in the unexhausted claims in evaluating those claims that had been exhausted. More fundamentally, according to the Court, it was wrong for the District Court even to consider the merits of the *exhausted* claims because the prisoner had included unexhausted claims in his pleading. Both of the Court's holdings are unsatisfactory for the same basic reason: the Court assumes that the character of all claims alleged in habeas corpus petitions is the same. Under the Court's analysis, *any* unexhausted claim asserted in a habeas corpus petition—no matter how frivolous—is sufficient to command the district judge to postpone relief on a meritorious exhausted claim, no matter how obvious and outrageous the constitutional violation may be.

In my opinion claims of constitutional error are not fungible. There are at least four types. The one most frequently encountered is a claim that attaches a constitutional label to a set of facts that does not disclose a violation of any constitutional right. In my opinion, each of the four claims asserted in this case falls in that category. The

---

[3] In his closing argument, the prosecutor stated:

"The only story we've heard about what happened from about 8:15 of the night of March 16th until about four o'clock in the morning of March 17th came from the state's witnesses."

[4] The judge instructed the jury:

"The jurors are the exclusive judges of the facts and the credibility of the witnesses. You are judges of the law under the direction of the court. If there are conflicts in the evidence, you must reconcile them, if you can, without hastily or rashly concluding that any witness has sworn falsely, for every witness is presumed to swear the truth."

second class includes constitutional violations that are not of sufficient import in a particular case to justify reversal even on direct appeal, when the evidence is still fresh and a fair retrial could be promptly conducted. Chapman v. California, 386 U.S. 18 (1967). A third category includes errors that are important enough to require reversal on direct appeal but do not reveal the kind of fundamental unfairness to the accused that will support a collateral attack on a final judgment. See, e.g., Stone v. Powell, 428 U.S. 465 (1976).[8] The fourth category includes those errors that are so fundamental that they infect the validity of the underlying judgment itself, or the integrity of the process by which that judgment was obtained. This category cannot be defined precisely; concepts of "fundamental fairness" are not frozen in time. But the kind of error that falls in this category is best illustrated by recalling the classic grounds for the issuance of a writ of habeas corpus—that the proceeding was dominated by mob violence; [9] that the prosecutor knowingly made use of perjured testimony; [10] or that the conviction was based on a confession extorted from the defendant by brutal methods.[11] Errors of this kind justify collateral relief no matter how long a judgment may have been final and even though they may not have been preserved properly in the original trial.[13]

In this case I think it is clear that neither the exhausted claims nor the unexhausted claims describe any error demonstrating that respondent's trial was fundamentally unfair. Since his lawyer found insufficient merit in the two unexhausted claims to object to the error at trial or to raise the claims on direct appeal, I would expect that the Tennessee courts will consider them to have been waived as a matter of state law; thereafter, under the teaching of Wainwright v. Sykes, 433 U.S. 72 (1977), they undoubtedly will not support federal relief. This

---

[8] In my opinion a claim generally belongs in this category if the purpose and significance of the constitutional rule is such that the Court enforces it prospectively but not retroactively, cf. Linkletter v. Walker, 381 U.S. 618 (1965), or if the probable significance of the claim is belied by the fact that otherwise competent defense counsel did not raise a timely objection, cf. Wainwright v. Sykes, 433 U.S. 72, 95–97 (1977) (Stevens, J., concurring). I recognize the apparent incongruity in suggesting that there is a class of constitutional error—not constitutionally harmless— that does not render a criminal proceeding fundamentally unfair. It may be argued, with considerable force, that a rule of procedure that is not necessary to ensure fundamental fairness is not worthy of constitutional status. The fact that such a category of constitutional error exists, however, is demonstrated by the jurisprudence of this Court concerning the retroactive application of newly recognized constitutional rights. See, e.g., *Linkletter v. Walker,* supra (exclusionary rule of *Mapp v. Ohio* not to be applied retroactively); Te-

han v. United States ex rel. Shott, 382 U.S. 406 (1966) (rule of *Griffin v. California* forbidding adverse comment on the defendant's failure to testify) [and others]. In ruling that a constitutional principle is not to be applied retroactively, the Court implicitly suggests that the right is not necessary to ensure the integrity of the underlying judgment: the Court certainly would not allow claims of such magnitude to remain unremedied. [These decisions] demonstrate that the Court's constitutional jurisprudence has expanded beyond the concept of ensuring fundamental fairness to the accused. My point here is simply that this expansion need not, and should not, be applied to collateral attacks on final judgments.

[9] Moore v. Dempsey, 261 U.S. 86 (1923).

[10] Mooney v. Holohan, 294 U.S. 103 (1935).

[11] See Brown v. Mississippi, 297 U.S. 278 (1936) (direct appeal).

[13] See Wainwright v. Sykes, 433 U.S. 72, 95–96 (1977) (Stevens, J., concurring). . . . .

case is thus destined to return to the federal District Court and the Court of Appeals where, it is safe to predict, those courts will once again come to the conclusion that the writ should issue. The additional procedure that the Court requires before considering the merits will be totally unproductive.

If my appraisal of respondent's exhausted claims is incorrect—if the trial actually was fundamentally unfair to the respondent—postponing relief until another round of review in the state and federal judicial systems has been completed is truly outrageous. The unnecessary delay will make it more difficult for the prosecutor to obtain a conviction on retrial if respondent is in fact guilty; if he is innocent, requiring him to languish in jail because he made a pleading error is callous indeed.

There are some situations in which a district judge should refuse to entertain a mixed petition until all of the petitioner's claims have been exhausted. If the unexhausted claim appears to involve error of the most serious kind and if it is reasonably clear that the exhausted claims do not, addressing the merits of the exhausted claims will merely delay the ultimate disposition of the case. Or if an evidentiary hearing is necessary to decide the merits of both the exhausted and unexhausted claims, a procedure that enables all the fact questions to be resolved in the same hearing should be followed. I therefore would allow district judges to exercise discretion to determine whether the presence of an unexhausted claim in a habeas corpus application makes it inappropriate to consider the merits of a properly pleaded exhausted claim. The inflexible, mechanical rule the Court adopts today arbitrarily denies district judges the kind of authority they need to administer their calendars effectively.

II

In recent years federal judges at times have lost sight of the true office of the great writ of habeas corpus. It is quite unlike the common-law writ of error that enabled a higher court to correct errors committed by a nisi prius tribunal in the trial of civil or criminal cases by ordering further proceedings whenever trial error was detected. The writ of habeas corpus is a fundamental guarantee of liberty.

The fact that federal judges have at times construed their power to issue writs of habeas corpus as though it were tantamount to the authority of an appellate court considering a direct appeal from a trial court judgment has had two unfortunate consequences. First, it has encouraged prisoners to file an ever-increasing volume of federal applications that often amount to little more than a request for further review of asserted grounds for reversal that already have been adequately considered and rejected on direct review. Second, it has led this Court into the business of creating special procedural rules for dealing with this flood of litigation. The doctrine of nonretroactivity, the emerging "cause and prejudice" doctrine,[b] and today's "total exhaustion" rule are examples of judicial lawmaking that might well have been avoided by confining the availability of habeas corpus relief to cases that truly involve fundamental fairness.

When that high standard is met, there should be no question about the retroactivity of the constitutional rule being enforced. Nor do I believe there is any need to fashion definitions of "cause" and "prejudice" to determine whether an error that was not preserved at trial or on direct appeal is subject to review in a collateral federal proceeding. The availability of habeas corpus relief should depend primarily on the character of the alleged constitutional violation and not on the procedural history underlying the claim.

The "total exhaustion" rule the Court crafts today demeans the high office of the great writ. Perhaps a rule of this kind would be an appropriate response to a flood of litigation requesting review of minor disputes. An assumption that most of these petitions are groundless might be thought to justify technical pleading requirements that would provide a mechanism for reducing the sheer number of cases in which the merits must be considered. But the Court's experience has taught us not only that most of these petitions lack merit, but also that there are cases in which serious injustice must be corrected by the issuance of the writ. In such cases, the statutory requirement that adequate state remedies be exhausted must, of course, be honored. When a person's liberty is at stake, however, there surely is no justification for the creation of needless procedural hurdles.

Procedural regularity is a matter of fundamental importance in the administration of justice. But procedural niceties that merely complicate and delay the resolution of disputes are another matter. In my opinion the federal habeas corpus statute should be construed to protect the former and, whenever possible, to avoid the latter.

I respectfully dissent.

NOTES ON EXHAUSTION OF STATE REMEDIES AND ABUSE OF THE WRIT

1. *Ex Parte Royall.* As the Court noted in *Lundy,* the exhaustion requirement originated in Ex parte Royall, 117 U.S. 241 (1886). At the time he sought federal habeas corpus, Royall was in jail awaiting

---

[b] The reference is to *Wainwright v. Sykes,* which appears as a main case at page 753, infra. That case concerned the rules that should apply to cases where the defendant did not raise his or her constitutional challenges at the state trial and no longer had any available procedure by which to do so. If the state court refuses to consider the merits of the defendant's claim, invoking the doctrine that claims not properly raised are lost, the question was what the federal courts should do. *Wainwright* held that the federal courts should hear the claim only if the defendant could show "cause" for why the claims were not raised in the state court and "prejudice" from the failure to have the claim considered in federal court. The meaning of these two terms is addressed in connection with *Wainwright* below. [Footnote by eds.]

trial on state criminal charges. The statutes under which he was being prosecuted were designed to prevent collection of certain bonds issued by the state of Virginia,[a] and Royall claimed that these laws violated the contract clause. The Supreme Court held that, absent special circumstances, the federal courts should not intervene until the state trial and appellate courts had an opportunity to rule on the constitutional claim. The federal trial court "was not at liberty . . . to presume that the decision of the state court[s] would be otherwise than is required by the fundamental law of the land, or that it would disregard the settled principles of constitutional law announced by this Court." The Court elaborated:

> "We are of opinion that while the [federal trial court] has the power to [issue habeas corpus], and may discharge the accused in advance of his trial if he is restrained of his liberty in violation of the national Constitution, it is not bound in every case to exercise such a power immediately upon application being made for the writ. We cannot suppose that Congress intended to compel those courts, by such means, to draw to themselves, in the first instance, the control of all criminal prosecutions commenced in state courts exercising authority within the same territorial limits, where the accused claims that he is held in custody in violation of the Constitution of the United States. The injunction to hear the case . . . does not deprive the court of discretion as to the time and mode in which it will exert the powers conferred upon it. That discretion should be exercised in light of the relations existing, under our system of government, between the judicial tribunals of the union and of the states, and in recognition of the fact that the public good requires that those relations be not disturbed by unnecessary conflict between courts equally bound to guard and protect rights secured by the Constitution."

The exhaustion requirement thus began as a judicially crafted limitation on the statutes authorizing the federal courts to hear habeas corpus claims by state prisoners. It became firmly entrenched in the succeeding years, and in 1948 was codified in 28 U.S.C. § 2254, which is quoted in *Lundy*.

2. The Nature of the Requirement: *Fay v. Noia*. Note that the *Lundy* case came to the Supreme Court after the defendant had been convicted, after the state appellate process had concluded, and after an effort to obtain state post-conviction relief had failed.[b] The context was unlike that in *Royall*, where the defendant sought federal habeas relief before the state trial had begun. In what sense, then, had Lundy failed to exhaust his state remedies?

---

[a] Specifically, Royall had been indicted for failing to pay a tax of $1000 before he sold a coupon worth $10.50 and for failing to pay a tax of $250 before he filed suit for a client trying to collect on several coupons.

[b] All states have some form of post-conviction procedure under which convicted prisoners can assert constitutional challenges to their convictions.

The answer is that the exhaustion doctrine requires that each claim raised in federal habeas be presented first to the state courts if it has not been presented previously and if there is an available opportunity to do so. Lundy had not asserted his "unexhausted" claims at any stage of the state proceedings, and presumably an avenue for asserting the claims remained open—probably by filing a second post-conviction proceeding in the state courts. The exhaustion requirement is satisfied with respect to a particular claim if it has been presented to the state courts and all appeals permitted within the state court system have been taken. It is not required that claims once presented be raised again. The defendant also need not go through the motions if it is completely clear that there is no available remedy under state law.

Fay v. Noia, 372 U.S. 391 (1963), held that Supreme Court review of the highest state court's decision need not be sought. *Fay* also made clear that the exhaustion requirement is not a doctrine of forfeitures. That is, the failure to present a constitutional claim to the state courts requires dismissal of a federal habeas petition only if the prisoner has a *currently* available avenue by which to submit the issue to the state courts. The fact that the defendant did not take advantage of an opportunity that is no longer available does not require dismissal of a habeas petition for failure to exhaust state remedies.[c]

As it has developed, the exhaustion requirement is one of the most difficult practical barriers to federal habeas corpus relief for state prisoners. Usually the defendant has presented some version of the claim to the state courts, but now wishes to present in federal court new facts or new arguments or a new twist on the old claim. The determination whether a given argument is so new as to require exhaustion or merely a restatement of an old claim is often a matter of some subtlety. Moreover, as *Lundy* illustrates, different claims can become so intertwined that it is difficult to separate the exhausted from the unexhausted. The result is a procedural morass that is a challenge to even the best of the pro se lawyers confined in state prisons, not to speak of law students.[d]

Did the *Lundy* Court come to the right answer? Note the announcement two years after *Lundy* that, "the exhaustion rule requiring dismissal of mixed petitions, though to be strictly enforced, is not jurisdictional." Strickland v. Washington, 466 U.S. 668, 684 (1984). In that case, the Court considered the merits of an exhausted claim even though the petitioner had also presented an unexhausted claim to the

[c] Note, however, that the failure to present a federal claim to the state courts may in certain circumstances foreclose subsequent habeas relief on other grounds. If the defendant's failure to raise a claim in state court means that the state courts will thereafter refuse to consider it on the merits, the exhaustion doctrine will have been satisfied but the defendant may still not be able to present the claim to a federal court. The issue in such a case will be whether the federal court should regard the claim as foreclosed by the refusal of the state courts to consider it. This problem is dealt with in detail beginning at page 753, infra.

[d] For a history of the exhaustion requirement, criticism of its development, and a citation to other literature, see Yackle, The Exhaustion Doctrine in Federal Habeas Corpus: An Argument For Return to First Principles, 44 Ohio St. L.J. 393 (1983).

District Court. The District Court had rejected the unexhausted claim on the merits, in part because the state had urged its consideration.

3. State Failure to Raise Exhaustion Issue. The consequences of the state's failure to raise the exhaustion requirement in the district court were considered in Granberry v. Greer, 481 U.S. 129 (1987). The District Court had dismissed the petition on the merits. On appeal, the state argued for the first time that the claim had not been exhausted. The Court of Appeals held that the state's failure to make that argument below did not waive the exhaustion requirement, and it ordered the case dismissed so that the claim could be presented in state court. In a unanimous opinion by Justice Stevens, the Supreme Court adopted a "middle course" between automatic waiver of the exhaustion requirement and automatic dismissal for failure to exhaust:

> "When the state answers a habeas corpus petition, it has a duty to advise the district court whether the prisoner has, in fact, exhausted all available state remedies. As this case demonstrates, however, there are exceptional cases in which the state fails, whether inadvertently or otherwise, to raise an arguably meritorious nonexhaustion defense. The state's omission in such a case makes it appropriate for the court of appeals to take a fresh look at the issue. The court should determine whether the interests of comity and federalism will be better served by addressing the merits forthwith or by requiring a series of additional state and federal court proceedings before reviewing the merits of the petitioner's claim."

The Court then gave examples of appropriate dispositions. If an "unresolved question of fact or state law" were relevant to the merits of the federal claim, exhaustion might be required. But if the federal claim were clearly meritorious or clearly without merit, then a decision on the merits might be called for. The Court remanded for application of this approach.

Is *Granberry* consistent with *Rose v. Lundy?* Why is ad hoc consideration of "the interests of comity and federalism" suitable in one case but not the other?

4. Repetitive Petitions: *Sanders v. United States.* One of the byproducts of state and federal post-conviction remedies is the opportunity for repetitive applications for relief. This raises the possibility that criminal convictions may never be final and the underlying controversy never settled. The exhaustion requirement in some contexts compounds the difficulty. Lundy's options were to re-file his unexhausted claims in state court and then return to federal court, to forego his unexhausted claims and re-file his federal petition, or to do both.

As mentioned in *Lundy,* the decision in Sanders v. United States, 373 U.S. 1 (1963), addressed the problem of repetitive applications in the context of a § 2255 proceeding. *Sanders* held that the standards governing federal and state prisoners on this question were the same.

It then said that relief can be denied on the ground of repetitive applications only if:

> "(1) the same ground presented in the subsequent application was determined adversely to the applicant on the prior application, (2) the prior determination was on the merits, and (3) the ends of justice would not be served by reaching the merits of the subsequent application."

The Court also held that a petition alleging new grounds for relief could be denied because of a prior petition only if an "abuse" of the writ had occurred, under standards quoted by Justice Brennan in *Lundy*.

There have been two subsequent legislative developments since the decision in *Sanders*. The first was the enactment in 1966 of 28 U.S.C. § 2244(b):

> "When after an evidentiary hearing on the merits of a material factual issue, or after a hearing on the merits of an issue of law, a person in custody pursuant to the judgment of a State court has been denied by a court of the United States . . . release from custody or other remedy on an application for a writ of habeas corpus, a subsequent application for a writ of habeas corpus in behalf of such person need not be entertained by a court of the United States . . . unless the application alleges and is predicated on a factual or other ground not adjudicated on the hearing of the earlier application for the writ, and unless the court . . . is satisfied that the applicant has not on the earlier application deliberately withheld the newly asserted ground or otherwise abused the writ."

The second was the adoption of separate rules governing § 2254 and § 2255 proceedings.[e] These rules were promulgated by the Court in 1976, postponed by Congress in that year, but subsequently enacted to become effective in 1977. Exactly what constitutes an "abuse" of the writ has not been clarified.[f]

NOTES ON THE CUSTODY REQUIREMENT

1. *Jones v. Cunningham.* From the beginning, habeas corpus has been available only to persons in "custody." For a long time, this meant jail or prison. The relaxation of this requirement began in Jones v. Cunningham, 371 U.S. 236 (1963). In 1953 Jones was sen-

[e] Rule 9(b) as quoted in *Lundy* is from the § 2254 Rules. The counterpart is Rule 9(b) in the § 2255 Rules, which is identical in all material respects. The rules for state prisoners are called the "§ 2254 Rules" because that statute elaborates the conditions under which the writ authorized by § 2241(c)(3) can be granted. For an extensive examination of Rule 9, see Robert Clinton, Rule 9 of the Federal Habeas Corpus Rules: A Case Study in the Need for Reform of the Rules Enabling Acts, 63 Iowa L.Rev. 15 (1977).

[f] For examination of this problem in one important context, see Steven M. Goldstein, Application of Res Judicata Principles to Successive Federal Habeas Corpus Petitions in Capital Cases: The Search for an Equitable Approach, 21 U.C.Davis L.Rev. 45 (1987).

tenced to 10 years' imprisonment, in part because he was a three-time offender. One of his prior convictions was for larceny in 1946. In 1961, he filed a habeas corpus petition alleging that his 1946 conviction was invalid because he had been denied the right to counsel. The District Court denied relief without inquiring into the truth of his allegations. Shortly before the case was to be argued before the Court of Appeals, Jones was paroled. The state then asked the Court of Appeals to dismiss the case on the ground that Jones was no longer in "custody" as required by the habeas corpus statutes. That court agreed, holding that the case had become moot as to the original respondent (the warden of the state penitentiary) and that the members of the parole board could not be substituted as proper respondents in the habeas action because they did not have "physical custody" of Jones.

The Supreme Court unanimously reversed. After a review of history and precedent, it reinterpreted the requirement of "custody" as follows:

"[I]n fact, as well as in theory, the custody and control of the parole board involve significant restraints on petitioner's liberty because of his conviction and sentence, which are in addition to those imposed by the state upon the public generally. Petitioner is confined by the parole order to a particular community, house, and job at the sufferance of his parole officer. He cannot drive a car without permission. He must periodically report to his parole officer, permit the officer to visit his home and job at any time, and follow the officer's advice. He is admonished to keep good company and good hours, work regularly, keep away from undesirable places, and live a clean, honest, and temperate life. Petitioner must not only faithfully obey these restrictions and conditions but he must live in constant fear that a single deviation, however slight, might be enough to result in his being returned to prison to serve out the very sentence he claims was imposed on him in violation of the United States Constitution. He can be rearrested at any time the Board or parole officer believes he has violated a term or condition of parole, and he might be thrown back in jail to finish serving the allegedly invalid sentence with few, if any, of the procedural safeguards that normally must be and are provided to those charged with crime. . . . While petitioner's parole releases him from immediate physical imprisonment, it imposes conditions which significantly confine and restrain his freedom; this is enough to keep him in the 'custody' of members of the Virginia Parole Board within the meaning of the habeas corpus statute. . . ."

Jones does not eliminate the requirement of "custody," but it does open the doors of habeas courts to persons who are not confined but who nonetheless suffer restraints on their liberty. Thus, a person on probation or one whose sentence has been suspended on condition of good behavior is in "custody" and may challenge the underlying conviction in a habeas corpus proceeding. The Court has also held that a person who is free on his own recognizance pending execution of sentence is in "custody" for this purpose. See Hensley v. Municipal Court, 411 U.S. 345 (1973).[a]

2. *Peyton v. Rowe* and The Prematurity Doctrine. Historically, the only appropriate relief in a federal habeas corpus proceeding was immediate release from custody. If the prisoner could be retained in custody for a reason independent of the challenged conviction, habeas was unavailable. In McNally v. Hill, 293 U.S. 131 (1934), this doctrine was applied to deny relief where a prisoner serving the first of two consecutive sentences sought to challenge the second. Because he was not yet serving the second sentence, and would not be entitled to immediate release even if the second sentence were invalidated, he was not entitled to habeas relief. The rule of *McNally* came to be called the "prematurity doctrine"—it was premature for McNally to seek habeas because he had not yet begun to serve the sentence he was seeking to attack.

The Catch–22 aspect of a strict application of this rule was strikingly revealed in Walker v. Wainwright, 390 U.S. 335 (1968). Walker was serving a life sentence for murder. He had also been given a consecutive five-year sentence for aggravated assault. He filed a habeas petition to challenge his murder conviction, but the lower courts dismissed on the ground that even if it were successful he would not be entitled to immediate release—he still would have to serve the five-year sentence for assault. As the Supreme Court put it, the lower courts in substance "held that [Walker] could not challenge his life sentence until after he had served it." The Supreme Court distinguished *McNally* and reversed in a per curiam decision.

Later that term, *McNally* was overruled in Peyton v. Rowe, 391 U.S. 54 (1968). Rowe had been sentenced to 30 years for rape, and subsequently was given a 20–year consecutive sentence. He challenged only the 20–year sentence. The District Court dismissed his habeas petition on the authority of *McNally,* holding that Rowe could not challenge the 20–year sentence until 1993, the year the rape sentence would be completed. The Court of Appeals reversed en banc. Speaking through Judge Haynsworth, it predicted unanimously that the Supreme Court would overrule *McNally.*

Judge Haynsworth's forecast proved accurate. The Supreme Court unanimously affirmed, holding that "immediate physical release" from confinement was not the only habeas remedy available and that, in effect, Rowe should be regarded as in "custody" under a single 50–year sentence, 20 years of which he sought to set aside. The Court buttressed its conclusion by an historical review of habeas corpus and by the practical conclusion that it served the interests of all concerned to

[a] For a history and discussion of the custody requirement, see Robbins and Newell, The Continuing Diminishing Availability of Federal Habeas Review to Challenge State Court Judgments: *Lehman v. Lycoming County Children's Services Agency,* 3 Am. U.L. Rev. 271 (1984).

settle the constitutionality of a criminal conviction while witnesses were available and retrial was still possible.

CONCLUDING PROBLEM: *BRADEN v. 30TH JUDICIAL CIRCUIT*

1. Introduction. Section 2241(a) provides that habeas corpus may be granted by district courts "within their respective jurisdictions." It was held in Ahrens v. Clark, 335 U.S. 188 (1948), that this phrase required "the presence within the territorial jurisdiction of the district court of the person detained [as a] prerequisite to filing a petition for [a] writ of habeas corpus." [a] The effect of this limitation in the context of interstate detainers came before the Court in Braden v. 30th Judicial Circuit Court of Kentucky, 410 U.S. 484 (1973).

2. *Smith v. Hooey.* On the merits, *Braden* involved the meaning of Smith v. Hooey, 393 U.S. 374 (1969). Smith had been indicted in Texas while serving a federal prison sentence at Leavenworth, Kansas. He wrote the Texas officials demanding a speedy trial and was notified that they were ready to try him "within two weeks of any date [he] might specify at which he could be present." He made additional demands for trial for six more years, during which the state made no formal efforts to bring him to trial. Finally, he sought mandamus in the Texas Supreme Court to get the charges dismissed. The writ was refused, and the Supreme Court granted certiorari.

The Court first noted the ways in which delayed trial on pending charges may affect persons imprisoned in another jurisdiction: the passage of time may make it impossible to present a defense; the defendant may be able to get a concurrent sentence if a new sentence is imposed before the old one expires; the chance of parole is often decreased by the existence of pending charges against the prisoner; and conditions of confinement are often influenced by the existence of pending charges. The Court also noted that Texas could easily have brought Smith to trial simply by asking the federal authorities to make him available. It held that Texas "had a constitutional duty to make a diligent, good faith effort" to bring Smith to trial, and reversed and remanded for proceedings not inconsistent with its opinion.[b]

3. The Problem in *Braden.* Braden was imprisoned in Alabama at a time when he was wanted in Kentucky on other charges. As is standard practice, the Kentucky prosecutor filed a detainer with the Alabama prison officials, thus notifying them that Kentucky planned to prosecute Braden at the conclusion of his Alabama sentence. Braden took the position that he wanted to be tried in Kentucky before the

---

[a] Section 2241(d), enacted in 1966, modified *Ahrens* in a narrow sense. In states which have multiple districts, § 2241(d) confers concurrent jurisdiction in the district where the prisoner is incarcerated and the district, if different, where the prisoner was convicted and sentenced. But it was thought that the *Ahrens* rule was otherwise unmodified by the 1966 legislation. See Nelson v. George, 399 U.S. 224, 228 n.5 (1970).

[b] The Court was not specific as to what those proceedings might be.

conclusion of his Alabama sentence. The Kentucky indictment had been returned three years earlier, and he claimed under *Smith* that Kentucky was denying him his right to a speedy trial if it did not make efforts to prosecute him promptly.

His problem was where to make the argument. He tried the Kentucky state courts first and was unable to obtain any relief. He then sought habeas corpus in a Kentucky federal district court, which granted relief but which was reversed by the Court of Appeals for the Sixth Circuit on the ground that, under *Ahrens v. Clark,* the Kentucky federal courts had no jurisdiction over a person incarcerated in Alabama. But the rule in the Fifth Circuit at the time appeared to be that, even though Alabama was the place of incarceration, it too was an inappropriate forum. The Sixth Circuit concluded: "Braden thus may find himself ensnared in what has aptly been termed 'Catch 2254'— unable to vindicate his constitutional rights in either of the only two states that could possibly afford a remedy. See Tuttle, Catch 2254: Federal Jurisdiction and Interstate Detainers, 32 U. Pitt. L. Rev. 489, 502–03 (1971)."

4. The Majority Opinion. The Supreme Court granted certiorari and reversed. Justice Brennan's opinion for the Court discussed three problems: whether the "custody" requirement was satisfied, whether Braden had exhausted his state remedies, and whether the rule of *Ahrens v. Clark* should be followed in this context.

(i) Custody. The Court held that Braden was "currently in 'custody' within the meaning of the federal habeas corpus statute." It noted that prior to *Rowe v. Peyton* the prematurity doctrine would have precluded relief. But the *Rowe* decision "opened the door to this action." The Court elaborated in a footnote:

> "In Smith v. Hooey, 393 U.S. 374 (1969), we considered a speedy trial claim similar to the one presented in the case before us, and we held that a state which had lodged a detainer against a petitioner in another state must, on the prisoner's demand, 'make a diligent, good-faith effort' to bring the prisoner to trial. But that case arose on direct review of the denial of relief by the state court, and we had no occasion to consider whether the same or similar claims could have been raised on federal habeas corpus. Yet it logically follows from Peyton v. Rowe, 391 U.S. 54 (1968), that the claims can be raised on collateral attack. In this context, as opposed to the situation presented in *Peyton,* the 'future custody' under attack will not be imposed by the same sovereign which holds the petitioner in his current confinement. Nevertheless, the considerations which were held in *Peyton* to warrant a prompt resolution of the claim also apply with full force in this context. Since the Alabama warden acts here as the agent of the Commonwealth of Kentucky in holding the petitioner pursuant to the Kentucky detainer, we have no difficulty concluding that petitioner is 'in custody' for purposes of 28 U.S.C. § 2241(c)(3). On the

facts of this case, we need not decide whether, if no detainer had been issued against him, petitioner would be sufficiently 'in custody' to attack the Kentucky indictment by an action in habeas corpus."

(ii) **Exhaustion.** On the exhaustion question, Justice Brennan noted that Braden had not yet been tried on the Kentucky charges and he was free to assert a speedy trial defense if and when he was finally brought to trial. He also reaffirmed the decision in *Ex parte Royall* that federal habeas normally does not lie "to adjudicate the merits of an affirmative defense to a state criminal charge prior to a judgment of conviction by a state court." But this case was different:

"Petitioner does not, however, seek at this time to litigate a federal defense to a criminal charge, but only to demand enforcement of the commonwealth's affirmative constitutional obligation to bring him promptly to trial. He has made repeated demands for trial to the courts of Kentucky, offering those courts an opportunity to consider on the merits his constitutional claim of the *present* denial of a speedy trial. Under these circumstances it is clear that he has exhausted all available state court remedies for consideration of that constitutional claim, even though Kentucky has not yet brought him to trial. . . .

"The fundamental interests underlying the exhaustion doctrine have been fully satisfied in petitioner's situation. He has already presented his federal constitutional claim of a *present* denial of a speedy trial to the courts of Kentucky. The state courts rejected the claim, apparently on the ground that since he had once escaped from custody the commonwealth should not be obligated to incur the risk of another escape by returning him for trial. Petitioner exhausted all available state court opportunities to establish his position that the prior escape did not obviate the commonwealth's duty under *Smith v. Hooey,* supra. Moreover, petitioner made no effort to abort a state proceeding or to disrupt the orderly functioning of state judicial processes. He comes to federal court, not in an effort to forestall a state prosecution, but to enforce the commonwealth's obligation to provide him with a state court forum. He delayed his application for federal relief until the state courts had conclusively determined that his prosecution was temporarily moribund. Since petitioner began serving the second of two 10–year Alabama sentences in March 1972, the revival of the prosecution may be delayed until as late as 1982. A federal habeas corpus action at this time and under these circumstances does not jeopardize any legitimate interest of federalism. . . .

"We emphasize that nothing we have said would permit the derailment of a pending state proceeding by an attempt to litigate constitutional defenses prematurely in federal court.

The contention in dissent that our decision converts federal habeas corpus into 'a pretrial-motion forum for state prisoners,' wholly misapprehends today's holding."

(iii) **The *Ahrens* Issue.** Having held that Braden's claim was ripe for consideration on federal habeas, the Court turned to the question of the appropriate forum. Justice Brennan noted that in terms of traditional venue considerations, Kentucky appeared to be the most desirable forum. He concluded that it was no longer appropriate to view *Ahrens* "as dictating the choice of an inconvenient forum . . . in a class of cases which could not have been foreseen at the time of our decision." c He read the language of § 2241(a) as requiring only that

"the court issuing the writ have jurisdiction over the custodian. So long as the custodian can be reached by service of process, the court can issue a writ 'within its jurisdiction' requiring that the prisoner be brought before the court for a hearing on his claim, or requiring that he be released outright from custody, even if the prisoner himself is confined outside the court's territorial jurisdiction."

5. **The Rehnquist Dissent.** Justice Rehnquist, joined by Chief Justice Burger and Justice Powell, dissented. He thought it inappropriate to overrule *Ahrens v. Clark,* arguing that this was an area of statutory interpretation where stare decisis should prevail. On the custody and exhaustion issues, he concluded that the majority had "explicitly" extended *Peyton v. Rowe* and "implicitly" rejected *Ex parte Royall.* He explained:

"It by no means follows [from *Smith v. Hooey*] that a state prisoner can assert the right to a speedy trial in a federal district court. The fundamental flaw in the reasoning of the Court is the assumption that since a prisoner has some 'right' under *Smith* he must have some forum in which affirmatively to assert that right, and that therefore the right may be vindicated in a federal district court under § 2241(c)(3). *Smith v. Hooey* did not, however, establish that a right distinct from the right to a speedy trial existed. It merely held that a state could not totally rely on the fact that it could not order that a prisoner be brought from another jurisdiction as a justification for not attempting to try the defendant as expeditiously as possible. The right to a speedy trial is, like other constitutional rights, a defense to a criminal charge, but one which, unlike others, increases in terms of potential benefit to the accused with the passage of time. The fact that a state must make an effort to obtain a defendant from another sovereign for trial but fails, after demand, to make an effort would weigh heavily in the defendant's favor. But *Smith v. Hooey* does not necessarily imply that federal courts may, as the District Court did

c In a footnote, he added that he did not mean to preclude the exercise of concurrent habeas corpus jurisdiction by a federal court in the district of confinement. If habeas were filed there, he added, "the court can, of course, transfer the suit to a more convenient forum. 28 U.S.C. § 1404(a)."

in this case, in effect, issue an injunction requiring a state court to conduct a criminal trial. If the state fails to perform its duty, it must face the consequences of possibly not obtaining a conviction. But the fact that the state has a duty by no means leads to the conclusion that the failure to perform that duty can be raised by a prospective defendant on federal habeas corpus in advance of trial. The history of habeas corpus and the principles of federalism strongly support the approach established by *Ex parte Royall* that, absent extraordinary circumstances, federal habeas corpus should not be used to adjudicate the merits of an affirmative defense to a state criminal charge prior to a judgment of conviction by a state court.

". . . Even though a person may be 'in custody' for purposes of §§ 2241(c)(3), or 2254, if he has not yet begun to serve a sentence entered after a judgment of conviction, as the Court held in *Peyton,* it by no means follows that he is similarly 'in custody' when no judgment of conviction has been entered or even any trial on the underlying charge conducted. The Court's suggestion that a person may challenge by way of federal habeas corpus any custody that might possibly be imposed at some time in the 'future,' which suggestion unwarrantedly assumes both that a constitutional defense will be rejected and that the jury will convict is not supported by the language or reasoning of *Peyton.*

"The Court here glosses over the disparate procedural posture of this case, and merely asserts, without analyzing the historical function of federal habeas corpus for state prisoners, that the rationale of *Peyton* is applicable to a pretrial, preconviction situation. Citation to that decision cannot obscure the fact that the Court here makes a significant departure from previous decisions . . . . What the Court here disregards . . . is almost a century of decisions of this Court to the effect that federal habeas corpus for state prisoners, prior to conviction, should not be granted absent truly extraordinary circumstances. . . . The situations in which pretrial or preconviction federal interference by way of habeas corpus with state criminal processes is justified involve the lack of jurisdiction, under the supremacy clause, for the state to bring any criminal charges against the petitioner. Wildenhus's Case, 120 U.S. 1 (1887); In re Loney, 134 U.S. 372 (1890); In re Neagle, 135 U.S. 1 (1890).

"The effect of today's ruling that federal habeas corpus prior to trial is appropriate because it will determine the validity of custody that *may* be imposed in actuality only sometime in the indefinite future constitutes an unjustifiable federal interference with the judicial administration of a state's criminal laws. The use of federal habeas corpus is, presumably, limited neither to the interstate detainer situation nor to the constitutional rights secured by the sixth and 14th amendments. The same reasoning would apply to a state prisoner who alleges that 'future custody' will result because the state plans to introduce at a criminal trial sometime in the future a confession allegedly obtained in violation of the fifth and 14th amendments, or evidence obtained in violation of the fourth and 14th amendments. I thoroughly disagree with this conversion of federal habeas corpus into a pretrial-motion forum for state prisoners."

SECTION 2: THE SCOPE OF REVIEW

STONE v. POWELL
United States Supreme Court, 1976.
428 U.S. 465.

MR. JUSTICE POWELL delivered the opinion of the Court.

Respondents in these cases were convicted of criminal offenses in state courts, and their convictions were affirmed on appeal. The prosecution in each case relied upon evidence obtained by searches and seizures alleged by respondents to have been unlawful. Each respondent subsequently sought relief in a federal district court by filing a petition for a writ of federal habeas corpus under 28 U.S.C. § 2254. The question presented is whether a federal court should consider, in ruling on a petition for habeas corpus relief filed by a state prisoner, a claim that evidence obtained by an unconstitutional search or seizure was introduced at his trial, when he has previously been afforded an opportunity for full and fair litigation of his claim in the state courts. The issue is of considerable importance to the administration of criminal justice.

I

We summarize first the relevant facts and procedural history of these cases.

A

Respondent Lloyd Powell was convicted of murder in June 1968 after trial in a California state court. At about midnight on February 17, 1968, he and three companions entered the Bonanza Liquor Store in San Bernardino, Cal., where Powell became involved in an altercation with Gerald Parsons, the store manager, over the theft of a bottle of wine. In the scuffling that followed Powell shot and killed Parsons' wife. Ten hours later an officer of the Henderson, Nev., Police Department arrested Powell for violation of the Henderson vagrancy ordinance, and in the search incident to the arrest discovered a .38–caliber revolver with six expended cartridges in the cylinder.

Powell was extradited to California and convicted of second-degree murder in the Superior Court of San Bernardino County. Parsons and Powell's accomplices at the liquor store testified against him. A criminologist testified that the revolver found on Powell was the gun that killed Parsons' wife. The trial court rejected Powell's contention that testimony by the Henderson police officer as to the search and the discovery of the revolver should have been excluded because the vagrancy ordinance was unconstitutional. In October 1969, the conviction was affirmed by a California District Court of Appeal. Although the issue was duly presented, that court found it unnecessary to pass upon the legality of the arrest and search because it concluded that the error, if any, in admitting the testimony of the Henderson officer was harmless beyond a reasonable doubt under Chapman v. California, 386 U.S. 18 (1967). The Supreme Court of California denied Powell's petition for habeas corpus relief.

In August 1971 Powell filed an amended petition for a writ of federal habeas corpus under 28 U.S.C. § 2254 . . ., contending that the testimony concerning the .38–caliber revolver should have been excluded as the fruit of an illegal search. He argued that his arrest had been unlawful because the Henderson vagrancy ordinance was unconstitutionally vague, and that the arresting officer lacked probable cause to believe that he was violating it. The District Court concluded that the arresting officer had probable cause and held that even if the vagrancy ordinance was unconstitutional, the deterrent purpose of the exclusionary rule does not require that it be applied to bar admission of the fruits of a search incident to an otherwise valid arrest. In the alternative, that court agreed with the California District Court of Appeal that the admission of the evidence concerning Powell's arrest, if error, was harmless beyond a reasonable doubt.

In December 1974, the Court of Appeals . . . reversed. The court concluded that the vagrancy ordinance was unconstitutionally vague, that Powell's arrest was therefore illegal, and that although exclusion of the evidence would serve no deterrent purpose with regard to police officers who were enforcing statutes in good faith, exclusion would serve the public interest by deterring legislators from enacting unconstitutional statutes. After an independent review of the evidence the court concluded that the admission of the evidence was not harmless error since it supported the testimony of Parsons and Powell's accomplices.

B

Respondent David Rice was convicted of murder in April 1971 after trial in a Nebraska state court. At 2:05 a.m. on August 17, 1970, Omaha police received a telephone call that a woman had been heard screaming at 2867 Ohio Street. As one of the officers sent to that address examined a suitcase lying in the doorway, it exploded, killing him instantly. By August 22 the investigation of the murder centered on Duane Peak, a 15–year old member of the National Committee to

Combat Fascism (NCCF), and that afternoon a warrant was issued for Peak's arrest. The investigation also focused on other known members of the NCCF, including Rice, some of whom were believed to be planning to kill Peak before he could incriminate them. In their search for Peak, the police went to Rice's home at 10:30 that night and found lights and a television on, but there was no response to their repeated knocking. While some officers remained to watch the premises, a warrant was obtained to search for explosives and illegal weapons believed to be in Rice's possession. Peak was not in the house, but upon entering the police discovered, in plain view, dynamite, blasting caps, and other materials useful in the construction of explosive devices. Peak subsequently was arrested, and on August 27, Rice voluntarily surrendered. The clothes Rice was wearing at that time were subjected to chemical analysis, disclosing dynamite particles.

Rice was tried for first-degree murder in the District Court of Douglas County. At trial Peak admitted planting the suitcase and making the telephone call, and implicated Rice in the bombing plot. As corroborative evidence the state introduced items seized during the search, as well as the results of the chemical analysis of Rice's clothing. The court denied Rice's motion to suppress this evidence. On appeal the Supreme Court of Nebraska affirmed the conviction, holding that the search of Rice's home had been pursuant to a valid search warrant.

In September 1972 Rice filed a petition for a writ of habeas corpus. . . . Rice's sole contention was that his incarceration was unlawful because the evidence underlying his conviction had been discovered as the result of an illegal search of his home. The District Court concluded that the search warrant was invalid, as the supporting affidavit was defective under Spinelli v. United States, 393 U.S. 410 (1969), and Aguilar v. Texas, 378 U.S. 108 (1964). The court also rejected the state's contention that even if the warrant was invalid the search was justified because of the valid arrest warrant for Peak and because of the exigent circumstances of the situation—danger to Peak and search for bombs and explosives believed in possession of the NCCF. The court reasoned that the arrest warrant did not justify the entry as the police lacked probable cause to believe Peak was in the house, and further concluded that the circumstances were not sufficiently exigent to justify an immediate warrantless search. The Court of Appeals . . . affirmed, substantially for the reasons stated by the District Court.

Petitioners Stone and Wolff, the wardens of the respective state prisons where Powell and Rice are incarcerated, petitioned for review of these decisions, raising questions concerning the scope of federal habeas corpus and the role of the exclusionary rule upon collateral review of cases involving fourth amendment claims. We granted their petitions for certiorari. We now reverse.

II

The authority of federal courts to issue the writ of habeas corpus ad subjiciendum was included in the first grant of federal-court jurisdiction, made by the Judiciary Act of 1789, with the limitation that the writ extend only to prisoners held in custody by the United States. The original statutory authorization did not define the substantive reach of the writ. It merely stated that the courts of the United States "shall have power to issue writs of . . . habeas corpus. . . ." The courts defined the scope of the writ in accordance with the common law and limited it to an inquiry as to the jurisdiction of the sentencing tribunal. See, e.g., Ex parte Watkins, 28 U.S. (3 Pet.) 193 (1830) (Marshall, C.J.).

In 1867 the writ was extended to state prisoners. Under the 1867 act federal courts were authorized to give relief in "all cases where any person may be restrained of his or her liberty in violation of the Constitution, or of any treaty or law of the United States. . . ." But the limitation of federal habeas corpus jurisdiction to consideration of the jurisdiction of the sentencing court persisted. And, although the concept of "jurisdiction" was subjected to considerable strain as the substantive scope of the writ was expanded,[7] this expansion was limited to only a few classes of cases [8] until Frank v. Mangum, 237 U.S. 309, in 1915. In *Frank,* the prisoner had claimed in the state courts that the proceedings which resulted in his conviction for murder had been dominated by a mob. After the state Supreme Court rejected his contentions, Frank unsuccessfully sought habeas corpus relief in the federal district court. This Court affirmed the denial of relief because Frank's federal claims had been considered by a competent and unbiased state tribunal. The Court recognized, however, that if a habeas corpus court found that the state had failed to provide adequate "corrective process" for the full and fair litigation of federal claims, whether or not "jurisdictional," the court could inquire into the merits to determine whether a detention was lawful.

In the landmark [decision] in Brown v. Allen, 344 U.S. 443 (1953), . . . the scope of the writ was expanded still further. [Brown] applied for federal habeas corpus relief claiming that the trial [court] had erred in failing to quash [his indictment] due to alleged discrimination in the selection of grand jurors and in ruling [a confession] admissible. [T]he highest court of the state had rejected these claims on direct appeal, and this Court had denied certiorari. Despite the apparent adequacy of the state corrective process, the Court reviewed the denial of the writ of habeas corpus and held that Brown was entitled to a full reconsideration of these constitutional claims, including, if appropriate, a hearing in the federal district court. . . .[10]

---

[7] Prior to 1889 there was, in practical effect, no appellate review in federal criminal cases. The possibility of Supreme Court review on certificate of division of opinion in the circuit court was remote because of the practice of single district judges' holding circuit court. Pressure naturally developed for expansion of the scope of habeas corpus to reach otherwise unreviewable decisions involving fundamental rights.

[8] The expansion occurred primarily with regard to (i) convictions based on assertedly unconstitutional statutes, e.g., Ex parte Siebold, 100 U.S. 371 (1879), or (ii) detentions based upon an allegedly illegal sentence, e.g., Ex parte Lange, 85 U.S. (18 Wall.) 163 (1873).

[10] Despite the expansion of the scope of the writ, there has been no change in the established rule with respect to nonconstitutional claims. The writ of habeas corpus

During the period in which the substantive scope of the writ was expanded, the Court did not consider whether exceptions to full review might exist with respect to particular categories of constitutional claims. Prior to the Court's decision in Kaufman v. United States, 394 U.S. 217 (1969), however, a substantial majority of the federal courts of appeals had concluded that collateral review of search-and-seizure claims was inappropriate on motions filed by federal prisoners under 28 U.S.C. § 2255, the modern postconviction procedure available to federal prisoners in lieu of habeas corpus. The primary rationale advanced in support of those decisions was that fourth amendment violations are different in kind from denials of fifth or sixth amendment rights in that claims of illegal search and seizure do not "impugn the integrity of the fact-finding process or challenge evidence as inherently unreliable; rather, the exclusion of illegally seized evidence is simply a prophylactic device intended generally to deter fourth amendment violations by law enforcement officers."

Kaufman rejected this rationale and held that search-and-seizure claims are cognizable in § 2255 proceedings. The Court noted that "the federal habeas remedy extends to state prisoners alleging that unconstitutionally obtained evidence was admitted against them at trial," and concluded, as matter of statutory construction, that there was no basis for restricting "access by federal prisoners with illegal search-and-seizure claims to federal collateral remedies, while placing no similar restriction on access by state prisoners." Although in recent years the view has been expressed that the Court should re-examine the substantive scope of federal habeas jurisdiction and limit collateral review of search-and-seizure claims "solely to the question of whether the petitioner was provided a fair opportunity to raise and have adjudicated the question in state courts," Schneckloth v. Bustamonte, 412 U.S. 218, 250 (1973) (Powell, J., concurring),[13] the Court, without discussion or consideration of the issue, has continued to accept jurisdiction in cases raising such claims. See Lefkowitz v. Newsome, 420 U.S. 283 (1975); Cady v. Dombrowski, 413 U.S. 433 (1973); Cardwell v. Lewis, 417 U.S. 583 (1974) (plurality opinion).

The discussion in *Kaufman* of the scope of federal habeas corpus rests on the view that the effectuation of the fourth amendment, as applied to the states through the 14th amendment, requires the granting of habeas corpus relief when a prisoner has been convicted in state court on the basis of evidence obtained in an illegal search or seizure since those amendments were held in Mapp v. Ohio, 367 U.S. 643 (1961), to require exclusion of such evidence at trial and reversal of conviction upon direct review. Until these cases we have not had occasion fully to consider the validity of this view. Upon examination, we conclude, in light of the nature and purpose of the fourth amend-

and its federal counterpart, 28 U.S.C. § 2255, "will not be allowed to do service for an appeal." Sunal v. Large, 332 U.S. 174, 178 (1947). For this reason, nonconstitutional claims that could have been raised on appeal, but were not, may not be asserted in collateral proceedings. . . .

[13] See, e.g., Friendly, Is Innocence Irrelevant? Collateral Attack on Criminal Judgments, 38 U. Chi. L. Rev. 142 (1970).

ment exclusionary rule, that this view is unjustified.[16] We hold, therefore, that where the state has provided an opportunity for full and fair litigation of a fourth amendment claim, the Constitution does not require that a state prisoner be granted federal habeas corpus relief on the ground that evidence obtained in an unconstitutional search or seizure was introduced at his trial.

III

The fourth amendment assures the "right of the people to be secure in their persons, houses, papers, and effects, against unreasonable searches and seizures." The amendment was primarily a reaction to the evils associated with the use of the general warrant in England and the writs of assistance in the Colonies, and was intended to protect the "sanctity of a man's home and the privacies of life" from searches under unchecked general authority.

The exclusionary rule was a judicially created means of effectuating the rights secured by the fourth amendment. Prior to the Court's decisions in Weeks v. United States, 232 U.S. 383 (1914), and Gouled v. United States, 255 U.S. 298 (1921), there existed no barrier to the introduction in criminal trials of evidence obtained in violation of the amendment. In *Weeks* the Court held that the defendant could petition before trial for the return of property secured through an illegal search or seizure conducted by federal authorities. In *Gouled* the Court held broadly that such evidence could not be introduced in a federal prosecution. Thirty-five years after *Weeks* the Court held in Wolf v. Colorado, 338 U.S. 25 (1949), that the right to be free from arbitrary intrusion by the police that is protected by the fourth amendment is "implicit in 'the concept of ordered liberty' and as such enforceable against the states through the [14th amendment] due process clause." The Court concluded, however, that the *Weeks* exclusionary rule would not be imposed upon the states as "an essential ingredient of [that] right." The full force of *Wolf* was eroded in subsequent decisions, and a little more than a decade later the exclusionary rule was held applicable to the states in Mapp v. Ohio, 367 U.S. 643 (1961).

Decisions prior to *Mapp* advanced two principal reasons for application of the rule in federal trials. The Court in Elkins v. United States, 364 U.S. 206 (1960), for example, in the context of its special supervisory role over the lower federal courts, referred to the "imperative of judicial integrity," suggesting that exclusion of illegally seized evidence prevents contamination of the judicial process. But even in that context a more pragmatic ground was emphasized:

"The rule is calculated to prevent, not to repair. Its purpose is to deter—to compel respect for the constitutional guaranty in

[16] The issue in *Kaufman* was the scope of § 2255. Our decision today rejects the dictum in *Kaufman* concerning the applicability of the exclusionary rule in federal habeas corpus review of state-court decisions pursuant to § 2254. To the extent the application of the exclusionary rule in *Kaufman* did not rely upon the supervisory role of this Court over the lower federal courts, the rationale for its application in that context is also rejected.

the only effectively available way—by removing the incentive to disregard it."

The *Mapp* majority justified the application of the rule to the states on several grounds, but relied principally upon the belief that exclusion would deter future unlawful police conduct.

Although our decisions often have alluded to the "imperative of judicial integrity," they demonstrate the limited role of this justification in the determination whether to apply the rule in a particular context. Logically extended this justification would require that courts exclude unconstitutionally seized evidence despite lack of objection by the defendant, or even over his assent. It also would require abandonment of the standing limitations on who may object to the introduction of unconstitutionally seized evidence, Alderman v. United States, 394 U.S. 165 (1969), and retreat from the proposition that judicial proceedings need not abate when the defendant's person is unconstitutionally seized, Gerstein v. Pugh, 420 U.S. 103, 119 (1975). Similarly, the interest in promoting judicial integrity does not prevent the use of illegally seized evidence in grand jury proceedings. United States v. Calandra, 414 U.S. 338 (1974). Nor does it require that the trial court exclude such evidence from use for impeachment of a defendant, even though its introduction is certain to result in conviction in some cases. Walder v. United States, 347 U.S. 62 (1954). The teaching of these cases is clear. While courts, of course, must ever be concerned with preserving the integrity of the judicial process, this concern has limited force as a justification for the exclusion of highly probative evidence. The force of this justification becomes minimal where federal habeas corpus relief is sought by a prisoner who previously has been afforded the opportunity for full and fair consideration of his search-and-seizure claim at trial and on direct review.

The primary justification for the exclusionary rule then is the deterrence of police conduct that violates fourth amendment rights. Post-*Mapp* decisions have established that the rule is not a personal constitutional right. It is not calculated to redress the injury to the privacy of the victim of the search or seizure, for any "[r]eparation comes too late." Linkletter v. Walker, 381 U.S. 618, 637 (1965). Instead, "the rule is a judicially created remedy designed to safeguard fourth amendment rights generally through its deterrent effect. . . ." *United States v. Calandra*, supra, at 348.

Mapp involved the enforcement of the exclusionary rule at state trials and on direct review. The decision in *Kaufman*, as noted above, is premised on the view that implementation of the fourth amendment also requires the consideration of search-and-seizure claims upon collateral review of state convictions. But despite the broad deterrent purpose of the exclusionary rule, it has never been interpreted to proscribe the introduction of illegally seized evidence in all proceedings or against all persons. As in the case of any remedial device, "the application of the rule has been restricted to those areas where its remedial objectives are thought most efficaciously served." *United*

States v. Calandra, supra, at 348.[24] Thus, our refusal to extend the exclusionary rule to grand jury proceedings was based on a balancing of the potential injury to the historic role and function of the grand jury by such extension against the potential contribution to the effectuation of the fourth amendment through deterrence of police misconduct:

> "Any incremental deterrent effect which might be achieved by extending the rule to grand jury proceedings is uncertain at best. Whatever deterrence of police misconduct may result from the exclusion of illegally seized evidence from criminal trials, it is unrealistic to assume that application of the rule to grand jury proceedings would significantly further that goal. Such an extension would deter only police investigation consciously directed toward the discovery of evidence solely for use in a grand jury investigation. . . . We therefore decline to embrace a view that would achieve a speculative and undoubtedly minimal advance in the deterrence of police misconduct at the expense of substantially impeding the role of the grand jury." 414 U.S., at 351 (footnote omitted).

The same pragmatic analysis of the exclusionary rule's usefulness in a particular context was evident earlier in Walder v. United States, 347 U.S. 62 (1954), where the Court permitted the government to use unlawfully seized evidence to impeach the credibility of a defendant who had testified broadly in his own defense. The Court held, in effect, that the interests safeguarded by the exclusionary rule in that context were outweighed by the need to prevent perjury and to assure the integrity of the trial process. The judgment in *Walder* revealed most clearly that the policies behind the exclusionary rule are not absolute. Rather, they must be evaluated in light of competing policies. In that case, the public interest in determination of truth at trial was deemed to outweigh the incremental contribution that might have been made to the protection of fourth amendment values by application of the rule.

The balancing process at work in these cases also finds expression in the standing requirement. Standing to invoke the exclusionary rule has been found to exist only when the government attempts to use illegally obtained evidence to incriminate the victim of the illegal search. Brown v. United States, 411 U.S. 223 (1973); Alderman v. United States, 394 U.S. 165 (1969). The standing requirement is premised on the view that the "additional benefits of extending the . . . rule" to defendants other than the victim of the search or seizure

---

[24] As Professor Amsterdam has observed:

"The rule is unsupportable as reparation or compensatory dispensation to the injured criminal; its sole rational justification is the experience of its indispensability in 'exert[ing] general legal pressures to secure obedience to the fourth amendment on the part of . . . law-enforcing officers.' As it serves this function, the rule is a needed, but grud[g]ingly taken, medicament; no more should be swallowed than is needed to combat the disease. Granted that so many criminals must go free as will deter the constables from blundering, pursuance of this policy of liberation beyond the confines of necessity inflicts gratuitous harm on the public interest . . . ." Search, Seizure, and Section 2255: A Comment, 112 U. Pa. L. Rev. 378, 388–89 (1964) (footnotes omitted).

are outweighed by the "further encroachment upon the public interest in prosecuting those accused of crime and having them acquitted or convicted on the basis of all the evidence which exposes the truth." *Alderman v. United States,* supra, at 174–75.[26]

IV

We turn now to the specific question presented by these cases. Respondents allege violations of fourth amendment rights guaranteed them through the 14th amendment. The question is whether state prisoners—who have been afforded the opportunity for full and fair consideration of their reliance upon the exclusionary rule with respect to seized evidence by the state courts at trial and on direct review— may invoke their claim again on federal habeas corpus review. The answer is to be found by weighing the utility of the exclusionary rule against the costs of extending it to collateral review of fourth amendment claims.

The costs of applying the exclusionary rule even at trial and on direct review are well known: the focus of the trial, and the attention of the participants therein, are diverted from the ultimate question of guilt or innocence that should be the central concern in a criminal proceeding. Moreover, the physical evidence sought to be excluded is typically reliable and often the most probative information bearing on the guilt or innocence of the defendant. As Mr. Justice Black emphasized in his dissent in *Kaufman* :

> "A claim of illegal search and seizure under the fourth amendment is crucially different from many other constitutional rights; ordinarily the evidence seized can in no way have been rendered untrustworthy by the means of its seizure and indeed often this evidence alone establishes beyond virtually any shadow of a doubt that the defendant is guilty."

Application of the rule thus deflects the truthfinding process and often frees the guilty. The disparity in particular cases between the error committed by the police officer and the windfall afforded a guilty defendant by application of the rule is contrary to the idea of proportionality that is essential to the concept of justice. Thus, although the rule is thought to deter unlawful police activity in part through the nurturing of respect for fourth amendment values, if applied indiscriminately it may well have the opposite effect of generating disrespect for the law and administration of justice.[30] These long-recognized costs of

[26] Cases addressing the question whether search-and-seizure holdings should be applied retroactively also have focused on the deterrent purpose served by the exclusionary rule, consistently with the balancing analysis applied generally in the exclusionary rule context. See Desist v. United States, 394 U.S. 244, 249–51, 253–54 and n. 21 (1969); Linkletter v. Walker, 381 U.S. 618, 636–37 (1965). The "attenuation-of-the-taint" doctrine also is consistent with the balancing approach. See Brown v. Illinois, 422 U.S. 590 (1975); Wong Sun v. United States, 371 U.S. 471, 491–92 (1963).

[30] In a different context, Dallin H. Oaks has observed:

"I am criticizing, not our concern with procedures, but our preoccupation, in which we may lose sight of the fact that our procedures are not the ultimate goals of our legal system. Our goals are truth and justice, and procedures are but means to these ends. . . ."

the rule persist when a criminal conviction is sought to be overturned on collateral review on the ground that a search-and-seizure claim was erroneously rejected by two or more tiers of state courts.[31]

Evidence obtained by police officers in violation of the fourth amendment is excluded at trial in the hope that the frequency of future violations will decrease. Despite the absence of supportive empirical evidence,[32] we have assumed that the immediate effect of exclusion will be to discourage law enforcement officials from violating the fourth amendment by removing the incentive to disregard it. More importantly, over the long term, this demonstration that our society attaches serious consequences to violation of constitutional rights is thought to encourage those who formulate law enforcement policies, and the officers who implement them, to incorporate fourth amendment ideals into their value system.

We adhere to the view that these considerations support the implementation of the exclusionary rule at trial and its enforcement on direct appeal of state-court convictions. But the additional contribution, if any, of the consideration of search-and-seizure claims of state prisoners on collateral review is small in relation to the costs. To be sure, each case in which such claim is considered may add marginally to an awareness of the values protected by the fourth amendment. There is no reason to believe, however, that the overall educative effect of the exclusionary rule would be appreciably diminished if search-and-seizure claims could not be raised in federal habeas corpus review of state convictions. Nor is there reason to assume that any specific disincentive already created by the risk of exclusion of evidence at trial or the reversal of convictions on direct review would be enhanced if there were the further risk that a conviction obtained in state court and affirmed on direct review might be overturned in collateral proceedings often occurring years after the incarceration of the defendant. The view that the deterrence of fourth amendment violations would be

---

"Truth and justice are ultimate values, so understood by our people, and the law and the legal profession will not be worthy of public respect and loyalty if we allow our attention to be diverted from these goals." Ethics, Morality and Professional Responsibility, 1975 B.Y.U. L. Rev. 591, 596.

[31] Resort to habeas corpus, especially for purposes other than to assure that no innocent person suffers an unconstitutional loss of liberty, results in serious intrusions on values important to our system of government. They include "(i) the most effective utilization of limited judicial resources, (ii) the necessity of finality in criminal trials, (iii) the minimization of friction between our federal and state systems of justice, and (iv) the maintenance of the constitutional balance upon which the doctrine of federalism is founded." Schneckloth v. Bustamonte, 412 U.S. 218, 250, 259 (1973) (Powell, J., concurring).

We nevertheless afford broad habeas corpus relief, recognizing the need in a free society for an additional safeguard against compelling an innocent man to suffer an unconstitutional loss of liberty. The Court in Fay v. Noia, 372 U.S. 391, 401, 441 (1963), described habeas corpus as a remedy for "whatever society deems to be intolerable restraints," and recognized that those to whom the writ should be granted "are persons whom society has grievously wronged." But in the case of a typical fourth amendment claim, asserted on collateral attack, a convicted defendant is usually asking society to redetermine an issue that has no bearing on the basic justice of his incarceration.

[32] The efficacy of the exclusionary rule has long been the subject of sharp debate. Until recently, scholarly empirical research was unavailable. And, the evidence derived from recent empirical research is still inconclusive. [Citing sources.]

furthered rests on the dubious assumption that law enforcement authorities would fear that federal habeas review might reveal flaws in a search or seizure that went undetected at trial and on appeal.[35] Even if one rationally could assume that some additional incremental deterrent effect would be present in isolated cases, the resulting advance of the legitimate goal of furthering fourth amendment rights would be outweighed by the acknowledged costs to other values vital to a rational system of criminal justice.

In sum, we conclude that where the state has provided an opportunity for full and fair litigation of a fourth amendment claim,[36] a state prisoner may not be granted federal habeas corpus relief on the ground that evidence obtained in an unconstitutional search or seizure was introduced at his trial.[37] In this context the contribution of the exclu-

---

[35] The policy arguments that respondents marshall in support of the view that federal habeas corpus review is necessary to effectuate the fourth amendment stem from a basic mistrust of the state courts as fair and competent forums for the adjudication of federal constitutional rights. The argument is that state courts cannot be trusted to effectuate fourth amendment values through fair application of the rule, and the oversight jurisdiction of this Court on certiorari is an inadequate safeguard. The principal rationale for this view emphasizes the broad differences in the respective institutional settings within which federal judges and state judges operate. Despite differences in institutional environment and the unsympathetic attitude to federal constitutional claims of some state judges in years past, we are unwilling to assume that there now exists a general lack of appropriate sensitivity to constitutional rights in the trial and appellate courts of the several states. State courts, like federal courts, have a constitutional obligation to safeguard personal liberties and to uphold federal law. Moreover, the argument that federal judges are more expert in applying federal constitutional law is especially unpersuasive in the context of search-and-seizure claims, since they are dealt with on a daily basis by trial level judges in both systems. In sum, there is "no intrinsic reason why the fact that a man is a federal judge should make him more competent or conscientious, or learned with respect to the [consideration of fourth amendment claims] than his neighbor in the state courthouse." Bator, Finality in Criminal Law and Federal Habeas Corpus for State Prisoners, 76 Harv. L. Rev. 441, 509 (1963).

[36] Cf. Townsend v. Sain, 372 U.S. 293 (1963).

[37] Mr. Justice Brennan's dissent characterizes the Court's opinion as laying the groundwork for a "drastic withdrawal of federal habeas jurisdiction, if not for all grounds . . ., then at least [for many]." It refers variously to our opinion as a "harbinger of future eviscerations of the habeas statutes;" as "rewrit[ing] Congress' jurisdictional statutes . . . and [barring] access to federal courts by state prisoners with constitutional claims distasteful to a majority" of the Court, and as a "denigration of constitutional guarantees [that] must appall citizens taught to expect judicial respect" of constitutional rights.

With all respect, the hyperbole of the dissenting opinion is misdirected. Our decision today is *not* concerned with the scope of the habeas corpus statute as authority for litigating constitutional claims generally. We do reaffirm that the exclusionary rule is a judicially created remedy rather than a personal constitutional right, and we emphasize the minimal utility of the rule when sought to be applied to fourth amendment claims in a habeas corpus proceeding. As Mr. Justice Black recognized in this context, "ordinarily the evidence seized can in no way have been rendered untrustworthy . . . and indeed often . . . alone establishes beyond virtually any shadow of a doubt that the defendant is guilty." *Kaufman v. United States,* supra at 237 (dissenting opinion). In sum, we hold only that a federal court need not apply the exclusionary rule on habeas review of a fourth amendment claim absent a showing that the state prisoner was denied an opportunity for a full and fair litigation of that claim at trial and on direct review. Our decision does not mean that the federal court lacks jurisdiction over such a claim, but only that the application of the rule is limited to cases in which there has been both such a showing and a fourth amendment violation.

sionary rule, if any, to the effectuation of the fourth amendment is minimal and the substantial societal costs of application of the rule persist with special force.

Accordingly, the judgments of the Courts of Appeals are

Reversed.

MR. CHIEF JUSTICE BURGER, concurring.

I concur in the Court's opinion. By way of dictum, and somewhat hesitantly, the Court notes that the holding in this case leaves undisturbed the exclusionary rule as applied to criminal trials. For reasons stated in my dissent in Bivens v. Six Unknown Named Federal Agents, 403 U.S. 388, 411 (1971), it seems clear to me that the exclusionary rule has been operative long enough to demonstrate its flaws. The time has come to modify its reach, even if it is retained for a small and limited category of cases. . . .

MR. JUSTICE BRENNAN, with whom MR. JUSTICE MARSHALL concurs, dissenting. . . .

Today's holding portends substantial evisceration of federal habeas corpus jurisdiction. . . . The Court's opinion does not specify the basis on which it denies federal habeas jurisdiction over claims of fourth amendment violations brought by state prisoners. The Court insists that its holding is based on the Constitution, but in light of the explicit language of 28 U.S.C. § 2254 (significantly not even mentioned by the Court), I can only presume that the Court intends to be understood to hold either that respondents are not, as a matter of statutory construction, "in custody in violation of the Constitution or laws . . . of the United States," or that " 'considerations of comity and concerns for the orderly administration of criminal justice,' " are sufficient to allow this Court to rewrite jurisdictional statutes enacted by Congress. Neither ground of decision is tenable; the former is simply illogical, and the latter is an arrogation of power committed solely to the Congress.

I

Much of the Court's analysis implies that respondents are not entitled to habeas relief because they are not being unconstitutionally detained. . . . Understandably the Court must purport to cast its holding in constitutional terms, because that avoids a direct confrontation with the incontrovertible facts that the habeas statutes have heretofore always been construed to grant jurisdiction to entertain fourth amendment claims of both state and federal prisoners, that fourth amendment principles have been applied in decisions on the merits in numerous cases on collateral review of final convictions, and that Congress has legislatively accepted our interpretation of congressional intent as to the necessary scope and function of habeas relief. Indeed, the Court reaches its result without explicitly overruling any of our plethora of precedents inconsistent with that ruling or even discussing principles of stare decisis. Rather, the Court asserts, in essence,

that the Justices joining those prior decisions or reaching the merits of
fourth amendment claims simply overlooked the obvious constitutional
dimension to the problem in adhering to the "view" that granting
collateral relief when state courts erroneously decide fourth amendment issues would effectuate the principles underlying that amendment.   But, shorn of the rhetoric of "interest balancing" used to
obscure what is at stake in this case, it is evident that today's attempt
to rest the decision on the Constitution must fail so long as Mapp v.
Ohio, 367 U.S. 643 (1961), remains undisturbed.

Under *Mapp,* as a matter of federal constitutional law, a state court
must exclude evidence from the trial of an individual whose fourth and
14th amendment rights were violated by a search or seizure that
directly or indirectly resulted in the acquisition of that evidence. . . .
When a state court admits such evidence, it has committed a *constitutional* error, and unless that error is harmless under federal standards,
it follows ineluctably that the defendant has been placed "in custody in
violation of the Constitution" within the comprehension of 28 U.S.C.
§ 2254.   In short, it escapes me as to what logic can support the
assertion that the defendant's unconstitutional confinement obtains
during the process of direct review, no matter how long that process
takes, but that the unconstitutionality then suddenly dissipates at the
moment the claim is asserted in a collateral attack on the conviction.

The only conceivable rationale upon which the Court's "constitutional" thesis might rest is the statement that "the [exclusionary] rule
is not a personal constitutional right. . . .   Instead, 'the rule is a
judicially created remedy designed to safeguard fourth amendment
rights generally through its deterrent effect.' " . . .   However the
Court reinterprets *Mapp,* and whatever the rationale now attributed to
Mapp 's holding or the purpose ascribed to the exclusionary rule, the
prevailing constitutional *rule* is that unconstitutionally seized evidence
cannot be admitted in the criminal trial of a person whose federal
constitutional rights were violated by the search or seizure.   The
erroneous admission of such evidence is a violation of the federal
Constitution—*Mapp* inexorably means at least this much, or there
would be no basis for applying the exclusionary rule in state criminal
proceedings—and an accused against whom such evidence is admitted
has been convicted in derogation of rights mandated by, and is "in
custody in violation of," the Constitution of the United States.   Indeed,
since state courts violate the strictures of the federal Constitution by
admitting such evidence, then even if federal habeas review did not
directly effectuate fourth amendment values, a proposition I deny, that
review would nevertheless serve to effectuate what is concededly a
constitutional principle concerning admissibility of evidence at trial.

The Court, assuming without deciding that respondents were convicted on the basis of unconstitutionally obtained evidence erroneously
admitted against them by the state trial courts, acknowledges that
respondents had the right to obtain a reversal of their convictions on
appeal in the state courts or on certiorari to this Court. [T]he basis for
reversing those convictions would of course have to be that the states,

in rejecting respondents' fourth amendment claims, had deprived them of a right in derogation of the federal Constitution. It is simply inconceivable that that constitutional deprivation suddenly vanishes after the appellate process has been exhausted. And as between this Court on certiorari, and federal district courts on habeas, it is for *Congress* to decide what the most efficacious method is for enforcing *federal* constitutional rights and asserting the primacy of federal law. The Court, however, simply ignores the settled principle that for purposes of adjudicating constitutional claims Congress, which has the power to do so under art. III of the Constitution, has effectively cast the district courts sitting in habeas in the role of surrogate Supreme Courts.[10]

Today's opinion itself starkly exposes the illogic of the Court's seeming premise that the rights recognized in *Mapp* somehow suddenly evaporate after all direct appeals are exhausted. For the Court would not bar assertion of fourth amendment claims on habeas if the defendant was not accorded "an opportunity for full and fair litigation of his claim in the state courts." But this "exception" is impossible if the Court really means that the "rule" that fourth amendment claims are not cognizable on habeas is constitutionally based. For if the Constitution mandates that "rule" because it is a "dubious assumption that law enforcement authorities would fear that federal habeas review might reveal flaws in a search or seizure that went undetected at trial and on appeal," is it not an equally "dubious assumption" that those same police officials would fear that federal habeas review might reveal that the state courts had denied the defendant an opportunity to have a full and fair hearing on his claim that went undetected at trial and on appeal? And to the extent the Court is making the unjustifiable assumption that our certiorari jurisdiction is adequate to correct "routine" condonation of fourth amendment violations by state courts,

[10] The failure to confront this fact forthrightly is obviously a core defect in the Court's analysis. For to the extent Congress has accorded the federal district courts a role in our constitutional scheme functionally equivalent to that of the Supreme Court with respect to review of state court resolutions of federal constitutional claims, it is evident that the Court's direct/collateral review distinction for constitutional purposes simply collapses. Indeed, logically extended, the Court's analysis, which basically turns on the fact that law enforcement officials cannot anticipate a second court's finding constitutional errors after one court has fully and fairly adjudicated the claim and found it to be meritless, would preclude any Supreme Court review on direct appeal or even state appellate review if the trial court fairly addressed the fourth amendment claim on the merits. . . .

The Court's arguments respecting the cost/benefit analysis of applying the exclusionary rule on collateral attack also have no merit. For all of the "costs" of applying the exclusionary rule on habeas *should already have been incurred* at the trial or on direct review if the state court had not misapplied federal constitutional principles. As such, these "costs" were evaluated and deemed to be outweighed when the exclusionary rule was fashioned. The only proper question on habeas is whether federal courts, acting under congressional directive to have the last say as to enforcement of federal constitutional principles, are to permit the states free enjoyment of the fruits of a conviction which by definition were only obtained through violations of the Constitution as interpreted in *Mapp.* And as to the question whether any "educative" function is served by such habeas review, today's decision will certainly provide a lesson that, tragically for an individual's constitutional rights, will not be lost on state courts. . . .

surely it follows a fortiori that our jurisdiction is adequate to redress the "egregious" situation in which the state courts did not even accord a fair hearing on the fourth amendment claim. The "exception" thus may appear to make the holding more palatable, but it merely highlights the lack of a "constitutional" rationale for today's constriction of habeas jurisdiction.

The Court adheres to the holding of *Mapp* that the Constitution "require[d] exclusion" of the evidence admitted at respondents' trials. However, the Court holds that the Constitution "does not require" that respondents be accorded habeas relief if they were accorded "an opportunity for full and fair litigation of [their] fourth amendment claim[s]" in state courts. Yet once the Constitution was interpreted by *Mapp* to require exclusion of certain evidence at trial, the Constitution became irrelevant to the manner in which the constitutional right was to be enforced in the federal courts; *that* inquiry is only a matter of respecting Congress' allocation of federal judicial power between this Court's appellate jurisdiction and a federal district court's habeas jurisdiction. Indeed, by conceding that today's "decision does not mean that the federal [district] court lacks jurisdiction over [respondents'] claim[s]," the Court admits that respondents have sufficiently alleged that they are "in custody in violation of the Constitution" within the meaning of § 2254 and that there is no "constitutional" rationale for today's holding. Rather, the constitutional "interest balancing" approach to this case is untenable, and I can only view the constitutional garb in which the Court dresses its result as a disguise for rejection of the longstanding principle that there are no "second class" constitutional rights for purposes of federal habeas jurisdiction; it is nothing less than an attempt to provide a veneer of respectability for an obvious usurpation of Congress' art. III power to delineate the jurisdiction of the federal courts.

II

Therefore, the real ground of today's decision—a ground that is particularly troubling in light of its portent for habeas jurisdiction generally—is the Court's novel reinterpretation of the habeas statutes; this would read the statutes as requiring the district courts routinely to deny habeas relief to prisoners "in custody in violation of the Constitution or laws . . . of the United States" as a matter of judicial "discretion"—a "discretion" judicially manufactured today contrary to the express statutory language—because such claims are "different in kind" from other constitutional violations in that they "do not 'impugn the integrity of the fact-finding process,'" and because application of such constitutional strictures "often frees the guilty." Much in the Court's opinion suggests that a construction of the habeas statutes to deny relief for non-"guilt-related" constitutional violations, based on this Court's vague notions of comity and federalism, is the actual premise for today's decision, and although the Court attempts to bury its underlying premises in footnotes, those premises mark this case as a harbinger of future eviscerations of the habeas statutes that plainly does violence to congressional power to frame the statutory contours of habeas jurisdiction. . . . Finally, we are provided a revisionist history of the genesis and growth of federal habeas corpus jurisdiction. If today's decision were only that erroneous state-court resolution of fourth amendment claims did not render the defendant's resultant confinement "in violation of the Constitution," these pronouncements would have been wholly irrelevant and unnecessary. I am therefore justified in apprehending that the groundwork is being laid today for a drastic withdrawal of federal habeas jurisdiction, if not for all grounds of alleged unconstitutional detention, then at least for claims—for example, of double jeopardy, entrapment, self-incrimination, *Miranda* violations and use of invalid identification procedures—that this Court later decides are not "guilt related."

To the extent the Court is actually premising its holding on an interpretation of 28 U.S.C. § 2241 or § 2254, it is overruling the heretofore settled principle that federal habeas relief is available to redress *any* denial of asserted constitutional rights, whether or not denial of the right affected the truth or fairness of the factfinding process. As Mr. Justice Powell recognized in proposing that the Court re-evaluate the scope of habeas relief as a statutory matter in *Schneckloth v. Bustamonte,* supra, at 251 (concurring opinion), "on petition for habeas corpus or collateral review filed in a federal district court, whether by state prisoners under 28 U.S.C. § 2254 or federal prisoners under § 2255, the present rule is that fourth amendment claims may be asserted and the exclusionary rule must be applied in precisely the same manner as on direct review." This Court has on numerous occasions accepted jurisdiction over collateral attacks by state prisoners premised on fourth amendment violations, often over dissents that as a statutory matter such claims should not be cognizable. Consideration of the merits in each of these decisions reaffirmed the unrestricted scope of habeas jurisdiction, but each decision must be deemed overruled by today's holding.

. . . This Court's precedents have been "premised in large part on a recognition that the availability of collateral remedies is necessary to insure the integrity of proceedings at and before trial where constitutional rights are at stake. Our decisions leave no doubt that the federal habeas remedy extends to state prisoners alleging that unconstitutionally obtained evidence was admitted against them at trial." Kaufman v. United States, 394 U.S. 217, 225 (1969). Some of those decisions explicitly considered and rejected the "policies" referred to by the Court. There were no "assumptions" with respect to the construction of the habeas statutes, but reasoned decisions that those policies were an insufficient justification for shutting the federal habeas door to litigants with federal constitutional claims in light of such countervailing considerations as "the necessity that federal courts have the 'last say' with respect to questions of federal law, the inadequacy of state procedures to raise and preserve federal claims, the concern that state judges may be unsympathetic to federally created rights, [and] the institutional constraints on the exercise of this Court's certiorari juris-

diction to review state convictions," as well as the fundamental belief
"that adequate protection of constitutional rights relating to the criminal trial process requires the continuing availability of a mechanism for
relief." Id. at 225, 226. As Mr. Justice Harlan, who had dissented
from many of the cases initially construing the habeas statutes, readily
recognized, habeas jurisdiction as heretofore accepted by this Court was
"not only concerned with those rules which substantially affect the factfinding apparatus of the original trial. Under the prevailing notions,
*the threat of habeas serves as a necessary additional incentive for trial
and appellate courts throughout the land to conduct their proceedings in
a manner consistent with established constitutional standards.*" Desist
v. United States, 394 U.S. 244, 262–263 (1969) (dissenting) (emphasis
supplied). The availability of collateral review assures "that the lower
federal and state courts toe the constitutional line." Id. at 264. . . .
In effect, habeas jurisdiction is a deterrent to unconstitutional actions
by trial and appellate judges, and a safeguard to ensure that rights
secured under the Constitution and federal laws are not merely
honored in the breach. . . .

At least since *Brown v. Allen,* detention emanating from judicial
proceedings in which constitutional rights were denied has been
deemed "contrary to fundamental law," and all constitutional claims
have thus been cognizable on federal habeas corpus. There is no
foundation in the language or history of the habeas statutes for discriminating between types of constitutional transgressions, and efforts to
relegate certain categories of claims to the status of "second-class
rights" by excluding them from that jurisdiction have been repulsed.
Today's opinion, however, marks the triumph of those who have sought
to establish a hierarchy of constitutional rights, and to deny for all
practical purposes a federal forum for review of those rights that this
Court deems less worthy or important. Without even paying the
slightest deference to principles of stare decisis or acknowledging Congress' failure for two decades to alter the habeas statutes in light of our
interpretation of congressional intent to render all federal constitutional contentions cognizable on habeas, the Court today rewrites Congress'
jurisdictional statutes as heretofore construed and bars access to federal
courts by state prisoners with constitutional claims distasteful to a
majority of my Brethren. But even ignoring principles of stare decisis
dictating that Congress is the appropriate vehicle for embarking on
such a fundamental shift in the jurisdiction of the federal courts, I can
find no adequate justification elucidated by the Court for concluding
that habeas relief for all federal constitutional claims is no longer
compelled . . . .

I would address the Court's concerns for effective utilization of
scarce judicial resources, finality principles, federal-state friction, and
notions of "federalism" only long enough to note that such concerns
carry no more force with respect to non-"guilt-related" constitutional
claims than they do with respect to claims that affect the accuracy of
the factfinding process. Congressional conferral of federal habeas
jurisdiction for the purpose of entertaining petitions from state prison-

ers necessarily manifested a conclusion that such concerns could not be controlling, and any argument for discriminating among constitutional rights must therefore depend on the nature of the constitutional right involved.

The Court, focusing on fourth amendment rights as it must to justify such discrimination, thus argues that habeas relief for non-"guilt-related" constitutional claims is not mandated because such claims do not affect the "basic justice" of a defendant's detention; this is presumably because the "ultimate goal" of the criminal justice system is "truth and justice." This denigration of constitutional guarantees and *constitutionally mandated procedures,* relegated by the Court to the status of mere utilitarian tools, must appall citizens taught to expect judicial respect and support for their constitutional rights. Even if punishment of the "guilty" were society's highest value—and procedural safeguards denigrated to this end—in a constitution that a majority of the members of this Court would prefer, that is not the ordering of priorities under the Constitution forged by the framers, and this Court's sworn duty is to uphold that Constitution and not to frame its own. The procedural safeguards mandated in the framers' Constitution are not admonitions to be tolerated only to the extent they serve functional purposes that ensure that the "guilty" are punished and the "innocent" freed; rather, every guarantee enshrined in the Constitution, our basic charter and the guarantor of our most precious liberties, is by it endowed with an independent vitality and value, and this Court is not free to curtail those constitutional guarantees even to punish the most obviously guilty. Particular constitutional rights that do not affect the fairness of factfinding procedures cannot for that reason be denied at the trial itself. What possible justification then can there be for denying vindication of such rights on federal habeas when state courts do deny those rights at trial? To sanction disrespect and disregard for the Constitution in the name of protecting society from lawbreakers is to make the government itself lawless and to subvert those values upon which our ultimate freedom and liberty depend. . . . Enforcement of *federal* constitutional rights that redress constitutional violations directed against the "guilty" is a particular function of *federal* habeas review, lest judges trying the "morally unworthy" be tempted not to execute the supreme law of the land. State judges popularly elected may have difficulty resisting popular pressures not experienced by federal judges given lifetime tenure designed to immunize them from such influences, and the federal habeas statutes reflect the congressional judgment that such detached federal review is a salutary safeguard against *any* detention of an individual "in violation of the Constitution or laws . . . of the United States."

Federal courts have the duty to carry out the congressionally assigned responsibility to shoulder the ultimate burden of adjudging whether detentions violate federal law, and today's decision substantially abnegates that duty. The Court does not, because it cannot, dispute that institutional constraints totally preclude any possibility that this Court can adequately oversee whether state courts have properly applied federal law, and does not controvert the fact that federal habeas jurisdiction is partially designed to ameliorate that inadequacy. Thus, although I fully agree that state courts "have a constitutional obligation to safeguard personal liberties and to uphold federal law," and that there is no "general lack of appropriate sensitivity to constitutional rights in the trial and appellate courts of the several states," I cannot agree that it follows that, as the Court today holds, federal court determination of almost all fourth amendment claims of state prisoners should be barred and that state court resolution of those issues should be insulated from the federal review Congress intended. . . .

Congress' action following Townsend v. Sain, 372 U.S. 293 (1963), and Fay v. Noia, 372 U.S. 391 (1963), emphasized "the choice of Congress how the superior authority of federal law should be asserted" in federal courts. *Townsend v. Sain* outlined the duty of federal habeas courts to conduct factfinding hearings with respect to petitions brought by state prisoners, and *Fay v. Noia* defined the contours of the "exhaustion of state remedies" prerequisite in § 2254 in light of its purpose of according state courts the first opportunity to correct their own constitutional errors. Congress expressly modified the habeas statutes to incorporate the *Townsend* standards so as to accord a limited and carefully circumscribed res judicata effect to the factual determinations of state judges. But Congress did not alter the principle . . . that collateral relief is to be available with respect to *any* constitutional deprivation and that federal district judges, subject to review in the courts of appeals and this Court, are to be the spokesmen of the supremacy of federal law. Indeed, subsequent congressional efforts to amend those jurisdictional statutes to effectuate the result that my Brethren accomplish by judicial fiat have consistently proved unsuccessful. . . .

In any event, respondents' contention that fourth amendment claims, like all other constitutional claims, must be cognizable on habeas, does not rest on the ground attributed to them by the Court— that the state courts are rife with animosity to the constitutional mandates of this Court. It is one thing to assert that state courts, as a general matter, accurately decide federal constitutional claims; it is quite another to generalize from that limited proposition to the conclusion that, despite congressional intent that federal courts sitting in habeas must stand ready to rectify any constitutional errors that are nevertheless committed, federal courts are to be judicially precluded from ever considering the merits of whole categories of rights that are to be accorded less procedural protection merely because the Court proclaims that they do not affect the accuracy or fairness of the factfinding process. . . . To the extent state trial and appellate judges faithfully, accurately, and assiduously apply federal law and the constitutional principles enunciated by the federal courts, such determinations will be vindicated on the merits when collaterally attacked. But to the extent federal law is erroneously applied by the state courts, there is no authority in this Court to deny defendants the right to have those errors rectified by way of federal habeas; indeed, the Court's reluctance to accept Congress' desires along these lines can only be a manifestation of this Court's mistrust for *federal* judges. Furthermore, some might be expected to dispute the academic's dictum seemingly accepted by the Court that a federal judge is not necessarily more skilled than a state judge in applying federal law. For the supremacy clause of the Constitution proceeds on a different premise, and Congress, as it was constitutionally empowered to do, made federal judges (and initially federal district court judges) "the *primary* and powerful reliances for vindicating every right given by the Constitution, the laws, and treaties of the United States." Zwickler v. Koota, 389 U.S. 241, 247 (1967). . . .

I would affirm the judgments of the Courts of Appeals.

MR. JUSTICE WHITE, dissenting.

For many of the reasons stated by Mr. Justice Brennan, I cannot agree that the writ of habeas corpus should be any less available to those convicted of state crimes where they allege fourth amendment violations than where other constitutional issues are presented to the federal court. Under the amendments to the habeas corpus statute, which . . . represented an effort by Congress to lend a modicum of finality to state criminal judgments, I cannot distinguish between fourth amendment and other constitutional issues.

Suppose, for example, that two confederates in crime, Smith and Jones, are tried separately for a state crime and convicted on the very same evidence, including evidence seized incident to their arrest allegedly made without probable cause. Their constitutional claims are fully aired, rejected, and preserved on appeal. Their convictions are affirmed by the state's highest court. Smith, the first to be tried, does not petition for certiorari, or does so but his petition is denied. Jones, whose conviction was considerably later, is more successful. His petition for certiorari is granted and his conviction reversed because this Court, without making any new rule of law, simply concludes that on the undisputed facts the arrests were made without probable cause and the challenged evidence was therefore seized in violation of the fourth amendment. The state must either retry Jones or release him, necessarily because he is deemed in custody in violation of the Constitution. It turns out that without the evidence illegally seized, the state has no case; and Jones goes free. Smith then files his petition for habeas corpus. He makes no claim that he did not have a full and fair hearing in the state courts, but asserts that his fourth amendment claim had been erroneously decided and that he is being held in violation of the federal Constitution. He cites this Court's decision in Jones' case to satisfy any burden placed on him by § 2254 to demonstrate that the state court was in error. Unless the Court's reservation, in its present opinion, of those situations where the defendant has not had a full and fair hearing in the state courts is intended to encompass all those circumstances under which a state criminal judgment may be re-examined under § 2254—in which event the opinion is essentially meaningless and the judgment erroneous—Smith's petition would be dismissed, and he would spend his life in prison while his colleague is a free man. I cannot believe that Congress intended this result.

Under the present habeas corpus statute, neither Rice's nor Powell's application for habeas corpus should be dismissed on the grounds now stated by the Court. I would affirm the judgments of the Courts of Appeals as being acceptable applications of the exclusionary rule applicable in state criminal trials by virtue of *Mapp v. Ohio*.

I feel constrained to say, however, that I would join four or more other Justices in substantially limiting the reach of the exclusionary rule as presently administered under the fourth amendment in federal and state criminal trials. . . . I am of the view that the rule should be substantially modified so as to prevent its application in those many circumstances where the evidence at issue was seized by an officer acting in the good-faith belief that his conduct comported with existing law and having reasonable grounds for this belief.

NOTES ON *STONE v. POWELL*

1. **History.** In Brown v. Allen, 344 U.S. 443 (1953), Justice Frankfurter said that the Habeas Corpus Act of 1867[a] required federal courts to redetermine the merits of federal constitutional claims already heard and decided in state courts. That this was not the clearly understood rule at the time is evidenced by the lively and continuing debate about the scope of federal habeas review before *Brown*.

In his influential article, Finality in Criminal Law and Federal Habeas Corpus for State Prisoners, 76 Harv. L. Rev. 441 (1963), Paul Bator argued that *Brown* made a major (and unwise) innovation in federal law. Bator began with the early "federal" cases, before the act of 1867 extended federal habeas corpus to state prisoners. He argued that these cases accepted the common law rule that habeas corpus was not available to one held pursuant to criminal conviction by a court of competent jurisdiction. See Ex parte Watkins, 28 U.S. (3 Pet.) 193 (1830). As a post-conviction remedy—that is, aside from its historic function of testing the legality of executive detention—habeas was largely limited to challenges to the jurisdiction of the sentencing court. Although certain expansions in the availability of the writ did take place, they were merely ad hoc responses to the fact that federal criminal convictions were generally not appealable. Against this background, Bator thought it would require "rather overwhelming evidence" to show that the purpose of the act of 1867 was "to tear habeas corpus entirely out of the context of its historical meaning and scope and convert it into an ordinary writ of error with respect to all federal questions in all criminal cases." He found no such evidence and therefore concluded that the 1867 act did not overturn the traditional rule that detention under judgment of a court of competent jurisdiction

---

[a] The act of 1867 gave the federal courts "power to grant writs of habeas corpus in all cases where any person may be re- strained of his or her liberty in violation of the Constitution, or of any treaty or law of the United States . . . ."

is not open to collateral attack simply on allegation of error in the original trial.

In the years following extension of federal habeas corpus to state prisoners, the scope of the writ continued an irregular expansion. In Bator's view, the key case was Frank v. Mangum, 237 U.S. 309 (1915). Frank was convicted of murder in a Georgia court. His contention that the trial was mob-dominated was rejected after an independent inquiry by the Georgia Supreme Court. The Supreme Court ruled that his subsequent petition for habeas corpus should be denied. The Court emphasized that there was no question concerning the jurisdiction of the Georgia court and that Frank's claim of a mob-dominated trial had been fully and fairly heard by a competent and unbiased court. Bator read *Frank*, therefore, as standing for the proposition that federal habeas corpus will issue either when "jurisdiction" is wanting *or* when the state has failed to supply adequate "corrective process" for litigation of the federal claim. The later case of Moore v. Dempsey, 261 U.S. 86 (1923), where another claim of mob-dominated trial resulted in granting the application for habeas, was distinguished on the ground of the inadequacy of the opportunity for consideration of the claim in the state courts. Bator concluded that the "central thrust" of the law just before *Brown v. Allen* could be stated as follows: "for purposes of habeas corpus a detention was not to be deemed 'unlawful' if based upon the judgment of a competent state court which had afforded full corrective process for the litigation of questions touching on federal rights."

This analysis has not gone unchallenged. Curtis Reitz identified a broader role for habeas corpus in an earlier article, and Bator's reading of history has been extensively criticized more recently by Gary Peller. See Reitz, The Abortive State Proceeding, 74 Harv. L. Rev. 1315 (1961); Peller, In Defense of Federal Habeas Corpus Relitigation, 16 Harv. C.R.-C.L. L. Rev. 579 (1982). A good deal of this dispute turns on the interpretation of several rather murky precedents decided by the Supreme Court in the years before *Brown v. Allen*. For Bator, *Frank v. Mangum* stated the norm; *Moore v. Dempsey* could be read as "entirely consistent" with the regime of *Frank*. For others, *Frank* was "substantially discredited" by *Moore* and later precedents. See Hart, Foreword: The Time Chart of the Justices, 73 Harv. L. Rev. 84, 105 (1959). Informed assessment of the matter would require more extensive review of these precedents than can be undertaken here. For present purposes, it may be enough to say that the meaning of the 1867 act and the state of the law prior to *Brown v. Allen* were and are unclear. *Brown v. Allen* made, therefore, at least a major clarification, and perhaps a major innovation, in the scope of federal habeas corpus.

2. Questions and Comments on *Stone v. Powell*. Whatever the actual scope of habeas review may have been before *Brown v. Allen*, after that decision federal courts were required to reexamine federal constitutional questions already heard and decided in state courts. *Stone v. Powell* makes an exception to that scheme. The decision in

Stone implicates two distinct lines of argument about the proper scope of federal habeas.

The first concerns the general value of finality in the criminal law: whether federal habeas corpus should ever be available to relitigate questions already heard and decided in the original trial and affirmed on appeal. Can relitigation be justified as a device for correcting error? Does the argument necessarily suppose that the second (i.e., federal) court is somehow better than its state counterparts? [b]

The second line of argument concerns the particular rights for which habeas corpus is an appropriate remedy. In his famous article, Is Innocence Irrelevant? Collateral Attack on Criminal Judgments, 38 U. Chi. L. Rev. 142 (1970), Judge Henry Friendly suggested that the availability of federal habeas relief should depend on the petitioner's ability to make a "colorable showing of innocence." Obviously, that requirement would distinguish the fourth amendment from most other constitutional rights. Is such a differentiation sound?

The same issues can be approached from another direction. Few would dispute the correctness of the proposition for which *Frank* is usually cited: federal habeas corpus should be available at least in instances where the state has not provided an adequate procedural opportunity to raise a federal constitutional claim. *Brown v. Allen* goes much farther: all federal constitutional challenges litigated in state court can be relitigated on federal habeas corpus. There is lively debate on whether *Frank* states the norm that should be followed today, whether *Brown* does, or whether the best position is somewhere in between. There is also debate as to whether *Stone v. Powell* should be viewed as a restriction on the scope of collateral review that approaches an intermediate position on the proper role of federal habeas corpus or as a curtailment of the fourth amendment exclusionary rule.

NOTES ON DEVELOPMENTS AFTER *STONE v. POWELL*

1. *Jackson v. Virginia.* Some critics feared that *Stone v. Powell* was only the first step in a broad dismantling of federal habeas review of state criminal convictions. So far, that fear has proved largely unfounded. The first case to consider the issue was Jackson v. Virginia, 443 U.S. 307 (1979).

[b] For the contention that sequential jurisdictional redundancy may be used to reduce error, as well as thoughtful comments on other possible uses of what he called the "complex concurrency" of American jurisdictional structures, see the essay by the late Robert M. Cover, The Uses of Jurisdictional Redundancy: Interest, Ideology, and Innovation, 22 Wm. & M.L.Rev. 639 (1981).

See also Larry W. Yackle, Explaining Habeas Corpus, 60 N.Y.U.L.Rev. 991 (1985). Yackle argues that habeas corpus should be used to assure a federal forum to those who claim federal rights. He acknowledges good reasons to postpone access to federal court until the state criminal process is over, but argues that at that point all federal claims should be open to litigation, or relitigation, in federal court.

Jackson was convicted of first degree murder following a bench trial. He admitted the killing, but contended that he was too drunk to have formed the specific intent to kill required by Virginia law. A petition for writ of error to the Virginia Supreme Court on grounds of insufficient evidence was denied. A federal District Court, however, granted Jackson's habeas petition on the ground that there was "no evidence" of the required mens rea and that his conviction was therefore unconstitutional under Thompson v. Louisville, 362 U.S. 199 (1960). The Court of Appeals found that there was "some" evidence and reversed. The Supreme Court affirmed the denial of habeas relief, but adopted a different standard. The Court held that the test was not whether there was "no evidence" to support conviction, but whether there was "sufficient evidence" to support a rational trier of fact in finding guilt beyond a reasonable doubt. See In re Winship, 397 U.S. 358 (1970). The Court expressly ruled, moreover, that this standard should be applied in habeas proceedings notwithstanding that the accused had a "full and fair opportunity" to litigate guilt or innocence in state court.

Justice Stevens concurred in the judgment in an opinion joined by Chief Justice Burger and Justice Rehnquist. Stevens thought that the extension of *Winship* to collateral review was unnecessary and potentially troublesome. In a footnote, Stevens gave his reasons for regarding sufficiency-of-the-evidence review as inappropriate for habeas corpus:

"In the past, collateral review of state proceedings has been justified largely on the grounds (1) that federal judges have special expertise in the federal issues that regularly arise in habeas corpus proceedings, and (2) that they are less susceptible than state judges to political pressures against applying constitutional rules to overturn convictions. But neither of these justifications has any force in the present context. State judges are more familiar with the elements of state offenses than are federal judges and should be better able to evaluate sufficiency claims. Moreover, of all decisions overturning convictions, the least likely to be unpopular and thus to distort state decisionmaking processes are ones based on the inadequacy of the evidence. Indeed, once federal courts were divested of authority to second-guess state courts on fourth amendment issues, which are far more likely to generate politically motivated state-court decisions, see *Stone v. Powell,* a like result in this case would seem to be a fortiori."

2. *Rose v. Mitchell. Jackson v. Virginia* expanded federal habeas review of claims of sufficiency of the evidence. The decision might be thought consistent with *Stone,* however, in that both focus on the relation of the particular constitutional right in issue to the defendant's factual guilt or innocence. By contrast, in Rose v. Mitchell, 443 U.S. 545 (1979), the Supreme Court declined to apply *Stone* to another constitutional violation that, like illegal search and seizure, is arguably not guilt-related.

Rose involved two black prisoners who had been convicted of first-degree murder for deaths occurring in the course of a robbery. After unsuccessful appeal in the state system, they sought federal habeas corpus on grounds of racial discrimination in the selection of the grand jury and its foreman. The Supreme Court ultimately found that no such discrimination had been shown, but it made two important preliminary rulings. First, the Court held that racial discrimination in the selection of a grand jury was not rendered harmless by subsequent conviction beyond a reasonable doubt by a properly constituted petit jury. Second, the Court refused to extend *Stone v. Powell* to foreclose habeas review of such claims.

Writing for the Court, Justice Blackmun distinguished *Stone* on several grounds. Here federal habeas review was "necessary to ensure that constitutional defects in the state judiciary's grand jury selection procedure are not overlooked by the very state judges who operate that system." The concern for "judicial integrity," deprecated in *Stone*, was more important where the integrity of the judicial system itself was put in issue. Moreover, quashing an indictment does not preclude retrial and therefore is less costly to the administration of justice than is suppression of evidence. Finally, a claim of racial discrimination in grand jury selection raised interests "substantially more compelling than those at issue in *Stone*."

Justice Powell, joined by Justice Rehnquist, dissented on the refusal to extend *Stone*. Powell noted that the prisoners "were found guilty of murder beyond a reasonable doubt by a petit jury whose composition is not questioned, following a trial that was fair in every respect" and that they had been "given a full and fair opportunity to litigate in the state courts their claim of discrimination." In these circumstances, he concluded, "allowing an attack on the selection of the grand jury in this case is an abuse of federal habeas corpus." [a]

[a] Justice Powell repeated this theme in *Vasquez v. Hillery*, 474 U.S. 254 (1986). The defendant had been convicted of murder in 1962. His petition for habeas corpus was granted by the District Court in 1983, on the ground of racial discrimination in selection of the grand jury that had indicted him. The Court of Appeals affirmed, as did the Supreme Court on the authority of *Rose*. Justice O'Connor concurred specially. Justice Powell's dissent was joined by Chief Justice Burger and Justice Rehnquist. Justice Powell concluded:

"Twenty-three years ago, respondent was fairly convicted of the most serious of crimes. Respondent's grand jury discrimination claim casts no doubt on the adequacy of the procedures used to convict him or on the sufficiency of the evidence of his guilt. For that reason alone, the Court should reverse the Court of Appeals' decision. Even assuming the harmlessness of the error is irrel-

evant, however, reversal is still required. The Court inappropriately applies a deterrence rule in a context where it is unlikely to deter, and where its costs to society are likely to be especially high. These considerations should at least lead the Court to remand for a determination of whether the long lapse of time since respondent's conviction would prejudice the state's ability to retry respondent."

The Court responded to Justice Powell's last point by noting that a committee of the Judicial Conference had proposed an amendment to the habeas rules that would permit dismissal in cases where the state's ability to reprosecute would be prejudiced by the delay between conviction and an effort to secure release on collateral attack. Congress had also declined to pass numerous bills that would have created a statute of limitations for habeas claims. The Court concluded: "We should not lightly create a new judicial rule, in the guise of

3.　*Kimmelman v. Morrison.* What happens if a defendant's lawyer neglects to raise a valid fourth amendment objection to the introduction of incriminating evidence? Federal habeas review of the fourth amendment claim is presumably precluded under *Stone.* But the lawyer's error may also give rise to a sixth amendment claim of ineffective assistance of counsel. Is the sixth amendment claim likewise precluded under *Stone,* or may the prisoner use ineffective assistance of counsel to obtain a new trial at which the fourth amendment error will be corrected? In Kimmelman v. Morrison, 477 U.S. 365 (1986), the Supreme Court ruled that habeas review was not foreclosed on such facts.

Morrison was convicted of raping a 15–year-old girl. The evidence included an incriminating bedsheet that had been taken from Morrison's apartment after an unlawful search. Morrison's lawyer failed to comply with a New Jersey rule requiring that suppression motions be made within 30 days of indictment, and his later attempt to raise the fourth amendment issue was held barred by that procedural default. Morrison then sought federal habeas corpus, alleging both that illegally seized evidence had been used against him and that he had been denied effective assistance of counsel. The fourth amendment claim was held barred by *Stone,* but the sixth amendment claim, although based on the lawyer's failure to raise the fourth amendment issue, led the lower court to order a new trial. The state argued that this procedure undermined *Stone,* but the Supreme Court disagreed.

Speaking for the Court, Justice Brennan differentiated fourth and sixth amendment rights:

> "The right to counsel is a fundamental right of criminal defendants; it assures the fairness, and thus the legitimacy, of our adversary process. The essence of an ineffective assistance claim is that counsel's unprofessional errors so upset the adversarial balance between defense and prosecution that the trial was rendered unfair and the verdict rendered suspect. See, e.g., Strickland v. Washington, 466 U.S. 668, 686 (1984). In order to prevail, the defendant must show both that counsel's representation fell below an objective standard of reasonableness and that there exists a reasonable probability that, but for counsel's unprofessional errors, the result of the proceeding would have been different. Where defense counsel's failure to litigate a fourth amendment claim competently is the principal allegation of ineffectiveness, the defendant must also prove that his fourth amendment claim is meritorious and that there is a reasonable probability that the verdict would have been different absent the excludable evidence in order to demonstrate actual prejudice. Thus, while respondent's defaulted fourth amendment claim is one element of proof of his sixth

constitutional interpretation, to achieve
the same end."

amendment claim, the two claims have separate identities and reflect different constitutional values."

Justice Brennan rejected the state's contention that the rationale of *Stone* applied to a sixth amendment claim based on counsel's failure to raise a fourth amendment issue:

"In *Stone* the Court . . . made clear that its 'decision [was] *not* concerned with the scope of the habeas corpus statute as authority for litigation of constitutional claims generally.' Rather, the Court simply 'reaffirm[ed] that the exclusionary rule is a judicially created remedy rather than a personal constitutional right . . . and . . . emphasiz[ed] the minimal utility of the rule' in the context of federal collateral proceedings.

"In contrast to the habeas petitioner in *Stone,* who sought merely to avail himself of the exclusionary rule, Morrison seeks direct federal habeas protection of his personal right to effective assistance of counsel. . . .

"A layman will ordinarily be unable to recognize counsel's errors and to evaluate counsel's professional performance; consequently a criminal defendant will rarely know that he has not been represented competently until after trial or appeal, usually when he consults another lawyer about his case. Indeed, an accused will often not realize that he has a meritorious ineffectiveness claim until he begins collateral review proceedings, particularly if he retained trial counsel on direct appeal. Were we to extend *Stone* and hold that criminal defendants may not raise ineffective assistance claims that are based primarily on incompetent handling of fourth amendment issues on federal habeas, we would deny most defendants whose trial attorneys performed incompetently in this regard the opportunity to vindicate their right to effective trial counsel. . . .

"While we have recognized that the ' "premise of our adversary system of criminal justice . . . that partisan advocacy . . . will best promote the ultimate objective that the guilty are convicted and the innocent go free" ' underlies and gives meaning to the right to effective assistance, we have never intimated that the right to counsel is conditioned upon actual innocence. The constitutional rights of criminal defendants are granted to the innocent and the guilty alike. Consequently, we decline to hold either that the guarantee of effective assistance of counsel belongs solely to the innocent or that it attaches only to matters affecting the determination of actual guilt."

Justice Powell, joined by Chief Justice Burger and Justice Rehnquist, concurred in the judgment. He agreed that *Stone* did not bar federal habeas review of a claim of ineffective assistance of counsel. The more difficult issue, as he saw it, was "whether the admission of illegally seized but reliable evidence can ever constitute 'prejudice' " for sixth amendment purposes under the test of Strickland v. Washington, 466 U.S. 668 (1984):

> "Applying *Strickland,* respondent must show both that his counsel fell below basic standards of competence and that he was sufficiently prejudiced by the resulting errors. . . . Respondent's sole claim of prejudice stems from the admission of evidence that is concededly reliable although arguably inadmissible under Mapp v. Ohio, 367 U.S. 643 (1961), and its progeny. The parties and the court below have assumed that if the evidence in question was in fact inadmissible, and if there is a 'reasonable probability' that its use at trial affected the verdict, *Strickland*'s prejudice prong is satisfied. In my view, that assumption is not justified. In *Strickland,* we emphasized that ineffective assistance claims were designed to protect defendants against fundamental unfairness. . . . This reasoning strongly suggests that only errors that call into question the basic justice of the defendant's conviction suffice to establish prejudice under *Strickland.* The question, in sum, must be whether the particular harm suffered by the defendant due to counsel's incompetence rendered the defendant's trial fundamentally unfair.

> "As many of our cases indicate, the admission of illegally seized but reliable evidence does not lead to an unjust or fundamentally unfair verdict. . . . Thus, the harm suffered by respondent in this case is not the denial of a fair and reliable adjudication of his guilt, but rather the absence of a windfall. Because the fundamental fairness of the trial is not affected, our reasoning in *Strickland* strongly suggests that such harm does not amount to prejudicial ineffective assistance of counsel under the sixth amendment."

Because this issue of the meaning of *Strickland* had not been raised by the parties, Powell was prepared to leave it for another day. He therefore concurred in the judgment on the ground that *Stone* "does not govern this case."

4. *Kuhlmann v. Wilson.* One other attempt to extend *Stone v. Powell* resulted, on this point, in a non-decision. Kuhlmann v. Wilson, 477 U.S. 436 (1986), involved the "ends of justice" standard articulated in Sanders v. United States, 373 U.S. 1 (1963), for consideration of successive habeas petitions on the same claim.[a] The *Stone* issue was whether the availability of such reconsideration should be made to turn on whether the petitioner could show a colorable claim of innocence.

Wilson was convicted of murder, based in part on statements made to a cellmate who had agreed to act as a police informant. Wilson's original habeas petition focused on Massiah v. United States, 377 U.S. 201 (1964), which held that admission of incriminating statements "deliberately elicited" from the accused by means of electronic eaves-

a See page 709, supra.

dropping denied the sixth amendment right to counsel. This petition was denied on the ground that the "deliberately elicited" language of *Massiah* required "something more than incriminating statements uttered in the absence of counsel." The Supreme Court then decided United States v. Henry, 447 U.S. 264 (1980), which invoked *Massiah* to suppress statements made to a jailhouse informant. After *Henry,* Wilson filed a second habeas petition. The District Court found that *Henry* was distinguishable, but the Second Circuit reversed, holding that *Massiah* had been violated and that the "ends of justice" required consideration of the petition, even though the same claim had previously been rejected on the merits.

The Supreme Court reversed. Justice Powell found two independently sufficient reasons for denying habeas relief. One of them was that, because Wilson's cellmate had not asked any questions but had merely made notes of the statements Wilson volunteered, *Massiah* and *Henry* did not apply. On this issue, Powell spoke for a majority. Additionally, Powell argued that in any event successive habeas petitions on the same claim should not be heard absent a colorable claim of innocence. On this issue, Powell spoke for a plurality consisting of himself, Chief Justice Burger, and Justices Rehnquist and O'Connor. After an extensive review of habeas precedents, he said:

> "We now consider the limited circumstances under which the interests of the prisoner in relitigating constitutional claims held meritless on a prior petition may outweigh the countervailing interests served by according finality to the prior judgment. We turn first to the interests of the prisoner.

> "The prisoner may have a vital interest in having a second chance to test the fundamental justice of his incarceration. Even where, as here, the many judges who have reviewed the prisoner's claims in several proceedings provided by the state and on his first petition for federal habeas corpus have determined that his trial was free from constitutional error, a prisoner retains a powerful and legitimate interest in obtaining his release from custody if he is innocent of the charge for which he was incarcerated. That interest does not extend, however, to prisoners whose guilt is conceded or plain. . . .

> "In the light of the historic purpose of habeas corpus and the interests implicated by successive petitions for federal habeas relief from a state conviction, we conclude that the 'ends of justice' require federal courts to entertain such petitions only where the prisoner supplements his constitutional claim with a colorable showing of factual innocence. This standard was proposed by Judge Friendly more than a decade ago as a prerequisite for federal habeas review generally. Friendly, Is Innocence Irrelevant? Collateral Attack on Criminal Judgments, 38 U. Chi. L. Rev. 142 (1970). As Judge Friendly persuasively argued then, a requirement that the prisoner come forward with a colorable showing of innocence

identifies those habeas petitioners who are justified in again seeking relief from incarceration. We adopt this standard now to effectuate the clear intent of Congress [in § 2244(b) [b]] that successive federal habeas review should be granted only in rare cases, but that it should be available when the ends of justice so require. The prisoner may make the requisite showing by establishing that under the probative evidence he has a colorable claim of factual innocence. The prisoner must make his evidentiary showing even though—as argued in this case—the evidence of guilt may have been unlawfully admitted."

Justice Brennan, joined by Justice Marshall, disagreed with both the rejection of the merits of the sixth amendment claim and with the plurality's proposed limitation on the scope of federal habeas review. On the habeas issue, Brennan disputed the relevance of *Stone* outside the fourth amendment context:

"Despite the plurality's intimations, we simply have never held that federal habeas review of properly presented, nondefaulted constitutional claims is limited either to constitutional protections that advance the accuracy of the factfinding process at trial or is available solely to prisoners who can make out a colorable showing of factual innocence."

In a separate dissent, Justice Stevens indicated that he agreed with Justice Brennan on the sixth amendment claim. On the habeas issue, he took a middle ground:

"When a district court is confronted with the question whether the 'ends of justice' would be served by entertaining a state prisoner's petition for habeas corpus raising a claim that has been rejected on a prior federal petition for the same relief, one of the facts that may properly be considered is whether the petitioner has advanced a 'colorable claim of innocence.' But I agree with Justice Brennan that this is not an essential element of every just disposition of a successive petition. More specifically, I believe that the District Court did not abuse its discretion in entertaining the petition in this case, although I would also conclude that this is one of those close cases in which the District Court could have properly decided that a

---

[b] The "ends of justice" language originally came from what is now 28 U.S.C. § 2244(a), which provides that successive habeas petitions on the same claim need not be considered if the judge is satisfied that "the ends of justice will not be served by such inquiry." In 1966, the statute was amended. The "ends of justice" language was left in § 2244(a), which now applies only to habeas petitions by federal prisoners. Section 2244(b) speaks to successive petitions by state prisoners. It declares, in pertinent part, that successive habeas applications by state prisoners "need not be entertained . . . unless the application alleges and is predicated on a factual or other ground not adjudicated on the hearing of the earlier application for the writ, and unless the court . . . is satisfied that the applicant has not on the earlier application deliberately withheld the newly asserted ground or otherwise abused the writ." The plurality carried forward the "ends of justice" concept in its application to state prisoners, even though that language does not appear in § 2244(b).

second review of the same contention was not required despite the intervening decision in the *Henry* case." [c]

5. Bibliography. *Stone v. Powell* has been widely discussed. Among the prominent criticisms is Louis Michael Seidman, Factual Guilt and the Burger Court: An Examination of Continuity and Change in Criminal Procedure, 80 Colum. L. Rev. 436 (1980). Seidman argues that *Stone* suffers from a basic confusion in its reliance on both lack of guilt-relatedness and finality as rationales for curtailing habeas review of fourth amendment claims. In Seidman's view, these premises are inconsistent. Guilt-relatedness addresses the correctness of outcomes. Finality (which surfaces in *Stone*'s requirement of an "opportunity for full and fair litigation") is concerned with the integrity of the process rather than the ultimately unknowable question of factual guilt. Is Seidman's criticism persuasive? Are guilt-relatedness and finality inconsistent, or can both concerns sensibly be taken into account?

A different line of criticism comes from Ira Robbins and James Sanders, authors of Judicial Integrity, the Appearance of Justice, and the Great Writ of Habeas Corpus: How to Kill Two Thirds (or More) with One Stone, 15 Am. Crim. L. Rev. 63 (1977). They take issue with the majority's focus on deterrence of police misconduct as the rationale for excluding illegal evidence and argue that federal habeas review of fourth amendment violations is in any event fully justified by a concern for judicial integrity. See also the related discussions by Sam Boyte, Federal Habeas Corpus After *Stone v. Powell*: A Remedy Only for the Arguably Innocent?, 11 U. Rich. L. Rev. 291 (1977) (contending that the availability of federal habeas relief should not depend on a showing that the petitioner is arguably innocent), and Brenda Soloff, Litigation and Relitigation: The Uncertain Status of Federal Habeas Corpus for State Prisoners, 6 Hofstra L. Rev. 297 (1978) (identifying and criticizing possible rationale(s) for the *Stone* holding). For additional criticism of *Stone* and an attempt to place the decision in a broader context of the purposes and values served by various procedural systems, see Judith Resnik's article, Tiers, 57 S. Cal. L. Rev. 837, 892–95 (1984).

Additionally, several commentators have criticized *Stone* on separation-of-powers grounds. The common theme is that restrictions on the availability of habeas review should be made by Congress, not the Court. Important articles in this line include J. Patrick Green, *Stone v. Powell*: The Hermeneutics of the Burger Court, 10 Creighton L. Rev. 655 (1977) (emphasizing that there is no basis in the habeas statute for differentiating among constitutional rights), and Mark Tushnet, Constitutional and Statutory Analyses in the Law of Federal Jurisdiction, 25 U.C.L.A. L. Rev. 1301 (1978) (criticizing *Stone*'s implicit reworking of the habeas statute). In the same vein, see R. Nils Olsen, Judicial Proposals to Limit the Scope of Federal Post-Conviction Habeas Corpus Consideration of the Claims of State Prisoners, 31 Buff. L. Rev. 301 (1982), which examines a number of proposed judicial restrictions on

[c] For a predictive analysis of *Stone*'s possible application to *Massiah* claims, see Schulhofer, Confessions and the Court, 79 Mich. L. Rev. 683 (1981).

habeas corpus and finds them neither legitimate nor feasible. Olsen concludes that the scope of federal review should be left to Congress, but that more information about the costs and benefits of current practice is needed before undertaking legislative reform.[d]

Qualified support for the *Stone* decision comes from Philip Halpern in Federal Habeas Corpus and the *Mapp* Exclusionary Rule After *Stone v. Powell,* 82 Colum. L. Rev. 1 (1982). Halpern identifies three premises underlying *Stone v. Powell*: "that exclusion of evidence seized in violation of the fourth amendment is not a personal constitutional right; that the exclusionary rule is a judicially created mechanism designed to deter fourth amendment violations generally; and that the deterrent benefits realizable from the rule's application in federal habeas corpus proceedings are outweighed by the attendant social costs." Halpern terms these propositions "plausible" and "defensible." The harder question, in his view, is to reconcile the limitation on federal habeas review with the *Stone* Court's explicit reaffirmation of the exclusionary rule in state courts and on direct review by the Supreme Court. Halpern's answer is that, once the exclusionary rule is correctly understood as a prophylactic measure to regulate law enforcement activities rather than as a personal constitutional right, the difference between direct and collateral enforcement of the exclusionary rule can be explained as "a prudential judgment about the relative utility of the rule's application in these contexts."

Additionally, reference should be made to Symposium: State Prisoner Use of Federal Habeas Corpus Procedures, 44 Ohio St. L. J. (1983), which includes articles by Lawrence Herman; Daniel Meador, Frank Remington, Max Rosenn, and Stephen Saltzburg; Pagano, Federal Habeas Corpus for State Prisoners: Present and Future, 49 Albany L. Rev. 1 (1984); Erwin Chemerinsky, Thinking About Federal Habeas Corpus, 37 Case W.Res.L.Rev. 748 (1986–87); and Frank Remington, Change in the Availability of Federal Habeas Corpus: Its Significance for State Prisoners and State Correctional Programs, 85 Mich.L.Rev. 570 (1986).

Finally, special mention should be made of an imaginative article by Robert Cover and Alexander Aleinikoff. In Dialectical Federalism: Habeas Corpus and the Court, 86 Yale L.J. 1035 (1977), Cover and Aleinikoff pursue a vision of federal habeas corpus as a continuing dialogue between state and federal courts about the nature and content of federal constitutional rights. In this dialogue, federal courts have typically taken a more "utopian" perspective, while state courts have maintained a more "pragmatic" approach. The tension between these two tendencies is not simply institutional in origin, but reflects a deep-seated ambiguity in society's attitude toward enforcement of the criminal law. In this frame of reference, *Stone* helps set the agenda for debate. By suggesting that habeas corpus should focus on guilt or

---

[d] On a related topic, see Robert Clinton, Rule 9 of the Federal Habeas Rules: A Case Study of the Need for Reform of the Rules Enabling Acts, 63 Iowa L.Rev. 15 (1977) (criticizing the rule on successive habeas petitions, see page 710, supra, as an inappropriate exercise of rule-making authority by the Supreme Court).

innocence, the *Stone* Court did not merely restrict the habeas remedy; it redirected the attention of both state and federal courts away from certain kinds of claims and toward others. In other words, the focus on guilt or innocence has substantive implications for the "disciplined articulation and refinement" of constitutional rights through federal habeas review of state court convictions.

NOTES ON HABEAS REVIEW OF QUESTIONS OF FACT

1. ***Brown v. Allen.*** Although Brown v. Allen, 344 U.S. 443 (1953), held that federal habeas courts should redetermine questions of law already heard and decided by state courts, it did not require retrial of all underlying issues of fact. Instead, the *Brown* Court stated that federal courts have the *power* to hold such hearings, but that the decision to do so is discretionary: "Where the record of the application affords an adequate opportunity to weigh the sufficiency of the allegations and the evidence, and no unusual circumstances calling for a hearing are presented, a repetition of the trial is not required." Writing for a majority of the Justices on this point, Justice Frankfurter further specified that a federal habeas court "may accept" the original factual determinations, unless "a vital flaw be found in the process of ascertaining such facts in the state court."

2. ***Townsend v. Sain.*** In the years following *Brown v. Allen,* the lower federal courts diverged widely in determining when it was necessary to hold an evidentiary hearing on an application for habeas corpus. The Supreme Court undertook to resolve these uncertainties in Townsend v. Sain, 372 U.S. 293 (1963).

Townsend was a 19–year-old drug addict sentenced to death for murder. Conviction was based chiefly on a confession. The confession had been obtained by the police shortly after an injection of phenobarbital and scopolamine (sometimes known as "truth serum") administered to relieve his withdrawal symptoms. At trial, Townsend objected to the introduction of the confession on the ground that it had been coerced by the injection. After a hearing, the trial judge denied the motion to suppress. He made no explicit findings of fact. In the subsequent federal habeas proceeding, there was substantial dispute about the facts surrounding the confession, but the District Court dismissed the petition without holding an evidentiary hearing. The Supreme Court reversed. Writing for the Court, Chief Justice Warren first reiterated that a federal habeas court has plenary power "to receive evidence and try the facts anew." He continued:

> "We turn now to the considerations which in certain cases may make exercise of that power mandatory. The appropriate standard—which must be considered to supersede, to the extent of any inconsistencies, the opinions in *Brown v. Allen*—is this: Where the facts are in dispute, the federal court in habeas corpus must hold an evidentiary hearing if the habeas applicant did not receive a full and fair evidentiary hearing in

a state court, either at the time of the trial or in a collateral proceeding. In other words a federal evidentiary hearing is required unless the state-court trier of fact has after a full hearing reliably found the relevant facts.

"It would be unwise to overly particularize this test. The federal district judges are more intimately familiar with state criminal justice, and with the trial of fact, than are we, and to their sound discretion must be left in very large part the administration of federal habeas corpus. But experience proves that a too general standard—the 'exceptional circumstances' and 'vital flaw' tests of the opinions in *Brown v. Allen*—does not serve adequately to explain the controlling criteria for the guidance of the federal habeas corpus courts. Some particularization may therefore be useful. We hold that a federal court must grant an evidentiary hearing to a habeas applicant under the following circumstances: If (1) the merits of the factual dispute were not resolved in the state hearing; (2) the state factual determination is not fairly supported by the record as a whole; (3) the fact-finding procedure employed by the state court was not adequate to afford a full and fair hearing; (4) there is a substantial allegation of newly discovered evidence; (5) the material facts were not adequately developed at the state court hearing; or (6) for any reason it appears that the state trier of fact did not afford the habeas applicant a full and fair fact hearing."

The Court discussed each of these circumstances in detail. It emphasized that the six enumerated circumstances were situations in which an evidentiary hearing was mandatory. "In all other cases where the material facts are in dispute, the holding of such a hearing is in the discretion of the district judge." Finally, the Court made plain that the district judge, although entitled in some cases to defer to a state court's findings of fact, could never defer to the state court's conclusions of law. "It is the district judge's duty to apply the applicable federal law to the state court fact findings independently."[a]

3. Section 2254(d). In 1966, Congress amended the habeas statutes by adding § 2254(d). This provision is often treated as a straightforward codification of *Townsend*, though that does not seem a fair reading of its terms. Section 2254(d) provides that a state court finding of fact, if "evidenced by a written finding, written opinion, or other reliable and adequate written indicia, shall be presumed to be correct," unless it appears:

[a] For an interesting analysis of *Townsend v. Sain* and its relation to *Stone v. Powell*, see Richard A. Michael, The New Federalism and the Burger Court's Deference to the States in Federal Habeas Proceedings, 64 Iowa L. Rev. 233 (1979). Michael believes that the concerns underlying *Stone* might have been vindicated more effectively by altering the rule of *Townsend v. Sain* rather than by cutting back on *Brown v. Allen*. In his view, the greater intrusion on principles of finality and federalism is occasioned by de novo federal factual determinations rather than by relitigation of pure questions of law.

"(1) that the merits of the factual dispute were not resolved in the state court hearing;

(2) that the factfinding procedure employed by the state court was not adequate to afford a full and fair hearing;

(3) that the material facts were not adequately developed at the state court hearing;

(4) that the state court lacked jurisdiction of the subject matter or over the person of the applicant in the state court proceeding;

(5) that the applicant was indigent and the state court, in deprivation of his constitutional right, failed to appoint counsel to represent him in the state court proceeding;

(6) that the applicant did not receive a full, fair, and adequate hearing in the state court proceeding; or

(7) that the applicant was otherwise denied due process of law in the state court proceeding;

(8) or unless that part of the record of the state court proceeding in which the determination of such factual issue was made, pertinent to a determination of the sufficiency of the evidence to support such factual determination, is produced as provided for hereinafter, and the federal court on a consideration of such part of the record as a whole concludes that such factual determination is not fairly supported by the record."

Unless one of the circumstances of paragraphs (1) through (7) appears, or unless the court concludes pursuant to paragraph (8) that the record does not fairly support the factual determination, "the burden shall rest on the applicant to establish by convincing evidence that the factual determination by the state court was erroneous."

4. Questions of Fact Under § 2254(d). The "presumption" of § 2254(d) applies to questions of fact, not to questions of law nor to mixed questions of law and fact. Thus, the federal habeas court must determine for itself not only what the federal Constitution may require but also, for example, whether on established facts a confession is "voluntary." See Miller v. Fenton, 474 U.S. 104 (1985).

Sometimes, it is hard to tell whether a given question is one of fact or of mixed law and fact. A good example is the issue of the death-qualified juror in Wainwright v. Witt, 469 U.S. 412 (1985). In Witherspoon v. Illinois, 391 U.S. 510 (1968), the Court held unconstitutional a statute authorizing challenge for cause of any juror who opposed capital punishment. *Witherspoon* was taken to mean that a potential juror could be challenged for cause only if he or she would "automatically" vote against the death penalty and only if that intention were "unambiguously" stated. In Adams v. Texas, 448 U.S. 38 (1980), the Court reexamined this issue and held that a juror could be challenged for cause if "his views about capital punishment . . . would prevent or substantially impair the performance of his duties as a juror in accordance with his instructions and his oath." This looser standard left the courts with the "difficult task" of distinguishing jurors "whose opposition to capital punishment will not allow them to apply the law or view the facts impartially" from jurors "who, though opposed to capital punishment, will nevertheless conscientiously apply the law to the facts adduced at trial."

At issue in *Witt* was the question whether a juror's exclusion for cause based on opposition to the death penalty was a question of fact subject to the presumption of § 2254(d) or a "mixed" question of law or fact open to de novo determination on habeas review. Speaking through Justice Rehnquist, the Court said:

> "[E]xcluding prospective capital sentencing jurors because of their opposition to capital punishment is no different from excluding jurors for innumerable other reasons which result in bias. . . . The trial judge is of course applying some kind of legal standard to what he sees and hears, but his predominant function in determining juror bias involves credibility findings whose basis cannot be easily discerned from an appellate record. These are 'factual issues' that are subject to § 2254(d)."

Justice Stevens concurred in the judgment on the particular facts presented. Justice Brennan, with whom Justice Marshall joined, filed a lengthy dissent condemning both the dilution of *Witherspoon* and the Court's interpretation of § 2254(d).

SECTION 3: PROCEDURAL FORECLOSURE

WAINWRIGHT v. SYKES
United States Supreme Court, 1977.
433 U.S. 72.

MR. JUSTICE REHNQUIST delivered the opinion of the Court.

We granted certiorari to consider the availability of federal habeas corpus to review a state convict's claim that testimony was admitted at his trial in violation of his rights under Miranda v. Arizona, 384 U.S. 436 (1966), a claim which the Florida courts have previously refused to consider on the merits because of noncompliance with a state contemporaneous-objection rule. Petitioner Wainwright, on behalf of the state of Florida, here challenges a decision of the Court of Appeals for the Fifth Circuit ordering a hearing in state court on the merits of respondent's contention.

Respondent Sykes was convicted of third-degree murder after a jury trial in the Circuit Court of DeSoto County. He testified at trial that on the evening of January 8, 1972, he told his wife to summon the police because he had just shot Willie Gilbert. Other evidence indicated that when the police arrived at respondent's trailer home, they found Gilbert dead of a shotgun wound, lying a few feet from the front porch. Shortly after their arrival, respondent came from across the road and volunteered that he had shot Gilbert, and a few minutes later respondent's wife approached the police and told them the same thing. Sykes was immediately arrested and taken to the police station.

Once there, it is conceded that he was read his *Miranda* rights, and that he declined to seek the aid of counsel and indicated a desire to talk. He then made a statement, which was admitted into evidence at trial through the testimony of the two officers who heard it, to the effect that he had shot Gilbert from the front porch of his trailer home. There were several references during the trial to respondent's consumption of alcohol during the preceding day and to his apparent state of intoxication, facts which were acknowledged by the officers who arrived at the scene. At no time during the trial, however, was the admissibility of any of respondent's statements challenged by his counsel on the ground that respondent had not understood the *Miranda* warnings.[2] Nor did the trial judge question their admissibility on his own motion or hold a factfinding hearing bearing on that issue.

Respondent appealed his conviction, but apparently did not challenge the admissibility of the inculpatory statements. He later filed [several post-conviction proceedings in state courts, in which], apparently for the first time, [he] challenged the statements made to police on grounds of involuntariness. In all of these efforts respondent was unsuccessful.

Having failed in the Florida courts, respondent initiated the present action under 28 U.S.C. § 2254, asserting the inadmissibility of his statements by reason of his lack of understanding of the *Miranda* warnings.[4] The United States District Court for the Middle District of Florida ruled that Jackson v. Denno, 378 U.S. 368 (1964), requires a hearing in a state criminal trial prior to the admission of an inculpatory out-of-court statement by the defendant. It held further that respondent had not lost his right to assert such a claim by failing to object at trial or on direct appeal, since only "exceptional circumstances" of "strategic decisions at trial" can create such a bar to raising federal constitutional claims in a federal habeas action. The court stayed issuance of the writ to allow the state court to hold a hearing on the "voluntariness" of the statements.

Petitioner warden appealed this decision to the United States Court of Appeals for the Fifth Circuit. That court first considered the nature of the right to exclusion of statements made without a knowing waiver of the right to counsel and the right not to incriminate oneself. It noted that *Jackson v. Denno,* supra, guarantees a right to a hearing on whether a defendant has knowingly waived his rights as described to

---

[2] At one point early in the trial defense counsel did object to admission of any statements made by respondent to the police, on the basis that the basic elements of an offense had not yet been established. The judge ruled that the evidence could be admitted "subject to [the crime's] being properly established later."

[4] Respondent expressly waived "any contention or allegation as regards ineffective assistance of counsel" at his trial. . . .

him in the *Miranda* warnings and stated that under Florida law "[t]he burden is on the state to secure [a] prima facie determination of voluntariness, not upon the defendant to demand it."

The court then directed its attention to the effect on respondent's right of Florida Rule Crim. Proc. 3.190(i);[5] which it described as "a contemporaneous objection rule" applying to motions to suppress a defendant's inculpatory statements. It focused on this Court's decisions in Henry v. Mississippi, 379 U.S. 443 (1965); Davis v. United States, 411 U.S. 233 (1973); and Fay v. Noia, 372 U.S. 391 (1963), and concluded that the failure to comply with the rule requiring objection at the trial would only bar review of the suppression claim where the right to object was deliberately bypassed for reasons relating to trial tactics. The Court of Appeals distinguished our decision in *Davis* (where failure to comply with a rule requiring pretrial objection to the indictment was found to bar habeas review of the underlying constitutional claim absent showing of cause for the failure and prejudice resulting), for the reason that "[a] major tenet of the *Davis* decision was that no prejudice was shown" to have resulted from the failure to object. It found that prejudice is "inherent" in any situation, like the present one, where the admissibility of an incriminating statement is concerned. Concluding that "[t]he failure to object in this case cannot be dismissed as a trial tactic, and thus a deliberate by-pass," the court affirmed the District Court order that the state hold a hearing on whether respondent knowingly waived his *Miranda* rights at the time he made the statements.

The simple legal question before the Court calls for a construction of the language of 28 U.S.C. § 2254(a), which provides that the federal courts shall entertain an application for a writ of habeas corpus "in behalf of a person in custody pursuant to the judgment of a state court only on the ground that he is in custody in violation of the Constitution or laws or treaties of the United States." But, to put it mildly, we do not write on a clean slate in construing this statutory provision. Its earliest counterpart, applicable only to prisoners detained by federal authority, is found in the Judiciary Act of 1789 . . . .

In 1867, Congress expanded the statutory language so as to make the writ available to one held in state as well as federal custody. For more than a century since the 1867 amendment, this Court has grappled with the relationship between the classical common-law writ of habeas corpus and the remedy provided in 28 U.S.C. § 2254. Sharp division within the Court has been manifested on more than one aspect

---

[5] Rule 3.190(i):

"Motion to Suppress a Confession or Admissions Illegally Obtained.

"(1) Grounds. Upon motion of the defendant or upon its own motion, the court shall suppress any confession or admission obtained illegally from the defendant.

"(2) Time for Filing. The motion to suppress shall be made prior to trial unless opportunity therefor did not exist or the defendant was not aware of the grounds for the motion, but the court in its discretion may entertain the motion or an appropriate objection at the trial.

"(3) Hearing. The court shall receive evidence on any issue of fact necessary to be decided in order to rule on the motion."

of the perplexing problems which have been litigated in this connection. Where the habeas petitioner challenges a final judgment of conviction rendered by a state court, this Court has been called upon to decide no fewer than four different questions, all to a degree interrelated with one another: (1) What types of federal claims may a federal habeas court properly consider? (2) Where a federal claim is cognizable by a federal habeas court, to what extent must that court defer to a resolution of the claim in prior state proceedings? (3) To what extent must the petitioner who seeks federal habeas exhaust state remedies before resorting to the federal court? (4) In what instances will an adequate and independent state ground bar consideration of otherwise cognizable federal issues on federal habeas review?

[Justice Rehnquist's canvass of prior cases dealing with the first three of these questions is omitted. He concluded that discussion by observing:]

There is no need to consider here in greater detail these first three areas of controversy attendant to federal habeas review of state convictions. Only the fourth area—the adequacy of state grounds to bar federal habeas review—is presented in this case. The foregoing discussion of the other three is pertinent here only as it illustrates this Court's historic willingness to overturn or modify its earlier views of the scope of the writ, even where the statutory language authorizing judicial action has remained unchanged.

As to the role of adequate and independent state grounds, it is a well-established principle of federalism that a state decision resting on an adequate foundation of state substantive law is immune from review in the federal courts. The application of this principle in the context of a federal habeas proceeding has therefore excluded from consideration any questions of state *substantive* law, and thus effectively barred federal habeas review where questions of that sort are either the only ones raised by a petitioner or are in themselves dispositive of his case. The area of controversy which has developed has concerned the reviewability of federal claims which the state court has declined to pass on because not presented in the manner prescribed by its *procedural* rules. The adequacy of such an independent state procedural ground to prevent federal habeas review of the underlying federal issue has been treated very differently than where the state law ground is substantive. The pertinent decisions marking the Court's somewhat tortuous efforts to deal with this problem are: Ex parte Spencer, 228 U.S. 652 (1913); Brown v. Allen, 344 U.S. 443 (1953); Fay v. Noia, 372 U.S. 391 (1963); Davis v. United States, 411 U.S. 233 (1973); and Francis v. Henderson, 425 U.S. 536 (1976).

In *Brown* [a] petitioner Daniels' lawyer had failed to mail the appeal papers to the state Supreme Court on the last day provided by law for filing, and hand delivered them one day after that date. Citing the

---

[a] The reference here is actually to a companion case, *Daniels v. Allen.* [Footnote by eds.]

state rule requiring timely filing, the Supreme Court of North Carolina refused to hear the appeal. This Court, relying in part on its earlier decision in *Ex parte Spencer,* held that federal habeas was not available to review a constitutional claim which could not have been reviewed on direct appeal here because it rested on an independent and adequate state procedural ground.

In *Fay v. Noia,* respondent Noia sought federal habeas to review a claim that his state-court conviction had resulted from the introduction of a coerced confession in violation of the fifth amendment to the United States Constitution. While the convictions of his two codefendants were reversed on that ground in collateral proceedings following their appeals, Noia did not appeal and the New York courts ruled that his subsequent coram nobis action was barred on account of that failure. This Court held that petitioner was nonetheless entitled to raise the claim in federal habeas, and thereby overruled its decision 10 years earlier in *Brown v. Allen*:

> "[T]he doctrine under which state procedural defaults are held to constitute an adequate and independent state law ground barring direct Supreme Court review is not to be extended to limit the power granted the federal courts under the federal habeas statute."

As a matter of comity but not of federal power, the Court acknowledged "a limited discretion in the federal judge to deny relief . . . to an applicant who had deliberately by-passed the orderly procedure of the state courts and in so doing has forfeited his state court remedies." In so stating, the Court made clear that the waiver must be knowing and actual—"'an intentional relinquishment or abandonment of a known right or privilege.'" Noting petitioner's "grisly choice" between acceptance of his life sentence and pursuit of an appeal which might culminate in a sentence of death, the Court concluded that there had been no deliberate bypass of the right to have the federal issues reviewed through a state appeal.

A decade later we decided *Davis v. United States,* in which a federal prisoner's application under 28 U.S.C. § 2255 sought for the first time to challenge the makeup of the grand jury which indicted him. The government contended that he was barred by the requirement of Fed. Rule Crim. Proc. 12(b)(2) providing that such challenges must be raised "by motion before trial." The rule further provides that failure to so object constitutes a waiver of the objection, but that "the court for cause shown may grant relief from the waiver." We noted that the rule "promulgated by this Court and, pursuant to 18 U.S.C. § 3771, 'adopted' by Congress, governs by its terms the manner in which the claims of defects in the institution of criminal proceedings may be waived," and held that this standard contained in the rule, rather than the *Fay v. Noia* concept of waiver, should pertain in federal habeas as on direct review. Referring to previous constructions of Rule 12(b)(2), we concluded that review of the claim should be barred on habeas, as on direct appeal, absent a showing of cause for the noncompliance and some showing of actual prejudice resulting from the alleged constitutional violation.

Last term, in *Francis v. Henderson,* the rule of *Davis* was applied to the parallel case of a state procedural requirement that challenges to grand jury composition be raised before trial. The Court noted that there was power in the federal courts to entertain an application in such a case, but rested its holding on "considerations of comity and concerns for the orderly administration of criminal justice. . . ." While there was no counterpart provision of the state rule which allowed an exception upon some showing of cause, the Court concluded that the standard derived from the federal rule should nonetheless be applied in that context since " '[t]here is no reason to . . . give greater preclusive effect to procedural defaults by federal defendants than to similar defaults by state defendants.' " As applied to the federal petitions of state convicts, the *Davis* cause-and-prejudice standard was thus incorporated directly into the body of law governing the availability of federal habeas corpus review.

To the extent that the dicta of *Fay v. Noia* may be thought to have laid down an all-inclusive rule rendering state contemporaneous-objection rules ineffective to bar review of underlying federal claims in federal habeas proceedings—absent a "knowing waiver" or a "deliberate bypass" of the right to so object—its effect was limited by *Francis,* which applied a different rule and barred a habeas challenge to the makeup of a grand jury. Petitioner Wainwright in this case urges that we further confine its effect by applying the principle enunciated in *Francis* to a claimed error in the admission of a defendant's confession.

Respondent . . . urges that a defendant has a right under Jackson v. Denno, 378 U.S. 368 (1964), to a hearing as to the voluntariness of a confession, even though the defendant does not object to its admission. But we do not read *Jackson* as creating any such requirement. In that case the defendant's objection to the use of his confession was brought to the attention of the trial court, and nothing in the Court's opinion suggests that a hearing would have been required even if it had not been. To the contrary, the Court prefaced its entire discussion of the merits of the case with a statement of the constitutional rule that was to prove dispositive—that a defendant has a "right at some stage in the proceeding *to object* to the use of the confession and to have a fair hearing and a reliable determination on the issue of voluntariness. . . ." Language in subsequent decisions of this Court has reaffirmed the view that the Constitution does not require a voluntariness hearing absent some contemporaneous challenge to the use of the confession.

We therefore conclude that Florida procedure did, consistently with the United States Constitution, require that respondent's confession be challenged at trial or not at all, and thus his failure to timely object to its admission amounted to an independent and adequate state procedural ground which would have prevented direct review here. We thus come to the crux of this case. Shall the rule of *Francis v. Henderson* barring federal habeas review absent a showing of "cause" and "prejudice" attendant to a state procedural waiver, be applied to a waived objection to the admission of a confession at trial?[11]　We answer that question in the affirmative.

[S]ince Brown v. Allen, 344 U.S. 443 (1953), it has been the rule that the federal habeas petitioner who claims he is detained pursuant to a final judgment of a state court in violation of the United States Constitution is entitled to have the federal habeas court make its own independent determination of his federal claim, without being bound by the determination on the merits of that claim reached in the state proceedings.　This rule of *Brown v. Allen* is in no way changed by our holding today.　Rather, we deal only with contentions of federal law which were *not* resolved on the merits in the state proceeding due to respondent's failure to raise them there as required by state procedure. We leave open for resolution in future decisions the precise definition of the "cause" and "prejudice" standard, and note here only that it is narrower than the standard set forth in dicta in Fay v. Noia, 372 U.S. 391 (1963), which would make federal habeas review generally available to state convicts absent a knowing and deliberate waiver of the federal constitutional contention.　It is the sweeping language of *Fay v. Noia,* going far beyond the facts of the case eliciting it, which we today reject.[12]

The reasons for our rejection of it are several.　The contemporaneous objection rule itself is by no means peculiar to Florida, and deserves greater respect than *Fay* gives it, both for the fact that it is employed by a coordinate jurisdiction within the federal system and for the many interests which it serves in its own right.　A contemporaneous objection enables the record to be made with respect to the constitutional claim when the recollections of witnesses are freshest, not years later in a federal habeas proceeding.　It enables the judge who observed the demeanor of those witnesses to make the factual determinations necessary for properly deciding the federal constitutional question.　While the 1966 amendment to § 2254 requires deference to be given to such determinations made by state courts, the determinations themselves are less apt to be made in the first instance if there is no contemporaneous objection to the admission of the evidence on federal constitutional grounds.

A contemporaneous objection rule may lead to the exclusion of the evidence objected to, thereby making a major contribution to finality in

---

[11] Petitioner does not argue, and we do not pause to consider, whether a bare allegation of a *Miranda* violation, without accompanying assertions going to the actual voluntariness or reliability of the confession, is a proper subject for consideration on federal habeas review, where there has been a full and fair opportunity to raise the argument in the state proceeding.　See Stone v. Powell, 428 U.S. 465 (1976).　We do not address the merits of that question because of our resolution of the case on alternative grounds.

[12] We have no occasion today to consider the *Fay* rule as applied to the facts there confronting the Court.　Whether the *Francis* rule should preclude federal habeas review of claims not made in accordance with state procedure where the criminal defendant has surrendered, other than for reasons of tactical advantage, the right to have all of his claims of trial error considered by a state appellate court, we leave for another day. . . .

criminal litigation. Without the evidence claimed to be vulnerable on federal constitutional grounds, the jury may acquit the defendant, and that will be the end of the case; or it may nonetheless convict the defendant, and he will have one less federal constitutional claim to assert in his federal habeas petition. If the state trial judge admits the evidence in question after a full hearing, the federal habeas court pursuant to the 1966 amendment to § 2254 will gain significant guidance from the state ruling in this regard. Subtler considerations as well militate in favor of honoring a state contemporaneous objection rule. An objection on the spot may force the prosecution to take a hard look at its hole card, and even if the prosecutor thinks that the state trial judge will admit the evidence he must contemplate the possibility of reversal by the state appellate courts or the ultimate issuance of a federal writ of habeas corpus based on the impropriety of the state court's rejection of the federal constitutional claim.

We think that the rule of *Fay v. Noia*, broadly stated, may encourage "sandbagging" on the part of defense lawyers, who may take their chances on a verdict of not guilty in a state trial court with the intent to raise their constitutional claims in a federal habeas court if their initial gamble does not pay off. The refusal of federal habeas courts to honor contemporaneous objection rules may also make state courts themselves less stringent in their enforcement. Under the rule of *Fay v. Noia*, state appellate courts know that a federal constitutional issue raised for the first time in the proceeding before them may well be decided in any event by a federal *habeas* tribunal. Thus, their choice is between addressing the issue notwithstanding the petitioner's failure to timely object, or else face the prospect that the federal habeas court will decide the question without the benefit of their views.

The failure of the federal habeas courts generally to require compliance with a contemporaneous objection rule tends to detract from the perception of the trial of a criminal case in state court as a decisive and portentous event. A defendant has been accused of a serious crime, and this is the time and place set for him to be tried by a jury of his peers and found either guilty or not guilty by that jury. To the greatest extent possible all issues which bear on this charge should be determined in this proceeding: the accused is in the courtroom, the jury is in the box, the judge is on the bench, and the witnesses, having been subpoenaed and duly sworn, await their turn to testify. Society's resources have been concentrated at that time and place in order to decide, within the limits of human fallibility, the question of guilt or innocence of one of its citizens. Any procedural rule which encourages the result that those proceedings be as free of error as possible is thoroughly desirable, and the contemporaneous objection rule surely falls within this classification.

We believe the adoption of the *Francis* rule in this situation will have the salutary effect of making the state trial on the merits the "main event," so to speak, rather than a "tryout on the road" for what will later be the determinative federal habeas hearing. There is nothing in the Constitution or in the language of § 2254 which requires that the state trial on the issue of guilt or innocence be devoted largely to the testimony of fact witnesses directed to the elements of the state crime, while only later will there occur in a federal habeas hearing a full airing of the federal constitutional claims which were not raised in the state proceedings. If a criminal defendant thinks that an action of the state trial court is about to deprive him of a federal constitutional right there is every reason for his following state procedure in making known his objection.

The "cause" and "prejudice" exception of the *Francis* rule will afford an adequate guarantee, we think, that the rule will not prevent a federal habeas court from adjudicating for the first time the federal constitutional claim of a defendant who in the absence of such an adjudication will be the victim of a miscarriage of justice. Whatever precise content may be given those terms by later cases, we feel confident in holding without further elaboration that they do not exist here. Respondent has advanced no explanation whatever for his failure to object at trial,[14] and, as the proceeding unfolded, the trial judge is certainly not to be faulted for failing to question the admission of the confession himself. The other evidence of guilt presented at trial, moreover, was substantial to a degree that would negate any possibility of actual prejudice resulting to the respondent from the admission of his inculpatory statement.

We accordingly conclude that the judgment . . . must be reversed, and the cause remanded . . . with instructions to dismiss respondent's petition for a writ of habeas corpus.

It is so ordered.

MR. CHIEF JUSTICE BURGER, concurring.

I concur fully in the judgment and in the Court's opinion. I write separately to emphasize one point which, to me, seems of critical importance to this case. In my view, the "deliberate bypass" standard enunciated in Fay v. Noia, 372 U.S. 391 (1963), was never designed for, and is inapplicable to, errors—even of constitutional dimension—alleged to have been committed during trial.

In *Fay v. Noia*, the Court applied the "deliberate bypass" standard to a case where the critical procedural decision—whether to take a criminal appeal—was entrusted to a convicted defendant. Although Noia, the habeas petitioner, was represented by counsel, he himself had to make the decision whether to appeal or not; the role of the attorney was limited to giving advice and counsel. In giving content to the new deliberate bypass standard, *Fay* looked to the Court's decision in John-

---

[14] In Henry v. Mississippi, 379 U.S., at 451, the Court noted that decisions of counsel relating to trial strategy, even when made without the consultation of the defendant, would bar direct federal review of claims thereby forgone, except where "the circumstances are exceptional."

Last term in Estelle v. Williams, 425 U.S. 501 (1976), the Court reiterated the burden on a defendant to be bound by the trial judgments of his lawyer: "Under our adversary system, once a defendant has the assistance of counsel the vast array of trial decisions, strategic and tactical, which must be made before and during trial rests with the accused and his attorney."

son v. Zerbst, 304 U.S. 458 (1938), a case where the defendant had been called upon to make the decision whether to request representation by counsel in his federal criminal trial. Because in both *Fay* and *Zerbst,* important rights hung in the balance of the *defendant's own decision,* the Court required that a waiver impairing such rights be a knowing and intelligent decision by the defendant himself. . . .

In contrast, the claim in the case before us relates to events during the trial itself. Typically, habeas petitioners claim that unlawfully secured evidence was admitted, or that improper testimony was adduced, or that an improper jury charge was given, or that a particular line of examination or argument by the prosecutor was improper or prejudicial. But unlike *Fay* and *Zerbst,* preservation of this type of claim under state procedural rules does not generally involve an assertion by the defendant himself; rather, the decision to assert or not to assert constitutional rights or constitutionally based objections at trial is necessarily entrusted to the defendant's attorney, who must make on-the-spot decisions at virtually all stages of a criminal trial. . . . Not only do these decisions rest with the attorney, but such decisions must as a practical matter, be made without consulting the client.[1] . . .

Since trial decisions are of necessity entrusted to the accused's attorney, the *Fay-Zerbst* standard of "knowing and intelligent waiver" is simply inapplicable. . . .

MR. JUSTICE STEVENS, concurring.

Although the Court's decision today may be read as a significant departure from the "deliberate bypass" standard announced in Fay v. Noia, 372 U.S. 391 (1963), I am persuaded that the holding is consistent with the way other federal courts have actually been applying *Fay.* [1] The notion that a client must always consent to a tactical decision not to assert a constitutional objection to a proffer of evidence has always seemed unrealistic to me.[2] Conversely, if the constitutional issue is

---

[1] Only such basic decisions as whether to plead guilty, waive a jury, or testify in one's behalf are ultimately for the accused to make. See ABA Project on Standards for Criminal Justice, The Prosecution Function and Defense Function § 5.2, pp. 237–38 (Approved Draft 1971).

[1] The suggestion in *Fay* that the decision must be made personally by the defendant has not fared well, although a decision by counsel may not be binding if made over the objection of the defendant. [The circuit courts] have generally found a "deliberate bypass" where counsel could reasonably have decided not to object, but they have not found a bypass when they consider the right "deeply embedded" in the Constitution or when the procedural default was not substantial. Sometimes, even a deliberate choice by trial counsel has been held not to be a "deliberate bypass" when the result would be unjust. In short, the

actual disposition of [cases under the *Fay* standard] seems to rest on the court's perception of the totality of the circumstances, rather than on mechanical application of the "deliberate bypass" test.

[2] "If counsel is to have the responsibility for conducting a contested criminal trial, quite obviously he must have the authority to make important tactical decisions promptly as a trial progresses. The very reasons why counsel's participation is of such critical importance in assuring a fair trial for the defendant . . . make it inappropriate to require that his tactical decisions always be personally approved, or even thoroughly understood, by his client. Unquestionably, assuming the lawyer's competence, the client must accept the consequences of his trial strategy. A rule which would require the client's participation in every decision to object, or not to object, to proffered evidence would make a

sufficiently grave, even an express waiver by the defendant himself may sometimes be excused.[3] Matters such as the competence of counsel, the procedural context in which the asserted waiver occurred, the character of the constitutional right at stake, and the overall fairness of the entire proceeding, may be more significant than the language of the test the Court purports to apply. I therefore believe the Court has wisely refrained from attempting to give precise content to its "cause" and "prejudice" exception to the rule of Francis v. Henderson, 425 U.S. 536 (1976).[4]

In this case I agree with the Court's holding that collateral attack on the state-court judgment should not be allowed. The record persuades me that competent trial counsel could well have made a deliberate decision not to object to the admission of the respondent's in-custody statement. That statement was consistent, in many respects, with the respondent's trial testimony. It even had some positive value, since it portrayed the respondent as having acted in response to provocation, which might have influenced the jury to return a verdict on a lesser charge. To the extent that it was damaging, the primary harm would have resulted from its effect in impeaching the trial testimony, but it would have been admissible for impeachment in any event. Harris v. New York, 401 U.S. 222 (1971). Counsel may well have preferred to have the statement admitted without objection when it was first offered rather than making an objection which, at best, could have been only temporarily successful.

Moreover, since the police fully complied with *Miranda,* the deterrent purpose of the *Miranda* rule is inapplicable to this case. Finally, there is clearly no basis for claiming that the trial violated any standard of fundamental fairness. Accordingly, no matter how the rule is phrased, this case is plainly not one in which a collateral attack should be allowed. I therefore join the opinion of the Court.

MR. JUSTICE WHITE, concurring in the judgment.

Under the Court's cases a state conviction will survive challenge in federal habeas corpus not only when there has been a deliberate bypass within the meaning of Fay v. Noia, 372 U.S. 391 (1963), but also when the alleged constitutional error is harmless beyond a reasonable doubt within the intendment of Harrington v. California, 395 U.S. 250 (1969), and similar cases. The petition for habeas corpus of respondent Sykes alleging the violation of his constitutional rights by the admission of certain evidence should be denied if the alleged error is deemed harmless. This would be true even had there been proper objection to

shambles of orderly procedure." United States ex rel. Allum v. Twomey, 484 F.2d 740, 744–45 (7th Cir. 1973).

[3] The test announced in *Fay* was not actually applied in that case. The Court held that habeas relief was available notwithstanding the client's participation in the waiver decision, and notwithstanding the fact that the decision was made on a tactical basis. The client apparently feared that the state might be able to convict him even without the use of his confession, and that he might be sentenced to death if reconvicted.

[4] As *Fay v. Noia,* makes clear, we are concerned here with a matter of equitable discretion rather than a question of statutory authority; and equity has always been characterized by its flexibility and regard for the necessities of each case.

the evidence and no procedural default whatsoever by either respondent or his counsel. . . .

In terms of the necessity for Sykes to show prejudice, it seems to me that the harmless error rule provides ample protection to the state's interest. If a constitutional violation has been shown and there has been no deliberate bypass—at least as I understand the rule as applied to alleged trial lapses of defense counsel—I see little if any warrant, having in mind the state's burden of proof, not to insist upon a showing that the error was harmless beyond a reasonable doubt. As long as there is acceptable cause for the defendant's not objecting to the evidence, there should not be shifted to him the burden of proving specific prejudice to the satisfaction of the habeas corpus judge.

With respect to the necessity to show cause for noncompliance with the state rule, I think the deliberate bypass rule of *Fay v. Noia* affords adequate protection to the state's interest in insisting that defendants not flout the rules of evidence. The bypass rule, however, as applied to events occurring during trial, cannot always demand that the defendant himself concur in counsel's judgment. Furthermore, if counsel is aware of the facts and the law (here the contemporaneous objection rule and the relevant constitutional objection that might be made) and yet decided not to object because he thinks the objection is unfounded, would damage his client's case, or for any other reason that flows from his exercise of professional judgment, there has been, as I see it, a deliberate bypass. It will not later suffice to allege in federal habeas corpus that counsel was mistaken, unless it is "plain error" appearing on the record or unless the error is sufficiently egregious to demonstrate that the services of counsel were not "within the range of competence demanded of attorneys in criminal cases." Other reasons not amounting to deliberate bypass, such as ignorance of the applicable rules, would be sufficient to excuse the failure to object to evidence offered during trial.

I do agree that it is the burden of the habeas corpus petitioner to negate deliberate bypass and explain his failure to object. Sykes did neither here, and I therefore concur in the judgment.

MR. JUSTICE BRENNAN, with whom MR. JUSTICE MARSHALL joins, dissenting.

Over the course of the last decade, the deliberate bypass standard announced in *Fay v. Noia*, 372 U.S. 391, 438–39 (1963), has played a central role in efforts by the federal judiciary to accommodate the constitutional rights of the individual with the state's interests in the integrity of their judicial procedural regimes. The Court today decides that this standard should no longer apply with respect to procedural defaults occurring during the trial of a criminal defendant. In its place, the Court adopts the two-part "cause" and "prejudice" test originally developed in Davis v. United States, 411 U.S. 233 (1973), and Francis v. Henderson, 425 U.S. 536 (1976). As was true with these earlier cases, however, today's decision makes no effort to provide concrete guidance as to the content of those terms. More particularly, left unanswered is the thorny question that must be recognized to be central to a realistic rationalization of this area of law: How should the federal habeas court treat a procedural default in a state court that is attributable purely and simply to the error or negligence of a defendant's trial counsel? Because this key issue remains unresolved, I shall attempt in this opinion a re-examination of the policies[2] that should inform—and in *Fay* did inform—the selection of the standard governing the availability of federal habeas corpus jurisdiction in the face of an intervening procedural default in the state court.

I

I begin with the threshold question: What is the meaning and import of a procedural default? If it could be assumed that a procedural default more often than not is the product of a defendant's conscious refusal to abide by the duly constituted, legitimate processes of the state courts, then I might agree that a regime of collateral review weighted in favor a state's procedural rules would be warranted. *Fay,* however, recognized that such rarely is the case; and therein lies *Fay's* basic unwillingness to embrace a view of habeas jurisdiction that results in "an airtight system of [procedural] forfeitures."

This, of course, is not to deny that there are times when the failure to heed a state procedural requirement stems from an intentional decision to avoid the presentation of constitutional claims to the state forum. *Fay* was not insensitive to this possibility. Indeed, the very purpose of its bypass test is to detect and enforce such intentional procedural forfeitures of outstanding constitutionally based claims.
. . .

But having created the bypass exception to the availability of collateral review, *Fay* recognized that intentional, tactical forfeitures are not the norm upon which to build a rational system of federal habeas jurisdiction. In the ordinary case, litigants simply have no incentive to slight the state tribunal, since constitutional adjudication on the state and federal levels are not mutually exclusive. Under the regime of collateral review recognized since the days of *Brown v. Allen,* and enforced by the *Fay* bypass test, no rational lawyer would risk the "sandbagging" feared by the Court.[5] If a constitutional challenge is not

[2] I use the term "policies" advisedly, for it is important to recognize the area of my disagreement with the Court. This Court has never taken issue with the foundation principle established by *Fay v. Noia*—that in considering a petition for the writ of habeas corpus, federal courts possess the *power* to look beyond a state procedural forfeiture in order to entertain the contention that a defendant's constitutional rights have been abridged. . . . Today's decision reconfirms this federal power by authorizing federal intervention under the "cause" and "prejudice" test. Were such power unavailable, federal courts would be bound by [the Florida contemporaneous ob-

jection rule], which contains no explicit provision for relief from procedural defaults. Our disagreement, therefore, centers upon the standard that should govern a federal district court in the exercise of this power to adjudicate the constitutional claims of a state prisoner—which, in turn, depends upon an evaluation of the competing policies and values served by collateral review weighted against those furthered through strict deference to a state's procedural rules. . . .

[5] In brief, the defense lawyer would face two options: (1) He could elect to present his constitutional claims to the state courts

properly raised on the state level, the explanation generally will be found elsewhere than in an intentional tactical decision.

In brief then, any realistic system of federal habeas corpus jurisdiction must be premised on the reality that the ordinary procedural default is born of the inadvertence, negligence, inexperience, or incompetence of trial counsel. The case under consideration today is typical. The Court makes no effort to identify a tactical motive for the failure of Sykes' attorney to challenge the admissibility or reliability of a highly inculpatory statement. While my Brother Stevens finds a possible tactical advantage, I agree with the Court of Appeals that this reading is most implausible: "We can find no possible advantage which the defense might have gained, or thought they might gain, from the failure to conform with [the Florida rule of procedure]." Indeed, there is no basis for inferring that Sykes or his state trial lawyer was even aware of the existence of his claim under the fifth amendment; for this is not a case where the trial judge expressly drew the attention of the defense to a possible constitutional contention or procedural requirement or where the defense signals its knowledge of a constitutional claim by abandoning a challenge previously raised. Rather, any realistic reading of the record demonstrates that we are faced here with a lawyer's simple error.

Fay's answer thus is plain: the bypass test simply refuses to credit what is essentially a lawyer's mistake as a forfeiture of constitutional rights. I persist in the belief that the interests of Sykes and the state of Florida are best rationalized by adherence to this test, and by declining to react to inadvertent defaults through the creation of an "airtight system of forfeitures."

II

What are the interests that Sykes can assert in preserving the availability of federal collateral relief in the face of his inadvertent state procedural default? Two are paramount.

. . . Congress explicitly chose to effectuate the federal court's primary responsibility for preserving federal rights and privileges by

in a proper fashion. If the state trial court is persuaded that a constitutional breach has occurred, the remedies dictated by the Constitution would be imposed, the defense would be bolstered, and the prosecution accordingly weakened, perhaps precluded altogether. If the state court rejects the properly tendered claims, the defense has lost nothing: Appellate review before the state courts and federal habeas consideration are preserved. (2) He could elect to "sandbag." This presumably means, first, that he would hold back the presentation of his constitutional claim to the trial court, thereby increasing the likelihood of a conviction would be able to present evidence that, while arguably constitutionally deficient, may be highly prejudicial to the defense. Second, he would thereby have forfeited all state review and remedies with respect to these claims (subject to whatever "plain error" rule is available). Third, to carry out his scheme, he would now be compelled to deceive the federal habeas court and to convince the judge that he did not "deliberately bypass" the state procedures. If he loses on this gamble, all federal review would be barred, and his "sandbagging" would have resulted in nothing but the forfeiture of all judicial review of his client's claims. The Court, without substantiation, apparently believes that a meaningful number of lawyers are induced into option two by *Fay.* I do not. That belief simply offends common sense.

authorizing the litigation of constitutional claims and defenses in a district court after the state vindicates its own interest through trial of the substantive criminal offense in the state courts.[7]　This, of course, was not the only course that Congress might have followed: As an alternative, it might well have decided entirely to circumvent all state procedure through the expansion of existing federal removal statutes . . . ., thereby authorizing the pretrial transfer of all state criminal cases to the federal courts whenever federal defenses or claims are in issue.　But liberal post-trial federal review is the redress that Congress ultimately chose to allow and the consequences of a state procedural default should be evaluated in conformance with this policy choice.　Certainly, we can all agree that once a state court has assumed jurisdiction of a criminal case, the integrity of its own process is a matter of legitimate concern.　The *Fay* bypass test, by seeking to discover intentional abuses of the rules of the state forum, is, I believe, compatible with this state institutional interest.　But whether *Fay* was correct in penalizing a litigant solely for his intentional forfeitures properly must be read in light of Congress' desired norm of widened post-trial access to the federal courts.　If the standard adopted today is later construed to require that the simple mistakes of attorneys are to be treated as binding forfeitures, it would serve to subordinate the fundamental rights contained in our constitutional charter to inadvertent defaults of rules promulgated by state agencies, and would essentially leave it to the states, through the enactment of procedure and the certification of the competence of local attorneys, to determine whether a habeas applicant will be permitted the access to the federal forum that is guaranteed him by Congress.[9]

Thus, I remain concerned that undue deference to local procedure can only serve to undermine the ready access to a federal court to which a state defendant otherwise is entitled.　But federal review is not the full measure of Sykes' interest, for there is another of even greater immediacy: assuring that his constitutional claims can be addressed to *some* court.　For the obvious consequence of barring Sykes from the federal courthouse is to insulate Florida's alleged constitutional violation from any and all judicial review because of a lawyer's mistake. From the standpoint of the habeas petitioner, it is a harsh rule indeed that denies him "any review at all where the state has granted none"— particularly when he would have enjoyed both state and federal consideration had his attorney not erred.

---

[7] Congress' grant of post-trial access to the federal courts was reconfirmed by its modification of 28 U.S.C. § 2254 following our decisions in *Fay* and Townsend v. Sain, 372 U.S. 293 (1963). This legislative amendment of the habeas statute essentially embraced the relitigation standards outlined in *Townsend* without altering the broad framework for collateral review contained in Brown v. Allen, 344 U.S. 443 (1953), *Fay,* and like cases.

[9] Of course, even under the Court's new standard, traditional principles continue to apply, and the federal judiciary is not bound by state rules of procedure that are unreasonable on their face, or that are either unreasonably or inconsistently applied. See, e.g., Henry v. Mississippi, 379 U.S. 443 (1965); NAACP v. Alabama, 377 U.S. 288 (1964); Staub v. Baxley, 355 U.S. 313 (1958); Williams v. Georgia, 349 U.S. 375 (1955).

Fay's answer to Sykes' predicament . . . is, I submit, a realistic one. The fifth amendment assures that no person "shall be compelled in any criminal case to be a witness against himself. . . ." A defendant like Sykes can forgo this protection in two ways: He may decide to waive his substantive self-incrimination right at the point that he gives an inculpatory statement to the police authorities or he and his attorney may choose not to challenge the admissibility of an incriminating statement when such a challenge would be effective under state trial procedure. With few exceptions in the past 40 years, this Court has required that the substantive waiver, to be valid, must be a knowing and intelligent one. It has long been established that such is the case for the waiver of the protections of the *Miranda* rule. *Fay* simply evaluates the procedural waiver of Sykes' fifth amendment rights by the same standard.

From the standpoint of the habeas petitioner this symmetry is readily understandable. To him, the inevitable consequence of either type of forfeiture—be it substantive or procedural—is that the protection of the fifth amendment is lost and his own words are introduced at trial to the prejudice of his defense. The defendant's vital interest in preserving his fifth amendment privilege entitles him to informed and intelligent consideration of any decision leading to its forfeiture. . . .

A procedural default should be treated accordingly. Indeed, a recent development in the law of habeas corpus suggests that adherence to the deliberate bypass test may be more easily justified today than it was when *Fay* was decided. It also suggests that the "prejudice" prong of the Court's new test may prove to be a redundancy. Last term the Court ruled that alleged violations of the fourth amendment in most circumstances no longer will be cognizable in habeas corpus. Stone v. Powell, 428 U.S. 465 (1976). While, for me, the principle that generated this conclusion was not readily apparent, I expressed my concern that the *Stone* decision contains the seeds for the exclusion from collateral review of a variety of constitutional rights that my Brethren somehow deem to be unimportant—perhaps those that they are able to conclude are not "guilt-related." If this trail is to be followed, it would be quite unthinkable that an unintentional procedural default should be allowed to stand in the way of vindication of constitutional rights bearing upon the guilt or innocence of a defendant. Indeed, if as has been argued, a key to decision in this area turns upon a comparison of the importance of the constitutional right at stake with the state procedural rule, Sandalow, Henry v. Mississippi and the Adequate State Ground: Proposals for a Revised Doctrine, 1965 Sup. Ct. Rev. 187, 236–37, then the Court's threshold effort to identify those rights of sufficient importance to be litigated collaterally should largely predetermine the outcome of this balance.

In sum, I believe that *Fay*'s commitment to enforcing intentional but not inadvertent procedural defaults offers a realistic measure of protection for the habeas corpus petitioner seeking federal review of federal claims that were not litigated before the state. The threatened creation of a more "airtight system of forfeitures" would effectively deprive habeas petitioners of the opportunity for litigating their constitutional claims before any forum and would disparage the paramount importance of constitutional rights in our system of government. Such a restriction of habeas corpus jurisdiction should be countenanced, I submit, only if it fairly can be concluded that *Fay*'s focus on knowing and voluntary forfeitures unduly interferes with the legitimate interests of state courts or institutions. The majority offers no suggestion that actual experience has shown that *Fay*'s bypass test can be criticized on this score. And, as I now hope to demonstrate, any such criticism would be unfounded.

III

A regime of federal habeas corpus jurisdiction that permits the reopening of state procedural defaults does not invalidate any state procedural rule as such;[10] Florida's courts remain entirely free to enforce their own rules as they choose, and to deny any and all state rights and remedies to a defendant who fails to comply with applicable state procedure. The relevant inquiry is whether more is required—specifically, whether the fulfillment of important interests of the state necessitates that federal courts be called upon to impose additional sanctions for inadvertent non-compliance with state procedural requirements such as the contemporaneous objection rule involved here.

Florida, of course, can point to a variety of legitimate interests in seeking allegiance to its reasonable procedural requirements, the contemporaneous objection rule included. As *Fay* recognized, a trial, like any organized activity, must conform to coherent process, and "there must be sanctions for the flouting of such procedure." The strict enforcement of procedural defaults, therefore, may be seen as a means of deterring any tendency on the part of the defense to slight the state forum, to deny state judges their due opportunity for playing a meaningful role in the evolving task of constitutional adjudication, or to mock the needed finality of criminal trials. All of these interests are referred to by the Court in various forms.[11]

The question remains, however, whether any of these policies or interests are efficiently and fairly served by enforcing both intentional

[10] This is not to suggest that the availability of collateral review has no bearing on the states' selection and enforcement of procedural requirements. On the contrary, to the extent that a state desires to have input into the process of developing federal law, and seeks to guarantee its primary factfinding role as authorized by § 2254 and Townsend v. Sain, 372 U.S. 293 (1963), the existence of broad federal habeas power will tend to encourage the liberalizing and streamlining of state rules that otherwise might serve to bar such state participation. From every perspective, I would suppose that any such effect of *Fay* would be considered a salutary one, although the Court implies the contrary.

[11] In my view, the strongest plausible argument for strict enforcement of a contemporaneous objection rule is one that the Court barely relies on at all: the possibility that the failure of timely objection to the admissibility of evidence may foreclose the making of a fresh record and thereby prejudice the prosecution in later litigation involving that evidence. There may be force to this contention, but it rests on the premise that the state in fact has suffered actual prejudice because of a procedural lapse. Florida demonstrates no such injury here. . . .

and inadvertent defaults pursuant to the identical stringent standard. I remain convinced that when one pierces the surface justifications for a harsher rule posited by the Court, no standard stricter than *Fay*'s deliberate bypass test is realistically defensible.

Punishing a lawyer's unintentional errors by closing the federal courthouse door to his client is both a senseless and misdirected method of deterring the slighting of state rules. It is senseless because unplanned and unintentional action of any kind generally is not subject to deterrence; and, to the extent that it is hoped that a threatened sanction addressed to the defense will induce greater care and caution on the part of trial lawyers, thereby forestalling negligent conduct or error, the potential loss of all valuable state remedies would be sufficient to this end. And it is a misdirected sanction because even if the penalization of incompetence or carelessness will encourage more thorough legal training and trial preparation, the habeas applicant, as opposed to his lawyer, hardly is the proper recipient of such a penalty. Especially with fundamental constitutional rights at stake, no fictional relationship of principal-agent or the like can justify holding the criminal defendant accountable for the naked errors of his attorney. This is especially true when so many indigent defendants are without any realistic choice in selecting who ultimately represents them at trial. Indeed, if responsibility for error must be apportioned between the parties, it is the state, through its attorney's admissions and certification policies, that is more fairly held to blame for the fact that practicing lawyers too often are ill-prepared or ill-equipped to act carefully and knowledgeably when faced with decisions governed by state procedural requirements.

Hence, while I can well agree that the proper functioning of our system of criminal justice, both federal and state, necessarily places heavy reliance on the professionalism and judgment of trial attorneys, I cannot accept a system that ascribes the absolute forfeiture of an individual's constitutional claims to situations where his lawyer manifestly exercises *no* professional judgment at all—where carelessness, mistake, or ignorance is the explanation for a procedural default. Of course, it is regrettable that certain errors that might have been cured earlier had trial counsel acted expeditiously must be corrected collaterally and belatedly. I can understand the Court's wistfully wishing for the day when the trial was the sole, binding and final "event" of the adversarial process—although I hesitate to agree that in the eyes of the criminal defendant it has ever ceased being the "main" one. But it should be plain that in the real world, the interest in finality is repeatedly compromised in numerous ways that arise with far greater frequency than do procedural defaults. Indeed, the very existence of the well-established right collaterally to reopen issues previously litigated before the state courts, Brown v. Allen, 344 U.S. 443 (1953), represents a congressional policy choice that is inconsistent with notions of strict finality—and probably more so than authorizing the litigation of issues that, due to inadvertence, were never addressed to any court. Ultimately, all of these limitations on the finality of criminal convictions emerge from the tension between justice and efficiency in a judicial system that hopes to remain true to its principles and ideals. Reasonable people may disagree on how best to resolve these tensions. But the solution that today's decision risks embracing seems to me the most unfair of all: the denial of any judicial consideration of the constitutional claims of a criminal defendant because of errors made by his attorney which lie outside the power of the habeas petitioner to prevent or deter and for which, under no view of morality or ethics, can he be held responsible.

In short, I believe that the demands of our criminal justice system warrant visiting the mistakes of a trial attorney on the head of a habeas corpus applicant only when we are convinced that the lawyer actually exercised his expertise and judgment in his client's service, and with his client's knowing and intelligent participation where possible. This, of course, is the precise system of habeas review established by *Fay v. Noia*.

IV

Perhaps the primary virtue of *Fay* is that the bypass test at least yields a coherent yardstick for federal district courts in rationalizing their power of collateral review. In contrast, although some four years have passed since its introduction in Davis v. United States, 411 U.S. 233 (1973), the only thing clear about the Court's "cause" and "prejudice" standard is that it exhibits the notable tendency of keeping prisoners in jail without addressing their constitutional complaints. Hence, as of today, all we know of the "cause" standard is its requirement that habeas applicants bear an undefined burden of explanation for the failure to obey the state rule. Left unresolved is whether a habeas petitioner like Sykes can adequately discharge this burden by offering the commonplace and truthful explanation for his default: attorney ignorance or error beyond the client's control. The "prejudice" inquiry, meanwhile, appears to bear a strong resemblance to harmless error doctrine. I disagree with the Court's appraisal of the harmlessness of the admission of respondent's confession, but if this is what is meant by prejudice, respondent's constitutional contentions could be as quickly and easily disposed of in this regard by permitting federal courts to reach the merits of his complaint. In the absence of a persuasive alternative formulation to the bypass test, I would simply affirm the judgment of the Court of Appeals and allow Sykes his day in court on the ground that the failure of timely objection in this instance was not a tactical or deliberate decision but stemmed from a lawyer's error that should not be permitted to bind his client.

One final consideration deserves mention. [M]ost courts, this one included, traditionally have resisted any realistic inquiry into the competency of trial counsel. . . . If the scope of habeas jurisdiction previously governed by *Fay v. Noia* is to be redefined so as to enforce the errors and neglect of lawyers with unnecessary and unjust rigor, the time may come when conscientious and fairminded federal and state courts . . . will have to reconsider whether they can continue to indulge the comfortable fiction that all lawyers are skilled or even competent craftsmen in representing the fundamental rights of their clients.

NOTES ON THE EFFECT OF PROCEDURAL DEFAULT

1. *Daniels v. Allen.* *Daniels* was a companion case to Brown v. Allen, 344 U.S. 443 (1953). Brown and Daniels were black defendants convicted, respectively, of rape and murder. Both were sentenced to death. They alleged racial discrimination in the selection of grand and petit juries and admission of coerced confessions. Brown's claims were rejected on the merits by the state courts and were also rejected, after reexamination of the merits, on federal habeas. Daniels' claims were rejected by the state Supreme Court without consideration of the merits, owing to the failure of Daniels' lawyer to perfect an appeal within the allotted time. On review of Daniels' federal habeas petition, the United States Supreme Court held that his claims were foreclosed by procedural default in the state system.

The doctrinal basis for this ruling was not made clear. Speaking for the Court, Justice Reed suggested at least three theories. Foreclosure might be required by the failure to exhaust state remedies. Alternatively, it might rest on a characterization of the untimely appeal as a waiver of the claims. Or it might be based on the theory that the procedural default provided an adequate and independent state ground for the judgment of conviction. Whatever the theory, the result was clear: if the state courts relied on the failure to follow reasonable procedures as the basis for failing to consider the merits of federal claims, review on federal habeas was also foreclosed. This prompted a dissent by Justice Black, who doubted "the soundness of a philosophy which prompts this Court to grant a second review where the state has granted one but to deny any review at all where the state has granted none."

2. *Fay v. Noia.* All three of the *Brown* theories were rejected in Fay v. Noia, 372 U.S. 391 (1963). Writing for the Court, Justice Brennan undertook to show, first, that habeas corpus historically had been available to remedy any restraint contrary to fundamental (i.e., constitutional) law and, second, that procedural default in the state system did not foreclose habeas review. This history has been bitterly criticized, not only in Justice Harlan's dissenting opinion, but also in several secondary sources.[a]

---

[a] See, e.g., Mayers, The Habeas Corpus Act of 1867: The Supreme Court as Legal Historian, 33 U. Chi. L. Rev. 31 (1965) (concluding that *Fay*'s interpretation of the 1867 Act is "without historical foundation"); Oaks, Legal History in the High Court—Habeas Corpus, 64 Mich. L. Rev. 451, 458–68 (1966) (characterizing *Fay* as "a regal patchwork of history that, on close examination, proves as embarrassingly illusory as the Emperor's new clothes"); Friendly, Is Innocence Irrelevant: Collateral Attack on Criminal Judgments, 38 U. Chi. L. Rev. 142, 170–71 (1970) (concluding that *Fay*'s history "has now been shown with as close to certainty as can ever be

Whatever the merits of *Fay*'s version of history, its rejection of procedural foreclosure established several important propositions.[b] First, *Fay* held that the exhaustion requirement,[c] as originated in *Ex parte Royall* and subsequently codified in § 2254, applies only to *currently* available state remedies. That an additional state remedy may once have been available does not foreclose federal habeas review for failure to exhaust state remedies. This aspect of *Fay* has not subsequently been questioned.

Second, *Fay* held that a waiver of constitutional rights could only be accomplished under the standard of Johnson v. Zerbst, 304 U.S. 458, 464 (1938), requiring the intentional relinquishment of a known right. This is the origin of the "deliberate bypass" test subsequently rejected in *Wainwright v. Sykes*.

Third, and perhaps most importantly, *Fay* established that, whatever the appropriate standard for the exercise of such authority, federal habeas courts have the *power* to hear a claim foreclosed in state court by procedural default. True, direct Supreme Court review of the state court judgment might, in such a case, be barred by the existence of an adequate and independent state ground for the decision below. But "the adequate state-ground rule," said Justice Brennan, "is a function of the limitations of *appellate* review":

"Most of the opinion in Murdock v. City of Memphis, 87 U.S. (20 Wall.) 590 (1875), is devoted to demonstrating the Court's lack of jurisdiction on direct review to decide questions of state law in cases also raising federal questions. It followed from this holding that if the state question was dispositive of the case, the Court could not decide the federal question. The federal question was moot; nothing turned on its resolution. And so we have held that the adequate state-ground rule is a consequence of the Court's obligation to refrain from rendering advisory opinions or passing upon moot questions.

"But while our appellate function is concerned only with the judgments or decrees of state courts, the habeas corpus jurisdiction of the lower federal courts is not so confined. The jurisdictional prerequisite is not the judgment of a state court but detention simpliciter. . . . Habeas lies to enforce the right of personal liberty; when that right is denied and a person confined, the federal court has the power to release him. . . .

"To be sure, this may not be the entire answer to the contention that the adequate state-ground principle should apply to the federal courts on habeas corpus as well as to the Supreme Court on direct review of state judgments. The *Murdock* decision may be supported not only by the factor of

expected in such matters" to be "simply wrong").

[b] *Fay*'s analysis of these issues follows an important early article by Curtis Reitz,

Federal Habeas Corpus: Impact of an Abortive State Proceeding, 74 Harv. L. Rev. 1315 (1961).

[c] See page 708, supra.

mootness, but in addition by certain characteristics of the federal system. The first question the Court had to decide in *Murdock* was whether it had the power to review state questions in cases also raising federal questions. It held that it did not, thus affirming the independence of the states in matters within the proper sphere of their lawmaking power from federal judicial interference. . . . But the problem [here] is crucially different from that posed in *Murdock* of the federal courts' deciding questions of substantive state law. In Noia's case the only relevant substantive law is federal—the 14th amendment. State law appears only in the procedural framework for adjudicating the substantive federal question. Cf. Dice v. Akron, Canton & Youngstown R.R., 342 U.S. 359 (1952). . . . Surely [the] state interest in an airtight system of forfeitures is of a different order from that, vindicated in *Murdock,* in the autonomy of state law within the proper sphere of its substantive regulation."

This declaration produced an anguished dissent by Justice Harlan, with whom Justices Clark and Stewart joined. Harlan argued that the doctrine of the adequate and independent state ground was constitutionally based—not merely in its relation to the ban against advisory opinions, but more fundamentally as an aspect of the constitutional structure of federalism illustrated by cases such as Erie Railroad Co. v. Tompkins, 304 U.S. 64 (1938). On direct review, the Supreme Court would be free to assess the "adequacy" and "independence" of the state ground, but not simply to ignore failure to comply with the state's procedures. To do so would be "to assume full control over a state's procedures for the administration of its own criminal justice," and the assertion of such authority "is and must be beyond our power if the federal system is to exist in substance as well as in form." For the Supreme Court simply to ignore the state law issue, said Harlan, was the same as deciding it sub silentio and thus subject to the same objection. For Harlan, therefore, the adequate and independent state ground doctrine imposed a *constitutional* limitation on direct review.

Moreover, Harlan argued, a federal district court exercising habeas jurisdiction was no more free than the Supreme Court on direct review "to 'ignore' the adequate state ground, proceed to the federal question, and order the prisoner's release":

"Of course, as the majority states, a judgment is a not a 'jurisdictional prerequisite' to a habeas corpus application, but that is wholly irrelevant. The point is that if the applicant is detained *pursuant* to a judgment, termination of the detention necessarily nullifies the judgment. . . . In habeas as on direct review, ordering the prisoner's release invalidates the judgment of conviction and renders ineffective the state rule relied upon to sustain that judgment."

Harlan therefore concluded that the rule of *Fay v. Noia* was an unconstitutional assertion of federal authority to disregard state procedural foreclosure.[d]

Harlan's view seems no longer to have adherents on the Court. Although the *Sykes* majority rejected broad application of *Fay*'s deliberate bypass test, Justice Brennan was correct in observing in footnote 2 of his *Sykes* opinion that "[t]his Court has never taken issue with the foundation principle established by *Fay v. Noia*—that in considering a petition for the writ of habeas corpus, federal courts possess the *power* to look beyond a state procedural forfeiture in order to entertain the contention that a defendant's constitutional rights have been abridged."

3. Questions and Comments on *Wainwright v. Sykes*. Is *Sykes* persuasive in the grounds it advances for rejecting *Fay v. Noia*? What are the values and assumptions underlying *Fay* with which the *Sykes* majority disagree?

Obviously, the import of *Sykes* depends in large measure on the content eventually given to "cause" and "prejudice." The possibilities are many, and the choices among them consequential. If, for example, the Court were to adopt Justice White's position that "cause" should mean anything short of "deliberate bypass" by the defendant or, in some cases, the lawyer and that "prejudice" should include any non-harmless error, *Sykes* would work only a minor change in the regime of *Fay*. If, by contrast, "prejudice" were construed to require prejudice to the integrity of the fact-finding process, *Sykes* would be brought into close conformity with *Stone v. Powell*, and the entire structure of federal habeas corpus would be reoriented toward a concern for factual guilt or innocence. And, if "cause" were read narrowly to exclude attorney error, forfeitures of rights would be common, and more attention would be drawn to the issue of lawyer competence.

4. Bibliography. A predictive discussion of the issues in *Wainwright v. Sykes*, focusing in particular on the implications of a system of forfeiture of constitutional claims based on attorney error, may be found in Cover and Aleinikoff, Dialectical Federalism: Habeas Corpus and the Court, 86 Yale L.J. 1035, 1069–86 (1977). An early explication of the possible meanings of "cause" and "prejudice" appears in Alfred Hill's article, The Forfeiture of Constitutional Rights in Criminal Cases, 78 Colum. L. Rev. 1050 (1978). For a preliminary survey of the reactions of lower courts, see Goodman and Sallett, *Wainwright v. Sykes*: The Lower Federal Courts Respond, 30 Hastings L.J. 1683 (1979). The effect of state waiver rules is explored by Lea Brilmayer in State Forfeiture Rules and Federal Review of State Criminal Convictions, 49 U. Chi. L. Rev. 741 (1982). The right-to-counsel dimension of the controversy is explored in Tague, Federal Habeas Corpus and Ineffective Representation of Counsel: The Supreme Court Has Work To Do, 31 Stan. L. Rev. 1 (1978).

[d] A more elaborate rendition of Harlan's rationale appears at pages 616–18, supra.

Perhaps the most dire prediction of the impact of *Sykes* appears in an article by Yale Rosenberg, Jettisoning *Fay v. Noia*: Procedural Defaults by Reasonably Incompetent Counsel, 62 Minn. L. Rev. 341 (1978). Rosenberg identifies several problems with the *Sykes* decision, but focuses in particular on the difficulty of expecting generally unrepresented habeas petitioners to explain the actions of their trial counsel. For a later work by the same author, see Constricting Federal Habeas Corpus: From Great Writ to Exceptional Remedy, 12 Hastings L.J. 597 (1985), in which Professor Rosenberg extends his criticisms to take account of more recent cases.

Special mention should be made of Maria Marcus' article, Federal Habeas Corpus After State Court Default: A Definition of Cause and Prejudice, 53 Ford. L. Rev. 663 (1985). Marcus examines the doctrinal and intellectual pedigree of *Sykes* and investigates the premises underlying the decision. She explores in detail the values and choices at stake in defining "cause" and "prejudice" and proposes carefully crafted definitions of the terms.

Finally, Judith Resnik has discussed *Sykes* and subsequent habeas decisions in the context of a broader review of procedural systems and the values they may be structured to serve. Her criticism of this line of cases appears in Tiers, 57 S. Cal. L. Rev. 837, 895–907 (1984).

For the Supreme Court's response to the blank canvas of "cause" and "prejudice," see the next main case and the notes following.

MURRAY v. CARRIER

Supreme Court of the United States, 1986.
477 U.S. 478.

JUSTICE O'CONNOR delivered the opinion of the Court.

We granted certiorari in this case to consider whether a federal habeas petitioner can show cause for a procedural default by establishing that competent defense counsel inadvertently failed to raise the substantive claim of error rather than deliberately withholding it for tactical reasons.

I

Respondent Clifford Carrier was convicted of rape and abduction by a Virginia jury in 1977. Before trial, respondent's court-appointed counsel moved for discovery of the victim's statements to police describing "her assailants, the vehicle the assailants were driving, and the location of where the alleged rape took place." The presiding judge denied the motion by letter to counsel after examining the statements in camera and determining that they contained no exculpatory evidence. Respondent's counsel made a second motion to discover the victim's statements immediately prior to trial, which the trial judge denied for the same reason after conducting his own in camera examination.

After respondent was convicted, his counsel filed a notice of appeal to the Virginia Supreme Court assigning seven errors, of which the fifth was:

"Did the trial judge err by not permitting defendant's counsel to examine the written statements of the victim prior to trial, and during the course of the trial?"

Without consulting respondent, counsel subsequently submitted the required petition for appeal but failed to include this claim, notwithstanding that Virginia Supreme Court Rule 5:21 provides that "[o]nly errors assigned in the petition for appeal will be noticed by this Court and no error not so assigned will be admitted as a ground for reversal of a decision below." The Virginia Supreme Court refused the appeal and this Court denied certiorari.

A year later respondent, by this time proceeding pro se, filed a state habeas corpus petition claiming that he had been denied due process of law by the prosecution's withholding of the victim's statements. The state sought dismissal of his petition on the ground that respondent was barred from presenting his due process discovery claim on collateral review because he failed to raise that claim on appeal. The state habeas court dismissed the petition "for the reasons stated in the motion to dismiss," and the Virginia Supreme Court denied certiorari.

Respondent next filed a pro se habeas petition in the District Court for the Eastern District of Virginia, renewing his due process discovery claim as grounds for relief. The state filed a motion to dismiss asserting that respondent's failure to raise the issue on direct appeal was a procedural default barring federal habeas review under Wainwright v. Sykes, 433 U.S. 72 (1977), and that respondent had not exhausted his state remedies because he could bring an ineffective assistance of counsel claim in the state courts to establish that his procedural default should be excused. The United States Magistrate to whom the case was referred recommended dismissal by virtue of the procedural default and also ruled that respondent had not exhausted his state remedies. In reply to the magistrate's report, respondent alleged that his procedural default was "due to ineffective assistance of counsel during the filing of his appeal." The District Court approved the magistrate's report, holding the discovery claim barred by the procedural default and indicating that respondent should establish cause for that default in the state courts.

At oral argument on appeal to the Court of Appeals for the Fourth Circuit, respondent abandoned any claim of ineffective assistance of counsel but asserted that counsel had mistakenly omitted his discovery claim from the petition for appeal and that this error was cause for his default. A divided panel of the Court of Appeals reversed and remanded. The court construed respondent's objection to the denial of discovery as having rested throughout on a contention that Brady v. Maryland, 373 U.S. 83 (1963), requires the prosecution to disclose any evidence that might be material to guilt whether or not it is exculpatory, and concluded that when respondent's counsel omitted this discovery claim from the petition for review "the issue was lost for purposes of direct and collateral review." The court framed the issue before it as whether "a single act or omission by counsel, insufficient by itself to contravene the sixth amendment, [can] satisfy the 'cause' prong of the exception to preclusive procedural default discussed in *Wainwright?*" In answering this question, the court drew a dispositive distinction between procedural defaults resulting from deliberate tactical decisions and those resulting from ignorance or inadvertence. The court determined that only in the latter category does an attorney's error constitute cause because, whereas a tactical decision implies that counsel has, at worst, "reasonably but incorrectly exercise[d] her judgment," ignorance or oversight implies that counsel "fail[ed] to exercise it at all, in dereliction of the duty to represent her client." Thus, in order to establish cause a federal habeas petitioner need only satisfy the district court "that the failure to object or to appeal his claim was the product of his attorney's ignorance or oversight, not a deliberate tactic." Accordingly, the Court of Appeals remanded to the District Court:

> "[A]lthough the likelihood of attorney error appears very great in this case, we lack testimony from Carrier's counsel which might disclose a strategic reason for failing to appeal the *Brady* issue. The question of counsel's motivation is one of fact for the District Court to resolve upon taking further evidence."

The court also ruled that the District Court erred in suggesting that respondent should establish cause for the default in the state courts. "The exhaustion requirement of 28 U.S.C. § 2254 pertains to independent claims for habeas relief, not to the proffer of *Wainwright* cause and prejudice." Since respondent did not allege ineffective assistance of counsel as an independent basis for habeas relief, the case presented no exhaustion question.

The dissenting judge believed that the petition should have been dismissed for failure to exhaust state remedies because respondent had never presented his discovery claim as a denial of due process in the state courts, and differed with the majority's interpretation of the cause standard because "[it] will ultimately allow the exception to swallow the rule." The state sought rehearing, and the en banc Court of Appeals adopted the panel majority's decision, with four judges dissenting. We now reverse and remand.

II

Wainwright v. Sykes held that a federal habeas petitioner who has failed to comply with a state's contemporaneous objection rule at trial must show cause for the procedural default and prejudice attributable thereto in order to obtain review of his defaulted constitutional claim. See also Francis v. Henderson, 425 U.S. 536 (1976). In so holding, the Court explicitly rejected the standard described in Fay v. Noia, 372 U.S. 391 (1963), under which a federal habeas court could refuse to review a defaulted claim only if "an applicant ha[d] deliberately by-passed the orderly procedure of the state courts," by personal waiver of the claim amounting to " 'an intentional relinquishment or abandonment of a known right or privilege.' "   At a minimum, then, *Wainwright v. Sykes* plainly implied that default of a constitutional claim by counsel pursuant to a trial strategy or tactical decision would, absent extraordinary circumstances, bind the habeas petitioner even if he had not personally waived that claim.   Beyond that, the Court left open "for resolution in future decisions the precise definition of the 'cause' and 'prejudice' standard."

We revisited the cause and prejudice test in Engle v. Isaac, 456 U.S. 107 (1982).   Like *Wainwright v. Sykes, Engle* involved claims that were procedurally defaulted at trial.   In seeking to establish cause for their defaults, the prisoners argued that "they could not have known at the time of their trials" of the substantive basis for their constitutional claims, which were premised on In re Winship, 397 U.S. 358 (1970). Without deciding "whether the novelty of a constitutional claim ever establishes cause for a failure to object," we rejected this contention because we could not conclude that the legal basis for framing the prisoners' constitutional claims was unavailable at the time.   In language that bears directly on the present case, we said:

> "We do not suggest that every astute counsel would have relied upon *Winship* to assert the unconstitutionality of a rule saddling criminal defendants with the burden of proving an affirmative defense.   Every trial presents a myriad of possible claims.   Counsel might have overlooked or chosen to omit respondents' due process argument while pursuing other avenues of defense.   We have long recognized, however, that the Constitution guarantees criminal defendants only a fair trial and a competent attorney.   It does not insure that defense counsel will recognize and raise every conceivable constitutional claim.   Where the basis of a constitutional claim is available, and other defense counsel have perceived and litigated that claim, the demands of comity and finality counsel against labeling alleged unawareness of the objection as a cause for a procedural default."

The thrust of this part of our decision in *Engle* is unmistakable: the mere fact that counsel failed to recognize the factual or legal basis for a claim, or failed to raise the claim despite recognizing it, does not constitute cause for a procedural default.   At least with respect to defaults that occur at trial, the Court of Appeals' holding that ignorant or inadvertent attorney error is cause for any resulting procedural default is plainly inconsistent with *Engle.*   It is no less inconsistent with the purposes served by the cause and prejudice standard.   That standard rests not only on the need to deter intentional defaults but on a judgment that the costs of federal habeas review "are particularly high when a trial default has barred a prisoner from obtaining adjudication of his constitutional claim in the state courts."   *Engle,* supra at 128.   Those costs, which include a reduction in the finality of litigation and the frustration of "both the states' sovereign power to punish offenders and their good-faith attempts to honor constitutional rights," are heightened in several respects when a trial default occurs: the default deprives the trial court of an opportunity to correct any error without retrial, detracts from the importance of the trial itself, gives state appellate courts no chance to review trial errors, and "exacts an extra charge by undercutting the state's ability to enforce its procedural rules." Clearly, these considerable costs do not disappear when the default stems from counsel's ignorance or inadvertence rather than from a deliberate decision, for whatever reason, to withhold a claim.

Indeed, the rule applied by the Court of Appeals would significantly increase the costs associated with a procedural default in many cases. In order to determine whether there was cause for a procedural default, federal habeas courts would routinely be required to hold evidentiary hearings to determine what prompted counsel's failure to raise the claim in question. While the federal habeas courts would no doubt strive to minimize the burdens to all concerned through the use of affidavits or other simplifying procedures, we are not prepared to assume that these costs would be negligible, particularly since, as we observed in Strickland v. Washington, 466 U.S. 668, 690 (1984), "[i]ntensive scrutiny of counsel . . . could dampen the ardor and impair the independence of defense counsel, discourage the acceptance of assigned cases, and undermine the trust between attorney and client." Nor will it always be easy to classify counsel's behavior in accordance with the deceptively simple categories propounded by the Court of Appeals. Does counsel act out of "ignorance," for example, by failing to raise a claim for tactical reasons after mistakenly assessing its strength on the basis of an incomplete acquaintance with the relevant precedent? The uncertain dimension of any exception for "inadvertence" or "ignorance" furnish an additional reason for rejecting it.

We think, then, that the question of cause for a procedural default does not turn on whether counsel erred or on the kind of error counsel may have made. So long as a defendant is represented by counsel whose performance is not constitutionally ineffective under the standard established in *Strickland v. Washington,* supra, we discern no inequity in requiring him to bear the risk of attorney error that results in a procedural default. Instead, we think that the existence of cause for a procedural default must ordinarily turn on whether the prisoner can show that some objective factor external to the defense impeded counsel's efforts to comply with the state's procedural rule. Without attempting an exhaustive catalog of such objective impediments to compliance with a procedural rule, we note that a showing that the factual or legal basis for a claim was not reasonably available to counsel, see Reed v. Ross, 468 U.S. 1, 16 (1984), or that "some interference by officials," Brown v. Allen, 344 U.S. 443, 486 (1953), made compliance impracticable, would constitute cause under this standard.

Similarly, if the procedural default is the result of ineffective assistance of counsel, the sixth amendment itself requires that responsibility for the default be imputed to the state, which may not "conduc[t] trials at which persons who face incarceration must defend themselves without adequate legal assistance." Cuyler v. Sullivan, 446 U.S. 335, 344 (1980). Ineffective assistance of counsel, then, is cause for a procedural default. However, we think that the exhaustion doctrine, which is "principally designed to protect the state courts' role in the enforcement of federal law and prevent disruption of state judicial proceedings," Rose v. Lundy, 455 U.S. 509, 518 (1982), generally requires that a claim of ineffective assistance be presented to the state courts as an independent claim before it may be used to establish cause for a procedural default. The question whether there is cause for a procedural default does not pose any occasion for applying the exhaustion doctrine when the federal habeas court can adjudicate the question of cause—a question of federal law—without deciding an independent and unexhausted constitutional claim on the merits. But if a petitioner could raise his ineffective assistance claim for the first time on federal habeas in order to show cause for a procedural default, the federal habeas court would find itself in the anomalous position of adjudicating an unexhausted constitutional claim for which state court review might still be available. The principle of comity that underlies the exhaustion doctrine would be ill-served by a rule that allowed a federal district court "to upset a state court conviction without an opportunity to the state courts to correct a constitutional violation," Darr v. Burford, 339 U.S. 200, 204 (1950), and that holds true whether an ineffective assistance claim is asserted as cause for a procedural default or denominated as an independent ground for habeas relief.

It is clear that respondent failed to show or even allege cause for his procedural default under this standard for cause, which *Engle* squarely supports. Respondent argues nevertheless that his case is not controlled by *Engle* because it involves a procedural default on appeal rather than at trial. Respondent does not dispute, however, that the cause and prejudice test applies to procedural defaults on appeal, as we plainly indicated in *Reed v. Ross,* supra. *Reed,* which involved a claim that was defaulted *on appeal,* held that a habeas petitioner could establish cause for a procedural default if his claim is "so novel that its legal basis is not reasonably available to counsel." That holding would have been entirely unnecessary to the disposition of the prisoner's claim if the cause and prejudice test were inapplicable to procedural defaults on appeal.

The distinction respondent would have us draw must therefore be made, if at all, in terms of the content of the cause requirement as applied to procedural defaults on appeal. Accordingly, respondent asks us to affirm the Court of Appeals' judgment on the narrow ground that even if counsel's ignorance or inadvertence does not constitute cause for a procedural default at trial, it does constitute cause for a procedural default on appeal. In support of this distinction, respondent asserts that the concerns that underlie the cause and prejudice test are not present in the case of defaults on appeal. A default on appeal, he maintains, does not detract from the significance of the trial or from the development of a full trial record, or deprive the trial court of an opportunity to correct error without the need for retrial. Moreover, unlike the rapid pace of trial, in which it is a matter of necessity that counsel's decisions bind the defendant, "the appellate process affords the attorney time for reflection, research, and full consultation with his client." Finally, respondent suggests that there is no likelihood that an attorney will preserve an objection at trial yet choose to withhold it on appeal in order to "sandbag" the prosecution by raising the claim on federal habeas if relief is denied by the state courts.

These arguments are unpersuasive. A state's procedural rules serve vital purposes at trial, on appeal, and on state collateral attack. The important role of appellate procedural rules is aptly captured by the Court's description in *Reed v. Ross* of the purposes served by the procedural rule at issue there, which required the defendant initially to raise his legal claims on appeal rather than on postconviction review:

> "It affords the state courts the opportunity to resolve the issue shortly after trial, while evidence is still available both to assess the defendant's claim and to retry the defendant effectively if he prevails in his appeal. See Friendly, Is Innocence Irrelevant? Collateral Attack on Criminal Judgments, 38 U. Chi. L. Rev. 142, 147 (1970). This type of rule promotes not only the accuracy and efficiency of judicial decisions, but also the finality of those decisions, by forcing the defendant to litigate all of his claims together, as quickly after trial as the docket will allow, and while the attention of the appellate court is focused on his case."

These legitimate state interests, which are manifestly furthered by the comparable procedural rule at issue in this case, warrant our adherence to the conclusion to which they led the Court in *Reed v. Ross*—that the cause and prejudice test applies to defaults on appeal as to those at trial.

We likewise believe that the standard for cause should not vary depending on the timing of a procedural default or on the strength of an uncertain and difficult assessment of the relative magnitude of the benefits attributable to the state procedural rules that attach at each successive stage of the judicial process. "Each state's complement of procedural rules . . . channel[s], to the extent possible, the resolution of various types of questions to the stage of the judicial process at which they can be resolved most fairly and efficiently." It is apparent that the frustration of the state's interests that occurs when an appellate procedural rule is broken is not significantly diminished when counsel's breach results from ignorance or inadvertence rather than a deliberate decision, tactical or not, to abstain from raising the claim. Failure to raise a claim on appeal reduces the finality of appellate proceedings, deprives the appellate court of an opportunity to review trial error, and "undercut[s] the state's ability to enforce its procedural rules." *Engle,* supra, at 129. As with procedural defaults at trial, these costs are imposed on the state regardless of the kind of attorney error that led to the procedural default. Nor do we agree that the possibility of "sandbagging" vanishes once a trial has ended in conviction, since appellate counsel might well conclude that the best strategy is to select a few promising claims for airing on appeal, while reserving others for federal habeas review should the appeal be unsuccessful. Moreover, we see little reason why counsel's failure to detect a colorable constitutional claim should be treated differently from a deliberate but equally prejudicial failure by counsel to raise such a claim. The fact that the latter error can be characterized as a misjudgment, while the former is more easily described as an oversight, is much too tenuous a distinction to justify a regime of evidentiary hearings into counsel's state of mind in failing to raise a claim on appeal.

The real thrust of respondent's arguments appear to be that on appeal it is inappropriate to hold defendants to the errors of their attorneys. Were we to accept that proposition, defaults on appeal would presumably be governed by a rule equivalent to *Fay v. Noia*'s "deliberate bypass" standard, under which only personal waiver by the defendant would require enforcement of a procedural default. We express no opinion as to whether counsel's decision not to take an appeal at all might require treatment under such a standard, but for the reasons already given, we hold that counsel's failure to raise a particular claim or claims on appeal is to be scrutinized under the cause and prejudice standard when that failure is treated as a procedural default by the state courts. Attorney error short of ineffective assistance of counsel does not constitute cause for a procedural default even when that default occurs on appeal rather than at trial. To the contrary, cause for a procedural default on appeal ordinarily requires a showing of some external impediment preventing counsel from constructing or raising the claim.

III

Concurring in the judgment, Justice Stevens contends that our decision today erects an unwarranted procedural barrier to the correction through federal habeas corpus of violations of fundamental constitutional rights that have resulted in a miscarriage of justice. The cause and prejudice test, in his view, "must be considered within an overall inquiry into justice," which requires consideration in every case of the character of the constitutional claim. If the federal right asserted is of "fundamental importance," or if a violation of that right "calls into question the accuracy of the determination of . . . guilt," Justice Stevens would then balance "the nature and strength of the constitutional claim" and "the nature and strength of the state procedural rule that has not been observed." . . .

The effect of such a reworking of the cause and prejudice test would essentially be to dispense with the requirement that the petitioner show cause and instead to focus exclusively on whether there has been a "manifest injustice" or a denial of "fundamental fairness." We are not told whether this inquiry would require the same showing of actual prejudice that is required by the cause and prejudice test as interpreted in *Engle* and in United States v. Frady, 456 U.S. 152 (1982), but the thrust of the concurrence leaves little doubt that this is so. The showing of prejudice required under *Wainwright v. Sykes* is significantly greater than that necessary under "the more vague inquiry suggested by the words 'plain error.'" *Engle,* supra, at 135; *Frady,* supra, at 166. See also Henderson v. Kibbe, 431 U.S. 145, 154 (1977). The habeas petitioner must show "not merely that the errors at . . . trial created a *possibility* of prejudice, but that they worked to his *actual* and substantial disadvantage, infecting his entire trial with error of constitutional dimensions." *Frady,* supra, at 170. Such a showing of pervasive actual prejudice can hardly be thought to constitute anything other than a showing that the prisoner was denied "fundamental fairness" at trial. Since, for Justice Stevens, a "constitutional claim that implicates 'fundamental fairness'. . . compels review regardless of possible procedural defaults," it follows that a showing of prejudice would invariably make a showing of cause unnecessary.

As the concurrence acknowledges, *Engle* expressly rejected this contention that a showing of actual prejudice "should permit relief even in the absence of cause." It may be true that the former Rule 12(b)(2) of the Federal Rules of Criminal Procedure, as interpreted in Shotwell Mfg. Co. v. United States, 371 U.S. 341 (1963), and Davis v. United States, 411 U.S. 233 (1973), treated prejudice as a component of the inquiry into whether there was cause for noncompliance with that rule. But, while the cause and prejudice test adopted in *Wainwright v. Sykes* finds its antecedents in cases interpreting Rule 12(b)(2), the Court in *Wainwright v. Sykes* declared that it was applying "the rule of *Francis v. Henderson* . . . barring federal habeas review absent a showing of 'cause' and 'prejudice' attendant to a state procedural waiver." In *Francis,* the Court could not have been clearer that both cause and prejudice must be shown, at least in a habeas corpus proceeding challenging a state court conviction. We deal here with habeas review of a state court conviction, and at least three decisions of this Court—*Francis, Sykes,* and *Engle*—are unambiguously contrary to the approach taken in the concurring opinion. We are unprepared, in the face of this weight of authority and in view of the principles of comity and finality these decisions reflect, to reduce the cause requirement to the vestigial role Justice Stevens envisions for it.

Moreover, although neither *Francis* nor *Wainwright v. Sykes* involved a constitutional claim that directly called into question the accuracy of the determination of the petitioner's guilt, the defaulted claims in *Engle,* no less than respondent's claim in this case, did involve issues bearing on the reliability of the verdict. In re Winship, 397 U.S. 358 (1970), which was "the basis for [the prisoners'] constitutional claim" in *Engle,* holds that "the due process clause protects the accused against conviction except upon proof beyond a reasonable doubt of every fact necessary to constitute the crime with which he is charged." In Ivan V. v. City of New York, 407 U.S. 203, 205 (1972) (per curiam), the Court held the rule in *Winship* to be retroactive, because "the major purpose of the constitutional standard of proof beyond a reasonable doubt announced in *Winship* was to overcome an aspect of a criminal trial that substantially impairs the truth-finding function." Consequently, our rejection in *Engle* of the contention advanced to-day—that cause need not be shown if actual prejudice is shown—is fully applicable to constitutional claims that call into question the reliability of an adjudication of legal guilt.

However, as we also noted in *Engle* "[i]n appropriate cases" the principles of comity and finality that inform the concepts of cause and prejudice "must yield to the imperative of correcting a fundamentally unjust incarceration." We remain confident that, for the most part, "victims of a fundamental miscarriage of justice will meet the cause-and-prejudice standard." But we do not pretend that this will always be true. Accordingly, we think that in an extraordinary case, where a constitutional violation has probably resulted in the conviction of one who is actually innocent, a federal habeas court may grant the writ even in the absence of a showing of cause for the procedural default.

There is an additional safeguard against miscarriages of justice in criminal cases, and one not yet recognized in state criminal trials when many of the opinions on which the concurrence relies were written. That safeguard is the right to effective assistance of counsel, which, as this Court has indicated, may in a particular case be violated by even an isolated error of counsel if that error is sufficiently egregious and prejudicial. *United States v. Cronic,* 466 U.S. 648, 657, n. 20 (1984). See also *Strickland v. Washington,* supra, at 693–96. The presence of such a safeguard may properly inform this Court's judgment in deter-mining "[w]hat standards should govern the exercise of the habeas court's equitable discretion" with respect to procedurally defaulted claims, *Reed v. Ross,* supra, at 9. The ability to raise ineffective assistance claims based in whole or in part on counsel's procedural defaults substantially undercuts any predictions of unremedied mani-fest injustices. We therefore remain of the view that adherence to the cause and prejudice test "in the conjunctive," *Engle,* supra, at 134, n.43, will not prevent federal habeas courts from ensuring the "fundamental fairness [that] is the central concern of the writ of habeas corpus." *Strickland v. Washington,* supra, at 697.

The cause and prejudice test may lack a perfect historical pedigree. But the Court acknowledged as much in *Wainwright v. Sykes,* noting its "historic willingness to overturn or modify its earlier views of the scope of the writ, even where the statutory language authorizing judicial action has remained unchanged." The cause and prejudice test as interpreted in *Engle* and in our decision today is, we think, a sound and workable means of channeling the discretion of federal habeas courts.

IV

Respondent has never alleged any external impediment that might have prevented counsel from raising his discovery claim in his petition for review, and has disavowed any claim that counsel's performance on appeal was so deficient as to make out an ineffective assistance claim.

Respondent's petition for federal habeas review of his procedurally defaulted discovery claim must therefore be dismissed for failure to establish cause for the default, unless it is determined on remand that the victim's statements contain material that would establish respondent's actual innocence.

The judgment of the Court of Appeals is reversed, and the case is remanded for further proceedings consistent with this opinion.

It is so ordered.

JUSTICE STEVENS, with whom JUSTICE BLACKMUN joins, concurring in the judgment.

The heart of this case is a prisoner's claim that he was denied access to material that might have established his innocence. The significance of such a claim can easily be lost in a procedural maze of enormous complexity.

The nature of the prisoner's claim, and its importance would be especially easy to overlook in this case because the case involves at least four possible procedural errors. A Virginia trial judge may have erroneously denied respondent's counsel access to statements that the victim had made to the police. The Virginia Supreme Court did not address this issue because, although respondent's counsel included it in the assignment of errors in his "notice of appeal," he omitted it from his "petition for appeal." In a subsequent federal habeas corpus proceeding, the District Court held that the procedural default in the state appellate court effected a waiver of any right to federal relief and therefore dismissed the petition without examining the victim's statements. The Court of Appeals, however, concluded that there was no waiver if counsel's omission was the consequence of inadvertence and ordered a remand for a hearing to determine whether the lawyer had made a deliberate decision to omit the error from the petition for appeal. We granted certiorari to review that decision.

I

The character of respondent's constitutional claim should be central to an evaluation of his habeas corpus petition. Before and during his trial on charges of rape and abduction, his counsel made timely motions for discovery of the statements made by the victim to the police. By denying those motions, the trial court significantly curtailed the defendant's ability to cross-examine the prosecution's most important witness, and may well have violated the defendant's right to review "evidence favorable to an accused upon request . . . where the evidence is material either to guilt or to punishment." Brady v. Maryland, 373 U.S. 83, 87 (1963). That right is unquestionably protected by the due process clause. See also United States v. Bagley, 473 U.S. 667 (1985); United States v. Agurs, 427 U.S. 97 (1976). Indeed, the Court has repeatedly emphasized the fundamental importance of that federal right.

The constitutional claim advanced by respondent calls into question the accuracy of the determination of his guilt. On the record before us, however, we cannot determine whether or not he is the victim of a miscarriage of justice. Respondent argues that the trial court's analysis was severely flawed. Even if the trial judge applied the correct standard, the conclusion that there was no "exculpatory" material in the victim's statements does not foreclose the possibility that inconsistencies between the statements and the direct testimony would have enabled an effective cross-examination to demonstrate that respondent is actually innocent. On the other hand, it is possible that other evidence of guilt in the record is so overwhelming that the trial judge's decision was clearly not prejudicial to the defendant. The important point is that we cannot evaluate the possibility that respondent may be the victim of a fundamental miscarriage of justice without any knowledge about the contents of the victim's statements.

In deciding whether the District Court should have examined these statements before dismissing respondent's habeas corpus petition, it is useful to recall the historic importance of the Great Writ. "The writ of habeas corpus is the fundamental instrument for safeguarding individual freedom against arbitrary and lawless state action." Harris v. Nelson, 394 U.S. 286, 290–91 (1969). Its well-known history bears repetition. The writ emerged in England several centuries ago, and was given explicit protection in our Constitution. The first Judiciary Act provided federal habeas corpus for federal prisoners. In 1867, Congress provided the writ of habeas corpus for state prisoners; the act gave federal courts "power to grant writs of habeas corpus in all cases where any person may be restrained of his or her liberty in violation of the Constitution, or any treaty or law of the United States." The current statute confers similar power, 28 U.S.C. § 2241(c)(3), and provides, "The court shall . . . dispose of the matter as law and justice require." 28 U.S.C. § 2243.

As the statute suggests, the central mission of the Great Writ should be the substance of "justice," not the form of procedures. . . .

Accordingly, the statutory mandate to "dispose of the matter as law and justice require" clearly requires at least some consideration of the character of the constitutional claim.

II

In my opinion, the "cause and prejudice" formula that the Court explicates in such detail today is not dispositive when the fundamental fairness of a prisoner's conviction is at issue. That formula is of recent vintage, particularly in comparison to the writ for which it is invoked. It is, at most, part of a broader inquiry into the demands of justice.

The Court cites Wainwright v. Sykes, 433 U.S. 72 (1977), as authority for its "cause and prejudice" standard. The actual source of the standard, however, is Rule 12(b)(2) of the Federal Rules of Criminal Procedure. For *Wainwright* relied on cases construing that rule in announcing the standard.

Rule 12(b)(2) specifies the procedure for asserting defenses and objections based on defects in the institution of a federal prosecution. Until part of the rule was shifted to Rule 12(f), Rule 12(b)(2) expressly provided that the failure to follow the specified procedure in presenting any such defense or objection "constitutes waiver thereof"; the rule included a proviso authorizing the court to grant relief from the waiver "for cause shown." Under the terms of the rule, the inquiry into "cause" was not made to ascertain whether a waiver occurred; rather, its function was to determine whether a waiver should be excused.

The term "prejudice" was not used in Rule 12(b)(2). In construing the rule in Shotwell Mfg. Co. v. United States, 371 U.S. 341 (1963), however, the Court decided that a consideration of the prejudice to the defendant, or the absence thereof, was an appropriate component of the inquiry into whether there was "cause" for excusing the waiver that had resulted from the failure to follow the rule. Thus, under the reasoning of the *Shotwell* case—as well as the text of the rule itself— "cause" and "prejudice" were not separate obstacles that a defendant was required to overcome to avoid a waiver. Rather, the cause component explicitly included an inquiry into "prejudice"—into the nature of the claim and its effect.

In Davis v. United States, 411 U.S. 233 (1973), the Court held that "the sort of express waiver provision contained in Rule 12(b)(2) which specifically provides for the waiver of a particular kind of constitutional claim if it be not timely asserted" bars a challenge, absent "cause," to the composition of the grand jury not only on direct federal review, but also in a federal habeas challenge to a federal conviction. Thus, in *Davis*, as in *Shotwell*, the Court simply enforced a federal rule that contained an express waiver provision. Notably, in *Davis*, the Court again considered both cause and prejudice as part of a single inquiry.

The *Davis* holding, in turn, provided the basis for the Court's decision in Francis v. Henderson, 425 U.S. 536 (1976). In that case, the Court reviewed a Louisiana rule similar to the federal rule at issue in *Francis* and a similar constitutional claim. Relying on *Davis*, the Court held that the state prisoner, having failed to make a timely challenge to the grand jury that indicted him, could not challenge his state conviction in a federal habeas corpus proceeding without making a showing of both "cause" for the failure and "actual prejudice." The Court cited the *Davis* cause and prejudice analysis in determining that prejudice had not been established.

Davis and *Francis* then provided the basis for the conclusion in *Wainwright v. Sykes*, supra, that the failure to make a contemporaneous objection to the admission of evidence at trial will ordinarily bar a post-conviction attack on the use of such evidence absent an appropriate showing of cause and prejudice. However, the Court's opinion in *Wainwright v. Sykes* carefully avoided any rigid definition of the terms "cause" and "prejudice"—terms which under Rule 12 had been used to identify two components of a single inquiry to determine whether an express waiver should be excused. Indeed, in *Wainwright*, the Court made very clear that, although "cause and prejudice" structured a court's inquiry, they were not rigid procedural rules that prevented the writ's fundamental mission—serving justice—from being realized: "The 'cause-and-prejudice' exception of the *Francis* rule will afford an adequate guarantee, we think, that the rule will not prevent a federal habeas court from adjudicating for the first time the federal constitutional claim of a defendant who in the absence of such an adjudication will be the victim of a miscarriage of justice." In *Wainwright* itself, the Court inquired into both cause and prejudice; the prejudice inquiry, of course, required some inquiry into the nature of the claim and its effect on the trial.

In a recent exposition of the "cause and prejudice" standard, moreover, the Court again emphasized that "cause and prejudice" must be considered within an overall inquiry into justice. In Engle v. Isaac, 456 U.S. 107 (1982), the Court closed its opinion with the assurance that it would not allow its judge-made "cause" and "actual prejudice" standard to become so rigid that it would foreclose a claim of this kind:

> "The terms 'cause' and 'actual prejudice' are not rigid concepts; they take their meaning from the principles of comity and finality discussed above. In appropriate cases those principles must yield to the imperative of correcting a fundamentally unjust incarceration. Since we are confident that victims of a fundamental miscarriage of justice will meet the cause-and-prejudice standard, see *Wainwright v. Sykes*, supra (Stevens, J., concurring), we decline to adopt the more vague inquiry suggested by the words 'plain error.'"

In order to be faithful to that promise, we must recognize that cause and prejudice are merely components of a broader inquiry which, in this case, cannot be performed without an examination of the victim's statements.[12]

III

An inquiry into the requirements of justice requires a consideration, not only of the nature and strength of the constitutional claim, but also of the nature and strength of the state procedural rule that has not been observed. In its opinion today, the Court relies heavily on cases in which the defendant failed to make a contemporaneous objection to an error that occurred during a trial. Most of the reasons for finding a waiver in that setting simply do not apply to the appellate process. Of special importance is the fact that the state interest in enforcing its contemporaneous objection rule is supported, not merely by the concern with finality that characterizes state appellate rules, but also by the

---

[12] Inconsistently, in *Engle v. Isaac*, alongside its references to fundamental fairness, the Court also emphasized that a failure to show cause could bar review regardless of the character of the claim. The Court's rigid invocation of the "cause" obstacle in an opinion that also emphasized the demand of "fundamental fairness" illustrates the confusion that has accompanied the Court's creation and imposition of the cause-and-prejudice standard.

concern with making the trial the "main event" in which the issue of guilt or innocence can be fairly resolved.

This Court has not often considered procedural defaults that have occurred at the appellate, rather than trial, level. In my view, it is not a coincidence that three of the most forceful and incisive analyses of the relationship between federal habeas corpus and state procedural defaults have emerged in the few cases involving appellate defaults. For, with an appellate default, the state interest in procedural rigor is weaker than at trial, and the transcendence of the Great Writ is correspondingly clearer. The opinions to which I refer are the dissenting opinions in Daniels v. Allen, 344 U.S. 443 (1953), and the Court's opinions in Fay v. Noia, 372 U.S. 391 (1963), and Reed v. Ross, 468 U.S. 1 (1984).

In *Daniels,* one of the three cases that gave rise to the opinions in Brown v. Allen, 344 U.S. 443 (1953), two petitioners challenged their convictions and death sentences on the ground that the trial judge had erroneously denied their timely objection to the admission of allegedly coerced confessions and to the alleged discrimination against blacks in the selection of both grand and petit jurors. After the trial court entered judgment and pronounced its sentence, the petitioners filed a notice of appeal and were granted 60 days in which to serve a statement of the case on opposing counsel. As a result of the negligence or inadvertence of petitioners' counsel, the statement was not served on the prosecutor until the 61st day and petitioners' right to appeal was lost. The state Supreme Court declined to exercise its discretion to review the merits of their appeal.

For reasons that are ambiguous at best, the Court held that the procedural default barred a subsequent federal habeas corpus petition unless the opportunity to appeal had been lost "because of lack of counsel, incapacity, or some interference by officials." Because the *Daniels* holding was repudiated in Fay v. Noia, 372 U.S. 391 (1963), Justice Black's penetrating dissent commands greater respect than Justice Reed's ambiguous opinion for the Court. Justice Black wrote:

> "Fourth. *Daniels v. Allen.* Here also evidence establishes an unlawful exclusion of Negroes from juries because of race. The state Supreme Court refused to review this evidence on state procedural grounds. Absence of state court review on this ground is now held to cut off review in federal habeas corpus proceedings. But in the two preceding cases where the state Supreme Court did review the evidence, this Court has also reviewed it. I find it difficult to agree with the soundness of a philosophy which prompts this Court to grant a second review where the state has granted one but to deny any review at all where the state has granted none. . . . ."

As noted, the view of the *Daniels* Court on the propriety of federal habeas proceedings after a procedural default was repudiated in Fay v. Noia, 372 U.S. 391 (1963), a case which also concerned an appellate default. Noia had made a timely objection to the admissibility of his confession in his trial on a charge of felony murder, but he allowed the time for a direct appeal to lapse without seeking review by a New York appellate court. In response to his subsequent application for a federal writ of habeas corpus, the state admitted that his conviction rested on a confession that had been obtained from him in violation of the 14th amendment, but contended that his failure to appeal foreclosed any relief in the federal courts. This Court rejected that contention. In a comprehensive opinion the Court restated three propositions of law that have not thereafter been questioned; the Noia opinion also, however, contained certain dicta that has been qualified by later opinions.

The propositions that *Noia* firmly established are these: First, the *power* of the federal district court to issue the writ of habeas corpus survives an adverse decision by a state court, whether the state judgment is based on a review of the merits of the federal claim or on the applicant's procedural default. Second, although a state's interest in orderly appellate procedure justifies a denial of appellate review in the state system when the inadvertence or neglect of defense counsel causes a procedural default, that state interest is not sufficient to bar a federal remedy in appropriate cases. Third, as the converse of the second proposition, Noia also holds that the federal district court had discretion to deny relief based on state procedural defaults in appropriate cases. None of these propositions has been questioned in any subsequent case.

The dicta in the *Noia* opinion that has been questioned was an attempt to prescribe a rather rigid limitation on the district court's discretion to deny habeas corpus relief based on the applicant's procedural default. The opinion set forth a standard that seemingly required federal judges to excuse every procedural default unless the habeas applicant had personally approved of his lawyer's deliberate decision to bypass an available state procedure. The breadth of that dicta was ultimately disavowed in *Wainwright v. Sykes,* but the Court has remained faithful to the specific holding in *Noia*—that appellate default in the state system need not bar federal habeas review—as well as to the basic principles announced in that opinion.

Finally, in Reed v. Ross, 468 U.S. 1 (1984), we again considered the consequences of an appellate procedural default. The defendant had not raised the constitutional error in his appeal to the North Carolina Supreme Court. Relying on *Fay v. Noia,* we reaffirmed that the federal court has power to look beyond the state procedural default and entertain the state prisoner's application for a writ of habeas corpus. In determining whether the power should be exercised, we found that the requirements of "cause" and "prejudice" that had been discussed in *Wainwright v. Sykes* had both been satisfied. The "cause" for the failure to object was the fact that counsel had not anticipated later decisions from this Court that supported the claim. We explained:

> "[T]he cause requirement may be satisfied under certain cir-
> cumstances when a procedural failure is not attributable to an
> intentional decision by counsel made in pursuit of his client's

interests. And the failure of counsel to raise a constitutional issue reasonably unknown to him is one situation in which the requirement is met."

In the *Reed* opinion we carefully identified the valid state interest that is served by enforcing a procedural default that forecloses state appellate review of a federal constitutional claim. But we squarely held that this interest is not sufficient to defeat a meritorious federal claim:

> "It is true that finality will be disserved if the federal courts reopen a state prisoner's case, even to review claims that were so novel when the cases were in state court that no one would have recognized them. *This Court has never held, however, that finality, standing alone, provides a sufficient reason for federal courts to compromise their protection of constitutional rights under § 2254.*" (Emphasis added.)

We thus concluded that the appellate default would not bar federal consideration of the constitutional claim.

Like the *Daniels* dissenters, then, in *Fay* and in *Reed,* against the backdrop of appellate defaults, the Court stressed that the state's interest in finality does not preclude review of the federal constitutional claim in a federal habeas court. To be sure, these opinions suggested that the power to hear claims which had been defaulted on appeal should be used sparingly—in "special circumstances," in the absence of "deliberate bypass," upon a showing of "cause." Even under such terms, however, our holding in *Reed* governs the case before us today. If the state's interest in the finality of its judgment is not sufficient to defeat a meritorious federal claim that was not raised on appeal because the prisoner's lawyer did not have the ability to anticipate a later development in the law, there is no reason why the same state interest should defeat a meritorious federal claim simply because the prisoner's lawyer did not exercise due care in prosecuting an appeal. There is no more reason to saddle an innocent prisoner with counsel's omission in one case than in the other.

IV

Procedural default that is adequate to foreclose appellate review of a claim of constitutional error in a state criminal trial should ordinarily also bar collateral review of such a claim in a federal district court. But the history of the Court's jurisprudence interpreting the acts of Congress authorizing the issuance of the writ of habeas corpus unambiguously requires that we carefully preserve the exception which enables the federal writ to grant relief in cases of manifest injustice. That exception cannot be adequately defined by a simply stated rule. The procedural default is always an important factor to be carefully reviewed. . . . But it is equally clear that the prisoner must always have some opportunity to reopen his case if he can make a sufficient showing that he is the victim of a fundamental miscarriage of justice. Whether the inquiry is channeled by the use of the terms "cause" and "prejudice"—or by the statutory duty to "dispose of the matter as law and justice require," 28 U.S.C. § 2243—it is clear to me that appellate procedural default should not foreclose habeas corpus review of a meritorious constitutional claim that may establish the prisoner's innocence.

The Court is therefore entirely correct in its decision to remand the case for further proceedings on the substance of respondent's claim. Because we did not grant certiorari to consider the proper standard that should govern the further proceedings in the District Court, and because we have not had the benefit of briefs or argument concerning that standard, I express no opinion on the Court's suggestion that the absence of "cause" for his procedural default requires respondent to prove that the "constitutional violation has probably resulted in the conviction of one who is actually innocent," or on the relationship of that standard to the principles explicated in *United States v. Bagley,* supra; *United States v. Agurs,* supra; and *Brady v. Maryland,* supra. There will be time enough to consider the proper standard after the District Court has examined the victim's statements and made whatever findings may be appropriate to determine whether "law and justice require" the issuance of the Great Writ in this case.

Accordingly, I concur in the judgment but not in the Court's opinion.

JUSTICE BRENNAN, with whom JUSTICE MARSHALL joins, dissenting. . . .

The particular question we must decide in this case is whether counsel's inadvertent failure to raise a substantive claim of error can constitute "cause" for the procedural default. Wainwright v. Sykes, 433 U.S. 72 (1977), held that defense counsel's tactical decision to by-pass a state procedure does not constitute cause. That result may arguably be defended on grounds similar to those which justified the result in Fay v. Noia, 372 U.S. 391 (1963), i.e., that the deterrent interests underlying the state's procedural default rule are at their apogee where counsel's decision to by-pass a state procedure is deliberate. However, to say that the petitioner should be bound to his lawyer's tactical decisions is one thing; to say that he must also bear the burden of his lawyer's inadvertent mistakes is quite another. Where counsel is unaware of a claim or of the duty to raise it at a particular time, the procedural default rule cannot operate as a specific deterrent to noncompliance with the state's procedural rules. Consequently, the state's interest in ensuring that the federal court help prevent circumvention of the state's procedural rules by imposing the same forfeiture sanction is much less compelling. To be sure, applying procedural default rules even to inadvertent defaults furthers the state's deterrent interests in a general sense by encouraging lawyers to be more conscientious on the whole. However, . . . such general deterrent interests are weak where the failure to follow a rule is accidental rather than intentional.

I believe that this incremental state interest simply is not sufficient to overcome the heavy presumption against a federal court's refusing to exercise jurisdiction clearly granted by Congress. This is especially so where the petitioner has satisfied the prejudice prong of the *Wainwright v. Sykes* test. That is, where a petitioner's constitutional rights have been violated and that violation may have affected the verdict, a federal court should not decline to entertain a habeas petition solely out of deference to the state's weak interest in punishing lawyers' inadvertent failures to comply with state procedures. I would therefore hold that "cause" is established where a procedural default resulted from counsel's inadvertence . . . .[4]

NOTES ON THE MEANING OF "CAUSE" AND "PREJUDICE"

1. ***Engle v. Isaac.*** The *Carrier* Court relied heavily on Engle v. Isaac, 456 U.S. 107 (1982). *Engle* involved three prisoners who had been convicted of various forms of assaultive behavior. Each had claimed self-defense and had been required, under the traditional Ohio rule, to carry the burden of persuasion on that issue by a preponderance of the evidence. No objection to this requirement was made at trial.

Subsequently, the Court decided Mullaney v. Wilbur, 421 U.S. 684 (1975), which seemed to require that the state prove beyond a reasonable doubt every fact relevant to the fact or grade of criminal liability.[a] The prisoners sought federal habeas relief under *Mullaney,* but that case was curtailed in Patterson v. New York, 432 U.S. 197 (1977). *Patterson* held that the state was required to prove beyond a reasonable doubt only "elements" of the offense charged; for facts relevant to an "affirmative defense," the burden of persuasion could be shifted to the

---

[4] I do not mean to suggest by this that I accept the Court's decision in *Wainwright v. Sykes* or that I think that a habeas petitioner should ever have to show "cause" and "prejudice" to gain access to the federal courts under § 2254. . . . I continue to believe that *Wainwright v. Sykes* represented an illegitimate exercise of this Court's very limited discretion to order federal courts to decline to entertain habeas petitions. My point is simply that, even accepting the validity of *Wainwright*'s "cause and prejudice" test, the Court must still carefully balance the relevant interests, and when this balancing is done properly, it is apparent that counsel's inadvertence should constitute "cause." Accordingly, I would affirm the decision of the Court of Appeals.

While reversing the holding of the Court of Appeals that counsel's inadvertence establishes "cause," the Court goes on to declare that "where a constitutional violation has probably resulted in the conviction of one who is actually innocent, a federal court may grant the writ even in the absence of a showing of cause for the procedural default." Under such circumstances, the Court explains, "the principles of comity and finality that inform the concepts of cause and prejudice 'must yield to the imperative of correcting a fundamentally unjust incarceration.'" Although I believe that principles of "comity" and "finality" yield upon far less than a showing of actual innocence, because this inquiry represents a narrowing of the "cause and prejudice" test, I agree it is proper.

[a] *Mullaney* was held retroactive in Hankerson v. North Carolina, 432 U.S. 233 (1977).

accused.[b] Since self-defense was an "affirmative defense" in Ohio, the Court held the *Mullaney-Patterson* claim without merit.

A closely related issue was whether the absence of self-defense was a constitutionally essential requirement for criminal liability. If that were so, the state could not place the burden of persuasion on the defendant no matter what the characterization of that issue. Speaking through Justice O'Connor, the Supreme Court found that this version of petitioners' argument stated "a colorable constitutional claim" on the merits. The question then became whether consideration of this claim was barred by the failure to object at trial. As is recounted more fully in *Carrier,* the *Engle* Court found that this claim (the constitutional indispensability of self-defense) could have been anticipated on the basis of precedents existing when the trials were held. Therefore, said *Engle,* no "cause" existed for the lawyers' failure to raise the issue, and federal habeas review was foreclosed by procedural default.

Justice Stevens objected to the Court's insistence on procedural foreclosure but agreed that petitioners' claims should be rejected on the merits. Justices Brennan and Marshall dissented.

2. *Reed v. Ross.* A similar question arose in Reed v. Ross, 468 U.S. 1 (1984). Ross had been convicted of first-degree murder under a North Carolina rule requiring the defendant to prove lack of malice and self-defense. No objection was made to the allocation of the burden of proof, either at trial or on appeal. Under state law, the latter failure barred post-conviction review.

After *Mullaney,* Ross filed a federal habeas petition raising the burden-of-proof issue. Habeas was denied in the lower courts, but the Supreme Court vacated for reconsideration in light of *Engle.* Relief was then granted, and the Supreme Court affirmed. "Actual prejudice" was conceded, and "cause" was based on the fact that the defense counsel had no reasonable basis for anticipating *Mullaney.*[c] "Accordingly," said Justice Brennan, "we hold that where a constitutional claim is so novel that its legal basis is not reasonably available to counsel, a defendant has cause for his failure to raise the claim in accordance with state procedures."

Justice Rehnquist dissented, in an opinion joined by the Chief Justice and by Justices Blackmun and O'Connor. Rehnquist argued that the majority had shown no convincing basis for distinguishing *Engle.*

3. **Questions and Comments on *Carrier.*** In *Murray v. Carrier,* the restrictive language of *Engle v. Isaac* was found to be controlling.

[b] Thus, under these precedents, the crucial issue was whether the absence of self-defense would be characterized, *under Ohio law,* as an element of the offense charged or as an affirmative defense. Why the state-law characterization should control the federal due process issue may well be thought puzzling, but the rule appears to be settled. See Jeffries and Stephan, Defenses, Presumptions, and Burden of Proof in the Criminal Law, 88 Yale L.J. 1325 (1979).

[c] The trial in *Ross* had occurred six years before the trial in *Engle,* and the developments leading up to *Mullaney* had occurred in the interim.

But *Engle* itself had left many questions in doubt. The confusion and uncertainty surrounding the merits of the claims raised in that case and the difficulty of reconciling its outcome with the later decision in *Reed v. Ross* might well have been seen as reasons for discounting its force. In *Carrier*, however, the *Engle* interpretation of "cause" is reiterated and confirmed in circumstances leaving little doubt as to its meaning: "Attorney error short of ineffective assistance of counsel does not constitute cause for a procedural default . . . ."

Is this rule wise? Is it fair? Is the potential for injustice adequately dealt with by the reservation that " '[i]n appropriate cases,' the principles of comity and finality that inform the concepts of cause and prejudice 'must yield to the imperative of correcting a fundamentally unjust incarceration' "?

4. *Smith v. Murray.* Smith v. Murray, 477 U.S. 527 (1986), was decided on the same day as *Murray v. Carrier* and was also written by Justice O'Connor. Smith was convicted of a brutal murder following the rape of his victim and was sentenced to death. In the course of preparing for trial, defense counsel obtained court appointment of a private psychiatrist to examine the defendant. Copies of his report were routinely sent to both the defense counsel and the prosecution. At the sentencing phase of the trial, the prosecution called the psychiatrist to the stand and elicited certain statements made to him by the defendant. Specifically, the psychiatrist reported that the defendant confessed to having once torn the clothes off a girl on a school bus before deciding not to carry out his intention to rape her. Over a defense objection, this information, along with the diagnosis of "sociopathic personality" and evidence of a prior rape conviction, was considered by the jury in determining sentence.

Both conviction and sentence were appealed to the Virginia Supreme Court, but no assignment of error was made regarding the psychiatrist's testimony. The issue was raised, however, in an amicus brief filed by the Post-Conviction Assistance Project of the University of Virginia Law School. The state Supreme Court nevertheless refused to address the question, noting that it would consider amicus' arguments only on issues specifically included in the defendant's assignments of error.

In a subsequent state habeas proceeding, the defendant claimed both that the psychiatrist's evidence should have been excluded and that he had been denied effective assistance of counsel. The former issue was deemed barred by the failure to raise it on appeal. On the latter issue, the court took evidence from the original defense counsel, who testified that he and an assistant had researched possible objections to the psychiatrist's testimony and determined under existing state precedents that no such objection was likely to succeed. Counsel therefore made a conscious decision not to raise the issue on appeal. The state court found that counsel had exercised "reasonable judgment" in deciding not to pursue the point and that defendant had enjoyed effective assistance of counsel.

The defendant next sought federal habeas relief. His claim was denied in the lower courts, and the Supreme Court affirmed on the ground that the claim was foreclosed by the failure to raise it on direct appeal to the Virginia Supreme Court. Defense counsel had made a conscious decision to forego the claim, and the fact that a later precedent suggested he may have underestimated the merits of the claim did not show "cause" for failure to appeal. Quoting *Carrier,* Justice O'Connor emphasized that "the mere fact that counsel failed to recognize the factual or legal basis for a claim, or failed to raise the claim despite recognizing it, does not constitute cause for a procedural default." Moreover, there was no indication of ineffective assistance of counsel: "After conducting a vigorous defense at both the guilt and sentencing phases of the trial, counsel surveyed the extensive transcript, researched a number of claims, and decided that, under the current state of the law, 13 were worth pursuing on direct appeal. This process of 'winnowing out weaker arguments on appeal and focusing on' those more likely to prevail, far from being evidence of incompetence, is the hallmark of effective appellate advocacy."

Justice O'Connor then turned to the "safety valve" preserved in both *Engle* and *Carrier*: "[W]here a constitutional violation has probably resulted in the conviction of one who is actually innocent, a federal habeas court may grant the writ even in the absence of a showing of cause for the procedural default":

> "We acknowledge the concept of 'actual,' as distinct from 'legal,' innocence does not translate easily into the context of an alleged error at the sentencing phase of a trial on a capital offense. Nonetheless, we think it clear on this record that application of the cause and prejudice test will not result in a 'fundamental miscarriage of justice.' There is no allegation that the testimony about the school bus incident was false or in any way misleading. Nor can it be argued that the prospect that Dr. Pile might later testify against him had the effect of foreclosing meaningful exploration of psychiatric defenses. While that concern is a very real one in the abstract, here the record clearly shows that Dr. Pile did ask petitioner to discuss the crime he stood accused of committing as well as prior incidents of deviant sexual conduct. Although initially reluctant to do so, ultimately petitioner was forthcoming on both subjects. In short, the alleged constitutional error neither precluded the development of true facts nor resulted in the admission of false ones. Thus, even assuming that, as a legal matter, Dr. Pile's testimony should not have been presented to the jury, its admission did not serve to pervert the jury's deliberations concerning the ultimate question whether *in fact* petitioner constituted a continuing threat to society. Under these circumstances, we do not believe that refusal to consider the defaulted claim on federal habeas corpus carries with it a risk of a manifest miscarriage of justice."

The suggestion that more liberal standards of habeas review should obtain in capital cases was specifically rejected.

Justice Stevens dissented in an opinion joined by Justices Marshall and Blackmun and in part by Justice Brennan. Stevens said:

"The Court concludes in this case that no miscarriage of justice will result from a refusal to entertain Smith's challenge to his death sentence. This conclusion is flawed in three respects. First, the Court mistakenly assumes that only a claim implicating 'actual innocence' rises to the level of a miscarriage of justice. Second, the Court does not properly assess the force of a claim that the death penalty is invalid. Finally, the Court vastly exaggerates the state interest in refusing to entertain this claim.

"The Court accurately quotes the holding in *Murray v. Carrier.* ' "[W]here a constitutional violation has probably resulted in the conviction of one who is actually innocent, a federal habeas court may grant the writ even in the absence of a showing of cause for the procedural default." ' The Court then seeks to transfer this 'actual innocence' standard to capital sentencing proceedings, and concludes that, in petitioner's sentencing hearing, 'the alleged constitutional error neither precluded the development of true facts nor results in the admission of false ones.' The Court does not explain, however, why *Carrier*'s clearly correct holding about the propriety of the writ in a case of innocence must also be a *limiting* principle on the federal court's ability to exercise its statutory authority to entertain federal habeas corpus actions; more specifically, the Court does not explain why the same principle should not apply when a constitutional violation is claimed to have resulted in a lack of fundamental fairness, either in a conviction or in a death sentence. . . .

"If accuracy in the determination of guilt or innocence were the only value of our criminal justice system, then the Court's analysis might have a great deal of force. . . . Our Constitution, however, and our decision to adopt an 'accusatorial,' rather than an 'inquisitorial' system of justice, reflect a different choice. That choice is to afford the individual certain protections—the right against compelled self-incrimination and the right against cruel and unusual punishments among them—even if those rights do not necessarily implicate the accuracy of the truth-finding proceedings. Rather, those protections are an aspect of the fundamental fairness, liberty, and individual dignity that our society affords to all, even those charged with heinous crimes.

"In my opinion, then, the Court's exaltation of accuracy as the only characteristic of 'fundamental fairness' is deeply flawed. . . .

"The Court similarly fails to give appropriate weight to the fact that capital punishment is at stake in this case. It is now well settled that 'death is a different kind of punishment from any other which may be imposed in this country.' It is of vital importance to the defendant and to the community that any decision to impose the death sentence be, and appear to be, the consequence of scrupulously fair procedures. When a condemned prisoner raises a substantial, colorable eighth amendment violation, there is a special obligation, consistent with the statutory mission to 'dispose of the matter as law and justice require,' to consider whether the prisoner's claim would render his sentencing proceeding fundamentally unfair. . . .

"Finally, as in every habeas corpus decision, the magnitude of the state's interest must be considered. In this case, several factors suggest that the state's interest is not adequate to obstruct federal habeas corpus consideration of petitioner's claim. First, petitioner made a timely objection at trial, and the state interest in enforcing procedural default rules at trial is far greater than the state's interest in enforcing procedural default rules on appeal. Second, the issue was raised before the state Supreme Court in an amicus curiae brief. Since this is a matter on which courts ordinarily may exercise discretion, the discretionary decision not to address the issue hardly rises to a state interest of sufficient magnitude that a man should die even though his [constitutional] rights were violated to achieve that objective. [M]ost importantly, the inadequacy of the state interest in this death penalty context is decisively shown by the prevailing practice in many states that appellate courts have a special duty in capital cases to overlook procedural defaults and review the trial record for reversible error, before affirming that most severe of all sentences."[d]

How would *Smith v. Murray* have been resolved under *Fay v. Noia*? Would defense counsel's conscious decision to forego a (possibly underestimated) claim on direct review have been a "deliberate bypass" of orderly state procedures? If so, would it bind the defendant?

Now consider the case under *Wainwright v. Sykes*. Would it make sense to treat defense counsel's conscious (but possibly mistaken) decision as "cause" for the procedural default? Only on appeal? Only in capital cases?

5. *United States v. Frady.* The preceding cases concern the meaning of "cause." The meaning of "prejudice" was at issue in United States v. Frady, 456 U.S. 152 (1982).

---

[d] For academic opinion that capital cases should be treated specially, see Robert Batey, Federal Habeas Corpus Relief and the Death Penalty: "Finality with a Capital F," 36 U. Fla. L. Rev. 252 (1984) (arguing that both limitations on the substantive scope of habeas review and rules of procedural foreclosure should be relaxed in capital cases); Robert Catz, Federal Habeas Corpus and the Death Penalty: Need for a Preclusion Doctrine Exception, 18 U.C. Davis L. Rev. 1177 (1985) (arguing for a return to the deliberate by-pass standard for procedural default in capital cases).

Frady was convicted of a brutal murder in 1963 and, although initially sentenced to death, later won a reduction of the sentence to life imprisonment. In the present case, one of a series of collateral attacks he had filed, he argued in a § 2255 proceeding that subsequent court of appeals decisions had demonstrated an error in the jury instructions on malice. He had not objected to these instructions at trial or on direct appeal.

In an opinion by Justice O'Connor, the Court first disposed of two preliminary issues. The conviction occurred in the District of Columbia, and Frady argued that a unique set of rules should apply to Supreme Court review of collateral attacks in the District. This argument was rejected. Secondly, Frady argued that the "plain error" standard governing appeals of federal criminal convictions[e] should apply in § 2255 proceedings. The Court held that the "plain error" standard was "out of place when a prisoner launches a collateral attack" and that "the proper standard for review of Frady's motion is the 'cause and actual prejudice' standard" applicable in habeas review of state convictions.

Applying this standard, the Court found it "unnecessary to determine whether Frady has shown cause, because we are confident he suffered no actual prejudice of a degree sufficient to justify collateral relief 19 years after his crime." As to the meaning "prejudice," the Court said:

> "While the import of the term in other situations . . . remains an open question, our past decisions . . . eliminate any doubt about its meaning for a defendant who has failed to object to jury instructions at trial.
>
> "Recently, for example, Justice Stevens, in his opinion without dissent in Henderson v. Kibbe, 431 U.S. 145 (1977), summarized the degree of prejudice we have required a prisoner to show before obtaining collateral relief for errors in the jury charge as ' "whether the ailing instruction by itself so infected the entire trial that the resulting conviction violates due process," not merely whether "the instruction is undesirable, erroneous, or even universally condemned." ' We reaffirm this formulation . . . ."

Frady was unable to meet this test. As the Court elaborated, Frady

> "must shoulder the burden of showing, not merely that the errors at his trial created a *possibility* of prejudice, but that they worked to his *actual* and substantial disadvantage, infecting his entire trial with error of constitutional dimensions. [W]e emphasize that this would be a different case had Frady brought before the District Court affirmative evidence indicating that he had been convicted wrongly of a crime of which he was innocent."

---

[e] Rule 52(b) of the Federal Rules of Criminal Procedure provides that "[plain errors or defects affecting substantial rights may be noticed although they were not brought to the attention of the court."

Frady's defense at trial had been that someone else committed the crime, although he admitted in subsequent collateral proceedings that he had committed it. Since the malice instruction did not concern his primary defense at trial, since there was uncontradicted evidence of malice in the record, and since Frady made no colorable claim that he acted without malice, the Court perceived "no risk of a fundamental miscarriage of justice in this case." Accordingly, "Frady has fallen far short of meeting his burden of showing that he has suffered the degree of actual prejudice necessary to overcome society's justified interests in the finality of criminal judgments."

Chief Justice Burger and Justice Marshall did not participate. Justice Stevens concurred in the opinion, Justice Blackmun concurred in the judgment, and Justice Brennan dissented.

6. State Court Forfeitures and Federal Common Law. It seems likely that a majority of all procedural defaults are failures to comply with requirements of contemporaneous objection. Whatever one's view of the appropriate scope of federal habeas review, the value to the state of a contemporaneous objection rule is easy to see. Some defaults, however, are occasioned by state procedures of less obvious importance. Both *Carrier* and *Smith,* for example, involved defaults on appeal, where the state's interest in timely presentation of claims is at least different and arguably less. Moreover, in *Smith* the claim was in fact timely raised, but by an amicus rather than by defense counsel. That counsel's failure to include the issue in the assignments of error should nonetheless bar all consideration of the merits may well be thought an unusually exacting implementation of state procedures.

Yet everyone in *Smith* seemed to agree that application of the procedural foreclosure in state court was constitutionally permissible. That is to say, the state's procedure did not violate due process of law, nor had it been manipulated to defeat a federal right. Presumably, therefore, the Virginia Supreme Court's refusal to hear Smith's objection to the psychiatrist's testimony constituted an adequate and independent state ground sufficient to bar direct Supreme Court review. And even if federal habeas review been allowed—that is, even if the dissenting opinion of Justice Stevens had prevailed—the state court would have been free to apply the same rule with the same severity in the next case. In other words, the common ground among all the competing positions on procedural foreclosure in federal habeas corpus is that "deliberate by-pass" or "cause" and "prejudice" govern access to the federal court; they do not speak to the permissibility of the procedures followed in state court.

Why should this be true? Would it be better if the usual state rules of procedure were displaced by federal rules when federal claims are in issue? Should the Supreme Court, in other words, impose on state courts a limited federal obligation to excuse procedural defaults that would otherwise bar consideration of a federal claim?

This intriguing line of questions is raised by Daniel Meltzer in State Court Forfeitures of Federal Rights, 99 Harv. L. Rev. 1130 (1986).

Meltzer argues that limitations on state procedural foreclosure would be justified as an exercise of the Supreme Court's power to make federal common law. Thus, in his view, the rules governing direct Supreme Court review of state criminal convictions and those governing the requirements for federal habeas review should be brought into conformity. More importantly, the same rules would also control in state court:

> "Viewing the rules governing state court defaults [on direct and collateral review] as a single body of federal common law carries another, and seemingly more radical implication: the rules applied by habeas courts to forgive state court procedural defaults should, like modern federal common law, apply in the state courts in the first instance. That is, if the federal common law requires the Supreme Court on direct review, or a federal habeas court, to excuse a procedural default in state court, it also requires a state court to hear the same claim if, for example, it is belatedly asserted in a post-trial motion, on appeal, or in state post-conviction proceedings. If the state's interest in imposing a forfeiture . . . is not sufficiently weighty to bar the Supreme Court or a federal habeas court from reviewing the federal issue, that interest is also not weighty enough to bar review of the federal issue in state court in the first instance."

Does the Supreme Court have the power to control the effect of procedural defaults in state courts? If so, should it be exercised? Or should the Court continue its practice of applying different standards on direct and collateral review? If a uniform set of standards were to govern both the practice in state courts and the terms of federal review (both direct and collateral), should the rules differ from the current meanings of "cause" and "prejudice"? Would *Sykes* itself be decided differently? *Smith v. Murray*? *United States v. Frady*? How about *Fay v. Noia*?[f]

---

[f] For an interesting criticism of *Fay* from this perspective, see Meltzer, supra, at 1193–95.

Chapter VIII

STATE SOVEREIGN IMMUNITY AND THE 11TH AMENDMENT

SECTION 1: NATURE OF THE LIMITATION

INTRODUCTORY NOTES ON THE ORIGINS AND MEANING OF THE 11TH AMENDMENT

1. *Chisholm v. Georgia.* Chisholm v. Georgia, 2 U.S. (2 Dall.) 419 (1793), was an action in assumpsit filed originally in the Supreme Court. It was brought by the executor of a South Carolina merchant to recover for supplies furnished under a contract with the state of Georgia. Jurisdiction was based on the article III specification of federal judicial power over "Controversies . . . between a State and Citizens of another State" and on its implementation in § 13 of the Judiciary Act of 1789.[a] The Court held that the suit could be filed against the state despite Georgia's claim of sovereign immunity.

In the manner of the time, each Justice wrote separately. Justices Blair and Cushing thought the suit authorized by the language of article III. Justice Wilson added that in any event state sovereign immunity would be incompatible with the ultimate sovereignty of the people. By creating the national government and vesting in its courts the power to hear controversies involving states, he said, the people bound the states to answer legal claims as would any individual. Wilson made particular reference to the art. I, § 10, prohibition against laws impairing the obligation of contracts: "What good purpose could this constitutional provision secure, if a state might pass a law impairing the obligation of its own contracts; and be amenable, for such a violation of right, to no controlling judiciary power?" Chief Justice Jay essentially agreed with Wilson.

Justice Iredell was the sole dissenter. He argued that Congress must pass an authorizing statute before any federal court can exercise jurisdiction,[b] and he found no federal statute authorizing a compulsory action for the recovery of money from a state. Section 13 of the Judiciary Act did not authorize such a suit, he thought, for it was meant to confer jurisdiction only over such "controversies of a civil

---

[a] "[T]he supreme court shall have exclusive jurisdiction of all controversies of a civil nature, where a state is a party, except between a state and its citizens; and except also, between a state and citizens of other states, or aliens, in which latter case it shall have original, but not exclusive jurisdiction."

[b] Today, it is widely accepted that the article III provisions on the original jurisdiction of the Supreme Court are self-executing.

803

nature" as were recognized by the principles and usages of the common law. Iredell found no precedent for an action of assumpsit against a state and therefore concluded that the Court lacked jurisdiction.

2. Reaction to *Chisholm*. The reaction to *Chisholm* was swift and hostile. The concern, according to Professor Warren, was not merely the affront to state sovereignty but a practical fear of exhausting state treasuries: "In the crucial condition of the finances of most of the states at that time, only disaster was to be expected if suits could be successfully maintained by holders of state issues of paper and other credits, or by Loyalist refugees to recover property confiscated or sequestered by the states; and that this was no theoretical danger was shown by the immediate institution of such suits against the states in South Carolina, Georgia, Virginia and Massachusetts." 1 C. Warren, The Supreme Court in United States History 99 (1922).[c] The state of Massachusetts adopted a resolution calling for the overturn of *Chisholm*, and the Georgia House of Representatives passed a bill to the effect that any persons attempting to execute process in the *Chisholm* case "are hereby declared to be guilty of felony, and shall suffer death, without the benefit of clergy, by being hanged." Id. at 100–01.

Constitutional amendments were proposed in the House of Representatives on the second and third days after *Chisholm* was announced. One became the basis for the resolution adopted by Congress in the next session and ultimately ratified as the 11th amendment to the Constitution:

> "The Judicial power of the United States shall not be construed to extend to any suit in law or equity, commenced or prosecuted against one of the United States by Citizens of another State, or by Citizens or Subjects of any Foreign State."[d]

3. The Next Hundred Years. For three-quarters of a century after its ratification, the 11th amendment was of little consequence. In Osborn v. Bank of the United States, 22 U.S. (9 Wheat.) 738 (1824), Chief Justice Marshall said that the amendment applied only when a state was "party of record." Thus, the effect of the amendment could be avoided simply by suing an appropriate state officer rather than the state itself.

[c] The significance of this factor is disputed in C. Jacobs, The Eleventh Amendment and Sovereign Immunity 67–74 (1972).

[d] The amendment as adopted differed from the original submission in referring to "suit" rather than "suits" in law and equity, and in adding the words "be construed to." The unsuccessful proposal was significantly different. It read as follows:

"That no state shall be liable to be made a party defendant in any of the judicial courts, established, or which shall be established under the authority of the United States, at the suit of any person or persons whether a citizen or citizens, or a foreigner or foreigners, of any body politic or corporate, whether within or without the United States."

For an account of these formulations and of the inferences that might be drawn from the choice among them, see Fletcher, A Historical Interpretation of the 11th Amendment: A Narrow Construction of an Affirmative Grant of Jurisdiction Rather than a Prohibition Against Jurisdiction, 35 Stan.L.Rev. 1033, 1058–62 (1983) and Amar, Of Sovereignty and Federalism, 96 Yale L.J. 1425, 1481–84 (1987).

This convenient evasion survived until the aftermath of Reconstruction. The Civil War had left the southern states economically destitute, yet saddled with debt. As the northern armies withdrew, one of the first items of business for the restored local leadership was to repudiate at least part of their public debts. The bondholders sought to hold the states to their obligations by resort to the federal courts. Given the rather similar history of *Chisholm,* the 11th amendment was an obvious problem, and the bondholders tried a variety of ways to avoid it. These included mandamus actions against state officials, Louisiana ex rel. Elliott v. Jumel, 107 U.S. 711 (1883); suits by other states, New Hampshire v. Louisiana and New York v. Louisiana, 108 U.S. 76 (1883); attachment of state property, Christian v. Atlantic & North Carolina R., 133 U.S. 233 (1890); and suit against a state by one of its own citizens, Hans v. Louisiana, 134 U.S. 1 (1890). None of these strategies worked. With some significant (and difficult to explain) exceptions, the Supreme Court refurbished and extended the 11th amendment to defeat recovery.

This history is recounted by John Orth in The Interpretation of the 11th Amendment, 1798–1908: A Case Study of Judicial Power, 1983 U.Ill.L.Rev. 423. Professor Orth's thesis is that the post-Reconstruction cases can most plausibly be explained as recognitions of the limited enforceability of judicial decisions:

> "The Civil War had resulted in victory for the federal government, and Reconstruction was a policy of coercion for the defeated states. So long as the national government was willing to coerce the states, there could be no danger of defiance of court orders directed to recalcitrant state officers. The Marshallian position could be thoughtlessly repeated. But the end of Reconstruction signaled the end of easy enforceability of orders to the states. A ruling in favor of the creditors of Louisiana and North Carolina would have required the collection of taxes and the disbursal of funds. The subjects of the orders would have been officers elected to prevent the payment of those very debts. Only overwhelming force could have availed, and the national will to coerce the South was lacking."

4. *Hans v. Louisiana.* The most famous case of this period remains a cornerstone of modern interpretation of the 11th amendment by the Supreme Court. Hans v. Louisiana, 134 U.S. 1 (1890), was a suit by a citizen of Louisiana to recover unpaid interest on bonds issued by the state. Louisiana had issued the bonds in 1874, but subsequently amended its Constitution to disclaim the obligation to pay the interest due in 1880. Hans claimed that the state constitutional amendment was a "Law impairing the Obligation of Contracts" and was therefore invalid under art. I, § 10, of the federal Constitution.

Justice Bradley stated the question before the Supreme Court as "whether a state can be sued in a Circuit Court of the United States by one of its own citizens upon a suggestion that the case is one that arises under the Constitution or laws of the United States." [e] Hans had argued that the statute authorizing the federal courts to hear cases "arising under" the Constitution or laws of the United States made "no exception" based on "the character of the parties, and, therefore, that a state can claim no exemption from suit, if the case is really one arising under the Constitution, laws or treaties of the United States." The Court responded:

"That a state cannot be sued by a citizen of another state, or of a foreign state, on the mere ground that the case is one arising under the Constitution or laws of the United States, is clearly established by the decisions of this Court in several recent cases. . . . This Court held that the suits were virtually against the states themselves and were consequently violative of the 11th amendment of the Constitution, and could not be maintained. It was not denied that they presented cases arising under the Constitution; but, notwithstanding that, they were held to be prohibited by the amendment referred to.

"In the present case [Hans] contends that he, being a citizen of Louisiana, is not embarrassed by the obstacle of the 11th amendment, inasmuch as that amendment only prohibits suits against a state which are brought by the citizens of another state, or by citizens or subjects of a foreign state. It is true, the amendment does so read: and if there were no other reason or ground for abating his suit, it might be maintainable; and then we should have this anomalous result, that in cases arising under the Constitution or laws of the United States, a state may be sued in the federal courts by its own citizens, though it cannot be sued for a like cause of action by the citizens of other states, or of a foreign state; and may be thus sued in the federal courts, although not allowing itself to be sued in its own courts. If this is the necessary consequence of the language of the Constitution and the law, the result is no less startling and unexpected than was the original decision of this Court [in] Chisholm v. Georgia, 2 U.S. (2 Dall.) 419 (1793), [which] created such a shock of surprise throughout the country that, at the first meeting of Congress thereafter, the 11th amendment was proposed, and was in due course adopted by the legislatures of the states. This amendment . . . did not in terms prohibit suits by individuals against the states, but declared that the Constitution should not be construed to import any power to authorize the bringing of such suits. The language of the amendment is that 'the Judicial power of the United States shall *not be construed to extend* to any suit in law or equity, commenced or prosecuted against one of the United States by Citizens of another State, or by Citizens or Subjects of any Foreign State.' The Supreme Court had con-

[e] Jurisdiction was based on the forerunner of 28 U.S.C. § 1331.

strued the judicial power as extending to such a suit, and its decision was thus overruled."

The Court embraced Justice Iredell's dissenting view in *Chisholm* "that it was not the intention [in the original Constitution] to create new and unheard of remedies, by subjecting sovereign states to actions at the suit of individuals, (which he conclusively showed was never done before,) but only, by proper legislation, to invest the federal courts with jurisdiction to hear and determine controversies and cases . . . that were properly susceptible of litigation in courts." Justice Bradley then quoted Hamilton, Madison, and Marshall to the effect that it is "inherent in the nature of sovereignty" that the state cannot be sued without its consent. Justice Bradley continued:

"It seems to us that these views of those great advocates and defenders of the Constitution were most sensible and just. [The argument by Hans] is an attempt to strain the Constitution and the law to a construction never imagined or dreamed of. Can we suppose that, when the 11th amendment was adopted, it was understood to be left open for citizens of a state to sue their own state in the federal courts, whilst the idea of suits by citizens of other states, or of foreign states, was indignantly repelled? Suppose that Congress, when proposing the 11th amendment, had appended to it a proviso that nothing therein contained should prevent a state from being sued by its own citizens in cases arising under the Constitution or laws of the United States: can we imagine that it would have been adopted by the states? The supposition that it would is almost an absurdity on its face.

"The truth is, that the cognizance of suits and actions unknown to the law, and forbidden by the law, was not contemplated by the Constitution when establishing the judicial power of the United States.. . . .

"To avoid misapprehension it may be proper to add that, although the obligations of a state rest for their performance upon its honor and good faith, and cannot be made the subjects of judicial cognizance unless the state consents to be sued, or comes itself into court; yet where property or rights are enjoyed under a grant or contract made by a state, they cannot wantonly be invaded. Whilst the state cannot be compelled by suit to perform its contracts, any attempt on its part to violate property or rights acquired under its contracts, may be judicially resisted; and any law impairing the obligation of contracts under which such property or rights are held is void and powerless to affect their enjoyment. . . ."

5. The Immunity Interpretation of the 11th Amendment. *Hans* might be read to adopt what can be called the immunity interpretation of the 11th amendment. This interpretation treats the 11th amendment as re-establishing the state sovereign immunity implicitly recognized by article III and erroneously abrogated by *Chisholm*. State sovereign immunity thus becomes a constitutional doctrine, embedded in the fabric of the original document and assertable at the option of the state.

There is, of course, a textual difficulty with this interpretation: the 11th amendment applies in terms only to suits by citizens of other states or of foreign countries; it does not mention immunity against suit by the state's own citizens. The *Hans* Court responded to this difficulty by suggesting that the supposition that the 11th amendment left the federal courts open to suit against a state by its own citizens was "almost an absurdity on its face." It therefore seemed to read the amendment as evidencing a comprehensive policy of state sovereign immunity in the federal courts.[f]

The *Hans* Court took Hamilton, Madison, and Marshall to say that state sovereign immunity was implicit in the original structure of article III. It should be noted, however, that they were not the only framers who spoke to the issue of state sovereign immunity under the proposed Constitution. Others reached exactly the opposite conclusion. Patrick Henry and George Mason, both of whom opposed the Constitution, saw in article III an abrogation of state sovereign immunity and based their opposition in part on that ground. But not all who took this view were opponents of the Constitution. James (later Justice) Wilson, argued for ratification and regarded it a virtue that the Constitution made states amenable to suits by individuals. Edmund Randolph, who while serving as Attorney General of the United States, argued the case for Chisholm, also read article III as abrogating state sovereign immunity and also approved that result.[g]

6. Concluding Comments. The stakes involved in interpreting the 11th amendment are very high. Virtually the entire class of modern civil rights litigation plausibly might be barred by an expansive reading of the immunity of states from suit in federal court. Note, for example, an extreme to which the "immunity" interpretation of the amendment might be taken. If broadly and literally applied, the immunity theory could prohibit any suit against a state in federal court. Since a state can only act through its officers, the immunity approach could readily be extended to prohibit suits against any state official. And it could easily be extended further to suits against cities,

[f] Later decisions have applied this policy in other contexts not covered by the language of the amendment. See, e.g., Ex parte New York, 256 U.S. 490 (1911) (state immunity may be invoked in admiralty actions, notwithstanding that the amendment applies in terms only to suits "in law or equity"); Monaco v. Mississippi, 292 U.S. 313 (1934) (immunity applies in action by foreign country). But see Rhode Island v. Massachusetts, 37 U.S. (12 Pet.) 657 (1838) (11th amendment does not bar suit by another state); United States v. Texas, 143 U.S. 621, 645 (1892) (federal court jurisdiction over suit by United States against an unconsenting state deemed "inherent in the constitutional plan").

[g] These and other statements of the framers are collected and discussed by Martha Field in The 11th Amendment and Other Sovereign Immunity Doctrines: Part One, 126 U.Pa.L.Rev. 515, 527–36 (1978). Field concluded that the *Chisholm* Court's construction of article III "was not therefore the clear contravention of a general understanding that it has long been said to be." See also Justice Brennan's extensive review of these materials in his dissent in Atascadero State Hospital v. Scanlon, 473 U.S. 234, 247 (1985).

counties, and other components of state government, as well as to suits against local officials. On this broad conception, the entire class of modern civil rights litigation would be excluded from the federal courts. There could be no *Brown v. Board of Education* (school desegregation) and no *Reynolds v. Sims* (reapportionment). There could be no damages against state officials for violation of the Constitution, and no injunction to secure future compliance with constitutional limitations. The Constitution could only be used as a shield against state actions sought to be enforced in court by the state; it could not operate as a sword to require the state to conduct its affairs consistently with constitutional requirements.

Modern litigation to enforce the 14th amendment could hardly have been in the minds of drafters acting 70 years before its adoption. Nor could the drafters of the 11th amendment have contemplated the revolution in federal-state relations that has occurred during the 19th and 20th centuries. The challenge facing the Supreme Court has been to adopt an interpretation of the 11th amendment that is plausible in light of these developments. One of the major responses of the Court to this challenge is the next main case.

EX PARTE YOUNG

Supreme Court of the United States, 1908.
209 U.S. 123.

[When Minnesota enacted legislation fixing railroad rates, shareholders of a railroad company brought a derivative suit in federal Circuit Court to challenge the rates as confiscatory under the 14th amendment. The federal court issued a preliminary injunction prohibiting the railroad from putting the new rates into effect and restraining Edward T. Young, Attorney General of the state of Minnesota, from taking any action to enforce the state law. Young nevertheless commenced a mandamus action in state court to compel compliance with the new rates and was promptly adjudged in contempt of the federal court. The dispute came to the Supreme Court on Young's original application for writs of habeas corpus and certiorari.]

MR. JUSTICE PECKHAM . . . delivered the opinion of the Court.
. . .

For disobedience to the freight act the officers, directors, agents and employees of the company are made guilty of a misdemeanor, and upon conviction each may be punished by imprisonment in the county jail for a period not exceeding 90 days. Each violation would be a separate offense, and therefore, might result in imprisonment of the various agents of the company who would dare disobey for a term of 90 days for each offense. Disobedience to the passenger rate act renders the party guilty of a felony and subject to a fine not exceeding $5,000 or imprisonment in the state prison for a period not exceeding five years, or both fine and imprisonment. The sale of each ticket above the price permitted by the act would be a violation thereof. It would be difficult, it not impossible, for the company to obtain officers, agents or employees willing to carry on its affairs except in obedience to the act and orders in question. . . .   The company, in order to test the validity of the acts, must find some agent or employee to disobey them at the risk stated. The necessary effect and result of such legislation must be to preclude a resort to the courts (either state or federal) for the purpose of testing its validity. The officers and employees could not be expected to disobey any of the provisions of the acts or orders at the risk of such fines and penalties being imposed upon them, in case the court should decide that the law was valid. The result would be a denial of any hearing to the company. . . .

We hold, therefore, that the provisions of the acts relating to the enforcement of the rates, either for freight or passengers, by imposing such enormous fines and possible imprisonment as a result of an unsuccessful effort to test the validity of the laws themselves, are unconstitutional on their face, without regard to the question of the insufficiency of the rates. . . .

We have, therefore, upon this record the case of an unconstitutional act of the state legislature and an intention by the Attorney General of the state to endeavor to enforce its provisions . . . .   The question that arises is whether there is a remedy that the parties interested may resort to, by going into a federal court of equity, in a case involving a violation of the federal Constitution, and obtaining a judicial investigation of the problem, and pending its solution obtain freedom from suits, civil or criminal, by a temporary injunction, and if the question be finally decided favorably to the contention of the company, a permanent injunction restraining all such actions or proceedings.

This inquiry necessitates an examination of the most material and important objection made to the jurisdiction of the Circuit Court, the objection being that the suit is, in effect, one against the state of Minnesota. . . .   This objection is to be considered with reference to the 11th [amendment] to the federal Constitution. The 11th amendment prohibits the commencement or prosecution of any suit against one of the United States by citizens of another state or citizens or subjects of any foreign state. . . .

[W]e naturally must give to the 11th amendment all the effect it naturally would have, without cutting it down or rendering its meaning any more narrow than the language, fairly interpreted, would warrant. [We have] ample justification for the assertion that individuals, who, as officers of the state, are clothed with some duty in regard to the enforcement of the laws of the state, and who threaten and are about to commence proceedings, either of a civil or criminal nature, to enforce against parties affected an unconstitutional act, violating the federal Constitution, may be enjoined by a federal court of equity from such action. . . .

It is contended that the complainants do not complain and they care nothing about any action which Mr. Young might take or bring as an ordinary individual, but that he was complained of as an officer, to whose discretion is confided the use of the name of the state of Minnesota so far as litigation is concerned, and that when or how he shall use it is a matter resting in his discretion and cannot be controlled by any court.

The answer to all this is the same as made in every case where an official claims to be acting under the authority of the state. The act to be enforced is alleged to be unconstitutional, and if it be so, the use of the name of the state to enforce an unconstitutional act to the injury of complainants is a proceeding without the authority of and one which does not affect the state in its sovereign or governmental capacity. It is simply an illegal act upon the part of a state official in attempting by the use of the name of the state to enforce a legislative enactment which is void because unconstitutional. If the act which the state Attorney General seeks to enforce be a violation of the federal Constitution, the officer in proceeding under such enactment comes into conflict with the superior authority of the Constitution, and he is in that case stripped of his official or representative character and is subjected in his person to the consequences of his individual conduct. The state has no power to impart to him any immunity from responsibility to the supreme authority of the United States. . . .

It is further objected (and the objection really forms part of the contention that the state cannot be sued) that a court of equity has no jurisdiction to enjoin criminal proceedings, by indictment or otherwise, under the state law. This, as a general rule, is true. But there are exceptions. When such indictment or proceeding is brought to enforce an alleged unconstitutional statute, which is the subject matter of inquiry in a suit already pending in a federal court, the latter court having first obtained jurisdiction over the subject matter, has the right, in both civil and criminal cases, to hold and maintain such jurisdiction, to the exclusion of all other courts, until its duty is fully performed. But the federal court cannot, of course, interfere in a case where the proceedings were already pending in a state court. . . .

It is further objected that there is a plain and adequate remedy at law open to the complainants and that a court of equity, therefore, has no jurisdiction in such case. It has been suggested that the proper way to test the constitutionality of the act is to disobey it, at least once, after which the company might obey the act pending subsequent proceedings to test its validity. But in the event of a single violation the prosecutor might not avail himself of the opportunity to make the test, as obedience to the law was thereafter continued, and he might think it unnecessary to start an inquiry. If, however, he should do so while the company was thereafter obeying the law, several years might elapse before there was a final determination of the question, and if it should be determined that the law was invalid the property of the company would have been taken during that time without due process of law, and there would be no possibility of its recovery.

Another obstacle to making the test on the part of the company might be to find an agent or employee who would disobey the law, with a possible fine and imprisonment staring him in the face if the act should be held valid. Take the passenger rate act, for instance: A sale of a single ticket above the price mentioned in that act might subject the ticket agent to a charge of felony, and upon conviction to a fine of $5,000 and imprisonment for five years. It is true the company might pay the fine, but the imprisonment the agent would have to suffer personally. It would not be wonderful if, under such circumstances, there would not be a crowd of agents offering to disobey the law. The wonder would be that a single agent should be found ready to take the risk. . . .

To await proceedings against the company in a state court grounded upon a disobedience of the act, and then, if necessary, obtain a review in this Court by writ of error to the highest state court, would place the company in peril of large loss and its agents in great risk of fines and imprisonment if it should be finally determined that the act was valid. This risk the company ought not to be required to take. . . .

[The supreme authority of the United States], which arises from the specific provisions of the Constitution itself, is nowhere more fully illustrated than in the series of decisions under the federal habeas corpus statute, in some of which cases persons in the custody of state officers for alleged crimes against the state have been taken from that custody and discharged by a federal court or judge, because the imprisonment was adjudged to be in violation of the federal Constitution. The right to so discharge has not been doubted by this Court, and it has never been supposed there was any suit against the state by reason of serving the writ upon one of the officers of the state in whose custody the person was found. In some of the cases the writ has been refused as a matter of discretion, but in others it has been granted, while the power has been fully recognized in all.

It is somewhat difficult to appreciate the distinction which, while admitting that the taking of such a person from the custody of the state by virtue of service of the writ on the state officer in whose custody he is found, is not a suit against the state, and yet service of a writ on the Attorney General to prevent his enforcing an unconstitutional enactment of a state legislature is a suit against the state. . . .

The rule to show cause is discharged and the petition for writs of habeas corpus and certiorari is dismissed.

MR. JUSTICE HARLAN, dissenting. . . .

Let it be observed that the suit instituted . . . in the Circuit Court of the United States was, as to the defendant Young, one against him *as, and only because he was,* Attorney General of Minnesota. No relief was sought against him individually but only in his capacity as Attorney General. And the manifest, indeed the avowed and admitted, object of seeking such relief was *to tie the hands* of the *state* so that it could not in any manner or by any mode of proceeding, *in its own courts,* test the validity of the statutes and orders in question. It would therefore seem clear that within the true meaning of the 11th amendment the suit brought in the federal court was one, in legal effect, against the state—as much so as if the state had been formally named on the record as a party—and therefore it was a suit to which, under the [11th] amendment, so far as the state or its Attorney General was concerned, the judicial power of the United States did not and could not extend. . . .

[T]he intangible thing, called a state, however extensive its powers, can never appear or be represented or known in any court in a litigated case, except by and through its officers. When, therefore, the federal court forbade the defendant Young, as Attorney General of Minnesota, from taking any action, suit, step or proceeding whatever looking to the enforcement of the statutes in question, it said in effect to the state of Minnesota: "It is true that the powers not delegated to the United States by the Constitution, nor prohibited by it to the states, are reserved to the states respectively or to its people, and it is true that under the Constitution the judicial power of the United States does not extend to any suit brought against a state by a citizen of another state or by a citizen or subject of a foreign state, yet the federal court adjudges that you, the state, although a sovereign for many important governmental purposes, shall not appear in your own courts, by your law officer, with the view of enforcing, or even for determining the validity of the state enactments which the federal court has, upon a preliminary hearing, declared to be in violation of the Constitution of the United States."

This principle, if firmly established, would work a radical change in our governmental system. It would inaugurate a new era in the American judicial system and in the relations of the national and state governments. It would enable the subordinate federal courts to supervise and control the official action of the states as if they were "dependencies" or provinces. It would place the states of the Union in a condition of inferiority never dreamed of when the Constitution was adopted or when the 11th amendment was made a part of the supreme law of the land. . . . Too little consequence has been attached to the fact that the courts of the states are under an obligation equally strong with that resting upon the courts of the Union to respect and enforce the provisions of the federal Constitution as the supreme law of the land, and to guard rights secured or guaranteed by that instrument. We must assume—a decent respect for the states requires us to assume—that the state courts will enforce every right secured by the Constitution. If they fail to do so, the party complaining has a clear remedy for the protection of his rights; for, he can come by writ of error, in an orderly, judicial way, from the highest court of the state to this tribunal for redress in respect of every right granted or secured by that instrument and denied by the state court . . . .

I dissent from the opinion and judgment.

———

NOTES ON ALTERNATIVE INTERPRETATIONS OF THE 11TH AMENDMENT

1. **Injunctive Relief Against State Officers.** *Ex parte Young* creates a substantial, if circumlocutory, exception to state sovereign immunity. For most purposes, the exception can be summarized in the proposition that a state can be sued in federal court for prospective relief by the simple expedient of naming the appropriate state officer as the defendant.[a] The official is "stripped" of any "official or representative character" if the enforcement of state law violates the federal Constitution, even though for purposes of the 14th amendment the official's conduct is regarded as "state action." [b] Indeed, if it were not, there would be no unconstitutionality of which to complain.

However desirable the result in *Ex parte Young,* the Court's theory rests on a fictional tour de force. By any measure, moreover, the full potential of an immunity interpretation of the 11th amendment was significantly curtailed in *Young.* Is it possible to reconcile the *Young* result with the theory of the 11th amendment adopted in *Hans*? If not, should the *Hans* interpretation be replaced with a different approach to the function of the 11th amendment? Consider the following notes in connection with these questions.

2. **The Diversity Interpretation.** One response to the difficulty of reconciling *Hans* with modern civil rights litigation is here labeled the "diversity" interpretation of the 11th amendment. This approach reads the amendment as a restriction on federal judicial power only when jurisdiction is based on the character of the parties. Under this interpretation, the 11th amendment does not enshrine state sovereign immunity as a constitutional concept. It only prohibits diversity suits *against* a state, and thus restricts the state-citizen diversity jurisdiction authorized by article III to cases where the state is the plaintiff. It does not prohibit suits based on other provisions of article III, such as cases arising under federal law. Thus, the function of the amendment under this view—and the reason it is limited to suits by out-of-state citizens—is to repeal a segment of the diversity jurisdiction originally authorized by article III.

This interpretation can be understood as faithful to the constitutional text. It begins with the assumption that article III was intended to be neutral with respect to sovereign immunity—that is, it neither adopted state sovereign immunity as a limitation on federal power, nor

---

[a] *Ex parte Young* was a watershed case in the sense that it clearly established for the first time a general basis for prospective relief against state officials. The older cases had permitted some forms of such relief, but not others. For example, it was settled before *Young* that a citizen could sue to recover specific property wrongfully seized by state officials. See, e.g., Osborn v. Bank of the United States, 22 U.S. (9 Wheat.) 738 (1824) (ordering the return of a large sum of money seized from the bank and kept separately in a trunk). But the Court had refused to permit a suit to enjoin the attorney general from instituting proceedings that, the plaintiff alleged, would have violated the contracts clause. In re Ayers, 123 U.S. 443 (1887).

[b] See, e.g., Home Telephone & Telegraph Co. v. City of Los Angeles, 227 U.S. 278 (1913), discussed infra, at pages 892–93.

did it abrogate the sovereign immunity available under state law simply because a case might be brought in federal court. In this view, the error of *Chisholm* was the treatment of the mere fact of state-citizen diversity as an abrogation of state sovereign immunity *for a claim based on state law*. Thus, the 11th amendment was designed, not to fix state sovereign immunity as a constitutional limitation on federal judicial power, but merely to repudiate the view that state sovereign immunity had been abrogated by the diversity provisions of article III. The failure of the amendment to prohibit suit by a state's own citizens is thus perfectly understandable; such a suit would not in any event have come within the state-citizen diversity provision of article III.

On the other hand, there is a textual difficulty in that the amendment, literally applied, precludes *all* suits against a state by a citizen of another state, apparently even those based on federal law. It is not limited on its face to situations where federal jurisdiction is based on diversity. The usual response to this point is that the failure to distinguish diversity from other grounds of jurisdiction is not surprising, given that there was at the time no statute generally authorizing the federal courts to hear cases based upon federal questions and no disposition by the national legislature to impose federal liability upon the states. The question whether a suit based on federal law should be prohibited by the 11th amendment, in other words, was simply not before the house when the amendment was debated.

In summary, the diversity interpretation sees in the 11th amendment only a desire to neutralize an erroneous construction of the effect of state-citizen diversity under article III. State sovereign immunity, the argument goes, survived only as a non-constitutional doctrine. It can be asserted against state causes of action to the extent permitted by state law. It can be asserted against federal causes of action to the extent permitted by federal law as fashioned by Congress or the courts. Under this view, *Ex parte Young* is not a difficult case. Since the plaintiff's case was based on federal and not state law, the 11th amendment was simply inapplicable. But can this view of the 11th amendment be reconciled with *Hans*?

No Justice of the Supreme Court wholly accepted the diversity interpretation until Justice Brennan's dissent, joined by Justices Marshall, Blackmun, and Stevens, in Atascadero State Hospital v. Scanlon, 473 U.S. 234, 289–90 (1985).[c] In Justice Brennan's view:

> "The language of the 11th amendment, its legislative history, and the attendant historical circumstances all strongly suggest that the amendment was intended to remedy an interpretation of the Constitution that would have had the state-citizen and state-alien diversity clauses of article III abrogating the state law of sovereign immunity on state-law causes of action brought in federal courts. . . . The original Constitution did not embody a principle of sovereign immunity as a

[c] See also Justice Brennan's dissent in Welch v. State Department of Highways and Public Transportation, ___ U.S. ___ (1987), page 852, infra.

limit on the federal judicial power. There is simply no reason to believe that the 11th amendment established such a broad principle for the first time.

". . . The *Chisholm* Court had interpreted the state-citizen clause of article III to work a major change in state law, or at least in those cases arising under state law that found their way to federal court. The 11th amendment corrected that error, and henceforth required that the party-based heads of jurisdiction in article III be construed not to work this kind of drastic modification of state law. . . .

"Article III grants a federal question jurisdiction to the federal courts that is as broad as is the lawmaking authority of Congress. If Congress acting within its article I or other powers creates a legal right and remedy, and if neither the right nor the remedy violates any provision of the Constitution outside article III, then Congress may entrust adjudication of claims based on the newly created right to the federal courts—even if the defendant is a state. Neither article III nor the 11th amendment impose an independent limit on the lawmaking authority of Congress. . . ." [d]

Additionally, several academics have endorsed this position, in part as an interpretation not foreclosed by the historical record and in part as a means of ensuring that state sovereign immunity does not defeat enforcement of federal rights. Perhaps the best known explication of this view is in Martha Field's article, The 11th Amendment and Other Sovereign Immunity Doctrines: Part One, 126 U.Pa.L.Rev. 515 (1977). See also Le Clercq, State Immunity and Federal Judicial Power—Retreat from National Supremacy, 27 Fla.L.Rev. 361 (1975), and Thornton, The 11th Amendment: An Endangered Species, 55 Ind.L.J. 293 (1980), both of which emphasize the importance of federal court vindication of federal rights. The most extensive historical investigation can be found in Fletcher, A Historical Intepretation of the Eleventh Amendment: A Narrow Construction of an Affirmative Grant of Jurisdiction Rather than a Prohibition Against Jurisdiction, 35 Stan.L.Rev. 1033 (1983), and Amar, Of Sovereignty and Federalism, 96 Yale L.J. 1425, 1466–92 (1987), both of which marshal the evidence in support of the view that the framers of the 11th amendment intended to limit only diversity jurisdiction. See also Gibbons, The 11th Amendment and State Sovereign Immunity: A Reinterpretation, 83 Colum.L.Rev. 1889 (1983). Further treatment of these questions and extensive comments on *Hans* may be found in McCormack, Intergovernmental Immunity and the 11th Amendment, 51 N.C.L.Rev. 486 (1973).

---

[d] At a later point in his opinion, Justice Brennan argued that *Hans* can "sensibly be read to have dismissed the suit before it on the ground that no federal cause of action supported the plaintiff's suit and that state-law causes of action would of course be subject to the ancient common-law doctrine of sovereign immunity." Brennan also argued that, if *Hans* was meant to enshrine sovereign immunity as a constitutional protection for state government, it was wrong because it "rested on misconceived history and misguided logic."

3. The Federalism/Separation of Powers Interpretation. A third view of the 11th amendment reads the provision as stating a limitation on the federal courts derived from principles of federalism and separation of powers. The error of *Chisholm,* according to this theory, lay in its judicial creativity. That creativity can be explained in either of two ways. One is that in enforcing a state-created cause of action, the Court set aside the accompanying state law of sovereign immunity. The other is that in effect the Court created a new federal cause of action to enforce the constitutional obligation of the states not to impair their contracts. The purpose of the 11th amendment, according to this view, was to curb the capacity of the federal courts to impose legal liabilities on the states in either manner.

This view holds that the 11th amendment was not designed to speak to the powers of Congress. The balance of power between the state and federal legislatures was struck in the Constitution by the relationship between article I and the 10th amendment. Article III, moreover—and particularly that part authorizing federal court jurisdiction over cases arising under federal law—was designed to permit the Congress to use the federal courts for any purpose legitimately within its article I powers.[e] The controversy surrounding the *Chisholm* case was not concerned with these matters, and the debates leading to the 11th amendment show no attention to whether these fundamental constitutional premises should be changed. The 11th amendment should therefore be interpreted as a limitation on the law-making capacity of the federal courts in cases where the state or a state official is the defendant. It should not be interpreted as a restriction of Congress' powers under the Constitution.

Aspects of this argument are explored in articles by John Nowak and Laurence Tribe. See Nowak, The Scope of Congressional Power to Create Causes of Action Against State Governments and the History of the 11th and 14th Amendments, 75 Colum.L.Rev. 1413 (1975); and Tribe, Intergovernmental Immunities in Litigation, Taxation, and Regulation: Separation of Powers Issues in Controversies About Federalism, 89 Harv.L.Rev. 682 (1976). Nowak's argument is grounded in part on historical investigation, and Tribe notes that the amendment in terms restricts only the judicial power. But in large measure both rely on the policy perception, as Nowak phrased it, "that the pragmatic problems of federalism posed by the 11th amendment should be resolved by Congress, not by the judiciary." Thus, both build on the premise, often associated with Herbert Wechsler,[f] that since the states as such are represented in the federal legislature, the courts should be reluctant to limit congressional power in the name of federalism. The federal judiciary, in contrast, is not politically responsive to the states

[e] Compare the passage quoted from Chief Justice Marshall's opinion in *Osborn v. Bank of the United States,* page 209, supra.

the Composition and Selection of the National Government, 54 Colum.L.Rev. 543 (1954).

[f] See Wechsler, The Political Safeguards of Federalism: The Role of the States in

and should be regarded as precluded by the 11th amendment from innovations that subject states to suit in federal court.

Martha Field has criticized the Nowak-Tribe position on the ground "that it derives from nothing peculiar to the 11th amendment." In her words, "[i]t is an argument for a *general* limitation upon judicial power in relation to legislative power, at least in areas involving federal-state relations." Field, The 11th Amendment and Other Sovereign Immunity Doctrines: Congressional Imposition of Suits Upon the States, 126 U.Pa.L.Rev. 1203, 1258–61 (1978).[g]

4. Concluding Comments. The Supreme Court has not adopted, in their pure forms, the "immunity" interpretation of the 11th amendment, the "diversity" interpretation, or the "federalism/separation of powers" interpretation. One reason, perhaps, is that both the diversity and federalism/separation of powers theories can, like the immunity theory, lead to results that might be regarded as unacceptable.

The diversity interpretation, for example, effectively reads the 11th amendment out of the picture in terms of suits that matter today. Under this view, suits against states or against state officials would be permitted if based on a federal question. The category of suits that would be precluded—those brought by citizens of another state to enforce state-created obligations—is of little modern significance.

In an important sense, therefore, the debate between the immunity and the diversity approaches to the 11th amendment puts an all-or-nothing choice. One response might be to adopt the "separation of powers" interpretation. Yet it too has a central difficulty. Taken to its extreme, it would limit the capacity of the federal courts to engage in creative law-making in order to enforce constitutional limitations on state government. It may explain *Hans,* but it is difficult to reconcile with *Ex parte Young.* More broadly speaking, the lines of cases based on *Mapp v. Ohio* (exclusionary rule), *Brown v. Board of Education* (school desegregation), and *Reynolds v. Sims* (reapportionment) involved the judicial development of remedies against state government, remedies the creation of which, if one adhered to a strict separation-of-powers limitation on judicial lawmaking, should have been left to the legislative process. Yet the necessities that led the Court to their development were in large part the result of legislative default.

The Court's response to this situation, as *Ex parte Young* illustrates and as is illustrated by subsequent materials in this chapter, has been to adopt an amalgam of fictions and theories that have turned the 11th amendment into "an arcane specialty of lawyers and federal judges" that is "replete with historical anomalies, internal inconsistencies, and senseless distinctions." [h]

---

[g] See also pages 1265–68 of the same article for an interesting attempt to rehabilitate *Hans* not as a construction of the 11th amendment but as a correct interpretation of the contract clause.

[h] J. Orth, The Judicial Power of the United States 11 (1987), quoted by Justice Brennan in Welch v. State Department of Highways and Public Transportation, ___ U.S. ___ (1987), page 855, infra.

ADDITIONAL NOTES ON *EX PARTE YOUNG*

1. The Anti–Injunction Act. The 11th amendment was not the only potential obstacle to the injunctive relief granted in *Ex parte Young*. There was also the Act of March 2, 1793, now codified in 28 U.S.C. § 2283. In its current form, the statute declares that "[a] court of the United States may not grant an injunction to stay proceedings in a state court except as expressly authorized by act of Congress, or where necessary in aid of its jurisdiction, or to protect or effectuate its judgments." The *Young* Court evidently assumed that this statute was inapplicable, for it was not discussed in the opinion. Under modern precedents, moreover, this assumption was correct, since the statute has been construed not to bar an injunction where a federal suit is commenced before state proceedings are actually under way. See, e.g., Dombrowski v. Pfister, 380 U.S. 479, 484 n.2 (1965).[a]

2. Subsequent Legislative Limitations on *Ex Parte Young*. Political reaction to *Ex parte Young* was not favorable. Particular objection was made to the power of a single federal judge to issue ex parte injunctive relief against enforcement of state law. Congress responded to this concern in 1910 by limiting the availability of temporary restraining orders and by requiring that applications for certain kinds of preliminary injunctive relief against state officials be heard by a special three-judge district court, with direct review by appeal to the United States Supreme Court.

The three-judge court requirement was extended in 1925 to the issuance of final injunctions against enforcement of unconstitutional state laws, and in 1937 an analogous provision ws enacted requiring three-judge courts for suits attacking the constitutionality of federal legislation. These provisions spawned an exceedingly complex body of law concerning such questions as the precise circumstances requiring the convening of a three-judge court, the powers of the single district judge before whom the case was initially filed, the kinds of additional claims that could be heard by the three-judge court once convened, the court to which issues that could have been resolved by a single judge should be appealed, etc.

Most of these questions have been mooted by repeal in 1976 of the general three-judge court provisions (formerly 28 U.S.C. §§ 2281 and 2282), a reform brought about in large part because of the burdens on lower court judges, the disproportionate share of the Supreme Court's docket consumed by appeals from three-judge courts, and by the percep-

---

For a practical guide to the 11th amendment, see John R. Pagan, Eleventh Amendment Analysis, 39 Ark.L.Rev. 447 (1986). Pagan dismisses as "pointless" additional attacks on the "distorted history and flawed reasoning" of the Court's 11th amendment precedents and attempts instead to provide a "step-by-step framework" for applying existing doctrine. See also Allen K. Easley, The Supreme Court and the Eleventh Amendment: Mourning the Lost Opportunity to Synthesize Conflicting Precedents, 64 Denver U.L.Rev. 485 (1988), which explores the doctrinal inconsistencies in the Court's 11th amendment jurisprudence.

[a] Section 2283 is considered in detail at pages 526–41, supra.

tion that such courts were no longer necessary. Today, outside of certain highly specific statutory cases, three-judge courts are required only "when an action is filed challenging the constitutionality of the apportionment of congressional districts or the apportionment of any statewide legislative body." 28 U.S.C. § 2284.[b]

3. Footnote on the Cause of Action. One issue not mentioned in *Ex parte Young* has nevertheless acquired some significance in retrospect. The complainants in that case sought affirmative relief to prevent violation of rights guaranteed by the 14th amendment to the federal Constitution. No statute was relied upon to authorize the suit. Where did the plaintiff's cause of action come from? The answer to this question is not clear. But *Ex parte Young* has come to be cited for the proposition that such a cause of action exists independent of explicit congressional authorization.[c]

EDELMAN v. JORDAN

Supreme Court of the United States, 1974.
415 U.S. 651.

[Respondent Jordan brought a class action to challenge the practices of certain Illinois officials in administering federal-state programs under the Aid to the Aged, Blind, or Disabled Act (AABD). The District Court found that the defendant officials had failed to process AABD applications within applicable time limits and had failed to make the benefits retroactive to the date of initial eligibility, as required by federal regulations issued by the Department of Health, Education and Welfare under the Social Security Act. The court enjoined any future violations and ordered the state officials to refund all wrongfully withheld past benefits. The Seventh Circuit affirmed over the defendants' objection that the 11th amendment barred the award of retroactive benefits. The Supreme Court granted certiorari.]

MR. JUSTICE REHNQUIST delivered the opinion of the Court. . . .

While the [11th] amendment by its terms does not bar suits against a state by its own citizens, this Court has consistently held that an unconsenting state is immune from suits brought in federal courts by her own citizens as well as by citizens of another state. Hans v.

---

[b] For the early history of the three-judge court statute, see Hutcheson, A Case for Three Judges, 47 Harv.L.Rev. 795 (1934). A more modern treatment is Currie, The Three-Judge District Court in Constitutional Litigation, 32 U.Chi.L.Rev. 1 (1964).

Two other statutes should be mentioned. They are more remote from *Ex parte Young* in time, but both limit the availability of the remedy it established. The first is the Johnson Act of 1934, now codified in 28 U.S.C. § 1342. This statute restricts federal court authority to enjoin state utility rate orders if specified conditions are met, including most notably the availabili-

ty of a "plain, speedy and efficient remedy" in state court. Second, the Tax Injunction Act of 1937, now 28 U.S.C. § 1341, forbids federal injunctions against the collection of state taxes, provided only that "a plain, speedy and efficient remedy may be had in the courts of such state."

[c] Cf. *Bivens v. Six Unknown Named Agents of Federal Bureau of Narcotics,* page 395, supra. The "presumed availability of federal equitable relief" to which Justice Harlan referred (see page 399, supra) was based on a line of cases beginning with *Ex parte Young.*

Louisiana, 134 U.S. 1 (1890); Parden v. Terminal R. Co., 377 U.S. 184 (1964); Employees v. Department of Public Health and Welfare, 411 U.S. 279 (1973). It is also well established that even though a state is not named a party to the action, the suit may nonetheless be barred by the 11th amendment. In Ford Motor Co. v. Department of the Treasury, 323 U.S. 459, 464 (1945), the Court said:

> "[W]hen the action is in essence one for the recovery of money from the state, the state is the real, substantial party in interest and is entitled to invoke its sovereign immunity from suit even though individual officials are nominal defendants."

Thus the rule has evolved that a suit by private parties seeking to impose a liability which must be paid from public funds in the state treasury is barred by the 11th amendment.

The Court of Appeals in this case, while recognizing that the *Hans* line of cases permitted the state to raise the 11th amendment as a defense to suit by its own citizens, nevertheless concluded that the amendment did not bar the award of retroactive payments of the statutory benefits found to have been wrongfully withheld. The Court of Appeals held that the above-cited cases, when read in light of this Court's landmark decision in Ex parte Young, 209 U.S. 123 (1908), do not preclude the grant of such a monetary award in the nature of equitable restitution.

Petitioner [the present Director of the Illinois Department of Public Aid] concedes that *Ex parte Young,* supra, is no bar to that part of the District Court's judgment that prospectively enjoined petitioner's predecessors for failing to process applications within the time limits established by the federal regulations. Petitioner argues, however, that *Ex parte Young* does not extend so far as to permit a suit which seeks the award of an accrued monetary liability which must be met from the general revenues of a state, absent consent or waiver by the state of its 11th amendment immunity, and that therefore the award of retroactive benefits by the District Court was improper.

Ex parte Young was a watershed case in which this Court held that the 11th amendment did not bar an action in the federal courts seeking to enjoin the Attorney General of Minnesota from enforcing a statute claimed to violate the 14th amendment of the United States Constitution. This holding has permitted the Civil War amendments to the Constitution to serve as a sword, rather than merely as a shield, for those whom they were designed to protect. But the relief awarded in *Ex parte Young* was prospective only; the Attorney General of Minnesota was enjoined to conform his future conduct of that office to the requirement of the 14th amendment. Such relief is analogous to that awarded by the District Court in the prospective portion of its order under review in this case.

But the retroactive portion of the District Court's order here, which requires the payment of a very substantial amount of money which that court held should have been paid, but was not, stands on quite a different footing. These funds will obviously not be paid out of the pocket of petitioner Edelman. Addressing himself to a similar situation in Rothstein v. Wyman, 467 F.2d 226 (2d Cir. 1972), cert. denied 411 U.S. 921 (1973), Judge McGowan observed for the court:

"It is not pretended that these payments are to come from the personal resources of these appellants. Appellees expressly contemplate that they will, rather, involve substantial expenditures from the public funds of the state. . . .

"It is one thing to tell the Commissioner of Social Services that he must comply with the federal standards for the future if the state is to have the benefit of federal funds in the programs he administers. It is quite another thing to order the Commissioner to use state funds to make reparation for the past. The latter would appear to us to fall afoul of the 11th amendment if that basic constitutional provision is to be conceived of has having any present force."

We agree with Judge McGowan's observations. The funds to satisfy the award in this case must inevitably come from the general revenues of the state of Illinois, and thus the award resembles far more closely the monetary award against the state itself, *Ford Motor Co. v. Department of Treasury*, supra, than it does the prospective injunctive relief awarded in *Ex parte Young*. . . .[11]

As in most areas of the law, the difference between the type of relief barred by the 11th amendment and that permitted under *Ex parte Young* will not in many instances be that between day and night. The injunction issued in *Ex parte Young* was not totally without effect on the state's revenues, since the state law which the Attorney General was enjoined from enforcing provided substantial monetary penalties against railroads which did not conform to its provisions. Later cases from this Court have authorized equitable relief which has probably had greater impact on state treasuries than did that awarded in *Ex parte Young*. In Graham v. Richardson, 403 U.S. 365 (1971), Arizona and Pennsylvania welfare officials were prohibited from denying welfare benefits to otherwise qualified recipients who were aliens. In Goldberg v. Kelly, 397 U.S. 254 (1970), New York City welfare officials were enjoined from following New York state procedures which authorized the termination of benefits paid to welfare recipients without prior hearing. But the fiscal consequences to state treasuries in these

---

[11] It may be true, as stated by our Brother Douglas in dissent, that "[m]ost welfare decisions by federal courts have a financial impact on the states." But we cannot agree that such a financial impact is the same where a federal court applies *Ex parte Young* to grant prospective declaratory and injunctive relief, as opposed to an order of retroactive payments as was made in the instant case. It is not necessarily true that "[w]hether the decree is prospective only or requires payments for the weeks or months wrongfully skipped over by the state officials, the nature of the impact on the state treasury is precisely the same." This argument neglects the fact that where the state has a definable allocation to be used in the payment of public aid benefits, and pursues a certain course of action such as the processing of applications within certain time periods as did Illinois here, the subsequent ordering by a federal court of retroactive payments to correct delays in such processing will invariably mean there is less money available for payments for the continuing obligations of the public aid system. . . .

cases were the necessary result of compliance with decrees which by their terms were prospective in nature. Such officials, in order to shape their official conduct to the mandate of the Court's decrees, would more likely have to spend money from the state treasury than if they had been left free to pursue their previous course of conduct. Such an ancillary effect on the state treasury is a permissible and often an inevitable consequence of the principle announced in *Ex parte Young,* supra.

But that portion of the District Court's decree which petitioner challenges on 11th amendment grounds goes much further than any of the cases cited. It requires payment of state funds, not as a necessary consequence of compliance in the future with a substantive federal-question determination, but as a form of compensation to those whose applications were processed on the slower time schedule at a time when petitioner was under no court-imposed obligation to conform to a different standard. While the Court of Appeals described this retroactive award of monetary relief as a form of "equitable restitution," it is in practical effect indistinguishable in many aspects from an award of damages against the state. It will to a virtual certainty be paid from state funds, and not from the pockets of the individual state officials who were the defendants in the action. It is measured in terms of a monetary loss resulting from a past breach of a legal duty on the part of the defendant state officials.

Were we to uphold this portion of the District Court's decree, we would be obligated to overrule the Court's holding in *Ford Motor Co. v. Department of Treasury,* supra. There a taxpayer, who had, under protest, paid taxes to the state of Indiana, sought a refund of those taxes from the Indiana state officials who were charged with their collection. The taxpayer claimed that the tax had been imposed in violation of the United States Constitution. The term "equitable restitution" would seem even more applicable to the relief sought in that case, since the taxpayer had at one time had the money, and paid it over to the state pursuant to an allegedly unconstitutional tax exaction. Yet this Court had no hesitation in holding that the taxpayer's action was a suit against the state, and barred by the 11th amendment. We reach a similar conclusion with respect to the retroactive portion of the relief awarded by the District Court in this case. . . .

Three fairly recent District Court judgments requiring state directors of public aid to make the type of retroactive payments involved here have been summarily affirmed by this Court notwithstanding 11th amendment contentions made by state officers who were appealing from the District Court judgments. Shapiro v. Thompson, 394 U.S. 618 (1969), is the only instance in which the 11th amendment objection to such retroactive relief was actually presented to this Court in a case which was orally argued. The three-judge District Court in that case had ordered the retroactive payment of welfare benefits found by that court to have been unlawfully withheld because of residence requirements held violative of equal protection. This Court, while affirming the judgment, did not in its opinion refer to or substantively treat the

11th amendment argument. Nor, of course, did the summary dispositions of the three District Court cases contain any substantive discussion of this or any other issues raised by the parties.

This case, therefore, is the first opportunity the Court has taken to
fully explore and treat the 11th amendment aspects of such relief in a
written opinion. *Shapiro v. Thompson* and these three summary affirmances obviously are of precedential value in support of the contention
that the 11th amendment does not bar the relief awarded by the
District Court in this case. Equally obviously, they are not of the same
precedential value as would be an opinion of this Court treating the
question on the merits. Since we deal with a constitutional question,
we are less constrained by the principle of stare decisis than we are in
other areas of the law. Having now had an opportunity to more fully
consider the 11th amendment issue after briefing and argument, we
disapprove the 11th amendment holdings of those cases to the extent
that they are inconsistent with our holding today.

The Court of Appeals held in the alternative that even if the 11th
amendment be deemed a bar to the retroactive relief awarded respondent in this case, the state of Illinois had waived its 11th amendment
immunity and consented to the bringing of such a suit by participating
in the federal AABD program. The Court of Appeals relied upon our
holdings in Parden v. Terminal R. Co., 377 U.S. 184 (1964), and Petty v.
Tennessee-Missouri Bridge Comm'n, 359 U.S. 275 (1959), and on the
dissenting opinion of Judge Bright in Employees v. Department of
Public Health and Welfare, 452 F.2d 820, 827 (8th Cir. 1971). While
the holding in the latter case was ultimately affirmed by this Court in
411 U.S. 279 (1973), we do not think that the answer to the waiver
question turns on the distinction between *Parden,* supra, and *Employees,* supra. Both *Parden* and *Employees* involved a congressional enactment which by its terms authorized suit by designated plaintiffs against
a general class of defendants which literally included states or state
instrumentalities. Similarly, *Petty v. Tennessee-Missouri Bridge
Comm'n,* supra, involved congressional approval, pursuant to the compact clause, of a compact between Tennessee and Missouri, which
provided that each compacting state would have the power "to contract,
to sue, and be sued in its own name." The question of waiver or
consent under the 11th amendment was found in those cases to turn on
whether Congress had intended to abrogate the immunity in question,
and whether the state by its participation in the program authorized by
Congress had in effect consented to the abrogation of that immunity.

But in this case the threshold fact of congressional authorization to
sue a class of defendants which literally includes states is wholly
absent. Thus respondent is not only precluded from relying on this
Court's holding in *Employees,* but on this Court's holdings in *Parden*
and *Petty* as well.

The Court of Appeals held that as a matter of federal law Illinois
had "constructively consented" to this suit by participating in the
federal AABD program and agreeing to administer federal and state

funds in compliance with federal law. Constructive consent is not a doctrine commonly associated with the surrender of constitutional rights, and we see no place for it here. In deciding whether a state has waived its constitutional protection under the 11th amendment, we will find waiver only where stated "by the most express language or by such overwhelming implications from the text as [will] leave no room for any other reasonable construction." Murray v. Wilson Distilling Co., 213 U.S. 151, 171 (1909). We see no reason to retreat from the Court's statement in Great Northern Life Ins. Co. v. Read, 322 U.S. 47, 54 (1944) (footnote omitted):

> "[W]hen we are dealing with the sovereign exemption from judicial interference in the vital field of financial administration a clear declaration of the state's intention to submit its fiscal problems to other courts than those of its own creation must be found."

The mere fact that a state participates in a program through which the federal government provides assistance for the operation by the state of a system of public aid is not sufficient to establish consent on the part of the state to be sued in the federal courts. And while this Court has, in cases such as J.I. Case Co. v. Borak, 377 U.S. 426 (1964), authorized suits by one private party against another in order to effectuate a statutory purpose, it has never done so in the context of the 11th amendment and a state defendant. Since *Employees,* supra, where Congress had expressly authorized suits against a general class of defendants and the only thing left to implication was whether the described class of defendants included states, was decided adversely to the putative plaintiffs on the waiver question, surely this respondent must also fail on that issue. The only language in the Social Security Act which purported to provide a federal sanction against a state which did not comply with federal requirements for the distribution of federal monies was found in former 42 U.S.C. § 1384 (now replaced by substantially similar provisions in 42 U.S.C. § 804), which provided for termination of future allocations of federal funds when a participating state failed to conform with federal law. This provision by its terms did not authorize suit against anyone, and standing alone, fell far short of a waiver by a participating state of its 11th amendment immunity.

Our Brother Marshall argues in dissent, and the Court of Appeals held, that although the Social Security Act itself does not create a private cause of action, the cause of action created by 42 U.S.C. § 1983, coupled with the enactment of the AABD program, and the issuance by HEW of regulations which require the states to make corrective payments after successful "fair hearings" and provide for federal matching funds to satisfy federal court orders of retroactive payments, indicate that Congress intended a cause of action for public aid recipients such as respondent. It is, of course, true that Rosado v. Wyman, 397 U.S. 397 (1970), held that suits in federal court under § 1983 are proper to secure compliance with the provisions of the Social Security Act on the part of participating states. But it has not heretofore been suggested that § 1983 was intended to create a waiver of a state's 11th amendment immunity merely because an action could be brought under that section against state officers, rather than against the state itself. Though a § 1983 action may be instituted by public aid recipients such as respondent, a federal court's remedial power, consistent with the 11th amendment, is necessarily limited to prospective injunctive relief, *Ex parte Young,* supra, and may not include a retroactive award which requires the payment of funds from the state treasury, *Ford Motor Co. v. Department of Treasury,* supra.

Respondent urges that since the various Illinois officials sued in the District Court failed to raise the 11th amendment as a defense to the relief sought by respondent, petitioner is therefore barred from raising the 11th amendment defense in the Court of Appeals or in this Court. The Court of Appeals apparently felt that the defense was properly presented, and dealt with it on the merits. We approve of this resolution, since it has been well settled since the decision in *Ford Motor Co. v. Department of Treasury,* supra, that the 11th amendment defense sufficiently partakes of the nature of a jurisdictional bar so that it need not be raised in the trial court:

> "[The Attorney General of Indiana] appeared in the federal District Court and the Circuit Court of Appeals and defended the suit on the merits. The objection to petitioner's suit as a violation of the 11th amendment was first made and argued by Indiana in this Court. This was in time, however. The 11th amendment declares a policy and sets forth an explicit limitation on federal judicial power of such compelling force that this Court will consider the issue arising under this amendment in this case even though urged for the first time in this Court."

For the foregoing reasons we decide that the Court of Appeals was wrong in holding that the 11th amendment did not constitute a bar to that portion of the District Court decree which ordered retroactive payment of benefits found to have been wrongfully withheld. The judgment of the Court of Appeals is therefore reversed and the cause remanded for further proceedings consistent with this opinion.

So ordered.

MR. JUSTICE DOUGLAS, dissenting.

Congress provided in 42 U.S.C. § 1983 that:

> "Every person who, under color of any statute, ordinance, regulation, custom, or usage, of any state or territory, subjects, or causes to be subjected, any citizen of the United States or other person within the jurisdiction thereof to the deprivation of any rights, privileges, or immunities secured by the Constitution and laws, shall be liable to the party injured in an action at law, suit in equity, or other proper proceeding for redress."

In this class action respondent sought to enforce against state aid officials of Illinois provisions of the Social Security Act, 42 U.S.C. §§ 1381–1385, known as the Aid to the Aged, Blind, or Disabled (AABD) program. The complaint alleges violations of the equal protection clause of the 14th amendment and also violations of the Social Security Act. Hence § 1983 is satisfied in haec verba, for a deprivation of "rights" which are "secured by the Constitution and laws" is alleged. The Court of Appeals, though ruling that the alleged constitutional violations had not occurred, sustained federal jurisdiction because federal "rights" were violated. The main issue tendered us is whether that ruling of the Court of Appeals is consistent with the 11th amendment. . . .

As the complaint in the instant case alleges violations by officials of Illinois of the equal protection clause of the 14th amendment, it seems that the case is governed by *Ex parte Young* so far as injunctive relief is concerned. The main thrust of the argument is that the instant case asks for relief which if granted would affect the treasury of the state.

Most welfare decisions by federal courts have a financial impact on the states. Under the existing federal state cooperative system, a state desiring to participate, submits a "state plan" to HEW for approval; once HEW approves the plan the state is locked into the cooperative scheme until it withdraws, all as described in King v. Smith, 392 U.S. 309, 316 (1968). The welfare cases coming here have involved ultimately the financial responsibility of the state to beneficiaries claiming they were deprived of federal rights. *King v. Smith* required payment to children even though their mother was cohabitating with a man who could not pass muster as a "parent." Rosado v. Wyman, 397 U.S. 397 (1970), held that under this state-federal cooperative program a state could not reduce its standard of need in conflict with the federal standard. It is true that *Rosado* did not involve retroactive payments as are involved here. But the distinction is not relevant or material because the result in every welfare case coming here is to increase or reduce the financial responsibility of the participating state. In no case when the responsibility of the state is increased to meet the lawful demand of the beneficiary, is there any levy on state funds. Whether the decree is prospective only or requires payments for the weeks or months wrongfully skipped over by the state officials, the nature of the impact on the state treasury is precisely the same.

We have granted relief in other welfare cases which included retroactive assistance benefits or payments. [Here Justice Douglas discussed *Shapiro v. Thompson* and the three summary affirmances mentioned in the majority opinion.]

It is said however, that the 11th amendment is concerned, not with immunity of states from suit, but with the jurisdiction of the federal courts to entertain the suit. The 11th amendment does not speak of "jurisdiction"; it withholds the "judicial power" of federal courts "to any suit in law or equity . . . against one of the United States . . . ." If that "judicial power," or "jurisdiction" if one prefers that concept, may not be exercised even in "any suit in . . . equity" then *Ex parte Young* should be overruled. But there is none eager to take the step.

Where a state has consented to join a federal-state cooperative project, it is realistic to conclude that the state has agreed to assume its obligations under that legislation. There is nothing in the 11th amendment to suggest a difference between suits at law and suits in equity, for it treats the two without distinction. If common sense has any role to play in constitutional adjudication, once there is a waiver of immunity it must be true that it is complete so far as effective operation of the state-federal joint welfare program is concerned. . . .

We have not always been unanimous in concluding when a state has waived its immunity. In Parden v. Terminal R. Co., 377 U.S. 184 (1964), where Alabama was sued by some of its citizens for injuries suffered in the interstate operation of an Alabama railroad, the state defended on the grounds of the 11th amendment. The Court held that Alabama was liable as a carrier under the Federal Employers' Liability Act, saying:

> "Our conclusion is simply that Alabama, when it began operation of an interstate railroad approximately 20 years after enactment of the FELA, necessarily consented to such suit as was authorized by that act."

The Court added:

> "Our conclusion that this suit may be maintained is in accord with the common sense of this nation's federalism. A state's immunity from suit by an individual without its consent has been fully recognized by the 11th amendment and by subsequent decisions of this Court. But when a state leaves the sphere that is exclusively its own and enters into activities subject to congressional regulation, it subjects itself to that regulation as fully as if it were a private person or corporation."

As the Court of Appeals in the instant case concluded, Illinois by entering into the joint federal-state welfare plan just as surely "[left] the sphere that is exclusively its own."

It is argued that participation in the program of federal financial assistance is not sufficient to establish consent on the part of the state to be sued in federal courts. But it is not merely participation which supports a finding of 11th amendment waiver, but participation in light of the existing state of the law as exhibited in such decisions as Shapiro v. Thompson, 394 U.S. 618 (1969), which affirmed judgments ordering retroactive payment of benefits. Today's holding that the 11th amendment forbids court-ordered retroactive payments, as the Court recognizes, necessitates an express overruling of several of our recent decisions. But it was against the background of those decisions that Illinois continued its participation in the federal program, and it can hardly be claimed that such participation was in ignorance of the possibility of court-ordered retroactive payments. The decision to participate against the background of precedent can only be viewed as a waiver of immunity from such judgments.

I would affirm the judgment of the Court of Appeals.

MR. JUSTICE BRENNAN, dissenting.

This suit is brought by Illinois citizens against Illinois officials. In that circumstance, Illinois may not invoke the 11th amendment, since that amendment bars only federal court suits against states by citizens of other states. Rather, the question is whether Illinois may avail itself of the nonconstitutional but ancient doctrine of sovereign immunity as a bar to respondent's claim for retroactive AABD payments. In my view Illinois may not assert sovereign immunity for the reason I expressed in dissent in Employees v. Department of Public Health and Welfare, 411 U.S. 279, 298 (1973): the states surrendered that immunity in Hamilton's words, "in the plan of the Convention," that formed the Union, at least insofar as the states granted Congress specifically enumerated powers. Congressional authority to enact the Social Security Act, of which AABD is a part, is to be found in art. I, § 8, cl. 1, one of the enumerated powers granted Congress by the states in the Constitution. I remain of the opinion that "because of its surrender, no immunity exists that can be the subject of a congressional declaration or a voluntary waiver," and thus have no occasion to inquire whether or not Congress authorized an action for AABD retroactive benefits, or whether or not Illinois voluntarily waived the immunity by its continued participation in the program against the background of precedents which sustained judgments ordering retroactive payments.

I would affirm the judgment of the Court of Appeals.

MR. JUSTICE MARSHALL, with whom MR. JUSTICE BLACKMUN joins, dissenting.

The Social Security Act's categorical assistance programs, including the Aid to the Aged, Blind, or Disabled (AABD) program involved here, are fundamentally different from most federal legislation. Unlike the Fair Labor Standards Act involved in last term's decision in Employees v. Department of Public Health and Welfare, 411 U.S. 279 (1973), or the Federal Employers' Liability Act at issue in Parden v. Terminal R. Co., 377 U.S. 184 (1964), the Social Security Act does not impose federal standards and liability upon all who engage in certain regulated activities, including often unwilling state agencies. Instead, the act seeks to induce state participation in the federal welfare programs by offering federal matching funds in exchange for the state's voluntary assumption of the act's requirements. I find this basic distinction crucial: it leads me to conclude that by participation in the programs, the states waive whatever immunity they might otherwise have from federal court orders requiring retroactive payment of welfare benefits.[1] . . .

In agreeing to comply with the requirements of the Social Security Act and HEW regulations, I believe that Illinois has also agreed to subject itself to suit in the federal courts to enforce these obligations. I

[1] In view of my conclusion on this issue, I find it unnecessary to consider whether the Court correctly treats this suit as one against the state rather than as a suit against a state officer permissible under the rationale of Ex parte Young, 209 U.S. 123 (1908).

recognize, of course, that the Social Security Act does not itself provide for a cause of action to enforce its obligations. As the Court points out, the only sanction expressly provided in the act for a participating state's failure to comply with federal requirements is the cutoff of federal funding by the Secretary of HEW.

But a cause of action is clearly provided by 42 U.S.C. § 1983, which in terms authorizes suits to redress deprivations of rights secured by the "laws" of the United States. And we have already rejected the argument that Congress intended the funding cutoff to be the sole remedy for noncompliance with federal requirements. In Rosado v. Wyman, 397 U.S. 397, 420–23 (1970), we held that suits in federal court were proper to enforce the provisions of the Social Security Act against participating states. . . .

I believe that Congress also intended the full panoply of traditional judicial remedies to be available to the federal courts in these § 1983 suits. There is surely no indication of any congressional intent to restrict the courts' equitable jurisdiction. . . . In particular I am firmly convinced that Congress intended the restitution of wrongfully withheld assistance payments to be a remedy available to the federal courts in these suits. Benefits under the categorical assistance programs "are a matter of statutory entitlement for persons qualified to receive them." Goldberg v. Kelly, 397 U.S. 254, 262 (1970). Retroactive payment of benefits secures for recipients this entitlement which was withheld in violation of federal law. Equally important, the courts' power to order retroactive payments is an essential remedy to insure future state compliance with federal requirements. No other remedy can effectively deter states from the strong temptation to cut welfare budgets by circumventing the stringent requirements of federal law. The funding cutoff is a drastic sanction, one which HEW has proved unwilling or unable to employ to compel strict compliance with the act and regulations. Moreover, the cutoff operates only prospectively; it in no way deters the states from even a flagrant violation of the act's requirements for as long as HEW does not discover the violation and threaten to take such action. . . .

Illinois chose to participate in the AABD program with its eyes wide open. Drawn by the lure of federal funds, it voluntarily obligated itself to comply with the Social Security Act and HEW regulations, with full knowledge that Congress had authorized assistance recipients to go into federal court to enforce these obligations and to recover benefits wrongfully denied. Any doubts on this score must surely have been removed by our decisions in *Rosado v. Wyman*, supra, and Shapiro v. Thompson, 394 U.S. 618 (1969), where we affirmed a district court retroactive payment order. I cannot avoid the conclusion that, by virtue of its knowing and voluntary decision to nevertheless participate in the program, the state necessarily consented to subject itself to these suits. I have no quarrel with the Court's view that the waiver of constitutional rights should not lightly be inferred. But I simply cannot believe that the state could have entered into this essentially contractual agreement with the federal government without recognizing that it was subjecting itself to the full scope of the § 1983 remedy provided by Congress to enforce the terms of the agreement.

Of course, § 1983 suits are nominally brought against state officers, rather than the state itself, and do not ordinarily raise 11th amendment problems in view of this Court's decision in Ex parte Young, 209 U.S. 123 (1908). But to the extent that the relief authorized by Congress in an action under § 1983 may be open to 11th amendment objections, these objections are waived when the state agrees to comply with federal requirements enforceable in such an action. I do not find persuasive the Court's reliance in this case on the fact that "congressional authorization to sue a class of defendants which literally includes states" is absent. While true, this fact is irrelevant here, for this is simply not a case "literally" against the state. While the Court successfully knocks down the strawman it has thus set up, it never comes to grips with the undeniable fact that Congress has "literally" authorized this suit within the terms of § 1983. Since there is every reason to believe that Congress intended the full panoply of judicial remedies to be available in § 1983 equitable actions to enforce the Social Security Act, I think the conclusion is inescapable that Congress authorized and the state consented to § 1983 actions in which the relief might otherwise be questioned on 11th amendment grounds. . . .

Congress undoubtedly has the power to insist upon a waiver of sovereign immunity as a condition of [the state's] consent to such a federal-state agreement. Since I am satisfied that Congress has in fact done so here, at least to the extent that the federal courts may do "complete rather than truncated justice," in § 1983 actions authorized by Congress against state welfare authorities, I respectfully dissent.

NOTES ON STATE IMMUNITY AGAINST AWARD OF DAMAGES

1. Questions and Comments on *Edelman v. Jordan.* *Edelman* accepts *Ex parte Young* but refuses to extend it to an action for wrongfully withheld welfare benefits. Why? Is the distinction supported by any plausible interpretation of the original meaning of the 11th amendment? Is it explained by the reasoning of *Ex parte Young*? Or is *Edelman* based on perceived policy differences between prospective and retrospective relief against a state? If so, what are they?

2. *Milliken v. Bradley (II)*. Even the *Edelman* majority admitted that "the difference between the type of relief barred by the 11th amendment and that permitted under *Ex parte Young* will not in many instances be that between day and night." Just how shadowy that line can become is suggested in Milliken v. Bradley (II), 433 U.S. 267 (1977), where the Court upheld a school desegregation order requiring the expenditure of state (as well as local) funds for several educational components of the desegregation decree, including remedial reading programs. The Court disposed of the state's 11th amendment objection as follows:

"The decree to share the future costs of educational components in this case fits squarely within the prospective-compliance exception reaffirmed by *Edelman*. That exception, which had its genesis in *Ex parte Young,* permits federal courts to enjoin state officials to conform their conduct to requirements of federal law, notwithstanding a direct and substantial impact on the state treasury. The order challenged here does no more than that. The decree requires state officials, held responsible for unconstitutional conduct, in findings which are not challenged, to eliminate a de jure segregated school system. . . . The educational components, which the District Court ordered into effect *prospectively,* are plainly designed to wipe out continuing conditions of inequality produced by the inherently unequal dual school system long maintained by Detroit. . . . That the programs are also 'compensatory' in nature does not change the fact that they are part of a plan that operates *prospectively* to bring about the delayed benefits of a unitary school system. We therefore hold that such prospective relief is not barred by the 11th amendment."

Could the award of past payments at issue in *Edelman* be fairly described as "part of a plan that operates *prospectively* to bring about the delayed benefits of" the federally required payment schedule? Is there a meaningful distinction between the two cases?[a]

3. *Quern v. Jordan.* In the aftermath of *Edelman v. Jordan,* attempts were made to secure reimbursement for past welfare benefits by resort to state remedies. To that end, the District Court ordered the state authorities to send to every member of the *Edelman* class a notice that "you were denied public assistance to which you were entitled in the amount of $_____," together with a form requesting a hearing on the denial of benefits. The Court of Appeals barred this procedure on the ground that it implicitly decided that state funds should be used to satisfy such claims. Jordan v. Trainor, 563 F.2d 873 (7th Cir. 1977). The court suggested, however, that a mere explanatory notice advising applicants of the existence of a state administrative procedure would be permissible. The District Court thereupon ordered that such a notice be mailed.

This requirement came to the Supreme Court in Quern v. Jordan, 440 U.S. 332 (1979). Speaking through Justice Rehnquist, the Court found that this notice of the availability of state procedures was "properly viewed as ancillary to the prospective relief already ordered by the court." The fact that the notice might encourage applications for retroactive benefits did not matter, as the availability of such

---

a For other cases in which the *Edelman* line of prospective and retrospective relief proved troublesome to the Court, see Cory v. White, 457 U.S. 85 (1982), and Papasan v. Allain, 478 U.S. 265 (1986).

benefits would rest "entirely with the state, its agencies, courts, and legislature, not with the federal court."

4. *Green v. Mansour.* A similar question arose in Green v. Mansour, 474 U.S. 64 (1985). Two class actions claimed that Michigan's calculation of benefits under the Aid to Families with Dependent Children legislation violated federal law. In one case, Congress amended the federal statute to validate the state procedure. In the other, the state changed its procedure to conform to federal law. The District Court thereupon dismissed the suits as moot, despite the plaintiffs' continuing insistence on declaratory and "notice" relief of the sort approved in *Quern v. Jordan.*

The Supreme Court affirmed the dismissals. Speaking through Justice Rehnquist, the Court held that "[b]ecause 'notice relief' is not the type of remedy designed to prevent ongoing violations of federal law, the 11th amendment limitation on the art. III power of federal courts prevents them from ordering it as an independent form of relief." Instead, notice could be ordered only when ancillary to some other form of relief. Here there was no other relief available:

> "There is no claimed continuing violation of federal law, and therefore no occasion to issue an injunction. . . . There is a dispute about the lawfulness of respondent's past actions, but the 11th amendment would prohibit the award of money damages or restitution if that dispute were resolved in favor of petitioners. We think that the award of a declaratory judgment in this situation would be useful in resolving the dispute over the past lawfulness of respondent's action only if it might be offered in state court proceedings as res judicata on the issue of liability, leaving to the state courts only a form of accounting proceeding whereby damages or restitution would be computed. But the issuance of a declaratory judgment in these circumstances would have much the same effect as a full-fledged award of damages or restitution by the federal court, the latter kinds of relief being of course prohibited by the 11th amendment. [A] declaratory judgment is not available when the result would be a partial 'end run' around our decision in *Edelman v. Jordan.* "

Four Justices dissented.

5. *Nevada v. Hall.* Consider, in connection with *Edelman* and its progeny, the decision in Nevada v. Hall, 440 U.S. 410 (1979). California residents were injured when their car was struck by a vehicle being driven on official business by an employee of the state of Nevada. The accident occurred in California. The plaintiffs sued in a California state court, naming as defendants the Nevada employee's estate (he was killed in the accident) and the state. Personal jurisdiction was acquired over the state based on provisions of the California statute authorizing service of process on nonresident motorists. The California courts upheld a jury verdict against Nevada for more than $1 million, notwithstanding a Nevada statute limiting recoveries

against the state to $25,000. The United States Supreme Court affirmed.

Speaking for the Court, Justice Stevens denied that California was bound by federal law to respect Nevada's sovereign immunity. The 11th amendment applied only in federal courts, and neither the full faith and credit clause nor the overall scheme of the Constitution prohibited California from following its own law.

Three justices dissented. Justice Blackmun, joined by Chief Justice Burger and by Justice Rehnquist, said that he would find "a constitutional doctrine of interstate sovereign immunity" implied as an essential component of the federal system. Justice Rehnquist, joined by the Chief Justice wrote separately, adding that the result reached by the majority "destroys the framers' careful allocation of responsibility among the state and federal judiciaries, and makes nonsense of the effort embodied in the 11th amendment to preserve the doctrine of sovereign immunity."

Is *Nevada v. Hall* consistent with *Edelman*? Can it be reconciled with *Hans*? Was it decided correctly?

6. 11th Amendment Immunity for Local Governments. On the same day that it handed down *Hans v. Louisiana*, the Supreme Court announced in Lincoln County v. Luning, 133 U.S. 529 (1890), that the 11th amendment did not protect a county from suit in federal court. Subsequent cases have extended this holding to other units of local government. See, e.g., Workman v. New York, 179 U.S. 552 (1900) (cities); Mount Healthy City School District v. Doyle, 429 U.S. 274 (1977) (school boards).

Today, the disparity between states and their political subdivisions may well seem anomalous, but it seems to have some foundation in history. At the time the 11th amendment was adopted, municipal corporations were analogized to private corporations and thus were deemed to lack the attributes of sovereignty possessed by states. By the time that the municipal corporation came to be seen as a distinct legal form exercising governmental powers delegated by the state, the amenability of local governments to suit in federal court had long been established. See generally Fletcher, A Historical Interpretation of the 11th Amendment: A Narrow Construction of an Affirmative Grant of Jurisdiction Rather than a Prohibition Against Jurisdiction, 35 Stan. L. Rev. 1033, 1044–45, 1099–1107 (1983).

In any event, the distinction between states and their political subdivisions was in most contexts inconsequential. Prospective relief could be had against either by resort to the fiction of *Ex parte Young*. Award of damages against a state was barred by the 11th amendment; in most instances, award of damages against a unit of local government was barred by the assumed unavailability of a cause of action authorizing such relief. All this changed in 1978, when the Supreme Court held, contrary to its earlier view, that the "person" against whom the cause of action created by 42 U.S.C. § 1983 may be asserted includes a municipal corporation. See Monell v. Department of Social Services,

436 U.S. 658 (1976), which is extensively treated at pages 927–41, infra. Today, therefore, the distinction matters a great deal. States and state agencies are protected against damage actions in federal court under the terms of *Edelman v. Jordan*. Local governments, by contrast, have no 11th amendment immunity and may be held liable in damages under § 1983 for violations of federal law.

Although this line is clear in principle, its application to particular situations is sometimes not obvious. The reason is that a unit of local government, although not in itself entitled to claim 11th amendment immunity, may be shielded by state sovereign immunity if an award of damages against it would operate directly against the state treasury. Thus, for example, in *Edelman v. Jordan,* the action was actually brought against both state and local welfare officials. Because the locality was merely disbursing state welfare funds according to state policy, both levels of government were deemed to be protected. In contrast, *Milliken v. Bradley (II)* also involved both state and local defendants. In this case, however, the locality was guilty of an independent constitutional violation, and no 11th amendment immunity could be claimed.

SECTION 2: CONSENT AND CONGRESSIONAL ABROGATION

INTRODUCTORY NOTES ON STATE CONSENT TO SUIT AND CONGRESSIONAL ABROGATION OF STATE SOVEREIGN IMMUNITY

1. **Jurisdiction, Immunity, and Consent.** As the *Edelman* Court noted, the 11th amendment issue in that case was raised for the first time on appeal. The Court of Appeals nevertheless considered the issue, and the Supreme Court approved on the ground that "the 11th amendment defense sufficiently partakes of the nature of a jurisdictional bar so that it need not be raised in the trial court." The basis for this view is apparently an analogy to subject matter jurisdiction, which can be raised by any party or by the court at any time. It is also well settled, however, that a state can waive its 11th amendment immunity and consent to suit in federal court.[a] Consent (although apparently revocable during the course of the litigation) may be given by the state's legal representative or by statute. Such statutes, however, will be narrowly construed, and the state is free to consent to suit only in its own courts.[b] Obviously, this rule departs from the model of subject

---

[a] Hans v. Louisiana, 134 U.S. 1, 17 (1890) ("Undoubtedly a state may be sued by its own consent"); Clark v. Barnard, 108 U.S. 436 (1883).

[b] See, e.g., Kennecott Copper Corp. v. State Tax Comm'n, 327 U.S. 573 (1946);

Ford Motor Co. v. Department of Treasury, 323 U.S. 459 (1945). See also page 845, footnote c, infra, and Pennhurst State School and Hospital v. Halderman, 465 U.S. 89, 102 n.12 (1984), page 861, infra.

matter jurisdiction, which consenting parties are powerless to confer, but is consistent with the tradition of sovereign immunity, which the sovereign may choose to waive.

2. Congressional Abrogation of State Sovereign Immunity. The remaining cases in this chapter concern the power of Congress to strip the state of sovereign immunity and the manner in which that power must be exercised. Preliminarily, two cases must be briefly examined.

(i) *Parden v. Terminal Ry.* Parden v. Terminal Ry., 377 U.S. 184 (1964), involved an FELA action against a state-owned railway. Writing for the Court, Justice Brennan found the 11th amendment "not in terms applicable," since suit was brought by the state's own citizens, but recognized nevertheless that "an unconsenting state is immune from federal-court suits brought by its own citizens," citing *Hans.* The Court found, in any event, that the FELA subjected the state to suit on the same terms as any other railroad in interstate commerce. Brennan advanced two seemingly independent rationales in support of this conclusion.

First, he said, "the states surrendered a portion of their sovereignty when they granted Congress the power to regulate commerce":

"By empowering Congress to regulate commerce, . . . the states necessarily surrendered any portion of their sovereignty that would stand in the way of such regulation. Since imposition of the FELA right of action upon interstate railroads is within the congressional regulatory power, it must follow that application of the act to such a railroad cannot be precluded by sovereign immunity."

Second, Brennan noted that Alabama had begun operation of the railroad some 20 years after the FELA was enacted and concluded that the state had thereby consented to suit:

"Congress conditioned the right to operate a railroad in interstate commerce upon amenability to suit in federal court as provided by the act; by thereafter operating a railroad in interstate commerce, Alabama must be taken to have accepted that condition and thus to have consented to suit."

Justice White, joined by Justices Douglas, Harlan, and Stewart, dissented. White agreed that "it is within the power of Congress to condition a state's permit to engage in the interstate transportation business on a waiver of the state's sovereign immunity from suits arising out of such business," but insisted that such a design must be clearly stated:

"A decent respect for the normally preferred position of constitutional rights dictates that if Congress decides to exercise its power to condition privileges within its control on the forfeiture of constitutional rights its intention to do so should appear with unmistakable clarity."

Since the FELA contained no express language on point, the dissenters voted to uphold the claim of immunity.

(ii) *Employees v. Department of Health and Welfare.* The implications of *Parden* were tested in Employees v. Department of Public Health and Welfare, 411 U.S. 279 (1973), a suit brought by state employees for overtime pay, liquidated damages, and attorneys fees under the Fair Labor Standards Act (FLSA). As originally enacted, that statute did not cover government employees, but in 1966 it was amended expressly to extend its wage and hour provisions to specified "employees of a state, or a political subdivision thereof."

Writing for the Court, Justice Douglas found that, although Congress intended that the act apply to the states, it did not intend to subject the states to private suits in federal court. Enforcement against states would be limited to actions brought by the Secretary of Labor. *Parden* was distinguished because it involved proprietary rather than governmental activity—a "rather isolated state activity," engaged in "for profit" in an area "where private persons and corporations normally ran the enterprise."

Justice Brennan dissented. He argued that *Parden* was indistinguishable and that Congress had in fact intended to make states suable in federal court under the FLSA. Brennan then embarked on an extended review of the 11th amendment in terms that are summarized in his dissent in *Edelman* and that later evolved to the views expressed in his dissents in Atascadero State Hospital v. Scanlon, 473 U.S. 234, 247 (1985), and Welch v. State Dept. of Highways and Public Transportation, ___ U.S. ___, ___ (1987).[c]

FITZPATRICK v. BITZER
Supreme Court of the United States, 1976.
427 U.S. 445.

MR. JUSTICE REHNQUIST delivered the opinion of the Court.

In the 1972 amendment to title VII of the Civil Rights Act of 1964, Congress, acting under § 5 of the 14th amendment, authorized federal courts to award money damages in favor of a private individual against a state government found to have subjected that person to employment discrimination on the basis of "race, color, religion, sex, or national origin." The principal question presented by these cases is whether, as against the shield of sovereign immunity afforded the state by the 11th amendment, Edelman v. Jordan, 415 U.S. 651 (1974), Congress has the power to authorize federal courts to enter such an award against the

[c] Still another interpretation of the 11th amendment was advanced in a concurrence by Justice Marshall. Marshall argued that a constitutional doctrine of state sovereign immunity prevented Congress from making states suable by private parties in *federal* court, but that Congress could compel a state to answer in *state* court for violations of federal rights. This suggestion has apparently been superseded by Justice Marshall's later endorsement of the "diversity interpretation," as articulated by Justice Brennan in his *Atascadero State Hospital* (see page 815, supra) and *Welch* (see page 852, infra) dissents.

state as a means of enforcing the substantive guarantees of the 14th amendment. The Court of Appeals for the Second Circuit held that the effect of our decision in *Edelman* was to foreclose Congress' power. We granted certiorari to resolve this important constitutional question. We reverse.

I

Petitioners sued in the United States District Court for the District of Connecticut on behalf of all present and retired male employees of the state of Connecticut. Their amended complaint asserted, inter alia, that certain provisions in the state's statutory retirement benefit plan discriminated against them because of their sex, and therefore contravened title VII of the 1964 act, as amended. Title VII, which originally did not include state and local governments, had in the interim been amended to bring the states within its purview.

The District Court held that the Connecticut State Employees Retirement Act violated title VII's prohibition against sex-based employment discrimination. It entered prospective injunctive relief in petitioners' favor against respondent state officials. Petitioners also sought an award of retroactive retirement benefits as compensation for losses caused by the state's discrimination, as well as "a reasonable attorney's fee as part of the costs." But the District Court held that both would constitute recovery of money damages from the state's treasury, and were therefore precluded by the 11th amendment and by this Court's decision in *Edelman v. Jordan,* supra.

On petitioners' appeal,[7] the Court of Appeals affirmed in part and reversed in part. It agreed with the District Court that the action, "insofar as it seeks damages, is in essence against the state and as such is subject to the 11th amendment." The Court of Appeals also found that under the 1972 amendments to title VII, "Congress intended to authorize a private suit for backpay by state employees against the state." Notwithstanding this statutory authority, the Court of Appeals affirmed the District Court and held that under *Edelman* a "private federal action for retroactive damages" is not a "constitutionally permissible method of enforcing 14th amendment rights." It reversed the District Court and remanded as to attorneys' fees, however, reasoning that such an award would have only an "ancillary effect" on the state treasury of the kind permitted under *Edelman* . . . .

II

In *Edelman* this Court held that monetary relief awarded by the District Court to welfare plaintiffs, by reason of wrongful denial of benefits which had occurred previous to the entry of the District Court's determination of their wrongfulness, violated the 11th amendment. Such an award was found to be indistinguishable from a monetary award against the state itself which had been prohibited in Ford Motor

---

[7] Respondent state officials did not appeal from the District Court's finding of a title VII violation and the entry of prospective injunctive relief.

Co. v. Department of Treasury, 323 U.S. 459, 464 (1945). It was therefore controlled by that case rather than by Ex parte Young, 209 U.S. 123 (1908), which permitted suits against state officials to obtain prospective relief against violations of the 14th amendment.

Edelman went on to hold that the plaintiffs in that case could not avail themselves of the doctrine of waiver expounded in cases such as Parden v. Terminal R. Co., 377 U.S. 184 (1964), and Employees v. Missouri Public Health Dept., 411 U.S. 279 (1973), because the necessary predicate for that doctrine was congressional intent to abrogate the immunity conferred by the 11th amendment. We concluded that none of the statutes relied upon by plaintiffs in *Edelman* contained any authorization by Congress to join a state as defendant. The Civil Rights Act of 1871, 42 U.S.C. § 1983, had been held in Monroe v. Pape, 365 U.S. 167, 187–91 (1961), to exclude cities and other municipal corporations from its ambit; that being the case, it could not have been intended to include states as parties defendant. The provisions of the Social Security Act relied upon by plaintiffs were held by their terms not to "authorize suit against anyone," and they, too, were incapable of supplying the predicate for a claim of waiver on the part of the state.

All parties in the instant litigation agree with the Court of Appeals that the suit for retroactive benefits by the petitioners is in fact indistinguishable from that sought to be maintained in *Edelman,* since what is sought here is a damages award payable to a private party from the state treasury.

Our analysis begins where *Edelman* ended, for in this title VII case the "threshold fact of congressional authorization," to sue the state as employer is clearly present. This is, of course, the prerequisite found present in *Parden* and wanting in *Employees.* We are aware of the factual differences between the type of state activity involved in *Parden* and that involved in the present case, but we do not think that difference is material for our purposes. The congressional authorization involved in *Parden* was based on the power of Congress under the commerce clause; here, however, the 11th amendment defense is asserted in the context of legislation passed pursuant to Congress' authority under § 5 of the 14th amendment.

As ratified by the states after the Civil War, that amendment quite clearly contemplates limitations on their authority. In relevant part, it provides:

> "Section 1. . . . No State shall make or enforce any law which shall abridge the privileges or immunities of citizens of the United States; nor shall any State deprive any person of life, liberty, or property, without due process of law; nor deny to any person within its jurisdiction the equal protection of the laws. . . .

> "Section 5. The Congress shall have power to enforce, by appropriate legislation, the provisions of this article."

The substantive provisions are by express terms directed at the states. Impressed upon them by those provisions are duties with respect to

their treatment of private individuals. Standing behind the imperatives is Congress' power to "enforce" them "by appropriate legislation."

The impact of the 14th amendment upon the relationship between
the federal government and the states, and the reach of congressional
power under § 5, were examined at length by this Court in Ex parte
Virginia, 100 U.S. 339 (1880). A state judge had been arrested and
indicted under a federal criminal statute prohibiting the exclusion on
the basis of race of any citizen from service as a juror in a state court.
The judge claimed that the statute was beyond Congress' power to
enact under either the 13th or the 14th amendment. The Court first
observed that these amendments "were intended to be, what they really
are, limitations of the power of the states and enlargements of the
power of Congress." It then addressed the relationship between the
language of § 5 and the substantive provisions of the 14th amendment:

> "The prohibitions of the 14th amendment are directed to the
> states, and they are to a degree restrictions of state power. It
> is these which Congress is empowered to enforce, and to
> enforce against state action, however put forth, whether that
> action be executive, legislative, or judicial. Such enforcement
> is no invasion of state sovereignty. No law can be, which the
> people of the states have, by the Constitution of the United
> States, empowered Congress to enact. . . . It is said that the
> selection of jurors for her courts and the administration of her
> laws belong to each state; that they are her rights. This is
> true in the general. But in exercising her rights, a state
> cannot disregard the limitations which the federal Constitution
> has applied to her power. Her rights do not reach to that
> extent. Nor can she deny to the general government the right
> to exercise all its granted powers, though they may interfere
> with the full enjoyment of rights she would have if those
> powers had not been thus granted. Indeed, every addition of
> power to the general government involves a corresponding
> diminution of the governmental powers of the state. It is
> carved out of them. . . ."

Ex parte Virginia's early recognition of this shift in the federal-
state balance has been carried forward by more recent decisions of this
Court. See, e.g., South Carolina v. Katzenback, 383 U.S. 301, 308
(1966); Mitchum v. Foster, 407 U.S. 225, 238–39 (1972).

There can be no doubt that this line of cases has sanctioned
intrusions by Congress, acting under the Civil War amendments, into
the judicial, executive, and legislative spheres of autonomy previously
reserved to the states. The legislation considered in each case was
grounded on the expansion of Congress' powers—with the corresponding diminution of state sovereignty—found to be intended by the
framers and made part of the Constitution upon the states' ratification
of those amendments, a phenomenon aptly described as a "carv[ing]
out" in Ex parte Virginia, supra, at 346.

It is true that none of these previous cases presented the question of the relationship between the 11th amendment and the enforcement power granted to Congress under § 5 of the 14th amendment. But we think that the 11th amendment, and the principle of state sovereignty which it embodies, see Hans v. Louisiana, 134 U.S. 1 (1890), are necessarily limited by the enforcement provisions of § 5 of the 14th amendment. In that section Congress is expressly granted authority to enforce "by appropriate legislation" the substantive provisions of the 14th amendment, which themselves embody significant limitations on state authority. When Congress acts pursuant to § 5, not only is it exercising legislative authority that is plenary within the terms of the constitutional grant, it is exercising that authority under one section of a constitutional amendment whose other sections by their own terms embody limitations on state authority. We think that Congress may, in determining what is "appropriate legislation" for the purpose of enforcing the provisions of the 14th amendment, provide for private suits against states or state officials which are constitutionally impermissible in other contexts. See Edelman v. Jordan, 415 U.S. 651 (1974); Ford Motor Co. v. Department of Treasury, 323 U.S. 459 (1945).

III

[T]he state officials contest the Court of Appeals' conclusion that an award of attorneys' fees in this case would under *Edelman* have only an "ancillary effect" on the state treasury and could therefore be permitted as falling outside the 11th amendment under the doctrine of Ex parte Young, 209 U.S. 123 (1908). We need not address this question, since, given the express congressional authority for such an award in a case brought under title VII, it follows necessarily from our holding . . . that Congress's exercise of power in this respect is also not barred by the 11th amendment. . . .

[The Court of Appeals' judgment as to damages was accordingly reversed, and its judgment as to attorneys' fees was affirmed.]

MR. JUSTICE BRENNAN, concurring in the judgment.

This suit was brought by present and retired employees of the state of Connecticut against the State Treasurer, the State Comptroller, and the Chairman of the State Employees' Retirement Commission. In that circumstance, Connecticut may not invoke the 11th amendment, since that amendment bars only federal-court suits against states by citizens of other states. Rather, the question is whether Connecticut may avail itself of the nonconstitutional but ancient doctrine of sovereign immunity as a bar to a claim for damages under title VII. In my view Connecticut may not assert sovereign immunity for the reason I expressed in dissent in Employees v. Missouri Public Health Dept., 411 U.S. 279, 298 (1973): The states surrendered that immunity, in Hamilton's words, "in the plan of the Convention" that formed the Union, at least insofar as the states granted Congress specifically enumerated powers. Congressional authority to enact the provisions of title VII at issue in this case is found in the commerce clause, art. I, § 8, cl. 3, and in § 5 of the 14th amendment, two of the enumerated powers granted in the Constitution. I remain of the opinion that "because of its surrender, no immunity exists that can be the subject of a congressional declaration or a voluntary waiver." *Employees,* supra.

I therefore concur in the judgment of the Court.

Mr. Justice Stevens, concurring in the judgment.

In my opinion the commerce power is broad enough to support federal legislation regulating the terms and conditions of state employment and, therefore, provides the necessary support for the 1972 amendments to title VII, even though Congress expressly relied on § 5 of the 14th amendment. But I do not believe plaintiffs proved a violation of the 14th amendment, and because I am not sure that the 1972 amendments were "needed to secure the guarantees of the 14th amendment," see Katzenback v. Morgan, 384 U.S. 641, 651 (1966), I question whether § 5 of that amendment is an adequate reply to Connecticut's 11th amendment defense. I believe the defense should be rejected for a different reason. . . .

The 11th amendment issue presented is whether the court has power to enter a judgment payable immediately out of trust assets which subsequently would be reimbursed from the general revenues of the state. . . . The holding in Edelman v. Jordan, 415 U.S. 651 (1974), does not necessarily require the same result in this case; this award will not be paid directly from the state treasury, but rather from two separate and independent pension funds. The fact that the state will have to increase its future payments into the funds as a consequence of this award does not, in my opinion, sufficiently distinguish this case from other cases in which a state may be required to conform its practices to the federal Constitution and thereby to incur additional expense in the future. Since the rationale of Ex parte Young, 209 U.S. 123 (1908), remains applicable to such cases, and since this case is not squarely covered by the holding in *Edelman,* I am persuaded that it is proper to reject the 11th amendment defense.

With respect to the fee issue, even if the 11th amendment were applicable, I would place fees in the same category as other litigation costs.

NOTES ON CONGRESSIONAL POWER TO ABROGATE STATE SOVEREIGN IMMUNITY

1. Questions and Comments on *Fitzpatrick v. Bitzer.* Does *Fitzpatrick v. Bitzer* support the proposition that the 14th amendment itself overrode state immunity from private suit in federal court to enforce its provisions? Or only that Congress has the power under § 5 to authorize such suits? Is there an important difference between these two formulations?

Two further lines of questions are implicated by *Fitzpatrick.* The first concerns the clarity with which Congress must spell out its intention to abrogate state sovereign immunity from suit in federal court. Must Congress do so in the language of the statute itself? Is there a role for congressional intent gleaned from legislative history and other similar sources? The second concerns congressional exercise of the original powers spelled out in article I, § 8, of the Constitution. What did the Court mean in *Fitzpatrick* when it said that Congress may, in the enforcement of 14th amendment guarantees, "provide for private suits against states or state officials which are constitutionally impermissible in other contexts"? Does this mean that Congress can override state immunity under the Civil War amendments but not, for example, under the commerce clause?

Both of these lines of questions are explored in the following notes and the next main case.

   2. *Hutto v. Finney*. The Civil Rights Attorney's Fees Awards Act of 1976, 42 U.S.C. § 1988, provides for an award of attorney's fees in successful actions under various civil rights statutes, including 42 U.S.C. § 1983. Although states are not explicitly mentioned, the act is in terms unqualified, and the legislative history indicates that fees may be assessed, in an appropriate case, against states and state officials.[a]

Hutto v. Finney, 437 U.S. 678 (1978), was a § 1983 action challenging conditions of confinement in Arkansas prisons. Those conditions were found to be violative of the eighth amendment, and attorney's fees were assessed against the state under § 1988. The Court rejected an 11th amendment challenge to that award, citing *Fitzpatrick*, both because the congressional intent was plain and because attorney's fees were imposed "as part of the costs" and thus were distinguishable from retroactive liability for prelitigation conduct. No express statutory abrogation of state immunity was required.

   Justice Powell, joined by the Chief Justice and Justices White and Rehnquist, dissented on the 11th amendment holding. Powell returned to the language of *Edelman* emphasizing that "the threshold fact of congressional authorization to sue a class of defendants which literally includes states is wholly absent" and insisted that congressional override of state immunity be clearly stated:

   "Absent such authorization, grounded in statutory language sufficiently clear to alert every voting member of Congress of the constitutional implications of particular legislation, we undermine the values of federalism served by the 11th amendment by inferring from congressional silence an intent to 'place new or even enormous fiscal burdens on the states.' [I]n this sensitive area of conflicting interests of constitutional dimension, we should not permit items of legislative history to substitute for explicit statutory language."

   In a concurrence, Justice Brennan responded to the dissenters by suggesting that there was in fact a statute authorizing suit against "a class of defendants which literally includes states"—namely, 42 U.S.C.

---

   [a] This part of § 1988 is quoted and discussed more fully at pages 1119–21, infra.   The legislative history is summarized in *Hutto*, 437 U.S. at 693–94.

§ 1983. *Edelman,* of course, had explicitly rejected that contention. Brennan noted that fact and quoted the explanation of *Edelman* given by Justice Rehnquist in *Fitzpatrick v. Bitzer*:

> "We concluded that none of the statutes relied upon by plaintiffs in *Edelman* contained any authorization by Congress to join a state as defendant. The Civil Rights Act of 1871, 42 U.S.C. § 1983, had been held in Monroe v. Pape, 365 U.S. 167, 187–91 (1961), to exclude cities and other municipal corporations from its ambit; that being the case, it could not have been intended to include states as parties defendant."

But, Brennan noted, subsequent to *Edelman* and *Fitzpatrick,* the Court had held in Monell v. Department of Social Services, 436 U.S. 658, 690 (1978), that Congress "*did* intend municipalities and other local government units to be included among those persons to whom § 1983 applies." Central to that conclusion was the so-called Dictionary Act, which defined "person," the word used in § 1983 to identify those who may be sued, to include "bodies politic and corporate." Thus, reasoned Brennan, *Monell* had destroyed the "essential premise" of *Edelman*'s treatment of § 1983—namely, that it was not a statute authorizing suit against "a class of defendants which literally includes states." Moreover, *Fitzpatrick* had made clear that Congress, acting under § 5 of the 14th amendment, "has plenary power to make states liable in damages." Section 1983 was enacted as "appropriate legislation" to enforce the 14th amendment. Therefore, Brennan concluded, "it is surely at least an open question whether § 1983 properly construed does not make the states liable for relief of all kinds, notwithstanding the 11th amendment."

3. *Quern v. Jordan.* The Court responded to Justice Brennan's suggestion in Quern v. Jordan, 440 U.S. 332 (1979). On remand from *Edelman v. Jordan,* an order had been entered requiring state officials to notify aid applicants of a state administrative procedure to determine eligibility for past benefits. The Court unanimously rejected the contention that this required notice violated the 11th amendment.[b]

Additionally, the majority, per Justice Rehnquist, reaffirmed *Edelman*'s conclusion that § 1983 did not abrogate state immunity. *Monell* had not undermined that conclusion, for it dealt only with local government units which in any event were not protected by the 11th amendment. *Hutto* was distinguished by the clear evidence in the legislative history of § 1988 that Congress meant to allow award of attorney's fees against states. Section 1983 was a different story:

> "[Section] 1983 does not explicitly and by clear language indicate on its face an intent to sweep away the immunity of the states; nor does it have a history which focuses directly on the question of state liability and which shows that Congress considered and firmly decided to abrogate the 11th amendment immunity of the states."

[b] The Court's rationale for this result is summarized at page 832, supra.

Justices Brennan and Marshall concurred in the judgment but objected to the Court's treatment of § 1983. Justice Brennan described the Court's discussion of that issue as "gratuitous" and its conclusion as "patently dicta." Brennan then endeavored to show, by a lengthy examination of the statutory language and history, that the majority's decision that a state was not a "person" within the meaning of § 1983 was "most likely incorrect."

4. *Atascadero State Hospital v. Scanlon.* The rigor of the Court's "clear statement" requirement was made plain in Atascadero State Hospital v. Scanlon, 473 U.S. 234 (1985). Scanlon claimed that he had been denied employment as a recreational therapist at a California state hospital because he was blind in one eye and a diabetic. He brought suit under § 504 of the Rehabilitation Act of 1973. That statute prohibits employment discrimination against "otherwise qualified" handicapped persons by "any recipient of federal assistance." It was undisputed that California was a recipient of federal assistance. Additionally, the legislative history seemed to indicate that Congress intended, or at least assumed, that the remedies authorized by the act would be available against states. Nonetheless, the Court found the action barred by the 11th amendment:

> "We . . . affirm that Congress may abrogate the states' constitutionally secured immunity from suit in federal court only by making its intention unmistakably clear in the language of the statute. . . . A general authorization for suit in federal court is not the kind of unequivocal statutory language sufficient to abrogate the 11th amendment. When Congress chooses to subject the states to federal jurisdiction, it must do so specifically."[c]

Justices Brennan, Marshall, Blackmun, and Stevens dissented.[d]

---

[c] The Court also rejected the argument that California's adoption of a general waiver of sovereign immunity in state courts permitted the suit in federal court, holding that "in order for a state statute or constitutional provision to constitute a waiver of 11th amendment immunity, it must specify the state's intention to subject itself to suit in *federal court.*"

In addition, it was argued that the Rehabilitation Act was enacted pursuant to the spending power, that this required a different analysis of the 11th amendment question, and that California had consented to suit in federal court by accepting funds under the Rehabilitation Act. The Court seemed to accept the fact that enactments under the spending power required a different analysis, but nonetheless rejected the argument:

"The act . . . falls far short of manifesting a clear intent to condition participation in the programs funded under the act on a state's consent to waive its constitutional immunity. Thus, were we to view this statute as an enactment pursuant to the spending clause, we would hold that there was no indication that the state of California consented to federal jurisdiction."

[d] For analysis of the implications of *Atascadero,* see George D. Brown, State Sovereignty under the Burger Court—How the Eleventh Amendment Survived the Death of the Tenth: Some Broader Implications of *Atascadero State Hospital v. Scanlon,* 74 Geo.L.J. 363 (1985).

WELCH v. STATE DEPARTMENT OF HIGHWAYS AND PUBLIC TRANSPORTATION

Supreme Court of the United States, 1987.
__ U.S. __.

JUSTICE POWELL announced the judgment of the Court and delivered an opinion in which THE CHIEF JUSTICE, JUSTICE WHITE, and JUSTICE O'CONNOR join.

The question in this case is whether the 11th amendment bars a state employee from suing the state in federal court under the Jones Act, 46 U.S.C. § 688.

I

The Texas Department of Highways and Public Transportation operates a free automobile and passenger ferry between Point Bolivar and Galveston, Texas. Petitioner Jean Welch, an employee of the state highway department, was injured while working on the ferry dock at Galveston. Relying on the Jones Act, she filed suit in the federal District Court for the Southern District of Texas against the highway department and the state of Texas.[1]

The District Court dismissed the action as barred by the 11th amendment. [T]he Court of Appeals affirmed . . .. [It] recognized that Parden v. Terminal Ry of Alabama State Docks Dept., 377 U.S. 184 (1964), held that an employee of a state-operated railroad company may bring an action in federal court under the Federal Employer's Liability Act (FELA), 45 U.S.C. §§ 51–60. *Parden* is relevant to this case because the Jones Act applied the remedial provisions of the FELA to seamen. The court nevertheless concluded that "the broad sweep of the *Parden* decision, although it has not been overruled, has overtly been limited by later decisions as its full implications have surfaced." The court relied on our holding that "Congress may abrogate the states' constitutionally secured immunity from suit in federal court only by making its intention unmistakably clear in the language of the statute." Atascadero State Hospital v. Scanlon, 473 U.S. 234, 242 (1985).[2] The Court of Appeals found no unmistakable expression of such an intention in the Jones Act. The court also held that Texas had not consented to suit under the Jones Act. We granted certiorari and now affirm.

---

[1] [T]he Jones Act provides in part:

"Any seaman who shall suffer personal injury in the course of his employment may, at his election, maintain an action for damages at law, with the right of trial by jury, and in such action all statutes of the United States modifying or extending the common-law right or remedy in cases of personal injury to railway employees shall apply. . . . Jurisdiction in such cases shall be under the court of the district in which the defendant employer resides or in which his principal office is located."

46 U.S.C. § 688(a).

[2] The question in *Scanlon* was whether § 504 of the Rehabilitation Act of 1973, 29 U.S.C. § 794, makes state agencies subject to suits for retroactive monetary relief in federal court. The Rehabilitation Act was passed pursuant to § 5 of the 14th amendment. Congress therefore had the power to subject unconsenting states to suit in federal court. See Fitzpatrick v. Bitzer, 427 U.S. 445 (1976).

II

[Part II of the opinion summarized prior 11th amendment decisions.]

III

We now apply these principles to the Jones Act. We note that the question whether the state of Texas has waived its 11th amendment immunity is not before us. Both the District Court and the Court of Appeals held that the state has not consented to Jones Act suits in federal court. The petition for certiorari does not address this issue, and we do not regard it as fairly included in the questions on which certiorari was granted. . . .

Petitioner's remaining argument is that Congress has abrogated the states' 11th amendment immunity from suit under the Jones Act. We assume, without deciding or intimating a view of the question, that the authority of Congress to subject unconsenting states to suit in federal court is not confined to § 5 of the 14th amendment.[5] Petitioner's argument fails in any event because Congress has not expressed in unmistakable statutory language its intention to allow states to be sued in federal court under the Jones Act. It is true that the act extends to "[a]ny seaman who shall suffer personal injury in the course of his employment." But the 11th amendment marks a constitutional distinction between the states and other employers of seamen. Because of the role of the states in our federal system, "[a] general authorization for suit in federal court is not the kind of unequivocal statutory language sufficient to abrogate the 11th amendment." *Atascadero State Hospital v. Scanlon,* supra at 246. In *Scanlon,* the Court held that § 504 of the Rehabilitation Act of 1973, that provides remedies for "any recipient of Federal assistance," does not contain the unmistakable language necessary to negate the states 11th amendment immunity. For the same reasons, we hold today that the general language of the Jones Act does not authorize suits against the states in federal court.[6]

IV

In Parden v. Terminal Ry of Alabama Docks Dept., 377 U.S. 184 (1964), the Court considered whether an employee of a state-owned railroad could sue the state in federal court under the FELA. The Court concluded that the state of Alabama had waived its 11th amendment immunity. It reasoned that Congress evidenced an intention to

---

[5] The argument for such an authority starts from the proposition that the Constitution authorizes Congress to regulate matters within the admiralty and maritime jurisdiction, either under the commerce clause or the necessary and proper clause. See D. Robertson, Admiralty and Federalism 142–45 (1970). By ratifying the Constitution, the argument runs, the states necessarily consented to suit in federal court with respect to enactments under either clause.

[6] Because 11th amendment immunity "partakes of the nature of a jurisdictional bar," Edelman v. Jordan, 415 U.S. 651, 678 (1974), we have no occasion to consider the state's additional argument that Congress did not intend to afford seamen employed by the states a remedy under the Jones Act.

abrogate 11th amendment immunity by making the FELA applicable to "every common carrier by railroad while engaging in commerce between any of the several States." . . .[7] But, as discussed above, the constitutional role of the states sets them apart from other employers and defendants. . . .

Although our later decisions do not expressly overrule *Parden,* they leave no doubt that *Parden's* discussion of congressional intent to negate 11th amendment immunity is no longer good law. . . . In subsequent cases the Court consistently has required an unequivocal expression that Congress intended to override 11th amendment immunity. *Atascadero State Hospital v. Scanlon,* supra at 242; Quern v. Jordan, 440 U.S. 332, 342–45 (1979). Accordingly, to the extent that *Parden* is inconsistent with the requirement that an abrogation of 11th amendment immunity by Congress must be expressed in unmistakably clear language, it is overruled.[8]

V

Today, for the fourth time in little more than two years, four members of the Court urge that we overrule Hans v. Louisiana, 134 U.S. 1 (1890), and the long line of cases that has followed it. The rule of law depends in large part on adherence to the doctrine of stare decisis. . . . Despite [this principle], the dissenters—on the basis of ambiguous historical evidence—would flatly overrule a number of major decisions of the Court, and cast doubt on others. See n. 27, infra. Once again, the dissenters have placed in issue the fundamental nature of our federal system.[9]

A

The constitutional foundation of state sovereign immunity has been well described by Justice Marshall in his separate opinion in Employees v. Missouri Dept. of Public Health and Welfare, 411 U.S. 279, 291–92 (1973):

> "It had been widely understood prior to ratification of the Constitution that the provision in art. III, § 2, concerning 'Controversies . . . between a State and Citizens of another State' would not provide a mechanism for making states unwilling defendants in federal court. The Court in Chisholm v. Georgia, 2 U.S. (2 Dall.) 419 (1793), however, considered the plain meaning of the constitutional provision to be controlling. The 11th amendment served effectively to reverse the particu-

---

[7] [Among the cases on which *Parden* relied was Petty v. Tennessee-Missouri Bridge Comm'n, 359 U.S. 275 (1959). That case, Justice Powell said, was distinguishable because it "involved an interstate compact that expressly permitted the bi-state corporation to sue and be sued."]

[8] [W]e have no occasion in this case to consider the validity of the additional holding in *Parden,* that Congress has the power to abrogate the states' 11th amendment immunity under the commerce clause to the extent that the states are engaged in interstate commerce.

[9] We address today only two principal arguments raised by the dissent: that citizens may bring federal question actions against the states in federal court and that citizens may bring admiralty suits against the states.

lar holding in *Chisholm,* and, more generally, to restore the original understanding. . . . Thus, despite the narrowness of the language of the amendment, its spirit has consistently guided this Court in interpreting the reach of the federal judicial power generally, and it 'has become established by repeated decisions of this Court that the entire judicial power granted by the Constitution does not embrace authority to entertain a suit brought by private parties against a state without consent given; not one brought by citizens of another state, because of the 11th amendment; and not even one brought by its own citizens, because of the fundamental rule of which the amendment is but an exemplification.' "

Although the dissent rejects the Court's reading of the historical record, there is ample support for the Court's rationale, that has provided the basis for many important decisions.

1

Justice Brennan has argued at length that "[a] close examination of the historical records" demonstrates that "[t]here simply is no constitutional principle of state sovereign immunity." *Atascadero State Hospital v. Scanlon,* 473 U.S., at 259 (Brennan, J. dissenting). In his dissent today, he repeats and expands this historical argument. [Justice Powell's response to Justice Brennan on the history has been omitted. He concluded:] At most, then, the historical materials show that—to the extent this question was debated—the intentions of the framers and ratifiers were ambiguous.

2

No one doubts that the 11th amendment nullified the Court's decision in Chisholm v. Georgia, 2 U.S. (2 Dall.) 419 (1793). . . . The dissent, observing that jurisdiction in *Chisholm* . . . was based solely on the fact that Chisholm was not a citizen of Georgia, argues that the 11th amendment does not apply to cases presenting a federal question. The text of the amendment states that "[t]he Judicial power of the United States *shall not be construed* to extend to *any* suit in law or equity, commenced or prosecuted against one of the United States by Citizens of another State, or by Citizens or Subjects of any Foreign State." Federal question actions unquestionably are suits "in law or equity"; thus the plain language of the amendment refutes this argument.[17] . . .

---

[17] The dissent's principal textual argument rests on the similarity between the language of the amendment and the language of the state-citizen diversity clauses in article III. This argument cannot explain why Congress chose to apply the amendment to "any suit in law or equity" rather than any suit where jurisdiction is predicated solely on diversity of citizenship. Instead, the dissent reads the amendment to accomplish even less than its plain language suggests. As the Court long has recognized, the speed and vigor of the nation's response to *Chisholm* suggests that the 11th amendment should be construed broadly so as to further the federal interests that the Court misapprehended in *Chisholm.* The dissent also has some difficulty explaining the clause in article III, § 2 that extends the federal judicial power

3

The Court's unanimous decision in Hans v. Louisiana, 134 U.S. 1 (1890), firmly established that the 11th amendment embodies a broad constitutional principle of sovereign immunity. . . .

Contrary to the suggestion in the dissent, the fundamental principle enunciated in *Hans* has been among the most stable in our constitutional jurisprudence. Moreover, the dissent is simply wrong in asserting that the doctrine lacks a clear rationale. Because of the sensitive problems "inherent in making one sovereign appear against its will in the courts of the other," Employees v. Missouri Dept. of Public Health and Welfare, 411 U.S., at 294 (Marshall, J., concurring in result), the doctrine of sovereign immunity plays a vital role in our federal system. The rationale has been set out most completely in the Court's unanimous opinion, per Chief Justice Hughes, in Monaco v. Mississippi, 292 U.S. 313 (1934). First, the United States may sue a state, because that is "inherent in the Constitutional plan." Absent such a provision, " 'the permanence of the Union might be endangered.' " Second, states may sue other states, because a federal forum for suits between states is "essential to the peace of the Union." Third, states may not be sued by foreign states, because "[c]ontroversies between a state and a foreign state may involve international questions in relation to which the United States has a sovereign prerogative." Fourth, the 11th amendment established "an absolute bar" to suits by citizens of other states or foreign states. Finally, "[p]rotected by the same fundamental principle [of sovereign immunity], the states, in the absence of consent, are immune from suits brought against them by their own citizens. . . ." The Court has never questioned this basic framework set out in *Monaco v. Mississippi.*

The dissenters offer their unsupported view that the principle of sovereign immunity is "pernicious" because it assertedly protects states from the consequences of their illegal conduct and prevents Congress from " 'tak[ing] steps it deems necessary and proper to achieve national goals within its constitutional authority.' " Of course, the dissent's assertion that our cases construing the 11th amendment deprive Congress of some of its constitutional power is simply question-begging. Moreover, . . . Congress clearly has authority to limit the 11th amendment when it acts to enforce the 14th amendment. Fitzpatrick v. Bitzer, 427 U.S. 445, 456 (1976). The dissent's statement that sovereign immunity "protect[s] the states from the consequences of their own illegal conduct" erroneously suggests that aggrieved individuals are left with no remedy for harmful state actions. Relief often may be obtained through suits against state officials rather than the state itself, or through injunctive or other prospective remedies. Edelman v. Jordan, 415 U.S. 651 (1974). Municipalities and other local government

---

"to Controversies to which the United States shall be a Party." Although arguments analogous to those in the dissent would suggest that this clause abrogated the sovereign immunity of the United States, the dissent stops short of such an extreme conclusion.

agencies may be sued under 42 U.S.C. § 1983. Monell v. New York City Dept. of Social Services, 436 U.S. 658 (1978). In addition, the states may provide relief by waiving their immunity from suit in state court on state-law claims.[19] That states are not liable in other circumstances is a necessary consequence of their role in a system of dual sovereignties. Although the dissent denies that sovereign immunity is "'required by the structure of the federal system,'" the principle has been deeply embedded in our federal system from its inception.

B

As a fall-back position, the dissent argues that the doctrine of sovereign immunity has no application to suits in admiralty against unconsenting states. This argument also is directly contrary to long-settled authority, as well as the Court's recognition that the 11th amendment affirms "the fundamental principle of sovereign immunity." . . .

C

In deciding yet another 11th amendment case, we do not write on a clean slate. The general principle of state sovereign immunity has been adhered to without exception by this Court for almost a century. The dissent nevertheless urges the Court to ignore stare decisis and overrule the long and unbroken series of precedents reaffirming this principle. If the Court were to overrule these precedents, a number of other major decisions also would have to be reconsidered.[27] As we have stated above, the doctrine of stare decisis is of fundamental importance to the rule of law. For this reason, "any departure from doctrine . . . demands special justification." Arizona v. Rumsey, 467 U.S. 203, 212 (1984). The arguments made in the dissent fall far short of justifying such a drastic repudiation of this Court's prior decisions.[28]

[19] In this case, for example, Welch is not without a remedy: She may file a workers' compensation claim against the state under the Texas Tort Claims Act. . . .

[27] The dissent is written as if the slate had been clean since Hans was decided 97 years ago. . . . Hans has been reaffirmed in case after case, often unanimously and by exceptionally strong Courts. The two principal holdings of Hans that the dissent challenges are that the federal judicial power does not extend either to suits against states that arise under federal law, or to suits brought against a state by its own citizens. If these holdings were rejected, the Court would overrule at least 17 cases, in addition to Hans itself. [Citations omitted.] . . .

[28] Apart from rhetoric, the dissent relies on two arguments: (i) the "historical record", and (ii) the perceived "perni-cious[ness]" of the principle of sovereign immunity. As we have noted, the fragments of historical evidence at the time of the adoption of the Constitution are as supportive of Hans as they are of the dissent. In attaching weight to this ambiguous history, it is not immaterial that we are a century further removed from the events at issue than were the justices who unanimously agreed in Hans. Not one of the 17 cases the dissent would overrule concludes that the historical evidence calls into question the principle of state sovereign immunity or justifies the ignoring of stare decisis. As for the view that it would be "pernicious" to protect states from liability for their "unlawful conduct", we have noted above that an aggrieved citizen such as petitioner in fact has a bundle of possible remedies.

VI

For the reasons we have stated, the judgment of the Court of Appeals . . . is affirmed.

It is so ordered.

JUSTICE WHITE, concurring in the opinion and judgment.

The Court expressly stops short of addressing the issue whether the Jones Act affords a remedy to seamen employed by the states. See n. 6, ante. The Court, however, has already construed the Jones Act to extend remedies to such seamen. Petty v. Tennessee-Missouri Bridge Comm'n, 359 U.S. 275, 282–83 (1959). Congress has not disturbed this construction, and the Court, as I understand it, does not now purport to do so.

JUSTICE SCALIA, concurring in part and concurring in the judgment.

The petitioner in this case did not assert as a basis for reversing the judgment that Hans v. Louisiana, 134 U.S. 1 (1890), had been wrongly decided. That argument was introduced by an amicus, addressed only briefly in respondent's brief, and touched upon only lightly at oral argument. I find both the correctness of *Hans* as an original matter, and the feasibility, if it was wrong, of correcting it without distorting what we have done in tacit reliance upon it, complex enough questions that I am unwilling to address them in a case whose presentation focused on other matters.

I find it unnecessary to do so in any event. Regardless of what one may think of *Hans,* it has been assumed to be the law for nearly a century. During that time, Congress has enacted many statutes— including the Jones Act and the provisions of the FELA which it incorporates—on the assumption that states were immune from lawsuits by individuals. Even if we were now to find that assumption to have been wrong, we could not, in reason, interpret the statutes as though the assumption never existed. Thus, although the terms of the Jones Act (through its incorporation of the FELA) apply to all common carriers by water, I do not read them to apply to states. For the same reason, I do not read the FELA to apply to states, and therefore agree with the Court that Parden v. Terminal Ry of Alabama Docks Dept., 377 U.S. 184 (1964), should be overruled. Whether or not, as *Hans* appears to have held, article III of the Constitution contains an implicit limitation on suits brought by individuals against states by virtue of a nearly universal "understanding" that the federal judicial power could not extend to such suits, such an understanding clearly underlay the Jones Act and the FELA.

JUSTICE BRENNAN, with whom JUSTICE MARSHALL, JUSTICE BLACKMUN, and JUSTICE STEVENS join, dissenting.

The Court overrules Parden v. Terminal Ry of Alabama Docks Dept., 377 U.S. 184 (1964), and thereby continues aggressively to expand its doctrine of 11th amendment sovereign immunity. I adhere to my belief that the doctrine "rests on flawed premises, misguided history, and an untenable vision of the needs of the federal system it purports to protect."   Atascadero State Hospital v. Scanlon, 473 U.S. 234, 248 (Brennan, J., dissenting).   In my view, the 11th amendment does not bar the District Court's jurisdiction over the Jones Act suit by Jean Welch against the state of Texas and the Texas Highway Department for four independent reasons.   First, the amendment does not limit federal jurisdiction over suits in admiralty.   Second, the amendment bars only actions against a state by citizens of another state or of a foreign nation.   Third, the amendment applies only to diversity suits. Fourth, even assuming the 11th amendment were applicable to the present case, Congress abrogated state immunity from suit under the Jones Act, which incorporates the FELA.   I therefore dissent.

I

Article III provides that the "Judicial power" assigned to federal courts extends not only to "Cases in Law and Equity," but also "to all Cases of admiralty and maritime jurisdiction."   In the instant case, the District Court stated that the "plaintiff brought this suit in admiralty." The 11th amendment limits the "Judicial power" in certain suits "in law or equity."   Therefore, even if the 11th amendment does bar federal jurisdiction over cases in which a state is sued by its own citizens, its express language reveals that it does so *only* in "Cases in Law and Equity," and not in "Cases of admiralty and maritime Jurisdiction."   . . .

[A] narrow holding allowing federal jurisdiction over Welch's suit in admiralty under the Jones Act against the state of Texas is consistent with precedent and the will of Congress,[9] and prevents further erosion of a legal distinction which is difficult, if not impossible, to rationalize.   It is patently improper to extend the 11th amendment doctrine of sovereign immunity any further.

II

The 11th amendment does not bar a suit under the Jones Act by a Texas citizen against the state of Texas.   The part of article III, § 2, that was affected by the amendment provides: "The judicial Power shall extend . . . to Controversies . . . between a State and Citizens of *another* State" and "between a State . . . and foreign . . . Citizens or Subjects."   The amendment uses language identical to that in article III to bar the extension of the judicial power to a suit "against one of the United States by Citizens of *another* State, or by Citizens or Subjects of any Foreign State."   The congruence of the language suggests that the amendment specifically limits only the jurisdiction conferred by the above-referenced part of article III.   Thus, the amend-

---

[9] In Petty v. Tennessee-Missouri Bridge Comm'n, 359 U.S. 275, 282 (1959), the Court considered the substantive applicability of the Jones Act to state employees: " 'When Congress wished to exclude state employees, it expressly so provided.' . . . The Jones Act . . . has no exceptions from the broad sweep of the words 'any seaman. . . .' "   The Court today does not disturb this holding.   See [Justice White's concurrence].

ment bars only federal actions brought against a state by citizens of another state or by foreign aliens.

Contrary to the Court's view, a proper assessment of the historical record of the Constitutional Convention and the debates surrounding the state ratification conventions confirms this interpretation. [Justice Brennan's discussion of the historical materials has been omitted.]

III

In my view, the 11th amendment applies only to diversity suits and not to federal question or admiralty suits. The parallel between the language of article III's grant of diversity jurisdiction . . . and the language in the 11th amendment . . . supports this view. The amendment prohibits federal jurisdiction over *all* such suits in law or equity which are based on diversity jurisdiction. Since Congress had not granted federal question jurisdiction to federal courts prior to the amendment's ratification, the amendment was not intended to restrict that type of jurisdiction. Furthermore, the controversy among the ratifiers . . . involved only *diversity* suits. Moreover, the Court recognizes that the immediate impetus for adoption of the 11th amendment was Chisholm v. Georgia, 2 U.S. (2 Dall.) 419 (1793). *Chisholm* was a *diversity* case brought in federal court upon a state cause of action against the state of Georgia by a citizen of South Carolina. The Court relies on Hans v. Louisiana, 134 U.S. 1 (1890), to hold that the 11th amendment bars Welch's suit in admiralty.

Hans, however, was a *federal question* suit brought by a Louisiana citizen against his own state. Ignoring this fact, the Court in *Hans* relied on materials that primarily addressed the question of state sovereign immunity in diversity cases, and not on federal question or admiralty cases. It is plain from the face of *Hans* that the Court misunderstood those materials. In particular, the Court in *Hans* heavily relied on two sources: a statement by Hamilton in The Federalist, No. 81, and the views of Justice Iredell, who wrote the dissent in *Chisholm.* A close examination of both of these sources indicates that they cannot serve as support for the holding of *Hans* or of the Court today. [Justice Brennan's examination of these sources has been omitted]

IV

The Court today overrules, in part, Parden v. Terminal Ry of Alabama Docks Dept., 377 U.S. 184 (1964). . . .

The Court's departure from normal rules of statutory construction frustrates the will of Congress. The Court's holding in *Parden* that Congress intended to abrogate the sovereign immunity of states in FELA has not been disturbed by Congress for the past two decades. In FELA, Congress not only indicated that "every common carrier . . . shall be liable . . . ," but also expressed in unequivocal language that the "action may be brought in a district court of the United States." 45 U.S.C. §§ 51, 56. The Court in *Parden* noted that the legislative history of FELA revealed that Congress meant to extend the scope to apply to "all commerce," without exception for state-owned carriers. . . .

The Court today repeatedly relies on a bare assertion that "the constitutional role of the states sets them apart from other employers and defendants." This may be true in many contexts, but it is not applicable in the sphere of interstate commerce. Congress has plenary authority in regulating this area. . . .

. . . I believe that *Parden* was correctly decided. . . . In my view, Congress abrogated state immunity to suits under the FELA, a statute incorporated by the Jones Act.

V

Sound precedent should produce progeny whose subsequent application of principle in light of experience confirms the original wisdom. Tested by this standard, *Hans* has proven to be unsound. The doctrine has been unstable, because it lacks a textual anchor, an established historical foundation, or a clear rationale.[19] We should not forget that the irrationality of doctrine has its costs. It has led to the development of a complex set of rules to avoid unfair results.[20] . . . The doctrine, based on a notion of kingship, intrudes impermissibly on Congress' lawmaking power. I adhere to my belief that:

> "[T]he doctrine that has thus been created is pernicious. In an era when sovereign immunity has been generally recognized by courts and legislatures as an anachronistic and unnecessary remnant of a feudal legal system, . . . the Court has aggressively expanded its scope. If this doctrine were required to enhance the liberty of our people in accordance with the Constitution's protections, I could accept it. If the doctrine were required by the structure of the federal system created by

[19] Today, only four members of the Court advocate adherence to *Hans.* Three factors counsel against continued reliance upon *Hans.* First, *Hans* misinterpreted the intent of the framers and those who ratified the 11th amendment. . . . Second, the progeny of *Hans* has produced erratic and irrational results. If a general principle of state sovereign immunity is based on the sensitive problems inherent in making one sovereign appear against its will in the courts of other sovereigns, then it is inexplicable why states can be sued in some cases (by other states, by the federal government or when prospective relief is sought) and not in other instances (by foreign countries, by citizens of the same state, or when retrospective relief is sought). The Court's recital of the rules of sovereign immunity in Monaco v. Mississippi, 292 U.S. 313 (1934), indicates the crazy-quilt pattern of the *Hans* doctrine. Third, the 11th amendment doctrine creates inconsistencies in constitutional interpretation. For example, under the seventh amendment, the Court has stated that a right to a jury trial does not extend to admiralty cases because these suits in admiralty are distinguishable from suits in law. Yet today, the Court ignores the distinction between suits in admiralty and in law in arriving at its decision.

[20] As Professor Orth concludes:

"By the late 20th century the law of the 11th amendment exhibited a baffling complexity. . . . 'The case law of the 11th amendment is replete with historical anomalies, internal inconsistencies, and senseless distinctions.' Marked by its history as were few other branches of constitutional law, interpretation of the amendment has become an arcane specialty of lawyers and federal judges." J. Orth, The Judicial Power of the United States 11 (1987).

the framers, I could accept it. Yet the current doctrine intrudes on the idea of liberty under law by protecting the states from the consequences of their illegal conduct. And the decision obstructs the sound operation of our federal system by limiting the ability of Congress to take steps it deems necessary and proper to achieve national goals within its constitutional authority." Atascadero State Hospital v. Scanlon, 473 U.S. 234, 302 (1985) (Brennan, J., dissenting).

By clinging to *Hans*, the Court today erases yet another traditional legal distinction and overrules yet another principle that defined the limits of that decision. In my view, we should at minimum confine *Hans* to its current domain. More fundamentally, however, it is time to begin a fresh examination of 11th amendment jurisprudence without the weight of that mistaken precedent. I therefore dissent.

FURTHER NOTES ON CONGRESSIONAL POWER TO ABROGATE STATE SOVEREIGN IMMUNITY

1. **Questions and Comments on *Welch v. State Department of Highways and Public Transportation*.** Three aspects of *Welch* merit separate attention. First, the plurality emphatically reaffirms the Court's prior cases indicating the need for "unequivocal statutory language" before an act of Congress will be held to have abrogated the sovereign immunity of the states embodied in the 11th amendment. The inconsistency of *Parden* is resolved, with Justice Scalia's concurrence, by the overruling of that decision. Has the Court finally settled on a sensible view of the 11th amendment?

Second, the plurality of four explicitly rejects the adoption by four Justices in dissent of the "diversity interpretation"[a] of the 11th amendment. Justice Scalia abstains from breaking the tie, observing that "the correctness of *Hans* as an original matter, and the feasibility, if it was wrong, of correcting it without distorting what we have done in tacit reliance upon it, [are] complex enough questions that I am unwilling to address them in a case whose presentation focused on other matters." Does Scalia mean to say that he may be willing to address these questions in another case? Does he imply that he thinks *Hans* wrongly decided? How might this issue be presented—that is, is it possible for a case to arise that is not amenable to the reasoning on which Justice Scalia disposed of *Welch*?

Finally, what does Justice White's concurrence mean? Does he mean to say that a suit against the state under the Jones Act may be brought in state court? Could those who joined Justice Powell's opinion have meant to preserve such an option?

2. ***United States v. Union Gas Co.*** United States v. Union Gas Co., 832 F.2d 1343 (3d Cir.1987), cert. granted, ___ U.S. ___ (1988), was a suit by the United States against a gas company to recover $720,000

---

[a] See page 814, supra.

that was expended by the commonwealth of Pennsylvania to clean up toxic waste and that was in turn reimbursed by the United States to Pennsylvania. The plant that discharged the waste had been closed and dismantled long before the commonwealth engaged in flood control excavations near a creek and struck a deposit of hazardous substances that then began to leak into the creek. The gas company responded to the suit by impleading Pennsylvania as a third-party defendant on the theory that it had "negligently caused, or contributed to, the discharge" and that it should therefore pay at least part of the clean-up costs. The District Court granted the commonwealth's motion to dismiss the third-party complaint. At that point the United States and the gas company settled their dispute and the gas company appealed the dismissal of its complaint against the state. The Court of Appeals affirmed, but the Supreme Court vacated the judgment and remanded in light of inter-vening amendments to the relevant federal statutes. The Third Circuit then reversed the dismissal of the complaint and the Supreme Court granted certiorari. The case was pending when this book went to press.

Both the complaint and the third-party complaint were filed under the Comprehensive Environmental Response Compensation and Liabili-ty Act (CERCLA, or Superfund), 42 U.S.C. § 9601 et seq. The interven-ing legislation was enacted in the Superfund Amendments and Reauthorization Act (SARA). In its initial decision, the Third Circuit held that CERCLA did not contain a sufficiently explicit statement of congressional intent to abrogate the state's 11th amendment immunity. After the remand by the Supreme Court, the Court of Appeals held that the text of SARA was clear and that abrogation of state immunity was intended. The court then faced the constitutional question left open in *Fitzpatrick* and *Welch*: whether the commerce power, under which both CERCLA and SARA were enacted, authorized the Congress to override the state's 11th amendment immunity. The court held, in accord with "every federal appellate court to have addressed the question," that "[b]y assenting to federal authority to regulate com-merce, the states necessarily surrendered their sovereignty over that area." The policies of the 11th amendment were sufficiently respected by "limiting the power to abrogate sovereign immunity to the freely elected legislative branch" and by "preventing the judiciary from independently using article III to do the same."

Did the Circuit Court reach the right conclusion? Will the Su-preme Court agree?

SECTION 3: THE *PENNHURST* PROBLEM

PENNHURST STATE SCHOOL AND HOSPITAL v.
HALDERMAN
Supreme Court of the United States, 1984.
465 U.S. 89.

JUSTICE POWELL delivered the opinion of the Court.

This case presents the question whether a federal court may award injunctive relief against state officials on the basis of state law.

I

This litigation, here for the second time, concerns the conditions of care at petitioner Pennhurst State School and Hospital, a Pennsylvania institution for the care of the mentally retarded. See Pennhurst State School & Hospital v. Halderman, 451 U.S. 1 (1981). Although the litigation's history is set forth in detail in our prior opinion, it is necessary for purposes of this decision to review that history.

This suit originally was brought in 1974 by respondent Terri Lee Halderman, a resident of Pennhurst, in the District Court for the Eastern District of Pennsylvania. Ultimately, plaintiffs included a class consisting of all persons who were or might become residents of Pennhurst; the Pennsylvania Association for Retarded Citizens; and the United States. Defendants were Pennhurst and various Pennhurst officials; the Pennsylvania Department of Public Welfare and several of its officials; and various county commissioners, county mental retardation administrators, and other officials of five Pennsylvania counties surrounding Pennhurst. Respondents' amended complaint charged that conditions at Pennhurst violated the class members' rights under the eighth and 14th amendments; § 504 of the Rehabilitation Act of 1973, as amended, 42 U.S.C. § 794; the Developmentally Disabled Assistance and Bill of Rights Act, 42 U.S.C. §§ 6001–6081; and the Pennsylvania Mental Health and Mental Retardation Act of 1966 (the "MH/MR Act"), Pa. Stat. Ann., Tit. 50, §§ 4101–4704. Both damages and injunctive relief were sought.

In 1977, following a lengthy trial, the District Court rendered its decision. As noted in our prior opinion, the court's findings were undisputed: "Conditions at Pennhurst are not only dangerous, with the residents often physically abused or drugged by staff members, but also inadequate for the 'habilitation' of the retarded. Indeed, the court found that the physical, intellectual, and emotional skills of some residents have deteriorated at Pennhurst." The District Court held that these conditions violated each resident's right to "minimally adequate habilitation" under the due process clause and the MH/MR Act; "freedom from harm" under the eighth and 14th amendments; and "non-discriminatory habilitation" under the equal protection clause and § 504 of the Rehabilitation Act. Furthermore, the court found that "due process demands that if a state undertakes the habilitation of a retarded person, it must do so in the *least restrictive setting* consistent with that individual's habilitative needs." (Emphasis added.) After concluding that the large size of Pennhurst prevented it from providing the necessary habilitation in the least restrictive environment, the court ordered "that immediate steps be taken to remove the retarded residents from Pennhurst." Petitioners were ordered "to provide suitable community living arrangements" for the class members, and the court appointed a special master "with the power and duty to plan, organize, direct, supervise and monitor the implementation of this and any further orders of the court."

The Court of Appeals for the Third Circuit affirmed most of the District Court's judgment. It agreed that respondents had a right to habilitation in the least restrictive environment, but it grounded this right solely on the "bill of rights" provision in the Developmentally Disabled Assistance and Bill of Rights Act, 42 U.S.C. § 6010. The court did not consider the constitutional issues or § 504 of the Rehabilitation Act, and while it affirmed the District Court's holding that the MH/MR Act provides a right to adequate habilitation, the court did not decide whether that state right encompassed a right to treatment in the least restrictive setting.

On the question of remedy, the Court of Appeals affirmed except as to the District Court's order that Pennhurst be closed. The court observed that some patients would be unable to adjust to life outside an institution, and it determined that none of the legal provisions relied on by plaintiffs precluded institutionalization. It therefore remanded for "individual determinations by the [District Court], or by the special master, as to the appropriateness of an improved Pennhurst for each such patient," guided by "a presumption in favor of placing individuals in [community living arrangements]."

On remand the District Court established detailed procedures for determining the proper residential placement for each patient. A team consisting of the patient, his parents or guardian, and his case manager must establish an individual habilitation plan providing for habilitation of the patient in a designated community living arrangement. The plan is subject to review by the special master. A second master, called the hearing master, is available to conduct hearings, upon request by the resident, his parents or his advocate, on the question whether the services of Pennhurst would be more beneficial to the resident than the community living arrangement provided in the resident's plan. The hearing master then determines where the patient should reside, subject to possible review by the District Court.

This Court reversed the judgment of the Court of Appeals, finding that 42 U.S.C. § 6010 did not create any substantive rights. We remanded the case to the Court of Appeals to determine if the remedial order could be supported on the basis of state law, the Constitution, or § 504 of the Rehabilitation Act. We also remanded for consideration of whether any relief was available under other provisions of the Developmentally Disabled Assistance and Bill of Rights Act.

On remand the Court of Appeals affirmed its prior judgment in its entirety. It determined that in a recent decision the Supreme Court of Pennsylvania had "spoken definitively" in holding that the MH/MR Act required the state to adopt the "least restrictive environment" approach for the case of the mentally retarded (citing In re Schmidt, 494 Pa. 86, 429 A.2d 631 (1981)). The Court of Appeals concluded that this state statute fully supported its prior judgment, and therefore did not reach the remaining issues of federal law. It also rejected petitioners' argument that the 11th amendment barred a federal court from considering this pendent state law claim. The court noted that the amendment did not bar a federal court from granting prospective injunctive relief against state officials on the basis of federal claims, Ex parte Young, 209 U.S. 123 (1908), and concluded that the same result obtained with respect to a pendent state law claim. It reasoned that because Siler v. Louisville & Nashville R. Co., 213 U.S. 175 (1909), an important case in the development of the doctrine of pendent jurisdiction, also involved state officials, "there cannot be . . . an 11th amendment exception to that rule."[5] Finally, the court rejected petitioners' argument that it should have abstained from deciding the state law claim under principles of comity, and refused to consider petitioners' objections to the District Court's use of a special master. Three judges dissented in part, arguing that under principles of federalism and comity the establishment of a special master to supervise compliance was an abuse of discretion.

We granted certiorari and now reverse and remand.

II

Petitioners raise three challenges to the judgment of the Court of Appeals: (i) the 11th amendment prohibited the District Court from ordering state officials to conform their conduct to state law; (ii) the doctrine of comity prohibited the District Court from issuing its injunctive relief; and (iii) the District Court abused its discretion in appointing two masters to supervise the decisions of state officials in implementing state law. We need not reach the latter two issues, for we find the 11th amendment challenge dispositive.

[The Court's review of 11th amendment precedents concluded as follows:]

This Court's decisions thus establish that "an unconsenting state is immune from suits brought in federal courts by her own citizens as well as by citizens of another state." . . .

The Court has recognized an important exception to this general rule: a suit challenging the constitutionality of a state official's action

[5] Judge Gibbons has expanded on his views of the 11th amendment in a recent law review article. Gibbons, The Eleventh Amendment and State Sovereign Immuni-ty: A Reinterpretation, 83 Colum. L. Rev. 1889 (1983). Judge Gibbons was the author of both the first and second opinions by the Court of Appeals in this case.

is not one against the state. This was the holding in Ex parte Young, 209 U.S. 123 (1908), in which a federal court enjoined the Attorney General of the state of Minnesota from bringing suit to enforce a state statute that allegedly violated the 14th amendment. This Court held that the 11th amendment did not prohibit issuance of this injunction. The theory of the case was that an unconstitutional enactment is "void" and therefore does not "impart to [the officer] any immunity from responsibility to the supreme authority of the United States." Since the state could not authorize the action, the official was "stripped of his official or representative character and [was] subjected to the consequence of his official conduct."

While the rule permitting suits alleging conduct contrary to "the supreme authority of the United States" has survived, the theory of *Young* has not been provided an expansive interpretation. Thus, in Edelman v. Jordan, 415 U.S. 651 (1974), the Court emphasized that the 11th amendment bars some forms of injunctive relief against state officials for violation of federal law. In particular, *Edelman* held that when a plaintiff sues a state official alleging a violation of federal law, the federal court may award an injunction that governs the official's future conduct, but not one that awards retroactive monetary relief. Under the theory of *Young,* such a suit would not be one against the state since the federal law allegation would strip the state officer of his official authority. Nevertheless, retroactive relief was barred by the 11th amendment.

III

With these principles in mind, we now turn to the question whether the claim that petitioners violated *state law* in carrying out their official duties at Pennhurst is one against the state and therefore barred by the 11th amendment. Respondents advance two principal arguments in support of the judgment below.[12] First, they contend that under the doctrine of *Edelman v. Jordan,* supra, the suit is not against the state because the courts below ordered only prospective injunctive relief. Second, they assert that the state law claim properly was decided under the doctrine of pendent jurisdiction. Respondents rely on decisions of this Court awarding relief against state officials on the basis of a pendent state law claim. See, e.g., Siler v. Louisville & Nashville R. Co., 213 U.S. 175 (1909).

A

We first address the contention that respondents' state law claim is not barred by the 11th amendment because it seeks only prospective

[12] We reject respondents' additional contention that Pennsylvania has waived its immunity from suit in federal court. At the time the suit was filed, suits against Pennsylvania were permitted only where expressly authorized by the legislature, see, e.g., French v. Commonwealth, 471 Pa. 558, 370 A.2d 1163 (1977), and respondents have not referred us to any provisions expressly waiving Pennsylvania's 11th amendment immunity. The state now has a statute governing sovereign immunity, including an express preservation of its immunity from suit in federal court. . . .

relief as defined in *Edelman v. Jordan,* supra. The Court of Appeals held that if the judgment below rested on federal law, it could be entered against petitioner state officials under the doctrine established in *Edelman* and *Young* even though the prospective financial burden was substantial and on-going. The court assumed, and respondents assert, that this reasoning applies as well when the official acts in violation of state law. This argument misconstrues the basis of the doctrine established in *Young* and *Edelman.*

As discussed above, the injunction in *Young* was justified, notwithstanding the obvious impact on the state itself, on the view that sovereign immunity does not apply because an official who acts unconstitutionally is "stripped of his official or representative character." This rationale, of course, created the "well recognized irony" that an official's unconstitutional conduct constitutes state action under the 14th amendment but not the 11th amendment. Nonetheless, the *Young* doctrine has been accepted as necessary to permit the federal courts to vindicate federal rights and hold state officials responsible to "the supreme authority of the United States." As Justice Brennan has observed, "*Ex parte Young* was the culmination of efforts by this Court to harmonize the principles of the 11th amendment with the effective supremacy of rights and powers secured elsewhere in the Constitution." Perez v. Ledesma, 401 U.S. 82, 106 (1971) (Brennan, J., concurring in part and dissenting in part). Our decisions repeatedly have emphasized that the *Young* doctrine rests on the need to promote the vindication of federal rights. See, e.g., Quern v. Jordan, 440 U.S. 332, 337 (1979); Scheuer v. Rhodes, 416 U.S. 232, 237 (1974); Georgia R. & Banking Co. v. Redwine, 342 U.S. 299, 304 (1952).

The Court also has recognized, however, that the need to promote the supremacy of federal law must be accommodated to the constitutional immunity of the states. This is the significance of *Edelman v. Jordan,* supra. We recognized that the prospective relief authorized by *Young* "has permitted the Civil War amendments to the Constitution to serve as a sword, rather than merely a shield, for those whom they were designed to protect." But we declined to extend the fiction of *Young* to encompass retroactive relief, for to do so would effectively eliminate the constitutional immunity of the states. Accordingly, we concluded that although the difference between permissible and impermissible relief "will not in many instances be that between day and night," an award of retroactive relief necessarily " 'fall[s] afoul of the 11th amendment if that basic constitutional provision is to be conceived of as having any present force.' " In sum *Edelman*'s distinction between prospective and retroactive relief fulfills the underlying purpose of *Ex parte Young* while at the same time preserving to an important degree the constitutional immunity of the states.

The need to reconcile competing interests is wholly absent, however, when a plaintiff alleges that a state official has violated *state* law. In such a case the entire basis for the doctrine of *Young* and *Edelman* disappears. A federal court's grant of relief against state officials on the basis of state law, whether prospective or retroactive, does not vindicate the supreme authority of federal law. On the contrary, it is difficult to think of a greater intrusion on state sovereignty than when a federal court instructs state officials on how to conform their conduct to state law. Such a result conflicts directly with the principles of federalism that underlie the 11th amendment. We conclude that *Young* and *Edelman* are inapplicable in a suit against state officials on the basis of state law.

B

The contrary view of Justice Stevens' dissent rests on fiction, is wrong on the law, and, most important, would emasculate the 11th amendment. Under his view, an allegation that official conduct is contrary to a state statute would suffice to override the state's protection under that amendment. The theory is that such conduct is contrary to the official's "instructions," and thus ultra vires his authority. Accordingly, official action based on a reasonable interpretation of any statute might, if the interpretation turned out to be erroneous, provide the basis for injunctive relief against the actors in their official capacities. In this case, where officials of a major state department, clearly acting within the scope of their authority, were found not to have improved conditions in a state institution adequately under state law, the dissent's result would be that the state itself has forfeited its constitutionally provided immunity.

This theory is out of touch with reality. The dissent does not dispute that the general criterion for determining when a suit is in fact against the sovereign is the *effect* of the relief sought. According to the dissent, the relief sought and ordered here—which in effect was that a major state institution be closed and smaller state institutions be created and expensively funded—did not operate against the state. This view would make the law a pretense. No other court or judge in the 10 year history of this litigation has advanced this theory. And the dissent's underlying view that the named defendants here were acting beyond and contrary to their authority cannot be reconciled with reality—or with the record. The District Court in this case held that the individual defendants "acted in the utmost good faith . . . *within the sphere of their official responsibilities*," and therefore were entitled to immunity from damages. The named defendants had nothing to gain personally from their conduct; they were not found to have acted wilfully or even negligently. The court expressly noted that the individual defendants "apparently took every means available to them to reduce the incidents of abuse and injury, but were constantly faced with staff shortages." It also found "that the individual defendants are dedicated professionals in the field of retardation who were given very little with which to accomplish the habilitation of the retarded at Pennhurst." As a result, all the relief ordered by the courts below was institutional and official in character. To the extent there was a violation of state law in this case, it is a case of the state itself not fulfilling its legislative promises.

The dissent bases its view on numerous cases from the turn of the century and earlier. [W]hile there is language in the early cases that advance the authority-stripping theory advocated by the dissent, this theory had never been pressed as far as Justice Stevens would do in this case. . . . The plain fact is that the dissent's broad theory, if it ever was accepted to the full extent to which it is now pressed, has not been the law for at least a generation.

The reason is obvious. Under the dissent's view of the ultra vires doctrine, the 11th amendment would have force only in the rare case in which a plaintiff foolishly attempts to sue the state in its own name, or where he cannot produce some state statute that has been violated to his asserted injury. Thus, the ultra vires doctrine, a narrow and questionable exception, would swallow the general rule that a suit is against the state if the relief will run against it. That result gives the dissent no pause presumably because of its view that the 11th amendment and sovereign immunity " 'undoubtedly ru[n] counter to modern democratic notions of the moral responsibility of the state.' " This argument has not been adopted by this Court. Moreover, the argument substantially misses the point with respect to 11th amendment sovereign immunity. As Justice Marshall has observed, the 11th amendment's restriction on the federal judicial power is based in large part on "the problems of federalism inherent in making one sovereign appear against its will in the courts of the other." Employees v. Missouri Public Health Dept., 411 U.S. 279, 294 (1973) (Marshall, J., concurring in the result). The dissent totally rejects the 11th amendment's basis in federalism.

C

The reasoning of our recent decisions on sovereign immunity thus leads to the conclusion that a federal suit against state officials on the basis of state law contravenes the 11th amendment when—as here—the relief sought and ordered has an impact directly on the state itself. In reaching a contrary conclusion, the Court of Appeals relied principally on a separate line of cases dealing with pendent jurisdiction. The crucial point for the Court of Appeals was that this Court has granted relief against state officials on the basis of a pendent state law claim. We therefore must consider the relationship between pendent jurisdiction and the 11th amendment.

This Court long has held generally that when a federal court obtains jurisdiction over a federal claim, it may adjudicate other related claims over which the court otherwise would not have jurisdiction. See, e.g., Mine Workers v. Gibbs, 383 U.S. 715, 726 (1966). The Court also has held that a federal court may resolve a case solely on the basis of a pendent state law claim, see Siler v. Louisville & Nashville R. Co., 213 U.S. 175, 192–93 (1909), and that in fact the court usually should do so in order to avoid federal constitutional questions, see id. at 193; Ashwander v. TVA, 297 U.S. 288, 347 (1936) (Brandeis, J., concurring) ("[I]f a case can be decided on either of two grounds, one involving a constitutional question, the other a question of statutory construction or general law, the Court will decide only the latter"). But pendent jurisdiction is a judge made doctrine inferred from the general language of article III. The question presented is whether the doctrine may be viewed as displacing the explicit limitation on federal jurisdiction contained in the 11th amendment.

As the Court of Appeals noted, in *Siler* and subsequent cases concerning pendent jurisdiction, relief was granted against state officials on the basis of state law claims that were pendent to federal constitutional claims. In none of these cases, however, did the Court so much as mention the 11th amendment in connection with the state law claim. Rather, the Court appears to have assumed that once jurisdiction was established over the federal law claim, the doctrine of pendent jurisdiction would establish power to hear the state law claims as well. The Court has not addressed whether that doctrine has a different scope when applied to suits against the state. . . .

As noted, the implicit view of these cases seems to have been that once jurisdiction is established on the basis of a federal question, no further 11th amendment inquiry is necessary with respect to other claims raised in the case. This is an erroneous view and contrary to the principles established in our 11th amendment decisions. "The 11th amendment is an explicit limitation on the judicial power of the United States." It deprives a federal court of power to decide certain claims against states that otherwise would be within the scope of article III's grant of jurisdiction. For example, if a lawsuit against state officials under 42 U.S.C. § 1983 alleges a constitutional claim, the federal court is barred from awarding damages against the state treasury even though the claim arises under the Constitution. See Quern v. Jordan, 440 U.S. 332 (1979). Similarly, if a § 1983 action alleging a constitutional claim is brought directly against a state, the 11th amendment bars a federal court from granting any relief on that claim. See Alabama v. Pugh, 438 U.S. 781 (1978) (per curiam). The amendment thus is a specific constitutional bar against hearing even *federal* claims that otherwise would be within the jurisdiction of the federal courts.

This constitutional bar applies to pendent claims as well. As noted above, pendent jurisdiction is a judge made doctrine of expediency and efficiency derived from the general article III language conferring power to hear all "cases" arising under federal law or between diverse parties. See Mine Workers v. Gibbs, 383 U.S. 715, 725 (1966). See also Hagans v. Lavine, 415 U.S. 528, 545 (1974) (terming pendent jurisdiction "a doctrine of discretion"). The 11th amendment should not be construed to apply with less force to this implied form of jurisdiction than it does to the explicitly granted power to hear federal claims. . . .

In sum, contrary to the view implicit in the [earlier decisions], neither pendent jurisdiction nor any other basis of jurisdiction may override the 11th amendment. A federal court must examine each claim in a case to see if the court's jurisdiction over that claim is barred by the 11th amendment. We concluded above that a claim that state officials violated state law in carrying out their official responsibilities is a claim against the state that is protected by the 11th amendment. We now hold that this principle applies as well to state law claims brought into federal court under pendent jurisdiction.

D

Respondents urge that application of the 11th amendment to pendent state law claims will have a disruptive effect on litigation against state officials. They argue that the "considerations of judicial economy, convenience, and fairness to litigants" that underlie pendent jurisdiction, see *Gibbs,* supra, 383 U.S. at 726, counsel against a result that may cause litigants to split causes of action between state and federal courts. They also contend that the policy of avoiding unnecessary constitutional decisions will be contravened if plaintiffs choose to forgo their state law claims and sue only in federal court or, alternatively, that the policy of *Ex parte Young* will be hindered if plaintiffs choose to forgo their right to a federal forum and bring all of their claims in state court.

It may be that applying the 11th amendment to pendent claims results in federal claims being brought in state court, or in bifurcation of claims. That is not uncommon in this area. Under *Edelman v. Jordan,* supra, a suit against state officials for retroactive monetary relief, whether based on federal or state law, must be brought in state court. Challenges to the validity of state tax systems under 42 U.S.C. § 1983 also must be brought in state court. Fair Assessment in Real Estate Ass'n v. McNary, 454 U.S. 100 (1981). Under the abstention doctrine, unclear issues of state law commonly are split off and referred to the state courts.

In any case, the answer to respondents' assertions is that such considerations of policy cannot override the constitutional limitation on the authority of the federal judiciary to adjudicate suits against a state. That a litigant's choice of forum is reduced "has long been understood to be a part of the tension inherent in our system of federalism." Employees v. Missouri Public Health & Welfare Dept., 411 U.S. 279, 298 (1973) (Marshall, J., concurring in result).

IV

Respondents contend that, regardless of the applicability of the 11th amendment to their state claims against petitioner state officials, the judgment may still be upheld against petitioner *county* officials. We are not persuaded. Even assuming that these officials are not immune from suit challenging their actions under the MH/MR Act,[34] it

---

[34] [W]e have applied the amendment to bar relief against county officials "in order to protect the state treasury from liability that would have had essentially the same practical consequences as a judgment against the state itself." Lake Country Estates, Inc. v. Tahoe Regional Planning Agency, 440 U.S. 391, 401 (1979). See, e.g., *Edelman v. Jordan,* supra (11th amendment bars suit against state and county officials for retroactive award of welfare benefits). . . .

is clear that without the injunction against the state institutions and officials in this case, an order entered on state law grounds necessarily would be limited. The relief substantially concerns Pennhurst, an arm of the state that is operated by state officials. Moreover, funding for the county mental retardation programs comes almost entirely from the state, and the costs of the masters have been borne by the state. Finally, the MH/MR Act contemplates that the state and county officials will cooperate in operating mental retardation programs. In short, the present judgment could not be sustained on the basis of the state law obligations of petitioner county officials. . . .

V

The Court of Appeals upheld the judgment of the District Court solely on the basis of Pennsylvania's MH/MR Act. We hold that these federal courts lacked jurisdiction to enjoin petitioner state institutions and state officials on the basis of this state law. The District Court also rested its decision on the eighth and 14th amendments and § 504 of the Rehabilitation Act of 1973. On remand the Court of Appeals may consider to what extent, if any, the judgment may be sustained on these bases. The court also may consider whether relief may be granted to respondents under the Developmentally Disabled Assistance and Bill of Rights Act, 42 U.S.C. §§ 6011, 6063. The judgment of the Court of Appeals is reversed, and the case remanded for further proceedings consistent with this opinion.

[The separate dissenting opinion of Justice Brennan is omitted.]

JUSTICE STEVENS, with whom JUSTICE BRENNAN, JUSTICE MARSHALL, and JUSTICE BLACKMUN join, dissenting.

This case has illuminated the character of an institution. The record demonstrates that the Pennhurst State School and Hospital has been operated in violation of state law. In 1977, after three years of litigation, the District Court entered detailed findings of fact that abundantly support that conclusion. In 1981, after four more years of litigation, this Court ordered the United States Court of Appeals for the Third Circuit to decide whether the law of Pennsylvania provides an independent and adequate ground which can support the District Court's remedial order. The Court of Appeals, sitting en banc, unanimously concluded that it did. This Court does not disagree with that conclusion. Rather, it reverses what this Court ordered it to do; the only error committed by the Court of Appeals was its faithful obedience to this Court's command.

This remarkable result is the product of an equally remarkable misapplication of the ancient doctrine of sovereign immunity. In a completely unprecedented holding, today the Court concludes that Pennsylvania's sovereign immunity prevents a federal court from enjoining the conduct that Pennsylvania itself has prohibited. No rational view of the sovereign immunity of the states supports this result. To the contrary, the question whether a federal court may award injunctive relief on the basis of state law has been answered affirmatively by this Court many times in the past. Yet the Court repudiates at least 28 cases, spanning well over a century of this Court's jurisprudence, proclaiming instead that federal courts have no power to enforce the will of the states by enjoining conduct because it violates state law. This new pronouncement will require the federal courts to decide federal constitutional questions despite the availability of state law grounds for decision, a result inimical to sound principles of judicial restraint. Nothing in the 11th amendment, the conception of state sovereignty it embodies, or the history of this institution, requires or justifies such a perverse result.

I

[Justice Stevens' review of the facts of the case and the history of the litigation concluded as follows:]

Thus, the District Court found that petitioners have been operating the Pennhurst facility in a way that is forbidden by state law, by federal statute, and by the federal Constitution. The en banc Court of Appeals for the Third Circuit unanimously concluded that state law provided a clear and adequate basis for upholding the District Court and that it was not necessary to address the federal questions decided by that court. That action conformed precisely to the directive issued by this Court when the case was here before. Petitioners urge this Court to make an unprecedented about face, and to hold that the 11th amendment prohibited the Court of Appeals from doing what this Court ordered it to do when we instructed it to decide whether respondents were entitled to relief under state law. Of course, if petitioners are correct, then error was committed not by the Court of Appeals, which after all merely obeyed the instructions of this Court, but rather by this Court in 1981 when we ordered the Court of Appeals to consider the state law issues.

Petitioners' position is utterly without support. The 11th amendment and the doctrine of sovereign immunity it embodies have never been interpreted to deprive a court of jurisdiction to grant relief against government officials who are engaged in conduct that is forbidden by their sovereign. On the contrary, this Court has repeatedly and consistently exercised the power to enjoin state officials from violating state law.

II

[In part II of his dissent, Justice Stevens examined prior cases and concluded that they rejected "the claim that the 11th amendment prohibits federal courts from issuing injunctive relief based on state law." In Stevens' view, the precedents supported the simple rule that "conduct that exceeds the scope of an official's lawful discretion is not conduct the sovereign has authorized and hence is subject to injunction."]

III

On its face, the 11th amendment applies only to suits against a state brought by citizens of other states and foreign nations. This textual limitation upon the scope of the states' immunity from suit in federal court was set aside in Hans v. Louisiana, 134 U.S. 1 (1890). . . . Thus, under our cases it is the doctrine of sovereign immunity, rather than the text of the amendment itself, which is critical to the analysis of any 11th amendment problem.

The doctrine of sovereign immunity developed in England, where it was thought that the king could not be sued. However, common law courts, in applying the doctrine, traditionally distinguished between the king and his agents, on the theory that the king would never authorize unlawful conduct, and that therefore the unlawful acts of the king's officers ought not to be treated as acts of the sovereign. See 1 W. Blackstone, Commentaries on the Laws of England *244 (J. Andrews ed., 1909). As early as the 15th century, Holdsworth writes, servants of the king were held liable for their unlawful acts. See 3 W. Holdsworth, A History of English Law 388 (1903). During the 17th century, this rule of law was used extensively to curb the king's authority. The king's officers

> "could do wrong, and if they committed wrongs, whether in the course of their employment or not, they could be made legally liable. The command or instruction of the king could not protect them. If the king really had given such commands or instructions, he must have been deceived."

In one famous case, it was held that although process would not issue against the sovereign himself, it could issue against officers. "For the warrant of no man, not even of the king himself, can excuse the doing of an illegal act." Sands v. Child, 83 Eng. Rep. 725, 726 (K.B. 1693). By the 18th century, this rule of law was unquestioned. And in the 19th century this view was taken by the court to be so well settled as to not require the citation of authority.

It was only natural, then that this Court, in applying the principles of sovereign immunity, recognized the distinction between a suit against a state and one against its officer. For example, while the Court did inquire as to whether a suit was "in essence" against the sovereign, it soon became settled law that the 11th amendment did not bar suits against state officials in their official capacities challenging unconstitutional conduct. This rule was reconciled with sovereign immunity principles by the use of the traditional rule that an action against an agent of the sovereign who had acted unlawfully was not considered to be against the sovereign. When an official acts pursuant to an unconstitutional statute, the Court reasoned, the absence of valid authority leaves the official ultra vires his authority, and thus a private actor stripped of his status as a representative of the sovereign. In Ex parte Young, 209 U.S. 123 (1908), the Court was merely restating a settled principle when it wrote:

"The act to be enforced is alleged to be unconstitutional, and if it be so, the use of the name of the state to enforce an unconstitutional act to the injury of complainants is a proceeding without the authority of and one which does not affect the state in its sovereign or governmental capacity. It is simply an illegal act upon the part of a state official in attempting by the use of the name of the state to enforce a legislative enactment which is void because unconstitutional. If the act which the state Attorney General seeks to enforce be a violation of the federal Constitution, the officer in proceeding under such enactment comes into conflict with the superior authority of that Constitution, and he is in that case stripped of his official or representative character and is subjected in his person to the consequences of his individual conduct."

The majority states that the holding of *Ex parte Young* is limited to cases in which relief is provided on the basis of federal law, and that it rests entirely on the need to protect the supremacy of federal law. That position overlooks the foundation of the rule of *Young*. . . .

The *Young* Court distinguished between the state and its Attorney General because the latter, in violating the Constitution, had engaged in conduct the sovereign could not authorize. The pivotal consideration was not that the conduct violated federal law, since nothing in the jurisprudence of the 11th amendment permits a suit against a sovereign merely because federal law is at issue. Indeed, at least since Hans v. Louisiana, 134 U.S. 1 (1890), the law has been settled that the 11th amendment applies even though the state is accused of violating the federal Constitution. In *Hans* the Court held that the 11th amendment applies to all cases within the jurisdiction of the federal courts including those brought to require compliance with federal law, and bars any suit where the state is the proper defendant under sovereign immunity principles. A long line of cases has endorsed that proposition, holding that irrespective of the need to vindicate federal law a suit is barred by the 11th amendment if the state is the proper defendant. It was clear until today that "the state [is not] divested of its immunity 'on the mere ground that the case is one arising under the Constitution or laws of the United States.'" Parden v. Terminal R. Co., 377 U.S. 184, 186 (1964) (quoting *Hans*).

The pivotal consideration in *Young* was that it was not conduct of the sovereign that was at issue. The rule that unlawful acts of an officer should not be attributed to the sovereign has deep roots in the history of sovereign immunity and makes *Young* reconcilable with the principles of sovereign immunity found in the 11th amendment, rather than merely an unprincipled accommodation between federal and state interests that ignores the principles contained in the 11th amendment.

This rule plainly applies to conduct of state officers in violation of state law. *Young* states that the significance of the charge of unconstitutional conduct is that it renders the state official's conduct "simply an illegal act," and hence the officer is not entitled to the sovereign's immunity. Since a state officer's conduct in violation of state law is certainly no less illegal than his violation of federal law, in either case the official, by committing an illegal act, is "stripped of his official or representative character." . . . The majority's position turns the *Young* doctrine on its head—sovereign immunity did not bar actions challenging unconstitutional conduct by state officers since the federal Constitution was also to be considered part of the state's law—and since the state could not and would not authorize a violation of its own law, the officers' conduct was considered individual and not sovereign. No doubt the [*Young* Court] would be shocked to discover that conduct authorized by state law but prohibited by federal law is not considered conduct attributable to the state for sovereign immunity purposes, but conduct prohibited by state law is considered conduct attributable to the very state which prohibited that conduct. [*Young* and other] cases are based on the simple idea that an illegal act strips the official of his state law shield, thereby depriving the official of the sovereign's immunity. The majority criticizes this approach as being "out of touch with reality" because it ignores the practical impact of an injunction on the state though directed at its officers. Yet that criticism cannot account for *Young*, since an injunction has the same effect on the state whether it is based on federal or state law. Indeed, the majority recognizes that injunctions approved by *Young* "have an obvious impact on the state itself." In the final analysis the distinction between the state and its officers, realistic or not, is one firmly embedded in the doctrine of sovereign immunity. It is that doctrine and not any theory of federal supremacy which the framers placed in the 11th amendment and which this Court therefore has a duty to respect.

It follows that the basis for the *Young* rule is present when the officer sued has violated the law of the sovereign; in all such cases the conduct is of a type that would not be permitted by the sovereign and hence is not attributable to the sovereign under traditional sovereign immunity principles. In such a case, the sovereign's interest lies with those who seek to enforce its laws, rather than those who have violated them. . . .

The majority's position that the 11th amendment does not permit federal courts to enjoin conduct that the sovereign state itself seeks to prohibit thus is inconsistent with both the doctrine of sovereign immunity and the underlying respect for the integrity of state policy which the 11th amendment protects. The issuance of injunctive relief which enforces state laws and policies, if anything, enhances federal courts' respect for the sovereign prerogatives of the states. The majority's approach, which requires federal courts to ignore questions of state law and to rest their decisions on federal bases, will create more rather than less friction between the states and the federal judiciary.

Moreover, the majority's rule has nothing to do with the basic reason the 11th amendment was added to the Constitution. There is general agreement that the amendment was passed because the states were fearful that federal courts would force them to pay their Revolutionary War debts, leading to their financial ruin. Entertaining a suit for injunctive relief based on state law implicates none of the concerns of the framers. Since only injunctive relief is sought there is no threat to the state treasury of the type that concerned the framers; and if the state wishes to avoid the federal injunction, it can easily do so simply by changing its law. The possibility of states left helpless in the face of disruptive federal decrees which led to the passage of the 11th amendment simply is not presented by this case. Indeed, the framers no doubt would have preferred federal courts to base their decisions on state law, which the state is then free to reexamine, rather than forcing courts to decide cases on federal grounds, leaving the litigation beyond state control.

In light of the preceding, it should come as no surprise that there is absolutely no authority for the majority's position that the rule of *Young* is inapplicable to violations of state law. . . .

In sum, a century and a half of this Court's 11th amendment jurisprudence has established the following. A suit alleging that the official had acted within his authority but in a manner contrary to state statutes was not barred because the 11th amendment prohibits suits against states; it does not bar suits against state officials for actions not permitted by the state under its own law. The sovereign could not and would not authorize its officers to violate its own law; hence an action against a state officer seeking redress for conduct not permitted by state law is a suit against the officer, not the sovereign. *Ex parte Young* concluded in as explicit a fashion as possible that unconstitutional action by state officials is not action by the state even if it purports to be authorized by state law, *because the federal Constitution strikes down the state law shield.* In the tort cases, if the plaintiff proves his case, there is by definition no state law defense to shield the defendant. Similarly, *when the state officer violates a state statute, the sovereign has by definition erected no shield against liability.* These precedents make clear that there is no foundation for the contention that the majority embraces—that *Ex parte Young* authorizes injunctive relief against state officials only on the basis of federal law. To the contrary, *Young* is as clear as a bell: the 11th amendment does not apply where there is no state law shield. That simple principle should control this case.

IV

The majority's decision in this case is especially unwise in that it overrules a long line of cases in order to reach a result that is at odds with the usual practices of this Court. In one of the most respected opinions ever written by a member of this Court, Justice Brandeis wrote:

"The Court [has] developed, for its own governance in the cases confessedly within its jurisdiction, a series of rules under which it has avoided passing upon a large part of all the constitutional questions pressed upon it for decision. They are:
. . . .

"The Court will not pass upon a constitutional question, although properly presented by the record, if there is also present some other ground upon which the case may be disposed of. This rule has found most varied application. Thus, if a case can be decided on either of two grounds, one involving a constitutional question, the other a question of statutory construction or general law, the Court will decide only the latter. Siler v. Louisville & Nashville R. Co., 213 U.S. 175, 191 (1909)." Ashwander v. Tennessee Valley Authority, 297 U.S. 288, 346–47 (1936) (Brandeis, J., concurring).

The *Siler* case, cited with approval by Justice Brandeis in *Ashwander,* employed a remarkably similar approach to that used by the Court of Appeals in this case. A privately owned railroad corporation brought suit against the members of the railroad commission of Kentucky to enjoin the enforcement of a rate schedule promulgated by the commission. The federal circuit court found that the schedule violated the plaintiff's federal constitutional rights and granted relief. This Court affirmed, but it refused to decide the constitutional question because injunctive relief against the state officials was adequately supported by state law. The Court held that the plaintiff's claim that the schedule violated the federal Constitution was sufficient to justify the assertion of federal jurisdiction over the case, but then declined to reach the federal question, deciding the case on the basis of state law instead:

"Where a case in this Court can be decided without reference to questions arising under the federal Constitution, that course is usually pursued and is not departed from without important reasons. In this case we think it much better to decide it with regard to the question of a local nature, involving construction of the state statute and the authority therein given to the commission to make the order in question, rather than to unnecessarily decide the various constitutional questions appearing in the record." Siler v. Louisville & Nashville R. Co., 213 U.S. 175, 193 (1909).

The *Siler* principle has been applied on numerous occasions; when a suit against state officials has presented both federal constitutional questions and issues of state law, the Court has upheld injunctive relief on state law grounds. [Citing cases.] . . .

Not only does the *Siler* rule have an impressive historical pedigree, but it is also strongly supported by the interest in avoiding duplicative litigation and the unnecessary decision of federal constitutional questions.

"The policy's ultimate foundations . . . lie in all that goes to make up the unique place and character, in our scheme, of judicial review of governmental action for constitutionality. They are found in the delicacy of that function, particularly in view of possible consequences for others stemming also from constitutional roots; the comparative finality of those consequences; the consideration due to the judgment of other repositories of constitutional power concerning the scope of their authority; the necessity, if government is to function constitutionally, for each to keep within its power, including the courts; the inherent limitations of the judicial process, arising especially from its largely negative character and limited resources of enforcement; withal in the paramount importance of constitutional adjudication in our system." Rescue Army v. Municipal Court, 331 U.S. 549, 571 (1947).

In addition, application of the *Siler* rule enhances the decisionmaking autonomy of the states. *Siler* directs the federal court to turn first to state law, which the state is free to modify or repeal. By leaving the policy determination underlying injunctive relief in the hands of the state, the Court of Appeals' approach gives appropriate deference to established state policies.

In contrast, the rule the majority creates today serves none of the interests of the state. The majority prevents federal courts from implementing state policies through equitable enforcement of state law. Instead, federal courts are required to resolve cases on federal grounds that no state authority can undo. Leaving violations of state law unredressed and ensuring that the decisions of federal courts may never be reexamined by the states hardly comports with the respect for states as sovereign entities commanded by the 11th amendment.

V

One basic fact underlies this case: far from immunizing petitioners' conduct, the state of Pennsylvania prohibited it. Respondents do not complain about the conduct of the state of Pennsylvania—it is Pennsylvania's commands which they seek to enforce. Respondents seek only to have Pennhurst run the way Pennsylvania envisioned that it be run. Until today, the Court understood that the 11th amendment does not shield the conduct of state officers which has been prohibited by their sovereign.

Throughout its history, this Court has derived strength from institutional self-discipline. Adherence to settled doctrine is presumptively the correct course. Departures are, of course, occasionally required by changes in the fabric of our society. When a court, rather than a legislature, initiates such a departure, it has a special obligation to explain and to justify the new course on which it has embarked. Today, however, the Court casts aside well settled respected doctrine that plainly commands affirmance of the Court of Appeals—the doctrine of the law of the case, the doctrine of stare decisis . . ., the doctrine of sovereign immunity, the doctrine of pendent jurisdiction, and the doctrine of judicial restraint. No sound reason justifies the further prolongation of this litigation or this Court's voyage into the sea of undisciplined lawmaking.

As I said at the outset, this case has illuminated the character of an institution.

I respectfully dissent.

NOTES ON THE *PENNHURST* PROBLEM

1. Questions and Comments on *Pennhurst*. Is the majority or the dissent more persuasive in its treatment of *Ex parte Young*? In particular, should the authority-stripping rationale of that case be taken seriously, as the dissenters suggest, or treated as a fiction designed only to secure the vindication of federal rights? Does either view of *Young* explain *Edelman*? Does either view fit into a coherent interpretation of the 11th amendment?

Consider also the practical effect of the two positions. Will the majority's view require bifurcated litigation? Will it require federal courts to decide federal constitutional questions unnecessarily? Is either of these concerns sufficient to call for a different interpretation of the 11th amendment? Or are they, as the majority implied, merely unexceptional features of the "tension inherent in our system of federalism"?

2. The Significance of the State Law of Sovereign Immunity. Footnote 12 of the *Pennhurst* opinion states that "[a]t the time the suit was filed, suits against Pennsylvania were permitted only where expressly authorized by the legislature," and further that Pennsylvania later enacted a statute on sovereign immunity, "including an express preservation of its immunity from suit in federal court." The dissent made no mention of this point, but as Professor Shapiro points out in Comment, Wrong Turns: The 11th Amendment and the *Pennhurst* Case, 98 Harv. L. Rev. 61, 76–78 (1984), the story is more complicated than at first appears.

The *Pennhurst* suit was filed in 1974. At that time, Pennsylvania's sovereign immunity was apparently intact. In 1978, however, the state Supreme Court abrogated the doctrine entirely. The legislature overturned that decision, but the Pennsylvania Supreme Court held that, although the judicial abrogation of sovereign immunity had applied retroactively, the statute could not bar litigation of any cause of action that had already accrued at the time of its passage. Thus, it is at least arguable that, under the decisions of the Pennsylvania Supreme Court (and despite the wishes of the legislature), there was no state doctrine of sovereign immunity applicable to the *Pennhurst* litigation.

The underlying question is whether state law should matter. *Erie* would seem to require that federal courts look to state law to determine state sovereign immunity from state law claims. Martha Field takes exactly that position. See Field, The 11th Amendment and Other Sovereign Immunity Doctrines: Congressional Imposition of Suit Upon the States, 126 U. Pa. L. Rev. 1203, 1254 n.240 (1978). However, as *Pennhurst* illustrates, the cases do not dwell on state law, but seem to regard federal law as controlling on the question of state liability in federal court. Is this sound? Is state law adequately taken into account by the notion of waiver or consent? Or is it possible that both the majority and the dissent focused on the wrong question?[a]

3. *Migra v. Warren City School District.* On the same day that it decided *Pennhurst,* the Court also handed down its decision in Migra v. Warren City School District Board of Education, 465 U.S. 75 (1984). Migra was a public school teacher, whom the school board declined to re-employ. She brought suit in an Ohio state court against the board and the three members who had voted not to re-employ her, alleging breach of contract by the board and wrongful interference with her contract of employment by the individual members. She won that suit and was awarded reinstatement and compensatory damages.

Migra then filed a second suit in federal court. She claimed that the board's action was in retaliation for a desegregation plan she had authored and a social studies curriculum she had designed. She alleged that her termination violated free speech, due process, and equal protection. She sought injunctive relief and both compensatory and punitive damages. The District Court granted summary judgment for the defendants, and the Court of Appeals affirmed.

Writing for a unanimous Supreme Court, Justice Blackmun referred to the full faith and credit clause and 28 U.S.C. § 1738,[b] noting that it "is now settled that a federal court must give to a state court judgment the same preclusive effect that would be given that judgment under the law of the state in which the judgment was rendered." He then discussed the holding in Allen v. McCurry, 449 U.S. 90 (1980):[c]

> "*Allen* . . . made clear that issues actually litigated in a state court proceeding are entitled to the same preclusive effect in a subsequent federal § 1983 suit as they enjoy in the courts of the state where the judgment was rendered.

> "The Court in *Allen* left open the possibility, however, that the preclusive effect of a state court judgment might be different as to a federal issue that a § 1983 litigant could have raised but did not raise in the earlier state court proceeding. That is the central issue to be resolved in the present case. Petitioner did not litigate her § 1983 claim in state court, and she asserts that the state court judgment should not preclude her suit in federal court simply because her federal claim could have been litigated in the state court proceeding. Thus, petitioner urges this Court to interpret the interplay of § 1738 and

---

[a] Note the Court's subsequent position in *Atascadero,* page 815, supra, on when a waiver of immunity under state law will permit a suit against the state in federal court.

[b] 28 U.S.C. § 1738 provides in part that "acts, records, and judicial proceeds [of any state] . . . shall have the same full faith and credit in every court within the United States . . . as they have by law or usage in the courts of such state . . . from which they are taken."

[c] *Allen* appears as a main case at page 1041, infra.

§ 1983 in such a way as to accord state-court judgments preclusive effect in § 1983 suits only as to issues actually litigated in state court.

"It is difficult to see how the policy concerns underlying § 1983 would justify a distinction between the issue preclusive and claim preclusive effects of state court judgments. The argument that state court judgments should have less preclusive effect in § 1983 suits than in other federal suits is based on Congress' expressed concern over the adequacy of state courts as protectors of federal rights. *Allen* recognized that the enactment of § 1983 was motivated partially out of such concern, but *Allen* nevertheless held that § 1983 did not open the way to relitigation of an issue that had been determined in a state criminal proceeding. Any distrust of state courts that would justify a limitation on the preclusive effect of state judgments in § 1983 suits would presumably apply equally to issues that actually were decided in a state court as well as to those that could have been. . . .

"Petitioner suggests that to give state court judgments full issue preclusive effect but no claim preclusive effect would enable litigants to bring their state claims in state court and their federal claims in federal court, thereby taking advantage of the relative expertise of both forums. Although such a division may seem attractive from a plaintiff's perspective, it is not the system established by § 1738. That statute embodies the view that it is more important to give full faith and credit to state court judgments than to ensure separate forums for federal and state claims. This reflects a variety of concerns, including notions of comity, the need to prevent vexatious litigation, and a desire to conserve judicial resources.

"In the present litigation, petitioner does not claim that the state court would not have adjudicated her federal claims had she presented them in her original suit in state court. Alternatively, petitioner could have obtained a federal forum for her federal claim by litigating it first in a federal court. Section 1983, however, does not override state preclusion law and guarantee petitioner a right to proceed to judgment in state court on her state claims and then turn to federal court for adjudication of her federal claims. We hold, therefore, that petitioner's state court judgment in this litigation has the same preclusive effect in federal court that the judgment would have had in the Ohio state courts."

Justice White, joined by Chief Justice Burger and Justice Powell, wrote a brief concurrence. He stated:

"In Union & Planters' Bank v. Memphis, 189 U.S. 71, 75 (1903), this Court held that a federal court 'can accord [a state judgment] no greater efficacy' than would the judgment rendering state. That holding has been adhered to on at least three occasions since that time. [Citing cases.] The Court has also indicated that the states are bound by a similar rule under the full faith and credit clause. Public Works v. Columbia College, 84 U.S. (17 Wall.) 521, 529 (1873). The Court is thus justified in this case to rule that preclusion in this case must be determined under state law, even if there would be preclusion under federal standards.

"This construction of § 1738 and its predecessors is unfortunate. In terms of the purpose of that section, which is to require federal courts to give effect to state-court judgments, there is no reason to hold that a federal court may not give preclusive effect to a state judgment simply because the judgment would not bar relitigation in the state courts. If the federal courts have developed rules of res judicata and collateral estoppel that prevent relitigation in circumstances that would not be preclusive in state courts, the federal courts should be free to apply them, the parties then being free to relitigate in the state courts. The contrary construction of § 1738 is nevertheless one of long standing, and Congress has not seen fit to disturb it, however justified such an action might have been."

What is the likely interaction between *Pennhurst* and *Migra*? Does the litigant who goes to state court for adjudication of state law claims that the federal court cannot hear lose the chance to have the federal claims adjudicated in federal court? How can this risk be avoided?

4. Bibliography. *Pennhurst* has sparked a good deal of comment, most of it critical. In addition to the criticism by David Shapiro already cited, see Ann Althouse, How to Build a Separate Sphere: Federal Courts and State Power, 100 Harv.L.Rev. 1485 (1987) (approving of *Pennhurst* because it strengthens state autonomy without interfering with the enforcement of federal rights; George Brown, Beyond *Pennhurst*—Protective Jurisdiction, the Eleventh Amendment, and the Power of Congress to Enlarge Federal Jurisdiction in Response to the Burger Court, 71 Va. L.Rev. 343 (1985) (analyzing *Pennhurst* at length and speculating about the power of Congress to overrule it); John Dwyer, Pendent Jurisdiction and the Eleventh Amendment, 75 Cal.L.Rev. 129 (1987) (analyzing *Pennhurst* in detail and suggesting that it ought to be confined to institutional reform litigation); David Rudenstine, *Pennhurst* and the Scope of Federal Judicial Power to Reform Social Institutions, 6 Cardozo L. Rev. 71 (1984) (analyzing the impact of *Pennhurst* on institutional litigation against state officers); Erwin Chemerinsky, State Sovereignty and Federal Court Power: The Eleventh Amendment after *Pennhurst v. Halderman,* 12 Hastings Con. L.Q. 643 (1985) (tracing the implications of *Pennhurst* and finding that the opinion casts some surprisingly long shadows); and Keith Werhan, *Pullman* Abstention after *Pennhurst:* A Comment on Judicial Federalism, 27 Wm. & M. L. Rev. 449 (1986) (relating the dispute in *Pennhurst* to a deeper division about the appropriate content of "judicial federalism," especially as practiced in *Pullman* abstention cases).

Chapter IX

REMEDIES AGAINST GOVERNMENT: THE CIVIL RIGHTS ACTS

SECTION 1: "UNDER COLOR OF" LAW

MONROE v. PAPE
Supreme Court of the United States, 1961.
365 U.S. 167.

MR. JUSTICE DOUGLAS delivered the opinion of the Court.

This case presents important questions concerning the construction of R.S. § 1979, 42 U.S.C. § 1983,[a] which reads as follows:

> "Every person who, under color of any statute, ordinance, regulation, custom, or usage, of any state or territory, subjects, or causes to be subjected, any citizen of the United States or other person within the jurisdiction thereof to the deprivation of any rights, privileges, or immunities secured by the Constitution and laws, shall be liable to the party injured in an action at law, suit in equity, or other proper proceeding for redress."

The complaint alleges that 13 Chicago police officers broke into petitioners' home in the early morning, routed them from bed, made them stand naked in the living room, and ransacked every room, emptying drawers and ripping mattress covers. It further alleges that Mr. Monroe was then taken to the police station and detained on "open" charges for 10 hours, while he was interrogated about a two-day-old murder, that he was not taken before a magistrate, though one was accessible, that he was not permitted to call his family or attorney, that he was subsequently released without criminal charges being preferred against him. It is alleged that the officers had no search warrant and no arrest warrant and that they acted "under color of the statutes, ordinances, regulations, customs and usages" of Illinois and of the city of Chicago. Federal jurisdiction was asserted under 42 U.S.C. § 1983, which we have set out above, and 28 U.S.C. § 1343[1] and 28 U.S.C. § 1331.

---

[a] Subsequent citations in the Court's opinion to § 1979 of the Revised Statutes have been replaced with the now more conventional reference to title 42 of the United States Code, § 1983. [Footnote by eds.]

[1] This section provides in material part:

"The district courts shall have original jurisdiction of any civil action authorized by law to be commenced by any person . . .

"(3) To redress the deprivation, under color of any state law, statute, ordinance, regulation, custom or usage, of any right,

The city of Chicago moved to dismiss the complaint on the ground that it is not liable under the Civil Rights Acts nor for acts committed in performance of its governmental functions. All defendants moved to dismiss, alleging that the complaint alleged no cause of action under those acts or the federal Constitution. The District Court dismissed the complaint. The Court of Appeals affirmed . . . .

I

Petitioners claim that the invasion of their home and the subsequent search without a warrant and the arrest and detention of Mr. Monroe without a warrant and without arraignment constituted a deprivation of their "rights, privileges, or immunities secured by the Constitution" within the meaning of § 1983. . . .

Section 1983 came onto the books as § 1 of the Ku Klux Act of April 20, 1871. . . . Its purpose is plain from the title of the legislation, "An Act to enforce the Provisions of the Fourteenth Amendment to the Constitution of the United States, and for other Purposes." Allegation of facts constituting a deprivation under color of state authority of a right guaranteed by the 14th amendment satisfies to that extent the requirement of § 1983. See Douglas v. City of Jeannette, 319 U.S. 157 (1943). So far petitioners are on solid ground. For the guarantee against unreasonable searches and seizures contained in the fourth amendment has been made applicable to the states by reason of the due process clause of the 14th amendment. Wolf v. Colorado, 338 U.S. 25 (1949).

II

There can be no doubt at least since Ex parte Virginia, 100 U.S. 339 (1879), that Congress has the power to enforce provisions of the 14th amendment against those who carry a badge of authority of a state and represent it in some capacity, whether they act in accordance with their authority or misuse it. See Home Tel. & Tel. Co. v. Los Angeles, 227 U.S. 278, 287–96 (1913). The question with which we now deal is the narrower one of whether Congress, in enacting § 1983, meant to give a remedy to parties deprived of constitutional rights, privileges and immunities by an official's abuse of his position. Cf. Williams v. United States, 341 U.S. 97 (1951); Screws v. United States, 325 U.S. 91 (1945); United States v. Classic, 313 U.S. 299 (1941). We conclude that it did so intend.

It is argued that "under color of" enumerated state authority excludes acts of an official or policeman who can show no authority under state law, state custom, or state usage to do what he did. In this case it is said that these policemen, in breaking into petitioners' apartment, violated the Constitution and laws of Illinois. It is pointed out that under Illinois law a simple remedy is offered for that violation

privilege or immunity secured by the Constitution of the United States or by any act of Congress providing for equal rights of citizens or of all person within the jurisdiction of the United States."

and that, so far as it appears, the courts of Illinois are available to give petitioners that full redress which the common law affords for violence done to a person; and it is earnestly argued that no "statute, ordinance, regulation, custom or usage" of Illinois bars that redress. . . .

The legislation—in particular the section with which we are now concerned—had several purposes. There are threads of many thoughts running through the debates. One who reads them in their entirety sees that the present section had three main aims.

First, it might, of course, override certain kinds of state laws. Mr. Sloss of Alabama, in opposition, spoke of that object and emphasized that it was irrelevant because there were no such laws:

> "The first section of this bill prohibits any invidious legislation by states against the rights or privileges of citizens of the United States. The object of this section is not very clear, as it is not pretended by its advocates on this floor that any state has passed any laws endangering the rights or privileges of colored people."

Second, it provided a remedy where state law was inadequate. That aspect of the legislation was summed up by Senator Sherman of Ohio:

> "[I]t is said the reason is that any offense may be committed upon a negro by a white man, and a negro cannot testify in any case against a white man, so that the only way by which any conviction can be had in Kentucky in those cases is in the United States courts, because the United States courts enforce the United States laws by which negroes may testify."

But the purposes were much broader. The third aim was to provide a federal remedy where the state remedy, though adequate in theory, was not available in practice. . . .

This Act of April 20, 1871, sometimes called "the third 'force bill,' " was passed by a Congress that had the Klan "particularly in mind." The debates are replete with references to the lawless conditions existing in the South in 1871. There was available to the Congress during these debates a report, nearly 600 pages in length, dealing with the activities of the Klan and the inability of the state governments to cope with it. This report was drawn on by many of the speakers. It was not the unavailability of state remedies but the failure of certain states to enforce the laws with an equal hand that furnished the powerful momentum behind this "force bill." Mr. Lowe of Kansas said:

> "While murder is stalking abroad in disguise, while whippings and lynchings and banishment have been visited upon unoffending American citizens, the local administrations have been found inadequate or unwilling to apply the proper corrective. Combinations, darker than the night that hides them, conspiracies, wicked as the worst of felons could devise, have gone unwhipped of justice. Immunity is given to crime, and

the records of the public tribunals are searched in vain for any evidence of effective redress." . . .

While one main scourge of the evil—perhaps the leading one—was the Ku Klux Klan, the remedy created was not a remedy against it or its members but against those who representing a state in some capacity were *unable* or *unwilling* to enforce a state law. . . . There was, it was said, no quarrel with the state laws on the books. It was their lack of enforcement that was the nub of the difficulty. . . .

Senator Pratt of Indiana spoke of the discrimination against Union sympathizers and Negroes in the actual enforcement of the laws:

"Plausibly and sophistically it is said [that] the laws of North Carolina do not discriminate against them; that the provisions in favor of rights and liberties are general; that the courts are open to all; that juries, grand and petit, are commanded to hear and redress without distinction as to color, race, or political sentiment.

"But it is a fact, asserted in the report, that of the hundreds of outrages committed upon loyal people through the agency of this Ku Klux organization not one has been punished. This defect in the administration of the laws does not extend to other cases. Vigorously enough are the laws enforced against Union people. They only fail in efficiency when a man of known Union sentiments, white or black, invokes their aid. Then Justice closes the door of her temple."

It was precisely that breadth of the remedy which the opposition emphasized. . . . Senator Thurman of Ohio [said] about the section we are now considering:

"It authorizes any person who is deprived of any right, privilege, or immunity secured to him by the Constitution of the United States, to bring an action against the wrongdoer in the federal courts, and that without any limit whatsoever as to the amount in controversy. The deprivation may be of the slightest conceivable character, the damages in the estimation of any sensible man may not be five dollars or even five cents; they may be what lawyers call merely nominal damages; and yet by this section jurisdiction of that civil action is given to the federal courts instead of its being prosecuted as now in the courts of the states."

The debates were long and extensive. It is abundantly clear that one reason the legislation was passed was to afford a federal right in federal courts because, by reason of prejudice, passion, neglect, intolerance or otherwise, state laws might not be enforced and the claims of citizens to the enjoyment of rights, privileges, and immunities guaranteed by the 14th amendment might be denied by the state agencies. . . .

Although the legislation was enacted because of the conditions that existed in the South at that time, it is cast in general language and is as applicable to Illinois as it is to the states whose names were mentioned over and again in the debates. It is no answer that the state has a law which if enforced would give relief. The federal remedy is supplementary to the state remedy, and the latter need not be first sought and refused before the federal one is invoked. Hence the fact that Illinois by its Constitution and laws outlaws unreasonable searches and seizures is no barrier to the present suit in the federal court.

We had before us in *United States v. Classic,* supra, 18 U.S.C. § 242, which provides a criminal punishment for anyone who "under color of any law, statute, ordinance, regulation, or custom" subjects any inhabitant of a state to the deprivation of "any rights, privileges, or immunities secured by the Constitution or laws of the United States." Section 242 first came into the law as § 2 of the Civil Rights Act, Act of April 9, 1866. After passage of the 14th amendment, this provision was re-enacted and amended by §§ 17, 18, Act of May 31, 1870. The right involved in the *Classic* case was the right of voters in a primary to have their votes counted. The laws of Louisiana required the defendants "to count the ballots, to record the result of the count, and to certify the result of the election." But according to the indictment they did not perform their duty. In an opinion written by Mr. Justice (later Chief Justice) Stone, in which Mr. Justice Roberts, Mr. Justice Reed, and Mr. Justice Frankfurter joined, the Court ruled, "Misuse of power, possessed by virtue of state law and made possible only because the wrongdoer is clothed with the authority of state law, is action taken 'under color of' state law." There was a dissenting opinion; but the ruling as to the meaning of "under color of" state law was not questioned.

That view of the meaning of the words "under color of" state law, 18 U.S.C. § 242, was reaffirmed in *Screws v. United States,* supra, [and] in *Williams v. United States,* supra. . . .

We conclude that the meaning given "under color of" law in the *Classic* case and in the *Screws* and *Williams* cases was the correct one; and we adhere to it.

In the *Screws* case we dealt with a statute that imposed criminal penalties for acts "wilfully" done. We construed that word in its setting to mean the doing of an act with "a specific intent to deprive a person of a federal right." We do not think that gloss should be placed on § 1983 which we have here. The word "wilfully" does not appear in § 1983. Moreover, § 1983 provides a civil remedy while in the *Screws* case we dealt with a criminal law challenged on the ground of vagueness. Section 1983 should be read against the background of tort liability that makes a man responsible for the natural consequences of his actions.

So far, then, the complaint states a cause of action. There remains to consider only a defense peculiar to the city of Chicago.

III

The city of Chicago asserts that it is not liable under § 1983. We do not stop to explore the whole range of questions tendered us on this issue at oral argument and in the briefs. For we are of the opinion that Congress did not undertake to bring municipal corporations within the ambit of § 1983.

When the bill that became the Act of April 20, 1871, was being debated in the Senate, Senator Sherman of Ohio proposed an amendment which would have made "the inhabitants of the county, city, or parish" in which certain acts of violence occurred liable "to pay full compensation" to the person damaged or his widow or legal representative. The amendment was adopted by the Senate. The House, however, rejected it. The Conference Committee reported another version. The House rejected the Conference report. In a second conference the Sherman amendment was dropped and in its place § 6 of the Act of April 20, 1871, was substituted. This new section, which is now 42 U.S.C. § 1986, dropped out all provision for municipal liability and extended liability in damages to "any person or person having knowledge that any" of the specified wrongs are being committed. Mr. Poland, speaking for the House Conferees about the Sherman proposal to make municipalities liable, said:

> "We informed the conferees on the part of the Senate that the House had taken a stand on that subject and would not recede from it; that that section imposing liability upon towns and counties must go out or we should fail to agree."

The objection to the Sherman amendment stated by Mr. Poland was that "the House had solemnly decided that in their judgment Congress had no constitutional power to impose any obligation upon county and town organizations, the mere instrumentality for the administration of state law." The question of constitutional power of Congress to impose civil liability on municipalities was vigorously debated with powerful arguments advanced in the affirmative.

Much reliance is placed on the Act of February 25, 1871, entitled "An Act prescribing the Form of enacting and resolving Clauses of Acts and Resolutions of Congress, and Rules for the Construction thereof." Section 2 of this Act provides that "the word 'person' may extend and be applied to bodies politic and corporate." It should be noted, however, that this definition is merely an allowable, not a mandatory, one. It is said that doubts should be resolved in favor of municipal liability because private remedies against officers for illegal searches and seizures are conspicuously ineffective, and because municipal liability will not only afford plaintiffs responsible defendants but cause those defendants to eradicate abuses that exist at the police level. We do not reach those policy considerations. Nor do we reach the constitutional question whether Congress has the power to make municipalities liable for acts of its officers that violate the civil rights of individuals.

The response of the Congress to the proposal to make municipalities liable for certain actions being brought within federal purview by the Act of April 20, 1871, was so antagonistic that we cannot believe that the word "person" was used in this particular act to include them. Accordingly we hold that the motion to dismiss the complaint against the city of Chicago was properly granted. But since the complaint should not have been dismissed against the officials the judgment must be and is

Reversed.

MR. JUSTICE HARLAN, whom MR. JUSTICE STEWART joins, concurring.

Were this case here as one of first impression, I would find the "under color of any statute" issue very close indeed. However, in *Classic* and *Screws* this Court considered a substantially identical statutory phrase to have a meaning which, unless we now retreat from it, requires that issue to go for the petitioners here. . . .

Those aspects of Congress' purpose which are quite clear in the earlier congressional debates, as quoted by my Brothers Douglas and Frankfurter in turn, seem to me to be inherently ambiguous when applied to the case of an isolated abuse of state authority by an official. One can agree with the Court's opinion that:

"It is abundantly clear that one reason the legislation was passed was to afford a federal right in federal courts because, by reason of prejudice, passion, neglect, intolerance or otherwise, state laws might not be enforced and the claims of citizens to the enjoyment of rights, privileges, and immunities guaranteed by the 14th amendment might be denied by the state agencies."

without being certain that Congress meant to deal with anything other than abuses so recurrent as to amount to "custom, or usage." One can agree with my Brother Frankfurter in dissent, that Congress had no intention of taking over the whole field of ordinary state torts and crimes, without being certain that the enacting Congress would not have regarded actions by an official, made possible by his position, as far more serious than an ordinary state tort, and therefore as a matter for federal concern. If attention is directed at the rare specific references to isolated abuses of state authority, one finds them neither so clear nor so disproportionately divided between favoring the positions of the majority or the dissent as to make either position seem plainly correct. . . .

The dissent considers that the "under color of" provision of § 1983 distinguishes between unconstitutional actions taken without state authority, which only the state should remedy, and unconstitutional actions authorized by the state, which the federal act was to reach. If so, then the controlling difference for the enacting legislature must have been either that the state remedy was more adequate for unauthorized actions than for authorized ones or that there was, in some sense, greater harm from unconstitutional actions authorized by the full panoply of state power and approval than from unconstitutional actions not so authorized or acquiesced in by the state. I find less than compelling the evidence that either distinction was important to that Congress.

I

If the state remedy was considered adequate when the official's unconstitutional act was unauthorized, why should it not be thought equally adequate when the unconstitutional act was authorized? . . .

Since the suggested narrow construction of § 1983 presupposes that state measures were adequate to remedy unauthorized deprivations of constitutional rights and since the identical state relief could be obtained for state-authorized acts with the aid of Supreme Court review, this narrow construction would reduce the statute to having merely a jurisdictional function, shifting the load of federal supervision from the Supreme Court to the lower courts and providing a federal tribunal for fact findings in cases involving authorized action. Such a function could be justified on various grounds. It could, for example, be argued that the state courts would be less willing to find a constitutional violation in cases involving "authorized action" and that therefore the victim of such action would bear a greater burden in that he would more likely have to carry his case to this Court, and once here, might be bound by unfavorable state court findings. But the legislative debates do not disclose congressional concern about the burdens of litigation placed upon the victims of "authorized" constitutional violations contrasted to the victims of unauthorized violations. Neither did Congress indicate an interest in relieving the burden placed on this Court in reviewing such cases.

The statute becomes more than a jurisdictional provision only if one attributes to the enacting legislature the view that a deprivation of a constitutional right is significantly different from and more serious than a violation of a state right and therefore deserves a different remedy even though the same act may constitute both a state tort and the deprivation of a constitutional right. This view, by no means unrealistic as a commonsense matter,[5] is, I believe, more consistent with the flavor of the legislative history than is a view that the primary purpose of the state was to grant a lower court forum for fact findings. . . .

[5] There will be many cases in which the relief provided by the state to the victim of a use of state power which the state either did not or could not constitutionally authorize will be far less than what Congress may have thought would be a fair reimbursement for deprivation of a constitutional right. I will venture only a few examples. There may be no damage remedy for the loss of voting rights or for the harm from psychological coercion leading to a confession. And what is the dollar value of the right to go to unsegregated schools? Even the remedy for such an unauthorized search and seizure as Monroe was allegedly subjected to may be only the nominal amount of damages to physical property allowable in an action for trespass to land. It would indeed be the purest coincidence if the state remedies for violation of common-law rights by private citizens were fully appropriate to redress those injuries which only a state official can cause and against which the Constitution provides protection.

II

I think this limited interpretation of § 1983 fares no better when viewed from the other possible premise for it, namely that state-approved constitutional deprivations were considered more offensive than those not so approved. For one thing, the enacting Congress was not unaware of the fact that there was a substantial overlap between the protections granted by state constitutional provisions and those granted by the 14th amendment. Indeed one opponent of the bill, Senator Trumbull, went so far as to state in a debate with Senators Carpenter and Edmunds that his research indicated a complete overlap in every state, at least as to the protections of the due process clause. Thus, in one very significant sense, there was no ultimate state approval of a large portion of otherwise authorized actions depriving a person of due-process rights. . . .

These difficulties in explaining the basis of a distinction between authorized and unauthorized deprivations of constitutional rights fortify my view that the legislative history does not bear the burden which stare decisis casts upon it. For this reason and for those stated in the opinion of the Court, I agree that we should not now depart from the holdings of the *Classic* and *Screws* cases.

MR. JUSTICE FRANKFURTER, dissenting except insofar as the Court holds that this action cannot be maintained against the city of Chicago. . . .

This case squarely presents the question whether the intrusion of a city policeman for which that policeman can show no such authority at state law as could be successfully interposed in defense to a state-law action against him, is nonetheless to be regarded as "under color" of state authority within the meaning of § 1983. Respondents, in breaking into the Monroe apartment, violated the laws of the state of Illinois. Illinois law appears to offer a civil remedy for unlawful searches; petitioners do not claim that none is available. Rather they assert that they have been deprived of due process of law and of equal protection of the laws under color of state law, although from all that appears the courts of Illinois are available to give them the fullest redress which the common law affords for the violence done them, nor does any "statute, ordinance, regulation, custom, or usage" of the state of Illinois bar that redress. Did the enactment by Congress of § 1 of the Ku Klux Act of 1871 encompass such a situation?

That section, it has been noted, was patterned on the similar criminal provision of § 2, Act of April 9, 1866 [now 18 U.S.C. § 242]. The earlier act had as its primary object the effective nullification of the Black Codes, those statutes of the Southern legislatures which had so burdened and disqualified the Negro as to make his emancipation appear illusory. The act had been vetoed by President Johnson, whose veto message describes contemporary understanding of its second section; the section, he wrote "seems to be designed to apply to some existing or future law of a state or territory which may conflict with the provisions of the bill . . . . It provides for counteracting such forbidden legislation by imposing fine and imprisonment upon the legislators who may pass such conflicting laws, or upon the officers or agents who shall put, or attempt to put, them into execution. It means an official offense, not a common crime committed against law upon the persons or property of the black race. Such an act may deprive the black man of his property, but not of the right to hold property. It means a deprivation of the right itself, either by the state judiciary or the state legislature."

And Senator Trumbull, then Chairman of the Senate Judiciary Committee, in his remarks urging its passage over the veto, expressed the intendment of the second section as those who voted for it read it:

"If an offense is committed against a colored person simply because he is colored, in a state where the law affords him the same protection as if he were white, this act neither has nor was intended to have anything to do with his case, because he has adequate remedies in the state courts; but if he is discriminated against under color of state laws because he is colored, then it becomes necessary to interfere for his protection." . . .

The original text of the present § 1983 contained words, left out in the Revised Statutes, which clarified the objective to which the provision was addressed:

"That any person who, under color of any law, statute, ordinance, regulation, custom, or usage of any state, shall subject or cause to be subjected, any person within the jurisdiction of the United States to the deprivation of any rights, privileges, or immunities secured by the Constitution of the United States, shall, *any such law, statute, ordinance, regulation, custom, or usage of the state to the contrary notwithstanding,* be liable to the party injured" . . . .

The Court now says, however, that "It was not the unavailability of state remedies but the failure of certain states to enforce the laws with an equal hand that furnished the powerful momentum behind this 'force bill.'" Of course, if the notion of "unavailability" of remedy is limited to mean an absence of statutory, paper right, this is in large part true. Insofar as the Court undertakes to demonstrate—as the bulk of its opinion seems to do—that § 1983 was meant to reach some instances of action not specifically authorized by the avowed, apparent, written law inscribed in the statute books of the states, the argument knocks at an open door. No one would or could deny this, for by its express terms the statute comprehends deprivations of federal rights under color of any "statute, ordinance, regulation, *custom, or usage*" of a state. (Emphasis added.) The question is, *what* class of cases other than those involving state statute law were meant to be reached. And, with respect to this question, the Court's conclusion is undermined by the very portions of the legislative debates which it cites. For surely the misconduct of individual municipal police officers, subject to the effective oversight of appropriate state administrative and judicial authorities, presents a situation which differs toto coelo from one in which "Immunity is given to crime, and the records of the public tribunals are searched in vain for any evidence of effective redress," or in which murder rages while a state makes "no successful effort to bring the guilty to punishment or afford protection or redress" . . . . These statements indicate that Congress—made keenly aware by the post-bellum conditions in the South that states through their authorities could sanction offenses against the individual by settled practice which established state law as truly as written codes—designed § 1983 to reach, as well, official conduct which, because engaged in "permanently and as a rule," or "systematically," came through acceptance by law-administering officers to constitute "custom, or usage" having the cast of law. They do not indicate an attempt to reach, nor does the statute by its terms include, instances of acts in defiance of state law and which no settled state practice, no systematic pattern of official action or inaction, no "custom, or usage, of any state," insulates from effective and adequate reparation by the state authorities.

Rather, all the evidence converges to the conclusion that Congress by § 1983 created a civil liability enforceable in the federal courts only in instances of injury for which redress was barred in the state courts because some "statute, ordinance, regulation, custom, or usage" sanctioned the grievance complained of. . . .

The present case comes here from a judgment sustaining a motion to dismiss petitioners' complaint. That complaint, insofar as it describes the police intrusion, makes no allegation that that intrusion was authorized by state law other than the conclusory and unspecific claim that "[d]uring all times herein mentioned the individual defendants and each of them were acting under color of the statutes, ordinances, regulations, customs, and usages of the state of Illinois, of the county of Cook and of the defendant city of Chicago." In the face of Illinois decisions holding such intrusions unlawful and in the absence of more precise factual averments to support its conclusion, such a complaint fails to state a claim under § 1983.

However, the complaint does allege, as to the 10–hour detention of Mr. Monroe, that "it was, and it is now, the custom or usage of the Police Department of the city of Chicago to arrest and confine individuals in the police stations and jail cells of the said department for long periods of time on 'open' charges." . . . Such averments do present facts which, admitted as true for purposes of a motion to dismiss, seem to sustain petitioners' claim that Mr. Monroe's detention—as contrasted with the night-time intrusion into the Monroe apartment—was "under color" of state authority. . . .

NOTES ON 42 U.S.C. § 1983

1. Background. Before *Monroe v. Pape,* § 1983 was remarkable for its insignificance. Indeed, one commentator found only 21 suits brought under this provision in the years between 1871 and 1920.[a] During the 1920's and 30's, the statute was invoked in a handful of cases involving racial discrimination and the franchise.[b] The prospect of broader application was signalled in Hague v. Committee for Industrial Organizations, 307 U.S. 496 (1939), where the Court affirmed an injunction against a local ordinance used to harass labor organizers. In all of these cases, however, the acts complained of were affirmatively authorized by statute or local ordinance and thus fit even the narrowest reading of "under color of" law. None raised the issue of unauthorized misconduct by state officials. *Monroe v. Pape* was the first Supreme Court vindication of the use of § 1983 as an independent federal remedy against acts violative of state law.

(i) The Mind-Set of the *Civil Rights Cases.* *Monroe* did not overrule precedent, but it did overturn a long-standing assumption that § 1983 reached only misconduct either officially authorized or so widely tolerated as to amount to "custom or usage." The origins of this assumption apparently lay in restrictive constitutional interpretations of the 19th century. In a number of cases, the Supreme Court insisted that federal legislative power to enforce the guarantees of the 14th amendment could be exercised only against "state action" and held unconstitutional Reconstruction-era efforts to reach private misconduct.[c] In the famous Civil Rights Cases, 109 U.S. 3 (1883), the Court struck down the attempt in the Civil Rights Act of 1875 to prohibit racial discrimination by private parties in the provision of public accommodations. The Court determined that Congress' power to protect civil rights was limited to the correction of defective state laws:

> "[U]ntil some state law has been passed or some state action through its officers and agents has been taken, adverse to the rights of citizens sought to be protected by the 14th amendment, no legislation of the United States under said amendment, nor any proceeding under such legislation, can be called into activity; for the prohibitions of the amendment are against state laws and acts done under state authority. . . .
> In this connection it is proper to state that civil rights, such as are guarantied by the Constitution against state aggression,

---

[a] Comment, The Civil Rights Act: Emergence of an Adequate Federal Civil Remedy?, 26 Ind. L.J. 361, 363 (1951).

[b] See, e.g., Nixon v. Herndon, 273 U.S. 536 (1927) (awarding damages against Texas officials for enforcing a statute barring blacks from the Democratic primary); Lane v. Wilson, 307 U.S. 268 (1939) (vindicating rights of blacks against enforcement of racially discriminatory laws governing the franchise).

[c] This was the fate of that part of § 2 of the Act of 1871 (of which § 1983 was originally § 1) that imposed criminal penalties for private conspiracy to deprive any person of "the equal protection of the laws, or of equal privileges or immunities under the law." United States v. Harris, 106 U.S. 629 (1882).

cannot be impaired by the wrongful acts of individuals, unsupported by state authority in the shape of laws, customs or
judicial or executive proceedings."

Nowhere did the Court explicitly say that the acts of a state officer in
violation of state law could not constitute the required state action, but
this decision, and others, seemed to imply as much.[d] In fact, several
lower courts explicitly so concluded.[e] In light of this background, a
19th-century observer might reasonably have thought that federal
legislative power was limited to the redress of official wrongdoing and
that § 1983 would be unconstitutional unless it were limited to acts
explicitly or impliedly authorized by state law.

(ii) *Home Telephone & Telegraph.* Of course, by 1961 the
notion of a *constitutional* incapacity to reach unauthorized misconduct
of state officials had long since died. In fact, the demise of this idea
dates from Home Telephone & Telegraph Co. v. City of Los Angeles, 227
U.S. 278 (1913) (cited in *Monroe*). In that case, the telephone company
went to federal court to enjoin enforcement of a city ordinance setting
telephone rates. The company charged that the rates were so unreasonably low as to be confiscatory and hence violative of the 14th
amendment guarantee of due process of law. The city answered that, if
that were true, the rates would also violate a parallel provision of the
state constitution. In that event, said the city, the rates would be
forbidden by state law and therefore their adoption would not constitute "state action." Since the 14th amendment guarantees due process
only against state action, the city argued, the federal court would have
no power to consider the matter "until, by final action of an appropriate state court, it was decided that such acts were authorized by the
state . . . ." The Supreme Court rejected this view in terms that
suggested a much broader interpretation of the "state action" concept:

> "To speak broadly, the difference between the proposition
> insisted upon and the true meaning of the amendment is this,
> that the one assumes that the amendment virtually contem-
> plates alone wrongs authorized by a state, and gives only power
> accordingly, while in truth the amendment contemplates the
> possibility of state officers abusing the powers lawfully con-
> ferred upon them by doing wrongs prohibited by the amend-
> ment. In other words, the amendment . . . proceeds not
> merely upon the assumption that states acting in their govern-
> mental capacity in a complete sense may do acts which conflict

---

[d] See, e.g., Virginia v. Rives, 100 U.S. 313
(1879), in which the Supreme Court considered a provision of the Civil Rights Act of
1866 authorizing removal to federal court
of a state criminal prosecution "[a]gainst
any person who is denied or cannot enforce
in the courts of such state a right under
any law providing for the equal civil rights
of citizens of the United States, or of all
persons within the jurisdiction thereof."
The Court held that the right to removal
applied only where such denial of equal

rights was accomplished by legislative acts
rather than by the unauthorized acts of a
state official. See also Barney v. City of
New York, 193 U.S. 430 (1904).

[e] See the cases cited in Developments in
the Law, Section 1983 and Federalism, 90
Harv. L. Rev. 1133, 1160–61 n.138 (1977),
which provides an excellent short discussion of the bases for the view that acts
violative of state law could not be state
action.

with its provisions, but, also conceiving, which was more normally to be contemplated, that state powers might be abused by those who possessed them and as a result might be used as the instrument for doing wrongs, provided against all and every such possible contingency."

Home Telephone & Telegraph established that conduct violative of state law could constitute state action within the meaning of the 14th amendment. This decision undermined the notion of a *constitutional* bar to a broad reading of § 1983, but it gave no indication whether the statute should in fact be so read. That possibility was first raised in *United States v. Classic* and *United States v. Screws,* both of which broadly interpreted the parallel "under color of" law language in 18 U.S.C. § 242 (quoted in *Monroe*). As the *Monroe* opinion recounts, 18 U.S.C. § 242 is a criminal provision, originally enacted as § 2 of the Civil Rights Act of 1866. The statute that ultimately became § 1983 was modeled on this earlier law, and provided civil remedies for conduct that had been prohibited by the penal statute. Given the close historical and textual association of the two provisions, it is not surprising that the interpretation placed on one would also be applied to the other.

The upshot of all this is that the degree of innovation involved in the *Monroe* decision is hard to pin down. The majority's reading of the statute may well have been consistent with the intent of its drafters, though that issue is certainly debatable. The decision was foreshadowed by *Classic* and *Screws* and should, therefore, have been predictable. On the other hand, during much of the life of the statute, the interpretation placed on it in *Monroe v. Pape* would have been thought at least surprising and probably unconstitutional. And it seems plain that the bar generally was not aware of the potentialities of § 1983 until *Monroe* pointed the way. Thus, in an important sense, and regardless of whether it restored or perverted the original intention, *Monroe v. Pape* began a new chapter in federal court supervision of state officials.

2. Questions and Comments on *Monroe v. Pape.* Justice Douglas' analysis of the origins of § 1983 identified three "main aims" for that legislation: (1) to "override certain kinds of state laws," (2) to provide "a remedy where state law was inadequate," and (3), and most importantly, "to provide a federal remedy where the state remedy, though adequate in theory, was not available in practice." Which of these purposes applies to the facts of *Monroe?* Was Illinois law "inadequate" to deal with this situation? In what respect?

More generally, if § 1983 was based on the inadequacy of state law, why did Justice Douglas declare that "the federal remedy is supplementary to the state remedy, and the latter need not be first sought and refused before the federal one is invoked?" What is the rationale for a federal remedy that is "supplementary" to state law? Is it the difficulty of determining whether state law is in fact adequate? Under Justice Frankfurter's view, the federal courts would have to distinguish between an isolated abuse of authority by a state official and an abuse so widely practiced or tolerated as to amount to a "custom or usage" forbidden by federal law. Do the difficulties in making this inquiry justify across-the-board federal relief?

A different rationale for an independent federal remedy was suggested by Justice Harlan. He "attribute[d] to the enacting legislature the view that a deprivation of a constitutional right is significantly different from and more serious than a violation of a state right and therefore deserves a different remedy even though the same act may constitute both a state tort and the deprivation of a constitutional right." Is this persuasive? Is deprivation of a constitutional right always "more serious" than the kinds of injuries against which state law protects?[f]

3. **Jurisdiction Over Civil Rights Actions.** The jurisdictional counterpart of § 1983 is 28 U.S.C. § 1343(3), which is quoted in footnote 1 of the *Monroe* opinion. A related provision is 28 U.S.C. § 1343(4), which contains a general grant of jurisdiction over suits brought under "any act of Congress providing for the protection of civil rights." Of course, these cases are also covered by the general "federal question" statute, 28 U.S.C. § 1331, but until 1980 that provision required a minimum amount in controversy. The elimination of that restriction has made the special jurisdictional provisions for civil rights actions unnecessary.

Under whatever statute, the plaintiff's option to bring suit in federal court is a matter of some significance. Comparison between state and federal judiciaries is inevitably suspect, but differences can arise. Federal judges may be more qualified, more expert in the adjudication of federal claims, more independent of popular sentiment, more sympathetic to federal rights, and less reluctant to award damages against state officials. Or they may be none of these things. For whatever reason, it seems clear that civil rights plaintiffs typically prefer federal court and that at certain times and in certain places the advantage of federal court may be very great. See generally Neuborne, The Myth of Parity, 90 Harv. L. Rev. 1105 (1977) (summarized at pages 202–03, supra); Wells, Is Disparity a Problem?, 22 Ga. L. Rev. 283 (1988) (examining the ambiguities in the Court's treatment of the parity issue and calling for a more candid reliance on differences between state and federal courts as a ground for allocating cases among them).

4. **Impact of *Monroe v. Pape*.** Some crude measure of the impact of *Monroe v. Pape* can be derived from the annual statistics on the business of the federal courts. In the year of the *Monroe* decision, fewer than 300 suits were brought in federal court under all the civil

---

[f] For discussion of these and related questions concerning the interpretation and impact of *Monroe*, see Shapo, Constitutional Tort: *Monroe v. Pape* and the Frontiers Beyond, 60 Nw. U.L. Rev. 277, 294–96 (1965); Whitman, Constitutional Torts, 79 Mich. L. Rev. 5, 21–25 (1980) (explicating and endorsing Justice Harlan's rationale). For extensive criticism of the decision, see Zagrans, "Under Color of" *What* Law: A Reconstructed Model of § 1983 Liability, 71 Va. L. Rev. 499 (1985) (concluding that, "[a]s a matter of statutory construction, *Monroe* is flatly wrong.")

rights acts. Ten years later, that figure had risen to 8,267, including 3,129 civil rights actions filed by prisoners. In 1981, nearly 32,000 suits were brought under the civil rights acts (chiefly § 1983), including more than 16,000 suits by prisoners.[g]

Qualitatively, the assessment is more difficult. Since *Ex parte Young,* injunctive relief against unconstitutional state action had been available simply by the expedient of naming the appropriate state officer as defendant. With respect to prospective relief, therefore, *Monroe* recharacterized rather than created the opportunity for federal litigation. What was really new was the prospect of damage actions against government officials. Of course, § 1983 applies only to persons acting under color of statute, etc., "of any state or territory or the District of Columbia."[h] It creates no right of action against federal officers, see Wheeldin v. Wheeler, 373 U.S. 647 (1963), unless they act in concert with state officials and under the authority of state law. See Dombrowski v. Eastland, 387 U.S. 82 (1967). Moreover, the states as such are immune from damages under the 11th amendment. See Edelman v. Jordan, 415 U.S. 651 (1974). And state officials enjoy various kinds of (usually qualified) immunity, as is detailed in the next section. Thus, although the damage remedy is importantly qualified, the availability of money damages for the unconstitutional acts of government officials is the heart of § 1983.

Finally, mention should be made that § 1983 is not limited to constitutional violations. It applies in terms to deprivation of rights, privileges, or immunities "secured by the Constitution *and laws* " of the United States. Thus, it seems to create a private right of action for every violation of federal statute or regulation by a person acting under color of state authority. The extent to which this is true is examined in *Maine v. Thiboutot,* and the notes following, pages 1017–40 infra.

NOTES ON OTHER CIVIL RIGHTS ACTS

Section 1983 is only the most important of the civil rights statutes. A number of other statutes, some from the Reconstruction era and others of modern origin, address related matters. There follows a summary of the Reconstruction laws, followed by a brief survey of successor provisions now in force.

[g] These figures are taken from the Annual Reports of the Director, Administrative Office of the United States Courts, for the years indicated.

For the results of one of the few empirical studies of § 1983 litigation, see Theodore Eisenberg and Stewart Schwab, The Reality of Constitutional Tort Litigation, 72 Corn.L.Rev. 641 (1987).

[h] In 1979, the statute was amended to treat the District of Columbia as a state for suit under § 1983. The amendment also declares that "any act of Congress applicable exclusively to the District of Columbia shall be considered to be a statute of the District of Columbia" for this purpose. Before that, the District of Columbia was outside the scope of § 1983, see District of Columbia v. Carter, 409 U.S. 418 (1973), even though the statute had been interpreted to cover acts under the laws of Puerto Rico. See Marin v. University of Puerto Rico, 377 F.Supp. 613 (D. P.R. 1974).

1. **Reconstruction Legislation.** In addition to approving the 13th, 14th, and 15th amendments to the Constitution, the Reconstruction Congresses also enacted a spate of civil rights laws. Pieces of this legislation remain in force today, although most have been rephrased slightly in the course of code revisions. Like 42 U.S.C. § 1983, many of these provisions lay dormant until they were rediscovered and reinvigorated in the modern civil rights era.

(i) **The Act of 1866.** The Civil Rights Act of 1866 was aimed chiefly at the elimination of the so-called Black Codes—racially restrictive laws designed to limit the effect of Emancipation. Section 1 overruled the famous *Dred Scott* case[1] by declaring that "all persons born in the United States are hereby declared to be citizens of the United States." Section 1 also protected "such citizens, of every race and color, without regard to previous condition of slavery or involuntary servitude," in the enjoyment of certain rights. Portions of this legislation survive as 42 U.S.C. §§ 1981 and 1982, as described below. Finally, § 2 of the 1866 statute provided criminal penalties for the deprivation of civil rights by persons acting "under color of law." This provision, which has been carried forward as 18 U.S.C. § 242, was the model on which the civil provision that is now 42 U.S.C. § 1983 was originally based.

(ii) **The Act of 1870.** Doubts about the constitutionality of the 1866 Act led to ratification of the 14th amendment in 1868. Two years later, the 15th amendment was ratified. Congress then passed the Enforcement Act of 1870, which made it criminal to obstruct the exercise of the right to vote. Most of the provisions of the 1870 Act were repealed in 1894, but an important remnant survives in 18 U.S.C. § 241, which punishes conspiracies to violate civil rights.

(iii) **The Act of 1871.** In 1871 Congress passed two additional statutes. The Act of February 28, 1971, amended the 1870 law. The Act of April 20, 1871, otherwise known as the Ku Klux Klan Act, was the origin of what is now 42 U.S.C. § 1983. Its history is recounted in *Monroe v. Pape.* In addition, the Ku Klux Klan Act included the predecessor of 42 U.S.C. § 1985(c), which provides a civil remedy for conspiracies to interfere with civil rights. Finally, Section 2 of the 1871 Act provided criminal penalties for private conspiracies to deny civil rights. It was declared unconstitutional in United States v. Harris, 106 U.S. 629 (1882), and eventually repealed in 1909.

(iv) **The Act of 1875.** The Civil Rights Act of 1875 provided civil and criminal remedies for denial of equal rights, without regard to race, color, or previous condition of servitude, in matters of public accommodation. It was held unconstitutional in the Civil Rights Cases, 109 U.S. 3 (1883).

2. **Successor Provisions.** In addition to § 1983, surviving remnants of Reconstruction-era legislation include:

---

[1] Dred Scott v. Sandford, 60 U.S. (19 How.) 393 (1857).

(i) 42 U.S.C. §§ 1981 and 1982. Sections 1981 and 1982 derive from the Civil Rights Act of 1866. Section 1981 secures to all persons the "same right . . . to make and enforce contracts, to sue, be parties, give evidence, [etc.] as is enjoyed by white citizens . . . ." Section 1982 provides in generally parallel terms that "[a]ll citizens of the United States shall have the same right, in every state and territory, as is enjoyed by white citizens thereof to inherit, purchase, lease, sell, hold, and convey real and personal property."

For a long time, these provisions were thought to create a right only against state action. So read, the right "enjoyed by white citizens" was the right to equal treatment under law—that is, the right to engage in contract or property transactions with other willing participants, free of governmental interference or discrimination. Then, in Jones v. Alfred H. Mayer Co., 392 U.S. 409 (1968), the Supreme Court held that § 1982 "bars *all* racial discrimination, private as well as public, in the sale or rental of property." The Court, speaking through Justice Stewart, based this conclusion on a lengthy review of the legislative history of the 1866 Act. Justice Harlan, in dissent, conducted an equally lengthy review in support of the narrower reading.

Several years later, in Runyon v. McCrary, 427 U.S. 160 (1976), the Court gave a similarly broad reading to § 1981. The Court found that the statute prohibited racial discrimination in admissions by a private school. Justices Powell and Stevens, neither of whom had been on the Court at the time of *Jones,* expressed doubts about the correctness of that decision but concluded that stare decisis required that it be followed with respect to this related statute.

(ii) 42 U.S.C. § 1985(c). Derived from § 1 of the Civil Rights Act of 1871, this statute has the same lineage as § 1983. It provides a civil remedy for conspiracies to violate civil rights. Specifically, it applies if two or more persons "conspire or go in disguise on the highway or on the premises of another, for the purpose of depriving, either directly or indirectly, any person or class of persons of the equal protection of the laws or of equal privileges and immunities under the laws." As late as 1951, the Court said that this provision covered only conspiracies under color of law. Since equal protection is guaranteed only against state action, reasoned the Court, the statute did not reach purely private conspiracies to discriminate. Collins v. Hardyman, 341 U.S. 651 (1951). This reading was reversed some years later in Griffin v. Breckenridge, 403 U.S. 88 (1971), where a unanimous Court concluded that § 1985(c) did reach private conspiracies to deny equal rights.

(iii) 18 U.S.C. § 241. This statute is the modern successor to the criminal provision on which § 1985(c) was based. Derived from the Civil Rights Act of 1870, § 241 punishes two or more persons who "conspire to injure, oppress, threaten, or intimidate any citizen in the free exercise or enjoyment of any right or privilege secured to him by the Constitution or laws of the United States" or who "go in disguise upon the highway" with intent to hinder enjoyment of such a right. The application of this provision to private conspiracies to deny equal rights was approved by a majority of the Court in United States v. Guest, 383 U.S. 745 (1966).

(iv) **18 U.S.C. § 242.**   Section 242 is a criminal provision derived from the Civil Rights Act of 1866.   As recounted in *Monroe v. Pape,* this was the model for what is now 42 U.S.C. § 1983.   It includes the "under color of law" language involved in *Classic* and *Screws.*   The current version punishes as a federal crime the willful deprivation by a person acting under color of law of "any rights, privileges, or immunities secured or protected by the Constitution or laws of the United States."

SECTION 2: OFFICIAL IMMUNITIES

SCHEUER v. RHODES
Supreme Court of the United States, 1974.
416 U.S. 232.

MR. CHIEF JUSTICE BURGER delivered the opinion of the Court.

We granted certiorari in these cases to resolve whether the District Court correctly dismissed civil damage actions, brought under 42 U.S.C. § 1983, on the ground that these actions were, as a matter of law, against the state of Ohio, and hence barred by the 11th amendment to the Constitution and, alternatively, that the actions were against state officials who were immune from liability for the acts alleged in the complaints.   These cases arise out of the . . . period of alleged civil disorder on the campus of Kent State University in Ohio during May 1970 . . . .

In these cases the personal representatives of the estates of three students who died in that episode seek damages against the governor, the adjutant general, and his assistant, various named and unnamed officers and enlisted members of the Ohio National Guard, and the president of Kent State University.   The complaints in both cases allege a cause of action under the Civil Rights Act of 1871, 42 U.S.C. § 1983. . . .

The District Court dismissed the complaints for lack of jurisdiction over the subject matter on the theory that these actions, although in form against the named individuals, were, in substance and effect, against the state of Ohio and thus barred by the 11th amendment.   The Court of Appeals affirmed the action of the District Court, agreeing that the suit was in legal effect one against the state of Ohio and, alternatively, that the common-law doctrine of executive immunity barred action against the state officials who are respondents here.   We are confronted with the narrow threshold question whether the District Court properly dismissed the complaints.   We hold that dismissal was inappropriate at this stage of the litigation and accordingly reverse the judgments and remand for further proceedings.   We intimate no view on the merits of the allegations since there is no evidence before us at this stage.

I

The complaints in these cases are not identical but their thrust is essentially the same. In essence, the defendants are alleged to have "intentionally, recklessly, wilfully and wantonly" caused an unnecessary deployment of the Ohio National Guard on the Kent State campus and, in the same manner, ordered the Guard members to perform allegedly illegal actions which resulted in the death of plaintiffs' decedents. Both complaints allege that the action was taken "under color of state law" and that it deprived the decedents of their lives and rights without due process of law. Fairly read, the complaints allege that each of the named defendants, in undertaking such actions, acted either outside the scope of his respective office, or, if within the scope, acted in an arbitrary manner, grossly abusing the lawful powers of office. . . .

II

The 11th amendment to the Constitution of the United States provides: "The Judicial power of the United States shall not be construed to extend to any suit in law or equity, commenced or prosecuted against one of the United States by Citizens of another State . . . ." It is well established that the amendment bars suits not only against the state when it is the named party but also when it is the party in fact. . . .

However, since Ex parte Young, 209 U.S. 123 (1908), it has been settled that the 11th amendment provides no shield for a state official confronted by a claim that he had deprived another of a federal right under the color of state law. *Ex parte Young* teaches that when a state officer acts under a state law in a manner violative of the federal Constitution, he

> "comes into conflict with the superior authority of that Constitution, and he is in that case stripped of his official or representative character and is subjected *in his person* to the consequences of his individual conduct. The state has no power to impart to him any immunity from responsibility to the supreme authority of the United States." [Emphasis supplied.]

Ex parte Young involved a question of the federal courts' injunctive power, not, as here, a claim for monetary damages. While it is clear that the doctrine of *Ex parte Young* is of no aid to a plaintiff seeking damages from the public treasury, Edelman v. Jordan, 415 U.S. 651 (1974), damages against individual defendants are a permissible remedy in some circumstances notwithstanding the fact that they hold public office. In some situations a damage remedy can be as effective a redress for the infringement of a constitutional right as injunctive relief might be in another.

Analyzing the complaints in light of these precedents, we see that petitioners allege facts that demonstrate they are seeking to impose individual and personal liability on the *named defendants* for what they claim—but have not yet established by proof—was a deprivation of federal rights by these defendants under color of state law. Whatever the plaintiffs may or may not be able to establish as to the merits of their allegations, their claims, as stated in the complaints, given the favorable reading required by the Federal Rules of Civil Procedure, are not barred by the 11th amendment. Consequently, the District Court erred in dismissing the complaints for lack of jurisdiction.

III

The Court of Appeals relied upon the existence of an absolute "executive immunity" as an alternative ground for sustaining the dismissal of the complaints by the District Court. If the immunity of a member of the executive branch is absolute and comprehensive as to all acts allegedly performed within the scope of official duty, the Court of Appeals was correct; if, on the other hand, the immunity is not absolute but rather one that is qualified or limited, an executive officer may or may not be subject to liability depending on all the circumstances that may be revealed by the evidence. The concept of the immunity of government officers from personal liability springs from the same root considerations that generated the doctrine of sovereign immunity. While the latter doctrine—that the "king can do no wrong"—did not protect all government officers from personal liability, the common law soon recognized the necessity of permitting officials to perform their official functions free from the threat of suits for personal liability. This official immunity apparently rested, in its genesis, on two mutually dependent rationales: (1) the injustice, particularly in the absence of bad faith, of subjecting to liability an officer who is required, by the legal obligations of his position, to exercise discretion; (2) the danger that the threat of such liability would deter his willingness to execute his office with the decisiveness and the judgment required by the public good. . . .

Although the development of the general concept of immunity, and the mutations which the underlying rationale has undergone in its application to various positions are not matters of immediate concern here, it is important to note, even at the outset, that one policy consideration seems to pervade the analysis: the public interest requires decisions and action to enforce laws for the protection of the public. Mr. Justice Jackson expressed this general proposition succinctly, stating "it is not a tort for government to govern." Public officials, whether governors, mayors or police, legislators or judges, who fail to make decisions when they are needed or who do not act to implement decisions when they are made do not fully and faithfully perform the duties of their offices. Implicit in the idea that officials have some immunity—absolute or qualified—for their acts, is a recognition that they may err. The concept of immunity assumes this and goes on to assume that it is better to risk some error and possible injury from such error than not to decide or act at all. In Barr v. Mateo, 360 U.S. 564, 572–73 (1959), the Court observed, in the somewhat parallel context of the privilege of public officers from defamation actions, "The privilege is not a badge or emolument of exalted office, but an expression of a policy designed to aid in the effective functioning of government."

For present purposes we need determine only whether there is an absolute immunity, as the Court of Appeals determined, governing the specific allegations of the complaint against the chief executive officer of a state, the senior and subordinate officers and enlisted personnel of that state's National Guard, and the president of a state-controlled university. If the immunity is qualified, not absolute, the scope of that immunity will necessarily be related to facts as yet not established either by affidavits, admissions or a trial record. Final resolution of this question must take into account the functions and responsibilities of these particular defendants in their capacities as officers of the state government, as well as the purposes of 42 U.S.C. § 1983. In neither of these inquiries do we write on a clean slate. It can hardly be argued, at this late date, that under no circumstances can the officers of state government be subject to liability under this statute. In Monroe v. Pape, 365 U.S. 167 (1961), Mr. Justice Douglas, writing for the Court, held that the section in question was meant "to give a remedy to parties deprived of constitutional rights, privileges and immunities by an official's abuse of his position." Through the civil rights statutes, Congress intended "to enforce provisions of the 14th amendment against those who carry a badge of authority of a state and represent it in some capacity, whether they act in accordance with their authority or misuse it."

Since the statute relied on thus included within its scope the " '[m]isuse of power, possessed by virtue of state law and made possible only because the wrongdoer is clothed with the authority of state law,' " government officials, as a class, could not be totally exempt, by virtue of some absolute immunity, from liability under its terms. Indeed, as the Court also indicated in *Monroe v. Pape,* supra, the legislative history indicates that there is no absolute immunity. Soon after *Monroe v. Pape,* Mr. Chief Justice Warren noted in Pierson v. Ray, 386 U.S. 547 (1967), that the "legislative record [of § 1983] gives no clear indication that Congress meant to abolish wholesale all common-law immunities." The Court had previously recognized that the Civil Rights Act of 1871 does not create civil liability for legislative acts by legislators "in a field where legislators traditionally have power to act." Tenney v. Brandhove, 341 U.S. 367 (1951). . . . .

In similar fashion, *Pierson v. Ray,* supra, examined the scope of judicial immunity under this statute. Noting that the record contained no "proof or specific allegation" that the trial judge had "played any role in these arrests and convictions other than to adjudge petitioners guilty when their cases came before his court," the Court concluded that, had the Congress intended to abolish the common-law "immunity of judges for acts within the judicial role," it would have done so specifically. A judge's

> "errors may be corrected on appeal, but he should not have to fear that unsatisfied litigants may hound him with litigation charging malice or corruption. Imposing such a burden on judges would contribute not to principled and fearless decision-making but to intimidation."

The *Pierson* Court was also confronted with whether immunity was available to that segment of the executive branch of a state government that is most frequently and intimately involved in day-to-day contacts with the citizenry and, hence, most frequently exposed to situations which can give rise to claims under § 1983—the local police officer. . . . The Court noted that the "common law has never granted police officers an absolute and unqualified immunity," but that "the prevailing view in this country [is that] a peace officer who arrests someone with probable cause is not liable for false arrest simply because the innocence of the suspect is later proved"; the Court went on to observe that a "policeman's lot is not so unhappy that he must choose between being charged with dereliction of duty if he does not arrest when he has probable cause, and being mulcted in damages if he does." The Court then held:

> "that the defense of good faith and probable cause, which the Court of Appeals found available to the officers in the common-law action for false arrest and imprisonment, is also available to them in the action under 1983."

When a court evaluates police conduct relating to an arrest its guideline is "good faith and probable cause." In the case of higher officers of the executive branch, however, the inquiry is far more complex since the range of decisions and choices—whether the formulation of policy, of legislation, of budgets, or of day-to-day decisions—is virtually infinite. In common with police officers, however, officials with a broad range of duties and authority must often act swiftly and firmly at the risk that action deferred will be futile or constitute virtual abdication of office. Like legislators and judges, these officers are entitled to rely on traditional sources for the factual information on which they decide and act. When a condition of civil disorder in fact exists, there is obvious need for prompt action, and decisions must be made in reliance on factual information supplied by others. While both federal and state laws plainly contemplate the use of force when the necessity arises, the decision to invoke military power has traditionally been viewed with suspicion and skepticism since it often involves the temporary suspension of some of our most cherished rights— government by elected civilian leaders, freedom of expression, of assembly, and of association. Decisions in such situations are more likely than not to arise in an atmosphere of confusion, ambiguity, and swiftly moving events and when, by the very existence of some degree of civil disorder, there is often no consensus as to the appropriate remedy. In short, since the options which a chief executive and his principal subordinates must consider are far broader and far more subtle than those made by officials with less responsibility, the range of discretion must be comparably broad. . . .

These considerations suggest that, in varying scope, a qualified immunity is available to officers of the executive branch of government, the variation being dependent upon the scope of discretion and responsibilities of the office and all the circumstances as they reasonably appeared at the time of the action on which liability is sought to be based. It is the existence of reasonable grounds for the belief formed at the time and in light of all the circumstances, coupled with good-faith belief, that affords a basis for qualified immunity of executive officers for acts performed in the course of official conduct. . . .

IV

These cases, in their present posture, present no occasion for a definitive exploration of the scope of immunity available to state executive officials nor, because of the absence of a factual record, do they permit a determination as to the applicability of the foregoing principles to the respondents here. The District Court acted before answers were filed and without any evidence other than the copies of the proclamations issued by respondent [Governor] Rhodes and brief affidavits of the adjutant general and his assistant. In dismissing the complaints, the District Court and the Court of Appeals erroneously accepted as a fact the good faith of the governor, and took judicial notice that "mob rule existed at Kent State University." There was no opportunity afforded petitioners to contest the facts assumed in that conclusion. There was no evidence before the courts from which such a finding of good faith could be properly made and, in the circumstances of these cases, such a dispositive conclusion could not be judicially noticed. We can readily grant that a declaration of emergency by the chief executive of a state is entitled to great weight but it is not conclusive.

The documents properly before the District Court at this early pleading stage specifically placed in issue whether the governor and his subordinate officers were acting within the scope of their duties under the Constitution and laws of Ohio; whether they acted within the range of discretion permitted the holders of such office under Ohio law and whether they acted in good faith both in proclaiming an emergency and as to the actions taken to cope with the emergency so declared. Similarly, the complaints place directly in issue whether the lesser officers and enlisted personnel of the Guard acted in good-faith obedience to the orders of their superiors. Further proceedings, either by way of summary judgment or by trial on the merits, are required. . . .

The judgments of the Court of Appeals are reversed and the cases are remanded for further proceedings consistent with this opinion.

MR. JUSTICE DOUGLAS took no part in the decision of these cases.[a]

---

[a] Following the Supreme Court's remand in *Scheuer,* the cases were tried on the merits. After a trial of nearly four months duration, the jury returned a verdict in favor of all defendants. This verdict was set aside on appeal because of threats

NOTES ON IMMUNITY FROM AWARD OF DAMAGES

1. **Background.** Liability of public officials under § 1983 involves two rather different types of immunity issues: immunity from award of damages and immunity from prospective relief. Of these two issues, the former has been litigated more frequently.

The *Scheuer* opinion discusses two important early cases. Tenney v. Brandhove, 341 U.S. 367 (1951), held that persons engaged in legitimate legislative activity are absolutely immune from civil liability under § 1983. The Court reasoned that legislative immunity was so well established at common law that Congress would have explicitly said so if it had meant to abolish such immunity under § 1983. Pierson v. Ray, 386 U.S. 547 (1967), extended this reasoning to judges, but held that police officers sued for unconstitutional arrest of civil rights demonstrators were entitled only to a "qualified" defense of "good faith and probable cause."

Thus, by the time of *Scheuer v. Rhodes*, it was established, despite the complete absence of statutory language to this effect, that liability for damages under § 1983 is limited by official immunity and that the immunity may be either absolute or qualified. Persons performing legislative or judicial functions are absolutely immune, and, as the Court has subsequently decided, so are prosecutors. Imbler v. Pachtman, 424 U.S. 409 (1976). Law enforcement personnel, however, are entitled only to a qualified defense.

2. **Questions and Comments on *Scheuer*.** *Scheuer v. Rhodes* was perhaps the first decision in which the Court devoted more attention to the merits of the immunity issue than to its common-law antecedents.[a] Is the opinion persuasive? Does it explain why damages liability under § 1983 should be limited by some level of official immunity? If so, does it demonstrate that the appropriate level of immunity for high executive officers is qualified rather than absolute? Why is absolute immunity less appropriate for a governor than for a judge or legislator?

Answers to these questions depend in part on the meaning of absolute and qualified immunity and on the way those defenses are applied in the courts. These matters are dealt with in the notes that follow.

3. **The Meaning of Absolute Immunity.** "Absolute" immunity typically refers to the level of immunity, not to its scope. For one thing, immunity from award of damages may not extend to declaratory or injunctive relief. Even with respect to damages, absolute immunity may not be completely comprehensive. There is always the require-

---

made against a juror by some unknown person. Krause v. Rhodes, 570 F.2d 563 (6th Cir. 1977). The cases were then remanded for a second trial, but were eventually settled out of court. See Krause v. Rhodes, 535 F. Supp. 338 (N.D. Ohio 1979).

[a] For criticism of the Court's reliance on history, see Richard A. Matasar, Personal Immunities under Section 1983: The Limits of the Court's Historical Analysis, 40 Ark.L.Rev. 741 (1987).

ment that the act complained of be within the sphere of activity for which the immunity has been recognized.

Generally speaking, the determinative factor is the function performed, not the office held. A judge acting as such is absolutely immune from award of damages, but a judge acting in an administrative capacity enjoys only a qualified defense from damages liability. See Forrester v. White, ___ U.S. ___ (1988) (holding that a state judge was not entitled to absolute immunity for the allegedly unconstitutional discharge of a court employee). And a judge who ordered a sandwich vendor to be handcuffed and brought before him for selling "putrid" coffee was held liable for compensatory and punitive damages on the sensible ground that monitoring matters of taste is no part of the business of judging. Zarcone v. Perry, 572 F.2d 52 (2d Cir. 1978). Similarly, prosecutors are absolutely immune from the award of damages for acts "intimately associated with the judicial phase of the criminal process"; but a prosecutor engaged in investigative or administrative activities has only a "good-faith defense comparable to a policeman's." Imbler v. Pachtman, 424 U.S. 409, 430 (1976). And individual city council members, although absolutely immune for legislative acts, were held amenable to an award of damages because they did not act in their legislative capacity when they urged discharge of the town's police chief. Miller v. City of Mission, 705 F.2d 368 (10th Cir. 1983).

It is sometimes necessary to make close distinctions concerning the particular function being performed. For example, in Cleavinger v. Saxner, 474 U.S. 193 (1985), the Supreme Court considered the status of senior corrections officers who sat as members of an "Institution Disciplinary Committee" to hear charges that inmates had violated prison disciplinary rules. The Court found that the committee was not fulfilling a "classic" adjudicatory function. The Court emphasized that these officers were not "independent" adjudicators, but only prison employees "temporarily diverted from their usual duties." As such, they were "under obvious pressure to resolve a disciplinary dispute in favor of the institution and their fellow employee." The officers were therefore entitled only to a qualified immunity from civil liability. Three Justices dissented.

Where applicable, however, absolute immunity protects against damage actions, no matter how wrongful the act or malicious the motivation. The results can be extreme. Thus, for example, a justice of the peace was held immune from damages, even though he had convicted the defendant of a non-existent crime. Turner v. Raynes, 611 F.2d 92 (5th Cir. 1980). And in Stump v. Sparkman, 435 U.S. 349 (1978), the Supreme Court upheld the immunity of a state judge who ordered a tubal ligation on a 15–year-old girl who was told she was having an appendectomy. Obviously, the effect of absolute immunity is to vindicate fully the public's interest in unintimidated decisionmaking by its officials, but only at a correspondingly complete sacrifice of the interests of those who may be disadvantaged by abuse.

4. The Meaning of Qualified Immunity. The meaning of "qualified" immunity is more problematic. Not only is there the same limitation as to scope of activity, but the level of protection is itself qualified. The immunity is often said to be qualified by the requirement that the defendant act in "good faith," but a good deal more must be said about what that formulation actually means.

In *Pierson v. Ray,* supra, the Court held that police charged with making unconstitutional arrests were entitled to a defense of "good faith and probable cause." Obviously, this formulation of the defense of immunity has particular relevance to a charge of false arrest by the police. In *Scheuer* the Court noted that "the inquiry is far more complex" for higher level executive officials. The Court said that, "since the options which a chief executive and his principal subordinates must consider are far broader and far more subtle than those made by officials with less responsibility, the range of discretion must be comparably broad." What does this mean? How is the jury supposed to evaluate "the scope of discretion and responsibilities of the office" in determining whether an executive official had "reasonable grounds for the belief formed at the time and in light of all the circumstances, coupled with good-faith belief"? And what sort of belief is in issue? Is it enough that the defendant reasonably and in good faith believed that conduct was appropriate under the circumstances? Or must there be a reasonable belief as to the content of the law? These and other questions about the meaning of the qualified defense of immunity have been explored in subsequent cases.

5. *Wood v. Strickland.* The Supreme Court returned to the issue of qualified immunity in Wood v. Strickland, 420 U.S. 308 (1975). Two teenage girls brought suit against school board members who ordered them expelled from high school for "spiking" the punch served at a school event. Under pressure from one of their teachers, the girls confessed to the principal, who suspended them from school for two weeks, subject to review by the school board. That night the school board met with neither the girls nor their parents in attendance. The board members heard recommendations of leniency and were preparing to act when they received a phone call stating that a third participant in the spiking incident had that evening been involved in a fight at a basketball game. The board then voted to expel all the girls for the rest of the semester, a period of about three months. Two weeks later, the board held another meeting with the girls, their parents, and counsel present, and affirmed its earlier decision.

The District Court instructed the jury that the school board members could be held liable only if they acted with "malice," defined to mean "ill will against a person—a wrongful act done intentionally without just cause or excuse." The jury were unable to agree, and the court entered judgment for defendants on the ground that there was no evidence from which such "malice" could be inferred. The Court of Appeals reversed. It ruled that no specific intent to do harm was required and that the defendants' liability should be determined by an "objective," rather than "subjective," test of good faith. The Supreme

Court, speaking through Justice White, dealt with the immunity issue as follows:

"The disagreement between the Court of Appeals and the District Court over the immunity standard in his case has been put in terms of an 'objective' versus a 'subjective' test of good faith. As we see it, the appropriate standard necessarily contains elements of both. The official himself must be acting sincerely and with a belief that he is doing right, but an act violating a student's constitutional rights can be no more justified by ignorance or disregard of settled, indisputable law on the part of one entrusted with supervision of students' daily lives than by the presence of actual malice. To be entitled to a special exemption from the categorical remedial language of § 1983 in a case in which his action violated a student's constitutional rights, a school board member, who has voluntarily undertaken the task of supervising the operation of the school and the activities of the students, must be held to a standard of conduct based not only on permissible intentions, but also on knowledge of the basic, unquestioned constitutional rights of his charges. Such a standard neither imposes an unfair burden upon a person assuming a responsible public office requiring a high degree of intelligence and judgment for the proper fulfillment of its duties, nor an unwarranted burden in light of the value which civil rights have in our legal system. Any lesser standard would deny much of the promise of § 1983. Therefore, in the specific context of school discipline, we hold that a school board member is not immune from liability for damages under § 1983 if he knew or reasonably should have known that the action he took within his sphere of official responsibility would violate the constitutional rights of the student affected, or if he took the action with the malicious intention to cause a deprivation of constitutional rights or other injury to the students."

These remarks prompted a dissent by Justice Powell, in which the Chief Justice and Justices Blackmun and Rehnquist joined. The dissenters objected particularly to the majority's insistence that liability could be based on a school official's lack of knowledge of constitutional rights, as distinct from subjective bad faith:

"This harsh standard, requiring knowledge of what is characterized as 'settled, indisputable law,' leaves little substance to the doctrine of qualified immunity. The Court's decision appears to rest on an unwarranted assumption as to what lay school officials know or can know about the law and constitutional rights. These officials will now act at the peril of some judge or jury subsequently finding that a good-faith belief as to the applicable law was mistaken and hence actionable.

"The Court states the standard of required knowledge in two cryptic phrases: 'settled, indisputable law' and 'unquestioned constitutional rights.' Presumably these are intended to mean the same thing, although the meaning of neither phrase is likely to be self-evident to constitutional law scholars—much less the average school board member. . . .

"There are some 20,000 school boards, each with five or more members, and thousands of school superintendents and school principals. Most of the school board members are popularly elected, drawn from the citizenry at large, and possess no unique competency in divining the law. Few cities and counties provide any compensation for service on school boards, and often it is difficult to persuade qualified persons to assume the burdens of this important function in our society. Moreover, even if counsel's advice constitutes a defense, it may safely be assumed that few school boards and school officials have ready access to counsel or indeed have deemed it necessary to consult counsel on the countless decisions that necessarily must be made.

"In view of today's decision significantly enhancing the possibility of personal liability, one must wonder whether qualified persons will continue in the desired numbers to volunteer for service in public education."

Application of the *Wood v. Strickland* standard raises some interesting problems. For one thing, how does one tell whether the law is "settled" and "indisputable?" Must there be a Supreme Court decision squarely on point? Does precedent from a circuit court of appeals suffice? Even if there is criticism of that view from other circuits? From state courts? From commentators?

Another difficult problem concerns the degree of knowledge of the law that a lay official should be expected to have. Obviously, it is not realistic to expect lay officials to have a lawyer's skills. On the other hand, it may be reasonable to demand that a lay official exercising government power know more about the limitations on the use of that power than would an ordinary citizen. Where is the line to be drawn? Will the jury have to decide in every case what that particular defendant reasonably should have known?

Of what importance is it that the official does or does not have ready access to a government lawyer? Is ignorance unreasonable if one fails to consult a lawyer when one is available? And if the official does consult a lawyer, is it automatically reasonable to rely on advice of counsel?[a]

For more detailed exploration of these and other questions concerning the qualified immunity standard and a review of the many lower-court decisions on these issues, see Casto, Innovations in the Defense of Official Immunity under Section 1983, 47 Tenn. L. Rev. 47, 85–104

[a] See, e.g., Dellums v. Powell, 566 F.2d 167 (D.C. Cir. 1977) (suggesting that advice of counsel must be sought in good faith and that all relevant facts must be disclosed in seeking such advice, but that reliance on advice of counsel may nevertheless be unreasonable if the issue is not highly technical or if the crucial issue is one of fact).

(1979).　For an earlier treatment with particular attention to the implications of *Scheuer,* see McCormack and Kirkpatrick, Immunities of State Officials under § 1983, 8 Rut.-Cam. L. J. 65 (1976).　See also Freed, Executive Official Immunity for Constitutional Violations: An Analysis and Critique, 72 Nw. U. L. Rev. 526 (1977) (proposing a reformulation of the qualified immunity standard in terms of overall reasonableness); Woolhandler, Patterns of Official Immunity and Accountability, 37 Case W.Res.L.Rev. 396 (1987) (suggesting that qualified immunity impairs the efficacious enforcement of federal rights).

6. *Harlow v. Fitzgerald.* Although the *Wood v. Strickland* dissenters anticipated difficulty with the "objective" branch of qualified immunity, the "subjective" inquiry proved, if anything, the more troublesome.　Specifically, the problem was the substantial pre-trial proceedings sometimes required to determine whether an allegation of subjective bad faith had adequate foundation to proceed to trial.　The Court addressed this problem in Harlow v. Fitzgerald, 457 U.S. 800 (1982).

A. Ernest Fitzgerald was a notorious "whistle-blower" in the Department of Defense.　Following the abolition of his job in an Air Force reorganization, Fitzgerald brought a damage action[b] against a number of people, including Bryce Harlow, a presidential aide primarily responsible for congressional relations.　Fitzgerald claimed that Harlow and others had participated in a conspiracy to discharge Fitzgerald in retaliation for testifying to Congress concerning cost overruns in the Air Force.　The alleged conspiracy took place in the years preceding Fitzgerald's dismissal in 1970.　Fitzgerald filed suit in 1973, and Harlow was added as a defendant in an amended complaint in 1978. Harlow denied any involvement in the decision to fire Fitzgerald, and at the conclusion of extensive discovery, the evidence of Harlow's involvement "remained inferential."　The trial court denied a motion for summary judgment, and a "collateral order" appeal was taken before trial to resolve the disputed issue of Harlow's immunity.　The Supreme Court discussed that issue as follows:

> "The resolution of immunity questions inherently requires a balance between the evils inevitable in any available alternative.　In situations of abuse of office, an action for damage may offer the only realistic avenue for vindication of constitutional guarantees.　It is this recognition that has required the denial of absolute immunity to most public officers.　At the same time, however, it cannot be disputed seriously that claims frequently run against the innocent as well as the guilty—at a cost not only to the defendant officials, but to society as a whole.　These social costs include the expenses of litigation,

[b] Since § 1983 applies in terms only to persons acting under color of "state" law, this action was not brought under that section but was a *Bivens*-type action brought directly under the Constitution. For present purposes, however, the distinction is immaterial, since the same concept of qualified immunity has been applied in both contexts. For a discussion of the immunity of federal officials, see Note 9, infra.

the diversion of official energy from pressing public issues, and the deterrence of able citizens from acceptance of public office. Finally, there is the danger that fear of being sued will 'dampen the ardor of all but the most resolute, or the most irresponsible [public officials] in the unflinching discharge of their duties.'

"In identifying qualified immunity as the best attainable accommodation of competing values, in Butz v. Economou, 438 U.S. 478 (1978)[holding federal executive officials entitled to qualified immunity in *Bivens*-type suits], and *Scheuer v. Rhodes,* supra, we relied on the assumption that this standard would permit '[i]nsubstantial lawsuits [to] be quickly terminated.' Yet petitioners advance persuasive arguments that the dismissal of insubstantial lawsuits without trial—a factor presupposed in the balance of competing interests struck by our prior cases—requires an adjustment of the 'good faith' standard established by our decisions.

"Qualified or 'good faith' immunity is an affirmative defense that must be pleaded by a defendant official. Decisions of this Court have established that the 'good faith' defense has both an 'objective' and a 'subjective' aspect. The objective element involves a presumptive knowledge of and respect for 'basic, unquestioned constitutional rights.' Wood v. Strickland, 420 U.S. 308, 322 (1975). The subjective component refers to 'permissible intentions.' Ibid. Characteristically, the Court has defined these elements by identifying the circumstances in which qualified immunity would *not* be available. Referring both to the objective and subjective elements, we have held that qualified immunity would be defeated if an official '*knew or reasonably should have known* that the action he took within his sphere of official responsibility would violate the constitutional rights of the [plaintiff], or if he took the action *with the malicious intention* to cause a deprivation of constitutional rights or other injury. . . .' Ibid. (emphasis added).

"The subjective element of the good-faith defense frequently has proved incompatible with our admonition in *Butz* that insubstantial claims should not proceed to trial. Rule 56 of the Federal Rules of Civil Procedure provides that disputed questions of fact ordinarily may not be decided on motions for summary judgment. And an official's subjective good faith has been considered to be a question of fact that some courts have regarded as inherently requiring resolution by a jury.

"In the context of *Butz* 's attempted balancing of competing values, it now is clear that substantial costs attend the litigation of the subjective good faith of government officials. Not only are there the general costs of subjecting officials to the risks of trial—distraction of officials from their governmental duties, inhibition of discretionary action, and deterrence of able people from public service. There are special costs to 'subjective' inquiries of this kind. Immunity generally is available only to officials performing discretionary functions. In contrast with the thought processes accompanying 'ministerial' tasks, the judgments surrounding discretionary action almost inevitably are influenced by the decisionmaker's experiences, values, and emotions. These variables explain in part why questions of subjective intent so rarely can be decided by summary judgment. Yet they also frame a background in which there often is no clear end to the relevant evidence. Judicial inquiry into subjective motivation therefore may entail broad-ranging discovery and the deposing of numerous persons, including an official's professional colleagues. Inquiries of this kind can be peculiarly disruptive of effective government.

"Consistently with the balance at which we aimed in *Butz*, we conclude today that bare allegations of malice should not suffice to subject government officials either to the costs of trial or to the burdens of broad-reaching discovery. We therefore hold that government officials performing discretionary functions generally are shielded from liability for civil damages insofar as their conduct does not violate clearly established statutory or constitutional rights of which a reasonable person would have known.

"Reliance on the objective reasonableness of an official's conduct, as measured by reference to clearly established law, should avoid excessive disruption of government and permit the resolution of many insubstantial claims on summary judgment. On summary judgment, the judge appropriately may determine, not only the currently applicable law, but whether that law was clearly established at the time an action occurred. If the law at that time was not clearly established, an official could not reasonably be expected to anticipate subsequent legal developments, nor could he fairly be said to 'know' that the law forbade conduct not previously identified as unlawful. Until this threshold immunity question is resolved, discovery should not be allowed. If the law was clearly established, the immunity defense ordinarily should fail, since a reasonably competent public official should know the law governing his conduct. Nevertheless, if the official pleading the defense claims extraordinary circumstances and can prove that he neither knew nor should have known of the relevant legal standard, the defense should be sustained."

The objective of the *Harlow* Court's reformulation of qualified immunity seems clear enough, but the reference to discovery is a bit puzzling. Does the Court mean that the defendant is entitled to summary judgment, in advance of discovery, whenever the law was unclear at the time the action was taken? Even if the official is alleged to have acted with malice? If so, the "subjective" branch of the defense of immunity has effectively been eliminated. Or does the Court mean only that something more than "bare allegations" of malice is required? How realistic is it to expect that the plaintiff can come up with more than "bare allegations" in advance of discovery?

Uncertainty on this point prompted a concurrence by Justice Brennan, with whom Justices Marshall and Blackmun joined:

> "I agree with the substantive standard announced by the Court today, imposing liability when a public-official defendant 'knew or should have known' of the constitutionally violative effect of his actions. . . . I write separately only to note that given this standard, it seems inescapable to me that some measure of discovery may sometimes be required to determine exactly what a public-official defendant did 'know' at the time of his actions. Of course, as the Court has already noted, summary judgment will be readily available to public-official defendants whenever the state of the law was so ambiguous at the time of the alleged violation that it could not have been 'known' then, and thus liability could not ensue. In my view, summary judgment will also be readily available whenever the plaintiff cannot prove, as a threshold matter, that a violation of his constitutional rights actually occurred. I see no reason why discovery of defendant's 'knowledge' should not be deferred by the trial judge pending decision of any motion of defendants for summary judgment on grounds such as these."

What is Brennan driving at? In what respect does he disagree with the majority opinion's treatment of discovery?

More generally, should the "subjective" branch of the qualified defense be restructured? The cost of doing so may be to allow an unscrupulous official to engage in malicious misuse of public authority whenever the relevant legal standards are objectively unclear. The cost of continuing the requirement of subjective good faith, on the other hand, may be to impose substantial costs of defending on the merits essentially meritless suits. Which is the lesser evil?

7. _Anderson v. Creighton._ The _Harlow_ problem was revisited in Anderson v. Creighton, ___ U.S. ___ (1987). Anderson was an FBI agent who was sued for conducting an unlawful search. He tried to have the action dismissed on a pre-trial motion for summary judgment. Ultimately, the Supreme Court ruled that Anderson was entitled to summary judgment if, in light of the clearly established principles on warrantless searches, a reasonable officer in Anderson's situation could have believed the search to be lawful.

Speaking through Justice Scalia, the Court acknowledged the "driving force behind _Harlow_'s substantial reformulation of qualified-immunity principles—that 'insubstantial claims' against government officials be resolved prior to discovery and on summary judgment if possible." It said that _Harlow_ required an inquiry into the "objective legal reasonableness" of the action taken, judged in light of "clearly established" legal rules. In the context of warrantless searches, this determination would "often require examination of the information possessed by the searching officials," but it would "not reintroduce into qualified immunity analysis the inquiry into officials' subjective intent that *Harlow* sought to minimize." Thus, in this case, the relevant issue was "the objective (albeit fact-specific) question whether a reasonable officer could have believed Anderson's warrantless search to be lawful, in light of clearly established law and the information the searching officers possessed." The Court explicitly noted that "Anderson's subjective beliefs about the search are irrelevant." In a concluding footnote, the Court added:

> "Thus, on remand, it should first be determined whether the actions the Creightons allege Anderson to have taken are actions that a reasonable officer could have believed lawful. If they are, then Anderson is entitled to dismissal prior to discovery. If they are not, and if the actions Anderson claims he took are different from those the Creightons allege (and are actions that a reasonable officer could have believed lawful), then discovery may be necessary before Anderson's motion for summary judgment on qualified immunity grounds can be resolved. Of course, any such discovery should be tailored specifically to the question of Anderson's qualified immunity."

Justice Stevens, joined by Justices Brennan and Marshall, dissented at length. First, Stevens disputed the applicability of *Harlow*. "The Court," he said, "makes the fundamental error of simply assuming that *Harlow* immunity is just as appropriate for federal law enforcement officers such as petitioner as it is for high government officials." Here there was no uncertainty in the applicable legal standards, but only in their application to particular facts. In this context, pre-trial summary judgment was inappropriate. Stevens explained:

> "In this Court, Anderson has not argued that any relevant rule of law—whether the probable-cause requirement or the exigent-circumstances exception to the warrant requirement— was not 'clearly established' in November 1983. Rather, he argues that a competent officer might have concluded that the particular set of facts he faced did constitute 'probable cause' and 'exigent circumstances,' and that his own reasonable belief that the conduct engaged in was within the law suffices to establish immunity. But the factual predicate for Anderson's argument is not found in the [plaintiffs'] complaint, but rather in the affidavits that he has filed in support of his motion for summary judgment. Obviously, the [plaintiffs] must be given an opportunity to have discovery to test the accuracy and completeness of the factual basis for the immunity claim."

Stevens also emphasized that denial of *Harlow* immunity would not necessarily mean that defendant would be liable. It would merely require that the case go to trial. The defendant official would still have a chance at trial to raise a reasonable good-faith defense, if adequately supported by the evidence. But discovery and trial were needed to resolve disputes about the factual matters on which the legal conclusions depend.

More fundamentally, Stevens argued that qualified immunity should not in any event be available to police officers accused of conducting unlawful searches. In his view, tolerance for reasonable police error was already built into the constitutional standard: "[T]he probable cause standard itself recognizes the fair leeway that law enforcement officers must have in carrying out their dangerous work. The concept of probable cause leaves room for mistakes, provided always that they are mistakes that could have been made by a reasonable officer." The extension to police of an additional immunity for reasonable mistakes about the existence of probable cause was unwise:

"The suggestion that every law enforcement officer should be given the same measure of immunity as a Cabinet officer or a senior aide to the President of the United States is not compelling. Testifying in court is a routine part of an officer's job; his or her participation in litigation does not occasion nearly as great a disruption of everyday duties as it would with those of a senior government official. Moreover, the political constraints that deter high government officials from violating the Constitution have only slight, if any, application to police officers, and may actually lead to more, rather than less, vigorous enforcement activity. It is thus quite wrong simply to assume that the considerations that justified the decision in *Harlow v. Fitzgerald* also justify an equally broad rule of immunity for police officers. . . .

"The argument that police officers need special immunity to encourage them to take vigorous enforcement action when they are uncertain about their right to make a forcible entry into a private home has already been accepted in our jurisprudence. We have held that the police act reasonably in entering a house when they have probable cause to believe a fugitive is in the house and exigent circumstances make it impracticable to obtain a warrant. This interpretation of the fourth amendment allows room for police intrusion, without a warrant, on the privacy of even innocent citizens. . . .

"Thus, until now the Court has not found intolerable the use of a probable-cause standard to protect the police officer from exposure to liability simply because his reasonable conduct is subsequently shown to have been mistaken. Today, however, the Court counts the law enforcement interest twice and the individual's privacy interest only once.

"The Court's double-counting approach reflects understandable sympathy for the plight of the officer and an overriding interest in unfettered law enforcement. It ascribes a far lesser importance to the privacy interest of innocent citizens than did the framers of the fourth amendment. The importance of that interest and the possible magnitude of its invasion are both illustrated by the facts of this case. The home of an innocent family was invaded by several officers without a warrant, without the owner's consent, with a substantial show of force, and with blunt expressions of disrespect for the law and for the rights of the family members. As the case comes to us, we must assume that the intrusion violated the fourth amendment. Proceeding on that assumption, I see no reason why the family's interest in the security of its own home should be accorded a lesser weight than the government's interest in carrying out an invasion that was unlawful. Arguably, if the government considers it important not to discourage such conduct, it should provide indemnity to its officers. Preferably, however, it should furnish the kind of training for its law enforcement agents that would entirely eliminate the necessity for the Court to distinguish between the conduct that a competent officer considers reasonable and the conduct that the Constitution deems reasonable. "Federal officials will not be liable for mere mistakes in judgment, whether the mistake is one of fact or of law." Butz v. Economou, 438 U.S. 478, 507 (1978). On the other hand, surely an innocent family should not bear the entire risk that a trial court, with the benefit of hindsight will find that a federal agent reasonably believed that he could break into their home equipped with force and arms but without probable cause or a warrant."

8. Appealability of Immunity Denials: *Mitchell v. Forsyth.* An important aspect of the administration of immunity defenses was settled in Mitchell v. Forsyth, 472 U.S. 511 (1985). Former Attorney General John Mitchell was sued by a person whose telephone conversations had been intercepted in a "national security" wiretap. Mitchell claimed at least a qualified immunity based on the uncertain legality of such wiretaps at the time of the authorization. The District Court rejected this claim, holding that Mitchell should have anticipated the Supreme Court's rejection of such wiretaps in United States v. United States District Court (the *Keith* case), 407 U.S. 297 (1972). The District Court then granted summary judgment against Mitchell on the question of liability and scheduled a trial on damages.

The important question was whether rejection of the immunity defense was immediately appealable. Mitchell sought to justify appeal under the "collateral order" doctrine of Cohen v. Beneficial Industrial Loan Corp., 337 U.S. 541 (1949).[c] The Supreme Court agreed that the appeal was proper:

"[T]he *Harlow* Court refashioned the qualified immunity doctrine in such a way as to 'permit the resolution of many

[c] *Cohen* held that a decision is "final" for purposes of appeal if it falls within "that small class which finally determines claims of right separable from, and collateral to, rights asserted in the action, too important to be denied review, and too independent of the cause itself to require that appellate consideration be deferred until the whole case is adjudicated." *Cohen* and the line of cases it spawned are discussed at pages 664–65, supra.

insubstantial claims on summary judgment' and to avoid 'subject[ing] government officials either to the costs of trial or to the burdens of broad-reaching discovery' in cases where the legal norms the officials are alleged to have violated were not clearly established at the time. Unless the plaintiff's allegations state a claim of violation of clearly established law, a defendant pleading qualified immunity is entitled to dismissal before the commencement of discovery. Even if the plaintiff's complaint adequately alleges the commission of acts that violated clearly established law, the defendant is entitled to summary judgment if discovery fails to uncover evidence sufficient to create a genuine issue as to whether the defendant in fact committed those acts. *Harlow* thus recognized an entitlement not to stand trial or face the other burdens of litigation, conditioned on the resolution of the essentially legal question whether the conduct of which the plaintiff complains violated clearly established law. The entitlement is an *immunity from suit* rather than a mere defense to liability; and like an absolute immunity, it is effectively lost if a case is erroneously permitted to go to trial. Accordingly, the reasoning that underlies the immediate appealability of an order denying absolute immunity indicates to us that the denial of qualified immunity should be similarly appealable: in each case, the district court's decision is effectively unreviewable on appeal from a final judgment."

On the merits, the Court overturned the District Court's ruling and held that Mitchell was entitled to summary judgment on his claim of qualified immunity.

Justice Brennan, with whom Justice Marshall joined, argued that the denial of the defense of qualified immunity was not immediately appealable and hence that the interpretation of that immunity was not properly before the Court.

9. Analogous Immunities for Federal Officials. As was mentioned in connection with *Wood v. Strickland*, § 1983 applies in terms only to persons acting under color of "state" law; federal officials are not covered. Under Bivens v. Six Unknown Named Agents of the Federal Bureau of Narcotics, 403 U.S. 388 (1971), and subsequent cases, however, damage actions may be brought against federal officers for violations of constitutional rights.[d] In Butz v. Economou, 438 U.S. 478, 504 (1978), the Court concluded that it would be "untenable to draw a distinction for purposes of immunity law between suits brought against state officials under § 1983 and suits brought directly under the Constitution against federal officers." For most purposes, therefore, the immunities accorded state and federal officers are the same. Indeed, the two lines of cases are often cited interchangeably.

There are, however, several respects in which federal officers are treated specially. First, members of Congress are protected by art. I,

---

[d] See pages 395–430, supra.

§ 6, which provides in part that senators and representatives "shall in all Cases, except Treason, Felony and Breach of the Peace, be privileged from Arrest during their Attendance at the Sessions of their respective Houses, and in going to and returning from the same; and for any Speech or Debate in either House, they shall not be questioned in any other Place." The privilege from arrest has been read narrowly to permit the operation against senators and congressmen of ordinary criminal laws, see Gravel v. United States, 408 U.S. 606 (1972), but the "speech or debate" clause had been construed quite broadly. Generally speaking, the "speech or debate" clause protects federal legislators and their aides from being prosecuted or punished in relation to any official acts.[e]

The second special feature of the law governing federal officers is the president's absolute immunity from award of damages for official misconduct. See Nixon v. Fitzgerald, 457 U.S. 731 (1982). No comparable immunity extends to state executives. In the *Nixon* case, the Court, speaking through Justice Powell, found that the "president occupies a unique position in the constitutional scheme" and is "entrusted with supervisory and policy responsibilities of utmost discretion and sensitivity" on a wide range of matters. In the Court's view, the president's "unique status under the Constitution" and the "singular importance" of the duties of the office called for a broader immunity than that enjoyed by state governors and other executive officials:

> "[D]iversion of [the president's] energies by concern with private lawsuits would raise unique risks to the effective functioning of government. . . . This concern is compelling where the officeholder must make the most sensitive and far-reaching decisions entrusted to any official under our constitutional system. Nor can the sheer prominence of the president's office be ignored. In view of the visibility of his office and the effect of his actions on countless people, the president would be an easily identifiable target for suits for civil damages. Cognizance of this personal vulnerability frequently could distract a president from his public duties, to the detriment not only of the president and his office but also the nation that the presidency was designed to serve."

The Court concluded, therefore, that the president should have an absolute immunity against award of damages and that this immunity should apply to all acts within the "outer perimeter" of presidential responsibility.

Justice White dissented in an opinion joined by Justices Brennan, Marshall, and Blackmun. The dissenters argued that the scope of

---

[e] The principal cases interpreting the "speech or debate" clause are Kilbourn v. Thompson, 103 U.S. 168 (1881); Williamson v. United States, 207 U.S. 425 (1908); United States v. Johnson, 383 U.S. 169 (1966); Dombrowski v. Eastland, 387 U.S. 82 (1967); United States v. Brewster, 408 U.S. 501 (1972); Gravel v. United States, 408 U.S. 606 (1972); and Eastland v. United States Servicemen's Fund, 421 U.S. 491 (1975). A general treatment of the subject is available in Reinstein and Silverglate, Legislative Privilege and the Separation of Powers, 86 Harv. L. Rev. 1113 (1973).

presidential immunity should be determined by function, not office. Thus, while absolute immunity might be appropriate for certain acts (e.g., presidential participation in prosecutorial decisions), qualified immunity should be applied to others. In the view of the dissenters, absolute immunity effectively placed the president above the law.

Aside from the somewhat broader immunity accorded federal legislators and the president's absolute immunity from damage actions, most federal officials are treated the same as are their state and local counterparts under § 1983. Thus, federal judges and law enforcement officers and executive personnel generally are entitled to the same absolute or qualified immunity, as the case may be, as exists under § 1983, and the meaning of those levels of immunity is generally the same in both contexts.

NOTES ON IMMUNITY FROM AWARD OF DAMAGES AND THE GOALS OF SECTION 1983

1. **Introduction.** Award of damages against public officials for the misuse of government power implicates a number of discrete objectives. Damage judgments compensate the victims of official misconduct and work to deter repetition of such misconduct in the future. Additionally, damage awards are one way of affirming legal rights and thus of educating the moral sentiments of the community. Obviously, these and other goals of damages under § 1983 are directly compromised by recognition of official immunity to damage liability. Thus, the immunity decisions provide a good context for exploring the objectives that award of damages might be thought to vindicate and the costs associated with pursuing those objectives.

2. **Compensation.** The Supreme Court has identified compensation of the victims of official misconduct as "the basic purpose of a § 1983 damages award." Carey v. Piphus, 435 U.S. 247, 254 (1978). Yet many factors, including the Court's own decisions, undercut the effectiveness of § 1983 as a compensatory remedy.

One restrictive factor is the 11th amendment protection of states and state agencies from award of damages. See Edelman v. Jordan, 415 U.S. 651 (1974). It is true that Congress can override this immunity, at least in the enforcement of rights secured by the 14th amendment, see Fitzpatrick v. Bitzer, 427 U.S. 445 (1976), but the Court has not found any such intent behind § 1983. See *Edelman v. Jordan*, supra; Quern v. Jordan, 440 U.S. 332 (1979). It is also true, after Monell v. Dept. of Social Services, 436 U.S. 658 (1978) (excerpted at pages 927–39, infra), that local governments may be held directly liable under § 1983, but only for acts done pursuant to some official policy or custom. Holding government liable on a theory of respondeat superior is not allowed. In most cases, therefore, compensation for official misconduct must be sought from the individual public official, rather than from the government itself. As is discussed in more detail in Note 5, below, individual officials may be reimbursed or indemnified for damage judgments under § 1983, but that is not dependably so. Thus, in the bulk of cases the named defendant in a damage action will be an individual official, and in some cases that is where liability will rest.

This fact has important implications. Plaintiffs may have trouble identifying the persons who should be sued. Where injury results from systemic failure rather than individual misconduct, the necessity of proceeding against named individuals may prove especially burdensome. Defendants who seem to face personal liability for government acts may well arouse the sympathy of juries. Perhaps most important of all, the fact that § 1983 actions ordinarily must be brought against public officials as individuals introduces the perceived unfairness of imposing personal liability for good faith error as a limitation on the plaintiff's claim to compensation. Thus, the *Scheuer* Court identified as the first rationale for official immunity "the injustice, particularly in the absence of bad faith, of subjecting to liability an officer who is required, by the legal obligations of his position, to exercise discretion." Because damage actions directly against government are typically unavailable under § 1983, the immunity of individual officials sharply curtails the availability of compensation. Where the immunity is absolute, the sacrifice of the compensation objective is complete. Even where the immunity is qualified, the obstacle to recovery may be substantial.

In light of these and other factors, the prospect of § 1983 as an effective scheme of compensation for official misconduct seems largely illusory. This perception has prompted criticism of decisions limiting the opportunity for compensation from public officials and has led to proposals to expand the direct monetary liability of government itself. (These suggestions are considered in more detail in the Notes on Compensation as a Value Under § 1983 following *City of St. Louis v. Praprotnik*, pages 988–92, infra.)

3. Deterrence. A second objective of money damages is to deter future misconduct. An award of damages against one official conveys to others a threat of similar treatment if they too misbehave. But to the extent that the standards of liability are uncertain or the mechanisms of enforcement unpredictable, the deterrent effect will be difficult to assess. Moreover, officials will have an incentive to avoid all acts that might lead to civil liability or to the necessity of litigation. This unintended inhibitory effect is what the *Scheuer* Court had in mind when it identified as the second rationale for official immunity "the danger that the threat of such liability would deter [the official's] willingness to execute his office with the decisiveness and the judgment required by the public good."

Of course, the problem of unintended deterrence is not unique to this context. In much the same way, ordinary tort liability will inhibit some non-tortious conduct that the actor finds difficult to segregate from potentially tortious activity. In most situations, society relies on private decision-makers to evaluate the expected costs and benefits of certain actions, including the possibility of civil liability, and to make decisions roughly congruent with the social interest. In the context of damage actions against government officials, however, many factors combine to make it likely that the prospect of personal liability will induce government officials to engage in excessive defensive activity and thus to sacrifice the public good in favor of individual protection. These factors are detailed in an analysis of the working environment of the street-level official by Peter H. Schuck in Suing Government: Citizen Remedies for Official Wrongs 60–77 (1983).

The person most likely to be sued under § 1983 is, in Schuck's parlance, the "street-level official." Examples include police officers, prison authorities, public school officials, and welfare administrators. Because these officials personally and directly deliver basic government services, they constantly interact with individual citizens on matters of intense concern. Many of these interactions are non-consensual and thus likely to be characterized by conflict and mutual suspicion. The goals that these officials are directed to pursue—maintaining order, educating students, and the like—are often complex and ambiguous, and the choice of means to attain them is irreducibly judgmental.

Moreover, the official often has a duty to act. While the private citizen is usually free to do nothing, if that seems the best course, the public official may be commanded by law to intervene on behalf of the public interest. Since government action is likely to be coercive, it is especially productive of conflict and harm. Indeed, as Professor Schuck notes, virtually any choice of action or inaction risks harm to someone. The decision to discipline a student risks unfairness to that student; the decision not to discipline may impair the educational opportunities of others. The decision to arrest may violate the rights of the arrestee; the decision not to arrest may sacrifice the protection of the public.

Not only are such decisions potentially harmful to others; they are also likely to be attended by significant risk of error. Many officials must act more or less instantly, in situations that border on emergency, and on the basis of inadequate information. Under such circumstances, it is difficult to capture appropriate decision-making in dependable rules. Not that the effort is lacking. As Schuck points out, the street-level official is typically required to administer and to abide by a host of rules, but rules "so voluminous, ambiguous, contradictory, and in flux that officials can only comply with or enforce them selectively." In short, says Schuck, the officials "are actually awash in discretion."

Most important of all, public officials are typically unable to appropriate to themselves the benefits that flow from their decisions. They are required to exercise discretion in ways that are likely to injure others and to carry significant risk of error. The costs of malfeasance or mistake can be visited upon the official by a suit for damages, but the benefits of good performance tend to run to the public at large. The resulting incentive structure may conduce to defensive, cost-minimizing behavior, even if it entails a net loss in social benefits. Professor Schuck explains the point as follows:[*]

---

[*] This excerpt and the one that follows are reprinted by permission of the author from P. Schuck, Suing Government: Citizen Remedies for Official Wrongs (1983).

> "Most private actors would decide to incur any cost if the expected value of the correlative benefit were great enough, but officials tend to reject any course of action that would drive their personal costs above some minimum level, what I call a 'duty threshold.' The duty threshold, of course, varies from official to official, for it is defined by one's idiosyncratic attitudes toward (and trade-offs among) certain values and interests, some altruistic, some more narrowly self-interested . . .—feelings of professionalism; moral duty; programmatic mission; fear of criticism, discipline, or reprisals for self-protective behavior; concern for professional reputation; habituation to routine; personal convenience; and the like. Officials tend to orient their decisions about whether, when, and how to act less toward maximizing . . . net benefits, which they cannot appropriate, than toward minimizing (subject to their duty threshold) those costs that they would incur personally." Id. at 68–69.

Among these costs is the risk of being sued. The magnitude of this risk depends not only on the expected cost of adverse judgments, but also on the expected cost of having to defend such actions and on the demoralization or other nonpecuniary cost of being sued. As Schuck points out, an important element of nonpecuniary cost is uncertainty— uncertainty concerning "the outcome of the case; its duration; its effect upon the official's creditworthiness; the circumstances under which the official may receive (or lose) free counsel and indemnification of any settlement or adverse judgment; the quality of legal representation that the defending agency will provide; and potential conflicts of interest on the part of the defending agency or assigned counsel." Id. at 69. Given the environments in which they work, decisions of street-level officials are likely to be especially risky. As Schuck concludes, these officials have strong incentives to minimize costs, including the risk of being sued, even if a strategy of cost-minimization means foregoing social benefits.

Finally, it is worth noting that the expected costs and benefits to officials of their own decisions are typically not symmetrical. To put the point very crudely, action is likely to be more costly than inaction. This imbalance is due in part to what Jerry Mashaw has termed a "cause of action" problem. See Mashaw, Civil Liability of Government Officers: Property Rights and Official Accountability, 42 Law & Contemp. Probs. 8 (1978). The individual who is injured by affirmative misconduct is likely to be able to state a cause of action against the responsible official. The harm to the citizen and its connection to the official's conduct are likely to be clear. By contrast, persons injured by an official's failure to act may find it more difficult to state a claim for relief. The connection between harm to the citizen and official inaction may be indirect and obscure, and causation therefore difficult to establish. Furthermore, enforcement authority is typically discretionary in nature. As a result, the official may be protected from liability for an omission by the absence of any duty to act. For these reasons, the likelihood of being sued for erroneous action exceeds the risk for erroneous inaction, and the incentives of government officials, given a realistic threat of civil liability, may therefore be skewed toward defensive behavior.

For these reasons, the prospect of unintended deterrence of legitimate government activity has loomed very large in the debates over official immunities. It is chiefly on this ground that the Supreme Court has established, both under § 1983 and under analogous *Bivens*-type actions against federal officers, that virtually every government official is entitled to at least a qualified defense of good faith and reasonable belief against actions for money damages. The result is a corresponding diminution in the deterrence of official misconduct, as well as a restriction in the availability of compensation for persons injured thereby.

4. **Qualified vs. Absolute Immunity.** Do the considerations discussed above suggest an explanation for the distinction between the absolute immunity from damages afforded judges, legislators, and prosecutors and the qualified immunity available to executive officials? The disparity has often been subject to adverse comment. Peter Schuck, for example, has examined the traditional arguments in favor of absolute judicial immunity and concluded that they apply with at least equal force to most executive officials:

"The Court has emphasized five justifications for absolute judicial immunity: (1) the need for a judge to 'be free to act upon his own conviction, without apprehension of personal consequences to himself'; (2) the controversiality and importance of the competing interests adjudicated by judges and the likelihood that the loser, feeling aggrieved, would wish to retaliate; (3) the record-keeping to which self-protective judges would be driven in the absence of immunity; (4) the availability of alternative remedies, such as appeal and impeachment, for judicial wrongdoing; and (5) the ease with which bad faith can be alleged and made the basis for 'vexatious litigation.'

"But these are not convincing reasons for the judiciary's privileged status. Bureaucrats, no less than judges, are expected and required to act objectively and without regard to personal considerations. Those disadvantaged by executive decisions are as likely to be aggrieved and litigious as those who lose in judicial forums. The interests at stake in the one are not obviously or importantly different from those at issue in the other. The propensity to 'build a record' in response to fear of liability is not limited to judges; indeed, . . . it is a tempting strategy for most street-level officials. Alternative remedies for controlling executive misconduct are far more numerous than those available against judges. Finally, . . . plaintiffs can allege bad faith—and force a trial on those allegations—quite as easily against executive officials. Indeed, when one contrasts the circumstances under which street-level officials must often act (momentarily;

with broad discretion and little guidance; with little information; under great stress and with uncertainty; in unfriendly surroundings; under severe resource constraints) with the conditions under which judges typically decide (at their own speed; with discretion narrowed and guidance provided by precedent and the wording of statutes, as well as by voluminous records and briefs; enjoying great deference; in friendly surroundings; able to treat time and information as 'free goods'), one must conclude that street-level officials would be far more vulnerable to litigation liability than judges, immunity rules being equal. If the slightest risk of suits against judges suffices to justify absolute immunity, a higher risk to street-level officials would seem to justify no less."

P. Schuck, Suing Government: Citizen Remedies for Official Wrongs 90–91 (1983). These considerations led Schuck to suggest that executive officials should also be absolutely immune from damages liability, but this recommendation was tied to an accompanying recommendation for expanded governmental liability for official misconduct. See the Notes on Compensation as a Value Under § 1983 following *City of St. Louis v. Praprotnik,* pages 988–92, infra. In the absence of expanded direct liability of government, the argument for expanded official immunity would obviously be more difficult to accept.

A more pointed comment was offered by Justice Rehnquist in Butz v. Economou, 438 U.S. 478, 517 (1978) (Rehnquist, J., dissenting). In disagreeing with the Court's decision to extend only qualified immunity to cabinet-level executive officers, Rehnquist added the following remark:

"The ultimate irony of today's decision is that in the area of common-law official immunity, a body of law fashioned and applied by judges, absolute immunity within the federal system is extended only to judges and prosecutors functioning in the judicial system. Similarly, where this Court has interpreted 42 U.S.C. § 1983 in the light of common-law doctrines of official immunity, again only judges and prosecutors are accorded absolute immunity. If one were to hazard an informed guess as to why such a distinction in treatment between judges and prosecutors, on the one hand, and other public officials on the other, obtains, mine would be that those who decide the common law know through personal experience the sort of pressures that might exist for such decision-makers in the absence of absolute immunity, but may not know or may have forgotten that similar pressures exist in the case of nonjudicial public officials to whom difficult decisions are committed. But the cynical among us might not unreasonably feel that this is simply another unfortunate example of judges treating those who are not part of the judicial machinery as 'lesser breeds without the law.' " [a]

[a] For an interesting, but admittedly speculative, attempt to explain this disparity in terms of possible differences in the non- liability incentives applicable to various classes of public officials, see Ronald A.

5. Indemnification and Insurance. Most damage actions under § 1983 are nominally against individual officials, but the extent to which those officials must actually face and bear the costs of civil liability is in fact uncertain. Government employers may choose to protect their employees against damage liability, either by themselves providing defense counsel and indemnifying the employees against loss or, less commonly, by purchasing insurance. No such arrangements are required by federal law. Thus, the availability of counsel, indemnification, and insurance depends on the statutes, ordinances, and practices obtaining in each jurisdiction. The overall picture is accordingly unclear, but most observers agree that indemnification or insurance is very generally available. See, e.g., Project, Suing the Police in Federal Court, 88 Yale L.J. 781, 811 (1979) (reporting that a survey of § 1983 actions against police showed that the officers were provided with counsel and indemnified, either by the municipality or by its insurance carrier, against the cost of a settlement or adverse judgment). In many states, however, there may be limits on the amount or availability of indemnification. Quite commonly, the act giving rise to liability must have been within the scope of employment and often must have been performed in good faith. Moreover, the availability of free legal counsel is often not guaranteed, but may depend on a decision by the state attorney general or some analogous local officer. See generally del Carmen and Veneziano, Legal Liabilities, Representation, and Indemnification of Probation and Parole Officers, 17 U.S.F.L. 227, 243–45 (1983).

In summary, the individual official who is sued for damages under § 1983 ordinarily can expect to be provided free counsel and to be indemnified against liability or settlement, but that expectation will often be hedged by doubt. In many respects, the protection available to the official will be uncertain or incomplete. As a result, although the prevailing pattern is for the costs of damage actions under § 1983 to fall on the government rather than on the individual official, a particular individual may have reason to feel less than fully confident that his or her interests are completely protected.

6. Affirmation of Rights. A different kind of justification for damage judgments focuses on the symbolic and educative functions of affirming legal rights. Christina Whitman has emphasized the symbolic message of providing a federal remedy for the protection of federal constitutional rights as an important justification for the "supplementary" cause of action provided by § 1983. See Whitman, Constitutional Torts, 79 Mich. L. Rev. 5, 21–25 (1980). One way of affirming the importance of federal rights (especially constitutional rights) and of demonstrating the federal commitment to protection of those rights is by an award of damages. In this view, the damage judgment has symbolic value independent of compensation and deterrent effect.

Obviously, affirmation of rights does not depend specifically on damage awards against public officials. The symbolic and educative

Cass, Damage Suits Against Public Officers, 129 U.Pa.L.Rev. 1110 (1981).

value of vindicating the plaintiff's rights can be accomplished by any kind of judgment in plaintiff's favor. Indeed, Professor Whitman has called for greater emphasis on equitable remedies as a better way to redress constitutional violations. See id. at 52–53.

This conclusion rests in part on the inadequacies of the current damage remedy as a vehicle for affirming legal rights. For one thing, official immunities severely curtail the availability of damage judgments. For another, the Supreme Court has held that damage judgments must be limited in amount to compensation for actual harm suffered; only nominal damages may be awarded to vindicate the declaration of rights. Carey v. Piphus, 435 U.S. 247 (1978).

Carey v. Piphus involved two children who had been suspended from school without procedural due process. The court of appeals ruled that the students were entitled to substantial damages without proof of injury. The Supreme Court reversed:

> "[T]he Court of Appeals [held] that respondents are entitled to recover substantial—although unspecified—damages to compensate them for 'the injury which is "inherent in the nature of the wrong,"' even if their suspensions were justified and even if they fail to prove that the denial of procedural due process actually caused them some real, if intangible, injury. Respondents, elaborating on this theme, submit that the holding is correct because injury fairly may be 'presumed' to flow from every denial of procedural due process. Their argument is that in addition to protecting against unjustified deprivations, the due process clause also guarantees the 'feeling of just treatment' by the government. They contend that the deprivation of protected interests without procedural due process, even where the premise for the deprivation is not erroneous, inevitably arouses strong feelings of mental and emotional distress. [Petitioners argue] that such injury cannot be presumed to occur, and that plaintiffs at least should be put to their proof on the issue, as plaintiffs are in most tort actions.

> "We agree with petitioners in this respect. . . . First, it is not reasonable to assume that every departure from procedural due process, no matter what the circumstances or how minor, inherently is . . . likely to cause distress . . . . Where the deprivation of a protected interest is substantively justified but procedures are deficient in some respect, there may well be those who suffer no distress over the procedural irregularities. Moreover, where a deprivation is justified but procedures are deficient, whatever distress a person feels may be attributable to the justified deprivation rather than to deficiencies in procedure. But as the Court of Appeals held, the injury caused by a justified deprivation, including distress, is not properly compensable under § 1983. This ambiguity in causation . . . provides additional need for requiring the plaintiff to convince the trier of fact that he actually suffered

distress because of the denial of procedural due process itself." [b]

The same approach was followed in Memphis Community School District v. Stachura, 477 U.S. 299 (1986). Plaintiff was a school teacher who had been improperly suspended following parental complaints about sex education. He claimed violations of procedural due process and a first amendment right of academic freedom. The trial judge instructed the jury that it could award not only ordinary compensatory and punitive damages, but also damages based on the value or importance of the constitutional right that had been violated:

> "You may wish to consider the importance of the right in our system of government, the role which this right has played in the history of our republic, [and] the significance of the right in the context of the activities which the plaintiff was engaged in at the time of the violation of the right."

The Supreme Court disapproved the instruction. Speaking through Justice Powell, the Court found it impossible to square with *Carey.* Non-punitive damages under § 1983 must be designed to compensate for actual injuries, the Court said, not simply to vindicate a "jury's perception of the abstract 'importance' of a constitutional right." Justice Marshall concurred in the judgment, agreeing that the jury had been invited to base its award on improper speculation about matters wholly detached from the actual injury.

Together, *Carey* and *Stachura* make it very difficult to use § 1983 damage actions to vindicate dignitary interests. Is this restriction wise? Would it be better to allow damage awards based on criteria such as those articulated by the *Stachura* trial court?

NOTE ON IMMUNITY FROM PROSPECTIVE RELIEF

Although most immunity decisions involve damages, questions occasionally arise concerning official immunity from prospective relief. The traditional view, dating at least from Ex parte Young, 209 U.S. 123 (1908), is that unconstitutional acts by state officials may be enjoined. State legislators, however, have absolute immunity against § 1983 injunctions. See Supreme Court of Virginia v. Consumers Union, 446 U.S. 719 (1980); Tenney v. Brandhove, 341 U.S. 367 (1951). This rule parallels the immunity from prospective relief granted federal legislators by the speech or debate clause. See, e.g., Eastland v. United States Servicemen's Fund, 421 U.S. 491, 502–03 (1975). The immunity applies only to legislative acts, not to all acts done by legislators.

In Pulliam v. Allen, 466 U.S. 522 (1984), the Supreme Court held that the same rule did not extend to judges. Like legislators, judges are absolutely immune from award of damages for their official acts.

---

[b] For analysis of *Carey* and a recommendation that presumed damages be used in constitutional tort litigation, see Jean C. Love, Damages: A Remedy for the Violation of Constitutional Rights, 67 Cal.L.Rev. 1242 (1979).

Unlike legislators, however, judges may be sued for injunctive or declaratory relief where appropriate. Under what circumstances such relief may be appropriate is difficult to say. *Pulliam* itself involved an unusual situation where suit was brought to enjoin a state magistrate from her practice of requiring bond for nonjailable offenses and incarcerating those who could not make bail. Because of the short duration of each pretrial detention and the recurring nature of the practice, arguably there was no adequate alternative remedy available to the *Pulliam* plaintiff. Ordinarily, of course, appeal or habeas corpus would be an "adequate" remedy sufficient to preclude equitable relief. If injunctive relief were limited to cases where there is no alternative remedy, *Pulliam* would have little practical significance. The opinion, however, does not make clear the extent to which the court relied on this factor.

SECTION 3: GOVERNMENTAL LIABILITY UNDER § 1983

MONELL v. DEPARTMENT OF SOCIAL SERVICES
Supreme Court of the United States, 1978.
436 U.S. 658.

MR. JUSTICE BRENNAN delivered the opinion of the Court.

Petitioners, a class of female employees of the Department of Social Services and of the Board of Education of the City of New York, commenced this action under 42 U.S.C. § 1983 in July, 1971. The gravamen of the complaint was that the board and the department had as a matter of official policy compelled pregnant employees to take unpaid leaves of absence before such leaves were required for medical reasons. Cf. Cleveland Board of Education v. LaFleur, 414 U.S. 632 (1974). The suit sought injunctive relief and backpay for periods of unlawful forced leave. Named as defendants in the action were the department and the commissioner, the board and its chancellor, and the city of New York and its mayor. In each case, the individual defendants were sued solely in their official capacities.

On cross-motions for summary judgment, the District Court for the Southern District of New York held moot petitioners' claims for injunctive and declaratory relief since the city of New York and the board, after the filing of the complaint, had changed their policies relating to maternity leaves so that no pregnant employee would have to take leave unless she was medically unable to perform her job. No one now challenges this conclusion. The court did conclude, however, that the acts complained of were unconstitutional under *LaFleur*, supra. Nonetheless plaintiffs' prayers for backpay were denied because any such damages would come ultimately from the city of New York and, therefore, to hold otherwise would be to "circumven[t]" the immunity conferred on municipalities by Monroe v. Pape, 365 U.S. 167 (1961). . . .

I

In *Monroe v. Pape,* we held that "Congress did not undertake to bring municipal corporations within the ambit of [§ 1983]." The sole basis for this conclusion was an inference drawn from Congress' rejection of the "Sherman amendment" to the bill which became the Civil Rights Act of 1871—the precursor of § 1983—which would have held a municipal corporation liable for damage done to the person or property of its inhabitants by *private* persons "riotously and tumultuously assembled." [8]

Although the Sherman amendment did not seek to amend § 1 of the Act, which is now § 1983, and although the nature of the obligation created by that amendment was vastly different from that created by § 1, the Court nonetheless concluded in *Monroe* that Congress must have meant to exclude municipal corporations from the coverage of § 1 because " 'the House [in voting against the Sherman amendment] had solemnly decided that in their judgment Congress had no constitutional power to impose any *obligation* upon county and town organizations, the mere instrumentality for the administration of state law,' " (emphasis added), quoting Rep. Poland. This statement, we thought, showed that Congress doubted its "constitutional power . . . to impose *civil liability* on municipalities" (emphasis added), and that such doubt would have extended to any type of civil liability.

A fresh analysis of debate on the Civil Rights Act of 1871, and particularly of the case law which each side mustered in its support, shows, however, that *Monroe* incorrectly equated the "obligation" of which Representative Poland spoke with "civil liability." . . .

House opponents of the Sherman amendment—whose views are particularly important since only the House voted down the amendment—. . . argued that the local units of government upon which the amendment fastened liability were not obligated to keep the peace at state law and further that the federal government could not constitutionally require local governments to create police forces, whether this requirement was levied directly, or indirectly by imposing damages for breach of the peace on municipalities. The most complete statement of this position is that of Representative Blair:

> "The proposition known as the Sherman amendment . . .
> is entirely new. It is altogether without a precedent in this
> country. . . . That amendment claims the power in the
> general government to go into the states of this union and lay
> such obligations as it may please upon the municipalities,
> which are the creatures of the states alone. . . .

---

[8] We expressly declined to consider "policy considerations" for or against municipal liability.

"Here it is proposed not to carry into effect an obligation which rests upon the municipalities, but to create that obligation, and that is the provision I am unable to assent to. . . .

"Now, only the other day, the Supreme Court . . . decided [in Collector v. Day, 78 U.S. (11 Wall.) 113 (1871)] that there is no power in the government of the United States, under its authority to tax, to tax the salary of a state officer. Why? Simply because the power to tax involves the power to destroy, and it was not the intent to give the government of the United States power to destroy the government of the states in any respect. It was also held in the case of Prigg v. Pennsylvania, 41 U.S. (16 Pet.) 539 (1842), that it is not within the power of the Congress of the United States to lay duties upon a state officer; that we cannot command a state officer to do any duty whatever, as such; and I ask . . . the difference between that and commanding a municipality, which is equally a creature of the state, to perform a duty."

Any attempt to impute a unitary constitutional theory to opponents of the Sherman amendment is, of course, fraught with difficulties, not the least of which is that most members of Congress did not speak to the issue of the constitutionality of the amendment. Nonetheless, two considerations lead us to conclude that opponents of the Sherman amendment found it unconstitutional substantially because of the reasons stated by Representative Blair: First, Blair's analysis is precisely that of Poland, whose views were quoted as authoritative in *Monroe*, and that analysis was shared in large part by all House opponents who addressed the constitutionality of the Sherman amendment. Second, Blair's exegesis of the reigning constitutional theory of his day, as we shall explain, was clearly supported by precedent—albeit precedent that has not survived . . . .

Collector v. Day, cited by Blair, was the clearest and, at the time of the debates, the most recent pronouncement of a doctrine of coordinate sovereignty that, as Blair stated, placed limits on even the enumerated powers of the national government in favor of protecting state prerogatives. There, the Court held that the United States could not tax the income of Day, a Massachusetts state judge, because the independence of the states within their legitimate spheres would be imperiled if the instrumentalities through which states executed their powers were "subject to the control of another and distinct government." [And in] Kentucky v. Dennison, 65 U.S. (24 How.) 66 (1861), . . . the Court was asked to require Dennison, the Governor of Ohio, to hand over Lago, a fugitive from justice wanted in Kentucky, as required by § 1 of the Act of Feb. 12, 1793, which implemented art. IV, § 2, cl. 2 of the Constitution. Mr. Chief Justice Taney, writing for a unanimous Court, refused to enforce that section of the act:

"[W]e think it clear, that the federal government, under the Constitution, has no power to impose on a state officer, as such, any duty whatever, and compel him to perform it; for if it possessed this power, it might overload the officer with duties which would fill up all his time, and disable him from performing his obligations to the state, and might impose on him duties of a character incompatible with the rank and dignity to which he was elevated by the state."

The rationale of *Dennison*—that the nation could not impose duties on state officers since that might impede states in their legitimate activities—is obviously identical to that which animated the decision in *Collector v. Day*. And, as Blair indicated, municipalities as instrumentalities through which states executed their policies could be equally disabled from carrying out state policies if they were also obligated to carry out federally imposed duties. Although no one cited *Dennison* by name, the principle for which it stands was well known to Members of Congress, many of whom discussed *Day,* as well as a series of state supreme court cases in the mid–1860's which had invalidated a federal tax on the process of state courts on the ground that the tax threatened the independence of a vital state function. Thus, there was ample support for Blair's view that the Sherman amendment, by putting municipalities to the Hobson's choice of keeping the peace or paying civil damages, attempted to impose obligations on municipalities by indirection that could not be imposed directly, thereby threatening to "destroy the government of the states."

If municipal liability under § 1 of the Civil Rights Act of 1871 created a similar Hobson's choice, we might conclude, as *Monroe* did, that Congress could not have intended municipalities to be among the "persons" to which that section applied. But that is not the case.

First, opponents expressly distinguished between imposing an obligation to keep the peace and merely imposing civil liability for damages on a municipality that was obligated by state law to keep the peace, but which had not in violation of the 14th amendment. Representative Poland, for example, reasoning from contract clause precedents, indicated that Congress could constitutionally confer jurisdiction on the federal courts to entertain suits seeking to hold municipalities liable for using their authorized powers in violation of the Constitution—which is as far as § 1 of the Civil Rights Act went:

> "I presume . . . that where a state had imposed a duty [to keep the peace] upon [a] municipality . . . an action would be allowed to be maintained against them in the courts of the United States under the ordinary restrictions as to jurisdiction. But enforcing a liability, existing by their own contract, or by a state law, in the courts, is a very widely different thing from devolving a new duty or liability upon them by the national government, which has no power either to create or destroy them, and no power or control over them whatever." . . .

Second, the doctrine of dual sovereignty apparently put no limit on the power of the federal courts to enforce the Constitution against municipalities that violated it. . . . The limits of the principles defined in *Dennison* and *Day* are not so well defined in logic, but are clear as a matter of history. It must be remembered that the same Court which rendered *Day* also vigorously enforced the contract clause against municipalities—an enforcement effort which included various forms of "positive" relief, such as ordering that taxes be levied and collected to discharge federal-court judgments, once a constitutional infraction was found. Thus, federal judicial enforcement of the Constitution's express limits on state power, since it was done so frequently, must, notwithstanding anything said in *Dennison* or *Day,* have been permissible. . . . Since § 1 of the Civil Rights Act simply conferred jurisdiction on the federal courts to enforce § 1 of the 14th amendment—a situation precisely analogous to the grant of diversity jurisdiction under which the contract clause was enforced against municipalities—there is no reason to suppose that opponents of the Sherman amendment would have found any constitutional barrier to § 1 suits against municipalities. . . .

From the foregoing discussion it is readily apparent that nothing said in the debates on the Sherman amendment would have prevented holding a municipality liable under § 1 of the Civil Rights Act for its own violations of the 14th amendment. The question remains, however, whether the general language describing those to be liable under § 1—"any person"—covers more than natural persons. An examination of the debate on § 1 and application of appropriate rules of construction show unequivocally that § 1 was intended to cover legal as well as natural persons. . . .

In both Houses, statements of the supporters of § 1 corroborated that Congress, in enacting § 1, intended to give a broad remedy for violations of federally protected civil rights. Moreover, since municipalities through their official acts could, equally with natural persons, create the harms intended to be remedied by § 1, and, further, since Congress intended § 1 to be broadly construed, there is no reason to suppose that municipal corporations would have been excluded from the sweep of § 1. One need not rely on this inference alone, however, for the debates show that members of Congress understood "persons" to include municipal corporations.

Representative Bingham, for example, in discussing § 1 of the bill, explained that he had drafted § 1 of the 14th amendment with the case of Barron v. Mayor of Baltimore, 32 U.S. (7 Pet.) 243 (1833), especially in mind. "In [that] case the *city* had taken private property for public use, without compensation . . . , and there was no redress for the wrong . . . ." (Emphasis added.) Bingham's further remarks clearly indicate his view that such takings by cities, as had occurred in *Barron,* would be redressable under § 1 of the bill. More generally, and as Bingham's remarks confirm, § 1 of the bill would logically be the vehicle by which Congress provided redress for takings, since that section provided the only civil remedy for 14th amendment violations and that amendment unequivocally prohibited uncompensated takings. Given this purpose, it beggars reason to suppose that Congress would have exempted municipalities from suit, insisting instead that compensation for a taking come from an officer in his individual capacity rather than from the government unit that had the benefit of the property taken.

In addition, by 1871, it was well understood that corporations should be treated as natural persons for virtually all purposes of constitutional and statutory analysis. . . .

That the "usual" meaning of the word "person" would extend to municipal corporations is also evidenced by an act of Congress which had been passed only months before the Civil Rights Act was passed. The act provided that

> "in all acts hereafter passed . . . the word 'person' may extend and be applied to bodies politic and corporate . . . unless the context shows that such words were intended to be used in a more limited sense."

Municipal corporations in 1871 were included within the phrase "bodies politic and corporate" and, accordingly, the "plain meaning" of § 1 is that local government bodies were to be included within the ambit of the persons who could be sued under § 1 of the Civil Rights Act. . . .

II

Our analysis of the legislative history of the Civil Rights Act of 1871 compels the conclusion that Congress *did* intend municipalities and other local government units to be included among those persons to whom § 1983 applies.[54] Local governing bodies, therefore, can be sued directly under § 1983 for monetary, declaratory, or injunctive relief where, as here, the action that is alleged to be unconstitutional implements or executes a policy statement, ordinance, regulation, or decision officially adopted and promulgated by that body's officers. Moreover, although the touchstone of the § 1983 action against a government body is an allegation that official policy is responsible for a deprivation of rights protected by the Constitution, local governments, like every other § 1983 "person," by the very terms of the statute, may be sued for constitutional deprivations visited pursuant to governmental "custom" even though such a custom has not received formal approval through the body's official decisionmaking channels. . . .

On the other hand, the language of § 1983, read against the background of the same legislative history, compels the conclusion that Congress did not intend municipalities to be held liable unless action pursuant to official municipal policy of some nature caused a constitutional tort. In particular, we conclude that a municipality cannot be held liable *solely* because it employs a tortfeasor—or, in other words, a

---

[54] There is certainly no constitutional impediment to municipal liability. "The 10th amendment's reservation of nondelegated powers to the states is not implicated by a federal-court judgment enforcing the express prohibitions of unlawful state conduct enacted by the 14th amendment." For this reason, National League of Cities v. Usery, 426 U.S. 833 (1976), is irrelevant to our consideration of this case. Nor is there any basis for concluding that the 11th amendment is a bar to municipal liability. See, e.g., Fitzpatrick v. Bitzer, 427 U.S. 445 (1976). Our holding today is, of course, limited to local government units which are not considered part of the state for 11th amendment purposes.

municipality cannot be held liable under § 1983 on a respondeat superior theory.

We begin with the language of § 1983 as passed:

> "*[A]ny person who,* under color of any law, statute, ordinance, regulation, custom, or usage of any state, *shall subject, or cause to be subjected,* any person . . . to the deprivation of any rights, privileges, or immunities secured by the Constitution of the United States, shall, any such law, statute, ordinance, regulation, custom, or usage of the state to the contrary notwithstanding, be liable to the party injured in any action at law, suit in equity, or other proper proceeding for redress . . . ." (emphasis added)

The italicized language plainly imposes liability on a government that, under color of some official policy "causes" an employee to violate another's constitutional rights. At the same time, the language cannot be easily read to impose liability vicariously on governing bodies solely on the basis of the existence of an employer-employee relationship with a tortfeasor. Indeed, the fact that Congress did specifically provide that *A*'s tort became *B*'s liability if *B* "caused" *A* to subject another to a tort suggests that Congress did not intend § 1983 liability to attach where such causation was absent.

Equally important, creation of a federal law of respondeat superior would have raised all the constitutional problems associated with the obligation to keep the peace, an obligation Congress chose not to impose because it thought imposition of such an obligation unconstitutional. To this day, there is disagreement about the basis for imposing liability on an employer for the torts of an employee when the sole nexus between the employer and the tort is the fact of the employer-employee relationship. Nonetheless, two justifications tend to stand out. First is the commonsense notion that no matter how blameless an employer appears to be in an individual case, accidents might nonetheless be reduced if employers had to bear the cost of accidents. Second is the argument that the cost of accidents should be spread to the community as a whole on an insurance theory.

The first justification is of the same sort that was offered for statutes like the Sherman amendment: "The obligation to make compensation for injury resulting from riot is, by arbitrary enactment of statutes, affirmatory law, and the reason of passing the statute is to secure a more perfect police protection." (Sen. Frelinghuysen) This justification was obviously insufficient to sustain the amendment against perceived constitutional difficulties and there is no reason to suppose that a more general liability imposed for a similar reason would have been thought less constitutionally objectionable. The second justification was similarly put forward as a justification for the Sherman amendment: "we do not look upon [the Sherman amendment] as a punishment . . . . It is a mutual insurance." (Rep. Butler) Again, this justification was insufficient to sustain the amendment.

We conclude, therefore, that a local government may not be sued under § 1983 for an injury inflicted solely by its employees or agents. Instead, it is when execution of a government's policy or custom, whether made by its lawmakers or by those whose edicts or acts may fairly be said to represent official policy, inflicts the injury that the government as an entity is responsible under § 1983. Since this case unquestionably involves official policy as a moving force of the constitutional violation found by the District Court, we must reverse the judgment below. . . .

III

Although we have stated before that stare decisis has more force in statutory analysis than in constitutional adjudication because, in the former situation, Congress can correct our mistakes through legislation, we have never applied stare decisis mechanically to prohibit overruling our earlier decisions determining the meaning of statutes. . . .

[Justice Brennan then gave four reasons why stare decisis should not be applied in this situation.

[First, he said, Monroe "was a departure from prior practice." He cited in support of this assertion a number of cases in which injunctive relief had been sought against municipalities. "Moreover," he continued, "the constitutional defect that led to the rejection of the Sherman amendment would not have distinguished between municipalities and school boards, each of which is an instrumentality of state administration." For this reason, prior cases decided both before and after Monroe holding school boards liable in § 1983 actions were inconsistent with Monroe.

[Second, "recent expressions of Congressional intent" indicated that a broad implementation of the principle of Monroe was unsound. Here he cited the rejection of efforts to strip the federal courts of jurisdiction over school boards, the enactment of legislation to assist school boards in complying with federal court decrees, and a passage in attorney-fee legislation indicating that Congress expected attorney fees in § 1983 suits to be collectable from state or local governments.

[Third, unlike in a commercial situation, "municipalities can assert no reliance claim." Surely, he said, Monroe cannot be read as allowing local governments to rely on their ability to adopt unconstitutional policies.

[And finally, he argued that even under the most stringent test for when a statutory interpretation should be overruled, Monroe qualified. It is "beyond doubt," he elaborated, that Monroe is wrong and "there is no justification" given the legislative history "for excluding municipalities from the 'persons' covered by § 1983."]

IV

Since the question whether local government bodies should be afforded some form of official immunity was not presented [or] briefed

. . . we express no views on the scope of any municipal immunity beyond holding that municipal bodies sued under § 1983 cannot be entitled to an absolute immunity, lest our decision that such bodies are subject to suit under § 1983 "be drained of meaning."

V

For the reasons stated above, the judgment of the Court of Appeals is

Reversed.

MR. JUSTICE POWELL, concurring. . . .

Few cases in the history of the Court have been cited more frequently than Monroe v. Pape, 365 U.S. 167 (1961), decided less than two decades ago. Focusing new light on 42 U.S.C. § 1983, that decision widened access to the federal courts and permitted expansive interpretations of the reach of the 1871 measure. But *Monroe* exempted local governments from liability at the same time it opened wide the courthouse door to suits against officers and employees of those entities— even where they act pursuant to express authorization. The oddness of that result and the weakness of the historical evidence relied on by the *Monroe* Court in support of it, are well demonstrated by the Court's opinion today. . . .

The Court correctly rejects a view of the legislative history that would produce the anomalous result of immunizing local government units from monetary liability for action directly causing a constitutional deprivation, even though such actions may be fully consistent with, and thus not remediable under, state law. No conduct of government comes more clearly within the "under color of" state law language of § 1983. It is most unlikely that Congress intended public officials acting under the command or the specific authorization of the government employer to be *exclusively* liable for resulting constitutional injury. . . .

[This is not] the usual case in which the Court is asked to overrule a precedent. Here considerations of stare decisis cut in both directions. On the one hand, we have a series of rulings that municipalities and counties are not "persons" for purposes of § 1983. On the other hand, many decisions of this Court have been premised on the amenability of school boards and similar entities to § 1983 suits. . . .

If now, after full consideration of the question, we continued to adhere to *Monroe,* grave doubt would be cast upon the Court's exercise of § 1983 jurisdiction over school boards. . . . Although there was an independent basis of jurisdiction in many of the school board cases because of the inclusion of individual public officials as nominal parties, the opinions of this Court make explicit reference to the school board party, particularly in discussions of the relief to be awarded. [T]he exercise of § 1983 jurisdiction over school boards . . . has been long-standing. Indeed, it predated *Monroe.* . . .

The Court of Appeals in this case suggested that we import, by analogy, the 11th amendment fiction of *Ex parte Young* into § 1983. That approach . . . would require "a bifurcated application" of "the generic word 'person' in § 1983" to public officials "depending on the nature of the relief sought against them." A public official sued in his official capacity for carrying out official policy would be a "person" for purposes of injunctive relief, but a non-"person" in an action for damages. The Court's holding avoids this difficulty.

Finally, if we continued to adhere to a rule of absolute municipal immunity under § 1983, we could not long avoid the question whether "we should, by analogy to our decision in *Bivens,* imply a cause of action directly from the 14th amendment. . . ." In light of the Court's persuasive re-examination in today's decision of the 1871 debates, I would have difficulty inferring from § 1983 "an explicit congressional declaration" against municipal liability for the implementation of official policies in violation of the Constitution. Rather than constitutionalize a cause of action against local government that Congress intended to create in 1871, the better course is to confess error and set the record straight, as the Court does today. . . .

MR. JUSTICE STEVENS, concurring in part.

[Justice Stevens declined to join those portions of the majority opinion dealing with respondeat superior on the ground that discussion of that issue was "merely advisory" and "not necessary to explain the Court's decision."]

MR. JUSTICE REHNQUIST, with whom THE CHIEF JUSTICE joins, dissenting.

Seventeen years ago in Monroe v. Pape, 365 U.S. 167 (1961), this Court held that the 42nd Congress did not intend to subject a municipal corporation to liability as a "person" within the meaning of 42 U.S.C. § 1983. Since then, the Congress has remained silent, but this Court has reaffirmed that holding on at least three separate occasions. Today, the Court abandons this long and consistent line of precedents, offering in justification only an elaborate canvass of the same legislative history which was before the Court in 1961. . . .

I

[O]ur only task is to discern the intent of the 42nd Congress. That intent was first expounded in *Monroe,* and it has been followed consistently ever since. This is not some esoteric branch of the law in which congressional silence might reasonably be equated with congressional indifference. Indeed, this very year, the Senate has been holding hearings on a bill which would remove the municipal immunity recognized by *Monroe.* In these circumstances, it cannot be disputed that established principles of stare decisis require this Court to pay the highest deference to its prior holdings. *Monroe* may not be overruled unless it has been demonstrated "beyond doubt from the legislative history of the 1871 statute that [*Monroe*] misapprehended the meaning of the controlling provision," [quoting Justice Harlan's remark in his

Monroe concurrence about overruling the interpretation of "under color of" law adopted in *Screws* and *Classic*]. The Court must show not only that Congress, in rejecting the Sherman amendment, concluded that municipal liability was not unconstitutional, but also that in enacting § 1, it intended to impose that liability. I am satisfied that no such showing has been made.

II

Any analysis of the meaning of the word "person" in § 1983, which was originally enacted as § 1 of the Ku Klux Klan Act of April 20, 1871, must begin, not with the Sherman amendment, but with the Dictionary Act. The latter act, which supplied rules of construction for all legislation, provided:

> "That in all acts hereafter passed . . . the word 'person' may extend and be applied to bodies politic and corporate . . . unless the context shows that such words were intended to be used in a more limited sense . . . ."

There are . . . factors . . . which suggest that the Congress which enacted § 1983 may well have intended the word "person" "to be used in a more limited sense," as *Monroe* concluded. It is true that this Court had held that both commercial corporations and municipal corporations were "citizens" of a state within the meaning of the jurisdictional provisions of art. III. Congress, however, also knew that this label did not apply in all contexts, since this Court had held commercial corporations not to be "citizens" within the meaning of the privileges and immunities clause, U.S. Const., art. IV, § 2. Thus, the Congress surely knew that, for constitutional purposes, corporations generally enjoyed a different status in different contexts. Indeed, it may be presumed that Congress intended that a corporation should enjoy the same status under the Ku Klux Klan Act as it did under the 14th amendment, since it had been assured that § 1 "was so very simple and really reenacting the Constitution." At the time § 1983 was enacted the only federal case to consider the status of corporations under the 14th amendment had concluded, with impeccable logic, that a corporation was neither a "citizen" nor a "person."

Furthermore, the state courts did not speak with a single voice with regard to the tort liability of municipal corporations. Although many members of Congress represented states which had retained absolute municipal tort immunity, other states had adopted the currently predominant distinction imposing liability for proprietary acts. Nevertheless, no state court had ever held that municipal corporations were always liable in tort in precisely the same manner as other persons.

The general remarks from the floor on the liberal purposes of § 1 offer no explicit guidance as to the parties against whom the remedy could be enforced. As the Court concedes, only Representative Bingham raised a concern which could be satisfied only by relief against governmental bodies. Yet he never directly related this concern to § 1 of the act. Indeed, Bingham stated at the outset, "I do not propose now to discuss the provisions of the bill in detail," and, true to his word, he launched into an extended discourse on the beneficent purposes of the 14th amendment. While Bingham clearly stated that Congress could "provide that no citizen in any state shall be deprived of his property by state law or the judgment of a state court without just compensation therefore," he never suggested that such a power was exercised in § 1.[4]

. . .

Thus, it ought not lightly to be presumed, as the Court does today, that § 1983 "should prima facie be construed to include 'bodies politic' among the entities that could be sued." Neither the Dictionary Act, the ambivalent state of judicial decisions, nor the floor debate on § 1 of the act gives any indication that any Member of Congress had any inkling that § 1 could be used to impose liability on municipalities.

. . .

The Court is probably correct that the rejection of the Sherman amendment does not lead ineluctably to the conclusion that Congress intended municipalities to be immune from liability under all circumstances. Nevertheless, it cannot be denied that the debate on that amendment, the only explicit consideration of municipal tort liability, sheds considerable light on the Congress' understanding of the status of municipal corporations in that context. . . . Whatever the merits of the constitutional arguments against it, the fact remains that Congress rejected the concept of municipal tort liability on the only occasion in which the question was explicitly presented. Admittedly this fact is not conclusive as to whether Congress intended § 1 to embrace a municipal corporation within the meaning of "person," and thus the reasoning of *Monroe* on this point is subject to challenge. The meaning of § 1 of the Act of 1871 has been subjected in this case to a more searching and careful analysis than it was in *Monroe,* and it may well be that on the basis of this closer analysis of the legislative debates a conclusion contrary to the *Monroe* holding could have been reached when that case was decided 17 years ago. But the rejection of the Sherman amendment remains instructive in that here alone did the legislative debates squarely focus on the liability of municipal corporations, and that liability was rejected. . . .

The decision in *Monroe v. Pape* was the fountainhead of the torrent of civil rights litigation of the last 17 years. Using § 1983 as a vehicle, the courts have articulated new and previously unforeseeable interpretations of the 14th amendment. At the same time, the doctrine of municipal immunity enunciated in *Monroe* has protected municipalities and their limited treasuries from the consequences of their officials' failure to predict the course of this Court's constitutional jurisprudence.

---

[4] It has not been generally thought, before today, that § 1983 provided an avenue of relief from unconstitutional takings. Those federal courts which have granted compensation against state and local governments have resorted to an implied right of action under the 5th and 14th amendments. Since the Court today abandons the holding of *Monroe* chiefly on the strength of Bingham's arguments, it is indeed anomalous that § 1983 will provide relief only when a local government, not the state itself, seizes private property. See note 54, supra.

None of the members of this Court can foresee the practical consequences of today's removal of that protection. Only the Congress,
which has the benefit of the advice of every segment of this diverse
nation, is equipped to consider the results of such a drastic change in
the law. It seems all but inevitable that it will find it necessary to do
so after today's decision. . . .

NOTES ON GOVERNMENTAL LIABILITY UNDER § 1983

1. Questions and Comments on *Monell*. Before *Monell*, damages could be obtained from a police officer who violated constitutional
rights but not from the city that ordered the officer to do so. Justice
Powell commented on the "oddness" of that result. There is something
odd, is there not, in holding an agent exclusively liable for acts
specifically authorized by the principal? And yet, exactly this situation
prevails with respect to state officials. They can be sued for damages
under § 1983, but the state itself is immune from suit. Does this make
sense? Is there any justification in policy for treating states and
municipalities differently? [a]

As a practical matter, the issue of state or municipal liability for
the *authorized* acts of its employees may be important only where the
official cannot be held personally liable. Where liability can be imposed on the official as an individual, the government will have a
strong incentive to indemnify its employees against loss incurred in
implementing official policy. Not only may the government feel a
moral obligation to hold its employee harmless for following orders; but
it is also likely to find that indemnification is necessary to recruit and
retain qualified employees. Few would be so bold as to accept government office without some protection against personal liability for government error. Perhaps for that reason, the states have very generally
followed a policy of defending state officers in actions under § 1983 and
reimbursing them for any damages assessed, despite the formal immunity of the 11th amendment.

Monell held that municipalities could be sued under § 1983, but
only for official policy or custom. The Court specifically rejected the
theory of respondeat superior. In essence, the *Monell* Court adopted
for municipalities the test proposed for all § 1983 defendants by Justice
Frankfurter's dissent in *Monroe*. Why? Is that result compelled by
the language of the statute? Is it indicated by the rejection of the
Sherman amendment? Is it consistent with the function of § 1983? [b]

---

[a] Note the argument of William D. Murphy, who suggests in Reinterpreting "Person" in Section 1983: The Hidden Influence of *Brown v. Board of Education*, 9
Black L.J. 97 (1985), that *Monell* was necessary to remove the "very serious danger"
of derailing desegregation suits against
school boards. By contrast, Murphy suggests, the exclusion of states from the concept of "person" in § 1983 has no large
impact on desegregation litigation.

[b] On the historical basis for rejection of
respondeat superior, see Levin, The Section
1983 Municipal Immunity Doctrine, 65
Geo. L.J. 1483 (1977) (analyzing the relevance of the Sherman Amendment to vicarious municipal liability). For an attack
on the Court's approach, see Comment,

2. Comment on Judicial Methodology Under § 1983. In holding that a municipality is a "person" within the meaning of § 1983, *Monell* overruled that part of *Monroe v. Pape.* Although the two decisions reach opposite conclusions on this point, they are very much alike in methodology. In both cases, the Supreme Court treated the issue as a straightforward exercise in statutory construction. Both decisions locate the question in the textual ambiguity of the word "person" as used in § 1983; both refer to the "Dictionary Act" for possible guidance as to the meaning of that term; and both purport to resolve the issue by resort to legislative history. The decisions read that history differently, but both seem to regard it as dispositive. Neither opinion discusses the policies involved nor acknowledges the relevance of such discussion. In fact, the *Monroe* Court specifically disavowed analysis of the "policy considerations" for or against municipal liability.

Perhaps this is just as it should be. Section 1983 is an act of Congress, and a traditional means of resolving statutory ambiguity is to refer to the intent of the enacting legislature. Indeed, the Court might have opened itself to criticism if it had taken any other approach. Conventional wisdom would say that the Court's job in interpreting acts of Congress (at least in the absence of constitutional infirmity) is to give effect to the legislative will, not to consult its own perceptions of sound public policy.

And yet there is something a bit unsettling about the relentless historicity of § 1983 opinions. For one thing, the legislative history is often less clear than it is made out to be. In *Monroe* and *Monell,* for example, despite a seemingly thorough search, neither side was able to produce the "smoking gun" that clearly demonstrated legislative intent one way or the other—not for the meaning of "under color of" law and not for the scope of the word "person." If, for example, the 42nd Congress had considered and rejected a proposal to exclude municipalities from the coverage of the word "person," the debates might have been more illuminating. But in fact the legislative history reveals no occasion for this kind of focused and collective consideration of the issue. Instead, inferences must be drawn from scattered statements of individual legislators, whose views may or may not have been representative and who may or may not have had this issue precisely in mind when they spoke. To treat such evidence as dispositive may be placing more reliance on history than it can fairly bear.[c]

Moreover, the uncertainty of historical reconstruction increases with remoteness in time. The legislators who spoke and voted in 1871 did so against a background of political experience and constitutional

---

Section 1983 Municipal Liability and the Doctrine of Respondeat Superior, 46 U. Chi. L. Rev. 935 (1979). For an effort to identify the kinds of official policy or custom for which municipalities may be held liable after *Monell,* see Schnapper, Civil Rights Litigation After *Monell,* 79 Colum. L. Rev. 213 (1979).

[c] For a similar argument with respect to official immunity, see Richard A. Matasar, Personal Immunities under Section 1983: The Limits of the Court's Historical Analysis, 40 Ark.L.Rev. 741 (1987).

interpretation vastly different from what we know today. Projecting their views forward in time inevitably invites distortion. Ultimately, what the Court is asking is not merely what the 42nd Congress thought with respect to the kinds of problems then before it, but also what it would have thought if confronted with the issues now at hand. The more radical the change between that day and this, the less likely that the question is susceptible to meaningful answer.

Finally, these problems are compounded by the accumulation of modern precedent. The original meaning of the statute may be obscured by layers of interpretation. Each decision builds on the others. At some point, the statutory scheme, although grounded in a legislative act, is more nearly the product of judicial construction. Reversion to expressions of original intent to resolve some remaining ambiguity may have the effect of projecting the utterances of original enactment onto a pattern of legal regulation that has been substantially altered by subsequent interpretation.

Whether these concerns warrant deemphasis of the traditional model of statutory interpretation is a matter of controversy, both on and off the Supreme Court. Some might feel that § 1983 should be treated as a specie of federal common law, with the Supreme Court setting the terms of federal court supervision of state officials as it thinks best, but leaving the matter open for Congressional correction. Others may think that the model of federal common law invites inappropriate innovation and that the wiser course is for the Court to stick close to the traditional tasks of statutory construction. Whatever the merits of this debate, this much is clear: From *Monroe* on, the Supreme Court has tended to anchor its interpretations of § 1983 in the traditional mode. Many decisions are explained chiefly, if not exclusively, in terms of statutory language, legislative history, and original intent. Often the policy justifications for deciding an issue one way or the other are slighted or ignored or refracted through the historical prism of what the framers "must have thought." As a result, students of § 1983 are often left to uncover for themselves the arguments on both sides and to reach their own conclusions substantially unaided by judicial explication.

OWEN v. CITY OF INDEPENDENCE
Supreme Court of the United States, 1980.
445 U.S. 622.

Mr. Justice Brennan delivered the opinion of the Court.

Monell v. New York City Dept of Social Services, 436 U.S. 658 (1978), overruled Monroe v. Pape, 365 U.S. 167 (1961), insofar as *Monroe* held that local governments were not among the "persons" to whom 42 U.S.C. § 1983 applies and were therefore wholly immune from suit under the statute. *Monell* reserved decision, however, on the question whether local governments, although not entitled to absolute immunity, should be afforded some form of official immunity in § 1983 suits.

In this action brought by petitioner in the District Court for the Western District of Missouri, the Court of Appeals for the Eighth Circuit held that respondent city of Independence, Mo., "is entitled to qualified immunity from liability" based on the good faith of its officials: "We extend the limited immunity the District Court applied to the individual defendants to cover the city as well, because its officials acted in good faith and without malice." We granted certiorari. We reverse.

I

The events giving rise to this suit are detailed in the District Court's findings of fact. On February 20, 1967, Robert L. Broucek, then city manager of respondent city of Independence, Mo., appointed George D. Owen to an indefinite term as chief of police.[2] In 1972, Owen and a new city manager, Lyle W. Alberg, engaged in a dispute over petitioner's administration of the police department's property room. In March of that year, a handgun, which the records of the department's property room stated had been destroyed, turned up in Kansas City in the possession of a felon. This discovery prompted Alberg to initiate an investigation of the management of the property room. Although the probe was initially directed by petitioner, Alberg soon transferred responsibility for the investigation to the city's department of law, instructing the city counselor to supervise its conduct and to inform him directly of its findings.

Sometime in early April 1972, Alberg received a written report on the investigation's progress, along with copies of confidential witness statements. Although the city auditor found that the police department's records were insufficient to permit an adequate accounting of the goods contained in the property room, the city counselor concluded that there was no evidence of any criminal acts or of any violation of state or municipal law in the administration of the property room. Alberg discussed the results of the investigation at an informal meeting with several city council members and advised them that he would take action at an appropriate time to correct any problems in the administration of the police department.

On April 10, Alberg asked petitioner to resign as chief of police and to accept another position within the department, citing dissatisfaction with the manner in which petitioner had managed the department, particularly his inadequate supervision of the property room. Alberg warned that if petitioner refused to take another position in the department his employment would be terminated, to which petitioner responded that he did not intend to resign.

On April 13, Alberg issued a public statement addressed to the mayor and the city council concerning the results of the investigation. After referring to "discrepancies" found in the administration, han-

[2] Under § 3.3(1) of the city's charter, the city manager has sole authority to "[a]ppoint, and when deemed necessary for the good of the service, lay off, suspend, demote, or remove all directors, or heads, of administrative departments and all other administrative officers and employees of the city . . . ."

dling, and security of public property, the release concluded that "[t]here appears to be no evidence to substantiate any allegations of a criminal nature" and offered assurances that "[s]teps have been initiated on an administrative level to correct these discrepancies." Although Alberg apparently had decided by this time to replace petitioner as police chief, he took no formal action to that end and left for a brief vacation without informing the city council of his decision.

While Alberg was away on the weekend of April 15 and 16, two developments occurred. Petitioner, having consulted with counsel, sent Alberg a letter demanding written notice of the charges against him and a public hearing with a reasonable opportunity to respond to those charges. At approximately the same time, city councilman Paul L. Roberts asked for a copy of the investigative report on the police department property room. Although petitioner's appeal received no immediate response, the acting city manager complied with Roberts' request and supplied him with the audit report and the witness statements.

On the evening of April 17, 1972, the city council held its regularly scheduled meeting. After completion of the planned agenda, councilman Roberts read a statement he had prepared on the investigation.[5] Roberts charged that petitioner had misappropriated police department property for his own use, that narcotics and money had "mysteriously disappeared" from his office, that traffic tickets had been manipulated, that high ranking police officials had made "inappropriate" requests affecting the police court, and that "things have occurred causing the unusual release of felons." At the close of his statement, Roberts

---

[5] Roberts' statement . . . in part recited:

"On April 2, 1972, the city council was notified of the existence of an investigative report concerning the activities of the chief of police of the city of Independence, certain police officers and activities of one or more other city officials. On Saturday, April 15th for the first time I was able to see these 27 voluminous reports. The contents of these reports are astoundingly shocking and virtually unbelievable. They deal with the disappearance of two or more television sets from the police department and [a] signed statement that they were taken by the chief of police for his own personal use.

"The reports show that numerous firearms properly in the police department custody found their way into the hands of others including undesirables and were later found by other law enforcement agencies.

"Reports whow [sic] that narcotics held by the Independence Missouri chief of police have mysteriously disappeared. Reports also indicate money has mysteriously disappeared. Reports show that traffic tickets have been manipulated. The reports show inappropriate requests affecting the police court have come from high ranking police officials. Reports indicate that things have occurred causing the unusual release of felons. The reports show gross inefficiencies on the part of a few of the high ranking officers of the police department.

"In view of the contents of these reports, I feel that the information in the reports backed up by signed statements taken by investigators is so bad that the council should immediately make available to the news media access to copies of all of these 27 voluminous investigative reports so the public can be told what has been going on in Independence. I further believe that copies of these reports should be turned over and referred to the prosecuting attorney of Jackson County, Missouri for consideration and presentation to the next grand jury. I further insist that the city manager immediately take direct and appropriate action, permitted under the charter, against such persons as are shown by the investigation to have been involved."

moved that the investigative reports be released to the news media and turned over to the prosecutor for presentation to the grand jury, and that the city manager "take all direct and appropriate action" against those persons "involved in illegal, wrongful, or gross inefficient activities brought out in the investigative reports." After some discussion, the city council passed Roberts' motion with no dissents and one abstention.

City manager Alberg discharged the petitioner the very next day. Petitioner was not given any reason for his dismissal; he received only a written notice stating that his employment as chief of police was "[t]erminated under the provisions of section 3.3(1) of the city charter." Petitioner's earlier demand for a specification of charges and a public hearing was ignored, and a subsequent request by his attorney for an appeal of the discharge decision was denied by the city on the grounds that "there is no appellate procedure or forum provided by the charter or ordinances of the city of Independence, Missouri, relating to the dismissal of Mr. Owen."

The local press gave prominent coverage both to the city council's action and petitioner's dismissal, linking the discharge to the investigation. As instructed by the city council, Alberg referred the investigative reports and witness statements to the prosecuting attorney of Jackson County, Mo., for consideration by a grand jury. The results of the audit and investigation were never released to the public, however. The grand jury subsequently returned a "no true bill," and no further action was taken by either the city council or city manager Alberg.

II

Petitioner named the city of Independence, city manager Alberg, and the present members of the city council in their official capacities as defendants in this suit.[9] Alleging that he was discharged without notice of reasons and without a hearing in violation of his constitutional rights to procedural and substantive due process, petitioner sought declaratory and injunctive relief, including a hearing on his discharge, backpay from the date of discharge, and attorney's fees. The District Court, after a bench trial, entered judgment for respondents.[10]

---

[9] Petitioner did not join former councilman Roberts in the instant litigation. A separate action seeking defamation damages was brought in state court against Roberts and Alberg in their individual capacities. Petitioner dismissed the state suit against Alberg and reached a financial settlement with Roberts.

[10] The District Court, relying on Monroe v. Pape, 365 U.S. 167 (1961), and City of Kenosha v. Bruno, 412 U.S. 507 (1973), held that § 1983 did not create a cause of action against the city, but that petitioner could base his claim for relief directly on the 14th amendment. On the merits, however, the court determined that petitioner's discharge did not deprive him of any con-

stitutionally protected property interest because, as an untenured employee, he possessed neither a contractual nor a de facto right to continued employment as chief of police. Similarly, the court found that the circumstances of petitioner's dismissal did not impose a stigma of illegal or immoral conduct on his professional reputation, and hence did not deprive him of any liberty interest.

The District Court offered three reasons to support its conclusion: First, because the actual discharge notice stated only that petitioner was "[t]erminated under the provisions of Section 3.3(1) of the city charter," nothing in his official record imputed any stigmatizing conduct to him. Second,

The Court of Appeals initially reversed the District Court. Although it agreed with the District Court that under Missouri law petitioner possessed no property interest in continued employment as police chief, the Court of Appeals concluded that the city's allegedly false public accusations had blackened petitioner's name and reputation, thus depriving him of liberty without due process of law. That the stigmatizing charges did not come from the city manager and were not included in the official discharge notice was, in the court's view, immaterial. What was important, the court explained, was that "the official actions of the city council released charges against [petitioner] contemporaneous and, in the eyes of the public, connected with that discharge." [12]

Respondents petitioned for review of the Court of Appeals' decision. Certiorari was granted, and the case was remanded for further consideration in light of our supervening decision in Monell v. New York City Dept. of Social Services, 438 U.S. 902 (1978). The Court of Appeals on the remand reaffirmed its original determination that the city had violated petitioner's rights under the 14th amendment, but held that all respondents, including the city, were entitled to qualified immunity from liability.

Monell held that "a local government may not be sued under § 1983 for an injury inflicted solely by its employees or agents. Instead, it is when execution of a government's policy or custom, whether made by its lawmakers or by those whose edicts or acts may fairly be said to represent official policy, inflicts the injury that the government as an entity is responsible under § 1983." The Court of Appeals held in the instant case that the municipality's official policy was responsible for the deprivation of petitioner's constitutional rights: "[T]he

the court found that the city council's actions had no causal connection to petitioner's discharge, for city manager Alberg had apparently made his decision to hire a new police chief before the council's April 17th meeting. Lastly, the District Court determined that petitioner was "completely exonerated" from any charges of illegal or immoral conduct by the city counselor's investigative report, Alberg's public statements, and the grand jury's return of a "no true bill."

As an alternative ground for denying relief, the District Court ruled that the city was entitled to assert, and had in fact established, a qualified immunity against liability based on the good faith of the individual defendants who acted as its agents: "[D]efendants have clearly shown by a preponderance of the evidence that neither they, nor their predecessors, were aware in April 1972, that, under the circumstances the 14th amendment accorded plaintiff the procedural rights of notice and a hearing at the time of his discharge. Defendants have further proven that they cannot reasonably be charged with con-

structive notice of such rights since plaintiff was discharged prior to the publication of the Supreme Court decisions in Roth v. Board of Regents, 408 U.S. 564 (1972) and Perry v. Sinderman, 408 U.S. 593 (1972)."

[12] As compensation for the denial of his constitutional rights, the Court of Appeals awarded petitioner damages in lieu of backpay. The court explained that petitioner's termination without a hearing must be considered a nullity, and that ordinarily he ought to remain on the payroll and receive wages until a hearing is held and a proper determination on his retention is made. But because petitioner had reached the mandatory retirement age during the course of the litigation, he could not be reinstated to his former position. Thus the compensatory award was to be measured by the amount of money petitioner would likely have earned to retirement had he not been deprived of his good name by the city's actions, subject to mitigation by the amounts actually earned, as well as by the recovery from Councilman Roberts in the state defamation suit. . . .

stigma attached to [petitioner] in connection with his discharge was caused by the official conduct of the city's lawmakers, or by those whose acts may fairly be said to represent official policy. Such conduct amounted to official policy causing the infringement of [petitioner's] constitutional rights, in violation of § 1983." [13]

Nevertheless, the Court of Appeals affirmed the judgment of the District Court denying petitioner any relief against the respondent city, stating:

> "The Supreme Court's decisions in Board of Regents v. Roth, 408 U.S. 564 (1972), and Perry v. Sinderman, 408 U.S. 593 (1972), crystallized the rule establishing the right to a name-clearing hearing for a government employee allegedly stigmatized in the course of his discharge. The Court decided those two cases two months after the discharge in the instant case. Thus, officials of the city of Independence could not have been aware of [petitioner's] right to a name-clearing hearing in connection with the discharge. The city of Independence should not be charged with predicting the future course of constitutional law. . . . We extend the limited immunity the district court applied to the individual defendants to the city as well, because its officials acted in good faith and without malice. We hold the city not liable for actions it could not reasonably have known violated [petitioner's] constitutional rights."

We turn now to the reasons for our disagreement with this holding.

III

Because the question of the scope of a municipality's immunity from liability under § 1983 is essentially one of statutory construction, the starting point in our analysis must be the language of the statute itself. By its terms, § 1983 "creates a species of tort liability that on its

---

[13] Although respondents did not cross-petition on this issue, they have raised a belated challenge to the Court of Appeal's ruling that petitioner was deprived of a protected "liberty" interest. We find no merit in their contention, however, and decline to disturb the determination of the court below.

Wisconsin v. Constantineau, 400 U.S. 433, 437 (1971), held that "[w]here a person's good name, reputation, honor, or integrity is at stake because of what the government is doing to him, notice and an opportunity to be heard are essential." In Board of Regents v. Roth, 408 U.S. 564, 573 (1972), we explained that the dismissal of a government employee accompanied by a "charge against him that might seriously damage his standing and associations in his community" would qualify as something "the government is doing to him," so as to trigger the due process right to a

hearing at which the employee could refute the charges and publicly clear his name. In the present case, the city—through the unanimous resolution of the city council—released to the public an allegedly false statement impugning petitioner's honesty and integrity. Petitioner was discharged the next day. The council's accusations received extensive coverage in the press, and even if they did not in point of fact "cause" petitioner's discharge, the defamatory and stigmatizing charges certainly "occur[red] in the course of the termination of employment." Yet the city twice refused petitioner's request that he be given written specification of the charges against him and an opportunity to clear his name. Under the circumstances, we have no doubt that the Court of Appeals correctly concluded that the city's actions deprived petitioner of liberty without due process of law.

face admits of no immunities." Imbler v. Pachtman, 424 U.S. 409, 417 (1976). Its language is absolute and unqualified; no mention is made of any privileges, immunities, or defenses that may be asserted. Rather, the act imposes liability upon "*every* person" who, under color of state law or custom, "subjects, or causes to be subjected, any citizen of the United States . . . to the deprivation of any rights, privileges, or immunities secured by the Constitution and laws." And *Monell* held that these words were intended to encompass municipal corporations as well as natural "persons."

Moreover, the congressional debates surrounding the passage of § 1 of the Civil Rights Act of 1871—the forerunner of § 1983—confirm the expansive sweep of the statutory language. . . .

However, notwithstanding § 1983's expansive language and the absence of any express incorporation of common-law immunities, we have, on several occasions, found that a tradition of immunity was so firmly rooted in the common law and was supported by such strong policy reasons that "Congress would have specifically so provided had it wished to abolish the doctrine." Pierson v. Ray, 386 U.S. 547, 555 (1967). . . . Subsequent cases have required that we consider the personal liability of various other types of government officials. . . .

In each of these cases, our finding of § 1983 immunity "was predicated upon a considered inquiry into the immunity historically accorded the relevant official at common law and the interests behind it." Where the immunity claimed by the defendant was well established at common law at the time § 1983 was enacted, and where its rationale was compatible with the purposes of the Civil Rights Act, we have construed the statute to incorporate that immunity. But there is no tradition of immunity for municipal corporations, and neither history nor policy [supports] a construction of § 1983 that would justify the qualified immunity accorded the city of Independence by the Court of Appeals. We hold, therefore, that the municipality may not assert the good faith of its officers or agents as a defense to liability under § 1983.

A

Since colonial times, a distinct feature of our nation's system of governance has been the conferral of political power upon public and municipal corporations for the management of matters of local concern. As *Monell* recounted, by 1871, municipalities—like private corporations—were treated as natural persons for virtually all purposes of constitutional and statutory analysis. In particular, they were routinely sued in both federal and state courts. Local governmental units were regularly held to answer in damages for a wide range of statutory and constitutional violations, as well as for common-law actions for breach of contract. And although, as we discuss below, a municipality was not subject to suit for all manner of tortious conduct, it is clear that at the time § 1983 was enacted, local governmental bodies did not enjoy the sort of "good-faith" qualified immunity extended to them by the Court of Appeals.

As a general rule, it was understood that a municipality's tort liability in damages was identical to that of private corporations and individuals:

> "There is nothing in the character of a municipal corporation which entitles it to an immunity from liability for such malfeasances as private corporations or individuals would be liable for in a civil action. A municipal corporation is liable to the same extent as an individual for any act done by the express authority of the corporation, or of a branch of its government, empowered to act for it upon the subject to which the particular act relates, and for any act which, after it has been done, has been lawfully ratified by the corporation." T. Shearman and A. Redfield, A Treatise on the Law of Negligence § 120, p. 139 (1869).

. . . Under this general theory of liability, a municipality was deemed responsible for any private losses generated through a wide variety of its operations and functions, from personal injuries due to its defective sewers, thoroughfares, and public utilities, to property damage caused by its trespasses and uncompensated takings.

Yet in the hundreds of cases from that era awarding damages against municipal governments for wrongs committed by them, one searches in vain for much mention of a qualified immunity based on the good faith of municipal officers. Indeed, where the issue was discussed at all, the courts had rejected the proposition that a municipality should be privileged where it reasonably believed its actions to be lawful. . . .

That municipal corporations were commonly held liable for damages in tort was also recognized by the 42nd Congress. See Monell v. New York City Dept of Social Services, 436 U.S. 658, 688 (1972). For example, Senator Stevenson, in opposing the Sherman amendment's creation of a municipal liability for the riotous acts of its inhabitants, stated the prevailing law: "Numberless cases are to be found where a statutory liability has been created against municipal corporations for injuries resulting from a neglect of corporate duty." Nowhere in the debates, however, is there a suggestion that the common law excused a city from liability on account of the good faith of its authorized agents, much less an indication of a congressional intent to incorporate such an immunity into the Civil Rights Act. . . .

To be sure, there were two doctrines that afforded municipal corporations some measure of protection from tort liability. The first sought to distinguish between a municipality's "governmental" and "proprietary" functions; as to the former, the city was held immune, whereas in its exercise of the latter, the city was held to the same standards of liability as any private corporation. The second doctrine immunized a municipality for its "discretionary" or "legislative" activities, but not for those which were "ministerial" in nature. A brief examination of the application and rationale underlying each of these doctrines demonstrates that Congress could not have intended them to limit a municipality's immunity under § 1983.

The governmental-proprietary distinction owed its existence to the dual nature of the municipal corporation. On the one hand, the municipality was a corporate body, capable of performing the same "proprietary" functions as any private corporation, and liable for its torts in the same manner and to the same extent, as well. On the other hand, the municipality was an arm of the state, and when acting in that "governmental" or "public" capacity, it shared the immunity traditionally accorded the sovereign. But the principle of sovereign immunity—itself a somewhat arid fountainhead for municipal immunity—is necessarily nullified when the state expressly or impliedly allows itself, or its creation, to be sued. Municipalities were therefore liable not only for their "proprietary" acts, but also for those "governmental" functions as to which the state had withdrawn their immunity. And, by the end of the 19th century, courts regularly held that in imposing a specific duty on the municipality either in the charter or by statute, the state had impliedly withdrawn the city's immunity from liability for the nonperformance or misperformance of its obligation. Thus, despite the nominal existence of an immunity for "governmental" functions, municipalities were found liable in damages in a multitude of cases involving such activities.

That the municipality's common-law immunity for "governmental" functions derives from the principle of sovereign immunity also explains why that doctrine could not have served as the basis for the qualified privilege respondent city claims under § 1983. First, because sovereign immunity insulates the municipality from unconsented suits altogether, the presence or absence of good faith is simply irrelevant. The critical issue is whether injury occurred while the city was exercising governmental, as opposed to proprietary, powers or obligations—not whether its agents reasonably believed they were acting lawfully in so conducting themselves. More fundamentally, however, the municipality's "governmental" immunity is obviously abrogated by the sovereign's enactment of a statute making it amenable to suit. Section 1983 was just such a statute. By including municipalities within the class of "persons" subject to liability for violations of the federal Constitution and laws, Congress—the supreme sovereign on matters of federal law—abolished whatever vestige of the state's sovereign immunity the municipality possessed.

The second common-law distinction between municipal functions—that protecting the city from suits challenging "discretionary" decisions—was grounded not on the principle of sovereign immunity, but on a concern for separation of powers. A large part of the municipality's responsibilities involved broad discretionary decisions on issues of public policy—decisions that affected large numbers of persons and called for a delicate balancing of competing considerations. For a court or jury, in the guise of a tort suit, to review the reasonableness of the city's judgment on these matters would be an infringement upon the powers properly vested in a coordinate and coequal branch of government. In order to ensure against any invasion into the legitimate sphere of the municipality's policymaking processes, courts therefore refused to entertain suits against the city "either for the nonexercise of, or for the manner in which in good faith it exercises, *discretionary powers* of a public or legislative character."

Although many, if not all, of a municipality's activities would seem to involve at least some measure of discretion, the influence of this doctrine on the city's liability was not as significant as might be expected. For just as the courts implied an exception to the municipality's immunity for its "governmental" functions, here, too, a distinction was made that had the effect of subjecting the city to liability for much of its tortious conduct. While the city retained its immunity for decisions as to whether the public interest required acting in one manner or another, once any particular decision was made, the city was fully liable for injuries incurred in the execution of its judgment. Thus, the municipalities remained liable in damages for a broad range of conduct implementing their discretionary decisions.

Once again, an understanding of the rationale underlying the common-law immunity for "discretionary" functions explains why that doctrine cannot serve as the foundation for a good-faith immunity under § 1983. That common-law doctrine merely prevented courts from substituting their own judgment on matters within the lawful discretion of the municipality. But a municipality has no "discretion" to violate the federal Constitution; its dictates are absolute and imperative. And when a court passes judgment on the municipality's conduct in a § 1983 action, it does not seek to second-guess the "reasonableness" of the city's decision nor to interfere with the local government's resolution of competing policy considerations. Rather, it looks only to whether the municipality has conformed to the requirements of the federal Constitution and statutes. . . .

In sum, we can discern no "tradition so well grounded in history and reason" that would warrant the conclusion that in enacting § 1 of the Civil Rights Act, the 42nd Congress sub silentio extended to municipalities a qualified immunity based on the good faith of their officers. Absent any clearer indication that Congress intended so to limit the reach of a statute expressly designed to provide a "broad remedy for violations of federally protected civil rights," *Monell,* we are unwilling to suppose that injuries occasioned by a municipality's unconstitutional conduct were not also meant to be fully redressable through its sweep.

B

Our rejection of a construction of § 1983 that would accord municipalities a qualified immunity for their good-faith constitutional violations is compelled both by the legislative purpose in enacting the statute and by considerations of public policy. The central aim of the Civil Rights Act was to provide protection to those persons wronged by the " '[m]isuse of power, possessed by virtue of state law and made possible only because the wrongdoer is clothed with the authority of state law.' " Monroe v. Pape, 365 U.S. 167, 184 (1961). By creating an express federal remedy, Congress sought to "enforce provisions of the 14th amendment against those who carry a badge of authority of a state and represent it in some capacity, whether they act in accordance with their authority or misuse it." Id. at 172.

How "uniquely amiss" it would be, therefore, if the government itself—"the social organ to which all in our society look for the promotion of liberty, justice, fair and equal treatment, and the setting of worthy norms and goals for social conduct"—were permitted to disavow liability for the injury it has begotten. A damages remedy against the offending party is a vital component of any scheme for vindicating cherished constitutional guarantees, and the importance of assuring its efficacy is only accentuated when the wrongdoer is the institution that has been established to protect the very rights it has transgressed. Yet owing to the qualified immunity enjoyed by most government officials, see Scheuer v. Rhodes, 416 U.S. 232 (1974), many victims of municipal malfeasance would be left remediless if the city were also allowed to assert a good-faith defense. Unless countervailing considerations counsel otherwise, the injustice of such a result should not be tolerated.[33]

Moreover, § 1983 was intended not only to provide compensation to the victims of past abuses, but to serve as a deterrent against future constitutional deprivations, as well. The knowledge that a municipality will be liable for all of its injurious conduct, whether committed in good faith or not, should create an incentive for officials who harbor doubts about the lawfulness of their intended actions to err on the side of protecting citizens' constitutional rights. Furthermore, the threat that damages might be levied against the city may encourage those in a policymaking position to institute internal rules and programs designed to minimize the likelihood of unintentional infringements on constitutional rights. Such procedures are particularly beneficial in preventing those "systemic" injuries that result not so much from the conduct of any single individual, but from the interactive behavior of several government officials, each of whom may be acting in good faith.[36]

Our previous decisions conferring qualified immunities on various government officials are not to be read as derogating the significance of the societal interest in compensating the innocent victims of governmental misconduct. Rather, in each case we concluded that overriding

[33] The absence of any damages remedy for violations of all but the most "clearly established" constitutional rights could also have the deleterious effect of freezing constitutional law in its current state of development, for without a meaningful remedy, aggrieved individuals will have little incentive to seek vindication of those constitutional deprivations that have not previously been clearly defined.

[36] In addition, the threat of liability against the city ought to increase the at-

tentiveness with which officials at the higher levels of government supervise the conduct of their subordinates. The need to institute system-wide measures in order to increase the vigilance with which otherwise indifferent municipal officials protect citizens' constitutional rights is, of course, particularly acute where the front-line officers are judgment-proof in their individual capacities.

considerations of public policy nonetheless demanded that the official be given a measure of protection from personal liability. The concerns that justified those decisions, however, are less compelling, if not wholly inapplicable, when the liability of the municipal entity is at issue.

In *Scheuer v. Rhodes,* supra, the Chief Justice identified the two "mutually dependent rationales" on which the doctrine of official immunity rested:

> "(1) the injustice, particularly in the absence of bad faith, of subjecting to liability an officer who is required, by the legal obligations of his position, to exercise discretion; (2) the danger that the threat of such liability would deter his willingness to execute his office with the decisiveness and the judgment required by the public good."

The first consideration is simply not implicated when the damages award comes not from the official's pocket, but from the public treasury. It hardly seems unjust to require a municipal defendant which has violated a citizen's constitutional rights to compensate him for the injury suffered thereby. Indeed, Congress enacted § 1983 precisely to provide a remedy for such abuses of official authority. Elemental notions of fairness dictate that one who causes a loss should bear the loss.

It has been argued, however, that revenue raised by taxation for public use should not be diverted to the benefit of a single or discrete group of taxpayers, particularly where the municipality has at all times acted in good faith. On the contrary, the accepted view is that stated in Thayer v. Boston, 36 Mass. 511, 515 (1837)—"that the city, in its corporate capacity, should be liable to make good the damage sustained by an [unlucky] individual, in consequence of the acts thus done." After all, it is the public at large which enjoys the benefits of the government's activities, and it is the public at large which is ultimately responsible for its administration. Thus, even where some constitutional development could not have been foreseen by municipal officials, it is fairer to allocate any resulting financial loss to the inevitable costs of government borne by all the taxpayers, than to allow its impact to be felt solely by those whose rights, albeit newly recognized, have been violated.[39]

The second rationale mentioned in *Scheuer* also loses its force when it is the municipality, in contrast to the official, whose liability is at

---

[39] *Monell v. New York Dept of Social Services* indicated that the principle of loss-spreading was an insufficient justification for holding the municipality liable under § 1983 on a respondeat superior theory. Here, of course, quite a different situation is presented. Petitioner does not seek to hold the city responsible for the unconstitutional actions of an individual official *"solely* because it employs a tortfeasor." Rather, liability is predicated on a determination that "the action that is alleged to be unconstitutional implements or executes a policy statement, ordinance, regulation, or decision officially adopted and promulgated by the body's officers." In this circumstance—when it is the local government itself that is responsible for the constitutional deprivation—it is perfectly reasonable to distribute the loss to the public as a cost of the administration of government, rather than to let the entire burden fall on the injured individual.

issue. At the heart of this justification for a qualified immunity for the individual official is the concern that the threat of *personal* monetary liability will introduce an unwarranted and unconscionable consideration into the decisionmaking process, thus paralyzing the governing official's decisiveness and distorting his judgment on matters of public policy. The inhibiting effect is significantly reduced, if not eliminated, however, when the threat of personal liability is removed. First, as an empirical matter, it is questionable whether the hazard of municipal loss will deter a public officer from the conscientious exercise of his duties; city officials routinely make decisions that either require a large expenditure of municipal funds or involve a substantial risk of depleting the public fisc. More important, though, is the realization that consideration of the *municipality's* liability for constitutional violations is quite properly the concern of its elected or appointed officials. Indeed, a decisionmaker would be derelict in his duties if, at some point, he did not consider whether his decision comports with constitutional mandates and did not weigh the risk that a violation might result in an award of damages from the public treasury. As one commentator aptly put it: "Whatever other concerns should shape a particular official's actions, certainly one of them should be the constitutional rights of individuals who will be affected by his actions. To criticize § 1983 liability because it leads decisionmakers to avoid the infringement of constitutional rights is to criticize one of the statute's raisons d'etre."[41]

IV

In sum, our decision holding that municipalities have no immunity from damages liability flowing from their constitutional violations harmonizes well with developments in the common law and our own pronouncements on official immunities under § 1983. Doctrines of tort law have changed significantly over the past century, and our notions of governmental responsibility should properly reflect that evolution. No longer is individual "blameworthiness" the acid test of liability; the principle of equitable loss-spreading has joined fault as a factor in distributing the costs of official misconduct.

We believe that today's decision, together with prior precedents in this area, properly allocates these costs among the three principals in the scenario of the § 1983 cause of action: the victim of the constitutional deprivation; the officer whose conduct caused the injury; and the public, as represented by the municipal entity. The innocent individual who is harmed by an abuse of governmental authority is assured that he will be compensated for his injury. The offending official, so long as he conducts himself in good faith, may go about his business secure in the knowledge that a qualified immunity will protect him from personal liability for damages that are more appropriately chargeable to the populace as a whole. And the public will be forced to

[41] Note, Developments in the Law: Section 1983 and Federalism, 90 Harv. L. Rev. 1133, 1224 (1977).

bear only the costs of injury inflicted by the "execution of a government's policy or custom, whether made by its lawmakers or by those whose edicts or acts may fairly be said to represent official policy." *Monell v. New York City Dept of Social Services,* supra.

Reversed.

MR. JUSTICE POWELL, with whom the CHIEF JUSTICE, MR. JUSTICE STEWART, and MR. JUSTICE REHNQUIST joined, dissenting.

The Court today holds that the city of Independence may be liable in damages for violating a constitutional right that was unknown when the events in this case occurred. It finds a denial of due process in the city's failure to grant petitioner a hearing to clear his name after he was discharged. But his dismissal involved only the proper exercise of discretionary powers according to prevailing constitutional doctrine. The city imposed no stigma on petitioner that would require a "name clearing" hearing under the due process clause.

On the basis of this alleged deprivation of rights, the Court interprets 42 U.S.C. § 1983 to impose strict liability on municipalities for constitutional violations. This strict liability approach inexplicably departs from this Court's prior decisions under § 1983 and runs counter to the concerns of the 42nd Congress when it enacted the statute. The Court's ruling also ignores the vast weight of common-law precedent as well as the current state law of municipal immunity. For these reasons, and because this decision will hamper local governments unnecessarily, I dissent.

I

The Court does not question the District Court's statement of the facts surrounding Owen's dismissal. It nevertheless rejects the District Court's conclusion that no due process hearing was necessary because "the circumstances of [Owen's] discharge did not impose a stigma of illegal or immoral conduct on his professional reputation." Careful analysis of the record supports the District Court's view that Owen suffered no constitutional deprivation. . . .[3]

Due process requires a hearing on the discharge of a government employee "if the employer creates and disseminates a false and defamatory impression about the employee in connection with his termination. . . ." Codd v. Velger, 429 U.S. 624, 628 (1977) (per curiam). This principle was first announced in Board of Regents v. Roth, 408 U.S. 564 (1972), which was decided in June 1972, 10 weeks *after* Owen was discharged. The pivotal question after *Roth* is whether the circumstances of the discharge so blackened the employee's name as to impair his liberty interest in his professional reputation.

The events surrounding Owen's dismissal "were prominently reported in local newspapers." Doubtless, the public received a negative impression of Owen's abilities and performance. But a "name clear-

---

[3] Owen initially claimed that his property interests in the job also were violated. The Court of Appeals affirmed the District Court's rejection of that contention, and petitioner has not challenged that ruling in this Court.

ing" hearing is not necessary unless the employer makes a public statement that "might seriously damage [the employee's] standing and associations in his community." Board of Regents v. Roth, 408 U.S. 564, 573 (1972). No hearing is required after the "discharge of a public employee whose position is terminable at the will of the employer when there is no public disclosure of the reasons for the discharge." Bishop v. Wood, 426 U.S. 341 (1976).

The city manager gave no specific reason for dismissing Owen. Instead, he relied on his discretionary authority to discharge top administrators "for the good of the service." Alberg did not suggest that Owen "had been guilty of dishonesty, or immorality." Board of Regents v. Roth, 408 U.S. 564, 573 (1972). Indeed, in his "property room" statement of April 13, Alberg said that there was "no evidence to substantiate any allegations of a criminal nature." This exoneration was reinforced by the grand jury's refusal to initiate a prosecution in the matter. Thus, nothing in the actual firing cast such a stigma on Owen's professional reputation that his liberty was infringed.

The Court does not address directly the question whether any stigma was imposed by the discharge. Rather, it relies on the Court of Appeals' finding that stigma derived from the events "connected with" the firing. That court attached great significance to the resolution adopted by the city council at its April 17 meeting. But the resolution merely recommended that Alberg take "appropriate action," and the District Court found no "causal connection" between events in the city council and the firing of Owen. Two days before the council met, Alberg already had decided to dismiss Owen. Indeed, councilman Roberts stated at the meeting that the city manager had asked for Owen's resignation.

Even if the council resolution is viewed as part of the discharge process, Owen has demonstrated no denial of his liberty. Neither the city manager nor the council cast any aspersions on Owen's character. Alberg absolved all connected with the property room of any illegal activity, while the council resolution alleged no wrongdoing. That events focused public attention upon Owen's dismissal is undeniable; such attention is a condition of employment—and of discharge—for high government officials. Nevertheless, nothing in the actions of the city manager or the city council triggered a constitutional right to a name-clearing hearing.

The statements by councilman Roberts were neither measured nor benign, but they provide no basis for this action against the city of Independence. Under Monell v. New York City Dept of Social Services, 436 U.S. 658, 691 (1978), the city cannot be held liable for Roberts' statements on a theory of respondeat superior. That case held that § 1983 makes municipalities liable for constitutional deprivations only if the challenged action was taken "pursuant to official municipal policy of some nature. . . ." As the Court noted, "a municipality cannot be held liable *solely* because it employs a tortfeasor. . . ." The statements of a single councilman scarcely rise to the level of municipal policy.

As the District Court concluded, "[a]t most, the circumstances . . . suggested that, as chief of police, [Owen] had been an inefficient administrator." This Court now finds unconstitutional stigma in the interaction of unobjectionable official acts with the unauthorized statements of a lone councilman who had no direct role in the discharge process. The notoriety that attended Owen's firing resulted not from any city policy, but solely from public misapprehension of the reasons for a purely discretionary dismissal. There was no constitutional injury.

II

Having constructed a constitutional deprivation from a valid exercise of governmental authority, the Court holds that municipalities are strictly liable for their constitutional torts. Until two years ago, municipal corporations enjoyed absolute immunity from § 1983 claims. Monroe v. Pape, 365 U.S. 167 (1961). But *Monell v New York City Dept of Social Services,* supra, held that local governments are "persons" within the meaning of the statute, and thus are liable in damages for constitutional violations inflicted by municipal policies. *Monell* did not address the question whether municipalities might enjoy a qualified immunity or good-faith defense against § 1983 actions.

After today's decision, municipalities will have gone in two short years from absolute immunity under § 1983 to strict liability. As a policy matter, I believe that strict municipal liability unreasonably subjects local governments to damages judgments for actions that were reasonable when performed. It converts municipal governance into a hazardous slalom through constitutional obstacles that are unknown and unknowable.

The Court's decision also impinges seriously on the prerogatives of municipal entities created and regulated primarily by the states. At the very least, this Court should not initiate a federal intrusion of this magnitude in the absence of explicit congressional action. Yet today's decision is supported by nothing in the text of § 1983. Indeed, it conflicts with the apparent intent of the drafters of the statute, with the common law of municipal tort liability, and with the current state law of municipal immunities.

A

1

Section 1983 provides a private right of action against "[e]very person" acting under color of state law who imposes or causes to be imposed a deprivation of constitutional rights. Although the statute does not refer to immunities, this Court has held that the law "is to be read in harmony with general principles of tort immunities and defenses rather than in derogation of them." Imbler v. Pachtman, 424 U.S. 409, 418 (1976). . . .

The Court today abandons any attempt to harmonize § 1983 with traditional tort law. It points out that municipal immunity may be abrogated by legislation. Thus, according to the Court, Congress "abolished" municipal immunity when it included municipalities "within the class of 'persons' subject to liability" under § 1983.

This reasoning flies in the face of our prior decisions under this statute. We have held repeatedly that "immunities 'well grounded in history and reason' [were not] abrogated 'by covert inclusion in the general language' of 1983." Imbler v. Pachtman, 424 U.S. 409, 418 (1976), quoting Tenney v. Brandhove, 341 U.S. 367, 376 (1951). The peculiar nature of the Court's position emerges when the status of executive officers under § 1983 is compared with that of local governments. State and local executives are personally liable for bad-faith or unreasonable constitutional torts. Although Congress had the power to make those individuals liable for all such torts, this Court has refused to find an abrogation of traditional immunity in a statute that does not mention immunities. Yet the Court now views the enactment of § 1983 as a direct abolition of traditional municipal immunities. Unless the Court is overruling its previous immunity decisions, the silence in § 1983 must mean that the 42nd Congress mutely accepted the immunity of executive officers, but silently rejected common-law municipal immunity. I find this interpretation of the statute singularly implausible.

2

Important public policies support the extension of qualified immunity to local governments. First, as recognized by the doctrine of separation of powers, some governmental decisions should be at least presumptively insulated from judicial review. . . . The allocation of public resources and the operational policies of the government itself are activities that lie peculiarly within the competence of executive and legislative bodies. When charting those policies, a local official should not have to gauge his employer's possible liability under § 1983 if he incorrectly—though reasonably and in good faith—forecasts the course of constitutional law. Excessive judicial intrusion into such decisions can only distort municipal decisionmaking and discredit the courts. Qualified immunity would provide presumptive protection for discretionary acts, while still leaving the municipality liable for bad faith or unreasonable constitutional deprivations. . . .

The Court now argues that local officials might modify their actions unduly if they face personal liability under § 1983, but that they are unlikely to do so when the locality itself will be held liable. This contention denigrates the sense of responsibility of municipal officers, and misunderstands the political process. Responsible local officials will be concerned about potential judgments against their municipalities for alleged constitutional torts. Moreover, they will be accountable within the political system for subjecting the municipality to adverse judgments. If officials must look over their shoulders at strict municipal liability for unknowable constitutional deprivations, the resulting degree of governmental paralysis will be little different from that caused by fear of personal liability.[9]

In addition, basic fairness requires a qualified immunity for municipalities. The good-faith defense recognized under § 1983 authorizes liability only when officials acted with malicious intent or when they "knew or should have known that their conduct violated the constitutional norm." The standard incorporates the idea that liability should not attach unless there was notice that a constitutional right was at issue. This idea applies to governmental entities and individual officials alike. Constitutional law is what the courts say it is, and—as demonstrated by today's decision and its precursor, *Monell*—even the most prescient lawyer would hesitate to give a firm opinion on matters not plainly settled. Municipalities, often acting in the utmost good faith, may not know or anticipate when their action or inaction will be deemed a constitutional violation.

The Court nevertheless suggests that, as a matter of social justice, municipal corporations should be strictly liable even if they could not have known that a particular action would violate the Constitution. After all, the Court urges, local governments can "spread" the costs of any judgment across the local population. The Court neglects, however, the fact that many local governments lack the resources to withstand substantial unanticipated liability under § 1983. Even enthusiastic proponents of municipal liability have conceded that ruinous judgments under the statute could imperil local governments. By simplistically applying the theorems of welfare economics and ignoring the reality of municipal finance, the Court imposes strict liability on the level of government least able to bear it. For some municipalities, the result could be a severe limitation on their ability to serve the public.

B

The Court searches at length—and in vain—for legal authority to buttress its policy judgment. Despite its general statements to the contrary, the Court can find no support for its position in the debates on the civil rights legislation that included § 1983. Indeed, the legislative record suggests that the members of the 42nd Congress would have been dismayed by this ruling. Nor, despite its frequent citation of authorities that are only marginally relevant, can the Court rely on the traditional or current law of municipal tort liability. Both in the 19th

---

[9] The Court's argument is not only unpersuasive, but also is internally inconsistent. The Court contends that strict liability is necessary to "create an incentive for officials . . . to err on the side of protecting citizens' constitutional rights." Yet the Court later assures us that such liability will not distort municipal decisionmaking because "[t]he inhibiting effect is significantly reduced, if not eliminated . . . when the threat of personal liability is removed." Thus, the Court apparently believes that strict municipal liability is needed to modify public policies, but will not have any impact on those policies anyway.

century and now, courts and legislatures have recognized the importance of limiting the liability of local governments for official torts. Each of these conventional sources of law points to the need for qualified immunity for local governments.

1

The modern dispute over municipal liability under § 1983 has focused on the defeat of the Sherman amendment during the deliberations on the Civil Rights Act of 1871. Senator Sherman proposed that local governments be held vicariously liable for constitutional deprivations caused by riots within their boundaries. As originally drafted, the measure imposed liability even if municipal officials had no actual knowledge of the impending disturbance. The amendment, which did not affect the part of the Civil Rights Act that we now know as § 1983, was approved by the Senate but rejected by the House of Representatives. After two revisions by conference committees, both houses passed what is now codified as 42 U.S.C. § 1986. The final version applied not just to local governments but to all "persons," and it imposed no liability unless the defendant knew that a wrong was "about to be committed."

Because Senator Sherman initially proposed strict municipal liability for constitutional torts, the discussion of his amendment offers an invaluable insight into the attitudes of his colleagues on the question now before the Court. Much of the resistance to the measure flowed from doubts as to Congress' power to impose vicarious liability on local governments. But opponents of the amendment made additional arguments that strongly support recognition of qualified municipal immunity under § 1983.

First, several legislators expressed trepidation that the proposal's strict liability approach could bankrupt local governments. . . .

Most significant, the opponents objected to liability imposed without any showing that a municipality knew of an impending constitutional deprivation. Senator Sherman defended this feature of the amendment as a characteristic of riot acts long in force in England and this country. But Senator Stevenson argued against creating "a corporate liability for personal injury which no prudence or foresight could have prevented." In the most thorough critique of the amendment, Senator Thurman carefully reviewed the riot acts of Maryland and New York. He emphasized that those laws imposed liability only when a plaintiff proved that the local government had both notice of the impending injury and the power to prevent it.

> "Is not that right? Why make the county, or town, or parish liable when it had no reason whatsoever to anticipate that any such crime was about to be committed, and when it had no knowledge of the commission of the crime until after it was committed? What justice is there in that?"

These concerns were echoed in the House of Representatives. . . .

Partly in response to these objections, the amendment as finally enacted conditioned liability on a demonstration that the defendant knew that constitutional rights were about to be denied. . . .

These objections to the Sherman amendment apply with equal force to strict municipal liability under § 1983. Just as the 42nd Congress refused to hold municipalities vicariously liable for deprivations that could not be known beforehand, this Court should not hold those entities strictly liable for deprivations caused by actions that reasonably and in good faith were thought to be legal. The Court's approach today, like the Sherman amendment, could spawn onerous judgments against local governments and distort the decisions of officers who fear municipal liability for their actions. Congress' refusal to impose those burdens in 1871 surely undercuts any historical argument that federal judges should do so now.

The Court declares that its rejection of qualified immunity is "compelled" by the "legislative purpose" in enacting § 1983. One would expect powerful documentation to back up such a strong statement. Yet the Court notes only three features of the legislative history of the Civil Rights Act. Far from "compelling" the Court's strict liability approach, those features of the congressional record provide scant support for its position.

First, the Court [relies on] statements by Congressmen attesting to the broad remedial scope of the law. In view of our many decisions recognizing the immunity of officers under § 1983, those statements plainly shed no light on the congressional intent with respect to immunity under the statute. Second, the Court cites Senator Stevenson's remark that frequently "a statutory liability has been created against municipal corporations for injuries resulting from a neglect of corporate duty." The Senator merely stated the unobjectionable proposition that municipal immunity could be qualified or abolished by statute. This fragmentary observation provides no basis for the Court's version of the legislative history.

Finally, the Court emphasizes the lack of comment on municipal immunity when opponents of the bill did discuss the immunities of government officers. "Had there been a similar common-law immunity for municipalities, the bill's opponents would have raised the spectre of its destruction as well." This is but another example of the Court's continuing willingness to find meaning in silence. This example is particularly noteworthy because the very next sentence in the Court's opinion concedes: "To be sure, there were two doctrines that afforded municipal corporations some measure of protection from tort liability." Since the opponents of the Sherman amendment repeatedly expressed their conviction that strict municipal liability was unprecedented and unwise, the failure to recite the theories of municipal immunity is of no relevance here. In any event, that silence cannot contradict the many contemporary judicial decisions applying that immunity.

2

The Court's decision also runs counter to the common law in the 19th century, which recognized substantial tort immunity for municipal actions. Nineteenth-century courts generally held that municipal corporations were not liable for acts undertaken in their "governmental," as opposed to their "proprietary," capacity. Most states now use other criteria for determining when a local government should be liable for damages. Still, the governmental/proprietary distinction retains significance because it was so widely accepted when § 1983 was enacted. It is inconceivable that a Congress thoroughly versed in current legal doctrines, see Monell v. New York City Dept of Social Services, 436 U.S. 658, 669 (1978), would have intended through silence to create the strict liability regime now imagined by this Court.

More directly relevant to this case is the common-law distinction between the "discretionary" and "ministerial" duties of local governments. This Court wrote in Harris v. District of Columbia, 256 U.S. 650, 652 (1921): "[W]hen acting in good faith municipal corporations are not liable for the manner in which they exercise their discretionary powers." The rationale for this immunity derives from the theory of separation of powers. . . .

That reasoning, frequently applied in the 19th century, parallels the theory behind qualified immunity under § 1983. This Court has recognized the importance of preserving the autonomy of executive bodies entrusted with discretionary powers. *Scheuer v. Rhodes* held that executive officials who have broad responsibilities must enjoy a "range of discretion [that is] comparably broad." Consequently, the immunities available under § 1983 [vary] directly with "the scope of discretion and responsibility of the office. . . ." Strict municipal liability can only undermine that discretion.[18] . . .

3

Today's decision also conflicts with the current law in 44 states and the District of Columbia. All of those jurisdictions provide municipal immunity at least analogous to a "good faith" defense against liability for constitutional torts. Thus, for municipalities in almost 90 per cent of our jurisdictions, the Court creates broader liability for constitutional deprivations than for state-law torts. . . .

---

[18] The Court cannot wash away these extensive municipal immunities. It quotes [a 19th-century treatise] as referring to municipal liability for some torts. [The passage, however, refers] to exceptions to the existing immunity rules. The . . . treatise cited by the Court concedes, though deplores, the fact that many jurisdictions embraced the governmental/proprietary distinction. T. Shearman and A. Redfield, A Treatise on the Law of Negligence § 120, pp. 140–41 (1869). The same volume notes that local governments could not be sued for injury caused by discretionary acts, id., § 127, at p. 154, or for officers' acts beyond the powers of the municipal corporation, id., § 140, at p. 169. . . .

The Court takes some solace in the absence in the 19th century of a qualified immunity for local governments. That absence, of course, was due to the availability of absolute immunity for governmental and discretionary acts. . . .

C

The Court turns a blind eye to this overwhelming evidence that municipalities have enjoyed a qualified immunity and to the policy considerations that for the life of this republic have justified its retention. This disregard of precedent and policy is especially unfortunate because suits under § 1983 typically implicate evolving constitutional standards. A good-faith defense is much more important for those actions than in those involving ordinary tort liability. The duty not to run over a pedestrian with a municipal bus is far less likely to change than is the rule as to what process, if any, is due the bus driver if he claims the right to a hearing after discharge.

The right of a discharged government employee to a "name clearing" hearing was not recognized until our decision in Board of Regents v. Roth, 408 U.S. 564 (1972). That ruling was handed down 10 weeks after Owen was discharged and eight weeks after the city denied his request for a hearing. By stripping the city of any immunity, the Court punishes it for failing to predict our decision in *Roth*. As a result, local governments and their officials will face the unnerving prospect of crushing damages judgments whenever a policy valid under current law is later found to be unconstitutional. I can see no justice or wisdom in that outcome.

NOTES ON *OWEN v. CITY OF INDEPENDENCE*

1. **The Due Process Issue.** In *Owen* the former police chief sought and received compensation for the period following his wrongful discharge. But why, exactly, was the discharge wrongful? The Court did not hold that Owen had a right to continued employment. As a discretionary employee, he was subject to termination for virtually any reason. The problem was apparently not the discharge itself, but rather the accompanying publicity. Of course, coverage by the media would have been beyond the city's power to control, so the crucial error seems to have been the public dissemination by city officials of statements harmful to Owen's reputation. Far and away the most injurious were the remarks of councilman Roberts, remarks that even the dissent admitted were "neither measured nor benign."

Does the *Owen* decision suggest that the city should have prevented those communications? Would the necessity for a hearing have been avoided if the city manager had refused to allow public disclosure of the charges in the investigative report? Or would it have been necessary as well to muzzle councilman Roberts? By what authority could the city have tried to silence a council member?

Suppose that such communications had been withheld and that Owen had been discharged without adverse publicity. Suppose further that Owen then went to a neighboring town and applied for appointment as chief of police. An officer of that town telephones the city manager of Independence and asks for a candid evaluation of Owen's character and abilities and for an explanation of the reasons for his dismissal. Should the city manager give an opinion? Or would it be wiser to refuse to cooperate? Would that be in the public interest?

One answer might be that a municipality should make no effort to restrict the flow of information to the public but should simply be prepared to grant a "name-clearing hearing" to any employee whose reputation is injured as a result. This seems to be the Court's position in *Owen*. Presumably, after councilman Roberts' remarks, the city should have held a hearing at which Owen would have had a chance to defend his record.

What would such a hearing look like? Would it lead to some sort of decision? Would the hearing officer attempt to adjudicate, whether, as councilman Roberts alleged, narcotics and money had "mysteriously disappeared"? Or whether "inappropriate requests" to the police court had in fact been made by "high ranking police officials"? Or whether, as councilman Roberts concluded, the investigative reports were "astoundingly shocking and virtually unbelievable"? By what standards would such issues be resolved? And if the determination were favorable to Owen, what relief would be given? Would he get his job back, or would he receive merely some sort of official certification of good character?

Alternatively, perhaps the Court envisions that the "name-clearing hearing" would not lead to any decisional outcome but would merely present an opportunity for the airing of views. Suppose such a hearing is held, and Owen makes a wide-ranging defense of his conduct in office. What should the city do in response? Is there any reason for city officials to say anything? Does the hearing officer simply thank Owen for his time and allow the city to get on with the business of selecting a new chief of police? If so, the "name-clearing hearing" would be little more than a press conference. The value to Owen would depend on the willingness of the media to give coverage and sympathetic attention to his side of the story. Of course, the media could do that without an official proceeding, and the city's role in mediating between Owen and the press seems at best obscure.

These issues did not surface in *Owen* because the time had already passed when the city might have attempted to restrain communication or to provide the necessary hearing. In the future, however, municipalities may be expected to attempt to structure their affairs so as to avoid civil liability, and the various possible inferences to be drawn from *Owen* may then come to the fore.

2. The Immunity Issue. *Owen* also illustrates the continuing evolution of § 1983. As the dissent points out, "in two short years" municipalities went from absolute immunity (by virtue of exclusion from the term "person") to strict liability. The opinion itself illustrates the by now familiar amalgam of statutory language, legislative history, common-law background, and public policy. Which of these factors seems to have been the most influential in *Owen*? Which should have

been? What are the appropriate inferences to be drawn from legislative silence on the subject of immunities? Should the answer hinge on
the law of municipal immunity as it stood in 1871? If so, which side
seems to have the better of the argument?

   3. *City of Newport v. Fact Concerts.* One year after *Owen* the
Supreme Court barred punitive damages against a municipality. Fact
Concerts had engaged musical groups to appear at the Newport Jazz
Festival. When a scheduled group cancelled, the promoter engaged
Blood, Sweat, and Tears to appear in its stead. The mayor and other
city officials objected on the ground that Blood, Sweat, and Tears was a
rock group and would attract the "wrong" sort of crowd. The promoter
disputed that characterization. At a meeting held the day before the
group's first appearance, the city council voted to cancel the contract.
The ostensible reason was the promoter's failure to live up to certain
contractual provisions, but it seems clear that this objection was pretextual. The promoter then obtained a state court injunction against the
city officials, and the event went off without incident. Owing to the
widespread publicity of the dispute, however, ticket sales were below
expectations.

   The promoter sued in federal court under § 1983 and state law.
The jury awarded compensatory damages of $72,910 and punitive
damages of $275,000, 75 per cent of which was assessed on the federal
claim. After the verdict had been returned, the city moved for a new
trial, claiming for the first time that municipalities were immune from
awards of punitive damages under § 1983. Despite the fact that this
claim was untimely raised, the District Court reached the merits and
upheld the punitive award, although with a remittitur reducing the
amount to $75,000.

   In City of Newport v. Fact Concerts, Inc., 453 U.S. 247 (1981), the
Supreme Court overturned the punitive award based on § 1983.
Speaking through Justice Blackmun, the Court surveyed the history of
municipal immunity from awards of punitive damages at the time
§ 1983 was enacted. The Court also considered the legislative history
of § 1983, and although punitive damages were not specifically debated,
the Court nevertheless inferred that the enacting legislature would not
have approved such awards. Finally, the Court turned to considerations of public policy:

   "Punitive damages by definition are not intended to compensate the injured party, but to punish the tortfeasor whose
   wrongful action was intentional or malicious, and to deter him
   and others from similar extreme conduct. Regarding retribution, it remains true that an award of punitive damages
   against a municipality 'punishes' only the taxpayers, who took
   no part in the commission of the tort. These damages are
   assessed over and above the amount necessary to compensate
   the injured party. Thus, there is no question of equitably
   distributing the losses resulting from official misconduct. Ow-
   en v. City of Independence, 445 U.S. 622, 657 (1980). Indeed,

punitive damages imposed on a municipality are in effect a windfall to a fully compensated plaintiff, and are likely accompanied by an increase in taxes or a reduction of public services for the citizens footing the bill.

"Under ordinary principles of retribution, it is the wrong-doer himself who is made to suffer for his unlawful conduct. If a government official acts knowingly and maliciously to deprive others of their civil rights, he may become the appropriate object of the community's vindictive sentiments. A municipality, however, can have no malice independent of the malice of its officials. Damages awarded for *punitive* purposes, therefore, are not sensibly assessed against the governmental entity itself."

As to the objective of deterrence, the Court concluded:

"By allowing juries and courts to assess punitive damages in appropriate circumstances against the offending official, based on his personal financial resources, the statute directly addresses the public's interest in preventing repeated constitutional deprivations. In our view, this provides sufficient protection against the prospect that a public official may commit recurrent constitutional violations by reason of his office."

Justice Brennan, joined by Justices Marshall and Stevens, dissented on the ground that the city's failure to object to submission of the issue of punitive damages to the jury should have barred its subsequent reconsideration.

INTRODUCTORY NOTES ON DETERMINING "OFFICIAL POLICY"

1. Introduction. *Monell* limited governmental liability to acts performed under an official policy or custom. This requirement has proved troublesome. Presumably, the issue is clear where, as in *Monell,* the decision is taken pursuant to a rule or regulation of general applicability. Much more difficult questions arise when govermental liability is sought for a single act or decision by government officials. The Supreme Court's most recent pronouncement on this issue appears as the next main case. Earlier attempts to define "official policy" are summarized below.

2. *Oklahoma City v. Tuttle.* In Oklahoma City v. Tuttle, 471 U.S. 808 (1985), a rookie police officer shot and killed Albert Tuttle as he tried to leave the scene of a reported robbery. The officer had already determined that the report was fictitious, and there seemed little reason to suspect that Tuttle was guilty of anything more serious than making the false report. Tuttle's widow sued both the officer and the city under § 1983. Her theory was that the city had a "policy" of inadequate training, which was responsible for the officer's precipitate reaction. The instructions allowed the jury to infer from a "single, unusually excessive use of force" that the officer's misconduct was "attributable to inadequate training or supervision amounting to 'deliberate indifference' or 'gross negligence' on the part of the officials in charge." The jury found in favor of the officer but returned a verdict against the city for $1.5 million.

This judgment was overturned by the Supreme Court. Speaking for a plurality of four, Justice Rehnquist said that proof of a single incident would not be enough to hold a municipality liable under *Monell*, "unless proof of the incident includes proof that it was caused by an existing, unconstitutional municipal policy, which policy can be attributed to a municipal policymaker." Rehnquist doubted whether a policy, not in itself unconstitutional could ever support liability under *Monell*, but said that "[a]t the very least there must be an affirmative link between the policy and the particular constitutional violation alleged."

Justice Brennan, joined by Justices Blackmun and Marshall, concurred in the judgment. Brennan argued that any municipal policy that caused a constitutional violation would support liability under *Monell*, but agreed that no such policy could properly be inferred from a single act of police misconduct.

Only Justice Stevens dissented.[a] He interpreted § 1983 to impose liability on a municipal employer on a theory of respondeat superior, without regard to any "policy or custom" of the city itself. The contrary indication in *Monell* was dismissed as "judicial legislation of the most blatant kind." [b]

3. *City of Springfield v. Kibbe.* The Court returned to the question of inadequate training in City of Springfield v. Kibbe, 480 U.S. 257 (1987). Ultimately, the writ of certiorari was dismissed as improvidently granted, because the city had not preserved the issue for appellate review. Justice O'Connor, joined by Chief Justice Rehnquist and Justices White and Powell, dissented. She thought the issue properly before the Court and therefore addressed the merits.

The case involved a protracted car chase of a person who had assaulted and abducted a woman. The chase ended when a motorcycle policeman moved abreast of the car and shot the driver in the head. Suit was filed by the administratrix of the driver against the police officer and the city. The jury awarded damages of $1 (compensatory) and $500 (punitive) against the officer and $50,000 (compensatory) against the city. The theory of liability was that the city "had a policy or custom of inadequately training its officers" in alternative methods of stopping a fleeing vehicle. Justice O'Connor responded:

> "Respondent does not contend that the city's police training
> program *authorizes* the use of deadly force in the apprehension
> of fleeing vehicles; rather, her argument is that the methods

---

[a] Justice Powell did not participate.

[b] For an analysis of the important questions left open by *Tuttle*, see Solomon Oliver, Municipal Liability for Police Misconduct under 42 U.S.C. § 1983 after *City of Oklahoma City v. Tuttle*, 64 Wash.U.L.Q. 151 (1986).

taught in the city's training program were 'inadequate,' and that if individual officers had received more complete training, they would have resorted to those alternative methods without engaging in the unconstitutional conduct. The difficulty with respondent's argument is that at the time of the officers' alleged misconduct, any number of other factors were also in operation that were equally likely to contribute or play a predominant part in bringing about the constitutional injury: the disposition of the individual officers, the extent of their experience with similar incidents, the actions of the other officers involved, and so forth. To conclude, in a particular instance, that omissions in a municipal training program constituted the 'moving force' in bringing about the officer's unconstitutional conduct, notwithstanding the large number of intervening causes also at work up to the time of the constitutional harm, appears to be largely a matter of speculation and conjecture.

"Because of the remote causal connection between omissions in a police training program and affirmative misconduct by individual officers in a particular instance, in my view the 'inadequacy' of police training may serve as the basis for § 1983 liability only where the failure to train amounts to a reckless disregard for or deliberate indifference to the rights of persons within the city's domain. The causation requirement of § 1983 is a matter of statutory interpretation rather than of common tort law. Analogy to traditional tort principles, however, shows that the law has been willing to trace more distant causation when there is a cognitive component to the defendant's fault than when the defendant's conduct results from simple or heightened negligence. Similarly, a jury should be permitted to find that the municipality's inadequate training 'caused' the plaintiff's injury only if the inadequacy of the training amounts to deliberate indifference or reckless disregard for the consequences. Negligence in training alone is not sufficient to satisfy the causation requirement of § 1983."

4. *Pembaur v. City of Cincinnati.* The next attempt to resolve the meaning of "official policy" came in Pembaur v. City of Cincinnati, 475 U.S. 469 (1986). The case arose from an investigation of alleged welfare fraud in Dr. Pembaur's medical clinic. During that investigation, a grand jury issued subpoenas for two of Pembaur's employees, both of whom failed to appear. The prosecutor then obtained warrants ordering the county sheriff to arrest and detain the two employees.

When deputy sheriffs arrived at the clinic to serve the warrants, Pembaur locked the door separating the reception area from the rest of the clinic and refused to let them enter. After consulting with the Cincinnati police, the deputies called their supervisor to ask for instructions. The supervisor told them to call William Whalen, assistant prosecutor of the county, and to follow his directions. Whalen conferred with his superior and relayed the instruction to "go in and get" the recalcitrant witnesses. When advised of these instructions, the city police officers on the scene obtained an axe and chopped down the door. The deputies then entered and searched for the witnesses. They arrested two individuals who fit the descriptions in the warrants but turned out to be the wrong persons.

Some four years after these events, Steagald v. United States, 451 U.S. 204 (1981), ruled that, absent exigent circumstances, the police cannot enter an individual's home or business without a search warrant, merely because they are seeking to execute an arrest warrant for a third person. *Steagald* was conceded to apply retroactively, and thus became the basis for Pembaur's § 1983 action against all involved. The issue that ultimately came to the Supreme Court was the liability of the county for the actions of its officers.

At trial, the evidence showed no prior instance where the sheriff had been denied access to property in an attempt to arrest a third person. There was also no written policy on the issue. The question of county's liability therefore turned on its responsibility for the decision of its officials on this particular occasion.

Speaking for the Court, Justice Brennan said:

"The Deputy Sheriffs who attempted to serve the [arrest warrants] at petitioner's clinic found themselves in a difficult situation. Unsure of the proper course of action to follow, they sought instructions from their supervisors. The instructions they received were to follow the orders of the County Prosecutor. The prosecutor made a considered decision based on his understanding of the law and commanded the officers forcibly to enter petitioner's clinic. That decision directly caused the violation of petitioner's fourth amendment rights.

"Respondent argues that the County Prosecutor lacked authority to establish municipal policy respecting law enforcement practices because only the County Sheriff may establish policy respecting such practices. Respondent suggests that the County Prosecutor was merely rendering 'legal advice' when he ordered the Deputy Sheriffs to 'go in and get' the witnesses. Consequently, the argument concludes, the action of the individual Deputy Sheriffs in following this advice and forcibly entering petitioner's clinic was not pursuant to a properly established municipal policy.

"We might be inclined to agree with respondent if we thought that the prosecutor had only rendered 'legal advice.' However, the Court of Appeals concluded, based upon its examination of Ohio law, that both the County Sheriff and the County Prosecutor could establish county policy under appropriate circumstances, a conclusion that we do not question here. Ohio Rev.Code Ann. § 309.09 provides that county officers may 'require . . . instructions from [the County Prosecutor] in matters connected with their official duties.' Pursuant to standard office procedure, the Sheriff's office referred this matter to the prosecutor and then followed his instructions. The Sheriff testified that his department followed this practice under appropriate circumstances and that it was 'the proper thing to do' in this case. We decline to accept respondent's invitation to overlook this delegation of authority by disingenuously labeling the prosecutor's clear command mere 'legal advice.' In ordering the Deputy Sheriffs to enter petitioner's clinic the County Prosecutor was acting as the final decisionmaker for the county, and the county may therefore be held liable under § 1983."

There were several separate opinions. Justice White concurred to suggest that liability was proper *only* because the search was not forbidden by any applicable law at the time it was made. If controlling law had plainly prohibited the search, he argued, the local officers could "not be said to have the authority to make contrary policy": "Had the sheriff or prosecutor in this case failed to follow an existing warrant requirement, it would be absurd to say that he was nevertheless executing county policy in authorizing the forceful entry. . . ." Here, however, the sheriff and the prosecutor exercised the discretion vested in them and "chose a course that was not forbidden by any applicable law." This decision therefore became "county policy" and was "no less so" because it later turned out to be unconstitutional.[c]

Justice Powell, joined by Chief Justice Burger and Justice Rehnquist, dissented. He argued that "no official county policy could have been created solely by an off-hand telephone response from a busy county prosecutor":

"Proper resolution of this case calls for identification of the applicable principles for determining when policy is created. The Court today does not do this, but instead focuses almost exclusively on the status of the decisionmaker. Its reasoning is circular: it contends that policy is what policymakers make, and policymakers are those who have authority to make policy. . . .

"In my view, the question whether official policy—in any normal sense of the term—has been made in a particular case is not answered by explaining who has final authority to make policy. The question here is not 'could the county prosecutor make policy?' but rather, 'did he make policy?' By focusing on the authority granted to the official under state law, the Court's test fails to answer the key federal question presented. The Court instead turns the question into one of state law. Under a test that focuses on the authority of the decisionmaker, the Court has only to look to state law for the resolution of this case. Here the Court of Appeals found that 'both the County Sheriff and the County Prosecutor had au-

c Justice O'Connor briefly endorsed these views in an opinion concurring in part and concurring in the judgment. Justice Ste- vens also wrote to reiterate his belief that county liability could be based on respondeat superior.

thority under Ohio law to establish county policy under appropriate circumstances.' Apparently that recitation of authority is all that is needed under the Court's test because no discussion is offered to demonstrate that the Sheriff or the Prosecutor actually used that authority to establish official county policy in this case. . . .

"In my view, proper resolution of the question whether official policy has been formed should focus on two factors: (i) the nature of the decision reached or the action taken, and (ii) the process by which the decision was reached or the action was taken.

"Focusing on the nature of the decision distinguishes between policies and mere ad hoc decisions. Such a focus also reflects the fact that most policies embody a rule of general applicability. That is the tenor of the Court's statement in *Monell* that local government units are liable under § 1983 when the action that is alleged to be unconstitutional 'implements or executes a policy statement, ordinance, regulation, or decision officially adopted and promulgated by the body's officers.' The clear implication is that policy is created when a rule is formed that applies to all similar situations. . . .[6] When a rule of general applicability has been approved, the government has taken a position for which it can be held responsible.

"Another factor indicating that policy has been formed is the process by which the decision at issue was reached. Formal procedures that involve, for example, voting by elected officials, prepared reports, extended deliberation or official records indicate that the resulting decisions taken 'may fairly be said to represent official policy.' Owen v. City of Independence, 445 U.S. 622 (1980), provides an example. . . .

"Applying these factors to the instant case demonstrates that no official policy was formulated. Certainly, no rule of general applicability was adopted. The Court correctly notes that the Sheriff 'testified that the department had no written policy respecting the serving of [arrest warrants] on the property of third persons and that the proper response in any given situation would depend upon the circumstances.' Nor could he recall a specific instance in which entrance had been denied and forcibly gained. The Court's result today rests on the implicit conclusion that the Prosecutor's response—'go in and get them'—altered the prior case-by-case approach of the department and formed a new rule to apply in all similar cases. Nothing about the Prosecutor's response to the inquiry over

---

[6] The focus on a rule of general applicability does not mean that more than one instance of its application is required. The local government unit may be liable for the first application of a duly constituted unconstitutional policy.

the phone, nor the circumstances surrounding the response, indicates that such a rule of general applicability was formed.

"Similarly, nothing about the way the decision was reached indicates that official policy was formed. The prosecutor, without time for thoughtful consideration or consultation, simply gave an off-the-cuff answer to a single question. There was no *process* at all. The Court's holding undercuts the basic rationale of *Monell* and unfairly increases the risk of liability on the level of government least able to bear it. I dissent."

CITY OF ST. LOUIS v. PRAPROTNIK

Supreme Court of the United States, 1988.
__ U.S. __.

JUSTICE O'CONNOR announced the judgment of the Court and delivered an opinion, in which CHIEF JUSTICE REHNQUIST, JUSTICE WHITE, and JUSTICE SCALIA join.

This case calls upon us to define the proper legal standard for determining when isolated decisions by municipal officials or employees may expose the municipality itself to liability under 42 U.S.C. § 1983.

I

The principal facts are not in dispute. Respondent James H. Praprotnik is an architect who began working for petitioner city of St. Louis in 1968. For several years, respondent consistently received favorable evaluations of his job performance, uncommonly quick promotions, and significant increases in salary. By 1980, he was serving in a management-level city planning position at petitioner's Community Development Agency (CDA).

The Director of CDA, Donald Spaid, had instituted a requirement that the agency's professional employees, including architects, obtain advance approval before taking on private clients. Respondent and other CDA employees objected to the requirement. In April 1980, respondent was suspended for 15 days by CDA's Director of Urban Design, Charles Kindleberger, for having accepted outside employment without prior approval. Respondent appealed to the city's Civil Service Commission, a body charged with reviewing employee grievances. Finding the penalty too harsh, the Commission reversed the suspension, awarded respondent back pay, and directed that he be reprimanded for having failed to secure a clear understanding of the rule.

The Commission's decision was not well received by respondent's supervisors at CDA. Kindleberger later testified that he believed respondent had lied to the Commission, and that Spaid was angry with respondent.

Respondent's next two annual job performance evaluations were markedly less favorable than those in previous years. In discussing one of these evaluations with respondent, Kindleberger apparently mentioned his displeasure with respondent's 1980 appeal to the Civil Service Commission. Respondent appealed both evaluations to the Department of Personnel. In each case, the Department ordered partial relief and was upheld by the city's Director of Personnel or the Civil Service Commission.

In April 1981, a new mayor came into office, and Donald Spaid was replaced as Director of CDA by Frank Hamsher. As a result of budget cuts, a number of layoffs and transfers significantly reduced the size of CDA and of the planning section in which respondent worked. Respondent, however, was retained.

In the spring of 1982, a second round of layoffs and transfers occurred at CDA. At that time, the city's Heritage and Urban Design Division (Heritage) was seeking approval to hire someone who was qualified in architecture and urban planning. Hamsher arranged with the Director of Heritage, Henry Jackson, for certain functions to be transferred from CDA to Heritage. This arrangement, which made it possible for Heritage to employ a relatively high-level "city planning manager," was approved by Jackson's supervisor, Thomas Nash. Hamsher then transferred respondent to Heritage to fill this position.

Respondent objected to the transfer, and appealed to the Civil Service Commission. The Commission declined to hear the appeal because respondent had not suffered a reduction in his pay or grade. Respondent then filed suit in federal district court, alleging that the transfer was unconstitutional. The city was named as a defendant, along with Kindleberger, Hamsher, Jackson (whom respondent deleted from the list before trial), and Deborah Patterson, who had succeeded Hamsher at CDA.

At Heritage, respondent became embroiled in a series of disputes with Jackson and Jackson's successor, Robert Killen. Respondent was dissatisfied with the work he was assigned, which consisted of unchallenging clerical functions far below the level of responsibilities that he had previously enjoyed. At least one adverse personnel decision was taken against respondent, and he obtained partial relief after appealing that decision.

In December 1983, respondent was laid off from Heritage. The lay off was attributed to a lack of funds, and this apparently meant that respondent's supervisors had concluded that they could create two lower-level positions with the funds that were being used to pay respondent's salary. Respondent then amended the complaint in his lawsuit to include a challenge to the layoff. He also appealed to the Civil Service Commission, but proceedings in that forum were postponed because of the pending lawsuit and have never been completed.

The case went to trial on two theories: (1) that respondent's first amendment rights had been violated through retaliatory actions taken in response to his appeal of his 1980 suspension; and (2) that respondent's layoff from Heritage was carried out for pretextual reasons in violation of due process. The jury returned special verdicts exonerating each of the three individual defendants, but finding the city liable under both theories. Judgment was entered on the verdicts, and the city appealed.

A panel of the Court of Appeals for the Eighth Circuit found that the due process claim had been submitted to the jury on an erroneous legal theory and vacated that portion of the judgment. With one judge dissenting, however, the panel affirmed the verdict holding the city liable for violating respondent's first amendment rights. Only the second of these holdings is challenged here.

The Court of Appeals found that the jury had implicitly determined that respondent's layoff from Heritage was brought about by an unconstitutional city policy. Applying a test under which a "policymaker" is one whose employment decisions are "final" in the sense that they are not subjected to de novo review by higher-ranking officials, the Court of Appeals concluded that the city could be held liable for adverse personnel decisions taken by respondent's supervisors. In response to petitioner's contention that the city's personnel policies are actually set by the Civil Service Commission, the Court of Appeals concluded that the scope of review before that body was too "highly circumscribed" to allow it fairly to be said that the Commission, rather than the officials who initiated the actions leading to respondent's injury, were the "final authority" responsible for setting city policy. . . .

We granted certiorari and we now reverse.

II

[Part II of Justice O'Connor's opinion concluded that the legal standard for municipal liability had been properly presented for review.]

III

A

. . . In the years since *Monell* was decided, the Court has considered several cases involving isolated acts by government officials and employees. We have assumed that an unconstitutional governmental policy could be inferred from a single decision taken by the highest officials responsible for setting policy in that area of the government's business. See Owen v. City of Independence, 445 U.S. 622 (1980); Newport v. Fact Concerts, Inc., 453 U.S. 247 (1981). At the other end of the spectrum, we have held that an unjustified shooting by a police officer cannot, without more, be thought to result from official policy. Oklahoma City v. Tuttle, 471 U.S. 808 (1985).

Two terms ago, in Pembaur v. Cincinnati, 475 U.S. 469 (1986), we undertook to define more precisely when a decision on a single occasion may be enough to establish an unconstitutional municipal policy. Although the Court was unable to settle on a general formulation, Justice Brennan's plurality opinion articulated several guiding principles. First, a majority of the Court agreed that municipalities may be held liable under § 1983 only for acts for which the municipality itself is actually responsible, "that is, acts which the municipality has officially sanctioned or ordered." Second, only those municipal officials who have "final policymaking authority" may by their actions subject the government to § 1983 liability. Third, whether a particular official has "final policymaking authority" is a question of *state law*. Fourth, the challenged action must have been taken pursuant to a policy adopted by the official or officials responsible under state law for making policy *in that area* of the city's business.

The Courts of Appeals have already diverged in their interpretation of these principles. Today, we set out again to clarify the issue that we last addressed in *Pembaur.*

B

We begin by reiterating that the identification of policymaking officials is a question of state law. "Authority to make municipal policy may be granted directly by a legislative enactment or may be delegated by an official who possesses such authority, and of course, whether an official had final policymaking authority is a question of state law." *Pembaur v. Cincinnati,* supra, at 483 (plurality opinion).[1] Thus, the identification of policymaking officials is not a question of federal law and it is not a question of fact in the usual sense. The states have extremely wide latitude in determining the form that local government takes, and local preferences have led to a profusion of distinct forms. . . . Without attempting to canvass the numberless factual scenarios that may come to light in litigation, we can be confident that state law (which may include valid local ordinances and regulations) will always direct a court to some official or body that has the responsibility for making law or setting policy in any given area of a local government's responsibility.[2]

[1] Unlike Justice Brennan, we would not replace this standard with a new approach in which state law becomes merely "an appropriate starting point" for an "assessment of a municipality's actual power structure." Municipalities cannot be expected to predict how courts or juries will assess their "actual power structures," and this uncertainty could easily lead to results that would be hard in practice to distinguish from the results of a regime governed by the doctrine of respondeat superior. It is one thing to charge a municipality with responsibility for the decisions of officials invested by law, or by a "custom or usage" having the force of law, with policymaking authority. It would be something else, and something inevitably more capricious, to hold a municipality responsible for every decision that is perceived as "final" through the lens of a particular factfinder's evaluation of the city's "actual power structure."

[2] Justice Stevens, who believes that *Monell* incorrectly rejected the doctrine of re-

spondeat superior, suggests a new theory that reflects his perceptions of the congressional purposes underlying § 1983. This theory would apparently ignore state law, and distinguish between "high" officials and "low" officials on the basis of an independent evaluation of the extent to which a particular official's actions have "the potential of controlling governmental decisionmaking," or are "perceived as the actions of the city itself." Whether this evaluation would be conducted by judges or juries, we think the legal test is too imprecise to hold much promise of consistent adjudication or principled analysis. We can see no reason, except perhaps a desire to come as close as possible to respondeat superior without expressly adopting that doctrine, that could justify introducing such unpredictability into a body of law that is already so difficult. . . .

We are not, of course, predicting that state law will always speak with perfect clarity. We have no reason to suppose, however, that federal courts will face greater difficulties here than those that they routinely address in other contexts. We are also aware that there will be cases in which policymaking responsibility is shared among more than one official or body. In the case before us, for example, it appears that the mayor or aldermen are authorized to adopt such ordinances relating to personnel administration as are compatible with the City Charter. See St. Louis City Charter, art. XVIII, § 7(b). The Civil Service Commission, for its part, is required to "prescribe . . . rules for the administration and enforcement of the provisions of this article, and of any ordinance adopted in pursuance thereof, and not inconsistent therewith." § 7(a). Assuming that applicable law does not make the decisions of the Commission reviewable by the mayor and aldermen, or vice versa, one would have to conclude that policy decisions made either by the mayor and aldermen or by the Commission would be attributable to the city itself. In any event, however, a federal court would not be justified in assuming that municipal policymaking authority lies somewhere other than where the applicable law purports to put it. And certainly there can be no justification for giving a jury the discretion to determine which officials are high enough in the government that their actions can be said to represent a decision of the government itself.

As the plurality in *Pembaur* recognized, special difficulties can arise when it is contended that a municipal policymaker has delegated his policymaking authority to another official. If the mere exercise of discretion by an employee could give rise to a constitutional violation, the result would be indistinguishable from respondeat superior liability. If, however, a city's lawful policymakers could insulate the government from liability simply by delegating their policymaking authority to others, § 1983 could not serve its intended purpose. It may not be possible to draw an elegant line that will resolve this conundrum, but certain principles should provide useful guidance.

First, whatever analysis is used to identify municipal policymakers, egregious attempts by local governments to insulate themselves from liability for unconstitutional policies are precluded by a separate doctrine. Relying on the language of § 1983, the Court has long recognized that a plaintiff may be able to prove the existence of a widespread practice that, although not authorized by written law or express municipal policy, is "so permanent and well settled as to constitute a 'custom or usage' with the force of law." Adickes v. S.H. Kress & Co., 398 U.S. 144, 167–68 (1970). That principle, which has not been affected by Monell v. N.Y. City Dept. of Social Services, 436 U.S. 658 (1978), or subsequent cases, ensures that most deliberate municipal evasions of the Constitution will be sharply limited.

Second, as the *Pembaur* plurality recognized, the authority to make municipal policy is necessarily the authority to make *final* policy. When an official's discretionary decisions are constrained by policies not of that official's making, those policies, rather than the subordinate's departures from them, are the act of the municipality. Similarly, when a subordinate's decision is subject to review by the municipality's authorized policymakers, they have retained the authority to measure the official's conduct for conformance with *their* policies. If the authorized policymakers approve a subordinate's decision and the basis for it, their ratification would be chargeable to the municipality because their decision is final.

C

Whatever refinements of these principles may be suggested in the future, we have little difficulty concluding that the Court of Appeals applied an incorrect legal standard in this case. In reaching this conclusion, we do not decide whether the first amendment forbade the city from retaliating against respondent for having taken advantage of the grievance mechanism in 1980. . . . .

The city cannot be held liable under § 1983 unless respondent proved the existence of an unconstitutional municipal policy. Respondent does not contend that anyone in city government ever promulgated, or even articulated, such a policy. Nor did he attempt to prove that such retaliation was ever directed against anyone other than himself. Respondent contends that the record can be read to establish that his supervisors were angered by his 1980 appeal to the Civil Service Commission; that new supervisors in a new administration chose, for reasons passed on through some informal means, to retaliate against respondent two years later by transferring him to another agency; and that this transfer was part of a scheme that led, another year and a half later, to his lay off. Even if one assumes that all this was true, it says nothing about the actions of those whom the law established as the makers of municipal policy in matters of personnel administration. The mayor and aldermen enacted no ordinance designed to retaliate against respondent or against similarly situated employees. On the contrary, the city established an independent Civil Service Commission and empowered it to review and correct improper personnel actions. Respondent does not deny that his repeated appeals from adverse personnel decisions repeatedly brought him at least partial relief, and the Civil Service Commission never so much as hinted that retaliatory transfers or lay offs were permissible. Respondent points to no evidence indicating that the Commission delegated to anyone its final authority to interpret and enforce the following policy set out in article XVIII of the city's Charter, § 2(a):

> "Merit and fitness. All appointments and promotions to positions in the service of the city and all measures for the control and regulation of employment in such positions, and separation therefrom, shall be on the sole basis of merit and fitness. . . . ."

The Court of Appeals concluded that "appointing authorities," like Hamsher and Killen were authorized to establish employment policy for the city with respect to transfers and layoffs. To the contrary, the

City Charter expressly states that the Civil Service Commission has the power and the duty:

> "To consider and determine any matter involved in the administration and enforcement of this [Civil Service] article and the rules and ordinances adopted in accordance therewith that may be referred to it for decision by the director [of personnel], or on appeal by any appointing authority, employe, or taxpayer of the city, from any act of the director of any appointing authority. The decision of the commission in all such matters shall be final, subject, however, to any right of action under law of the state or of the United States."

This case therefore resembles the hypothetical example in *Pembaur*: "[I]f [city] employment policy was set by the [mayor and aldermen and by the Civil Service Commission], only [those] bod[ies'] decisions would provide a basis for [city] liability. This would be true even if the [mayor and aldermen and the Commission] left the [appointing authorities] discretion to hire and fire employees and [they] exercised that discretion in an unconstitutional manner. . . ." A majority of the Court of Appeals panel determined that the Civil Service Commission's review of individual employment actions gave too much deference to the decisions of appointing authorities like Hamsher and Killen. Simply going along with discretionary decisions made by one's subordinates, however, is not a delegation to them of the authority to make policy. It is equally consistent with a presumption that the subordinates are faithfully attempting to comply with the policies that are supposed to guide them. It would be a different matter if a particular decision by a subordinate was cast in the form of a policy statement and expressly approved by the supervising policymaker. It would also be a different matter if a series of decisions by a subordinate official manifested a "custom or usage" of which the supervisor must have been aware. In both those cases, the supervisor could realistically be deemed to have adopted a policy that happened to have been formulated or initiated by a lower-ranking official. But the mere failure to investigate the basis of a subordinate's discretionary decisions does not amount to a delegation of policymaking authority, especially where (as here) the wrongfulness of the subordinate's decision arises from a retaliatory motive or other unstated rationale. In such circumstances, the purposes of § 1983 would not be served by treating a subordinate employee's decision as if it were a reflection of municipal policy.

Justice Brennan's opinion, concurring in the judgment, finds implications in our discussion that we do not think necessary or correct. We nowhere say or imply, for example, that "a municipal charter's precatory admonition against discrimination or any other employment practice not based on merit and fitness effectively insulates the municipality from any liability based on acts inconsistent with that policy." Rather, we would respect the decisions, embodied in state and local law, that allocate policymaking authority among particular individuals and bodies. Refusals to carry out stated policies could obviously help to show that a municipality's actual policies were different from the ones that had been announced. If such a showing were made, we would be confronted with a different case than the one we decide today.

Nor do we believe that we have left a "gaping" hole in § 1983 that needs to be filled with the vague concept of "de facto final policymaking authority." Except perhaps as a step towards overruling *Monell* and adopting the doctrine of respondeat superior, ad hoc searches for officials possessing such "de facto" authority would serve primarily to foster needless unpredictability in the application of § 1983.

IV

[T]he decision of the Court of Appeals is reversed, and the case is remanded for further proceedings consistent with this opinion.

It is so ordered.

JUSTICE KENNEDY took no part in the consideration or decision of this case.

JUSTICE BRENNAN, with whom JUSTICE MARSHALL and JUSTICE BLACKMUN join, concurring.

[T]his case at bottom presents a relatively straightforward question: whether respondent's supervisor at the Community Development Agency, Frank Hamsher, possessed the authority to establish final employment policy for the city of St. Louis such that the city can be held liable under 42 U.S.C. § 1983 for Hamsher's allegedly unlawful decision to transfer respondent to a dead-end job. Applying the test set out two terms ago by the plurality in Pembaur v. Cincinnati, 475 U.S. 469 (1986), I conclude that Hamsher did not possess such authority and I therefore concur in the Court's judgment reversing the decision below. I write separately, however, because I believe that the commendable desire of today's plurality to "define more precisely when a decision on a single occasion may be enough" to subject a municipality to § 1983 liability has led it to embrace a theory of municipal liability that is both unduly narrow and unrealistic, and one that ultimately would permit municipalities to insulate themselves from liability for the acts of all but a small minority of actual city policymakers.

I

. . . The District Court instructed the jury that generally a city is not liable under § 1983 for the acts of its employees, but that it may be held to answer for constitutional wrongs "committed by an official high enough in the government so that his or her actions can be said to represent a government decision.". . . The Court of Appeals for the Eighth Circuit [affirmed, reasoning] that the city could be held accountable for an improperly motivated transfer and layoff if it had delegated to the responsible officials, either directly or indirectly, the authority to act on behalf of the city, and if the decisions made within the scope of this delegated authority were essentially final. Applying this test, the court noted that under the City Charter, "appointing authorities," or department heads, such as Hamsher could undertake transfers and layoffs subject only to the approval of the Director of Personnel, who undertook no substantive review of such decisions and simply conditioned his approval on formal compliance with city procedures. Moreover, because the Civil Service Commission engaged in highly circumscribed and deferential review of layoffs and, at least so far as this case reveals, no review whatever of lateral transfers, the court concluded that an appointing authority's transfer and layoff decisions were final.

Having found that Hamsher was a final policymaker whose acts could subject petitioner to § 1983 liability, the court determined that the jury had ample evidence from which it could find that Hamsher transferred respondent in retaliation for the latter's exercise of first amendment rights, and that the transfer in turn precipitated respondent's layoff. . . .

II

. . . Municipalities, of course, conduct much of the business of governing through human agents. Where those agents act in accordance with formal policies, or pursuant to informal practices "so permanent and well settled as to constitute a 'custom or usage' with the force of law," Adickes v. S.H. Kress & Co., 398 U.S. 144, 167–68 (1970), we naturally ascribe their acts to the municipalities themselves and hold the latter responsible for any resulting constitutional deprivations. Monell v. N.Y. City Dept. of Social Services, 436 U.S. 658 (1978), which involved a challenge to a city-wide policy requiring all pregnant employees to take unpaid leave after their fifth month of pregnancy, was just such a case. Nor have we ever doubted that a single decision of a city's properly constituted legislative body is a municipal act capable of subjecting the city to liability. See, e.g., Newport v. Fact Concerts, Inc., 453 U.S. 247 (1981) (city council canceled concert permits for content-based reasons); Owen v. City of Independence, 445 U.S. 622 (1980) (city council passed resolution firing police chief without any pretermination hearing). In these cases we neither required, nor as the plurality suggests, assumed that these decisions reflected generally applicable "policies" as that term is commonly understood, because it was perfectly obvious that the actions of the municipalities' policymaking organs, whether isolated or not, were properly charged to the municipalities themselves. And, in *Pembaur* we recognized that "the power to establish policy is no more the exclusive province of the legislature at the local level than at the state or national level," and that the isolated decision of an executive municipal policymaker, therefore, could likewise give rise to municipal liability under § 1983.

In concluding that Frank Hamsher was a policymaker, the Court of Appeals relied on the fact that the city had delegated to him "the authority, either directly or indirectly, to act on [its] behalf," and that his actions within the scope of this delegated authority were effectively final. In *Pembaur*, however, we made clear that a municipality is not liable merely because the official who inflicted the constitutional injury had the final authority to *act* on its behalf; rather, as four of us explained, the official in question must possess "final authority to establish municipal policy with respect to the [challenged] action." Thus, we noted, "[t]he fact that a particular official—even a policymaking official—has discretion in the exercise of particular functions does not, without more, give rise to municipal liability based on an exercise of that discretion." [J]ust as in *Owen* and *Fact Concerts* we deemed it fair to hold municipalities liable for the isolated, unconstitutional acts of their legislative bodies, regardless of whether those acts were meant to establish generally applicable "policies," so too in *Pembaur* four of us concluded that it is equally appropriate to hold municipalities accountable for the isolated constitutional injury inflicted by an executive final municipal policymaker, even though the decision giving rise to the injury is not intended to govern future situations. In either case, as long as the contested decision is made in an area over which the official or legislative body *could* establish a final policy capable of governing future municipal conduct, it is both fair and consistent with the purposes of § 1983 to treat the decision as that of the municipality itself, and to hold it liable for the resulting constitutional deprivation.

In my view, *Pembaur* controls this case. As an "appointing authority," Hamsher was empowered under the City Charter to initiate lateral transfers such as the one challenged here, subject to the approval of both the Director of Personnel and the appointing authority of the transferee agency. The Charter, however, nowhere confers upon agency heads any authority to establish city *policy,* final or otherwise, with respect to such transfers. Thus, for example, Hamsher was not authorized to promulgate binding guidelines or criteria governing how or when lateral transfers were to be accomplished. Nor does the record reveal that he in fact sought to exercise any such authority in these matters. There is no indication, for example, that Hamsher ever purported to institute or announce a practice of general applicability concerning transfers. Instead, the evidence discloses but one transfer decision—the one involving respondent—which Hamsher ostensibly undertook pursuant to a city-wide program of fiscal restraint and budgetary reductions. At most, then the record demonstrates that Hamsher had the authority to determine how best to *effectuate* a policy announced by his superiors, rather than the power to *establish* that policy. . . . Because the court identified only one unlawfully motivated municipal employee involved in respondent's transfer and layoff, and because that employee did not possess final policymaking authority with respect to the contested decision, the city may not be held accountable for any constitutional wrong respondent may have suffered.

III

These determinations, it seems to me, are sufficient to dispose of this case, and I therefore think it unnecessary to decide, as the plurality does, who the actual policymakers in St. Louis are. I question more than the mere necessity of these determinations, however, for I believe that in the course of passing on issues not before us, the plurality announces legal principles that are inconsistent with our earlier cases and unduly restrict the reach of § 1983 in cases involving municipalities.

The plurality begins its assessment of St. Louis' power structure by asserting that the identification of policymaking officials is a question of state law, by which it means that the question is neither one of federal law nor of fact, at least "not in the usual sense." Instead, the plurality explains, courts are to identify municipal policymakers by referring exclusively to applicable state statutory law. Not surprisingly, the plurality cites no authority for this startling proposition, nor could it, for we have never suggested that municipal liability should be determined in so formulaic and unrealistic a fashion. In any case in which the policymaking authority of a municipal tortfeasor is in doubt, state law will naturally be the appropriate starting point, but ultimately the factfinder must determine where such policymaking authority actually resides, and not simply "where the applicable law purports to put it.". . . Thus, although I agree with the plurality that juries should not be given open-ended "*discretion* to determine which officials are high enough in the government that their actions can be said to represent a decision of the government itself," (emphasis added), juries can and must find the predicate facts necessary to a determination of whether a given official possesses final policymaking authority. While the jury instructions in this case were regrettably vague, the plurality's solution tosses the baby out with the bath water. The identification of municipal policymakers is an essentially factual determination "in the usual sense," and is therefore rightly entrusted to a properly instructed jury.

Nor does the "custom or usage" doctrine adequately compensate for the inherent inflexibility of a rule that leaves the identification of policymakers exclusively to state statutory law. That doctrine, under which municipalities and states can be held liable for unconstitutional practices so well settled and permanent that they have the force of law has little if any bearing on the question whether a city has delegated de facto final policymaking authority to a given official. A city practice of delegating final policymaking authority to a subordinate or mid-level official would not be unconstitutional in and of itself, and an isolated unconstitutional act by an official entrusted with such authority would obviously not amount to a municipal "custom or usage." Under *Pembaur,* of course, such an isolated act *should* give rise to municipal liability. Yet a case such as this would fall through the gaping hole the plurality's construction leaves in § 1983, because state statutory law would not identify the municipal actor as a policymaking official, and a single constitutional deprivation, by definition, is not a well settled and permanent municipal practice carrying the force of law.

For these same reasons, I cannot subscribe to the plurality's narrow and overly rigid view of when a muncipal official's policymaking authority is "final." Attempting to place a gloss on *Pembaur*'s finality requirement, the plurality suggests that whenever the decisions of an official are subject to some form of review—however limited—that official's decisions are nonfinal. Under the plurality's theory, therefore, even where an official wields policymaking authority with respect to a challenged decision, the city would not be liable for that official's policy decision unless *reviewing* officials affirmatively approved both the "decision and the basis for it." Reviewing officials, however, may as a matter of practice never invoke their plenary oversight authority, or their review powers may be highly circumscribed. Under such circumstances, the subordinate's decision is in effect the final municipal pronouncement on the subject. Certainly a § 1983 plaintiff is entitled to place such considerations before the jury, for the law is concerned not with the niceties of legislative draftsmanship but with the realities of municipal decisionmaking, and any assessment of a municipality's actual power structure is necessarily a factual and practical one.[7]

Accordingly, I cannot endorse the plurality's determination, based on nothing more than its own review of the city charter, that the mayor, the aldermen, and the CSC are the only policymakers for the city of St. Louis. While these officials may well have policymaking authority, that hardly ends the matter; the question before us is whether the officials responsible for respondent's allegedly unlawful transfer were final policymakers. As I have previously indicated, I do not believe that CDA Director Frank Hamsher possessed any policymaking authority with respect to lateral transfers and thus I do not believe that his allegedly improper decision to transfer respondent could, without more, give rise to municipal liability. Although the plurality reaches the same result, it does so by reasoning that because others could have reviewed the decisions of Hamsher and Killen, the latter officials simply could not have been final policymakers.

This analysis, however, turns a blind eye to reality, for it ignores not only the lower court's determination, nowhere disputed, that CSC review was highly circumscribed and deferential, but that in this very case the Commission *refused* to judge the propriety of Hamsher's transfer decision because a lateral transfer was not an "adverse" employment action falling within its jurisdiction. Nor does the plurality account for the fact that Hamsher's predecessor, Donald Spaid,

---

[7] The plurality also asserts that "[w]hen an official's discretionary decisions are constrained by policies not of that official's making, those policies, rather than the subordinate's departures from them, are the act of the municipality." While I have no quarrel with such a proposition in the abstract, I cannot accept the plurality's apparent view that a municipal charter's precatory admonition against discrimination or any other employment practice not based on merit and fitness effectively insulates the municipality from any liability based on acts inconsistent with that policy. Again, the relevant inquiry is whether the policy in question is actually and effective- ly enforced through the city's review mechanisms. Thus in this case, a policy prohibiting lateral transfers for unconstitutional or discriminatory reasons would not shield the city from liability if an official possessing final policymaking authority over such transfers acted in violation of the prohibition, because the CSC would lack jurisdiction to review the decision and thus could not enforce the policy. Where as here, however, the official merely possesses discretionary authority over transfers, the city policy is irrelevant, because the official's actions cannot subject the city to liability in any event.

promulgated what the city readily acknowledges was a binding policy regarding secondary employment; [8] although the CSC ultimately modified the sanctions respondent suffered as a result of his apparent failure to comply with that policy, the record is devoid of any suggestion that the Commission reviewed the substance or validity of the policy itself. Under the plurality's analysis, therefore, even the hollowest promise of review is sufficient to divest all city officials save the mayor and governing legislative body of final policymaking authority. . . . Because the plurality's mechanical "finality" test is fundamentally at odds with the pragmatic and factual inquiry contemplated by *Monell,* I cannot join what I perceive to be its unwarranted abandonment of the traditional factfinding process in § 1983 actions involving municipalities.

Finally, I think it necessary to emphasize that despite certain language in the plurality opinion suggesting otherwise, the Court today need not and therefore does not decide that a city can only be held liable under § 1983 where the plaintiff "prove[s] the existence of an unconstitutional municipal policy." Just last term, we left open for the second time the question whether a city can be subjected to liability for a policy that, while not unconstitutional in and of itself, may give rise to constitutional deprivations. See Springfield v. Kibbe, 480 U.S. ___ (1987); see also Oklahoma City v. Tuttle, 471 U.S. 808 (1985). That question is certainly not presented by this case, and nothing we say today forecloses its future consideration. . . .

JUSTICE STEVENS, dissenting.

If this case involved nothing more than a personal vendetta between a municipal employee and his superiors, it would be quite wrong to impose liability on the City of St. Louis. In fact, however, the jury found the top officials in the city administration relying on pretextual grounds, had taken a series of retaliatory actions against respondent because he had testified truthfully on two occasions, one relating to personnel policy and the other involving a public controversy of importance to the mayor and the members of his cabinet. No matter how narrowly the Court may define the standards for imposing liability upon municipalities in § 1983 litigation, the judgment entered by the District Court in this case should be affirmed.

In order to explain why I believe that affirmance is required by this Court's precedents,[1] it is necessary to begin with a more complete

---

[8] Although the plurality is careful in its discussion of the facts to label Director Spaid's directive a "requirement" rather than a "policy," the city itself draws no such fine semantic distinctions. Rather, it states plainly that Spaid "promulgated a 'secondary employment' *policy* that sought to control outside employment by CDA architects," and that "[respondent] resented the policy. . . ."

[1] This would, of course, be an easy case if the Court disavowed its dicta in part II of its opinion in Monell v. N.Y. City Dept. of Social Services, 436 U.S. 658, 691–95 (1978). Like many commentators who have confronted the question, I remain convinced that Congress intended the doctrine of respondeat superior to apply in § 1983 litigation. Given the Court's reiteration of the contrary ipse dixit in *Monell* and subsequent opinions, however, I shall join the Court's attempt to draw an intelligible boundary between municipal agents' actions that bind and those that do not. . . .

statement of the disputed factual issues that the jury resolved in respondent's favor. . . .

The City of St. Louis hired respondent as a licensed architect in 1968. During the ensuing decade, he was repeatedly promoted and consistently given "superior" performance ratings. In April of 1980, while serving as the Director of Urban Design in the Community Development Agency (CDA), he was recommended for a two-step salary increase by his immediate superior.

Thereafter, on two occasions he gave public testimony that was critical of official city policy. In 1980 he testified before the Civil Service Commission (CSC) in support of his successful appeal from a 15-day suspension. In that testimony he explained that he had received advance oral approval of his outside employment and voiced his objections to the requirement of prior written approval. The record demonstrates that this testimony offended his immediate superiors at the CDA.

In 1981 respondent testified before the Heritage and Urban Design Commission (HUD) in connection with a proposal to acquire a controversial rusting steel sculpture by Richard Serra. In his testimony he revealed the previously undisclosed fact that an earlier city administration had rejected an offer to acquire the same sculpture, and also explained that the erection of the sculpture would require the removal of structures on which the city had recently expended about $250,000. This testimony offended top officials of the city government, possibly including the mayor, who supported the acquisition of the Serra sculpture, as well as respondent's agency superiors. They made it perfectly clear that they believed that respondent had violated a duty of loyalty to the mayor by expressing his personal opinion about the sculpture. . . .

After this testimony respondent was the recipient of a series of adverse personnel actions that culminated in his transfer from an important management level professional position to a rather menial assignment for which he was "grossly overqualified" and his eventual layoff. [E]vidence in the record amply supports the conclusion that respondent was first transferred and then laid off, not for fiscal and administrative reasons, but in retaliation for his public testimony before the CSC and HUD. It is undisputed that respondent's right to testify in support of his civil service appeal and his right to testify in opposition to the city's acquisition of the Serra sculpture were protected by the first amendment to the federal Constitution. Given the jury's verdict, the case is therefore one in which a municipal employee's federal constitutional rights were violated by officials of the city government. . . .

In Monell v. N.Y. Dept. of Social Services, 436 U.S. 658 (1978), we held that municipal corporations are "persons" within the meaning of 42 U.S.C. § 1983. Since a corporation is incapable of doing anything except through the agency of human beings, that holding necessarily gave rise to the question of what human activity undertaken by agents of the corporation may create municipal liability in § 1983 litigation.[19]

[In *Monell* and subsequent cases] the Court has permitted a municipality to be held liable for the unconstitutional actions of its agents when those agents: enforced a rule of general applicability, *Monell*; were of sufficiently high stature and acted through a formal process, Owen v. City of Independence, 445 U.S. 622 (1980); or were authorized to establish policy in the particular area of city government in which the tort was committed, Pembaur v. Cincinnati, 475 U.S. 469 (1986). Under these precedents, the City of St. Louis should be held liable in this case.

Both *Pembaur* and the plurality and concurring opinions today acknowledge that a high official who has ultimate control over a certain area of city government can bind the city through his unconstitutional actions even though those actions are not in the form of formal rules or regulations. Although the Court has explained its holdings by reference to the nonstatutory term "policy," it plainly has not embraced the standard understanding of that word as covering a rule of general applicability. Instead it has used that term to include isolated acts not intended to be binding over a class of situations. But when one remembers that the real question in cases such as this is not "what constitutes city policy?" but rather "when should a city be liable for the acts of its agents?", the inclusion of single acts by high officials makes sense, for those acts bind a municipality in a way that the misdeeds of low officials do not.

Every act of a high official constitutes a kind of "statement" about how similar decisions will be carried out; the assumption is that the same decision would have been made, and would again be made, across a class of cases. Lower officials do not control others in the same way. Since their actions do not dictate the responses of various subordinates, those actions lack the potential of controlling governmental decisionmaking; they are not perceived as the actions of the city itself. If a county police officer had broken down Dr. Pembaur's door on the officer's own initiative, this would have been seen as the action of an overanxious officer, and would not have sent a message to other officers that similar actions would be countenanced. . . . Here, the mayor, those working for him, and the agency heads are high-ranking officials; accordingly, we must assume that their actions have city-wide ramifications, both through their similar response to a like class of situations, and through the response of subordinates who follow their lead.

[19] The "theme" of *Monell*—"that some basis for government liability other than vicarious liability for the acts of individuals must be found"—has proved to be a "difficult" one largely because "there is no obvious way to distinguish the acts of a municipality from the acts of the individuals whom it employs." Whitman, Government Responsibility for Constitutional Torts, 85 Mich.L.Rev. 225, 236 (1986). In other words, every time a municipality is held liable in tort, even in a case like *Monell*, actions of its human agents are necessarily involved. Accordingly, our task is not to draw a line between the actions of the city and the actions of its employees, but rather to develop a principle for determining *which* human acts should bind a municipality.

Just as the actions of high-ranking and low-ranking municipal employees differ in nature, so do constitutional torts differ. An illegal search, *Pembaur,* or seizure, Oklahoma City v. Tuttle, 471 U.S. 808 (1985), is quite different from a firing without due process, *Owen*; the retaliatory personnel action involved in today's case is in still another category. One thing that the torts in *Pembaur, Tuttle,* and *Owen* had in common is that they occurred "in the open"; in each of those cases, the ultimate judgment of unconstitutionality was based on whether undisputed events (the breaking-in in *Pembaur,* the shooting in *Tuttle,* the firing in *Owen*) comported with accepted constitutional norms. But the typical retaliatory personnel action claim pits one story against another; although everyone admits that the transfer and discharge of respondent occurred, there is sharp, and ultimately central, dispute over the reasons—the motivation—behind the actions. *The very nature of the tort is to avoid a formal process. Owen*'s relevance should thus be clear. For if the Court is willing to recognize the existence of municipal policy in a non-rule case as long as high enough officials engaged in a formal enough process, it should not deny the existence of such a policy merely because those same officials act "underground," as it were. It would be a truly remarkable doctrine for this Court to recognize municipal liability in an employee discharge case when high officials are foolish enough to act through a "formal process," but not when similarly high officials attempt to avoid liability by acting on the pretext of budgetary concerns, which is what the jury found based on the evidence presented at trial.

Thus, holding St. Louis liable in this case is supported by both *Pembaur* and *Owen.* We hold a municipality liable for the decisions of its high officials in large part because those decisions, by definition, would be applied across a class of cases. Just as we assume in *Pembaur* that the county prosecutor (or his subordinate) would issue the same break-down-the-door order in similar cases, and just as we assume in *Owen* that the city council (or those following its lead) would fire an employee without notice of reasons or opportunity to be heard in similar cases, so too must we assume that whistleblowers like respondent would be dealt with in similar retaliatory fashion if they offend the mayor, his staff, and relevant agency heads, or if they offend those lower-ranking officials who follow the example of their superiors. Furthermore, just as we hold a municipality liable for discharging an employee without due process when its city council acts formally—for a due process violation is precisely the *type* of constitutional tort that a city council might commit when it acts formally—so too must we hold a municipality liable for discharging an employee in retaliation against his public speech when similarly high officials act informally—for a first amendment retaliation tort is precisely the *type* of constitutional tort that high officials might commit when they act in concert and informally.

Whatever difficulties the Court may have with binding municipalities on the basis of the unconstitutional conduct of individuals, it should have no such difficulties binding a city when many of its high officials—including officials directly under the mayor, agency heads, and possibly the mayor himself—cooperate to retaliate against a whistleblower for the exercise of his first amendment rights.

I would affirm the judgment of the Court of Appeals.

————

FURTHER NOTES ON GOVERNMENTAL LIABILITY

1. **Questions and Comments on *Praprotnik*.** The opinions in *Praprotnik* suggest three different ways of distinguishing between those acts for which the municipality will be liable and those for which it will not. Justice O'Connor emphasizes state law as the crucial inquiry. Does that mean, as Justice Brennan charged, that a municipality could insulate itself from liability by issuing "precatory statements" against unconstitutional employment policies? By providing adequate internal review of personnel decisions? How will a court distinguish between self-protective window dressing and genuine attempts to set one's own house in order by adopting appropriate employment policies?

Justice Brennan would distinguish between final authority to act on behalf of the municipality and final authority to make official policy with respect to that act. Is this distinction clear? Does it aim at something important, or is it mere characterization?

Justice Stevens suggests that municipalities should be liable for the acts of high-ranking officials but not for those of low-ranking officials. Why? Does the rank of the official necessarily correlate with the official status of that person's actions? Why should the decisive factor be the position held by the *person* who acted unlawfully rather than the relation between the government and the act itself?

Which of these approaches seems the best way of addressing the official policy requirement? Is there some better way of going about it?

2. **Bibliography.** The line of cases stretching from *Monell* through *Praprotnik* has spawned substantial comment. A comprehensive attempt to implement *Monell*'s "policy or custom" requirement is made in Barbara Rook Snyder, The Final Authority Analysis: A Unified Approach to Municipal Liability under § 1983, 1986 Wis.L.Rev. 633. Snyder argues that municipalities should be held liable for the acts of an official or employee vested with "final authority" over the matter in question. She explicates this analysis over a wide range of circumstances and concludes that its adoption would bring consistency and predictability to municipal liability under § 1983.

For a different perspective, see Christina Whitman, Government Responsibility for Constitutional Torts, 85 Mich.L.Rev. 225 (1986). Whitman sees an essential problem in the application of traditional tort concepts to the sphere of government wrongs. In her view, the Supreme Court has focused too closely on individual attitude and responsibility as determinants of governmental liability. This leads to the post-*Monell* search for individual decisionmakers with sufficient authority to "speak for" the municipality. Neglected are questions about "how institutions can, as institutions, cause injuries." A focus on institutional structures, rather than individual responsibility, could "expand our sensitivity to previously disregarded harms." "Our struggle with the consequences of racism and sexism has made us aware that injuries do not flow solely from the acts of evil or careless persons." They may also be the "consequence of social structures and expectations." Thus, "a law that addresses only the isolated behavior of individuals, whether private or official, sees only some of the ways in which power can be abused. . . ."

For further analysis of this important issue, see Susan Bandes, *Monell, Parratt, Daniels,* and *Davidson*: Distinguishing a Custom or Policy from a Random, Unauthorized Act, 72 Iowa L.Rev. 101 (1986); George D. Brown, Municipal Liability under § 1983 and the Ambiguities of Burger Court Federalism: A Comment on *City of Oklahoma City v. Tuttle* and *Pembaur v. City of Cincinnati*—the "Official Policy" Cases, 27 B.C.L.Rev. 883 (1986), which analyzes this line of cases in light of the continuing tension between nationalist and federalist tendencies on the Supreme Court; and Susanah M. Mead, 42 U.S.C. § 1983 Municipal Liability: The *Monell* Sketch Becomes a Distorted Picture, 65 N.C.L.Rev. 518 (1987), which urges reconsideration of *Monell*'s rejection of respondeat superior.

NOTES ON COMPENSATION AS A VALUE
UNDER § 1983

1. **A Step Toward Enterprise Liability?** The line of cases beginning with *Monell* can be seen as a first step toward the imposition of enterprise liability under § 1983. To be sure, it is a small step. Without Congressional action, the 11th amendment stands as a barrier to the direct liability of states or state agencies. Even with respect to local government, the decisions only apply to actions taken pursuant to an official policy or custom. Whatever this may ultimately come to mean, it at least seems to exclude liability for the routine case of unauthorized misconduct by an individual government official. Nonetheless, where the unconstitutionality can be said to result from an "official policy," liability for money damages will be imposed directly on the government itself, without reference to the immunities that might be claimed by individual officials. The result is a limited imposition of enterprise liability for governmental misconduct.

This step responds to the demand of many commentators for reform of § 1983 to allow direct governmental liability. See, e.g., Bermann, Integrating Governmental and Officer Tort Liability, 77 Colum. L. Rev. 1175 (1977) (exploring alternative models for integrating official and governmental liability and endorsing a scheme of direct governmental liability with a right of indemnification against miscreant officials); Davis, An Approach to Legal Control of the Police, 52 Tex. L. Rev. 703 (1974) (arguing that administrative control of the police will be facilitated by holding government itself liable for the tortious misconduct of its officials); Newman, Suing the Lawbreakers: Proposals to Strengthen the Section 1983 Damage Remedy for Law Enforcers' Misconduct, 87 Yale L.J. 447, 445–58 (1978) (calling for authorization of damage actions directly against both state and federal governments and their agencies).

These arguments vary significantly in scope and emphasis, but several themes recur. Most prominent among them is the idea that enterprise liability would facilitate effective compensation:

> "Governmental liability would clearly maximize the probability that officially inflicted harms would be adequately compensated. Victims could more readily identify an appropriate defendant against whom suit might be brought, would receive a more sympathetic hearing from juries unconcerned about imposing liability upon officials of modest means, could obtain judgments that better reflected the significance of the rights infringed, and would be able to satisfy those judgments fully."
> P. Schuck, Suing Government: Citizen Remedies for Official Wrongs 101 (1983).

Underlying this discussion is the assumption, vindicated in *Owen* and *Pembaur,* that the direct liability of government would not be limited by an immunity for actions taken in good faith. If it were, compensation would be effectively foreclosed in many cases. A truly effective compensatory remedy requires abrogation of the good faith immunity, and this might most plausibly be done by transferring liability from the errant official to the government itself. Of course, the government might then seek indemnification from its employee, but presumably only where the official acted in deliberate contravention of established policy.

It is against this background that references to "loss spreading" arise. Effective compensation for official misconduct obviously would increase the cost of government. A scheme of enterprise liability would distribute those costs over the entire tax-paying population. The result would be higher taxation in order to compensate those harmed by government or a contraction in government activity in order to avoid these (and other) costs, or both. Not only might this result seem, as it did to the *Owen* majority, fair and "equitable," but it might also have important redistributive effects. Predicting those effects would be extremely difficult, as they would depend in part on the political response to the increased costs of maintaining a given level of government services, but it seems plausible that the distributive effects of enterprise liability might be substantial.

Finally, establishment of enterprise liability would affect the incentive structure of government officials, although in exactly what way is open to dispute. A closely related point concerns the effect of enterprise liability on the internal procedures of government. Recall that the majority in *Owen* argued that enterprise liability would induce policymakers to devise administrative controls over the acts of government employees. In the majority's view, such procedures would be "particularly beneficial in preventing those 'systemic' injuries that result not so much from the conduct of any single individual, but from the interactive behavior of several government officials, each of whom may be acting in good faith." Such "systemic" injuries are particularly likely to involve government failures to provide adequate services or protections rather than affirmative misconduct. Does this suggest that the courts should be asked to evaluate the failures of government, as well as its affirmative acts? Or is the *Owen* majority merely suggesting that shifting the focus away from the blameworthiness of individual officials would be a desirable simplification in determining when compensation is due?

These and many other questions are suggested by the prospect of direct governmental liability for official misconduct. These issues have been explored in detail by the commentators, but have not received much attention from the courts. Now that *Monell, Owen,* and subsequent cases have laid the doctrinal foundations, however, judicial consideration of enterprise liability might be expected to increase.

2. Questions and Comments on Compensation as a Remedy for Unconstitutional Acts. The Supreme Court has frequently identified compensation of the victims of official misconduct as an important goal of damage actions under § 1983. Yet for a long time, little was done to make that remedy effective. Taken together *Monell, Owen,* and *Pembaur* raise the prospect that effective compensation for government misconduct may begin to be taken seriously. The move in that direction poses interesting questions about the meaning of compensation as a remedy for unconstitutional acts.

Section 1983 applies to the deprivation of "rights, privileges, or immunities secured by the Constitution and laws" of the United States. Enforcement of this provision through damage actions would create a comprehensive compensatory scheme for all unconstitutional (or otherwise illegal) acts of government.[a] Differences among the rights that would be included in that scheme may make compensation as a comprehensive remedy for unconstitutional acts more problematic than at first appears.

The civil liberties provisions of the federal Constitution consist of a series of prohibitions of acts by government. Some of these (e.g., "nor shall private property be taken for public use without just compensation") necessarily imply a cause of action for money damages. Others (e.g., "Congress shall make no law respecting an establishment of religion") impose systemic restraints that cannot as readily be translated into compensation of individuals. In most cases, constitutional guarantees can be enforced by money damages, but not without raising difficult questions concerning the nature and scope of the compensatory objective in various contexts.

[a] Discussion of § 1983 as a vehicle for compensating violations of non-constitutional rights is postponed until *Maine v.* *Thiboutot* and the notes following, infra at pages 1017–40.

Consider the fourth amendment. A search in violation of the constitutional prohibition of "unreasonable searches and seizures" seems an obvious situation where compensation is appropriate. The constitutional limitation protects an individual's interest in freedom from government intrusion; invasions of that right could be (but generally are not now) occasions for government compensation. Yet questions do arise. The Constitution only protects against "unreasonable" searches and seizures—generally speaking, those conducted without probable cause to believe that the individual has committed a crime. But from the point of view of the person whose home is invaded and searched, the existence of probable cause says little or nothing about the extent of the government intrusion or the injury inflicted thereby. If compensation of the innocent victims of government intrusion were deemed the chief purpose of § 1983 enforcement of the fourth amendment, then perhaps damages should be awarded whenever the objects of a search are not discovered, whether or not the search is unlawful.

On the other hand, one could argue that for the truly innocent victim, an unlawful (or merely unsuccessful) search is likely to be little more than an inconvenience. Much more grievously injured by unlawful search and seizure are those found to possess incriminating evidence. If a person who is unlawfully but successfully searched should be entitled to recover damages for the injury of arrest, for the stigma and humiliation of being named as a criminal defendant, for the expenses of litigation, etc., such damages obviously may be quite substantial. The trouble is that although such injuries may have been "caused" by the unlawful search, they also flow from the actor's own unlawful conduct. In a sense, therefore, a completely compensatory scheme would indemnify the individual for the consequences of his or her own misconduct.

Compensation for violations of other constitutional rights would raise significantly different—and perhaps more difficult—questions. Consider, for example, the first amendment prohibition of laws "abridging the freedom of speech." Would damages for violation of this provision be measured by the private value of the activity suppressed, or by its public worth? The societal importance of free speech notwithstanding, many individuals may place a relatively low valuation on the opportunity to participate in political debate. Would that mean that only insignificant sums would be available as compensation? Or should some system of liquidated damages be devised in order to reflect in compensatory judgments the societal importance of unfettered political debate?

On the other hand, some individuals may have a sizeable financial stake in certain activities in which the societal interest seems more attenuated. In Schad v. Mt. Ephraim, 452 U.S. 61 (1981), for example, the Court struck down an anti-entertainment zoning ordinance used to bar nude dancing from a small locality. The economic interest of the impresario may be substantially greater (or conceivably less) than the societal interest in maintaining a free flow of nude dancing. Would the appropriate measure of compensation in such a case be the value of such activity as a business or as a component of a system of freedom of expression? Does the answer turn on what one takes to be the essential rationales for protecting freedom of speech? If so the compensatory remedy might require the courts to distinguish more carefully than heretofore among the several competing conceptions of freedom of speech.

These and similar questions have largely been avoided by the recognition of official immunities and by other limitations on damage actions under § 1983. The move toward enterprise liability, however, suggests that these issues may surface in the future.

SECTION 4: FOR WHAT WRONGS?

PARRATT v. TAYLOR
Supreme Court of the United States, 1981.
451 U.S. 527.

JUSTICE REHNQUIST delivered the opinion of the Court.

The respondent is an inmate at the Nebraska Penal and Correctional Complex who ordered by mail certain hobby materials valued at $23.50. The hobby materials were lost and respondent brought suit under 42 U.S.C. § 1983 to recover their value. . . . Respondent claimed that his property was negligently lost by prison officials in violation of his rights under the 14th amendment to the United States Constitution. More specifically, he claimed that he had been deprived of property without due process of law.

The United States District Court for the District of Nebraska entered summary judgment for respondent, and the United States Court of Appeals for the Eighth Circuit affirmed in a per curiam order. We granted certiorari.

I

The facts underlying this dispute are not seriously contested. Respondent paid for the hobby materials he ordered with two drafts drawn on his inmate account by prison officials. The packages arrived at the complex and were signed for by two employees who worked in the prison hobby center. One of the employees was a civilian and the other was an inmate. Respondent was in segregation at the time and was not permitted to have the hobby materials. Normal prison procedures for the handling of mail packages is that upon arrival they are either delivered to the prisoner who signs a receipt for the package or the prisoner is notified to pick up the package and to sign a receipt. No inmate other than the one to whom the package is addressed is supposed to sign for a package. After being released from segregation, respondent contacted several prison officials regarding the whereabouts of his packages. The officials were never able to locate the packages or to determine what caused their disappearance.

In 1976, respondent commenced this action against the petitioners, the warden and hobby manager of the prison, in the District Court seeking to recover the value of the hobby materials which he claimed had been lost as a result of the petitioners' negligence. Respondent alleged that petitioners' conduct deprived him of property without due process of law in violation of the 14th amendment of the United States Constitution. Respondent chose to proceed in the United States District Court under 28 U.S.C. § 1343 and 42 U.S.C. § 1983, even though the state of Nebraska had a tort claims procedure which provided a remedy to persons who suffered tortious losses at the hands of the state.

On October 25, 1978, the District Court granted respondent's motion for summary judgment. The District Court ruled that negligent actions by state officials can be a basis for an action under 42 U.S.C. § 1983; petitioners were not immune from damages actions of this kind; and the deprivation of the hobby kit "implicate[d] due process rights." The District Court explained:

"This is not a situation where prison officials confiscated contraband. The negligence of the officials in failing to follow their own policies concerning the distribution of mail resulted in a loss of personal property for [respondent], which loss should not go without redress."

II

In the best of all possible worlds, the District Court's above-quoted statement that respondent's loss should not go without redress would be an admirable provision to be contained in a code which governed the administration of justice in a civil-law jurisdiction. For better or for worse, however, our traditions arise from the common law of case-by-case reasoning and the establishment of precedent. In 49 of the 50 states the common-law system, as modified by statute, constitutional amendment, or judicial decision governs. Coexisting with the 50 states which make it up, and supreme over them to the extent of its authority under article IV of the Constitution, is the national government. At an early period in the history of this nation, it was held that there was no federal common law of crimes, United States v. Hudson & Goodwin, 11 U.S. (7 Cranch) 32 (1812), and since Erie R. Co. v. Tompkins, 304 U.S. 64 (1938), there has been no general common law applicable in federal courts merely by reason of diversity-of-citizenship jurisdiction. Therefore, in order properly to decide this case we must deal not simply with a single, general principle, however just that principle may be in the abstract, but with the complex interplay of the Constitution, statutes, and the facts which form the basis for this litigation. . . .

Section 1983 provided at the year in question:

"Every person who, under color of any statute, ordinance, regulation, custom, or usage of any state or territory, subjects, or causes to be subjected, any citizen of the United States or other person within the jurisdiction thereof to the deprivation of any rights, privileges, or immunities secured by the Constitution and laws, shall be liable to the party injured in an action at law, suit in equity, or other proper proceeding for redress."

While we have twice granted certiorari in cases to decide whether mere negligence will support a claim for relief under § 1983, see Procunier v. Navarette, 434 U.S. 555 (1978), and Baker v. McCollan, 443 U.S. 137 (1979), we have in each of those cases found it unnecessary to decide the issue. In *Procunier,* we held that regardless of whether the § 1983 complaint framed in terms of negligence stated a claim for relief, the defendants would clearly have been entitled to qualified immunity and therefore not liable for damages. In *Baker,* we held that no deprivation of any rights, privileges, or immunities secured by the Constitution and laws of the United States had occurred, and therefore it was unnecessary to decide whether mere negligence on the part of the actor would have rendered him liable had there been such a deprivation. These two decisions, however, have not aided the various courts of appeals and district courts in their struggle to determine the correct manner in which to analyze claims such as the present one which allege facts that are commonly thought to state a claim for a common-law tort normally dealt with by state courts, but instead are couched in terms of a constitutional deprivation and relief is sought under § 1983. The diversity of approaches is legion. We, therefore, once more put our shoulder to the wheel hoping to be of greater assistance to courts confronting such a fact situation than it appears we have been in the past.

Nothing in the language of § 1983 or its legislative history limits the statute solely to intentional deprivation of constitutional rights. In *Baker v. McCollan,* supra, we suggested that simply because a wrong was negligently as opposed to intentionally committed did not foreclose the possibility that such action could be brought under § 1983. We explained:

"[T]he question whether an allegation of simple negligence is sufficient to state a cause of action under § 1983 is more elusive than it appears at first blush. It may well not be susceptible of a uniform answer across the entire spectrum of conceivable constitutional violations which might be the subject of a § 1983 action."

Section 1983, unlike its criminal counterpart, 18 U.S.C. § 242, has never been found by this court to contain a state-of-mind requirement. The Court recognized as much in Monroe v. Pape, 365 U.S. 167 (1961), when we explained after extensively reviewing the legislative history of § 1983, that

"[i]t is abundantly clear that one reason the legislation was passed was to afford a federal right in federal courts because, by reason of prejudice, passion, neglect, intolerance or otherwise, state laws might not be enforced and the claims of

citizens to the enjoyment of rights, privileges and immunities
guaranteed by the 14th amendment might be denied by the
state agencies."

In distinguishing the criminal counterpart which had earlier been at
issue in Screws v. United States, 325 U.S. 91 (1945), the *Monroe* Court
stated:

"In the *Screws* case we dealt with a statute that imposed
criminal penalties for acts 'willfully' done. We construed that
word in its setting to mean the doing of an act with 'a specific
intent to deprive a person of a federal right.' We do not think
that gloss should be put on § 1983 which we have here. The
word 'willfully' does not appear in § 1983. Moreover, § 1983
provides a civil remedy, while in the *Screws* case we dealt with
a criminal law challenged on the grounds of vagueness. Section 1983 should be read against the background of tort liability that makes a man responsible for the natural consequences
of his actions."

Both *Baker v. McCollan* and *Monroe v. Pape* suggest that § 1983
affords a "civil remedy" for deprivations of federally protected rights
caused by persons acting under color of state law without any express
requirement of a particular state of mind. Accordingly, in any § 1983
action the initial inquiry must focus on whether the two essential
elements to a § 1983 action are present: (1) whether the conduct
complained of was committed by a person acting under color of state
law; and (2) whether this conduct deprived a person of rights, privileges, or immunities secured by the Constitution or laws of the United
States.

III

Since this Court's decision in *Monroe v. Pape,* supra, it can no
longer be questioned that the alleged conduct by the petitioners in this
case satisfies the "under color of state law" requirement. Petitioners
were, after all, state employees in positions of considerable authority.
They do not seriously contend otherwise. Our inquiry, therefore, must
turn to the second requirement—whether respondent has been deprived
of any right, privilege, or immunity secured by the Constitution or laws
of the United States.

The only deprivation respondent alleges in his complaint is that
"his rights under the 14th amendment of the Constitution of the United
States were violated. That he was deprived of his property and due
process of law." . . . The pertinent text of the 14th amendment
provides:

"Section 1. All persons born or naturalized in the United
States, and subject to the jurisdiction thereof, are citizens of
the United States and the State wherein they reside. No State
shall make or enforce any law which shall abridge the privileges or immunities of citizens of the United States; *nor shall
any State deprive any person of life, liberty, or property, without*

due process of law; nor deny to any person within its jurisdiction the equal protection of the laws." (Emphasis supplied.)

Unquestionably, respondent's claim satisfies three prerequisites of a valid due process claim: the petitioners acted under color of state law; the hobby kit falls within the definition of property; and the alleged loss, even though negligently caused, amounted to a deprivation. Standing alone, however, these three elements do not establish a violation of the 14th amendment. Nothing in that amendment protects against all deprivations of life, liberty, or property by the state. The 14th amendment protects only against deprivations "without due process of law." Our inquiry therefore must focus on whether the respondent has suffered a deprivation of property without due process of law. In particular, we must decide whether the tort remedies which the state of Nebraska provides as a means of redress for property deprivations satisfy the requirements of procedural due process.

The Court has never directly addressed the question of what process is due a person when an employee of a state negligently takes his property. In some cases this Court has held that due process requires a predeprivation hearing before the state interferes with any liberty or property interest enjoyed by its citizens. In most of these cases, however, the deprivation of property was pursuant to some established state procedure and "process" could be offered before any actual deprivation took place. For example, in Mullane v. Central Hanover Trust Co., 339 U.S. 306 (1950), the Court struck down on due process grounds a New York statute that allowed a trust company, when it sought a judicial settlement of its trust accounts, to give notice by publication to all beneficiaries even if the whereabouts of the beneficiaries were known. The Court held that personal notice in such situations was required and stated that "when notice is a person's due, process which is a mere gesture is not due process." More recently, in Bell v. Burson, 402 U.S. 535 (1971), we reviewed a state statute which provided for the taking of the driver's license and registration of an uninsured motorist who had been involved in an accident. We recognized that a driver's license is often involved in the livelihood of a person and as such could not be summarily taken without a prior hearing. In Fuentes v. Shevin, 407 U.S. 67 (1972), we struck down the Florida prejudgment replevin statute which allowed secured creditors to obtain writs in ex parte proceedings. We held that due process required a prior hearing before the state authorized its agents to seize property in a debtor's possession. See also Goldberg v. Kelly, 397 U.S. 254 (1970); and Sniadach v. Family Finance Corp., 395 U.S. 337 (1969). In all these cases, deprivations of property were authorized by an established state procedure and due process was held to require predeprivation notice and hearing in order to serve as a check on the possibility that a wrongful deprivation would occur.

We have, however, recognized that postdeprivation remedies made available by the state can satisfy the due process clause. In such cases, the normal predeprivation notice and opportunity to be heard is pretermitted if the state provides a postdeprivation remedy. In North

American Cold Storage Co. v. Chicago, 211 U.S. 306 (1908), we upheld the right of a state to seize and destroy unwholesome food without a preseizure hearing. The possibility of erroneous destruction of property was outweighed by the fact that the public health emergency justified immediate action and the owner of the property could recover his damages in an action at law after the incident. In Ewing v. Mytinger & Casselberry, Inc., 339 U.S. 594 (1950), we upheld under the fifth amendment due process clause the summary seizure and destruction of drugs without a preseizure hearing. . . . These cases recognize that either the necessity of quick action by the state or the impracticality of providing any meaningful predeprivation process can, when coupled with the availability of some meaningful means by which to assess the propriety of the state's action at some time after the initial taking, satisfy the requirements of procedural due process. As we stated in Mitchell v. W.T. Grant Co., 416 U.S. 600 (1974):

> "Petitioner asserts that his right to a hearing before his possession is in any way disturbed is nonetheless mandated by a long line of cases in this Court, culminating in Sniadach v. Family Finance Corp., 395 U.S. 337 (1969), and Fuentes v. Shevin, 407 U.S. 67 (1972). The pre-*Sniadach* cases are said by petitioner to hold that 'the opportunity to be heard must precede any actual deprivation of private property.' Their import, however, is not so clear as petitioner would have it; they merely stand for the proposition that a hearing must be had before one is finally deprived of his property and do not deal at all with the need for a pre-termination hearing where a full and immediate post-termination hearing is provided. The usual rule has been '[w]here only property rights are involved, mere postponement of the judicial enquiry is not a denial of due process, if the ultimate judicial determination of liability is adequate.' "

Our past cases mandate that some kind of hearing is required at some time before a state finally deprives a person of his property interests. The fundamental requirement of due process is the opportunity to be heard and it is an "opportunity which must be granted at a meaningful time and in a meaningful manner." However, as many of the above cases recognize, we have rejected the proposition that "at a meaningful time and in a meaningful manner" *always* requires the state to provide a hearing prior to the initial deprivation of property. This rejection is based in part on the impracticability in some cases of providing any preseizure hearing under a state-authorized procedure, and the assumption that at some point a full and meaningful hearing will be available.

The justifications which we have found sufficient to uphold takings of property without any predeprivation process are applicable to a situation such as the present one involving a tortious loss of a prisoner's property as a result of a random and unauthorized act by a state employee. In such a case, the loss is not a result of some established state procedure and the state cannot predict precisely when the loss will occur. It is difficult to conceive of how the state could provide a meaningful hearing before the deprivation takes place. The loss of property, although attributable to the state as action under "color of law," is in almost all cases beyond the control of the state. Indeed, in most cases it is not only impracticable, but impossible to provide a meaningful hearing before deprivation. That does not mean, of course, that the state can take property without providing a meaningful postdeprivation hearing. The prior cases which have excused the prior-hearing requirement have rested in part on the availability of some meaningful opportunity subsequent to the initial taking for a determination of rights and liabilities. . . .

IV

Application of the principles recited above to this case leads us to conclude the respondent has not alleged a violation of the due process clause of the 14th amendment. Although he has been deprived of property under color of state law, the deprivation did not occur as a result of some established state procedure. Indeed, the deprivation occurred as a result of the unauthorized failure of agents of the state to follow established state procedure. There is no contention that the procedures themselves are inadequate nor is there any contention that it was practicable for the state to provide a predeprivation hearing. Moreover, the state of Nebraska has provided respondent with the means by which he can receive redress for the deprivation. The state provides a remedy to persons who believe they have suffered a tortious loss at the hands of the state. See Neb. Rev. Stat. § 81–8.209 et seq. (1976). Through this tort claims procedure the state hears and pays claims of prisoners housed in its penal institutions. This procedure was in existence at the time of the loss here in question but respondent did not use it. It is argued that the state does not adequately protect the respondent's interests because it provides only for an action against the state as opposed to its individual employees, it contains no provisions for punitive damages, and there is no right to a trial by jury. Although the state remedies may not provide the respondent with all the relief which may have been available if he could have proceeded under § 1983, that does not mean that the state remedies are not adequate to satisfy the requirements of due process. The remedies provided could have fully compensated the respondent for the property loss he suffered, and we hold that they are sufficient to satisfy the requirements of due process.

Our decision today is fully consistent with our prior cases. To accept respondent's argument that the conduct of the state officials in this case constituted a violation of the 14th amendment would almost necessarily result in turning every alleged injury which may have been inflicted by a state official acting under "color of law" into a violation of the 14th amendment cognizable under § 1983. It is hard to perceive any logical stopping place to such a line of reasoning. Presumably, under this rationale any party who is involved in nothing more than an automobile accident with a state official could allege a constitutional violation under § 1983. Such reasoning "would make the 14th amendment a font of tort law to be superimposed upon whatever systems may already be administered by the states." Paul v. Davis, 424 U.S. 693, 701 (1976). We do not think the drafters of the 14th amendment intended the amendment to play such a role in our society.

Accordingly, the judgment of the Court of Appeals is reversed.

JUSTICE STEWART, concurring.

It seems to me extremely doubtful that the property loss here, even though presumably caused by the negligence of state agents, is the kind of deprivation of property to which the 14th amendment is addressed. If it is, then so too would be damages to a person's automobile resulting from a collision with a vehicle negligently operated by a state official. To hold that this kind of loss is a deprivation of property within the meaning of the 14th amendment seems not only to trivialize, but grossly to distort the meaning and intent of the Constitution.

But even if Nebraska has deprived the respondent of his property in the constitutional sense, it has not deprived him of it without due process of law. By making available to the respondent a reparations remedy, Nebraska has done all that the 14th amendment requires in this context.

On this understanding, I join the opinion of the Court.

JUSTICE WHITE, concurring.

I join the opinion of the Court but with the reservations stated by my brother Blackmun in his concurring opinion.

JUSTICE BLACKMUN, concurring.

While I join in the Court's opinion in this case, I write separately to emphasize my understanding of its narrow reach. This suit concerns the deprivation only of property and was brought only against supervisory personnel, whose simple "negligence" was assumed but, on this record, not actually proved. I do not read the Court's opinion as applicable to a case concerning deprivation of life or liberty. I also do not understand the Court to intimate that the sole content of the due process clause is procedural regularity. I continue to believe that there are certain governmental actions that, even if undertaken with a full panoply of procedural protection, are, in and of themselves, antithetical to fundamental notions of due process. See, e.g., Boddie v. Connecticut, 401 U.S. 371 (1971); Roe v. Wade, 410 U.S. 113 (1973).

Most importantly, I do not understand the Court to suggest that the provision of "postdeprivation remedies" within a state system would cure the unconstitutional nature of a state official's intentional act that deprives a person of property. While the "random and unauthorized" nature of negligent acts by state employees makes it difficult for the state to "provide a meaningful hearing before the deprivation takes place," it is rare that the same can be said of intentional acts by state employees. When it is possible for a state to institute procedures to contain and direct the intentional actions of its officials, it should be required, as a matter of due process, to do so. See

Sniadach v. Family Finance Corp., 395 U.S. 337 (1969); Fuentes v Shevin, 407 U.S. 67 (1972); Goldberg v. Kelly, 397 U.S. 354 (1970). In the majority of such cases, the failure to provide adequate process prior to inflicting the harm would violate the due process clause. The mere availability of a subsequent tort remedy before tribunals of the same authority that, through its employees, deliberately inflicted the harm complained of, might well not provide the due process of which the 14th amendment speaks.

JUSTICE POWELL, concurring in the result.

This case presents the question whether a state prisoner may sue to recover damages under 42 U.S.C. § 1983, alleging that a violation of the due process clause of the 14th amendment occurred when two shipments mailed to him were lost due to the negligence of the prison's warden and "hobby manager." Unlike the Court, I do not believe that such negligent acts by state officials constitute a deprivation of property within the meaning of the 14th amendment, regardless of whatever subsequent procedure a state may or may not provide. I therefore concur only in the result.

The Court's approach begins with three "unquestionable" facts concerning respondent's due process claim: "the petitioners acted under color of state law; the hobby kit falls within the definition of property; and the alleged loss, even though negligently caused, amounted to a deprivation." It then goes on to reject respondent's claim on the theory that procedural due process is satisfied in such a case where a state provides a "postdeprivation" procedure for seeking redress—here a tort claims procedure. I would not decide this case on that ground for two reasons. First, the Court passes over a threshold question—whether a negligent act by a state official that results in loss of or damage to property constitutes a deprivation of property for due process purposes. Second, in doing so, the Court suggests a narrow, wholly procedural view of the limitation imposed on the states by the due process clause.

The central question in this case is whether *unintentional* but negligent acts by state officials, causing respondent's loss of property, are actionable under the due process clause. In my view, this question requires the Court to determine whether intent is an essential element of a due process claim, just as we have done in cases applying the equal protection clause[2] and the eighth amendment's prohibition of "cruel and unusual punishment."[3] The intent question cannot be given "a

[2] Washington v. Davis, 426 U.S. 229 (1976); Arlington Heights v. Metropolitan Housing Dev. Corp., 429 U.S. 252 (1977) (invidious discriminatory purpose required for claim of racial discrimination under the equal protection clause).

[3] In Estelle v. Gamble, 429 U.S. 97 (1976), we held that "deliberate indifference to a prisoner's serious illness or injury" on the part of prison officials is sufficient to constitute an "infliction" of cruel

and unusual punishment under the eighth amendment. We also stated that an "accident, although it may produce added anguish, is not on that basis alone to be characterized as wanton infliction of unnecessary pain." Ibid. *Estelle v. Gamble* thus supports my view of the due process clause—which requires consideration not only of the *effect* of an injury or loss on a citizen but also of the *intent* of the state

uniform answer across the entire spectrum of conceivable constitutional violations which might be the subject of a § 1983 action," Baker v. McCollan, 443 U.S. 137 (1979). Rather, we must give close attention to the nature of the particular constitutional violation asserted, in determining whether intent is a necessary element of such a violation.

In the due process area, the question is whether intent is required before there can be a "deprivation" of life, liberty, or property. In this case, for example, the negligence of the prison officials caused respondent to lose his property. Nevertheless, I would not hold that such a negligent act, causing unintended loss of or injury to property, works a deprivation in the *constitutional sense.* Thus, no procedure for compensation is constitutionally required.

A "deprivation" connotes an intentional act denying something to someone, or, at the very least, a deliberate decision not to act to prevent a loss. The most reasonable interpretation of the 14th amendment would limit due process claims to such active deprivations. This is the view adopted by an overwhelming number of lower courts, which have rejected due process claims premised on negligent acts without inquiring into the existence or sufficiency of the subsequent procedures provided by the states. In addition, such a rule would avoid trivializing the right of action provided in § 1983. That provision was enacted to deter real *abuses* by state officials in the exercise of governmental powers. It would make no sense to open the federal courts to lawsuits where there has been no affirmative abuse of power, merely a negligent deed by one who happens to be acting under color of state law.

The Court appears unconcerned about this prospect, probably because of an implicit belief in the availability of state tort remedies in most cases. In its view, such remedies will satisfy procedural due process, and relegate cases of official negligence to nonfederal forums. But the fact is that this rule would "make of the 14th amendment a font of tort law," Paul v. Davis, 424 U.S. 693, 701 (1976), whenever a state has failed to provide a remedy for negligent invasions of liberty or property interests.[8] Moreover, despite the breadth of state tort remedies, such claims will be more numerous than might at first be supposed. In Kent v. Prasse, 385 F.2d 406 (3d Cir. 1967) (per curiam), for example, a state prisoner was forced to work on a faulty machine, sustained an injury, and brought suit against prison officials. The United States Court of Appeals for the Third Circuit noted that the

official whose actions caused the injury or loss.

[8] One additional problem with the Court's purely procedural approach is worth noting. In Kent v. Prasse, 385 F.2d 406 (3rd Cir. 1967), the Third Circuit faced a claimed deprivation of procedural due process by prison officials based on the failure of a state to provide a tort remedy for official negligence—the exact claim validated by the Court today. The court noted that "[i]n any event, such a deprivation would be the work of the state, not these defendants." Arguably, if the absence of a tort remedy is the heart of one's constitutional claim, the defendant in the § 1983 suit must be the state itself, or its lawmakers, both of whom are immune from suit. See Tenney v. Brandhove, 341 U.S. 367 (1951); Edelman v. Jordan, 415 U.S. 651 (1974). If so, the only remedy available to plaintiffs would be a more substantive due process claim—where grounds for such claim exist. The Court does not discuss this possibility.

state, unfortunately, did not provide compensation for this injury, but stated:

> "Nor are we able to perceive that a tort committed by a state official acting under color of law is, in and of itself, sufficient to show an invasion of a person's right under [§ 1983]. While not dispositive, we note that there is no allegation that defendants violated any state criminal law or acted out of bad motive. Nor [is it] alleged that any state law was not enforced by the defendants."

Rather than reject this reasoning, I would adopt the view that negligent official acts do not provide any basis for inquiries by federal courts into the existence, or procedural adequacy, of applicable state tort remedies.

Such an approach has another advantage; it avoids a somewhat disturbing implication in the Court's opinion concerning the scope of due process guarantees. The Court analyzes this case solely in terms of the procedural rights created by the due process clause. Finding state procedures adequate, it suggests that no further analysis is required of more substantive limitations on state action located in this clause.

The due process clause imposes substantive limitations on state action, and under proper circumstances these limitations may extend to intentional and malicious deprivations of liberty and property even where compensation is available under state law. The Court, however, fails altogether to discuss the possibility that the kind of state action alleged here constitutes a violation of the substantive guarantees of the due process clause. As I do not consider a negligent act the kind of deprivation that implicates the procedural guarantees of the due process clause, I certainly would not view negligent acts as violative of these substantive guarantees. But the Court concludes that there has been such a deprivation. And yet it avoids entirely the question whether the due process clause may place substantive limitations on this form of government conduct.

In sum, it seems evident that the reasoning and decision of the Court today, even if viewed as compatible with our precedents, creates new uncertainties as well as invitations to litigate under a statute that already has burst its historical bounds.

JUSTICE MARSHALL, concurring in part and dissenting in part.

I join the opinion of the Court insofar as it holds that negligent conduct by persons acting under color of state law may be actionable under 42 U.S.C. § 1983. I also agree with the majority that in cases involving claims of *negligent* deprivation of property without due process of law, the availability of an adequate postdeprivation cause of action for damages under state law may preclude a finding of a violation of the 14th amendment. I part company with the majority, however, over its conclusion that there was an adequate state-law remedy available to respondent in this case. My disagreement with the majority is not because of any shortcomings in the Nebraska tort claims procedure. Rather, my problem is with the majority's application of its legal analysis to the facts of this case.

It is significant, in my view, that respondent is a state prisoner whose access to information about his legal rights is necessarily limited by his confinement. Furthermore, there is no claim that either petitioners or any other officials informed respondent that he could seek redress for the alleged deprivation of his property by filing an action under the Nebraska tort claims procedure. This apparent failure takes on additional significance in light of the fact that respondent pursued his complaint about the missing hobby kit through the prison's grievance procedure. In cases such as this, I believe prison officials have an affirmative obligation to inform a prisoner who claims that he is aggrieved by official action about the remedies available under state law. If they fail to do so, then they should not be permitted to rely on the existence of such remedies as adequate alternatives to a § 1983 action for wrongful deprivation of property. Since these prison officials do not represent that respondent was informed about his rights under state law, I cannot join in the judgment of the Court in this case.

Thus, although I agree with much of the majority's reasoning, I would affirm the judgment of the Court of Appeals.

NOTES ON CONSTITUTIONAL RIGHTS ENFORCEABLE UNDER § 1983

1. Background. The issue of the "state of mind" required under § 1983 has a long history.[a] Before 1961, many courts looked to the defendant's motive or purpose in determining whether a § 1983 claim was made out. In *Monroe v. Pape,* however, the Supreme Court rejected a specific intent requirement for § 1983 and said, in language quoted in *Parratt v. Taylor,* that the statute "should be read against the background of tort liability that makes a man responsible for the natural consequences of his actions." The reaction of the lower courts was diverse. Some continued to require a specific motive or purpose, at least for certain kinds of cases. Others moved toward various less demanding formulations of culpability. Over time, the issue came to be seen as whether liability under § 1983 could be based on simple negligence.

The issue is complicated by the fact that there are at least three analytically distinct reasons why state of mind might be relevant in an action under § 1983:

> First, a state-of-mind requirement might be implicit in the particular constitutional right being enforced. The equal protection clause, for example, requires a discriminatory purpose.

[a] See Kirkpatrick, Defining a Constitutional Tort under Section 1983: The State-of-Mind Requirement, 46 U. Cinn. L. Rev. 45 (1977) (reviewing the history of the question and suggesting that "the standard of liability under § 1983 should vary depending upon the constitutional claim being asserted"); and Gildin, The Standard of Culpability in Section 1983 and *Bivens* Actions: The Prima Facie Case, Qualified Immunity and the Constitution, 11 Hof. L. Rev. 557 (1983) (distinguishing and analyzing interactions among the various sources of a fault requirement in § 1983 and *Bivens*-type actions).

Government action taken without such a purpose is not unconstitutional, even though a racial or ethnic minority is disproportionately affected thereby. Similarly, culpability is required to demonstrate cruel and unusual punishment. A burn suffered in an accidental fire would not be a constitutional violation, but the same injury would be unconstitutional if inflicted intentionally. In these and other instances, state of mind must be proved in order to show that a constitutional violation occurred.

Second, state of mind might be required as a component of the cause of action under § 1983. If the statute itself were the source of the fault requirement, then culpability would be necessary for all § 1983 actions, including those seeking to enforce rights containing no such requirement.

Third, culpability becomes relevant when the defendant is entitled to assert a qualified immunity from damages liability. No such issue arises, however, when the suit is against a municipality or when it concerns only prospective relief.

As the *Parratt* opinion recounts, the Supreme Court had made previous attempts to unravel these issues. The most notable was Baker v. McCollan, 443 U.S. 137 (1979), a case of mistaken identity between two brothers, Leonard and Linnie. Leonard procured a duplicate of his brother's driver's license. When he was subsequently arrested on narcotics charges, he identified himself as Linnie and was released on bail under that name. When he did not return as promised, a warrant for his arrest was issued under the name of Linnie Carl McCollon. Shortly thereafter, the real Linnie McCollon was caught running a red light. A routine warrant check landed him in jail, where he remained until someone took the trouble to compare his appearance to the file photograph of the wanted man. The error was then recognized, and Linnie was released.

Linnie then filed what was characterized as a "§ 1983 false imprisonment action," the elements of which were determined by reference to the common-law tort. The issue in the lower courts was whether the defendant sheriff was entitled to the defense of qualified immunity, "which in turn depended on the reasonableness of his failure to institute an identification procedure that would have discovered the error." The Supreme Court, however, concluded that in any event no constitutional wrong had been done. The arrest warrant was concededly valid, and there had been no prolonged detention that might violate the right to speedy trial. Whatever might be actionable at common law, said the Court, "we do not think a sheriff executing an arrest warrant is required by the Constitution to investigate independently every claim of innocence."

In reaching this conclusion, the *Baker* Court made clear that the issue whether a constitutional right has been violated is logically antecedent to statutory requirements for relief under § 1983. The Court therefore once again declined to reach the question whether simple negligence could support damages liability under § 1983. "Of course," the Court added, "the state of mind of the defendant may be relevant on the issue of whether a constitutional violation has occurred in the first place, quite apart from the issue of whether § 1983 contains some additional qualification of that nature . . . ."

2. Questions and Comments on *Parratt v. Taylor.* Nowhere in the *Parratt* opinion did the Court explicitly say whether § 1983 actions require culpability. The answer, however, was implied in the Court's summary of the "two essential ingredients" of a § 1983 action: (1) conduct under color of law that (2) violates the Constitution or laws of the United States. No mention was made of culpability as an ingredient of the cause of action. This reading was confirmed by the Court's later reference to *Parratt* as "deciding that § 1983 contains no independent state-of-mind requirement." Daniels v. Williams, 474 U.S. 327, 328 (1986).

The fact that *Parratt* involves due process is not entirely accidental, for the interpretation of that guarantee has been the underlying issue in many arguments about the scope of § 1983. The due process clause provides at least some level of protection for a wide range of individual interests. The emergence of § 1983 as a comprehensive remedy against misconduct by public officers therefore threatened to turn virtually every grievance against state or local government into a federal constitutional issue. Requiring state of mind under § 1983 would be one way of responding to this prospect. Another is a more rigorous definition of the right itself.

The opinions in *Parratt* identify two possible limitations on the due process right protected by § 1983. The majority holds that due process was satisfied by Nebraska's provision of an adequate postdeprivation remedy in the form of a tort claims procedure for prison inmates. Presumably, lack of an adequate compensatory remedy would convert official negligence into a procedural due process violation. Is it surprising, after *Monroe v. Pape*, to find that the focus returns to the adequacy of remedies under state law? Is *Parratt v. Taylor* a belated triumph for Justice Frankfurter's dissent in *Monroe*? Of course, the *Parratt* decision explicitly addresses only procedural due process claims. Does the Court's analysis have application outside that context? If not, does it make sense that the adequacy of state law should be the central issue in § 1983 claims based on procedural due process, but irrelevant elsewhere?[b]

An alternative justification for the result in *Parratt* is Justice Powell's suggestion that negligent acts by government officials do not constitute a "deprivation" within the meaning of due process. In his view, a deprivation requires an intentional act or a deliberate decision not to act. Destruction of property through mere inadvertence would not be a constitutional violation in the first place and hence would not

---

[b] For comment on these and other questions and an argument that *Parratt* should be read narrowly, see Friedman, *Parratt v.* *Taylor*: Opening and Closing the Door on Section 1983, 9 Hast. Con. L.Q. 545 (1982).

support an action under § 1983. The Court adopted this view in *Daniels v. Williams.*

3. *Daniels v. Williams,* **State Sovereign Immunity, and the Meaning of "Deprivation."** The *Parratt* decision gave rise to an interesting line of speculation about the continued vitality of state sovereign immunity for garden-variety tortious acts by state employees. Traditionally, states have asserted the right to claim sovereign immunity in their own courts when sued for torts committed by their employees. The attempt to evade this restriction by resort to federal court was cut short by the 11th amendment. As a result, garden-variety torts by government employees have been subject to compensation by the state only to the extent that the state explicitly waived its right not to be sued in its own courts.

Parratt suggested a possible way to evade such restrictions. If a state fails to provide an adequate compensatory remedy for the negligent acts of its employees, then presumably such acts become procedural due process violations. The individuals injured thereby can bring suit under § 1983 by characterizing the tort claim as an instance of procedural inadequacy. Of course, the action must be brought against the employee rather than directly against the state, but that may not matter. Once the procedural due process right to adequate state procedures is "clearly established," the defense of qualified immunity presumably would become unavailable to the employee, and the employee would very likely be indemnified by the state for any adverse judgment.

The Court addressed this issue in Daniels v. Williams, 474 U.S. 327 (1986). Daniels was a prisoner in the Richmond, Va., city jail. He tripped over a pillow allegedly left on a staircase by Williams, a corrections officer. Daniels asserted that the resulting injury was a "deprivation" of his "liberty" interest in freedom from bodily hurt. Since sovereign immunity arguably blocked ordinary tort recovery, Daniels claimed that he had no "adequate" state remedy and therefore that the deprivation of liberty was without due process of law and hence compensable under § 1983.

The Supreme Court disagreed. Speaking through Justice Rehnquist, the Court adopted Justice Powell's suggestion that "the due process clause is simply not implicated by a *negligent* act of an official causing unintended loss of or injury to life, liberty, or property." *Parratt v. Taylor* was explicitly overruled "to the extent that it states that mere lack of due care by a state official may 'deprive' an individual of life, liberty or property under the 14th amendment." The Court reasoned that the due process clause was "intended to secure the individual from the arbitrary exercise of the powers of government":

> "By requiring the government to follow appropriate procedures when its agents decide to 'deprive any person of life, liberty, or property,' the due process clause promotes fairness in such decisions. And by barring certain government actions regardless of the fairness of the procedures used to implement them,

it serves to prevent governmental power from being 'used for purposes of oppression.'

"We think that the actions of prison custodians in leaving a pillow on the prison stairs, or mislaying an inmate's property, are quite remote from the concerns just discussed. Far from an abuse of power, lack of due care suggests no more than a failure to measure up to the conduct of a reasonable person. To hold that injury caused by such conduct is a deprivation within the meaning of the 14th amendment would trivialize the centuries-old principle of due process of law."

Justices Marshall, Blackmun, and Stevens concurred in the result.

4. *Davidson v. Cannon.* Mention should also be made of a companion case, Davidson v. Cannon, 474 U.S. 344 (1986). Inmate Davidson sued state prison officials for failure to protect him from another inmate. Prior to the assault, the victim had sent a note to prison authorities warning of the possibility, but they neglected to take timely action. The Court, per Justice Rehnquist, rejected his claim on the authority of *Daniels.*

Justice Blackmun, joined by Justice Marshall, dissented. He agreed that mere negligence by government officials *"ordinarily"* would not be actionable under § 1983, but argued that the Court erred "in elevating this sensible rule of thumb to the status of inflexible constitutional dogma." In some cases, Blackmun concluded, governmental negligence was the kind of abuse of power at which the due process clause was aimed. He thought this was such a case.

Justice Brennan dissented separately on the narrower ground that the prison authorities may have been reckless, rather than merely negligent, in not acting. He voted to remand for further consideration of that issue.

5. *Hudson v. Palmer* and State Law Remedies for Intentional Wrongs. In *Parratt v. Taylor*, Justice Blackmun concurred specially to say that, with respect to intentional misconduct by a government employee, postdeprivation remedies might well be inadequate to satisfy due process. The question whether the analysis of *Parratt* should be extended to intentional wrongs came before the Court in Hudson v. Palmer, 468 U.S. 517 (1984).

Hudson was an officer at a correctional institution. He conducted a "shakedown" search of inmate Palmer's cell, where he discovered a ripped pillowcase. Disciplinary proceedings were brought against Palmer, who was made to pay for the cost of the pillowcase. Subsequently, Palmer filed a § 1983 action claiming, inter alia, that Hudson had intentionally and without justification destroyed noncontraband personal property during the shakedown. Hudson denied the allegation and won a summary judgment, which in due course was affirmed by the Supreme Court. Indeed, on this issue, the decision was unanimous. Speaking through Chief Justice Burger, the Court said:

"While *Parratt* is necessarily limited by its facts to negligent deprivations of property, it is evident, as the Court of Appeals recognized, that its reasoning applies as well to intentional deprivations of property. The underlying rationale of *Parratt* is that when deprivations of property are effected through random and unauthorized conduct of a state employee, predeprivation procedures are simply 'impracticable' since the state cannot know when such deprivations will occur. We can discern no logical distinction between negligent and intentional deprivations of property insofar as the 'practicablity' of affording pre-deprivation process is concerned. The state can no more anticipate and control in advance the random and unauthorized intentional conduct of its employees than it can anticipate similar negligent conduct. . . .

"Accordingly, we hold that an unauthorized intentional deprivation of property by a state employee does not constitute a violation of the procedural requirements of the due process clause of the 14th amendment if a meaningful postdeprivation remedy for the loss is available. For intentional, as for negligent deprivations of property by state employees, the state's action is not complete until and unless it provides or refuses to provide a suitable postdeprivation remedy."

At the same time the Court was careful to note that the *Parratt* analysis does not apply to deprivations of property caused pursuant to established state procedure. Such an act violates due process regardless of the postdeprivation remedies available. See Logan v. Zimmerman Brush Co., 455 U.S. 422 (1982).

Is *Hudson v. Palmer* sound? The Court is right, is it not, in suggesting that the analysis of *Parratt* applies equally well to all random and unauthorized behavior, whether negligent or intentional? Yet the extension of that reasoning to intentional misconduct highlights its ironic relation to *Monroe v. Pape.* Does *Hudson* suggest that *Monroe* may, after all, have been misguided? Or that *Parratt* and *Hudson* are mistaken? Or can these cases be reconciled?

For recent commentary on these questions, see Rosalie Berger Levinson, Due Process Challenges to Governmental Actions: The Meaning of *Parratt* and *Hudson,* 18 Urb. Law. 189 (1986) (advocating a narrow construction of *Parratt* and *Hudson* and suggesting reliance on substantive due process as a way of preserving access to federal court); and Stephen Shapiro, Keeping Civil Rights Actions Against State Officials in Federal Court: Avoiding the Reach of *Parratt v. Taylor* and *Hudson v. Palmer,* 3 J. Law & Inequality 161 (1985) (analyzing *Parratt* and *Hudson* as a partial retreat from *Monroe v. Pape* and arguing that these cases should be confined to procedural due process claims where no prior hearing is possible).

See also Mark R. Brown, De-Federalizing Common Law Torts: Empathy for *Parratt, Hudson,* and *Daniels,* 28 B.C.L.Rev. 813 (1987) (concluding that the Court has adopted a "sound premise in attempting to deflect certain cases from the federal courts" and proposing that the problem be addressed through a narrowing construction of procedural due process); Henry Paul Monaghan, State Law Wrongs, State Law Remedies, and the 14th Amendment, 86 Colum.L.Rev. 979 (1986) (criticizing *Parratt* and *Hudson* as based on a theory of "state action" inconsistent with constitutional precedents); Susanah M. Mead, Evolution of the "Species of Tort Liability" Created by 42 U.S.C. § 1983: Can Constitutional Tort Be Saved From Extinction?, 55 Fordham L.Rev. 1 (1986) (analyzing these cases from the perspective of a torts scholar); Frederic S. Schwartz, The Postdeprivation Remedy Doctrine of *Parratt v. Taylor* and Its Application to Cases of Land Use Regulation, 21 Ga.L. Rev. 601 (1987) (analyzing interesting questions concerning the application of *Parratt* in a specialized context); and Kathryn R. Urbonya, Establishing a Deprivation of a Constitutional Right to Personal Security Under Section 1983: The Use of Unjustified Force by State Officials in Violation of the Fourth, Eighth, and Fourteenth Amendments, 51 Albany L.Rev. 171 (1987) (examining the constitutional basis for claims of invasion of personal security and arguing that reckless or grossly negligent conduct should be actionable).

Finally, two recent articles relate the *Parratt* line of cases to the policy-or-custom requirement of *Monell.* See Susan Bandes, *Monell, Parratt, Daniels,* and *Davidson:* Distinguishing a Custom or Policy from a Random, Unauthorized Act, 72 Iowa L.Rev. 101 (1986) (analyzing *Monell* and *Parratt* as "correlatives that distinguish random, unauthorized acts of government employees from the customs and policies of the government"); and Christina Whitman, Government Responsibility for Constitutional Torts, 85 Mich.L.Rev. 225 (1986) (examining both lines of cases with a focus on systemic or structural harms as bases for institutional liability).

6. *Paul v. Davis* and the Protection of Liberty. The due process clause of the 14th amendment protects "life, liberty, or property" against deprivation without due process of law. As has been noted, this formulation covers a wide range of individual interests. At one time, the criterion for determining whether a particular interest was protected was simply its "importance" to the individual. See, e.g., Bell v. Burson, 402 U.S. 535 (1971). This approach proved so inclusive that, in the words of one authority, "there seems to have been an overriding consensus that every individual 'interest' worth talking about [was] encompassed within the 'liberty' and 'property' secured by the due process clause and thus entitled to some constitutional protection. . . ." Monaghan, Of "Liberty" and "Property," 62 Corn. L. Rev. 405, 406–07 (1977).

Then the Supreme Court took a new approach. In Board of Regents of State Colleges v. Roth, 408 U.S. 564 (1972), the Court for the first time rejected a procedural due process claim on the ground that the individual interest there affected (continued employment as a non-tenured teacher) did not qualify as "life, liberty, or property." In subsequent years, the Court rejected several procedural due process claims for lack of a protectible interest. One particularly famous, and controversial, illustration of this approach came in Paul v. Davis, 424 U.S. 693 (1976).

Edward Charles Davis was arrested for shoplifting in Louisville, Kentucky. He pleaded not guilty, and the case was continued without disposition. Shortly thereafter, his name and "mug shot" appeared on a local police flyer under the heading "active shoplifters." Davis brought a § 1983 action, claiming that his inclusion on the list without any form of hearing on the merits of the charge violated his right to procedural due process. The Supreme Court, per Justice Rehnquist, disagreed:

"Respondent's due process claim is grounded upon his assertion that the flyer, and in particular the phase 'Active Shoplifters' appearing at the head of the page upon which his name and photograph appear, impermissibly deprived him of some 'liberty' protected by the 14th amendment. His complaint asserted that the 'active shoplifter' designation would inhibit him from entering business establishments for fear of being suspected of shoplifting and possibly apprehended, and would seriously impair his future employment opportunities. Accepting that such consequences may flow from the flyer in question, respondent's complaint would appear to state a classical claim for defamation actionable in the courts of virtually every state. Imputing criminal behavior to an individual is generally considered defamatory per se, and actionable without proof of special damages.

"Respondent brought his action, however, not in the state courts of Kentucky, but in a United States district court for that state. He asserted not a claim for defamation under the laws of Kentucky, but a claim that he had been deprived of rights secured to him by the 14th amendment of the United States Constitution. Concededly if the same allegations had been made about respondent by a private individual, he would have nothing more than a claim for defamation under state law. But, he contends, since petitioners are respectively an official of city and of county governments, his action is transmuted into one for deprivation by the state of rights secured under the 14th amendment. . . .

"Respondent, however, has pointed to no specific constitutional guarantee safeguarding the interest he asserts has been invaded. Rather, he apparently believes that the 14th amendment's due process clause should ex proprio vigore extend to him a right to be free of injury wherever the state may be characterized as the tortfeasor. But such a reading would make of the 14th amendment a font of tort law to be superimposed upon whatever systems may already be administered by the states. [T]he due process clause cannot be the source for such law. . . .

"The words 'liberty' and 'property' as used in the 14th amendment do not in terms single out reputation as a candidate for special protection over and above other interests that may be protected by state law. While we have in a number of our prior cases pointed out the frequently drastic effect of the 'stigma' which may result from defamation by the government in a variety of contexts, this line of cases does not establish the proposition that reputation alone, apart from some more tangible interests such as employment, is either 'liberty' or 'property' by itself sufficient to invoke the procedural protection of the due process clause. As we have said, the court of appeals, in reaching a contrary conclusion, relied primarily upon Wisconsin v. Constantineau, 400 U.S. 433 (1971). We think the correct import of that decision, however, must be derived from an examination of the precedents upon which it relied . . . ."

After reviewing a number of earlier cases, the Court returned to its discussion of *Constantineau*:

"It was against this backdrop that the Court in 1971 decided *Constantineau*. There the Court held that a Wisconsin statute authorizing the practice of 'posting' was unconstitutional because it failed to provide procedural safeguards of notice and an opportunity to be heard, prior to an individual's being 'posted.' Under the statute 'posting' consisted of forbidding in writing the sale or delivery of alcoholic beverages to certain persons who were determined to have become hazards to themselves, to their family, or to the community by reason of their 'excessive drinking.' The statute also made it a misdemeanor to sell or give liquor to any person so posted.

"There is undoubtedly language in *Constantineau*, which is sufficiently ambiguous to justify the reliance upon it by the court of appeals:

'Yet certainly where the state attaches "a badge of infamy" to the citizen, due process comes into play. "[T]he right to be heard before being condemned to suffer grievous loss of any kind, even though it may not involve the stigma and hardships of a criminal conviction, is a principle basic to our society.'

'Where a person's good name, reputation, honor, or integrity is at stake *because of what the government is doing to him,* notice and an opportunity to be heard are essential.' (Emphasis supplied.)

"The last paragraph of the quotation could be taken to mean that if a government official defames a person, without more, the procedural requirements of the due process clause of the 14th amendment are brought into play. If read that way, it would represent a significant broadening of the holdings of [earlier cases]. We should not read this language as significantly broadening those holdings without in any way adverting to the fact if there is any other possible interpretation of *Constantineau*'s language. We believe there is.

"We think that the italicized language in the last sentence quoted, 'because of what the government is doing to him,' referred to the fact that the government action taken in that case deprived the individual of a right previously held under state law—the right to purchase or obtain liquor in common with the rest of the citizenry. 'Posting,' therefore, significantly altered his status as a matter of state law, and it was alteration of legal status which, combined with the injury resulting from the defamation, justified the invocation of procedural safeguards. The 'stigma' resulting from the defamatory character of the posting was doubtless an important factor in evaluating the extent of harm worked by that act, but we do not think that such defamation, standing alone, deprived Constantineau of any 'liberty' protected by the procedural guarantees of the 14th amendment. . . .

"It is apparent from our decisions that there exists a variety of interests which are difficult of definition but are nevertheless comprehended within the meaning of either 'liberty' or 'property' as meant in the due process clause. These interests attain this constitutional status by virtue of the fact that they have been initially recognized and protected by state law, and we have repeatedly ruled that the procedural guarantees of the 14th amendment apply whenever the state seeks to remove or significantly alter that protected status. . . . But the interest in reputation alone which respondent seeks to vindicate in this action in federal court is quite different from the 'liberty' and 'property' recognized in those decisions. Kentucky law does not extend to respondent any legal guarantee of present enjoyment of reputation which has been altered as a result of petitioners' actions. Rather his interest in reputation is simply one of a number which the state may protect against injury by virtue of its tort law, providing a forum for vindication of those interests by means of damages actions. And any harm or injury to that interest, even where as here inflicted by an officer of the state, does not result in a deprivation of any 'liberty' or 'property' recognized by state or federal law, nor has it worked any change of respondent's status as theretofore recognized under the state's laws. For these reasons we hold that the interest in reputation asserted in this case is neither 'liberty' nor 'property' guaranteed against state deprivation without due process of law. . . ."

This conclusion prompted an extensive dissent by Justice Brennan, with whom Justices White and Marshall joined:[c]

---

[c] Justice Stevens took no part in the consideration or decision of the case.

"The Court today holds that police officials, acting in their official capacities as law enforcers, may on their own initiative and without trial constitutionally condemn innocent individuals as criminals and thereby brand them with one of the most stigmatizing and debilitating labels in our society. If there are no constitutional restraints on such oppressive behavior, the safeguards constitutionally accorded an accused in a criminal trial are rendered a sham, and no individual can feel secure that he will not be arbitrarily singled out for similar ex parte punishment by those primarily charged with fair enforcement of the law. The Court accomplishes this result by excluding a person's interest in his good name and reputation from all constitutional protection, regardless of the character of or necessity for the government's actions. The result, which is demonstrably inconsistent with our prior case law and unduly restrictive in its construction of our precious bill of rights, is one in which I cannot concur. . . .

"The stark fact is that the police here have officially imposed on respondent the stigmatizing label 'criminal' without the salutary and constitutionally mandated safeguards of a criminal trial. [B]ut the Court by mere fiat and with no analysis wholly excludes personal interest in reputation from the ambit of 'life, liberty, or property' under the fifth and 14th amendments, thus rendering due process concerns *never* applicable to the official stigmatization, however arbitrary, of an individual. The logical and disturbing corollary of this holding is that no due process infirmities would inhere in a statute constituting a commission to conduct ex parte trials of individuals, so long as the only official judgment pronounced was limited to the public condemnation and branding of a person as a Communist, a traitor, an 'active murderer,' a homosexual, or any other mark that 'merely' carries social opprobrium. The potential of today's decision is frightening for a free people. That decision surely finds no support in our relevant constitutional jurisprudence. . . ."

The dissent then discussed a number of precedents, including *Constantineau*:

"Moreover, Wisconsin v. Constantineau, 400 U.S. 433 (1971), which was relied on by the Court of Appeals in this case, did not rely at all on the fact asserted by the Court today as controlling—namely, upon the fact that 'posting' denied Ms. Constantineau the right to purchase alcohol for a year. Rather, *Constantineau* stated: 'The *only* issue present here is whether the label or characterization given a person by 'posting,' though a mark of serious illness to some, is to others such a stigma or badge of disgrace that procedural due process requires notice and an opportunity to be heard.' (Emphasis supplied.) In addition to the statements quoted by the Court, the Court in *Constantineau* continued: ' "Posting" under the

Wisconsin act may to some be merely the mark of illness, to others it is a stigma, an official branding of a person. The label is a degrading one. Under the Wisconsin act, a resident of Hartford is given no process at all. This appellee was not afforded a chance to defend herself. She may have been the victim of an official's caprice. Only when the whole proceedings leading to the pinning of an unsavory label on a person are aired can oppressive results be prevented.' '[T]he right to be heard before being condemned to suffer grievous loss of any kind, *even though it may not involve the stigma and hardships of a criminal conviction,* is a principle basic to our society.' (Emphasis supplied.) There again, the fact that government stigmatization of an individual implicates constitutionally protected interests was made plain. . . .

"It is inexplicable how the Court can say that a person's status is 'altered' when the state suspends him from school, revokes his driver's license, fires him from a job, or denies him the right to purchase a drink of alcohol, but is in no way 'altered' when it officially pins upon him the brand of a criminal, particularly since the Court recognizes how deleterious will be the consequences that inevitably flow from its official act. Our precedents clearly mandate that a person's interest in his good name and reputation is cognizable as a 'liberty' interest within the meaning of the due process clause, and the Court has simply failed to distinguish those precedents in any rational manner in holding that no invasion of a 'liberty' interest was effected in the official stigmatizing without any 'process' whatsoever.

"I had always thought that one of this Court's most important roles is to provide a formidable bulwark against governmental violation of the constitutional safeguards securing in our free society the legitimate expectations of every person to innate human dignity and sense of worth. It is a regrettable abdication of that role and a saddening denigration of our majestic bill of rights when the Court tolerates arbitrary and capricious official conduct branding an individual as a criminal without compliance with constitutional procedures designed to ensure the fair and impartial ascertainment of criminal culpability. Today's decision must surely be a short-lived aberration."

7. Commentary on *Paul v. Davis*. The reaction to the *Paul v. Davis* opinion has been almost uniformly hostile. In particular, the opinion has been criticized for its allegedly disingenuous treatment of precedent. See, e.g., Shapiro, Mr. Justice Rehnquist: A Preliminary View, 90 Harv. L. Rev. 293, 324–28 (1976) (concluding that it is "simply impossible" to reconcile *Paul* with prior decisions); Monaghan, Of "Liberty" and "Property," 62 Corn. L. Rev. 405, 423–29 (1977) (describing as "wholly startling" the Court's re-rationalization of its earlier cases).

Additionally, the decision has been criticized on the merits. Henry Monaghan, for example, found it "an unsettling conception of 'liberty' that protects an individual against state interference with his access to liquor but not with his reputation in the community." See also the views expressed by Frank McClellan and Phoebe Northcross in Remedies and Damages for Violations of Constitutional Rights, 18 Duq. L. Rev. 409, 422–33 (1980), in which the *Paul v. Davis* Court's blanket removal of reputation from protected liberty interests is criticized as "unwise and short-sighted."

In a similar vein, Robert Jerome Glennon has argued for a narrow construction of *Paul* and related cases in order to preserve a minimum federal content for the "liberty" and "property" interests protected by due process of law. In Glennon's view, it is critical that the content of those terms not be limited to interests as defined by state law. Instead, state law definitions of "liberty" and "property" should be treated as federal common law, adopted by the federal courts to enforce federal rights and therefore subject to minimum federal standards. See Glennon, Constitutional Liberty and Property: Federal Common Law and § 1983, 51 S. Cal. L. Rev. 355 (1978) (also examining the role of § 1983 in enforcing due process rights).

Other commentators have focused on how one might articulate a persuasive basis for limiting the intrusion of federal civil rights actions into state tort law. Efforts in this direction have been of two sorts. Some have suggested limits on the availability of remedies under § 1983. Others have focused directly on the content of the rights guaranteed by the 14th amendment.

Illustrative of the former approach is Monaghan, Of "Liberty" and "Property," 62 Corn. L. Rev. 405 (1977). Monaghan identified *Paul v. Davis* and other restrictive due process decisions as responses to the "staggering array of complaints" brought under § 1983. "Rightly or wrongly," he observed, "a majority of the present Court is struggling to place limits on the federal superintendence of the operations of state and local government, a struggle which has occurred largely in the context of '§ 1983' actions." In Monaghan's view, that effort was "understandable, if not acceptable," but the Court erred in addressing the problem by narrowing the scope of procedural due process. Instead, he speculated, perhaps it would have been better to read § 1983 "less than literally . . . so as not to embrace all the interests encompassed by the 'liberty' (and 'property') of the due process clause." This suggestion was echoed by Gerald Gunther, who noted that "a limiting statutory interpretation [of § 1983] would have made the Court's extensive discussion of constitutionally protected liberty interests unnecessary." G. Gunther, Cases and Materials on Constitutional Law 581 (11th ed. 1985).

What kind of limiting statutory construction did Monaghan and Gunther have in mind? One possibility was suggested by Melvyn Durchslag in Federalism and Constitutional Liberties: Varying the Remedy to Save the Right, 54 N.Y.U.L. 723, 734–48 (1979). Durchslag argued that the federalism concern vindicated in *Paul v. Davis* should have been handled through an elaboration of official immunity under § 1983 rather than by redefinition of the underlying constitutional right.

A substantive approach to the content of 14th amendment rights was taken by Rodney Smolla in The Displacement of Federal Due Process Claims by State Tort Remedies: *Parratt v. Taylor* and *Logan v. Zimmerman Brush Co.,* 1982 U. Ill. L. Rev. 831. Smolla argued that the *Parratt* Court's concern for the adequacy of state-law remedies is an essentially sound interpretation of procedural due process and justifies the result, though not the opinion, in *Paul v. Davis.* According to Smolla, "[t]he critics of *Paul v. Davis* have never explained satisfactorily how a § 1983 action is in any substantive law sense an improvement on the law of libel." The state's provision of an adequate post-deprivation remedy, therefore, satisfies due process, and leaves the injured plaintiff with no federal claim to pursue.

Finally, still another approach was explored by Michael Wells and Thomas Eaton in Substantive Due Process and the Scope of Constitutional Torts, 18 Ga. L. Rev. 201 (1984). They suggested that both *Parratt v. Taylor* and *Paul v. Davis* may have been correctly decided, but on an analysis very different from that advanced in the Court's opinions. Specifically, they argued that these cases should not have been treated as procedural due process claims but as questions of substantive due process. All such cases turn on a basic substantive issue: "Within the universe of state actions that harm individuals, which of those actions should the Court proscribe as deprivations of constitutionally protected life, liberty, or property, and which should be left for the states to grant or deny remedies for at their discretion?" The decisive factor in determining the reach of the constitutional tort, they suggested, is not whether the plaintiff was harmed, but rather "whether the defendant's conduct has passed the boundary of acceptable governmental behavior toward individuals." If not, then the individual injured by government conduct should be remitted to whatever remedies may be provided by state law, including, where state sovereign immunity applies, no remedy at all.

Of these several suggestions for reinterpreting *Paul v. Davis,* which seems the most promising? Is the decision wholly wrong, or does it address a genuine problem? And if the latter, is that problem better addressed by some sort of limiting construction of § 1983, or by a restrictive formulation of the underlying right, or by an extension of official immunity?

MAINE v. THIBOUTOT

Supreme Court of the United States, 1980.
448 U.S. 1.

MR. JUSTICE BRENNAN delivered the opinion of the Court.

This case presents two related questions arising under 42 U.S.C. §§ 1983 and 1988. Respondents brought this suit in the Maine Superior Court alleging that petitioners, the state of Maine and its Commissioner of Human Services, violated § 1983 by depriving respondents of welfare benefits to which they were entitled under the federal Social Security Act, specifically 42 U.S.C. § 602(a)(7). The petitioners present two issues: (1) whether § 1983 encompasses claims based on purely statutory violations of federal law, and (2) if so, whether attorney's fees under § 1988 may be awarded to the prevailing party in such an action.[1]

I

Respondents, Lionel and Joline Thiboutot, are married and have eight children, three of whom are Lionel's by a previous marriage. The Maine Department of Human Services notified Lionel that, in computing the aid to families with dependent children (AFDC) benefits to which he was entitled for the three children exclusively his, it would no longer make allowance for the money spent to support the other five children, even though Lionel is legally obligated to support them. Respondents, challenging the state's interpretation of 42 U.S.C. § 602(a)(7), exhausted their state administrative remedies and then sought judicial review of the administrative action in the state Superior Court. By amended complaint, respondents also claimed relief under § 1983 for themselves and others similarly situated. The Superior Court's judgment enjoined petitioners from enforcing the challenged rule and ordered them to adopt new regulations, to notify class members of the new regulations, and to pay the correct amounts retroactively to eligible class members.[2] The court, however, denied respondents' motion for attorney's fees. The Supreme Judicial Court of Maine concluded that respondents had no entitlement to attorney's fees under state law, but were eligible for attorney's fees pursuant to the Civil Rights Attorney's Fees Awards Act of 1976. We granted certiorari. We affirm.

---

[1] Petitioners also argue that jurisdiction to hear § 1983 claims rests exclusively with the federal courts. Any doubt that state courts may also entertain such actions was dispelled by Martinez v. California, 444 U.S. 277, 283–84 n.7 (1980). There, while reserving the question whether state courts are *obligated* to entertain § 1983 actions, we held that Congress has not barred them from doing so.

[2] The state did not appeal the judgment against it.

II

Section 1983 provides:

"Every person who, under color of any statute, ordinance, regulation, custom, or usage, of any state or territory, subjects, or causes to be subjected, any citizen of the United States or other person within the jurisdiction thereof to the deprivation of any rights, privileges, or immunities secured by the Constitution *and laws,* shall be liable to the party injured in an action at law, suit in equity, or other proper proceeding for redress." (Emphasis added.)

The question before us is whether the phrase "and laws," as used in § 1983, means what it says, or whether it should be limited to some subset of laws. Given that Congress attached no modifiers to the phrase, the plain language of the statute undoubtedly embraces respondents' claim that petitioners violated the Social Security Act.

Even were the language ambiguous, however, any doubt as to its meaning has been resolved by our several cases suggesting, explicitly or implicitly, that the § 1983 remedy broadly encompasses violations of federal statutory as well as constitutional law. Rosado v. Wyman, 397 U.S. 397 (1970), for example, "held that suits in federal court under § 1983 are proper to secure compliance with the provisions of the Social Security Act on the part of participating states." Edelman v. Jordan, 415 U.S. 651, 675 (1974). Monell v. New York City Dept. of Social Services, 436 U.S. 658 (1978), as support for its conclusion that municipalities are "persons" under § 1983, reasoned that "there can be no doubt that § 1 of the Civil Rights Act [of 1871] was intended to provide a remedy, to be broadly construed, against all forms of official violation of federally protected rights." Similarly, Owen v. City of Independence, 445 U.S. 622 (1980), in holding that the common-law immunity for discretionary functions provided no basis for according municipalities a good-faith immunity under § 1983, noted that a court "looks only to whether the municipality has conformed to the requirements of the federal Constitution and statutes." . . . Greenwood v. Peacock, 384 U.S. 808, 829–30 (1966), observed that under § 1983 state "officers may be made to respond in damages not only for violations of rights conferred by federal equal civil rights laws, but for violations of other federal constitutional and statutory rights as well." . . .

While some might dismiss as dictum the foregoing statements, numerous and specific as they are, our analysis in several § 1983 cases involving Social Security Act claims has relied on the availability of a § 1983 cause of action for statutory claims. Constitutional claims were also raised in these cases, providing a jurisdictional base, but the statutory claims were allowed to go forward, and were decided on the merits, under the court's pendent jurisdiction. In each of the following cases § 1983 was necessarily the exclusive statutory cause of action because, as the Court held in *Edelman v. Jordan,* the Social Security

Act affords no private right of action against a state. [Citations omitted.]

In the face of the plain language of § 1983 and our consistent treatment of that provision, petitioners nevertheless persist in suggesting that the phrase "and laws" should be read as limited to civil rights or equal protection laws. Petitioners suggest that when § 1 of the Civil Rights Act of 1871, which accorded jurisdiction and a remedy for deprivations of rights secured by "the Constitution of the United States" was divided by the 1874 statutory revision into a remedial section, Rev. Stat. § 1979, and jurisdictional sections, Rev. Stat. §§ 563(12) and 629(16), Congress intended that the same change made in § 629(16) be made as to each of the new sections as well. Section 629(16), the jurisdictional provision for the circuit courts and the model for the current jurisdictional provision, 28 U.S.C. § 1343(3), applied to the deprivation of rights secured by "the Constitution of the United States, or of any right secured by any law providing for equal rights." On the other hand, the remedial provision, the predecessor of § 1983, was expanded to apply to deprivations of rights secured by "the Constitution and laws" and § 563(12), the provision granting jurisdiction to the district courts, to deprivations of rights secured by "the Constitution of the United States, or of any right secured by any law of the United States."

We need not repeat at length the detailed debate over the meaning of the scanty legislative history concerning the addition of the phrase "and laws." See Chapman v. Houston Welfare Rights Org., 441 U.S. 600 (1979). One conclusion which emerges clearly is that the legislative history does not permit a definitive answer. There is no express explanation offered for the insertion of the phrase "and laws." On the one hand, a principal purpose of the added language was to "ensure that federal legislation providing specifically for equality of rights would be brought within the ambit of the civil action authorized by that statute." Id. at 637 (Powell, J., concurring). On the other hand, there are no indications that that was the only purpose, and Congress' attention was specifically directed to this new language. Representative Lawrence, in a speech to the House of Representatives that began by observing that the revisers had very often changed the meaning of existing statutes, referred to the civil rights statutes as "possibly [showing] verbal modifications bordering on legislation." He went on to read to Congress the original and revised versions. In short, Congress was aware of what it was doing, and the legislative history does not demonstrate that the plain language was not intended.[5] Petition-

---

[5] In his concurring opinion in Chapman v. Houston Welfare Rights Org., 441 U.S. 600 (1979), Mr. Justice Powell's argument proceeds on the basis of the flawed premise that Congress did not intend to change the meaning of existing laws when it revised the statutes in 1874. He assumed that Congress had instructed the revisers not to make changes, and that the revisers had obeyed those instructions. In fact, the sec-ond section of the statute creating the revision commission mandated that the commissioners "mak[e] such alterations as may be necessary to reconcile the contradictions, supply the omissions, and amend the imperfections of the original text." Furthermore, it is clear that Congress understood this mandate to authorize the commission to do more than merely "copy and arrange in proper order, and classify in

ers' arguments amount to the claim that had Congress been more careful, and had it fully thought out the relationships among the various sections,[6] it might have acted differently. That argument, however, can best be addressed to Congress, which, it is important to note, has remained quiet in the face of our many pronouncements on the scope of § 1983.

III

Petitioners next argue that, even if this claim is within § 1983, Congress did not intend statutory claims to be covered by the Civil Rights Attorney's Fees Awards Act of 1976, which added the following sentence to 42 U.S.C. § 1988 (emphasis added):

> "In *any action* or proceeding *to enforce* a provision of §§ 1981, 1982, 1983, 1985, and 1986 of this title . . ., the court, in its discretion, may allow the prevailing party, other than the United States, a reasonable attorney's fee as part of the costs."

Once again, given our holding in part II, supra, the plain language provides an answer. The statute states that fees are available in *any* § 1983 action. Since we hold that this statutory action is properly brought under § 1983, and since § 1988 makes no exception for statutory § 1983 actions, § 1988 plainly applies to this suit.

The legislative history is entirely consistent with the plain language. As was true with § 1983, a major purpose of the Civil Rights Attorney's Fees Act was to benefit those claiming deprivations of constitutional and civil rights. Principal sponsors of the measure in both the House and the Senate, however, explicitly stated during the floor debate that the statute would make fees available more broadly. Representative Drinan explained that the act would apply to § 1983 and that § 1983 "authorizes suits against state and local officials based upon federal statutory as well as constitutional rights. . . ." Senator Kennedy also included a Social Security Act case as an example of the cases "enforc[ing] the rights promised by Congress or the Constitution" which the act would embrace. In short, there can be no question that Congress passed the Fees Act anticipating that it would apply to statutory § 1983 claims.

Several states, participating as amicus curiae, argue that even if § 1988 applies to § 1983 claims alleging deprivations of statutory rights, it does not apply in state courts. There is no merit to this argument. [We have] held that § 1983 actions may be brought in state courts. Representative Drinan described the purpose of the Civil Rights Attorney's Fees Act as "authoriz[ing] the award of a reasonable attorney's fee in actions brought in state or federal courts." And

---

heads the actual text of statutes in force." . . .

[6] There is no inherent illogic in construing § 1983 more broadly than § 1343(3) was construed in *Chapman v. Houston Welfare Rights Org.*, supra. It would only mean that there are statutory rights which Congress has decided cannot be enforced in the federal courts unless 28 U.S.C. § 1331(a)'s $10,000 jurisdictional amount is satisfied. [The jurisdictional amount was repealed on December 1, 1980—addition to footnote by eds.]

Congress viewed the fees authorized by § 1988 as "an integral part of the remedies necessary to obtain" compliance with § 1983. It follows from this history and from the supremacy clause that the fee provision is part of the § 1983 remedy whether the action is brought in federal or state court.[12]

Affirmed.

MR. JUSTICE POWELL, with whom the CHIEF JUSTICE and MR. JUSTICE REHNQUIST join, dissenting.

The Court holds today, almost casually, that 42 U.S.C. § 1983 creates a cause of action for deprivations under color of state law of any federal statutory right. Having transformed purely statutory claims into "civil rights" actions under § 1983, the Court concludes that 42 U.S.C. § 1988 permits the "prevailing party" to recover his attorney's fees. These two holdings dramatically expand the liability of state and local officials and may virtually eliminate the "American rule" in suits against those officials.

The Court's opinion reflects little consideration of the consequences of its judgment. It relies upon the "plain" meaning of the phrase "and laws" in § 1983 and upon this Court's assertedly "consistent treatment" of that statute. But the reading adopted today is anything but "plain" when the statutory language is placed in historical context. Moreover, until today this Court never had held that § 1983 encompasses all purely statutory claims. Past treatment of the subject has been incidental and far from consistent. The only firm basis for decision is the historical evidence, which convincingly shows that the phrase the Court now finds so clear was—and remains—nothing more than a shorthand reference to equal rights legislation enacted by Congress. To read "and laws" more broadly is to ignore the lessons of history, logic, and policy. . . .

I

Section 1983 provides in relevant part that "[e]very person who, under color of [state law] subjects . . . any . . . person . . . to the deprivation of any rights, privileges, or immunities secured by the Constitution and laws, shall be liable to the party injured. . . ." The Court asserts that "the phrase 'and laws' . . . means what it says," because "Congress attached no modifiers to the phrase. . . ." Finding no "definitive" contrary indications in the legislative history of § 1983, the Court concludes that that statute provides a remedy for violations of the Social Security Act. The Court suggests that those who would read the phrase "and laws" more narrowly, should address their arguments to Congress.

---

[12] If fees were not available in state courts, federalism concerns would be raised because most plaintiffs would have no choice but to bring their complaints concerning state actions in federal courts. Moreover, given that there is a class of cases stating causes of action under § 1983 but not cognizable in federal court absent the $10,000 jurisdictional minimum of § 1331(a), some plaintiffs would be forced to go to state courts, but contrary to congressional intent, would still face financial disincentives to asserting their claimed deprivations of federal rights.

If we were forbidden to look behind the language in legislative enactments, there might be some force to the suggestion that "and laws" must be read to include all federal statutes.[1] But the "plain meaning" rule is not as inflexible as the Court imagines. . . . We have recognized consistently that statutes are to be interpreted " 'not only by a consideration of the words themselves, but by considering, as well, the context, the purposes of the law, and the circumstances under which the words were employed.' "

The rule is no different when the statute in question is derived from the civil rights legislation of the Reconstruction era. . . .

Blind reliance on plain meaning is particularly inappropriate where, as here, Congress inserted the critical language without explicit discussion when it revised the statutes in 1874. Indeed, not a single shred of evidence in the legislative history of the adoption of the 1874 revision mentions this change. Since the legislative history also shows that the revision generally was not intended to alter the meaning of existing law, this Court previously has insisted that apparent changes be scrutinized with some care. . . .

II

The origins of the phrase "and laws" in § 1983 were discussed in detail in two concurring opinions last term. Compare Chapman v. Houston Welfare Rights Org., 441 U.S. 600, 623 (Powell, J., concurring) with id. at 646 (White, J., concurring in judgment). I shall not recount the full historical evidence presented in my *Chapman* opinion. Nevertheless, the Court's abrupt dismissal of the proposition that "Congress did not intend to change the meaning of existing laws when it revised the statutes in 1874" reflects a misconception so fundamental as to require a summary of the historical record.

A

Section 1983 derives from § 1 of the Civil Rights Act of 1871, which provided a cause of action for deprivation of constitutional rights only. "Laws" were not mentioned. The phrase "and laws" was added in 1874, when Congress consolidated the laws of the United States into a single volume under a new subject-matter arrangement. Consequently, the intent of Congress in 1874 is central to this case.

In addition to creating a cause of action, § 1 of the 1871 act conferred concurrent jurisdiction upon "the district or circuit courts of the United States. . . ." In the 1874 revision, the remedial portion of § 1 was codified as § 1979 of the Revised Statutes, which provided for a

---

[1] The "plain meaning" of "and laws" may be more elusive than the Court admits. One might expect that a statute referring to all rights secured either by the Constitution or by the laws would employ the disjunctive "or." . . .

In contrast, a natural reading of the conjunctive "and" in § 1983 would require that the right at issue be secured both by the Constitution and by the laws. In 1874, this would have included the rights set out in the Civil Rights Act of 1866, which had been incorporated in the 14th amendment and re-enacted in the Civil Rights Act of 1870. . . .

cause of action in terms identical to the present § 1983. The jurisdictional portion of § 1 was divided into § 563(12), conferring district court jurisdiction, and § 629(16), conferring circuit court jurisdiction. Although §§ 1979, 563(12), and 629(16) came from the same source, each was worded differently. Section 1979 referred to deprivations of rights "secured by the Constitution and laws"; § 563(12) described rights secured "by the Constitution of the United States, or . . . by any law of the United States"; and § 629(16) encompassed rights secured "by the Constitution of the United States, or . . . by any law providing for equal rights of citizens of the United States." When Congress merged the jurisdiction of circuit and district courts in 1911, the narrower language of § 629(16) was adopted and ultimately became the present 28 U.S.C. § 1343(3).

B

In my view, the legislative history unmistakably shows that the variations in phrasing were inadvertent, and that each section was intended to have precisely the same scope. Moreover, the only defensible interpretation of the contemporaneous legislative record is that the reference to "laws" in each section was intended "to do no more than ensure that federal legislation providing specifically for equality of rights would be brought within the ambit of the civil action authorized by [§ 1979]." Careful study of the available materials leaves no serious doubt that the Court's contrary conclusion is completely at odds with the intent of Congress in 1874.

The Court holds today that the foregoing reasoning is based on a "flawed premise," because Congress instructed the revision commission to change the statutes in certain respects. But it is the Court's premise that is flawed. The revision commission, which worked for six years on the project, submitted to Congress a draft that did contain substantive changes. But a joint congressional committee, which was appointed in early 1873 to transform the draft into a bill, concluded that it would be "utterly impossible to carry the measure through, if it was understood that it contained new legislation." Therefore, the committee employed Thomas Jefferson Durant to "strike out . . . modifications of the existing law" "wherever the meaning of the law had been changed." On December 10, 1873 Durant's completed work was introduced in the House with the solemn assurance that the bill "embodies the law as it is."

The House met in a series of evening sessions to review the bill and to restore original meaning where necessary. During one of these sessions, Representative Lawrence delivered the speech upon which the Court now relies. Lawrence explained that the revisers often had separated existing statutes into substantive, remedial, and criminal sections to accord with the new organization of the statutes by topic. He read both the original and revised versions of the civil rights statutes to illustrate the arrangement, and "possibly [to] show verbal modifications bordering on legislation." After reading § 1979 without mentioning the addition of "and laws," Lawrence stated that "[a] comparison of all these will present a fair specimen of the manner in which the work has been done, and from these all can judge of the accuracy of the translation." Observing that "[t]his mode of classifying . . . to some extent duplicates in the revision portions of statutes" that previously were one, Lawrence praised "the general accuracy" of the revision. Nothing in this sequence of remarks supports the decision of the Court today. There was no mention of the addition of "and laws" nor any hint that the reach of § 1983 was to be extended. If Lawrence had any such intention, his statement to the House was a singularly disingenuous way of proposing a major piece of legislation.

In context, it is plain that Representative Lawrence did not mention changes "bordering on legislation" as a way of introducing substantive changes in § 1 of the 1871 act. Rather, he was emphasizing that the revision was not intended to modify existing statutes, and that his reading might reveal errors that should be eliminated. No doubt Congress "was aware of what it was doing." It was meeting specially in one last attempt to detect and strike out legislative changes that may have remained in the proposed revision despite the best efforts of Durant and the joint committee. No representative challenged those sections of the revised statutes that derived from § 1 of the Civil Rights Act of 1871. That silence reflected the understanding of those present that "and laws" did not alter the original meaning of the statute.[6] The members of Congress who participated in the year long effort to expunge all substantive alterations from the revised statutes evince no intent whatever to enact a far-reaching modification of § 1 of the Civil Rights Act of 1871. The relevant evidence, largely ignored by the Court today, shows that Congress painstakingly sought to avoid just such changes.

III

The legislative history alone refutes the Court's assertion that the 43rd Congress intended to alter the meaning of § 1983. But there are other compelling reasons to reject the Court's interpretation of the phrase "and laws." First, by reading those words to encompass every federal enactment, the Court extends § 1983 beyond the reach of its jurisdictional counterpart. Second, that reading creates a broad program for enforcing federal legislation that departs significantly from the purposes of § 1983. Such unexpected and plainly unintended consequences should be avoided whenever a statute reasonably may be given an interpretation that is consistent with the legislative purpose.

A

The Court acknowledges that its construction of § 1983 creates federal "civil rights" for which 28 U.S.C. § 1343(3) supplies no federal

---

[6] The addition of "and laws" did not change the meaning of § 1 because Congress assumed that that phrase referred only to federal equal rights legislation. In 1874, the only such legislation was contained in the 1866 and 1870 Civil Rights Acts, which conferred rights also secured by the recently adopted 14th amendment.

jurisdiction. The Court finds no "inherent illogic" in this view. But the gap in the Court's logic is wide indeed in light of the history and purpose of the civil rights legislation we consider today. Sections 1983 and 1343(3) derive from the same section of the same act. As originally enacted the two sections were necessarily coextensive. And this Court has emphasized repeatedly that the right to a federal forum in every case was viewed as a crucial ingredient in the federal remedy afforded by § 1983. . . . Since § 1343(3) covers statutory claims only when they arise under laws providing for the equal rights of citizens, the same limitation necessarily is implicit in § 1983. The Court's decision to apply that statute without regard to the scope of its jurisdictional counterpart is at war with the plainly expressed intent of Congress.

B

The Court's opinion does not consider the nature or scope of the litigation it has authorized. In practical effect, today's decision means that state and local governments, officers, and employees now face liability whenever a person believes he has been injured by the administration of *any* federal-state cooperative program, whether or not that program is related to equal or civil rights. . . .

Even a cursory survey of the United States code reveals that literally hundreds of cooperative regulatory and social welfare enactments may be affected. The states now participate in the enforcement of federal laws governing migrant labor, noxious weeds, historic preservation, wildlife conservation, anadromous fisheries, scenic trails, and strip mining. Various statutes authorize federal-state cooperative agreements in most aspects of federal land management. In addition, federal grants administered by state and local governments now are available in virtually every area of public administration. Unemployment, Medicaid, school lunch subsidies, food stamps, and other welfare benefits may provide particularly inviting subjects of litigation. Federal assistance also includes a variety of subsidies for education, housing, health care, transportation, public works, and law enforcement. Those who might benefit from these grants now will be potential § 1983 plaintiffs.

No one can predict the extent to which litigation arising from today's decision will harass state and local officials; nor can one foresee the number of new filings in our already overburdened courts. But no one can doubt that these consequences will be substantial. And the Court advances no reason to believe that any Congress—from 1874 to the present day—intended this expansion of federally imposed liability on state defendants.

Moreover, state and local governments will bear the entire burden of liability for violations of statutory "civil rights" even when federal officials are involved equally in the administration of the affected program. Section 1983 grants no right of action against the United States, and few of the foregoing cooperative programs provide expressly for private actions to enforce their terms. Thus, private litigants may sue responsible federal officials only in the relatively rare case in which a cause of action may be implied from the governing substantive statute. Cf. Transamerica Mtg. Advisors v. Lewis, 444 U.S. 11 (1979); Touche Ross & Co. v. Redington, 442 U.S. 560 (1979). It defies reason to believe that Congress intended—without discussion—to impose such a burden only upon state defendants.

Even when a cause of action against federal officials is available, litigants are likely to focus efforts upon state defendants in order to obtain attorney's fees under the liberal standard of 42 U.S.C. § 1988. There is some evidence that § 1983 claims already are being appended to complaints solely for the purpose of obtaining fees in actions where "civil rights" of any kind are at best an afterthought. . . .

IV

The Court finally insists that its interpretation of § 1983 is foreordained by a line of precedent so strong that further analysis is unnecessary. It is true that suits against state officials alleging violations of the Social Security Act have become commonplace in the last decade. The instant action follows that pattern. Thus, the Court implies, today's decision is a largely inconsequential reaffirmation of a statutory interpretation that has been settled authoritatively for many years.

This is a tempting way to avoid confronting the serious issues presented by this case. But the attempt does not withstand analysis. Far from being a long-accepted fact, purely statutory § 1983 actions are an invention of the last 20 years. And the Court's seesaw approach to § 1983 over the last century leaves little room for certainty on any question that has not been discussed fully and resolved explicitly by this Court. Yet, until last term, neither this Court nor any justice ever had undertaken—directly and thoroughly—a consideration of the question presented in this case. . . .

The issue did not arise with any frequency until the late 1960's, when challenges to state administration of federal social welfare legislation became commonplace. The lower courts responded to these suits with conflicting conclusions. Some found § 1983 applicable to all federal statutory claims. Others refused to apply it to statutory rights. Yet others believed that § 1983 covered some but not all rights derived from nonconstitutional sources. Numerous scholarly comments discussed the possible solutions, without reaching a consensus. . . .

The Court quotes the statement in Edelman v. Jordan, 415 U.S. 651, 675 (1974), that Rosado v. Wyman, 397 U.S. 397 (1970), " 'held that suits in federal court under § 1983 are proper to secure compliance with the provisions of the Social Security Act on the part of participating states.' " If that statement were true, the confusion remaining after Rosado is simply inexplicable. In fact, of course, Rosado established no such proposition of law. The plaintiffs in that case challenged a state welfare provision on constitutional grounds premising jurisdiction upon § 1343(3), and added a pendent statutory claim. This Court held first that the District Court retained its power to adjudicate the statutory claim even after the constitutional claim, on which § 1343(3) jurisdiction was based, became moot. The opinion then considered the merits of the plaintiffs' argument that New York law did not comport with the Social Security Act. Although the Court had to assume the existence of a private right of action to enforce that act, the opinion did not discuss or purport to decide whether § 1983 applies to statutory claims.

Rosado is not the only case to have assumed sub silentio that welfare claimants have a cause of action to challenge the adequacy of state programs under the Social Security Act. As the Court observes, many of our recent decisions construing the act made the same unspoken assumption. It does not necessarily follow that the Court in those cases assumed that the cause of action was provided by § 1983 rather than the Social Security Act itself. But even if it did, these cases provide no support for the Court's ruling today. "[W]hen questions of jurisdiction have been passed on in prior decisions sub silentio, this Court has never considered itself bound when a subsequent case finally brings the jurisdictional issue before us." Hagans v. Lavine, 415 U.S. 528, 535 n.5 (1974). This rule applies with even greater force to questions involving the availability of a cause of action, because the question whether a cause of action exists—unlike the existence of federal jurisdiction—may be assumed without being decided. Thus, the Court's ruling finds no support in past cases in which the issue was not squarely raised. . . .

The Court also relies upon "numerous and specific" dicta in prior decisions. But none of the cited cases contains anything more than a bare assertion of the proposition that is to be proved. Most say much less than that. For example, the Court occasionally has referred to § 1983 as a remedy for violations of "federally protected rights" or of "the federal Constitution and statutes," Monell v. New York City Dept. of Social Services, 436 U.S. 658, 700–01 (1978); Owen v. City of Independence, 445 U.S. 622, 649, 650 (1980). These generalized references merely restate the language of the statute. They shed no light on the question whether all or only some statutory rights are protected. To the extent they have any relevance to the issue at hand, they could be countered by the frequent occasions on which the Court has referred to § 1983 as a remedy for constitutional violations without mentioning statutes. But the debate would be meaningless, for none of these off-hand remarks provides the remotest support for the positions taken in this case.

The only remaining decision in the Court's "consistent" line of precedents are Greenwood v. Peacock, 384 U.S. 808, 829–30 (1966), and Edelman v. Jordan, 415 U.S. 651, 675 (1974). In each case, the Court asserted—without discussion and in the course of disposing of other issues—that § 1983's coverage of statutory rights extended beyond federal equal rights laws. Neither contains any discussion of the question; neither cites relevant authority. Nor has this Court always uncritically assumed the proposition for which *Greenwood* and *Edelman* now are said to stand. On the same day the Court decided *Edelman*, it refused to express a view on the question whether § 1983 creates a cause of action for purely statutory claims. Hagans v. Lavine, 415 U.S. 528, 534 n.5 (1974). The point was reserved again in Southeastern Community College v. Davis, 442 U.S. 397, 404–05 n.5 (1979).

To rest a landmark decision of this Court on two statements made in dictum without critical examination would be extraordinary in any case. In the context of § 1983, it is unprecedented. Our decisions construing the civil rights legislation of the Reconstruction era have repudiated "blind adherence to the principle of stare decisis. . . ." As Mr. Justice Frankfurter once observed, the issues raised under § 1983 concern "a basic problem of American federalism" that "has significance approximating constitutional dimension." *Monroe v. Pape,* supra, at 222 (dissenting opinion). Although Mr. Justice Frankfurter's view did not prevail in *Monroe,* we have heeded consistently his admonition that the ordinary concerns of stare decisis apply less forcefully in this than in other areas of the law. E.g., *Monell v. New York City Dept. of Social Services,* supra. Against this backdrop, there is no justification for the Court's reliance on unexamined dicta as the principal support for a major extension of liability under § 1983.

V

In my view, the Court's decision today significantly expands the concept of "civil rights" and creates a major new intrusion into state sovereignty under our federal system. There is no probative evidence that Congress intended to authorize the pervasive judicial oversight of state officials that will flow from the Court's construction of § 1983. Although today's decision makes new law with far-reaching consequences, the Court brushes aside the critical issues of congressional intent, national policy, and the force of past decisions as precedent. I would reverse the judgment of the Supreme Judicial Court of Maine.

NOTES ON NON–CONSTITUTIONAL RIGHTS ENFORCEABLE UNDER § 1983

1. *Chapman v. Houston Welfare Rights Org.* As the *Thiboutot* opinions mention, the issue before the Court was first extensively discussed in Chapman v. Houston Welfare Rights Org., 441 U.S. 600 (1979). That case involved challenges to state welfare regulations on the ground that they violated the Social Security Act. The question was whether federal courts had jurisdiction over such claims under the jurisdictional counterpart to § 1983, 28 U.S.C. § 1343(3). Section 1343(3) confers subject matter jurisdiction on federal district courts over actions to redress the deprivation under color of law "of any right, privilege or immunity secured by the Constitution of the United States or by any act of Congress *providing for equal rights* of citizens or of all persons within the jurisdiction of the United States." (Emphasis added.)

The Court held that this statute did not include claims of incompatibility between state welfare regulations and the Social Security Act.[a]

The Court's opinion was written by Justice Stevens, who was joined by Chief Justice Burger, and Justices Blackmun, Powell, and Rehnquist. The majority considered and rejected three theories for bringing such claims within the coverage of § 1343(3). First, the Court held that "secured by the Constitution," as these words are used in § 1343(3), did not include rights secured by the supremacy clause of article VI. To hold otherwise would go too far, for every federal right, whether created by treaty, statute, or regulation, is "secured" against state interference by the supremacy clause. If rights "secured" by the supremacy clause qualified, every conceivable federal claim against a state agent would be "secured by the Constitution" within the meaning of § 1343(3) and the additional language providing for jurisdiction over claims "secured . . . by any act of Congress providing for equal rights" would be rendered superfluous and without meaning.

Second, the Court rejected the argument that § 1343(3) should be read as congruent with the broader "and laws" language of § 1983, either directly or by treating § 1983 as a law "providing for equal rights" within the meaning of § 1343(3). The Court found it unnecessary to decide whether the two statutes covered the same behavior, but concluded that the limiting language in § 1343(3) could in any event not be ignored. Additionally, the Court noted that § 1983 does not secure any rights, equal or otherwise, but merely provides a cause of action for rights secured elsewhere. Third and finally, the Court held that the Social Security Act was not itself a law "providing for equal rights" within the meaning of § 1343(3).

Justice Stewart dissented in an opinion joined by Justices Brennan and Marshall. He argued that § 1983 was in fact an "act of Congress providing for equal rights" and therefore that § 1343(3) created federal jurisdiction for every claim brought under § 1983. Stewart pointed to *Rosado v. Wyman* and other cases treating § 1983 as the source of a cause of action to enforce the Social Security Act and rejected as anomalous the "conclusion that Congress intended § 1983 to create some causes of action which could not be heard in a federal court under § 1343(3)." That conclusion would be contrary to the Court's understanding that "the common origin of §§ 1983 and 1343(3) in § 1 of the 1871 Act suggests that the two provisions were meant to be, and are, complementary." The correct result, therefore, would be to bring the two provisions into alignment by reading § 1983 as a law "providing for equal rights" under § 1343(3):

> "The Court's reasoning to the contrary seems to rely solely on the fact that § 1983 does not create any rights. Section 1343(3) does not require, however, that the act create rights.

---

[a] The Court also found no jurisdiction under 28 U.S.C. § 1343(4), a provision which originated in the Civil Rights Act of 1957 and which gives the district courts jurisdiction over actions to enforce "any act of Congress providing for the protection of civil rights, including the right to vote." Because of its different origin, the meaning of § 1343(4) has no relevance to the interpretation of § 1983.

Nor does it require that the act 'provide' them. It refers to any act of Congress that provides 'for' equal rights. Section 1983 provides for rights when it creates a cause of action for deprivation of those rights under color of state law. It is, therefore, one of the statutes for which § 1343(3), by its terms, confers jurisdiction upon the federal district courts."

By far the most elaborate opinions in *Chapman* were the concurrences of Justices Powell and White. Powell, who was joined by Chief Justice Burger and Justice Rehnquist, wrote separately to say that §§ 1983 and 1343(3) should be read as having the same scope and that the better interpretation would be to limit § 1983 to the reach of its jurisdictional counterpart. Powell supported this claim by an extensive review of the legislative history, the highlights of which are restated in his *Thiboutot* dissent.

Justice White concurred in the result. He wrote separately to address the issue avoided by the majority and concluded that §§ 1983 and 1343(3) were in fact not coextensive. White began by saying that the majority's construction of § 1343(3) was "compelled" by the "plain terms of that statute and the absence of any overriding indication in the legislative history that these plain terms should be ignored." At the same time, White found nothing in the history of § 1983 indicating that its equally "plain terms" should not also be given effect. White argued that the history of revision and recodification of various civil rights statutes yielded so many "ambiguities, contradictions, and uncertainties" that there was "no satisfactory basis" for overriding the literal terms of these laws. He concluded, therefore, that §§ 1983 and 1343(3) "cannot be read as though they were but one statute," but that each should be accorded the meaning indicated by its language. Ironically, although Justice White was alone in finding that §§ 1983 and 1343(3) could be read independently, it was his position that ultimately prevailed in *Thiboutot*.

2. **Questions and Comments on *Maine v. Thiboutot*.** Compare with *Thiboutot* the Court's recent decisions "implying" private rights of action from federal regulatory statutes, considered at pages 365–89, supra. On the one hand, the Court has become increasingly restrictive of attempts to read into federal statutes remedies that they do not expressly provide. See, e.g., Touche Ross & Co. v. Redington, 442 U.S. 560 (1979) (refusing to allow private suits to enforce the record and reporting requirements imposed on broker-dealers by § 17(a) of the Securities Exchange Act of 1934); Transamerica Mtg. Advisors, Inc. v. Lewis, 444 U.S. 11 (1979) (finding no implied private right of action for a client defrauded by acts in violation of the Investment Advisors Act of 1940). By contrast, *Thiboutot* reads § 1983 to provide a comprehensive private right of action for all violations of federal law by state and local officials. Are these developments reconcilable?

The potential reach of *Thiboutot* is suggested by an appendix to the dissenting opinion of Justice Powell. The appendix lists a number of federal statutes that do not provide for private enforcement but that typically will involve state and local officials in their administration. The examples fall into three broad categories: (1) joint federal-state regulatory programs—e.g., the Historic Sites, Buildings, and Antiquities Act, the Fish and Wildlife Coordination Act, and the Surface Mining Control and Reclamation Act; (2) resource management programs administered cooperatively by federal and state agencies—e.g., laws involving the administration of national parks and forest lands, the construction and management of water projects, and oil leasing; and (3) federal grant programs that either subsidize state or local activities or provide matching funds for state and local programs that meet federal standards.

Of these categories, the last is probably the most important. It includes not only the welfare, unemployment, and medical assistance programs administered under the Social Security Act, but also grant programs under the Food Stamp Act, the Small Business Investment Act, the National School Lunch Act, the Public Works and Economic Development Act, the Energy Conservation and Production Act, the Developmentally Disabled Assistance and Bill of Rights Act, and the Urban Mass Transportation Act, among others. These statutes typically provide only for enforcement by federal agencies, but *Thiboutot* says that they may also be enforced by private damage actions under § 1983. The potential significance is hard to overstate. As noted in Cappalli, Federal Grants and the New Statutory Tort: State and Local Officials Beware!, 12 Urb. Law. 445, 446 (1980):

> "[W]hen state and local officials act (and many hospital, university, and nonprofit organization officials), the likelihood of finding an applicable federal standard of conduct is great. The officials are involved in a program activity which is aided by the federal government. The aid carries a series of standards imposed by the grant statute and its implementing regulations. While these standards are usually expressed at a high level of generality, they are readily usable in evaluating the 'legality' of the officials' conduct in a wide variety of circumstances."

The enforcement of grant-in-aid standards by private damage actions raises a number of potential problems. See generally Sunstein, Section 1983 and the Private Enforcement of Federal Law, 49 U. Chi. L. Rev. 394, 416–18 (1982). In some instances, Congress may have intended that the specified enforcement mechanism be exclusive. The addition of a private right of action may lead to over-enforcement of the federal standards. In some cases, the provision of a judicial remedy may invade agency specialization in the elaboration of statutory standards. Judicial enforcement, which tends to be decentralized and which depends on the agenda of private litigants, may also impair an agency's ability to devise a consistent and coordinated policy of enforcement. And finally, judicial supervision may diminish the political accountability of those who administer federal programs.

For all of these reasons, judicial enforcement of federal statutes under § 1983 may provide needed judicial oversight of state compliance with federal statutes, but may in other instances be disruptive of federal regulatory objectives. The question therefore arises whether and to what extent the courts will attempt to integrate *Thiboutot*'s recognition of a comprehensive private right of action with the enforcement structures and underlying policies of the particular statutory scheme being enforced. The Supreme Court's initial reactions to such issues are revealed in the cases that follow.

3. *Pennhurst State School.* Pennhurst State School and Hospital v. Halderman, 451 U.S. 1 (1981), involved a class action brought to challenge the administration of a state-run hospital for the mentally retarded. Among the many issues involved in that case was whether a private cause of action could be asserted to enforce certain provisions of the Developmentally Disabled Assistance and Bill of Rights Act. These provisions required assurances of compliance with federal standards as a condition of federal funding. The Supreme Court ultimately decided to remand for further consideration of the private-right-of-action issue. Speaking through Justice Rehnquist, the Court ventured the following comment on the relevance of *Maine v. Thiboutot*:

> "[I]t must be determined whether respondents have a private cause of action to compel state compliance with those conditions. In legislation enacted pursuant to the spending power, the typical remedy for state noncompliance with federally imposed conditions is not a private cause of action for noncompliance but rather action by the federal government to terminate funds to the state. Just last term, however, in *Maine v. Thiboutot,* we held that 42 U.S.C. § 1983 provides a cause of action for state deprivations of 'rights secured' by 'the laws' of the United States. Whether *Thiboutot* controls this case depends on two factors. First, respondents here, unlike the plaintiff in *Thiboutot* who alleged that state law prevented him from receiving federal funds to which he was entitled, can only claim that the state plan has not provided adequate 'assurances' to the Secretary [of Health and Human Services]. It is at least an open question whether an individual's interest in having a state program provide those 'assurances' is a 'right secured' by the laws of the United States within the meaning of 1983. Second, Justice Powell in dissent in *Thiboutot* suggested that § 1983 would not be available where the 'governing statute provides an exclusive remedy for violations of its terms.' It is unclear whether the express remedy contained in this act is exclusive."

The suggestion of Rehnquist's second factor is that the express provision for termination of federal funding—a remedy attached to virtually all grant programs—might be preclusive of private enforcement, whether under an implied right of action or under § 1983.[b]

---

[b] This implication proved unsettling to Justice Blackmun, who joined the Court's conclusion on the merits, but disassociated himself from the majority's "negative attitude" toward private enforcement.

Justice White, in a dissent joined by Justices Brennan and Marshall, offered his own appraisal of the appropriate integration of § 1983 with more specific statutory remedies. "In essence," said White, "*Thiboutot* creates a presumption that a federal statute creating federal rights may be enforced in a § 1983 action." It is true that "Congress may explicitly direct otherwise," but as a general matter, "the fact that a federal administrative agency has the power to oversee a cooperative state-federal venture does not mean that Congress intended such oversight to be the exclusive remedy for enforcing statutory rights." Since there was no express indication that Congress intended defunding to be the exclusive remedy for violations of the act, White concluded, private enforcement should be available under § 1983.

4. *National Sea Clammers.* The Court returned to the implications of *Thiboutot* in Middlesex County Sewerage Authority v. National Sea Clammers Association, 453 U.S. 1 (1981). In that case an organization of commercial fisherman brought suit against various governmental authorities to stop the discharge of sewage and other pollutants into New York Harbor and the Hudson River. The plaintiffs sought injunctive and declaratory relief, as well as damages. Among other grounds, the plaintiffs alleged that the pollution violated the Federal Water Pollution Control Act and the Marine Protection, Research, and Sanctuaries Act. Both statutes authorize "citizen suits," but only after 60-days notice to both federal and state authorities and to the alleged violators. Additionally, the statutes authorize only prospective relief.

Plaintiffs failed to give the required notice, and the District Court entered summary judgment on that ground. The Court of Appeals reversed on the theory that the statutorily authorized "citizen suits" were not the only causes of action available to these plaintiffs. The court emphasized that both statutes have "savings clauses" that preserve "any right which any person (or class of persons) may have under any statute or common law." The Court of Appeals reasoned that the savings clauses preserved implied rights of action that were not burdened by procedural requirements.

The Supreme Court reversed. Speaking through Justice Powell, the Court reiterated that the implied right of action inquiry turns on legislative intent and concluded that the legislative provision of "unusually elaborate enforcement mechanisms," including citizen suits for injunctive relief, precluded any finding of implied authorization of additional judicial remedies. The Court then turned to the question whether an "*express* congressional authorization of private suits under these acts" might be found in § 1983. The analysis of this issue closely tracked the earlier rejection of implied rights of action:

"When the remedial devices provided in a particular act are sufficiently comprehensive, they may suffice to demonstrate congressional intent to preclude the remedy of suits under § 1983. . . . As discussed above, the Federal Water Pollution Control Act and the Marine Protection, Research, and Sanctuaries Act do provide quite comprehensive enforcement mechanisms. It is hard to believe that Congress intended to preserve the § 1983 right of action when it created so many specific statutory remedies including the two citizen-suit provisions. We therefore conclude that the existence of these express remedies demonstrates not only that Congress intended to foreclose implied private actions but also that it intended to supplant any remedy that otherwise would be available under § 1983."

Justice Stevens, joined by Justice Blackmun, dissented. Stevens agreed with the Court's refusal to find an implied right of action under these regulatory statutes, but disagreed with the conclusion that the same analysis should preclude resort to § 1983. In Stevens' view, the savings clauses and the legislative history indicated a congressional desire to preserve all otherwise available remedies, including § 1983. More fundamentally, he asserted that question was "not whether Congress 'intended to preserve the § 1983 right of action,' but rather whether Congress intended to withdraw that right of action." As he explained in a footnote, the difference between the two formulations is consequential:

"As the Court formulates the inquiry, the burden is placed on the § 1983 plaintiff to show an explicit or implicit congressional intention that violations of the substantive statute at issue be redressed in private § 1983 actions. The correct formulation, however, places the burden on the defendant to show that Congress intended to foreclose access to the § 1983 remedy as a means of enforcing the substantive statute. Because the § 1983 plaintiff is invoking an express private remedy that is, on its face, applicable any time a violation of a federal statute is alleged, see *Maine v. Thiboutot,* the burden is properly placed on the defendant to show that Congress, in enacting the particular substantive statute at issue, intended an exception to the general rule of § 1983. A defendant may carry this burden by identifying express statutory language or legislative history revealing Congress' intent to foreclose the § 1983 remedy, or by establishing that Congress intended that the remedies provided in the substantive statute itself be exclusive."

The Court responded that "contrary to Justice Steven's argument, we do not suggest that the burden is on a plaintiff to demonstrate congressional intent to preserve § 1983." No further explanation was forthcoming. In particular, the Court did not say what kind of showing would be required to establish the continuing availability of a § 1983 remedy, nor did the Court respond directly to the "presumption" approach of Justice Stevens.

5. *Wright v. City of Roanoke Redevelopment and Housing Authority.* The Court returned to the *Sea Clammers* problem in Wright v. City of Roanoke Redevelopment and Housing Authority, 479 U.S. 418 (1987). The case involved a suit by low-income tenants against their landlord, a public housing authority, alleging that they had been overbilled for their utilities and that the overbilling violated a federal rent ceiling. The question was whether the federal rent ceiling could be enforced in a § 1983 action.

Justice White's opinion for the Court began by summarizing *Pennhurst* and *Sea Clammers:*

"[These cases] recognized two exceptions to the application of § 1983 to remedy statutory violations: where Congress has foreclosed such enforcement of the statute in the enactment itself and where the statute did not create enforceable rights, privileges, or immunities within the meaning of § 1983. . . . Under these cases, if there is a state deprivation of a 'right' secured by a federal statute, § 1983 provides a remedial cause of action unless the state actor demonstrates by express provision or other specific evidence from the statute itself that Congress intended to foreclose such private enforcement. 'We do not lightly conclude that Congress intended to preclude reliance on § 1983 as a remedy' for the deprivation of a federally secured right. Smith v. Robinson, 468 U.S. 992, 1012 (1984)."

Applying this standard, the Court held that "the remedial mechanisms provided [are not] sufficiently comprehensive and effective to raise a clear inference that Congress intended to foreclose a § 1983 cause of action for the enforcement of tenants' rights secured by federal law."

Justice O'Connor, joined by Chief Justice Rehnquist and Justices Powell and Scalia, dissented. She would have held that the federal statute did not create an enforceable right to reasonable utilities and that, even if such a right could be created by agency regulations, the regulations at issue were "not susceptible of judicial enforcement."

Note the *Wright* Court's insistence on "express provision or other specific evidence from the statute itself that Congress intended to foreclose . . . private enforcement." Under that standard, very few federal statutes will be found to have foreclosed a private right of action under § 1983. Indeed, it is instructive to ask whether the statutes in *Sea Clammers* meet that test. If not, did *Wright* overrule *Sea Clammers?* Or is the issue too contextual to support generalization?

6. *Smith v. Robinson.* Smith v. Robinson, 468 U.S. 992 (1984), cited by the Court in *Wright,* raised a different problem. The case involved the right of a handicapped child to a "free appropriate public education." The plaintiffs claimed this right under four different theories: state law, a provision of the federal Education of the Handicapped Act (EHA), a provision of the federal Rehabilitation Act of 1973, and the equal protection clause of the 14th amendment. Plaintiffs prevailed on the EHA theory. That statute provides an express remedy, enforceable in federal court, for the rights it protects.

The question then was whether the plaintiffs were entitled to attorney's fees. The EHA does not authorize attorney's fees, but the

Rehabilitation Act does. Moreover, the plaintiffs had asserted their constitutional claim under § 1983, and plaintiffs who prevail in § 1983 actions, or who assert a "substantial but unaddressed" § 1983 claim and who prevail on other grounds, are entitled to attorney's fees under 42 U.S.C. § 1988.[c]

In an opinion by Justice Blackmun, the Court had "little difficulty concluding that Congress intended the EHA to be the exclusive avenue through which a plaintiff may assert an equal protection claim to a publicly financed education." Although the Court could "not lightly conclude that Congress intended to preclude reliance on § 1983 for a substantial equal protection claim, . . . § 1983 is a statutory remedy and Congress retains the authority to repeal it or replace it with an alternative remedy." The "crucial consideration" was what Congress intended, and here the Court thought Congress clearly intended to make the EHA remedy exclusive. It followed from this conclusion that attorney's fees were not available under either § 1988 or the Rehabilitation Act of 1973. Justice Brennan, joined by Justices Marshall and Stevens, dissented.

The issue in *Smith* was whether the EHA was intended by Congress to provide an exclusive mechanism for the assertion of the plaintiffs' constitutional rights and thereby to displace their ability to assert these rights under § 1983. Is there a case to be made that the standard by which to judge whether a *constitutional* right can be asserted under § 1983 should be different from the standard that should control whether a *statutory* right can be asserted? What is the significance of the *Wright* Court's reliance on *Smith?*

7. Confusion in the Lower Courts. The progression from *Thiboutot* to *Pennhurst* to *Sea Clammers* is hardly a model of clarity. On its face, *Thiboutot* appears to be a major precedent. Yet the approach suggested in *Pennhurst* and followed in *Sea Clammers* makes a significant retrenchment. Not surprisingly, the lower courts have found in these decisions very uncertain guidance. Their responses are summarized by George D. Brown in Whither *Thiboutot* ?: Section 1983, Private Enforcement, and the Damages Dilemma, 33 DePaul L. Rev. 31, 46–53 (1983).

Brown reports that relatively uniform results have been achieved where the regulatory statutes "contain explicit provision for judicial enforcement against the specific defendants before the court." In such situations, most courts follow *Sea Clammers* in concluding that § 1983 is not independently available. More difficult questions arise where the underlying statute provides a less comprehensive remedial scheme. In such cases, plaintiffs typically argue both an implied private right of action under the underlying statute and an express right of action under § 1983. The reactions of the lower courts are predictably diverse.

[c] See Maher v. Gagne, 448 U.S. 122 (1980), discussed at page 1129, infra.

Some courts appear to believe that the two inquiries are basically the same. The result of this approach is to deprive § 1983 of any independent significance. In other cases, the courts recognize a theoretical difference between the implied right and § 1983 inquiries, but resolve both by reference to the same aspects of the underlying statute.

Other courts have followed Justices White and Stevens in creating a "presumption analysis." Under this approach, the § 1983 remedy promised by *Thiboutot* is deemed presumptively available, even where analysis of the underlying statute does not support the finding of an implied right of action. As one court put it, "the court must presume a § 1983 right of action to exist unless there is evidence in the underlying statute which suggests an intent on the part of Congress to *foreclose* such an action." Ryans v. New Jersey Commission for the Blind and Visually Impaired, 542 F. Supp. 841, 848 (D.N.J. 1982) (emphasis in original).

Finally, some courts have taken a very different approach, namely that valid inference of a private cause of action from the underlying statute precludes enforcement under § 1983. An example is Ruth Anne M. v. Alvin Independent School District, 532 F. Supp. 460 (S.D. Tex. 1982), which involved § 504 of the Rehabilitation Act of 1973. That statute provides that no "otherwise qualified" handicapped individual shall "solely by reason of his handicap, be excluded from the participation in, be denied the benefits of, or be subjected to discrimination under any program or activity receiving federal financial assistance." The court's analysis of the legislative history led it to conclude that Congress must have envisioned some means of private judicial enforcement. The court limited this implied cause of action to prospective relief, however, and refused to imply a damage remedy from the federal act. It noted that damage awards would place a drain on the funds provided for the program in question and that the prospect of unpredictably large damage judgments would be a disincentive to state participation in a federal grant program under this statute. The argument that a private damage action was nevertheless available under *Thiboutot* was rejected on the ground that the implied private right of action for equitable relief precluded a damages action under § 1983. Brown commented as follows:

> "The court's conclusion with respect to the availability of § 1983 is remarkable in several respects. Analytically, it would seem that the express § 1983 cause of action takes precedence over any potential implied right to sue. Moreover, a fundamental assumption of the exclusive remedy exception to the *Thiboutot* principle is that Congress has spoken with respect to the nature and types of remedies to be available for the enforcement of a particular statute. In the § 504 context Congress had indicated nothing at all about private judicial remedies. Yet the *Ruth Anne* court was able to infer, from silence, an intent to create and also an intent to limit remedies, thereby precluding actions under § 1983. This conclusion rests on double conjecture by the court, because Congress had

addressed neither the existence of private judicial relief, nor its possible relationship to relief under § 1983. Apart from possible doubts about the validity of *Thiboutot* itself, the court was obviously swayed by the grave questions which would be raised by awarding damages for violations of conditions attached to federal grant programs. A number of other district courts have followed the example set in *Ruth Anne*, and have ruled that once an implied cause of action for injunctive relief has been found in a federal grant statute, § 1983 is inapplicable."

Which of the three approaches described above is most defensible? Does the answer depend on whether the underlying federal statute is simply a general regulatory statute or a grant provision? Or should the same approach apply across the board?

8. Commentary and Bibliography. *Thiboutot* and its progeny have prompted a good deal of comment. Most commentators follow Justices White and Stevens in suggesting that the § 1983 remedy be presumptively available, absent "clear evidence" of a congressional intent to withdraw it. See, e.g., Wartelle and Louden, Private Enforcement of Federal Statutes: The Role of the Section 1983 Remedy, 9 Hast. Con. L.Q. 487, 543 (1982). In practice, this approach would read *Thiboutot* very broadly, for it would be rare indeed to find express indication of a legislative intent to preclude enforcement under § 1983. As Cass Sunstein noted:

> "[I]n almost all cases there will be virtually no evidence of such intent. It has only been in unusual circumstances that Congress has explicitly precluded private remedies in designing a regulatory scheme. It has also been rare that the issue has been addressed in the legislative history. The question of the continued availability of § 1983 is almost invariably one to which Congress devoted little or no thought, for Congress has not as an institution generally been aware that § 1983 creates a remedy for all federal statutory violations."

Sunstein, Section 1983 and the Private Enforcement of Federal Law, 49 U. Chi. L. Rev. 394, 418 (1982).

The general availability of a private damage action under § 1983 has been defended as an appropriate implementation of the statutory language and as a good way to deter abuses, compensate victims, and ensure access to a federal forum. Additionally, *Thiboutot* has been welcomed as a means of securing extensive judicial oversight over federal grant programs. Such oversight would ensure that national policies are not defeated by unsupervised local administration. See Wartelle and Lauden, supra, at 538–40.

A radically different position is taken in Brown, Whither *Thiboutot*?: Section 1983, Private Enforcement, and the Damages Dilemma, 33 Depaul L. Rev. 31 (1983). Brown's assessment of the potentialities of *Thiboutot* is decidedly negative. As he put it, "the lesson of *Thiboutot* is that bad decisions made hard law." *Pennhurst* and *Sea Clammers* have blunted the harmful impact, but left courts and litigants with the "impossible task" of integrating those decisions. The problem, as Brown sees it, is that "the Supreme Court's decision to apply, in a cursory fashion, a plain meaning approach to an exceedingly complex area was doomed from the start." The solution, he suggests, is "to admit the mistake and start over."

An intermediate position is advanced by Cass Sunstein in Section 1983 and the Private Enforcement of Federal Law, 49 U. Chi. L. Rev. 394 (1982). Sunstein is reluctant to apply § 1983 across the board, but equally uncomfortable with the view that statutory specification of any other remedy results in repeal by implication of § 1983. The appropriate test, he suggests, is whether there is "manifest inconsistency" between the statutory enforcement scheme and a private right of action. If so, the § 1983 remedy should be precluded, notwithstanding the absence of explicit legislative intent to accomplish that result. If not, a damage action under § 1983 should be freely available.

Sunstein goes on to categorize the contexts in which such manifest inconsistency is likely to exist. Clearest of all are statutes, such as those involved in *Sea Clammers*, that create independent private causes of action against state officials. In Sunstein's view, preclusion of § 1983 in such cases is equally justified, whether the private right of action arising from the underlying statute is express or implied.

Second, preclusion of § 1983 may be indicated where the statute involves open-ended substantive standards. In such a case, Congress may be relying on agency specialization to spell out what the law requires. Further, Congress may desire that the agency's policies be subject to influence by politically accountable branches of government. In such circumstances, the courts may "seriously distort" the regulatory scheme by interpreting statutory standards in advance of agency determination. Judicial review of agency decisions does not pose the same danger, for the courts ordinarily defer to non-arbitrary agency action.

Third, preclusion of § 1983 may be justified where the federal statute demands consistency and coordination in enforcement. Only an administrative agency can develop and implement a coherent system of enforcement priorities. He argues that judicial enforcement at the behest of private litigants is inevitably decentralized and potentially disruptive. Therefore, private actions should be precluded whenever "it appears that a rational enforcement scheme requires the exercise of prosecutorial discretion."

Sunstein goes on to discuss and give examples of several other situations. These include statutes where the gravity of the authorized sanction has been calibrated by the expected level of enforcement; statutes that provide remedies against the federal government to compel state compliance with federal standards; statutes that were intended to be enforced exclusively by informal methods; and statutes protecting collective interests. The common theme is a rejection of any per se rule in favor of a judicial inquiry that is inevitably contextual and ad hoc.

Is this approach sound? Or is a categorical solution to be preferred? If so, what should it be?

9. Footnote on § 1983 Actions in State Court. Note that *Maine v. Thiboutot* involved a § 1983 action brought in state court. In footnote 1 of its opinion, the Court restated that federal jurisdiction over such actions is not exclusive. While most § 1983 actions are nevertheless brought in federal court, resort to state court is increasingly common. A thorough analysis of this development, including possible tactical advantages in the choice of state court and specific issues that may arise there, may be found in Steven H. Steinglass, The Emerging State Court § 1983 Action: A Procedural Review, 38 U. Miami L. Rev. 381 (1984).

SECTION 5: ADMINISTRATION OF THE CIVIL RIGHTS ACTS: INTERSECTIONS OF STATE AND FEDERAL LAW

INTRODUCTORY NOTE

Administration of the civil rights acts implicates a number of discrete topics. The materials that follow present three topics of particular importance and controversy. They are: the application to civil rights actions of the principles of res judicata (Subsection A); the question whether federal civil rights plaintiffs should be required to exhaust state administrative and judicial remedies (Subsection B); and the enforceability of agreements whereby a state criminal defendant agrees to release state officials from liability for alleged civil rights violations in return for dismissal of the criminal charge (Subsection C).

Several related topics might also have been considered. They include: the incorporation of state law to remedy "deficiencies" in federal law, as required by 42 U.S.C. § 1988; the choice of a statute of limitations for federal civil rights actions that carry no express limitation; and the availability of punitive damages in civil rights actions. Space constraints preclude inclusion of these topics here. Those with a special interest in these issues may wish to consult Low and Jeffries, Civil Rights Actions: Section 1983 and Related Statutes (Foundation Press, 1988), which covers these matters in some detail.

SUBSECTION A: RES JUDICATA

ALLEN v. MCCURRY
Supreme Court of the United States, 1980.
449 U.S. 90.

JUSTICE STEWART delivered the opinion of the Court.

At a hearing before his criminal trial in a Missouri court, the respondent, Willie McCurry, invoked the fourth and 14th amendments to suppress evidence that had been seized by the police. The trial court denied the suppression motion in part, and McCurry was subsequently convicted after a jury trial. The conviction was later affirmed on appeal. Because he did not assert that the state courts had denied him a "full and fair opportunity" to litigate his search and seizure claim, McCurry was barred by this Court's decision in Stone v. Powell, 428 U.S. 465 (1976), from seeking a writ of habeas corpus in a federal district court. Nevertheless, he sought federal-court redress for the alleged constitutional violation by bringing a damages suit under 42 U.S.C. § 1983 against the officers who had entered his home and seized the evidence in question. We granted certiorari to consider whether the unavailability of federal habeas corpus prevented the police officers from raising the state courts' partial rejection of McCurry's constitutional claim as a collateral estoppel defense to the § 1983 suit against them for damages.

I

In April 1977, several undercover police officers, following an informant's tip that McCurry was dealing in heroin, went to his house in St. Louis, Mo., to attempt a purchase. Two officers, petitioners Allen and Jacobsmeyer, knocked on the front door, while the other officers hid nearby. When McCurry opened the door, the two officers asked to buy some heroin "caps." McCurry went back into the house and returned soon thereafter, firing a pistol at and seriously wounding Allen and Jacobsmeyer. After a gun battle with the other officers and their reinforcements, McCurry retreated into the house; he emerged again when the police demanded that he surrender. Several officers then entered the house without a warrant, purportedly to search for other persons inside. One of the officers seized drugs and other contraband that lay in plain view, as well as additional contraband found in dresser drawers and in auto tires on the porch.

McCurry was charged with possession of heroin and assaults with intent to kill. At the pretrial suppression hearing, the trial judge excluded the evidence seized from the dresser drawers and tires, but denied suppression of the evidence found in plain view. McCurry was convicted of both the heroin and assault offenses.

McCurry subsequently filed the present § 1983 action for $1 million in damages against petitioners Allen and Jacobsmeyer, other unnamed individual police officers, and the city of St. Louis and its police department. The complaint alleged a conspiracy to violate McCurry's fourth amendment rights, an unconstitutional search and seizure of his house, and an assault on him by unknown police officers after he had been arrested and handcuffed. The petitioners moved for summary judgment. The District Court apparently understood the gist of the complaint to be the allegedly unconstitutional search and seizure and granted summary judgment, holding that collateral estoppel prevented McCurry from relitigating the search-and-seizure question already decided against him in the state courts.[2]

The Court of Appeals reversed the judgment and remanded the case for trial. The appellate court said it was not holding that collateral estoppel was generally inapplicable in a § 1983 suit raising issues determined against the federal plaintiff in a state criminal trial. But noting that *Stone v. Powell,* supra, barred McCurry from federal habeas corpus relief, and invoking "the special role of the federal courts in protecting civil rights," the court concluded that the § 1983 suit was McCurry's only route to a federal forum for his constitutional claim and directed the trial court to allow him to proceed to trial unencumbered by collateral estoppel.

II

The federal courts have traditionally adhered to the related doctrines of res judicata and collateral estoppel. Under res judicata, a final judgment on the merits of an action precludes the parties or their privies from relitigating issues that were or could have been raised in that action. Under collateral estoppel, once a court has decided an issue of fact or law necessary to its judgment, that decision may preclude relitigation of the issue in a suit on a different cause of action involving a party to the first case.[5] As this Court and other courts have

---

[2] The merits of the fourth amendment claim are discussed in the opinion of the Missouri Court of Appeals. State v. McCurry, 587 S.W.2d 337 (1979). The state courts upheld the entry of the house as a reasonable response to emergency circumstances, but held illegal the seizure of any evidence discovered as a result of that entry except what was in plain view. McCurry therefore argues here that even if the doctrine of collateral estoppel generally applies to this case, he should be able to proceed to trial to obtain damages for the part of the seizure declared illegal by the state courts. The petitioners contend, on the other hand, that the complaint alleged essentially an illegal entry, adding that only the entry could possibly justify the $1 million prayer. Since the state courts upheld the entry, the petitioners argue that if collateral estoppel applies here at all, it removes from trial all issues except the

alleged assault. The United States Court of Appeals, however, addressed only the broad question of the applicability of collateral estoppel to § 1983 suits brought by plaintiffs in McCurry's circumstances, and questions as to the scope of collateral estoppel with respect to the particular issues in this case are not now before us.

[5] The Restatement of Judgments now speaks of res judicata as "claim preclusion" and collateral estoppel as "issue preclusion." Restatement (2d) of Judgments § 74 (Tent. Draft No. 3, April 1976). Some courts and commentators use "res judicata" as generally meaning both forms of preclusion.

Contrary to a suggestion in the dissenting opinion, this case does not involve the question whether a § 1983 claimant can litigate in federal court an issue he might

often recognized, res judicata and collateral estoppel relieve parties of the cost and vexation of multiple lawsuits, conserve judicial resources, and, by preventing inconsistent decisions, encourage reliance on adjudication.

In recent years, this Court has reaffirmed the benefits of collateral estoppel in particular, finding the policies underlying it to apply in contexts not formerly recognized at common law. Thus, the Court has eliminated the requirement of mutuality in applying collateral estoppel to bar relitigation of issues decided earlier in federal-court suits, Blonder-Tongue Laboratories, Inc. v. University of Illinois Foundation, 402 U.S. 313 (1971), and has allowed a litigant who was not a party to a federal case to use collateral estoppel "offensively" in a new federal suit against the party who lost on the decided issue in the first case. Parklane Hosiery Co. v. Shore, 439 U.S. 322 (1979). But one general limitation the Court has repeatedly recognized is that the concept of collateral estoppel cannot apply when the party against whom the earlier decision is asserted did not have a "full and fair opportunity" to litigate that issue in the earlier case. Montana v. United States, 440 U.S. 147, 153 (1979).[7]

The federal courts generally have also consistently accorded preclusive effect to issues decided by state courts. Thus, res judicata and collateral estoppel not only reduce unnecessary litigation and foster reliance on adjudication, but also promote the comity between state and federal courts that has been recognized as a bulwark of the federal system. See Younger v. Harris, 401 U.S. 37, 43–45 (1971).

Indeed, though the federal courts may look to the common law or to the policies supporting res judicata and collateral estoppel in assessing the preclusive effect of decisions of other federal courts, Congress has specifically required all federal courts to give preclusive effect to state-court judgments whenever the courts of the state from which the judgments emerged would do so:

> "[J]udicial proceedings [of any court of any state] shall have the same full faith and credit in every court within the United States and its Territories and Possessions as they have by law or usage in the courts of such State. . . ." 28 U.S.C. § 1738.

It is against this background that we examine the relationship of § 1983 and collateral estoppel, and the decision of the Court of Appeals in this case.

have raised but did not raise in previous litigation.

[7] Other factors, of course, may require an exception to the normal rules of collateral estoppel in particular cases.

Contrary to the suggestion of the dissent, our decision today does not "fashion" any new, more stringent doctrine of collateral estoppel, nor does it hold that the collateral-estoppel effect of a state-court decision turns on the single factor of whether the state gave the federal claimant a full and fair opportunity to litigate a federal question. Our decision does not "fashion" any doctrine of collateral estoppel at all. Rather, it construes § 1983 to determine whether the conventional doctrine of collateral estoppel applies to the case at hand. It must be emphasized that the question whether any exceptions or qualifications within the bounds of that doctrine might ultimately defeat a collateral-estoppel defense in this case is not before us.

III

This Court has never directly decided whether the rules of res judicata and collateral estoppel are generally applicable to § 1983 actions. But in Preiser v. Rodriguez, 411 U.S. 475, 497 (1973), the Court noted with implicit approval the view of other federal courts that res judicata principles fully apply to civil rights suits brought under that statute. And the virtually unanimous view of the courts of appeals since *Preiser* has been that § 1983 presents no categorical bar to the application of res judicata and collateral estoppel concepts.[10] These federal appellate court decisions have spoken with little explanation or citation in assuming the compatibility of § 1983 and rules of preclusion, but the statute and its legislative history clearly support the courts' decisions.

Because the requirement of mutuality of estoppel was still alive in the federal courts until well into this century, the drafters of the 1871 Civil Rights Act, of which § 1983 is a part, may have had less reason to concern themselves with rules of preclusion than a modern Congress would. Nevertheless, in 1871 res judicata and collateral estoppel could certainly have applied in federal suits following state-court litigation between the same parties or their privies, and nothing in the language of § 1983 remotely expresses any congressional intent to contravene the common-law rules of preclusion or to repeal the express statutory requirements of the predecessor of 28 U.S.C. § 1738. Section 1983 creates a new federal cause of action. It says nothing about the preclusive effect of state-court judgments.[12]

Moreover, the legislative history of § 1983 does not in any clear way suggest that Congress intended to repeal or restrict the traditional doctrines of preclusion. The main goal of the act was to override the corrupting influence of the Ku Klux Klan and its sympathizers on the governments and law enforcement agencies of the southern states, see Monroe v. Pape, 365 U.S. 167, 174 (1961), and of course the debates show that one strong motive behind its enactment was grave congressional concern that the state courts had been deficient in protecting federal rights. But in the context of the legislative history as a whole, this congressional concern lends only the most equivocal support to any argument that, in cases where the state courts have recognized the constitutional claims asserted and provided fair procedures for deter-

---

[10] A very few courts have suggested that the normal rules of claim preclusion should not apply in § 1983 suits in one peculiar circumstance: Where a § 1983 plaintiff seeks to litigate in federal court a federal issue which he could have raised but did not raise in an earlier state-court suit against the same adverse party. These cases present a narrow question not now before us, and we intimate no view as to whether they were correctly decided.

[12] By contrast, the roughly contemporaneous statute extending the federal writ of habeas corpus to state prisoners expressly rendered "null and void" any state-court proceeding inconsistent with the decision of a federal habeas court, Act of Feb. 5, 1867, ch. 28 (current version at 28 U.S.C. § 2254) . . . . In any event the traditional exception to res judicata for habeas corpus review provides no analogy to § 1983 cases, since that exception finds its source in the unique purpose of habeas corpus—to release the applicant for the writ from unlawful confinement.

mining them, Congress intended to override § 1738 or the common-law rules of collateral estoppel and res judicata. Since repeals by implication are disfavored, much clearer support than this would be required to hold that § 1738 and the traditional rules of preclusion are not applicable to § 1983 suits.

As the Court has understood the history of the legislation, Congress realized that in enacting § 1983 it was altering the balance of judicial power between the state and federal courts. See Mitchum v. Foster, 407 U.S. 225, 241 (1972). But in doing so, Congress was adding to the jurisdiction of the federal courts, not subtracting from that of the state courts. See *Monroe v. Pape,* supra, at 183 ("The federal remedy is supplementary to the state remedy . . . ."). The debates contain several references to the concurrent jurisdiction of the state courts over federal questions, and numerous suggestions that the state courts would retain their established jurisdiction so that they could, when the then current political passions abated, demonstrate a new sensitivity to federal rights.

To the extent that it did intend to change the balance of power over federal questions between the state and federal courts, the 42d Congress was acting in a way thoroughly consistent with the doctrines of preclusion. In reviewing the legislative history of § 1983 in *Monroe v. Pape,* the Court inferred that Congress had intended a federal remedy in three circumstances: where state substantive law was facially unconstitutional, where state procedural law was inadequate to allow full litigation of a constitutional claim, and where state procedural law, though adequate in theory, was inadequate in practice. In short, the federal courts could step in where the state courts were unable or unwilling to protect federal rights. This understanding of § 1983 might well support an exception to res judicata and collateral estoppel where state law did not provide fair procedures for the litigation of constitutional claims, or where a state court failed to even acknowledge the existence of the constitutional principle on which a litigant based his claim. Such an exception, however, would be essentially the same as the important general limit on rules of preclusion that already exists: Collateral estoppel does not apply where the party against whom an earlier court decision is asserted did not have a full and fair opportunity to litigate the claim or issue decided by the first court. But the Court's view of § 1983 in *Monroe* lends no strength to any argument that Congress intended to allow relitigation of federal issues decided after a full and fair hearing in a state court simply because the state court's decision may have been erroneous.[17]

---

[17] The dissent suggests that the Court's decision in England v. Medical Examiners, 375 U.S. 411 (1964), demonstrates the impropriety of affording preclusive effect to the state-court decision in this case. The *England* decision is inapposite to the question before us. In the *England* case, a party first submitted to a federal court his claim that a state statute violated his constitutional rights. The federal court abstained and remitted the plaintiff to the state courts, holding that a state-court decision that the statute did not apply to the plaintiff would moot the federal question. The plaintiff submitted both the state- and federal-law questions to the state courts, which decided both questions adversely to him. This Court held that in such a circumstance, a plaintiff who properly reserved the federal issue by informing the

The Court of Appeals in this case acknowledged that every court of appeals that has squarely decided the question has held that collateral estoppel applies when § 1983 plaintiffs attempt to relitigate in federal court issues decided against them in state criminal proceedings. But the court noted that the only two federal appellate decisions invoking collateral estoppel to bar relitigation of fourth amendment claims decided adversely to the § 1983 plaintiffs in state courts came before this Court's decision in Stone v. Powell, 428 U.S. 465 (1976). It also noted that some of the decisions holding collateral estoppel applicable to § 1983 actions were based at least in part on the estopped party's access to another federal forum through habeas corpus. The Court of Appeals thus concluded that since *Stone v. Powell* had removed McCurry's right to a hearing of his fourth amendment claim in federal habeas court, collateral estoppel should not deprive him of a federal judicial hearing of that claim in a § 1983 suit.

Stone v. Powell does not provide a logical doctrinal source for the court's ruling. This Court in *Stone* assessed the costs and benefits of the judge-made exclusionary rule within the boundaries of the federal courts' statutory power to issue writs of habeas corpus, and decided that the incremental deterrent effect that the issuance of the writ in fourth amendment cases might have on police conduct did not justify the cost the writ imposed upon the fair administration of criminal justice. The *Stone* decision concerns only the prudent exercise of federal-court jurisdiction under 28 U.S.C. § 2254. It has no bearing on § 1983 suits or on the question of the preclusive effect of state-court judgments.

The actual basis of the Court of Appeals' holding appears to be a generally framed principle that every person asserting a federal right is entitled to one unencumbered opportunity to litigate that right in a federal district court, regardless of the legal posture in which the federal claim arises. But the authority for this principle is difficult to discern. It cannot lie in the Constitution, which makes no such guarantee, but leaves the scope of the jurisdiction of the federal district courts to the wisdom of Congress. And no such authority is to be found in § 1983 itself. For reasons already discussed at length, nothing in the language or legislative history of § 1983 proves any congressional intent to deny binding effect to a state-court judgment or decision when the state court, acting within its proper jurisdiction, has given the parties a full and fair opportunity to litigate federal claims, and thereby has shown itself willing and able to protect federal rights. And nothing in the legislative history of § 1983 reveals any purpose to afford less deference to judgments in state criminal proceedings than to

state court of his intention to return to federal court, if necessary, was not precluded from litigating the federal question in federal court. The holding in *England* depended entirely on this Court's view of the purpose of abstention in such a case: Where a plaintiff properly invokes federal-court jurisdiction in the first instance on a federal claim, the federal court has a duty to accept that jurisdiction. Abstention may serve only to postpone, rather than to abdicate, jurisdiction, since its purpose is to determine whether resolution of the federal question is even necessary, or to obviate the risk of a federal court's erroneous construction of state law. These concerns have no bearing whatsoever on the present case.

those in state civil proceedings. There is, in short, no reason to believe that Congress intended to provide a person claiming a federal right an unrestricted opportunity to relitigate an issue already decided in a state court simply because the issue arose in a state proceeding in which he would rather not have been engaged at all.

Through § 1983, the 42nd Congress intended to afford an opportunity for legal and equitable relief in a federal court for certain types of injuries. It is difficult to believe that the drafters of the act considered it a substitute for a federal writ of habeas corpus, the purpose of which is not to redress civil injury, but to release the applicant from unlawful physical confinement, Preiser v. Rodriguez, 411 U.S. 475, 484 (1973); Fay v. Noia, 372 U.S. 391, 399 n.5 (1963), particularly in light of the extremely narrow scope of federal habeas relief for state prisoners in 1871.

The only other conceivable basis for finding a universal right to litigate a federal claim in a federal district court is hardly a legal basis at all, but rather a general distrust of the capacity of state courts to render correct decisions on constitutional issues. It is ironic that *Stone v. Powell* provided the occasion for the expression of such an attitude in the present litigation, in view of this Court's emphatic reaffirmation in that case of the constitutional obligation of the state courts to uphold federal law, and its expression of confidence in their ability to do so.

The Court of Appeals erred in holding that McCurry's inability to obtain federal habeas corpus relief upon his fourth amendment claim renders the doctrine of collateral estoppel inapplicable to his § 1983 suit.[25] Accordingly, the judgment is reversed, and the case is remanded to the Court of Appeals for proceedings consistent with this opinion.

JUSTICE BLACKMUN, with whom JUSTICE BRENNAN and JUSTICE MARSHALL join, dissenting.

The legal principles with which the Court is concerned in this civil case obviously far transcend the ugly facts of respondent's criminal convictions in the courts of Missouri for heroin possession and assault.

The Court today holds that notions of collateral estoppel apply with full force to this suit brought under 42 U.S.C. § 1983. In my view, the Court, in so ruling, ignores the clear import of the legislative history of that statute and disregards the important federal policies that underlie its enforcement. It also shows itself insensitive both to the significant differences between the § 1983 remedy and the exclusionary rule, and to the pressures upon a criminal defendant that make a free choice of forum illusory. I do not doubt that principles of preclusion are to be given such effect as is appropriate in a § 1983 action. In many cases, the denial of res judicata or collateral estoppel effect would serve no purpose and would harm relations between federal and state tribunals. Nonetheless, the Court's analysis in this particular case is unacceptable to me. It works injustice on this § 1983 plaintiff, and it makes more

---

[25] We do not decide *how* the body of collateral-estoppel doctrine of 28 U.S.C. § 1738 should apply in this case.

difficult the consistent protection of constitutional rights, a consideration that was at the core of the enactors' intent. Accordingly, I dissent.

In deciding whether a common-law doctrine is to apply to § 1983 when the statute itself is silent, prior cases uniformly have accorded the intent of the legislators great weight. . . . In the present case, however, the Court minimizes the significance of the legislative history and discounts its own prior explicit interpretations of the statute. Its discussion is limited to articulating what it terms the single fundamental principle of res judicata and collateral estoppel.

Respondent's position merits a quite different analysis. Although the legislators of the 42nd Congress did not expressly state whether the then existing common-law doctrine of preclusion would survive enactment of § 1983, they plainly anticipated more than the creation of a federal statutory remedy to be administered indifferently by either a state or a federal court. The legislative intent, as expressed by supporters and understood by opponents, was to restructure relations between the state and federal courts. Congress deliberately opened the federal courts to individual citizens in response to the states' failure to provide justice in their own courts. Contrary to the view presently expressed by the Court, the 42nd Congress was not concerned solely with procedural regularity. Even where there was procedural regularity, which the Court today so stresses, Congress believed that substantive justice was unobtainable. The availability of the federal forum was not meant to turn on whether, in an individual case, the state procedures were adequate. Assessing the state of affairs as a whole, Congress specifically made a determination that federal oversight of constitutional determinations through the federal courts was necessary to ensure the effective enforcement of constitutional rights.

That the new federal jurisdiction was conceived of as concurrent with state jurisdiction does not alter the significance of Congress' opening the federal courts to these claims. Congress consciously acted in the broadest manner possible. The legislators perceived that justice was not being done in the states then dominated by the Klan, and it seems senseless to suppose that they would have intended the federal courts to give full preclusive effect to prior state adjudications. That supposition would contradict their obvious aim to right the wrongs perpetuated in those same courts.

I agree that the legislative history is capable of alternative interpretations. I would have thought, however, that our prior decisions made very clear which reading is required. The Court repeatedly has recognized that § 1983 embodies a strong congressional policy in favor of federal courts' acting as the primary and final arbiters of constitutional rights. In Monroe v. Pape, 365 U.S. 167 (1961), the Court held that Congress passed the legislation in order to substitute a federal forum for the ineffective, although plainly available, state remedies:

"It is abundantly clear that one reason the legislation was passed was to afford a federal right in federal courts because, by reason of prejudice, passion, neglect, intolerance or otherwise, state laws might not be enforced and the claims of citizens to the enjoyment of rights, privileges, and immunities guaranteed by the 14th amendment might be denied by the state agencies." Id. at 180.[10]

The Court appears to me to misconstrue the plain meaning of *Monroe*. It states that in that case "the Court inferred that Congress had intended a federal remedy in three circumstances: where state substantive law was facially unconstitutional, where state procedural law was inadequate to allow full litigation of a constitutional claim, and where state procedural law, though adequate in theory, was inadequate in practice." It is true that the Court in *Monroe* described those three circumstances as the "three main aims" of the legislation. Yet in that case, the Court's recounting of the legislative history and its articulation of these three purposes were intended only as illustrative of *why* the 42nd Congress chose to establish a federal remedy in federal court, not as a delineation of *when* the remedy would be available. The Court's conclusion was that this remedy was to be available no matter what the circumstances of state law:

> "It is no answer that the state has a law which if enforced would give relief. The federal remedy is supplementary to the state remedy, and the latter need not be first sought and refused before the federal one is invoked. Hence the fact that Illinois by its constitution and laws outlaws unreasonable searches and seizures is no barrier to the present suit in the federal court." Id. at 183.

In Mitchum v. Foster, 407 U.S. 225 (1972), the Court reiterated its understanding of the effect of § 1983 upon state and federal relations:

> "Section 1983 was thus a product of a vast transformation from the concepts of federalism that had prevailed in the late 18th century. . . . The very purpose of § 1983 was to interpose the federal courts between the states and the people, as guardians of the people's federal rights—to protect the people from unconstitutional action under color of state law, 'where that action be executive, legislative, or judicial.'" Id. at 242.

At the very least, it is inconsistent now to narrow, if not repudiate, the meaning of *Monroe* and *Mitchum* and to alter our prior understanding of the distribution of power between the state and federal courts.

One should note also that in England v. Medical Examiners, 375 U.S. 411 (1964), the Court had affirmed the federal courts' special role in protecting constitutional rights under § 1983. In that case it held that a plaintiff required by the abstention doctrine to submit his constitutional claim first to a state court could not be precluded entirely from having the federal court, in which he initially had sought relief, pass on his constitutional claim. The Court relied on "the

---

[10] To the extent that *Monroe v. Pape* held that a municipality was not a "person" within the meaning of § 1983, it was overruled by the Court in *Monell v. New York* *City Dept. of Social Services*, supra, at 664–89. That ruling, of course, does not affect *Monroe*'s authoritative pronouncement of the legislative purposes of § 1983.

unqualified terms in which Congress, pursuant to constitutional authorization, has conferred specific categories of jurisdiction upon the federal courts," and on its "fundamental objections to any conclusion that a litigant who has properly invoked the jurisdiction of a federal district court to consider federal constitutional claims can be compelled, without his consent and through no fault of his own, to accept instead a state court's determination of those claims." Id., at 415. The Court set out its understanding as to when a litigant in a § 1983 case might be precluded by prior litigation, holding that "if a party freely and without reservation submits his federal claims for decision by the state courts, litigates them there, and has them decided there, then—whether or not he seeks direct review of the state decision in this Court—he has elected to forgo his right to return to the district court." Id., at 419. I do not understand why the Court today should abandon this approach.

The Court now fashions a new doctrine of preclusion, applicable only to actions brought under § 1983, that is more strict and more confining than the federal rules of preclusion applied in other cases. In Montana v. United States, 440 U.S. 147 (1979), the Court pronounced three major factors to be considered in determining whether collateral estoppel serves as a barrier in the federal court:

> "[W]hether the issues presented . . . are in substance the same . . .; whether controlling facts or legal principles have changed significantly since the state-court judgment; and finally, whether other special circumstances warrant an exception to the normal rules of preclusion." Id., at 155.

But now the Court states that the collateral-estoppel effect of prior state adjudication should turn on only one factor, namely, what it considers the "one general limitation" inherent in the doctrine of preclusion: "that the concept of collateral estoppel cannot apply when the party against whom the earlier decision is asserted did not have a 'full and fair opportunity' to litigate that issue in the earlier case." If that one factor is present, the Court asserts, the litigant properly should be barred from relitigating the issue in federal court.[12] One cannot deny that this factor is an important one. I do not believe, however, that the doctrine of preclusion requires the inquiry to be so narrow, and my understanding of the policies underlying § 1983 would lead me to consider all relevant factors in each case before concluding that the preclusion was warranted.

In this case, the police officers seek to prevent a criminal defendant from relitigating the constitutionality of their conduct in searching his house, after the state trial court had found that conduct in part violative of the defendant's fourth amendment rights and in part justified by the circumstances. I doubt that the police officers, now defendants in this § 1983 action, can be considered to have been in

---

[12] This articulation of the preclusion doctrine of course would bar a § 1983 litigant from relitigating any issue he *might* have raised, as well as any issue he actually litigated in his criminal trial.

privity with the state in its role as prosecutor. Therefore, only "issue preclusion" is at stake.

The following factors persuade me to conclude that this respondent should not be precluded from asserting his claim in federal court. First, at the time § 1983 was passed, a non-party's ability, as a practical matter, to invoke collateral estoppel was non-existent. One could not preclude an opponent from relitigating an issue in a new cause of action, though that issue had been determined conclusively in a prior proceeding, unless there was "mutuality." Additionally, the definitions of "cause of action" and "issue" were narrow. As a result, and obviously, no preclusive effect could arise out of a criminal proceeding that would affect subsequent *civil* litigation. Thus, the 42nd Congress could not have anticipated or approved that a criminal defendant, tried and convicted in state court, would be precluded from raising against police officers a constitutional claim arising out of his arrest.

Also, the process of deciding in a state criminal trial whether to exclude or admit evidence is not at all the equivalent of a § 1983 proceeding. The remedy sought in the latter is utterly different. In bringing the civil suit the criminal defendant does not seek to challenge his conviction collaterally. At most, he wins damages. In contrast, the exclusion of evidence may prevent a criminal conviction. A trial court, faced with the decision whether to exclude relevant evidence, confronts institutional pressures that may cause it to give a different shape to the fourth amendment right from what would result in civil litigation of a damages claim. Also, the issue whether to exclude evidence is subsidiary to the purpose of a criminal trial, which is to determine the guilt or innocence of the defendant, and a trial court, at least subconsciously, must weigh the potential damage to the truth-seeking process caused by excluding relevant evidence. See Stone v. Powell, 428 U.S. 465, 489–95 (1976).

A state criminal defendant cannot be held to have chosen "voluntarily" to litigate his fourth amendment claim in the state court. The risk of conviction puts pressure upon him to raise all possible defenses. He also faces uncertainty about the wisdom of foregoing litigation on *any* issue, for there is the possibility that he will be held to have waived his right to appeal on that issue. The "deliberate bypass" of state procedures, which the imposition of collateral estoppel under these circumstances encourages, surely is not a preferred goal. To hold that a criminal defendant who raises a fourth amendment claim at his criminal trial "freely and without reservation submits his federal claims for decision by the state courts," *England v. Medical Examiners*, supra, at 419, is to deny reality. The criminal defendant is an involuntary litigant in the state tribunal, and against him all the forces of the state are arrayed. To force him to a choice between foregoing either a potential defense or a federal forum for hearing his constitutional civil claim is fundamentally unfair.

I would affirm the judgment of the Court of Appeals.

NOTES ON RES JUDICATA IN CIVIL RIGHTS ACTIONS

1. **Access to the Federal Courts in State Criminal Cases.**
Even the *McCurry* dissenters agreed that state-court judgments should
be given preclusive effect in some § 1983 actions. The easiest case is
where a civil plaintiff submits a § 1983 claim to state court, loses, and
then attempts to relitigate that same claim in federal court. In such
circumstances, there would seem to be no reason to allow two bites at
the apple. The plaintiff made a choice to submit the claim to state
court, and presumably should be bound by the consequences. A less
obvious case arises where the plaintiff submits a civil state-law claim to
state court and litigates therein some issue of fact relevant to a later
§ 1983 action. Even in this situation an argument could be made that
the usual application of collateral estoppel, or issue preclusion, should
be followed. Again the plaintiff is in control of the choice of forum and
can anticipate, or perhaps should be required to anticipate, the consequences of the choice of a state court on any subsequent § 1983
litigation.

The issue presented in *McCurry* is made more difficult by the fact
that the federal claimant was an involuntary litigant in state criminal
proceedings. Of course, McCurry could have elected not to raise the
fourth amendment issue and perhaps could thereby have preserved his
right to bring a later § 1983 suit. The cost of doing so, however, would
be to forego a potential defense to the criminal charges. Realistically,
therefore, McCurry did not have "a free choice of forum" in which to
litigate his federal claim.

It is this denial of access to a federal forum that underlies the
argument against applying ordinary preclusion principles in § 1983
suits. Since this concern is abated where the federal claimant volunteers to go to state court, the dispute involves chiefly those cases in
which, for one reason or another, the federal claimant is forced to
litigate in state court. The paridigm case is where, as in *McCurry*, the
federal claimant is a defendant in state criminal proceedings.[a] Obviously relevant to the strength of the federal claimant's argument in
this context are the alternative methods by which access to a federal
forum may be gained by a state criminal defendant.

(i) **Pre-trial Access to Federal Court.** One strategy might
be to attempt litigation in a federal court *before* any state-court adjudi-

[a] There are situations, though they are
far less frequent, where a federal claimant
may be forced to litigate non-criminal
claims in a state court. For an example,
see *Trainor v. Hernandez* and the notes
following, pages 1213–33, infra. As the
Court itself develops in footnote 17 of its
McCurry opinion, England v. Board of Medical Examiners, 375 U.S. 411 (1964), does
not present such a situation. In *England*,
plaintiffs who filed claims in federal court
were required to submit certain issues of
state law to a state court for authoritative
resolution. They remained free to return
to federal court to litigate their federal
claims, however, and thus were not denied
access to a federal forum. The *England*
case is treated in detail at pages 1148–58,
infra.

cation of the federal claim. For reasons that are developed in more detail elsewhere in these materials, that strategy is likely to fail.[b]

An effort to secure pre-trial habeas corpus on the grounds that the statute on which the prosecution is based is unconstitutional or that illegally obtained evidence will be used in the upcoming trial will surely fail. Habeas corpus requires exhaustion of state remedies— which includes the state criminal proceedings themselves.[c]

Similarly, a pretrial § 1983 action is also likely to be unavailable. In Younger v. Harris, 401 U.S. 37 (1971), and companion cases, the Supreme Court held that neither declaratory nor injunctive relief could be obtained with respect to issues that might arise in a pending state criminal prosecution, absent the most flagrant sort of unconstitutionality or a showing of bad faith harassment. A subsequent decision extended *Younger* to state criminal prosecutions begun after a federal suit but before substantial proceedings on the merits of the federal action. Hicks v. Miranda, 422 U.S. 332 (1975).[d] It is likely, moreover, that an effort to get damages in a federal § 1983 suit prior to the state-court adjudication will be forestalled, either because the state criminal trial is likely to be concluded before the federal civil case comes to trial or because the federal court will invoke *Younger* as a reason for delaying federal court resolution of the issue.[e]

(ii) Post-Trial Habeas Corpus. After trial, the situation is very different. Insofar as incarceration is at issue, the state-court judgment in a criminal case typically has no preclusive effect. That is, most federal constitutional claims remain open for relitigation on an application for federal habeas corpus.[f] For that reason, habeas corpus and § 1983 might be thought of as alternative post-trial routes of access to the federal courts. And so long as one door remains open, it might be argued, it may not matter that the other is shut. Indeed, some such notion seems to have animated the Court of Appeals in *McCurry*, which allowed relitigation of the fourth amendment claim precisely because it was barred from habeas review. Otherwise, presumably, the availability of habeas review would have been taken as a reason to bar relitigation under § 1983.

Would such an approach be sensible? Consider the remarks in Comment, The Collateral-Estoppel Effect to be Given State-Court Judgments in Federal § 1983 Damage Actions, 128 U. Pa. L. Rev. 1471, 1494–95 (1980):

> "Section 1983 damages are designed to be compensatory . . . . In contrast, the habeas mechanism does not even attempt to compensate for past sufferings; rather the habeas

---

[b] Another strategy might be to seek removal of the case to federal court under 28 U.S.C. § 1443. That effort is likely to fail for reasons developed at pages 572–93, supra.

[c] See pages 691–710, supra.

[d] The *Younger* decision and its progeny are treated in detail at pages 1158–1243, infra.

[e] See, e.g., Hadley v. Werner, 753 F.2d 514 (6th Cir. 1985) (per curiam); Guerro v. Mulhearn, 498 F.2d 1249 (1st Cir. 1974).

[f] See pages 718–53, supra, for a full development of this proposition.

remedy begins where the § 1983 remedy leaves off. By releasing a defendant from custody, habeas corpus can prevent only future injury. Thus, the habeas-corpus and § 1983 damage remedies do not overlap. They are mutually exclusive, yet complementary, remedies that *together* operate to render the injured party whole. Because they should not be interpreted simply as alternative means of access to a federal forum, it is difficult to see why the availability of habeas should preempt the applicability of § 1983."

Is this argument sound?

(iii) **The Significance of** *Stone v. Powell.* Of course, the actual point of the *McCurry* Court of Appeals was not that the availability of habeas should bar relitigation under § 1983, but that the unavailability of habeas in this context should allow such relitigation. This argument focuses on *Stone v. Powell,* where the Supreme Court restricted habeas relitigation of fourth amendment claims. The *McCurry* Court of Appeals relied on *Stone* to support its position. Is that plausible? Or is it more plausible to view *McCurry* as a necessary corollary of the majority's position in *Stone*?

One way of analyzing this issue is to ask what would have happened to *Stone* had *McCurry* gone the other way. In that event, a defendant who lost a fourth amendment claim in state court could obtain de novo consideration in federal court via § 1983. If the federal court agreed with the federal claimant, what should a federal court do if a habeas proceeding were subsequently filed? Should it, consistent with *Stone v. Powell,* continue to regard the state-court judgment as determinative of the legality of confinement, even though that confinement was based on a search or seizure now found to be unconstitutional?

One commentator has suggested that this result is in fact exactly consistent with the rationale of *Stone v. Powell.* See Comment, The Collateral-Estoppel Effect to be Given State-Court Judgments in Federal § 1983 Damage Suits, 128 U. Pa. L. Rev. 1471, 1493–94, 1502 (1980): *

> "*Stone v. Powell,* which mandates unfavorable treatment for fourth-amendment habeas claims, in no way denigrates the constitutional right itself. *Stone* merely holds that the benefits of vindicating fourth-amendment rights through habeas corpus are outweighed by the costs: the incremental deterrence of illegal police behavior by means of this tardy application of the exclusionary rule is not worth the price of freedom for the guilty.

> "If we view *Stone* as a comment on the costs of the 'remedy' rather than a statement on the quality of the rights, then a § 1983 proceeding should be embraced by a majority of

* Reprinted by permission of The University of Pennsylvania Law Review and Fred B. Rothman & Company from The   University of Pennsylvania Law Review, Vol. 128, pp. 1493–94, 1502.

the Court. A § 1983 suit for damages is not nearly as intrusive as habeas relief; because even the successful § 1983 litigant would not gain early release from jail as a direct consequence of his suit, there can be no claim that the federal courts are undoing the efforts of the state criminal-justice system. Further, to the extent a federal court is concerned with vindicating constitutional rights, a § 1983 proceeding is preferable to habeas corpus. The habeas remedy—release from custody—bears no rational relationship to the constitutional wrong committed, while a damage award under § 1983 is theoretically tailored to the actual degree of harm. [Furthermore] continued incarceration even in the light of a proven fourth-amendment violation can, if one accepts the holding of *Stone v. Powell,* no longer be considered unjust. Current fourth-amendment jurisprudence makes no link between the validity of the fourth-amendment claim and the defendant's guilt or innocence. Thus, there is no fear that, by continuing to detain the successful fourth-amendment § 1983 damage litigant, society is unfairly incarcerating an innocent man."

Is this argument persuasive? Does it depend on how the exclusionary rule is viewed? On how *Stone v. Powell* is interpreted? Is *Allen v. McCurry* at bottom a dispute over the real meaning of *Stone v. Powell*?

2. *Mitchum v. Foster.* The Anti-Injunction Act, 28 U.S.C. § 2283, provides that a federal court "may not grant an injunction to stay proceedings in a state court except as expressly authorized by act of Congress, or where necessary in aid of its jurisdiction, or to protect or effectuate its judgments." In Mitchum v. Foster, 407 U.S. 225 (1972), the Court considered whether § 1983 was an "expressly authorized" exception within this language.[g] The Court found that it was:

"[The] legislative history [of § 1983] makes evident that Congress clearly conceived that it was altering the relationship between the states and the nation with respect to the protection of federally created rights; it was concerned that state instrumentalities could not protect those rights; it realized that state officers might, in fact, be antipathetic to the vindication of those rights; and it believed that these failings extended to the state courts. . . . The very purpose of § 1983 was to interpose the federal courts between the states and the people, as guardians of the people's federal rights—to protect the people from unconstitutional action under color of state law, 'whether that action be executive, legislative or judicial.' Ex parte Virginia, 100 U.S. 339, 346 (1879)."

Is *McCurry* consistent with this understanding of the purpose of § 1983?

3. *Kremer v. Chemical Construction Corp.* Two years after *McCurry,* the Supreme Court applied the same approach to the rather

---

[g] *Mitchum* appears as a main case at page 1179, infra.

complicated facts of Kremer v. Chemical Construction Corp., 456 U.S. 461 (1982). Kremer filed a charge with the Equal Employment Opportunity Commission, alleging employment discrimination in violation of title VII of the Civil Rights Act of 1964. That statute prohibits EEOC action until any comparable state agency has had at least 60 days to resolve the matter. Kremer's complaint was therefore referred to the New York State Division of Human Rights, which in due course concluded that the charge was unfounded. Kremer then returned to the EEOC, but simultaneously sought judicial review in state court of the state agency's action. The EEOC found that there was no reasonable cause to believe that Kremer's charge was true and issued a right-to-sue notice, after which Kremer brought a title VII action in federal court. By this time, however, the New York agency determination had been affirmed in the state courts. The District Court dismissed the title VII complaint on grounds of res judicata.

The Supreme Court, speaking through Justice White, found § 1738 fully applicable to title VII cases: "Section 1738 requires federal courts to give the same preclusive effect to state court judgments that those judgments would be given in the courts of the state from which the judgments emerged." Under title VII neither EEOC action nor a determination by any state agency would bar de novo trial in federal court. But Kremer had sought *judicial* review of the state agency's action, and the judgment of that reviewing court was entitled to full faith and credit under § 1738. The fact that the state court was reviewing an administrative determination did not matter, for "[t]here is no requirement that judicial review must proceed de novo if it is to be preclusive." Justice Blackmun, joined by Justices Brennan and Marshall, dissented.[h]

4. *Migra v. Board of Education.* *Allen v. McCurry* involved issue preclusion; in footnote 10 of its opinion the majority expressly declined to address the operation of claim preclusion in § 1983 actions. That question arose a few years later in Migra v. Warren City School District Board of Education, 465 U.S. 75 (1984).

(i) Claim vs. Issue Preclusion. Ethel Migra worked under successive annual contracts as supervisor of elementary schools in Warren City, Ohio. She accepted an offer of re-employment for a given year, but the school board subsequently reversed itself and decided not to renew her contract. Migra brought suit in state court, claiming breach of contract by the board and wrongful interference with her contract of employment by the board members who voted against her. She won that suit and was awarded reinstatement and compensatory damages.

Migra then filed a § 1983 action in federal court. She alleged that the non-renewal was in retaliation for a desegregation plan she had authored and a social studies curriculum she had designed. She

[h] For an analysis of the impact of *Kremer* in title VII cases, see Cataria, Access to the Federal Courts for Title VII Claimants in the Post-*Kremer* Era: Keeping the Doors Open, 16 Loy.-Chi. L.J. 209 (1985).

claimed that the non-renewal was intended to punish her for the exercise of her right of free speech and also claimed violations of due process and equal protection. The District Court dismissed the complaint, and the Court of Appeals affirmed.

Speaking for a unanimous Supreme Court, Justice Blackmun reviewed *Allen v. McCurry* and *Kremer v. Chemical Const. Corp.* and concluded that the same approach applied to claims that should have been raised in a prior state court proceeding. "It is difficult," he said, "to see how the policy concerns underlying § 1983 would justify a distinction between the issue preclusive and claim preclusive effects of state-court judgments." The argument that § 1983 should be an exception to the usual principles of preclusion was based on "concern over the adequacy of state courts as protectors of federal rights." Any such distrust, however, "would presumably apply equally to issues that actually were decided in a state court as well as to those that could have been."[i] Therefore, there was no basis for distinguishing the situations, and *McCurry* controlled.[j]

Is this reasoning sound? Consider the contrary argument of Stephen J. Shapiro in The Application of State Claim Preclusion Rules in a Federal Civil Rights Action, 10 Ohio Northern L. Rev. 223 (1983). Shapiro suggested that there are good reasons to differentiate issue from claim preclusion and to allow an exception for the latter. First, allowing relitigation of issues already adjudicated in state court "calls the correctness of the state court decision into question" and thereby offends the interest in comity between state and federal courts. Allowing a claimant to present a federal claim not heard in state court, by contrast, "not only shows no disrespect for the state court decision, but actually furthers the principles of comity by encouraging litigants to bring state claims in the state courts." As a corollary, an exception for claim preclusion would reduce the burden on the federal courts by allowing litigants to present their state claims to state court without risking loss of access to a federal forum. Finally, issue and claim preclusion were thought to have different benefits: Whereas issue preclusion "avoids duplicative legal effort and therefore conserves judicial resources," claim preclusion, "although reducing the number of lawsuits, does not usually reduce the total judicial effort expended by the parties or the court." Professor Shapiro therefore argued that *Migra* and *McCurry* should be treated differently.

Is this reasoning persuasive? What about Justice Blackmun's argument that *Migra* is actually a better case for preclusion than *McCurry*?

[i] Additional excerpts from Justice Blackmun's opinion appear at pages 876–78, supra.

[j] In a footnote, Justice Blackmun noted that he had dissented in *McCurry*, but explained that the "rationale of that dissent . . . was based largely on the fact that the § 1983 plaintiff in that case first litigated his constitutional claim in state court in the posture of his being a *defendant* in a criminal proceeding." Here, by contrast, "petitioner was in an offensive posture in her state court proceeding, and could have proceeded first in federal court had she wanted to litigate her federal claim in a federal forum." Additional excerpts from *Migra* appear at pages 876–78, supra.

(ii) **The Significance of State Law.** In *Migra* the Court quoted *Kremer v. Chemical Const. Corp.* to the effect that "§ 1738 requires federal courts to give the same preclusive effect to state court judgments that those judgments would be given in the courts of the state from which the judgments emerged." It was not clear, however, whether Ohio law would regard Migra's breach of contract suit and her later § 1983 action as based on the same "claim" or "cause of action" for purposes of preclusion. The lower courts seemed to have resolved that question according to general preclusion principles rather than by specific reference to Ohio law. The Supreme Court said that Ohio law should govern and remanded the case for further inquiry into the controlling state law.

This point prompted an interesting concurrence by Justice White, with whom the Chief Justice and Justice Powell joined. Justice White noted that § 1738 had long been construed to mean that a federal court could accord a state-court judgment "no greater efficacy" than would a court of the rendering state, but found that construction nevertheless "unfortunate":

> "In terms of the purposes of that section, which is to require federal courts to give effect to state-court judgments, there is no reason to hold that a federal court may not give preclusive effect to a state judgment simply because the judgment would not bar relitigation in the state courts. If the federal courts have developed rules of res judicata and collateral estoppel that prevent relitigation in circumstances that would not be preclusive in state courts, the federal courts should be free to apply them, the parties then being free to relitigate in the state courts. The contrary construction of § 1738 is nevertheless one of long standing, and Congress has not seen fit to disturb it, however justified such an action might have been."

Is White's suggestion sound? Professor Shapiro thinks not. He suggested that according greater preclusive effect than would a state court might be unfair to the plaintiff, who may have relied on state preclusion law in bringing the original suit. Additionally, he thought that White's approach "may interfere with state substantive policies by giving too great a preclusive effect" to state-court judgments. Shapiro, The Application of State Claim Preclusion Rules in a Federal Civil Rights Action, 10 Ohio Northern L. Rev. 223, 237–38 (1983). Are these arguments persuasive? Are they adequately answered by White's observation that the litigant would remain free to return to state court?

5. *Haring v. Prosise.* Consider also the facts of Haring v. Prosise, 462 U.S. 306 (1983). After pleading guilty to a charge of manufacturing a controlled substance, Prosise filed a § 1983 action against the police officers who had searched his apartment. The District Court held this claim barred, but the Supreme Court disagreed. Speaking through Justice Marshall, a unanimous Court held that the issue under § 1738 was simply whether state law would regard the

conviction as preclusive. It would not, first because the fourth amendment claim was not actually litigated in the criminal prosecution, and second because the prosecution did not actually resolve any issue relevant to the § 1983 suit: The only issue determined by the guilty plea was whether Prosise had manufactured a controlled substance, and "[t]his question is simply irrelevant to the legality of the search under the fourth amendment or to Prosise's right to compensation from state officials under § 1983."

The Court also refused to embrace any notion of waiver. True, a defendant who pleads guilty cannot later raise a fourth amendment claim in a habeas proceeding. The guilty plea is a "break in the chain of events," Tollett v. Henderson, 411 U.S. 258, 267 (1973), and renders an alleged fourth amendment violation irrelevant to the legality of the conviction. In such a case, the conviction rests on the defendant's plea of guilty and not on allegedly unlawful evidence. By contrast, the § 1983 action does not test the validity of the conviction, but "challenges directly the legality of police conduct." Therefore, the fourth amendment issue is open to litigation in a civil rights action, even though it is barred from consideration on habeas.

6. *McDonald v. City of West Branch.* All of the preceding cases involved the preclusive effect of judgments by state courts. The preclusive effect of an arbitration award was considered in McDonald v. City of West Branch, Michigan, 466 U.S. 284 (1984). There a discharged police officer filed a grievance under a collective bargaining agreement. The dispute went to arbitration, and the arbitrator found just cause for the discharge. The officer did not appeal the arbitrator's decision, but instead filed a § 1983 action in federal district court. Speaking through Justice Brennan, the Supreme Court held unanimously that § 1738 did not apply. The Court also declined to fashion any judicial rule of preclusion for arbitration awards. The Court reasoned that, "although arbitration is well suited to resolving contractual disputes, . . . it cannot provide an adequate substitute for a judicial proceeding in protecting the federal statutory and constitutional rights that § 1983 was designed to safeguard."

7. Bibliography. The issue of the preclusive effect of state-court judgments in subsequent § 1983 actions has spawned a considerable literature. In addition to the sources already cited, see the comprehensive survey of this subject by Robert H. Smith in Full Faith and Credit and § 1983: A Reappraisal, 63 N.C.L. Rev. 59 (1984). Smith argues that the preclusive effect of state-court judgments in § 1983 suits should be subject to some exceptions, and he suggests consideration of five variables to determine whether an exception is warranted. These variables include: (i) whether the party facing preclusion had a choice of forum in the first instance; (ii) whether the federal action would relitigate claims or issues already determined by the state court and thus risk inconsistent rulings; (iii) whether the state court's consideration was limited in scope or procedure or tangential to the federal claim; (iv) whether allowing relitigation would unduly burden other litigants; and (v) whether specially important federal policies are at stake.

Reference should also be made to Burbank, Interjurisdictional Preclusion: A General Approach, 71 Cornell L. Rev. 733, 817–22 (1986) (suggesting an approach to problems of preclusion in the federal-state context and applying it to § 1983 litigation); Luneburg, The Opportunity to be Heard and the Doctrines of Preclusion: Federal Limits on State Law, 31 Vill.L.Rev. 81 (1986) (considering the role of federal law in an extensive discussion of claim and issue preclusion); Mahoney, A Sword as Well as a Shield: The Offensive Use of Collateral Estoppel in Civil Rights Litigation, 69 Iowa L. Rev. 469 (1984) (suggesting that recent decisions may encourage resort to federal court in order to take advantage of success by the offensive assertion of collateral estoppel in subsequent state-court actions); and Atwood, State Court Judgments in Federal Litigation: Mapping the Contours of Full Faith and Credit, 58 Ind. L.J. 59 (1982) (analyzing the recent decisions with particular reference to the impact of exclusive federal jurisdiction on issue and claim preclusion under § 1738).

Many of the problems dealt with in the recent cases were anticipated in Torke, Res Judicata in Federal Civil Rights Actions Following State Litigation, 9 Ind. L. Rev. 543 (1976). Also of interest are the provocative comments in Currie, Res Judicata: The Neglected Defense, 45 U. Chi. L. Rev. 317 (1978). See also the still useful, though inevitably dated, discussions in Theis, Res Judicata in Civil Rights Act Cases: An Introduction to the Problem, 70 Nw. U. L. Rev. 859 (1976); Vestal, State Court Judgment as Preclusive in § 1983 Litigation in a Federal Court, 27 Okla. L. Rev. 185 (1974); and the excellent early treatment in McCormack, Federalism and § 1983: Limitations on Judicial Enforcement of Constitutional Claims, Part II, 60 Va. L. Rev. 250 (1974).

SUBSECTION B: EXHAUSTION OF REMEDIES

PATSY v. FLORIDA INTERNATIONAL UNIVERSITY
United States Court of Appeals, Fifth Circuit, 1981.
634 F.2d 900.

RONEY, CIRCUIT JUDGE.

This § 1983 sex and race discrimination suit was dismissed on motion for failure to allege exhaustion of state administrative remedies. A panel of this court reversed on the ground that exhaustion of administrative remedies is not a prerequisite of a § 1983 suit. Patsy v. Florida International University, 612 F.2d 946 (5th Cir. 1980). We took this case en banc for the purpose of considering whether to adhere to an automatic rule that no § 1983 plaintiff need pursue state administrative procedures before asserting federal court jurisdiction, regardless of the adequacy of relief that might be there available, or whether to adopt a more flexible rule that would require such exhaustion in appropriate cases. Deciding to take the latter course, we remand the case to the District Court for it to consider the adequacy of the administrative procedures available to this plaintiff in light of the rule here adopted.

Plaintiff is a white female employed as a secretary at Florida International University (FIU). [P]laintiff alleges that during her employment with FIU, she has applied for numerous employment openings in the university for which she was clearly qualified, but has been uniformly rejected because FIU has discriminated against her on the basis of race and sex. Plaintiff contends that by seeking out individuals from minority groups to hire and promote and by segregating applicants' files according to race and sex, FIU is engaged in a pattern and practice of discrimination, in violation of the Constitution and laws of the United States. . . .

I. The Exhaustion Doctrine

It has long been established that a party will normally be denied judicial relief for injury until available administrative remedies have been exhausted. As the Supreme Court stated in one of the leading cases dealing with the exhaustion doctrine, Myers v. Bethlehem Shipbuilding Corp., 303 U.S. 41, 50–51 (1938):

> "[T]he long settled rule of judicial administration [is] that no one is entitled to judicial relief for a supposed or threatened injury until the prescribed administrative remedy has been exhausted." . . .

Many of the important policy purposes of the doctrine requiring exhaustion of federal administrative proceedings as a precedent to judicial relief were articulated by the Supreme Court in McKart v. United States, 395 U.S. 185, 193–95 (1969): (1) to avoid premature interruption of the administrative process; (2) to let the agency develop the necessary factual background upon which decisions should be based; (3) to permit the agency to exercise its discretion or apply its expertise; (4) to improve the efficiency of the administrative process; (5) to conserve scarce judicial resources, since the complaining party may be successful in vindicating rights in the administrative process and the courts may never have to intervene; (6) to give the agency a chance to discover and correct its own errors; and (7) to avoid the possibility that "frequent and deliberate flouting of administrative processes could weaken the effectiveness of an agency by encouraging people to ignore its procedures."

When the complaining party seeks federal court review of state action, the reasons stated in *McKart* are overlaid by forceful considerations of federalism and comity which counsel the exhaustion of administrative relief before the intervention of the federal judiciary into the dispute. Cf. Younger v. Harris, 401 U.S. 37 (1971) (non-intervention of federal courts in pending state court action absent exceptional circumstances); Railroad Commission v. Pullman Co., 312 U.S. 496, 501 (1949) (abstention because of "scrupulous regard for the rightful independence of the state governments").

Like most judicial doctrines, the requirement of exhaustion of administrative remedies is subject to numerous practical exceptions which result from the efforts of the courts to balance the rights of the claimants against the substantial policy factors favoring the rule. Briefly the traditional exceptions are first, exhaustion is not required when the prescribed administrative remedy is plainly inadequate because either no remedy is available, the available remedy will not give relief commensurate with the claim, or the remedy would be so unreasonably delayed as to create a serious risk of irreparable injury.

Second, when the claimant seeks to have a legislative act declared unconstitutional and administrative action will leave standing the constitutional question, exhaustion is not required.

Third, courts do not require exhaustion when the question of the adequacy of the administrative remedy is for all practical purposes coextensive with the merits of the plaintiff's claim, such as when, for example, the plaintiff contends that the administrative system itself is unlawful or unconstitutional in form or purpose.

Fourth, exhaustion of administrative remedies is not required if it would be futile to comply with the administrative procedures because it is clear that the claim will be rejected.

It should be noted that the application of the exhaustion doctrine with its traditional exceptions is far from an exact science. Indeed, as Professor Davis has stated, in applying the exhaustion rule, "judicial action is variable and difficult or impossible to predict." K. Davis, Administrative Law § 20.01 (1958). This is because "[a]pplication of the doctrine to specific cases requires an understanding of its purposes and of the particular administrative scheme involved." *McKart v. United States*, supra, at 193. In most situations the decision to require exhaustion or not comes after careful analysis and thoughtful balancing of the interests for and against exhaustion. The question presented in this case is whether the court in § 1983 cases should take the analytical approach normally applied whenever administrative remedies are available or whether it should automatically except every § 1983 case from the requirement, as seems to have been done in many cases.

II. Exhaustion in § 1983 Cases

The initial inquiry in this determination is whether the point is open for decision under cases that have been decided by the Supreme Court. Although the simple statement that "exhaustion of administrative remedies is not required in § 1983 cases" has support in the language of some opinions, a careful analysis of the holdings of the Supreme Court leads us to conclude that there is room for this court to develop an analytical rule.

The Supreme Court held in Monroe v. Pape, 365 U.S. 167 (1961), that it is not a prerequisite to filing an action under 42 U.S.C. § 1983 that state judicial remedies be exhausted. The question of administrative remedies was not before the Court. In McNeese v. Board of Education, 373 U.S. 668 (1963), a subsequent § 1983 case, the Supreme Court was confronted with the issue of exhaustion of both judicial and administrative remedies. *McNeese* was a school desegregation case in which the primary administrative remedy available was that the residents of the school district could file a complaint with the Superintendent of Public Instruction alleging racial segregation. He could then set a hearing and, after the hearing, if he decided the allegations were substantially correct he could request the Illinois Attorney General to file suit. Alternatively, it was suggested that the Superintendent could refuse to certify the school and then withhold state funds.

The Court first stated that it had "previously indicated that relief under the Civil Rights Act may not be defeated because relief was not sought under state law," and quoted the language from *Monroe v. Pape* which held that state judicial remedies need not be exhausted. . . . Upon reaching the question of administrative remedies, the Court said:

> "Moreover, it is by no means clear that Illinois law provides petitioner with an administrative remedy sufficiently adequate to preclude prior resort for protection of their federal rights."

After examining the administrative remedies at some length and noting their ineffectiveness in responding to petitioners' complaints, the Court concluded that "[w]hen federal rights are subject to such tenuous protection, prior resort to a state proceeding is not necessary."

It is quite clear that exhaustion of administrative remedies would not have been required in *McNeese* under the traditional rule because a clear-cut exception—inadequacy of administrative remedy—was applicable. In fact, the administrative process could afford no direct relief. Nevertheless, from *McNeese* and subsequent Supreme Court pronouncements relying on *McNeese* has grown the rule, following by a majority of the circuits, that exhaustion of state administrative remedies is absolutely never required in § 1983 suits. . . .

We are aware of the numerous instances in which the Court has stated in opinions, apparently quite categorically, that exhaustion is not required in § 1983 cases. But the simple fact of the matter, as one commentator has noted, is that "in all the cases in which the Supreme Court has articulated its no-exhaustion rule, the state administrative remedies were sufficiently inadequate that exhaustion would not have been appropriate in any event." Developments in the Law—Section 1983 and Federalism, 90 Harv.L.Rev. 1133, 1274 (1977). Individual examination of each § 1983 case mentioning exhaustion of state administrative remedies bears this out. . . .

III. Objections and Policy Considerations

Having determined that under relevant Supreme Court authority this court *may* take an analytical approach to the question of exhaustion of state administrative remedies in § 1983 cases, . . . we must now decide whether we *should* take such an approach.

There are two basic arguments for a blanket rule that no exhaustion of administrative remedies is required in any § 1983 case. First, it is argued that an exhaustion requirement would thwart the purposes of Congress in enacting § 1983. Second, it is argued that the elimination of an exhaustion prerequisite is justified because, given the nature of the rights protected by § 1983, claims for their protection are entitled to be adjudicated in federal courts.

Although an additional argument could be made that a mechanical rule is easy to understand and apply, we reject it out of hand because of the important interests that might be unthinkingly sacrificed on that altar of expediency. Instead, we examine the two principal arguments that could reasonably support a no-exhaustion rule.

In *Monroe v. Pape*, the Supreme Court examined at length the historical background and legislative intent of Congress in enacting § 1983. The Court discerned three main aims for the legislation: (1) to override certain kinds of state laws that were inconsistent with federal law; (2) to provide a federal remedy where state law was inadequate; and (3) to provide a federal remedy where the state remedy was available in theory but not in practice. . . . Discriminatory state statutes present . . . the strongest case for not requiring exhaustion, because in such cases administrative procedures are unlikely to provide any significant relief. But as one commentator has persuasively argued, even in the case of discriminatory state laws,

> "categorical rejection of exhaustion is inappropriate. Assuming a state statute is inconsistent with federal law, exhaustion may be appropriate for the purpose of developing a factual record, receiving the benefit of agency expertise in the administration of its statutes and rules, and allowing the agency to limit the application of the statute consistently with federal law. Only where a factual record is irrelevant and the statute is both facially unconstitutional and incapable of any appropriate construction is exhaustion without value."

Comment, Exhaustion of State Administrative Remedies in § 1983 Cases, 41 U.Chi.L.Rev. 537, 553 (1974).

Far from thwarting congressional intent, a requirement of exhaustion of adequate state remedies is wholly consistent with the second and third congressional purposes identified in *Monroe v. Pape*, that is, the provision of a federal remedy where the state remedy is inadequate on its face or in practice. "If Congress sought to provide a federal remedy where the state remedy is not adequate in fact, it follows that the legislative intent required adequate remedies to be exhausted." Comment, supra, at 553. Although the federal courts must inquire into the actual efficacy of the state administrative process, once it is found to provide an adequate remedy, an exhaustion requirement is consistent with a § 1983 purpose to provide a federal remedy where a state remedy is inadequate or not available in practice.

Regardless of congressional purpose or intent, however, the question remains as to whether the nature of every § 1983 claim entitles it to immediate adjudication in the federal courts. It must be kept in mind that we are here dealing with state administrative remedy exhaustion, not state judicial exhaustion. Unlike judicial actions, state administrative proceedings carry no res judicata or collateral estoppel baggage into federal court. Resorting to appropriate and adequate state administrative remedies in no way precludes federal court protection of federal constitutional and statutory rights. At most it can only delay federal court action, at best it could eliminate the need for such action. The proper focus should be on relief from wrong, and the adequacy of the administrative system to provide a remedy, not on the federal origin of the right that was violated.

There are important policy reasons for requiring a potential § 1983 plaintiff to exhaust adequate and appropriate state administrative remedies. . . .

First, exhaustion promotes a wiser allocation of judicial resources, and does so in a variety of ways. To begin with the most obvious, the administrative process may resolve the dispute in a manner wholly satisfactory to the complainant. In that case, no judicial action at all will be required. The administrative process may also serve to focus the contentions of the parties and eliminate extraneous issues, thereby simplifying any resulting litigation. In cases where the facts are significant, during the administrative process the agency can sift through complicated factual matters and reduce issues of fact, thus aiding the court in making its findings of fact. Yet another potential benefit is that the agency may be able to construe or interpret statutes or regulations in such a way as to resolve the complainant's grievance or to avoid a constitutional conflict. Permitting the administrative process to function may also allow the agency to define the contours of a yet uninterpreted statute or regulation and alleviate the necessity of having the federal courts guess about its meaning.

Second, a reasonable exhaustion requirement will assure that "the action complained of is final within the institution in the sense that it is ripe for adjudication." If the university or the board of regents is being sued, it should be clear that the university or the board of regents is responsible for the alleged wrong, instead of some first echelon functionary. As then Chief Judge Brown stated:

> "[It] must be clear that the *body* having responsibility, in response to specific complaints, has for the legal entity involved, failed or refused to take corrective action. The street light in my block may be inadequate, and unequal to another neighborhood, but until I can seek a § 1983 order from a federal judge, I must at least allow the *city* of Houston to turn

me down. This is good sense. It is good federalism. It is good
nineteen eighty-threeism."

Hawkins v. Town of Shaw, 461 F.2d 1171, 1177 (5th Cir. 1972) (en banc)
(Brown, C.J., concurring). Involved in the ripeness concept are notions
of fairness. Many would think it simply unfair to be summoned into
federal court to defend against a constitutional claim where they have
contrary policies and machinery to right alleged wrongs in an orderly
fashion, but are given no reasonable opportunity for that machinery to
operate.

Third, a reasonable exhaustion requirement will improve the administrative process itself. Prompted by appropriate judicial decisions,
the state administrative agency will have the incentive and be able to
hone its procedures to comply with federal requirements, both procedural and substantive, without losing the advantage of the agency's
expertise, its familiarity with local conditions and awareness of the
impact of particular action on related areas, and its desire to correct
errors of lower level functionaries within the agency. The proper roles
of the officials within the agency will be solidified when the errors of
lower level functionaries are corrected within the agency instead of by
the courts.

Fourth, administrative remedies are generally simpler, speedier
and less expensive for the parties themselves. Under a no-exhaustion
rule, plaintiffs, of course, would have a choice between court and
administrative procedures. Defendants, however, have a genuine interest in solving conflicts with the least court cost and attorney fees.
Failure to require utilization of administrative remedies which might
well achieve the same or a better remedy than could be obtained in
court is wasteful of a litigant's resources.

Fifth, of serious importance to the judicial system's response to the
concept of dual constitutional government, a requirement that a plaintiff complaining of state action must first exhaust state administrative
remedies is supported by fundamental notions of federalism and comity.
The policy here has at least three significant bases. First, the citizens
of a state have a constitutionally based interest in autonomously
running the state business and government to the fullest extent possible, until it collides with the federal Constitution. The constitutional
collision should come, if at all, at the end of state action, not at the
beginning. . . . Second, much of the work of the federal courts . . .
has been to establish rules and regulations under which the states must
operate to meet due process and other constitutional requirements.
That effort is of little practical value of the parties the courts have
sought to protect by improving the state procedural structure can turn
their backs on state administrative remedies and go directly into a
federal forum. Good faith efforts by the states to provide protection for
such parties are discouraged when federal courts encourage ignoring
state administrative remedies. Third, plaintiffs are required to exhaust
federal administrative remedies. As Professor Davis queried, "Why are
not the reasons for requiring exhaustion of state remedies stronger

than the reasons for requiring exhaustion of federal remedies, on account of all the reasons behind the abstention doctrine?" K. Davis, Administrative Law § 20.01 at 646 (Supp.1970). In terms of comity, why should not state defendants have at least the same right as federal defendants in suits against them for alleged governmental wrongs?

IV. The Decision

Considering the policy factors which so heavily favor the imposition of an exhaustion requirement, we are compelled to conclude that adequate and appropriate state administrative remedies must be exhausted before a § 1983 action is permitted to proceed in federal court, absent any of the traditional exceptions to the general exhaustion rule. In so holding, we make it clear that we deal only with the question of what must be done procedurally before a § 1983 action is prosecuted in federal court. This decision in no way limits the range of substantive rights for which § 1983 provides a remedy.

In determining whether the administrative remedies available to a particular plaintiff are adequate and appropriate, the courts should look to the large body of law applying the exhaustion requirement in non § 1983 contexts. In view of the importance of the rights protected by § 1983, however, certain minimum conditions must be met before resort to state administrative remedies can be made a prerequisite to proceeding under § 1983. First, an orderly system of review or appeal must be provided by statute or written agency rule. Second, the agency must be able to grant relief more or less commensurate with the claim. Third, relief must be available within a reasonable period of time. Fourth, the procedures must be fair, and not unduly burdensome, and must not be used to harass or otherwise discourage those with legitimate claims. Fifth, interim relief must be available, in appropriate cases, to prevent irreparable injury and to preserve the litigant's rights under § 1983 until the administrative process has been concluded.

Where these minimum standards are met, the court will need to further consider the particular administrative scheme, the nature of the interest the plaintiff seeks to protect, the values served by the exhaustion doctrine, and the proper balance of these interests in this type of case. See *McKart v. United States*, supra.

Contrary to the suggestion that the adoption of an exhaustion of administrative remedies requirement will somehow "turn back the clock" on civil rights law, we think that a carefully devised, well-monitored exhaustion requirement might well advance the cause of potential civil rights litigants. The resulting development of speedy and effective state administrative procedures for the vindication of 1983 transgressions could make available less expensive, less time consuming, more accessible, easily understandable procedures. For all litigants alike, but most particularly for those potential litigants who are neither so poor that they lose nothing by protracted federal court litigation nor so rich they can afford the risk of loss without financial worry, carefully constructed procedures within their own state and especially within their own agency should be a step forward, not backward. . . .

We therefore remand the case to the District Court with directions . . . to apply the principles set forth in this opinion in determining whether plaintiff should be required to exhaust state administrative remedies before bringing this action. . . .

ALVIN B. RUBIN, CIRCUIT JUDGE, with whom VANCE, FRANK M. JOHNSON, JR., HATCHETT, and SAM D. JOHNSON, CIRCUIT JUDGES, join, dissenting.

The majority opinion is both a scholarly and pragmatic exposition of the reasons why § 1983 claimants should in some cases be required to resort to administrative remedies before entering federal court. The evident fault lies not in its logic but in its eventual, albeit respectful, disregard for the numerous instances in which the Supreme Court has stated, "apparently quite categorically, that exhaustion is not required in § 1983 cases". . . .

KRAVITCH, CIRCUIT JUDGE, dissenting.

The majority, in a comprehensive opinion, advances compelling arguments for requiring exhaustion of state administrative remedies, where adequate, as a prerequisite to a § 1983 action. I do not agree, however, that the language in any Supreme Court opinion cited authorizes a lower court to adopt this change. In my judgment, we are bound by the present rule of non-exhaustion until Congress amends the statute or the Supreme Court alters its interpretation.

I therefore dissent.

HATCHETT, CIRCUIT JUDGE, with whom ALVIN B. RUBIN, VANCE, FRANK M. JOHNSON, JR. and THOMAS A. CLARK, CIRCUIT JUDGES, join, dissenting. . . .

The majority holds that "adequate and appropriate state administrative remedies must be exhausted before a § 1983 action is permitted to proceed in federal court absent any of the traditional exceptions to the general exhaustion rule." I dissent because this holding contravenes numerous decisions of the nation's highest Court; presumes a congressional intent never articulated by Congress; usurps authority delegated to Congress; and turns the clock back to the 1950's by creating a procedural nightmare that can only have a "chilling effect" on civil rights litigation. In short, I dissent because I believe the majority opinion is both legally unsound and judicially inappropriate. . . .

There are many reasons why this court should not abolish the no-exhaustion rule. First, and fundamentally, the Supreme Court has enunciated and continually followed the no-exhaustion rule. . . .

Second, . . . Congress did not intend to require exhaustion of state administrative remedies. . . .

Third, although it is often argued that administrative remedies should be exhausted because of the "expertise" of an administrative body, where federal issues are involved no such "expertise" resides in state administrative agencies. . . .

Fourth, there is a very real danger that the delay inherent in requiring use of state administrative processes may discourage aggrieved individuals from seeking vindication of their rights. . . .

Fifth, the majority opinion may create a time-consuming procedural nightmare, the curse of both litigants and federal trial judges. After the filing of a § 1983 complaint, the defendant will likely move to dismiss on the ground that the state administrative remedies are adequate. To rule on this motion, the district court will not only have to examine state remedies, but also take testimony from knowledgeable persons as to how the administrative process really works. If the state administrative remedy is found adequate, the court will have to decide whether to dismiss the suit or retain jurisdiction. Presumably, the state's statute of limitations will be tolled during the ensuing period of exhaustion since the majority makes pursuit of state administrative remedies a prerequisite to federal suit. If the plaintiff loses on every point of the state administrative claim, since neither res judicata nor collateral estoppel [applies], the plaintiff may then, having exhausted administrative remedies, return to the federal court to continue the suit.

Sixth, the typical state administrative process is not constituted to provide adequately for the award of costs and attorney's fees. Thus, even when a litigant prevails in the state administrative process, he will still need to return to federal court for an award of costs and attorney's fees. By the time the prevailing plaintiff completes the procedural nightmare dictated by the majority opinion, costs and attorney's fees will be staggering.

Seventh, most administrative processes cannot adequately entertain class action claims. In the typical administrative setting, when an individual plaintiff is a member of a class and is suing to protect the rights of the class, an individual settlement[, a]lthough satisfactory to the individual plaintiff, . . . may not protect other class members from like deprivations.

Eighth, assuming that considerations of federal-state friction avoidance are relevant, friction between the states and the federal judiciary can only increase under a system that requires federal courts to judge the adequacy of state administrative remedies. Moreover, the majority opinion will in fact interfere with orderly state procedures. What will be the effect of a federal court ruling that a particular state administrative scheme is not adequate for the protections of litigants' constitutional rights? Will the state be under any duty to amend its statutes and regulations for the next litigant? If the state disagrees with this finding, may it appeal? May the state participate in the hearing regarding the adequacy of state remedies? . . .

Exhaustion of state administrative remedies simply has no place in the civil rights context. I agree with Judge Friendly's conclusion that "[i]t is hard to conceive a task more appropriate for federal courts than to protect civil rights guaranteed by the Constitution against invasion by the states." H. Friendly, Federal Jurisdiction: A General View 90 (1973). Today's institution of an exhaustion requirement can only interfere with our performance of that most appropriate task.

PATSY v. BOARD OF REGENTS

Supreme Court of the United States, 1982.
457 U.S. 496.

JUSTICE MARSHALL delivered the opinion of the Court.

This case presents the question whether exhaustion of state administrative remedies is a prerequisite to an action under 42 U.S.C. § 1983. . . .

I

[The Court's summary of the proceedings below is omitted.]

II

The question whether exhaustion of administrative remedies should ever be required in a § 1983 action has promoted vigorous debate and disagreement. Our resolution of this issue, however, is made much easier because we are not writing on a clean slate. This Court has addressed this issue, as well as related issues, on several prior occasions.

Respondent suggests that our prior precedents do not control our decision today, arguing that these cases can be distinguished on their facts or that this Court did not "fully" consider the question whether exhaustion should be required. This contention need not detain us long. Beginning with McNeese v. Board of Education, 373 U.S. 668, 671–73 (1963), we have on numerous occasions rejected the argument that a § 1983 action should be dismissed where the plaintiff has not exhausted state administrative remedies. Respondent may be correct in arguing that several of these decisions could have been based on traditional exceptions to the exhaustion doctrine. Nevertheless, this Court has stated categorically that exhaustion is not a prerequisite to an action under § 1983, and we have not deviated from that position in the 19 years since *McNeese*. Therefore, we do not address the question presented in this case as one of first impression.

III

Respondent argues that we should reconsider these decisions and adopt the Court of Appeals' exhaustion rule, which was based on McKart v. United States, 395 U.S. 185 (1969). This Court has never announced a definitive formula for determining whether prior decisions should be overruled or reconsidered. However, in Monell v. New York City Dept. of Social Services, 436 U.S. 658, 695–701 (1978), we articulated four factors that should be considered. Two of these factors— whether the decisions in question misconstrued the meaning of the statute as revealed in its legislative history and whether overruling these decisions would be inconsistent with more recent expressions of congressional intent—are particularly relevant to our decision today.[3]

. . .

A

In determining whether our prior decisions misconstrued the meaning of § 1983, we begin with a review of the legislative history to § 1 of the Civil Rights Act of 1871, the precursor to § 1983. Although we recognize that the 1871 Congress did not expressly contemplate the exhaustion question, we believe that the tenor of the debates over § 1 supports our conclusion that exhaustion of administrative remedies in § 1983 actions should not be judicially imposed.

The Civil Rights Act of 1871, along with the 14th amendment it was enacted to enforce, were crucial ingredients in the basic alteration of our federal system accomplished during the Reconstruction Era. During that time, the federal government was clearly established as a guarantor of the basic federal rights of individuals against incursions by state power. . . .

At least three recurring themes in the debates over § 1 cast serious doubt on the suggestion that requiring exhaustion of state administrative remedies would be consistent with the intent of the 1871 Congress. First, in passing § 1, Congress assigned to the federal courts a paramount role in protecting constitutional rights. . . . The 1871 Congress intended § 1 to "throw open the doors of the United States courts" to individuals who were threatened with, or who had suffered, the deprivation of constitutional rights and to provide these individuals immediate access to the federal courts notwithstanding any provision of state law to the contrary. . . .

A second theme in the debates further suggests that the 1871 Congress would not have wanted to impose an exhaustion requirement. A major factor motivating the expansion of federal jurisdiction through §§ 1 and 2 of the bill was the belief of the 1871 Congress that the state authorities had been unable or unwilling to protect the constitutional rights of individuals or to punish those who violated these rights. Of primary importance to the exhaustion question was the mistrust that the 1871 Congress held for the factfinding processes of state institutions. This Congress believed that federal courts would be less susceptible to local prejudice and to the existing defects in the factfinding processes of the state courts. This perceived defect in the states' factfinding processes is particularly relevant to the question of exhaustion of administrative remedies: exhaustion rules are often applied in

---

[3] The other factors discussed in *Monell*—whether the decisions in question constituted a departure from prior decisions and whether overruling these decisions would frustrate legitimate reliance on their holdings—do not support overruling these decisions. *McNeese* was not a departure from prior decisions—this Court had not previously addressed the application of the exhaustion rule to § 1983 actions. Overruling these decisions might injure those § 1983 plaintiffs who had forgone or waived their state administrative remedies in reliance on these decisions.

deference to the superior factfinding ability of the relevant administrative agency.

A third feature of the debates relevant to the exhaustion question is the fact that many legislators interpreted the bill to provide dual or concurrent forums in the state and federal system, enabling the plaintiff to choose the forum in which to seek relief. . . .

This legislative history supports the conclusion that our prior decisions, holding that exhaustion of state administrative remedies is not a prerequisite to an action under § 1983, did not misperceive the statutory intent: it seems fair to infer that the 1871 Congress did not intend that an individual be compelled in every case to exhaust state administrative remedies before filing an action under § 1 of the Civil Rights Act. We recognize, however, that drawing such a conclusion from this history alone is somewhat precarious: the 1871 Congress was not presented with the question of exhaustion of administrative remedies, nor was it aware of the potential role of state administrative agencies. Therefore, we do not rely exclusively on this legislative history in deciding the question presented here. Congress addressed the question of exhaustion under § 1983 when it recently enacted 42 U.S.C. § 1997e. The legislative history of § 1997e provides strong evidence of congressional intent on this issue.

B

The Civil Rights of Institutionalized Persons Act, 42 U.S.C. § 1997 et seq., was enacted primarily to ensure that the United States Attorney General has "legal standing to enforce existing constitutional rights and federal statutory rights of institutionalized persons." H.R.Conf.Rep. No. 96-897, 9 (1980). In § 1997e, Congress also created a specific, limited exhaustion requirement for adult prisoners bringing actions pursuant to § 1983. Section 1997e and its legislative history demonstrate that Congress understood that exhaustion is not generally required in § 1983 actions, and that it decided to carve out only a narrow exception to this rule. A judicially imposed exhaustion requirement would be inconsistent with Congress' decision to adopt § 1997e and would usurp policy judgments that Congress has reserved for itself.

In considering whether an exhaustion requirement should be incorporated into the bill, Congress clearly expressed its belief that a decision to require exhaustion for certain § 1983 actions would work a change in the law. Witnesses testifying before the subcommittee that drafted the bill discussed the decisions of this Court holding that exhaustion was not required. . . .

The debates over adopting an exhaustion requirement also reflect this understanding. With the understanding that exhaustion generally is not required, Congress decided to adopt the limited exhaustion requirement of § 1997e in order to relieve the burden on the federal courts by diverting certain prisoner petitions back through state and local institutions, and also to encourage the states to develop appropriate grievance procedures. Implicit in this decision is Congress' conclusion that the no-exhaustion rule should be left standing with respect to other § 1983 suits. . . .

In sum, the exhaustion provisions of the [Civil Rights of Institutionalized Persons] Act make sense, and are not superfluous, only if exhaustion could not be required before its enactment and if Congress intended to carve out a narrow exception to this no-exhaustion rule. The legislative history of § 1997e demonstrates that Congress has taken the approach of carving out specific exceptions to the general rule that federal courts cannot require exhaustion under § 1983. It is not our province to alter the balance struck by Congress in establishing the procedural framework for bringing actions under § 1983.

C

Respondent and the Court of Appeals argue that exhaustion of administrative remedies should be required because it would further various policies. They argue that an exhaustion requirement would lessen the perceived burden that § 1983 actions impose on federal courts, would further the goal of comity and improve federal-state relations by postponing federal-court review until after the state administrative agency had passed on the issue; and would enable the agency, which presumably has expertise in the area at issue, to enlighten the federal court's ultimate decision.

As we noted earlier, policy considerations alone cannot justify judicially imposed exhaustion unless exhaustion is consistent with congressional intent. Furthermore, . . . the relevant policy considerations do not invariably point in one direction, and there is vehement disagreement over the validity of the assumptions underlying many of them. The very difficulty of these policy considerations, and Congress' superior institutional competence to pursue this debate, suggest that legislative not judicial solutions are preferable.

Beyond the policy issues that must be resolved in deciding *whether* to require exhaustion, there are equally difficult questions concerning the design and scope of an exhaustion requirement. These questions include how to define those categories of § 1983 claims in which exhaustion might be desirable; how to unify and centralize the standards for judging the kinds of administrative procedures that should be exhausted; what tolling requirements and time limitations should be adopted; what is the res judicata and collateral estoppel effect of particular administrative determinations; what consequences should attach to the failure to comply with procedural requirements of administrative proceedings; and whether federal courts could grant necessary interim injunctive relief and hold the action pending exhaustion, or proceed to judgment without requiring exhaustion even though exhaustion might otherwise be required, where the relevant administrative agency is either powerless or not inclined to grant such interim relief. These and similar questions might be answered swiftly and surely by legislation, but would create costly, remedy-delaying, and court-burdening litigation if answered incrementally by the judiciary in the context of diverse constitutional claims relating to thousands of different state agencies.

The very variety of claims, claimants, and state agencies involved in § 1983 cases argues for congressional consideration of the myriad of policy considerations. . . .

IV

Based on the legislative histories of both § 1983 and § 1997e, we conclude that exhaustion of state administrative remedies should not be required as a prerequisite to bringing an action pursuant to § 1983. We decline to overturn our prior decisions holding that such exhaustion is not required. The decision of the Court of Appeals is reversed, and the case is remanded for proceedings consistent with this opinion.

It is so ordered.

JUSTICE O'CONNOR, with whom JUSTICE REHNQUIST, joins, concurring.

As discussed in Justice Powell's dissenting opinion, as well as in the opinion of the court below, considerations of sound policy suggest that a § 1983 plaintiff should be required to exhaust adequate state administrative remedies before filing his complaint. At the very least, prior state administrative proceedings would resolve many claims, thereby decreasing the number of § 1983 actions filed in the federal courts, which are now straining under excessive caseloads. However, for the reasons set forth in the Court's opinion, this Court already has ruled that, in the absence of additional congressional legislation, exhaustion of administrative remedies is not required in § 1983 actions. Perhaps Congress' enactment of the Civil Rights of Institutionalized Persons Act, which creates a limited exhaustion requirement for prisoners bringing § 1983 suits, will prompt it to reconsider the possibility of requiring exhaustion in the remainder of § 1983 cases. Reluctantly, I concur.

JUSTICE WHITE, concurring in all but part III–B.

I fully agree with the Court that our frequent and unequivocal statements on exhaustion cannot be explained or distinguished away as the Fifth Circuit attempted to do. For nearly 20 years and on at least 10 occasions, this Court has clearly held that no exhaustion of administrative remedies is required in a § 1983 suit. Whether or not this initially was a wise choice, these decisions are stare decisis, and in a statutory case, a particularly strong showing is required that we have misread the relevant statute and its history. . . . I accordingly join the judgment and all but part III–B of the opinion of the Court.

In part III–B, the Court unnecessarily and unwisely ventures further to find support where none may be had. The wisdom of a general no-exhaustion rule in § 1983 suits was not at issue when Congress considered and passed the Civil Rights of Institutionalized Persons Act. As Justice Powell persuasively points out in his dissenting opinion, and as reflected in the title of the act, congressional attention was narrowly focused on procedures concerning the legal rights of prisoners and other institutionalized persons. Unsurprisingly, the legislation which emerged addressed only the specific problem under investigation; it indicates neither approval of a no-exhaustion rule nor an intent to preclude us from reconsidering the issue.

As the Court acknowledges, the policy arguments cut in both directions. The Court concludes that "the very difficulty of these policy considerations, and Congress' superior institutional competence . . . suggest that legislative not judicial decisions are preferable." To be sure, exhaustion is a statutory issue and the dispositive word on the matter belongs to Congress. It does not follow, however, that, were the issue not foreclosed by earlier decisions, we would be institutionally incompetent to formulate an exhaustion rule. The lack of an exhaustion requirement in § 1983 actions is itself an exception to the general rule, judicially formulated, that exhaustion of administrative remedies is required in a civil action. Myers v. Bethlehem Shipbuilding Corp., 303 U.S. 41 (1938); McKart v. United States, 395 U.S. 185 (1969). Unlike other statutory questions, exhaustion is "a rule of judicial administration," *Myers v. Bethlehem Shipbuilding Corp.*, supra, at 50, and unless Congress directs otherwise, rightfully subject to crafting by judges. Our resolution of this case as governed by stare decisis, reinforced by the legislative history of § 1983, should not be taken as undercutting the general exhaustion principle of long standing. The result today is also fully consistent with our decisions that a defendant in a civil or administrative enforcement proceeding may not enjoin and sidetrack that proceeding by resorting to a § 1983 action in federal court, Huffman v. Pursue, Ltd., 420 U.S. 592 (1975); Juidice v. Vail, 430 U.S. 327 (1977); Trainor v. Hernandez, 431 U.S. 434 (1977); Moore v. Sims, 442 U.S. 415 (1979), and that a federal action should be stayed pending determination of state-law issues central to the constitutional dispute. Railroad Comm'n v. Pullman Co., 312 U.S. 496 (1941). On this understanding, I join all but part III–B of the opinion of the Court.

JUSTICE POWELL, dissenting.[a] . . .

Seventeen judges joined in the Court of Appeals' persuasive opinion adopting a rule of "flexible" exhaustion of administrative remedies in § 1983 suits. Other Courts of Appeals have adopted a similar rule. The opinion for the en banc court carefully reviewed the exhaustion doctrine in general and as applied to § 1983 actions. It found that the prior decisions of this Court did not clearly decide the question. And it concluded that the exhaustion of adequate and appropriate state administrative remedies would promote the achievement of the rights protected by § 1983.

I agree with the Court of Appeals' opinion. The requirement that a § 1983 plaintiff exhaust adequate state administrative remedies was the accepted rule of law until quite recently. The rule rests on sound considerations. It does not defeat federal-court jurisdiction, it merely

---

[a] Chief Justice Burger joined the portion of the dissent from which these excerpts are taken. He did not join Justice Powell's discussion of an unrelated 11th amendment issue. [Footnote by eds.]

defers it. It permits the states to correct violations through their own procedures, and it encourages the establishment of such procedures. It is consistent with the principles of comity that apply whenever federal courts are asked to review state action or supersede state proceedings. See Younger v. Harris, 401 U.S. 37 (1971).

Moreover, and highly relevant to the effective functioning of the over-burdened federal court system, the rule conserves and supplements scarce judicial resources. In 1961, the year that Monroe v. Pape, 365 U.S. 167 (1961), was decided, only 270 civil rights actions were begun in the federal district courts. In 1981, over 30,000 such suits were commenced.[20] The result of this unprecedented increase in civil rights litigation is a heavy burden on the federal courts to the detriment of all federal-court litigants, including others who assert that their constitutional rights have been infringed.

The Court argues that past decisions of the Court categorically hold that there is no exhaustion requirement in § 1983 suits. But as the Court of Appeals demonstrates, and as the Court recognizes, many of these decisions can be explained as applications of traditional exceptions to the exhaustion requirement. See McNeese v. Board of Education, 373 U.S. 668 (1963). Other decisions speak to the question in an off-hand and conclusory fashion without full briefing and argument. Moreover, a categorical no-exhaustion rule would seem inconsistent with the decision in *Younger v. Harris*, supra, prescribing abstention when state criminal proceedings are pending. At least where administrative proceedings are pending, *Younger* would seem to suggest the appropriateness of exhaustion. Yet the Court today adopts a flat rule without exception.

The Court seeks to support its no-exhaustion rule with indications of congressional intent. Finding nothing directly on point in the history of the Civil Rights Act itself, the Court places primary reliance on the recent Civil Rights of Institutionalized Persons Act, 42 U.S.C. § 1997 et seq. This legislation was designed to authorize the Attorney General to initiate civil rights actions on behalf of institutionalized persons. § 1997a. The act also placed certain limits on the existing authority of the Attorney General to intervene in suits begun by institutionalized persons. See § 1997c. In addition, in § 1997e, the act sets forth an exhaustion requirement but only for § 1983 claims brought by prisoners.

On the basis of the exhaustion provision in § 1997e . . ., the Court contends that Congress has endorsed a *general* no-exhaustion rule. The irony in this reasoning should be obvious. A principal concern that prompted the Department of Justice to support, and the Congress to adopt, § 1997e was the vast increase in § 1983 suits brought by state prisoners in federal courts. There has been a year-by-year increase in these suits since the mid-1960's. The increase in fiscal

[20] Of the approximately 30,000 civil rights suits filed in fiscal year 1981, 15,639 were filed by state prisoners under § 1983.

The remainder involved a variety of civil rights suits.

1981 over fiscal 1980 was some 26%, resulting in a total of 15,639 such suits filed in 1981 as compared with 12,397 in 1980. The 1981 total constituted over 8.6% of the total federal district court civil docket. Although most of these cases present frivolous claims, many are litigated through the courts of appeals to this Court. The burden on the system fairly can be described as enormous with few, if any, benefits that would not be available in meritorious cases if exhaustion of appropriate administrative remedies were required prior to any federal-court litigation. It was primarily this problem that prompted enactment of § 1997e.

Moreover, it is clear from the legislative history that Congress simply was not addressing the exhaustion problem in any general fashion. The concern focused on the problem of prisoner petitions. The new act had a dual purpose in this respect. In addition to requiring prior exhaustion of adequate state remedies, Congress wished to authorize the Attorney General to act when necessary to protect the constitutional rights of prisoners, but at the same time minimize the need for federal action of any kind by requiring prior exhaustion. . . .

In short, in enacting the Civil Rights of Institutionalized Persons Act Congress was focusing on the powers of the Attorney General, and the particular question of prisoners' suits, not on the general question of exhaustion in § 1983 actions. Also revealing as to the limited purpose of § 1997e is Congress' consistent refusal to adopt legislation imposing a general no-exhaustion requirement. Thus, for example, in 1979, a bill was introduced into the Senate providing:

"No court of the United States shall stay or dismiss any civil action brought under this act on the ground that the party bringing such action failed to exhaust the remedies available in the courts or the administrative agencies of any state." S.1983, 96th Cong., 1st Sess., § 5 (1979).

The bill was never reported out of committee.

The requirement that plaintiffs exhaust available and adequate administrative remedies—subject to well-developed exceptions—is firmly established in virtually every area of the law. This is dictated in § 1983 actions by common sense, as well as by comity and federalism, where adequate state administrative remedies are available.

[On the exhaustion issue] I would affirm the Court of Appeals.

NOTES ON EXHAUSTION OF STATE REMEDIES

1. **Questions and Comments on *Patsy*.** Was the Supreme Court right in *Patsy*? If so, on what ground? Is it decisive that the Court had previously ruled on the issue? Or that Congress in enacting § 1997e obviously was aware of the Court's prior rulings? Or that endorsing an exhaustion requirement would have raised a number of difficult questions of administration?

Note that at least four Justices indicated that they would endorse an exhaustion requirement as a matter of policy, even though only two of them felt free to vote that way. The majority opinion, on the other hand, did not fully engage in a debate on the merits of the question. If they were freed from the constraints of precedent and legislative history, how should the questions be resolved? Do the purposes advanced by the Fifth Circuit majority justify an exhaustion requirement? Or, as claimed by the dissent, would it "turn the clock back" and create a "procedural nightmare" for civil rights litigation?

2. The Civil Rights of Institutionalized Persons Act. A good deal of the debate in *Patsy* turns on the inferences, if any, that can be drawn from the enactment in 1980 of the Civil Rights of Institutionalized Persons Act, now codified at 42 U.S.C. § 1997. The main purpose of that legislation was to confer standing on the Attorney General to file civil suits on behalf of institutionalized persons. Additionally, § 1997e imposes a limited exhaustion requirement for adult prisoners bringing suit under § 1983. That requirement is subject to elaborate conditions.

Specifically, the statute spells out minimum standards to which state administrative remedies must adhere if they are to qualify for mandatory exhaustion. These standards include such requirements as priority processing of emergency grievances, safeguards against reprisals against participants in the procedure, and independent review of the disposition of grievances by a person not under the direct supervision or control of the institution. Perhaps the most important limitation is that there be "an advisory role" for both employees and inmates "in the formulation, implementation, and operation of the system." Finally, the statute directs that the Attorney General promulgate more detailed regulations consistent with these statutory standards.

In order to qualify for exhaustion under the statute, a state grievance procedure must be certified by the Attorney General or by a court to be in "substantial compliance" with the statutory standards. Additionally, the court must find in the individual case that requiring exhaustion would be "appropriate and in the interest of justice." If these findings are made, the court may require resort to the state remedies, but the case is not dismissed from the federal docket. The litigation is simply held in abeyance for a period not to exceed 90 days.

Experience so far under § 1997e has drawn mixed reactions. Judge James Turk of the Western District of Virginia has termed the statute "a viable mechanism for unburdening the federal courts of trivial and non-serious prisoner litigation." Turk, The Nation's First Application of the Exhaustion Requirement of 42 U.S.C. § 1997e: "The Virginia Experience," 7 Am.J. Trial Adv. 1 (1983). Judge Kevin Thomas Duffy of the Southern District of New York, by contrast, describes § 1997e as so hedged about with limitations as to be "incapable of fulfilling congressional expectations." Duffy, The Civil Rights Act: A Need for Re-evaluation of the Non-Exhaustion Doctrine Applied to Prisoner Section 1983 Lawsuits, 4 Pace L.Rev. 61, 74 (1983). Perhaps the most elaborate analysis appears in an article by Donald Lay, Chief Judge of the Eighth Circuit. In Exhaustion of Grievance Procedures for State Prisoners Under Section 1997e of the Civil Rights Act, 71 Iowa L.Rev. 935 (1986), Judge Lay describes the operation of the statute and examines the procedures adopted in Virginia, Wyoming, and Iowa. The article also discusses reasons why many states have not applied for certification of prisoner grievance procedures. Lay concludes that the kind of procedure contemplated by § 1997e can provide "an effective mechanism within correctional institutions for the prompt and fair resolution of inmate grievances" and that the states "have much to gain" by adopting such procedures.

3. Challenges to State Taxes. Fair Assessment in Real Estate Association, Inc. v. McNary, 454 U.S. 100 (1981), was a § 1983 damage action brought by taxpayers who alleged defects in the administration of local property taxes. Specifically, they claimed that recently improved properties were unfairly taxed at a higher percentage of market value and that taxpayers who successfully challenged their assessments were specifically targeted for reassessment the next year. The District Court dismissed the action, and the Supreme Court ultimately affirmed. Although the Justices agreed on the outcome, they were sharply divided on the rationale.

(i) Exhaustion of State Judicial Remedies. Writing for the Court, Justice Rehnquist characterized the case as a conflict between "two divergent lines of authority respecting access to federal courts for adjudication of the constitutionality of state tax laws." On the one hand, § 1983 ordinarily requires no exhaustion of state remedies, whether administrative or judicial. On the other hand, a line of federal cases restricted federal injunctive interference with state tax laws, thus relegating some federal claimants to litigation in state courts. This principle was codified in the Tax Injunction Act of 1937, 28 U.S.C. § 1341, which provides: "The district courts shall not enjoin, suspend or restrain the assessment, levy or collection of any tax under State law where a plain, speedy and efficient remedy may be had in the court of such State." Although this statute might have been read to reach only injunctions, in Great Lakes Dredge & Dock Co. v. Huffman, 319 U.S. 293 (1943), the Court held that it barred declaratory relief as well.

Nevertheless, doubt remained as to whether the statute applied where, as was true in *Fair Assessment*, the taxpayers sought damages for taxes already paid rather than any form of anticipatory relief. The Court therefore based its decision not on the precise terms of the Tax Injunction Act but on the more general principle of federal-state comity, as exemplified by Younger v. Harris, 401 U.S. 37 (1971):

> "Petitioners will not recover damages under § 1983 unless a district court first determines that respondents' administration of the county tax system violated petitioners' constitutional rights. In effect, the district court must first enter a declaratory judgment like that barred in *Great Lakes*. We are convinced that such a determination would be fully as intru-

sive as the equitable actions that are barred by principles of comity. Moreover, the intrusiveness of such § 1983 actions would be exacerbated by the nonexhaustion doctrine of Monroe v. Pape, 365 U.S. 167 (1961). Taxpayers such as petitioners would be able to invoke federal judgments without first permitting the state to rectify any alleged impropriety. . . .

"This intrusion, although undoubtedly present in every § 1983 claim, is particularly highlighted by the facts of this case. Defendants are not one or two isolated administrators, but virtually every key tax official in St. Louis County. . . . In addition, the actions challenged in the complaint—unequal assessment of new and old property and retaliatory assessment of property belonging to those who successfully appeal to the Board of Equalization—may well be the result of policies or practicalities beyond the control of any individual officer. [A] judicial determination of official liability for the acts complained of, even though necessarily based upon a finding of bad faith, would have an undeniable chilling effect upon the actions of all county officers governed by the same practicalities or required to implement the same policies. There is little doubt that such officials, faced with the prospect of personal liability to numerous taxpayers, not to mention the assessment of attorney's fees under § 1988, would promptly cease the conduct found to have infringed petitioners' constitutional rights, whether or not those officials were acting in good faith. In short, petitioners' actions would 'in every practical sense operate to suspend collection of the state taxes . . .,' *Great Lakes*, supra, at 299, a form of federal court interference previously rejected by this Court on principles of federalism. . . .

"Therefore, despite the ready access to federal courts provided by *Monroe* and its progeny, we hold that taxpayers are barred by the principle of comity from asserting § 1983 actions against the validity of state tax systems in federal courts. Such taxpayers must seek protection of their federal rights by state remedies, provided of course that those remedies are plain, adequate and complete, and may ultimately seek review of the state decisions in this Court."

The Court noted that the adequacy of the available state remedies was not at issue in this case and that the state supreme court had "expressly held that plaintiffs such as petitioners may assert a § 1983 claim in state court."

　　(ii) Exhaustion of State Administrative Remedies. Justices Brennan, Marshall, Stevens, and O'Connor concurred in the judgment. Speaking for the minority, Brennan attacked the Court's conclusion that the comity principles of *Younger v. Harris* could oust a federal court of jurisdiction over an action for damages:

"While the 'principle of comity' may be source of judicial policy, it is emphatically no source of judicial *power* to renounce jurisdiction. The application of the comity principle has thus been limited to a relatively narrow class of cases: Only where a federal court is asked to employ its historic powers as a court of equity, and is called upon to decide whether to exercise the broadest and potentially most intrusive form of judicial authority, does 'comity' have an established and substantial role in informing the exercise of the court's discretion. There is little room for the 'principle of comity' in actions at law where, apart from matters of administration, judicial discretion is at a minimum."

Brennan interpreted the Tax Injunction Act to apply only to actions for anticipatory relief. He thus concluded that Congress had not excepted this case from the ordinary jurisdictional statutes, and the Court had no power to do so.

Nonetheless, Brennan agreed that this particular suit should have been dismissed. The reason was the taxpayers' failure to exhaust the state *administrative* opportunities for challenging their tax assessments:

"[W]hile this Court has repeatedly reaffirmed that exhaustion of administrative remedies is not a precondition to a suit brought under the Civil Rights Acts, that conclusion rests firmly on the understanding that such was the intention of Congress in enacting § 1983. Where Congress has provided that in a particular class of cases the federal courts should refrain from hearing suits brought under § 1983 until administrative remedies have been exhausted, see, e.g., 42 U.S.C. § 1997e, there is no doubt that the federal courts are bound by that limitation. Cf. Preiser v. Rodriguez, 411 U.S. 475, 489–90 (1973). My view has always been that displacement of § 1983 remedies can only 'be justified by a clear statement of congressional intent, or, at the very least, by the presence of the most persuasive considerations of policy.' Id. at 518 (Brennan, J., dissenting). Surely a somewhat lesser showing is required where, as here, we are concerned not with the displacement of the § 1983 remedy, but with deferral of federal court consideration pending exhaustion of the state *administrative* process. Where the obligation to require exhaustion of administrative remedies may be fairly understood from congressional action, or is in accord with congressional policy, not only is § 1983 no bar, but the federal courts should be alert to further these policies.

"We plainly have sufficient evidence of such congressional policy here. [I]n enacting the Tax Injunction Act, Congress sought to assure that the federal court would remain open to suits for monetary relief in state tax cases 'if the requisite elements of federal jurisdiction existed.' In 1937 the requirement of exhaustion of state administrative remedies was certainly a mandatory precondition to suit, and in that sense a 'jurisdictional prerequisite.' Nevertheless, we need not reach the conclusion that Congress intended by enactment of the Tax Injunction Act to freeze the then-operative jurisdictional practice of the federal courts in order to recognize that the administrative-exhaustion requirement is entirely consonant with the principal purposes of the act: to provide assurance that federal courts exercise at least the same restraint in dealing with questions of state tax administration as the courts of the state that levied that tax. Where administrative remedies are a precondition to suit for monetary relief in state court, absent some substantial consideration compelling a contrary result in a particular case, those remedies should be deemed a precondition to suit in federal court as well."

(iii) **Questions and Comments on** *Fair Assessment.* The minority position in *Fair Assessment* seems odd in light of *Patsy.* At the least, the broad holding of *Patsy* is called into question by Justice Brennan's pronouncement in *Fair Assessment*: "Where administrative remedies are a precondition to suit for monetary relief in state court, absent some substantial consideration compelling a contrary result in a particular case, those remedies should be deemed a precondition to suit in federal court as well." Does this mean that, if exhaustion of state administrative remedies is required prior to bringing a state suit, such exhaustion is also required before a § 1983 suit can be brought? If so, what is left of *Patsy*?

The *Fair Assessment* majority, by contrast, embraced a different set of problems. Justice Rehnquist does not directly address *McNeese v. Board of Education* and subsequent cases dealing with exhaustion of state *administrative* remedies, but presumably any state requirement of exhaustion of administrative remedies would be enforced in state court. More fundamentally, however, Rehnquist's view creates a tension with *Monroe v. Pape* and its rejection of any requirement of exhaustion of state *judicial* remedies for § 1983 claims.

The *Fair Assessment* decision is extensively criticized on this ground by Daan Braveman in *Fair Assessment* and Federal Jurisdiction in Civil Rights Cases, 45 U.Pitt.L.Rev. 351 (1984). Braveman argues that both the Tax Injunction Act and the policies underlying that statute apply only to anticipatory interference with the administration of state tax laws. In his view, the extension of *Younger* comity principles to an action for damages threatens to undermine the no-exhaustion   principle of *Monroe v. Pape.* As Braveman puts it, the Court "fails to explain any real difference between [*Fair Assessment*] and every other § 1983 case." What principle, he asks, prevents the doctrine of *Fair Assessment* "from completely eroding the congressional intent underlying § 1983, which places the federal courts between the people and the states as guardians of federal constitutional rights?" Read broadly, *Fair Assessment* "moves the Court closer to the notion the [*Younger*] requires litigants to exhaust state judicial remedies whenever they seek to challenge the constitutionality of a state practice or policy."

Is this criticism persuasive? What about the Court's asserted grounds for differentiating this case from other § 1983 actions? Should it matter that suit was brought not against one or two offending officials but against "virtually every key tax official" in the country? That other tax officials might be "chilled" from engaging in similar practices? In short, on what ground, if any, can *Fair Assessment* be reconciled with the principle that state judicial remedies need not be asserted prior to resort to § 1983?

4. Notice-of-Claim Statutes. A Wisconsin statute provided that before a suit could be filed against a state or local government or officer, the plaintiff was required to give the government notice of the amount and circumstances of the claim within 120 days of the occurrence and to forbear filing suit for 120 days after providing such notice. The application of this statute to § 1983 claims filed in state court was disapproved in Felder v. Casey, ___ U.S. ___ (1988).

Speaking for the Court, Justice Brennan reasoned that the purpose of the statute to minimize governmental liability was "manifestly inconsistent" with the remedial purposes of § 1983. Moreover, the special four-month statute of limitations only for those tort victims who sue governmental defendants was thought to discriminate against federal rights. And the notice-of-claim statute was regarded as in effect an exhaustion requirement and on that ground inconsistent with *Patsy*. Justice White concurred on the view that the notice-of-claim statute was inconsistent with the policies underlying Wilson v. Garcia, 471 U.S. 261 (1985), namely the uniformity and certainty of applicable statutes of limitation and the absence of discrimination against federal claims.

Justice O'Connor, with whom Justice Rehnquist joined, dissented. She argued that § 1983 plaintiffs should take the state courts as they found them. There was no conflict between the notice-of-claim law and § 1983, as the latter could always be enforced, without regard to such statutes, in federal court. She concluded, therefore, that to construe § 1983 both to allow resort to a state courts and to require that those courts to abandon the usual forum requirements of litigation was a misuse of statutory preemption.

SUBSECTION C: RELEASE–DISMISSAL AGREEMENTS

NEWTON v. RUMERY
Supreme Court of the United States, 1987.
480 U.S. 386.

JUSTICE POWELL announced the judgment of the Court and delivered the opinion of the Court with respect to parts I, II, III–A, IV, and V, and an opinion with respect to part III–B in which THE CHIEF JUSTICE, JUSTICE WHITE, and JUSTICE SCALIA join.

The question in this case is whether a court properly may enforce an agreement in which a criminal defendant releases his right to file a § 1983 action in return for a prosecutor's dismissal of pending criminal charges.

I

In 1983, a grand jury in Rockingham County, New Hampshire, indicted David Champy for aggravated felonious sexual assault. Respondent Bernard Rumery, a friend of Champy's, read about the charges in a local newspaper. Seeking information about the charges, he telephoned Mary Deary, who was acquainted with both Rumery and Champy. Coincidentally, Deary had been the victim of the assault in question and was expected to be the principal witness against Champy. The record does not reveal directly the date or substance of this conversation between Rumery and Deary, but Deary apparently was disturbed by the call. On March 12, according to police records, she called David Barrett, the Chief of Police for the town of Newton. She told him that Rumery was trying to force her to drop the charges against Champy. Rumery talked to Deary again on May 11. The substance of this conversation also is disputed. Rumery claims that Deary called him and that she raised the subject of Champy's difficulties. According to the police records, however, Deary told Chief Barrett that Rumery had threatened that, if Deary went forward on the Champy case, she would "end up like" two women who recently had been murdered in Lowell, Massachusetts. Barrett arrested Rumery and accused him of tampering with a witness in violation of N.H.Rev. Stat.Ann. § 641:5, I(b) (1986), a Class B felony.

Rumery promptly retained Stephen Woods, an experienced criminal defense attorney. Woods contacted Brian Graf, the Deputy County Attorney for Rockingham County. He warned Graf that he "had better [dismiss] these charges, because we're going to win them and after that we're going to sue." After further discussions, Graf and Woods reached an agreement, under which Graf would dismiss the charges against Rumery if Rumery would agree not to sue the town, its officials, or Deary for any harm caused by the arrest. All parties agreed that one factor in Graf's decision not to prosecute Rumery was Graf's desire to protect Deary from the trauma she would suffer if she were forced to testify. As the prosecutor explained in the District Court:

> "I had been advised by Chief Barrett that Mary Deary did not want to testify against Mr. Rumery. The witness tampering charge would have required Mary Deary to testify. . . .
>
> "I think that was a particularly sensitive type of case where you are dealing with a victim of an alleged aggravated felonious sexual assault."

Woods drafted an agreement in which Rumery agreed to release any claims he might have against the town, its officials, or Deary if

Graf agreed to dismiss the criminal charges (the release-dismissal agreement). After Graf approved the form of the agreement, Woods presented it to Rumery. Although Rumery's recollection of the events was quite different, the District Court found that Woods discussed the agreement with Rumery in his office for about an hour and explained to Rumery that he would forgo all civil actions if he signed the agreement. Three days later, on June 6, 1983, Rumery returned to Woods' office and signed the agreement. The criminal charges were dropped.

Ten months later, on April 13, 1984, Rumery filed an action under 42 U.S.C. § 1983 in the federal District Court for the District of New Hampshire. He alleged that the town and its officers had violated his constitutional rights by arresting him, defaming him, and imprisoning him falsely. The defendants filed a motion to dismiss, relying on the release-dismissal agreement as an affirmative defense. Rumery argued that the agreement was unenforceable because it violated public policy. The court rejected Rumery's argument and concluded that a "release of claims under § 1983 is valid . . . if it results from a decision that is voluntary, deliberate and informed." The court found that Rumery

> "is a knowledgeable, industrious individual with vast experience in the business world. [H]e intelligently and carefully, after weighing all the factors, concluded that it would be in his best interest and welfare to sign the covenant. He was also represented by a very competent attorney with more than ordinary expertise in the sometimes complex area of criminal law."

The court then dismissed Rumery's suit.

On appeal, the Court of Appeals for the First Circuit reversed. It adopted a per se rule invalidating release-dismissal agreements. [W]e granted the town's petition for a writ of certiorari. We reverse.

II

We begin by noting the source of the law that governs this case. The agreement purported to waive a right to sue conferred by a federal statute. The question whether the policies underlying that statute may in some circumstances render that waiver unenforceable is a question of federal law. We resolve this question by reference to traditional common-law principles, as we have resolved other questions about the principles governing § 1983 actions. E.g., Pulliam v. Allen, 466 U.S. 522, 539–40 (1984). The relevant principle is well-established: a promise is unenforceable if the interest in its enforcement is outweighed in the circumstances by a public policy harmed by enforcement of the agreement.

III

The Court of Appeals concluded that the public interests related to release-dismissal agreements justified a per se rule of invalidity. We think the court overstated the perceived problems and also failed to credit the significant public interests that such agreements can further. Most importantly, the Court of Appeals did not consider the wide variety of factual situations that can result in release-dismissal agreements. Thus, although we agree that in some cases these agreements may infringe important interests of the criminal defendant and of society as a whole, we do not believe that the mere possibility of harm to these interests calls for a per se rule.

A

Rumery's first objection to release-dismissal agreements is that they are inherently coercive. He argues that it is unfair to present a criminal defendant with a choice between facing criminal charges and waiving his right to sue under § 1983. We agree that some release-dismissal agreements may not be the product of an informed and voluntary decision. The risk, publicity, and expense of a criminal trial may intimidate a defendant, even if he believes his defense is meritorious. But this possibility does not justify invalidating all such agreements. In other contexts criminal defendants are required to make difficult choices that effectively waive constitutional rights. For example, it is well settled that plea bargaining does not violate the Constitution even though a guilty plea waives important constitutional rights.[3] See Brady v. United States, 397 U.S. 742, 752–53 (1970); Santobello v. New York, 404 U.S. 257, 264 (1971) (Douglas, J. concurring). We see no reason to believe that release-dismissal agreements pose a more coercive choice than other situations we have accepted. E.g., Corbitt v. New Jersey, 439 U.S. 212 (1978) (upholding a statute that imposed higher sentences on defendants who went to trial than on those who entered guilty pleas). . . .

In many cases a defendant's choice to enter into a release-dismissal agreement will reflect a highly rational judgment that the certain benefits of escaping criminal prosecution exceed the speculative benefits of prevailing in a civil action. Rumery's voluntary decision to enter this agreement exemplifies such a judgment. Rumery is a sophisticated businessman. He was not in jail and was represented by an experienced criminal lawyer, who drafted the agreement. Rumery considered the agreement for three days before signing it. The benefits of the agreement to Rumery are obvious: he gained immunity from criminal prosecution in consideration of abandoning a civil suit that he may well have lost.

Because Rumery voluntarily waived his right to sue under § 1983, the public interest opposing involuntary waiver of constitutional rights

[3] We recognize that the analogy between plea bargains and release-dismissal agreements is not complete. The former are subject to judicial oversight. Moreover, when the state enters a plea bargain with a criminal defendant, it receives immediate and tangible benefits, such as promptly imposed punishment without the expenditure of prosecutorial resources. Also, the defendant's agreement to plead to some crime tends to ensure some satisfaction of the public interest in the prosecution of crime and confirms that the prosecutor's charges have a basis in fact. The benefits the state may realize in particular cases from release-dismissal agreements may not be as tangible, but they are not insignificant.

is no reason to hold this agreement invalid. Moreover, we find that the possibility of coercion in the making of similar agreements insufficient by itself to justify a per se rule against release-dismissal bargains. If there is such a reason, it must lie in some external public interest necessarily injured by release-dismissal agreements.

B

[T]he Court of Appeals held that all release-dismissal agreements offend public policy because it believed these agreements "tempt prosecutors to trump up charges in reaction to a defendant's civil rights claim, suppress evidence of police misconduct, and leave unremedied deprivations of constitutional rights." We can agree that in some cases there may be a substantial basis for this concern. It is true, of course, that § 1983 actions to vindicate civil rights may further significant public interests. But it is important to remember that Rumery had no public duty to institute a § 1983 action merely to further the public's interest in revealing police misconduct. Congress has confided the decision to bring such actions to the injured individuals, not to the public at large. Thus, we hesitate to elevate more diffused public interests above Rumery's considered decision that he would benefit personally from the agreement.

We also believe the Court of Appeals misapprehended the range of public interests arguably affected by a release-dismissal agreement. The availability of such agreements may threaten important public interests. They may tempt prosecutors to bring frivolous charges, or to dismiss meritorious charges, to protect the interests of other officials.[4] But a per se rule of invalidity fails to credit other relevant public interests and improperly assumes prosecutorial misconduct.[5]

The vindication of constitutional rights and the exposure of official misconduct are not the only concerns implicated by § 1983 suits. No one suggests that all such suits are meritorious. Many are marginal and some are frivolous. Yet even when the risk of ultimate liability is negligible, the burden of defending such lawsuits is substantial. Counsel may be retained by the official, as well as the governmental entity. Preparation for trial, and the trial itself, will require the time and attention of the defendant officials, to the detriment of their public duties. In some cases litigation will extend over a period of years. This diversion of officials from their normal duties and the inevitable expense of defending even unjust claims is distinctly not in the public interest. To the extent release-dismissal agreements protect public

---

[4] Actions taken for these reasons properly have been recognized as unethical. See Model Code of Professional Responsibility, Disciplinary Rule 7–105 (1980).

[5] Prosecutors themselves rarely are held liable in § 1983 actions. See Imbler v. Pachtman, 424 U.S. 409 (1976) (discussing prosecutorial immunity). Also, in many states and municipalities—perhaps in most—prosecutors are elected officials and are entirely independent of the civil authorities likely to be defendants in § 1983 suits. There may be situations, of course, when a prosecutor is motivated to protect the interests of such officials or of police. But the constituency of an elected prosecutor is the public, and such a prosecutor is likely to be influenced primarily by the general public interest.

officials from the burdens of defending such unjust claims, they further this important public interest.

A per se rule invalidating release-dismissal agreements also assumes that prosecutors will seize the opportunity for wrongdoing. In recent years the Court has considered a number of claims that prosecutors have acted improperly. E.g., Wayte v. United States, 470 U.S. 598 (1985); United States v. Goodwin, 457 U.S. 368 (1982); Bordenkircher v. Hayes, 434 U.S. 357 (1978). Our decisions in those cases uniformly have recognized that courts normally must defer to prosecutorial decisions as to whom to prosecute. The reasons for judicial deference are well-known. Prosecutorial charging decisions are rarely simple. In addition to assessing the strength and importance of a case, prosecutors also must consider other tangible and intangible factors, such as government enforcement priorities. Finally, they also must decide how best to allocate the scarce resources of a criminal justice system that simply cannot accommodate the litigation of every serious charge. . . .

Against this background of discretion, the mere opportunity to act improperly does not compel an assumption that all—or even a significant number of—release-dismissal agreements stem from the prosecutors abandoning "the independence of judgment required by [their] public trust," Imbler v. Pachtman, 424 U.S. 409, 423 (1976).[7] Rather, tradition and experience justify our belief that the great majority of prosecutors will be faithful to their duty. Indeed, the merit of this view is illustrated by this case, where the only evidence of prosecutorial misconduct is the agreement itself.

Because release-dismissal agreements may further legitimate prosecutorial and public interests, we reject the Court of Appeals' holding that all such agreements are invalid per se.[8]

IV

Turning to the agreement presented by this case, we conclude that the District Court's decision to enforce the agreement was correct. As we have noted, it is clear that Rumery voluntarily entered the agreement. Moreover, in this case the prosecutor had an independent, legitimate reason to make this agreement directly related to his prose-

---

[7] Of course, the Court has found that certain actions are so likely to result from prosecutorial misconduct that it has " 'presume[d]' an improper vindictive motive," United States v. Goodwin, 457 U.S. 368, 373 (1982). E.g., Blackledge v. Perry, 417 U.S. 21 (1974) (holding that it violates the due process clause for a prosecutor to increase charges in response to a defendant's exercise of his right to appeal). But the complexity of pretrial decisions by prosecutors suggests that judicial evaluation of those decisions should be especially deferential. Thus, the Court has never accepted such a blanket claim with respect to pretrial decisions. See United States v. Good-win, supra; Bordenkircher v. Hayes, 434 U.S. 357 (1978).

[8] Justice Stevens' evaluation of the public interests associated with release-dismissal agreements relies heavily on his view that Rumery is a completely innocent man. He rests this conclusion on the testimony Rumery and his attorney presented to the District Court, but fails to acknowledge that the District Court's factual findings gave little credence to this testimony. Justice Stevens also gives great weight to the fact that Rumery "must be presumed to be innocent." But this is not a criminal case. This is a civil case, in which Rumery bears the ultimate burden of proof.

cutorial responsibilities. The agreement foreclosed both the civil and criminal trials concerning Rumery, in which Deary would have been a key witness. She therefore was spared the public scrutiny and embarrassment she would have endured if she had to testify in either of those cases. Both the prosecutor and the defense attorney testified in the District Court that this was a significant consideration in the prosecutor's decision.

In sum, we conclude that this agreement was voluntary, that there is no evidence of prosecutorial misconduct, and that enforcement of this agreement would not adversely affect the relevant public interests.[10]

V

We reverse the judgment of the Court of Appeals and remand the case to the District Court for dismissal of the complaint.

It is so ordered.

JUSTICE O'CONNOR, concurring in part and in the judgment.

I join in parts I, II, III–A, IV, and V of the Court's opinion. More particularly, I join the Court in disapproving the Court of Appeal's broad holding that a criminal defendant's promise not to sue local governments and officials for constitutional violations arising out of his arrest and prosecution, given in exchange for the prosecutor's agreement to dismiss pending criminal charges, is void, as against public policy under all circumstances. I agree with the Court that a case-by-case approach appropriately balances the important interests on both sides of the question of the enforceability of these agreements, and that on the facts of this particular case Bernard Rumery's covenant not to sue is enforceable. I write separately, however, in order to set out the factors that lead me to conclude that this covenant should be enforced and to emphasize that it is the burden of those relying upon such covenants to establish that the agreement is neither involuntary nor the product of an abuse of the criminal process.

As the Court shows, there are substantial policy reasons for permitting release-dismissal bargains to be struck in appropriate cases. Certainly some § 1983 litigation is meritless, and the inconvenience and distraction of public officials caused by such suits is not inconsiderable. Moreover, particular release-dismissal agreements may serve bona fide criminal justice goals. Here, for example, the protection of Mary Deary, the complaining witness in an aggravated sexual assault case, was an important, legitimate criminal justice objective served by the release-dismissal agreement. Similarly, prosecutors may legitimately believe that, though the police properly defused a volatile situation by arresting a minor misdemeanant, the public interest in further prosecution is outweighed by the cost of litigation. Sparing the local communi-

---

[10] . . . We have no occasion in this case to determine whether an inquiry into voluntariness alone is sufficient to determine the enforceability of release-dismissal agreements. We also note that it would be helpful to conclude release-dismissal agreements under judicial supervision. Although such supervision is not essential to the validity of an otherwise proper agreement, it would help ensure that the agreements did not result from prosecutorial misconduct.

ty the expense of litigation associated with some minor crimes for which there is little or no public interest in prosecution may be a legitimate objective of a release-dismissal agreement.

On the other hand, as the Court acknowledges, release-dismissal agreements potentially threaten the integrity of the criminal process and preclude vindication of federal civil rights. Permitting such releases may tempt public officials to bring frivolous criminal charges in order to deter meritorious civil complaints. The risk and expense of a criminal trial can easily intimidate even an innocent person whose civil and constitutional rights have been violated. The coercive power of criminal process may be twisted to serve the end of suppressing complaints against official abuse, to the detriment not only of the victim of such abuse, but also of society as a whole.

In addition, the availability of the release option may tempt officials to ignore their public duty by dropping meritorious criminal prosecutions in order to avoid the risk, expense and publicity of a § 1983 suit. The public has an interest in seeing its laws faithfully executed. But, officials may give more weight to the private interest in seeing a civil claim settled than to the public interest in seeing the guilty convicted. By introducing extraneous considerations into the criminal process, the legitimacy of that process may be compromised. Release-dismissal bargains risk undermining faith in the fairness of those who administer the criminal process. Finally, the execution of release-dismissal agreements may result in having to determine whether the prosecutor violated any of his ethical obligations as a lawyer.

As the Court indicates, a release-dismissal agreement is not directly analogous to a plea-bargain. The legitimacy of plea bargaining depends in large measure upon eliminating extraneous considerations from the process. See Santobello v. New York, 404 U.S. 257, 260–61 (1971); Brady v. United States, 397 U.S. 742, 753 (1970); ALI, Model Code of Pre-Arraignment Procedure § 350.5(2) (1975). No court would knowingly permit a prosecutor to agree to accept a defendant's plea to a lesser charge in exchange for the defendant's cash payment to the police officers who arrested him. Rather, the prosecutor is permitted to consider only legitimate criminal justice concerns in striking his bargain—concerns such as rehabilitation, allocation of criminal justice resources, the strength of the evidence against the defendant, and the extent of his cooperation with the authorities. The central problem with the release-dismissal agreement is that public criminal justice interests are explicitly traded against the private financial interest of the individuals involved in the arrest and prosecution. Moreover, plea bargaining takes place only under judicial supervision, an important check against abuse. Release-dismissal agreements are often reached between the prosecutor and defendant with little or no judicial oversight.

Nevertheless, the dangers of the release-dismissal agreement do not preclude its enforcement in all cases. The defendants in a § 1983 suit may establish that a particular release executed in exchange for the dismissal of criminal charges was voluntarily made, not the product of prosecutorial overreaching, and in the public interest. But they must prove that this is so; the courts should not presume it as I fear portions of part III–B of the Court's opinion may imply.

Many factors may bear on whether a release was voluntary and not the product of overreaching, some of which come readily to mind. The knowledge and experience of the criminal defendant and the circumstances of the execution of the release, including, importantly, whether the defendant was counseled, are clearly relevant. The nature of the criminal charges that are pending is also important, for the greater the charge, the greater the coercive effect. The existence of a legitimate criminal justice objective for obtaining the release will support its validity. And, importantly, the possibility of abuse is clearly mitigated if the release-dismissal agreement is executed under judicial supervision.

Close examination of all the factors in this case leads me to concur in the Court's decision that this covenant not to sue is enforceable. There is ample evidence in the record concerning the circumstances of the execution of this agreement. Testimony of the prosecutor, defense counsel and Rumery himself leave little doubt that the agreement was entered into voluntarily. While the charge pending against Rumery was serious—subjecting him to up to seven years in prison—it is one of the lesser felonies under New Hampshire law, and a long prison term was probably unlikely given the absence of any prior criminal record and the weaknesses in the case against Rumery. Finally, as the Court correctly notes, the prosecutor had a legitimate reason to enter into this agreement directly related to his criminal justice function. The prosecutor testified that:

> "I had been advised by Chief Barrett that Mary Deary did not want to testify against Mr. Rumery. The witness tampering charge would have required Mary Deary to testify. She would have been the primary source of evidence against Mr. Rumery. There was still considerable concern about Mary Deary because the David Champy case was still pending.

> "I think that was a particular sensitive type of case where you are dealing with a victim of an alleged aggravated felonious sexual assault. And I think I was taking into consideration the fact that I had her as a victim of one case, and now, the state was in a position of perhaps having to force her to testify against her will perhaps causing more trauma or upset to her forcing her to go through more things than what I felt comfortable with doing. So that was one of the considerations I was taking into play at that time, that I had been informed that Mary Deary did not want to go forward with the prosecution, that she felt she had gone through enough."

Thus, Mary Deary's emotional distress, her unwillingness to testify against Rumery, presumably in later civil as well as criminal proceedings, and the necessity of her testimony in the pending sexual assault case against David Champy all support the prosecutor's judgment that the charges against Rumery should be dropped if further injury to Deary, and therefore the Champy case, could thereby be avoided.

Against the convincing evidence that Rumery voluntarily entered into the agreement and that it served the public interest, there is only Rumery's blanket claim that agreements such as this one are inherently coercive. While it would have been preferable, and made this an easier case, had the release-dismissal agreement been concluded under some form of judicial supervision, I concur in the Court's judgment, and all but part III–B of its opinion, that Rumery's § 1983 suit is barred by his valid, voluntary release.

JUSTICE STEVENS, with whom JUSTICE BRENNAN, JUSTICE MARSHALL, and JUSTICE BLACKMUN join, dissenting.

The question whether the release-dismissal agreement signed by the respondent is unenforceable is much more complex than the Court's opinion indicates. A complete analysis of the question presented by this case cannot end with the observation that respondent made a knowing and voluntary choice to sign a settlement agreement. Even an intelligent and informed, but completely innocent, person accused of crime should not be required to choose between a threatened indictment and trial, with their attendant publicity and the omnipresent possibility of wrongful conviction, and surrendering the right to a civil remedy against individuals who have violated his or her constitutional rights. Moreover, the prosecutor's representation of competing and possibly conflicting interests compounds the dangerous potential of release-dismissal agreements. To explain my disagreement with the majority, I shall first discuss the dilemma confronted by respondent at the time his lawyer advised him to sign the agreement, then comment on the three different interests the prosecutor represented, and finally discuss the plurality's evaluation of the relevant public interests in this case.

I

Respondent is an innocent man. As a matter of law, he must be presumed to be innocent. As a matter of fact, the uncontradicted sworn testimony of respondent, and his lawyer, buttressed by the circumstantial evidence, overwhelmingly attest to his innocence. There was no written statement by the alleged victim, sworn or unsworn, implicating respondent in any criminal activity. The charge that respondent had threatened the victim was reported to the police by the victim's daughter, and the substance of the conversation as summarized in Chief Barrett's report was based in part on conversations between another police officer and the victim, and in part on his own conversation with the victim when she was in a state of extreme emotional distress. Respondent was never indicted, and the warrant for his arrest was issued on the basis of a sketchy statement by Chief Barrett. Even the assistant prosecutor who was in charge of the case was surprised to learn that Chief Barrett had arrested respondent on the basis of the information in the police report. Thus, when the Newton police officers arrested respondent in his home they had not even obtained a written statement from the complaining witness. Prior to the arrest, and prior to the police chief's press conference concerning it, respondent was a respected member of a small community who had never been arrested, even for a traffic offense.

A few days before respondent was scheduled for a probable cause hearing on the charge of witness tampering, respondent's attorney advised him to sign a covenant not to sue the town of Newton, its police officers or the witness Deary in exchange for dismissal of the charge against him. The advice was predicated on the lawyer's judgment that the value of a dismissal outweighed the harmful consequences of an almost certain indictment on a felony charge together with the risk of conviction in a case in which the outcome would depend on the jury's assessment of the relative credibility of respondent and his alleged victim. The lawyer correctly advised respondent that even if he was completely innocent, there could be no guarantee of acquittal. He therefore placed a higher value on his client's interest in terminating the criminal proceeding promptly than on the uncertain benefits of pursuing a civil remedy against the town and its police department.[9] After delaying a decision for three days, respondent reluctantly followed his lawyer's advice.

From respondent's point of view, it is unquestionably true that the decision to sign the release-dismissal agreement was, as the Court emphasizes, "voluntary, deliberate, and informed." It reflected "a highly rational judgment that the certain benefits of escaping criminal prosecution exceed the speculative benefits of prevailing in a civil action." As the plurality iterates and reiterates, respondent made a "considered decision that he would benefit personally from the agreement." I submit, however, that the deliberate and rational character of respondent's decision is not a sufficient reason for concluding that the agreement is enforceable. Otherwise, a promise to pay a state trooper $20 for not issuing a ticket for a traffic violation, or a promise to contribute to the police department's retirement fund in exchange for the dismissal of a felony charge, would be enforceable. Indeed, I would suppose that virtually all contracts that courts refuse to enforce nevertheless reflect perfectly rational decisions by the parties who entered into them. There is nothing irrational about an agreement to bribe a police officer, to enter into a wagering arrangement, to pay usurious rates of interests, or to threaten to indict an innocent man in order to induce him to surrender something of value.

The "voluntary, deliberate, and informed" character of a defendant's decision generally provides an acceptable basis for upholding the validity of a plea bargain. But it is inappropriate to assume that the same standard determines the validity of a quite different agreement to

---

[9] Although the witness Deary was a covenantee, she was not named as a defendant in the civil case.

forego a civil remedy for the violation of the defendant's constitutional rights in exchange for complete abandonment of a criminal charge.

The net result of every plea bargain is an admission of wrongdoing by the defendant and the imposition of a criminal sanction with its attendant stigma. Although there may be some cases in which an innocent person pleads guilty to a minor offense to avoid the risk of conviction on a more serious charge, it is reasonable to presume that such cases are rare and represent the exception rather than the rule. See Fed.Rule Crim.Procedure 11(f) (court may not enter judgment on a guilty plea unless it is satisfied the plea has a factual basis). Like a plea bargain, an agreement by the suspect to drop § 1983 charges and to pay restitution to the victim in exchange for the prosecutor's termination of criminal proceedings involves an admission of wrongdoing by the defendant. The same cannot be said about an agreement that completely exonerates the defendant. Not only is such a person presumptively innocent as a matter of law; as a factual matter the prosecutor's interest in obtaining a covenant not to sue will be strongest in those cases in which he realizes that the defendant was innocent and was wrongfully accused. Moreover, the prosecutor will be most willing—indeed, he is ethically obligated—to drop charges when he believes that probable cause as established by the available, admissible evidence is lacking.

The plea bargain represents a practical compromise between the prosecutor and the defendant that takes into account the burdens of litigation and its probable outcome, as well as society's interest in imposing appropriate punishment upon an admitted wrongdoer. The defendant admits wrongdoing for conduct upon which the guilty plea is based and avoids further prosecution; the prosecutor need not go to trial; and an admitted wrongdoer is punished, all under close judicial supervision. By simultaneously establishing and limiting the defendant's criminal liability, plea bargains strike a delicate balance of individual and social advantage. This mutuality of advantage does not exist in release-dismissal agreements. A defendant entering a release-dismissal agreement is forced to waive claims based on official conduct under color of state law, in exchange merely for the assurance that the state will not prosecute him for conduct for which he has made no admission of wrongdoing. The state is spared the necessity of going to trial, but its willingness to drop the charge completely indicates that it might not have proceeded with the prosecution in any event. No social interest in the punishment of wrongdoers is satisfied; the only interest vindicated is that of resolving once and for all the question of § 1983 liability.

Achieving this result has no connection with the give-and-take over the defendant's wrongdoing that is the essence of the plea-bargaining process, and thus cannot be justified by reference to the principles of mutual advantage that support plea bargaining. Although the outcome of a criminal proceeding may affect the value of the civil claim, as a matter of law the claims are quite distinct. Even a guilty defendant may be entitled to receive damages for physical abuse, and conversely, the fact that a defendant is ultimately acquitted is entirely consistent with the possibility that the police had probable cause to arrest him and did not violate any of his constitutional rights.

The plurality assumes that many § 1983 suits "are marginal and some are frivolous." Whether that assumption is correct or incorrect, the validity of each ought to be tested by the adversary process. Experience teaches us that some § 1983 suits in which release-dismissal agreements are sought are meritorious. Whatever the true value of a § 1983 claim may be, a defendant who is required to give up such a claim in exchange for a dismissal of a criminal charge is being forced to pay a price that is unrelated to his possible wrongdoing as reflected in that charge. Indeed, if the defendant is forced to abandon a claim that has a value of $1000, the price that he pays is the functional equivalent of a $1000 payment to a police department's retirement benefit fund.

Thus, even though respondent's decision in this case was deliberate, informed, and voluntary, this observation does not address two distinct objections to enforcement of the release-dismissal agreement. The prosecutor's offer to drop charges if the defendant accedes to the agreement is inherently coercive; moreover, the agreement exacts a price unrelated to the character of the defendant's own conduct.

II

When the prosecutor negotiated the agreement with respondent, he represented three potentially conflicting interests. His primary duty, of course, was to represent the sovereign's interests in the evenhanded and effective enforcement of its criminal laws. In addition, as the covenant demonstrates, he sought to represent the interests of the town of Newton and its police department in connection with their possible civil liability to respondent. Finally, as the inclusion of Mary Deary as a covenantee indicates, the prosecutor also represented the interest of a potential witness who allegedly accused both respondent and a mutual friend of separate instances of wrongdoing.

If we view the problem from the standpoint of the prosecutor's principal client, the state of New Hampshire, it is perfectly clear that the release-dismissal agreement was both unnecessary and unjustified. For both the prosecutor and the state of New Hampshire enjoy absolute immunity from common-law and § 1983 liability arising out of a prosecutor's decision to initiate criminal proceedings. See Imbler v. Pachtman, 424 U.S. 409, 427 (1976). The agreement thus gave the state and the prosecutor no protection that the law did not already provide.

The record in this case indicates that an important reason for obtaining the covenant was "[t]o protect the police department." There is, however, an obvious potential conflict between the prosecutor's duty to enforce the law and his objective of protecting members of the police department who are accused of unlawful conduct. The public is entitled to have the prosecutor's decision to go forward with a criminal case, or to dismiss it, made independently of his concerns about the potential damages liability of the police department. It is equally clear that this separation of functions cannot be achieved if the prosecutor may use the threat of criminal prosecution as a weapon to obtain a favorable termination of a civil claim against the police.

In negotiating a release-dismissal agreement, the prosecutor inevitably represents both the public and the police. When release agreements are enforceable, consideration of the police interest in avoiding damages liability severely hampers the prosecutor's ability to conform to the strictures of professional responsibility in deciding whether to prosecute. In particular, the possibility that the suspect will execute a covenant not to sue in exchange for a decision not to prosecute may well encourage a prosecutor to bring or to continue prosecutions in violation of his or her duty to "refrain from prosecuting a charge that the prosecutor knows is not supported by probable cause." ABA Model Rules of Professional Conduct, Rule 3.8(a) (1984).

This ethical obligation of every prosecutor is consistent with the general and fundamental rule that "[a] lawyer should exercise independent professional judgment on behalf of a client." ABA Model Code of Professional Responsibility, Canon 5 (1980). Every attorney should avoid situations in which he is representing potentially conflicting interests. As we noted in *Imbler v. Pachtman,* prosecutorial immunity from § 1983 lawsuits "does not leave the public powerless to deter misconduct or to punish that which occurs," in large part because "a prosecutor stands perhaps unique, among officials whose acts could deprive persons of constitutional rights, in his amenability to professional discipline by an association of his peers."

The prosecutor's potential conflict of interest increases in magnitude in direct proportion to the seriousness of the charges of police wrongdoing. Yet a rule that determines the enforceability of a release-dismissal agreement by focusing entirely on the quality of the defendant's decision to sign the agreement cannot detect the seriousness of this conflict of interest because it cannot distinguish the meritorious § 1983 claims from the frivolous ones. On the other hand, if the merits of the claim must be evaluated in each case in order to decide whether the agreement should be enforced, the agreement would not serve the goal of saving the litigation costs associated with a trial of the claim itself. The efficiency argument on behalf of enforcing a release-dismissal agreement thus requires inattention to conflicts of interest in precisely those circumstances in which the agreement to be enforced is most likely to have been exacted by a prosecutor serving the interests of more than one constituency.

At bottom, the Court's holding in this case seems to rest on concerns related to the potential witness, Mary Deary.[18] As is true with the prosecutor's concerns for police liability, there is a potential

---

[18] Despite a good deal of unfortunate language in its opinion, in the final analysis the Court merely rejects a per se rule invalidating all release-dismissal agreements and holds that this particular agreement is enforceable. If the interest in protecting the potential witness were not present, presumably the author of the Court's opinion would adhere to the views he expressed in Bordenkircher v. Hayes, 434 U.S. 357, 372–73 (1978) (Powell, J., dissenting).

conflict between the public interest represented by the prosecutor and the private interests of a recalcitrant witness. As a general matter there is no reason to fashion a rule that either requires or permits a prosecutor always to defer to the interests of a witness. The prosecutor's law enforcement responsibilities will sometimes diverge from those interests; there will be cases in which the prosecutor has a plain duty to obtain critical testimony despite the desire of the witness to remain anonymous or to avoid a courtroom confrontation with an offender. There may be other cases in which a witness has given false or exaggerated testimony for malicious reasons. It would plainly be unwise for the Court to hold that a release-dismissal agreement is enforceable simply because it affords protection to a potential witness.

Arguably a special rule should be fashioned for witnesses who are victims of sexual assaults. The trauma associated with such an assault leaves scars that may make it especially difficult for a victim to press charges or to testify publicly about the event. It remains true, however, that uncorroborated, unsworn statements by persons who claim to have been victims of any crime, including such an assault, may be inaccurate, exaggerated or incomplete—and sometimes even malicious. It is even more clear that hearsay descriptions of statements by such persons may be unreliable. Rather than adopting a general rule that upholds a release-dismissal agreement whenever the criminal charge was based on a statement by the alleged victim of a sexual assault, I believe the Court should insist upon a "close examination" of the facts that purportedly justified the agreement.

Thus, in this case Justice O'Connor has suggested that three special facts support the conclusion that the prosecutor was legitimately interested in protecting the witness Deary from "further injury": (1) her "emotional distress"; (2) her unwillingness to testify against Rumery; and (3) the necessity of her testimony in the pending sexual assault case against Champy. Each of these facts merits a brief comment.

The only evidence of Deary's emotional distress in the record is found in Chief Barrett's report of his telephone conversation on the afternoon of May 11, 1983. While he was talking to Deary's daughter he "could hear an intense argument and sobbing in the background"; after he was finally able to talk to Deary herself, he characterized her conversation as "hysterical, distra[u]ght, and terrified." It is, of course, reasonable to assume that Deary's emotional distress may have affected her unwillingness to testify against either Champy or Rumery, and thereby influenced the prosecutor's decision to dismiss the witness tampering charge. But the testimony of the prosecutor, who appears only to have talked to her about the sexual assault charge, does not even mention the possibility that she might have to testify in any civil litigation.

Deary's unwillingness to testify against Rumery is perfectly obvious.[19] That fact unquestionably supports the prosecutor's decision to

---

[19] Indeed, that fact must have been obvious to the police before they arrested respondent. For it was Deary's daughter, not Deary herself, who advised the police

dismiss the charge against respondent, but it is not a sufficient reason for exonerating police officers from the consequences of actions that they took when they must have known that Deary was unwilling to testify. For it was the precipitous character of the police decision to make an arrest without first obtaining a written statement from the witness and contrary to the expectations—and presumably the advice— of the prosecutor that created the risk that the victim might have to testify in open court.[20]

The need for Deary's testimony in the pending sexual assault case against Champy simply cannot justify denying this respondent a reme- dy for a violation of his fourth amendment rights. Presumably, if there had been an actual trial of the pending charge against Champy,[21] that trial would have concluded long before Deary would have been required to testify in any § 1983 litigation.

It may well be true that a full development of all the relevant facts would provide a legitimate justification for enforcing the release-dismis- sal agreement. In my opinion, however, the burden of developing those facts rested on the defendants in the § 1983 litigation, and that burden has not been met by mere conjecture and speculation concerning the emotional distress of one reluctant witness.

III

Because this is the first case of this kind that the Court has reviewed, I am hesitant to adopt an absolute rule invalidating all such agreements.[22] I am, however, persuaded that the federal policies re-

---

of Deary's call to respondent on May 11. Since the allegedly incriminating version of that call is based on two police officers' summary of what they had been told by Deary and her daughter—rather than a coherent statement by Deary herself—it is reasonable to assume that Deary was un- willing to provide the police with a state- ment of her recollection of exactly what was said in her conversation with respon- dent.

[20] Moreover, it is by no means apparent that testimony in a § 1983 action arising out of Rumery's telephone conversations with Deary would require any inquiry about the facts of the underlying assault or about the victim's relationship with Champy, the alleged assailant.

[21] Champy pleaded guilty to a lesser in- cluded offense and the felony charge against him was dismissed without a trial.

[22] It seems likely, however, that the costs of having courts determine the validity of release-dismissal agreements will outweigh the benefits that most agreements can be expected to provide. A court may enforce such an agreement only after a careful inquiry into the circumstances under which the plaintiff signed the agreement

and into the legitimacy of the prosecutor's objective in entering into the agreement. This inquiry will occupy a significant amount of the court's and the parties' time, and will subject prosecutorial deci- sionmaking to judicial review. But the only benefit most of these agreements will provide is another line of defense for prose- cutors and police in § 1983 actions. This extra protection is unnecessary because prosecutors already enjoy absolute immu- nity and because police have been afforded qualified immunity, see Harlow v. Fitzger- ald, 457 U.S. 800 (1982). Thus, the vast majority of "marginal or frivolous" § 1983 suits can be dismissed under existing stan- dards with little more burden on the defen- dants than is entailed in defending a re- lease-dismissal agreement. Moreover, there is an oddly suspect quality to this extra protection; the agreement is one that a public official signs, presumably in good faith, but that a court must conclude is invalid unless that official proves other- wise. In most cases, if social and judicial resources are to be expended at all, they would seem better spent on an evaluation of the merits of the § 1983 claim rather than on a detour into the enforceability of a release-dismissal agreement.

flected in the enactment and enforcement of § 1983 mandate a strong presumption against the enforceability of such agreements and that the presumption is not overcome in this case by the facts or by any of the policy concerns discussed by the plurality.[23] The very existence of the statute identifies the important federal interests in providing a remedy for the violation of constitutional rights and in having the merits of such claims resolved openly by an impartial adjudicator rather than sub silentio by a prosecutor whose primary objective in entering release-dismissal agreements is definitely not to ensure that all meritorious § 1983 claims prevail. The interest in vindication of constitutional violations unquestionably outweighs the interest in avoiding the expense and inconvenience of defending unmeritorious claims. Paradoxically, the plurality seems more sensitive to that burden than to the cost to the public and the individual of denying relief in meritorious cases. In short, the plurality's decision seems to rest on the unstated premise that § 1983 litigation imposes a net burden on society. If that were a correct assessment of the statute, it should be repealed. Unless that is done, however, we should respect the congressional decision to attach greater importance to the benefits associated with access to a federal remedy than to the burdens of defending these cases.[24]

The plurality also suggests that these agreements must be enforced in order to give proper respect to the prosecutor's exercise of discretion. I must confess that I do not understand this suggestion. The prosecu-

[23] The Courts of Appeals which have found agreements not to sue void as against public policy demonstrate, in my view, much more sensitivity to the possibility of prosecutorial abuse than does the Court's opinion today. As the Seventh Circuit has held:

"[W]e think that the release is void as against public policy. . . . As well stated in Dixon v. District of Columbia, 394 F.2d 966, 968–69 (D.C.Cir.1968), a case where the arrestee violated his 'tacit' agreement not to sue and the prosecutor retaliated by filing the traffic charges, which had been held in abeyance pursuant to the tacit agreement:

" 'The government may not prosecute for the purpose of deterring people from exercising their right to protest official misconduct and petition for redress of grievances. . . .

" 'The major evil of these agreements is not that charges are sometimes dropped against people who probably should be prosecuted. Much more important, these agreements suppress complaints against police misconduct which should be thoroughly aired in a free society. And they tempt the prosecutor to trump up charges for use in bargaining for suppression of the complaint. The danger of concocted charges is particularly great because complaints against the police usually arise in connection with arrests for extremely vague offenses such as disorderly conduct or resisting arrest.' "

Boyd v. Adams, 513 F.2d 83, 88–89 (7th Cir. 1975).

[24] Justice O'Connor suggests that these agreements might serve a legitimate purpose when the charges dismissed are misdemeanors rather than felonies. "Sparing the local community the expense of litigation associated with some minor crimes for which there is little or no public interest in prosecution may be a legitimate objective of a release-dismissal agreement." Implicit in this reasoning, I think, is the assumption that the court has independently determined that the arrest was proper. Otherwise, a valid § 1983 claim could be barred under this reasoning because of a factor wholly unrelated to the merits of the claim—the public's lack of interest in prosecuting the misdemeanor charges that were dismissed. These agreements could then be routinely upheld in circumstances where they were improperly employed. For example, one would expect that an officer attempting to cover up an illegal arrest would find it easier to trump up misdemeanor charges (such as resisting arrest) than felony charges.

tor is adequately protected by the shield of absolute immunity. Moreover, in this case it is police misconduct—not that of the prosecutor—that is challenged in the § 1983 litigation. A holding that the agreement is unenforceable need not rest on an assumption that "prosecutors will seize the opportunity for wrongdoing." On the contrary, it would merely respect the wholly unrelated premise that undergirds § 1983 itself—that law enforcement officers sometimes violate the constitutional rights of individual citizens. The public interest in identifying and redressing such violations is, in my judgment, paramount to the prosecutor's interest in using the threat of a felony indictment and trial as a means of avoiding an independent appraisal of the merits of a § 1983 claim.

Accordingly, although I am not prepared to endorse all of the reasoning of the Court of Appeals, I would affirm its judgment.

NOTES ON *NEWTON v. RUMERY*

1. **The Legitimacy of Release-Dismissal Agreements.** Should release-dismissal agreements be tolerated? The following comments may help to identify some of the relevant issues.

(i) **Unequal Bargaining Power: The Analogy of Plea Bargains.** Rumery contended, and the dissenters agreed, that release-dismissal agreements are "inherently coercive" and should for that reason be disallowed. The underpinning of this view would seem to be a perception of unequal bargaining power between the authorities and the accused. As the Court said, "[t]he risk, publicity, and expense of a criminal trial may intimidate a defendant, even if he believes his defense is meritorious." If, as seems plausible, the defendant's threat to bring a civil rights action is not comparably intimidating to the public official, there may be a systemic inequality of bargaining power that renders release-dismissal agreements inherently suspect.

Consider in this respect the analogy of the plea bargain. For better or for worse, the great majority of criminal prosecutions are resolved by plea bargains. While many distrust this practice, the judicial attitude has been largely supportive, and the constitutionality of such agreements is well established. At least at first blush, the negotiations underlying the plea bargain would seem to feature the same inequality of bargaining power that arguably infects release-dismissal agreements. And to the extent that such inequality yields "wrong" results, the evil is arguably more severe where the defendant agreeds to plead guilty to a charge of crime rather than merely to forego a civil remedy. The question, therefore, is why the "inherently coercive" aspect of release-dismissal agreements should be a matter of concern to a system that tolerates, indeed encourages, prosecution by plea bargain.

One answer is that the plea bargain is subject to judicial supervision. Typically, the judge inquires whether the defendant understands the nature of the charge, the penalties associated with that offense, and the rights waived by a plea of guilty. See Boykin v. Alabama, 395 U.S. 238 (1969). The judge further seeks to determine that the plea is voluntary. The cases are clear, however, that a plea is voluntary if it results from an informed choice among known alternatives, no matter how unpleasant the alternatives or how difficult the choice between them. See, e.g., Brady v. United States, 397 U.S. 742 (1970). Additionally, at least in the federal system, the judge must determine that there is a sufficient factual basis to support a finding of guilt. See Fed.Rule of Crim.Proc. 11(f).[a]

No doubt procedures of this sort are helpful in identifying pleas based on ignorance, confusion, or prosecutorial overreaching. One may wonder, however, whether they are equally relevant to the problem of unequal bargaining power. The prosecutorial threat used to produce a plea bargain seems fundamentally similar to that involved in release-dismissal agreements. Whether the "inherently coercive" nature of that threat is significantly reduced by judicial supervision may, perhaps, be doubted.

In dissent, Justice Stevens suggested other reasons for distinguishing plea bargains. Among other things he focused on "the principles of mutual advantage that support plea bargaining" and argued that this "mutuality of advantage" is lacking in release-dismissal agreements. Why is this so? Is it not clear that each side has something to gain (as well as something to lose) by concluding such an agreement?

(ii) The Nature of the Government's Interest. Perhaps Stevens means to say that the government's objective in obtaining release-dismissal agreements is not legitimate—that is, that the defendant's willingness to forego a § 1983 claim is not the kind of benefit for which the prosecutor can validly bargain. Under this view, the problem with release-dismissal agreements is not so much the process of their negotiation, but rather that the government is pursuing an interest that does not deserve vindication. Is this plausible? Are the government's interests in plea bargains substantially different from those involved in release-dismissal agreements?

At other points, Stevens approaches the same idea somewhat differently. The problem, he says, with the release-dismissal agreement is that it "exacts a price unrelated to the character of the defendant's own conduct." In plea bargaining, the terms of the bargain are presumably related to the strength of each side's position. Of course, the same is true in a release-dismissal agreement. The difference lies in relation between the two sides. In a plea bargain, the strength of the prosecution's position and the strength of the defendant's position are inversely related; both sides cannot have a strong case on the same facts. In a release-dismissal agreement, however, the strength of the two claims may be entirely unrelated; the civil rights claim may be based on police misconduct having no bearing on the

---

[a] Procedures of this sort were probably what the Court and Justice O'Connor had in mind when they suggested judicial supervision of release-dismissal agreements.

defendant's guilt or innocence. Thus, in Stevens' words, the defendant who relinquishes a § 1983 claim in return for dismissal of a criminal charge is "forced to pay a price that is unrelated to the possible wrongdoing as reflected in that charge."

Does this line of reasoning show that the government's interest in concluding release-dismissal agreements is illegitimate? Does it explain why plea bargaining and release-dismissal agreements should be treated differently?

(iii) **Prosecutorial Misconduct.** Finally, Justice Stevens says that release-dismissal agreements create, or exacerbate, prosecutorial conflicts of interest. "There is," said Stevens, "an obvious potential conflict between the prosecutor's duty to enforce the law and his objective of protecting members of the police department who are accused of unlawful conduct." "In negotiating a release-dismissal agreement, the prosecutor inevitably represents both the public and the police," a duality of interest that "severely hampers" the prosecutor's conformance to ethical obligations. Moreover, in this case, the prosecutor's loyalties were further divided by a concern for the complaining witness.

Are these concerns persuasive? It is unethical for a prosecutor to consider the interests of both the public at large and the law enforcement community?

2. Standards for the Acceptance of Release-Dismissal Agreements. *Newton v. Rumery* was the Supreme Court's first encounter with release-dismissal agreements in civil rights actions, but it is unlikely to be the last. The Court rejected a per se rule against the practice, but it stopped short of a blanket acceptance of all such agreements. Instead, it adopted an intermediate position allowing enforcement of release-dismissal agreements in some circumstances. Further litigation will doubtless be required to spell out what those circumstances may be.

The Court emphasized that the agreement was voluntary—at least in the sense that Rumery had a meaningful choice and that he exercised that choice in a rational and informed manner. Relevant to that conclusion were the facts that Rumery was a sophisticated businessman, that he was represented by experienced counsel, and that he took time to consider the decision.

What if these factors are missing? If they are critical to the validity of an agreement, then *Rumery* may have a very limited application. Presumably this would mean that a valid agreement could not be made with an unrepresented arrestee. In that event, the utility to the authorities of concluding such agreements would be greatly reduced, as would the prospect of systematic avoidance of civil rights actions by routinely inducing arrestees to release their claims.

On the other hand, it is far from clear that individual sophistication and advice of counsel are prerequisites to voluntary choice. Under *Miranda*, for example, a suspect who has been told of the options may validly waive both the right to counsel during interrogation *and* the fifth amendment privilege against self-incrimination. Such waivers must be informed and voluntary, but they are not deemed involuntary simply because the suspect was not a sophisticated individual with an experienced lawyer and ample time to consider the matter. Should the same standard of voluntariness be adopted for release-dismissal agreements? Or does *Rumery* imply a different inquiry?

3. Bibliography. For commentary on *Rumery*, see Seth F. Kreimer, Releases, Redress, and Police Misconduct: Reflections on Agreements to Waive Civil Rights Actions in Exchange for Dismissal of Criminal Charges, 136 U. Pa. L. Rev. 851 (1988); and Michael E. Solimine, Enforcement and Interpretation of Settlements of Federal Civil Rights Actions, 19 Rutgers L.J. 295 (1988). Kreimer emphasizes the unusual facts of *Rumery* (including the role of counsel and the sophistication of the accused) and argues that enforcing release-dismissal agreements in other contexts would have substantial costs. Prominent among them is the threat to prosecutorial integrity that would be posed by "a continuing incentive to modify criminal prosecution decisions in the interests of goals extraneous to the criminal process," such as protecting the police. Kreimer reports interviews with several prosecutors, most of whom disapprove release-dismissal agreements as a matter of policy. He also argues that release-dismissal agreements could undermine the role of § 1983 in deterring official misconduct and vindicating constitutional rights.

Solimine criticizes *Rumery* on choice-of-law grounds. He argues that the validity of the release-dismissal agreement should have been determined under the contract law of New Hampshire. Solimine argues that a federal common law rule is unnecessary since this is not, in his view, an issue requiring a uniform solution.

SECTION 6: ATTORNEY'S FEES

CITY OF RIVERSIDE v. RIVERA
Supreme Court of the United States, 1986.
477 U.S. 561.

JUSTICE BRENNAN announced the judgment of the Court and delivered an opinion in which JUSTICE MARSHALL, JUSTICE BLACKMUN, and JUSTICE STEVENS join.

The issue presented in this case is whether an award of attorney's fees under 42 U.S.C. § 1988 is per se "unreasonable" within the meaning of the statute if it exceeds the amount of damages recovered by the plaintiff in the underlying civil rights action.

I

Respondents, eight Chicano individuals, attended a party on the evening of August 1, 1975, at the Riverside, California, home of respondents Santos and Jennie Rivera. A large number of unidentified police officers, acting without a warrant, broke up the party using tear gas and, as found by the District Court, "unnecessary physical force." Many of the guests, including four of the respondents, were arrested. The District Court later found that "[t]he party was not creating a disturbance in the community at the time of the break-in." Criminal charges against the arrestees were ultimately dismissed for lack of probable cause.

On June 4, 1976, respondents sued the city of Riverside, its chief of police, and 30 individual police officers under 42 U.S.C. §§ 1981, 1983, 1985(3), and 1986 for allegedly violating their first, fourth, and 14th amendment rights. The complaint, which also alleged numerous state-law claims, sought damages, and declaratory and injunctive relief. On August 5, 1977, 23 of the individual police officers moved for summary judgment; the District Court granted summary judgment in favor of 17 of these officers. The case against the remaining defendants proceeded to trial in September 1980. The jury returned a total of 37 individual verdicts in favor of the respondents and against the city and five individual officers, finding 11 violations of § 1983, four instances of false arrest and imprisonment, and 22 instances of negligence. Respondents were awarded $33,350 in compensatory and punitive damages: $13,300 for their federal claims, and $20,050 for their state-law claims.[1]

Respondents also sought attorney's fees and costs under § 1988. They requested compensation for 1,946.75 hours expended by their two attorneys at a rate of $125 per hour, and for 84.5 hours expended by law clerks at a rate of $25.00 per hour, a total of $245,456.25. The District Court found both the hours and rates reasonable, and awarded respondents $245,456.25 in fees. The court rejected respondents' request for certain additional expenses, and for a multiplier sought by respondents to reflect the contingent nature of their success and the high quality of their attorneys' efforts.

Petitioners appealed only the attorney's fees award, which the Court of Appeals for the Ninth Circuit affirmed. Petitioners sought a writ of certiorari from this Court. We granted the writ, vacated the Court of Appeals' judgment, and remanded the case for reconsideration in light of Hensley v. Eckerhart, 461 U.S. 424 (1983). On remand, the District Court held two additional hearings, reviewed additional briefing, and reexamined the record as a whole. The court made extensive findings of fact and conclusions of law, and again concluded that

---

[1] Counsel for respondents explained to the District Court that respondents had not pursued their request for injunctive relief because "the bottom line of what we would ask for is that the police officers obey the law. And that is virtually always denied by a court because a court properly, I think, says that for the future we will assume that all police officers will abide by the law, including the Constitution." The District Court's response to this explanation is significant:

"[I]f you [respondents] had asked for [injunctive relief] against some of the officers I think I would have granted it. . . . I would agree with you that there is a problem about telling the officers that they have to obey the law. But if you want to know what the court thought about some of the behavior, it was—it would have warranted an injunction."

respondents were entitled to an award of $245,456.25 in attorney's fees, based on the same total number of hours expended on the case and the same hourly rates. The court again denied respondents' request for certain expenses and for a multiplier.

Petitioners again appealed the fee award. And again, the Court of Appeals affirmed, finding that "the District Court correctly reconsidered the case in light of *Hensley* . . . ."

Petitioners again sought a writ of certiorari from this Court, alleging that the District Court's fee award was not "reasonable" within the meaning of § 1988, because it was disproportionate to the amount of damages recovered by respondents. We granted the writ, and now affirm the Court of Appeals.

II

A

In Alyeska Pipeline Service Co. v. Wilderness Society, 421 U.S. 240 (1975), the Court reaffirmed the "American rule" that, at least absent express statutory authorization to the contrary, each party to a lawsuit ordinarily shall bear its own attorney's fees. In response to *Alyeska*, Congress enacted the Civil Rights Attorney's Fees Awards Act of 1976, 42 U.S.C. § 1988, which authorized the district courts to award reasonable attorney's fees to prevailing parties in specified civil rights litigation. While the statute itself does not explain what constitutes a reasonable fee, both the House and Senate Reports accompanying § 1988 expressly endorse the analysis set forth in Johnson v. Georgia Highway Express, Inc., 488 F.2d 714 (5th Cir. 1974). See S. Rep. No. 94–1011, p. 6 (1976) (hereafter Senate Report); H.R.Rep.No. 94–1558, p. 8 (1976) (hereafter House Report). *Johnson* identifies 12 factors to be considered in calculating a reasonable attorney's fee.[3]

Hensley v. Eckerhart, 461 U.S. 424 (1983), announced certain guidelines for calculating a reasonable attorney's fee under § 1988. *Hensley* stated that "[t]he most useful starting point for determining the amount of a reasonable fee is the number of hours reasonably expended on the litigation multiplied by a reasonable hourly rate." This figure, commonly referred to as the "lodestar," is presumed to be the reasonable fee contemplated by § 1988. The opinion cautioned that "[t]he district court . . . should exclude from this initial fee calculation hours that were not 'reasonably expended'" on the litigation.

Hensley then discussed other considerations that might lead the district court to adjust the lodestar figure upward or downward, including the "important factor of the 'results obtained.'" The opinion noted

---

[3] These factors are: (1) the time and labor required; (2) the novelty and difficulty of the questions; (3) the skill requisite to perform the legal service properly; (4) the preclusion of employment by the attorney due to acceptance of the case; (5) the customary fee; (6) whether the fee is fixed or contingent; (7) time limitations imposed by the client or the circumstances; (8) the amount involved and the results obtained; (9) the experience, reputation, and ability of the attorneys; (10) the "undesirability" of the case; (11) the nature and length of the professional relationship with the client; and (12) awards in similar cases.

that where a prevailing plaintiff has succeeded on only some of his claims, an award of fees for time expended on unsuccessful claims may not be appropriate. In these situations, the Court held that the judge should consider whether or not the plaintiff's unsuccessful claims were related to the claims on which he succeeded, and whether the plaintiff achieved a level of success that makes it appropriate to award attorney's fees for hours reasonably expended on unsuccessful claims:

> "In [some] cases the plaintiff's claims for relief will involve a common core of facts or will be based on related legal theories. Much of counsel's time will be devoted generally to the litigation as a whole, making it difficult to divide the hours expended on a claim-by-claim basis. Such a lawsuit cannot be viewed as a series of discrete claims. Instead the district court should focus on the significance of the overall relief obtained by the plaintiff in relation to the hours reasonably expended on the litigation."

Accordingly, *Hensley* emphasized that "[w]here a plaintiff has obtained excellent results, his attorney should recover a fully compensatory fee," and that "the fee award should not be reduced simply because the plaintiff failed to prevail on every contention raised in the lawsuit."

B

Petitioners argue that the District Court failed properly to follow *Hensley* in calculating respondents' fee award. We disagree. The District Court carefully considered the results obtained by respondents pursuant to the instructions set forth in *Hensley,* and concluded that respondents were entitled to recover attorney's fees for all hours expended on the litigation. First, the court found that "[t]he amount of time expended by counsel in conducting this litigation was reasonable and reflected sound legal judgment under the circumstances."[4] The court also determined that counsels' excellent performances in this case entitled them to be compensated at prevailing market rates, even though they were relatively young when this litigation began.

The District Court then concluded that it was inappropriate to adjust respondents' fee award downward to account for the fact that respondents had prevailed only on some of their claims, and against only some of the defendants. The court first determined that "it was never actually clear what officer did what until we had gotten through with the whole trial," so that "[u]nder the circumstances of this case, it

---

[4] *Hensley* stated that a fee applicant should "exercise 'billing judgment' with respect to hours worked." Petitioners maintain that respondents failed to exercise "billing judgment" in this case, since they sought compensation for all time spent litigating this case. We think this argument misreads the mandate of *Hensley*. *Hensley* requires a fee applicant to exercise "billing judgment" not because he should necessarily be compensated for less than the actual number of hours spent litigating a case, but because the hours he does seek compensation for must be reasonable. "Counsel for the prevailing party should make a good-faith effort to exclude from a fee request hours that are excessive, redundant, or otherwise unnecessary . . . ." In this case, the District Court found that the number of hours expended by respondents' counsel was reasonable. Thus, counsel did, in fact, exercise the "billing judgment" recommended in *Hensley*. . . .

was reasonable for plaintiffs initially to name 31 individual defendants . . . as well as the city of Riverside as defendants in this action." The court remarked:

> "I think every one of the claims that were made were related and if you look at the common core of facts that we had here that you had total success. . . . There was a problem about who was responsible for what and that problem was there all the way through to the time that we concluded the case. Some of the officers couldn't agree about who did what and it is not at all surprising that it would, in my opinion, have been wrong for you not to join all those officers since you yourself did not know precisely who were the officers that were responsible."

The court then found that the lawsuit could not "be viewed as a series of discrete claims," *Hensley,* supra, at 435:

> "All claims made by plaintiffs were based on a common core of facts. The claims on which plaintiffs did not prevail were closely related to the claims on which they did prevail. The time devoted to claims on which plaintiffs did not prevail cannot reasonably be separated from time devoted to claims on which plaintiffs did prevail."

The District Court also considered the amount of damages recovered, and determined that the size of the damages award did not imply that respondent's success was limited:

> "[T]he size of the jury award resulted from (a) the general reluctance of jurors to make large awards against police officers, and (b) the dignified restraint which the plaintiffs exercised in describing their injuries to the jury. For example, although some of the actions of the police would clearly have been insulting and humiliating to even the most insensitive person and were, in the opinion of the court, intentionally so, plaintiffs did not attempt to play up this aspect of the case."[5]

The court paid particular attention to the fact that the case "presented complex and interrelated issues of fact and law," and that "[a] fee award in this civil rights action will . . . advance the public interest":

> "Counsel for plaintiffs . . . served the public interest by vindicating important constitutional rights. Defendants had engaged in lawless, unconstitutional conduct, and the litigation of plaintiffs' case was necessary to remedy defendants' misconduct. Indeed, the court was shocked at some of the acts of the police officers in this case and was convinced from the testimony that these acts were motivated by a general hostility to the

---

[5] At the second hearing on remand, the court also remarked:

"I have tried several civil rights violation cases in which police officers have figured and in the main they prevailed because juries do not bring in verdicts against police officers very readily nor against cities. The size of the verdicts against the individuals is not at all surprising because juries are very reluctant to bring in large verdicts against police officers who don't have the resources to answer those verdicts. The relief here I think was absolutely complete."

Chicano community in the area where the incident occurred. The amount of time expended by plaintiffs' counsel in conducting this litigation was clearly reasonable and necessary to serve the public interest as well as the interests of plaintiffs in the vindication of their constitutional rights."

Finally, the District Court "focus[ed] on the significance of the overall relief obtained by [respondents] in relation to the hours reasonably expended on the litigation." *Hensley,* supra, at 435. The court concluded that respondents had "achieved a level of success in this case that makes the total number of hours expended by counsel a proper basis for making the fee award":

"Counsel for plaintiffs achieved excellent results for their clients, and their accomplishment in this case was outstanding. The amount of time expended by counsel in conducting this litigation was reasonable and reflected sound legal judgment under the circumstances."

Based on our review of the record, we agree with the Court of Appeals that the District Court's findings were not clearly erroneous. We conclude that the District Court correctly applied the factors announced in Hensley in calculating respondents' fee award, and that the court did not abuse its discretion in awarding attorney's fees for all time reasonably spent litigating the case.

III

Petitioners, joined by the Solicitor General as amicus curiae, maintain that *Hensley*'s lodestar approach is inappropriate in civil rights cases where a plaintiff recovers only monetary damages. In these cases, so the argument goes, use of the lodestar may result in fees that exceed the amount of damages recovered and that are therefore unreasonable. Likening such cases to private tort actions, petitioners and the Solicitor General submit that attorney's fees in such cases should be proportionate to the amount of damages a plaintiff recovers. Specifically, they suggest that fee awards in damages cases should be modeled upon the contingent fee arrangements commonly used in personal injury litigation. In this case, assuming a 33 per cent contingency rate, this would entitle respondents to recover approximately $11,000 in attorney's fees.

The amount of damages a plaintiff recovers is certainly relevant to the amount of attorney's fees to be awarded under § 1988. It is, however, only one of many factors that a court should consider in calculating an award of attorney's fees. We reject the proposition that fee awards under § 1988 should necessarily be proportionate to the amount of damages a civil rights plaintiff actually recovers.

A

As an initial matter, we reject the notion that a civil rights action for damages constitutes nothing more than a private tort suit benefiting only the individual plaintiffs whose rights were violated. Unlike most private tort litigants, a civil rights plaintiff seeks to vindicate important civil and constitutional rights that cannot be valued solely in monetary terms. See Carey v. Piphus, 435 U.S. 247, 266 (1978). And, Congress has determined that "the public as a whole has an interest in the vindication of the rights conferred by the statutes enumerated in § 1988, over and above the value of a civil rights remedy to a particular plaintiff. . . ." *Hensley,* supra, at 444 n.4 (Brennan, J., concurring in part and dissenting in part). Regardless of the form of relief he actually obtains, a successful civil rights plaintiff often secures important social benefits that are not reflected in nominal or relatively small damages awards. In this case, for example, the District Court found that many of petitioners' unlawful acts were "motivated by a general hostility to the Chicano community," and that this litigation therefore served the public interest:

> "The institutional behavior involved here . . . had to be stopped and . . . nothing short of having a lawsuit like this would have stopped it. [T]he improper motivation which appeared as a result of all of this seemed to me to have pervaded a very broad segment of police officers in the department."

In addition, the damages a plaintiff recovers [contribute] significantly to the deterrence of civil rights violations in the future. This deterrent effect is particularly evident in the area of individual police misconduct, where injunctive relief generally is unavailable.

Congress expressly recognized that a plaintiff who obtains relief in a civil rights lawsuit " 'does so not for himself alone but also as a "private attorney general," vindicating a policy that Congress considered of the highest importance.' " House Report, at 2 (quoting Newman v. Piggie Park Enterprises, Inc., 390 US. 400, 402 (1968)). "If the citizen does not have the resources, his day in court is denied him; the congressional policy which he seeks to assert and vindicate goes unvindicated; and the entire nation, not just the individual citizen, suffers." 122 Cong. Rec. 33313 (1976) (remarks of Sen. Tunney).

Because damages awards do not reflect fully the public benefit advanced by civil rights litigation, Congress did not intend for fees in civil rights cases, unlike most private law cases, to depend on obtaining substantial monetary relief. Rather, Congress made clear that it "intended that the amount of fees awarded under [§ 1988] be governed by the same standards which prevail in other types of equally complex federal litigation, such as antitrust cases and *not be reduced because the rights involved may be nonpecuniary in nature."* Senate Report, at 6 (emphasis added). . . . The Senate report specifically approves of the fee awards made in cases such as Stanford Daily v. Zurcher, 64 F.R.D. 680 (N.D. Cal. 1974); and Swann v. Charlotte-Mecklenburg Board of Education, 66 F.R.D. 483 (W.D.N.C. 1975). In each of these cases, counsel received substantial attorney's fees despite the fact the plaintiffs sought no monetary damages. Thus, Congress recognized that reasonable attorney's fees under § 1988 are not conditioned upon and need not be proportionate to an award of money damages. The lower courts have generally eschewed such a requirement.

B

A rule that limits attorney's fees in civil rights cases to a proportion of the damages awarded would seriously undermine Congress' purpose in enacting § 1988. Congress enacted § 1988 specifically because it found that the private market for legal services failed to provide many victims of civil rights violations with effective access to the judicial process. These victims ordinarily cannot afford to purchase legal services at the rates set by the private market. Moreover, the contingent fee arrangements that make legal services available to many victims of personal injuries would often not encourage lawyers to accept civil rights cases, which frequently involve substantial expenditures of time and effort but produce only small monetary recoveries. As the House Report states:

> "[W]hile damages are theoretically available under the statutes covered by [§ 1988], it should be observed that, in some cases, immunity doctrines and special defenses, available only to public officials, preclude *or severely limit the damage remedy.* Consequently, awarding counsel fees to prevailing plaintiffs in such litigation is particularly important and necessary if federal civil and constitutional rights are to be adequately protected." House Report, at 9 (Emphasis added; footnote omitted).

Congress enacted § 1988 specifically to enable plaintiffs to enforce the civil rights laws even where the amount of damages at stake would not otherwise make it feasible for them to do so . . . .

A rule of proportionality would make it difficult, if not impossible, for individuals with meritorious civil rights claims but relatively small potential damages to obtain redress from the courts. This is totally inconsistent with the Congress' purpose in enacting § 1988. Congress recognized that private-sector fee arrangements were inadequate to ensure sufficiently vigorous enforcement of civil rights. In order to ensure that lawyers would be willing to represent persons with legitimate civil rights grievances, Congress determined that it would be necessary to compensate lawyers for all time reasonably expended on a case.

This case illustrates why the enforcement of civil rights laws cannot be entrusted to private-sector fee arrangements. The District Court observed that "[g]iven the nature of this lawsuit and the type of defense presented, many attorneys in the community would have been reluctant to institute and to continue to prosecute this action." The court concluded, moreover, that "[c]ounsel for plaintiffs achieved excellent results for their clients, and their accomplishment in this case was outstanding. The amount of time expended by counsel in conducting this litigation was reasonable and reflected sound legal judgment under the circumstances." Nevertheless, petitioners suggest that respondents' counsel should be compensated for only a small fraction of the actual time spent litigating the case. In light of the difficult nature of the issues presented by this lawsuit and the low pecuniary value of . . . the rights respondents sought to vindicate, it is highly unlikely that the prospect of a fee equal to a fraction of the damages respondents might recover would have been sufficient to attract competent counsel.[10] Moreover, since counsel might not have found it economically feasible to expend the amount of time respondents' counsel found necessary to litigate the case properly, it is even less likely that counsel would have achieved the excellent results that respondents' counsel obtained here. Thus, had respondents had to rely on private-sector fee arrangements, they might well have been unable to obtain redress for their grievances. It is precisely for this reason that Congress enacted § 1988.

IV

We agree with petitioners that Congress intended that statutory fee awards be "adequate to attract competent counsel, but . . . not produce windfalls to attorneys." Senate Report, at 6. However, we find no evidence that Congress intended that, in order to avoid "windfalls to attorneys," attorney's fees be proportionate to the amount of damages a civil rights plaintiff might recover. Rather, there already exists a wide range of safeguards designed to protect civil rights defendants against the possibility of excessive fee awards. Both the House and Senate Reports identify standards for courts to follow in awarding and calculating attorney's fees; these standards are designed to insure that attorneys are compensated only for time *reasonably expended* on a case. The district court has the discretion to deny fees to prevailing plaintiffs under special circumstances, see *Hensley,* supra, at 429 (citing Senate Report, at 4), and to award attorney's fees against plaintiffs who litigate frivolous or vexatious claims. See Christiansburg Garment Co. v. EEOC, 434 U.S. 412, 416–17 (1978); Hughes v. Rowe, 449 U.S. 5, 14–16 (1980) (per curiam); House Report, at 6–7. Furthermore, we have held that a civil rights defendant is not liable for attorneys' fees incurred after a pretrial settlement offer, where the judgment recovered by the plaintiff is less than the offer. Marek v. Chesny, 473 U.S. __ (1985).[11] We believe that these safeguards adequately protect against the possibility that § 1988 might produce a "windfall" to civil rights attorneys.

[10] The Solicitor General suggests that "[t]he prospect of recovering $11,000 for representing [respondents] in a damages suit (assuming a contingency rate of 33 per cent) is likely to attract a substantial number of attorneys." Brief for United States as Amicus Curiae 22–23. However, the District Court found that the 1,946.75 hours respondents' counsel spent litigating the case was reasonable and that "[t]here was not any possible way that you could have avoided putting in that amount of time . . . ." We reject the Solicitor General's suggestion that the prospect of working nearly 2,000 hours at a rate of $5.65 an hour, to be paid more than 10 years after the work began, is "likely to attract a substantial number of attorneys."

[11] Thus, petitioners could have avoided liability for the bulk of the attorney's fees for which they now find themselves liable by making a reasonable settlement offer in a timely manner. . . .

In the absence of any indication that Congress intended to adopt a strict rule that attorney's fees under § 1988 be proportionate to damages recovered, we decline to adopt such a rule ourselves.[12]   The judgment of the Court of Appeals is hereby

Affirmed.

JUSTICE POWELL, concurring in the judgment.

I join only the Court's judgment. The plurality opinion reads our decision in Hensley v. Eckerhart, 461 U.S. 424 (1983), more expansively than I would, and more expansively than is necessary to decide this case. For me affirmance—quite simply—is required by the District Court's detailed findings of fact, which were approved by the Court of Appeals. On its face, the fee award seems unreasonable. But I find no basis for this Court to reject the findings made and approved by the courts below.

I

. . . On remand [for reconsideration of the fee award in light of *Hensley*], the District Court heard oral argument and "reconsidered the memoranda, affidavits, and exhibits previously filed by the parties, as well the record as a whole." That court then made explicit findings of fact, including the following that are relevant to the fee award:

> 1. "All claims made by plaintiffs were based on a common core of facts. The claims on which plaintiffs did not prevail were closely related to the claims on which they did prevail. The time devoted to claims on which plaintiffs did not prevail cannot reasonably be separated from time devoted to claims on which plaintiffs did prevail."

> 2. "Counsel demonstrated outstanding skill and experience in handling this case."

> 3. "[M]any attorneys in the community would have been reluctant to institute and to continue to prosecute this action."

> 4. The number of hours claimed to have been expended by the two lawyers was "fair and reasonable."

> 5. "Counsel for plaintiffs achieved excellent results for their clients, and their accomplishment in this case was outstanding. The amount of time expended by counsel . . . was reasonable and reflected sound legal judgment under the circumstances."

> 6. Counsel "also served the public interest by vindicating important constitutional rights."

> 7. The "hourly rate [of $125 per hour is] typical of the prevailing market rate for similar services by lawyers of com-

---

[12] We note that Congress has been urged to amend § 1988 to prohibit the award of attorney's fees that are disproportionate to monetary damages recovered. See, e.g., The Legal Fees Equity Act, S. 2802, 98th Cong., 2d Sess. (1984); S. 1580, 99th Cong., 1st Sess. (1985). These efforts have thus far not been persuasive.

parable skill, experience and reputation within the Central District at the time these services were performed."

8. Finally, in view of the level of success attained in this case, "the total number of hours expended by counsel [is] a proper basis for making the fee award."

Federal Rule of Civil Procedure 52(a) provides that "[f]indings of fact [by a district court] shall not be set aside unless clearly erroneous . . . ." The Court of Appeals did not disagree with any of the foregoing findings by the District Court. I see no basis on which this Court now could hold that these findings are clearly erroneous. To be sure, some of the findings fairly can be viewed as conclusions or matters of opinion, but the findings that are critical to the judgments of the courts below are objective facts. Justice Rehnquist's arguments in dissent suggest that the District Court may have been mistaken. But . . . "a reviewing court [may not] reverse the finding of the trier of fact simply because it is convinced that it would have decided the case differently." . . .

II

. . . Petitioners argue for a rule of proportionality between the fee awarded and the damages recovered in a civil rights case. Neither the decisions of this Court nor the legislative history of § 1988 support such a "rule." The facts and circumstances of litigation are infinitely variable. Under *Hensley,* of course, "the most critical factor [in the final determination of fee awards] is the degree of success obtained." Where recovery of private damages is the purpose of a civil rights litigation, a district court, in fixing fees, is obligated to give primary consideration to the amount of damages awarded as compared to the amount sought. In some civil rights cases, however, the court may consider the vindication of constitutional rights in addition to the amount of damages recovered. In this case, for example, the District Court made an explicit finding that the "public interest" had been served by the jury's verdict that the warrantless entry was lawless and unconstitutional. Although the finding of a fourth amendment violation hardly can be considered a new constitutional ruling, in the special circumstances of this case, the vindication of the asserted fourth amendment right may well have served a public interest, supporting the amount of the fees awarded. As the District Court put it, there were allegations that the police misconduct was "motivated by a general hostility to the Chicano community in the area. . . ." The record also contained evidence of racial slurs by some of the police.

Finally, petitioners also contend that in determining a proper fee under § 1988 in a suit for damages the court should consider the prevailing contingent fee rate charged by counsel in personal injury cases. The use of contingent fee arrangements in many types of tort cases was customary long before Congress enacted § 1988. It is clear from the legislative history that § 1988 was enacted because existing fee arrangements were thought not to provide an adequate incentive to lawyers particularly to represent plaintiffs in unpopular civil rights cases. I therefore find petitioners' asserted analogy to personal injury claims unpersuasive in this context.

III

In sum, despite serious doubts as to the fairness of the fees awarded in this case, I cannot conclude that the detailed findings made by the District Court, and accepted by the Court of Appeals, were clearly erroneous, or that the District Court abused its discretion in making this fee award.

CHIEF JUSTICE BURGER, dissenting.

I join Justice Rehnquist's dissenting opinion. I write only to add that it would be difficult to find a better example of legal nonsense than the fixing of attorney's fees by a judge at $245,456.25 for the recovery of $33,350 damages.

The two attorneys receiving this nearly quarter-million dollar fee graduated from law school in 1973 and 1974; they brought this action in 1975, which resulted in the $33,350 jury award in 1980. Their total professional experience when this litigation began consisted of Gerald Lopez' one-year service as a law clerk to a judge and Roy Cazares' two years' experience as a trial attorney in the Defenders' Program of San Diego County. For their services the District Court found that an hourly rate of $125 per hour was reasonable.

Can anyone doubt that no private party would ever have dreamed of paying these two novice attorneys $125 per hour in 1975, which, considering inflation, would represent perhaps something more nearly a $250 per hour rate today? For example, as Justice Rehnquist points out, would any private litigant be willing to pay a total of $17,875 simply for preparation of a pretrial order?

This fee award plainly constitutes a grave abuse of discretion which should be rejected by this Court—particularly when we have already vacated and remanded this identical fee award previously—rather than simply affirming the District Court's findings as not being either "clearly erroneous" or an "abuse of discretion." The Court's result will unfortunately only add fuel to the fires of public indignation over the costs of litigation.

JUSTICE REHNQUIST, with whom THE CHIEF JUSTICE, JUSTICE WHITE, and JUSTICE O'CONNOR join, dissenting.

In Hensley v. Eckerhart, 461 U.S. 424, 433 (1983), our leading case dealing with attorney's fees awarded pursuant to 42 U.S.C. § 1988, we said that "[t]he most useful starting point for determining the amount of a reasonable fee is the number of hours reasonably expended on the litigation multiplied by a reasonable hourly rate." As if we had foreseen the case now before us, we went on the emphasize that "[t]he district court . . . should exclude from this initial fee calculation hours that were not 'reasonably expended' " on the litigation. Id. at 434, quoting S. Rep. No. 94–1011, p. 6 (1976). Today, despite its adoption of a revisionist interpretation of *Hensley,* the plurality none-theless acknowledges that "*Hensley* requires a fee applicant to exercise 'billing judgment' not because he should necessarily be compensated for less than the actual number of hours spent litigating a case, but because the hours he does seek compensation for must be *reasonable.*" (Emphasis in original.) I see no escape from the conclusion that the District Court's finding that respondents' attorneys "reasonably" spent 1,946.75 hours to recover a money judgment of $33,350 is clearly erroneous, and that therefore the District Court's award of $245,456.25 in attorney's fees to respondents should be reversed. The Court's affirmance of the fee award emasculates the principles laid down in *Hensley,* and turns § 1988 into a relief act for lawyers.

A brief look at the history of this case reveals just how "unreasonable" it was for respondents' lawyers to spend so much time on it. Respondents filed their initial complaint in 1976, seeking injunctive and declaratory relief and compensatory and punitive damages from the city of Riverside, its chief of police, and 30 police officers, based on 256 separate claims allegedly arising out of the police breakup of a single party. Prior to trial, 17 of the police officers were dismissed from the case on motions for summary judgment, and respondents dropped their requests for injunctive and declaratory relief. More significantly, respondents also dropped their original allegation that the police had acted with discriminatory intent. The action proceeded to trial, and the jury completely exonerated nine additional police officers. Respondents ultimately prevailed against only the city and five police officers on various § 1983, false arrest and imprisonment, and common negligence claims. No restraining orders or injunctions were ever issued against petitioners, nor was the city ever compelled to change a single practice or policy as a result of respondents' suit. The jury awarded respondents a total of $33,350 in compensatory and punitive damages. Only about one-third of this total, or $13,300 was awarded to respondents based on violations of their federal constitutional rights.

Respondents then filed a request for $495,713.51 in attorney's fees, representing approximately 15 times the amount of the underlying money judgment. In April 1981, the District Court made its initial fee award of $245,456.25, declining to apply respondents' requested "multiplier," but awarding, to the penny, the entire "lodestar" claimed by respondents and their attorneys. The Ninth Circuit affirmed. We granted certiorari, vacated, and remanded, in light of *Hensley,* supra. On remand, the District Court convened a hearing, at which the court promptly announced, "I tell you now that I will not change the award. I will simply go back and be more specific about it." The court ultimately proved true to its word. After reviewing the record and the submissions of the parties, the court convened a second hearing, at which it approved exactly the same award as before: $245,456.25 in attorney's fees. The only noticeable change was that, the second time around, the court created a better "paper trail" by including in its order a discussion of those factors in Hensley and Johnson v. Georgia

Highway Express, Inc., 488 F.2d 714 (5th Cir. 1974), which it believed supported such a huge fee award. The Ninth Circuit again affirmed.

It is obvious to me that the District Court viewed *Hensley* not as a constraint on its discretion, but instead as a blueprint for justifying, in an after-the-fact fashion, a fee award it had already decided to enter solely on the basis of the "lodestar." In fact, the District Court failed at almost every turn to apply any kind of "billing judgment," or to seriously consider the "results obtained," which we described in *Hensley* as "the important factor" in determining a "reasonable" fee award. A few examples should suffice: (1) The court approved almost 209 hours of "prelitigation time," for a total of $26,118.75. (2) The court approved some 197 hours of time spent in conversations between respondents' two attorneys, for a total of $24,625. (3) The court approved 143 hours for preparation of a pre-trial order, for a total of $17,875.00. (4) Perhaps most egregiously, the court approved 45.50 hours of "stand-by time," or time spent by one of respondents' attorneys, who was then based in San Diego, to wait in a Los Angeles hotel room for a jury verdict to be rendered in Los Angeles, where his co-counsel was then employed by the U.C.L.A. School of Law, less than 40 minutes' driving time from the courthouse. The award for "stand-by-time" totaled $5,687.50. I find it hard to understand how any attorney can be said to have exercised "billing judgment" in spending such huge amounts of time on a case ultimately worth only $33,350.

Indeed, on the basis of some of the statements made by the District Court in this case, I reluctantly conclude that the court may have attempted to make up to respondents in attorney's fees what it felt the jury had wrongfully withheld from them in damages. As the court noted in its opinion, apparently believing that the observation supported the entry of a huge award of attorney's fees:

> "[T]he size of the jury award resulted from (a) the general reluctance of jurors to make large awards against police officers, and (b) the dignified restraint which the plaintiffs exercised in describing their injuries to the jury. For example, although some of the actions of the police would clearly have been insulting and humiliating to even the most insensitive person and were, in the opinion of the court, intentionally so, plaintiffs did not attempt to play up this aspect of the case."

But a District Court, in awarding attorney's fees under § 1988, does not sit to retry questions submitted to and decided by the jury. If jurors are reluctant to make large awards against police officers, this is a fact of life that plaintiffs, defendants, and district courts must live with, and a district court simply has no business trying to correct what it regards as an unfortunate tendency in the award of damages by granting inflated attorney's fees.

The analysis of whether the extraordinary number of hours put in by respondents' attorneys in this case was "reasonable" must be made in light of both the traditional billing practices in the profession, and the fundamental principle that the award of a "reasonable" attorney's fee under § 1988 means a fee that would have been deemed reasonable if billed to affluent plaintiffs by their own attorneys. This latter principle was stressed in the legislative history of § 1988, and by this Court in *Hensley*:

> "Counsel for the prevailing party should make a good faith effort to exclude from a fee request hours that are excessive, redundant, or otherwise unnecessary, just as a lawyer in private practice ethically is obligated to exclude such hours from his fee submission. 'In the private sector, "billing judgment" is an important component in fee setting. It is no less important here. Hours that are not properly billed to one's *client* also are not properly billed to one's *adversary* pursuant to statutory authority.'"

I think that this analysis, which appears nowhere in the plurality's opinion, leads inexorably to the conclusion that the District Court's fee award of $245,456.25, based on a prevailing hourly rate of $125 multiplied by the number of hours which respondents' attorneys claim to have spent on the case, is not a "reasonable" attorney's fee under § 1988.

Suppose that *A* offers to sell Blackacre to *B* for $10,000. It is commonly known and accepted that Blackacre has a fair market value of $10,000. *B* consults an attorney and requests a determination whether *A* can convey good title to Blackacre. The attorney writes an elaborate memorandum concluding that *A*'s title to Blackacre is defective, and submits a bill to *B* for $25,000. *B* refuses to pay the bill, the attorney sues, and the parties stipulate that the attorney spent 200 hours researching the title issue because of an extraordinarily complex legal and factual situation, and that the prevailing rate at which the attorney billed, which was also a "reasonable" rate, was $125. Does anyone seriously think that a court should award the attorney the full $25,000 which he claims? Surely a court would start from the proposition that, unless special arrangements were made between the client and the attorney, a "reasonable" attorney's fee for researching the title to a piece of property worth $10,000 could not exceed the value of the property. Otherwise the client would have been far better off never going to an attorney in the first place, and simply giving *A* $10,000 for a worthless deed. The client thereby would have saved himself $15,000.

Obviously the billing situation in a typical litigated case is more complex than in this bedrock example of a defective title claim, but some of the same principles are surely applicable. If *A* has a claim for contract damages in the amount of $10,000 against *B*, and retains an attorney to prosecute the claim, it would be both extraordinary and unjustifiable, in the absence of any special arrangement, for the attorney to put in 200 hours on the case and send the client a bill for $25,000. Such a bill would be "unreasonable," regardless of whether *A* obtained a judgment against *B* for $10,000 or obtained a take-nothing judgment. And in such a case, where the prospective recovery is limited, it is exactly this "billing judgment" which enables the parties to achieve a settlement; any competent attorney, whether prosecuting or defending a contract action for $10,000, would realize that the case simply cannot justify a fee in excess of the potential recovery on the part of either the plaintiff's or the defendant's attorney. All of these examples illuminate the point made in *Hensley* that "the important factor" in determining a "reasonable" fee is the "results obtained." The very "reasonableness" of the hours expended on a case by a plaintiff's attorney necessarily will depend, to a large extent, on the amount that may reasonably be expected to be recovered if the plaintiff prevails.

The amount of damages which a jury is likely to award in a tort case is of course more difficult to predict than the amount it is likely to award in a contract case. But even in a tort case some measure of the kind of "billing judgment" previously described must be brought to bear in computing a "reasonable" attorney's fee. Again, a hypothetical example will illustrate the point. If, at the time respondents filed their lawsuit in 1976, there had been in the Central District of California a widely publicized survey of jury verdicts in this type of civil rights action which showed that successful plaintiffs recovered between $10,000 and $75,000 in damages, could it possibly be said that it would have been "reasonable" for respondents' attorneys to put in on the case hours which, when multiplied by the attorneys' prevailing hourly rate, would result in an attorney's fee of over $245,000? In the absence of such a survey, it might be more difficult for a plaintiff's attorney to accurately estimate the amount of damages likely to be recovered, but this does not absolve the attorney of the responsibility for making such an estimate and using it as a guide in the exercise of "billing judgment."

In the context of § 1988, there would obviously be some exceptions to the general rules of "billing judgment" which I have been discussing, but none of these exceptions [is] applicable here. If the litigation is unnecessarily prolonged by the bad-faith conduct of the defendants, or if the litigation produces significant, identifiable benefits for persons other than the plaintiffs, then the purpose of Congress in authorizing attorney's fees under § 1988 should allow a larger award of attorney's fees than would be "reasonable" where the only relief is the recovery of monetary damages by individual plaintiffs. Nor do we deal with a case such as Carey v. Piphus, 435 U.S. 247, 266 (1978), in which the deprivation of a constitutional right necessarily results in only nominal pecuniary damages. Here, respondents successfully claimed both compensatory and punitive damages for false arrest and imprisonment, negligence, and violations of their constitutional rights under the fourth and 14th amendments, and the jury assessed damages as juries do in such cases. In short, this case shares none of the special aspects of certain civil rights litigation which the plurality suggests, in part III of its opinion, would justify an award of attorney's fees totally divorced from the amount of damages awarded by the jury.

The plurality explains the position advanced by petitioner and the Solicitor General concerning fee awards in a case such as this, and then goes on to "reject the proposition that fee awards under § 1988 should necessarily be proportionate to the amount of damages a civil rights plaintiff actually recovers." I agree with the plurality that the importation of the contingent-fee model to govern fee awards under § 1988 is not warranted by the terms and legislative history of the statute. But I do not agree with the plurality if it means to reject the kind of "proportionality" that I have previously described. Nearly 2,000 attorney-hours spent on a case in which the total recovery was only $33,000, in which only $13,300 of that amount was recovered for the federal claims, and in which the District Court expressed the view that, in such cases, juries typically were reluctant to award substantial damages against police officers, is simply not a "reasonable" expenditure of time. The snippets of legislative history which the plurality relies upon to dismiss *any* relationship between the amount of time put in on a case and the amount of damages awarded are wholly unconvincing. One may agree with all of the glowing rhetoric contained in the plurality's opinion about Congress' noble purpose in authorizing attorney's fees under § 1988 without concluding that Congress intended to turn attorneys loose to spend as many hours as possible to prepare and try a case that could reasonably be expected to result only in a relatively minor award of monetary damages.

In *Hensley,* we noted that "complex civil rights litigation involving numerous challenges to institutional practices or conditions" might well require "many hours of lawyers' services," and thus justify a large award of attorney's fees. This case is a far cry from the situation we referred to in *Hensley.* I would reverse the judgment of the Ninth Circuit affirming the District Court's award of attorney's fees, and remand the case to the District Court for recomputation of the fee award in light of both *Hensley* and the principles set forth in this opinion.

NOTES ON ATTORNEY'S FEES IN CIVIL RIGHTS ACTIONS

1. **Introduction.** The Civil Rights Attorneys' Fees Award Act of 1976 was a response to Alyeska Pipeline Service Co. v. Wilderness Society, 421 U.S. 240 (1975). In that case, environmentalists sued under the Mineral Leasing Act of 1920 to bar the Secretary of the Interior from authorizing construction of the Alaskan oil pipeline. Although their victory on the merits was almost immediately overturned by Congress, the plaintiffs persuaded the D.C. Circuit to award attorney's fees. This award departed from the traditional "American rule," which ordinarily requires each party to pay its own lawyers. The exception was thought justified on the ground that plaintiffs had acted as private attorneys general in vindicating public interests, but the Supreme Court disagreed:

"We are asked to fashion to far-reaching exception to the 'American rule'; but having considered its origin and development, we are convinced that it would be inappropriate for the judiciary, without legislative guidance, to reallocate the burdens of litigation . . . ."

The chief consequence of the decision to bar fee-shifting absent specific legislation was to preclude award of attorney's fees in § 1983 actions. Since attorney's fees were specifically authorized by several modern civil rights laws, the disparity seemed anomalous. Congress responded by passing the Civil Rights Attorneys' Fees Awards Act of 1976, now codified in 42 U.S.C. § 1988:[a]

"In any action or proceeding to enforce a provision of §§ 1981, 1982, 1983, 1985, and 1986 of this title, title IX of Public Law 92–318 [the Education Amendments of 1972, 20 U.S.C. §§ 1681 et seq.], or title VI of the Civil Rights Act of 1964 [42 U.S.C. § 2000d et seq.], the court, in its discretion, may allow the prevailing party, other than the United States, a reasonable attorney's fee as part of the costs."

Congress based this statute on analogous provisions in titles II and VII of the 1964 Civil Rights Act. The legislative history indicates that Congress intended that the standard for awarding fees under these provisions "be generally the same." S. Rep. No. 1011, 94th Cong., 2d Sess., at 3 (1976). This history accounts for two important glosses on the text of the statute.

(i) **"In its Discretion."** The text of § 1988 seems to make fee awards discretionary with the court. In fact, award of fees to the successful civil rights plaintiff is required, absent "special circumstances [that] would render such an award unjust." This interpretation comes from Newman v. Piggie Park Enterprises, Inc., 390 U.S. 400 (1968), which found in the 1964 Civil Rights Act a legislative intention routinely to award attorney's fees in order to encourage and reward private enforcement of civil rights. *Piggie Park* was specially referenced in the legislative history of § 1988, and its limitation of judicial discretion is taken to control the application of § 1988.

The "special circumstances" that might justify denial of fees to a prevailing plaintiff are not entirely settled, but it is clear that the category is extremely narrow. George Cochran's survey of Fifth Circuit cases found that each of the following circumstances had been found insufficient to justify a denial of fees:

"A prevailing party's independent ability to pay counsel; a defendant's good faith; the fact that ultimate responsibility for payment falls on innocent taxpayers or a public or private entity with a limited budget which has already incurred substantial legal expenses; the fact that plaintiff's counsel is court appointed or a salaried attorney with a public interest organi-

---

[a] Also codified in 42 U.S.C. § 1988 is an unrelated provision that originated in the Civil Rights Act of 1866.

zation; the fact that more time was spent litigating the issue of fees than the merits; and the fact that the claim is essentially one sounding in tort for private monetary damages or outside the ambit of seeking relief for discrimination based on race, sex, or other inherently offensive criteria."

Cochran, Section 1988 Attorney Fee Awards in the Fifth Circuit, 15 Tex. Tech. L. Rev. 1, 19–20 (1984). Indeed, the only circumstance found to justify denial of fees was the fact that plaintiff litigated pro se. Results in other circuits may vary in detail, but it appears quite generally true that prevailing plaintiffs almost always recover their fees.

(ii) **"Prevailing Party."** Section 1988 could be read to say that, depending on outcome, either plaintiff or defendant would be equally entitled to recover fees as a "prevailing party." Such balanced incentives, however, presumably would do little to encourage private enforcement of the civil rights acts. The literal reading has therefore been rejected in favor of a differentiation between plaintiffs and defendants. A prevailing plaintiff "should ordinarily recover an attorney's fee unless special circumstances would render such an award unjust." Newman v. Piggie Park Enterprises, Inc., 390 U.S. 400, 402 (1968). A prevailing defendant, by contrast, may recover fees only when the litigation is unreasonable, frivolous, meritless, or vexatious. The term "meritless" has been construed by the Court to mean "groundless or without foundation, rather than [that] the plaintiff has ultimately lost his case." Christiansburg Garment Co. v. Equal Employment Opportunity Commission, 434 U.S. 412, 421 (1978) (involving an unsuccessful charge of racial discrimination in employment in violation of title VII of the 1964 Civil Rights Act).

The *Christiansburg Garment Co.* opinion also explicates the basis for distinguishing plaintiffs from defendants under title VII:

"[A] moment's reflection reveals that there are at least two strong equitable considerations counselling an attorney's fee award to a prevailing title VII plaintiff that are wholly absent in the case of a prevailing title VII defendant.

"First as emphasized so forcefully in *Piggie Park*, the plaintiff is the chosen instrument of Congress to vindicate 'a policy that Congress considered of the highest priority.' Second, when a district court awards counsel fees to a prevailing plaintiff, it is awarding them against a violator of federal law. As the Court of Appeals clearly perceived, 'these policy considerations which support the award of fees to a prevailing plaintiff are not present in the case of a prevailing defendant.' "

This reasoning was adopted for § 1988 in Hughes v. Rowe, 449 U.S. 5 (1980).[b]

---

[b] For a window on the complexities to which the requirement of a "prevailing party" can occasionally give rise, see Hew- itt v. Helms, ___ U.S. ___ (1987). Plaintiff was a prisoner who sought damages for allegedly unlawful disciplinary confine-

2. Questions and Comments on *City of Riverside*. Of the several issues that have arisen since passage of the 1976 act, none is more important than the question of proportionality. Under the statute, a party may recover fees only by prevailing on the merits. The question is: Should the size of the fee be limited by the value of the victory? Should plaintiff's recovery of attorney's fees include all time validly spent in litigating the claim, no matter how trivial, or should there be some implicit deflator of the fee to match the size or importance of the judgment obtained?

In *City of Riverside,* the Solicitor General proposed that fee awards in damage actions be conformed to the model of a contingent fee. Under this approach, where plaintiff obtained only monetary damages, the maximum fee award would be some fraction (typically one-third) of the amount of judgment. Note that none of the nine Justices endorsed this view. Is the Court's unanimity on this point surprising?

Given the Court's rejection of the contingent fee model, the question then becomes whether some looser notion of proportionality is in order. Consider the facts of *City of Riverside.* The dissenters thought that the 197 hours of conversation between plaintiffs' attorneys and the $5,687.50 of hotel "stand-by time" were not "reasonable" in view of the judgment obtained. Would these expenses have been (more nearly?) "reasonable" had the jury returned a larger verdict? Does the answer depend on the degree to which the approximate dollar value of the lawsuit could have been predicted? Does it depend on the judge's assessment of the public interest served by the litigation? Recall that in *City of Riverside* the trial judge would have issued an injunction had he been asked, and that he apparently would have preferred a larger verdict. Are these appropriate considerations in determining a "reasonable" fee award?

3. Multi-Claim Litigation. A variant of the proportionality issue arises in multi-claim litigation. Where plaintiff prevails on one of several claims, should the fee award include work on the others? This question is not difficult where time is spent on issues common to all claims. If it takes 100 hours to develop the factual basis underlying five related claims, victory on any one of them presumably should lead to award of fees for the full 100 hours. But what of time spent researching a particular legal theory applicable to only one of several claims? Should success on one claim or theory entitle plaintiff to recover fees for all colorable claims or theories arising from the same facts?

The question is especially difficult where the unsuccessful claims were brought against other defendants. In *City of Riverside,* for exam-

ment. Ultimately, he was denied relief because of the defendants' immunity, but the court agreed with plaintiff's interpretation of the Constitution. The state corrections authority therefore revised its regulations. Plaintiff then sought attorney's fees, presenting, in the words of Justice Scalia, "the peculiar-sounding question whether a party who litigates to judgment and loses on all of his claims can nonetheless be a 'prevailing party' for purposes of an award of attorney's fees." The Court determined that he could not and upheld the denial of fees. Justice Marshall dissented, in an opinion joined by Justices Brennan, Blackmun, and Stevens.

ple, the losing defendants had to bear plaintiff's lawyers' expense in litigating against defendants who won on summary judgment. Is that justified? Under what circumstances?

Some of these issues were addressed in Hensley v. Eckerhart, 461 U.S. 424 (1983), where the Court said:

> "Where the plaintiff has failed to prevail on a claim that is distinct in all respects from his successful claims, the hours spent on the unsuccessful claim should be excluded in considering the amount of a reasonable fee. Where a lawsuit consists of related claims, a plaintiff who has won substantial relief should not have his attorney's fee reduced simply because the district court did not adopt each contention raised. But where the plaintiff achieved only limited success, the district court should award only that amount of fee that is reasonable in relation to the results obtained."

What do these comments mean? Do they suggest a workable test for determining when to compensate for time spent on unsuccessful claims?

4. Multipliers. Another important issue in awarding attorney's fees is the use of multipliers. Some courts have awarded some multiple of the lodestar as a way of compensating successful attorneys for the risk of not being paid. The use of such multipliers was conditionally approved by a badly fractured Supreme Court in Pennsylvania v. Delaware Valley Citizens' Council for Clean Air, ___ U.S. ___ (1987).

Delaware Valley involved litigation to compel Pennsylvania to comply with certain provisions of the Clean Air Act. After ultimately prevailing on the merits, the plaintiff organization sought attorney's fees, as authorized by that statute. The District Court computed the lodestar for each of several phases of the litigation, then doubled some figures to reflect the risk that plaintiff might not have prevailed on those issues. The Third Circuit affirmed, but the Supreme Court reversed.

Justice White spoke for a plurality consisting of himself, Chief Justice Rehnquist, and Justices Powell and Scalia. The plurality read the attorney's fees provision of the Clean Air Act, and by extension 42 U.S.C. § 1988, to preclude enhancement of fee awards through use of multipliers. Justice White emphasized the lack of clear evidence that Congress intended to authorize such awards. He also pointed out that the effect of enhancement was to require losing defendants to compensate plaintiffs' lawyers for not prevailing against other defendants in other cases. Finally, Justice White suggested that even if the fee-shifting provisions were construed to authorize multipliers in appropriate cases, the enhancement should ordinarily not exceed one-third of the lodestar.

Justice Blackmun, joined by Justices Brennan, Marshall, and Stevens, dissented. Blackmun argued that denying fee enhancement for contingency cases would undermine the purpose behind the fee-shifting statutes—namely, to attract competent counsel for cases that otherwise might not be litigated. In Blackmun's view, the legislative history of § 1988 indicated Congressional approval of the risk of nonrecovery as a factor in computing "reasonable" fee awards:

"Thus, a statutory fee cannot be computed solely by reference to rates charged by corporate firms, which obtain many payments from their clients through monthly billings. Rather, in order to arrive at a 'reasonable' attorney's fee, a court must incorporate a premium for the risk of nonrecovery, for the delay in payment, and for any economic risks aggravated by the contingency of payment, at a level similar to the premium incorporated in market rates. The risk premium can be reflected in the hourly rate that goes into the lodestar calculation, or, if the hourly rate does not include consideration of risk, in an enhancement of the lodestar."

Turning to the facts of this case, Blackmun found that the District Court had not adequately justified the doubling of several lodestar figures and therefore suggested that the case should be remanded for further findings.

The decisive vote was cast by Justice O'Connor. She agreed with the dissenters that Congress had not intended to foreclose consideration of contingency in setting reasonable attorney's fees. She also agreed with the dissent's suggestion that "compensation for contingency must be based on the difference in market treatment of contingent fee cases as a class, rather than on an assessment of the 'riskiness' of any particular case." However, O'Connor agreed with the plurality that the multiplier award in this case was improper. She gave the following guidance as to her view of appropriate fee awards:

"First, district courts and courts of appeals should treat a determination of how a particular market compensates for contingency as controlling future cases involving the same market. . . . Second, at all times the fee applicant bears the burden of proving the degree to which the relevant market compensates for contingency. I would also hold that a court may not enhance a fee award any more than necessary to bring the fee within the range that would attract competent counsel. I agree with the plurality that no enhancement for risk is appropriate unless the applicant can establish that without an adjustment for risk the prevailing party 'would have faced substantial difficulties in finding counsel in the local or other relevant market.'

"Finally, a court should not award any enhancement based on 'legal' risks or risks peculiar to the case. The lodestar—'the product of reasonable hours times a reasonable rate'—is flexible enough to account for great variation in the nature of the work performed in, and the challenges presented by, different cases. . . . The same can be said for most other problems posed by litigation, such as the tenacity of the defendant. . . . Thus, it is presumed that when counsel demon-

strates considerable ability in overcoming unusual difficulties
that have arisen in a case, counsel will be compensated for
those accomplishments by means of an appropriate hourly rate
multiplied by the hours expended."

Based on these factors, she found the fee award inadequate. It was not
based on findings regarding compensation for contingency in the relevant market nor by findings indicating that large enhancements were
necessary to attract competent counsel in the relevant community.
Therefore, she concurred in the judgment.

**5. Fee Awards for Time Spent in Administrative Proceed-
ings.** Section 1983 actions lie against persons acting "under color of"
state law, chiefly state officers. Often state law provides administrative remedies for official misconduct. Where a claimant successfully
invokes such a remedy, can attorney's fees be awarded under § 1988 for
time spent in the agency proceedings?

In New York Gaslight Club, Inc. v. Carey, 447 U.S. 54 (1980), the
Court held that the provision authorizing attorney's fees in an "action
or proceeding" under title VII of the 1964 Civil Rights Act covered state
administrative hearings. Under title VII, however, a claimant *must*
resort to available state remedies before seeking federal relief. Under
§ 1983, by contrast, exhaustion of state remedies normally is not
required. Patsy v. Board of Regents of the State of Florida, 457 U.S.
496 (1982). A § 1983 claimant usually can by-pass state administrative
opportunities and go directly to federal court.

In Webb v. Board of Education, 471 U.S. 234 (1985), this difference
was found decisive. A black school teacher sought and obtained local
administrative review of his dismissal. When the school board eventually decided to adhere to its decision, the teacher brought a federal civil
rights action. A partial record of the administrative hearing was filed
with the District Court. After some litigation, a consent order was
entered granting the plaintiff some $15,400 in damages. The issue of
attorney's fees was reserved for later resolution. In subsequent negotiations, plaintiff claimed a fee of $21,000, but the school board would
offer only $5,000. Plaintiff then filed a motion for award of fees under
§ 1988. One of the disputed issues was whether the fee should include
time spent in the state administrative proceedings. The trial court
decided to exclude such time, but accepted plaintiff's representations on
all other points and awarded a fee of nearly $10,000. The Court of
Appeals affirmed, and the Supreme Court granted certiorari to determine whether state administrative proceedings should be covered under
§ 1988.

Speaking through Justice Stevens, the Court ruled that since a
§ 1983 claimant could go straight to federal court, a state administrative hearing did not qualify as an "action or proceeding to enforce
[§ 1983]," as specified in § 1988. The Court noted, however, that some
services performed by an attorney before filing a complaint might be
compensable as time spent on the litigation. Thus, if a "discrete
portion" of work done in the administrative proceeding were "both

useful and of a type ordinarily necessary to advance the civil rights litigation," it would be covered by the fee award.[c] In this case, the District Court's decision to deny fees for time spent in the administrative process was found to be reasonable.

Justice Brennan, with whom Justice Blackmun joined, wrote separately. He argued that the case called for a remand to the trial court to consider whether some of the time spent in the administrative hearing contributed directly to the success in federal court. Justice Marshall did not participate.[d]

6. Fee Awards for Disputes Settled Prior to Litigation. A related question concerns the award of fees for time spent in resolving a civil rights dispute that is settled prior to litigation. Can a civil rights claimant whose dispute is settled without litigation sue for attorney's fees?

In North Carolina Dept. of Transportation v. Crest St. Community Council, Inc., 479 U.S. 6 (1986), the Supreme Court said "no." The case involved a proposed highway through a black neighborhood in Durham, N.C. A community group claimed that the routing decision would violate title VI of the 1964 Civil Rights Act, 42 U.S.C. § 2000d. That statute forbids racial discrimination in any federally funded program or activity and authorizes the cut-off of federal funds as a sanction. The statute also has been construed to create a private right of action, and such lawsuits are among the civil rights actions for which attorney's fees are authorized under 42 U.S.C. § 1988.

The community group took their complaint to the United States Department of Transportation, which, after investigation, advised the North Carolina agency that there was "reasonable cause" to believe that the proposed highway location would violate title VI. Ensuing discussions resulted in modification of the plan and a settlement accepted by all parties.

The dispute lasted for some five years, and the lawyer for the community group spent more than 12,000 hours on the project. According to the Supreme Court, "[t]he result of this diligent labor was both substantial and concrete." Nonetheless, the Court barred the group's effort to collect attorney's fees. Speaking through Justice O'Connor, the Court reasoned that § 1988 authorized fees only in an "action or proceeding to enforce" the listed civil rights laws. Here there had been no judicial complaint filed on the underlying civil rights claim; the independent action brought to collect the fees did not qualify.

[c] For implementation of this approach in the context of the attorney fee provisions of the Clean Air Act, see Pennsylvania v. Delaware Valley Citizens' Council for Clear Air, 478 U.S. 546 (1986).

[d] For pre-*Webb* criticism of the denial of § 1988 attorney's fees for time spent in state administrative proceedings, see Jeffrey Parness and Gigi Woodruff, Federal District Court Proceedings to Recover At-torney's Fees for Prevailing Parties on Section 1983 Claims in State Administrative Agencies, 18 Ga. L. Rev. 83 (1983). The authors argue that allowing such fees would encourage resort to available state remedies, thus taking advantage of the expertise of state agencies, relieving some of the caseload of the federal courts, and contributing to good federal-state relations.

The Court recognized that dicta in some earlier decisions had suggested that it would be anomalous to award fees only when the dispute leads to litigation, but concluded that "the paradoxical nature of this result may have been exaggerated":

"There are many types of behavior that may lead others to comply with civil rights laws. For example, an employee, after talking to his lawyer, may choose to discuss hiring or promotion practices with an employer, and as a result of this discussion the employer may alter those practices to comply more fully with employment discrimination laws. In some sense it may be considered anomalous that this employee's initiative would not be awarded with attorney's fees. But an award of attorney's fees under § 1988 depends not only on results obtained, but also on what actions were needed to obtain those results. It is entirely reasonable to limit the award of attorney's fees to those parties who, in order to obtain relief, found it necessary to file a complaint in court."

The Court also rejected a suggestion found in prior cases that "today's holding would create an incentive to file protective lawsuits in order to obtain attorney's fees":

"[W]e think that the better view was expressed by our conclusion in *Webb* that 'competent counsel will be motivated by the interests of the client to pursue . . . administrative remedies when they are available and counsel believes that they may prove successful.' An interpretation of § 1988 cannot be based on the assumption that 'an attorney would advise the client to forgo an available avenue of relief solely because § 1988 does not provide for attorney fees. . . .' Moreover, our holding creates a legitimate incentive for potential civil rights defendants to resolve disputes expeditiously, rather than risk the attorney's fees liability connected to civil rights litigation."

Justice Brennan, joined by Justices Marshall and Blackmun, dissented. "What today's holding ensures," he said, "is that no challenge brought under a statute covered by § 1988 will ever be settled without a court action." Brennan also spelled out the extent to which *Crest St. Council* had gone beyond *Webb:*

"In Webb v. Dyer County Board of Education, 471 U.S. 234 (1985), the Court held that § 1988 does not mandate an automatic award of fees to a civil rights claimant who prevails in an administrative proceeding. Specifically, the Court required that the proceeding involved be one 'to enforce' the underlying civil rights statute. But here the Court has not determined whether the administrative scheme promulgated by the United States Department of Transportation is a 'proceeding to enforce . . . title VI.' Instead, the Court sweeps aside the possibility of fees in *any* administrative proceeding—whether mandatory or optional, whether integral or peripheral to an enforcement scheme—unless the complainant files a concurrent lawsuit alleging the same civil rights violations. Unless such a complaint is filed in court, success at the administrative level automatically precludes any subsequent action for fees."

The lesson for civil rights lawyers, said Brennan, was "that they must file a civil lawsuit to have any hope of obtaining attorney's fees upon prevailing in an administrative enforcement proceeding." This, he said, will place a "pointless burden" on federal district courts, particularly in cases where claimants are "unfettered by a requirement that they exhaust administrative remedies" prior to filing such a suit.

7. Bibliography. The best general source is the symposium on attorney's fee shifting in volume 47 of Law and Contemporary Problems. In addition to providing a complete bibliography, see Christie, Attorney Fee Shifting: A Bibliography, 47 Law & Contemp. Prob. 347 (1984), the symposium features articles from a variety of perspectives. Included are the following: Schwartz, Foreword, at 1; Leubsdorf, Toward a History of the American Rule on Attorney Fee Recovery, at 9; Pfenningstorf, The European Experience with Attorney Fee Shifting, at 37; Kritzer, Fee Arrangements and Fee Shifting: Lessons from the Experience in Ontario, at 125; Rowe, Predicting the Effects of Attorney Fee Shifting, at 139; Braeutigam, Owen, and Panzar, An Economic Analysis of Alternative Fee Shifting Systems, at 173; Zemans, Fee Shifting and the Implementation of Public Policy, at 187; Fein, Citizen Suit Attorney Fee Shifting Awards: A Critical Examination of Government-"Subsidized" Litigation, at 211; Percival and Miller, The Role of Attorney Fee Shifting in Public Interest Litigation, at 233; Breger, Compensation Formulas for Court-Awarded Attorneys Fees, at 249; Conard, Winnowing Derivative Suits Through Attorneys Fees, at 269; and Wolfram, The Second Set of Players: Lawyers, Fee Shifting, and the Limits of Professional Discipline, at 293.

In addition to the sources already cited, see Berger, Court Awarded Attorney's Fees: What is "Reasonable"?, 126 U.Pa.L.Rev. 281 (1977) (discussing a number of practical problems in implementing fee awards); Diamond, The Firestorm Over Attorney Fees Awards, 69 A.B. A.J. 1420 (1983) (focusing on fee awards to nonprofit organizations); Feinberg and Gomperts, Attorneys' Fees in the Agent Orange Litigation: Modifying the Lodestar Analysis for Mass Tort Cases, 14 N.Y.U. Rev. of Law & Social Change 613 (1986) (recounting the experience of a special master in the Agent Orange litigation); Green, From Here to Attorney's Fees: Certainty, Efficiency, and Fairness in the Journey to the Appellate Courts, 69 Corn.L.Rev. 207 (1984) (examining issues of appellate jurisdiction in cases involving attorney's fees); Larson, Current Proposals in Congress to Limit and to Bar Court-Awarded Attorneys' Fees in Public Interest Litigation, 14 N.Y.U.Rev. of Law & Social Change 523 (1986) (reviewing and criticizing a number of hostile legislative proposals); Rowe, The Legal Theory of Attorney Fee Shifting: A Critical Overview, 1982 Duke L.J. 651 (analyzing the various rationales that might be advanced to support fee shifting); Rowe, The Supreme Court on Attorney Fee Awards, 1985 and 1986 Terms: Economics, Ethics, and Ex Ante Analysis, 1 Geo.J. Legal Ethics 621 (1988) (analyzing the economic reasoning in recent attorney's fee cases and the likely impact of those decisions on future behavior).

NOTES ON ATTORNEY'S FEES AND SETTLEMENT NEGOTIATIONS

1. **Attorney's Fees Upon Settlement.** Maher v. Gagne, 448 U.S. 122 (1980), was a § 1983 action to bring state welfare regulations into compliance with federal requirements. Substantial relief was obtained in a consent decree based on a negotiated settlement in which the defendants did not concede the illegality of past practice. Plaintiff then sought attorney's fees as a "prevailing party" under § 1988. The Supreme Court upheld the award of fees:

> "The fact that [plaintiff] prevailed through a settlement rather than through litigation does not weaken her claim to fees. Nothing in the language of § 1988 conditions the district court's power to award fees on full litigation of the issues or on a judicial determination that the plaintiff's rights have been violated."

Under *Maher* a settlement that does not include attorney's fees leaves the defendant's total exposure unsettled. Defendants therefore have an obvious incentive to include the issue of attorney's fees in settlement negotiations. The impact of settlement negotiations on the implementation of § 1988 raises a number of problems, some of which are dealt with in the notes that follow.

2. **Settlement Offers and Rule 68:** *Marek v. Chesny.* Rule 68 of the Federal Rules of Civil Procedure authorizes offer of settlement to be made "[a]t any time more than 10 days before the trial begins." If the offer is accepted, judgment is entered according to its terms. If the offer is rejected, the trial goes forward, but with an important proviso: "If the judgment finally obtained by the offeree is not more favorable than the offer, the offeree must pay the costs incurred after the making of the offer." Does the term "costs" as used in Rule 68 include the attorney's fees awarded to the successful civil rights plaintiff under § 1988? Or will the fee award include time spent both before and after the settlement offer?

In Marek v. Chesny, 437 U.S. 1 (1985), plaintiff brought § 1983 and state tort claims against three police officers who, in answering a call, shot and killed plaintiff's adult son. Defendants made a timely offer of settlement for $100,000, including attorney's fees and accrued costs. Plaintiff refused, but eventually recovered only $5,000 on the state-law claim, $52,000 under § 1983, and $3,000 in punitive damages. Plaintiff then filed a motion for $171,692.47 in costs and fees. Defendants invoked Rule 68, and it was later agreed that costs and fees accrued prior to the offer of settlement totalled $32,000. The District Court disallowed all other costs and fees, a position subsequently endorsed by the Supreme Court.

(i) **The Majority.** Speaking for the Court, Chief Justice Burger noted that at the time Rule 68 was adopted, there were already many statutes authorizing award of attorney's fees. Nevertheless, the drafters did not specify whether the limitation of post-offer "costs" covered attorney's fees. The Chief Justice interpreted this silence as follows:

> "In this setting, given the importance of 'costs' to the rule, it is very unlikely that this omission was mere oversight; on the contrary, the most reasonable inference is that the term 'costs' in Rule 68 was intended to refer to all costs properly awardable under the relevant substantive statute or other authority. In other words, all costs properly awardable in an action are to be considered within the scope of Rule 68 'costs.' Thus, absent Congressional expressions to the contrary, where the underlying statute defines 'costs' to include attorney's fees, we are satisfied that such fees are to be included as costs for purposes of Rule 68."

Plaintiff argued that this "plain meaning" application of Rule 68 would undermine § 1988's purpose to recruit and encourage civil rights plaintiffs, but the Court was not persuaded:

> "Rule 68's policy of encouraging settlements is neutral, favoring neither plaintiffs nor defendants; it expresses a clear policy of favoring settlement of all lawsuits. Civil rights plaintiffs—along with other plaintiffs—who reject an offer more favorable than what is thereafter recovered at trial will not recover attorney's fees for services performed after the offer is rejected. But, since the rule is neutral, many civil rights plaintiffs will benefit from the offers of settlement encouraged by Rule 68. Some plaintiffs will receive compensation in settlement where, on trial, they might not have recovered, or would have recovered less than what was offered. And, even for those who would prevail at trial, settlement will provide them with compensation at an earlier date without the burdens, stress, and time of litigation. In short, settlements rather than litigation will serve the interests of plaintiffs as well as defendants."

There was, therefore, no inconsistency between the two provisions:

> "Section 1988 encourages plaintiffs to bring meritorious civil rights suits; Rule 68 simply encourages settlements. There is nothing incompatible in these two objectives."[a]

---

[a] Justice Rehnquist had earlier taken the position that Rule 68 "costs" did not include attorney's fees awarded under title VII. Delta Airlines v. August, 450 U.S. 346 (1981). In *Marek v. Chesny,* he joined the Court opinion with the notation that "[f]urther examination of the question has convinced me that this view was wrong."

Justice Powell also joined the *Marek* majority and with a similar disavowal of prior views. In *Delta Airlines,* he had written specially to say that an offer of settlement should not qualify under Rule 68 unless it explicitly differentiated between the substantive relief proposed and the costs, including attorney's fees. The amount of the fee would ultimately be within the discretion of the court if the offer were accepted on other grounds. In *Marek,* Justice Powell noted that his *Delta Airlines* opinion

(ii) **The Dissent.** Justice Brennan, joined by Justices Marshall and Blackmun, dissented. He argued that the Court's interpretation of "costs" to include all costs authorized by an underlying substantive statute would produce "absurd variations in Rule 68's operation based on nothing more than picayune differences in statutory phraseology." Some statutes seem to identify attorney's fees as part of the "costs"; others refer to "costs *and* a reasonable attorney's fee"; and still others authorize award of fees without any mention of "costs." Brennan charged that the majority's "plain language" approach to Rule 68 would lead to a "senseless patchwork of fee-shifting," depending on the phrasing of the underlying statute. For these and other reasons, Brennan thought that Rule 68's reference to "costs" should be read to exclude attorney's fees no matter what the terms of the underlying statute authorizing such awards.

Among other arguments, Brennan focused on the asserted compatibility of Rule 68 and § 1988:

"The Court is wrong. Congress has instructed that attorney's fee entitlement under § 1988 be governed by a *reasonableness* standard. Until today the Court always has recognized that this standard precludes reliance on any mechanical 'bright-line' rules automatically denying a portion of fees, acknowledging that such 'mathematical approach[es]' provide 'little aid in determining what is a reasonable fee in light of all the relevant factors.' Hensley v. Eckerhart, 461 U.S. 424, 435–36 n.11 (1983). . . .

"Rule 68, on the other hand, . . . is a mechanical per se provision automatically shifting 'costs' incurred after an offer is rejected, and it deprives a district court of *all* discretion with respect to the matter . . . . The potential for conflict between § 1988 and Rule 68 could not be more apparent.

"Of course, a civil-rights plaintiff who *unreasonably* fails to accept a settlement offer, and who thereafter recovers less than the proffered amount in settlement, is barred under § 1988 itself from recovering fees for unproductive work performed in the wake of the rejection. This is because 'the extent of a plaintiff's success is *a* crucial factor in determining the proper amount of an award of attorney's fees,' *Hensley v. Eckerhart*, supra, at 440 (emphasis added); hours that are 'excessive, redundant, or otherwise unnecessary must be excluded from the calculation. To this extent, the results might sometimes be the same either under § 1988's reasonableness inquiry or the Court's wooden application of Rule 68. [But today's] decision necessarily will require the disallowance of some fees that otherwise would have passed muster under § 1988's reasonableness standard, and there is *nothing* in

had attracted no support, and he joined the majority on the ground that "it is important to have a Court for a clear interpretation of Rule 68."

§ 1988's legislative history even vaguely suggesting that Congress intended such a result.

"The Court argues, however, that its interpretation of Rule 68 'is neutral, favoring neither plaintiffs nor defendants.' This contention is also plainly wrong. . . . Interpreting Rule 68 in its current version to include attorney's fees will lead to a number of skewed settlement incentives that squarely conflict with Congress' intent. To discuss but one example, Rule 68 allows an offer to be made any time after the complaint is filed and gives the plaintiff only 10 days to accept or reject. The Court's decision inevitably will encourage defendants who know they have violated the law to make 'low-ball' offers immediately after suit is filed and before plaintiffs have been able to obtain the information they are entitled to by way of discovery to assess the strength of their claims and the reasonableness of the offers. The result will put severe pressure on plaintiffs to settle on the basis of inadequate information in order to avoid the risk of bearing all of their fees even if reasonable discovery might reveal that the defendants were subject to far greater liability. . . . This sort of so-called 'incentive' is fundamentally incompatible with Congress' goals."

(iii) **Questions and Comments on *Marek v. Chesny*.** For present purposes, the most important aspect of *Marek v. Chesny* is whether the Court's "plain meaning" interpretation of Rule 68 is or is not compatible with the purposes underlying § 1988. Who has the better side of this argument?[b]

3. **Settlement Conditioned on Waiver of Fees: *Evans v. Jeff D.*** What happens if defendant conditions an offer of settlement on waiver of attorney's fees? Plaintiff's counsel may feel obliged to accept an offer that is favorable to the client's interests, even though it requires that the lawyer forego compensation. Can the defendant force such a choice, or is plaintiff's statutory right to a "reasonable" attorney's fee exempt from settlement negotiations? These issues were addressed in Evans v. Jeff D., 475 U.S. 717 (1986).

Evans was a class action brought on behalf of emotionally and mentally handicapped children to contest the provision of educational and health care services by the state of Idaho. The class was represented by Charles Johnson, a lawyer with the Idaho Legal Aid Society, Inc. One week before trial, the state offered to settle the action by granting

---

[b] The literature on the question is mixed. The result in *Marek* was anticipated and approved in Simon, Rule 68 at the Crossroads: The Relationship Between Offers of Judgment and Statutory Attorney's Fees, 53 U. Cin. L. Rev. 889 (1984) (arguing that Rule 68's policy of encouraging settlement will benefit both plaintiffs and defendants). For a general analysis of the administration of Rule 68, including special attention to the problem of attorney's fees and some proposals for reform, see Branham, Offer of Judgment and Rule 68: A Response to the Chief Justice, 18 John Marshall L. Rev. 341 (1985). For some skeptical comments about the general wisdom of encouraging settlements rather than trial, see Fiss, Against Settlement, 93 Yale L.J. 1073 (1984).

plaintiffs "virtually all of the injunctive relief [they] had sought in their complaint." The offer, however, was conditioned on waiver of any claim to fees or costs. Settlement on these terms was unacceptable to the Legal Aid Society, but Johnson nonetheless concluded that he was ethically obligated to accept the offer. The settlement was then presented to the court, as is required under Rule 23, but at this point Johnson asked that he be allowed to present a bill of costs and fees. He argued that the defendant's offer had forced him to forego his fee by exploiting his ethical duty to his clients. The District Court rejected this claim, and the Supreme Court ultimately agreed.

(i) **The Majority.** Speaking for the Court, Justice Stevens noted that the Rule 23 requirement of court approval for settlement of class actions does not give the court the power to force a settlement on terms not agreed to by the parties. The judge could accept or reject a proposed settlement, but not enforce it as modified: "The District Court could not enforce the settlement on the merits and award attorney's fees anymore than it could, in a situation in which the attorney had negotiated a large fee at the expense of the plaintiff class, preserve the fee award and order greater relief on the merits." Therefore, the question was whether the judge had a duty to reject the proposed settlement because it included a waiver of fees. The Court found that § 1988 imposed no such obligation:

"The statute and its legislative history nowhere suggest that Congress intended to forbid *all* waivers of attorney's fees—even those insisted upon by a civil rights plaintiff in exchange for some other relief to which he is indisputably not entitled—anymore than it intended to bar a concession on damages to secure broader injunctive relief. Thus, while it is undoubtedly true that Congress expected fee-shifting to attract competent counsel to represent citizens deprived of their civil rights, it neither bestowed fee awards upon attorneys nor rendered them nonwaivable or nonnegotiable; instead, it added them to the arsenal of remedies available to combat violations of civil rights, a goal not invariably inconsistent with conditioning settlement on the merits on a waiver of statutory attorney's fees.

"Indeed, we believe that a general proscription against negotiated waiver of attorney's fees in exchange for a settlement on the merits would itself impede vindication of civil rights, at least in some cases, by reducing the attractiveness of settlement. . . .

"[D]efendants are unlikely to settle unless the cost of the predicted judgment, discounted by its probability, plus the transactions costs of further litigation, are greater than the cost of the settlement package. If fee waivers cannot be negotiated, the settlement package must either contain an attorney's fee component of potentially large and typically uncertain magnitude, or else the parties must agree to have the fee fixed by the court. Although either of these alternatives may well be acceptable in many cases, there surely is a significant number in which neither alternative will be as satisfactory as a decision to try the entire case.

"The adverse impact of removing attorney's fees and costs from bargaining might be tolerable if the uncertainty introduced into settlement negotiations were small. But it is not. The defendants' potential liability for fees in this kind of litigation can be as significant as, and sometime even more significant than, their potential liability on the merits. . . . Indeed, in this very case '[c]ounsel for defendants view[ed] the risk of an attorney's fees award as the most significant liability in the case.' Brief of Defendants. Undoubtedly there are many other civil rights actions in which potential liability for attorney's fees may overshadow the potential cost of relief on the merits and darken prospects for settlement if fees cannot be negotiated. . . .

"It is therefore not implausible to anticipate that parties to a significant number of civil rights cases will refuse to settle if liability for attorney's fees remains open, thereby forcing more cases to trial, unnecessarily burdening the judicial system, and disserving civil rights litigants. Respondents' own waiver of attorney's fees and costs to obtain settlement of their educational claims is eloquent testimony to the utility of fee waivers in vindicating civil rights claims. We conclude, therefore, that it is not necessary to construe [§ 1988] as embodying a general rule prohibiting settlements conditioned on waiver of fees in order to be faithful to the purposes of that act."

Finally, Justice Stevens turned to the issue whether, on the facts of this case, the trial court's approval of settlement conditioned on complete fee waiver constituted an abuse of discretion. He emphasized the trial court's finding that the extensive injunctive relief obtained on behalf of plaintiffs was a quid pro quo for the waiver of fees. Approval of the settlement could plausibly be attacked, therefore, only on the erroneous supposition that plaintiffs were somehow entitled to reject the fee waiver but retain the relief on the merits. Stevens concluded, therefore, that it should be left to the district courts to "appraise the reasonableness of particular class-action settlements on a case-by-case basis, in the light of all the relevant circumstances."

(ii) The Dissent. Justice Brennan, joined by Justices Marshall and Blackmun, dissented. Brennan criticized the majority for failing to distinguish between a simultaneous negotiation of fees and merits and a waiver of fees. "As a matter of logic, either of these practices may be permitted without the other." Brennan agreed that simultaneous negotiation should be permitted, but he strenuously objected to allowing waiver of fees. In his view, waiver was inconsistent with the overriding purpose of § 1988 to secure "enforcement of civil rights laws by ensuring that lawyers would be willing to take civil rights cases":

> "[I]t does not require a sociological study to see that permitting fee waivers will make it more difficult for civil rights plaintiffs to obtain legal assistance. It requires only common sense. Assume that a civil rights defendant makes a settlement offer that includes a demand for waiver of statutory attorney's fees. The decision whether to accept or reject the offer is the plaintiff's alone, and the lawyer must abide by the plaintiff's decision. See, e.g., ABA, Model Rules of Professional Conduct 1.2(a) (1984); ABA, Model Code of Professional Responsibility EC 7–7 to EC 7–9 (1982). As a formal matter, of course, the statutory fee belongs to the plaintiff, and thus technically the decision to waive entails a sacrifice only by the plaintiff. As a practical matter, however, waiver affects only the lawyer. Because 'a vast majority of the victims of civil rights violations' have no resources to pay attorney's fees, lawyers cannot hope to recover fees from the plaintiff and must depend entirely on the fees act for compensation. The plaintiff has no real stake in the statutory fee and is unaffected by its waiver. Consequently, plaintiffs will readily agree to waive fees if this will help them to obtain other relief they desire. . . .

> "Of course, from the lawyer's standpoint, things could scarcely have turned out worse. He or she invested considerable time and effort in the case, won, and has exactly nothing to show for it. [Is there reason to doubt] that this lawyer will be reluctant when, the following week, another civil rights plaintiff enters his office and asks for representation? . . .

> "Because making it more difficult for civil rights plaintiffs to obtain legal assistance is precisely the opposite of what Congress sought to achieve by enacting the fees act, fee waivers should be prohibited. . . ."

Justice Brennan then analyzed the impact that prohibiting fee waivers would likely have on settlements. He agreed that some settlements might be deterred, but argued that the majority had greatly exaggerated that effect. He further suggested that any incidental discouragement of settlements was in any event necessary in order to recruit lawyers for civil rights plaintiffs.

Additionally, Justice Brennan noted that several local bar associations had declared it unethical for defense counsel to seek waiver of fees. See, e.g., Committee on Professional Ethics of the Association of the Bar of the City of New York Op. No. 82–80 (1985). He expressed the hope that such rulings "will be followed by other state and local organizations concerned with respecting the intent of Congress and with protecting civil rights."

Finally, Brennan suggested that civil rights attorneys could obtain agreements from their clients not to waive attorney's fees. Such agreements would "enable civil rights practitioners to make it economically feasible—as Congress hoped—to expend time and effort litigating civil rights claims."

(iii) **Questions and Comments on *Evans*.** In his dissent, Justice Brennan drew a line between simultaneous negotiation of fees and merits, which he would allow, and waiver of fees, which he would forbid. Are the two really separable? How could a fee settlement be negotiated if plaintiff were not allowed to waive the right to a "reasonable" attorney's fee? Would not an agreed fee be a waiver of any claim to a greater amount? Brennan's answer is that the parties should be permitted to negotiate about the fee "so long as whatever fee the parties agree to is found by the court to be a 'reasonable' one under the fees act." Is this workable? What kinds of negotiating incentives would it create?

Note also Brennan's suggestion that civil rights lawyers have their clients agree not to waive attorney's fees. Would that work? Is there an ethical problem with a lawyer limiting the client's right to settle? Would there have been an ethical problem if, on the facts of *Evans*, Charles Johnson had followed the direction of the Legal Aid Society and refused the settlement offer on the ground that it omitted his compensation?

Should there be, as Justice Brennan suggested, an ethical prohibition against defense lawyers asking for fee waivers? Why? Would it also be unethical for the defense lawyer to negotiate a fee at the low end of the range of "reasonableness"? Should a defense lawyer be ethically obligated to ensure that plaintiff's counsel be adequately compensated?[c]

4. **Bibliography.** In addition to the sources already cited, see Berger, Court Awarded Attorney's Fees: What is "Reasonable"?, 126 U. Pa. L. Rev. 281 (1977) (discussing a number of practical problems in implementing fee awards); Diamond, The Firestorm Over Attorney

[c] For a discussion of the ethical problem presented by conditioning settlement on waiver of fees, see Kraus, Ethical and Legal Concerns in Compelling the Waiver of Attorney's Fees by Civil Rights Litigants in Exchange for Favorable Settlement of Cases Under the Civil Rights Attorneys' Fees Awards Act of 1976, 29 Vill. L. Rev. 597 (1984).

For a more wide-ranging discussion of a variety of ethical problems than can arise in settlement negotiations in civil rights cases, see Emily Calhoun's discussion in Attorney-Client Conflicts of Interest and the Concept of Non-Negotiable Fee Awards Under 42 U.S.C. § 1988, 55 U. Colo. L. Rev. 341 (1984). Professor Calhoun surveys the potential problems and discusses a number of attempted palliatives, including retainer agreements, judicial scrutiny of civil rights settlements, bifurcated negotiation of fees and merits, and the use of various trial stratagems to achieve the effects of non-negotiability. She concludes that none of these solutions is satisfactory and therefore urges that civil rights attorney's fees should be made non-negotiable. Otherwise, the implicit conflict of interest between attorney and client will be subject to various forms of exploitation in the settlement process. Calhoun admits that it is "unlikely" that § 1988 itself could be construed to forbid fee negotiations, but she contends that the courts have inherent discretion to make fees non-negotiable.

See also Charles W. Wolfram, The Second Set of Players: Lawyers, Fee Shifting, and the Limits of Professional Discipline, 47 Law & Contemp. Prob. 293 (1984). Wolfram focuses on the ethical dimensions of negotiating over attorney's fees and argues that fee waivers should be banned as against public policy.

Fees Awards, 69 A.B.A.J. 1420 (1983) (focusing on fee awards to non-profit organizations).

For an economic analysis of the case for awarding attorney's fees in civil rights cases, see Robert Percival and Geoffrey Miller, The Role of Attorney Fee Shifting in Public Interest Litigation, 47 Law & Contemp. Prob. 233 (1984). The authors argue that public interest litigation presents a free rider problem because many non-parties benefit from such litigation. As a result, market forces do not produce a societally optimal amount of public interest litigation. On this analysis, fee awards therefore function as a corrective to market failure.

———

Chapter X

ABSTENTION IN CIVIL RIGHTS CASES

INTRODUCTORY NOTE ON ABSTENTION IN CIVIL RIGHTS CASES

There are many contexts in which a federal trial court will decline to decide a case within its jurisdiction in favor of adjudication in the state courts. Some involve postponement of decision. In these cases there will be a subsequent opportunity for the litigation to return to a federal trial court. Some, however, involve abdication of decision. In these cases the only subsequent opportunity for federal intervention will be on review of the state court proceedings in the United States Supreme Court.

The generic term for these practices is "abstention." Abstention is not a unitary concept. It refers to many doctrines of different origins and with vastly different rationales. In some situations abstention is mandated by statute, the most important of which are the Anti-Injunction Act,[a] the Tax-Injunction Act,[b] the Johnson Act,[c] and the exhaustion of available state remedies required for federal habeas corpus.[d] Most abstention doctrines, however, are judicially crafted exceptions to jurisdictional statutes. Examples are the exclusion of domestic relations and probate cases from the diversity jurisdiction;[e] deference to state adjudication when a federal court decision would substantially interfere with a complex state administrative structure;[f] and the stay of federal civil proceedings in favor of an ongoing state suit concerning the same subject matter.[g]

The present concern is the intersection of abstention with the litigation of civil rights cases under 42 U.S.C. § 1983. Two abstention formulas are most commonly invoked in this context. The first is based on Railroad Comm'n of Texas v. Pullman, 312 U.S. 496 (1941), which deferred federal adjudication to give state courts an opportunity to decide whether an allegedly unconstitutional state practice was authorized by an ambiguous state law. The second derives from Younger v. Harris, 401 U.S. 37 (1971). *Younger* itself involved an unsuccessful effort to enjoin a pending state criminal prosecution under an allegedly

[a] 28 U.S.C. § 2283. See pages 526–41, supra.

[b] 28 U.S.C. § 1341. See pages 571–72, supra.

[c] 28 U.S.C. § 1342. See page 572, supra.

[d] The requirement of exhaustion in habeas cases was initially developed by the courts, but has subsequently been codified. See pages 689–710, supra.

[e] See page 470, supra.

[f] The major cases are Burford v. Sun Oil Co., 319 U.S. 315 (1943), and Alabama Public Service Comm'n v. Southern Ry Co., 341 U.S. 341 (1951). See pages 564–66, supra.

[g] See the *Colorado River* case and its notes, pages 541–58, supra.

unconstitutional statute. Today, however, the significance of *Younger* extends far beyond this context.

SECTION 1. *PULLMAN* ABSTENTION

RAILROAD COMMISSION OF TEXAS v. PULLMAN COMPANY
Supreme Court of the United States, 1941.
312 U.S. 496.

MR. JUSTICE FRANKFURTER delivered the opinion of the Court.

In those sections of Texas where the local passenger traffic is slight, trains carry but one sleeping car. These trains, unlike trains having two or more sleepers, are without a Pullman conductor; the sleeper is in charge of a porter who is subject to the train conductor's control. As is well known, porters on Pullmans are colored and conductors are white. Addressing itself to this situation, the Texas Railroad Commission after due hearing ordered that "no sleeping car shall be operated on any line of railroad in the state of Texas . . . unless such cars are continuously in the charge of an employee . . . having the rank and position of Pullman conductor." Thereupon, the Pullman Company and the railroads affected brought this action in a federal district court to enjoin the commission's order. Pullman porters were permitted to intervene as complainants, and Pullman conductors entered the litigation in support of the order. Three judges having been convened, the court enjoined enforcement of the order. From this decree, the case came here directly.[a]

The Pullman Company and the railroads assailed the order as unauthorized by Texas law as well as violative of the equal protection, the due process and the commerce clauses of the Constitution. The intervening porters adopted these objections but mainly objected to the order as a discrimination against Negroes in violation of the 14th amendment.

The complaint of the Pullman porters undoubtedly tendered a substantial constitutional issue. It is more than substantial. It touches a sensitive area of social policy upon which the federal courts ought not to enter unless no alternative to its adjudication is open. Such constitutional adjudication plainly can be avoided if a definitive ruling on the state issue would terminate the controversy. It is therefore our duty to turn to a consideration of questions under Texas law.

[a] A three-judge district court, followed by direct appeal to the Supreme Court, was required by a statute—since repealed—enacted in the wake of Ex parte Young, 209 U.S. 123 (1908). See pages 819–20, supra. [Footnote by eds.]

The commission found justification for its order in a Texas statute which we quote in the margin.[1] It is common ground that if the order is within the commission's authority its subject matter must be included in the commission's power to prevent "unjust discrimination . . . and to prevent any and all other abuses" in the conduct of railroads. Whether arrangements pertaining to the staffs of Pullman cars are covered by the Texas concept of "discrimination" is far from clear. What practices of the railroads may be deemed to be "abuses" subject to the commission's correction is equally doubtful. Reading the Texas statutes and the Texas decisions as outsiders without special competence in Texas law, we would have little confidence in our independent judgment regarding the application of that law to the present situation. The lower court did deny that the Texas statutes sustained the commission's assertion of power. And this represents the view of an able and experienced circuit judge of the circuit which includes Texas and of two capable district judges trained in Texas law. Had we or they no choice in the matter but to decide what is the law of the state, we should hesitate long before rejecting their forecast of Texas law. But no matter how seasoned the judgment of the District Court may be, it cannot escape being a forecast rather than a determination. The last word on the meaning of article 6445 of the Texas Civil Statutes, and therefore the last word on the statutory authority of the Railroad Commission in this case, belongs neither to us nor to the District Court but to the Supreme Court of Texas. In this situation a federal court of equity is asked to decide an issue by making a tentative answer which may be displaced tomorrow by a state adjudication. The reign of law is hardly promoted if an unnecessary ruling of a federal court is thus supplanted by a controlling decision of a state court. The resources of equity are equal to an adjustment that will avoid the waste of a tentative decision as well as the friction of a premature constitutional adjudication.

An appeal to the chancellor . . . is an appeal to the "exercise of the sound discretion, which guides the determination of courts of equity." The history of equity jurisdiction is the history of regard for public consequences in employing the extraordinary remedy of the injunction. There have been as many and as variegated applications of this supple principle as the situations that have brought it into play. . . . Few public interests have a higher claim upon the discretion of a federal chancellor than the avoidance of needless friction with state policies, whether the policy relates to the enforcement of the criminal law, Fenner v. Boykin, 271 U.S. 240 (1926); Spielman Motor Co. v.

---

[1] Vernon's Anno. Texas Civil Statutes, Article 6445:

"Power and authority are hereby conferred upon the Railroad Commission of Texas over all railroads . . . and it is hereby made the duty of the said Commission to adopt all necessary rates, charges and regulations, to govern and regulate such railroads . . . and to correct abuses and prevent unjust discrimination in the rates, charges and tolls of such railroads . . . and to fix division of rates, charges and regulations between railroads and other utilities and common carriers where a division is proper and correct, and to prevent any and all other abuses in the conduct of their business and to do and perform such other duties and details in connection therewith as may be provided by law."

Dodge, 295 U.S. 89 (1935); or the administration of a specialized scheme for liquidating embarrassed business enterprises, Pennsylvania v. Williams, 294 U.S. 176 (1935); or the final authority of a state court to interpret doubtful regulatory laws of the state, Gilchrist v. Interborough Co., 279 U.S. 159 (1929); cf. Hawks v. Hamill, 288 U.S. 52, 61 (1933). These cases reflect a doctrine of abstention appropriate to our federal system whereby the federal courts, "exercising a wise discretion," restrain their authority because of "scrupulous regard for the rightful independence of the state governments" and for the smooth working of the federal judiciary. This use of equitable powers is a contribution of the courts in furthering the harmonious relation between state and federal authority without the need of rigorous congressional restriction of those powers. Compare [the Three-Judge Court Act, the Tax-Injunction Act, the Johnson Act, and the Norris-LaGuardia Act.]

Regard for these important considerations of policy in the administration of federal equity jurisdiction is decisive here. If there was no warrant in state law for the commission's assumption of authority there is an end of the litigation; the constitutional issue does not arise. The law of Texas appears to furnish easy and ample means for determining the commission's authority. Article 6453 of the Texas Civil Statutes gives a review of such an order in the state courts. Or, if there are difficulties in the way of this procedure of which we have not been apprised, the issue of state law may be settled by appropriate action on the part of the state to enforce obedience to the order. In the absence of any showing that these obvious methods for securing a definitive ruling in the state courts cannot be pursued with full protection of the constitutional claim, the District Court should exercise its wise discretion by staying its hands.

We therefore remand the cause to the District Court, with directions to retain the bill pending a determination of proceedings, to be brought with reasonable promptness, in the state court in conformity with this opinion.

Reversed.

MR. JUSTICE ROBERTS took no part in the consideration or decision of this case.

NOTES ON *PULLMAN* ABSTENTION

1. *Siler v. Louisville & Nashville RR.* Siler v. Louisville & Nashville RR. Co., 213 U.S. 175 (1909), involved a suit by a railroad to enjoin enforcement of an order of the Kentucky railroad commission fixing maximum rates on commodities transported to and from points within the state. There was no diversity. Jurisdiction was based on the presence of a federal question in the complaint. It was argued that the rates violated various provisions of the federal Constitution and also that they were unauthorized under the applicable state statutes.

The lower court enjoined enforcement of the rates on federal constitutional grounds.

The Supreme Court first held that the lower court had jurisdiction:

> "The federal questions . . . gave the Circuit Court jurisdiction, and, having properly obtained it, that court had the right to decide all the questions in the case, even though it decided the federal questions adversely to the party raising them, or even if it omitted to decide them at all, but decided the case on local or state questions only."

The Court then addressed the order in which the questions in the case should be decided:

> "Where a case in this Court can be decided without reference to questions arising under the federal Constitution, that course is usually pursued and is not departed from without important reasons. In this case we think it much better to decide it with regard to the question of a local nature, involving the construction of the state statute and the authority therein given to the commission to make the order in question, rather than to unnecessarily decide the various constitutional questions appearing in the record. . . .

> "In this case we are without the benefit of a construction of the statute by the highest state court of Kentucky, and we must proceed in the absence of state adjudication upon the subject. Nevertheless, we are compelled to the belief that the statute does not grant to the commission any such great and extensive power as it has assumed to exercise in making the order in question. . . ."

The Court then explained why it thought the state statute' did not authorize the rate-making at issue, and upheld the injunction.

2. Questions and Comments on *Pullman*. Why did the *Pullman* Court decline to follow *Siler*? Note that the decree in *Siler* could have been modified by the trial court if, in light of subsequent state court decisions, the "forecast" of state law turned out to be wrong.[a] At that point, of course, the federal constitutional issue would have to be resolved and the injunction reissued if the state practice were found unconstitutional.

[a] See, e.g., Field, Abstention in Constitutional Cases: The Scope of the *Pullman* Abstention Doctrine, 122 U. Pa. L. Rev. 1071, 1094 n.90 (1974):

"When a federal court rests its decision on a state question and thereby avoids a federal constitutional question, the decree will often include a provision expressly authorizing reopening in the event that the question of state law is subsequently decided differently in the state court. See Lee v. Bickell, 292 U.S. 415 (1934); Wald Transfer & Storage Co. v. Smith, 290 U.S. 602 (1933); Glenn v. Field Packing Co., 290 U.S. 177 (1933). Even if the federal judge neglects to insert such a provision, the decree can be modified when the state court has authoritatively spoken. It is this possibility of modification that led Justice Frankfurter to fear in *Pullman* that a federal ruling on the state issue would be 'tentative.' "

Consider, however, the state's perspective. If a federal injunction were issued in *Siler*, the rate structure could not be put into effect until the state obtained an authoritative ruling on the state law question. If it turned out that the state practice was both authorized and constitutional, the state would have been deprived of the chance to implement its valid legislative authority in the interim. On the other hand, if the state practice in *Pullman* was unconstitutional and was allowed to be implemented during the period that the issue of state authority was being litigated, the plaintiffs would have been subjected to an avoidable period of unconstitutional regulation.

What should be done in these situations? Would it be better to assume that state law authorizes the practice in question and decide the federal constitutional issue? Should the plaintiff be entitled to interim relief if abstention is to be ordered?[b] Is there any other option?[c]

3. *Wisconsin v. Constantineau.* The Supreme Court has held that *Pullman* abstention can be invoked in suits based on § 1983.[d] Note, moreover, that the decree in *Pullman* was a remand to the district court "with directions to retain the bill" pending determination of the state questions in state court. The contemplation of this order is that the case can then return to the district court, if necessary, for resolution of the federal constitutional question. Can this result be reconciled with the position that exhaustion of state remedies is not required in § 1983 suits? Can it be reconciled with the rejection of Justice Frankfurter's argument in *Monroe v. Pape* [e] that § 1983 should only be available to attack practices authorized by state law? Consider Wisconsin v. Constantineau, 400 U.S. 433 (1971), in connection with these questions.

Acting under authority of a state statute, the Chief of Police, without notice or a hearing, "posted" the plaintiff's name in all retail liquor outlets in a Wisconsin town. The consequence was that the plaintiff was unable to purchase liquor for a period of one year. She sought a federal injunction against the practice of "posting." On appeal, the Court, in an opinion by Justice Douglas, held that she had been denied procedural due process and was entitled to injunctive relief. On the question of abstention, Justice Douglas wrote:

[b] For an extensive treatment of this issue, see Wells, Preliminary Injunctions and Abstention: Some Problems in Federalism, 63 Corn. L. Rev. 65 (1977).

[c] In The Abstention Doctrine Today, 125 U. Pa. L. Rev. 590, 605–06 & n.56 (1977), Martha Field suggests that certification of unclear questions of state law to the state supreme courts may be the answer. For states without a certification procedure,

"Congress could dispense with the need for state authorization and require states to entertain certified questions. . . .

Congressional power would stem from article III in conjunction with the necessary and proper clause. It may also be that article III gives the federal courts power, without any congressional authorization, to compel certification."

Are these viable suggestions?

[d] See, e.g., Askew v. Hargrave, 401 U.S. 476 (1971); Harrison v. NAACP, 360 U.S. 167 (1959).

[e] See pages 888–90, supra.

"Congress could, of course, have routed all federal constitutional questions through the state court systems, saving to this Court the final say when it came to review of the state court judgments. But our first Congress resolved differently and created the federal court system and in time granted the federal courts various heads of jurisdiction, which today involve most federal constitutional rights. Once that jurisdiction was granted, the federal courts resolved those questions even when they were enmeshed with state law questions. In 1941 we gave vigor to the so-called abstention doctrine in *Railroad Comm'n of Texas v. Pullman.* . . .

"In the present case [t]here is no ambiguity in the state statute. . . . The act on its face gives the Chief of Police the power to do what he did to the appellee. Hence the naked question, uncomplicated by an unresolved state law, is whether that act on its face is unconstitutional. [A]bstention should not be ordered merely to await an attempt to vindicate the claim in a state court."

Chief Justice Burger, joined by Justice Blackmun, dissented on the abstention issue. He argued:

"Very likely we reach the correct result since the Wisconsin statute appears, on its face and in its application, to be in conflict with accepted concepts of due process.

"The reason for my dissent is that it seems to me a very odd business to strike down a state statute, on the books for 40 years more or less, without any opportunity for the state courts to dispose of the problem either under the Wisconsin Constitution or the U.S. Constitution. For all we know, the state courts would find this statute invalid under the state Constitution . . . . Since no one could reasonably think that the judges of Wisconsin have less fidelity to due process requirements of the federal Constitution than we do, this case is, for me, a classic illustration of one in which we should decline to act until resort to state courts has been exhausted. . . .

"It is no answer to contend that there is no ambiguity in the Wisconsin statute and hence no need to abstain . . . . [I]n furtherance of this Court's firm policy to steer around head-on collisions with the states by avoiding unnecessary constitutional decisions, we [should reverse] the District Court and [remand] with instructions to stay its hand while the litigants [exhaust] state court remedies for resolution of their challenge to the statute.

"I quite agree that there is no absolute duty to abstain—to stay our hand—until the state courts have at least been asked to construe their own statute, but for me, it is the negation of sound judicial administration—and an unwarranted use of a limited judicial resource—to impose this kind of case on a three-judge federal district court, and then by direct appeal, on this Court. . . .

"This Court has an abundance of important work to do, which, if it is to be done well, should not be subject to the added pressures of non-urgent state cases which the state courts have never been called on to resolve. . . ."[f]

Chief Justice Burger was plainly concerned with the burden placed on the courts by the three-judge court requirement,[g] which has since been repealed for this class of cases. It may be that he would have taken a different view in the absence of that procedure. But if one reads his opinion for what it says, it moves towards an exhaustion requirement for some § 1983 cases.[h] Is this wise? Should the federal courts invoke *Pullman* in cases where the challenged practice may be invalid under the state constitution?

Compare Justice Douglas' opinion. He argues that Congress has conferred jurisdiction on the federal courts and that the courts should exercise the jurisdiction as conferred.[i] Can *Pullman* itself be reconciled with that premise? In Abstention, Separation of Powers, and the Limits of the Judicial Function, 94 Yale L.J. 71 (1984), Martin Redish argues that it cannot be. Redish contends that abstention is unacceptable "as a matter of legal process and separation of powers, wholly apart from the practical advisability . . . of the doctrine." In his view, abstention involves "precisely the same dangers" as the creation of federal common law and the implication of private remedies from statutes. "[A] far greater judicial encroachment upon the legislative prerogative takes place," he continues,

"when the federal courts directly undermine enforcement of an existing legislative program by declining to enforce federal rights in situations not authorized by Congress. Judge-made

[f] Justice Black, also joined by Justice Blackmun, filed a dissent in which he noted that he agreed "substantially" with the Chief Justice and that it seemed to him "wholly uncertain that the state law has the meaning it purports to have."

[g] The three-judge court act, a reaction by Congress to *Ex parte Young,* disrupted both district and circuit court dockets by requiring trial of cases seeking injunctions against statutes of state-wide applicability to be heard before three judges, usually two district judges and a circuit judge. The only available review was a direct appeal to the Supreme Court. The Chief Justice noted in an omitted portion of his opinion that the plaintiff's lawyer admitted that he chose to go to federal court because that was the fastest way to the Supreme Court.

[h] The Court has ordered abstention to resolve whether the challenged practice was invalid under the state constitution in at least two § 1983 actions. See Harris

County Commissioners Court v. Moore, 420 U.S. 77 (1975) (abstention appropriate in a reapportionment case where "the uncertain status of local law stems from the unsettled relationship between the state constitution and a statute"); Reetz v. Bozanich, 397 U.S. 82 (1970) (abstention ordered in challenge to Alaska program for fishing licenses where "the nub of the whole controversy may be the state constitution. The constitutional provision relates to fish resources, an asset unique in its abundance in Alaska. The statute and regulations relate to that same unique resource, the management of which is a matter of great state concern.").

[i] Cf. Chief Justice Marshall in Cohens v. Virginia, 19 U.S. (6 Wheat.) 264, 404 (1821): "We have no more right to decline the exercise of jurisdiction which is given, than to usurp that which is not given. The one or the other would be treason to the Constitution."

abstention, then, constitutes judicial lawmaking of the most sweeping nature. The principle of separation of powers would be better protected by the Court's application of the same cautious scrutiny used to review the creation of federal common law to the development of judge-made abstention."

Michael Wells has responded to this argument in Why Professor Redish Is Wrong About Abstention, 19 Ga. L. Rev. 1097 (1985). Wells argues that Redish relies on a "faulty premise," namely "that Congress is responsible for the modern federal cause of action under 42 U.S.C. § 1983 against state actors to redress constitutional violations." Wells continues:

"Once this premise is accepted, it is easy to show that the abstention rules violate Congress' intent. The problem . . . is that the statute was never intended to create such a broad cause of action. [T]he holding in *Monroe* cannot be credibly defended as the result of a successful search for the intent of the framers of the statute. Abstention is more accurately viewed as a judge-made forum rule for a judge-made cause of action and hence can withstand the attack mounted against it by Professor Redish."[j]

Who has the better of the debate?

4. Administration of the *Pullman* Doctrine. The debate in most *Pullman* cases is whether state law is "unclear" enough to justify abstention.[k] Other considerations are whether an adequate state remedy is available to the federal plaintiff,[l] whether a single state proceeding is likely to clear up the difficulty,[m] and whether there are special reasons for prompt federal intervention.[n] *Pullman* abstention is usual-

---

[j] Wells also addresses two further questions: "[I]f both the cause of action and abstention are judge-made, then is it possible to defend either of them against the contention that the scope of federal jurisdiction is a matter delegated to Congress in article III of the Constitution? [I]s it possible to distinguish between the expansive and restrictive rules, and to uphold judge-made rules that broaden federal jurisdiction but not those that restrict it?" His answers are "yes to the first of these questions and no to the second."

[k] For an extensive discussion of this requirement, see Sidney Shapiro, Abstention and Primary Jurisdiction: Two Chips off the Same Block?—A Comparative Analysis, 60 Corn. L. Rev. 75, 83–91 (1974). Shapiro concludes:

"What [the] cases make clear is that the requirement of state law uncertainty is relative. It is variously influenced by comity, by the nature of the rights involved, and by the other reasons for abstention. Because of the variability of

such influences, the rule is uncertain and prediction of outcomes is difficult."

[l] For discussion of this requirement, see Justice Powell's concurring opinion in Houston v. Hill, __ U.S. __ (1987).

[m] See, in this respect, Dombrowski v. Pfister, 380 U.S. 479 (1965) (first amendment vagueness and overbreadth challenge), and Baggett v. Bullitt, 377 U.S. 360 (1964) (vagueness challenge to loyalty oath). Both cases involved state statutes that could only have been clarified in a series of lawsuits. Accordingly, the Court held that abstention was inappropriate.

[n] See, e.g., Pike v. Bruce Church, Inc., 397 U.S. 137, 140 n.3 (1970): "In view of the emergency situation presented, and the fact that only a narrow and specific application of the act was challenged as unconstitutional, the court was fully justified in not abstaining . . . ." The suit concerned the validity of packing regulations for the shipping of cantaloupes. The emergency was that if the regulations were enforced, a $700,000 crop would be lost.

ly thought to be a doctrine that finds its roots in equity and hence to be limited to efforts to obtain an injunction.[o]

Beyond these generalizations, it is hard to identify a consistent pattern in the cases. The propriety of abstention in any given situation is therefore likely to be unclear.[p] This, in fact, is one of the major difficulties in the administration of the doctrine. *Pullman* abstention is not discretionary with the trial court. Deference is not given to a decision to abstain or not to abstain made at the outset of the case. Instead, the question is reviewed de novo on appeal and can even be raised sua sponte. Abstention may thus be ordered even though time and money have been expended in litigating the merits in lower federal courts.[q]

One of the consequences of *Pullman* abstention is substantial delay in the adjudication of federal claims. Indeed, Martha Field has suggested that:

"A survey of abstention decisions . . . raises the question whether delay is not sometimes the *aim* of the abstention procedure, and the desirability of obtaining a clarifying state decision simply the *excuse* for the delay. When, for example, a lawsuit presents a federal constitutional attack on a state program that does not seem politic at the moment to resolve, abstention may appear a convenient device for removing the parties from federal court, for the time being at least. Even if they persist in demanding a federal forum to resolve their federal claims, abstention will put them off for a number of years."[r]

For these reasons, as well as the problems developed in connection with the next main case, many are opposed to the idea of *Pullman* abstention.[s] Invocation of the doctrine has ebbed and flowed over the years—in response, some have contended, to the Court's view of the importance of the constitutional values at stake.[t]

---

[o] There are, however, a few damages cases in which it has been invoked. See, e.g., Fornaris v. Ridge Tool Co., 400 U.S. 41 (1970); United Gas Pipe Line Co. v. Ideal Cement Co., 369 U.S. 134 (1962). See also Louisiana Power & Light Co. v. City of Thibodaux, 360 U.S. 25 (1959).

[p] Extensive consideration of *Pullman* cases can be found in Bezanson, Abstention: The Supreme Court and Allocation of Judicial Power, 27 Vand. L. Rev. 1107 (1974), and Field, Abstention in Constitutional Cases: The Scope of the *Pullman* Abstention Doctrine, 122 U. Pa. L. Rev. 1071 (1974).

[q] See Field, The Abstention Doctrine Today, 125 U. Pa. L. Rev. 590, 599 (1977).

[r] Field, The Abstention Doctrine Today, 125 U. Pa. L. Rev. 590, 602 (1977).

[s] See, e.g., McMillan, Abstention—The Judiciary's Self-Inflicted Wound, 56 N.C.L. Rev. 527 (1978); Field, The Abstention Doctrine Today, 125 U. Pa. L. Rev. 590 (1977); Currie, The Federal Courts and the American Law Institute, 36 U. Chi. L. Rev. 268 (1969); Kurland, Toward a Co-operative Judicial Federalism: The Federal Court Abstention Doctrine, 24 F.R.D. 481 (1959).

[t] In *Pullman* and *Burford* Abstention: Clarifying the Roles of State and Federal Courts in Constitutional Cases, 20 U.C. Davis L.Rev. 1 (1986), Julie Davies discusses the extent to which the ebb and flow of *Pullman* abstention has responded to changing views of substantive federal rights and the values of federalism and analyzes the costs of this practice. She argues that *Pullman* and *Burford* (see page 564, supra) abstention "are not the proper

ENGLAND v. LOUISIANA STATE BOARD OF
MEDICAL EXAMINERS

Supreme Court of the United States, 1964.
375 U.S. 411.

MR. JUSTICE BRENNAN delivered the opinion of the Court.

Appellants are graduates of schools of chiropractic who seek to practice in Louisiana without complying with the educational requirements of the Louisiana Medical Practice Act, title 37, La. Rev. Stat. §§ 1261–1290. They brought this action against respondent Louisiana State Board of Medical Examiners in the federal District Court for the Eastern District of Louisiana, seeking an injunction and a declaration that as applied to them, the act violated the 14th amendment. A statutory three-judge court[1] invoked, sua sponte, the doctrine of abstention . . . .

Appellants thereupon brought proceedings in the Louisiana courts. They did not restrict those proceedings to the question whether the Medical Practice Act applied to chiropractors. They unreservedly submitted for decision, and briefed and argued, their contention that the act, if applicable to chiropractors, violated the 14th amendment. The state proceedings terminated with a decision by the Louisiana Supreme Court declining to review an intermediate appellate court's holding both that the Medical Practice Act applied to chiropractors and that, as so applied, it did not violate the 14th amendment.

Appellants then returned to the District Court,[4] where they were met with a motion by appellees to dismiss the federal action. This motion was granted, on the ground that

"since the courts of Louisiana have passed on all issues raised, including the claims of deprivation under the federal Constitution, this court, having no power to review those proceedings, must dismiss the complaint. The proper remedy was by appeal to the Supreme Court of the United States." . . .

vehicles for effectuating large-scale changes in the allocation of power between the state and federal judicial systems or state and federal governments." While she does not advocate abandonment of the doctrines, she does argue that they should be implemented "without regard to the sensitivity or the local character of an issue." In particular, *Pullman* abstention, in her view, should be limited to consideration of whether "the underlying and potentially dispositive question of state law is so unclear that federal courts would run a substantial risk of error in deciding it, and deciding the case on a state ground would avoid the risk of a premature decision of a constitutional question." See also Schoenfeld, American Federalism and the Absten-

tion Doctrine in the Supreme Court, 73 Dick. L. Rev. 605, 606–18 (1969); Comment, I Used to Love You But It's All Over Now: Abstention and the Federal Courts' Retreat from Their Role as Primary Guardians of First Amendment Freedoms, 45 S. Cal. L. Rev. 847 (1972).

[1] The action was brought in 1957. The District Court initially dismissed the complaint. The Court of Appeals for the Fifth Circuit reversed. We denied certiorari. On remand the three-judge District Court was convened.

[4] Appellants made no attempt to obtain appellate review of the state court decision in this Court.

Appellants appealed directly to this Court . . . and we noted probable jurisdiction. We reverse and remand to the District Court for decision, on the merits, of appellants' 14th amendment claims.

There are fundamental objections to any conclusion that a litigant who has properly invoked the jurisdiction of a federal district court to consider federal constitutional claims can be compelled, without his consent and through no fault of his own, to accept instead a state court's determination of those claims.[5] Such a result would be at war with the unqualified terms in which Congress, pursuant to constitutional authorization, has conferred specific categories of jurisdiction upon the federal courts, and with the principle that "[w]hen a federal court is properly appealed to in a case over which it has by law jurisdiction, it is its duty to take such jurisdiction. . . . The right of a party plaintiff to choose a federal court where there is a choice cannot be properly denied." Willcox v. Consolidated Gas Co., 212 U.S. 19, 40 (1909). Nor does anything in the abstention doctrine require or support such a result. Abstention is a judge-fashioned vehicle for according appropriate deference to the "respective competence of the state and federal court systems." Louisiana P. & L. Co. v. Thibodaux, 360 U.S. 25, 29 (1959). Its recognition of the role of state courts as the final expositors of state law implies no disregard for the primacy of the federal judiciary in deciding questions of federal law. Accordingly, we have on several occasions explicitly recognized that abstention "does not, of course, involve the abdication of federal jurisdiction, but only the postponement of its exercise." Harrison v. NAACP, 360 U.S. 167, 177 (1959).

It is true that, after a post-abstention determination and rejection of his federal claims by the state courts, a litigant could seek direct review in this Court. But such review, even when available by appeal rather than only by discretionary writ of certiorari, is an inadequate substitute for the initial district court determination—often by three judges—to which the litigant is entitled in the federal courts. This is true as to issues of law; it is especially true as to issues of fact. Limiting the litigant to review here would deny him the benefit of a federal trial court's role in constructing a record and making fact findings. How the facts are found will often dictate the decision of federal claims. "It is the typical, not the rare, case in which constitutional claims turn upon the resolution of contested actual issues." Townsend v. Sain, 372 U.S. 293, 312 (1963). "There is always in litigation a margin of error, representing error in factfinding. . . ." Speiser v. Randall, 357 U.S. 513, 525 (1958). Thus in cases where, but for the application of the abstention doctrine, the primary fact determination would have been by the district court, a litigant may not be unwillingly deprived of that determination.[8] The possibility of appel-

---

[5] At least this is true in a case, like the instant one, not involving the possibility of unwarranted disruption of a state administrative process. Compare Burford v. Sun Oil Co., 319 U.S. 315 (1943); Alabama Public Service Comm'n v. Southern R. Co., 341 U.S. 341 (1951).

[8] Even where fact findings on federal constitutional contentions are for state tribunals to make in the first instance, as

late review by this Court of a state court determination may not be substituted, against a party's wishes, for his right to litigate his federal claims fully in the federal courts. . . .

We made clear in NAACP v. Button, 371 U.S. 415 (1963), however, that a party may elect to forgo that right. Our holding in that case was that a judgment of the Virginia Supreme Court of Appeals upon federal issues submitted to the state tribunals by parties remitted there under the abstention doctrine was "final" for purposes of our review under 28 U.S.C. § 1257. In so determining, we held that the petitioner had elected "to seek a complete and final adjudication of [its] rights in the state courts" and thus not to return to the District Court, and that it had manifested this election "by seeking from the Richmond Circuit Court 'a binding adjudication' of all its claims and a permanent injunction as well as declaratory relief, by making no reservation to the disposition of the entire case by the state courts, and by coming here directly on certiorari." We fashioned the rule recognizing such an election because we saw no inconsistency with the abstention doctrine in allowing a litigant to decide, once the federal court has abstained and compelled him to proceed in the state courts in any event, to abandon his original choice of a federal forum and submit his entire case to the state court, relying on the opportunity to come here directly if the state decision on his federal claims should go against him. Such a choice by a litigant serves to avoid much of the delay and expense to which application of the abstention doctrine inevitably gives rise; when the choice is voluntarily made, we see no reason why it should not be given effect.

In *Button* we had no need to determine what steps, if any, short of those taken by the petitioner there would suffice to manifest the election. The instant case, where appellants did not attempt to come directly to this Court but sought to return to the District Court, requires such a determination. The line drawn should be bright and clear, so that litigants shunted from federal to state courts by application of the abstention doctrine will not be exposed, not only to unusual expense and delay, but also to procedural traps operating to deprive them of their right to a district court determination of their federal claims. It might be argued that nothing short of what was done in *Button* should suffice—that a litigant should retain the right to return to the district court unless he not only litigates his federal claims in the state tribunals but seeks review of the state decision in this Court. But we see no reason why a party, after unreservedly litigating his federal claims in the state courts although not required to do so, should be allowed to ignore the adverse state decision and start all over again in the district court. Such a rule would not only countenance an unnecessary increase in the length and cost of the litigation; it would also be a potential source of friction between the state and federal judiciaries. . . . We now explicitly hold that if a party freely and without

in state criminal prosecutions, they are not immune, when brought into question in federal habeas corpus, from district court consideration and, in proper cases, from de novo consideration. Townsend v. Sain, 372 U.S. 293, 312–19 (1963).

reservation submits his federal claims for decision by the state courts, litigates them there, and has them decided there, then—whether or not he seeks direct review of the state decision in this Court—he has elected to forgo his right to return to the district court.

This rule requires clarification of our decision in Government Employees v. Windsor, 353 U.S. 364 (1957). . . . On oral argument in the instant case, we were advised that appellants' submission of their federal claims to the state courts had been motivated primarily by a belief that *Windsor* required this. The District Court likewise thought that under *Windsor* a party is required to litigate his federal question in the state courts and "dare not restrict his state court case to local law issues." Others have read *Windsor* the same way. It should not be so read. The case does not mean that a party must litigate his federal claims in the state courts, but only that he must inform those courts what his federal claims are, so that the state statute may be construed "in light of" those claims. Thus mere compliance with *Windsor* will not support a conclusion, much less create a presumption, that a litigant has freely and without reservation litigated his federal claims in the state courts and so elected not to return to the district court.

We recognize that in the heat of litigation a party may find it difficult to avoid doing more than is required by *Windsor*. This would be particularly true in the typical case, such as the instant one, where the state courts are asked to construe a state statute against the backdrop of a federal constitutional challenge. The litigant denying the statute's applicability may be led not merely to state his federal constitutional claim but to argue it, for if he can persuade the state court that application of the statute to him would offend the federal Constitution, he will ordinarily have persuaded it that the statute should not be construed as applicable to him. In addition, the parties cannot prevent the state court from rendering a decision on the federal question if it chooses to do so; and even if such a decision is not explicit, a holding that the statute is applicable may arguably imply, in view of the constitutional objections to such a construction, that the court considers the constitutional challenge to be without merit.

Despite these uncertainties arising from application of *Windsor*— which decision, we repeat, does not require that federal claims be actually litigated in the state courts—a party may readily forestall any conclusion that he has elected not to return to the district court. He may accomplish this by making on the state record the "reservation to the disposition of the entire case by the state courts" that we referred to in *Button*. That is, he may inform the state courts that he is exposing his federal claims there only for the purpose of complying with *Windsor,* and that he intends, should the state courts hold against him on the question of state law, to return to the district court for disposition of his federal contentions. Such an explicit reservation is not indispensable; the litigant is in no event to be denied his right to return to the district court unless it clearly appears that he voluntarily did more than *Windsor* required and fully litigated his federal claims in the state courts.[12] When the reservation has been made, however, his right to return will in all events be preserved.[13]

On the record in the instant case, the rule we announce today would call for affirmance of the District Court's judgment. But we are unwilling to apply the rule against these appellants. As we have noted, their primary reason for litigating their federal claims in the state courts was assertedly a view that *Windsor* required them to do so. That view was mistaken, and will not avail other litigants who rely upon it after today's decision. But we cannot say, in the face of the support given the view by respectable authorities, including the court below, that appellants were unreasonable in holding it or acting upon it. We therefore hold that the District Court should not have dismissed their action. The judgment is reversed, and the case is remanded for further proceedings consistent with this opinion.

It is so ordered.

Mr. Justice Douglas, concurring.

The judge-made rule we announce today promises to have such a serious impact on litigants who are properly in the federal courts that I think a reappraisal of Railroad Comm'n v. Pullman Co., 312 U.S. 496 (1941), from which today's decision stems, is necessary. . . .

I

The *Pullman* case, decided a little over 20 years ago, launched an experiment in the management of federal-state relations that has inappropriately been called the "abstention doctrine." There are numerous occasions when a federal court abstains, dismissing an action or declining to entertain it because a state tribunal is a more appropriate one for resolving the controversy. A bankruptcy court commonly sends its trustee into state courts to have complex questions of local law adjudicated. Thompson v. Magnolia Co., 309 U.S. 478 (1940). A federal court refuses to exercise its equity powers by appointing receivers to take charge of a failing business, where state procedures afford adequate protection to all private rights. Pennsylvania v. Williams, 294

[12] It has been suggested that state courts may "take no more pleasure than do federal courts in deciding cases piecemeal . . ." and "probably prefer to determine their questions of law with complete records of cases in which they can enter final judgments before them." Clay v. Sun Ins. Office, 363 U.S. 207, 227 (1960) (dissenting opinion). We are confident that state courts, sharing the abstention doctrine's purpose of "[f]urthering the harmonious relation between state and federal authority," Railroad Comm'n v. Pullman Co., 312 U.S. 496, 501 (1941), will respect a litigant's reservation of his federal claims for decision by the federal courts. However, evidence that a party has been compelled by the state courts to litigate his federal claims there will of course preclude a finding that he has voluntarily done so. And if the state court has declined to decide the state question because of the litigant's refusal to submit without reservation the federal question as well, the district court will have no alternative but to vacate its order of abstention.

[13] The reservation may be made by any party to the litigation. Usually the plaintiff will have made the original choice to litigate in the federal court, but the defendant also, by virtue of the removal jurisdiction, 28 U.S.C. § 1441(b), has a right to litigate the federal question there. Once issue has been joined in the federal court, no party is entitled to insist, over another's objection, upon a binding state court determination of the federal question. . . .

U.S. 176 (1935). A federal court will normally not entertain a suit to enjoin criminal prosecutions in state tribunals, with review of such convictions by this Court being restricted to constitutional issues. Beal v. Missouri Pac. R. Co., 312 U.S. 45 (1941). A federal court declines to entertain an action for declaratory relief against state taxes because of the federal policy against interfering with them by injunction. Great Lakes Co. v. Huffman, 319 U.S. 293 (1943). Where state administrative action is challenged, a federal court will normally not intervene where there is an adequate state court review which is protective of any federal constitutional claim. Burford v. Sun Oil Co., 319 U.S. 315 (1943); Alabama Comm'n v. Southern R. Co., 341 U.S. 341 (1951). The examples could be multiplied where the federal court adopts a hands-off policy and remits the litigants to a state tribunal.

Railroad Comm'n v. Pullman Co., supra, is a different kind of case. There the federal court does not abstain; it does not dismiss the complaint; it retains jurisdiction while the parties go to a state tribunal to obtain a preliminary ruling—a declaratory judgment—on state law questions. The reason for requiring them to repair to the state tribunal for a preliminary ruling on a question of state law is because the state law is challenged on federal constitutional grounds; if the state law is construed one way, the constitutional issue may disappear; the federal constitutional question will survive only if one of two or more state-law constructions is adopted. . . .

II

I was a member of the Court that launched *Pullman* and sent it on its way. But if I had realized the creature it was to become, my doubts would have been far deeper than they were.

Pullman from the start seemed to have some qualities of a legal research luxury. As I said in Clay v. Sun Ins. Office, 363 U.S. 207, 228 (1960) (dissenting opinion):

> "Some litigants have long purses. Many, however, can hardly afford one lawsuit, let alone two. Shuttling the parties between state and federal tribunals is a sure way of defeating the ends of justice. The pursuit of justice is not an academic exercise. There are no foundations to finance the resolution of nice state law questions involved in federal court litigation. The parties are entitled—absent unique and rare situations— to adjudication of their rights in the tribunals which Congress has empowered to act."

As recently stated by the late Judge Charles E. Clark of the Second Circuit Court of Appeals, "[a]s a result of this doctrine, individual litigants have been shuffled back and forth between state and federal courts, and cases have been dragged out over eight-and 10-year periods." Federal Procedural Reform and States' Rights, 40 Tex. L. Rev. 211, 221 (1961).

Professor Charles A. Wright described the results that occurred when this doctrine was applied to a suit to enjoin the enforcement of a state statute restricting the rights of state employees to join unions:[1] ". . . after five years of litigation, including two trips to the Supreme Court of the United States and two to the highest state court, the parties still had failed to obtain a decision on the merits of the statute." The Abstention Doctrine Reconsidered, 37 Tex. L. Rev. 815, 818 (1959).

This case raises a question so simple that it at least verges on the insubstantial. The question is whether Louisiana's Medical Practice Act includes chiropractors as practitioners of medicine. The State Board of Medical Examiners, representing the state, says that they are included. The chiropractors say they are not and, if they are, that the act is unconstitutional. The case was started in May 1957, and here we are nearly seven years later without a decision on the merits.

That seems like an unnecessary price to pay for our federalism. Referral to state courts for declaratory rulings on state law questions is said to encourage a smooth operation of our federalism, as it may avoid clashes between the two systems. But there always have been clashes and always will be; and the influence of the *Pullman* doctrine has, I think, been de minimis. Moreover, the complexity of local law to federal judges is inherent in the federal court system as designed by Congress. Resolution of local law questions is implicit in diversity of citizenship jurisdiction. Since Erie R. Co. v. Tompkins, 304 U.S. 64 (1938), the federal courts under that head of jurisdiction daily have the task of determining what the state law is. The fact that those questions are complex and difficult is no excuse for a refusal by the district court to entertain the suit. . . .

What we do today makes the *Pullman* case something of a Frankenstein. Any presumption should work the other way—that he who is *required* to go to the state courts and does what we *require* him to do when he gets there, is not there voluntarily and does not forsake his federal suit, unless he does something in the state courts that he is not required to do and that evinces an election to litigate the matter finally and not preliminarily in the state courts.

As, if, and when he exhausts the state procedure and decides to come here, . . . he has elected to abandon the federal for the state forum. But short of that, he seldom can be said to have made such an election. For when he pursues the matter through the hierarchy of the state courts, he is doing only what he is *required* to do. The only time when he goes beyond that requirement is when he takes the fork in the road leading here rather than the one to the district court.

III

If the *Pullman* doctrine is to be preserved, we should lighten rather than make more ponderous the procedures which we have been imposing. We have made *Pullman* mandatory, not discretionary, with the district courts. . . . So, no matter the ease with which the whole controversy can be resolved, parties are sent their weary and expensive

[1] Government Employees v. Windsor, 353 U.S. 364 (1957).

way into the state tribunals. Whether or not we agree with Mr. Justice Black that the present case involves no substantial federal question, it certainly borders on the insubstantial; and a district court, if it has that view of a case, should be allowed in its discretion to decide the whole case at once, avoiding the state litigation completely—free of interference here or in the court of appeals. . . .

IV

. . . If we are to retain the *Pullman* doctrine, I think with all deference, we should make it less of a mandatory procedure and lighten its requirements, rather than make them stricter. [W]e should not weight it down with procedures, which, like today's decision, make it a trap for the unwary.

The *Pullman* doctrine, as it has evolved, is the least desirable alternative. It is better, I think, for the federal courts to decide the local law questions, as they customarily do in the diversity cases, adding at the foot of the decree [a provision for return to the federal court if the state law is mistakenly construed.]

Another alternative is for the district court to follow the certificate route, when one is available. . . . We cannot require the states to provide such a procedure; but by asserting the independence of the federal courts and insisting on prompt adjudications we will encourage its use.

V

. . . I mention the time element as one of the evils spun by the *Pullman* doctrine. Time has a particularly noxious effect on explosive civil rights questions, where the problem only festers as grievances pile high and the law takes its slow, expensive pace to decide in years what should be decided promptly.

The late Judge Charles E. Clark made an apt and pertinent observation on the impact of the *Pullman* doctrine. At times, he said "the upshot inevitably seems to be a negative decision or, in plain language, a defendant's judgment."[12] Delay which the *Pullman* doctrine sponsors, keeps the status quo entrenched and renders a "defendant's judgment" even in the face of constitutional requirements. These evils are all compounded by what we do today, making it likely that litigants seeking the protection of the federal courts for assertion of their civil rights will be ground down slowly by the passage of time and the expenditure of money in state proceedings, leaving the ultimate remedy here, at least in many cases, an illusory one.

MR. JUSTICE BLACK, concurring in part and dissenting in part.

I join in the judgment and in the opinion insofar as the Court holds that the District Court erred in the reasons it gave for dismissing appellants' action. I am of the opinion, however, that the dismissal

[12] Clark, The Limits of Judicial Objectivity, 12 Am. U.L. Rev. 1, 5 (1963).

should be affirmed on the grounds relied upon by Judge J. Skelly Wright sitting alone in the District Court when the action first was brought: that the complaint failed to state a substantial federal question warranting exercise of jurisdiction.[a]

NOTES ON THE PROCEDURAL CONSEQUENCES OF *PULLMAN* ABSTENTION

1. *Government Employees v. Windsor.* As noted in *England,* Government and Civil Employees Organizing Committee v. Windsor, 353 U.S. 364 (1957), caused considerable confusion over how state law questions should be submitted to the state courts after a *Pullman* abstention. The suit in *Windsor* was filed in 1953, and a three-judge court abstained. That decision was affirmed by the Supreme Court, after which proceedings were begun in the state courts. The state trial court held the challenged statute applicable to the plaintiffs' activity, and the state Supreme Court affirmed. The plaintiffs then returned to the three-judge federal court. That court held the statute constitutional as applied, and dismissed the case. The case then came back to the Supreme Court, which in a unanimous per curiam opinion (Justice Black not participating) said:

> "We do not reach the constitutional issues. . . . The bare adjudication by the Alabama Supreme Court . . . does not suffice, since that court was not asked to interpret the statute in light of the constitutional objections presented to the District Court. If appellants' [constitutional] arguments had been presented to the state court, it might have construed the statute in a different manner. Accordingly, the judgment of the District Court is vacated, and this cause is remanded to it with directions to retain jurisdiction until efforts to obtain an appropriate adjudication in the state courts have been exhausted."

Apparently the plaintiffs were themselves exhausted by the Supreme Court's disposition. See Field, Abstention in Constitutional Cases: The Scope of the *Pullman* Abstention Doctrine, 122 U. Pa. L. Rev. 1071, 1086 n.65 (1974), which reports that the District Court remanded the "case to state court a second time, after which the plaintiff abandoned suit, having failed to obtain a decision on the merits after four years of litigation, including one trip to the Alabama Supreme Court and two to the United States Supreme Court."

2. *Harris County Commissioners v. Moore.* Harris County Commissioners Court v. Moore, 420 U.S. 77 (1975), involved a suit by three justices of the peace and two constables who lost their jobs because of a redistricting plan. Two local voters also joined as plain-

---

[a] The suit in *England* was finally dismissed by a three-judge federal court in November of 1965. See England v. Louisiana State Board of Medical Examiners, 246 F. Supp. 993 (E.D. La. 1965). The opinion was again written by Judge Wright, who again concluded that the constitutional claims lacked merit. [Footnote by eds.]

tiffs. A three-judge court granted relief, but the Supreme Court held that the lower court should have abstained. The Court's opinion concluded:

> "In order to remove any possible obstacles to state court jurisdiction, we direct the District Court to dismiss the complaint. The dismissal should be without prejudice so that any remaining federal claim may be raised in a federal forum after the Texas courts have been given the opportunity to address the state law questions in the case. England v. Louisiana State Board of Medical Examiners, 375 U.S. 411 (1964)."

The Court then added in a footnote:

> "Ordinarily the proper course in ordering '*Pullman* abstention' is to remand with instructions to retain jurisdiction but to stay the federal suit pending determination of the state law questions in state court. The Texas Supreme Court has ruled, however, that it cannot grant declaratory relief under state law if a federal court retains jurisdiction over the federal claim. United Services Life Ins. Co. v. Delaney, 396 S.W.2d 855 (Tex. 1965).[a]

> "We have adopted the unusual course of dismissing in this case solely in order to avoid the possibility that some state law remedies might otherwise be foreclosed to appellees on their return to state court. Obviously, the dismissal must not be used as a means to defeat the appellees' federal claims if and when they return to federal court."[b]

3. Questions and Comments on the Procedural Consequences of Abstention. *England* requires a procedure that substantially increases the delay, complexity, and expense of litigation. Is the problem worth such an elaborate solution? If not, what should be done?

Justice Brennan said in *England* that "[l]imiting the litigant to review here would deny him the benefit of a federal trial court's role in constructing a record and making fact findings." Suppose the state court must resolve factual disputes before it can determine the precise question of state law presented for decision. Is the plaintiff then entitled to a retrial of the facts on return to federal court? If so, what is to be done if the issues of state law might have been differently resolved in light of differences in the facts as found in federal court? Or should the state-court findings of fact be given collateral estoppel effect in subsequent federal court proceedings?

Another aspect of the problem is how the state courts are likely to react to litigants who make the kind of explicit reservation contemplat-

[a] *Delaney* held that declaratory relief could not be obtained because it would require an advisory opinion. [Footnote by eds.]

[b] Justice Douglas was the lone dissenter. He pointed out that the suit had already been in litigation for two years, that the term of office of the three justices of the peace had expired before the lower court rendered its judgment, and that the term of the two constables would expire ten months after the Supreme Court's remand. He argued that they had suffered enough delay.

ed by *England.* Is the reaction of the Texas court in *Delaney* surprising? Does *England* promote harmonious federal-state relations?[c]

SECTION 2: *YOUNGER* ABSTENTION

SUBSECTION A: ORIGINS

INTRODUCTORY NOTES ON FEDERAL INJUNCTIONS AGAINST STATE CRIMINAL PROCEEDINGS

1. Introduction. Current thought about federal injunctions against state criminal prosecutions begins with *Younger v. Harris,* the next main case. *Younger* held that, absent prosecutorial bad faith or harassment, a federal court cannot enjoin a pending state criminal prosecution on the ground that the statute on which the prosecution is based is unconstitutional. Two earlier cases provide necessary background.

2. *Douglas v. City of Jeannette.* A group of Jehovah's Witnesses distributed religious literature without a permit in Jeannette, Pennsylvania, in violation of a local criminal ordinance. Some were prosecuted and convicted. They appealed their convictions through the state court system, and certiorari was granted by the Supreme Court. In Murdock v. Pennsylvania, 319 U.S. 105 (1943), the Court held the ordinance unconstitutional as applied and reversed.

In the meantime, the individuals who were before the Court in *Murdock,* together with other members of the group, had filed a class action in federal District Court seeking an injunction against any further prosecutions under the ordinance. The District Court held the ordinance unconstitutional as applied and enjoined its enforcement. The Court of Appeals reversed, and the Supreme Court granted certiorari. This case, styled Douglas v. City of Jeannette, 319 U.S. 157 (1943), was argued with *Murdock* and decided on the same day.

The Court easily could have decided *Douglas* on the ground that, given the decision in *Murdock* that the statute was unconstitutional as applied to these plaintiffs, no injunction was necessary.[a] But Chief

---

[c] There are numerous other procedural problems caused by *Pullman* abstention. One problem is whether decisions to abstain or not to abstain are subject to appellate review. As a technical matter, neither would seem to be "final" within the requirement of 28 U.S.C. § 1291. For discussion of this issue, see Field, The Abstention Doctrine Today, 125 U. Pa. L. Rev. 590, 592–601 (1977).

Another problem is whether an abstaining federal court can nonetheless give preliminary relief against enforcement of the state statute during the pendency of the state proceedings. This issue is extensively considered in Wells, Preliminary Injunctions and Abstention: Some Problems in Federalism, 63 Corn. L. Rev. 65 (1977).

[a] Cf. Roe v. Wade, 410 U.S. 113, 166 (1973). The plaintiffs in *Roe* had sought

Justice Stone, speaking for the Court, took the occasion to state a broader rationale for withholding injunctive relief:

"It is a familiar rule that courts of equity do not ordinarily restrain criminal prosecutions. No person is immune from prosecution in good faith for his alleged criminal acts. Its imminence, even though alleged to be in violation of constitutional guarantees, is not a ground for equity relief since the lawfulness or constitutionality of the statute or ordinance may be determined as readily in the criminal case as in a suit for an injunction. Where the threatened prosecution is by state officers for alleged violations of a state law, the state courts are the final arbiters of its meaning and application, subject only to review by this Court on federal grounds appropriately asserted. Hence the arrest by the federal courts of the processes of the criminal law within the states, and the determination of questions of criminal liability under state law by a federal court of equity, are to be supported only on a showing of danger of irreparable injury 'both great and immediate.' . . . It does not appear from the record that petitioners have been threatened with any injury other than that incidental to every criminal proceeding brought lawfully and in good faith, or that a federal court of equity by withdrawing the determination of guilt from the state courts could rightly afford the petitioners any protection which they could not secure by prompt trial and appeal pursued to this Court. . . ."

3. *Dombrowski v. Pfister.* Dombrowski v. Pfister, 380 U.S. 479 (1965), was a § 1983 suit brought by a civil rights organization, the Southern Conference Educational Fund (SCEF), and several of its officers. The plaintiffs sought to enjoin enforcement of two Louisiana statutes, the Subversive Activities and Communist Control Law and the Communist Propaganda Control Law, on the ground that they were unconstitutionally overbroad. The complaint alleged that state authorities were threatening prosecution of the plaintiffs under these laws, not with any expectation of securing valid convictions, but in order to harass the SCEF and to dissuade its members from civil rights activities. A three-judge District Court [b] dismissed the complaint without reaching the merits, partially on the ground that it "did not present a case of threatened irreparable injury to federal rights which warranted

declaratory and injunctive relief against future prosecution under the Texas abortion statutes. Declaratory relief was awarded to one of them, but an injunction was denied: "We find it unnecessary to decide whether the District Court erred in withholding injunctive relief, for we assume the Texas prosecutorial authorities will give full credence to this decision that the present criminal abortion statutes are unconstitutional." See also Fiss, *Dombrowski*, 86 Yale L.J. 1103, 1106 (1977); Gibbons, Our Federalism, 12 Suffolk Univ. L. Rev. 1087, 1093 (1978).

[b] Congress passed the Three-Judge Court Act in 1910 in response to the decision in *Ex parte Young,* page 809, supra. The statute required three federal judges—usually two district judges and a circuit judge—to act as the trial court in cases brought to seek an injunction against a statute of statewide applicability. Appeal in such cases was available directly to the Supreme Court. These provisions were repealed in 1976.

cutting short the normal adjudication of constitutional defenses in the course of state criminal prosecutions." The case was then appealed to the Supreme Court.

Justice Brennan's opinion for the Court stated the general rule in terms consistent with *Douglas v. City of Jeannette*:

> "In Ex parte Young, 209 U.S. 123 (1908), the fountainhead of federal injunctions against state prosecutions, the Court characterized the power and its proper exercise in broad terms: it would be justified where state officers '. . . threaten and are about to commence proceedings, either of a civil or criminal nature, to enforce against parties affected an unconstitutional act, violating the federal Constitution . . . .' Since that decision, however, considerations of federalism have tempered the exercise of equitable power, for the Court has recognized that federal interference with a state's good faith administration of its criminal laws is peculiarly inconsistent with our federal framework. It is generally to be assumed that state courts and prosecutors will observe constitutional limitations as expounded by this Court, and that the mere possibility of erroneous initial application of constitutional standards will usually not amount to the irreparable injury necessary to justify a disruption of orderly state proceedings."

Brennan then went on to explain why this case should be decided differently:

> "[T]he allegations of this complaint depict a situation in which defense of the state's criminal prosecution will not assure adequate vindication of constitutional rights. They suggest that a substantial loss or impairment of freedoms of expression will occur if appellants must await the state court's disposition and ultimate review in this Court of any adverse determination. These allegations, if true, clearly show irreparable injury."

Justice Brennan then examined the allegations. Four aspects of his opinion and the thrust of Justice Harlan's dissent are worth special attention:

(i) **Effect of Allegations of Overbreadth.** The opinion stated that "[t]he assumption that defense of a criminal prosecution will generally assure ample vindication of constitutional rights is unfounded" in cases where a statute is challenged on first-amendment overbreadth grounds. "The chilling effect upon the exercise of first amendment rights may derive from the fact of the prosecution, unaffected by the prospects of its success or failure." The opinion thus appeared to hold that the restraints established in *Douglas* do not apply to challenges based on first-amendment overbreadth grounds.

(ii) **Effect of Harassment Allegations.** Brennan looked in detail at the allegations of harassment and concluded that, if true, they stated an independent basis for equitable intervention. Since the case had been dismissed before trial in the court below, a remand was necessary in order to determine whether the prosecuting authorities were in fact using the statutes to harass the plaintiffs.

(iii) Disposition. Certain portions of the Louisiana statutes were held unconstitutionally overbroad on their face, although the Court declined to consider overbreadth challenges against other portions of the statutes. The lower court was ordered to enter an injunction without further proceedings against enforcement of those portions of the statutes held fatally overbroad. Since the injunction was to be issued *before* the hearings on the harassment allegations, this aspect of the decision reinforced interpretation of *Dombrowski* as holding that the first-amendment overbreadth challenge was an independently sufficient basis for an exception to *Douglas.*

(iv) Resurrection of Invalidated Statute. Finally, note should be taken of a subsidiary aspect of the *Dombrowski* opinion on which Justice Black relied in *Younger.* The question was whether a statute held unconstitutionally overbroad could ever be used as the basis for a subsequent prosecution. Justice Brennan said:

> "The state must, if it is to invoke the statute after injunctive relief has been sought, assume the burden of obtaining a permissible narrow construction in a noncriminal proceeding before it may seek modification of the injunction to permit future prosecutions.[7] [T]he settled rule of our cases is that district courts retain power to modify injunctions in light of changed circumstances. Our view of the proper operation of the vagueness doctrine does not preclude district courts from modifying injunctions to permit prosecutions in light of subsequent state court interpretation clarifying the application of the statute to particular conduct."

(v) The Harlan Dissent. Justice Harlan, joined by Justice Clark, dissented. "In practical effect," he said, "the Court's decision means that a state may no longer carry on prosecutions under statutes challengeable for vagueness on 'first amendment' grounds without the prior approval of the federal courts." Harlan found such supervision unwarranted:

> "Underlying the Court's major premise that criminal enforcement of an overly broad statute affecting rights of speech and association is in itself a deterrent to the free exercise thereof seems to be the unarticulated assumption that state courts will not be as prone as federal courts to vindicate constitutional rights promptly and effectively. Such an assumption should not be indulged in the absence of a showing that such is apt to be so in a given case."

4. Conclusion. Justice Brennan's opinion in *Dombrowski* was premised on the view that *Douglas* correctly stated the general rule governing the availability of federal injunctive relief against a state

---

[7] "Our cases indicate that once an acceptable limiting construction is obtained, it may be applied to conduct occurring prior to the construction, provided such application affords fair warning to the defendants."

criminal prosecution.[c] In Brennan's view, the facts of *Dombrowski* justified an exception to this general rule. Civil rights plaintiffs and their attorneys shared this view of the case. *Dombrowski* was regarded as signalling a new receptivity by federal courts to suits seeking injunctions against criminal proceedings based on overbroad state statutes. Many suits—literally hundreds, though few were successful— were brought to exploit this new opportunity.[d] One of those suits was *Younger v. Harris.*

YOUNGER v. HARRIS

United States Supreme Court, 1971.
401 U.S. 37.

MR. JUSTICE BLACK delivered the opinion of the Court.

Appellee, John Harris, Jr., was indicted in a California state court, charged with violation of the California Penal Code §§ 11400 and 11401, known as the California Criminal Syndicalism Act.[a] . . . He then filed a complaint in the federal District Court, asking that court to enjoin the appellant, Younger, the District Attorney of Los Angeles County, from prosecuting him, and alleging that the prosecution and even the presence of the act inhibited him in the exercise of his rights of free speech and press, rights guaranteed him by the first and 14th amendments. Appellees Jim Dan and Diane Hirsch intervened as plaintiffs in the suit, claiming that the prosecution of Harris would inhibit them as members of the Progressive Labor Party from peacefully advocating the program of their party, which was to replace capitalism with socialism and to abolish the profit system of production in this country. Appellee Farrell Broslawsky, an instructor in history at Los Angeles Valley College, also intervened claiming that the prosecution of Harris made him uncertain as to whether he could teach about the doctrines of Karl Marx or read from the Communist Manifesto as part

[c] Subsequent research has challenged this view. See Laycock, Federal Interference with State Prosecutions: The Cases *Dombrowski* Forgot, 46 U. Chi. L. Rev. 636 (1979); Soifer and Macgill, The *Younger* Doctrine: Reconstructing Reconstruction, 55 Texas L. Rev. 1141 (1977); B. Wechsler, Federal Courts, State Criminal Law and the First Amendment, 49 N.Y.U.L. Rev. 740 (1974). These articles argue that *Douglas* did not represent a settled view against the issuance of injunctions in this context and that in fact such injunctions had routinely been issued by lower courts and approved by the Supreme Court.

It was apparently settled during this period that the "adequate remedy at law" prerequisite to a federal injunction referred to an adequate remedy in a federal court, not a state court. See Field, The Uncertain Nature of Federal Jurisdiction, 22 W. & M. L. Rev. 683, 705–06 (1981).

[d] See Maraist, Federal Injunctive Relief Against State Court Proceedings: The Significance of *Dombrowski*, 48 Tex. L. Rev. 535, 606 (1970).

[a] Cal. Penal Code § 11400 defined "criminal syndicalism" to include "any doctrine or precept advocating, teaching or aiding and abetting the commission of crime, sabotage . . ., or unlawful acts of force and violence . . . as a means of accomplishing a change in industrial organization or control, or effecting any political change." Section 11401 punished, inter alia, one who "[b]y spoken or written words or personal conduct advocates, teaches or aids and abets criminal syndicalism . . .," or who "[p]rints, publishes, edits, issues or circulates or publicly displays any book, paper, pamphlet, document, poster or written or printed matter in any other form "advocating or advising criminal syndicalism. [Footnote by eds.]

of his classwork. All claimed that unless the United States court restrained the state prosecution of Harris each would suffer immediate and irreparable injury. A three-judge federal District Court . . . held that it had jurisdiction and power to restrain the District Attorney from prosecuting, held that the state's Criminal Syndicalism Act was void for vagueness and overbreadth in violation of the first and 14th amendments, and accordingly restrained the District Attorney from "further prosecution of the currently pending action against plaintiff Harris for alleged violation of the act."

The case is before us on [direct] appeal by the state's District Attorney Younger . . . . In his notice of appeal and his jurisdictional statement appellant presented two questions: (1) whether the decision of this Court in Whitney v. California, 274 U.S. 357 (1927), holding California's law constitutional in 1927 was binding on the District Court and (2) whether the state's law is constitutional on its face. In this Court the brief for the state of California, filed at our request, also argues that only Harris, who was indicted, has standing to challenge the state's law, and that issuance of the injunction was a violation of a longstanding judicial policy and of 28 U.S.C. § 2283, which provides:

> "A court of the United States may not grant an injunction to stay proceedings in a State court except as expressly authorized by Act of Congress, or where necessary in aid of its jurisdiction, or to protect or effectuate its judgments."

Without regard to the questions raised about *Whitney v. California,* supra, since overruled by Brandenburg v. Ohio, 395 U.S. 444 (1969), or the constitutionality of the state law, we have concluded that the judgment of the District Court, enjoining appellant Younger from prosecuting under these California statutes, must be reversed as a violation of the national policy forbidding federal courts to stay or enjoin pending state court proceedings except under special circumstances. We express no view about the circumstances under which federal courts may act when there is no prosecution pending in state courts at the time the federal proceeding is begun.

I

Appellee Harris has been indicted, and was actually being prosecuted by California for a violation of its Criminal Syndicalism Act at the time this suit was filed. He thus has an acute, live controversy with the state and its prosecutor. But none of the other parties plaintiff in the District Court, Dan, Hirsch, or Broslawsky, has such a controversy. None has been indicted, arrested, or even threatened by the prosecutor. About these three the three-judge court said:

> "Plaintiffs Dan and Hirsch allege that they are members of the Progressive Labor Party, which advocates change in industrial ownership and political change, and that they feel inhibited in advocating the program of their political party through peaceful, non-violent means, because of the presence of the act 'on the books,' and because of the pending criminal prosecution

against Harris. Plaintiff Broslawsky is a history instructor, and he alleges that he is uncertain as to whether his normal practice of teaching his students about the doctrines of Karl Marx and reading from the Communist Manifesto and other revolutionary works may subject him to prosecution for violation of the act."

Whatever right Harris, who is being prosecuted under the state syndicalism law may have, Dan, Hirsch, and Broslawsky cannot share it with him. If these three had alleged that they would be prosecuted for the conduct they planned to engage in, and if the District Court had found this allegation to be true—either on the admission of the state's District Attorney or on any other evidence—then a genuine controversy might be said to exist. But here appellees Dan, Hirsch, and Broslawsky do not claim that they have ever been threatened with prosecution, that a prosecution is likely, or even that a prosecution is remotely possible. They claim the right to bring this suit solely because, in the language of their complaint, they "feel inhibited." We do not think this allegation, even if true, is sufficient to bring the equitable jurisdiction of the federal courts into play to enjoin a pending state prosecution. A federal lawsuit to stop a prosecution in a state court is a serious matter. And persons having no fears of state prosecution except those that are imaginary or speculative, are not to be accepted as appropriate plaintiffs in such cases. Since Harris is actually being prosecuted under the challenged laws, however, we proceed with him as a proper party.

II

Since the beginning of this country's history Congress has, subject to few exceptions, manifested a desire to permit state courts to try state cases free from interference by federal courts. In 1793 an act unconditionally provided: "[N]or shall a writ of injunction be granted to stay proceedings in any court of a state. . . ." 1 Stat. 335, c. 22, § 5. A comparison of the 1793 act with 28 U.S.C. § 2283, its present-day successor, graphically illustrates how few and minor have been the exceptions granted from the flat, prohibitory language of the old act. During all this lapse of years from 1793 to 1970 the statutory exceptions to the 1793 congressional enactment have been only three: (1) "except as expressly authorized by Act of Congress"; (2) "where necessary in aid of its jurisdiction"; and (3) "to protect or effectuate its judgments." In addition, a judicial exception to the longstanding policy evidenced by the statute has been made where a person about to be prosecuted in a state court can show that he will, if the proceeding in the state court is not enjoined, suffer irreparable damages. See Ex parte Young, 209 U.S. 123 (1908).

The precise reasons for this longstanding public policy against federal court interference with state court proceedings have never been specifically identified but the primary sources of the policy are plain. One is the basic doctrine of equity jurisprudence that courts of equity should not act, and particularly should not act to restrain a criminal prosecution, when the moving party has an adequate remedy at law and will not suffer irreparable injury if denied equitable relief. The doctrine may originally have grown out of circumstances peculiar to the English judicial system and not applicable in this country, but its fundamental purpose of restraining equity jurisdiction within narrow limits is equally important under our Constitution, in order to prevent erosion of the role of the jury and avoid a duplication of legal proceedings and legal sanctions where a single suit would be adequate to protect the rights asserted. This underlying reason for restraining courts of equity from interfering with criminal prosecutions is reinforced by an even more vital consideration, the notion of "comity," that is, a proper respect for state functions, a recognition of the fact that the entire country is made up of a Union of separate state governments, and a continuance of the belief that the national government will fare best if the states and their institutions are left free to perform their separate functions in their separate ways. This, perhaps for lack of a better and clearer way to describe it, is referred to by many as "Our Federalism," and one familiar with the profound debates that ushered our federal Constitution into existence is bound to respect those who remain loyal to the ideals and dreams of "Our Federalism." The concept does not mean blind deference to "states' rights" any more than it means centralization of control over every important issue in our national government and its courts. The framers rejected both these courses. What the concept does represent is a system in which there is sensitivity to the legitimate interests of both state and national governments, and in which the national government, anxious though it may be to vindicate and protect federal rights and federal interests, always endeavors to do so in ways that will not unduly interfere with the legitimate activities of the state. It should never be forgotten that this slogan, "Our Federalism," born in the early struggling days of our union of states, occupies a highly important place in our nation's history and its future.

This brief discussion should be enough to suggest some of the reasons why it has been perfectly natural for our cases to repeat time and time again that the normal thing to do when federal courts are asked to enjoin pending proceedings in state courts is not to issue such injunctions. In Fenner v. Boykin, 271 U.S. 240 (1926), suit had been brought in the federal District Court seeking to enjoin state prosecutions under a recently enacted state law that allegedly interfered with the free flow of interstate commerce. The Court, in a unanimous opinion made clear that such a suit, even with respect to state criminal proceedings not yet formally instituted, could be proper only under very special circumstances:

> "*Ex parte Young* and following cases have established the doctrine that when absolutely necessary for protection of constitutional rights courts of the United States have power to enjoin state officers from instituting criminal actions. But this may not be done except under extraordinary circumstances where the danger of irreparable loss is both great and immedi-

CIVIL RIGHTS ABSTENTION Ch. 10

ate. Ordinarily, there should be no interference with such officers; primarily, they are charged with the duty of prosecuting offenders against the laws of the state and must decide when and how this is to be done. The accused should first set up and rely upon his defense in the state courts, even though this involves a challenge of the validity of some statute, unless it plainly appears that this course would not afford adequate protection."

These principles, made clear in the *Fenner* case, have been repeatedly followed and reaffirmed in other cases involving threatened prosecutions. See, e.g., Watson v. Buck, 313 U.S. 387 (1941); Douglas v. City of Jeannette, 319 U.S. 157 (1943).

In all of these cases the Court stressed the importance of showing irreparable injury, the traditional prerequisite to obtaining an injunction. In addition, however, the Court also made clear that in view of the fundamental policy against federal interference with state criminal prosecutions, even irreparable injury is insufficient unless it is "both great and immediate." Certain types of injury, in particular, the cost, anxiety, and inconvenience of having to defend against a single criminal prosecution, could not by themselves be considered "irreparable" in the special legal sense of that term. Instead, the threat to the plaintiff's federally protected rights must be one that cannot be eliminated by his defense against a single criminal prosecution. Thus, in the *Buck* case, supra, at 400, we stressed:

"Federal injunctions against state criminal statutes, either in their entirety or with respect to their separate and distinct prohibitions, are not to be granted as a matter of course, even if such statutes are unconstitutional. 'No citizen or member of the community is immune from prosecution, in good faith, for his alleged criminal acts. The imminence of such a prosecution even though alleged to be unauthorized and hence unlawful is not alone ground for relief in equity which exerts its extraordinary powers only to prevent irreparable injury to the plaintiff who seeks its aid.' "

And similarly, in *Douglas,* supra, at 164, we made clear, after reaffirming this rule, that:

"It does not appear from the record that petitioners have been threatened with any injury other than that incidental to every criminal proceeding brought lawfully and in good faith. . . . ."

This is where the law stood when the Court decided Dombrowski v. Pfister, 380 U.S. 479 (1965), and held that an injunction against the enforcement of certain state criminal statutes could properly issue under the circumstances presented in that case. In *Dombrowski,* unlike many of the earlier cases denying injunctions, the complaint made substantial allegations that:

"the threats to enforce the statutes against appellants are not made with any expectation of securing valid convictions, but rather are part of a plan to employ arrests, seizures, and threats of prosecution under color of the statutes to harass appellants and discourage them and their supporters from asserting and attempting to vindicate the constitutional rights of Negro citizens of Louisiana."

The appellants in *Dombrowski* had offered to prove that their offices had been raided and all their files and records seized pursuant to search and arrest warrants that were later summarily vacated by a state judge for lack of probable cause. They also offered to prove that despite the state court order quashing the warrants and suppressing the evidence seized, the prosecutor was continuing to threaten to initiate new prosecutions of appellants under the same statutes, was holding public hearings at which photostatic copies of the illegally seized documents were being used, and was threatening to use other copies of the illegally seized documents to obtain grand jury indictments against the appellants on charges of violating the same statutes. These circumstances, as viewed by the Court, sufficiently establish the kind of irreparable injury, above and beyond that associated with the defense of a single prosecution brought in good faith, that had always been considered sufficient to justify federal intervention. Indeed, after quoting the Court's statement in *Douglas* concerning the very restricted circumstances under which an injunction could be justified, the Court in *Dombrowski* went on to say:

"But the allegations in this complaint depict a situation in which defense of the state's criminal prosecution will not assure adequate vindication of constitutional rights. They suggest that a substantial loss of or impairment of freedoms of expression will occur if appellants must await the state court's disposition and ultimate review in this Court of any adverse determination. These allegations, if true, clearly show irreparable injury."

And the Court made clear that even under these circumstances the district court issuing the injunction would have continuing power to lift it at any time and remit the plaintiffs to the state courts if circumstances warranted. Similarly, in Cameron v. Johnson, 390 U.S. 611 (1968), a divided Court denied an injunction after finding that the record did not establish the necessary bad faith and harassment; the dissenting Justices themselves stressed the very limited role to be allowed for federal injunctions against state criminal prosecutions and differed with the Court only on the question whether the particular facts of that case were sufficient to show that the prosecution was brought in bad faith.

It is against the background of these principles that we must judge the propriety of an injunction under the circumstances of the present case. Here a proceeding was already pending in the state court, affording Harris an opportunity to raise his constitutional claims. There is no suggestion that this single prosecution against Harris is brought in bad faith or is only one of a series of repeated prosecutions to which he will be subjected. In other words, the injury that Harris faces is solely "that incidental to every criminal proceeding brought lawfully and in good faith," *Douglas,* supra, and therefore under the settled doctrine we have already described he is not entitled to equitable relief "even if such statutes are unconstitutional," *Buck,* supra.

The District Court, however, thought that the *Dombrowski* decision substantially broadened the availability of injunctions against state criminal prosecutions and that under that decision the federal courts may give equitable relief, without regard to any showing of bad faith or harassment, whenever a state statute is found "on its face" to be vague or overly broad, in violation of the first amendment. We recognize that there are some statements in the *Dombrowski* opinion that would seem to support this argument. But, as we have already seen, such statements were unnecessary to the decision of that case, because the Court found that the plaintiffs had alleged a basis for equitable relief under the long-established standards. In addition, we do not regard the reasons adduced to support this position as sufficient to justify such a substantial departure from the established doctrines regarding the availability of injunctive relief. It is undoubtedly true, as the Court stated in *Dombrowski* that "[a] criminal prosecution under a statute regulating expression usually involves imponderables and contingencies that themselves may inhibit the full exercise of first amendment freedoms." But this sort of "chilling effect," as the Court called it, should not by itself justify federal intervention. In the first place, the chilling effect cannot be satisfactorily eliminated by federal injunctive relief. In *Dombrowski* itself the Court stated that the injunction to be issued there could be lifted if the state obtained an "acceptable limiting construction" from the state courts. The Court then made clear that once this was done, prosecutions could then be brought for conduct occurring before the narrowing construction was made, and proper convictions could stand so long as the defendants were not deprived of fair warning. The kind of relief granted in *Dombrowski* thus does not effectively eliminate uncertainty as to the coverage of the state statute and leaves most citizens with virtually the same doubts as before regarding the danger that their conduct might eventually be subjected to criminal sanctions. The chilling effect can, of course, be eliminated by an injunction that would prohibit any prosecution whatever for conduct occurring prior to a satisfactory rewriting of the statute. But the states would then be stripped of all power to prosecute even the socially dangerous and constitutionally unprotected conduct that had been covered by the statute, until a new statute could be passed by the state legislature and approved by the federal courts in potentially lengthy trial and appellate proceedings. Thus, in *Dombrowski* itself the Court carefully reaffirmed the principle that even in the direct prosecution in the state's own courts, a valid narrowing construction can be applied to conduct occurring prior to the date when the narrowing construction was made, in the absence of fair warning problems.

Moreover, the existence of a "chilling effect," even in the area of first amendment rights, has never been considered a sufficient basis, in and of itself, for prohibiting state action. Where a statute does not directly abridge free speech, but—while regulating a subject within the state's power—tends to have the incidental effect of inhibiting first amendment rights, it is well settled that the statute can be upheld if the effect on speech is minor in relation to the need for control of the conduct and the lack of alternative means for doing so. Just as the incidental "chilling effect" of such statutes does not automatically render them unconstitutional, so the chilling effect that admittedly can result from the very existence of certain laws on the statute books does not in itself justify prohibiting the state from carrying out the important and necessary task of enforcing these laws against socially harmful conduct that the state believes in good faith to be punishable under its laws and the Constitution.

Beyond all this is another, more basic consideration. Procedures for testing the constitutionality of a statute "on its face" in the manner apparently contemplated by *Dombrowski*, and for then enjoining all action to enforce the statute until the state can obtain court approval for a modified version, are fundamentally at odds with the function of the federal courts in our constitutional plan. The power and duty of the judiciary to declare laws unconstitutional is in the final analysis derived from its responsibility for resolving concrete disputes brought before the courts for decision; a statute apparently governing a dispute cannot be applied by judges, consistently with their obligations under the supremacy clause, when such an application of the statute would conflict with the Constitution. But this vital responsibility, broad as it is, does not amount to an unlimited power to survey the statute books and pass judgment on laws before the courts are called upon to enforce them. Ever since the constitutional convention rejected a proposal for having members of the Supreme Court render advice concerning pending legislation it has been clear that, even when suits of this kind involve a "case or controversy" sufficient to satisfy the requirements of article III of the Constitution, the task of analyzing a proposed statute, pinpointing its deficiencies, and requiring correction of these deficiencies before the statute is put into effect, is rarely if ever an appropriate task for the judiciary. The combination of the relative remoteness of the controversy, the impact on the legislative process of the relief sought, and above all the speculative and amorphous nature of the required line-by-line analysis of detailed statutes, ordinarily results in a kind of case that is wholly unsatisfactory for deciding constitutional questions, whichever way they might be decided. In light of this fundamental conception of the framers as to the proper place of the federal courts in the governmental processes of passing and enforcing laws, it can seldom be appropriate for these courts to exercise any such power of prior approval or veto over the legislative process.

For these reasons, fundamental not only to our federal system but also to the basic functions of the judicial branch of the national government under our Constitution, we hold that the *Dombrowski* decision should not be regarded as having upset the settled doctrines that have always confined very narrowly the availability of injunctive relief against state criminal prosecutions. We do not think that opinion stands for the proposition that a federal court can properly enjoin enforcement of a statute solely on the basis of a showing that the statute "on its face" abridges first amendment rights. There may, of course, be extraordinary circumstances in which the necessary irreparable injury can be shown even in the absence of the usual prerequisites of bad faith and harassment. For example, as long ago as the *Buck* case, supra, we indicated:

> "It is of course conceivable that a statute might be flagrantly and patently violative of express constitutional prohibitions in every clause, sentence and paragraph, and in whatever manner and against whomever an effort might be made to apply it."

Other unusual situations calling for federal intervention might also arise, but there is no point in our attempting now to specify what they might be. It is sufficient for purposes of the present case to hold, as we do, that the possible unconstitutionality of a statute "on its face" does not in itself justify an injunction against good-faith attempts to enforce it, and that appellee Harris has failed to make any showing of bad faith, harassment, or any other unusual circumstance that would call for equitable relief. Because our holding rests on the absence of the factors necessary under equitable principles to justify federal intervention, we have no occasion to consider whether 28 U.S.C. § 2283, which prohibits an injunction against state court proceedings "except as expressly authorized by Act of Congress" would in and of itself be controlling under the circumstances of this case.

The judgment of the District Court is reversed, and the case is remanded for further proceedings not inconsistent with this opinion.

Reversed.

MR. JUSTICE STEWART, with whom MR. JUSTICE HARLAN joins, concurring.

The questions the Court decides today are important ones. Perhaps as important, however, is a recognition of the areas into which today's holdings do not necessarily extend. In all of these cases,[b] the Court deals only with the proper policy to be followed by a federal court when asked to intervene by injunction or declaratory judgment in a criminal prosecution which is contemporaneously pending in a state court.

In basing its decisions on policy grounds, the Court does not reach any questions concerning the independent force of the federal anti-injunction statute, 28 U.S.C. § 2283. Thus we do not decide whether the word "injunction" in § 2283 should be interpreted to include a declaratory judgment, or whether an injunction to stay proceedings in a state court is "expressly authorized" by § 1 of the Civil Rights Act of 1871, now 42 U.S.C. § 1983. And since all of these cases involve state criminal prosecutions, we do not deal with the considerations that

---

[b] Stewart was referring to *Younger* and to five companion cases decided on the same day. [Footnote by eds.]

should govern a federal court when it is asked to intervene in state civil proceedings, where, for various reasons, the balance might be struck differently.[2] Finally, the Court today does not resolve the problems involved when a federal court is asked to give injunctive or declaratory relief from *future* state criminal prosecutions.

The Court confines itself to deciding the policy considerations that in our federal system must prevail when federal courts are asked to interfere with pending state prosecutions. Within this area, we hold that a federal court must not, save in exceptional and extremely limited circumstances, intervene by way of either injunction or declaration in an existing state criminal prosecution. Such circumstances exist only when there is a threat of irreparable injury "both great and immediate." A threat of this nature might be shown if the state criminal statute in question were patently and flagrantly unconstitutional on its face, or if there has been bad faith and harassment—official lawlessness—in a statute's enforcement. In such circumstances the reasons of policy for deferring to state adjudication are outweighed by the injury flowing from the very bringing of the state proceedings, by the perversion of the very process that is supposed to provide vindication, and by the need for speedy and effective action to protect federal rights.

MR. JUSTICE BRENNAN, with whom MR. JUSTICE WHITE and MR. JUSTICE MARSHALL join, concurring in the result.

I agree that the judgment of the District Court should be reversed. Appellee Harris had been indicted for violations of the California Criminal Syndicalism Act before he sued in federal court. He has not alleged that the prosecution was brought in bad faith to harass him. His constitutional contentions may be adequately adjudicated in the state criminal proceeding, and federal intervention at his instance was therefore improper.

Appellees Hirsch and Dan have alleged that they "feel inhibited" by the statute and the prosecution of Harris from advocating the program of the Progressive Labor Party. Appellee Broslawsky has alleged that he "is uncertain" whether as an instructor in college history he can under the statute give instruction relating to the Communist Manifesto and similar revolutionary works. None of these appellees has stated any ground for a reasonable expectation that he will actually be prosecuted under the statute for taking the actions contemplated. The court below expressly declined to rely on any finding "that . . . Dan, Hirsch or Broslawsky stand[s] in any danger of prosecution by the [state], because of the activities that they ascribed to themselves in complaint. . . ." It is true, as the court below pointed out, that "[w]ell-intentioned prosecutors and judicial safeguards do not neutralize the vice of a vague law," but still there must be a live

---

[2] Courts of equity have traditionally shown greater reluctance to intervene in criminal prosecutions than in civil cases. The offense to state interests is likely to be less in a civil proceeding. A state's decision to classify conduct as criminal provides some indication of the importance it has ascribed to prompt and unencumbered enforcement of its law. By contrast, the state might not even be a party in a proceeding under a civil statute. . . .

controversy under art. III.   No threats of prosecution of these appellees are alleged.   Although Dan and Hirsch have alleged that they desire to advocate doctrines of the Progressive Labor Party, they have not asserted that their advocacy will be of the same genre as that which brought on the prosecution of Harris.   In short, there is no reason to think that California has any ripe controversy with them.

MR. JUSTICE DOUGLAS, dissenting.

The fact that we are in a period of history when enormous extrajudicial sanctions are imposed on those who assert their first amendment rights in unpopular causes emphasizes the wisdom of Dombrowski v. Pfister, 380 U.S. 479 (1965).   There we recognized that in times of repression, when interests with powerful spokesmen generate symbolic pogroms against nonconformists, the federal judiciary, charged by Congress with special vigilance for protection of civil rights, has special responsibilities to prevent an erosion of the individual's constitutional rights.

Dombrowski represents an exception to the general rule that federal courts should not interfere with state criminal prosecutions.   The exception does not arise merely because prosecutions are threatened to which the first amendment will be the proffered defense.   *Dombrowski* governs statutes which are a blunderbuss by themselves or when used en masse—those that have an "overbroad" sweep.   "If the rule were otherwise, the contours of regulation would have to be hammered out case by case—and tested only by those hardy enough to risk criminal prosecution to determine the proper scope of regulation."   Ibid., at 487. It was in the context of overbroad state statutes that we spoke of the "chilling effect upon the exercise of first amendment rights" caused by state prosecutions. . . .

The special circumstances when federal intervention in a state criminal proceeding is permissible are not restricted to bad faith on the part of state officials or the threat of multiple prosecutions.   They also exist where for any reason the state statute being enforced is unconstitutional on its face . . . .

In *Younger,* "criminal syndicalism" is defined so broadly as to jeopardize "teaching" that socialism is preferable to free enterprise.

Harris' "crime" was distributing leaflets advocating change in industrial ownership through political action.   The statute under which he was indicted was the one involved in Whitney v. California, 274 U.S. 357 (1927), a decision we overruled in Brandenburg v. Ohio, 395 U.S. 444, 449 (1969).

If the "advocacy" which Harris used was an attempt at persuasion through the use of bullets, bombs, and arson, we would have a different case.   But Harris is charged only with distributing leaflets advocating political action toward his objective.   He tried unsuccessfully to have the state court dismiss the indictment on constitutional grounds.   He resorted to the state appellate court for writs of prohibition to prevent the trial, but to no avail.   He went to the federal court as a matter of last resort in an effort to keep this unconstitutional trial from being saddled on him. . . .

——————

NOTES ON *YOUNGER v. HARRIS*

1. **Introduction.** Five companion cases were decided on the same day as *Younger*. Two were per curiam reversals,[a] but three produced signed opinions. Each is considered below.

2. ***Boyle v. Landry.*** In Boyle v. Landry, 401 U.S. 77 (1971), various Illinois statutes and Chicago ordinances were challenged on the ground that they had been used to harass and intimidate blacks. As the case reached the Supreme Court, only a portion of a single statute was in issue, and none of the plaintiffs had been prosecuted or even threatened with prosecution under that provision. "[I]t appears," said Justice Black, "that those who originally brought this suit made a search of state statutes and city ordinances with a view to picking out certain ones that they thought might possibly be used by the authorities as devices for bad-faith prosecutions against them." Such "speculation," the Court held, could not support equitable relief.

Justices Brennan and White concurred in the result. Justice Douglas dissented.

3. ***Samuels v. Mackell.*** The issue in Samuels v. Mackell, 401 U.S. 66 (1971), was whether the policies of *Younger* also foreclosed federal *declaratory* relief against a state criminal statute under which prosecutions were then pending. Again Justice Black spoke for the Court:

> "In our opinion in the *Younger* case, we set out in detail the historical and practical basis for the settled doctrine of equity that a federal court should not enjoin a state criminal prosecution begun prior to the institution of the federal suit except in very unusual situations, where necessary to prevent immediate irreparable injury. The question presented here is whether under ordinary circumstances the same considerations that require the withholding of injunctive relief will make declaratory relief equally inappropriate. . . .

> "[O]rdinarily a declaratory judgment will result in precisely the same interference with and disruption of state proceedings that the longstanding policy limiting injunctions was designed to avoid. This is true for at least two reasons. In the first place the Declaratory Judgment Act provides that after a declaratory judgment is issued the district court may enforce it by granting 'further necessary or proper relief,' and therefore a declaratory judgment issued while state proceedings are pending might serve as the basis for a subsequent injunction against those proceedings to 'protect or effectuate' the declara-

———

[a] Dyson v. Stein, 401 U.S. 200 (1971), and Byrne v. Karalexis, 401 U.S. 216 (1971).

tory judgment, 28 U.S.C. § 2283, and thus result in a clearly improper interference with the state proceedings. Secondly, even if the declaratory judgment is not used as a basis for actually issuing an injunction, the declaratory relief alone has virtually the same practical impact as a formal injunction would. As we said in Public Service Comm'n of Utah v. Wycoff Co., 344 U.S. 237, 247 (1952):

> 'Is the declaration contemplated here to be res judicata, so that the [state court] cannot hear evidence and decide any matter for itself? If so, the federal court has virtually lifted the case out of the state [court] before it could be heard. If not, the federal judgment serves no useful purpose as a final determination of rights.'

We therefore hold that, in cases where the state criminal prosecution was begun prior to the federal suit, the same equitable principles relevant to the propriety of an injunction must be taken into consideration by federal district courts in determining whether to issue a declaratory judgment, and that where an injunction would be impermissible under these principles, declaratory relief should ordinarily be denied as well." [b]

Justice Douglas concurred on the ground that the challenged state statute was not unconstitutional on its face and its constitutionality as applied to the federal plaintiffs depended on the facts, which should be developed in the state criminal trial. Justices Brennan, White, and Marshall concurred in the result.

4. *Perez v. Ledesma.* The last and most complicated of the *Younger* companions was Perez v. Ledesma, 401 U.S. 82 (1971). Ledesma and other plaintiffs had been charged in state court with violating both a state obscenity statute and a local obscenity ordinance. They sought declaratory and injunctive relief against these prosecutions. A three-judge court, which was convened to hear the challenge to the state-wide statute, ruled that the statute was not unconstitutional on its face, but that the arrest of the defendants and the seizure of allegedly obscene materials to be used in evidence were constitutionally invalid. The court therefore ordered that the materials be suppressed from use at trial and returned to the defendants. This ruling was appealed directly to the Supreme Court.

---

[b] Justice Black added:

"We do not mean to suggest that a declaratory judgment should never be issued in cases of this type if it has been concluded that injunctive relief would be improper. There may be unusual circumstances in which an injunction might be withheld because, despite a plaintiff's strong claim for relief under the established standards, the injunctive remedy seemed particularly intrusive or offensive; in such a situation, a declaratory judgment might be appropriate and might not be contrary to the basic equitable doctrines governing the availability of relief. Ordinarily, however, the practical effect of the two forms of relief will be virtually identical, and the basic policy against federal interference with pending state criminal prosecutions will be frustrated as much by a declaratory judgment as it would be by an injunction.

". . . We, of course, express no views on the propriety of declaratory relief when no state proceeding is pending at the time the federal suit is begun."

Speaking for the Court, Justice Black disapproved these orders as inconsistent with the principles underlying *Younger* and Stefanelli v. Minard, 342 U.S. 117 (1951).[c] He said:

"The propriety of arrests and the admissibility of evidence in state criminal prosecutions are ordinarily matters to be resolved by state tribunals, subject, of course, to review by certiorari or appeal to this Court or, in a proper case, on federal habeas corpus. Here Ledesma was free to present his federal constitutional claims concerning arrest and seizure of materials or other matters to the Louisiana courts in the manner permitted in that state. Only in cases of proven harassment or prosecutions undertaken by state officials in bad faith without hope of obtaining a valid conviction and perhaps in other extraordinary circumstances where irreparable injury can be shown is federal injunctive relief against pending state prosecutions appropriate. There is nothing in the record before us to suggest that these Louisiana officials undertook these prosecutions other than in a good-faith attempt to enforce the state's criminal laws. We therefore hold that the three-judge court improperly intruded into the state's own criminal process and reverse its orders suppressing evidence in the pending state prosecution and directing the return of all seized materials."

Only Justice Douglas dissented from this aspect of the case.

The local obscenity ordinance presented a different problem. The three-judge court had declared it unconstitutional. The Supreme Court ruled, however, that this judgment was not properly before it on direct appeal from the three-judge court.[d] The majority therefore refused to consider the merits.

Justice Brennan, joined by Justices White and Marshall, dissented from this aspect of the Court's decision. He thought that the ruling on the local ordinance was properly before the Court on a theory of pendent jurisdiction and that the declaratory judgment was properly issued. Crucial to his position was the fact that prosecution of Ledesma under the local ordinance had been dismissed by the state court before the hearing in the three-judge federal court. Since *Younger* applied

[c] *Stefanelli* involved a state criminal defendant who sought a federal injunction against the admissibility at trial of evidence allegedly seized in violation of the fourth and 14th amendments. The suit was filed 10 years before the exclusionary rule was applied to the states in Mapp v. Ohio, 367 U.S. 643 (1961). The defendant was therefore trying to do indirectly what he could not do directly—that is, require suppression of illegally seized evidence by a state court. The Supreme Court held that this could not be done. *Stefanelli* spawned a line of cases declining to interfere by injunction with the admissibility of evidence in state criminal proceedings. See Cleary v. Bolger, 371 U.S. 392 (1963); Pugach v. Dollinger, 365 U.S. 458 (1961); Wilson v. Schnettler, 365 U.S. 381 (1961); but see Rea v. United States, 350 U.S. 214 (1956).

[d] A three-judge court was required only where an injunction was sought against a statute of state-wide applicability. Since the municipal ordinance applied only locally, the attack on its constitutionality did not come within the direct-appeal provision of the three-judge court statute.

only to *pending* state prosecutions and since criminal charges were no longer pending, he thought it appropriate for the lower court to consider the questions of declaratory and injunctive relief free of the constraints of *Younger.* [e]

5. Questions and Comments on *Younger v. Harris.* The *Younger* decision is controversial on a number of grounds, including its treatment of precedent. In particular, one might ask whether Justice Black was entirely correct in recounting the holding of *Dombrowski.* Recall, for example, his assertion that "there are some statements in the *Dombrowski* opinion that would seem to support" the District Court's reading of the case, but that "such statements were unnecessary to the decision." Is this accurate?

There were at least two narrower grounds on which the case could have been decided. The first involves the timing of the decision. The three-judge District Court decided *Younger* on March 11, 1968. The case was argued for the first time during the Court's 1968 term, but was set down for reargument the following year. After the reargument during the 1969 term, it was again set down for reargument during the 1970 term, when it was finally decided. The Court had decided Brandenburg v. Ohio, 395 U.S. 444 (1969), on June 9, 1969. *Brandenburg* explicitly overruled *Whitney v. California,* the 1927 decision that had upheld the statute at issue in *Younger.* Since *Whitney* had been overruled, the Supreme Court could have remanded the case to the three-judge court for reconsideration in light of *Brandenburg* or could have taken the position, see page 1158, footnote a supra, that injunctive relief was no longer needed.

Secondly, there was precedent for the proposition that federal equitable relief should be withheld where the only relief sought was an injunction against a pending state criminal prosecution.[f] By contrast, Black's evocation of "Our Federalism" is not in any obvious way limited to federal injunctions against pending state criminal prosecutions. His rhetoric might well be taken to suggest a broader prohibition of federal injunctive relief against unconstitutional state laws. It is this broader application, or perhaps implication, that has excited criticism.[g]

---

[e] This suggestion was addressed by the Court in *Steffel v. Thompson,* the next main case.

[f] E.g., Cline v. Frink Dairy Co., 274 U.S. 445 (1927). See Soifer and Macgill, The *Younger* Doctrine: Reconstructing Reconstruction, 55 Texas L. Rev. 1141, 1147 (1977): "If Justice Black's opinion actually had been confined to the situation of a pending prosecution presented in *Younger,* the decision would have represented little more than finetuning, perhaps portentous, of established doctrine." See also Field, The Uncertain Nature of Federal Jurisdiction, 22 W. & M. L. Rev. 683, 706 (1981). But see B. Wechsler, Federal Courts, State Criminal Law and the First Amendment, 49 N.Y.U.L. Rev. 740, 885 (1974) (conclud-

ing that, at least with respect to first amendment cases, "the decision in *Younger* was out of joint").

[g] See, for example, the remarks of Aviam Soifer and H.C. Macgill in The *Younger* Doctrine: Reconstructing Reconstruction, 55 Tex. L. Rev. 1141 (1977). They assert that Justice Black "rewrote history" by "ignoring a body of . . . cases in which the Court regularly reached the merits of suits for injunctive and declaratory relief." They conclude that prior to *Dombrowski* and *Younger,* at least where state prosecutions were not already pending, federal courts did not adhere to any categorical rule of non-intervention, but instead exercised discretion "in light of the balance struck between the competing public inter-

6. The Policies of *Younger*. Whatever one thinks Black's agenda might have been, the fact remains that the judgment in *Younger* was supported by eight of the nine Justices, including Justice Brennan, the author of *Dombrowski*. Why was there such near unanimity of result? What are the policies that underlie the result in *Younger*?

Consider a simple case. Assume a pending *federal* criminal prosecution under an arguably overbroad statute for conduct the defendant has committed once and does not propose to engage in again. The defendant seeks an injunction against the prosecution from a different federal district judge sitting in the same district. Should the injunction be issued if the second judge thinks the statute unconstitutional? Should it matter if the criminal case is pending in a *state* court and an injunction is sought from a federal judge? On what policies should the answer to these questions be based? Are they unique to the federal-state context?[h]

7. The *Younger* Exceptions. Even in the context of the pending state criminal prosecution, *Younger* recognized an exception for cases of bad-faith harassment. In *Dombrowski*, 86 Yale L.J. 1103 (1977), Owen Fiss reported the results of his attempt to assess the practical importance of the *Younger* exceptions. He found only five post-*Younger* cases where the lower courts found bad faith and only two more where allegations of bad faith were thought to require a hearing. Moreover, in the one case that had gone to the Supreme Court as of the time of his writing, the finding of bad faith had been reversed. Fiss concluded that "the universe of bad-faith harassment claims that can be established is virtually empty."[i] Why might this be so?

Younger also recognized an exception for a law "flagrantly and patently violative of express constitutional prohibitions in every clause, sentence and paragraph, in whatever manner and against whomever an effort might be made to apply it." Reported instances of the successful assertion of this ground are also rare. See Soifer and Macgill, The *Younger* Doctrine: Reconstructing Reconstruction, 55 Texas L. Rev. 1141, 1204–06 n.259 (1977). Why, in any event, should patent unconstitutionality be a ground for immediate federal intervention? Is it unlikely that a state court will afford prompt and adequate relief in

ests and private rights presented in the facts of each case." See also Burton Wechsler, Federal Courts, State Criminal Law and the First Amendment, 49 N.Y. U.L. Rev. 740, 875 (1974), which surveys pre-*Younger* cases and concludes that "to the extent the Court based *Younger* on prior law, it relied upon sheer mythology, a total misconception of pre-*Dombrowski* history and precedent."

h For a pungent "dialogue" attacking the policies behind *Younger,* see B. Wechsler, Federal Courts, State Criminal Law and the First Amendment, 49 N.Y.U.L. Rev. 740, 888–96 (1974). For an effort to articu-

late the policies of *Younger,* see Redish, The Doctrine of *Younger v. Harris*: Deference in Search of a Rationale, 63 Corn. L. Rev. 463, 465–66 (1977). For wide-ranging criticism of *Younger* abstention in relation to the history and contemporary uses of 42 U.S.C. § 1983, see Gene R. Nichol, Jr., Federalism, State Courts and Section 1983, 73 Va.L.Rev. 959 (1987).

i See also C. Keith Wingate's treatment of this question in The Bad Faith Harassment Exception to the *Younger* Doctrine: Exploring the Empty Universe, 5 Rev. Litigation 123 (1986).

such a case? If such an exception is to exist, why did the statute at issue in *Younger* not come within it?

8. Bibliography. *Younger* is the subject of a large body of comment. A partial listing would include, in addition to those already cited, the following articles.

A critical assumption underlying the *Younger* decision is attacked by Douglas Laycock in Federal Interference with State Prosecutions: The Need for Prospective Relief, 1977 Sup. Ct Rev. 193. Laycock argues that the opportunity to raise a defense in a state criminal prosecution is, in many cases, not an adequate remedy for the violation of federal rights. Quite apart from any supposed lack of sympathy for federal rights, state criminal courts typically cannot grant interlocutory, prospective, or class-wide relief. Thus, in Laycock's view, "even if one accepts the core of *Younger*—that federal relief should be withheld where the pending state remedy is adequate—a pending prosecution should not be a near automatic bar to a federal action. The federal court should consider whether the state remedy is actually adequate on each set of facts and provide supplementary relief where needed."

Younger is also examined by Donald H. Zeigler in An Accommodation of the *Younger* Doctrine and the Duty of the Federal Court to Enforce Constitutional Safeguards in the State Criminal Process, 125 U.Pa.L.Rev. 266 (1976), by Louise Weinberg in The New Judicial Federalism, 29 Stan.L.Rev. 1191 (1977), and by Ralph Whitten in Federal Declaratory and Injunctive Interference with State Court Proceedings: The Supreme Court and the Limits of Judicial Discretion, 53 N.C.L.Rev. 591 (1975). Zeigler attempts to chart "a workable middle course" by carefully analyzing situations in which *Younger* should and should not apply and suggesting appropriate content for the *Younger* exceptions.[j] Weinberg agrees that *Younger*, or some equivalent rule, is an essential accommodation of federal civil rights enforcement and established patterns of judicial federalism. In her view, "real compromise" is necessary to avert the collision course between § 1983 and the dual court system. Weinberg argues, however, that *Younger's* "principles of comity and federalism" should not apply to cases seeking injunctions against state *officials*. Cf. Rizzo v. Goode, 423 U.S. 362 (1976). She sees *Younger* as part of a broad post-Warren Court assault on federal judicial power in civil rights cases. Whitten regards the "trend" of *Younger* as "salutary." He accepts "the legitimacy of the Court's role in settling the conflict between the federal courts' obligation to adjudicate controversies within their jurisdiction and their obligation to avoid emasculating interference with the state court systems," but criticizes the Court's reliance on "outmoded chancery concepts" in striking the balance. Instead, Whitten proposes a "functional standard" for granting federal anticipatory relief. His standard would include the principle that "federal anticipatory relief should not

---

[j] In a more recent article, Zeigler calls for reevaluation of all abstention doctrines, including *Younger*, with a presumption favoring enforcement of federal rights. See Zeigler, Rights Require Remedies: A New Approach to the Enforcement of Rights in the Federal Courts, 38 Hast.L.J. 665, 682–708 (1987).

issue against state action unless that relief is the only effective remedy for denial of a constitutional right."

For an extensive analysis of the relation of *Younger* and its progeny to other forms of federal court intervention into ongoing state proceedings, see Michael G. Collins, The Right to Avoid Trial: Justifying Federal Court Intervention into Ongoing State Court Proceedings, 66 N.C.L.Rev. 49 (1987). A detailed analysis of the history surrounding modern jurisdictional statutes is undertaken in David Logan, Judicial Federalism in the Court of History, 66 Ore.L.Rev. 453 (1987). Logan concludes that "the notions of parity and 'Our Federalism' used by the Supreme Court to justify curtailing national judicial power are simply inconsistent with the historical record. As such, they are illegitimate bases for construing the jurisdiction of federal courts when a litigant seeks a federal forum to protect national rights from state infringements." In Is Disparity a Problem?, 22 Ga.L.Rev. 283 (1988), Michael Wells identifies *Younger* as the beginning of a contraction of federal court jurisdiction in constitutional litigation. He attributes the change to a substantive agenda which, although he does not share the values it reflects, he does not regard as illegitimate.

Finally, a summary of the *Younger* line of cases and an effort to identify the "thread of logical consistency" among them may be found in Dittfurth, The *Younger* Abstention Doctrine: Primary State Jurisdiction over Law Enforcement, 10 St. Mary's L.J. 445 (1979).

MITCHUM v. FOSTER
United States Supreme Court, 1972.
407 U.S. 225.

MR. JUSTICE STEWART delivered the opinion of the Court.

The federal anti-injunction statute provides that a federal court "may not grant an injunction to stay proceedings in a State court except as expressly authorized by Act of Congress, or where necessary in aid of its jurisdiction, or to protect or effectuate its judgments." [2] An act of Congress, 42 U.S.C. § 1983, expressly authorizes a "suit in equity" to redress "the deprivation," under color of state law, "of any rights, privileges, or immunities secured by the Constitution. . . ." The question before us is whether this "Act of Congress" comes within the "expressly authorized" exception of the anti-injunction statute so as to permit a federal court in a § 1983 suit to grant an injunction to stay a proceeding pending in a state court. This question, which has divided the federal courts, has lurked in the background of many of our recent cases, but we have not until today explicitly decided it. [4]

The prosecuting attorney of Bay County, Florida brought a proceeding in a Florida court to close down the appellant's bookstore as a

---

[2] 28 U.S.C. § 2283.

[4] In Younger v. Harris, 401 U.S. 37 (1971), Mr. Justice Douglas was the only member of the Court who took a position on the question now before us. He expressed the view that § 1983 is included in the "expressly authorized exception to § 2283. . . ."

public nuisance under the claimed authority of Florida law. The state court entered a preliminary order prohibiting continued operation of the bookstore. After further inconclusive proceedings in the state courts, the appellant filed a complaint in the United States District Court for the Northern District of Florida, alleging that the actions of the state judicial and law enforcement officials were depriving him of rights protected by the first and 14th amendments. Relying upon 42 U.S.C. § 1983, he asked for injunctive and declaratory relief against the state court proceedings, on the ground that Florida laws were being unconstitutionally applied by the state court so as to cause him great and irreparable harm. A single federal district judge issued temporary restraining orders, and a three-judge court was convened. . . . After a hearing, the three-judge court dissolved the temporary restraining orders and refused to enjoin the state court proceeding, holding that the "injunctive relief sought here as to the proceedings pending in the Florida courts does not come under any of the exceptions set forth in § 2283. It is not expressly authorized by act of Congress, it is not necessary in the aid of this court's jurisdiction, and it is not sought in order to protect or effectuate any judgment of this court." An appeal was brought directly here . . ., and we noted probable jurisdiction.

II

In denying injunctive relief, the District Court relied on this Court's decision in Atlantic Coast Line R. Co. v. Brotherhood of Locomotive Engineers, 398 U.S. 281 (1970). The *Atlantic Coast Line* case did not deal with the "expressly authorized" exception of the anti-injunction statute,[7] but the Court's opinion in that case does bring into sharp focus the critical importance of the question now before us. For in that case we expressly rejected the view that the anti-injunction statute merely states a flexible doctrine of comity, and made clear that the statute imposes an absolute ban upon the issuance of a federal injunction against a pending state court proceeding, in the absence of one of the recognized exceptions:

> "On its face the present act is an absolute prohibition against enjoining state court proceedings, unless the injunction falls within one of three specifically defined exceptions. The respondents here have intimated that the act only establishes a 'principle of comity,' not a binding rule on the power of the federal courts. The argument implies that in certain circumstances a federal court may enjoin state court proceedings even if that action cannot be justified by any of the three exceptions. We cannot accept any such contention. [We] hold that any injunction against state court proceedings otherwise proper under general equitable principles must be based on one of the specific statutory exceptions to § 2283 if it is to be upheld. . . ." 398 U.S., at 286–87.

[7] At issue were the other two exceptions of the anti-injunction statute: "where necessary in aid of its jurisdiction, or to protect or effectuate its judgments."

It follows, in the present context, that if 42 U.S.C. § 1983 is not within the "expressly authorized" exception of the anti-injunction statute, then a federal equity court is wholly without power to grant any relief in a § 1983 suit seeking to stay a state court proceeding. In short, if a § 1983 action is not an "expressly authorized" statutory exception, the anti-injunction law absolutely prohibits in such an action all federal equitable intervention in a pending state court proceeding, whether civil or criminal, and regardless of how extraordinary the particular circumstances may be.

Last term, in Younger v. Harris, 401 U.S. 37 (1971), and its companion cases, the Court dealt at length with the subject of federal judicial intervention in pending state criminal prosecutions. In *Younger*, a three-judge federal district court in a § 1983 action had enjoined a criminal prosecution pending in a California court. In asking us to reverse that judgment, the appellant argued that the injunction was in violation of the federal anti-injunction statute. But the Court carefully eschewed any reliance on the statute in reversing the judgment, basing its decision instead upon what the Court called "Our Federalism"—upon "the national policy forbidding federal courts to stay or enjoin pending state court proceedings except under special circumstances."

In *Younger*, this Court emphatically reaffirmed "the fundamental policy against federal interference with state criminal prosecutions." It made clear that even "the possible unconstitutionality of a statute 'on its face' does not in itself justify an injunction against good-faith attempts to enforce it." At the same time, however, the Court clearly left room for federal injunctive intervention in a pending state court prosecution in certain exceptional circumstances—where irreparable injury is "both great and immediate," where the state law is " 'flagrantly and patently violative of express constitutional prohibitions,' " or where there is a showing of "bad faith, harassment, or . . . other unusual circumstances that would call for equitable relief." In the companion case of Perez v. Ledesma, 401 U.S. 82, 85 (1971), the Court said that "[o]nly in cases of proven harassment or prosecutions undertaken by state officials in bad faith without hope of obtaining a valid conviction and perhaps in other extraordinary circumstances where irreparable injury can be shown is federal injunctive relief against pending state prosecutions appropriate."

While the Court in *Younger* and its companion cases expressly disavowed deciding the question now before us—whether § 1983 comes within the "expressly authorized" exception of the anti-injunction statute—it is evident that our decisions in those cases cannot be disregarded in deciding this question. In the first place, if § 1983 is not within the statutory exception, then the anti-injunction statute would have absolutely barred the injunction issued in *Younger*, as the appellant in that case argued, and there would have been no occasion whatever for the Court to decide that case upon the "policy" ground of "Our Federalism." Secondly, if § 1983 is not within the "expressly authorized" exception of the anti-injunction statute, then we must overrule *Younger* and its companion cases insofar as they recognized the permissibility of injunctive relief against pending criminal prosecutions in certain limited and exceptional circumstances. For, under the doctrine of *Atlantic Coast Line,* the anti-injunction statute would, in a § 1983 case, then be an "absolute prohibition" against federal equity intervention in a pending state criminal *or* civil proceeding—under any circumstances whatever.

The *Atlantic Coast Line* and *Younger* cases thus serve to delineate both the importance and the finality of the question now before us. And it is in the shadow of those cases that the question must be decided.

III

The anti-injunction statute goes back almost to the beginnings of our history as a nation. In 1793, Congress enacted a law providing that no "writ of injunction be granted [by any federal court] to stay proceedings in any court of a state. . . ." Act of March 2, 1793, 1 Stat. 335. The precise origins of the legislation are shrouded in obscurity, but the consistent understanding has been that its basic purpose is to prevent "needless friction between state and federal courts." Oklahoma Packing Co. v. Gas Co., 309 U.S. 4, 9 (1940). The law remained unchanged until 1874, when it was amended to permit a federal court to stay state court proceedings that interfered with the administration of a federal bankruptcy proceeding. The present wording of the legislation was adopted with the enactment of title 28 of the United States Code in 1948.

Despite the seemingly uncompromising language of the anti-injunction statute prior to 1948, the Court soon recognized that exceptions must be made to its blanket prohibition if the import and purpose of other acts of Congress were to be given their intended scope. So it was that, in addition to the bankruptcy law exception that Congress explicitly recognized in 1874, the Court through the years found that federal courts were empowered to enjoin state court proceedings, despite the anti-injunction statute, in carrying out the will of Congress under [numerous federal statutes that seemed to contemplate the stay of state court proceedings].

In addition to the exceptions to the anti-injunction statute found to be embodied in these various acts of Congress, the Court recognized other "implied" exceptions to the blanket prohibition of the anti-injunction statute. One was an "in rem" exception, allowing a federal court to enjoin a state court proceeding in order to protect its jurisdiction of a res over which it had first acquired jurisdiction. Another was a "relitigation" exception, permitting a federal court to enjoin relitigation in a state court of issues already decided in federal litigation. Still a third exception, more recently developed, permits a federal injunction of state court proceedings when the plaintiff in the federal court is the United States itself, or a federal agency asserting "superior federal interests."

In Toucey v. New York Life Ins. Co., 314 U.S. 118 (1941), the Court in 1941 issued an opinion casting considerable doubt upon the approach to the anti-injunction statute reflected in its previous decisions. The Court's opinion expressly disavowed the "relitigation" exception to the statute, and emphasized generally the importance of recognizing the statute's basic directive "of 'hands off' by the federal courts in the use of the injunction to stay litigation in a state court." The congressional response to *Toucey* was the enactment in 1948 of the anti-injunction statute in its present form in 28 U.S.C. § 2283, which, as the Reviser's Note makes evident, served not only to overrule the specific holding of *Toucey*, but to restore "the basic law as generally understood and interpreted prior to the *Toucey* decision."

We proceed, then, upon the understanding that in determining whether § 1983 comes within the "expressly authorized" exception of the anti-injunction statute, the criteria to be applied are those reflected in the Court's decisions prior to *Toucey*. A review of those decisions makes reasonably clear what the relevant criteria are. In the first place, it is evident that, in order to qualify under the "expressly authorized" exception of the anti-injunction statute, a federal law need not contain an express reference to that statute. As the Court has said, "no prescribed formula is required; an authorization need not expressly refer to § 2283." *Amalgamated Clothing Workers v. Richman Bros. Co.*, 348 U.S. 511, 516 (1955). Indeed, none of the previously recognized statutory exceptions contains any such reference. Secondly, a federal law need not expressly authorize an injunction of a state court proceeding in order to qualify as an exception. [Some of the] previously recognized statutory exceptions contain no such authorization.[a] Thirdly, it is clear that, in order to qualify as an "expressly authorized" exception to the anti-injunction statute, an act of Congress must have created a specific and uniquely federal right or remedy, enforceable in a federal court of equity, that could be frustrated if the federal court were not empowered to enjoin a state court proceeding. This is not to say that in order to come within the exception an act of Congress must, on its face and in every one of its provisions, be totally incompatible with the prohibition of the anti-injunction statute. The test, rather, is whether an act of Congress, clearly creating a federal right or remedy enforceable in a federal court of equity, could be given its intended scope only by the stay of a state court proceeding.

With these criteria, in view, we turn to consideration of 42 U.S.C. § 1983.

IV

Section 1983 was originally § 1 of the Civil Rights Act of 1871. It was "modeled" on § 2 of the Civil Rights Act of 1866, and was enacted for the express purpose of "enforc[ing] the provisions of the 14th

---

[a] One of the Court's illustrations of this proposition was the provision in 28 U.S.C. § 1446(e) that, following the removal of a case from state to federal court, the "State court shall proceed no further unless and until the case is remanded." [Footnote by eds.]

amendment." The predecessor of § 1983 was thus an important part of the basic alteration in our federal system wrought in the Reconstruction era through federal legislation and constitutional amendment. As a result of the new structure of law that emerged in the post-Civil War era—and especially of the 14th amendment, which was its centerpiece—the role of the federal government as a guarantor of basic federal rights against state power was clearly established. Monroe v. Pape, 365 U.S. 167 (1961); H. Flack, The Adoption of the Fourteenth Amendment (1908); J. TenBroek, The Anti-Slavery Origins of the Fourteenth Amendment (1951).[29] Section 1983 opened the federal courts to private citizens, offering a uniquely federal remedy against incursions under the claimed authority of state law upon rights secured by the Constitution and laws of the Nation.

It is clear from the legislative debates surrounding passage of § 1983's predecessor that the act was intended to enforce the provisions of the 14th amendment "against state action, . . . whether that action be executive, legislative, or *judicial*." Ex parte Virginia, 100 U.S. 339, 346 (1879) (emphasis supplied). Proponents of the legislation noted that state courts were being used to harass and injure individuals, either because the state courts were powerless to stop deprivations or were in league with those who were bent upon abrogation of federally protected rights.

As Representative Lowe stated, the "records of the [state] tribunals are searched in vain for evidence of effective redress [of federally secured rights]. What less than this [the Civil Rights Act of 1871] will afford an adequate remedy? The federal government cannot serve a writ of mandamus upon state executives or upon state courts to compel them to protect the rights, privileges and immunities of citizens. . . . The case has arisen . . . when the federal government must resort to its own agencies to carry its own authority into execution. Hence this bill throws open the doors of the United States courts to those whose rights under the Constitution are denied or impaired." Cong. Globe, 42nd Cong., 1st Sess., 374–76 (1871). This view was echoed by Senator Osborn: "If the state courts had proven themselves competent to suppress the local disorders, or to maintain law and order, we should not have been called upon to legislate. . . . We are driven by existing facts to provide for the several states in the South what they have been unable to fully provide for themselves; i.e., the full and complete administration of justice in the courts. And the courts with reference to which we legislate must be the United States courts." Id. at 653. And Representative Perry concluded: "Sheriffs, having eyes to

---

[29] See generally Gressman, The Unhappy History of Civil Rights Legislation, 50 Mich.L.Rev. 1323 (1952); Note, 75 Yale L.J. 1007 (1966); F. Frankfurter & J. Landis, The Business of the Supreme Court: A Study in the Federal Judicial System 65 (1928). As one commentator has put it: "That statutory plan [of the 14th amendment and acts of Congress to enforce it] did supply the means of vindicating those rights [of person and property] through the instrumentalities of the federal government. . . . It did constitute the federal government the protector of the civil rights. . . ." TenBroek, at 185. See also K. Stampp, The Era of Reconstruction (1965).

see, see not; judges, having ears to hear, hear not; witnesses conceal the truth or falsify it; grand and petit juries act as if they might be accomplices. [A]ll the apparatus and machinery of civil government, all the processes of justice, skulk away as if government and justice were crimes and feared detection. Among the most dangerous things an injured party can do it to appeal to justice." Id. at App. 78.[31]

Those who opposed the act of 1871 clearly recognized that the proponents were extending federal power in an attempt to remedy the state courts' failure to secure federal rights. The debate was not about whether the predecessor of § 1983 extended to actions of state courts, but whether this innovation was necessary or desirable.

This legislative history makes evident that Congress clearly conceived that it was altering the relationship between the states and the nation with respect to the protection of federally created rights; it was concerned that state instrumentalities could not protect those rights; it realized that state officers might, in fact, be antipathetic to the vindication of those rights; and it believed that these failings extended to the state courts.

V

Section 1983 was thus a product of a vast transformation from the concepts of federalism that had prevailed in the late 18th century when the anti-injunction statute was enacted. The very purpose of § 1983 was to interpose the federal courts between the states and the people, as guardians of the people's federal rights—to protect the people from unconstitutional action under color of state law, "whether that action be executive, legislative, or judicial." *Ex parte Virginia*, supra at 346. In carrying out that purpose, Congress plainly authorized the federal courts to issue injunctions in § 1983 actions, by expressly authorizing a "suit in equity" as one of the means of redress. And this Court long ago recognized that federal injunctive relief against a state court proceeding can in some circumstances be essential to prevent great, immediate, and irreparable loss of a person's constitutional rights. Ex parte Young, 209 U.S. 123 (1908). For these reasons we conclude that, under the criteria established in our previous decisions construing the anti-injunction statute, § 1983 is an act of Congress that falls within the "expressly authorized" exception of that law.

In so concluding, we do not question or qualify in any way the principles of equity, comity, and federalism that must restrain a federal court when asked to enjoin a state court proceeding. These principles, in the context of state criminal prosecutions, were canvassed at length last Term in Younger v. Harris, 401 U.S. 37 (1971), and its companion

---

[31] Representative Coburn stated: "the United States courts are further above mere local influence than the county courts; their judges can act with more independence, cannot be put under terror as local judges can; their sympathies are not so nearly identified with those of the vicinage; the jurors are taken from the state, and not the neighborhood; they will be able to rise above prejudices or bad passions or terror more easily. . . ." Cong. Globe, 42nd Cong., 1st Sess., 460 (1871).

cases. They are principles that have been emphasized by this Court many times in the past. Today we decide only that the District Court in this case was in error in holding that, because of the anti-injunction statute, it was absolutely without power in this § 1983 action to enjoin a proceeding pending in a state court under any circumstances whatsoever.

The judgment is reversed and the case is remanded to the District Court for further proceedings consistent with this opinion.

It is so ordered.

MR. JUSTICE POWELL and MR. JUSTICE REHNQUIST took no part in the consideration or decision of this case.

MR. CHIEF JUSTICE BURGER, with whom MR. JUSTICE WHITE and MR. JUSTICE BLACKMUN join, concurring.

I concur in the opinion of the Court and add a few words to emphasize what the Court is and is not deciding today as I read the opinion. The Court holds only that 28 U.S.C. § 2283, which is an absolute bar to injunctions against state court proceedings in most suits, does not apply to a suit brought under 42 U.S.C. § 1983 seeking an injunction of state proceedings. But, as the Court's opinion has noted, it does nothing to "question or qualify in any way the principles of equity, comity, and federalism that must restrain a federal court when asked to enjoin a state court proceeding." In the context of pending state criminal proceedings, we held in Younger v. Harris, 401 U.S. 37 (1971), that these principles allow a federal court properly to issue an injunction in only a narrow class of circumstances. We have not yet reached or decided exactly how great a restraint is imposed by these principles on a federal court asked to enjoin state *civil* proceedings. Therefore, on remand in this case, it seems to me the District Court, before reaching a decision on the merits of appellant's claim, should properly consider whether general notions of equity or principles of federalism, similar to those invoked in *Younger*, prevent the issuance of an injunction against the state "nuisance abatement" proceedings in the circumstances of this case.

NOTES ON *MITCHUM v. FOSTER*

1. **Questions and Comments on *Mitchum*.** The Court's opinion in *Mitchum* emphasizes the extent to which § 1983 was intended to change the role of the federal courts vis-a-vis the state courts. Its third criterion for determining when an exception to the anti-injunction statute was "expressly authorized" was whether the statute under consideration "created a specific and uniquely federal right or remedy, enforceable in a federal court of equity, that could be frustrated if the federal court were not empowered to enjoin a state court proceeding." The Court noted that the proponents of § 1983 observed that "state courts were being used to harass and injure individuals, either because the state courts were powerless to stop deprivations or were in league

with those who were bent upon abrogation of federally protected rights." Representative Lowe was quoted approvingly to the effect that "this bill throws open the doors of the federal courts to those whose rights under the Constitution are denied or impaired." And the Court concluded:

> "This legislative history makes evident that Congress clearly conceived that it was altering the relationship between the states and the nation with respect to the protection of federally created rights; it was concerned that state instrumentalities could not protect those rights; it realized that state officers might, in fact, be antipathetic to the vindication of those rights; and it believed that these failings extended to the state courts."

Does this legislative history, and the Court's unanimous acceptance of its importance in interpreting § 2283, cast doubt on the correctness of the holding in *Younger*? Specifically, what is the Court's authority, given *Mitchum*, for limiting the occasions for federal intervention in state criminal proceedings to the "exceptions" recognized in *Younger* and its companions? To ask the same question from the other direction, could it be argued on the basis of the policies articulated in *Younger* that *Mitchum* was wrongly decided?

2. Relation to Other Remedies. Consider also the other federal remedies available to persons charged with state crimes at the time § 1983 was enacted. Direct review in the Supreme Court had been authorized since the First Judiciary Act in 1789, and the habeas corpus jurisdiction of the lower federal courts had been extended in 1867 to "all cases where any person may be restrained of his or her liberty in violation of the Constitution." The effect of the 1867 statute was to make habeas corpus available for the first time to persons held under state law. Habeas corpus for federal prisoners had been available since the First Judiciary Act.[a]

Today, virtually any federal ground on which an injunction against a state criminal proceeding might be thought justified would be cognizable in a habeas corpus petition to a federal district court. It has been clear at least since Ex parte Royall, 117 U.S. 241 (1886), however, that state remedies must be exhausted before relief can be granted by a federal court in a habeas corpus proceeding.[b] See Preiser v. Rodriguez, 411 U.S. 475 (1973), considered at page 1202, infra. Indeed, on one view, *Younger* can be regarded as merely an implementation of the policies that require exhaustion of state remedies before resort to federal habeas corpus.

Is it plausible to conclude, as the Court apparently did in *Mitchum*, that the Congress meant federal injunctive relief against state court

---

[a] Note, however, that in 1867 habeas may have been available to persons held under the judgment of a court only where the court lacked jurisdiction. The use of habeas to test the constitutionality of the statute on the basis of which a conviction had been rendered by a court dates at least from Ex parte Siebold, 100 U.S. 371 (1879).

[b] Although initially developed by the judiciary, the exhaustion requirement was codified in 1948. See 28 U.S.C. § 2254(b).

proceedings under § 1983 to be supplementary to remedies available on direct review by the Supreme Court and habeas corpus in the lower federal courts? Do the modern criteria for the availability of habeas corpus justify the Court's contemporary limitations on the availability of injunctive relief? In other words, can the historicity of *Mitchum* be reconciled with the policy-orientation of *Younger* and modern habeas corpus?

Of what relevance is the pendency of state proceedings to these questions? Note that § 2283 has been interpreted not to preclude federal court interference with the *institution* of litigation in the state courts. It is a prohibition on interference with state proceedings that are pending or that have been concluded when the federal suit is filed.[c] If this reading of § 2283 is correct, does the fact that § 1983 is an "express exception" to § 2283 mean that it is precisely in pending or concluded state proceedings that federal injunctive relief *ought* to be available? In other words, could one reasonably conclude that injunctive relief ought to be available under § 1983: (1) against the institution of state court proceedings (because § 2283 is not applicable) and (2) against the continuation of pending state proceedings or the implementation of concluded state proceedings (because § 1983 is an "express exception" to § 2283)?

3. Application of *Younger* to Civil Proceedings. Chief Justice Burger's concurrence in *Mitchum* noted that the Court had not yet decided "how great a restraint is imposed by [*Younger*] principles on a federal court asked to enjoin state *civil* proceedings" and that this was one of the issues that remained open for litigation on remand. This issue is postponed in these materials to subsection D, which begins at page 1223, infra. The next two subsections deal with additional questions that have arisen in the application of *Younger* to criminal proceedings.

SUBSECTION B: APPLICATION TO CRIMINAL PROCEEDINGS

STEFFEL v. THOMPSON
United States Supreme Court, 1974.
415 U.S. 452.

MR. JUSTICE BRENNAN delivered the opinion of the Court.

. . . This case presents the important question reserved in Samuels v. Mackell, 401 U.S. 66 (1971), whether declaratory relief is precluded when a state prosecution has been threatened, but is not pending, and a showing of bad-faith enforcement or other special circumstances has not been made.

----

[c] See Dombrowski v. Pfister, 380 U.S. 479, 484 n. 2 (1965).

Petitioner . . . filed a complaint in the District Court for the Northern District of Georgia [seeking] a declaratory judgment . . . that [the Georgia criminal trespass statute] was being applied in violation of petitioner's first and 14th amendment rights, and an injunction restraining respondents—the solicitor of the Civil and Criminal Court of DeKalb County, the chief of the DeKalb County Police, the owner of the North DeKalb Shopping Center, and the manager of that shopping center—from enforcing the statute so as to interfere with petitioner's constitutionally protected activities.

The parties stipulated to the relevant facts: On October 8, 1970, while petitioner and other individuals were distributing handbills protesting American involvement in Vietnam on an exterior sidewalk of the North DeKalb Shopping Center, shopping center employees asked them to stop handbilling and leave. They declined to do so, and police officers were summoned. The officers told them that they would be arrested if they did not stop handbilling. The group then left to avoid arrest. Two days later petitioner and a companion returned to the shopping center and again began handbilling. The manager of the center called the police, and petitioner and his companion were once again told that failure to stop their handbilling would result in their arrests. Petitioner left to avoid arrest. His companion stayed, however, continued handbilling, and was arrested and subsequently arraigned on a charge of criminal trespass . . . .[3] Petitioner alleged in his complaint that, although he desired to return to the shopping center to distribute handbills, he had not done so because of his concern that he, too, would be arrested . . . .

After hearing, the District Court denied all relief and dismissed the action . . . . The Court of Appeals . . . affirmed . . . . We granted certiorari and now reverse.

I

At the threshold we must consider whether petitioner presents an "actual controversy," a requirement imposed by art. III of the Constitution and the express terms of the Federal Declaratory Judgment Act, 28 U.S.C. § 2201.[9]

Unlike three of the appellees in *Younger v. Harris,* supra, petitioner has alleged threats of prosecution that cannot be characterized as "imaginary or speculative." He has been twice warned to stop handbil-

---

[3] We were advised at oral argument that the trial of petitioner's companion, Sandra Lee Becker, has been stayed pending decision of this case.

[9] Section 2201 provides:

"In a case of actual controversy within its jurisdiction, except with respect to Federal taxes, any court of the United States, upon the filing of an appropriate pleading, may declare the rights and other legal relations of any interested party seeking such declaration, whether or not further relief is or could be sought. Any such declaration shall have the force and effect of a final judgment or decree and shall be reviewable as such."

Section 2202 further provides:

"Further necessary or proper relief based on a declaratory judgment or decree may be granted, after reasonable notice and hearing, against any adverse party whose rights have been determined by such judgment."

ling that he claims is constitutionally protected and has been told by the police that if he again handbills at the shopping center and disobeys a warning to stop he will likely be prosecuted. The prosecution of petitioner's handbilling companion is ample demonstration that petitioner's concern with arrest has not been "chimerical." In these circumstances, it is not necessary that petitioner first expose himself to actual arrest or prosecution to be entitled to challenge a statute that he claims deters the exercise of his constitutional rights. Moreover, petitioner's challenge is to those specific provisions of state law which have provided the basis for threats of criminal prosecution against him. . . .

II

We now turn to the question of whether the District Court and the Court of Appeals correctly found petitioner's request for declaratory relief inappropriate.

Sensitive to principles of equity, comity, and federalism, we recognized in *Younger v. Harris,* supra, that federal courts should ordinarily refrain from enjoining ongoing state criminal prosecutions. We were cognizant that a pending state proceeding, in all but unusual cases, would provide the federal plaintiff with the necessary vehicle for vindicating his constitutional rights, and, in that circumstance, the restraining of an ongoing prosecution would entail an unseemly failure to give effect to the principle that state courts have the solemn responsibility, equally with the federal courts "to guard, enforce, and protect every right granted or secured by the Constitution of the United States. . . ." Robb v. Connolly, 111 U.S. 624 (1884). In *Samuels v. Mackell,* supra, the Court also found that the same principles ordinarily would be flouted by issuance of a federal declaratory judgment when a state proceeding was pending, since the intrusive effect of declaratory relief "will result in precisely the same interference with and disruption of state proceedings that the long-standing policy limiting injunctions was designed to avoid."[11] We therefore held in *Samuels* that, "in cases where the state criminal prosecution was begun prior to the federal suit, the same equitable principles relevant to the propriety of an injunction must be taken into consideration by federal district courts in determining whether to issue a declaratory judgment. . . ."

Neither *Younger* nor *Samuels,* however, decided the question whether federal intervention might be permissible in the absence of a pending state prosecution. . . . When no state criminal proceeding is pending at the time the federal complaint is filed, federal intervention does not result in duplicative legal proceedings or disruption of the state criminal justice system; nor can federal intervention, in that circumstance, be interpreted as reflecting negatively upon the state court's ability to enforce constitutional principles. In addition, while a

---

[11] The Court noted that under 28 U.S.C. § 2202 a declaratory judgment might serve as the basis for issuance of a later injunction to give effect to the declaratory judgment, see n.9, supra, and that a declaratory judgment might have a res judicata effect on the pending state proceeding.

pending state prosecution provides the federal plaintiff with a concrete opportunity to vindicate his constitutional rights, a refusal on the part of the federal courts to intervene when no state proceeding is pending may place the hapless plaintiff between the Scylla of intentionally flouting state law and the Charybdis of forgoing what he believes to be constitutionally protected activity in order to avoid becoming enmeshed in a criminal proceeding.

When no state proceeding is pending and thus considerations of equity, comity, and federalism have little vitality, the propriety of granting federal declaratory relief may properly be considered independently of a request for injunctive relief. Here, the Court of Appeals held that, because injunctive relief would not be appropriate since petitioner failed to demonstrate irreparable injury—a traditional prerequisite to injunctive relief—it followed that declaratory relief was also inappropriate. Even if the Court of Appeals correctly viewed injunctive relief as inappropriate—a question we need not reach today since petitioner has abandoned his request for that remedy—the court erred in treating the requests for injunctive and declaratory relief as a single issue. "[W]hen no state prosecution is pending and the only question is whether declaratory relief is appropriate, . . . the congressional scheme that makes the federal courts the primary guardians of constitutional rights, and the express congressional authorization of declaratory relief, afforded because it is a less harsh and abrasive remedy than the injunction, become the factors of primary significance." Perez v. Ledesma, 401 U.S. 82, 104 (1971) (separate opinion of Brennan, J.).

. . . That Congress plainly intended declaratory relief to act as an alternative to the strong medicine of the injunction and to be utilized to test the constitutionality of state criminal statutes in cases where injunctive relief would be unavailable is amply evidenced by the legislative history of the act . . . . The highlights of that history, particularly pertinent to our inquiry today, emphasize that:

> "[I]n 1934, without expanding or reducing the subject matter jurisdiction of the federal courts, or in any way diminishing the continuing vitality of *Ex parte Young* with respect to federal injunctions, Congress empowered the federal courts to grant a new remedy, the declaratory judgment. . . .

> "The express purpose of the Federal Declaratory Judgment Act was to provide a milder alternative to the injunction remedy. . . . Of particular significance on the question before us, the Senate report makes it even clearer that the declaratory judgment was designed to be available to test state criminal statutes in circumstances where an injunction would not be appropriate.

> ". . . Much of the hostility to federal injunctions referred to in the Senate report was hostility to their use against state officials seeking to enforce state regulatory statutes carrying criminal sanctions; this was the strong feeling that

produced the Three Judge Court Act in 1910, the Johnson Act of 1934, 28 U.S.C. § 1342, and the Tax Injunction Act of 1937, 28 U.S.C. § 1341. The Federal Declaratory Judgment Act was intended to provide an alternative to injunctions against state officials, except where there was a federal policy against federal adjudication of the class of litigation altogether. . . . Moreover, the Senate report's clear implication that declaratory relief would have been appropriate in Pierce v. Society of Sisters, 268 U.S. 510 (1925), and Village of Euclid v. Ambler Realty Co., 272 U.S. 365 (1926), both cases involving federal adjudication of the constitutionality of a state statute carrying criminal penalties, and the report's quotation from [another case which] involved anticipatory federal adjudication of the constitutionality of a state criminal statute, make it plain that Congress anticipated that the declaratory judgment procedure would be used by the federal courts to test the constitutionality of state criminal statutes." Perez v. Ledesma, 401 U.S. 82, 111–12, 115 (1971) (Separate opinion of Brennan, J.).[18]

It was this history that formed the backdrop to our decision in Zwickler v. Koota, 389 U.S. 241 (1967), where a state criminal statute was attacked on grounds of unconstitutional overbreadth and no state prosecution was pending against the federal plaintiff. There, we found error in a three-judge district court's considering, as a single question, the propriety of granting injunctive and declaratory relief. Although we noted that injunctive relief might well be unavailable under principles of equity jurisprudence canvassed in Douglas v. City of Jeannette, 319 U.S. 157 (1943), we held that "a federal district court has the duty to decide the appropriateness and the merits of the declaratory request irrespective of its conclusion as to the propriety of the issuance of the injunction." Only one year ago, we reaffirmed the *Zwickler v. Koota* holding in Roe v. Wade, 410 U.S. 113 (1973), and Doe v. Bolton, 410 U.S. 179 (1973). In those two cases, we declined to decide whether the district courts had properly denied to the federal plaintiffs, against whom no prosecutions were pending, injunctive relief restraining enforcement of the Texas and Georgia criminal abortion statutes; instead, we affirmed the issuance of declaratory judgments of unconstitutionality, anticipating that these would be given effect by state authorities. We said:

[18] As Professor Borchard, a principal proponent and author of the Federal Declaratory Judgment Act, said in a written statement introduced at the hearings on the act:

"It often happens that courts are unwilling to grant injunctions to restrain the enforcement of penal statutes or ordinances, and relegate the plaintiff to his option, either to violate the statute and take his chances in testing constitutionality on a criminal prosecution, or else to forgo, in the fear of prosecution, the exercise of his claimed rights. Into this dilemma no civilized legal system operating under a constitution should force any person. The court, in effect, by refusing an injunction informs the prospective victim that the only way to determine whether the suspect is a mushroom or a toadstool, is to eat it. Assuming that the plaintiff has a vital interest in the enforcement of the challenged statute or ordinance, there is no reason why a declaratory judgment should not be issued, instead of compelling a violation of the statute as a condition precedent to challenging its constitutionality."

"The Court has recognized that *different considerations* enter into a federal court's decision as to declaratory relief, on the one hand, and injunctive relief, on the other. Zwickler v. Koota, 389 U.S. 241, 252–255 (1967); Dombrowski v. Pfister, 380 U.S. 479 (1965)." *Roe v. Wade,* supra, at 166 (emphasis added).

The "different considerations" entering into a decision whether to grant declaratory relief have their origins in the preceding historical summary. First, as Congress recognized in 1934, a declaratory judgment will have a less intrusive effect on the administration of state criminal law. As we observed in Perez v. Ledesma, 401 U.S., at 124–26 (separate opinion of Brennan, J.):

"Of course, a favorable declaratory judgment may nevertheless be valuable to the plaintiff though it cannot make even an unconstitutional statute disappear. [T]he declaration does not necessarily bar prosecutions under the statute, as a broad injunction would. Thus, where . . . a federal court declares the statute unconstitutionally vague or overbroad, it may well be open to a state prosecutor, after the federal court decision, to bring a prosecution under the statute if he reasonably believes that the defendant's conduct is not constitutionally protected and that the state courts may give the statute a construction so as to yield a constitutionally valid conviction. . . . The persuasive force of the court's opinion and judgment may lead state prosecutors, courts, and legislators to reconsider their respective responsibilities toward the statute. Enforcement policies or judicial construction may be changed, or the legislature may repeal the statute and start anew. Finally, the federal court judgment may have some res judicata effect, though this point is not free from difficulty and the governing rules remain to be developed with a view to the proper workings of a federal system. What is clear, however, is that even though a declaratory judgment has 'the force and effect of a final judgment' it is a much milder form of relief than an injunction. Though it may be persuasive, it is not ultimately coercive; noncompliance with it may be inappropriate, but is not contempt."[19]

Second, engrafting upon the Declaratory Judgment Act a requirement that all of the traditional equitable prerequisites to the issuance of an injunction be satisfied before the issuance of a declaratory judgment is considered would defy Congress' intent to make declaratory relief available in cases where an injunction would be inappropriate. . . . Thus, the Court of Appeals was in error when it ruled that a

---

[19] The pending prosecution of petitioner's handbilling companion does not affect petitioner's action for declaratory relief. In Roe v. Wade, 410 U.S. 113 (1973), while the pending prosecution of Dr. Hallford under the Texas abortion law was found to render his action for declaratory and injunctive relief impermissible, this did not prevent our granting plaintiff Roe, against whom no action was pending, a declaratory judgment that the statute was unconstitutional.

failure to demonstrate irreparable injury—a traditional prerequisite to injunctive relief, having no equivalent in the law of declaratory judgments—precluded the granting of declaratory relief.

The only occasions where this Court has disregarded these "different considerations" and found that a preclusion of injunctive relief inevitably led to a denial of declaratory relief have been cases in which principles of federalism militated altogether against federal intervention in a class of adjudications. See Great Lakes Co. v. Huffman, 319 U.S. 293 (1943) (federal policy against interfering with the enforcement of state tax laws);[20] Samuels v. Mackell, 401 U.S. 66 (1971). In the instant case, principles of federalism not only do not preclude federal intervention, they compel it. Requiring the federal courts totally to step aside when no state criminal prosecution is pending against the federal plaintiff would turn federalism on its head. When federal claims are premised on 42 U.S.C. § 1983 and 28 U.S.C. § 1343(3)—as they are here—we have not required exhaustion of state judicial or administrative remedies, recognizing the paramount role Congress has assigned to the federal courts to protect constitutional rights. See, e.g., McNeese v. Board of Education, 373 U.S. 668 (1963); Monroe v. Pape, 365 U.S. 167 (1961). But exhaustion of state remedies is precisely what would be required if both federal injunctive and declaratory relief were unavailable in a case where no state prosecution had been commenced.

III

Respondents, however, . . . argue that, although it may be appropriate to issue a declaratory judgment when no state criminal proceeding is pending and the attack is upon the *facial validity* of a state criminal statute, such a step would be improper where, as here, the attack is merely upon the constitutionality of the statute as applied, since the state's interest in unencumbered enforcement of its laws outweighs the minimal federal interest in protecting the constitutional rights of only a single individual. We reject the argument.

[T]he state's concern with potential interference in the administration of its criminal laws is of lesser dimension when an attack is made upon the constitutionality of a state statute as applied. A declaratory judgment of a lower federal court that a state statute is invalid in toto—and therefore incapable of any valid application—or is overbroad or vague—and therefore no person can properly be convicted under the statute until it is given a narrowing or clarifying construction—will

---

[20] In *Great Lakes Co. v. Huffman*, employers sought a declaration that a state unemployment compensation scheme imposing a tax upon them was unconstitutional as applied. Although not relying on the precise terms of 28 U.S.C. § 41(1) (1940 ed.), now 28 U.S.C. § 1341, which ousts the district courts of jurisdiction to "enjoin, suspend or restrain the assessment, levy or collection of any tax under State law where a plain, speedy and efficient remedy may be had in the courts of such State," the Court, recognizing the unique effects of anticipatory adjudication on tax administration, held that declaratory relief should be withheld when the taxpayer was provided an opportunity to maintain a refund suit after payment of the disputed tax. "In contrast, there is no statutory counterpart of 28 U.S.C. § 1341 applicable to intervention in state criminal prosecutions." Perez v. Ledesma, 401 U.S. 82, 128 (1971) (separate opinion of Brennan, J.).

likely have a more significant potential for disruption of state enforcement policies than a declaration specifying a limited number of impermissible applications of the statute. While the federal interest may be greater when a state statute is attacked on its face, since there exists the potential for eliminating any broad-ranging deterrent effect on would-be actors, we do not find this consideration controlling. The solitary individual who suffers a deprivation of his constitutional rights is no less deserving of redress than one who suffers together with others.

We therefore hold that, regardless of whether injunctive relief may be appropriate, federal declaratory relief is not precluded when no state prosecution is pending and a federal plaintiff demonstrates a genuine threat of enforcement of a disputed state criminal statute, whether an attack is made on the constitutionality of the statute on its face or as applied. The judgment of the Court of Appeals is reversed, and the case is remanded for further proceedings consistent with this opinion.

It is so ordered.

MR. JUSTICE STEWART, with whom THE CHIEF JUSTICE joins, concurring.

While joining the opinion of the Court, I add a word by way of emphasis.

Our decision today must not be understood as authorizing the invocation of federal declaratory judgment jurisdiction by a person who thinks a state criminal law is unconstitutional, even if he genuinely feels "chilled" in his freedom of action by the law's existence, and even if he honestly entertains the subjective belief that he may now or in the future be prosecuted under it.

As the Court stated in Younger v. Harris, 401 U.S. 37, 52 (1971):

> "The power and duty of the judiciary to declare laws unconstitutional is in the final analysis derived from its responsibility for resolving concrete disputes brought before the courts for decision. . . ."

The petitioner in this case has succeeded in objectively showing that the threat of imminent arrest, corroborated by the actual arrest of his companion, has created an actual concrete controversy between himself and the agents of the state. He has, therefore, demonstrated "a genuine threat of enforcement of a disputed state criminal statute. . . ." Cases where such a "genuine threat" can be demonstrated will, I think, be exceedingly rare.

MR. JUSTICE WHITE, concurring.

I offer the following few words in light of Mr. Justice Rehnquist's concurrence in which he discusses . . . whether a federal court may enjoin a state criminal prosecution under a statute the federal court has earlier declared unconstitutional at the suit of the defendant now being prosecuted, and the question whether that declaratory judgment is res judicata in such a later filed state criminal action. . . .

At this writing at least, I would anticipate that a final declaratory judgment entered by a federal court holding particular conduct of the federal plaintiff to be immune on federal constitutional grounds from prosecution under state law should be accorded res judicata effect in any later prosecution of that very conduct. . . .

Neither can I at this stage agree that the federal court, having rendered a declaratory judgment in favor of the plaintiff, could not enjoin a later state prosecution for conduct that the federal court has declared immune. The Declaratory Judgment Act itself provides that a "declaration shall have the force and effect of a final judgment or decree," 28 U.S.C. § 2201; eminent authority anticipated that declaratory judgments would be res judicata, E. Borchard, Declaratory Judgments 10–11 (2d ed. 1941); and there is every reason for not reducing declaratory judgments to mere advisory opinions. . . . The statute provides for "[f]urther necessary or proper relief . . . against any adverse party whose rights have been determined by such judgment," 28 U.S.C. § 2202, and it would not seem improper to enjoin local prosecutors who refuse to observe adverse federal judgments. . . .

MR. JUSTICE REHNQUIST, with whom THE CHIEF JUSTICE joins, concurring.

I concur in the opinion of the Court. . . . Congress apparently was aware at the time it passed the [Declaratory Judgment Act] that persons threatened with state criminal prosecutions might choose to forgo the offending conduct and instead seek a federal declaration of their rights. Use of the declaratory judgment procedure in the circumstances presented by this case seems consistent with that congressional expectation.

. . . The Court quite properly leaves for another day whether the granting of a declaratory judgment by a federal court will have any subsequent res judicata effect or will perhaps support the issuance of a later federal injunction. But since possible resolutions of those issues would substantially undercut the principles of federalism reaffirmed in Younger v. Harris, 401 U.S 37 (1971), and preserved by the decision today, I feel it appropriate to add a few remarks.

First, the legislative history of the Declaratory Judgment Act and the Court's opinion in this case both recognize that the declaratory judgment procedure is an alternative to pursuit of the arguably illegal activity. There is nothing in the act's history to suggest that Congress intended to provide persons wishing to violate state laws with a federal shield behind which they could carry on their contemplated conduct. . . .

Second, I do not believe that today's decision can properly be raised to support the issuance of a federal injunction based upon a favorable declaratory judgment. The Court's description of declaratory relief as "'a milder alternative to the injunction remedy,'" having a "less intrusive effect on the administration of state criminal laws" than an injunction, indicates to me critical distinctions which make declaratory relief appropriate where injunctive relief would not be. . . .

A declaratory judgment is simply a statement of rights, not a binding order supplemented by continuing sanctions. State authorities may choose to be guided by the judgment of a lower federal court, but they are not compelled to follow the decision by threat of contempt or other penalties. If the federal plaintiff pursues the conduct for which he was previously threatened with arrest and is in fact arrested, he may not return the controversy to federal court, although he may, of course, raise the federal declaratory judgment in the state court for whatever value it may prove to have.[3] In any event, the defendant at that point is able to present his case for full consideration by a state court charged, as are the federal courts, to preserve the defendant's constitutional rights. Federal interference with this process would involve precisely the same concerns discussed in *Younger* and recited in the Court's opinion in this case.

Third, attempts to circumvent *Younger* by claiming that enforcement of a statute declared unconstitutional by a federal court is per se evidence of bad faith should not find support in the Court's decision in this case. . . .

If the declaratory judgment remains, as I think the Declaratory Judgment Act intended, a simple declaration of rights without more, it will not be used merely as a dramatic tactical maneuver on the part of any state defendant seeking extended delays. Nor will it force state officials to try cases time after time, first in the federal courts and then in the state courts. I do not believe Congress desired such unnecessary results, and I do not think that today's decision should be read to sanction them. Rather the act, and the decision, stand for the sensible proposition that both a potential state defendant, threatened with prosecution but not charged, and the state itself, confronted by a possible violation of its criminal laws, may benefit from a procedure which provides for a declaration of rights without activation of the criminal process. If the federal court finds that the threatened prosecution would depend upon a statute it judges unconstitutional, the state may decide to forgo prosecution of similar conduct in the future, believing the judgment persuasive. Should the state prosecutors not find the decision persuasive enough to justify forbearance, the successful federal plaintiff will at least be able to bolster his allegations of unconstitutionality in the state trial with a decision of the federal district court in the immediate locality. The state courts may find the reasoning convincing even though the prosecutors did not. Finally, of course, the state legislature may decide, on the basis of the federal decision, that the statute would be better amended or repealed. All these possible avenues of relief would be reached voluntarily by the states and would be completely consistent with . . . concepts of

---

[3] The Court's opinion notes that the possible res judicata effect of a federal declaratory judgment in a subsequent state court prosecution is a question " 'not free from difficulty.' " I express no opinion on that issue here. However, I do note that the federal decision would not be accorded the stare decisis effect in state court that it would have in a subsequent proceeding within the same federal jurisdiction. Although the state court would not be compelled to follow the federal holding, the opinion might, of course, be viewed as highly persuasive.

federalism . . . . Other more intrusive forms of relief should not be routinely available.

These considerations should prove highly significant in reaching future decisions based upon the decision rendered today. For the present it is enough to say, as the Court does, that petitioner . . . may maintain an action for a declaratory judgment in the District Court.

NOTES ON DECLARATORY AND EQUITABLE RELIEF AFTER *STEFFEL*

1. *Hicks v. Miranda.* *Steffel* made the availability of declaratory relief turn on whether a state prosecution was pending at the time federal intervention was sought. This rule was significantly adjusted in Hicks v. Miranda, 422 U.S. 332 (1975). The dispute began when the police, acting pursuant to warrants, seized four copies of the film "Deep Throat" from an adult theater in Orange County. Criminal charges were brought against two employees of the cinema, and judicial proceedings were begun to have the film declared legally obscene. After a hearing, the court determined that the film was obscene and ordered seized all copies that might be found at the theater. The theater owners did not appeal this judgment but went straight to federal court for a declaration of the obscenity statute's unconstitutionality, an injunction against its continued enforcement, and an order requiring return of the films. A three-judge court was convened to consider the constitutionality of the statute, at which point the state court amended the criminal complaint to name the theater owners as additional defendants in the criminal charges. The federal court nevertheless proceeded to judgment and granted the relief sought.

The Supreme Court reversed. Speaking through Justice White, the Court gave alternative grounds for requiring the dismissal of the federal proceedings. First, when the federal complaint was filed, the theater owners' interest was already at stake in a pending state prosecution: "[They] had a substantial stake in the state proceedings, so much so that they sought federal relief, demanding that the state statute be declared void and their films be returned to them." Under these circumstances, the owners could not avoid the rule of *Younger* merely because they had not been formally named as defendants prior to the federal suit.

The Court's second ground for decision was more far-reaching:

> "[O]n the day following the completion of service of the complaint, [the owners] were charged along with their employees in Municipal Court. Neither *Steffel v. Thompson* nor any other case in this Court has held that for *Younger v. Harris* to apply, the state criminal proceedings must be pending on the day the federal case is filed. Indeed, the issue has been left open; and we now hold that where state criminal proceedings are begun against the federal plaintiffs after the federal com-

plaint is filed but before any proceedings of substance on the merits have taken place in the federal court, the principles of *Younger v. Harris* should apply in full force. . . ."

This pronouncement sparked a dissent from Justice Stewart, joined by Justices Douglas, Brennan, and Marshall:

"There is, to be sure, something unseemly about having the applicability of the *Younger* doctrine turn solely on the outcome of a race to the courthouse. The rule the Court adopts today, however, does not eliminate that race; it merely permits the state to leave the mark later, run a shorter course, and arrive first at the finish line. This rule seems to me to result from a failure to evaluate the state and federal interests as of the time the state prosecution was commenced.

"As of the time when its jurisdiction is invoked in a *Steffel* situation, a federal court is called upon to vindicate federal constitutional rights when no other remedy is available to the federal plaintiff. The Court has recognized that at this point in the proceedings no substantial state interests counsel the federal court to stay its hand. . . . But there is nothing in our decision in *Steffel* that requires a state to stay its hand during the pendency of the federal litigation. If, in the interest of efficiency, the state wishes to refrain from actively prosecuting the criminal charge pending the outcome of the federal declaratory judgment suit, it may, of course, do so. But no decision of this Court requires it to make the choice.

"The Court today, however, goes much further than simply recognizing the right of the state to proceed with the orderly administration of its criminal law; it ousts the federal courts from their historic role as the 'primary reliances' for vindicating constitutional freedoms. This is no less offensive to 'Our Federalism' than the federal injunction restraining pending state criminal proceedings condemned in *Younger v. Harris*.

"The Court's new rule creates a reality which few state prosecutors can be expected to ignore. It is an open invitation to state officials to institute state proceedings in order to defeat federal jurisdiction. One need not impugn the motives of state officials to suppose that they would rather prosecute a criminal suit in state court than defend a civil case in a federal forum.

. . .

"The doctrine of *Younger v. Harris* reflects an accommodation of competing interests. The rule announced today distorts that balance beyond recognition."

2. *Doran v. Salem Inn.* Doran v. Salem Inn, Inc., 422 U.S. 922 (1975), was decided six days after *Hicks v. Miranda*. It involved three corporations operating topless bars in North Hempstead, Long Island. The town passed an ordinance against topless dancing, after which the corporations clad their dancers in bikini tops and brought a federal suit under § 1983 for a declaration of the invalidity of the ordinance and an injunction against its enforcement. The day after the complaint was filed, one of the bars resumed topless entertainment and was prosecuted under the ordinance. The District Court thereafter ruled the ordinance unconstitutional on its face under the first amendment and issued a preliminary injunction restraining its enforcement against all three corporations. The Court of Appeals affirmed, and the Supreme Court granted certiorari.

Justice Rehnquist wrote the opinion for the Court. With respect to the corporation that had been prosecuted, the Court held that *Younger* and *Hicks* were fully applicable, and that both injunctive and declaratory relief were therefore barred. That the federal action was actually begun first did not matter, for it was still "in an embryonic stage and no contested matter had been decided." Only Justice Douglas dissented from this portion of the opinion.

With respect to the other two corporations, the Court unanimously held that they were entitled to relief:

> "Under *Steffel* they . . . could at least have obtained a declaratory judgment upon an ordinary showing of entitlement to that relief. The District Court, however, did not grant declaratory relief . . ., but instead granted them preliminary injunctive relief. . . . We now hold that on the facts of this case the issuance of a preliminary injunction is not subject to the restrictions of *Younger*. [P]rior to final judgment there is no established declaratory remedy comparable to a preliminary injunction; unless preliminary relief is available upon a proper showing, plaintiffs in some situations may suffer unnecessary and substantial irreparable harm. Moreover, neither declaratory nor injunctive relief can directly interfere with enforcement of contested statutes or ordinances except with respect to the particular federal plaintiffs, and the state is free to prosecute others who may violate the statute.

> "The traditional standard for granting a preliminary injunction requires the plaintiff to show that in the absence of its issuance he will suffer irreparable injury and also that he is likely to prevail on the merits. . . . Although only temporary, the injunction does prohibit state and local enforcement activities against the federal plaintiff pending final resolution of his case in the federal court. [W]hile the standard to be applied by the District Court in deciding whether a plaintiff is entitled to a preliminary injunction is stringent, the standard of appellate review is simply whether the issuance of the injunction . . . constituted an abuse of discretion. . . ."

The Court then held that, while the question was "a close one," the District Court did not abuse its discretion as to either of the two elements that justified relief. The two corporations had sufficiently shown that they would suffer a substantial loss of business—"and perhaps even bankruptcy"—if they were not able to resume topless entertainment. And the ordinance was sufficiently broad so as to make out a "sufficient showing of the likelihood of ultimate success on the merits."[a]

3. Questions and Comments. The Court was nearly unanimous on the facts of both *Younger* and *Steffel,* though the Justices disagreed as to rationale. It was *Hicks* that produced the first close split. How should that case have been resolved? Does it create improper incentives for state prosecutors? Does it undermine the authority of the federal courts?

Given *Hicks,* the unanimity of the Court in *Doran* may be the most surprising result of all. It would appear—assuming that irreparable harm and the likelihood of success on the merits can be shown—that a person who has not yet violated a criminal statute may obtain a preliminary injunction and then engage in the conduct under the protection of the injunction until the federal case is resolved on the merits. Of course, the plaintiff risks prosecution if the federal case is lost. But if declaratory relief is ultimately obtained, the plaintiff has successfully avoided state court resolution of the controversy and at the same time enjoyed the benefits of engaging in the conduct prohibited by the state statute. Is this consistent with *Hicks*? Would the same strategy be permitted by one who has violated the statute but seeks to repeat his or her conduct?

4. The Relevance of State Appellate Proceedings. In Huffman v. Pursue, Ltd., 420 U.S. 592 (1975), the Court concluded that there was a pending state proceeding, even though final judgment had been entered in the trial court. Justice Rehnquist explained:

> "Virtually all of the evils at which *Younger* is directed would inhere in federal intervention prior to completion of state appellate proceedings, just as surely as they would if such intervention occurred at or before trial. Intervention at the later stage is if anything more highly duplicative, since an entire trial has already taken place, and it is also a direct aspersion on the capabilities and good faith of state appellate courts. Nor, in these state-initiated nuisance proceedings, is federal intervention at the appellate stage any the less a disruption of the state's efforts to protect interests which it deems important. Indeed, it is likely to be even more disruptive and offensive because the state has already won a nisi prius determination that its valid policies are being violated in a fashion which justifies judicial abatement."[b]

5. *Wooley v. Maynard.* *Huffman* was distinguished on this point in Wooley v. Maynard, 430 U.S. 705 (1977). George and Maxine Maynard had religious objections to the "Live Free or Die" motto displayed on state license plates. George put tape over those words and

---

[a] The Court noted that the District Court judgment "spoke in terms of actually holding the ordinance unconstitutional, but in the context of a preliminary injunction the court must have intended to refer only to the likelihood that [the corporations] ulti- mately would prevail. The Court of Appeals properly clarified this point."

[b] This aspect of *Huffman* is criticized in Soifer and Macgill, The *Younger* Doctrine: Reconstructing Reconstruction, 55 Tex. L. Rev. 1141, 1182–85 (1977).

was three times convicted of obscuring a license. None of these convictions was appealed. The Maynards then sued in federal court under § 1983 to enjoin future enforcement of the state statute. A temporary restraining order was issued, and was eventually followed by permanent injunctive relief.

In the Supreme Court, the state invoked *Huffman* for the proposition that the state prosecution remained pending until the defendant exhausted state appellate remedies, but the Court disagreed. Speaking for the Court, Chief Justice Burger noted that in *Huffman*, the plaintiff had sought to prevent enforcement of the state court judgment declaring the theater a public nuisance. In *Wooley,* by contrast, plaintiffs sought only prospective relief. Mr. Maynard's sentences had been served, and he sought no revision of his record or other retrospective relief. Since the Maynards sought "only to be free from prosecutions for future violations," the fact that he had been prosecuted in the past did not bar federal relief.

Justice White, joined by Justices Rehnquist and Blackmun, dissented. He appeared to accept the proposition that a declaratory judgment would have been proper under *Steffel v. Thompson,* but argued that no "unusual circumstances" had been shown to justify injunctive relief. Cf. Doran v. Salem Inn, Inc., 422 U.S. 922 (1975), discussed in note 2, supra.

Is the line between *Huffman* and *Wooley* clear? Does *Wooley* follow from *Steffel?*

SUBSECTION C: DAMAGES SUITS AND HABEAS CORPUS

PREISER v. RODRIGUEZ
United States Supreme Court, 1973.
411 U.S. 475.

MR. JUSTICE STEWART delivered the opinion of the Court.

The respondents in this case were state prisoners who were deprived of good-conduct-time credits by the New York State Department of Correctional Services as a result of disciplinary proceedings. They then brought actions in a federal district court, pursuant to the Civil Rights Act of 1871, 42 U.S.C. § 1983. Alleging that the department had acted unconstitutionally in depriving them of the credits, they sought injunctive relief to compel restoration of the credits, which in each case would result in their immediate release from confinement in prison. [The District Court granted the requested relief, the Court of Appeals affirmed, and the Supreme Court granted certiorari.] The question before us is whether state prisoners seeking such redress may obtain equitable relief under the Civil Rights Act, even though the federal habeas corpus statute, 28 U.S.C. § 2254, clearly provides a specific federal remedy.

The question is of considerable practical importance. For if a remedy under the Civil Rights Act is available, a plaintiff need not first seek redress in a state forum. If, on the other hand, habeas corpus is the exclusive federal remedy in these circumstances, then a plaintiff cannot seek the intervention of a federal court until he has first sought and been denied relief in the state courts, if a state remedy is available and adequate. 28 U.S.C. § 2254(b). . . .

The problem involves the interrelationship of two important federal laws. The relevant habeas corpus statutes are 28 U.S.C. §§ 2241 and 2254. Section 2241(c)(3) provides that "[t]he writ of habeas corpus shall not extend to a prisoner unless [h]e is in custody in violation of the Constitution or laws or treaties of the United States. . . ." Section 2254 provides in pertinent part:

"(a) [A] district court shall entertain an application for a writ of habeas corpus in behalf of a person in custody pursuant to the judgment of a State court only on the ground that he is in custody in violation of the Constitution or laws or treaties of the United States.

"(b) An application for a writ of habeas corpus in behalf of a person in custody pursuant to the judgment of a state court shall not be granted unless it appears that the applicant has exhausted the remedies available in the courts of the State, or that there is either an absence of available state corrective process or the existence of circumstances rendering such process ineffective to protect the rights of the prisoner.

"(c) An applicant shall not be deemed to have exhausted the remedies available in the courts of the State, within the meaning of this section, if he has the right under the law of the State to raise, by any available procedure, the question presented."

The Civil Rights Act, 42 U.S.C. § 1983, provides:

"Every person who, under color of any statute, ordinance, regulation, custom, or usage, of any State or Territory, subjects, or causes to be subjected, any citizen . . . or other person . . . to the deprivation of any rights, privileges, or immunities secured by the Constitution and laws, shall be liable to the party injured in an action at law, suit in equity, or other proper proceeding for redress."

It is clear, not only from the language of §§ 2241(c)(3) and 2254(a), but also from the common-law history of the writ, that the essence of habeas corpus is an attack by a person in custody upon the legality of that custody, and that the traditional function of the writ is to secure release from illegal custody. . . .

By the time the American colonies achieved independence, the use of habeas corpus to secure release from unlawful physical confinement

. . . was . . . an integral part of our common-law heritage. The writ was given explicit recognition in the suspension clause of the Constitution, art. I, § 9, cl. 2; was incorporated in the first congressional grant of jurisdiction to the federal courts; and was early recognized by this Court as a "great constitutional privilege."

The original view of a habeas corpus attack upon detention under a judicial order was a limited one. The relevant inquiry was confined to determining simply whether or not the committing court had been possessed of jurisdiction. But, over the years, the writ of habeas corpus evolved as a remedy available to effect discharge from any confinement contrary to the Constitution or fundamental law, even though imposed pursuant to conviction by a court of competent jurisdiction. Thus, whether the petitioner's challenge to his custody is that the statute under which he stands convicted is unconstitutional; that he has been imprisoned prior to trial on account of a defective indictment against him; that he is unlawfully confined in the wrong institution; that he was denied his constitutional rights at trial; that his guilty plea was invalid; that he is being unlawfully detained by the executive or the military; or that his parole was unlawfully revoked, causing him to be reincarcerated in prison—in each case his grievance is that he is being unlawfully subjected to physical restraint, and in each case habeas corpus has been accepted as the specific instrument to obtain release from such confinement.

In the case before us, the respondents' suits in the District Court fell squarely within this traditional scope of habeas corpus. They alleged that the deprivation of their good-conduct-time credits was causing or would cause them to be in illegal physical confinement, i.e., that once their conditional-release date had passed, any further detention of them in prison was unlawful; and they sought restoration of those good-time credits, which, by the time the District Court ruled on their petitions, meant their immediate release from physical custody.

Even if the restoration of the respondents' credits would not have resulted in their immediate release, but only in shortening in length of their actual confinement in prison, habeas corpus would have been their appropriate remedy. For recent cases have established that habeas corpus relief is not limited to immediate release from illegal custody, but that the writ is available as well to attack future confinement and obtain future releases. . . . So, even if restoration of respondents' good-time credits had merely shortened the length of their confinement, rather than required immediate discharge from that confinement, their suits would still have been within the core of habeas corpus in attacking the very duration of their physical confinement itself. It is beyond doubt, then, that the respondents could have sought and obtained fully effective relief through federal habeas corpus proceedings.

Although conceding that they could have proceeded by way of habeas corpus, the respondents argue that the Court of Appeals was correct in holding that they were nonetheless entitled to bring their suits under § 1983 so as to avoid the necessity of first seeking relief in a state forum. Pointing to the broad language of § 1983, they argue that since their complaints plainly came within the literal terms of that statute, there is no justifiable reason to exclude them from the broad remedial protection provided by that law. According to the respondents, state prisoners seeking relief under the Civil Rights Act should be treated no differently from any other civil rights plaintiffs, when the language of the act clearly covers their causes of action.

The broad language of § 1983, however, is not conclusive of the issue before us. The statute is a general one, and, despite the literal applicability of its terms, the question remains whether the specific federal habeas corpus statute, explicitly and historically designed to provide the means for a state prisoner to attack the validity of his confinement, must be understood to be the exclusive remedy available in a situation like this where it so clearly applies. The respondents' counsel acknowledged at oral argument that a state prisoner challenging his underlying conviction and sentence on federal constitutional grounds in a federal court is limited to habeas corpus. It was conceded that he cannot bring a § 1983 action, even though the literal terms of § 1983 might seem to cover such a challenge, because Congress has passed a more specific act to cover that situation, and, in doing so, has provided that a state prisoner challenging his conviction must first seek relief in a state forum, if a state remedy is available. It is clear to us that the result must be the same in the case of a state prisoner's challenge to the fact or duration of his confinement, based, as here, upon the alleged unconstitutionality of state administrative action. Such a challenge is just as close to the core of habeas corpus as an attack on the prisoner's conviction, for it goes directly to the constitutionality of his physical confinement itself and seeks either immediate release from that confinement or the shortening of its duration.

In amending the habeas corpus laws in 1948, Congress clearly required exhaustion of adequate state remedies as a condition precedent to the invocation of federal judicial relief under those laws. It would wholly frustrate explicit congressional intent to hold that the respondents in the present case could evade this requirement by the simple expedient of putting a different label on their pleadings. In short, Congress has determined that habeas corpus is the appropriate remedy for state prisoners attacking the validity of the fact or length of their confinement, and that specific determination must override the general terms of § 1983.

The policy reasons underlying the habeas corpus statute support this conclusion. The respondents concede that the reason why only habeas corpus can be used to challenge a state prisoner's underlying conviction is the strong policy requiring exhaustion of state remedies in that situation—to avoid the unnecessary friction between the federal and state court systems that would result if a lower federal court upset a state court conviction without first giving the state court system an opportunity to correct its own constitutional errors. But they argue that this concern applies only to federal interference with state court convictions; and to support this argument, they quote from Ex parte Royall, 117 U.S. 241 (1886), the case that first mandated exhaustion of state remedies as a precondition to federal habeas corpus:

"The injunction to hear the case summarily, and thereupon 'to dispose of the party as law and justice require' does not deprive the court of discretion as to the time and mode in which it will exert the powers conferred upon it. That discretion should be exercised in the light of the relations existing, under our system of government, *between the judicial tribunals of the union and of the states,* and in recognition of the fact that the public good requires that those relations be not disturbed by *unnecessary conflict between courts* equally bound to guard and protect rights secured by the Constitution." (Emphasis added).

In the respondents' view, the whole purpose of the exhaustion requirement, now codified in § 2254(b), is to give state *courts* the first chance at remedying *their own* mistakes, and thereby to avoid "the unseemly spectacle of federal district courts trying the regularity of proceedings had in *courts* of coordinate jurisdiction." This policy, the respondents contend, does not apply when the challenge is not to the action of a state court, but, as here, to the action of a state administrative body. In that situation, they say, the concern with avoiding unnecessary interference by one court with the courts of another sovereignty with concurrent powers, and the importance of giving state courts the first opportunity to correct constitutional errors made by them, do not apply; and hence the purpose of the exhaustion requirement of the habeas corpus statute is inapplicable.

We cannot agree. The respondents, we think, view the reasons for the exhaustion requirement of § 2254(b) far too narrowly. The rule of exhaustion in federal habeas corpus actions is rooted in considerations of federal-state comity. That principle was defined in Younger v. Harris, 401 U.S. 37, 44 (1971), as "a proper respect for state functions," and it has as much relevance in areas of particular state administrative concern as it does where state judicial action is being attacked. . . .

It is difficult to imagine an activity in which a state has a stronger interest, or one that is more intricately bound up with state laws, regulations, and procedures, than the administration of its prisoners. The relationship of state prisoners and the state officers who supervise their confinement is far more intimate than that of a state and a private citizen. For state prisoners, eating, sleeping, dressing, washing, working, and playing are all done under the watchful eye of the state, and so the possibilities for litigation under the 14th amendment are boundless. What for a private citizen would be a dispute with his landlord, with his employer, with his tailor, with his neighbor, or with his banker becomes, for the prisoner, a dispute with the state. Since these internal problems of state prisons involve issues so peculiarly within state authority and expertise, the states have an important interest in not being bypassed in the correction of these problems. Moreover, because most potential litigation involving state prisoners arises on a day-to-day basis, it is most efficiently and properly handled by the state administrative bodies and state courts, which are, for the most part, familiar with the grievances of state prisoners and in a better physical and practical position to deal with those grievances. In New York, for example, state judges sit on a regular basis at all but one of the state's correctional facilities, and thus inmates may present their grievances to a court at the place of their confinement, where the relevant records are available and where potential witnesses are located. The strong considerations of comity that require giving a state court system that has convicted a defendant the first opportunity to correct its own errors thus also require giving the states the first opportunity to correct the errors made in the internal administration of their prisons.[10]

[T]he respondents contend that confining state prisoners to federal habeas corpus, after first exhausting state remedies, could deprive those prisoners of any damages remedy to which they might be entitled for their mistreatment, since damages are not available in federal habeas corpus proceedings, and New York provides no damages remedy at all for state prisoners. In the respondents' view, if habeas corpus is the exclusive federal remedy for a state prisoner attacking his confinement, damages might never be obtained, at least where the state makes no provision for them. They argue that even if such a prisoner were to bring a subsequent federal civil rights action for damages, that action could be barred by principles of res judicata where the state courts had previously made an adverse determination of his underlying claim, even though a federal habeas court had later granted him relief on habeas corpus.

The answer to this contention is that the respondents here sought no damages, but only equitable relief—restoration of their good-time credits—and our holding today is limited to that situation. If a state prisoner is seeking damages, he is attacking something other than the fact or length of his confinement, and he is seeking something other than immediate or more speedy release—the traditional purpose of habeas corpus. In the case of a damages claim, habeas corpus is *not* an appropriate or available federal remedy. Accordingly, as petitioners themselves concede, a damages action by a state prisoner could be brought under the Civil Rights Act in federal court without any requirement of prior exhaustion of state remedies. . . .

[10] The dissent argues that the respondents' attacks on the actions of the prison administration here are no different, in terms of the potential for exacerbating federal-state relations, from the attacks made by the petitioners in McNeese v. Board of Education, 373 U.S. 668 (1963), Damico v. California, 389 U.S. 416 (1967), and Monroe v. Pape, 365 U.S. 167 (1961), on the various state administrative actions there. Thus, it is said, since exhaustion of state remedies was not required in those cases, it is anomalous to require it here. The answer, of course, is that in those cases, brought pursuant to § 1983, no other, more specific federal statute was involved that might have reflected a different congressional intent. In the present case, however, the respondents' actions fell squarely within the traditional purpose of federal habeas corpus, and Congress has made the specific determination in § 2254(b) that requiring the exhaustion of adequate state remedies in such cases will best serve the policies of federalism.

Principles of res judicata are, of course, not wholly applicable to habeas corpus proceedings. 28 U.S.C. § 2254(d). Hence, a state prisoner in the respondents' situation who has been denied relief in the state courts is not precluded from seeking habeas relief on the same claims in federal court. On the other hand, res judicata has been held to be fully applicable to a civil rights action brought under § 1983. Accordingly, there would be an inevitable incentive for a state prisoner to proceed at once in federal court by way of a civil rights action, lest he lose his right to do so. This would have the unfortunate dual effect of denying the state prison administration and the state courts the opportunity to correct the errors committed in the state's own prisons, and of isolating those bodies from an understanding of and hospitality to the federal claims of state prisoners in situations such as those before us. Federal habeas corpus, on the other hand, serves the important function of allowing the state to deal with these peculiarly local problems on its own, while preserving for the state prisoner an expeditious federal forum for the vindication of his federally protected rights, if the state has denied redress.

The respondents place a great deal of reliance on our recent decisions upholding the right of state prisoners to bring federal civil rights actions to challenge the conditions of their confinement. Cooper v. Pate, 378 U.S. 546 (1964); Houghton v. Shafer, 392 U.S. 639 (1968); Wilwording v. Swenson, 404 U.S. 249 (1971); Haines v. Kerner, 404 U.S. 519 (1972). But none of the state prisoners in those cases was challenging the fact or duration of his physical confinement itself, and none was seeking immediate release or a speedier release from that confinement—the heart of habeas corpus. In *Cooper,* the prisoner alleged that, solely because of his religious beliefs, he had been denied permission to purchase certain religious publications and had been denied other privileges enjoyed by his fellow prisoners. In *Houghton,* the prisoner's contention was that prison authorities had violated the Constitution by confiscating legal materials which he had acquired for pursuing his appeal, but which, in violation of prison rules, had been found in the possession of another prisoner. In *Wilwording,* the prisoners' complaints related solely to their living conditions and disciplinary measures while confined in maximum security. And in *Haines,* the prisoner claimed that prison officials had acted unconstitutionally by placing him in solitary confinement as a disciplinary measure, and he sought damages for claimed physical injuries sustained while so segregated. It is clear then, that in all those cases, the prisoners' claims related solely to the states' alleged unconstitutional treatment of them while in confinement. None sought, as did the respondents here, to challenge the very fact or duration of the confinement itself. Those cases, therefore, merely establish that a § 1983 action is a proper remedy for a state prisoner who is making a constitutional challenge to the conditions of his prison life, but not to the fact or length of his custody. Upon that understanding, we reaffirm those holdings.[14]

[14] If a prisoner seeks to attack both the conditions of his confinement and the fact or length of that confinement, his latter claim, under our decision today, is cogniza-

This is not to say that habeas corpus may not also be available to challenge such prison conditions. See Johnson v. Avery, 393 U.S. 483 (1969); *Wilwording v. Swenson,* supra. When a prisoner is put under additional and unconstitutional restraints during his lawful custody, it is arguable that habeas corpus will lie to remove the restraints making the custody illegal. See Note, Developments in the Law—Habeas Corpus, 83 Harv. L. Rev. 1038, 1084 (1970).

But we need not in this case explore the appropriate limits of habeas corpus as an alternative remedy to a proper action under § 1983. That question is not before us. What is involved here is the extent to which § 1983 is a permissible alternative to the traditional remedy of habeas corpus. Upon that question, we hold today that when a state prisoner is challenging the very fact or duration of his physical imprisonment, and the relief he seeks is a determination that he is entitled to immediate release or a speedier release from that imprisonment, his sole federal remedy is a writ of habeas corpus. Accordingly, we reverse the judgment before us.

It is so ordered.

MR. JUSTICE BRENNAN with whom MR. JUSTICE DOUGLAS and MR. JUSTICE MARSHALL join, dissenting.

The question presented by this case is one that I, like the Court of Appeals, had thought already resolved by our decision last term in Wilwording v. Swenson, 404 U.S. 249 (1971). We held there that the Ku Klux Klan Act of 1871, 42 U.S.C. § 1983; 28 U.S.C. § 1343(3), confers jurisdiction on the United States district courts to entertain a state prisoner's application for injunctive relief against allegedly unconstitutional conditions of confinement. At the same time, we held that "[t]he remedy provided by these acts 'is supplementary to the state remedy, and the latter need not be first sought and refused before the federal one is invoked.' State prisoners are not held to any stricter standard of exhaustion than other civil rights plaintiffs."

Regrettably, the Court today eviscerates that proposition by drawing a distinction that is both analytically unsound and, I fear, unworkable in practice. The net effect of the distinction is to preclude respondents from maintaining these actions under § 1983, leaving a petition for writ of habeas corpus the only available federal remedy. As a result, respondents must exhaust state remedies before their claims can be heard in a federal district court. I remain committed to the principles set forth in *Wilwording v. Swenson* and I therefore respectfully dissent. . . .

The Court's conclusion that *Wilwording* is not controlling is assertedly justified by invocation of a concept, newly invented by the Court today, variously termed the "core of habeas corpus," the "heart of habeas corpus," and the "essence of habeas corpus." In the Court's

ble only in federal habeas corpus, with its attendant requirement of exhaustion of state remedies. But, consistent with our prior decisions, that holding in no way precludes him from simultaneously litigating in federal court, under § 1983, his claim relating to the conditions of his confinement.

view, an action lying at the "core of habeas corpus" is one that "goes directly to the constitutionality of [the prisoner's] physical confinement itself and seeks either immediate release from that confinement or the shortening of its duration." With regard to such actions, habeas corpus is now considered the prisoner's exclusive remedy. . . .

At bottom, the Court's holding today rests on an understandable apprehension that the no-exhaustion rule of § 1983 might, in the absence of some limitation, devour the exhaustion rule of the habeas corpus statute. The problem arises because the two statutes necessarily overlap. Indeed, every application by the state prisoner for federal habeas corpus relief against his jailers could, as a matter of logic and semantics, be viewed as an action under the Ku Klux Klan Act to obtain injunctive relief against "the deprivation," by one acting under color of state law, "of any rights, privileges, or immunities secured by the Constitution and laws" of the United States. 42 U.S.C. § 1983. To prevent state prisoners from nullifying the habeas corpus exhaustion requirement by invariably styling their petitions as pleas for relief under § 1983, the Court today devises an ungainly and irrational scheme that permits some prisoners to sue under § 1983, while others may proceed only by way of petition for habeas corpus. And the entire scheme operates in defiance of the purposes underlying both the exhaustion requirement of habeas corpus and the absence of a comparable requirement under § 1983.

II[a]

Putting momentarily to one side the grave analytic shortcomings of the Court's approach, it seems clear that the scheme's unmanageability is sufficient reason to condemn it. For the unfortunate but inevitable legacy of today's opinion is a perplexing set of uncertainties and anomalies. And the nub of the problem is the definition of the Court's new-found and essentially ethereal concept, the "core of habeas corpus." . . .

Between a suit for damages and an attack on the conviction itself or on the deprivation of good-time credits are cases where habeas corpus is an appropriate and available remedy, but where the action falls outside the "core of habeas corpus" because the attack is directed at the conditions of confinement, not at its fact or duration. Notwithstanding today's decision, a prisoner may challenge, by suit under § 1983, prison living conditions and disciplinary measures, or confiscation of legal materials, or impairment of the right to free exercise of religion, even though federal habeas corpus is available as an alternative remedy. It should be plain enough that serious difficulties will arise whenever a prisoner seeks to attack in a single proceeding both the conditions of his confinement and the deprivation of good-time credits. And the addition of a plea for monetary damages exacerbates the problem.

---

[a] Part I of Justice Brennan's opinion, in which he noted that the majority left *Wilwording* "unimpaired" where the challenge is merely to the conditions of confinement, has been omitted. [Footnote by eds.]

If a prisoner's sole claim is that he was placed in solitary confinement pursuant to an unconstitutional disciplinary procedure, he can obtain federal injunctive relief and monetary damages in an action under § 1983. The unanswered question is whether he loses the right to proceed under § 1983 if, as punishment for his alleged misconduct, his jailers have not only subjected him to unlawful segregation and thereby inflicted an injury that is compensable in damages, but have compounded the wrong by improperly depriving him of good-time credits. Three different approaches are possible.

First, we might conclude that jurisdiction under § 1983 is lost whenever good-time credits are involved, even where the action is based primarily on the need for monetary relief or an injunction against continued segregation. If that is the logic of the Court's opinion, then the scheme creates an undeniable, and in all likelihood irresistible, incentive for state prison officials to defeat the jurisdiction of the federal courts by adding the deprivation of good-time credits to whatever other punishment is imposed. And if all of the federal claims must be held in abeyance pending exhaustion of state remedies, a prisoner's subsequent effort to assert a damages claim under § 1983 might arguably be barred by principles of res judicata. To avoid the loss of his damages claim, a prisoner might conclude that he should make no mention of the good-time issue and instead seek only damages in a § 1983 action. That approach (assuming it would not be disallowed as a subterfuge to circumvent the exhaustion requirement) creates its own distressing possibilities. For, having obtained decision in federal court on the issue of damages, the prisoner would presumably be required to repair to state court in search of his lost good-time credits, returning once again to federal court if his state court efforts should prove unavailing.

Moreover, a determination that no federal claim can be raised where good-time credits are at stake would give rise to a further anomaly. If the prisoner is confined in an institution that does not offer good-time credits, and therefore cannot withdraw them, his prison-conditions claims could always be raised in a suit under § 1983. On the other hand, an inmate in an institution that uses good-time credits as reward and punishment, who seeks a federal hearing on the identical legal and factual claims, would normally be required to exhaust state remedies and then proceed by way of federal habeas corpus. The rationality of that difference in treatment is certainly obscure. Yet that is the price of permitting the availability of a federal forum to be controlled by the happenstance (or stratagem) that good-time credits are at stake.

As an alternative, we might reject outright the premises of the first approach and conclude that a plea for money damages or for an injunction against continued segregation is sufficient to bring all related claims, including the question of good-time credits, under the umbrella of § 1983. That approach would, of course, simplify matters considerably. And it would make unnecessary the fractionation of the prisoner's claims into a number of different issues to be resolved in duplicative proceedings in state and federal courts. Nevertheless, the approach would seem to afford a convenient means of sidestepping the basic thrust of the Court's opinion, and we could surely expect state prisoners routinely to add to their other claims a plea for monetary relief. So long as the prisoner could formulate at least a colorable damages claim, he would be entitled to litigate all issues in federal court without first exhausting state remedies.

In any event, the Court today rejects, perhaps for the reasons suggested above, both of the foregoing positions. Instead, it holds that insofar as a prisoner's claim relates to good-time credits, he is required to exhaust state remedies; but he is not precluded from simultaneously litigating in federal court, under § 1983, his claim for monetary damages or an injunction against continued segregation. Under that approach, state correctional authorities have no added incentive to withdraw goodtime credits, since that action cannot, standing alone, keep the prisoner out of federal court. And, at the same time, it does not encourage a prisoner to assert an unnecessary claim for damages or injunctive relief as a means of bringing his good-time claim under the purview of § 1983. Nevertheless, this approach entails substantial difficulties—perhaps the greatest difficulties of the three. In the first place, its extreme inefficiency is readily apparent. For in many instances a prisoner's claims will be under simultaneous consideration in two distinct forums, even though the identical legal and factual questions are involved in both proceedings. Thus, if a prisoner's punishment for some alleged misconduct is both a term in solitary and the deprivation of good-time credits, and if he believes that the punishment was imposed pursuant to unconstitutional disciplinary procedures, he can now litigate the legality of those procedures simultaneously in state court (where he seeks restoration of good-time credits) and in federal court (where he seeks damages or an injunction against continued segregation). Moreover, if the federal court is the first to reach decision, and if that court concludes that the procedures are, in fact, unlawful, then the entire state proceeding must be immediately aborted, even though the state court may have devoted substantial time and effort to its consideration of the case. By the same token, if traditional principles of res judicata are applicable to suits under § 1983, the prior conclusion of the state court suit would effectively set at naught the entire federal court proceeding. This is plainly a curious prescription for improving relations between state and federal courts.

Since some of the ramifications of this new approach are still unclear, the unfortunate outcome of today's decision—an outcome that might not be immediately surmised from the seeming simplicity of the basic concept, the "core of habeas corpus"—is almost certain to be the further complication of prison-conditions litigation. In itself that is disquieting enough. But it is especially distressing that the remaining questions will have to be resolved on the basis of pleadings, whether in habeas corpus or suit under § 1983, submitted by state prisoners, who will often have to cope with these questions without even minimal assistance of counsel.

III

. . . The concern that § 1983 not be used to nullify the habeas corpus exhaustion doctrine is, of course, legitimate. But our effort to preserve the integrity of the doctrine must rest on an understanding of the purposes that underlie it. In my view, the Court misapprehends these fundamental purposes and compounds the problem by paying insufficient attention to the reasons why exhaustion of state remedies is not required in suits under § 1983. As a result, the Court mistakenly concludes that allowing suit under § 1983 would jeopardize the purposes of the exhaustion rule.

By enactment of the Ku Klux Klan Act in 1871, and again by the grant in 1875 of original federal-question jurisdiction to the federal courts, Congress recognized important interests in permitting a plaintiff to choose a federal forum in cases arising under federal law. . . .

This grant of jurisdiction was designed to preserve and enhance the expertise of federal courts in applying federal law; to achieve greater uniformity of results; and, since federal courts are "more likely to apply federal law sympathetically and understandingly than are state courts," to minimize misapplications of federal law.

In the service of the same interests, we have taken care to emphasize that there are

"fundamental objections to any conclusion that a litigant who has properly invoked the jurisdiction of a federal district court to consider federal constitutional claims can be compelled, without his consent and through no fault of his own, to accept instead a state court's determination of those claims. Such a result would be at war with the unqualified terms in which Congress, pursuant to constitutional authorization, has conferred specific categories of jurisdiction upon the federal courts, and with the principle that 'When a federal court is properly appealed to in a case over which it has by law jurisdiction, it is its duty to take such jurisdiction . . . . The right of a party plaintiff to choose a federal court where there is a choice cannot be properly denied.'" England v. Louisiana State Board of Medical Examiners, 375 U.S. 411, 415 (1964).

We have also recognized that review by this Court of state decisions, "even when available by appeal rather than only by discretionary writ of certiorari, is an inadequate substitute for the initial district court determination . . . to which the litigant is entitled in the federal courts." The federal courts are, in short, the "primary and powerful reliances for vindicating every right given by the Constitution, the laws, and treaties of the United States." F. Frankfurter and J. Landis, The Business of the Supreme Court: A Study in the Federal Judicial System 65 (1928).

These considerations, applicable generally in cases arising under federal law, have special force in the context of the Ku Klux Klan Act of 1871. In a suit to enforce fundamental constitutional rights, the plaintiff's choice of a federal forum has singular urgency. The statutory predecessor to § 1983 was, after all, designed "to afford a federal right in federal courts because, by reason of prejudice, passion, neglect, intolerance or otherwise, state laws might not be enforced and the claims of citizens to the rights, privileges, and immunities guaranteed by the 14th amendment might be denied by the state agencies." Monroe v. Pape, 365 U.S. 167, 180 (1961). And the statute's legislative history

> "makes evident that Congress clearly conceived that it was altering the relationship between the states and the nation with respect to the protection of federally created rights; it was concerned that state instrumentalities could not protect those rights; it realized that state officers might, in fact, be antipathetic to the vindication of those rights; and it believed that these failings extended to the state courts. . . . The very purpose of § 1983 was to interpose the federal courts between the states and the people, as guardians of the people's federal rights—to protect the people from unconstitutional action under color of state law, 'whether that action be executive, legislative or judicial.' " Mitchum v. Foster, 407 U.S. 225, 242 (1972).

It is against this background that we have refused to require exhaustion of state remedies by civil rights plaintiffs. . . .

Our determination that principles of federalism do not require the exhaustion of state remedies in cases brought under the Ku Klux Klan Act holds true even where the state agency or process under constitutional attack is intimately tied to the state judicial machinery. Indeed, only last term we held in *Mitchum v. Foster,* supra, that § 1983 operates as an exception to the federal anti-injunction statute, 28 U.S.C. § 2283, which prohibits federal court injunctions against ongoing state judicial proceedings and which is designed to prevent "needless friction between state and federal courts." Although the anti-injunction statute rests in part on considerations as fundamental as the "constitutional independence of the states and their courts," and although exceptions will "not be enlarged by loose statutory construction," we nevertheless unanimously concluded that § 1983 is excepted from the statute's prohibition—that the anti-injunction statute does not, in other words, displace federal jurisdiction under the Ku Klux Klan Act.

In sum, the absence of an exhaustion requirement in § 1983 is not an accident of history or the result of careless oversight by Congress or this Court. On the contrary, the no-exhaustion rule is an integral feature of the statutory scheme. Exhaustion of state remedies is not required precisely because such a requirement would jeopardize the purposes of the act. For that reason, the imposition of such a requirement, even if done indirectly by means of a determination that jurisdiction under § 1983 is displaced by an alternative remedial device, must be justified by a clear statement of congressional intent, or, at the very least, by the presence of the most persuasive considerations of policy. In my view, no such justification can be found.

Crucial to the Court's analysis of the case before us is its understanding of the purposes that underlie the habeas corpus exhaustion requirement. But just as the Court pays too little attention to the reasons for a no-exhaustion rule in actions under § 1983, it also misconceives the purposes of the exhaustion requirement in habeas corpus. As a result, the Court reaches what seems to me the erroneous conclusion that the purposes of the exhaustion requirement are fully implicated in respondents' actions, even though respondents sought to bring these actions under § 1983.

"The rule of exhaustion in federal habeas corpus actions is," according to today's opinion, "rooted in considerations of federal-state comity. That principle was defined in Younger v. Harris, 401 U.S. 37, 44 (1971), as 'a proper respect for state functions,' and it has as much relevance in areas of particular state administrative concern as it does where state judicial action is being attacked." Moreover, the Court reasons that since the relationship between state prisoners and state officers is especially intimate, and since prison issues are peculiarly within state authority and expertise, "the states have an important interest in not being bypassed in the correction of those problems." With all respect, I cannot accept either the premises or the reasoning that lead to the Court's conclusion.

Although codified in the habeas corpus statute in 1948, the exhaustion requirement is a "judicially crafted instrument which reflects a careful balance between important interests of federalism and the need to preserve the writ of habeas corpus as a 'swift and imperative remedy in all cases of illegal restraint or confinement.'" Braden v. 30th Judicial Circuit, 410 U.S. 484, 490 (1973). The indisputable concern of all our decisions concerning the doctrine has been the relationship "between the *judicial tribunals* of the union and of the states. [T]he public good requires that those relations be not disturbed by unnecessary conflict between *courts* equally bound to guard and protect rights secured by the Constitution." *Ex parte Royall,* supra, at 251 (emphasis added). . . .

That is not to say, however, that the purposes of the doctrine are implicated only where an attack is directed at a state court *conviction* or *sentence*. *Ex parte Royall* itself did not involve a challenge to a state conviction, but rather an effort to secure a prisoner's release on habeas corpus "in advance of his trial in the [state] court in which he [was] indicted." But there, too, the focus was on relations between the state and federal *judiciaries*. It is a fundamental purpose of the exhaustion doctrine to preserve the "orderly administration of state judicial business, preventing the interruption of state adjudication by federal habeas proceedings. It is important that petitioners reach state appellate courts, which can develop and correct errors of state and federal law and most effectively supervise and impose uniformity on trial courts." . . .

With these considerations in mind, it becomes clear that the Court's decision does not serve the fundamental purposes behind the exhaustion doctrine. For although respondents were confined pursuant to the judgment of a state judicial tribunal, their claims do not relate to their convictions or sentences, but only to the administrative action of prison officials who subjected them to allegedly unconstitutional treatment, including the deprivation of good-time credits. This is not a case, in other words, where federal intervention would interrupt a state proceeding or jeopardize the orderly administration of state judicial business. Nor is it a case where an action in federal court might imperil the relationship between state and federal courts. The "regularity of proceedings had in courts of coordinate jurisdiction" is not in any sense at issue.

To be sure, respondents do call into question the constitutional validity of action by state officials, and friction between those officials and the federal court is by no means an inconceivable result. But standing alone, that possibility is simply not enough to warrant application of an exhaustion requirement. First, while we spoke in Younger v. Harris, 401 U.S. 37, 44 (1971), of the need for federal courts to maintain a "proper respect for state functions," neither that statement nor our holding there supports the instant application of the exhaustion doctrine. Our concern in *Younger* was the "longstanding public policy against federal court interference with *state court proceedings*" by means of a federal injunction against the continuation of those proceedings. *Younger* is thus an instructive illustration of the very proposition that the Court regrettably misconstrues. It does not in any sense demand, or even counsel, today's decision.

Second, the situation that exists in the case before us—an attack on state administrative rather than judicial action—is the stereotypical situation in which relief under § 1983 is authorized. See, e.g., McNeese v. Board of Education, 373 U.S. 668 (1963) (attack on school districting scheme); Damico v. California, 389 U.S. 416 (1967) (attack on welfare requirements); Monroe v. Pape, 365 U.S., at 183 (attack on police conduct). In each of these cases the exercise of federal jurisdiction was potentially offensive to the state and its officials. In each of these cases the attack was directed at an important state function in an area in which the state has wide powers of regulation. Yet in each of these cases we explicitly held that exhaustion of state remedies was not required. And in comparable cases we have taken pains to insure that the abstention doctrine is not used to defeat the plaintiff's initial choice of a federal forum, even though the plaintiff could reserve the right to litigate the federal claim in federal court at the conclusion of the state proceeding. England v. Louisiana State Board of Medical Examiners, 375 U.S. 411 (1964). Like Judge Kaufman, who concurred in the affirmance of the cases now before us, "I cannot believe that federal jurisdiction in cases involving prisoner rights is any more offensive to the state than federal jurisdiction in the areas" where the exhaustion requirement has been explicitly ruled inapplicable.

Third, if the Court is correct in assuming that the exhaustion requirement must be applied whenever federal jurisdiction might be a source of substantial friction with the state, then I simply do not understand why the Court stops where it does in rolling back the district courts' jurisdiction under § 1983. Application of the exhaustion doctrine now turns on whether or not the action is directed at the fact or duration of the prisoner's confinement. It seems highly doubtful to me that a constitutional attack on prison conditions is any less disruptive of federal-state relations than an attack on prison conditions joined with a plea for restoration of good-time credits. . . . Yet the Court holds today that exhaustion is required where a prisoner attacks the deprivation of good-time credits, but not where he challenges only the conditions of his confinement. It seems obvious to me that both of those propositions cannot be correct.

Finally, the Court's decision may have the ironic effect of turning a situation where state and federal courts are not initially in conflict into a situation where precisely such conflict does result. Since respondents' actions would neither interrupt a state judicial proceeding nor, even if successful, require the invalidation of a state judicial decision, "[t]he question is simply whether one court or another is going to decide the case." Note, Exhaustion of State Remedies Under the Civil Rights Act, 68 Colum. L. Rev. 1201, 1205–06 (1968). If we had held, consistently with our prior cases, that the plaintiff has the right to choose a federal forum, the exercise of that right would not offend or embarrass a state court with concurrent jurisdiction. Now, however, a prisoner who seeks restoration of good-time credits must proceed first in state court, although he has the option of petitioning the federal court for relief if his state suit is unsuccessful. If the prisoner does resort to a federal habeas corpus action, the potential for friction with the state is certain to increase. The state is likely, after all, to derive little pleasure from the federal court's effort to determine whether there was "either an absence of available state corrective process or the existence of circumstances rendering such process ineffective to protect the rights of the prisoner." 28 U.S.C. § 2254(b). And since it is the validity of the state court's decision that is placed in issue, the state will have to endure a federal court inquiry into whether the state's factfinding process was adequate to afford a full and fair hearing, 28 U.S.C. § 2254(d)(2), whether the petitioner was denied due process of law in the state court proceeding, § 2254(d)(7), and whether the state court's factual determinations were fairly supported by the record, § 2254(d)(8). Cf. Townsend v. Sain, 372 U.S. 293 (1963). Since none of these questions would even arise if the Court had held these actions properly brought under § 1983, it seems a good deal premature to proclaim today's decision a major victory in our continuing effort to achieve a harmonious and healthy federal-state system.

IV

In short, I see no basis for concluding that jurisdiction under § 1983 is, in this instance, pre-empted by the habeas corpus remedy.

Respondents' effort to bring these suits under the provisions of the Ku Klux Klan Act should not be viewed as an attempted circumvention of the exhaustion requirement of the habeas corpus statute, for the effort does not in any sense conflict with the policies underlying that requirement. By means of these suits, they demand an immediate end to action under color of state law that has the alleged effect of violating fundamental rights guaranteed by the federal Constitution. The Ku Klux Klan Act was designed to afford an expeditious federal hearing for the resolution of precisely such claims as these. Since I share the Court's view that exhaustion of state judicial remedies is not required in any suit properly brought in federal court under § 1983 and since I am convinced that respondents have properly invoked the jurisdictional grant of § 1983, I would affirm the judgment of the Court of Appeals.

NOTES ON DAMAGES SUITS AND HABEAS CORPUS

1. Questions and Comments on the Relation of § 1983 and Habeas Corpus. Federal habeas corpus requires that available state judicial remedies be exhausted before resort to federal court. One consequence of this requirement is that federal habeas is generally unavailable until state criminal proceedings have been concluded.[a] *Younger* is consistent with this aspect of the law of habeas corpus. It too, as a general matter, forecloses federal judicial relief that would pretermit or undermine pending state criminal proceedings.

As *Preiser* illustrates, however, there is a tension between § 1983 and habeas corpus. Where *Younger* is inapplicable, § 1983 does not require exhaustion of state remedies.[b] Thus, after state criminal proceedings have been completed, there would be no reason—considering *Younger* and the law of § 1983 alone—for resort to further state proceedings before seeking an injunction to set aside a prison sentence that resulted from a criminal conviction. But it is the major function of habeas corpus to provide comparable relief. If § 1983 were available in such a case, the habeas exhaustion requirement would become a dead letter. Some boundary line must thus be drawn between the two regimes if both are to retain independent functions. Does *Preiser* draw the right line?[c] Of what relevance is *Younger* to the issues in *Preiser*?

2. Relation of *Younger* and *Preiser* to § 1983 Actions for Damages. *Preiser* contemplates the possibility of simultaneous state and federal litigation where a prisoner seeks relief from the terms and conditions of confinement and also seeks money damages. Is simultaneous litigation also possible where a defendant in a pending state criminal trial seeks damages in federal court for conduct of an official

---

[a] For elaboration of this requirement, see pages 689–710, supra.

[b] For elaboration of this proposition, see pages 1060–83, supra.

[c] For commentary on *Preiser*, see Note, A Comparison of § 1983 and Federal Habeas Corpus in State Prisoner's Litigation, 59 Notre Dame Law. 1315; Note, State Prisoners' Suits Brought on Issues Dispositive of Confinement: The Aftermath of *Preiser v. Rodriguez* and *Wolff v. McDonald*, 77 Colum.L.Rev. 742 (1977).

that will be at issue during the criminal trial? Consider the following cases in connection with this question.

3. *Guerro v. Mulhearn.* In Guerro v. Mulhearn, 498 F.2d 1249 (1st Cir. 1974), Guerro had been convicted of a state criminal offense. The validity of the conviction was pending on appeal within the state system. He sought damages under § 1983 for alleged misconduct by state officials that was also at issue in the state proceedings. The defendants argued that the federal suit should be stayed or dismissed until the issues had been finally decided by the state courts. The Court of Appeals held:

> "Requests for relief in the form of money damages under § 1983 are not controlled by *Preiser*, but . . . the reasoning and policy of that case, as well as the policy considerations underlying Younger v. Harris, 401 U.S. 37 (1971), require a federal court to stay its hand where disposition of the damages action would involve a ruling implying that a state conviction is or would be illegal. . . .

> "Where the federal court, in dealing with the question of damages caused by violation of civil rights, would have to make rulings by virtue of which the validity of a conviction in contemporary state proceedings would be called in question, the potential for federal-state friction is obvious. The federal ruling would embarrass, and could even intrude into, the state proceedings. Questions concerning the effect to be given the federal ruling in the state courts might be difficult ones and could lead to delay, or even derailment of the course of the state action. It is not impossible that circumstances might arise where a federal judgment for damages could be used by a state defendant to obtain his release from, or prevent, his incarceration, thus presuming upon, if not preempting, the province of the Great Writ. . . ."

The court added that the "touchstone for any decision to defer a civil rights damage action which is parallel to state criminal proceedings is whether the federal court will be making rulings whose necessary implication would be to call in question the validity of the state conviction."

4. *Deakins v. Monaghan.* Deakins v. Monaghan, ___ U.S. ___ (1988), involved the propriety of an eight-hour search of business premises during which hundreds of documents were seized. Various proceedings ensued before the state judge who had issued a warrant for the search in his capacity as supervisor of a state grand jury. A suit for damages and attorney's fees was then filed in federal court under § 1983.[d] The District Court dismissed the damages claim in deference to the pending state grand jury proceedings. The Court of Appeals reversed, holding that dismissal was inappropriate but that the District

---

[d] The plaintiffs also sought injunctive relief, but later withdrew this aspect of their complaint.

Court should have stayed its hand until the state proceedings concluded. An indictment was then returned (without reliance on the disputed materials) against some of the persons who had filed the federal suit. After the indictment, the state court to which the case was assigned for trial took jurisdiction over the question whether the disputed documents should be returned or whether they would be available for use in the pending criminal trial. The question decided by the Supreme Court was whether the District Court had properly dismissed the damages complaint.

(i) **Justice Blackmun's Opinion.** Justice Blackmun wrote for the Court:

"Petitioners argue that the *Younger* doctrine—which requires a federal court to abstain where a plaintiff's federal claims could be adjudicated in a pending state judicial proceeding—applies to complaints seeking only monetary relief. Petitioners further argue that it is within the district court's discretion to dismiss rather than stay a federal complaint for damages and fees where abstention is required. We need not decide the extent to which the *Younger* doctrine applies to a federal action seeking only monetary relief, however, because even if the *Younger* doctrine requires abstention here, the District Court had no discretion to dismiss rather than to stay claims for monetary relief that cannot be redressed in the state proceeding.[6]

"In reversing the District Court's dismissal of the claims for damages and attorney's fees, the Court of Appeals applied the Third Circuit rule that requires a district court to stay rather than dismiss claims that are not cognizable in the parallel state proceeding. The Third Circuit rule is sound. It allows a parallel state proceeding to go forward without interference from its federal sibling, while enforcing the duty of federal courts 'to assume jurisdiction where jurisdiction properly exists.'[7] This Court repeatedly has stated that the federal courts have a 'virtually unflagging obligation' to exercise their jurisdiction except in those extraordinary circumstances ' "where the order to the parties to repair to the state court

[6] "In his concurring opinion in this case, Justice White urges that we reach the question—not considered at any stage below, and not the subject of our grant of certiorari—whether the *Younger* doctrine applies to cases in which only money damages are sought in the federal forum. Apparently, Justice White also finds it appropriate to conclude that *Younger* requires abstention in this particular case, although he does not analyze this question separately. Because all respondents have represented that they will seek a stay of their damages claim on remand, we see no reason to reach issues so awkwardly presented for review."

[Certiorari was granted by the Court to consider whether *Younger* required a federal court to defer to ongoing state grand jury proceedings. This question was mooted by the subsequent indictment of some of the respondents and by the representation of the others that they wished to drop their plea for equitable relief.—Addition to footnote by eds.]

[7] "In [prior decisions], the Court of Appeals recognized that unless it retained jurisdiction during the pendency of the state proceeding, a plaintiff could be barred permanently from asserting his claims in the federal forum by the running of the applicable statute of limitations."

would clearly serve an important countervailing interest." '
Colorado River Water Conservation District v. United States,
424 U.S. 800 (1976).

"We are unpersuaded by petitioners' suggestion that this
case presents such extraordinary circumstances. [P]etitioners'
speculation that the District Court, if allowed to retain jurisdiction, would 'hover' about the state proceeding, ready to lift its
stay whenever it concluded that things were proceeding unsat-
isfactorily, is groundless. Petitioners seem to assume that the
District Court would not hold up its end of the comity bargain—an assumption as inappropriate as the converse assumption that the states cannot be trusted to enforce federal rights
with adequate diligence. See Stone v. Powell, 428 U.S. 465,
493–94 n.35 (1976). . . .

"[P]etitioners [also] argue that allowing the District Court
to dismiss the complaint will prevent the piecemeal litigation
of the dispute between the parties. But the involvement of the
federal courts cannot be blamed for the fragmentary nature of
the proceedings in this litigation. Because the state criminal
proceeding can provide only equitble relief, any action for
damages would necessarily be separate. Indeed, the state
forum in which petitioners invite respondents to pursue their
claims for monetary relief clearly would require the initiation
of a separate action. Piecemeal litigation of the issues involved in this case is thus inevitable.

"In sum, none of the circumstances cited by petitioners to
justify the District Court's dismissal of respondents' claims for
damages and attorney's fees constitutes the kind of extraordinary circumstances that we have held may justify abdication of
the 'virtually unflagging obligation . . . to exercise the jurisdiction given' the federal courts. *Colorado River Water Conservation District v. United States*, supra, at 817."

(ii) **Justice White's Concurrence.** Justice White, joined by
Justice O'Connor, concurred. He agreed that dismissal of the damages
claim was inappropriate. But he faulted the Court for not adequately
explaining "why the federal courts must or may stay, rather than
proceed to adjudicate, the federal constitutional claims for damages."
"After all," he continued, "the Court's opinion cites the 'virtually
unflagging obligation' of the federal courts to adjudicate claims within
their jurisdiction absent extraordinary circumstances . . . . Why,
then, stay the § 1983 damages claim asserting a violation of federal
constitutional rights? Why does not the District Court's 'unflagging
obligation' require it to proceed on that claim?"

Justice White's answer to these questions began with the observation that "[t]he Third Circuit rule, which the Court endorses, appears to
rest on 'prudential considerations' and not on the view that *Younger*
requires that a damages action be stayed when there is a parallel state
criminal (or 'quasi-criminal') proceeding underway." He continued:

"To affirm the Court of Appeals' judgment ordering a stay requires a more substantial basis than 'prudential consideration[s]' and that basis is not difficult to find: it is that *Younger* requires, not only dismissal of the equitable claim in the case, but also that the damages action not go forward. . . .

"The reasons for such an approach are obvious. As the *Younger* decision itself recognized, it has long been the rule that the federal courts should not interfere with or pre-empt the progress of state criminal proceedings. A judgment in the federal damages action may decide several questions at issue in the state criminal proceeding. . . . If the claims the Court remands today were disposed of on the merits by the District Court, this decision would presumably be owed res judicata effect in the forthcoming state criminal trial of respondents. '[T]he potential for federal-state friction is obvious.' Guerro v. Mulhearn, 498 F.2d 1249, 1253 (1st Cir. 1974).

"It was for these same reasons that we held that a federal court should not entertain a declaratory judgment action aimed at adjudicating a federal issue involved in a state criminal proceeding. See Samuels v. Mackell, 401 U.S. 66 (1971). As was true in *Samuels*, here, 'the practical effect of the two forms of relief [here, damages and injunction] will be virtually identical, and the basic policy against federal interference with pending state criminal prosecutions will be frustrated as much by a declaratory judgment [or, I believe, a damage award] as it would be by an injunction.' See id., at 73. Under *Samuels*, for example, if a state criminal prosecution is ongoing, a federal court cannot adjudicate a plaintiff's request for a declaration that evidence being used in that prosecution was seized contrary to the fourth amendment. Yet if *Younger* does not apply to damages claims, that same court in the same circumstances *could* rule the search unconstitutional as long as the federal plaintiff was seeking damages *in addition to* a determination of the unconstitutionality of the seizure—a prerequisite of any damages award. Why the latter action should be considered *less* problematic for purposes of comity or 'Our Federalism' escapes me. If anything, I would have thought just the opposite to be true.

"In light of . . . our decisions in *Younger* and *Samuels*, it is clear that the District Court should not dismiss the damages claims, yet must not proceed to judgment on them either. Consequently, I would couple our remand of this case with a holding that, pursuant to *Younger*, the lower courts *may not* adjudicate respondents' damges claims until the conclusion of the pending state criminal proceedings.[5]"

---

[5] "While three of the respondents have been indicted, three others have not. Even if *Younger* does not apply to their claims for damages, the District Court would be prudent, under *Colorado River*, supra, to stay the adjudication of these claims—virtually indistinguishable from the substance

5. Questions and Comments on *Guerro* and *Deakins*. What did Justice Blackmun mean by stating that the Court was not deciding whether *Younger* applied, but in the next paragraph of his opinion approving the Third Circuit rule requiring a stay of the District Court proceedings? In this connection, consider Justice Brennan's observations for the Court in Moses H. Cone Memorial Hospital v. Mercury Constr. Corp., 460 U.S. 1 (1983), quoted in context at pages 555–58 supra, that "a stay is just as much a refusal to exercise jurisdiction as a dismissal." The point of Justice Brennan's remark was the Court's holding that neither a stay nor a dismissal of federal proceedings is appropriate unless the case meets the *Colorado River* "extraordinary circumstances" exception to the "unflagging obligation" of district courts to exercise their jurisdiction. In light of *Moses H. Cone*, how can the Court's decision in *Deakins* be justified? On the merits of the *Younger* question, do *Guerro* and Justice White reach the right result?

Consider also the res judicata effect of the state criminal prosecution on the pending federal litigation. Under either the Court's or Justice White's solution, would the determination in the state criminal proceeding that a search and seizure was constitutional require dismissal of the federal action? If the search were held unconstitutional, what issues would remain for determination in the federal court?

Finally, consider the intersection of *Preiser* with these problems. Suppose a criminal defendant did not raise a federal constitutional issue in the state criminal trial or on direct appeal, but asserted it after conviction in a § 1983 action for damages. If it were possible to use the claim as the basis for a collateral attack on the conviction in the state courts, should federal relief be withheld until the state remedy had been exhausted? If so, would the combination of *Deakins* and *Preiser* mean that a federal damages action must be stayed until *both* the criminal proceedings themselves *and* any available collateral attack have been pursued? If not, why is simultaneous litigation in state and federal court permitted at the stage of collateral attack but not while the criminal proceedings themselves are pending?

SUBSECTION D: APPLICATION TO CIVIL PROCEEDINGS

TRAINOR v. HERNANDEZ
Supreme Court of the United States, 1977.
431 U.S. 434.

MR. JUSTICE WHITE delivered the opinion of the Court.

The Illinois Department of Public Aid (IDPA) filed a lawsuit in the Circuit Court of Cook County, Ill., on October 30, 1974, against

of the ongoing state criminal proceedings involving the other respondents—as well."

appellees Juan and Maria Hernandez, alleging that they had fraudulently concealed assets while applying for and receiving public assistance. Such conduct is a crime under Illinois law. The IDPA, however, proceeded civilly and sought only return of the money alleged to have been wrongfully received. The IDPA simultaneously instituted an attachment proceeding against appellees' property. Pursuant to the Illinois Attachment Act, the IDPA filed an affidavit setting forth the nature and amount of the underlying claim and alleging that the appellees had obtained money from the IDPA by fraud. The writ of attachment was issued automatically by the clerk of the court upon receipt of this affidavit. The writ was then given to the sheriff who executed it, on November 5, 1974, on money belonging to appellees in a credit union. Appellees received notice of the attachment, freezing their money in the credit union, on November 8, 1974, when they received the writ, the complaint, and the affidavit in support of the writ. The writ indicated a return date for the attachment proceeding of November 18, 1974. Appellees appeared in court on November 18, 1974, and were informed that the matter would be continued until December 19, 1974. Appellees never filed an answer either to the attachment or to the underlying complaint. They did not seek a prompt hearing, nor did they attempt to quash the attachment on the ground that the procedures surrounding its issuance rendered it and the act unconstitutional. Instead appellees filed the instant lawsuit in the United States District Court for the Northern District of Illinois on December 2, 1974, seeking, inter alia, return of the attached money. The federal complaint alleged that the appellees' property had been attached pursuant to the act and that the act was unconstitutional in that it provided for the deprivation of debtors' property without due process of law. Appellees as plaintiffs sought to represent a class of those "who have had or may have their property attached without notice or hearing upon the creditor's mere allegation of fraudulent conduct pursuant to the Illinois Attachment Act." They named as defendants appellants Trainor and O'Malley, officials of the IDPA, and sought declaration of a defendant class made up of all the court clerks in the Circuit Courts of Illinois, and of another defendant class of all sheriffs in Illinois. They sought an injunction against Trainor and O'Malley forbidding them to seek attachments under the act and an injunction against the clerks and sheriffs forbidding them to issue or serve writs of attachment under the act. . . .

In an opinion dated December 19, 1975, almost one year after the return date of the attachment in state court, [the District Court] declined to dismiss the case under the doctrine of Younger v. Harris, 401 U.S. 37 (1971), and Huffman v. Pursue, Ltd., 420 U.S. 592 (1975), stating:

> "In *Huffman*, the state of Ohio proceeded under a statute which gave an exclusive right of action to the state. By contrast, the Illinois Attachment Act provides a cause of action

for any person, public or private. It is mere happenstance that the state of Illinois was the petitioner in this attachment proceeding. It is likewise coincidental that the pending state proceedings may arguably be quasi-criminal in nature; under the Illinois Attachment Act, they need not be. These major distinctions preclude this court from extending the principles of *Younger,* based considerations of equity, comity and federalism, beyond the quasi-criminal situation set forth in *Huffman.* "

Proceeding to the merits, it held [various provisions] of the act to be "on their face patently violative of the due process clause of the 14th amendment to the United States Constitution." It ordered the clerk of the court and the Sheriff of Cook County to return to appellees . . . their attached property; it enjoined all clerks and all sheriffs from issuing or serving attachment writs pursuant to the act and ordered them to release any currently held attached property to its owner; and it enjoined appellants Trainor and O'Malley from authorizing applications for attachment writs pursuant to the act. Appellants [claim] that under *Younger* and *Huffman* principles the District Court should have dismissed the suit without passing on the constitutionality of the act and that the act is in any event constitutional. Since we agree with appellants that *Younger* and *Huffman* principles do apply here, we do not reach their second claim. . . .

Because our federal and state legal systems have overlapping jurisdiction and responsibilities, we have frequently inquired into the proper role of a federal court, in a case pending before it and otherwise within its jurisdiction, when litigation between the same parties and raising the same issues is or apparently soon will be pending in a state court. More precisely, when a suit is filed in federal court challenging the constitutionality of a state law under the federal Constitution and seeking to have state officers enjoined from enforcing it, should the federal court proceed to judgment when it appears that the state has already instituted proceedings in the state court to enforce the challenged statute against the federal plaintiff and the latter could tender and have his federal claims decided in the state court?

Younger v. Harris, supra, and Samuels v. Mackell, 401 U.S. 66 (1971), [involved situations] where the already pending state proceeding was a criminal prosecution and the federal plaintiff sought to invalidate the statute under which the state prosecution was brought. In these circumstances, the Court ruled that the federal district court should issue neither a declaratory judgment nor an injunction but should dismiss the case. The first justification the Court gave for this rule was simply the "basic doctrine of equity jurisprudence that courts of equity should not act, and particularly should not act to restrain a criminal prosecution, when the moving party has an adequate remedy at law and will not suffer irreparable injury if denied equitable relief." *Younger v. Harris,* supra, at 43–44.

Beyond the accepted rule that equity will ordinarily not enjoin the prosecution of a crime, however, the Court voiced a "more vital consideration," namely, that in a union where both the states and the federal government are sovereign entities, there are basic concerns of federalism which counsel against interference by federal courts, through injunctions or otherwise, with legitimate state functions, particularly with the operation of state courts. Relying on cases that declared that courts of equity should give "scrupulous regard [to] the rightful independence of state governments," Beal v. Missouri Pacific R. Co., 312 U.S. 45 (1941), the Court held, that in this intergovernmental context, the two classic preconditions for the exercise of equity jurisdiction assumed new dimensions. Although the existence of an adequate remedy at law barring equitable relief normally would be determined by inquiring into the remedies available in the federal rather than in the state courts, Great Lakes Co. v. Huffman, 319 U.S. 293, 297 (1943), here the inquiry was to be broadened to focus on the remedies available in the pending state proceeding. . . .   "The policy of equitable restraint . . . is founded on the premise that ordinarily a pending state prosecution provides the accused a fair and sufficient opportunity for vindication of federal constitutional rights." Kugler v. Helfant, 421 U.S. 117, 124 (1975).

The Court also concluded that the other precondition for equitable relief—irreparable injury—would not be satisfied unless the threatened injury was both great and immediate. The burden of conducting a defense in the criminal prosecution was not sufficient to warrant interference by the federal court with legitimate state efforts to enforce state laws; only extraordinary circumstances would suffice. As the Court later explained, to restrain a state proceeding that afforded an adequate vehicle for vindicating the federal plaintiff's constitutional rights "would entail an unseemly failure to give effect to the principle that state courts have the solemn responsibility equally with the federal courts" to safeguard constitutional rights and would "reflec[t] negatively upon the state court's ability" to do so. Steffel v. Thompson, 415 U.S. 454, 460–61 (1974). The state would be prevented not only from "effectuating its substantive policies, but also from continuing to perform the separate function of providing a forum competent to vindicate any constitutional objections interposed against those policies." *Huffman v. Pursue, Ltd.,* supra, at 604.

Huffman involved the propriety of a federal injunction against the execution of a judgment entered in a pending state court suit brought by the state to enforce a nuisance statute. Although the state suit was a civil rather than a criminal proceeding, *Younger* principles were held to require dismissal of the federal suit. Noting that the state was a party to the nuisance proceeding and that the nuisance statute was "in aid of and closely related to criminal statutes," the Court concluded that a federal injunction would be "an offense to the state's interest in the nuisance litigation [which] is likely to be every bit as great as it would be were this a criminal proceeding." Thus, while the traditional maxim that equity will not enjoin a criminal prosecution strictly speaking did not apply to the nuisance proceeding in *Huffman,* the "more vital consideration" of comity, id. at 601, quoting *Younger v. Harris,* supra, at 44, counseled restraint as strongly in the context of the pending state civil enforcement action as in the context of a pending criminal proceeding. In these circumstances, it was proper that the federal court stay its hand.

We have recently applied the analysis of *Huffman* to proceedings similar to state civil enforcement actions—judicial contempt proceedings. Juidice v. Vail, 430 U.S. 327 (1977). The Court again stressed the "more vital consideration" of comity underlying the *Younger* doctrine and held that the state interest in vindicating the regular operation of its judicial system through the contempt process—whether that process was labeled civil, criminal, or quasi-criminal—was sufficiently important to preclude federal injunctive relief unless *Younger* standards were met.

These cases control here. An action against appellees was pending in state court when they filed their federal suit. The state action was a suit by the state to recover from appellees welfare payments that allegedly had been fraudulently obtained. The writ of attachment issued as part of that action. The District Court thought that *Younger* policies were irrelevant because suits to recover money and writs of attachment were available to private parties as well as the state; it was only because of the coincidence that the state was a party that the suit was "arguably" in aid of the criminal law. But the fact remains that the state was a party to the suit in its role of administering its public assistance programs. Both the suit and the accompanying writ of attachment were brought to vindicate important state policies such as safeguarding the fiscal integrity of those programs. The state authorities also had the option of vindicating those policies through criminal prosecutions. Although, as in *Juidice,* the state's interest here is "[p]erhaps . . . not quite as important as is the state's interest in the enforcement of its criminal laws . . . or even its interest in the maintenance of a quasi-criminal proceeding . . .," the principles of *Younger* and *Huffman* are broad enough to apply to interference by a federal court with an ongoing civil enforcement action such as this, brought by the state in its sovereign capacity.[8]

[8] Title 28 U.S.C. § 2283 provides that "[a] court of the United States may not grant an injunction to stay proceedings in a state court except as expressly authorized by act of Congress, or where necessary in aid of its jurisdiction, or to protect or effectuate its judgments." The section is not applicable here because this § 1983 action is an express statutory exception to its application, Mitchum v. Foster, 407 U.S. 225 (1972); but it is significant for present purposes that the section does not discriminate between civil and criminal proceedings pending in state courts. Furthermore, 28 U.S.C. § 1341 provides that district courts shall not enjoin, suspend, or restrain the levy or collection of any tax under state law where there are adequate remedies available in state tribunals.

Prior cases in this Court that at the time counseled restraint in actions seeking to enjoin state officials from enforcing state statutes or implementing public policies, did not necessarily distinguish between the type of proceedings—civil or criminal—pending or contemplated by state officers. [Citing cases.]

As in Juidice v. Vail, 430 U.S. 327, 336 n. 13 (1977), we have no occasion to decide whether *Younger* principles apply to all civil litigation.

For a federal court to proceed with its case rather than to remit appellees to their remedies in a pending state enforcement suit would confront the state with a choice of engaging in duplicative litigation, thereby risking a temporary federal injunction, or of interrupting its enforcement proceedings pending decision of the federal court at some unknown time in the future. It would also foreclose the opportunity of the state court to construe the challenged statute in the face of the actual federal constitutional challenges that would also be pending for decision before it, a privilege not wholly shared by the federal courts. Of course, in the case before us the state statute was invalidated and a federal injunction prohibited state officers from using or enforcing the attachment statute for any purpose. The eviscerating impact on many state enforcement actions is readily apparent.[9] This disruption of suits by the state in its sovereign capacity, when combined with the negative reflection on the state's ability to adjudicate federal claims that occurs whenever a federal court enjoins a pending state proceeding, leads us to the conclusion that the interests of comity and federalism on which *Younger* and *Samuels v. Mackell* primarily rest apply in full force here. The pendency of the state court action called for restraint by the federal court and for the dismissal of appellees' complaint unless extraordinary circumstances were present warranting federal interference or unless their state remedies were inadequate to litigate their federal due process claim.

No extraordinary circumstances warranting equitable relief were present here. There is no suggestion that the pending state action was brought in bad faith or for the purpose of harassing appellees. It is urged that this case comes within the exception that we said in *Younger* might exist where a statute is "flagrantly and patently violative of express constitutional prohibitions in every clause, sentence and paragraph, and in whatever manner and against whomever an effort might be made to apply it." 401 U.S., at 53–54, quoting Watson v. Buck, 313 U.S. 387, 402 (1941). Even if such a finding were made below, which we doubt, it would not have been warranted in light of our cases. Compare North Georgia Finishing, Inc. v. Di-Chem, Inc., 419 U.S. 601 (1975), with Mitchell v. W.T. Grant Co., 416 U.S. 600 (1974).

As for whether appellees could have presented their federal due process challenge to the attachment statute in the pending state proceeding, that question, if presented below, was not addressed by the District Court, which placed its rejection of *Younger* and *Huffman* on

---

[9] Appellees argue that the injunction issued below in no way interfered with a pending state case. They point to the fact that only the attachment proceeding was interfered with—the underlying fraud action may continue unimpeded—and claim that the attachment proceeding is not a court proceeding within the doctrine of *Younger* and *Huffman*. . . .

[T]he attachment was issued by a court clerk and is very much a part of the under-

lying action for fraud. Moreover, the attachment in this case contained a return date on which the parties were to appear in *court* and at which time the appellees would have had an opportunity to contest the validity of the attachment. Thus the attachment proceeding was "pending" *in the state courts* within the *Younger* and *Huffman* doctrine at the time of the federal suit.

broader grounds. The issue is heavily laden with local law, and we do not rule on it here in the first instance.

The grounds on which the District Court refused to apply the principles of *Younger* and *Huffman* were infirm; it was therefore error, on those grounds, to entertain the action on behalf of either the named or the unnamed plaintiffs and to reach the issue of the constitutionality of the Illinois attachment statute.[11]

The judgment is therefore reversed, and the case is remanded to the District Court for further proceedings consistent with this opinion.

It is so ordered.

MR. JUSTICE STEWART substantially agrees with the views expressed in the dissenting opinions of Mr. Justice Brennan and Mr. Justice Stevens. Accordingly, he respectfully dissents from the opinion and judgment of the Court.

MR. JUSTICE BLACKMUN, concurring.

I join the Court's opinion and write only to stress that the substantiality of the state's interest in its proceeding has been an important factor in abstention cases under Younger v. Harris, 401 U.S. 37 (1971), from the beginning. . . . I emphasize the importance of the fact that the state interest in the pending state proceeding was substantial. In my view, the fact that the state had the option of proceeding either civilly or criminally to impose sanctions for a fraudulent concealment of assets while one applies for and receives public assistance demonstrates that the underlying state interest is of the same order of importance as the interests in *Younger* and *Huffman*. The propriety of abstention should not depend on the state's choice to vindicate its interests by a less drastic, and perhaps more lenient, route. In addition, as the Court notes, the state court proceeding played an important role in safeguarding the fiscal integrity of the public assistance programs. Since the benefits of the recovery of fraudulently obtained funds are enjoyed by all the taxpayers of the state, it is reasonable to recognize a distinction between the state's status as creditor and the status of private parties using the same procedures. . . .

MR. JUSTICE BRENNAN, with whom MR. JUSTICE MARSHALL joins, dissenting.

The Court continues on, to me, the wholly improper course of extending *Younger* principles to deny a federal forum to plaintiffs invoking 42 U.S.C. § 1983 for the decision of meritorious federal constitutional claims when a *civil* action that might entertain such claims is pending in a state court. Because I am of the view that the decision patently disregards Congress' purpose in enacting § 1983—to open federal courts to the decision of such claims without regard to the pendency of such state civil actions—and because the decision indefen-

---

[11] Appellees have argued here that the relief granted in favor of other class members is not barred by *Younger* and *Huffman* because state cases were not pending against some of them. Since the class should never have been certified, we need not address this argument.

sibly departs from prior decisions of this Court, I respectfully dissent.
. . .

[T]he Court apparently desires once more to leave "for another day" the question of the applicability of *Younger* abstention principles to civil suits generally. But the Court's insistence that "the interests of comity and federalism on which *Younger* and *Samuels v. Mackell* primarily rest apply in full force here" is the signal that "merely the formal announcement is being postponed," Juidice v. Vail, 430 U.S. 327, 345 (1977) (Brennan, J., dissenting). *Younger* and Samuels v. Mackell, 401 U.S. 66 (1971), dismissed federal court suits because the plaintiffs sought injunctions against pending criminal prosecutions. I agreed with those results because "[p]ending state criminal prosecutions have always been viewed as paradigm cases involving paramount state interests." Juidice v. Vail, 430 U.S. 327, 345 (1977) (Brennan, J., dissenting). But abstention principles developed to avoid interfering with state criminal prosecutions are manifestly inapplicable here.

In this case the federal plaintiffs seek an injunction only against the use of statutory attachment proceedings which, properly speaking, are not part of the pending civil suit at all. The relief granted here in no way interfered with or prevented the state from proceeding with its suit in state court. It merely enjoined the use of an unconstitutional mechanism for attaching assets from which the state hoped to satisfy its judgment if it prevailed on the merits of the underlying lawsuit. To say that the interest of the state in continuing to use an unconstitutional attachment mechanism to insure payment of a liability not yet established brings into play "in full force" "all the interests of comity and federalism" present in a state criminal prosecution is simply wrong. . . .

The application of *Younger* principles here is also inappropriate because even in the underlying lawsuit the state seeks only a civil recovery of money allegedly fraudulently received. The Court relies on the state's fortuitous presence as a plaintiff in the state court suit to conclude that the suit is closely related to a criminal suit, but I am hard pressed to understand why the "mere happenstance" that the state of Illinois rather than a private party invoked the attachment act makes this so. The Court's reliance on the presence of the state here may suggest that it might view differently an attachment under the same act at the instance of a private party, but no reason is advanced why the state as plaintiff should enjoy such an advantage in its own courts over the ordinary citizen plaintiff. Under any analysis, it seems to me that this solicitousness for the state's use of an unconstitutional ancillary proceeding to a civil lawsuit is hardly compelled by the great principles of federalism, comity, and mutual respect between federal and state courts that account for *Younger* and its progeny.

The principles that give strength to *Younger* simply do not support an inflexible rule against federal courts' enjoining state civil proceedings. *Younger* was justified primarily on the basis of the longstanding rule that "courts of equity . . . particularly should not act to restrain a criminal prosecution." A comparably rigid rule against enjoining civil proceedings was never suggested until *Huffman,* for in civil proceedings it cannot be assumed that state interests of compelling importance outweigh the interests of litigants seeking vindication of federal rights in federal court, particularly under a statute expressly enacted by Congress to provide a federal forum for that purpose. Even assuming that federal abstention might conceivably be appropriate in some civil cases, the transformation of what I must think can only be an exception into an absolute rule crosses the line between abstention and abdication.

When it enacted § 1983, Congress weighed the competing demands of "Our Federalism," and consciously decided to protect federal rights in the federal forum. As we have previously recognized, § 1983 was enacted for the express purpose of altering the federal-state judicial balance that had theretofore existed, and of "offering a uniquely federal remedy against incursions under the claimed authority of state law upon rights secured by the Constitution and the laws of the nation." Mitchum v. Foster, 407 U.S. 225, 239 (1972). State courts are, of course, bound to follow the federal Constitution equally with federal courts, but Congress has clearly ordained, as constitutionally it may, that the federal courts are to be the *"primary* and powerful reliances" for vindicating federal rights under § 1983. Steffel v. Thompson, 415 U.S. 452, 464 (1974) (emphasis in original). If federal courts are to be flatly prohibited, regardless of the circumstances of the individual claim of violation of federal rights, from implementing this "uniquely federal remedy" because of deference to purported state interests in the maintenance of state civil suits, the Court has "effectively cripple[d] the congressional scheme enacted in § 1983." *Juidice v. Vail,* supra, at 343 (Brennan, J., dissenting). . . .

Even assuming, arguendo, the applicability of *Younger* principles, I agree with the District Court that the Illinois Attachment Act falls within one of the established exceptions to those principles. As an example of an "extraordinary circumstance" that might justify federal court intervention, *Younger* referred to a statute that "might be flagrantly and patently violative of express constitutional prohibitions in every clause, sentence and paragraph, and in whatever manner and against whomever an effort might be made to apply it." 401 U.S. at 53–54, quoting Watson v. Buck, 313 U.S. 387, 402 (1941). . . .

Obviously, a requirement that the *Watson v. Buck* formulation must be literally satisfied renders the exception meaningless, and . . . elevates to a literalistic definitional status what was obviously meant only to be illustrative and nonexhaustive. The human mind does not possess a clairvoyance that can foresee whether "every clause, sentence and paragraph" of a statute will be unconstitutional "in whatever manner and against whomever an effort might be made to apply it." The only sensible construction of the test is to treat the "every clause, etc." wording as redundant, at least when decisions of this Court make clear that the challenged statute is "patently and flagrantly violative of the Constitution." . . .

Clearly the Illinois Attachment Act is "patently and fragrantly violative of express constitutional prohibitions" under the relevant decisions of this Court. *North Georgia Finishing, Inc. v. Di-Chem, Inc.,* 419 U.S. 601 (1975), struck down a Georgia garnishment statute that permitted the issuance of a writ of garnishment by the court clerk upon the filing of an affidavit containing only conclusory allegations, and under which there was "no provisions for an early hearing at which the creditor would be required to demonstrate at least probable cause for the garnishment." The Illinois Attachment Act is constitutionally indistinguishable from the Georgia statute struck down in *North Georgia Finishing.* . . . No one could seriously contend that the Illinois act even remotely resembles that sustained in Mitchell v. W.T. Grant Co., 416 U.S. 600 (1974) . . . . *W.T. Grant* upheld a Louisiana . . . statute under which [t]he showing of grounds for the issuance of the writ was made before a judge rather than a court clerk, and the debtor was entitled "immediately [to] have a full hearing on the matter of possession following the execution of the writ." None of these procedural safeguards is provided by the Illinois act. The [District Court] correctly concluded that the act "is on its face patently violative of the due process clause of the 14th amendment."

The Court gives only bare citation to *North Georgia Finishing* and *W.T. Grant* and declines to discuss or analyze them in even the most cursory manner. These decisions so clearly support the District Court's holding under any sensible construction of the *Younger* exception that the Court's silence, and its insistence upon compliance with the literal wording of *Watson v. Buck,* only confirms my conviction that the Court is determined to extend to "state *civil* proceedings generally the holding of *Younger,* " *Huffman v. Pursue, Ltd.,* supra, at 613, and to give its exceptions the narrowest possible reach. I respectfully dissent.

MR. JUSTICE STEVENS, dissenting. . . .

The Court's decision to remand this litigation to the District Court to decide whether the Illinois attachment procedure provides a debtor with an appropriate forum in which to challenge the constitutionality of the Illinois attachment procedure is ironic. For that procedure includes among its undesirable features a set of rules which effectively foreclose any challenge to its constitutionality in the Illinois courts.

Although it is true that § 27 of the Illinois Attachment Act allows the defendant to file a motion to quash the attachment, the purpose of such a motion is to test the sufficiency and truth of the facts alleged in the affidavit or the adequacy of the attachment bond. Section 28 of the act precludes consideration of any other issues. Even if—contrary to a fair reading—the statute might be construed to allow consideration of a constitutional challenge on a motion to quash, a trial judge may summarily reject such a challenge without fear of reversal; for an order denying such a motion is interlocutory and nonappealable. The ruling on the validity of an attachment does not become final until the underlying tort or contract claim is resolved. At that time, the attachment issue will, of course, be moot because the prevailing party will then be entitled to the property regardless of the validity of the attachment.

Because it is so clear that the proceeding pending in the state court did not afford the appellees in this case an adequate remedy for the violation of their federal constitutional rights, the Court's disposition points up the larger problem confronting litigants who seek to challenge any state procedure as violative of the due process clause of the 14th amendment.

As I suggested in my separate opinion in Juidice v. Vail, 430 U.S. 339 (1977), principled application of the rationale of Younger v. Harris, 401 U.S. 37 (1971), forecloses abstention in cases in which the federal challenge is to the constitutionality of the state procedure itself. Since this federal plaintiff raised a serious question about the fairness of the Illinois attachment procedure, and since that procedure does not afford a plain, speedy, and efficient remedy for his federal claim, it necessarily follows that *Younger* abstention is inappropriate. . . .

NOTES ON THE APPLICATION OF *YOUNGER* TO CIVIL PROCEEDINGS

1. *Huffman v. Pursue, Ltd.* *Younger* was first applied to non-criminal proceedings in Huffman v. Pursue, Ltd., 420 U.S. 592 (1975). Local officials had sued to close down an adult theater as a public nuisance. The theater owner lost in the trial court but did not appeal. Instead, it filed a § 1983 action in federal court seeking an injunction against enforcement of the nuisance statute. A three-judge District Court granted the requested relief, but the Supreme Court reversed.

Speaking for the Court, Justice Rehnquist emphasized the similarities between criminal prosecution and the public nuisance action: "[W]e deal here with a state proceeding which in important respects is more akin to a criminal prosecution than are most civil cases." The state was a party to the action, which was "both in aid of and closely related to" criminal obscenity statutes. Thus, the offense to the state's interest occasioned by the federal court injunction was "likely to be every bit as great as it would be were this a criminal proceeding."

There was, however, one clear difference between the nuisance proceeding and a criminal prosecution: "[W]hereas a state court criminal defendant may, after exhaustion of his state remedies, present his constitutional claims to the federal courts through habeas corpus, no analogous remedy is available" for the defendant in a state civil action. The theater owner argued, therefore, that this suit should be permitted in order to vindicate a right of access to the federal courts. Justice Rehnquist responded:

"The issue of whether federal courts should be able to interfere with ongoing state proceedings is quite distinct and separate from the issue of whether litigants are entitled to subsequent federal review of state court dispositions of federal questions. *Younger* turned on considerations of comity and federalism peculiar to the fact that state proceedings were pending; it did not turn on the fact that in any event a criminal defendant could eventually have obtained federal habeas consideration of his federal claims. The propriety of federal court interference with an Ohio nuisance proceeding must likewise be controlled by application of those same considerations of comity and federalism."

Justice Brennan dissented in an opinion joined by Justices Douglas and Marshall. He saw the result as "obviously only the first step" toward extending *Younger* to all civil proceedings. *Younger* was "basically an application, in the context of the relation of federal courts to pending state criminal prosecutions, of 'the basic doctrine of equity jurisprudence that courts of equity . . . particularly should not act to restrain a criminal prosecution.'" With respect to civil proceedings, the tradition was "quite the opposite." Moreover, Brennan saw functional differences between criminal and civil actions:

> "The extension [of *Younger*] threatens serious prejudice to the potential federal court plaintiff not present when the pending state proceeding is a criminal prosecution. That prosecution does not come into existence until completion of steps designed to safeguard him against spurious prosecution—arrest, charge, information, or indictment. In contrast, the civil proceeding, as in this case, comes into existence merely upon the filing of a complaint whether or not well founded. To deny by fiat of this Court the potential federal plaintiff a federal forum in that circumstance is obviously to arm his adversary (here the public authorities) with an easily wielded weapon to strip him of a forum and a remedy that federal statutes were enacted to assure him."

2. *Juidice v. Vail.* Two years later, the Court applied *Huffman* to a § 1983 action challenging New York's statutory contempt procedures. In Juidice v. Vail, 430 U.S. 327 (1977), the federal plaintiff was a state judgment debtor. He had been held in contempt for failing to honor a subpoena designed to uncover his assets. At first he was merely fined, but when he did not pay the fine, the judge issued an ex parte commitment order. The debtor then brought a federal class action against the judge to enjoin enforcement of the contempt procedures. Speaking for the Court, Justice Rehnquist found that the principles of federalism and comity developed in *Younger* and *Huffman* also applied to contempt proceedings:

> "A state's interest in the contempt process, through which it vindicates the regular operation of its judicial system, so long as that system itself affords the opportunity to pursue federal claims within it, is surely an important interest. Perhaps it is not quite as important as the state's interest in the enforcement of its criminal laws, *Younger*, supra, or even its interest in the maintenance of a quasi-criminal proceeding

such as was involved in *Huffman,* supra. But we think it is of sufficiently great import as to require application of the principles of those cases. The contempt power lies at the core of the administration of a state's judicial system. Whether disobedience of a court-sanctioned subpoena, and the resulting process leading to a finding of contempt of court, is labeled civil, quasi-criminal, or criminal in nature, we think the salient fact is that federal-court interference with the state's contempt process is 'an offense to the state's interest . . . likely to be every bit as great as it would be were this a criminal proceeding,' *Huffman,* supra. Moreover, such interference with the contempt process . . . also can readily be interpreted 'as reflecting negatively upon the state's ability to enforce constitutional principles.' *Huffman,* supra."

Justice Brennan, joined by Justice Marshall, dissented. He restated his opposition to *Huffman* and complained of its extension to this case:

"[W]hereas in *Huffman* state officials were parties in the state-court suit, here those suits are between purely private parties. Whatever the importance of the state's direct interest in *Huffman* in closing theaters exhibiting alleged obscene films, one must strain hard to discover any comparable state interest here in having federal rights adjudicated in a state rather than a federal forum. Thus *Huffman* 's 'quasi-criminal' rationale and today's reliance on state 'contempt power' are revealed to be only covers for the ultimate goal of denying § 1983 plaintiffs the federal forum in any case, civil or criminal, when a pending state proceeding may hear the federal plaintiff's federal claims."

Justice Stewart dissented separately.

3. Questions and Comments on the Extension of *Younger* to Civil Proceedings. In *Trainor v. Hernandez,* as in *Huffman* and *Juidice,* the Court explicitly declined to "decide whether *Younger* principles apply to all civil litigation." [a] Is this reservation realistic? Are there good reasons to differentiate these cases from civil litigation generally?

If not, the question becomes whether *Younger* should be confined to criminal cases or extended, as Justice Brennan plainly fears, to all civil litigation. What would be the rationale for confining *Younger* to criminal cases? Is it enough that equity traditionally observed this

[a] In Pennzoil Co. v. Texaco, Inc., 481 U.S. 1 (1987), the Court again explicitly declined to hold "that *Younger* abstention is always appropriate whenever a civil proceeding is pending in state court." But it relied on *Juidice* to require *Younger* abstention when Texaco sued in federal court to attack the methods by which Pennzoil sought to enforce a state-court judgment. There were also numerous state grounds on which Texaco's challenge might have been resolved, and the Court added that "[a]nother important reason for abstention is to avoid unwarranted determination of federal constitutional questions." The case was unanimous in result, though four Justices disagreed with the Court's reliance on *Younger.*

distinction? Are there functional justifications for treating pending criminal prosecutions differently from pending civil litigation?

4. Commentary and Bibliography. The Court held in Mitchum v. Foster, 407 U.S. 225 (1972), that § 1983 was an express exception to the prohibition in 28 U.S.C. § 2283 of injunctions against state court proceedings. *Younger* and its progeny are not technically inconsistent because they relied on principles of equity, comity, and federalism rather than on the anti-injunction statute. Still, one might ask what has become of *Mitchum* in light of *Huffman, Juidice,* and *Trainor.* Professors Soifer and Macgill say that *Mitchum* "might never have been written." See The *Younger* Doctrine: Reconstructing Reconstruction, 55 Tex. L. Rev. 1141, 1174 (1977). Is that accurate? Can the policies underlying *Younger* abstention be reconciled with the result in *Mitchum*?

Consider the remarks of Soifer and Macgill:

"[The Court's] view of 'comity and federalism' reflects an obsessive concern with conflict between the state and national sovereigns. It addresses problems of the structure of the Republic, not the rights of people who live in it. The 'comity' of Our Federalism, purportedly an approach to balance judicial power between state and federal judicial power, turns out in practice to be a mandate to federal courts to give way. It places scant weight upon federal jurisdiction, on the statutes conferring it, or on the rights of individuals who seek to invoke federal protection. . . .

"Our Federalism has taken on many of the attributes of substantive due process. It is a creature of pure judicial will, superior to statute and to constitutional and political philosophy developed over a century. [In short, the] present Court legislates as freely toward the diminution of the power of the federal judiciary to secure civil liberties as the Warren Court ever did on behalf of civil rights."

In addition to the articles already cited, reference should be made to Bartels, Avoiding a Comity of Errors: A Model for Adjudicating Federal Civil Rights Suits That "Interfere" with State Civil Proceedings, 29 Stan. L. Rev. 27 (1976), which examines the extension of *Younger* principles to civil cases and proposes a detailed analysis for determining when abstention is appropriate.

For an unqualifiedly critical evaluation of *Younger* abstention, see Zeigler, Federal Court Reform of State Criminal Justice Systems: A Reassessment of the *Younger* Doctrine from a Modern Perspective, 19 U.C.D.L.Rev. 31 (1985). Professor Zeigler argues for direct federal intervention in order to achieve systemic reform of state criminal justice and calls for abolition of *Younger* abstention. He also sets forth detailed guidelines for the kinds of federal injunctive reform of state criminal systems that he would endorse. See also Zeigler, Rights Require Remedies: A New Approach to the Enforcement of Rights in the Federal Courts, 38 Hast.L.J. 665 (1987).

Finally, consider the views of Michael Wells. In The Role of Comity in the Law of Federal Courts, 60 N.C.L. Rev. 59 (1981), Wells surveys the Court's invocation of the notion of comity in a wide range of cases, including *Younger* and its progeny. He summarizes his evaluation of the increasingly elaborate body of *Younger* law as follows:

"The Court asserts that it has identified good reasons for deferring to state courts in these cases [e.g., *Younger*] while continuing to permit access to federal courts in other constitutional cases [e.g., *Steffel*]. Critics . . . charge that the Court's reasoning in the recent comity cases within the *Younger* doctrine undermines virtually all federal jurisdiction to the constitutional challenges to the actions of state officers. [B]oth the Court and its critics are wrong. . . . The role of comity in these cases is not to identify good reasons for federal court restraint in particular areas nor to undermine access to federal court in general. Rather, the Court makes arbitrary distinctions between cases, assigning some to federal courts and others to state courts. It uses comity as a device to obscure the lack of good reasons for these distinctions."

Why would the Court do this? Because, says Wells, at a general level the Court is unable to decide which is stronger, "the state's interest in having the issues adjudicated in a state forum" or "the individuals' interest in a federal forum." In short, Wells concludes, the Court "makes arbitrary distinctions because it cannot find good ones."

Is this criticism apt? Are the distinctions drawn by the Court as arbitrary as Wells suggests?

NOTES ON THE APPLICATION OF *YOUNGER* TO ADMINISTRATIVE PROCEEDINGS

1. *Middlesex County.* The applicability of *Younger* to state bar disciplinary proceedings was at issue in Middlesex County Ethics Committee v. Garden State Bar Association, 457 U.S. 423 (1982). New Jersey had an elaborate administrative system for reviewing charges of attorney misconduct. Ultimate authority rested with the New Jersey Supreme Court, which issued rules governing the administrative procedure and which reviewed all serious sanctions. Lennox Hinds was executive director of the National Conference of Black Lawyers and a member of the New Jersey bar. He had represented one Joanne Chesimard in certain civil proceedings concerning the conditions of her confinement in jail. When she went to trial in state court for murdering a policeman, Hinds held a news conference at which he questioned the judge's fairness and denounced the trial as a "travesty," a "legalized lynching," and a "kangaroo court." These remarks were reported in the press and led to a charge of conduct "prejudicial to the administration of justice" in violation of DR1–102(A)(5) of the Disciplinary rules of the Code of Professional Responsibility. Additionally, Hinds was

charged with violating DR7–107(D), which forbids extra-judicial statements by prosecution and defense counsel in a criminal trial.

Rather than contest the charges in the state system, Hinds and certain bar organizations sued in federal court to have the disciplinary rules declared invalid. The District Court dismissed the suit so that the state would have an opportunity to interpret its rules in light of the constitutional challenge. The Third Circuit reversed on the ground that the state proceedings were administrative in nature and therefore did not provide an adequate opportunity for litigation of the federal claim. The New Jersey Supreme Court then announced that it would nevertheless hear Hinds' constitutional challenges, but the Third Circuit declined to reconsider.

Speaking for the Court, Chief Justice Burger began with the proposition that the policies underlying *Younger* are "fully applicable" to civil proceedings "when important state interests are involved." The importance of the state interests might be demonstrated by a close relationship between civil and criminal enforcement proceedings, as in *Huffman v. Pursue, Ltd.*, or by a showing that the civil proceedings were "necessary" for the vindication of "important state policies," as in *Trainor v. Hernandez*, or for "the functioning of the state judicial system," as in *Juidice v. Vail*.

Having endorsed a broad application of *Younger* to civil proceedings, Burger then turned to the specifics of the case. He determined first that the disciplinary proceedings were "judicial" in nature. They were conducted under the authority of the New Jersey Supreme Court, and the local administrative bodies functioned in a way analogous to special masters. Thus, the proceedings were "of such a character as to warrant federal-court deference." Second, Burger identified "important state interests" in "maintaining and assuring the professional conduct of the attorneys it licenses" and noted that the named defendant in the federal suit was the Middlesex County Ethics Committee, "an agency of the Supreme Court of New Jersey." Finally, the Court found that the bar disciplinary proceedings gave Hinds ample opportunity to raise his federal constitutional claim. Therefore, *Younger* abstention was appropriate.

Four Justices agreed only as to the result. Justice Brennan concurred in the judgment with the notation that "[t]he traditional and primary responsibility of state courts for establishing and enforcing standards for members of their bars and the quasi-criminal nature of bar disciplinary proceedings call for exceptional deference by the federal court." Justice Marshall wrote separately on behalf of himself and Justices Brennan, Blackmun, and Stevens to say that, whatever might have been true at the outset of the proceedings, the disciplinary action had now been certified to the New Jersey Supreme Court and that *Younger* abstention was therefore appropriate.

Is it surprising that *Middlesex County* was unanimous as to result? Is a bar disciplinary proceeding a better case for invoking *Younger* abstention than a public nuisance action, a contempt proceeding, or an attachment procedure?

Another line of inquiry concerns the relation of *Younger* abstention to pending state administrative proceedings. Would *Middlesex County* have come out differently if it had not been possible to characterize the disciplinary proceedings as "judicial" in nature? What if the federal court had begun proceedings on the merits before the bar disciplinary proceeding had been certified to the state supreme court? Would *Younger* abstention nevertheless have been appropriate?

2. *Hawaii Housing Authority v. Midkiff.* A negative answer to the last of these questions might be inferred from Hawaii Housing Authority v. Midkiff, 467 U.S. 229 (1984). The case involved a just compensation challenge to Hawaii legislation. The law provided for condemnation of residential property held by large landowners, for resale by the Hawaii Housing Authority to current lessees, and for compulsory arbitration if that agency and the landowners could not agree as to price. The federal suit challenging this scheme was brought after compulsory arbitration was ordered but before any judicial proceedings in state court. The Supreme Court, speaking through Justice O'Connor, found *Younger* abstention inapplicable, despite *Middlesex County*. "Since *Younger* is not a bar to federal action when state judicial proceedings have not themselves commenced, abstention [in favor of the] administrative proceedings was not required."

Does *Hawaii Housing Authority* undermine *Middlesex County*? Does it mean that *Middlesex County* only applies when state bar disciplinary proceedings have been scheduled for judicial determination before a federal court has begun to hear the merits? If so, can other sorts of professional disciplinary proceedings be interrupted by resort to federal court?

3. *Moore v. Sims.* An additional dimension of *Younger* abstention arose in Moore v. Sims, 442 U.S. 415 (1979). The dispute began with a report of suspected child abuse. The Texas Department of Human Resources promptly seized the affected children, and a state court issued an emergency ex parte order giving the Department temporary custody. After some inconclusive proceedings in state court, the parents went to federal court. Further procedural maneuvers in both the state and federal courts ensued, after which a three-judge District Court finally reached the merits of the parents' claims. That court examined virtually every aspect of the state's child-protection procedures and found them in important respects unconstitutional. Specifically, the District Court held that Texas law was defective in failing to provide allegedly abusive parents with adequate notice and a sufficiently prompt hearing prior to removing their children from parental custody.

(i) The Majority. On direct appeal, the Supreme Court ruled that the District Court should not have reached the merits. First, Justice Rehnquist noted that *Younger* is "fully applicable to civil proceedings in which important state interests are involved." As in

Huffman, the state's child-protection procedures were "in aid of and closely related to" criminal statutes. Rehnquist then turned to the lower court's reasons for not abstaining:

> "The District Court . . . concluded that *Younger* absten-
> tion was not warranted because . . . 'there is no single state
> proceeding to which the plaintiffs may look for relief on
> constitutional or any other grounds'[:]

> > 'Many of the challenged actions taken by the state do not
> > and will not involve any judicial proceeding. Certainly as
> > to these, there is no pending state civil litigation about
> > which even to consider abstention.'

> The Court specifically alluded to . . . the appellees' challenge
> on constitutional grounds to the state's computerized collection
> and dissemination of child-abuse information . . . where that
> information is not the product of a judicial determination of
> abuse or neglect.

> ". . . Under established principles of equity, the exer-
> cise of equitable powers is inappropriate if there is an adequate
> remedy at law. Restated in the abstention context, the federal
> court should not exert jurisdiction if the plaintiffs 'had an
> *opportunity* to present their federal claims in the state proceed-
> ings.' Juidice v. Vail, 430 U.S. 327, 337 (1977). The pertinent
> issue is whether appellees' constitutional claims could have
> been raised in the pending state court proceedings. The Dis-
> trict Court's reference to the child-abuse reporting system
> reflects a misunderstanding of the nature of the inquiry. That
> the Department's suit does not necessarily implicate [this sys-
> tem] is not determinative. The question is whether that chal-
> lenge can be raised in the pending state proceedings subject to
> conventional limits on justiciability. On this point, Texas law
> is apparently as accommodating as the federal forum. Certain-
> ly, abstention is appropriate unless state law clearly bars the
> interposition of the constitutional claim.[a]

> "There are also intimations in the District Court's opinion
> that its decision to exert jurisdiction was influenced by a
> broader and novel consideration—the breadth of appellees'
> challenge to [the Texas statutes]. Thus, the District Court
> suggests that the more sweeping the challenge the more inap-
> propriate is abstention, and thereby inverts traditional absten-
> tion reasoning. The breadth of a challenge to a complex state
> statutory scheme has traditionally militated in *favor* of absten-
> tion, not *against* it. . . ."

Justice Rehnquist added that "[t]here are three distinct considerations that counsel abstention when broad-based challenges are made to

[a] Justice Rehnquist emphasized in a subsequent footnote that the important factor
was an "opportunity" to present the claims
in the pending state proceeding. This "opportunity" was apparently available under
Texas law by virtue of liberal provisions
governing permissive counterclaims.
[Footnote by eds.]

state statutes." The first was the concern that arose in Railroad Comm'n of Texas v. Pullman, 312 U.S. 496 (1941), namely:

"that a federal court will be forced to interpret state law without the benefit of state court consideration and therefore under circumstances where a constitutional determination is predicated on a reading of the statute that is not binding on state courts and may be discredited at any time—thus essentially rendering the federal court decision advisory and the litigation underlying it meaningless. These dangers increase with the breadth of the challenge."

The second was "the need for a concrete case or controversy—a concern also obviously enhanced by the scope of the challenge." Here the plaintiffs challenged numerous aspects of the Texas procedure that had not yet been applied to them and "consequently [they] can point to no injury in fact."

The third concern

"prompted by broad facial attacks on state statutes is the threat to our federal system of government posed by 'the needless obstruction of the domestic policy of the states by forestalling state action in construing and applying its own statutes.' Alabama State Federation of Labor v. McAdory, 325 U.S. 450, 471 (1945). . . . State courts are the principal expositors of state law. Almost every constitutional challenge—and particularly one as far ranging as that involved in this case—offers the opportunity for narrowing constructions that might obviate the constitutional problem and intelligently mediate federal constitutional concerns and state interests. When federal courts disrupt that process of mediation while interjecting themselves in such disputes, they prevent the informed evolution of state policy by state tribunals. The price exacted in terms of comity would only be outweighed if state courts were not competent to adjudicate federal constitutional claims—a postulate we have repeatedly and emphatically rejected."

Finally, the Court concluded that the inconclusive proceedings in state court, although clearly evidencing "confusion," did not demonstrate bad faith or other "extraordinary circumstances" making *Younger* inapplicable.

(ii) The Dissent. Justice Stevens dissented in an opinion joined by Justices Brennan, Stewart, and Marshall. In his view, *Younger* was "simply inapplicable" where "there is no single pending state proceeding in which the constitutional claims may be raised 'as a defense' and effective relief secured." The only proceeding pending in state court was a suit to determine custody. But the parents' federal action "did not go to their fitness as parents or to their rights to permanent custody of their children." Instead, the "thrust of their federal complaint was that the procedures employed by the state to gather information and to seize and retain the children pending the formal adversary hearing" were constitutionally inadequate:

> "As to these constitutional claims, the hearing to be afforded in state court on parental fitness and permanent custody was virtually as irrelevant as a hearing on a traffic violation. It is clearly the case, and the majority does not suggest otherwise, that the Sims could not avoid losing custody of their children at that point by successfully arguing that the state had acted unconstitutionally in its initial seizure of the children, or that a hearing should have been afforded earlier. These claims could not be raised 'as a defense to the ongoing proceedings,' Juidice v. Vail, 430 U.S. 327, 330 (1977). . . .

> "It may well be, as the majority suggests, that the Sims could have raised their constitutional claims against the state, not in defense, but in the nature of permissive counterclaims. . . . But even if Texas law does allow a party to raise any and all claims against the other party—no matter how unrelated—in a single proceeding, it certainly does not mandate that he do so. . . . The considerations of comity, equity, and federalism underlying [*Younger*] are no more implicated by the Sims' decision that claims unrelated to a pending state proceeding should be brought in federal rather than state court than they are by a similar decision in the absence of an unrelated state proceeding. If there is no requirement that federal plaintiffs initiate constitutional litigation in state rather than federal court in the first instance—and this Court has repeatedly held that there is not—then the coincidence of an unrelated state proceeding provides no justification for imposing such a requirement."

Additionally, the dissenters argued that the procedural inadequacies of the state scheme made *Younger* inapplicable. The state "did not afford plaintiffs the sufficient opportunity to vindicate their constitutional rights that is not only a predicate to a *Younger* dismissal, but also their entitlement under the Constitution." Hence the District Court's finding that the plaintiffs did not have a fair opportunity to pursue their claims in state court should have foreclosed any reliance on *Younger*.

   (iii) Questions and Comments on *Moore v. Sims*. *Moore v. Sims* provides a useful test of the complexities of *Younger* abstention in the context of institutional litigation. Anticipatory challenges to complex regulatory schemes will often be wide-ranging. By contrast, state enforcement actions will likely focus on a discrete decision. It often may happen, therefore, that a state defendant may wish to raise in federal court a far broader range of issues than will necessarily be determined in a pending state proceeding.

What should *Younger* mean in such a case? Should the federal court abstain from deciding *all* challenges to state law simply because *some* of them are involved in a pending proceeding? Would that rule effectively create an exhaustion requirement for federal constitutional claims? Or should the federal court invoke *Younger* only for those precise issues involved in the state proceeding? Would that lead to an inefficient splitting of related claims between state and federal court? Or, as the District Court apparently thought in *Moore,* should the breadth and scope of the federal claims be regarded as a ground for not applying *Younger*?

*

Appendix A

THE CONSTITUTION OF THE UNITED STATES OF AMERICA

We the People of the United States, in Order to form a more perfect Union, establish Justice, insure domestic Tranquility, provide for the common defence, promote the general Welfare, and secure the Blessings of Liberty to ourselves and our Posterity, do ordain and establish this Constitution for the United States of America.

ARTICLE I.

SECTION 1. All legislative Powers herein granted shall be vested in a Congress of the United States, which shall consist of a Senate and House of Representatives.

SECTION 2. The House of Representatives shall be composed of Members chosen every second Year by the People of the several States, and the Electors in each State shall have the Qualifications requisite for Electors of the most numerous Branch of the State Legislature.

No Person shall be a Representative who shall not have attained to the Age of twenty five Years, and been seven Years a Citizen of the United States, and who shall not, when elected, be an Inhabitant of that State in which he shall be chosen.

Representatives and direct Taxes shall be apportioned among the several States which may be included within this Union, according to their respective Numbers, which shall be determined by adding to the whole Number of free Persons, including those bound to Service for a Term of Years, and excluding Indians not taxed, three fifths of all other Persons. The actual Enumeration shall be made within three Years after the first Meeting of the Congress of the United States, and within every subsequent Term of ten Years, in such Manner as they shall by Law direct. The Number of Representatives shall not exceed one for every thirty Thousand, but each State shall have at Least one Representative; and until such enumeration shall be made, the State of New Hampshire shall be entitled to chuse three, Massachusetts eight, Rhode Island and Providence Plantations one, Connecticut five, New-York six, New Jersey four, Pennsylvania eight, Delaware one, Maryland six, Virginia ten, North Carolina five, South Carolina five, and Georgia three.

When vacancies happen in the Representation from any State, the Executive Authority thereof shall issue Writs of Election to fill such Vacancies.

The House of Representatives shall chuse their Speaker and other Officers; and shall have the sole Power of Impeachment.

SECTION 3. The Senate of the United States shall be composed of two Senators from each State, chosen by the Legislature thereof, for six Years; and each Senator shall have one Vote.

Immediately after they shall be assembled in Consequence of the first Election, they shall be divided as equally as may be into three Classes. The Seats of the Senators of the first Class shall be vacated at the Expiration of the second Year, of the second Class at the Expiration of the fourth Year, and of the third Class at the Expiration of the sixth Year, so that one third may be chosen every second Year; and if Vacancies happen by Resignation, or otherwise, during the Recess of the Legislature of any State, the Executive thereof may make temporary Appointments until the next Meeting of the Legislature, which shall then fill such Vacancies.

No Person shall be a Senator who shall not have attained to the Age of thirty Years, and been nine Years a Citizen of the United States, and who shall not, when elected, be an Inhabitant of that State for which he shall be chosen.

The Vice President of the United States shall be President of the Senate, but shall have no Vote, unless they be equally divided.

The Senate shall chuse their other Officers, and also a President pro tempore, in the Absence of the Vice President, or when he shall exercise the Office of President of the United States.

The Senate shall have the sole Power to try all Impeachments. When sitting for that Purpose, they shall be on Oath or Affirmation. When the President of the United States is tried, the Chief Justice shall preside: And no Person shall be convicted without the Concurrence of two thirds of the Members present.

Judgment in Cases of Impeachment shall not extend further than to removal from Office, and disqualification to hold and enjoy any Office of honor, Trust or Profit under the United States: but the Party convicted shall nevertheless be liable and subject to Indictment, Trial, Judgment and Punishment, according to Law.

SECTION 4. The Times, Places and Manner of holding Elections for Senators and Representatives, shall be prescribed in each State by the Legislature thereof; but the Congress may at any time by Law make or alter such Regulations, except as to the Places of chusing Senators.

The Congress shall assemble at least once in every Year, and such Meeting shall be on the first Monday in December, unless they shall by Law appoint a different Day.

SECTION 5. Each House shall be the Judge of the Elections, Returns and Qualifications of its own Members, and a Majority of each shall constitute a Quorum to do Business; but a smaller Number may adjourn from day to day, and may be authorized to compel the Attendance of absent Members, in such Manner, and under such Penalties as each House may provide.

Each House may determine the Rules of its Proceedings, punish its Members for disorderly Behaviour, and, with the Concurrence of two thirds, expel a Member.

Each House shall keep a Journal of its Proceedings, and from time to time publish the same, excepting such Parts as may in their Judgment require Secrecy; and the Yeas and Nays of the Members of either House on any question shall, at the Desire of one fifth of those Present, be entered on the Journal.

Neither House, during the Session of Congress, shall, without the Consent of the other, adjourn for more than three days, nor to any other Place than that in which the two Houses shall be sitting.

SECTION 6. The Senators and Representatives shall receive a Compensation for their Services, to be ascertained by Law, and paid out of the Treasury of the United States. They shall in all Cases, except Treason, Felony and Breach of the Peace, be privileged from Arrest during their Attendance at the Session of their respective Houses, and in going to and returning from the same; and for any Speech or Debate in either House, they shall not be questioned in any other Place.

No Senator or Representative shall, during the Time for which he was elected, be appointed to any civil Office under the Authority of the United States, which shall have been created, or the Emoluments whereof shall have been encreased during such time; and no Person holding any Office under the United States, shall be a Member of either House during his Continuance in Office.

SECTION 7. All Bills for raising Revenue shall originate in the House of Representatives; but the Senate may propose or concur with amendments as on other Bills.

Every Bill which shall have passed the House of Representatives and the Senate, shall, before it become a Law, be presented to the President of the United States; If he approve he shall sign it, but if not he shall return it, with his Objections to that House in which it shall have originated, who shall enter the Objections at large on their Journal, and proceed to reconsider it. If after such Reconsideration two thirds of that House shall agree to pass the Bill, it shall be sent, together with the Objections, to the other House, by which it shall likewise be reconsidered, and if approved by two thirds of that House, it shall become a Law. But in all such Cases the Votes of both Houses shall be determined by Yeas and Nays, and the Names of the Persons voting for and against the Bill shall be entered on the Journal of each House respectively. If any Bill shall not be returned by the President within ten Days (Sunday excepted) after it shall have been presented to him, the Same shall be a Law, in like Manner as if he had signed it, unless the Congress by their Adjournment prevent its Return, in which Case it shall not be a Law.

Every Order, Resolution, or Vote to which the Concurrence of the Senate and House of Representatives may be necessary (except on a question of Adjournment) shall be presented to the President of the United States; and before the Same shall take Effect, shall be approved by him, or being disapproved by him, shall be repassed by two thirds of the Senate and House of Representatives, according to the Rules and Limitations prescribed in the Case of a Bill.

SECTION 8.   The Congress shall have Power To lay and collect Taxes, Duties, Imposts and Excises, to pay the Debts and provide for the common Defence and general Welfare of the United States; but all Duties, Imposts and Excises shall be uniform throughout the United States;

To borrow Money on the credit of the United States;

To regulate Commerce with foreign Nations, and among the several States, and with the Indian Tribes;

To establish an uniform Rule of Naturalization, and uniform Laws on the subject of Bankruptcies throughout the United States;

To coin Money, regulate the Value thereof, and of foreign Coin, and fix the Standard of Weights and Measures;

To provide for the Punishment of counterfeiting the Securities and current Coin of the United States;

To establish Post Offices and post Roads;

To promote the Progress of Science and useful Arts, by securing for limited Times to Authors and Inventors the exclusive Right to their respective Writings and Discoveries;

To constitute Tribunals inferior to the supreme Court;

To define and punish Piracies and Felonies committed on the high Seas, and Offences against the Law of Nations;

To declare War, grant Letters of Marque and Reprisal, and make Rules concerning Captures on Land and Water;

To raise and support Armies, but no Appropriation of Money to that Use shall be for a longer Term than two Years;

To provide and maintain a Navy;

To make Rules for the Government and Regulation of the land and naval Forces;

To provide for calling forth the Militia to execute the Laws of the Union, suppress Insurrections and repel Invasions;

To provide for organizing, arming, and disciplining, the Militia, and for governing such Part of them as may be employed in the Service of the United States, reserving to the States respectively, the Appointment of the Officers, and the Authority of training the Militia according to the discipline prescribed by Congress;

To exercise exclusive Legislation in all Cases whatsoever, over such District (not exceeding ten Miles square) as may, by Cession of particular States, and the Acceptance of Congress, become the Seat of the Government of the United States, and to exercise like Authority over all Places purchased by the Consent of the Legislature of the State in which the Same shall be, for the Erection of Forts, Magazines, Arsenals, dock-Yards, and other needful Buildings;—And

To make all Laws which shall be necessary and proper for carrying into Execution the foregoing Powers, and all other Powers vested by this Constitution in the Government of the United States, or in any Department or Officer thereof.

SECTION 9. The Migration or Importation of such Persons as any of the States now existing shall think proper to admit, shall not be prohibited by the Congress prior to the Year one thousand eight hundred and eight, but a Tax or duty may be imposed on such Importation, not exceeding ten dollars for each Person.

The Privilege of the Writ of Habeas Corpus shall not be suspended, unless when in Cases of Rebellion or Invasion the public Safety may require it.

No Bill of Attainder or ex post facto Law shall be passed.

No Capitation, or other direct, Tax shall be laid, unless in Proportion to the Census or Enumeration herein before directed to be taken.

No Tax or Duty shall be laid on Articles exported from any State.

No Preference shall be given by any Regulation of Commerce or Revenue to the Ports of one State over those of another; nor shall Vessels bound to, or from, one State, be obliged to enter, clear, or pay Duties in another.

No Money shall be drawn from the Treasury, but in Consequence of Appropriations made by Law; and a regular Statement and Account of the Receipts and Expenditures of all public Money shall be published from time to time.

No Title of Nobility shall be granted by the United States: And no Person holding any Office of Profit or Trust under them, shall, without the Consent of the Congress, accept of any present, Emolument, Office, or Title, of any kind whatever, from any King, Prince or foreign State.

SECTION 10. No State shall enter into any Treaty, Alliance, or Confederation; grant Letters of Marque and Reprisal; coin Money; emit Bills of Credit; make any Thing but gold and silver Coin a Tender in Payment of Debts; pass any Bill of Attainder, ex post facto Law, or Law impairing the Obligation of Contracts, or grant any Title of Nobility.

No State shall, without the Consent of the Congress, lay any Imposts or Duties on Imports or Exports, except what may be absolutely necessary for executing its inspection Laws: and the net Produce of all Duties and Imposts, laid by any State on Imports or Exports, shall be for the Use of the Treasury of the United States; and all such Laws shall be subject to the Revision and Controul of the Congress.

No State shall, without the Consent of Congress, lay any Duty of Tonnage, keep Troops, or Ships of War in time of Peace, enter into any

Agreement or Compact with another State, or with a foreign Power, or engage in War, unless actually invaded, or in such imminent Danger as will not admit of delay.

ARTICLE II.

SECTION 1. The executive Power shall be vested in a President of the United States of America. He shall hold his Office during the Term of four Years, and, together with the Vice President, chosen for the same Term, be elected, as follows:

Each State shall appoint, in such Manner as the Legislature thereof may direct, a Number of Electors, equal to the whole Number of Senators and Representatives to which the State may be entitled in the Congress: but no Senator or Representative, or Person holding an Office of Trust or Profit under the United States, shall be appointed an Elector.

The Electors shall meet in their respective States, and vote by Ballot for two Persons, of whom one at least shall not be an Inhabitant of the same State with themselves. And they shall make a List of all the Persons voted for, and of the Number of Votes for each; which List they shall sign and certify, and transmit sealed to the Seat of the Government of the United States, directed to the President of the Senate. The President of the Senate shall, in the Presence of the Senate and House of Representatives, open all the Certificates, and the Votes shall then be counted. The Person having the greatest Number of Votes shall be the President, if such Number be a Majority of the whole Number of Electors appointed; and if there be more than one who have such Majority, and have an equal Number of Votes, then the House of Representatives shall immediately chuse by Ballot one of them for President; and if no Person have a Majority, then from the five highest on the List the said House shall in like Manner chuse the President. But in chusing the President, the Votes shall be taken by States, the Representation from each State having one Vote; a quorum for this Purpose shall consist of a Member or Members from two thirds of the States, and a Majority of all the States shall be necessary to a Choice. In every Case, after the Choice of the President, the Person having the greatest Number of Votes of the Electors shall be the Vice President. But if there should remain two or more who have equal Votes, the Senate shall chuse from them by Ballot the Vice President.

The Congress may determine the Time of chusing the Electors, and the Day on which they shall give their Votes; which Day shall be the same throughout the United States.

No Person except a natural born Citizen, or a Citizen of the United States, at the time of the Adoption of this Constitution, shall be eligible to the Office of President; neither shall any Person be eligible to that Office who shall not have attained to the Age of thirty five Years, and been fourteen Years a Resident within the United States.

In Case of the Removal of the President from Office, or of his Death, Resignation, or Inability to discharge the Powers and Duties of the said Office, the Same shall devolve on the Vice President, and the Congress may by Law provide for the Case of Removal, Death, Resignation or Inability, both of the President and Vice President, declaring what Officer shall then act as President, and such Officer shall act accordingly, until the Disability be removed, or a President shall be elected.

The President shall, at stated Times, receive for his Services, a Compensation, which shall neither be encreased nor diminished during the Period for which he shall have been elected, and he shall not receive within that Period any other Emolument from the United States, or any of them.

Before he enter on the Execution of his Office, he shall take the following Oath or Affirmation:—"I do solemnly swear (or affirm) that I will faithfully execute the Office of President of the United States, and will to the best of my Ability, preserve, protect and defend the Constitution of the United States."

SECTION 2. The President shall be Commander in Chief of the Army and Navy of the United States, and of the Militia of the several States, when called into the actual Service of the United States; he may require the Opinion, in writing, of the principal Officer in each of the executive Departments, upon any Subject relating to the Duties of their respective Offices, and he shall have Power to grant Reprieves and Pardons for Offences against the United States, except in Cases of Impeachment.

He shall have Power, by and with the Advice and Consent of the Senate, to make Treaties, provided two thirds of the Senators present concur; and he shall nominate, and by and with the Advice and Consent of the Senate, shall appoint Ambassadors, other public Ministers and Consuls, Judges of the supreme Court, and all other Officers of the United States, whose Appointments are not herein otherwise provided for, and which shall be established by Law: but the Congress may by Law vest the Appointment of such inferior Officers, as they think proper, in the President alone, in the Courts of Law, or in the Heads of Departments.

The President shall have Power to fill up all Vacancies that may happen during the Recess of the Senate, by granting Commissions which shall expire at the End of their next Session.

SECTION 3. He shall from time to time give to the Congress Information of the State of the Union, and recommend to their Consideration such Measures as he shall judge necessary and expedient; he may, on extraordinary Occasions, convene both Houses, or either of them, and in Case of Disagreement between them, with Respect to the Time of Adjournment, he may adjourn them to such Time as he shall think proper; he shall receive Ambassadors and other public Ministers;

he shall take Care that the Laws be faithfully executed, and shall Commission all the Officers of the United States.

SECTION 4. The President, Vice President and all Civil Officers of the United States, shall be removed from Office on Impeachment for, and Conviction of, Treason, Bribery, or other high Crimes and Misdemeanors.

ARTICLE III.

SECTION 1. The judicial Power of the United States, shall be vested in one supreme Court, and in such inferior Courts as the Congress may from time to time ordain and establish. The Judges, both of the supreme and inferior Courts, shall hold their Offices during good Behaviour, and shall, at stated Times, receive for their Services, a Compensation, which shall not be diminished during their Continuance in Office.

SECTION 2. The judicial Power shall extend to all Cases, in Law and Equity, arising under this Constitution, the Laws of the United States, and Treaties made, or which shall be made, under their Authority;—to all Cases affecting Ambassadors, other public Ministers and Consuls;—to all Cases of admiralty and maritime Jurisdiction;—to Controversies to which the United States shall be a Party;—to Controversies between two or more States;—between a State and Citizens of another State;—between Citizens of different States;—between Citizens of the same State claiming Lands under Grants of different States, and between a State, or the Citizens thereof, and foreign States, Citizens or Subjects.

In all Cases affecting Ambassadors, other public Ministers and Consuls, and those in which a State shall be Party, the Supreme Court shall have original Jurisdiction. In all the other Cases before mentioned, the supreme Court shall have appellate Jurisdiction, both as to Law and Fact, with such Exceptions, and under such Regulations as the Congress shall make.

The Trial of all Crimes, except in Cases of Impeachment, shall be by Jury; and such Trial shall be held in the State where the said Crimes shall have been committed; but when not committed within any State, the Trial shall be at such Place or Places as the Congress may by Law have directed.

SECTION 3. Treason against the United States, shall consist only in levying War against them, or in adhering to their Enemies, giving them Aid and Comfort. No Person shall be convicted of Treason unless on the Testimony of two Witnesses to the same overt Act, or on Confession in open Court.

The Congress shall have Power to declare the Punishment of Treason, but no Attainder of Treason shall work Corruption of Blood, or Forfeiture except during the Life of the Person attainted.

ARTICLE IV.

SECTION 1.   Full Faith and Credit shall be given in each State to the public Acts, Records, and judicial Proceedings of every other State. And the Congress may by general Laws prescribe the Manner in which such Acts, Records and Proceedings shall be proved, and the Effect thereof.

SECTION 2.   The Citizens of each State shall be entitled to all Privileges and Immunities of Citizens in the several States.

A Person charged in any State with Treason, Felony, or other Crime, who shall flee from Justice, and be found in another State, shall on Demand of the executive Authority of the State from which he fled, be delivered up, to be removed to the State having Jurisdiction of the Crime.

No Person held to Service or Labour in one State, under the Laws thereof, escaping into another, shall, in Consequence of any Law or Regulation therein, be discharged from such Service or Labour, but shall be delivered up on Claim of the Party to whom such Service or Labour may be due.

SECTION 3.   New States may be admitted by the Congress into this Union; but no new State shall be formed or erected within the Jurisdiction of any other State; nor any State be formed by the Junction of two or more States, or Parts of States, without the Consent of the Legislatures of the States concerned as well as of the Congress.

The Congress shall have Power to dispose of and make all needful Rules and Regulations respecting the Territory or other Property belonging to the United States; and nothing in this Constitution shall be so construed as to Prejudice any Claims of the United States, or of any particular State.

SECTION 4.   The United States shall guarantee to every State in this Union a Republican Form of Government, and shall protect each of them against Invasion; and on Application of the Legislature, or of the Executive (when the Legislature cannot be convened) against domestic Violence.

ARTICLE V.

The Congress, whenever two thirds of both Houses shall deem it necessary, shall propose Amendments to this Constitution, or, on the Application of the Legislatures of two thirds of the several States, shall call a Convention for proposing Amendments, which, in either Case, shall be valid to all Intents and Purposes, as Part of this Constitution, when ratified by the Legislatures of three fourths of the several States, or by Conventions in three fourths thereof, as the one or the other Mode of Ratification may be proposed by the Congress; Provided that no Amendment which may be made prior to the Year One thousand eight hundred and eight shall in any Manner affect the first and fourth

Clauses in the Ninth Section of the first Article; and that no State, without its Consent, shall be deprived of its equal Suffrage in the Senate.

ARTICLE VI.

All Debts contracted and Engagements entered into, before the Adoption of this Constitution, shall be as valid against the United States under this Constitution, as under the Confederation.

This Constitution, and the Laws of the United States which shall be made in Pursuance thereof; and all Treaties made, or which shall be made, under the Authority of the United States, shall be the supreme Law of the Land; and the Judges in every State shall be bound thereby, any Thing in the Constitution or Laws of any State to the Contrary notwithstanding.

The Senators and Representatives before mentioned, and the Members of the several State Legislatures, and all executive and judicial Officers, both of the United States and of the several States, shall be bound by Oath or Affirmation, to support this Constitution; but no religious Test shall ever be required as a Qualification to any Office or public Trust under the United States.

ARTICLE VII.

The Ratification of the Conventions of nine States, shall be sufficient for the Establishment of this Constitution between the States so ratifying the Same.

. . .

ARTICLES IN ADDITION TO, AND AMENDMENT OF, THE CONSTITUTION OF THE UNITED STATES OF AMERICA, PROPOSED BY CONGRESS, AND RATIFIED BY THE SEVERAL STATES, PURSUANT TO THE FIFTH ARTICLE OF THE ORIGINAL CONSTITUTION.

AMENDMENT I [1791].

Congress shall make no law respecting an establishment of religion, or prohibiting the free exercise thereof; or abridging the freedom of speech, or of the press; or the right of the people peaceably to assemble, and to petition the Government for a redress of grievances.

AMENDMENT II [1791].

A well regulated Militia, being necessary to the security of a free State, the right of the people to keep and bear Arms, shall not be infringed.

AMENDMENT III [1791].

No Soldier shall, in time of peace be quartered in any house, without the consent of the Owner, nor in time of war, but in a manner to be prescribed by law.

AMENDMENT IV [1791].

The right of the people to be secure in their persons, houses, papers, and effects, against unreasonable searches and seizures, shall not be violated, and no Warrants shall issue, but upon probable cause, supported by Oath or affirmation, and particularly describing the place to be searched, and the persons or things to be seized.

AMENDMENT V [1791].

No person shall be held to answer for a capital, or otherwise infamous crime, unless on a presentment or indictment of a Grand Jury, except in cases arising in the land or naval forces, or in the Militia, when in actual service in time of War or public danger; nor shall any person be subject for the same offence to be twice put in jeopardy of life or limb; nor shall be compelled in any criminal case to be a witness against himself, nor be deprived of life, liberty, or property, without due process of law; nor shall private property be taken for public use, without just compensation.

AMENDMENT VI [1791].

In all criminal prosecutions, the accused shall enjoy the right to a speedy and public trial, by an impartial jury of the State and district wherein the crime shall have been committed, which district shall have been previously ascertained by law, and to be informed of the nature and cause of the accusation; to be confronted with the witnesses against him; to have compulsory process for obtaining Witnesses in his favor, and to have the Assistance of Counsel for his defence.

AMENDMENT VII [1791].

In Suits at common law, where the value in controversy shall exceed twenty dollars, the right of trial by jury shall be preserved, and no fact tried by a jury, shall be otherwise re-examined in any Court of the United States, than according to the rules of the common law.

AMENDMENT VIII [1791].

Excessive bail shall not be required, nor excessive fines imposed, nor cruel and unusual punishments inflicted.

AMENDMENT IX [1791].

The enumeration in the Constitution, of certain rights, shall not be construed to deny or disparage others retained by the people.

AMENDMENT X [1791].

The powers not delegated to the United States by the Constitution, nor prohibited by it to the States, are reserved to the States respectively, or to the people.

AMENDMENT XI [1798].

The Judicial power of the United States shall not be construed to extend to any suit in law or equity, commenced or prosecuted against one of the United States by Citizens of another State, or by Citizens or Subjects of any Foreign State.

AMENDMENT XII [1804].

The Electors shall meet in their respective states and vote by ballot for President and Vice-President, one of whom, at least, shall not be an inhabitant of the same state with themselves; they shall name in their ballots the person voted for as President, and in distinct ballots the person voted for as Vice-President, and they shall make distinct lists of all persons voted for as President, and of all persons voted for as Vice-President, and of the number of votes for each, which lists they shall sign and certify, and transmit sealed to the seat of the government of the United States, directed to the President of the Senate;—The President of the Senate shall, in the presence of the Senate and House of Representatives, open all the certificates and the votes shall then be counted;—The person having the greatest number of votes for President, shall be the President, if such number be a majority of the whole number of Electors appointed; and if no person have such majority, then from the persons having the highest numbers not exceeding three on the list of those voted for as President, the House of Representatives shall choose immediately, by ballot, the President. But in choosing the President, the votes shall be taken by states, the representation from each state having one vote; a quorum for this purpose shall consist of a member or members from two-thirds of the states, and a majority of all the states shall be necessary to a choice. And if the House of Representatives shall not choose a President whenever the right of choice shall devolve upon them, before the fourth day of March next following, then the Vice-President shall act as President, as in the case of the death or other constitutional disability of the President—The person having the greatest number of votes as Vice-President, shall be the Vice-President, if such number be a majority of the whole number of Electors appointed, and if no person have a majority, then from the two highest numbers on the list, the Senate shall choose the Vice-President; a quorum for the purpose shall consist of two-thirds of the whole number of Senators, and a majority of the whole number shall be necessary to a choice. But no person constitutionally ineligible to the office of President shall be eligible to that of Vice-President of the United States.

AMENDMENT XIII [1865].

SECTION 1. Neither slavery nor involuntary servitude, except as a punishment for crime whereof the party shall have been duly convicted, shall exist within the United States, or any place subject to their jurisdiction.

SECTION 2. Congress shall have power to enforce this article by appropriate legislation.

AMENDMENT XIV [1868].

SECTION 1. All persons born or naturalized in the United States, and subject to the jurisdiction thereof, are citizens of the United States and of the State wherein they reside. No State shall make or enforce any law which shall abridge the privileges or immunities of citizens of the United States; nor shall any State deprive any person of life, liberty, or property, without due process of law; nor deny to any person within its jurisdiction the equal protection of the laws.

SECTION 2. Representatives shall be apportioned among the several States according to their respective numbers, counting the whole number of persons in each State, excluding Indians not taxed. But when the right to vote at any election for the choice of electors for President and Vice President of the United States, Representatives in Congress, the Executive and Judicial officers of a State, or the members of the Legislature thereof, is denied to any of the male inhabitants of such State, being twenty-one years of age, and citizens of the United States, or in any way abridged, except for participation in rebellion, or other crime, the basis of representation therein shall be reduced in the proportion which the number of such male citizens shall bear to the whole number of male citizens twenty-one years of age in such State.

SECTION 3. No person shall be a Senator or Representative in Congress, or elector of President and Vice President, or hold any office, civil or military, under the United States, or under any State, who, having previously taken an oath, as a member of Congress, or as an officer of the United States, or as a member of any State legislature, or as an executive or judicial officer of any State, to support the Constitution of the United States, shall have engaged in insurrection or rebellion against the same, or given aid or comfort to the enemies thereof. But Congress may by a vote of two-thirds of each House, remove such disability.

SECTION 4. The validity of the public debt of the United States, authorized by law, including debts incurred for payment of pensions and bounties for services in suppressing insurrection or rebellion, shall not be questioned. But neither the United States nor any State shall assume or pay any debt or obligation incurred in aid of insurrection or rebellion against the United States, or any claim for the loss of emancipation of any slave; but all such debts, obligations and claims shall be held illegal and void.

SECTION 5. The Congress shall have power to enforce, by appropriate legislation, the provisions of this article.

AMENDMENT XV [1870].

SECTION 1. The right of citizens of the United States to vote shall not be denied or abridged by the United States or by any State on account of race, color, or previous condition of servitude.

SECTION 2. The Congress shall have power to enforce this article by appropriate legislation.

AMENDMENT XVI [1913].

The Congress shall have power to lay and collect taxes on incomes, from whatever source derived, without apportionment among the several States, and without regard to any census or enumeration.

AMENDMENT XVII [1913].

The Senate of the United States shall be composed of two Senators from each State, elected by the people thereof, for six years; and each Senator shall have one vote. The electors in each State shall have the qualifications requisite for electors of the most numerous branch of the State legislatures.

When vacancies happen in the representation of any State in the Senate, the executive authority of such State shall issue writs of election to fill such vacancies: *Provided,* That the legislature of any State may empower the executive thereof to make temporary appointments until the people fill the vacancies by election as the legislature may direct.

This amendment shall not be so construed as to affect the election or term of any Senator chosen before it becomes valid as part of the Constitution.

AMENDMENT XVIII [1919].

SECTION 1. After one year from the ratification of this article the manufacture, sale, or transportation of intoxicating liquors within, the importation thereof into, or the exportation thereof from the United States and all territory subject to the jurisdiction thereof for beverage purposes is hereby prohibited.

SECTION 2. The Congress and the several States shall have concurrent power to enforce this article by appropriate legislation.

SECTION 3. This article shall be inoperative unless it shall have been ratified as an amendment to the Constitution by the legislatures of the several States, as provided in the Constitution, within seven years from the date of the submission hereof to the States by the Congress.

AMENDMENT XIX [1920].

The right of citizens of the United States to vote shall not be denied or abridged by the United States or by any State on account of sex.

Congress shall have power to enforce this article by appropriate legislation.

AMENDMENT XX [1933].

SECTION 1. The terms of the President and Vice President shall end at noon on the 20th day of January, and the terms of Senators and Representatives at noon on the 3d day of January, of the years in which such terms would have ended if this article had not been ratified; and the terms of their successors shall then begin.

SECTION 2. The Congress shall assemble at least once in every year, and such meeting shall begin at noon on the 3d day of January, unless they shall by law appoint a different day.

SECTION 3. If, at the time fixed for the beginning of the term of the President, the President elect shall have died, the Vice President elect shall become President. If a President shall not have been chosen before the time fixed for the beginning of his term, or if the President elect shall have failed to qualify, then the Vice President elect shall act as President until a President shall have qualified; and the Congress may by law provide for the case wherein neither a President elect nor a Vice President elect shall have qualified, declaring who shall then act as President, or the manner in which one who is to act shall be selected, and such person shall act accordingly until a President or Vice President shall have qualified.

SECTION 4. The Congress may by law provide for the case of the death of any of the persons from whom the House of Representatives may choose a President whenever the right of choice shall have devolved upon them, and for the case of the death of any of the persons from whom the Senate may choose a Vice President whenever the right of choice shall have devolved upon them.

SECTION 5. Sections 1 and 2 shall take effect on the 15th day of October following the ratification of this article.

SECTION 6. This article shall be inoperative unless it shall have been ratified as an amendment to the Constitution by the legislatures of three-fourths of the several States within seven years from the date of its submission.

AMENDMENT XXI [1933].

SECTION 1. The eighteenth article of amendment to the Constitution of the United States is hereby repealed.

SECTION 2. The transportation or importation into any State, Territory, or possession of the United States for delivery or use therein of intoxicating liquors, in violation of the laws thereof, is hereby prohibited.

SECTION 3. This article shall be inoperative unless it shall have been ratified as an amendment to the Constitution by conventions in the several States, as provided in the Constitution, within seven years from the date of the submission hereof to the States by the Congress.

AMENDMENT XXII [1951].

SECTION 1. No person shall be elected to the office of the President more than twice, and no person who has held the office of President, or acted as President, for more than two years of a term to which some other person was elected President shall be elected to the office of the President more than once. But this Article shall not apply to any person holding the office of President when this Article was proposed by the Congress, and shall not prevent any person who may be holding the office of President, or acting as President, during the term within which this Article becomes operative from holding the office of President or acting as President during the remainder of such term.

SECTION 2. This article shall be inoperative unless it shall have been ratified as an amendment to the Constitution by the legislatures of three-fourths of the several States within seven years from the date of its submission to the States by the Congress.

AMENDMENT XXIII [1961].

SECTION 1. The District constituting the seat of Government of the United States shall appoint in such manner as the Congress may direct:

A number of electors of President and Vice President equal to the whole number of Senators and Representatives in Congress to which the District would be entitled if it were a State, but in no event more than the least populous State; they shall be in addition to those appointed by the States, but they shall be considered, for the purposes of the election of President and Vice President, to be electors appointed by a State; and they shall meet in the District and perform such duties as provided by the twelfth article of amendment.

SECTION 2. The Congress shall have power to enforce this article by appropriate legislation.

AMENDMENT XXIV [1964].

SECTION 1. The right of citizens of the United States to vote in any primary or other election for President or Vice President, for electors for President or Vice President, or for Senator or Representative in Congress, shall not be denied or abridged by the United States or any State by reason of failure to pay any poll tax or other tax.

SECTION 2. The Congress shall have power to enforce this article by appropriate legislation.

AMENDMENT XXV [1967].

SECTION 1. In case of the removal of the President from office or of his death or resignation, the Vice President shall become President.

SECTION 2. Whenever there is a vacancy in the office of the Vice President, the President shall nominate a Vice President who shall take office upon confirmation by a majority vote of both Houses of Congress.

SECTION 3. Whenever the President transmits to the President pro tempore of the Senate and the Speaker of the House of Representatives his written declaration that he is unable to discharge the powers and duties of his office, and until he transmits to them a written declaration to the contrary, such powers and duties shall be discharged by the Vice President as Acting President.

SECTION 4. Whenever the Vice President and a majority of either the principal officers of the executive departments or of such other body as Congress may by law provide, transmit to the President pro tempore of the Senate and the Speaker of the House of Representatives their written declaration that the President is unable to discharge the powers and duties of his office, the Vice President shall immediately assume the powers and duties of the office as Acting President.

Thereafter, when the President transmits to the President pro tempore of the Senate and the Speaker of the House of Representatives his written declaration that no inability exists, he shall resume the powers and duties of his office unless the Vice President and a majority of either the principal officers of the executive department or of such other body as Congress may by law provide, transmit within four days to the President pro tempore of the Senate and the Speaker of the House of Representatives their written declaration that the President is unable to discharge the powers and duties of his office. Thereupon Congress shall decide the issue, assembling within forty-eight hours for that purpose if not in session. If the Congress, within twenty-one days after receipt of the latter written declaration, or, if Congress is not in session, within twenty-one days after Congress is required to assemble, determines by two-thirds vote of both Houses that the President is unable to discharge the powers and duties of his office, the Vice President shall continue to discharge the same as Acting President;

otherwise, the President shall resume the powers and duties of his office.

AMENDMENT XXVI [1971].

SECTION 1. The right of citizens of the United States, who are eighteen years of age or older, to vote shall not be denied or abridged by the United States or by any State on account of age.

SECTION 2. The Congress shall have power to enforce this article by appropriate legislation.

———

Appendix B

SELECTED FEDERAL STATUTES

I. Title 18, U.S.C.:

§ 241. Conspiracy against rights of citizens

If two or more persons conspire to injure, oppress, threaten, or intimidate any citizen in the free exercise or enjoyment of any right or privilege secured to him by the Constitution or laws of the United States, or because of his having so exercised the same; or

If two or more persons go in disguise on the highway, or on the premises of another, with intent to prevent or hinder his free exercise or enjoyment of any right or privilege so secured—

They shall be fined not more than $10,000 or imprisoned not more than ten years, or both; and if death results, they shall be subject to imprisonment for any term of years or for life.

§ 242. Deprivation of rights under color of law

Whoever, under color of any law, statute, ordinance, regulation, or custom, willfully subjects any inhabitant of any State, Territory, or District to the deprivation of any rights, privileges, or immunities secured or protected by the Constitution or laws of the United States, or to different punishments, pains, or penalties, on account of such inhabitant being an alien, or by reason of his color, or race, than are prescribed for the punishment of citizens, shall be fined not more than $1,000 or imprisoned not more than one year, or both; and if death results shall be subject to imprisonment for any term of years or for life.

§ 3231. District courts

The district courts of the United States shall have original jurisdiction, exclusive of the courts of the States, of all offenses against the laws of the United States.

Nothing in this title shall be held to take away or impair the jurisdiction of the courts of the several States under the laws thereof.

§ 3731. Appeal by United States

In a criminal case an appeal by the United States shall lie to a court of appeals from a decision, judgment, or order of a district court dismissing an indictment or information or granting a new trial after verdict or judgment, as to any one or more counts, except that no appeal shall lie where the double jeopardy clause of the United States Constitution prohibits further prosecution.

An appeal by the United States shall lie to a court of appeals from a decision or order of a district court suppressing or excluding evidence or requiring the return of seized property in a criminal proceeding, not made after the defendant has been put in jeopardy and before the verdict or finding on an indictment or information, if the United States attorney certifies to the district court that the appeal is not taken for purpose of delay and that the evidence is a substantial proof of a fact material in the proceeding.

An appeal by the United States shall lie to a court of appeals from a decision or order, entered by a district court of the United States, granting the release of a person charged with or convicted of an offense, or denying a motion for revocation of, or modification of the conditions of, a decision or order granting release.

The appeal in all such cases shall be taken within thirty days after the decision, judgment or order has been rendered and shall be diligently prosecuted.

Pending the prosecution and determination of the appeal in the foregoing instances, the defendant shall be released in accordance with chapter 207 of this title.

The provisions of this section shall be liberally construed to effectuate its purposes.

II. Title 28, U.S.C.:

§ 1251. Original jurisdiction

(a) The Supreme Court shall have original and exclusive jurisdiction of all controversies between two or more States.

(b) The Supreme Court shall have original but not exclusive jurisdiction of:

(1) All actions or proceedings to which ambassadors, other public ministers, consuls, or vice consuls of foreign states are parties;

(2) All controversies between the United States and a State;

(3) All actions or proceedings by a State against the citizens of another State or against aliens.

§ 1252. Direct appeals from decisions invalidating Acts of Congress

Any party may appeal to the Supreme Court from an interlocutory or final judgment, decree or order of any court of the United States, the United States District Court for the District of the Canal Zone, the District Court of Guam and the District Court of the Virgin Islands and any court of record of Puerto Rico, holding an Act of Congress unconstitutional in any civil action, suit, or proceeding to which the United States or any of its agencies, or any officer or employee thereof, as such officer or employee, is a party.

A party who has received notice of appeal under this section shall take any subsequent appeal or cross appeal to the Supreme Court.

All appeals or cross appeals taken to other courts prior to such notice shall be treated as taken directly to the Supreme Court.

§ 1253. Direct appeals from decisions of three-judge courts

Except as otherwise provided by law, any party may appeal to the Supreme Court from an order granting or denying, after notice and hearing, an interlocutory or permanent injunction in any civil action, suit or proceeding required by any Act of Congress to be heard and determined by a district court of three judges.

§ 1254. Courts of appeals; certiorari; certified questions

Cases in the courts of appeals may be reviewed by the Supreme Court by the following methods:

(1) By writ of certiorari granted upon the petition of any party to any civil or criminal case, before or after rendition of judgment or decree;

(2) By certification at any time by a court of appeals of any question of law in any civil or criminal case as to which instructions are desired, and upon such certification the Supreme Court may give binding instructions or require the entire record to be sent up for decision of the entire matter in controversy.

§ 1257. State courts; certiorari.

(a) Final judgments or decrees rendered by the highest court of a State in which a decision could be had, may be reviewed by the Supreme Court by writ of certiorari where the validity of a treaty or statute of the United States is drawn in question or where the validity of a statute of any State is drawn in question on the ground of it being repugnant to the Constitution, treaties, or laws of the United States, or where any title, right, privilege, or immunity is specially set up or claimed under the Constitution or the treaties or statutes of, or any commission held or authority exercised under, the United States.

(b) For purposes of this section, the term "highest court of s State" includes the district of Columbia Court of Appeals.

§ 1291. Final decisions of district courts

The courts of appeals (other than the United States Court of Appeal for the Federal Circuit) shall have jurisdiction of appeals from all final decisions of the district courts of the United States, the United States District Court for the District of the Canal Zone, the District Court of Guam, and the District Court of the Virgin Islands, except where a direct review may be had in the Supreme Court. The jurisdiction of the United States Court of Appeals for the Federal Circuit shall be limited to the jurisdiction described in sections 1292(c) and (d) and 1295 of this title.

§ 1292. Interlocutory decisions

(a) Except as provided in subsections (c) and (d) of this section, the courts of appeals shall have jurisdiction of appeals from:

(1) Interlocutory orders of the district courts of the United States, the United States District Court for the District of the Canal Zone, the District Court of Guam, and the District Court of the Virgin Islands, or of the judges thereof, granting, continuing, modifying, refusing or dissolving injunctions, or refusing to dissolve or modify injunctions, except where a direct review may be had in the Supreme Court;

(2) Interlocutory orders appointing receivers, or refusing orders to wind up receiverships or to take steps to accomplish the purposes thereof, such as directing sales or other disposals of property;

(3) Interlocutory decrees of such district courts on the judges thereof determining the rights and liabilities of the parties to admiralty cases in which appeals from final decrees are allowed.

(b) When a district judge, in making in a civil action an order not otherwise appealable under this section, shall be of the opinion that such order involves a controlling question of law as to which there is substantial ground for difference of opinion and that an immediate appeal from the order may materially advance the ultimate termination of the litigation, he shall so state in writing in such order. The Court of Appeals which would have jurisdiction of an appeal of such action may thereupon, in its discretion, permit an appeal to be taken from such order, if application is made to it within ten days after the entry of the order: Provided, however, That application for an appeal hereunder shall not stay proceedings in the district court unless the district judge or the Court of Appeals or a judge thereof shall so order.

(c) The United States Court of Appeals for the Federal Circuit shall have exclusive jurisdiction—

(1) of an appeal from an interlocutory order or decree described in subsection (a) or (b) of this section in any case over which the court would have jurisdiction of an appeal under section 1295 of this title; and

(2) of an appeal from a judgment in a civil action for patent infringement which would otherwise be appealable to the United States Court of Appeals for the Federal Circuit and is final except for an accounting.

(d)(1) When the chief judge of the Court of International Trade issues an order under the provisions of section 256(b) of this title, or when any judge of the Court of International Trade, in issuing any other interlocutory order, includes in the order a statement that a controlling question of law is involved with respect to which there is a substantial ground for difference of opinion and that an immediate appeal from that order may materially advance the ultimate termination of the litigation, the United States Court of Appeals for the Federal

Circuit may, in its discretion, permit an appeal to be taken from such order, if application is made to that Court within ten days after the entry of such order.

(2) When any judge of the United States Claims Court, in issuing an interlocutory order, includes in the order a statement that a controlling question of law is involved with respect to which there is a substantial ground for difference of opinion and that an immediate appeal from that order may materially advance the ultimate termination of the litigation, the United States Court of Appeals for the Federal Circuit may, in its discretion, permit an appeal to be taken from such order, if application is made to that Court within ten days after the entry of such order.

(3) Neither the application for nor the granting of an appeal under this subsection shall stay proceedings in the Court of International Trade or in the Claims Court, as the case may be, unless a stay is ordered by a judge of the Court of International Trade or of the Claims Court or by the United States Court of Appeals for the Federal Circuit or a judge of that court.

(4)(A) The United States Court of Appeals for the Federal Circuit shall have exclusive jurisdiction of an appeal from an interlocutory order of a district court of the United States, the District Court of Guam, the District Court of the Virgin Islands, or the District Court for the Northern Mariana Islands, granting or denying, in whole or in part, a motion to transfer an action to the United States Claims Court under section 1631 of this title.

(B) When a motion to transfer an action to the Claims Court is filed in a district court, no further proceedings shall be taken in the district court until 60 days after the court has ruled upon the motion. If an appeal is taken from the district court's grant or denial of the motion, proceedings shall be further stayed until the appeal has been decided by the Court of Appeals for the Federal Circuit. The stay of proceedings in the district court shall not bar the granting of preliminary or injunctive relief, where appropriate and where expedition is reasonably necessary. However, during the period in which proceedings are stayed as provided in this subparagraph, no transfer to the Claims Court pursuant to the motion shall be carried out.

§ 1330. Actions against foreign states

(a) The district courts shall have original jurisdiction without regard to amount in controversy of any nonjury civil action against a foreign state as defined in section 1603(a) of this title as to any claim for relief in personam with respect to which the foreign state is not entitled to immunity either under sections 1605–1607 of this title or under any applicable international agreement.

(b) Personal jurisdiction over a foreign state shall exist as to every claim for relief over which the district courts have jurisdiction under subsection (a) where service has been made under section 1608 of this title.

(c) For purposes of subsection (b), an appearance by a foreign state does not confer personal jurisdiction with respect to any claim for relief not arising out of any transaction or occurrence enumerated in sections 1605–1607 of this title.

§ 1331. Federal question; amount in controversy; costs

The district courts shall have original jurisdiction of all civil actions arising under the Constitution, laws, or treaties of the United States.

§ 1332. Diversity of citizenship; amount in controversy; costs

(a) The district courts shall have original jurisdiction of all civil actions where the matter in controversy exceeds the sum or value of $50,000, exclusive of interest and costs, and is between— .

  (1) citizens of different States; *complete diversity*

  (2) citizens of a State and citizens or subjects of a foreign state;

  (3) citizens of different States and in which citizens or subjects of a foreign state are additional parties; and

  (4) a foreign state, defined in section 1603(a) of this title, as plaintiff and citizens of a State or of different States.

For the purposes of this section, section 1335, and section 1441, an alien admitted to the United States for permanent residence shall be deemed a citizen of the State in which such alien is domiciled.

(b) Except when express provision therefor is otherwise made in a statute of the United States, where the plaintiff who files the case originally in the Federal courts is finally adjudged to be entitled to recover less than the sum or value of $50,000, computed without regard to any setoff or counterclaim to which the defendant may be adjudged to be entitled, and exclusive of interest and costs, the district court may deny costs to the plaintiff and, in addition, may impose costs on the plaintiff.

(c) For the purposes of this section and section 1441 of this title—

  (1) a corporation shall be deemed to be a citizen of any State by which it has been incorporated and of the State where it has its principal place of business, except that in any direct action against the insurer of a policy or contract of liability insurance, whether incorporated or unincorporated, to which action the insured is not joined as a party-defendant, such insurer shall be deemed a citizen of the State of which the insured is a citizen, as well as of any State by which the insurer has been incorporated and of the State where it has its principal place of business; and

  (2) the legal representative of the estate of a decedent shall be deemed to be a citizen only of the same State as the decedent, and

the legal representative of an infant or incompetent shall be deemed to be a citizen only of the same State as the infant or incompetent.

(d) The word "States", as used in this section, includes the Territories, the District of Columbia, and the Commonwealth of Puerto Rico.

§ 1334. Bankruptcy cases and proceedings

(a) Except as provided in subsection (b) of this section, the district court shall have original and exclusive jurisdiction of all cases under title 11.

(b) Notwithstanding any Act of Congress that confers exclusive jurisdiction on a court or courts other than the district courts, the district courts shall have original but not exclusive jurisdiction of all civil proceedings arising under title 11, or arising in or related to cases under title 11.

(c)(1) Nothing in this section prevents a district court in the interest of justice, or in the interest of comity with State courts or respect for State law, from abstaining from hearing a particular proceeding arising under title 11 or arising in or related to a case under title 11.

(2) Upon timely motion of a party in a proceeding based upon a State law claim or State law cause of action, related to a case under title 11 but not arising under title 11 or arising in a case under title 11, with respect to which an action could not have been commenced in a court of the United States absent jurisdiction under this section, the district court shall abstain from hearing such proceeding if an action is commenced, and can be timely adjudicated, in a State forum of appropriate jursidiction. Any decision to abstain made under this subsection is not reviewable by appeal or otherwise. This subsection shall not be construed to limit the applicability of the stay provided for by section 362 of title 11, United States Code, as such section applies to an action affecting the property of the estate in bankruptcy.

(d) The district court in which a case under title 11 is commenced or is pending shall have exclusive jurisdiction of all of the property, wherever located, of the debtor as of the commencement of such case, and of the estate.

§ 1335. Interpleader

(a) The district courts shall have original jurisdiction of any civil action of interpleader or in the nature of interpleader filed by any person, firm, or corporation, association, or society having in his or its custody or possession money or property of the value of $500 or more, or having issued a note, bond, certificate, policy of insurance, or other instrument of value or amount of $500 or more, or providing for the delivery or payment or the loan of money or property of such amount or value, or being under any obligation written or unwritten to the amount of $500 or more, if

(1) Two or more adverse claimants, of diverse citizenship as defined in section 1332 of this title, are claiming or may claim to be entitled to such money or property, or to any one or more of the benefits arising by virtue of any note, bond, certificate, policy or other instrument, or arising by virtue of any such obligation; and if (2) the plaintiff has deposited such money or property or has paid the amount of or the loan or other value of such instrument or the amount due under such obligation into the registry of the court, there to abide the judgment of the court, or has given bond payable to the clerk of the court in such amount and with such surety as the court or judge may deem proper, conditioned upon the compliance by the plaintiff with the future order or judgment of the court with respect to the subject matter of the controversy.

(b) Such an action may be entertained although the titles or claims of the conflicting claimants do not have a common origin, or are not identical, but are adverse to and independent of one another.

§ 1338. Patents, plant variety protection, copyrights, trademarks, and unfair competition

(a) The district courts shall have original jurisdiction of any civil action arising under any Act of Congress relating to patents, plant variety protection, copyrights and trade-marks. Such jurisdiction shall be exclusive of the courts of the states in patent, plant variety protection and copyright cases.

(b) The district courts shall have original jurisdiction of any civil action asserting a claim of unfair competition when joined with a substantial and related claim under the copyright, patent, plant variety protection, or trade-mark laws.

§ 1341. Taxes by States

The district courts shall not enjoin, suspend or restrain the assessment, levy or collection of any tax under State law where a plain, speedy and efficient remedy may be had in the courts of such State.

§ 1342. Rate orders of State agencies

The district courts shall not enjoin, suspend or restrain the operation of, or compliance with, any order affecting rates chargeable by a public utility and made by a State administrative agency or a rate-making body of a State political subdivision, where:

(1) Jurisdiction is based solely on diversity of citizenship or repugnance of the order to the Federal Constitution; and,

(2) The order does not interfere with interstate commerce; and,

(3) The order has been made after reasonable notice and hearing; and,

(4) A plain, speedy and efficient remedy may be had in the courts of such State.

§ 1343. Civil rights and elective franchise

(a) The district courts shall have original jurisdiction of any civil action authorized by law to be commenced by any person:

(1) To recover damages for injury to his person or property, or because of the deprivation of any right or privilege of a citizen of the United States, by any act done in furtherance of any conspiracy mentioned in section 1985 of Title 42;

(2) To recover damages from any person who fails to prevent or to aid in preventing any wrongs mentioned in section 1985 of Title 42 which he had knowledge were about to occur and power to prevent;

(3) To redress the deprivation, under color of any State law, statute, ordinance, regulation, custom or usage, of any right, privilege or immunity secured by the Constitution of the United States or by any Act of Congress providing for equal rights of citizens or of all persons within the jurisdiction of the United States;

(4) To recover damages or to secure equitable or other relief under any Act of Congress providing for the protection of civil rights, including the right to vote.

(b) For purposes of this section—

(1) the District of Columbia shall be considered to be a State; and

(2) any Act of Congress applicable exclusively to the District of Columbia shall be considered to be a statute of the District of Columbia.

§ 1345. United States as plaintiff

Except as otherwise provided by Act of Congress, the district courts shall have original jurisdiction of all civil actions, suits or proceedings commenced by the United States, or by any agency or officer thereof expressly authorized to sue by Act of Congress.

§ 1346. United States as defendant

(a) The district courts shall have original jurisdiction, concurrent with the United States Claims Court, of:

(1) Any civil action against the United States for the recovery of any internal-revenue tax alleged to have been erroneously or illegally assessed or collected, or any penalty claimed to have been collected without authority or any sum alleged to have been excessive or in any manner wrongfully collected under the internal-revenue laws;

(2) Any other civil action or claim against the United States, not exceeding $10,000 in amount, founded either upon the Constitution, or any Act of Congress, or any regulation of an executive department, or upon any express or implied contract with the

United States, or for liquidated or unliquidated damages in cases not sounding in tort, except that the district courts shall not have jurisdiction of any civil action or claim against the United States founded upon any express or implied contract with the United States or for liquidated or unliquidated damages in cases not sounding in tort which are subject to sections 8(g)(1) and 10(a)(1) of the Contract Disputes Act of 1978. For the purpose of this paragraph, an express or implied contract with the Army and Air Force Exchange Service, Navy Exchanges, Marine Corps Exchanges, Coast Guard Exchanges, or Exchange Councils of the National Aeronautics and Space Administration shall be considered an express or implied contract with the United States.

(b) Subject to the provisions of chapter 171 of this title, the district courts, together with the United States District Court for the District of the Canal Zone and the District Court of the Virgin Islands, shall have exclusive jurisdiction of civil actions on claims against the United States, for money damages, accruing on and after January 1, 1945, for injury or loss of property, or personal injury or death caused by the negligent or wrongful act or omission of any employee of the Government while acting within the scope of his office or employment, under circumstances where the United States, if a private person, would be liable to the claimant in accordance with the law of the place where the act or omission occurred.

(c) The jurisdiction conferred by this section includes jurisdiction of any set-off, counterclaim, or other claim or demand whatever on the part of the United States against any plaintiff commencing an action under this section.

(d) The district courts shall not have jurisdiction under this section of any civil action or claim for a pension.

(e) The district courts shall have original jurisdiction of any civil action against the United States provided in section 6226, 6228(a), 7426, or 7428 (in the case of the United States district court for the District of Columbia) of the Internal Revenue Code of 1954.

(f) The district courts shall have exclusive original jurisdiction of civil actions under section 2409a to quiet title to an estate or interest in real property in which an interest is claimed by the United States.

§ 1359. Parties collusively joined or made

A district court shall not have jurisdiction of a civil action in which any party, by assignment or otherwise, has been improperly or collusively made or joined to invoke the jurisdiction of such court.

§ 1361. Action to compel an officer of the United States to peform his duty

The district courts shall have original jurisdiction of any action in the nature of mandamus to compel an officer or employee of the United States or any agency thereof to perform a duty owed to the plaintiff.

§ 1364. Construction of references to laws of the United States or Acts of Congress

For the purposes of this chapter, references to laws of the United States or Acts of Congress do not include laws applicable exclusively to the District of Columbia.

§ 1391. Venue generally

(a) A civil action wherein jurisdiction is founded only on diversity of citizenship may, except as otherwise provided by law, be brought only in the judicial district where all plaintiffs or all defendants reside, or in which the claim arose.

(b) A civil action wherein jurisdiction is not founded solely on diversity of citizenship may be brought only in the judicial district where all defendants reside, or in which the claim arose, except as otherwise provided by law.

(c) A corporation may be sued in any judicial district in which it is incorporated or licensed to do business or is doing business, and such judicial district shall be regarded as the residence of such corporation for venue purposes.

(d) An alien may be sued in any district.

(e) A civil action in which a defendant is an officer or employee of the United States or any agency thereof acting in his official capacity or under color of legal authority, or an agency of the United States, or the United States, may, except as otherwise provided by law, be brought in any judicial district in which (1) a defendant in the action resides, or (2) the cause of action arose, or (3) any real property involved in the action is situated, or (4) the plaintiff resides if no real property is involved in the action. Additional persons may be joined as parties to any such action in accordance with the Federal Rules of Civil Procedure and with such other venue requirements as would be applicable if the United States or one of its officers, employees, or agencies were not a party.

The summons and complaint in such an action shall be served as provided by the Federal Rules of Civil Procedure except that the delivery of the summons and complaint to the officer or agency as required by the rules may be made by certified mail beyond the territorial limits of the district in which the action is brought.

(f) A civil action against a foreign state as defined in section 1603(a) of this title may be brought—

(1) in any judicial district in which a substantial part of the events or omissions giving rise to the claim occurred, or a substantial part of property that is the subject of the action is situated;

(2) in any judicial district in which the vessel or cargo of a foreign state is situated, if the claim is asserted under section 1605(b) of this title;

(3) in any judicial district in which the agency or instrumentality is licensed to do business or is doing business, if the action is brought against an agency or instrumentality of a foreign state as defined in section 1603(b) of this title; or

(4) in the United States District Court for the District of Columbia if the action is brought against a foreign state or political subdivision thereof.

§ 1397. Interpleader

Any civil action of interpleader or in the nature of interpleader under section 1335 of this title may be brought in the judicial district in which one or more of the claimants reside.

§ 1404. Change of venue

(a) For the convenience of parties and witnesses, in the interest of justice, a district court may transfer any civil action to any other district or division where it might have been brought.

(b) Upon motion, consent or stipulation of all parties, any action, suit or proceeding of a civil nature or any motion or hearing thereof, may be transferred, in the discretion of the court, from the division in which pending to any other division in the same district. Transfer of proceedings in rem brought by or on behalf of the United States may be transferred under this section without the consent of the United States where all other parties request transfer.

(c) A district court may order any civil action to be tried at any place within the division in which it is pending.

(d) As used in this section, "district court" includes the United States District Court for the District of the Canal Zone; and "district" includes the territorial jurisdiction of that court.

§ 1406. Cure or waiver of defects

(a) The district court of a district in which is filed a case laying venue in the wrong division or district shall dismiss, or if it be in the interest of justice, transfer such case to any district or division in which it could have been brought.

(b) Nothing in this chapter shall impair the jurisdiction of a district court of any matter involving a party who does not interpose timely and sufficient objection to the venue.

(c) As used in this section, "district court" includes the United States District Court for the District of the Canal Zone; and "district" includes the territorial jurisdiction of that court.

§ 1441. Actions removable generally

(a) Except as otherwise expressly provided by Act of Congress, any civil action brought in a State court of which the district courts of the United States have original jurisdiction, may be removed by the defendant or the defendants, to the district court of the United States for the district and division embracing the place where such action is pending.

(b) Any civil action of which the district courts have original jurisdiction founded on a claim or right arising under the Constitution, treaties or laws of the United States shall be removable without regard to the citizenship or residence of the parties. Any other such action shall be removable only if none of the parties in interest properly joined and served as defendants is a citizen of the State in which such action is brought.

(c) Whenever a separate and independent claim or cause of action, which would be removable if sued upon alone, is joined with one or more otherwise non-removable claims or causes of action, the entire case may be removed and the district court may determine all issues therein, or, in its discretion, may remand all matters not otherwise within its original jurisdiction.

(d) Any civil action brought in a State court against a foreign state as defined in section 1603(a) of this title may be removed by the foreign state to the district court of the United States for the district and division embracing the place where such action is pending. Upon removal the action shall be tried by the court without jury. Where removal is based upon this subsection, the time limitations of section 1446(b) of this chapter may be enlarged at any time for cause shown.

(e) The court to which such civil action is removed is not precluded from hearing and determining any claim in such civil action because the State court from which such civil action is removed did not have jurisdiction over that claim.

§ 1442. Federal officers sued or prosecuted

(a) A civil action or criminal prosecution commenced in a State court against any of the following persons may be removed by them to the district court of the United States for the district and division embracing the place wherein it is pending:

(1) Any officer of the United States or any agency thereof, or person acting under him, for any act under color of such office or on account of any right, title or authority claimed under any Act of Congress for the apprehension or punishment of criminals or the collection of the revenue.

(2) A property holder whose title is derived from any such officer, where such action or prosecution affects the validity of any law of the United States.

(3) Any officer of the courts of the United States, for any Act under color of office or in the performance of his duties:

(4) Any officer of either House of Congress, for any act in the discharge of his official duty under an order of such House.

(b) A personal action commenced in any State court by an alien against any citizen of a State who is, or at the time the alleged action accrued was, a civil officer of the United States and is a non-resident of such State, wherein jurisdiction is obtained by the State court by personal service of process, may be removed by the defendant to the district court of the United States for the district and division in which the defendant was served with process.

§ 1443. Civil rights cases

Any of the following civil actions or criminal prosecutions, commenced in a State court may be removed by the defendant to the district court of the United States for the district and division embracing the place wherein it is pending:

(1) Against any person who is denied or cannot enforce in the courts of such State a right under any law providing for the equal civil rights of citizens of the United States, or of all persons within the jurisdiction thereof;

(2) For any act under color of authority derived from any law providing for equal rights, or for refusing to do any act on the ground that it would be inconsistent with such law.

§ 1445. Nonremovable actions

(a) A civil action in any State court against a railroad or its receivers or trustees, arising under sections 51–60 of Title 45, may not be removed to any district court of the United States.

(b) A civil action in any State court against a common carrier or its receivers or trustees to recover damages for delay, loss, or injury of shipments, arising under section 11707 of title 49, may not be removed to any district court of the United States unless the matter in controversy exceeds $10,000, exclusive of interest and costs.

(c) A civil action in any State court arising under the workmen's compensation laws of such State may not be removed to any district court of the United States.

§ 1451. Definitions

For purposes of this chapter—

(1) The term "State court" includes the Superior Court of the District of Columbia.

(2) The term "State" includes the District of Columbia.

§ 1651. Writs

(a) The Supreme Court and all courts established by Act of Congress may issue all writs necessary or appropriate in aid of their respective jurisdictions and agreeable to the usages and principles of law.

(b) An alternative writ or rule nisi may be issued by a justice or judge of a court which has jurisdiction.

§ 1652. State laws as rules of decision

The laws of the several states, except where the Constitution or treaties of the United States or Acts of Congress otherwise require or provide, shall be regarded as rules of decision in civil actions in the courts of the United States, in cases where they apply.

§ 1738. State and Territorial statutes and judicial proceedings; full faith and credit

The Acts of the legislature of any State, Territory, or Possession of the United States, or copies thereof, shall be authenticated by affixing the seal of such State, Territory or Possession thereto.

The records and judicial proceedings of any court of any such State, Territory or Possession, or copies thereof, shall be proved or admitted in other courts within the United States and its Territories and Possessions by the attestation of the clerk and seal of the court annexed, if a seal exists, together with a certificate of a judge of the court that the said attestation is in proper form.

Such Acts, records and judicial proceedings or copies thereof, so authenticated, shall have the same full faith and credit in every court within the United States and its Territories and Possessions as they have by law or usage in the courts of such State, Territory or Possession from which they are taken.

§ 2071. Rule-making power generally

The Supreme Court and all courts established by Act of Congress may from time to time prescribe rules for the conduct of their business. Such rules shall be consistent with Acts of Congress and rules of practice and procedure prescribed by the Supreme Court.

§ 2072. Rules of procedure and evidence; power to prescribe

(a) The Supreme Court shall have the power to prescribe general rules of practice and procedure and rules of evidence for cases in the United States district courts (including proceedings before magistrates thereof) and courts of appeals.

(b) Such rules shall not abridge, enlarge or modify any substantive right. All laws in conflict with such rules shall be of no further force or effect after such rules have taken effect.

§ 2073. Rules of procedure and evidence; method of prescribing

(a)(1) The Judicial Conference shall prescribe and publish the procedures for the consideration of proposed rules under this section.

(2) The Judicial Conference may authorize the appointment of committees to assist the Conference by recommending rules to be prescribed under section 2072 of this title. Each such committee shall consist of members of the bench and the professional bar, and trial and appellate judges.

(b) The Judicial Conference shall authorize the appointment of a standing committee on rules of practice, procedure, and evidence under subsection (a) of this section. Such standing committee shall review each recommendation of any other committees so appointed and recommend to the Judicial Conference rules of practice, procedure, and evidence and such changes in rules proposed by a committee appointed under subsection (a)(2) of this section as may be necessary to maintain consistency and otherwise promote the interest of justice.

(c)(1) Each meeting for the transaction of business under this chapter by any committee appointed under this section shall be open to the public, except when the committee so meeting, in open session and with a majority present, determines that it is in the public interest that all or part of the remainder of the meeting on that day shall be closed to the public, and states the reason for so closing the meeting. Minutes of each meeting for the transaction of business under this chapter shall be maintained by the committee and made available to the public, except that any portion of such minutes, relating to a closed meeting and made available to the public, may contain such deletions as may be necessary to avoid frustrating the purposes of closing the meeting.

(2) Any meeting for the transaction of business under this chapter, by a committee appointed under this section, shall be preceded by sufficient notice to enable all interested persons to attend.

(d) In making a recommendation under this section or under section 2072, the body making that recommendation shall provide a proposed rule, an explanatory note on the rule, and a written report explaining the body's action, including any minority or other separate views.

(e) Failure to comply with this section does not invalidate a rule prescribed under § 2072 of this title.

§ 2074. Rules of procedure and evidence; submission to Congress; effective date

(a) The Supreme Court shall transmit to the Congress not later than May 1 of the year in which a rule prescribed under section 2072 is to become effective a copy of the proposed rule. Such rule shall take effect no earlier than December 1 of the year in which such rule is so transmitted unless otherwise provided by law. The Supreme Court may fix the extent such rule shall apply to proceedings then pending, except that the Supreme Court shall not require the application of such rule to further proceedings then pending to the extent that, in the opinion of the court in which such proceedings are pending, the application of such rule in such proceedings would not be feasible or would work injustice, in which event the former rule applies.

(b) Any such rule creating, abolishing, or modifying an evidentiary privilege shall have no force or effect unless approved by Act of Congress.

§ 2111. Harmless error

On the hearing of any appeal or writ of certiorari in any case, the court shall give judgment after an examination of the record without regard to errors or defects which do not affect the substantial rights of the parties.

§ 2201. Creation of remedy

(a) In a case of actual controversy within its jurisdiction, except with respect to Federal taxes other than actions brought under section 7428 of the Internal Revenue Code of 1954 or a proceeding under section 505 or 1146 of title 11, any court of the United States, upon the filing of an appropriate pleading, may declare the rights and other legal relations of any interested party seeking such declaration, whether or not further relief is or could be sought. Any such declaration shall have the force and effect of a final judgment or decree and shall be reviewable as such. . . .

§ 2202. Further relief

Further necessary or proper relief based on a declaratory judgment or decree may be granted, after reasonable notice and hearing, against any adverse party whose rights have been determined by such judgment.

§ 2241. Power to grant writ

(a) Writs of habeas corpus may be granted by the Supreme Court, any justice thereof, the district courts and any circuit judge within their respective jurisdictions. The order of a circuit judge shall be entered in the records of the district court of the district wherein the restraint complained of is had.

(b) The Supreme Court, any justice thereof, and any circuit judge may decline to entertain an application for a writ of habeas corpus and may transfer the application for hearing and determination to the district court having jurisdiction to entertain it.

(c) The writ of habeas corpus shall not extend to a prisoner unless—

(1) He is in custody under or by color of the authority of the United States or is committed for trial before some court thereof; or

(2) He is in custody for an act done or omitted in pursuance of an Act of Congress, or an order, process, judgment or decree of a court or judge of the United States; or

(3) He is in custody in violation of the Constitution or laws or treaties of the United States; or

(4) He, being a citizen of a foreign state and domiciled therein is in custody for an act done or omitted under any alleged right, title, authority, privilege, protection, or exemption claimed under

the commission, order or sanction of any foreign state, or under color thereof, the validity and effect of which depend upon the law of nations; or

(5) It is necessary to bring him into court to testify or for trial.

(d) Where an application for a writ of habeas corpus is made by a person in custody under the judgment and sentence of a State court of a State which contains two or more Federal judicial districts, the application may be filed in the district court for the district wherein such person is in custody or in the district court for the district within which the State court was held which convicted and sentenced him and each of such district courts shall have concurrent jurisdiction to entertain the application. The district court for the district wherein such an application is filed in the exercise of its discretion and in furtherance of justice may transfer the application to the other district court for hearing and determination.

§ 2242. Application

Application for a writ of habeas corpus shall be in writing signed and verified by the person for whose relief it is intended or by someone acting in his behalf.

It shall allege the facts concerning the applicant's commitment or detention, the name of the person who has custody over him and by virtue of what claim or authority, if known.

It may be amended or supplemented as provided in the rules of procedure applicable to civil actions.

If addressed to the Supreme Court, a justice thereof or a circuit judge it shall state the reasons for not making application to the district court of the district in which the applicant is held.

§ 2243. Issuance of writ; return; hearing; decision

A court, justice or judge entertaining an application for a writ of habeas corpus shall forthwith award the writ or issue an order directing the respondent to show cause why the writ should not be granted, unless it appears from the application that the applicant or person detained is not entitled thereto.

The writ, or order to show cause shall be directed to the person having custody of the person detained. It shall be returned within three days unless for good cause additional time, not exceeding twenty days, is allowed.

The person to whom the writ or order is directed shall make a return certifying the true cause of the detention.

When the writ or order is returned a day shall be set for hearing, not more than five days after the return unless for good cause additional time is allowed.

Unless the application for the writ and the return present only issues of law the person to whom the writ is directed shall be required to produce at the hearing the body of the person detained.

The applicant or the person detained may, under oath, deny any of the facts set forth in the return or allege any other material facts.

The return and all suggestions made against it may be amended, by leave of court, before or after being filed.

The court shall summarily hear and determine the facts, and dispose of the matter as law and justice require.

§ 2244. Finality of determination

(a) No circuit or district judge shall be required to entertain an application for a writ of habeas corpus to inquire into the detention of a person pursuant to a judgment of a court of the United States if it appears that the legality of such detention has been determined by a judge or court of the United States on a prior application for a writ of habeas corpus and the petition presents no new ground not theretofore presented and determined, and the judge or court is satisfied that the ends of justice will not be served by such inquiry.

(b) When after an evidentiary hearing on the merits of a material factual issue, or after a hearing on the merits of an issue of law, a person in custody pursuant to the judgment of a State court has been denied by a court of the United States or a justice or judge of the United States release from custody or other remedy on an application for a writ of habeas corpus, a subsequent application for a writ of habeas corpus in behalf of such person need not be entertained by a court of the United States or a justice or judge of the United States unless the application alleges and is predicated on a factual or other ground not adjudicated on the hearing of the earlier application for the writ, and unless the court, justice, or judge is satisfied that the applicant has not on the earlier application deliberately withheld the newly asserted ground or otherwise abused the writ.

(c) In a habeas corpus proceeding brought in behalf of a person in custody pursuant to the judgment of a State court, a prior judgment of the Supreme Court of the United States on an appeal or review by a writ of certiorari at the instance of the prisoner of the decision of such State court, shall be conclusive as to all issues of fact or law with respect to an asserted denial of a Federal right which constitutes ground for discharge in a habeas corpus proceeding, actually adjudicated by the Supreme Court therein, unless the applicant for the writ of habeas corpus shall plead and the court shall find the existence of a material and controlling fact which did not appear in the record of the proceeding in the Supreme Court and the court shall further find that the applicant for the writ of habeas corpus could not have caused such fact to appear in such record by the exercise of reasonable diligence.

§ 2254. State custody; remedies in Federal courts

(a) The Supreme Court, a Justice thereof, a circuit judge, or a district court shall entertain an application for a writ of habeas corpus in behalf of a person in custody pursuant to the judgment of a State court only on the ground that he is in custody in violation of the Constitution or laws or treaties of the United States.

(b) An application for a writ of habeas corpus in behalf of a person in custody pursuant to the judgment of a State court shall not be granted unless it appears that the applicant has exhausted the remedies available in the courts of the State, or that there is either an absence of available State corrective process or the existence of circumstances rendering such process ineffective to protect the rights of the prisoner.

(c) An applicant shall not be deemed to have exhausted the remedies available in the courts of the State, within the meaning of this section, if he has the right under the law of the State to raise, by any available procedure, the question presented.

(d) In any proceeding instituted in a Federal court by an application for a writ of habeas corpus by a person in custody pursuant to the judgment of a State court, a determination after a hearing on the merits of a factual issue, made by a State court of competent jurisdiction in a proceeding to which the applicant for the writ and the State or an officer or agent thereof were parties, evidenced by a written finding, written opinion, or other reliable and adequate written indicia, shall be presumed to be correct, unless the applicant shall establish or it shall otherwise appear, or the respondent shall admit—

(1) that the merits of the factual dispute were not resolved in the State court hearing;

(2) that the factfinding procedure employed by the State court was not adequate to afford a full and fair hearing;

(3) that the material facts were not adequately developed at the State court hearing;

(4) that the State court lacked jurisdiction of the subject material or over the person of the applicant in the State court proceeding;

(5) that the applicant was an indigent and the State court, in deprivation of his constitutional right, failed to appoint counsel to represent him in the State court proceeding;

(6) that the applicant did not receive a full, fair, and adequate hearing in the State court proceeding; or

(7) that the applicant was otherwise denied due process of law in the State court proceeding;

(8) or unless that part of the record of the State court proceeding in which the determination of such factual issue was made, pertinent to a determination of the sufficiency of the evidence to

support such factual determination, is produced as provided for hereinafter, and the Federal court on a consideration of such part of the record as a whole concludes that such factual determination is not fairly supported by the record:

And in an evidentiary hearing in the proceeding in the Federal court, when due proof of such factual determination has been made, unless the existence of one or more of the circumstances respectively set forth in paragraphs numbered (1) to (7), inclusive, is shown by the applicant, otherwise appears, or is admitted by the respondent, or unless the court concludes pursuant to the provisions of paragraph numbered (8) that the record in the State court proceeding, considered as a whole, does not fairly support such factual determination, the burden shall rest upon the applicant to establish by convincing evidence that the factual determination by the State court was erroneous.

(e) If the applicant challenges the sufficiency of the evidence adduced in such State court proceeding to support the State court's determination of a factual issue made therein, the applicant, if able, shall produce that part of the record pertinent to a determination of the sufficiency of the evidence to support such determination. If the applicant, because of indigency or other reason is unable to produce such part of the record, then the State shall produce such part of the record and the Federal court shall direct the State to do so by order directed to an appropriate State official. If the State cannot provide such pertinent part of the record, then the court shall determine under the existing facts and circumstances what weight shall be given to the State court's factual determination.

(f) A copy of the official records of the State court, duly certified by the clerk of such court to be a true and correct copy of a finding, judicial opinion, or other reliable written indicia showing such a factual determination by the State court shall be admissible in the Federal court proceeding.

§ 2255. Federal custody; remedies on motion attacking sentence

A prisoner in custody under sentence of a court established by Act of Congress claiming the right to be released upon the ground that the sentence was imposed in violation of the Constitution or laws of the United States, or that the court was without jurisdiction to impose such sentence, or that the sentence was in excess of the maximum authorized by law, or is otherwise subject to collateral attack, may move the court which imposed the sentence to vacate, set aside or correct the sentence.

A motion for such relief may be made at any time.

Unless the motion and the files and records of the case conclusively show that the prisoner is entitled to no relief, the court shall cause notice thereof to be served upon the United States attorney, grant a prompt hearing thereon, determine the issues and make findings of fact and conclusions of law with respect thereto. If the court finds that the judgment was rendered without jurisdiction, or that the sentence imposed was not authorized by law or otherwise open to collateral attack, or that there has been such a denial or infringement of the constitutional rights of the prisoner as to render the judgment vulnerable to collateral attack, the court shall vacate and set the judgment aside and shall discharge the prisoner or resentence him or grant a new trial or correct the sentence as may appear appropriate.

A court may entertain and determine such motion without requiring the production of the prisoner at the hearing.

The sentencing court shall not be required to entertain a second or succesive motion for similar relief on behalf of the same prisoner.

An appeal may be taken to the court of appeals from the order entered on the motion as from a final judgment on application for a writ of habeas corpus.

An application for a writ of habeas corpus in behalf of a prisoner who is authorized to apply for relief by motion pursuant to this section, shall not be entertained if it appears that the applicant has failed to apply for relief, by motion, to the court which sentenced him, or that such court has denied him relief, unless it also appears that the remedy by motion is inadequate or ineffective to test the legality of his detention.

§ 2283. Stay of State court proceedings

A court of the United States may not grant an injunction to stay proceedings in a State court except as expressly authorized by Act of Congress, or where necessary in aid of its jurisdiction, or to protect or effectuate its judgments.

§ 2674. Liability of United States

The United States shall be liable, respecting the provisions of this title relating to tort claims, in the same manner and to the same extent as a private individual under like circumstances, but shall not be liable for interest prior to judgment or for punitive damages. . . .

§ 2676. Judgment as bar

The judgment in an action under section 1346(b) of this title shall constitute a complete bar to any action by the claimant, by reason of the same subject matter, against the employee of the government whose act or omission gave rise to the claim.

§ 2680. Exceptions

The provisions of this chapter and section 1346(b) of this title shall not apply to—

(a) Any claim based upon an act or omission of an employee of the Government, exercising due care, in the execution of a statute or regulation, whether or not such statute or regulation be valid, or based upon the exercise or performance or the failure to exercise or perform a discretionary function or duty on the part of a federal agency or an employee of the Government, whether or not the discretion involved be abused. . . .

(h) Any claim arising out of assault, battery, false imprisonment, false arrest, malicious prosecution, abuse of process, libel, slander, misrepresentation, deceit, or interference with contract rights: *Provided,* That, with regard to acts or omissions of investigative or law enforcement officers of the United States Government, the provisions of this chapter and section 1346(b) of this title shall apply to any claim arising, on or after the date of the enactment of this proviso, out of assault, battery, false imprisonment, false arrest, abuse of process, or malicious prosecution. For the purpose of this subsection, "investigative or law enforcement officer" means any officer of the United States who is empowered by law to execute searches, to seize evidence, or to make arrests for violations of Federal law. . . .

III. Title 42, U.S.C.:

§ 1981. Equal rights under the law

All persons within the jurisdiction of the United States shall have the same right in every State and Territory to make and enforce contracts, to sue, be parties, give evidence, and to the full and equal benefit of all laws and proceedings for the security of persons and property as is enjoyed by white citizens, and shall be subject to like punishment, pains, penalties, taxes, licenses, and exactions of every kind, and to no other.

§ 1982. Property rights of citizens

All citizens of the United States shall have the same right, in every State and Territory, as is enjoyed by white citizens thereof to inherit, purchase, lease, sell, hold, and convey real and personal property.

§ 1983. Civil action for deprivation of rights

Every person who, under color of any statute, ordinance, regulation, custom, or usage, of any State or Territory or the District of Columbia, subjects, or causes to be subjected, any citizen of the United States or other person within the jurisdiction thereof to the deprivation of any rights, privileges, or immunities secured by the Constitution and laws, shall be liable to the party injured in an action at law, suit in equity, or other proper proceeding for redress. For the purposes of this section, any Act of Congress applicable exclusively to the District of Columbia shall be considered to be a statute of the District of Columbia.

§ 1985. Conspiracy to interfere with civil rights

Preventing officer from performing duties

(1) If two or more persons in any State or Territory conspire to prevent, by force, intimidation, or threat, any person from accepting or holding any office, trust, or place of confidence under the United States, or from discharging any duties thereof; or to induce by like means any officer of the United States to leave any State, district, or place, where his duties as an officer are required to be performed, or to injure him in his person or property on account of his lawful discharge of the duties of his office, or while engaged in the lawful discharge thereof, or to injure his property so as to molest, interrupt, hinder, or impede him in the discharge of his official duties;

Obstructing justice; intimidating party, witness, or juror

(2) If two or more persons in any State or Territory conspire to deter, by force, intimidation, or threat, any party or witness in any court of the United States from attending such court, or from testifying to any matter pending therein, freely, fully, and truthfully, or to injure such party or witness in his person or property on account of his having so attended or testified, or to influence the verdict, presentment, or indictment of any grand or petit juror in any such court, or to injure such juror in his person or property on account of any verdict, presentment, or indictment lawfully assented to by him, or of his being or having been such juror; or if two or more persons conspire for the purpose of impeding, hindering, obstructing, or defeating, in any manner, the due course of justice in any State or Territory, with intent to deny to any citizen the equal protection of the laws, or to injure him or his property for lawfully enforcing, or attempting to enforce, the right of any person, or class of persons, to the equal protection of the laws;

Depriving persons of rights or privileges

(3) If two or more persons in any State or Territory conspire to go in disguise on the highway or on the premises of another, for the purpose of depriving, either directly or indirectly, any person or class of persons of the equal protection of the laws, or of equal privilges and immunities under the laws; or for the purpose of preventing or hindering the constituted authorities of any State or Territory from giving or securing to all persons within such State or Territory the equal protection of the laws; or if two or more persons conspire to prevent by force, intimidation, or threat, any citizen who is lawfully entitled to vote, from giving his support or advocacy in a legal manner, toward or in favor of the election of any lawfully qualified person as an elector for Preisdent or Vice President, or as a Member of Congress of the United States; or to injure any citizen in person or property on account of such support or advocacy; in any case of conspiracy set forth in this section, if one or more persons engaged therein do, or cause to be done, any act

in furtherance of the object of such conspiracy, whereby another is injured in his person or property, or deprived of having and exercising any right or privilege of a citizen of the United States, the party so injured or deprived may have an action for the recovery of damages occasioned by such injury or deprivation, against any one or more of the conspirators.

§ 1986. Action for neglect to prevent

Every person who, having knowledge that any of the wrongs conspired to be done, and mentioned in section 1985 of this title, are about to be committed, and having power to prevent or aid in preventing the commission of the same, neglects or refuses so to do, if such wrongful act be committed, shall be liable to the party injured, or his legal representatives, for all damages caused by such wrongful act, which such person by reasonable diligence could have prevented; and such damages may be recovered in an action on the case; and any number of persons guilty of such wrongful neglect or refusal may be joined as defendants in the action; and if the death of any party be caused by any such wrongful act and neglect, the legal representatives of the deceased shall have such action therefor, and may recover not exceeding $5,000 damages therein, for the benefit of the widow of the deceased, if there be one, and if there be no widow, then for the benefit of the next of kin of the deceased. But no action under the provisions of this section shall be sustained which is not commenced within one year after the cause of action has accrued.

§ 1988. Proceedings in vindication of civil rights; attorney's fees

The jurisdiction in civil and criminal matters conferred on the district courts by the provisions of this Title, and of Title "CIVIL RIGHTS," and of Title "CRIMES," for the protection of all persons in the United States in their civil rights, and for their vindication, shall be exercised and enforced in conformity with the laws of the United States, so far as such laws are suitable to carry the same into effect; but in all cases where they are not adapted to the object, or are deficient in the provisions necessary to furnish suitable remedies and punish offenses against law, the common law, as modified and changed by the constitution and statutes of the State wherein the court having jurisdiction of such civil or criminal cause is held, so far as the same is not inconsistent with the Constitution and laws of the United States, shall be extended to and govern the said courts in the trial and disposition of the cause, and, if it is of a criminal nature, in the infliction of punishment on the party found guilty. In any action or proceeding to enforce a provision of sections 1981, 1982, 1983, 1985, and 1986 of this title, title IX of Public Law 92–318 [20 U.S.C. 1681 et seq.], or title VI of the Civil Rights Act of 1964 [42 U.S.C. 2000d et seq.], the court, in its discretion, may allow the prevailing party, other than the United States, a reasonable attorney's fee as part of the costs.

§ 1997e. Exhaustion of remedies

Applicability of administrative remedies

(a)(1) Subject to the provisions of paragraph (2), in any action brought pursuant to section 1983 of this title by an adult convicted of a crime confined in any jail, prison, or other correctional facility, the court shall, if the court believes that such a requirement would be appropriate and in the interests of justice, continue such case for a period of not to exceed ninety days in order to require exhaustion of such plain, speedy, and effective administrative remedies as are available.

(2) The exhaustion of administrative remedies under paragraph (1) may not be required unless the Attorney General has certified or the court has determined that such administrative remedies are in substantial compliance with the minimum acceptable standards promulgated under subsection (b) of this section.

Minimum standards for development and implementation of system for resolution of grievances of confined adults; consultation, promulgation, submission, etc., by Attorney General of standards

(b)(1) No later than one hundred eighty days after May 23, 1980, the Attorney General shall, after consultation with persons, State and local agencies, and organizations with background and expertise in the area of corrections, promulgate minimum standards for the development and implementation of a plain, speedy, and effective system for the resolution of grievances of adults confined in any jail, prison, or other correctional facility. The Attorney General shall submit such proposed standards for publication in the Federal Register in accordance with section 553 of title 5. Such standards shall take effect thirty legislative days after publication unless, within such period, either House of Congress adopts a resolution of disapproval of such standards.

(2) The minimum standards shall provide—

(A) for an advisory role for employees and inmates of any jail, prison, or other correctional institution (at the most decentralized level as is reasonably possible), in the formulation, implementation, and operation of the system;

(B) specific maximum time limits for written replies to grievances with reasons thereto at each decision level within the system;

(C) for priority processing of grievances which are of an emergency nature, including matters in which delay would subject the grievant to substantial risk of personal injury or other damages;

(D) for safeguards to avoid reprisals against any grievant or participant in the resolution of a grievance; and

(E) for independent review of the disposition of grievances, including alleged reprisals, by a person or other entity not under the direct supervision or direct control of the institution.

Procedure for review and certification of systems for resolution of grievances of confined adults for determination of compliance with minimum standards; suspension or withdrawal of certification for noncompliance; development, etc., by Attorney General

(c)(1) The Attorney General shall develop a procedure for the prompt review and certification of systems for the resolution of grievances of adults confined in any jail, prison, or other correctional facility, or pretrial detention facility, to determine if such systems, as voluntarily submitted by the various States and political subdivisions, are in substantial compliance with the minimum standards promulgated under subsection (b) of this section.

(2) The Attorney General may suspend or withdraw the certification under paragraph (1) at any time that he has reasonable cause to believe that the grievance procedure is no longer in substantial compliance with the minimum standards promulgated under subsection (b) of this section.

———

*

Appendix C

A BRIEF HISTORY OF THE FEDERAL JUDICIAL SYSTEM

1. The Constitution. Important features of the federal judicial system were settled in the Constitution itself. Article III declares that the judicial power "shall be vested" in one Supreme Court and specifies the categories of cases to which the federal judicial power shall extend. Article III also provides tenure and salary protection to assure the independence of federal judges. Under art. II, § 2, these judges are to be appointed by the President "with the Advice and Consent of the Senate."

Equally important were the powers withheld from the article III courts. Several attempts were made in the Constitutional Convention to involve federal judges in a Council of Revision with power to veto federal legislation. These efforts were defeated, as was a proposal to authorize advisory opinions at the request of a coordinate branch.[a] The result was the important separation-of-powers principle limiting the federal judiciary to decision of matters presented in a "case" or "controversy."

The most controversial question, however, was left unresolved. Article III states that the judicial power "shall be vested . . . in such inferior Courts as the Congress may from time to time ordain and establish." This was a compromise between those who urged and those who opposed the creation of lower federal courts. It is generally understood to have given Congress the choice of whether to create lower federal courts. As summarized in M. Farrand, The Framing of the Constitution of the United States 79–80 (1913):

> "That there should be a national judiciary was readily accepted by all. . . . The most serious question was that of the inferior courts. The difficulty lay in the fact that they were regarded as an encroachment upon the rights of the individual states. It was claimed that the state courts were perfectly competent for the work required, and that it would be quite sufficient to grant an appeal from them to the national supreme court. The decision that was reached was characteristic . . . . [T]he matter was compromised: inferior courts were not required, but the national legislature was *permitted* to establish them."[b]

[a] The general source for the deliberations of the Constitutional Convention is M. Farrand, The Records of the Federal Convention (1911). See also J. Goebel, History of the Supreme Court of the United States: Antecedents and Beginnings to 1801 (1971). Specific references to the Council of Revision may be found in 1 Farrand 21, 97–104, 108–110, 138–40; 2 Farrand 73–80, 298.

[b] This is, at least, the conventional view of the matter. In 1 J. Goebel, History of the Supreme Court: Antecedents and Be-

2. The First Judiciary Act. Congress exercised the power to create lower federal courts in the First Judiciary Act passed on September 24, 1789.[c] The Congress that adopted this legislation contained many members who had participated in the constitutional debates. The statute was so nearly contemporaneous with the adoption of the Constitution itself as to have been accorded special significance by many constitutional historians as an authoritative rendition of the original understanding. Some attention to its provisions is accordingly appropriate.

In broad outline, the following system was established. Two levels of courts were created below the Supreme Court. The statute established 13 districts, each with one district court staffed by one judge. As is still the case today, no district extended beyond the borders of a single state. Eleven of the districts[d] were grouped into three circuits, each with a circuit court that met twice annually in each district within the circuit. The circuit courts were staffed by two Supreme Court Justices and the district judge of the district in which the court met. The circuit courts doubled as trial and appellate courts. They were empowered to try federal criminal cases and three categories of civil cases subject to a $500 jurisdictional amount: where the United States was a plaintiff, where an alien was a party, and diversity cases. Cases filed in state court against an alien "or by a citizen of the state in which the suit is brought against a citizen of another state" could be removed by the defendant to a circuit court, again subject to a $500 jurisdictional amount. Circuit courts also were empowered to hear appeals from district courts. District courts had trial jurisdiction over minor crimes and heard admiralty and maritime cases as well as several other categories of civil actions.

There were, of course, very few cases that could have arisen under federal law in 1789, and whether for this reason or another, no general

ginnings to 1801 at 247 (1971), it is argued that a change in the language of the operative phrases in art. III was designed "to assure that federal inferior courts must be created, and further that designation of state tribunals would not do." Specifically, when submitted to the Committee of Style, art. III read "in such Inferior Courts as shall, when necessary, from time to time, be constituted by the Legislature." The Committee changed this language to read "in such inferior courts as Congress may from time to time ordain and establish." Professor Goebel argues that the words "ordain and establish," which had been used in four important state constitutions and in the preamble to the new federal Constitution, were "the most forceful words in the contemporary constitutional vocabulary." The discretion left to Congress, he concludes, was only to "settle the institutional pattern" of the lower federal courts and to distribute the art. III jurisdiction among the courts that were created.

For a recent defense of the conventional view, see, e.g., Redish, Congressional Power to Control the Jurisdiction of Lower Federal Courts: A Critical Review and a New Synthesis, 124 U.Pa.L.Rev. 45, 52–56 (1975). For an analysis of the understanding on this point of the Congress that enacted the first Judiciary Act, see Casto, The First Congress's Understanding of its Authority over the Federal Courts' Jurisdiction, 26 B.C.L.Rev. 1101 (1985).

[c] Act of Sept. 24, 1789, 1 Stat. 73. For a careful historical analysis of the First Judiciary Act and the composition of the Congress that enacted it, see Clinton, A Mandatory View of Federal Court Jurisdiction: Early Implementation of and Departures from the Constitutional Plan, 86 Colum.L.Rev. 1515 (1986).

[d] Special provisions were made for the other two districts.

federal question jurisdiction was initially conferred on the federal trial courts. Instead, the pattern arose that Congress appended specific jurisdictional provisions to substantive legislation. Even today this pattern prevails. Although a general federal question statute was enacted in 1875, most federal-question litigation still may be heard under special jurisdictional statutes scattered throughout the various titles of the United States Code.

Although their configuration and the range of their jurisdiction have changed as the country matured, lower federal courts have been in continuous existence since 1789. While it is generally assumed that Congress has the authority to abolish the lower federal courts, that is no longer a realistic possibility. As is illustrated throughout this book, Congress needs the enforcement powers of the lower federal courts to carry out its substantive policies.

The First Judiciary Act also established a Supreme Court of six justices. The Supreme Court was given jurisdiction by writ of error over "final judgments and decrees in civil actions, and suits in equity in a circuit court, brought there by original process, or removed there from courts of the several States, or removed there by appeal from a district court where the matter in dispute exceeds the sum or value of two thousand dollars." There was no provision for appellate review of criminal cases in the Supreme Court. Review by writ of error was available from "a final judgment or decree in any suit, in the highest court in law or equity of a State in which a decision in the suit could be had." Such review was limited to federal questions, and only to cases in which the decision by the state court was *against* the federal claimant.

3. Subsequent Structural Changes. The system established at the outset of the Republic proved cumbersome. Objections were raised to the fact that district judges sat on appeals from their own judgments and Supreme Court Justices found the task of riding the circuits oppressive. In 1793 the requirement of two Justices for each circuit court was relaxed to one,[e] but this created the anomaly of a two-judge court and exacerbated the problem of district judges reviewing their own decisions. In the last days of the Adams administration, the Federalists responded to these problems and to the prospect of political oblivion by authorizing creation of several new districts and the appointment of permanent judges for the circuit courts.[f] The Republicans, who objected to the political sympathies of the recent appointments, promptly repealed the law and abolished the positions.[g]

Some weeks later, Congress passed the Judiciary Act of 1802.[h] This legislation returned to the system of circuit-riding. It created six

[e] Act of March 2, 1793, 1 Stat. 333.

[f] Act of Feb. 13, 1801, 2 Stat. 89. This was the so-called Midnight Judges' Act, which led to the decision in Marbury v. Madison, 5 U.S. (1 Cranch) 137 (1803). The history is described in 1 C. Warren, The Supreme Court in United States History 185–93 (1926). For a more recent account, see Turner, Federalist Policy and the Judiciary Act of 1801, 22 Wm. & Mary Q. 3 (1965).

[g] Act of Mar. 8, 1802, 2 Stat. 132.

[h] Act of Apr. 29, 1802, 2 Stat. 156.

circuits and assigned to each a single Justice. In consideration of the Justices' complaints, however, the act allowed the circuit court to be held by a single district judge. Thereafter, circuit-riding became less regular, and the opportunity for meaningful appellate review of district court judgments declined accordingly.

So matters stood for most of the 19th century. As the country grew, new circuits were created, and a new Justice was authorized for each. This process led eventually to the appointment of a tenth Justice in 1863.[i] Three years later, however, Congress regrouped the districts into nine circuits and deprived President Johnson of the chance of filling vacancies by prospectively reducing the Supreme Court to seven Justices.[j] After Johnson left office, the number was restored to nine,[k] where it has remained despite the subsequent creation of additional circuits.

The Act of 1869 also took the first step toward independent staffing of the circuit courts by authorizing a permanent judge for every circuit.[l] By this time, however, both the Supreme Court and the lower federal courts found themselves increasingly unable to keep up with their work. The appointment of nine circuit judges was inadequate to resolve the problem. The situation was made worse by enactment of general federal question jurisdiction in 1875.[m] Thereafter, things continued to deteriorate until finally, in 1891, Congress created nine circuit courts of appeals, each staffed by two permanent circuit judges and a third judge drawn either from the Supreme Court or from the district bench.[n] The district judges at long last were precluded from hearing appeals from their own judgments. Additionally, the 1891 legislation introduced discretionary Supreme Court review by writ of certiorari, but appeal as of right to the circuit courts of appeals and thereafter to the Supreme Court remained for many cases. Partly for that reason and partly owing to a great increase in public litigation, the Supreme Court again fell behind in its work in the years following World War I.

The appointment of William Howard Taft as Chief Justice brought to the Court a student of judicial administration with political background and influence. Taft lobbied both publicly and privately for judicial reform and named three Justices to a committee to draft legislation. Eventually, their proposals were endorsed by all of the Justices and enacted by Congress in the Judges' Bill of 1925.[o] Its main feature was sharply to reduce appeals as of right to the Supreme Court

---

[i] Act of Mar. 3, 1863, 12 Stat. 794. The addition of a tenth Justice was responsive to the creation of a tenth Circuit (including California and later Oregon) in 1855. Act of Mar. 2, 1855, 10 Stat. 631.

[j] Act of July 23, 1866, 14 Stat. 209.

[k] Act of April 10, 1869, 16 Stat. 44.

[l] Id.

[m] Act of Mar. 3, 1875, 18 Stat. 470.

[n] Act of Mar. 3, 1891, 26 Stat. 826. This legislation is popularly known as the Evarts Act. Although the Evarts Act created circuit courts of appeals, it did not abolish the old circuit courts, which continued an anachronistic existence until finally abolished by the Act of Mar. 3, 1911, 36 Stat. 1087.

[o] 43 Stat. 936.

and to substitute for most cases the new mechanism of discretionary review by writ of certiorari.[p]

This system has remained largely intact to the present day. New judges have been added from time to time, and in 1980 the Eleventh Circuit was created out of territory formerly in the Fifth.[q]

4. The Federal Circuit. Perhaps the most important modern innovation has been the creation in 1982 of the Court of Appeals for the Federal Circuit.[r] Acting under the leadership of then Assistant Attorney General Daniel J. Meador, the Department of Justice proposed creation of a new court of appeals, not superior to the existing courts of appeals but on a par with them, and exercising a jurisdiction geographically national in scope but limited as to subject matter.[s] This proposal was forwarded to the Congress, where it eventually matured, with significant alteration, into the Federal Courts Improvement Act of 1982.[t]

The result was creation of the Court of Appeals for the Federal Circuit. This court superseded, in their appellate functions, the Court of Customs and Patent Appeals and the Court of Claims. The trial division of the old Court of Claims was reconstituted as a new court, organized as an article I court. The Federal Circuit emerged with exclusive appellate jurisdiction over patent, trademark, and plant variety protection cases, although not, as had originally been proposed, over civil tax litigation. Additionally, the Federal Circuit hears appeals in cases involving government employment and international trade.[u]

5. Judicial Improvements and Access to Justice Act. In 1988 Congress enacted the Judicial Improvements and Access to Justice Act, which made a great many detailed changes in title 28. Prominent among them are amendment of the general diversity statute to require claims in excess of $50,000, see 28 U.S.C. § 1332, and certain amendments to the Rules Enabling Act, see 28 U.S.C. § 2072 et seq. Additionally, title I of the statute, entitled the Federal Courts Study Act, created a Federal Courts Study Committee to "examine problems and issues currently facing the courts of the United States" and "to develop a long-range plan for the future of the Federal judiciary," including assessments on a number of

---

[p] Id. Previously, Congress had extended the Supreme Court's certiorari jurisdiction to the review of state court judgments *upholding* a claim of federal right. Act of Dec. 23, 1914, 38 Stat. 790.

[q] Omnibus Judgeship Act, Pub. L. No. 95–486, 92 Stat. 1629 (1978).

[r] Federal Courts Improvement Act of 1982, Pub. L. No. 97–164, 96 Stat. 25 (1982).

[s] Office for Improvements in the Administration of Justice, U.S. Dep't of Justice, A Proposal to Improve the Federal Appellate System (July 21, 1978).

[t] Pub. L. No. 97–164, 96 Stat. 25 (1982). See House Report No. 97–312, 97th Cong., 1st Sess. (1981).

[u] A detailed statement of the Court's jurisdiction appears in 28 U.S.C. § 1295. The background and workings of the new Federal Circuit are summarized and potential problems explored in Petrowitz, Federal Court Reform: The Federal Courts Improvement Act of 1982—And Beyond, 32 Am.U.L.Rev. 543 (1983); and Adams, The Court of Appeals for the Federal Circuit: More than a National Patent Court, 49 Mo.L.Rev. 43 (1984).

specific issues. For the full provisions of this legislation, see Pub.L. 100–702, § 101 et seq.

6. The National Court of Appeals Movement. More ambitious modern reform efforts have so far not succeeded. In 1971 the Federal Judicial Center began a series of studies of federal appellate litigation. An immediate consequence was issuance of the Freund Commission Report,[v] which recommended creation of a National Court of Appeals. This court was to consist of seven court of appeals' judges serving staggered three-year terms. The court was to screen all petitions for review by the Supreme Court and to refer to that body the most meritorious cases. The National Court of Appeals would retain jurisdiction over cases presenting a genuine conflict between circuits and would render a decision on the merits. Additionally, the National Court of Appeals would decide on the merits cases remanded to it by the Supreme Court.

Despite the impressive membership of the Freund Commission[w] and the strong support it received in some quarters,[x] the proposed National Court of Appeals excited much opposition, including that of some Supreme Court Justices.[y] The main features of concern were that the Supreme Court would be weakened by interposition of another court with authority to screen cases for review and, secondarily, that the courts of appeal would be reduced in influence and prestige by the introduction of a superior body between them and the Supreme Court.

During the deliberations of the Freund Commission, Congress established a Commission on Revision of the Federal Court Appellate System, otherwise known as the Hruska Commission. The report of the Hruska Commission[z] tried to meet some of the objections to the Freund recommendations by proposing a National Court of Appeals without authority to screen cases for Supreme Court review. Instead, the Hruska Commission's court would hear cases referred to it by the Supreme Court, or transferred to it from other courts of appeals or from the Court of Customs and Patent Appeals or the Court of Claims. The court would be staffed by seven permanent article III judges.

[v] Federal Judicial Center, Report of the Study Group on the Caseload of the Supreme Court (1972), reported in 57 F.R.D. 573 (1972). The proposals were defended by Professor Freund in Why We Need the National Court of Appeals, 59 A.B.A.J. 247 (1973).

[w] The chairman was Paul Freund of the Harvard Law School. Members were the late Alexander M. Bickel of the Yale Law School; Charles Alan Wright of the University of Texas Law School; Dr. Russell D. Niles, Director of the Institute of Judicial Administration; Peter D. Ehrenhaft, of the D.C. Bar; Bernard G. Segal, of the Philadelphia Bar; and Robert L. Stern, of the Chicago Bar.

[x] See, e.g., Haynsworth, A New Court to Improve the Administration of Justice, 59 A.B.A.J. 841 (1973).

[y] See, e.g., Black, The National Court of Appeals: An Unwise Proposal, 83 Yale L.J. 883 (1974); Brennan, Justice Brennan Calls National Court of Appeals Proposal "Fundamentally Unnecessary and Ill Advised," 59 A.B.A.J. 835 (1973); Warren, Let's Not Weaken the Supreme Court, 60 A.B.A.J. 677 (1974).

[z] Commission on Revision of the Federal Court Appellate System, Structure and Internal Procedures: Recommendations for Change (1975), reported in 67 F.R.D. 195 (1975).

Despite substantial support,[a] the Hruska Commission report also failed to attract sufficient backing for political action. The chief question seems to have been whether the National Court of Appeals, as proposed, would actually solve the problems to which it was addressed. Some observers even thought that the new court would increase the burdens on the Supreme Court by requiring its decision on cases to be referred by it to the National Court of Appeals and by the increased necessity for Supreme Court review of nationally binding decisions.[b]

More recently, attention has been given to a proposed Intercircuit Tribunal of the United States Courts of Appeals.[c] This proposal was advanced by Chief Justice Burger in a 1983 address to the American Bar Association.[d] He called for immediate establishment of a temporary court, organized as a special panel of the Federal Circuit, to hear intercircuit conflicts. This proposal has been debated publicly for some time, as have others. But as yet no action has been taken.[e]

[a] Perhaps most notable was an influential article by Judge Harold Leventhal, A Modern Proposal for a Multi-Circuit Court of Appeals, 24 Am.U.L.Rev. 881 (1975), in which he endorsed the basic principles of the Hruska proposal, but with significant refinements and qualifications.

[b] See Alsup, Reservations on the Proposal of the Hruska Commission to Establish a National Court of Appeals, 7 U.Tol.L.Rev. 431 (1976).

[c] The original proposal was made by Senators Dole, Heflin, and Thurmond. S.645, 98th Cong., 1st Sess. (1983).

[d] Burger, Annual Report on the State of the Judiciary, 69 A.B.A.J. 442 (1983). For consideration of the idea, see the Symposium in 11 Hastings Const. L.Q. 353–504 (1984).

[e] These various proposals have generated an enormous literature, reviewing not only the details of specific suggestions but more generally the state of the federal appellate courts. Many of the most distinguished persons in the profession have addressed these issues, often in informative and insightful ways.

In addition to the sources already cited on the original Freund Commission, see Brennan, The National Court of Appeals: Another Dissent, 40 U.Chi.L.Rev. 473 (1973); Freund, A National Court of Appeals, 25 Hastings L.J. 1301 (1974); Friendly, Averting the Flood by Lessening the Flow, 59 Cornell L. Rev. 634 (1974); Gressman, The National Court of Appeals: A Dissent, 59 A.B.A.J. 253 (1973); Poe, Schmidt & Whalen, A National Court of Appeals: A Dissenting View, 67 Nw.U.L.Rev. 842 (1973).

More recent participation in this debate comes from Brennan, Some Thoughts on the Supreme Court's Workload, 66 Judicature 230 (1983); Cameron, Federal Review, Finality of State Court Decisions, and a Proposal for a National Court of Appeals—A State Judge's Solution to a Continuing Problem, 1981 B.Y. U.L.Rev. 545; Feinberg, A National Court of Appeals?, 42 Brooklyn L. Rev. 611 (1976); Haworth and Meador, A Proposed New Federal Intermediate Appellate Court, 12 U. Mich. J.L. Ref. 201 (1979); Meador, A Comment on the Chief Justice's Proposals, 69 A.B.A.J. 448 (1983); Rx for an Overburdened Supreme Court: Is Relief in Sight?, 66 Judicature 394 (1983) (panel discussion with Judges Alvin Rubin and Patrick Higginbotham, Professors Paul Freund, Arthur Hellman, and Daniel Meador, attorney Robert L. Stern, and the Honorable Roman Hruska). For a recent restatement of the need for some form of a new national appellate body, see Thomas E. Baker and Douglas D. McFarland, Commentary, The Need for a New National Court, 100 Harv.L.Rev. 1400 (1987). Baker and McFarland emphasize the "unreasonably heavy" workload of the Supreme Court and the need to improve the system's capacity to achieve "a satisfactory measure of uniformity in our national law."

Finally, special mention must be made of an important and interesting review of these proposals and an attempt to make systematic quantitative assessment of the Supreme Court's workload by Samuel Estreicher and John E. Sexton of the New York University Law School. Their conclusions are reported in Estreicher and Sexton, A Managerial Theory of the Supreme Court's Responsibilities: An Empirical Study, 59 N.Y.U.L.Rev. 681 (1984).

†